Mastercam® 2018

TRAINING GUIDE

LATHE

By Matthew Manton and Duane Weidinger

camInstructor

Mastercam® 2018 Training Guide Lathe
Published by
CamInstructor Inc.
330 Chandos Crt.
Kitchener, Ontario
N2A 3C2
www.caminstructor.com

Date: June 1, 2016
Author: Matthew Manton and Duane Weidinger
ISBN: 978-1-988766-02-7

National Library of Canada Cataloguing in Publication

To order additional copies of the book contact CamInstructor at:

Canadian Office	Phone 1-877-873-6867
330 Chandos Crt	Fax 1-866-741-8421
Kitchener, ON	email sales@caminstructor.com
N2A 3C2	

Printed in Canada

Requirements

Use of this book requires Mastercam 2018 Lathe.
June 1, 2017

camInstructor

TRAINING GUIDE

IMPORTANT – please read

Starting with our Mastercam 2018 Training Guides we will no longer include CD/DVDs. Instead we are providing **FREE** one year access to the **CamInstructor Course Site**, which contains all the relevant videos for this book and a link to access the software required for this book.

By providing you with access to the **CamInstructor Course Site,** you will always have the latest most up to date video content.

IF YOU PURCHASED THIS BOOK FROM A BOOKSTORE

A **Registration Card** has been included with this book. It contains a unique code and instructions on how to register for the relevant content on the **CamInstructor Course Site**.

camInstructor
Mastercam 2018 Lathe
TRAINING GUIDE VIDEOS
Required for Access to Online Videos

Instructions:

To register your Access Code go to www.caminstructor.com/student-registration

1. Type the Redemption Code (found on the bottom right) into the Redemption Code* space. Click Continue.
2. Select your instructor and Click Continue.
3. Fill in the required information on the Check-Out Information page. **NOTE, be sure to enter an accurate email address or you will not receive your username and password.**
4. Click on **Complete Purchase**. You will NOT be charged.
5. Your username and password will be emailed to the email address you listed in the Check-Out page. If you already have a username and password for the CamInstructor course site you will NOT be emailed a new username and password. Use your existing username and password to log into the Course Site.

WARNING: Access to the Online Course Material is limited to students who have purchased a Book and/or Student Access Code. Attempting to share User Name and Password will result in termination of your account and access to the CamInstructor Course site, without refund.

To download the Mastercam HLE Software

1. Log into the CamInstructor course site at **www.caminstructor.com** (after you receive your username and password)
2. Click on **Select a Category** and then select your Mastercam Version
3. Select the course from the list.
4. Click on Mastercam Software

Web: www.caminstructor.com
E-Mail: customer.service@caminstructor.com

Redemption Code: AE234567
Mastercam 2018 Lathe

Registration is free and once completed you will receive an email containing your password.

IF YOU PURCHASED THIS BOOK ONLINE

You will have already received an email with your password to access the **CamInstructor Course Site** and you should already have logged in and accessed the video content on the site.

If you have not received an email with a Password it will be for one of the following reasons;

1. You misspelled your email address when purchasing the book online and the email was sent to the wrong email address. In this case email customer.service@caminstructor.com and ask for your log-in information.
2. You already have an account and a password for the **CamInstructor Course Site** in which case you can log into the site and access your content. If you have forgotten your password just go to the Login Page and click on the **Reset a Lost Password** link.

Should you still require a CD/DVD with the video content on it, please email customer.service@caminstructor.com and be sure to provide the following in the email:

Full name
Email
Registration Code on the accompanying card
Title of Book including Version
ISBN (found on top of copyright page)

Please note, a fee of $30.00 will be charged for the CD/DVD's which covers production and shipping.

Contents at a Glance

Setting the Environment 1

Lesson 1 9

Exercise 1 51

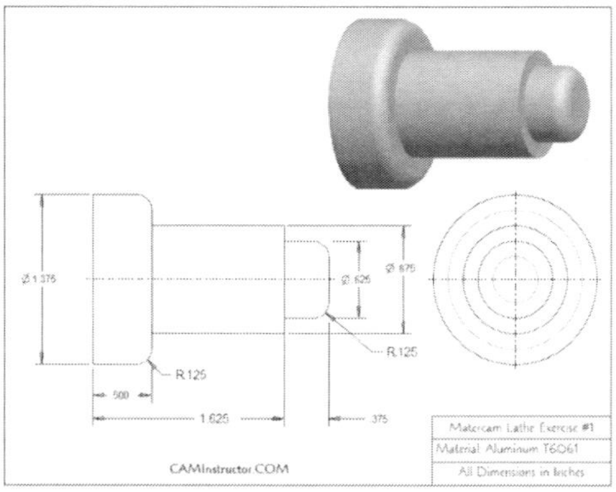

Lesson 2 53

Exercise 2.. 100

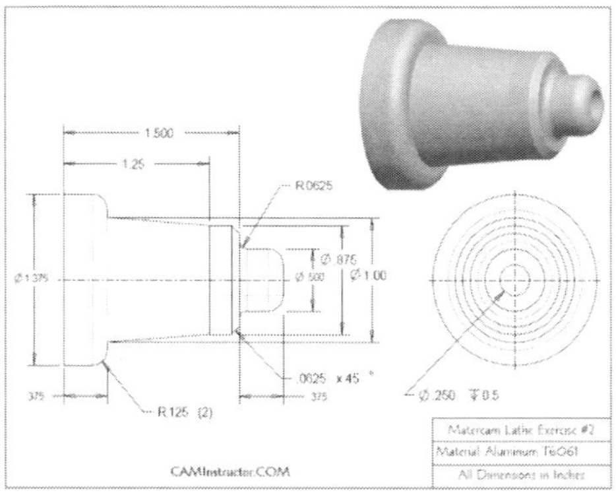

Lathe

Lesson 3 101

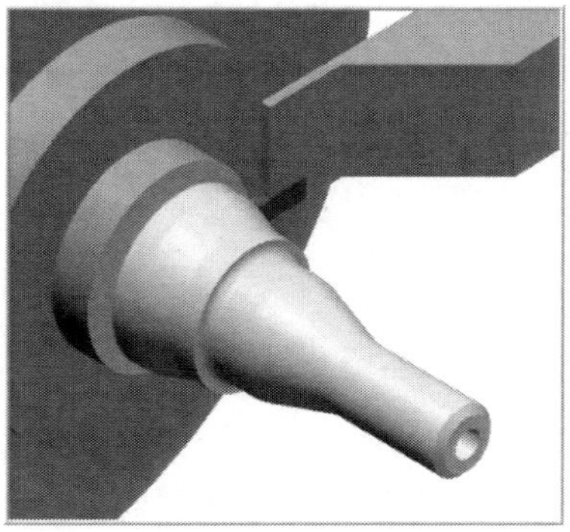

Exercise 3.. 150

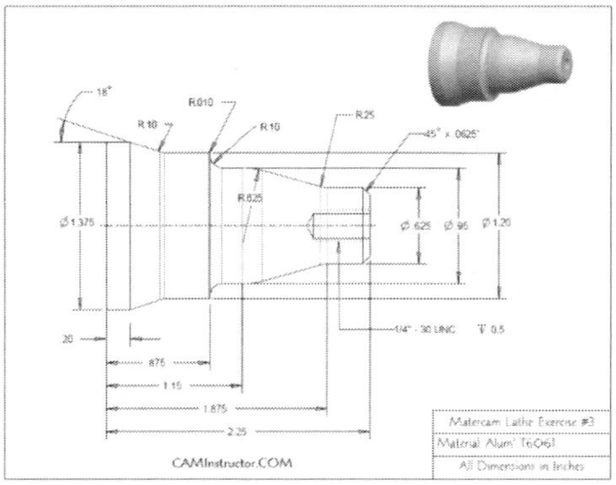

Lesson 4 151

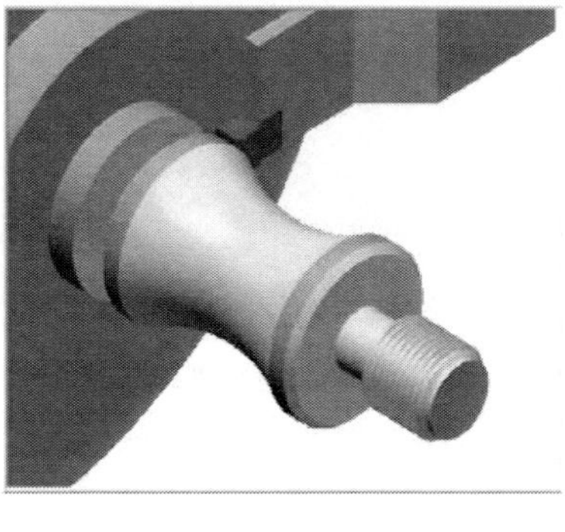

Exercise 4.. 203

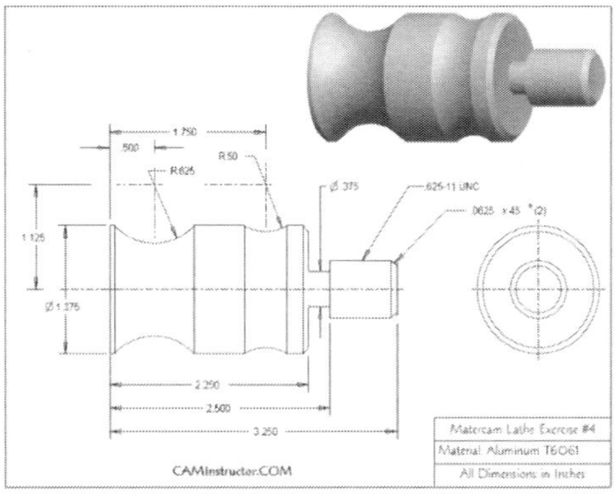

Lesson 5 CAD/CAM 205

Exercise 5.......... 261

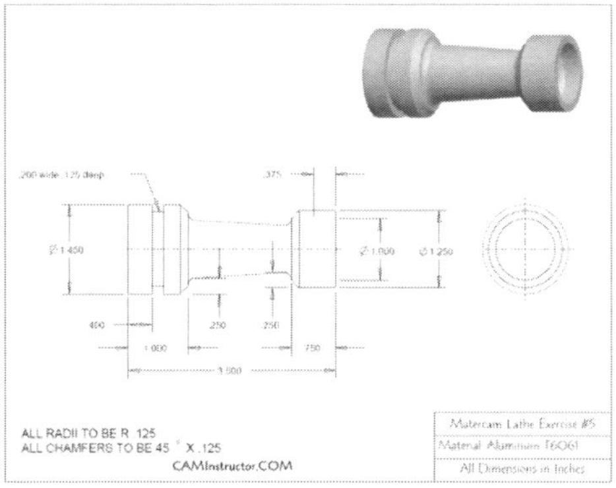

Lesson 5B – Import a CAD Solid Part File 263

Lathe

Lesson 6 265

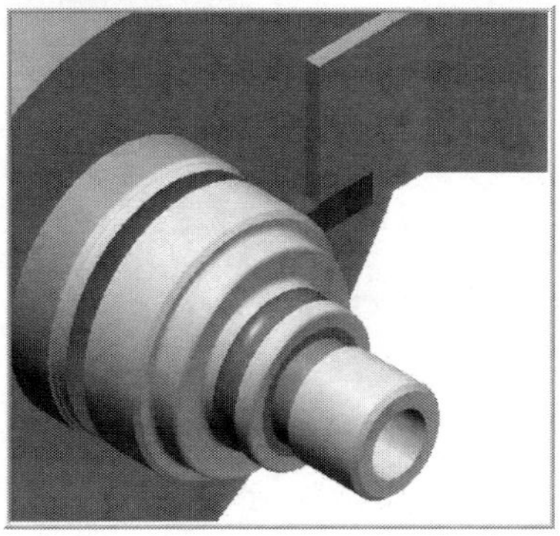

Exercise 6 321

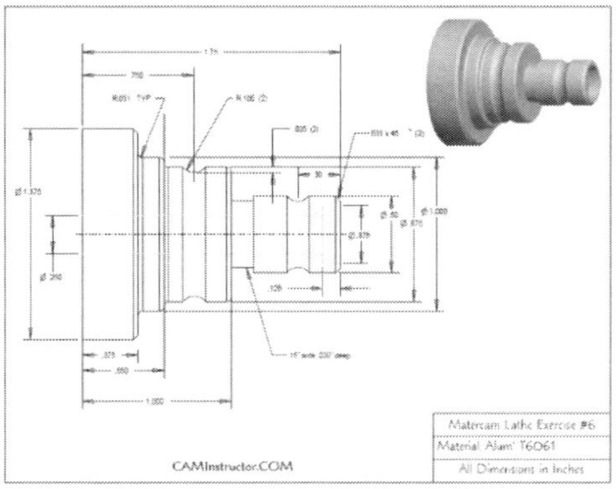

Lesson 7 323

Exercise 7 382

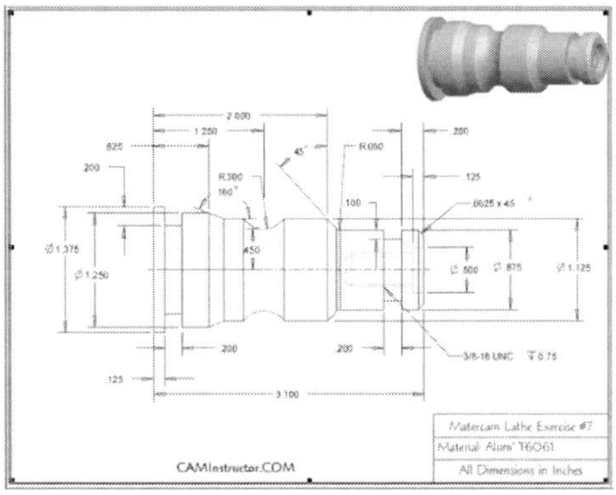

Lesson 8 383

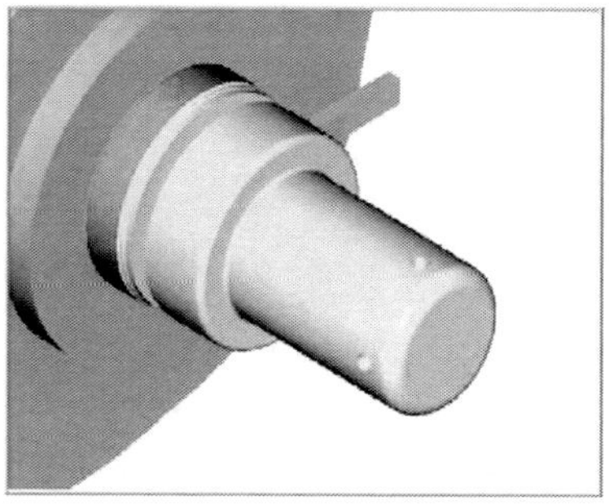

Exercise 8 407

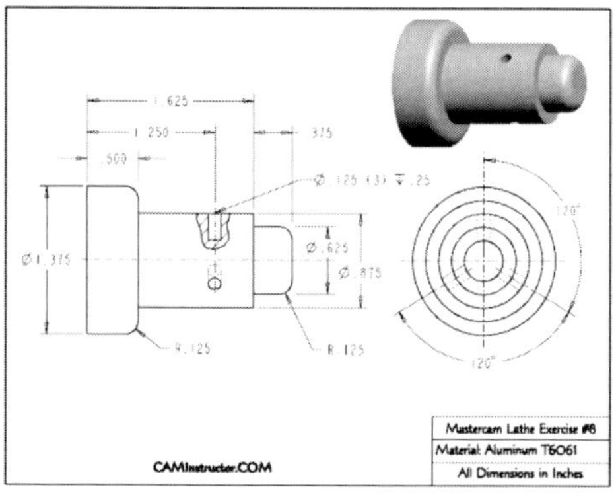

Lesson 9 409

Exercise 9 471

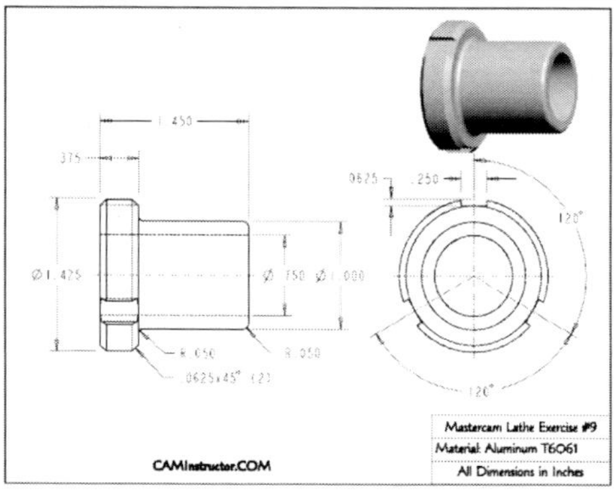

Lathe

Lesson 10 473

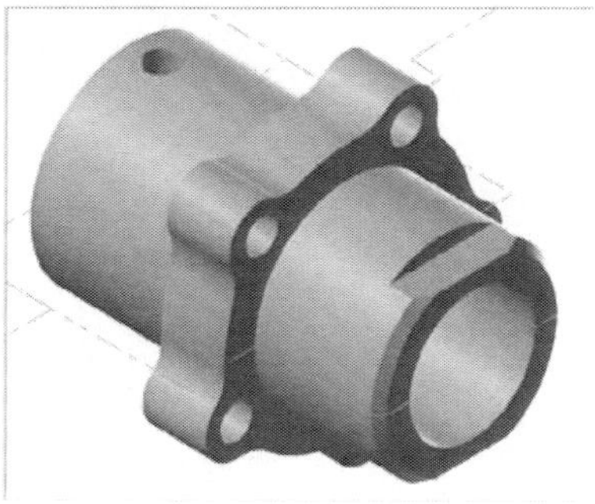

Mastercam® 2018
TRAINING
GUIDE

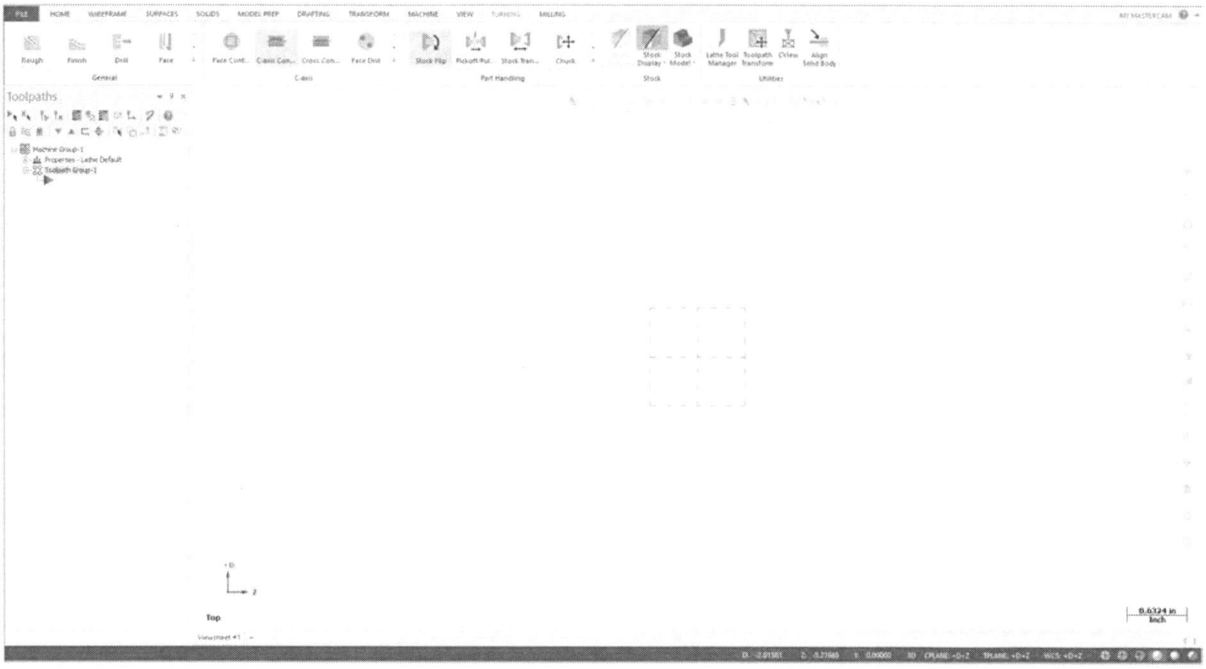

LATHE
SETTING THE ENVIRONMENT

camInstructor

SETTING THE ENVIRONMENT
COMPLETE THESE STEPS BEFORE STARTING EACH MODULE

Before starting the geometry creation and generating the toolpaths you should:

- ➲ Set the Grid. This will help identify the location of the origin.
- ➲ Set the machine type to Lathe Default.

SETTING THE GRID:

1. Launch **Mastercam**.
2. Select **File** in the upper left corner of your screen.

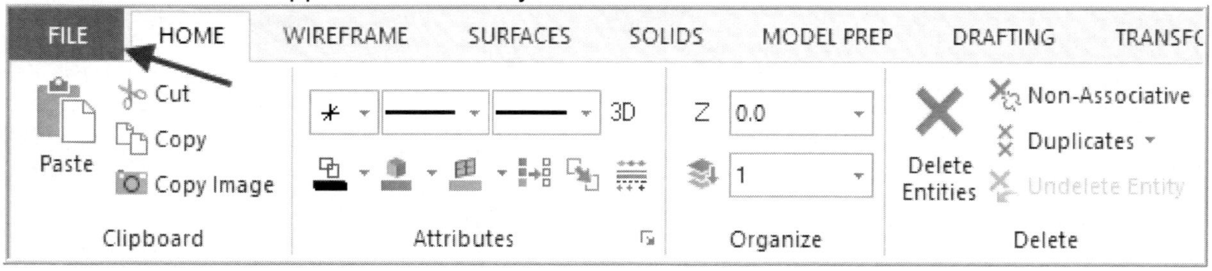

3. From the selections on the left of your screen select **Configuration.**

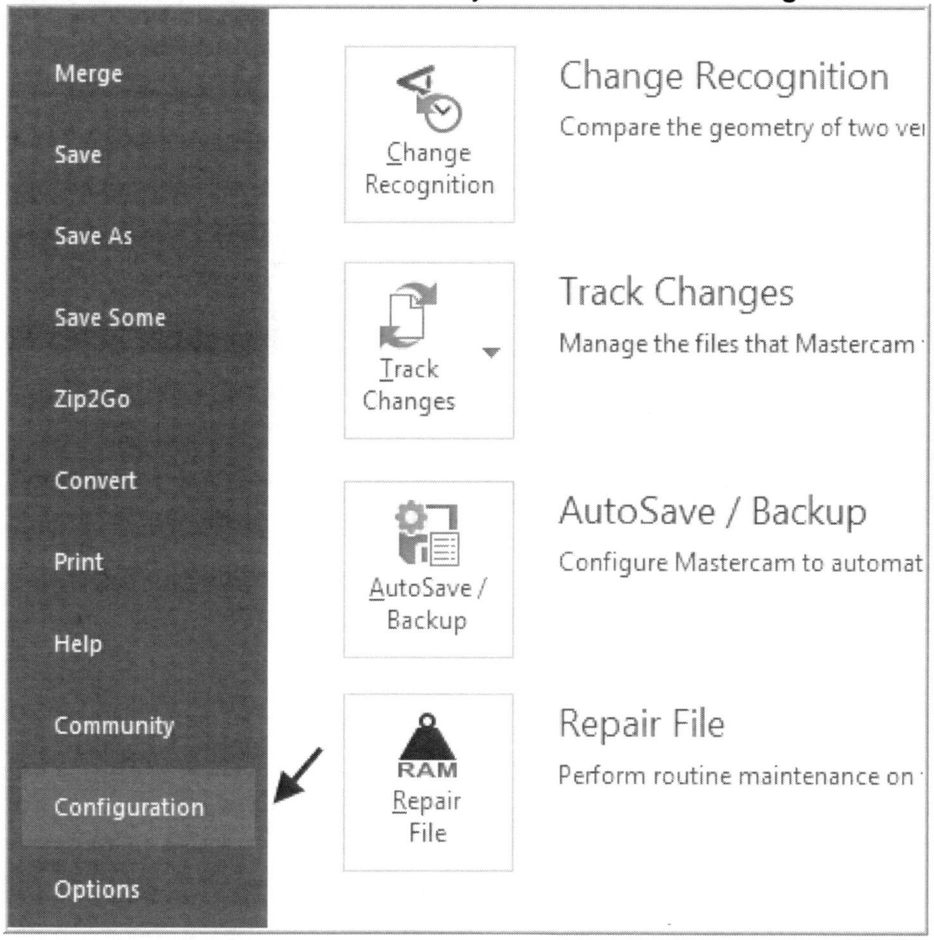

4. From the window on the left side of this window expand the **Screen** topic by selecting the **+ sign** and then select **Grid Settings**.

5. Change the **Size to 1**.

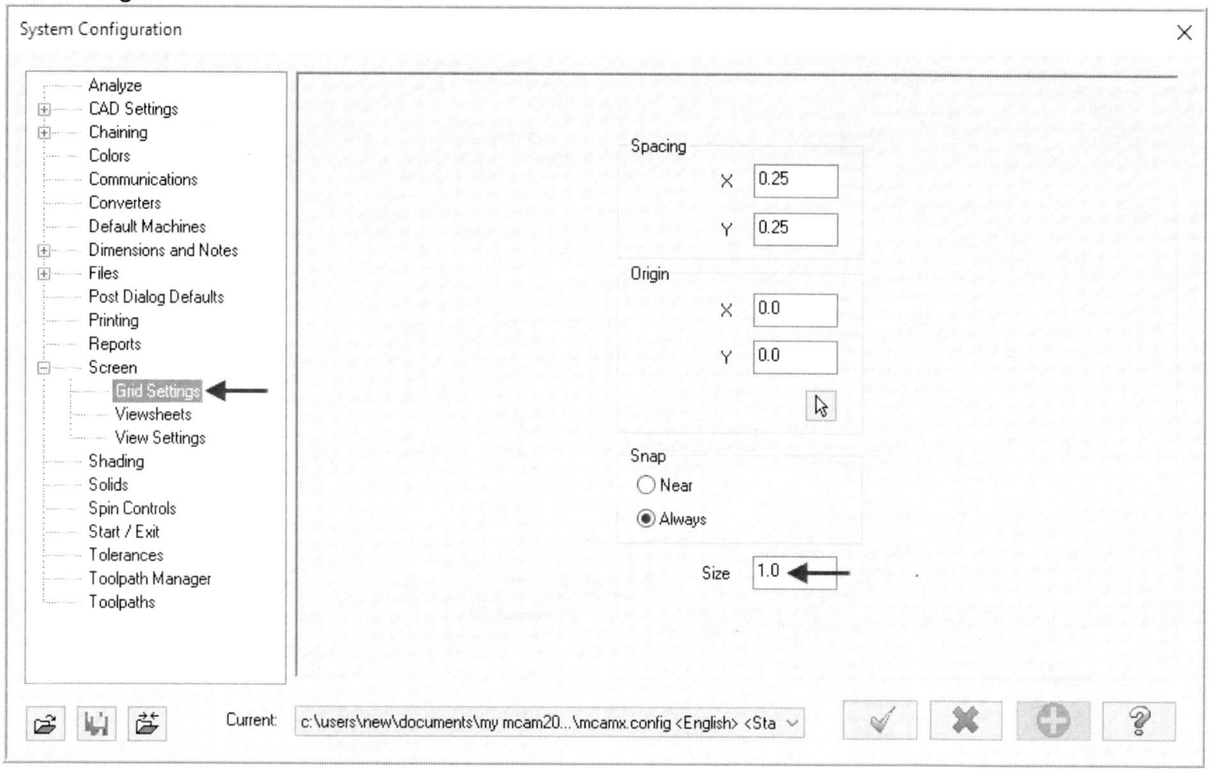

6. Select the **OK** button to complete this function.
7. When prompted to **"Save settings to configuration file"** select **Yes.**

> **Grid Settings**
> Use the Grid Settings page to configure the default settings for Mastercam's grid function.
>
> Activate the grid using the **Show Grid** and **Snap to Grid** controls on the **View tab**.
>
> The selection grid is a matrix of reference points that the cursor snaps to when you sketch a point. Snapping to the selection grid provides a finer level of precision than sketching points freehand. For example, to draw entities whose locations and dimensions are always multiples of a half inch, set your grid X and Y values to 0.5.

8. Now select the **View** tab and click on **Show Grid** to display the grid on the screen.

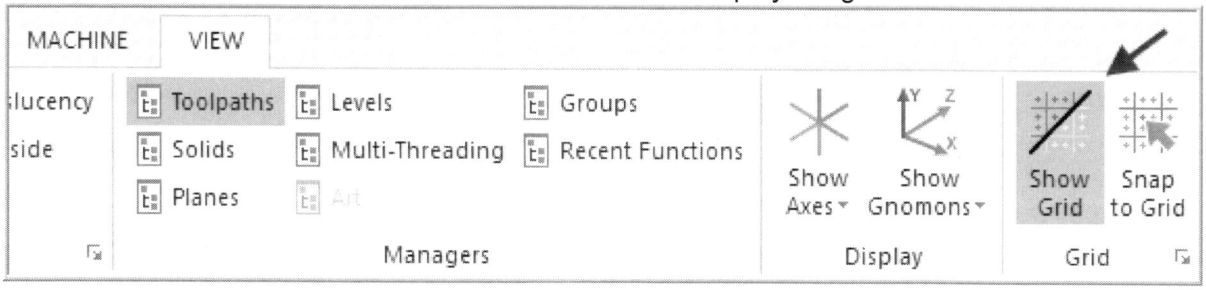

9. In the lower right corner of the **Grid** section click on the arrow.

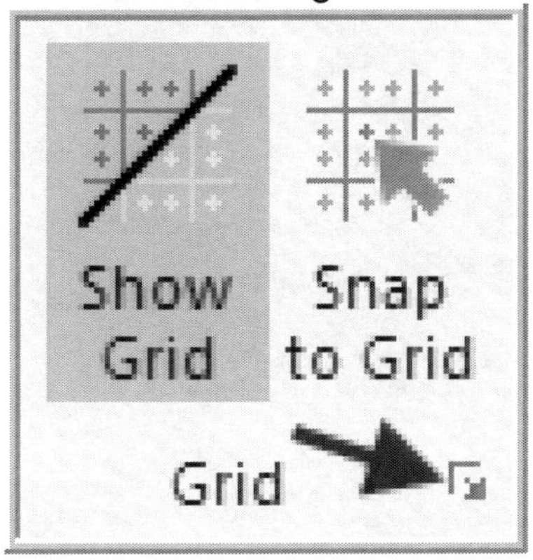

This opens up the **Grid Settings** page – **no changes are required here**.

You can save grid parameters to the Mastercam configuration file as you did earlier or you can make **temporary changes only for the current session** on this page.

Saved grid parameters are loaded when you start a new Mastercam session.

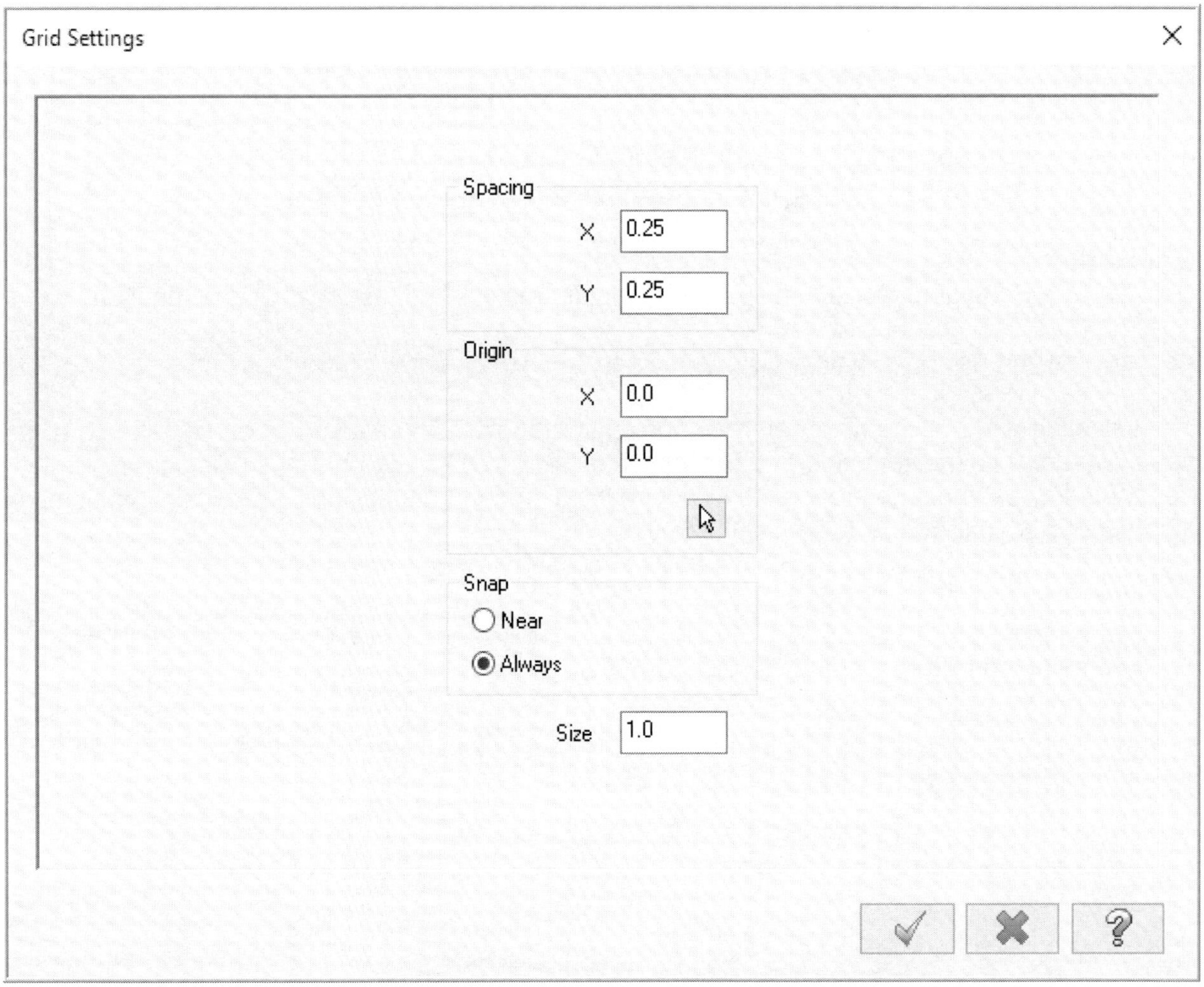

10. Select the **Cancel** button  as no changes are required.

SELECTING THE TYPE OF MACHINE:

- For Lathe-Lessons 1 through 7 you will use the **Default Lathe** to machine the part.
- For Lathe-Lessons 8 thru 10 you will use the **C-AXIS SLANT BED** Lathe to machine the part.
- To set the machine type to **Default Lathe** do the following:

1. Select the **MACHINE** tab at the top of the screen.

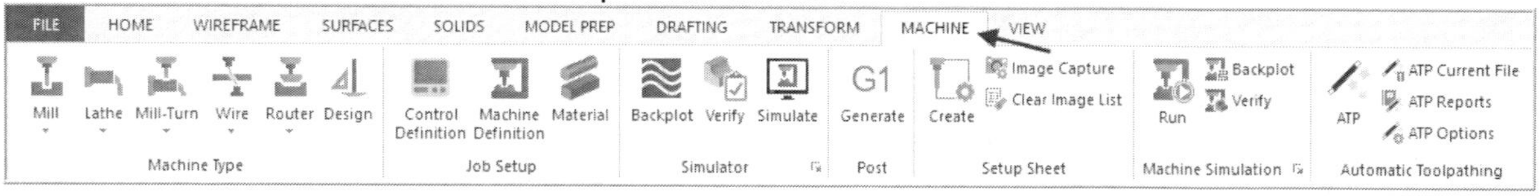

2. Now click on **Lathe** on the left of your screen to open the drop down menu. Click on **Default** as shown below.

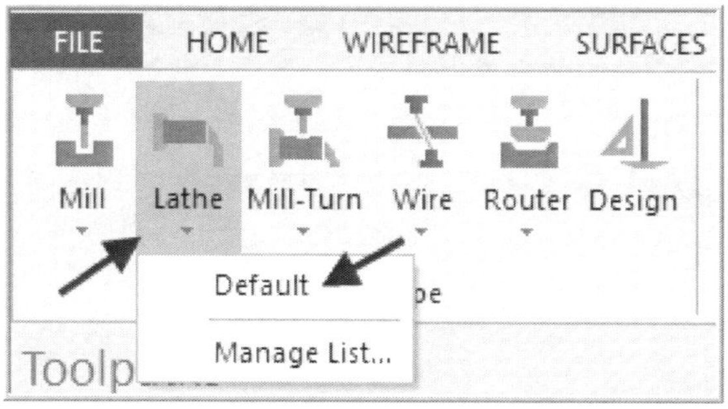

- Your screen should look like the image shown below:

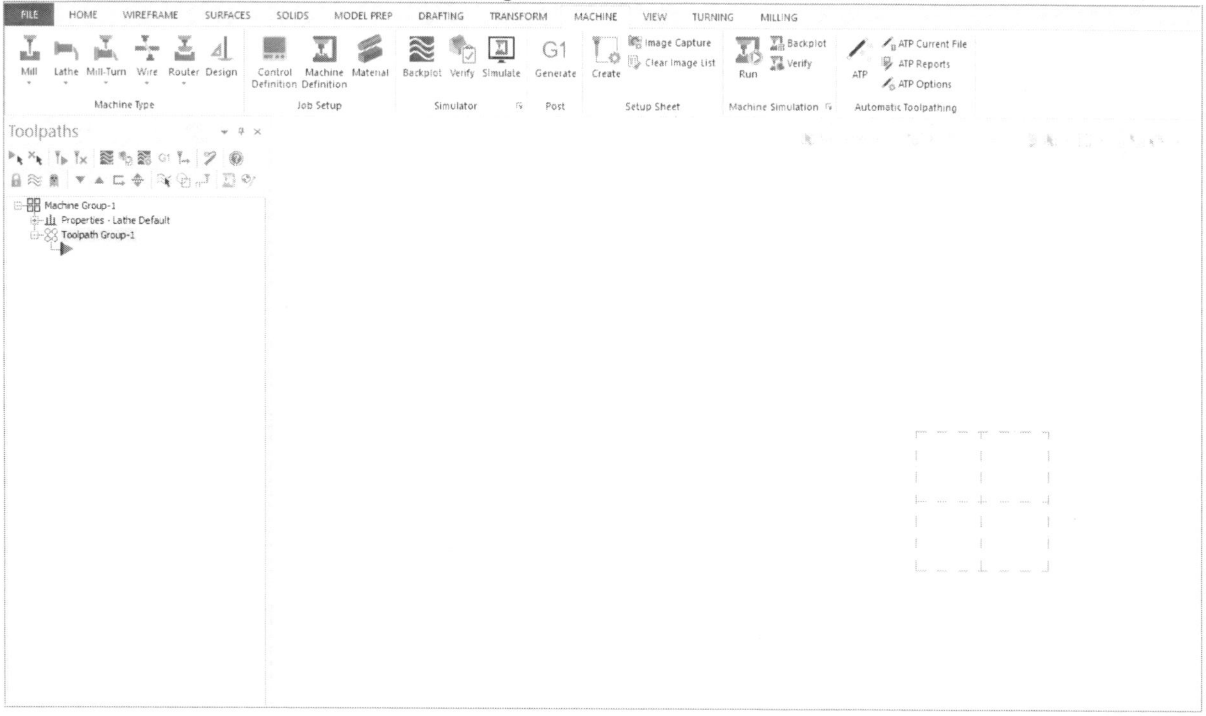

SETTING THE CONSTRUCTION PLANES:

➲ **Set the Construction Plane to Lathe diameter +D +Z**

1. Select the **View tab** and click on **Toolpaths** and **Solids** in the **Managers** section to **hide** them and toggle the **Planes Manager to display**.

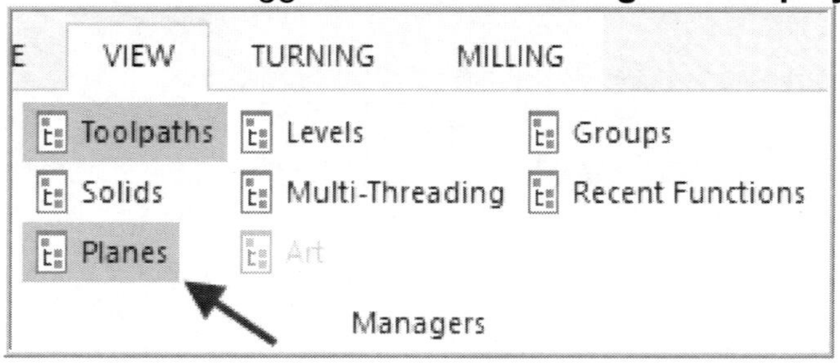

2. Ensure the **C column** (Construction Plane) and **T column** (Tool Plane) are set to the **+D +Z Plane**. Just click in the C and T columns in the **+D +Z** row.

➲ Take note at the lower part of the screen **CPLANE: +D +Z TPLANE: +D +Z WCS:TOP** as shown below right.

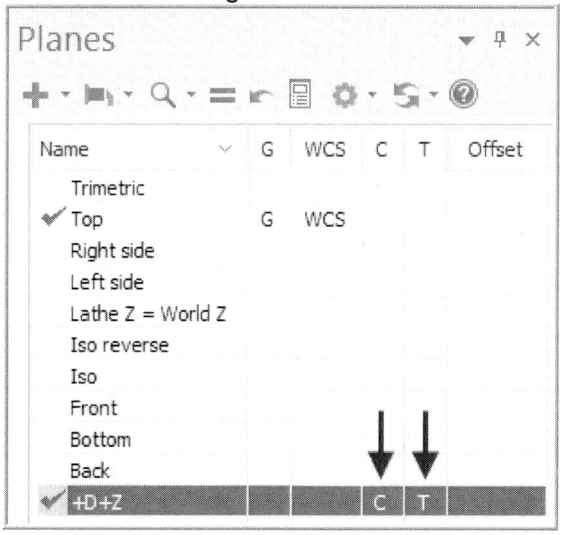

3. To change the **Lathe Plane** open up the drop down menu for **Select lathe plane** and click on the required coordinate system

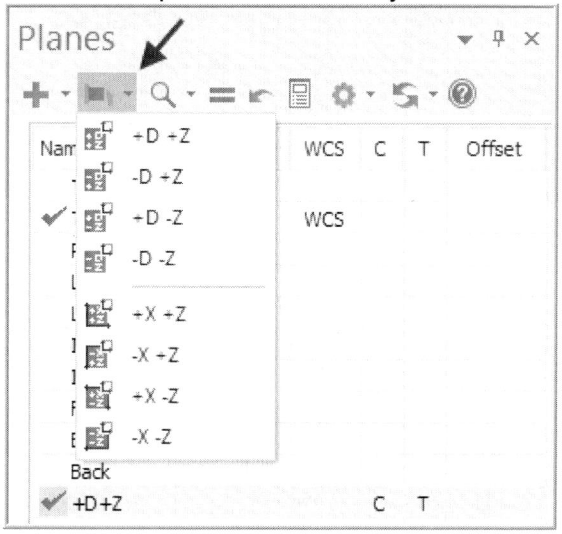

Once your machine is set up, Mastercam includes special lathe construction planes that let you work in radius or diameter coordinates.

For conventional 2D turning applications, use the Planes Manager to select the desired coordinate system, as shown on the left. Choose to use either radius or diameter coordinates, then choose the desired X/D and Z directions.

DISPLAYING THE TOOLPATHS MANAGER:

1. You can close the **Toolpaths/Solids/Planes Manager** by clicking the **Close** button in the **upper right corner for each manager panel**. To open the Toolpaths Manager again, choose the **View tab**, and select **Toolpaths**.

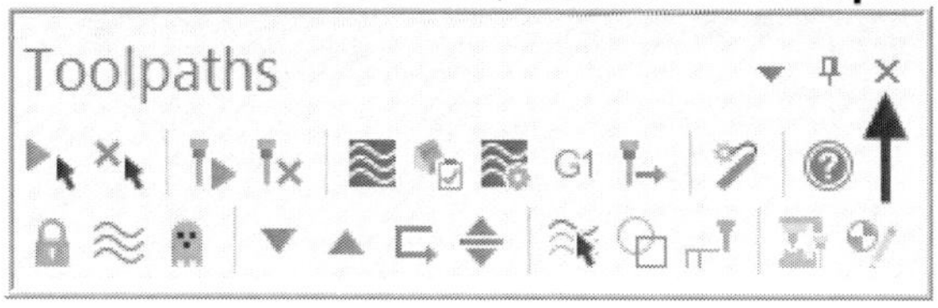

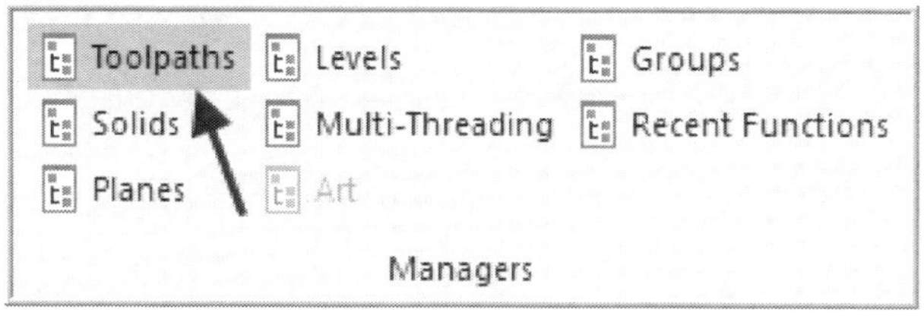

Note:
Your settings for the Managers are modal between Mastercam sessions. This means that Mastercam "remembers" and maintains the position and size of the Managers, even if you close and re-open Mastercam.

2. When all three **Toolpaths and Solids Manager** are activated you can display a particular manager panel by selecting the relevant tab at the lower left of the screen

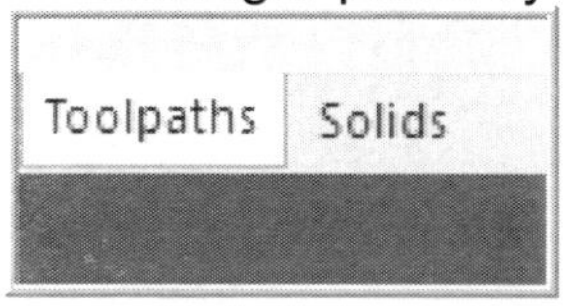

Toolpaths/Solids/Planes Manager Hidden

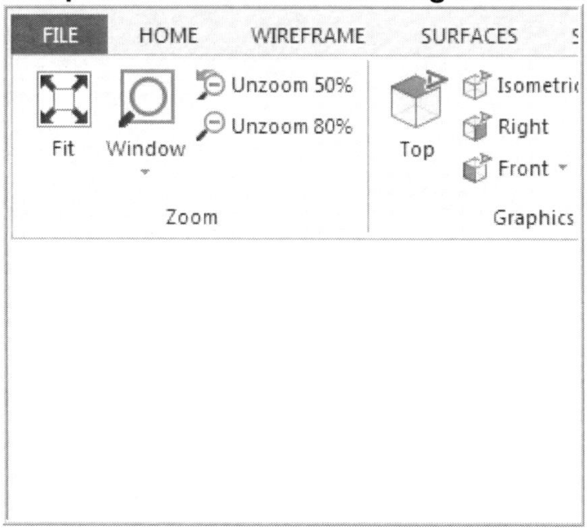

Toolpaths Manager Displayed

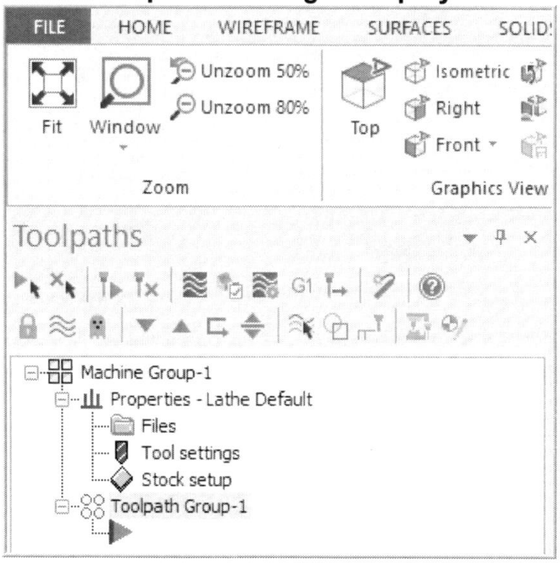

Mastercam allows you to move the Toolpath Manager and Solids Manager to a different location, re-size their window, and close or re-open them whenever you want.
By default, the Toolpath and Solids Manger are docked to the left side of the graphics window. You can undock the Managers and dock them where you like. To do so, drag the Manager pane to a screen position or to one of the docking icons that appear as you drag.

For more information on the Toolpaths Manager refer to the Tips and Techniques content in the Online Course Instruction.

Mastercam® 2018

TRAINING

GUIDE

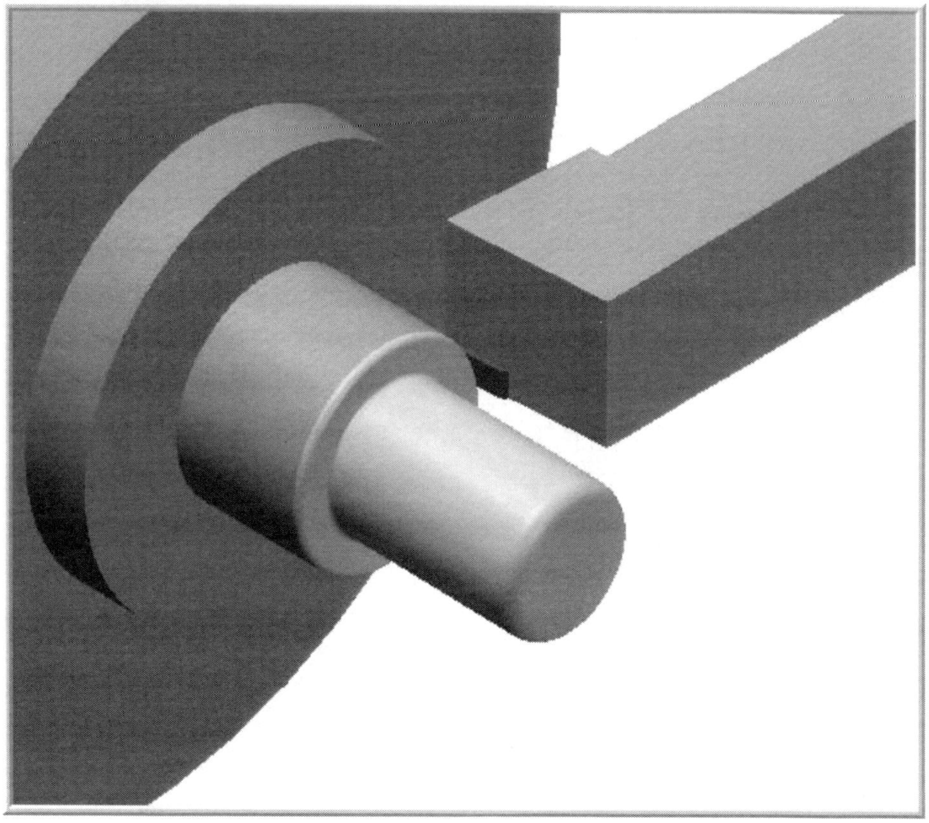

LATHE-LESSON-1

FACE, ROUGH, FINISH AND CUTOFF

camInstructor

Objectives

You will create the geometry for Lathe-Lesson-1, and then generate a toolpath to machine the part on a CNC lathe. This lesson covers the following topics:

➲ **Create a 2-dimensional drawing by:**
Creating lines.
Creating fillets.

➲ **Establish Stock and Chuck settings:**
Stock size.
Chuck Configuration.
Material for the part.
Feed calculation.

➲ **Generate a 2-dimensional lathe toolpath consisting of:**
Lathe Face.
Lathe Rough.
Lathe Finish.
Lathe Cutoff.

➲ **Inspect the toolpath using Mastercam's Verify and Backplot by:**
Launching the Verify function to machine the part on the screen.
Using Backplot to identify the correctness of the toolpaths.
Generating the NC- code.

LATHE-LESSON-1 DRAWING

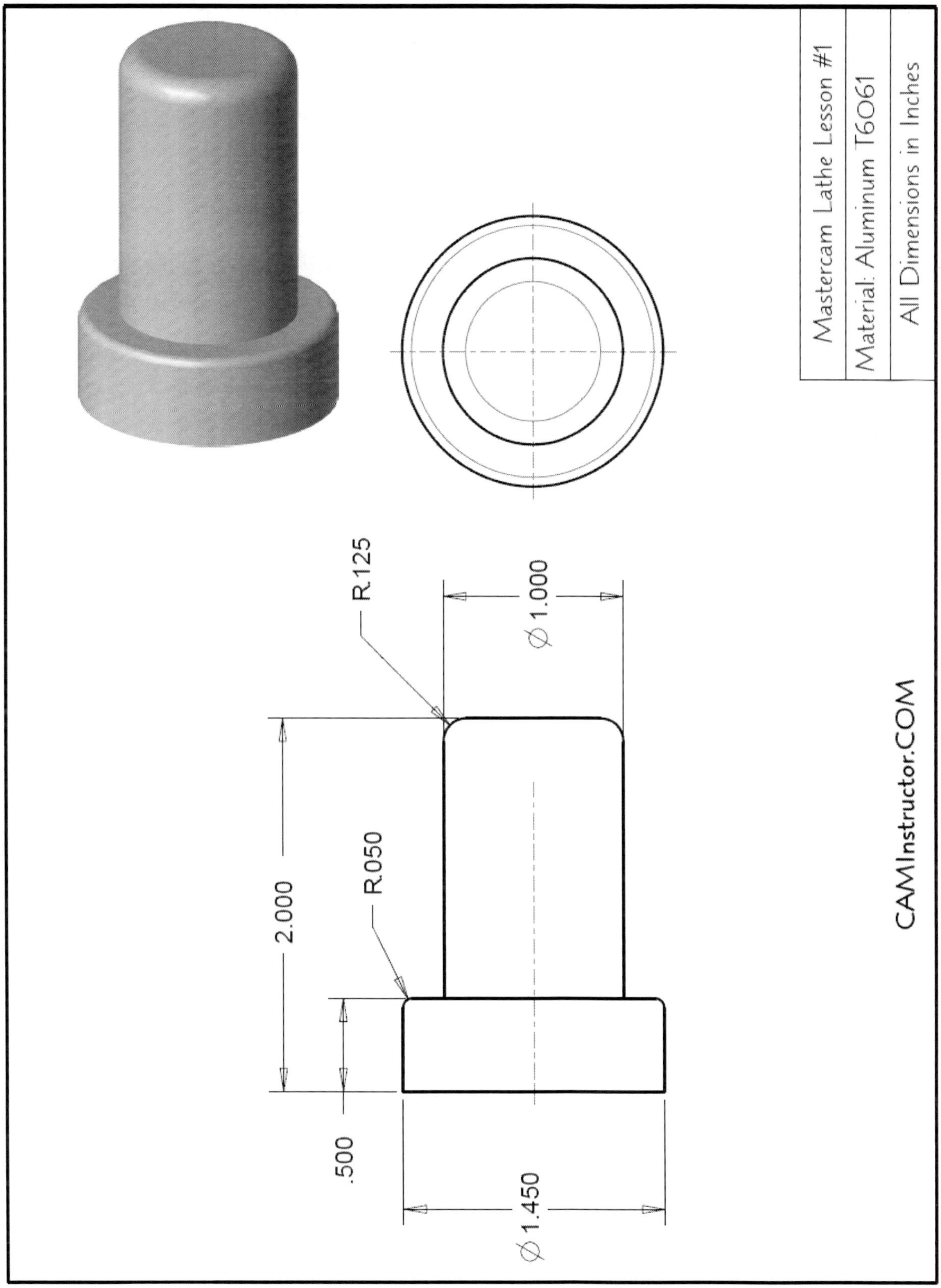

TOOL LIST

Two tools will be used to create this part.

➲ **Tool #1 Face, Rough and Finish the outside diameters**
Holder: Outside Diameter Rough Right Hand - DCGNR-164D.
Insert: 80 Degree Diamond Insert – CNMG-432.

➲ **Tool #2 Cutoff the part**
Holder: Outside Diameter Cut-off Right Hand.
Insert: 0.125" Wide.

LATHE - LESSON - 1 - THE PROCESS

Geometry Creation

TASK 1: Setting the Environment
TASK 2: Setting the Construction Planes
TASK 3: Create the Geometry
TASK 4: Create the Fillets (Radius)
TASK 5: Save the Drawing

Toolpath Creation

TASK 6: Define the Stock and Chuck Parameters
TASK 7: Face the Front of the Part
TASK 8: Rough the Outside Diameters
TASK 9: Finish the Outside Diameters
TASK 10: Cut off the Part
TASK 11: Backplot the Toolpath
TASK 12: Verify the Toolpath
TASK 13: Save the Updated Mastercam File
TASK 14: Post and Create the CNC Code File

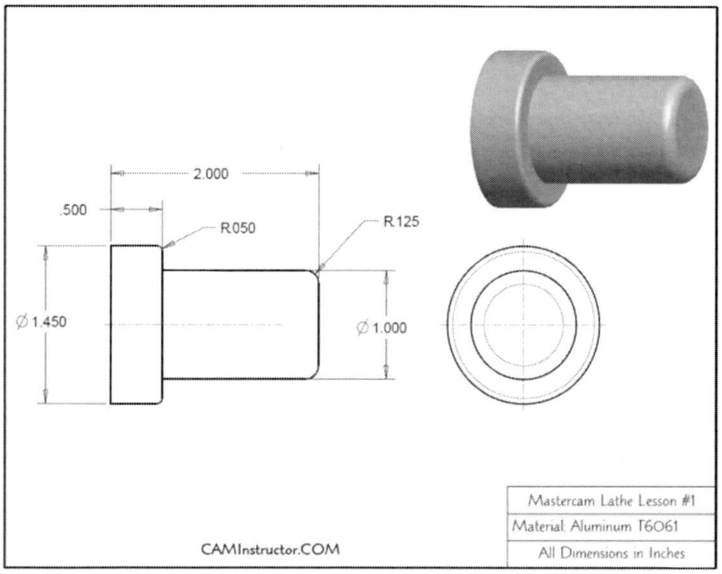

Geometry Creation

TASK 1:
SETTING THE ENVIRONMENT

Before starting the geometry creation you should set up the grid machine type as outlined in the **Setting the Environment** section at the beginning of this text:

1. Set up the **Grid**. This will help identify the location of the origin.
2. Set the **MACHINE TYPE** to the **Lathe Default**.

TASK 2:
SETTING THE CONSTRUCTION PLANES:

➲ **Set the Construction Plane to Lathe diameter +D +Z**

1. Select the **View tab** and click on **Toolpaths** and **Solids** in the **Managers** section to **hide** them and toggle **only** the **Planes Manager to display**.

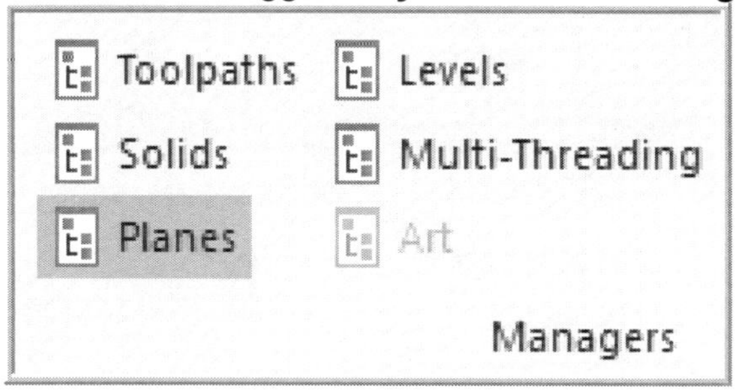

Once your machine is set up, Mastercam includes special lathe construction planes that let you work in **radius or diameter coordinates**.

For conventional 2D turning applications, use the Planes Manager to select the desired coordinate system, as shown below right.

Choose to use either radius or diameter coordinates and then choose the desired X/D and Z directions.

2. Ensure the **C column** (Construction Plane) and **T column** (Tool Plane) are set to the **+D +Z Plane**. Just click in the C and T columns in the **+D +Z** row.

➲ Take note of the **Status bar** at the bottom of the screen **CPLANE: +D +Z TPLANE: +D +Z WCS:TOP** as shown below right.

3. To change the **Lathe Plane** open up the drop down menu for **Select lathe plane** and click on the required coordinate system as shown below right.

4. Select the **Close** button ☒ in the top right hand corner to close the Planes Manager.

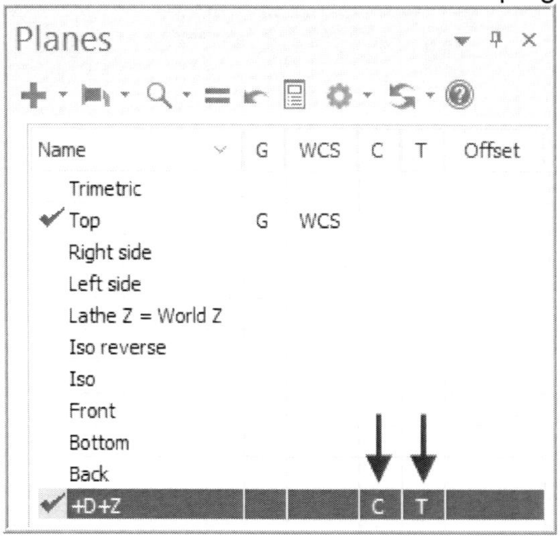

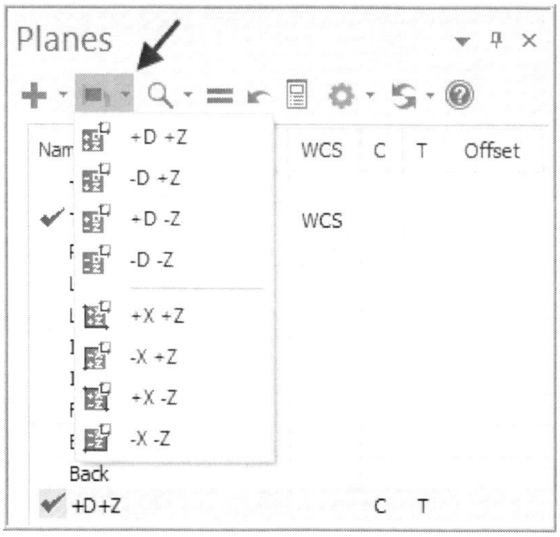

TASK 3:
CREATE THE GEOMETRY – THE RIGHT HAND FACE IS AT Z0

- This task explains how to create the geometry of this part. In this lathe part you only need to create **half of the geometry**, the geometry above the center line.
- Lines 1 through 5 will be created first and then the fillet and chamfer will be created.

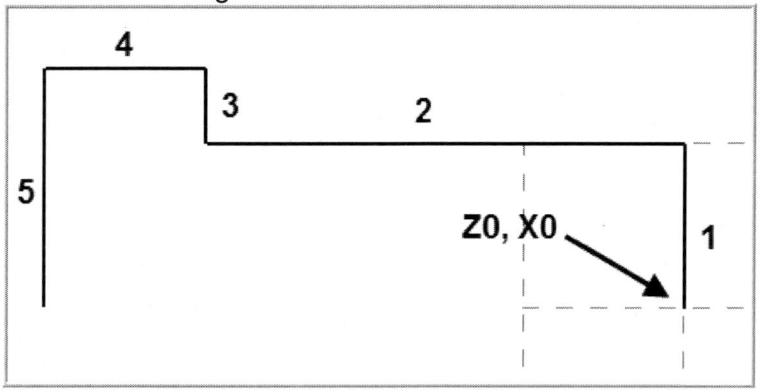

- **Create Line #1**

1. Select the **WIREFRAME** tab at the top of the screen and in the **Lines** section click on **Line Endpoints**.

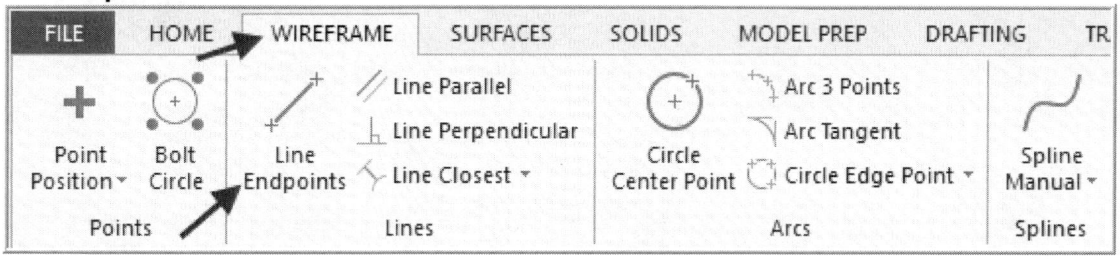

- On the graphics screen you are prompted: **Specify the first endpoint** and the Line panel appears.

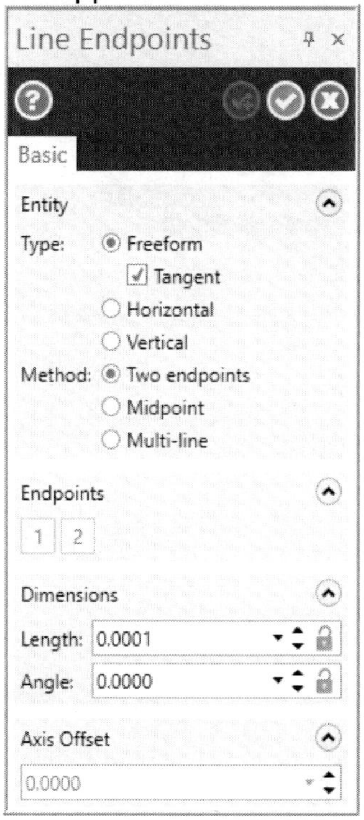

Line Endpoints
Use this function to create single lines with two endpoints, or multiple lines connected at their endpoints.

Simply click in the graphics window to set the two endpoints; or enter values in the Length and Angle fields, and then click in the graphics window to position the line.

2. Move the cursor over the **center of the grid** and as you get close to the origin a visual cue appears.  With this visual cue highlighted click the **left mouse** button.

➲ The following are Mastercam Visual Cues:

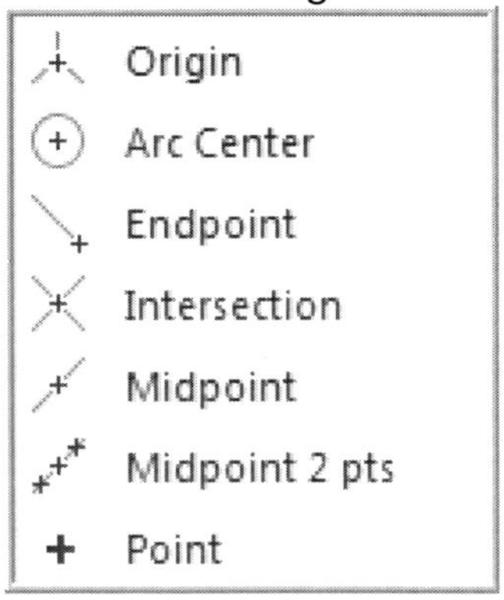

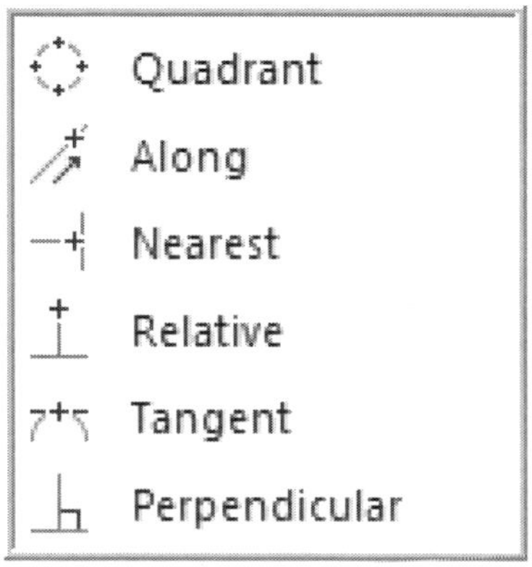

3. You are prompted to **"Specify the second endpoint"**. To satisfy this prompt **click the middle mouse button** and then **hit the spacebar** on your keyboard.
4. The **Fastpoint** box now opens. Input **1.0,0** and hit the **Enter** key. This is **D1.0 Z0.**

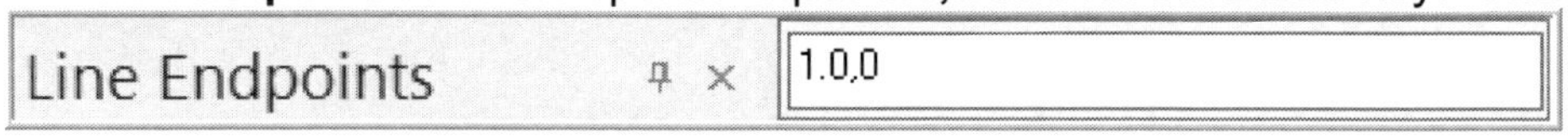

➲ A vertical line should be visible as shown below:

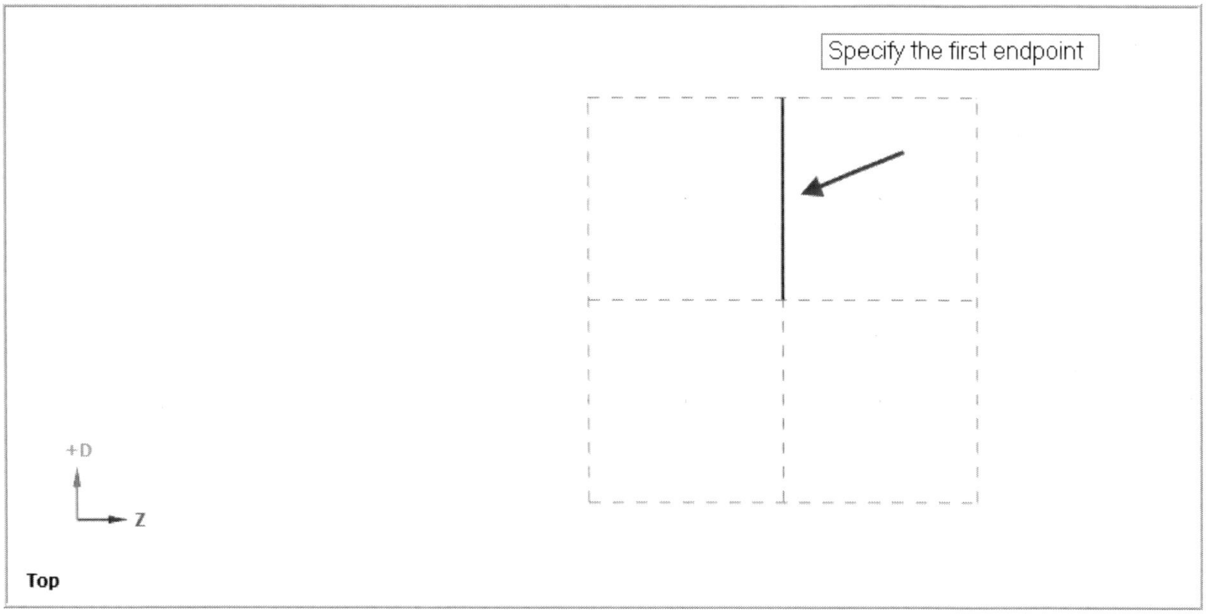

NOTE: If you make a mistake creating lines, click on the **OK** icon  and click on the **Undo** icon 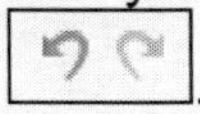. Then re-create the Line.

➲ **Create Line #2.**

5. You are next prompted to **"Specify the first endpoint".** Click on the **end of the line** that was just created as shown below and as you get close to the end point a visual cue appears.  This is the cue that will allow you to snap to the endpoint of this line. With this visual cue highlighted pick the end point of the line.

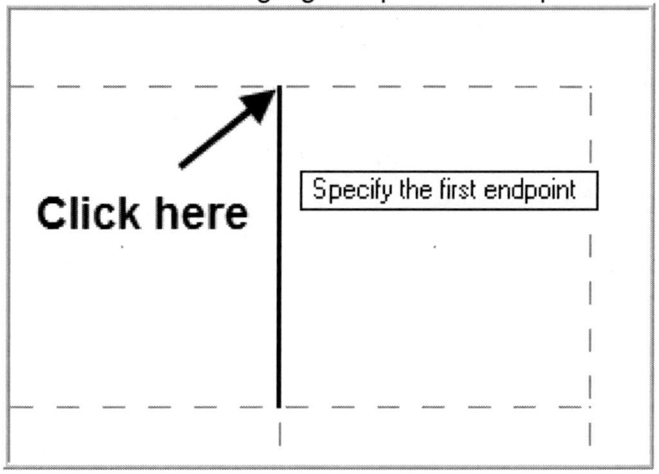

6. You are next prompted to **"Specify the second endpoint.** To satisfy this prompt **just type** the coordinate, **type 1.0,-1.5** and hit the Enter key. This is **D1.0 Z-1.5**.

➲ **Create Line #3**

7. You are next prompted to **"Specify the first endpoint"**. Click on the **end of the line** that was just created as shown below:

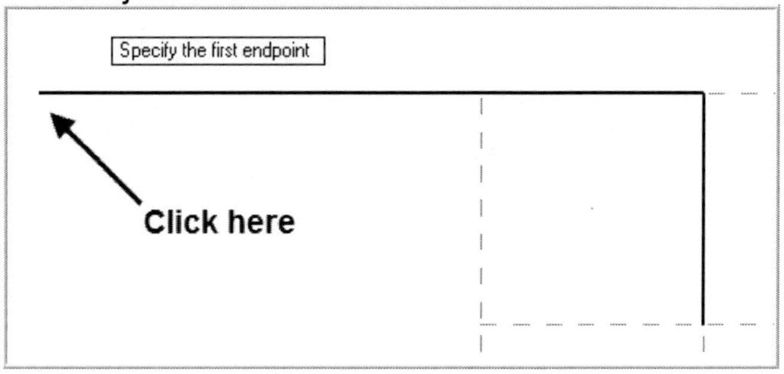

8. You are next prompted to **"Specify the second endpoint.** To satisfy this prompt **just type** the coordinate, **type 1.45,-1.5** and hit the Enter key. This is **D1.45 Z-1.5**.

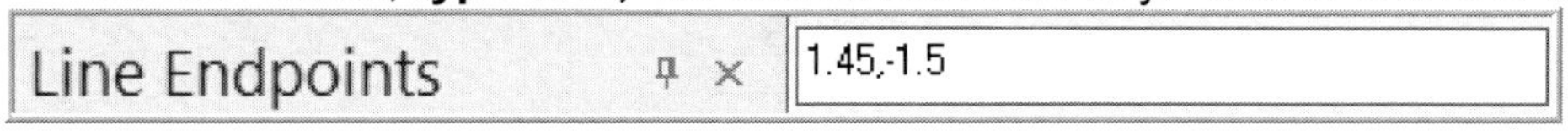

➲ **Create Line #4**

9. You are next prompted to **"Specify the first endpoint"**. Click on the **end of the line** that was just created as shown below:

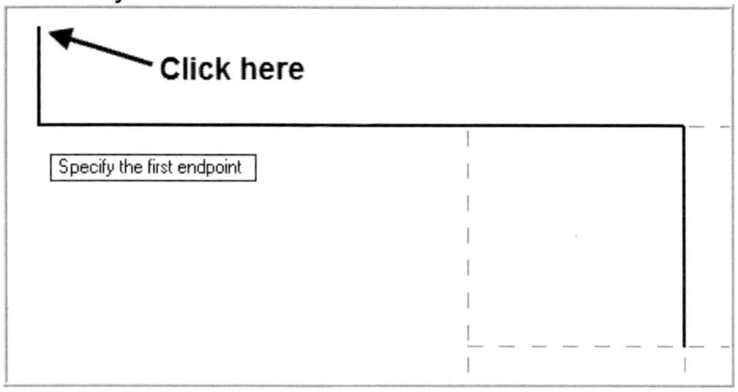

10. You are next prompted to **"Specify the second endpoint.** To satisfy this prompt **just type** the coordinate, **type 1.45,-2.0** and hit the Enter key. This is **D1.45 Z-2.0**.

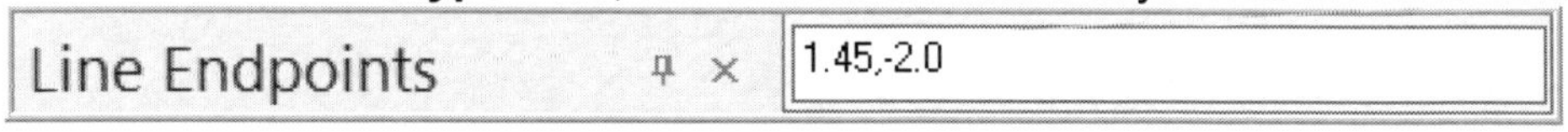

11. Select the **VIEW** tab at the top of the screen
12. Select the **Fit** icon in the **Zoom** section.
13. Next select **Unzoom 80%** to shrink the display.

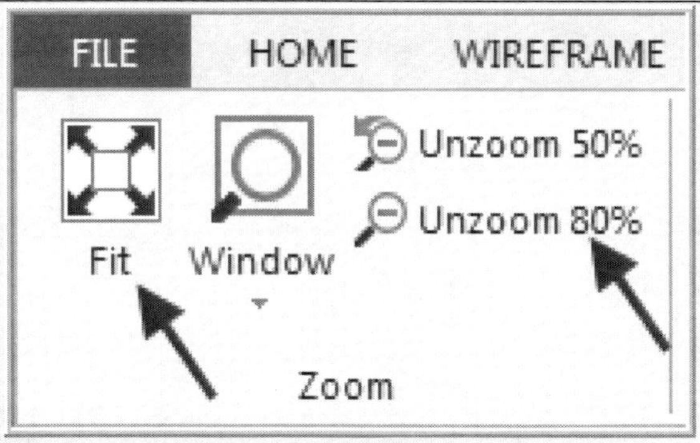

Fit
Use this function to maximize your view of visible geometry in the graphics window. When you use this function, the system positions and sizes the displayed geometry to fill as much of the graphics area as possible.

Unzoom 80%
This reduces the size of the displayed geometry to 80% of its current size.

Fit
In addition to using the View menu, you can access **Fit** from the **right-click menu**.

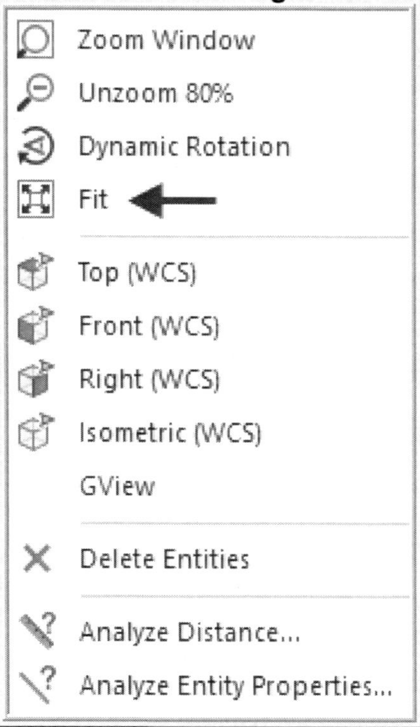

➲ **Create Line #5**

14. You are next prompted to **"Specify the first endpoint"**. Click on the **end of the line** that was just created as shown below:

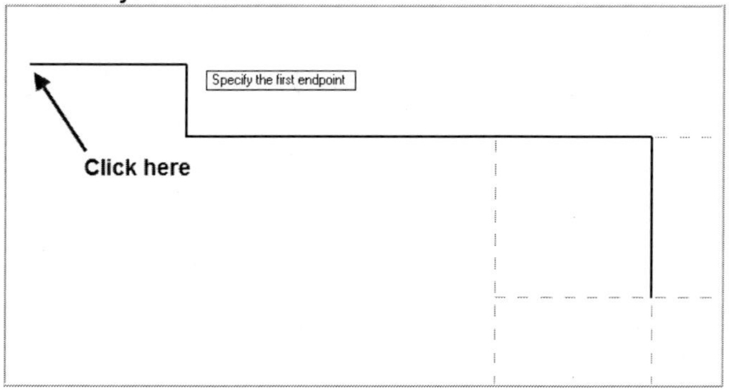

15. You are next prompted to **"Specify the second endpoint.** To satisfy this prompt **just type** the coordinate, **type 0,-2.0** and hit the Enter key. This is **D0 Z-2.0**.

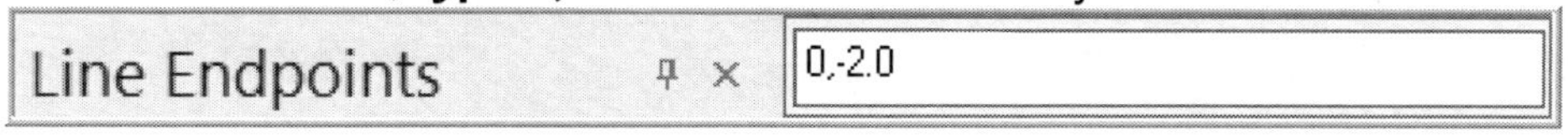

16. Click on the **OK** icon  to complete this feature.
17. Right mouse click in the graphics area and click on the **Fit** icon .

➲ Your geometry should look like the figure below:

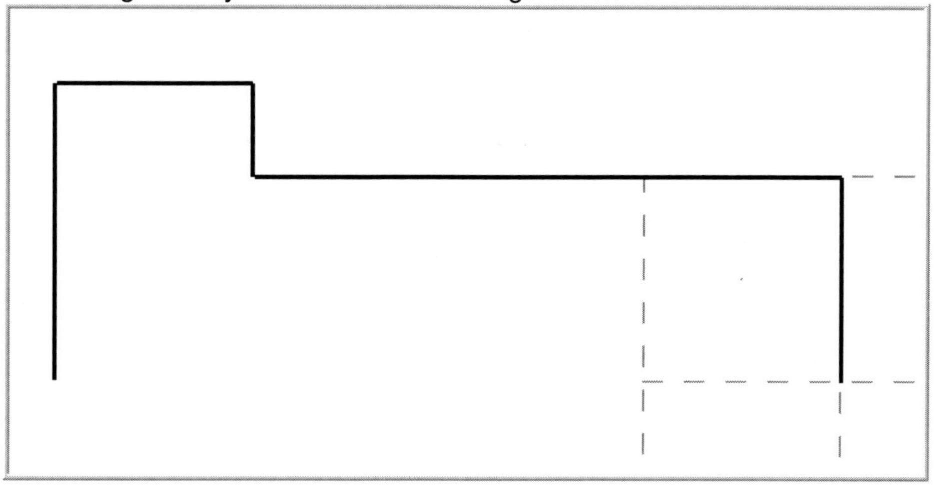

TASK 4:
CREATE THE FILLETS

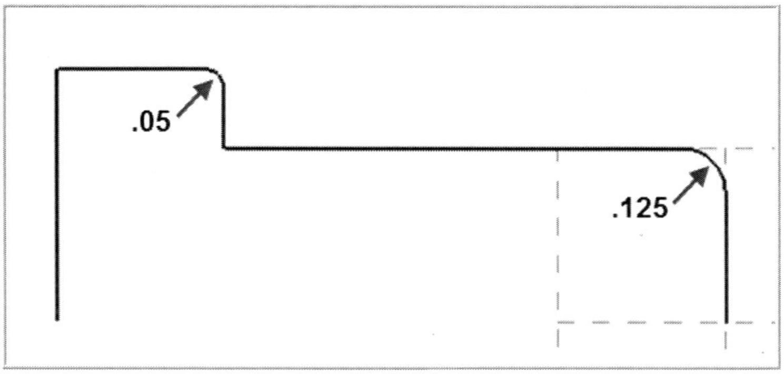

➲ **Create the .050 fillet radius.**

1. Select the **WIREFRAME** tab at the top of the screen and in the **Modify** section click on **Fillet Entities**.

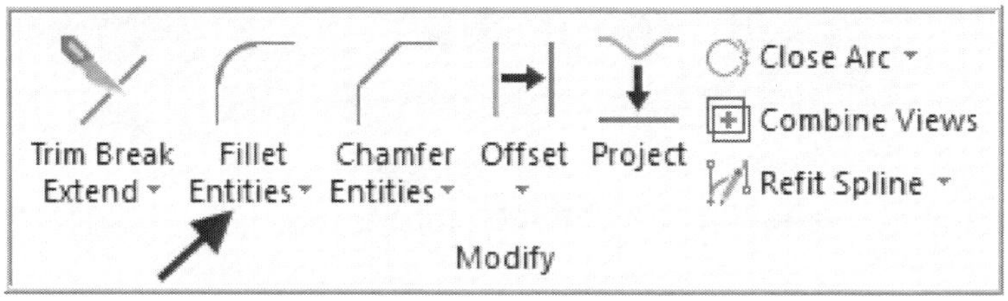

2. The **Fillet Entities** panel appears. If required activate the **Style** to **Normal** and enter a value of **0.05** for **Radius**.
3. Ensure the **Trim** entities box at the bottom of the panel is check marked to turn the trim on.

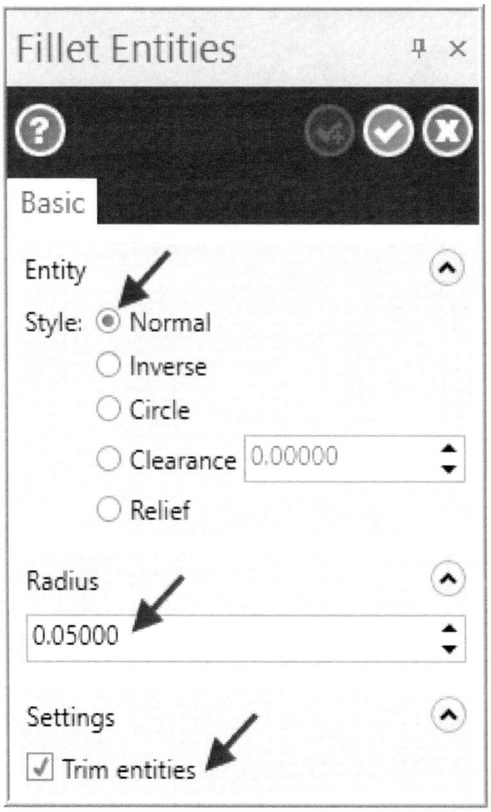

Use **Fillet Entities** to apply fillets to existing entities.

Before selecting the entities to fillet, choose the fillet style (Normal, Inverse, Circle, Clearance, Relief), and enter the desired radius value. Then choose the first and second entities.

Mastercam's auto-preview feature displays a temporary fillet at the selected location.

You can also choose to trim to the fillet or to leave the selected lines untrimmed.

Trimming is the default, so for no trimming, un-check **Trim entities**.

4. Click on **line 1** and then click on **Line 2** as shown below:

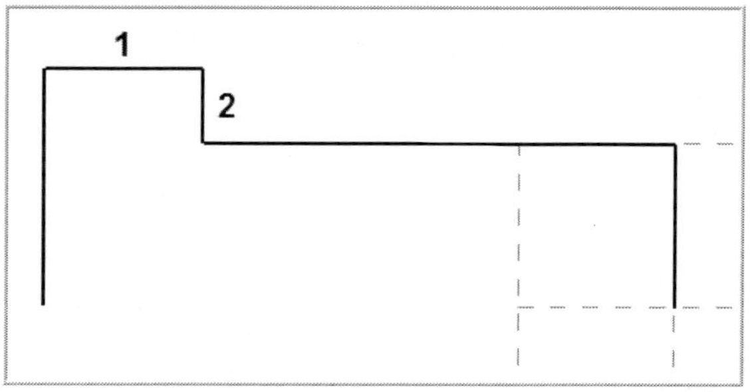

5. Click on the **OK and Create New Operation** icon .
6. The completed fillet is shown below:

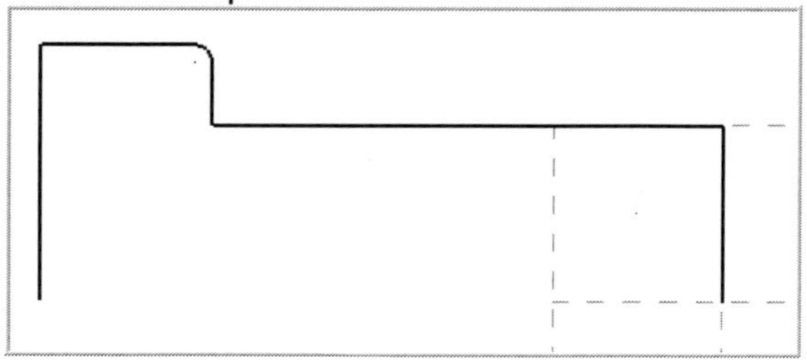

➲ **Create the .125 radius**

7. Click in the space for radius and input 0**.125** and then hit the enter key.

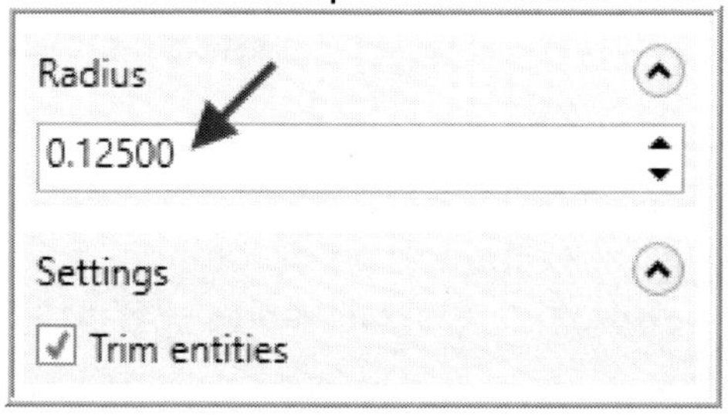

8. Click on **Line 1** and then click on **Line 2** as shown below:

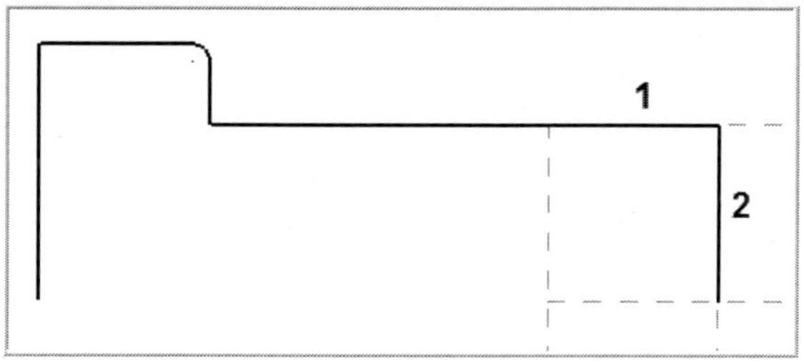

9. Click on the **OK** icon  to complete this feature.

➲ The completed fillet is shown below:

➲ This completes the geometry for this part.

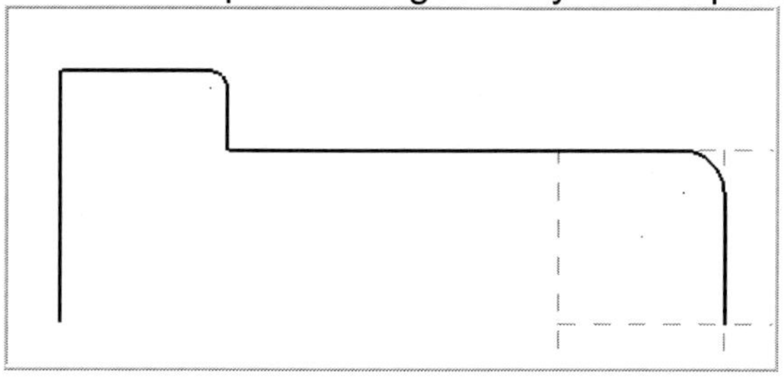

TASK 5:
SAVE THE DRAWING

1. Select **File** at the top left corner of the screen.
2. Select **Save As**.

3. Click on the Browse icon.

4. In the **File name** box, type **LATHE-LESSON-1**.
5. Browse to an appropriate location.
6. Select the **Save** button to save the file and complete this function.

Toolpath Creation

TASK 6:
DEFINING THE STOCK AND CHUCK PARAMETERS

1. Select the **VIEW** tab at the top of the screen.
2. Select the **Fit** icon in the **Zoom** section. Next select **Unzoom 50%** to shrink the display.

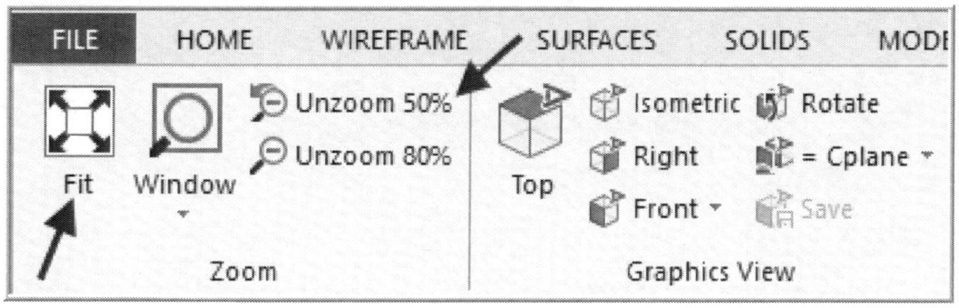

3. Still on the **View tab** and click on **Toolpaths** to display the Toolpaths Manager.

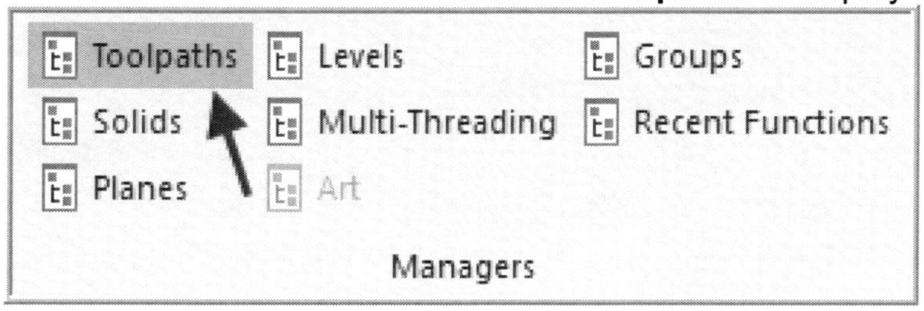

4. Ensure your screen looks like the image below:
   A. The Toolpaths Manager is open.
   B. The Properties icon displays **Lathe Default**. If it is not turn to the section titled **Setting the Environment** at the beginning of this book.
   C. The **Lathe - Lesson-1** Geometry is displayed.

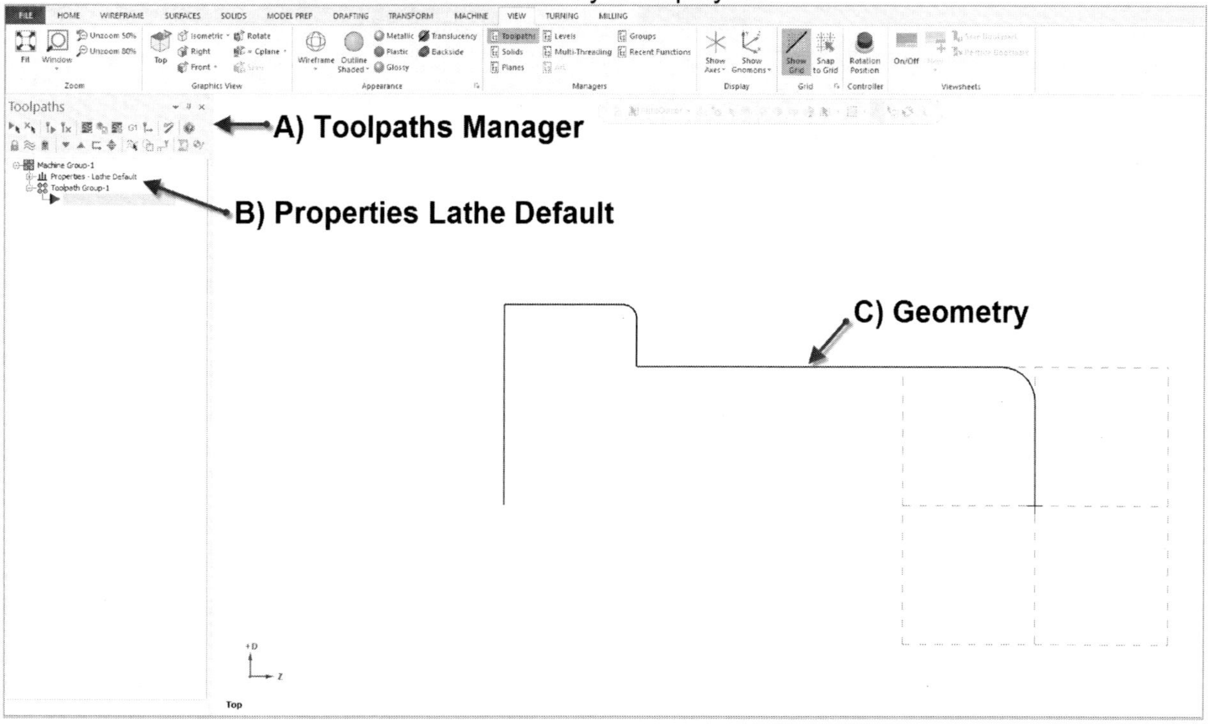

5. Select the plus in front of **Properties** to expand the Machine Group Properties, if required.

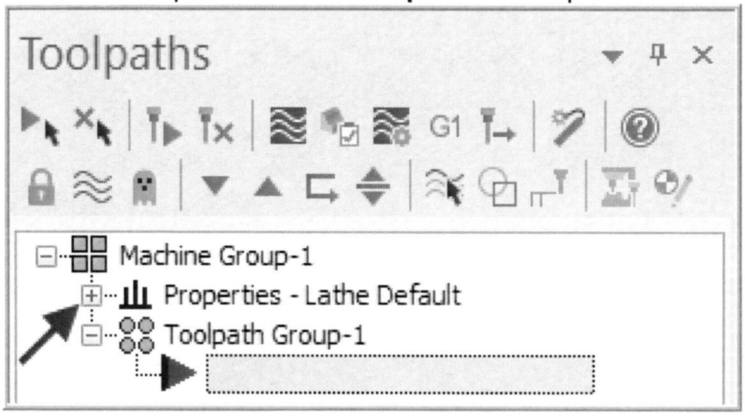

6. **This is optional** - To expand the toolpaths manager window, click on the outside of the window with the left mouse button (hold the button down) and drag it to the right.

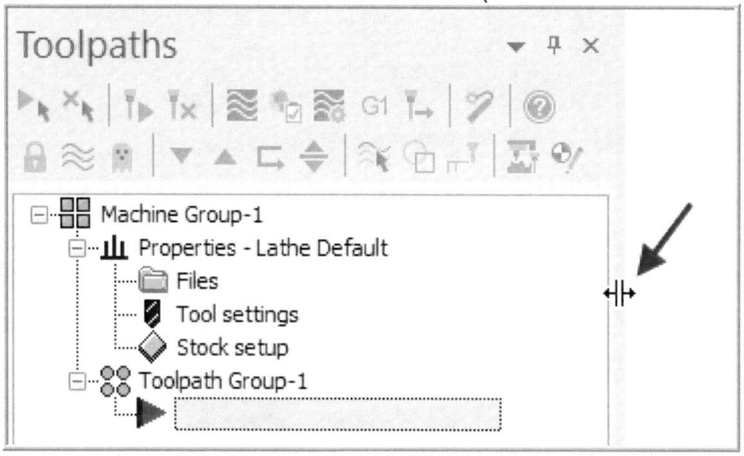

7. Select **Stock setup** in the Toolpaths Manager window.

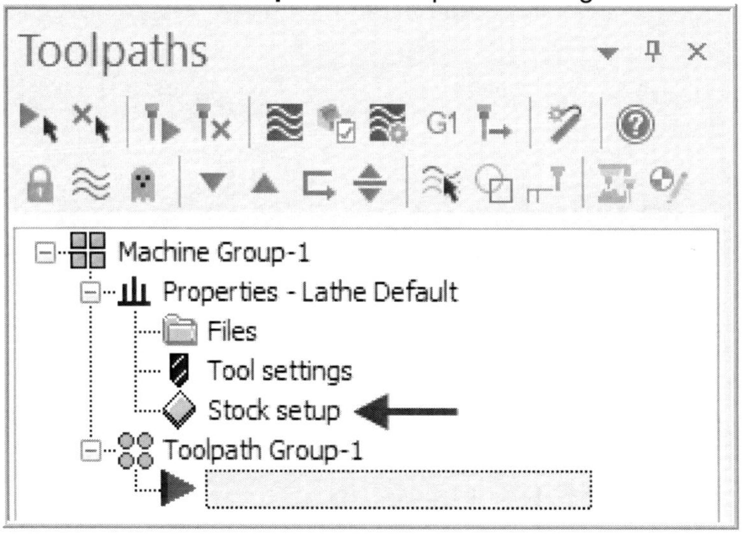

8. Select the **Stock Properties** button in the Stock Setup page as shown in the screenshot below:

Note: To learn more about Stock Setup refer to the Tips and Techniques content in the Online Course Instruction.

9. In the **Machine Component Manager-Stock** window click on the **Geometry** button and select **Cylinder** as shown below, if required:

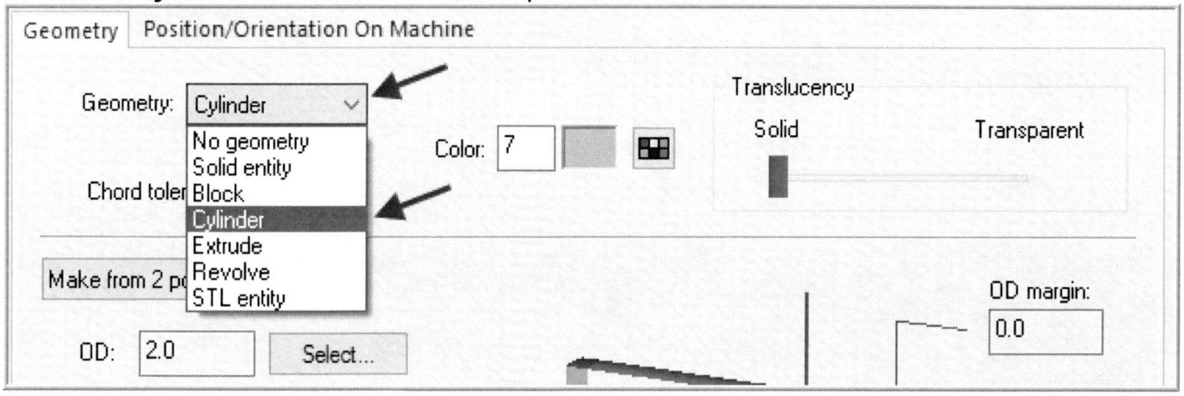

10. In the **Stock** setup activate **Use Margins** and set the values as shown below. **Note** that **Axis** is set to **–Z**.

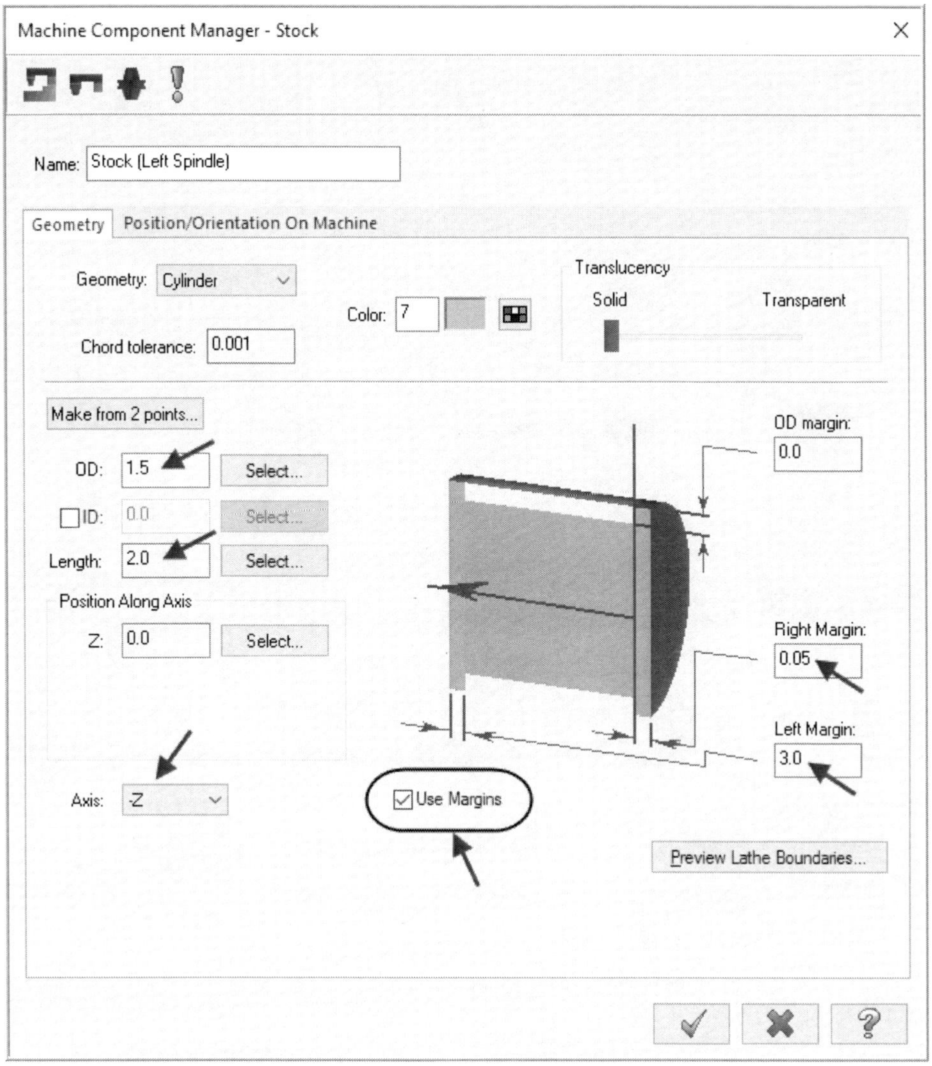

11. Click on the **OK** icon  to complete this feature.
12. Still on the Stock Setup page activate **Fit screen to boundaries**.

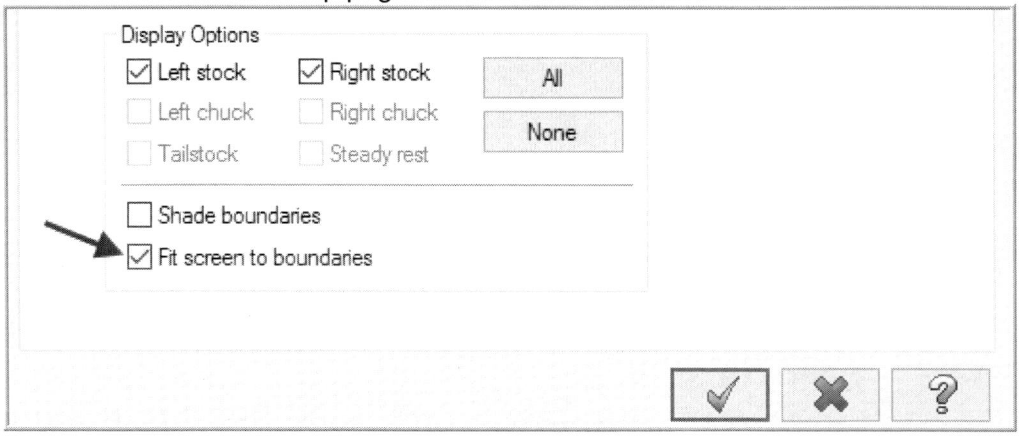

Fit screen to boundaries
Check to determine that the stock, chuck, and tailstock boundaries are included when fitting geometry to the graphics window

13. Select the **Chuck Jaws Properties** button in the Stock Setup page as shown below.

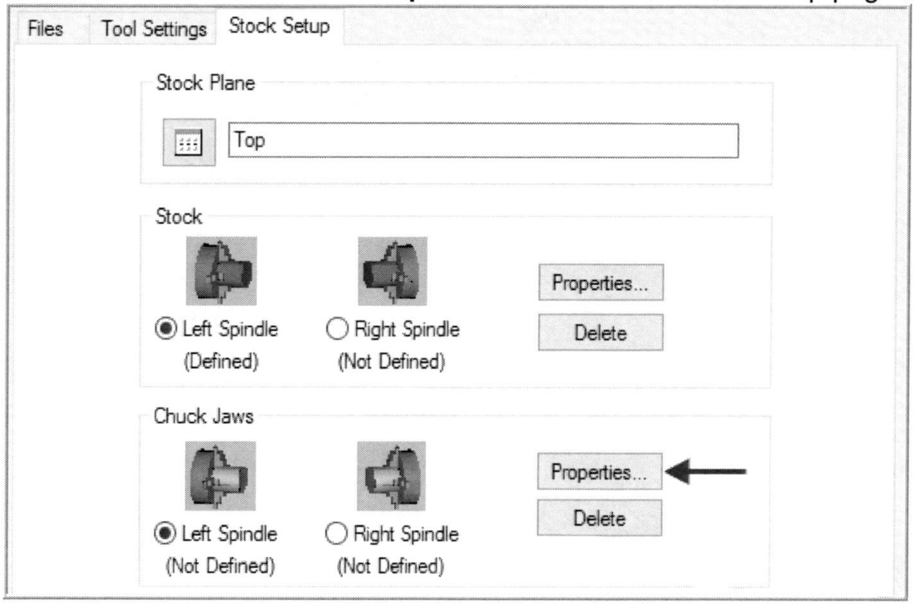

14. In the **Chuck Jaws** setup set the values as shown below:

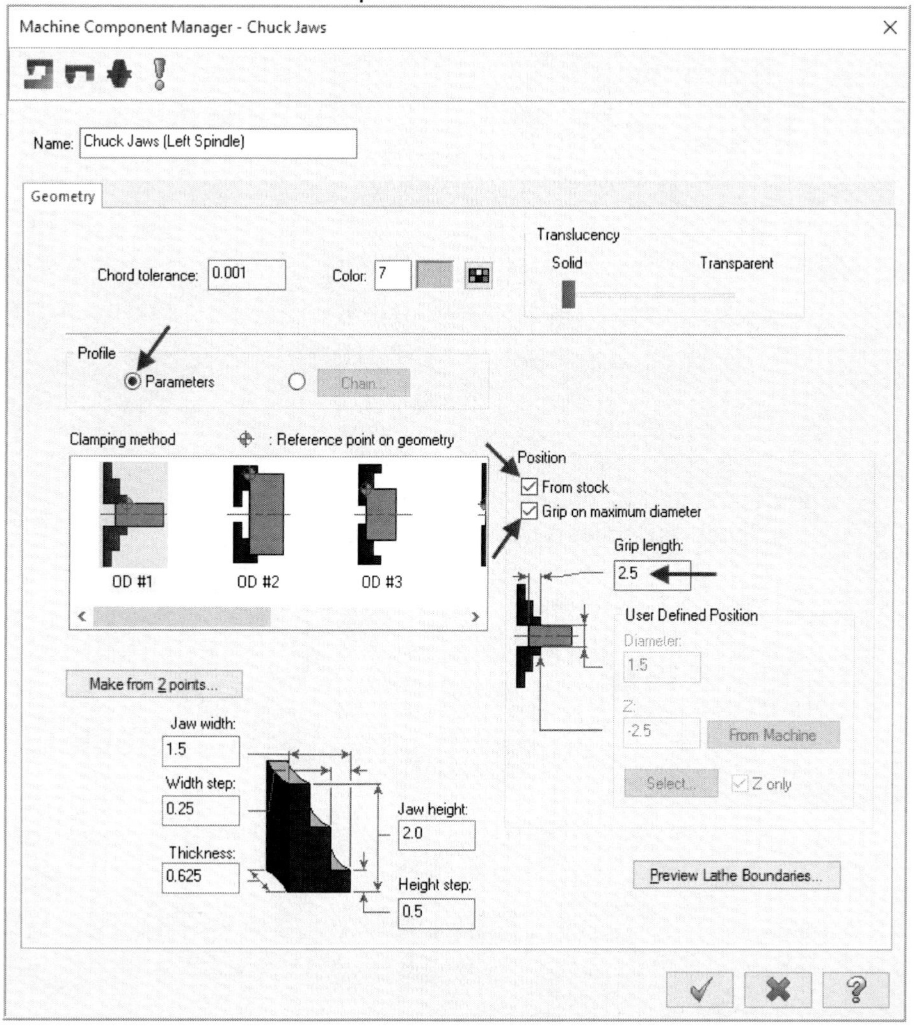

15. Click on the **OK** icon [✓] to complete this feature.

16. Click on the **Tool Settings** page:

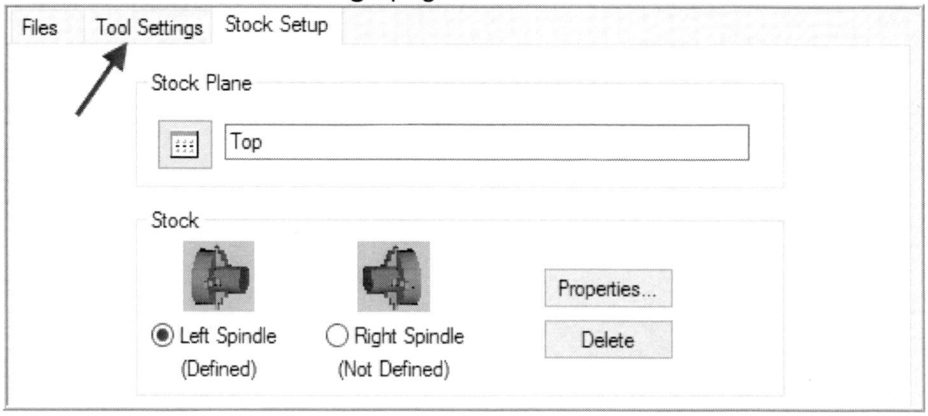

17. Make changes as shown below then click on the **Select** button:

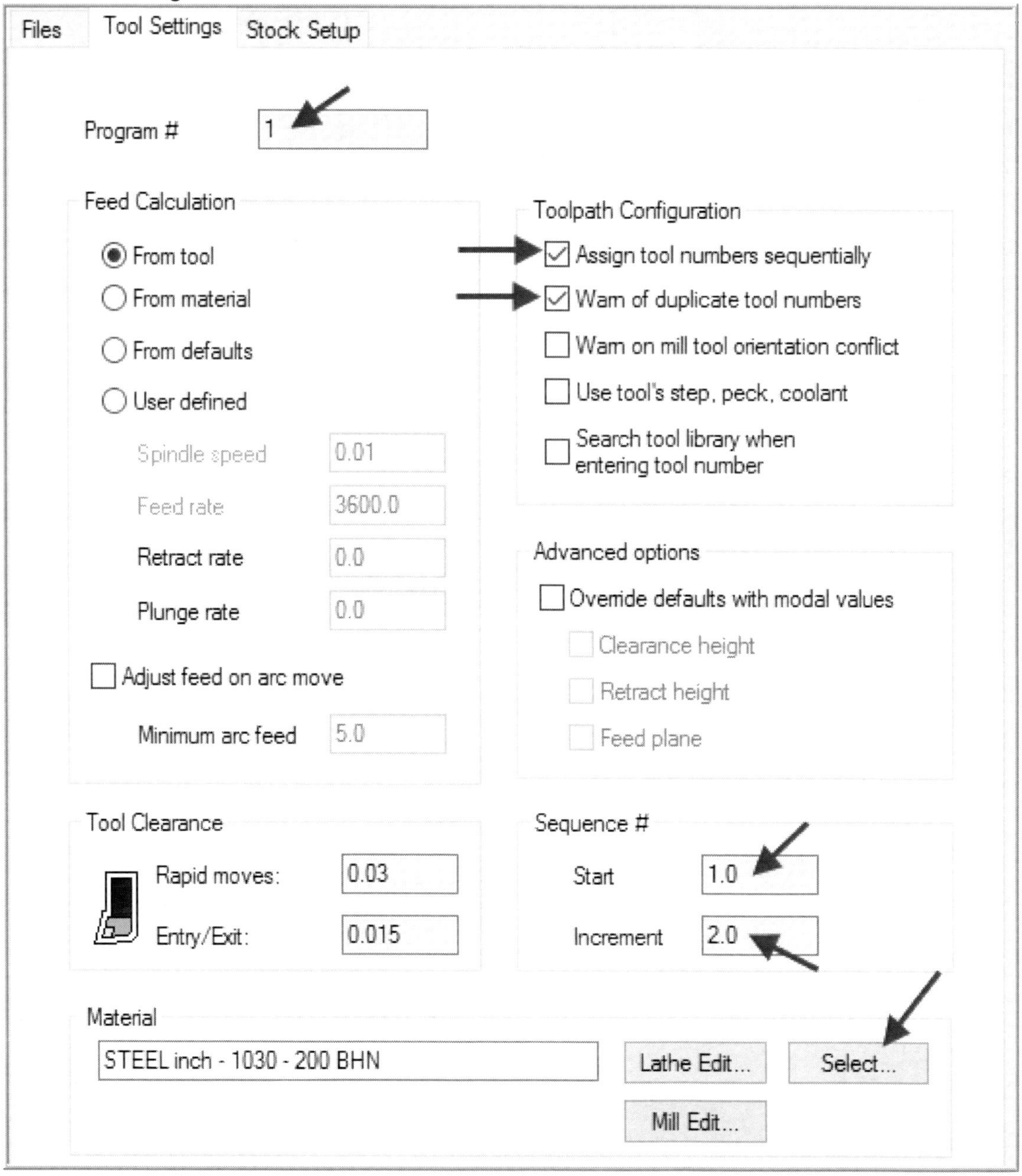

18. Select **Lathe – library** from the drop down **Material List** dialog box as shown below:

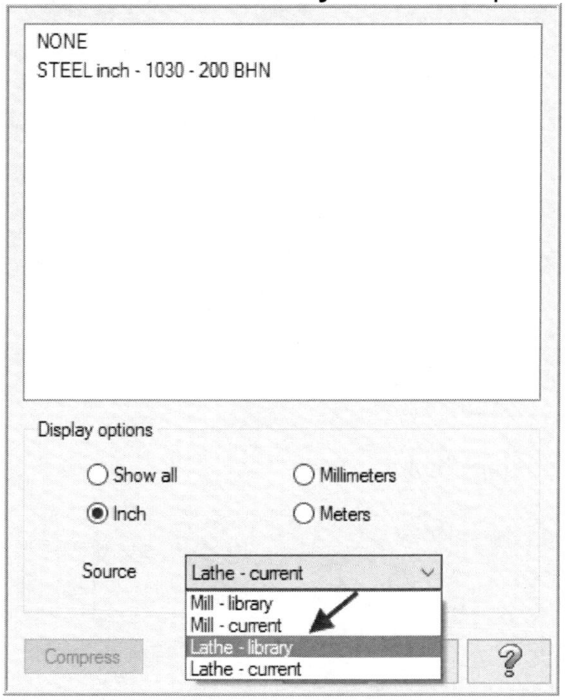

19. Select ALUMINUM inch - 6061 from the Default Materials list.

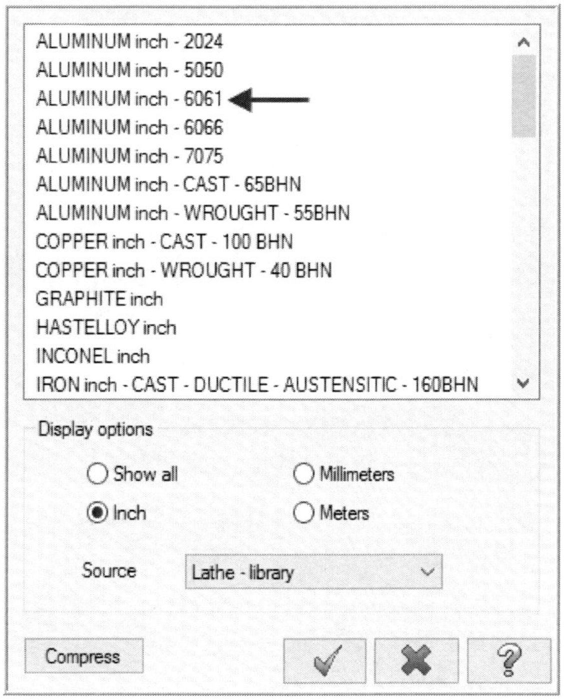

20. Select the OK button .
21. Select the OK button again to complete this Stock Setup function.

22. Right mouse click in the graphics area and click on the **Fit** icon .

➲ Notice the stock setup outline as indicated by broken lines as shown below:

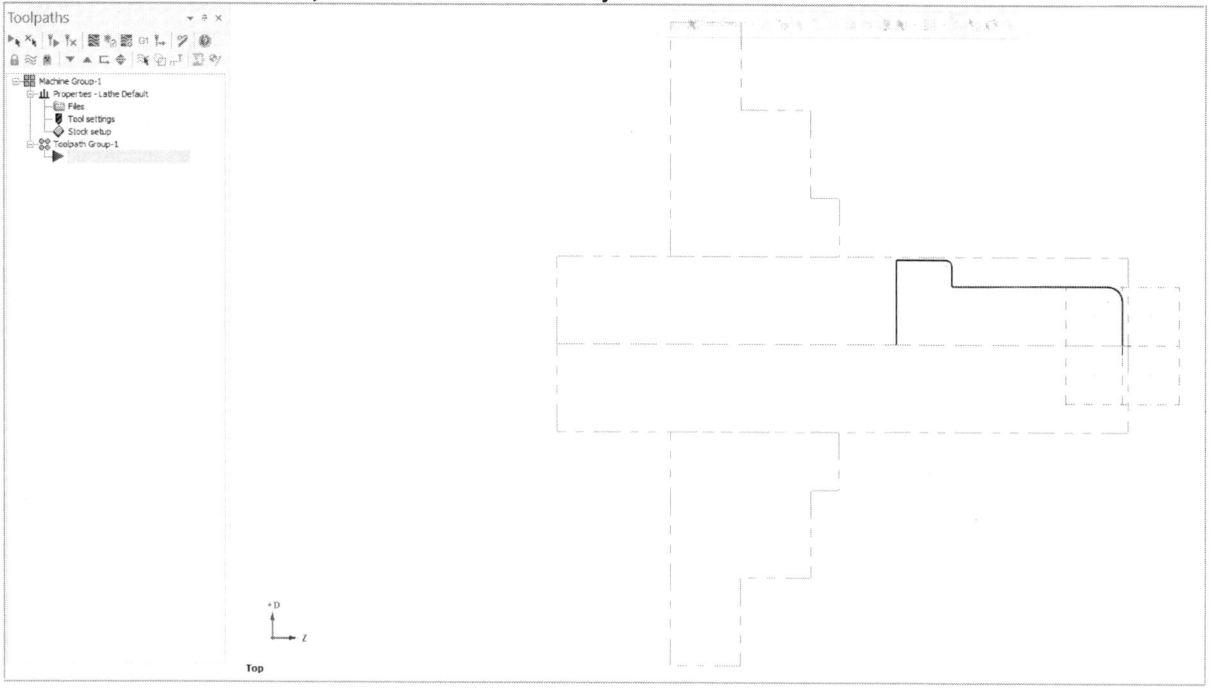

TASK 7:
FACE THE FRONT OF THE PART:

➲ In this task you will use a facing tool to face the front of the part in one cut.

1. If required right mouse click in the graphics area and click on the **Fit** icon.
2. Select the **TURNING** tab at the top right side of the screen.
3. Now select **Face** in the **General** section.

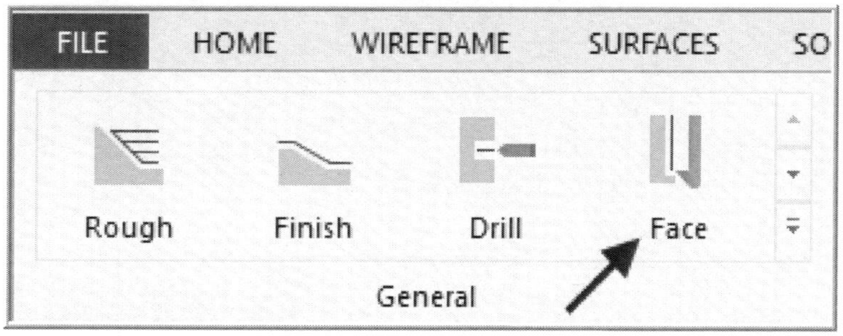

Face Toolpaths
Face toolpaths prepare the face of the part for further machining. Once the face of the part is clean, you can use it to set tools or determine tool offsets.

You do not need to chain any geometry to create the toolpath. Instead, the Face Parameters tab gives you two ways to specify how much stock to remove:

- Choose Select Points to return to the graphic window and select two points which represent opposite corners of a rectangle.
- Use the stock boundary. If you do so, you must enter the Z coordinate of the finished face of the part in the Finish Z text box. This option is available only if you have defined the stock boundary in Job Setup.

➲ After selecting the OK button you are confronted with **Toolpath parameters** page. The first task here will be to select **Tool #1 an OD Rough- Right – 80 deg.**

4. Click on **Tool #1 OD ROUGH RIGHT** and make changes in the Toolpath parameters page as shown below.
5. Click on **Coolant,** open up the drop down menu for **Flood** and set it to **On.**

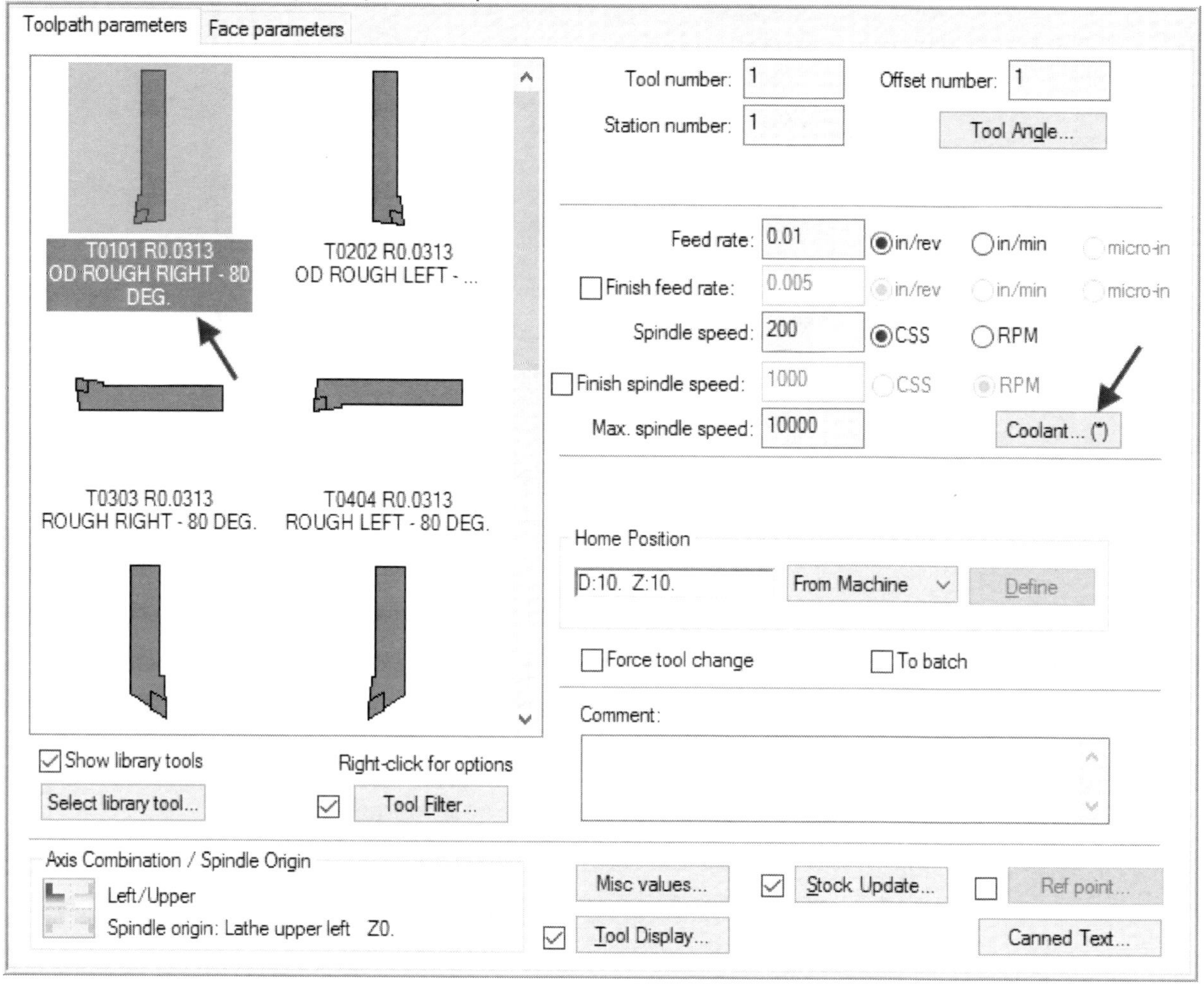

6. Select the **Face parameters** page as shown below:

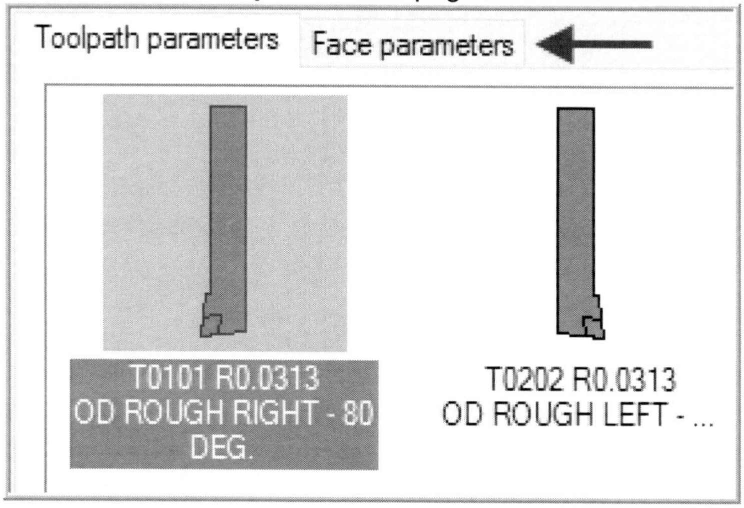

7. Make changes as shown below. **Finish Z** is set to **Zero**.

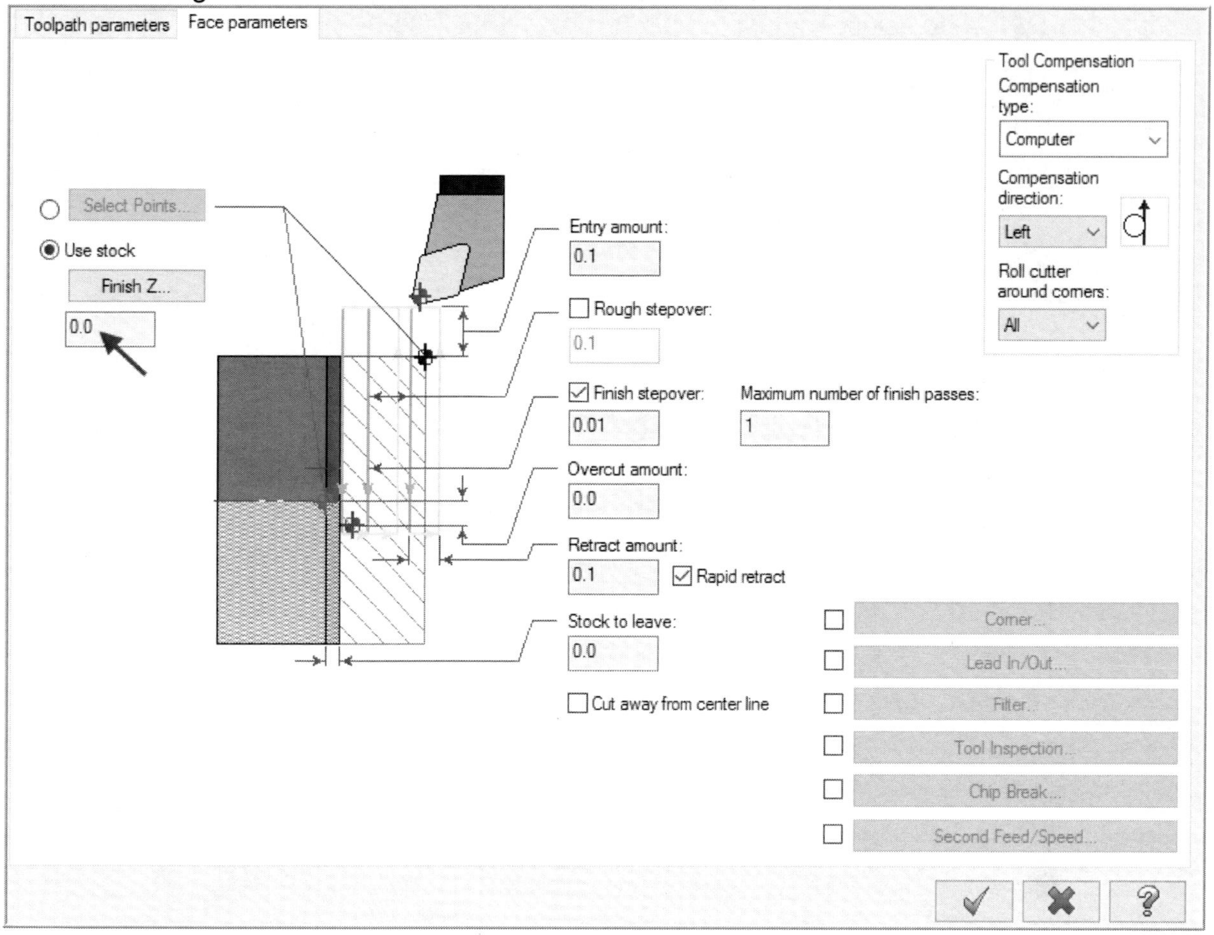

8. Select the OK button  to complete this **Lathe Face** operation.

➲ Your screen should look like the image below:

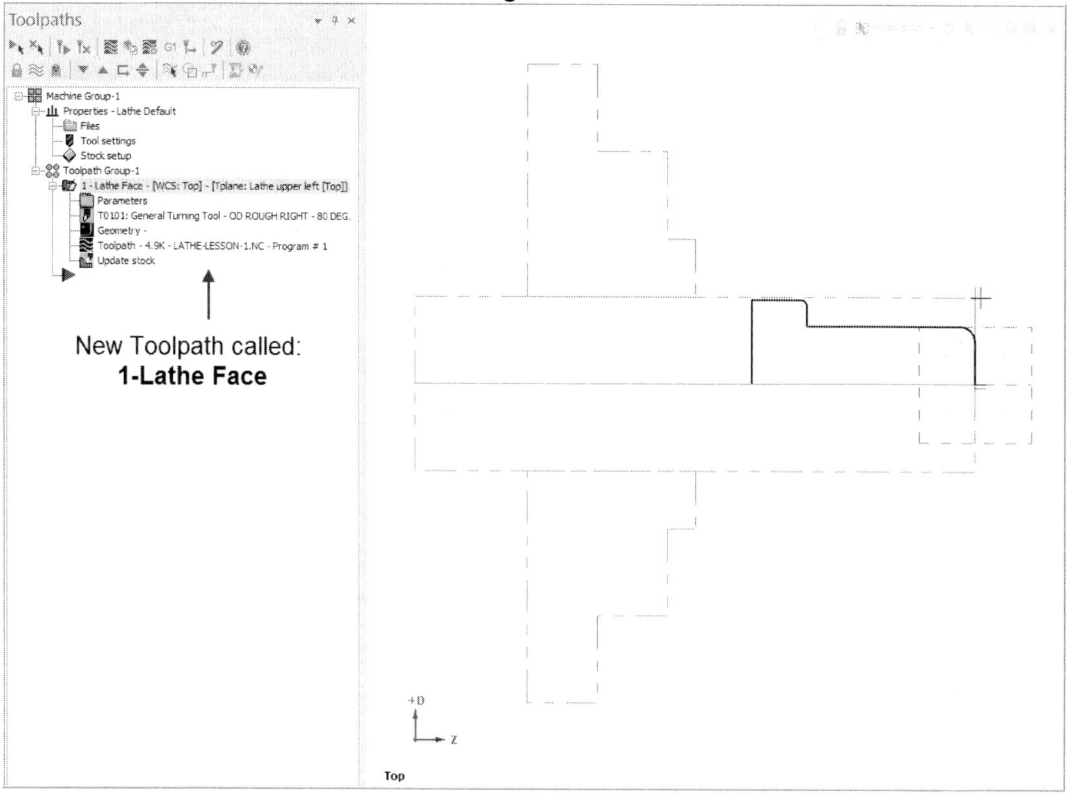

➲ **Note:** the new Toolpath called **1-Lathe Face**. This is where all the toolpath information is kept. If changes are required to this toolpath just click on the parameter icon 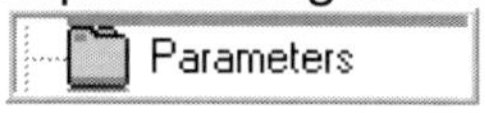 and the Screens from steps 4 through 8 will be available. This is handy in case a mistake was made in setting the toolpath parameters or in case a modification needs to be made.

9. To experience how this works, click on the **Parameters** icon for this Face toolpath.

10. Click on the **Toolpath parameters** tab or the **Face parameters** tab as shown below:

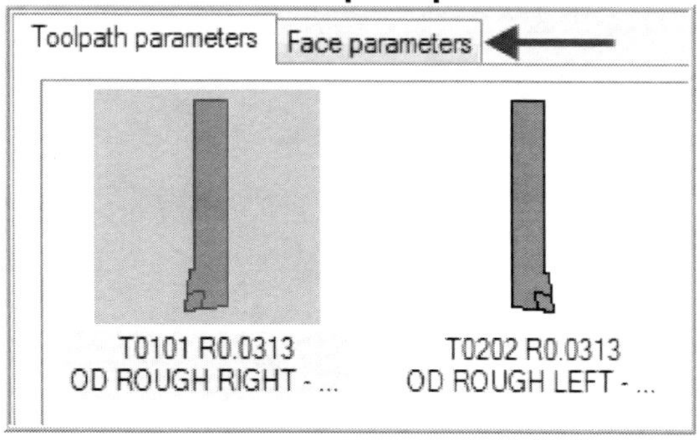

➲ As you can see, all the toolpath settings (parameters) are available in case a change or correction is required.

11. Click on the OK button  to return to the main screen.

TASK 8:
ROUGH THE OUTSIDE DIAMETERS

➲ In this task you will use the same tool as used for the previous facing operation **Tool #1 an OD Rough- Right – 80 deg.**

1. On the **TURNING** tab select **Rough** in the **General** section.

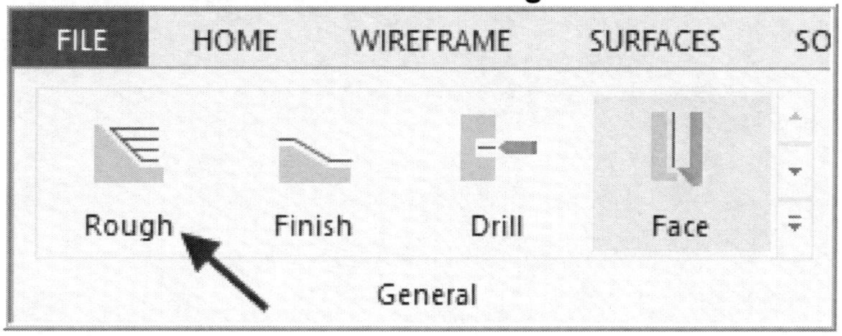

Rough toolpaths
Use rough toolpaths to quickly remove large amounts of stock in preparation for a finish pass. Roughing passes are typically straight cuts parallel to the Z-axis; however, you can set options for plunging into undercut areas.

Standard rough toolpaths also include a semi-finish option, in which the roughing tool makes a final pass which follows the part contour, like a finish pass.

2. In the **Chaining** window the Chaining mode is set to **Partial** by default.

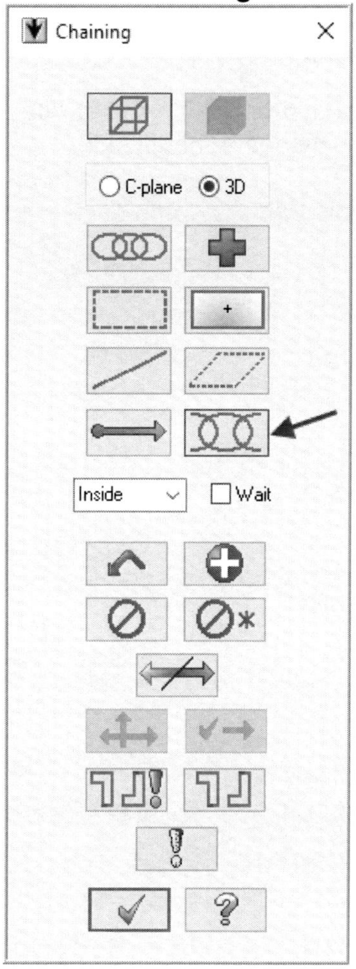

3. Select **Arc 1** as the start of the **Partial chain**.

After you have selected the arc **ensure** that the arrows are pointing up and to the left of the part.

If not select the reverse button in the Chaining dialog box: 

4. Then select **Line 2** as the end entity in this chain.

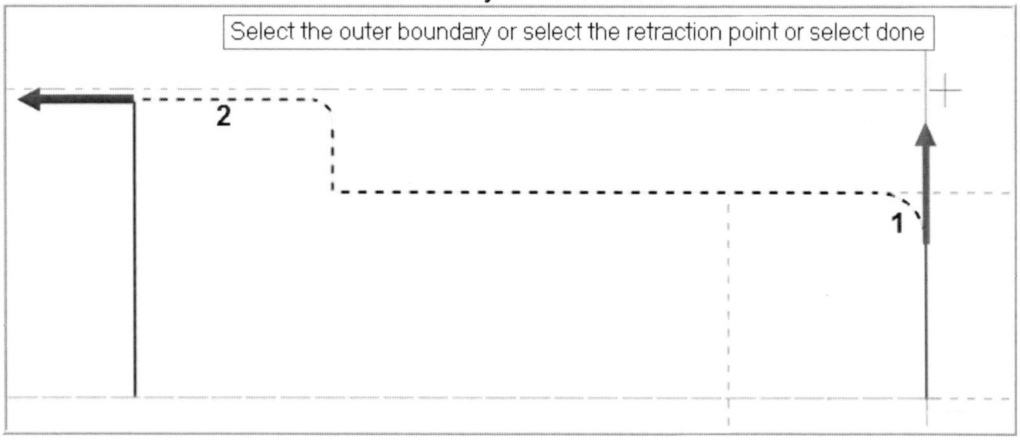

5. Select the **OK** button  to exit the Chaining dialog window.
6. In the **Toolpath parameters** page select the same tool used to face the part **Tool #1 OD ROUGH RIGHT** and make sure the settings are the same as shown below.
7. Click on **Coolant,** open up the drop down menu for **Flood** and set it to **On.**

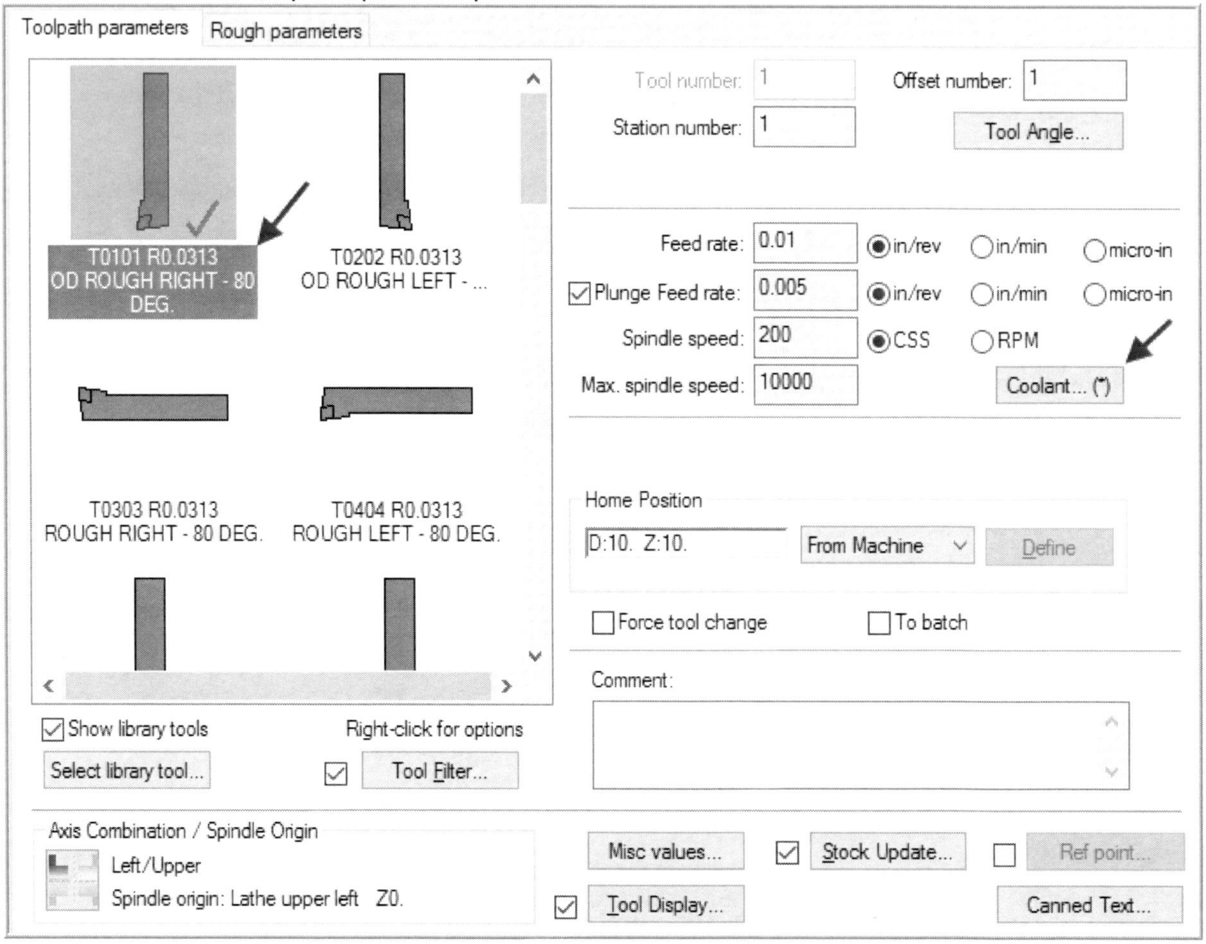

8. Select the **Rough parameters** page and make changes as shown below:

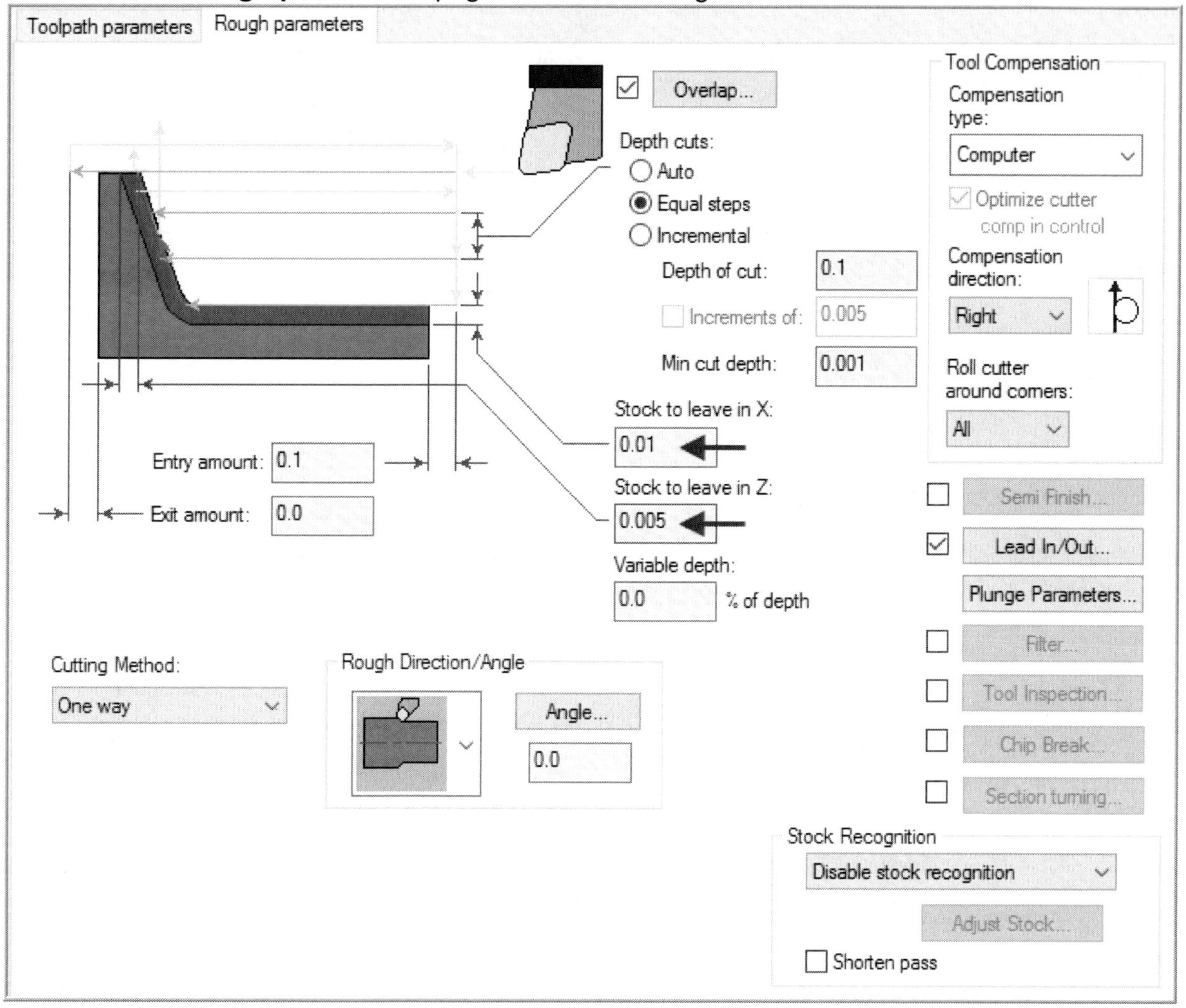

Rough parameters tab
Use this tab to create a lathe rough toolpath. Compared to other types of lathe roughing toolpaths, this tab offers you the most complete set of roughing options.

-Select whether the cutting direction is one-way or zig-zag.

-Select a toolpath orientation from the Rough Direction/Angle drop-down.

-Use the pictures as a guide for entering the different toolpath dimensions.

-Use the options on the right side of the tab to select the type of cutter compensation.

- Complete the toolpath by adding advanced features such as a semi-finish pass, lead in/out moves, and toolpath filtering.

9. Select the **Lead In/Out** button select the **Lead out** page and extend the contour by **.2** as shown below:

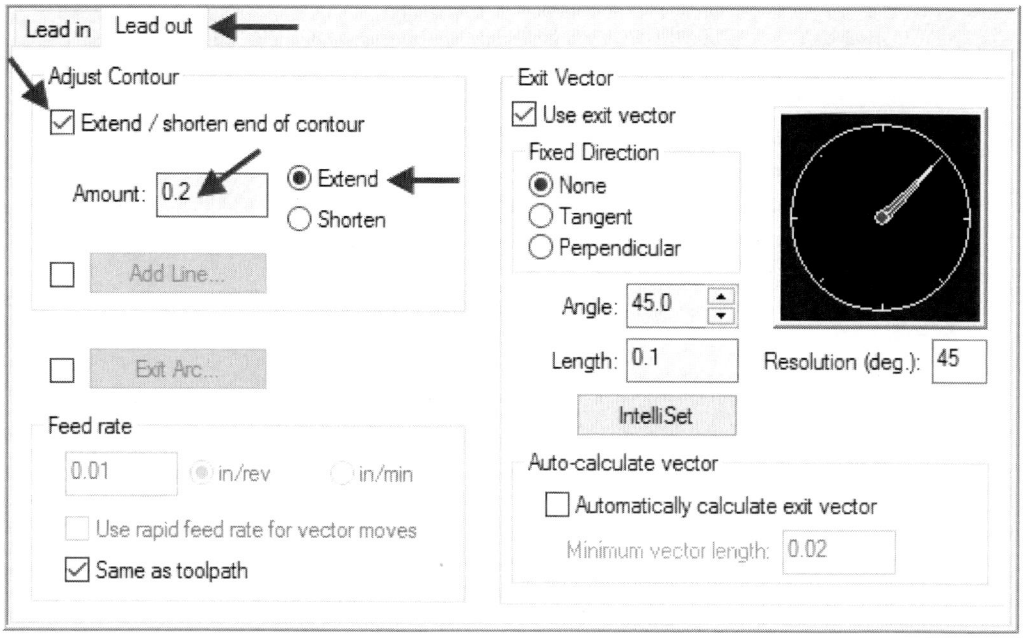

Lead In/Out dialog box
Use this dialog box to control how the tool approaches or retracts from the part for each pass in the toolpath. This eliminates the need to create extra geometry for this purpose.

You can also combine different types of moves. For example, you can extend a contour and lead in to it with a tangent arc.

The Lead In and Lead Out tabs have identical options for creating entry and exit moves, letting you set different values for each move.

10. Select the **OK** button  to exit this function.
11. Select the **OK** button  to exit Rough Parameters.

TASK 9:
FINISH THE OUTSIDE DIAMETERS

➲ In this task you will finish the outside diameters in one cut using **Tool #1 an OD Rough-Right – 80 deg.**

1. On the **TURNING** tab select **Finish** in the **General** section.

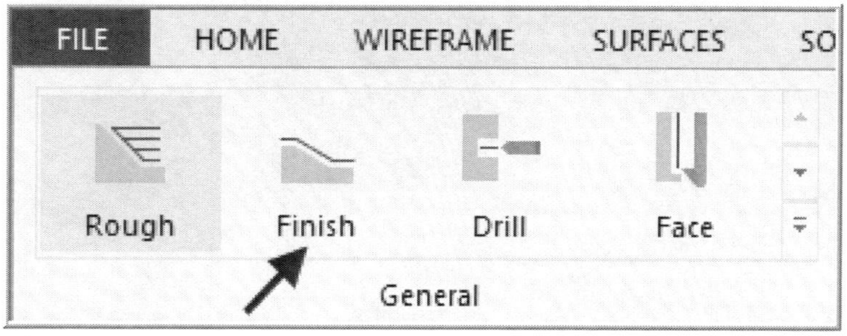

Finish toolpaths
Use finish toolpaths to have the tool follow the contour of chained geometry.

Typically, a finish toolpath follows a roughing toolpath, but this is not required.

You can create a finish toolpath even if no roughing operation has been created.

2. Select **Last** in the Chaining dialog box.

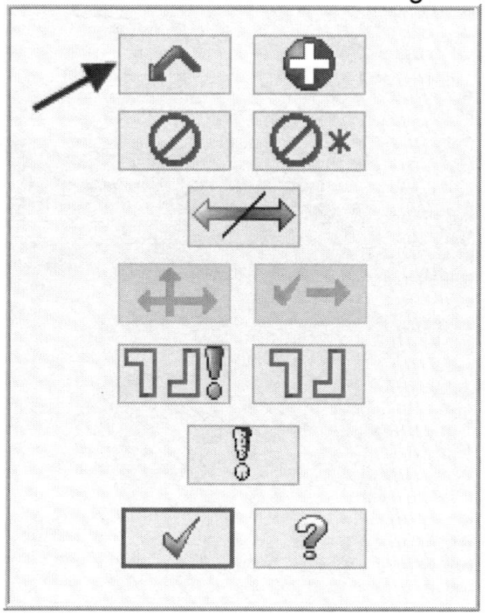

3. Select the **OK** button  to complete the selection.

4. Select the same tool used to rough the part; **Tool #1 OD Rough Right** tool from the tool list and make changes as shown below if required.
5. Click on **Coolant,** open up the drop down menu for **Flood** and set it to **On.**

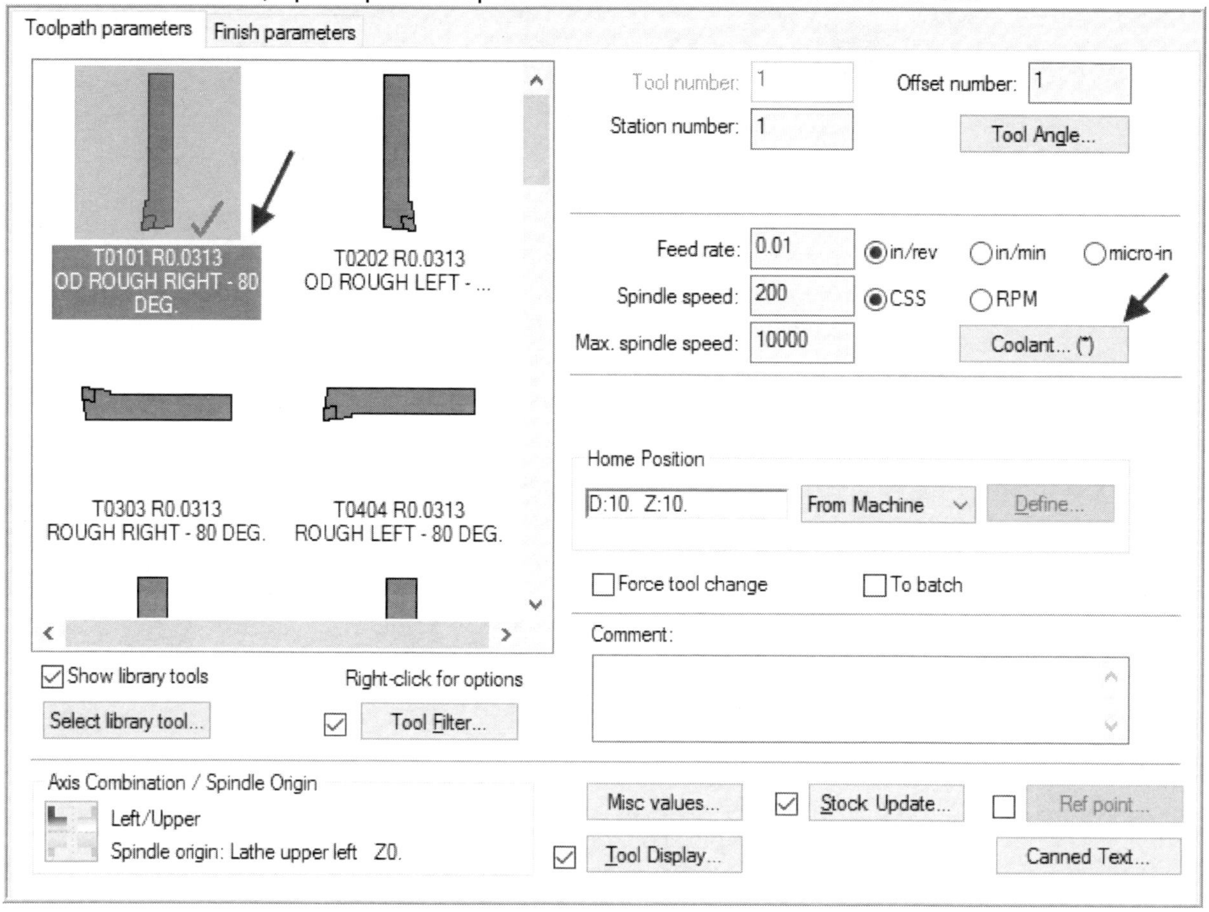

6. Select the **Finish parameters** page and make changes as shown below:

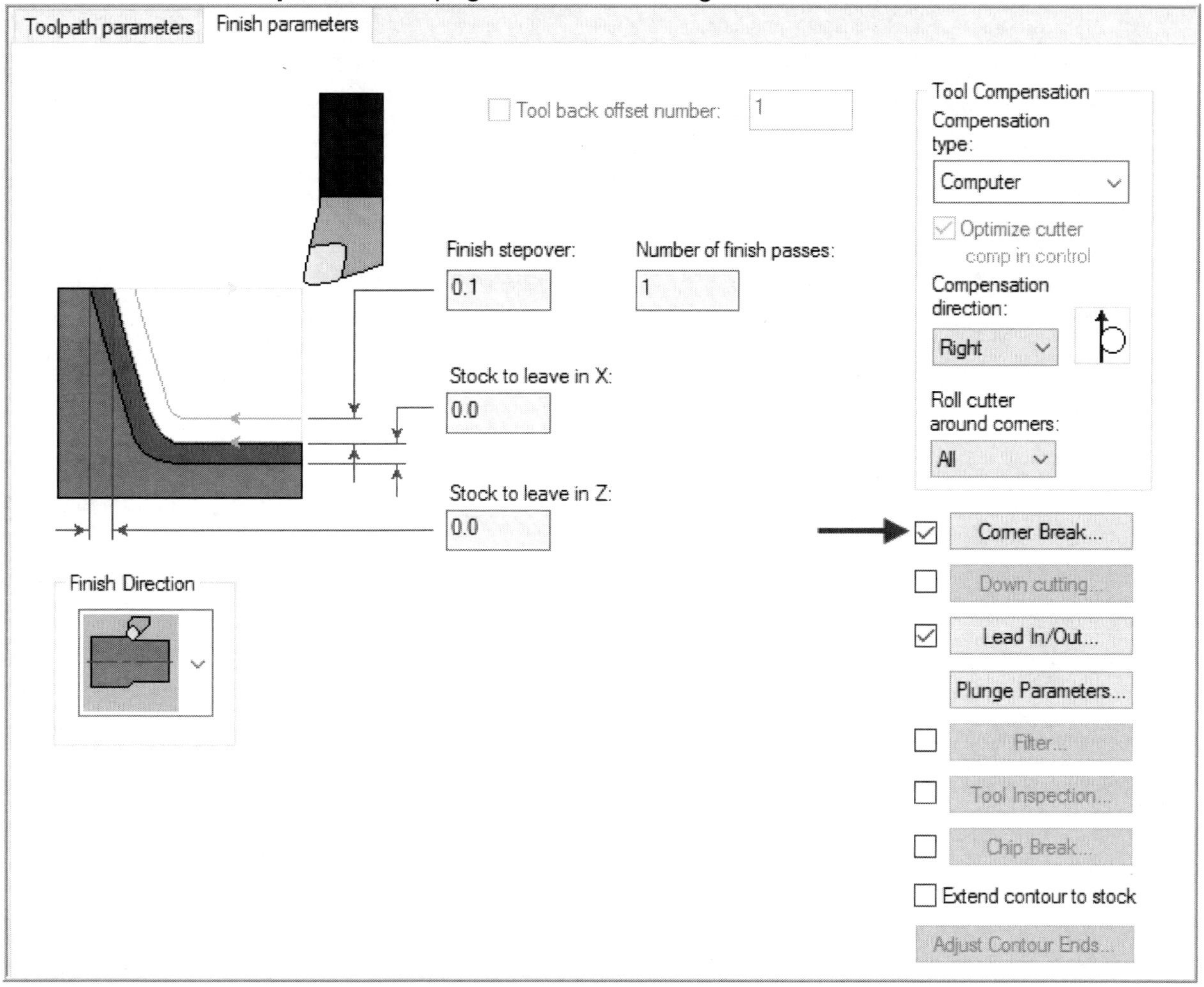

Corner Break:
Select the check box to automatically create radii or chamfers on all outer corners of the toolpath. Click the button to edit the corner break settings.

7. Select the **Corner Break** button and make changes as shown below if required:

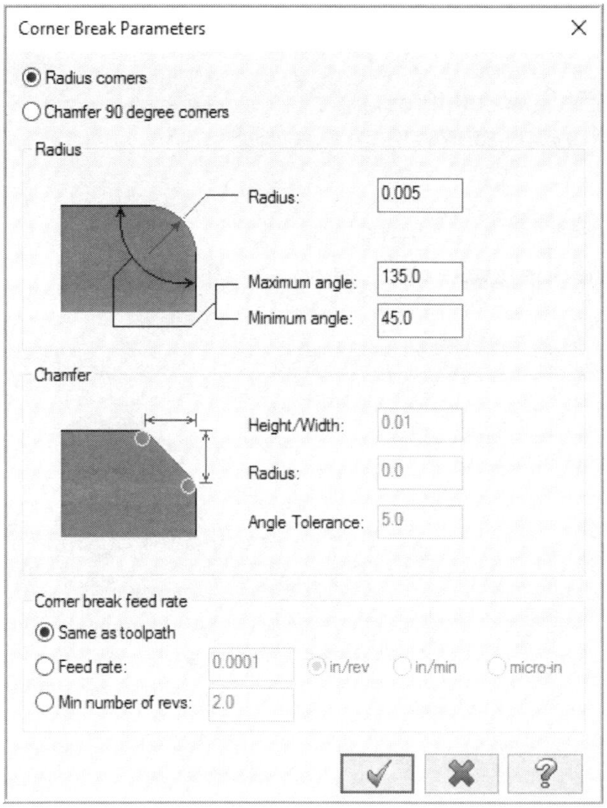

Corner Break
Use this dialog box to automatically create radii or chamfers on all outer corners of lathe finish toolpaths.

You can also set the feed rate when the tool creates the radii or chamfers.

8. Select the **OK** button to complete this feature and exit **Corner Break**.
9. Select the **Lead In/Out** button select the **Lead out** page and extend the contour by **0.2** as shown below:

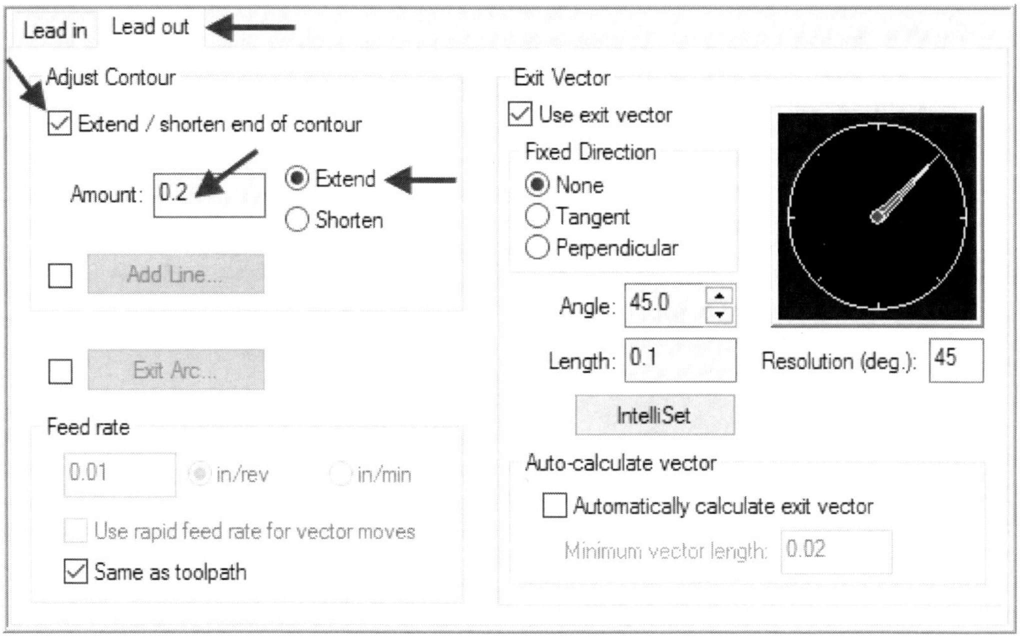

10. Select the **OK** button to exit this function.
11. Select the **OK** button to exit **Finish parameters.**

TASK 10:
CUTOFF THE PART

➲ In this task you will cutoff the part using a .125 wide cutoff tool.
➲ To begin with you will turn off the display of the toolpaths.

1. Click on the **Select all operations** icon .
2. Now click on the **Toggle display on selected operations**  button **or ALT and T** to show/hide the tool path.

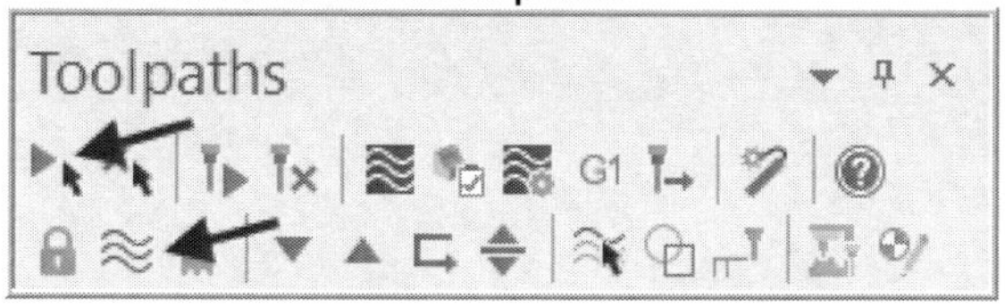

Toolpath Lines visible:

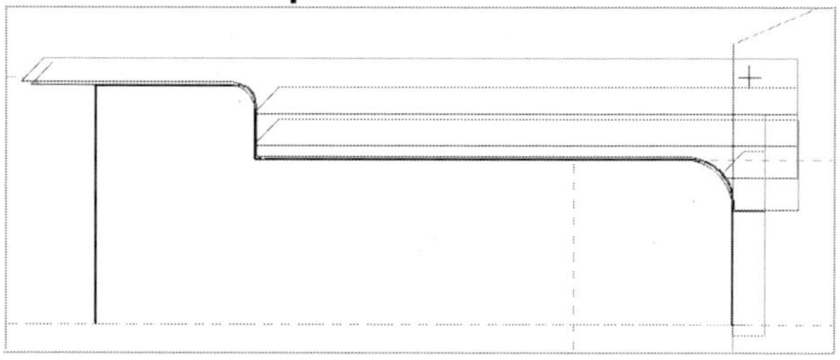

Press Alt T to hide toolpath Lines:

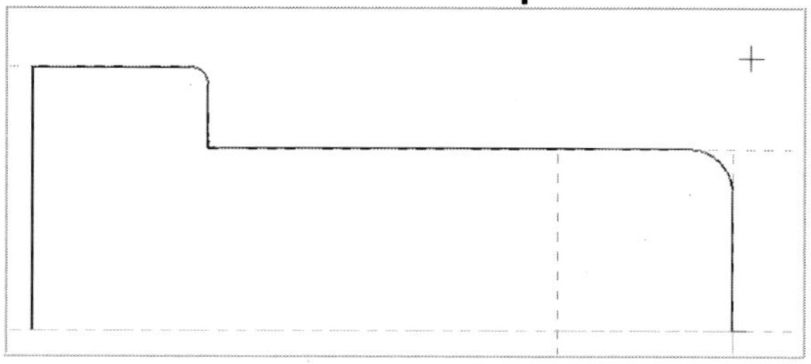

3. Click on the **Expand gallery** down arrow to view additional options in the **General** toolpath section.

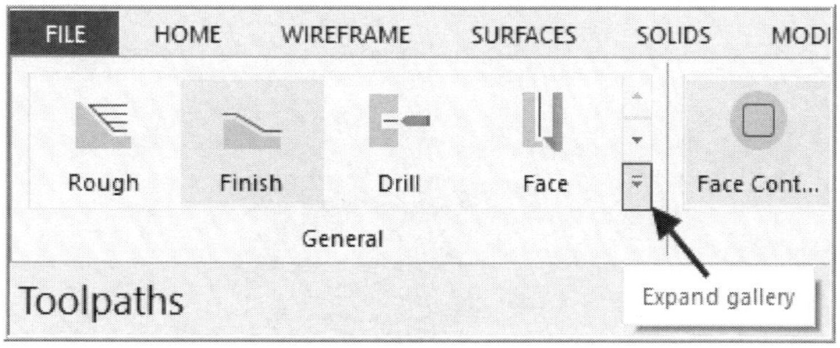

4. In the **General** section select **Cutoff.**

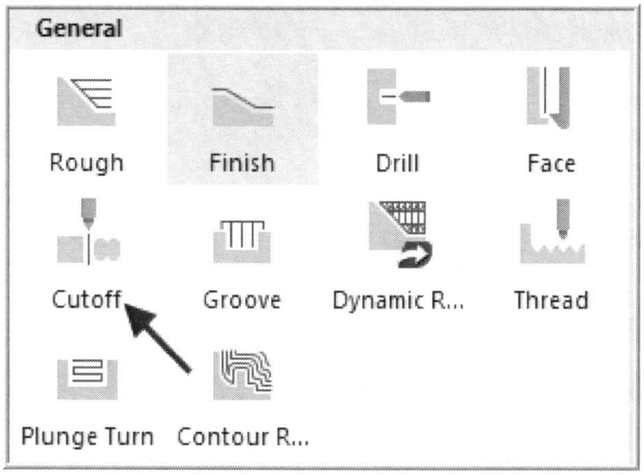

Cutoff toolpaths
Cutoff toolpaths vertically cut off pieces of the part, such as sections of bar stock.

You do not need to chain any geometry for a cutoff toolpath. Instead, you select the point where the part is cut off.

5. Move the cursor over the corner (where **Line 1** and **Line 2** meet) until the visual cue  for End point displays and then click on this point as shown below:

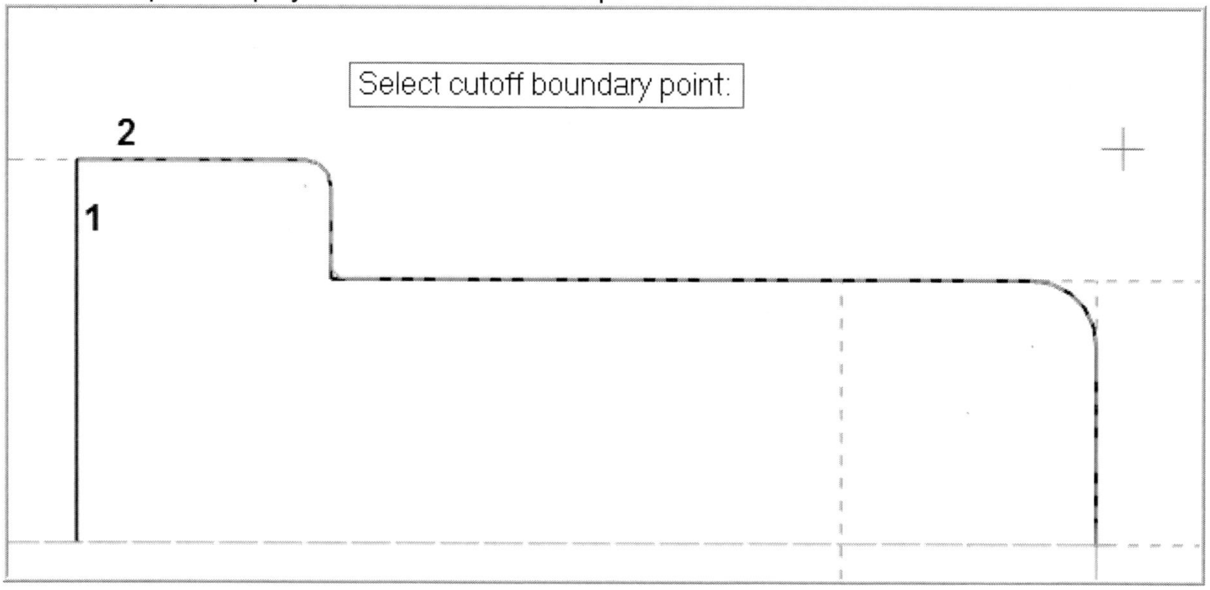

6. Scroll down in the tool window and select the **OD Cutoff Right Width .125** tool and make changes as shown below in the **Toolpath parameters** page.
7. Click on **Coolant,** open up the drop down menu for **Flood** and set it to **On.**

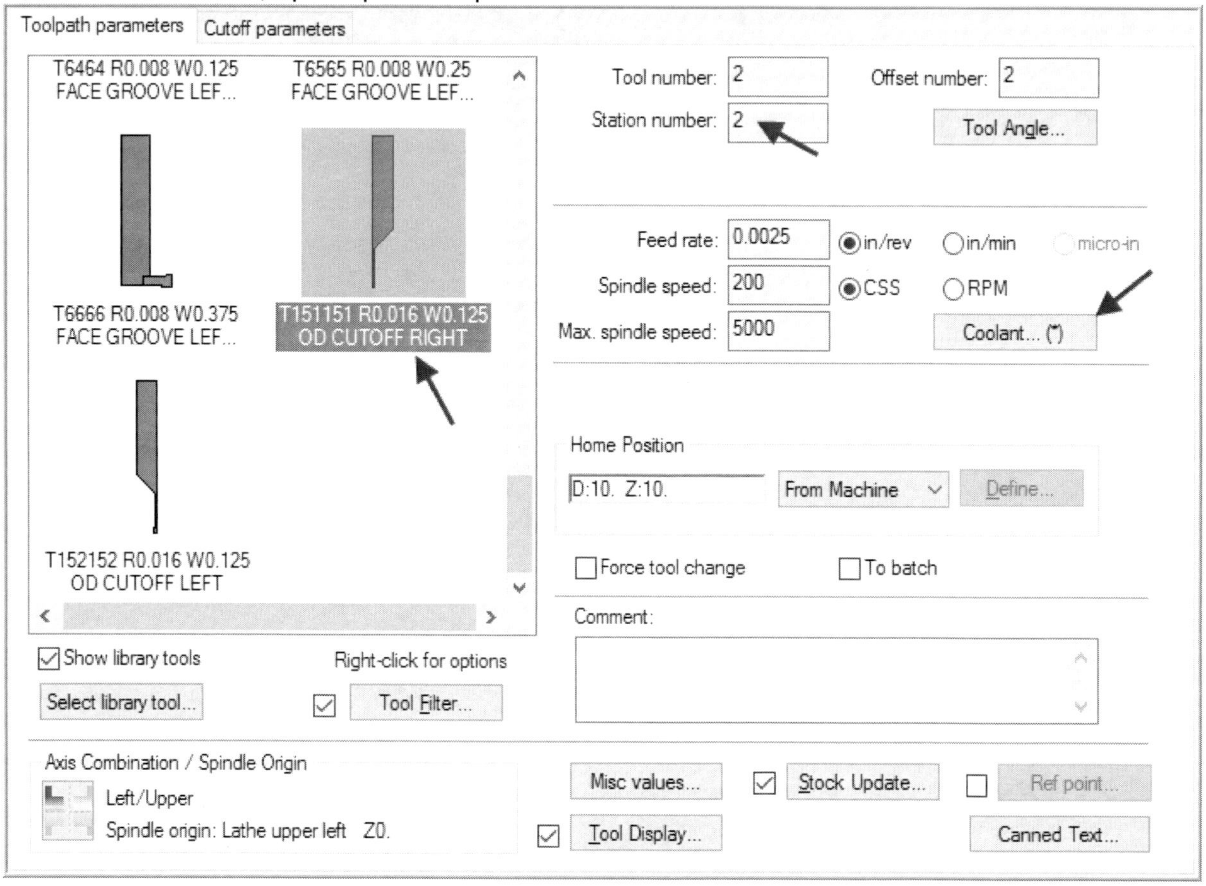

8. Click on the **Stock Update...** button.

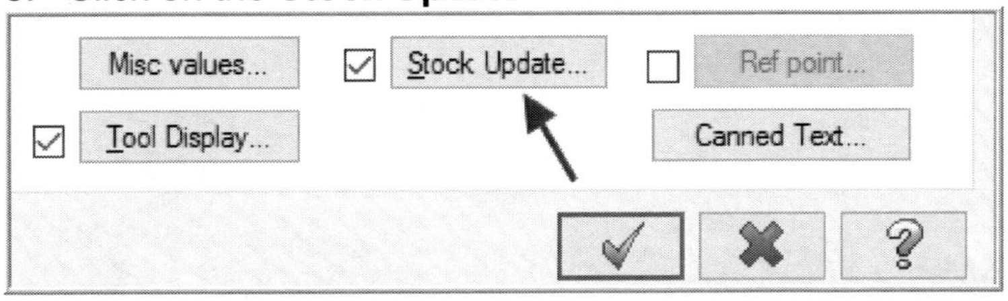

9. Activate **Keep both pieces**.

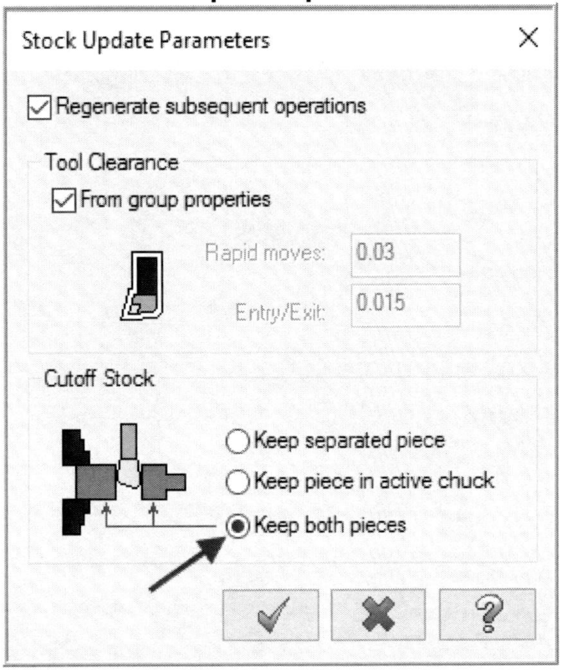

Keep separated piece
Select to display the part boundary after the part is cut off.

Keep piece in active chuck
Select to display the stock boundary after the part is cut off.

Keep both pieces
Select to display both the separated piece and the leftover piece. This is useful when the separated piece will be transferred to a sub spindle and you will be machining on both spindles at the same time.

These options are available only with cutoff operations.

10. Select the **OK** button  to exit **Stock Update Parameters.**

11. Select the **Cutoff parameters** page and make changes if required as shown below:

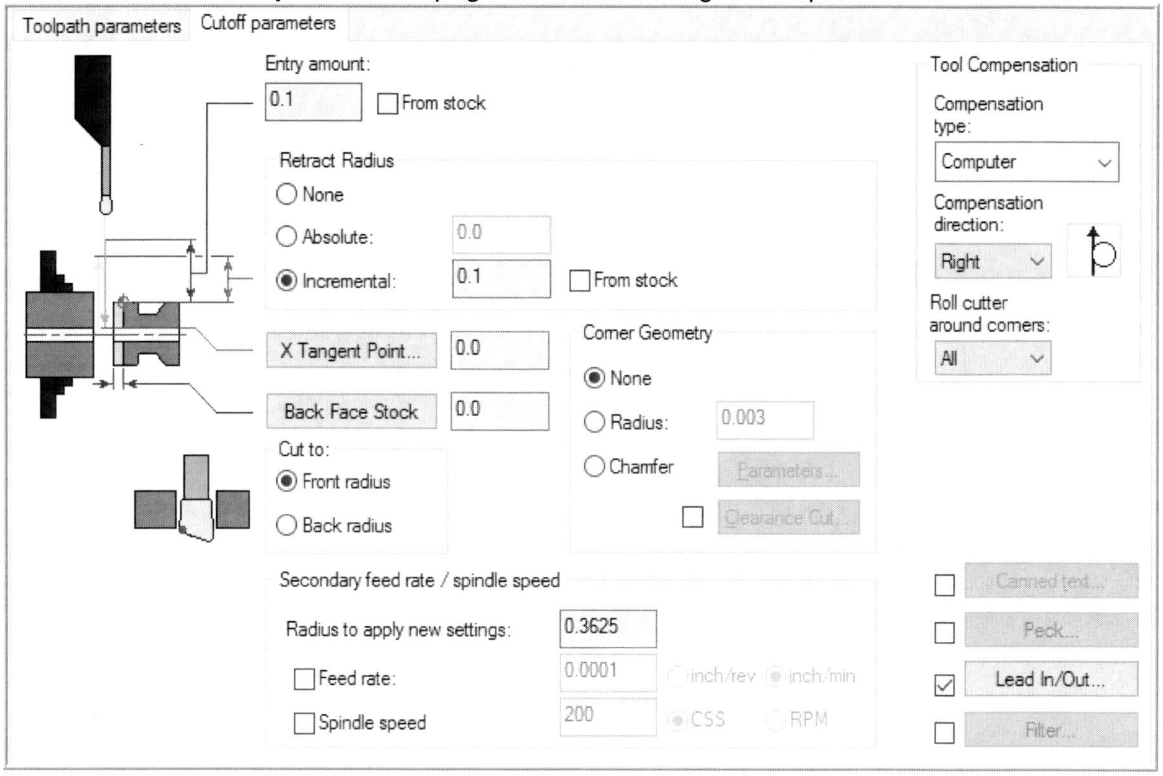

12. Select the **OK** button to exit **Cutoff parameters.**

TASK 11:
BACKPLOT THE TOOLPATH

- In this task you will use Mastercam's Backplot function to view the path the tools take to cut this part.
- Backplot will enable you to review the cutting motions and identify any problem areas when cutting the part.
- When the toolpaths are being Backplotted Mastercam displays tool path information on the right of the screen. Information such as the current tool position in X and Z coordinates.
- **For more information on Backplot refer to the Tips and Techniques content in the Online Course Instruction.**

1. To pick all the operations to Backplot pick the **Select All** icon  circled below:

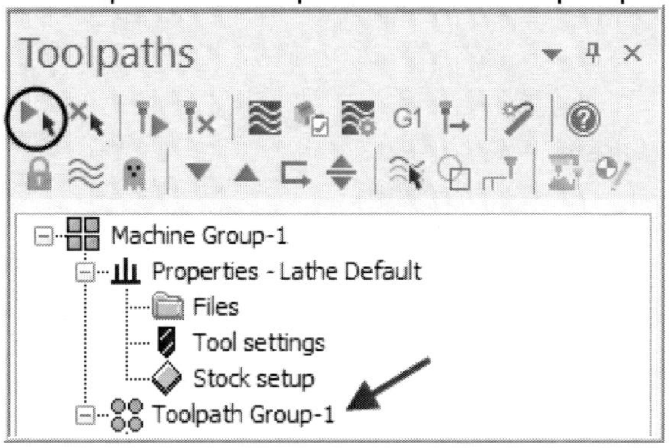

- Another method to **Select all** the operations is by clicking on the **Toolpath Group-1** in the Toolpaths Manager as shown by the arrow above.

2. The next step is to select the **Backplot selected operations** icon shown below:

3. **Maximize** the Backplot/Verify window if required.
4. Select the **Home** tab if required.

5. Activate the options shown below in the **Visibility** section of the **Home** tab.

Initial Stock
This displays the stock before machining.
Click to cycle through three states:
On
Translucent
Off

Tool
This displays the tool during Backplot or Verification. Click to cycle through three states as mentioned above

6. Activate the **Both** option in the **Toolpath section** of the **Home** tab.

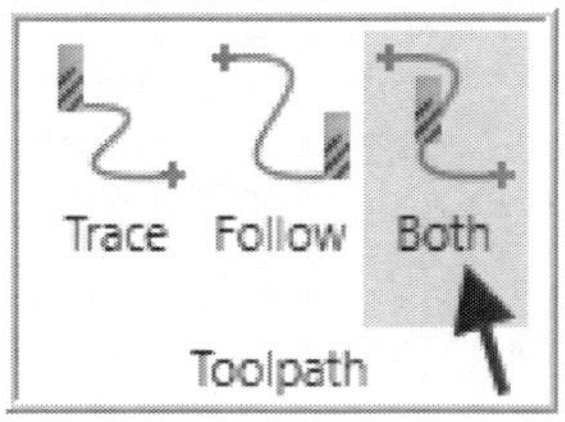

Both
This displays the entire toolpath and the tool as it travels over the displayed toolpath.

7. At the top of the screen select the **View** tab, the **Isometric** icon and then select **Fit**.

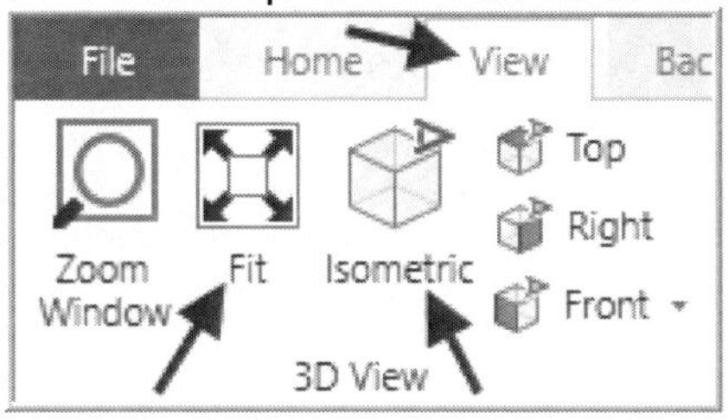

8. In the lower part of the screen now set the run **Speed** to slow by moving the slider bar pointer over to the left as shown below.

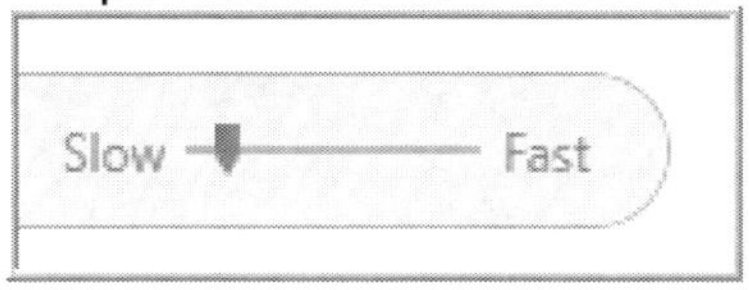

9. Now select the **Play Simulation** button to review the toolpaths.

10. After reviewing the Backplot of the toolpaths select the **Close** button 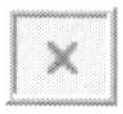 in the top right hand corner to exit Backplot.

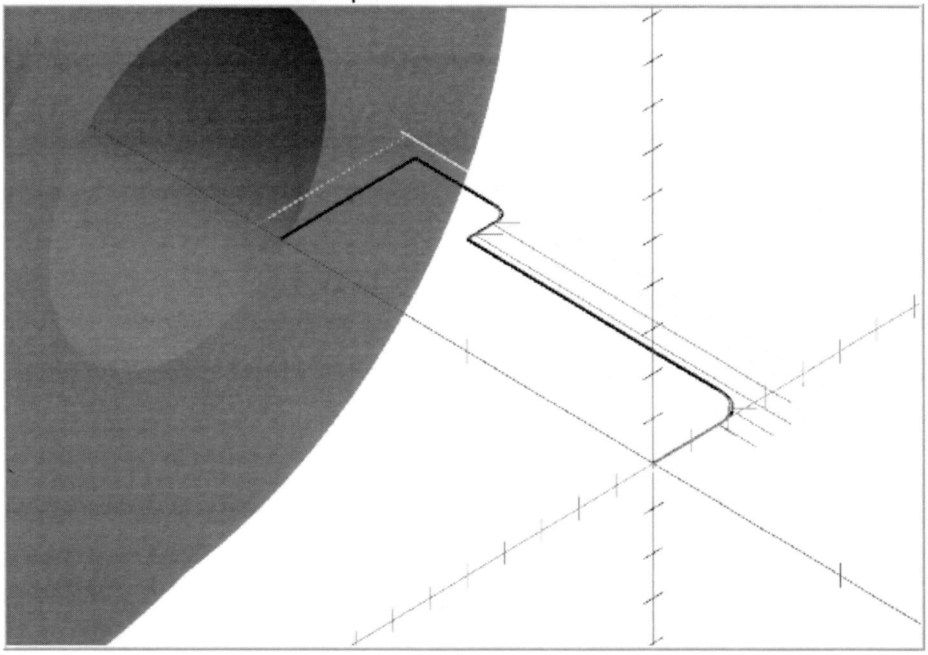

TASK 12:
VERIFY THE TOOLPATH

- Mastercam's Verify utility allows you to use solid models to simulate the machining of a part. The model created by the verification represents the surface finish, and shows collisions, if any exist.
- This allows you to identify and correct program errors before they reach the shop floor.
- Backplot and Verify are very similar. The differences between these two functions are that Backplot offers basic simulation options. Whereas Verify offers material removal, collision checking and precision control.
- **For more information on Verify refer to the Tips and Techniques content in the Online Course Instruction.**

1. In the **Toolpaths Manager** pick all the operations to verify by picking the **Select All** icon .
2. Select the **Verify selected operations** icon shown below:

3. **Maximize** the Backplot/Verify window if required.
4. Now select the **Home** Tab if required.

5. Activate the options shown below in the **Visibility** section of the Home tab. **Initial Stock not activated.**

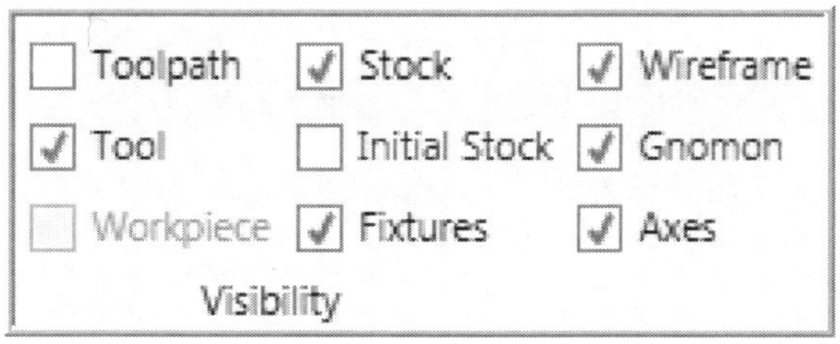

6. At the top of the screen select the **View** tab, the **Isometric** icon and then select **Fit**.

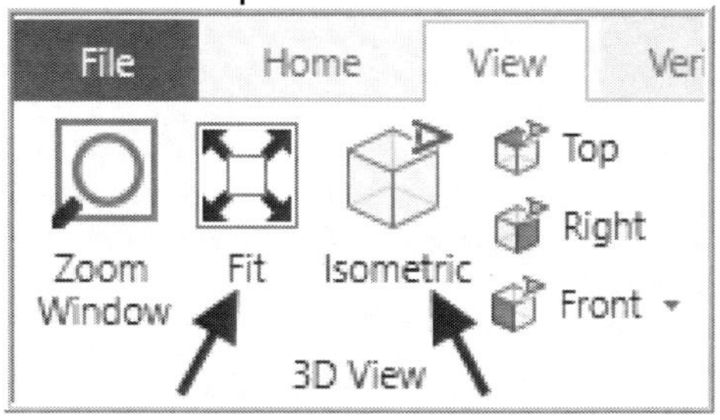

7. Select the **Verify** tab and activate the **Color Loop** to change the color of the tools for the verified part.

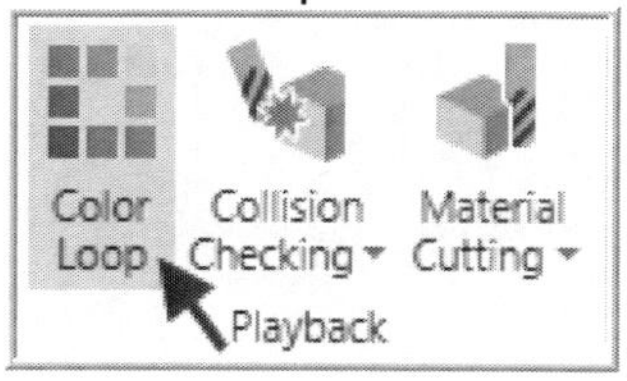

Color Loop
Changes the color of the toolpath or cut stock by operation or by tool change.

Choose **File Options** to set the colors.

8. In the lower part of the screen now set the run **Speed** to slow by moving the slider bar pointer over to the left as shown below.

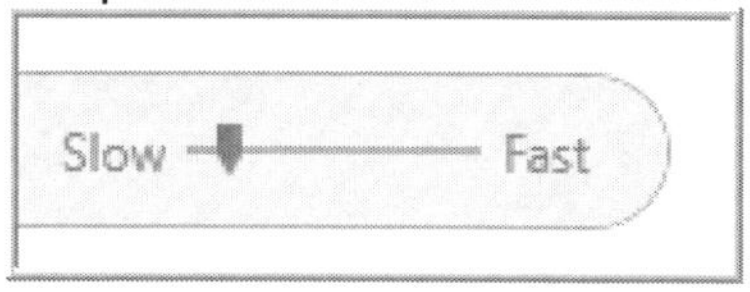

9. Now select the **Play Simulation** button to review the toolpaths.

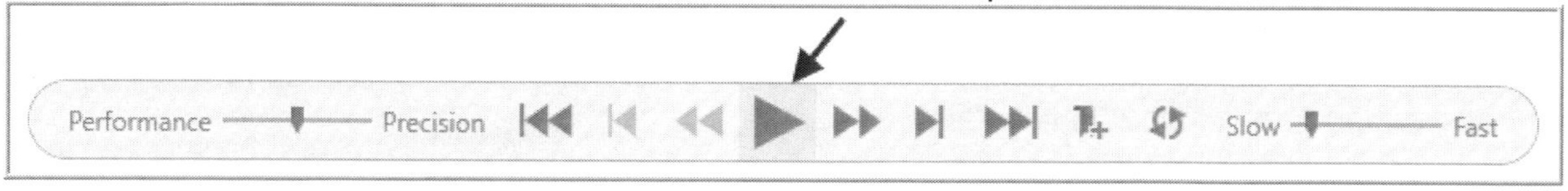

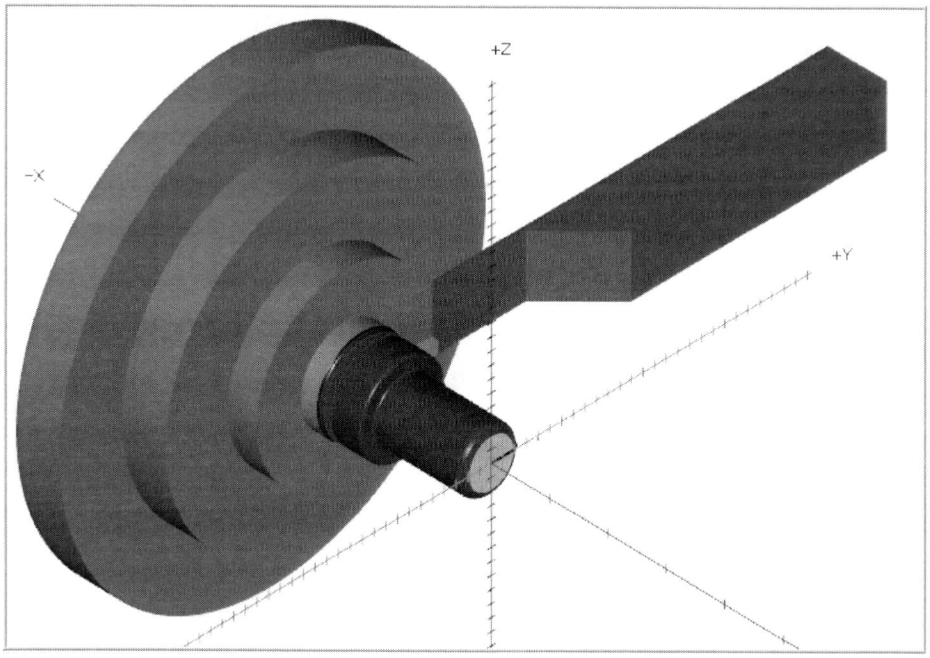

10. Select the **Close** button  in the top right hand corner to exit Verify.

TASK 13:
SAVE THE UPDATED MASTERCAM FILE

1. Select the **Save** icon from the **Quick Access** toolbar at the top left of the screen.

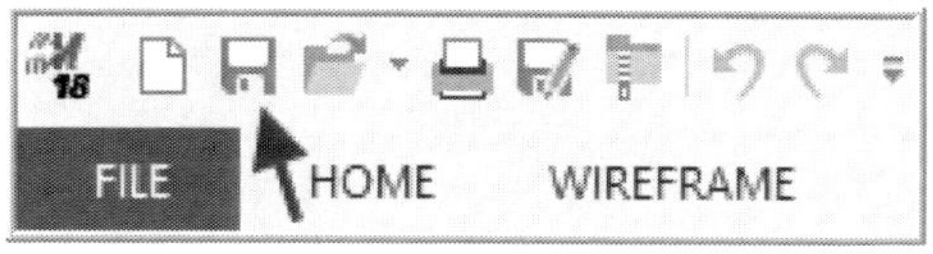

TASK 14:
POST AND CREATE THE CNC CODE FILE

Please Note:
Users of the Mastercam **Home Learning Edition** (HLE) will not be able to Post and Create the CNC code file.

1. Ensure all the operations are selected by picking the **Select All** icon  from the Toolpaths manager.

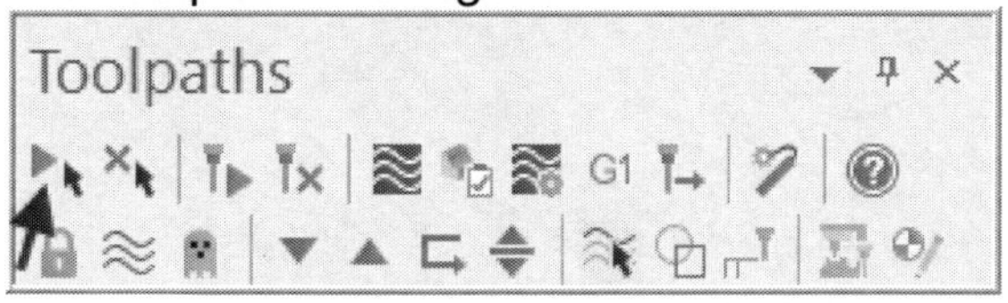

2. Select the **Post selected operations** button from the Toolpaths manager.

➲ **Please Note:** If you cannot see **G1** click on the right pane of the Toolpaths manager window and expand the window to the right.

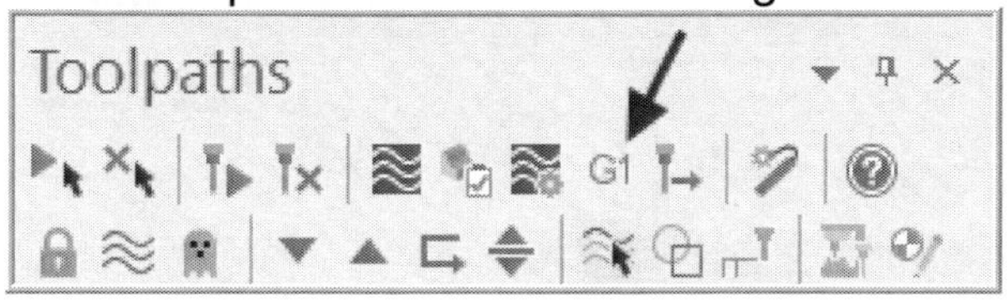

3. In the Post processing window, make the necessary changes as shown below, if required.

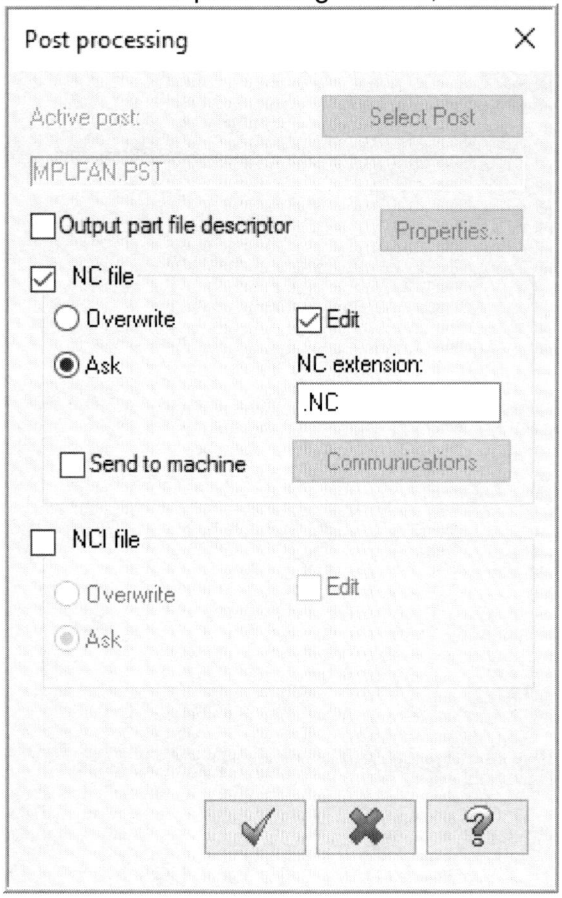

About Post Processing

NC file:
Select this option to save the NC file. The file name and extension are stored in the machine group properties for the selected operation. If you are posting operations from different machine groups or Mastercam files, or batch processing, Mastercam will create several files according to the settings for each machine group.

Edit:
When checked, automatically launches the default text editor with the file displayed so that you can review or modify it.

4. Select the OK button to continue.
5. Ensure the same name as your Mastercam part file name is displayed in the **NC File name** field as shown below:

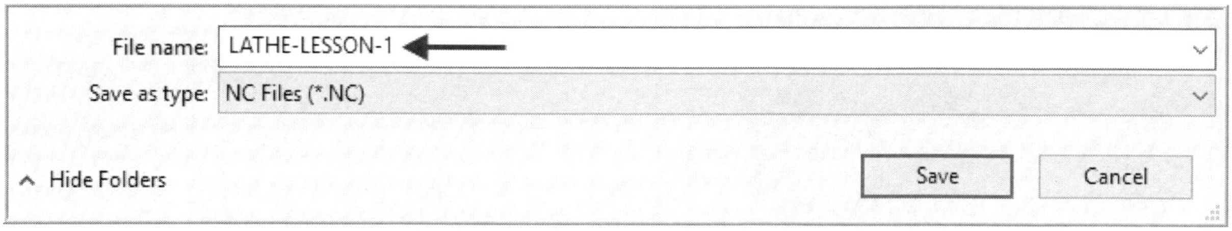

6. Select the **Save** button.

➲ The CNC code file opens up in the default editor.

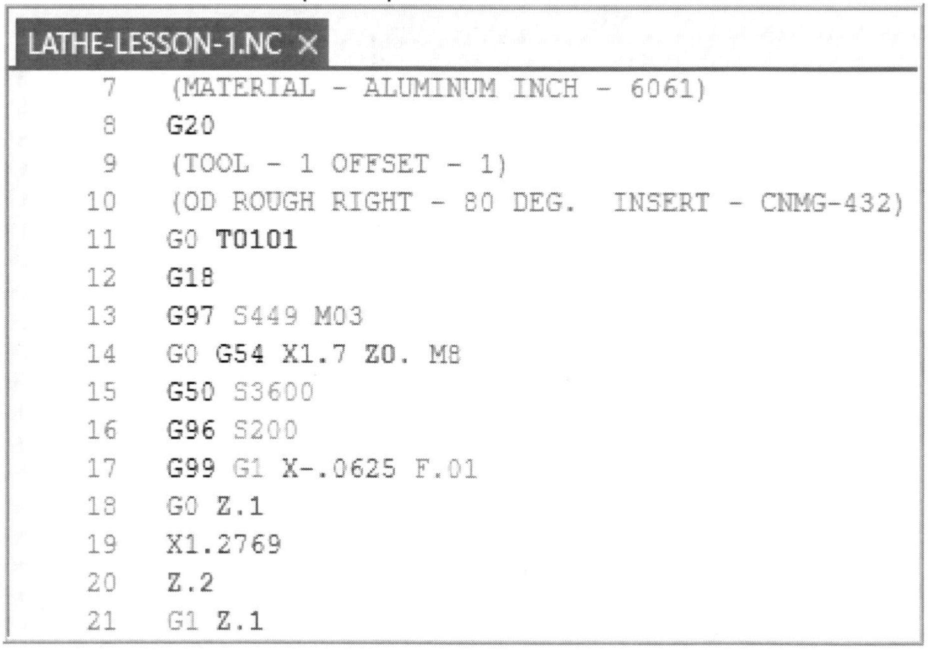

7. Select the in the top right corner to exit the CNC editor.

➲ This completes LATHE-LESSON -1.

LATHE-LESSON-1 EXERCISE

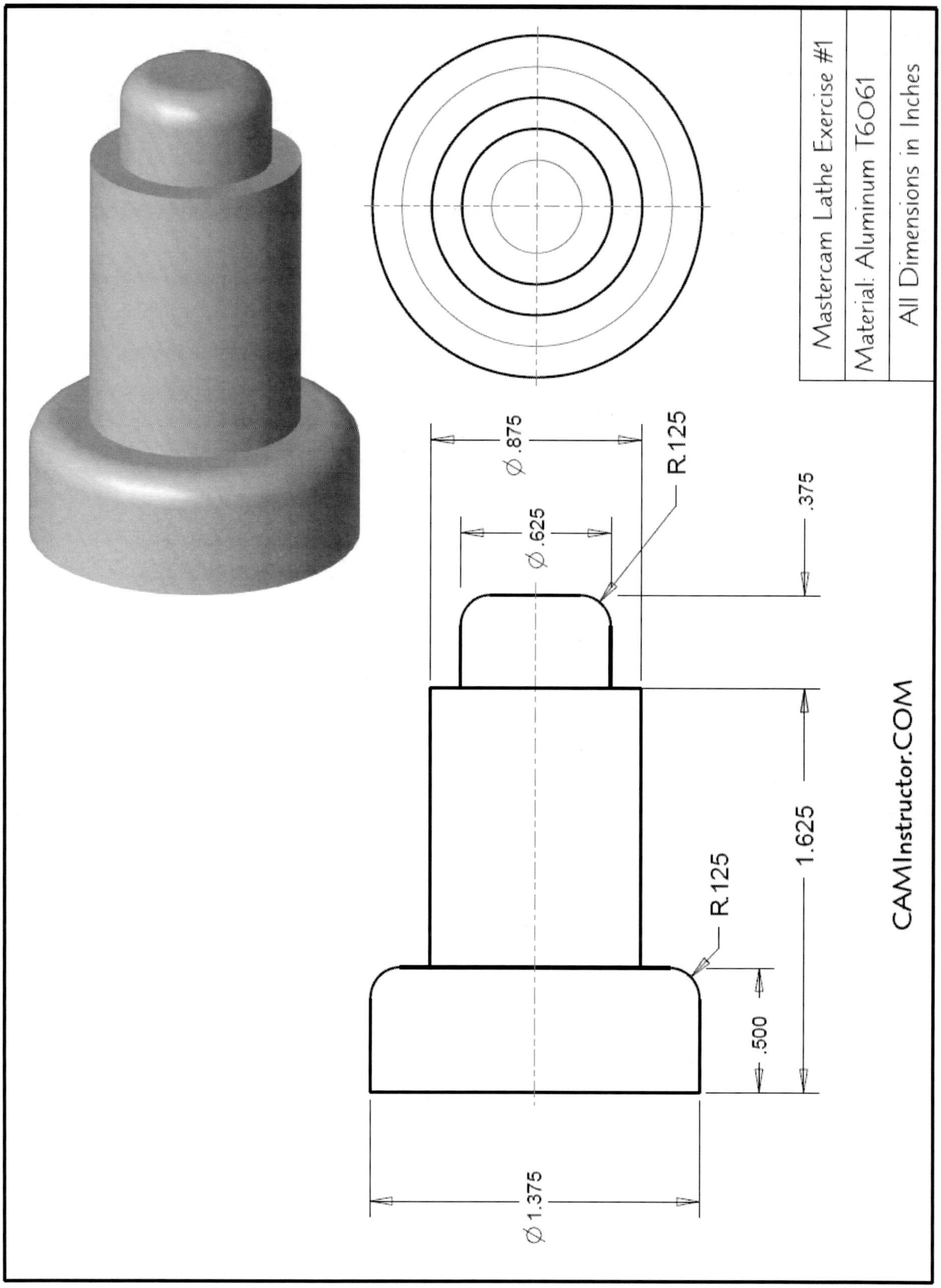

Mastercam® 2018

TRAINING GUIDE

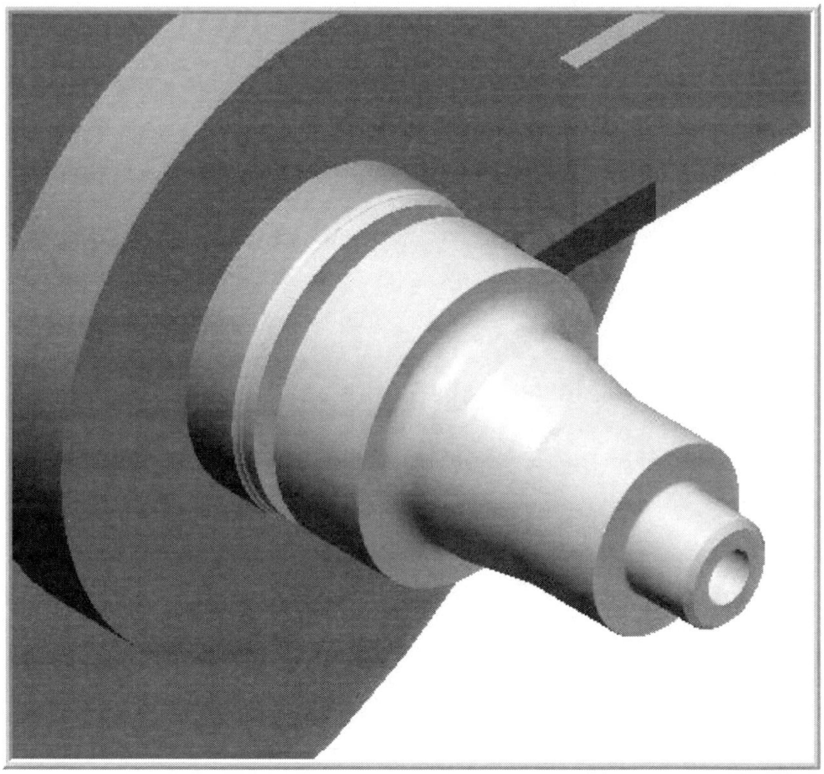

LATHE-LESSON-2

FACE, ROUGH, FINISH, DRILL AND CUTOFF

camInstructor

Objectives

You will create the geometry for Lathe Lesson 2, and then generate a toolpath to machine the part on a CNC lathe. This lesson covers the following topics:

➲ **Create a 2-dimensional drawing by:**
Creating lines.
Creating fillets.
Creating chamfers.

➲ **Establish Stock and Chuck Setup settings:**
Stock size.
Chuck Configuration.
Material for the part.
Feed calculation.

➲ **Generate a 2-dimensional lathe toolpath consisting of:**
Lathe Face.
Lathe Rough.
Lathe Finish.
Lathe Drill.
Lathe Cutoff.

➲ **Inspect the toolpath using Mastercam's Verify and Backplot by:**
Launching the Verify function to machine the part on the screen.
Using Backplot to identify the accuracy of the toolpaths.
Generating the NC- code.

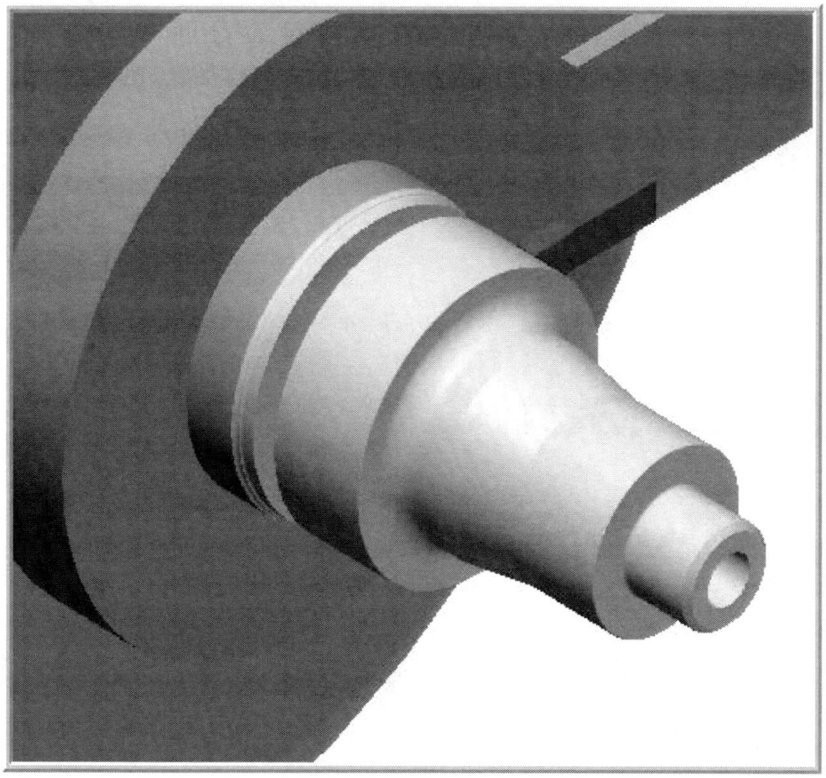

LATHE - LESSON - 2 DRAWING

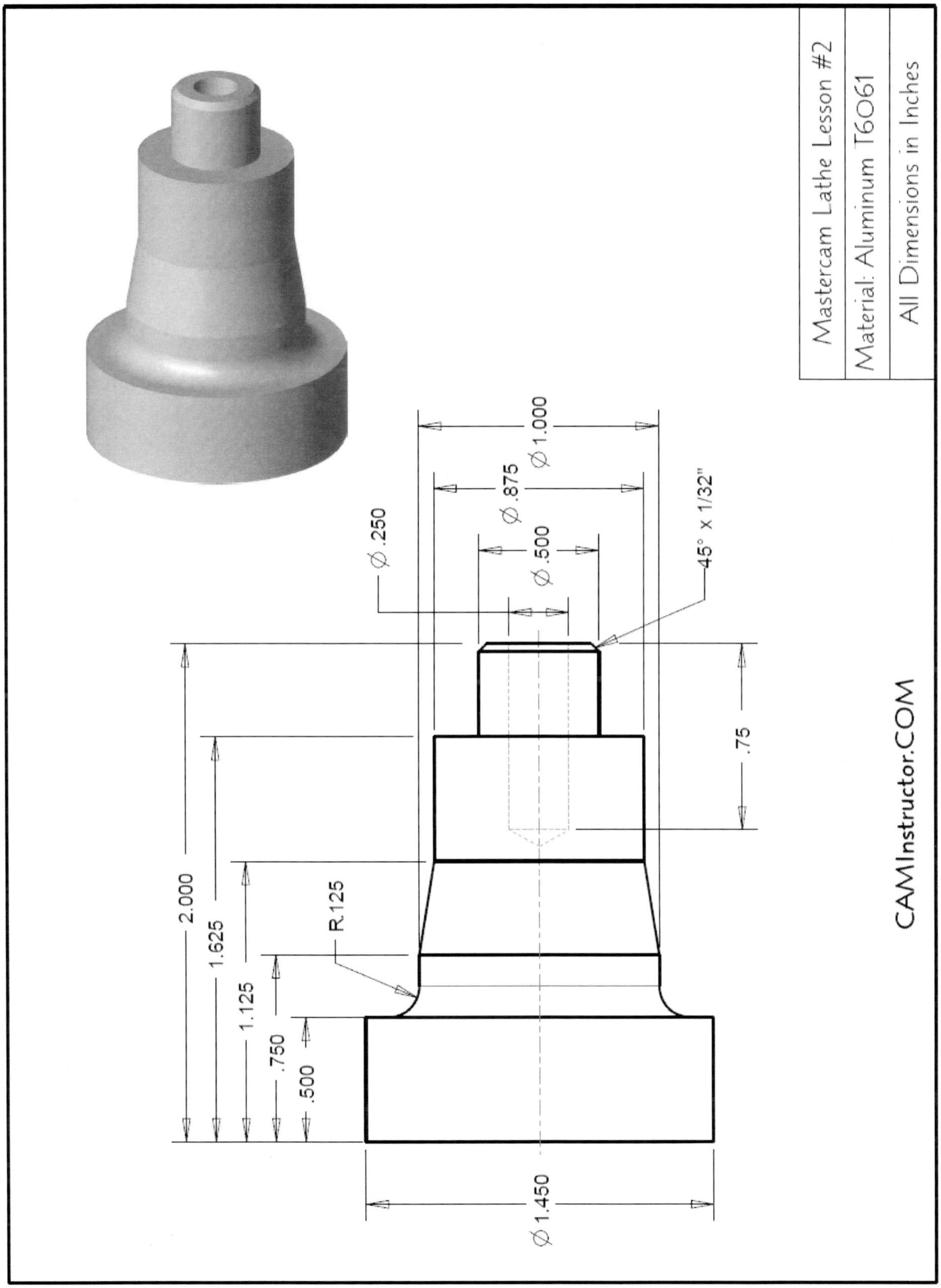

TOOL LIST

Five tools will be used to create this part.

- **Tool #1 Face and Rough the outside diameters**
  Holder: Outside Diameter Rough Right Hand - DCGNR-164D.
  Insert: 80 Degree Diamond Insert – CNMG-432.

- **Tool #2 Finish the outside diameters**
  Holder: Outside Diameter Finish Right Hand - MVJNR-164D.
  Insert: 35 Degree Diamond Insert – VNMG-431.

- **Tool #3 Centre drill the hole**
  Centre Drill – body diameter 0.250”

- **Tool #4 Drill the .25 diameter hole**
  Drill 0.25” diameter

- **Tool #5 Cutoff the part**
  Holder: Outside Diameter Cut-off Right Hand.
  Insert: 0.125” Wide.

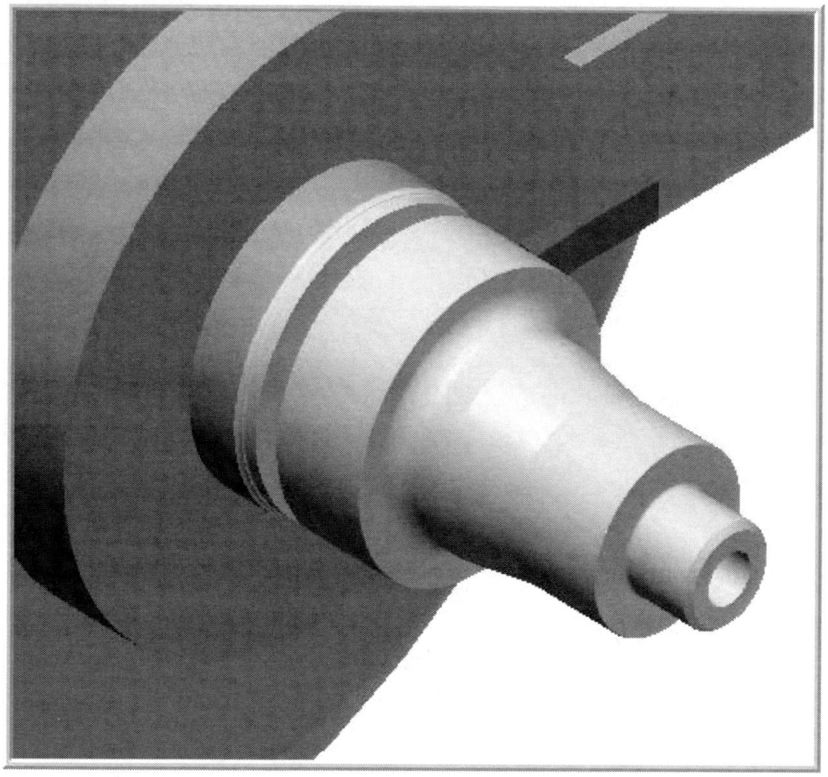

LESSON #2 - THE PROCESS

Geometry Creation

TASK 1:	Setting the Environment
TASK 2:	Setting the Construction Planes
TASK 3:	Create the Geometry
TASK 4:	Create the.125 Fillet radius and 45° x 1/32" –Chamfer
TASK 5:	Save the Drawing

Toolpath Creation

TASK 6:	Define the Stock and Chuck parameters
TASK 7:	Face the Front of the Part
TASK 8:	Rough the Outside Diameters
TASK 9:	Finish the Outside Diameters
TASK 10:	Center Drill the .25" Hole
TASK 11:	Drill the .25" Hole
TASK 12:	Cut off the Part
TASK 13:	Backplot the Toolpath
TASK 14:	Verify the Toolpath
TASK 15:	Save the Updated Mastercam File
TASK 16:	Post and Create the CNC Code File

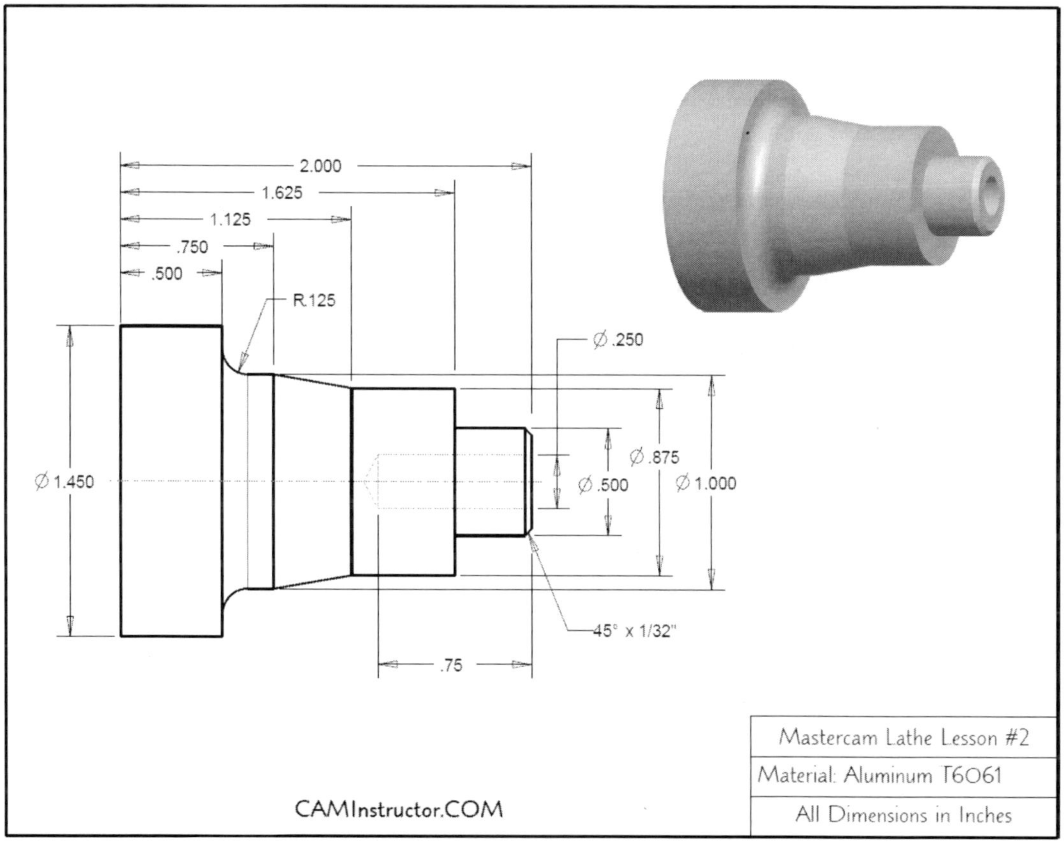

Geometry Creation

TASK 1:
SETTING THE ENVIRONMENT

Before starting the geometry creation you should set up the grid machine type as outlined in the **Setting the Environment** section at the beginning of this text:

1. Set up the **Grid**. This will help identify the location of the origin.
2. Set the **MACHINE TYPE** to the **Lathe Default**.

TASK 2:
SETTING THE CONSTRUCTION PLANES:

➲ **Set the Construction Plane to Lathe diameter +D +Z (WCS).**

1. Select the **View tab** and click on **Toolpaths** and **Solids** in the **Managers** section to **hide** them and toggle **only** the **Planes Manager to display**.

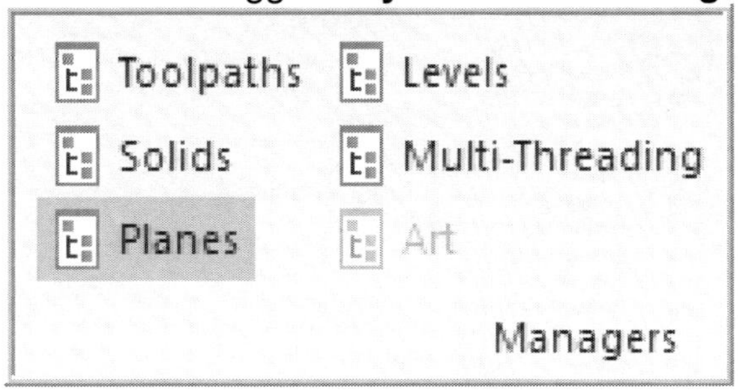

Once your machine is set up, Mastercam includes special lathe construction planes that let you work in **radius or diameter coordinates**.

For conventional 2D turning applications, use the Planes Manager to select the desired coordinate system, as shown below right.

Choose to use either radius or diameter coordinates and then choose the desired X/D and Z directions.

2. Ensure the **C column** (Construction Plane) and **T column** (Tool Plane) are set to the **+D +Z Plane**. Just click in the C and T columns in the **+D +Z** row.

➲ Take note of the **Status bar** at the bottom of the screen **CPLANE: +D +Z TPLANE: +D +Z WCS:TOP** as shown below right.

3. To change the **Lathe Plane** open up the drop down menu for **Select lathe plane** and click on the required coordinate system as shown below right.

4. Select the **Close** button ☒ in the top right hand corner to close the Planes Manager.

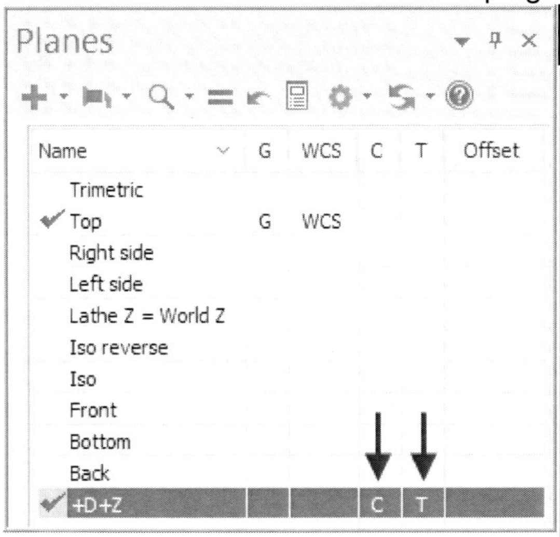

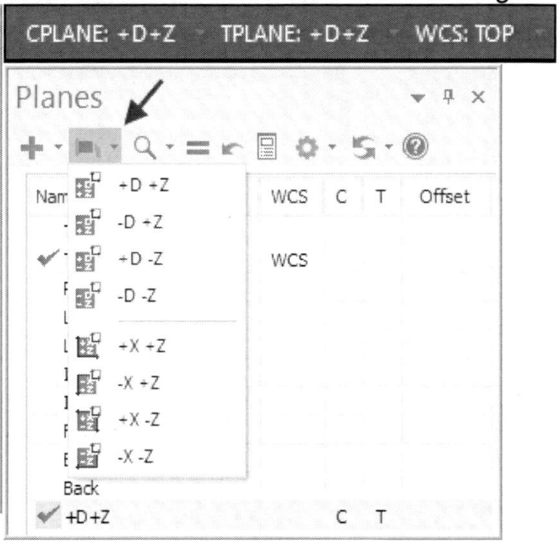

TASK 3:
CREATE THE GEOMETRY – THE LEFT HAND FACE IS AT Z0

- This task explains how to create the geometry of this part. In this lathe part you only need to create **half of the geometry**, the geometry above the center line.
- Lines 1 through 9 will be created first and then the fillet and chamfer will be created.

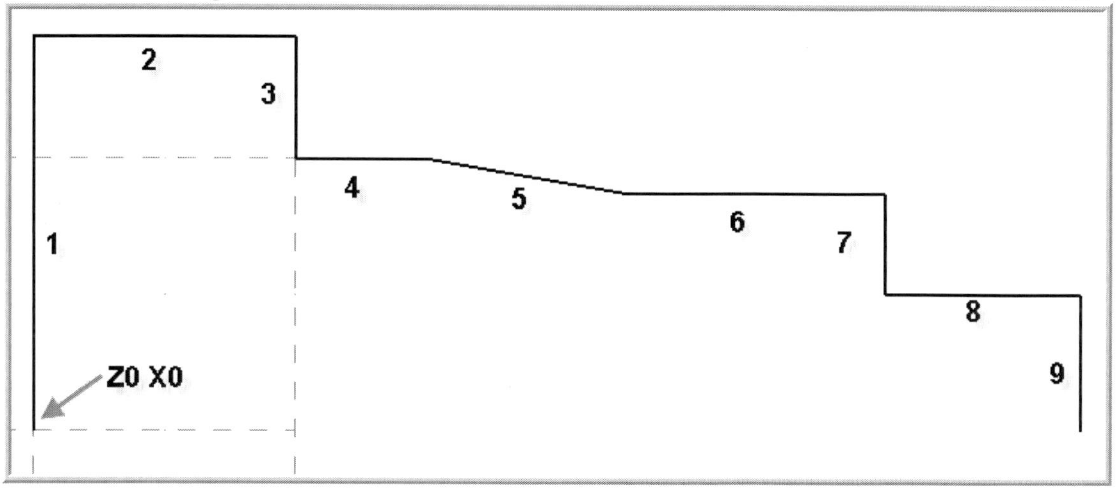

- **Create Line #1**

1. Select the **WIREFRAME** tab at the top of the screen and in the **Lines** section click on **Line Endpoints**.

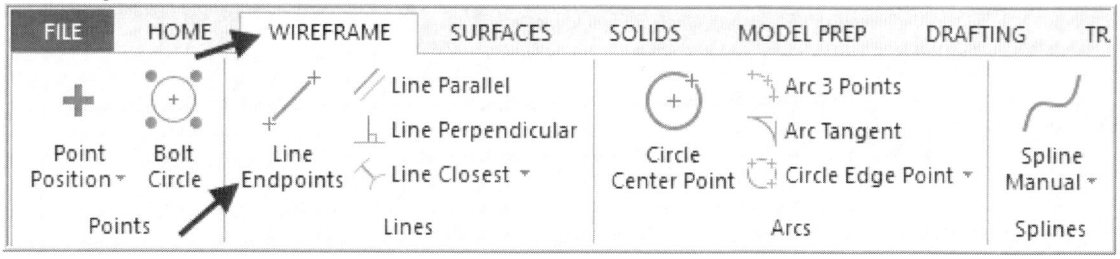

- On the graphics screen you are prompted: **Specify the first endpoint** and the Line Endpoints panel appears.

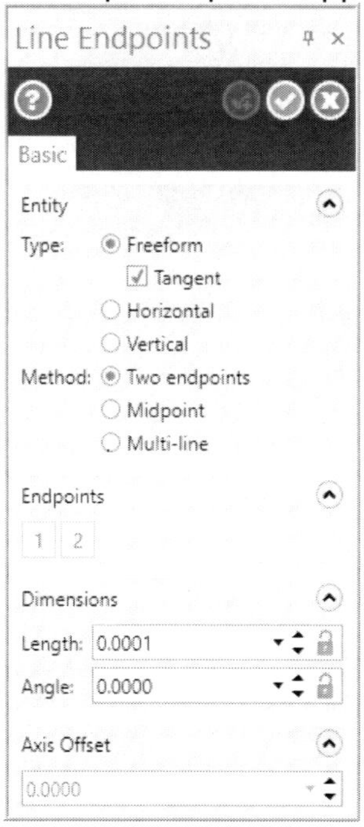

Line Endpoints
Use this function to create single lines with two endpoints, or multiple lines connected at their endpoints.

Simply click in the graphics window to set the two endpoints; or enter values in the Length and Angle fields, and then click in the graphics window to position the line.

2. Move the cursor over the **center of the grid** and as you get close to the origin a visual cue appears.  This is the cue that will allow you to snap to the **origin**. With this visual cue highlighted click on the **origin.**

AutoCursor: Visual Cues detects and highlights endpoints and midpoints of curves, lines, arc center points, and point entities. In addition, AutoCursor can snap to angle, nearest, tangent, perpendicular, horizontal, and vertical conditions.

➲ The following are Mastercam Visual Cues:

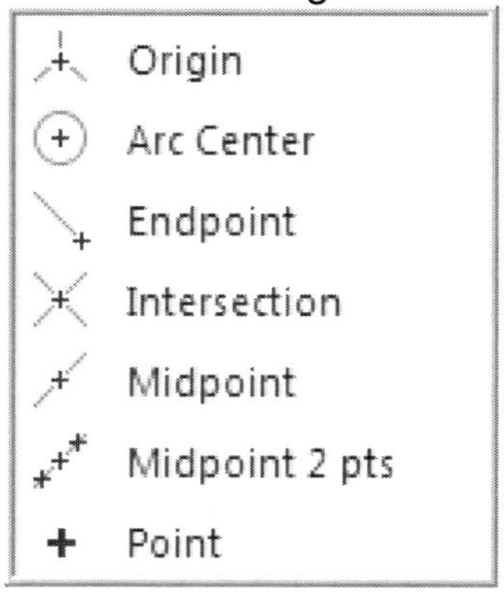

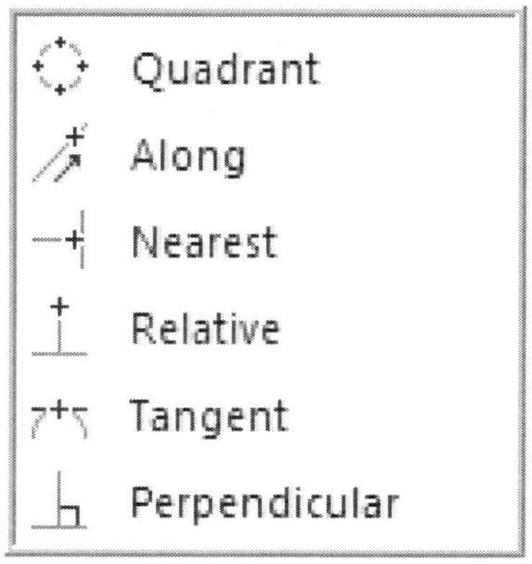

3. You are next prompted to **"Specify the second endpoint".** In the Line Endpoints panel activate **Multi-line and Freeform**.

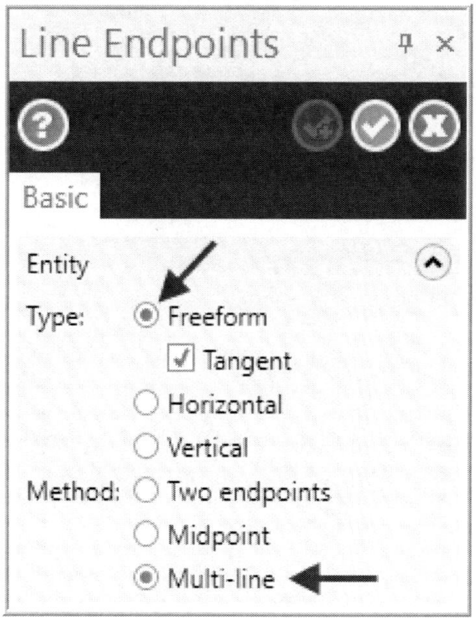

Multi-line Let's you create multiple lines connected at their endpoints. Enter a point for the first endpoint of the first line and then a point for the second endpoint of the line. That second point becomes the first endpoint of the next line that you create. Double-click the last point or press Escape to end this function. **Freeform** Allows you to create the line anywhere on the plane.

4. You are still prompted to **"Specify the second endpoint"**. To satisfy this prompt **click the middle mouse button** and then **hit the spacebar** on your keyboard.
5. The **Fastpoint** box now opens. Input **1.45,0** and hit the **Enter** key. This is **D1.45 Z0.**

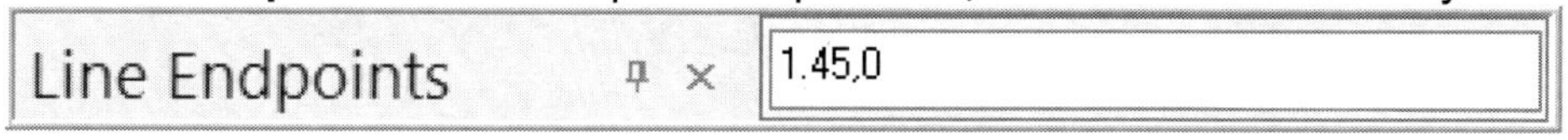

➲ A vertical line should be visible as shown below:

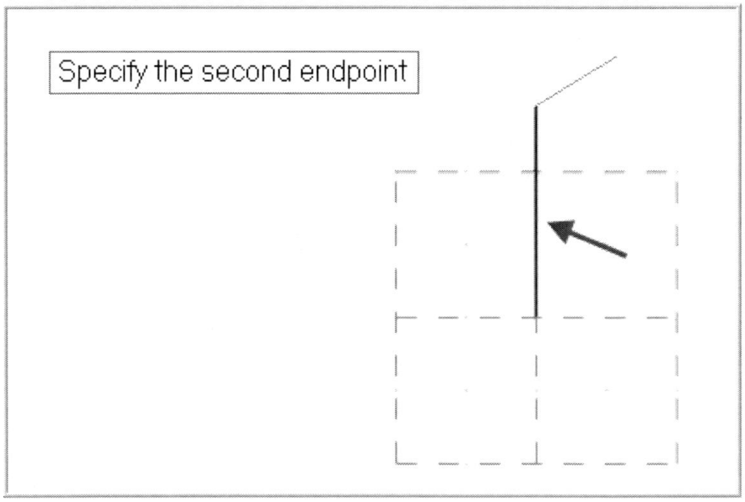

NOTE: If you make a mistake creating lines, click on the **Undo** icon at the top of the screen.

Then redo the Line.

➲ **Create Line #2**

6. You are next prompted to **"Specify the second endpoint.** To satisfy this prompt **just type** the coordinate, **type 1.45,0.5** and hit the Enter key. This is **D1.45 Z0.5**.

➲ **Create Line #3**

7. To satisfy the prompt **"Specify the second endpoint" just type** the coordinate, **type 1.0,0.5** and hit the Enter key to complete this line. This is **D1.0 Z0.5**.

➲ **Create Line #4**

8. To satisfy the prompt **"Specify the second endpoint" just type** the coordinate, **type 1.0,0.75** and hit the Enter key to complete this line. This is **D1.0 Z0.75**.

➲ **Create Line #5**

9. To satisfy the prompt **"Specify the second endpoint" just type** the coordinate, **type 0.875,1.125** and hit the Enter key to complete this line. This is **D0.875 Z1.125**.

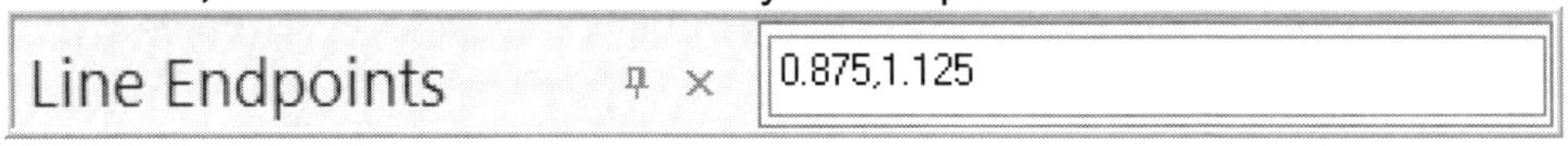

➲ **Create Line #6**

10. To satisfy the prompt **"Specify the second endpoint" just type** the coordinate, **type 0.875,1.625** and hit the Enter key to complete this line. This is **D0.875 Z1.625**.

11. Right mouse click in the graphics area and click on the **Fit** icon.
12. Right mouse click in the graphics area and click on **Unzoom 80%** to shrink the display.

➲ **Create Line #7**

13. To satisfy the prompt **"Specify the second endpoint" just type** the coordinate, **type 0.5,1.625** and hit the Enter key to complete this line. This is **D0.5 Z1.625**.

➲ **Create Line #8**

14. To satisfy the prompt **"Specify the second endpoint" just type** the coordinate, **type 0.5,2.0** and hit the Enter key to complete this line. This is **D0.5 Z2.0**.

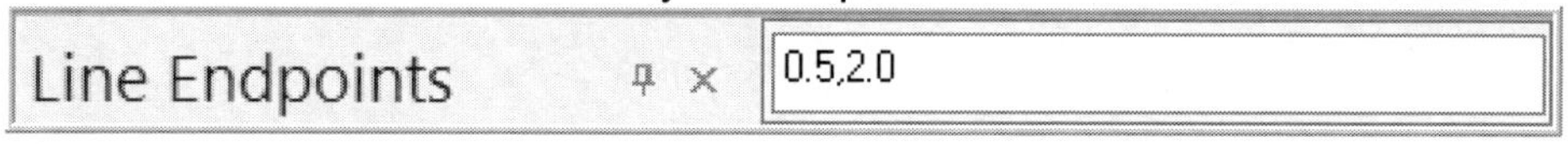

➲ **Create Line #9**

15. To satisfy the prompt **"Specify the second endpoint" just type** the coordinate, **type 0,2.0** and hit the Enter key to complete this line. This is **D0 Z2.0**.

16. Click on the **OK** icon to complete this feature.
17. Right mouse click in the graphics area and click on the **Fit** icon.

➲ Your geometry should look like the figure below:

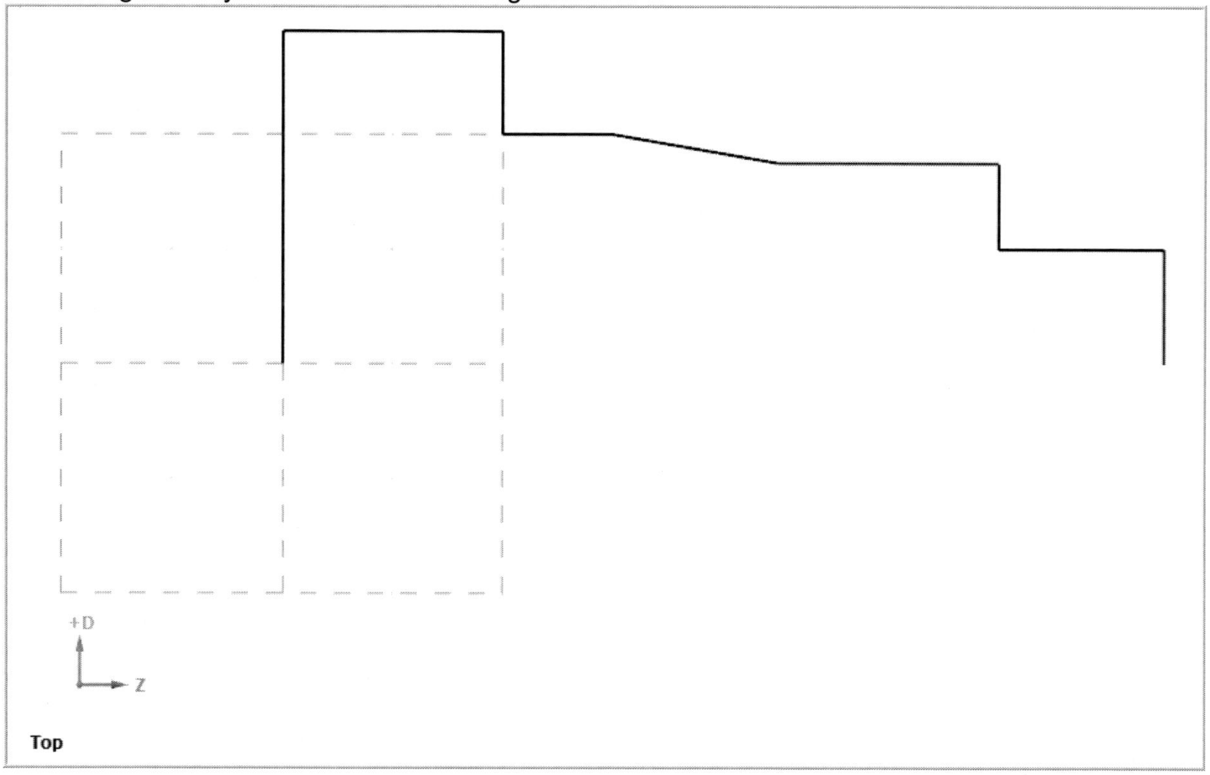

TASK 4:
CREATE THE .125 FILLET RADIUS AND 45° X 1/32" –CHAMFER

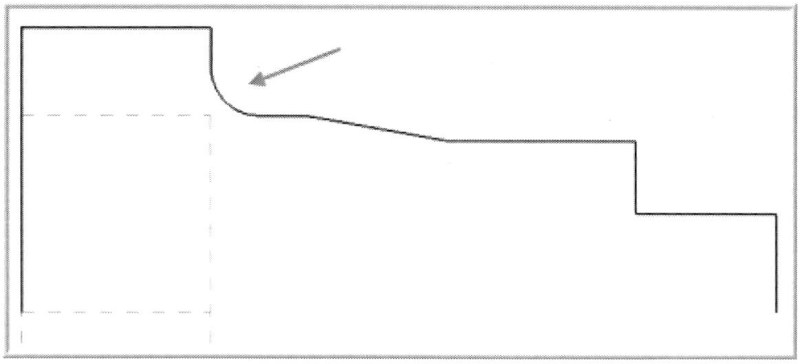

➲ **Create the .125 fillet radius.**

1. Select the **WIREFRAME** tab at the top of the screen and in the **Modify** section click on **Fillet Entities**.

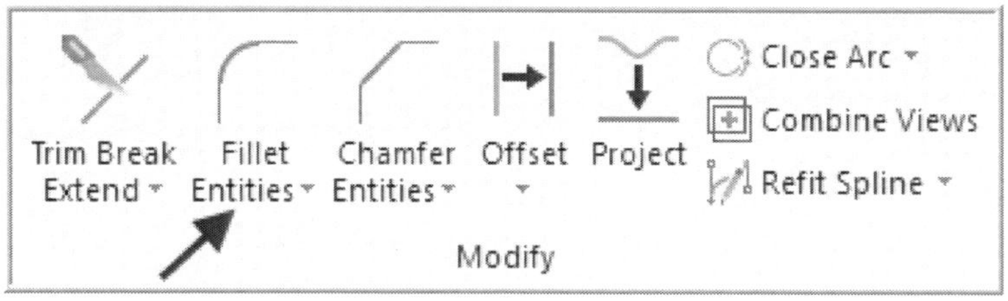

2. The **Fillet Entities** panel appears. If required activate the **Style** to **Normal** and enter a value of **0.125** for **Radius**.
3. Ensure the **Trim** entities box at the bottom of the panel is check marked to turn the trim on.

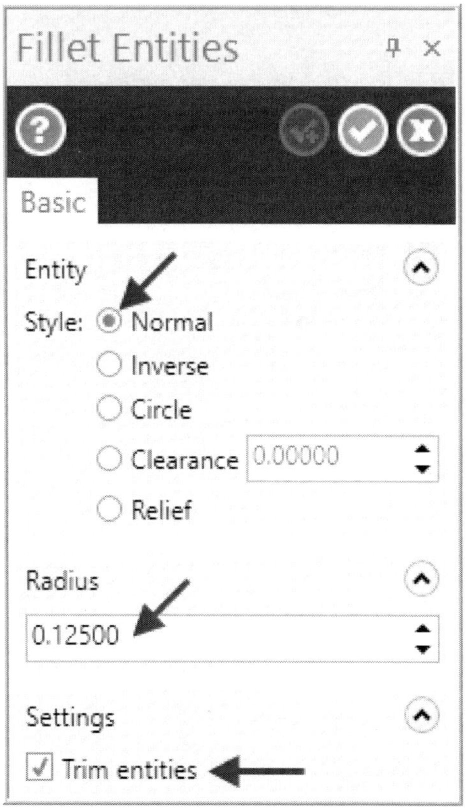

Style:
Sets the fillet style to be created.
The following styles are:
Normal = creates normal fillets on the corners of a contour, resulting in rounded corners.

Inverse = creates inverted arcs on the corners of a contour.

Circle = creates full circles in each of the corners of a contour.

Clearance = creates fillets on inside corners of a contour so that the tool will reach completely into the corner to remove material.

Relief = Creates a fillet that puts the clearance on only one entity. Only lines can be selected for this fillet style.

4. Move over to the graphic screen and for the prompt **"Fillet: Select an entity"** click on **Line 1** and then for the prompt **"Fillet: Select another entity"** click on **Line 2** as shown below:

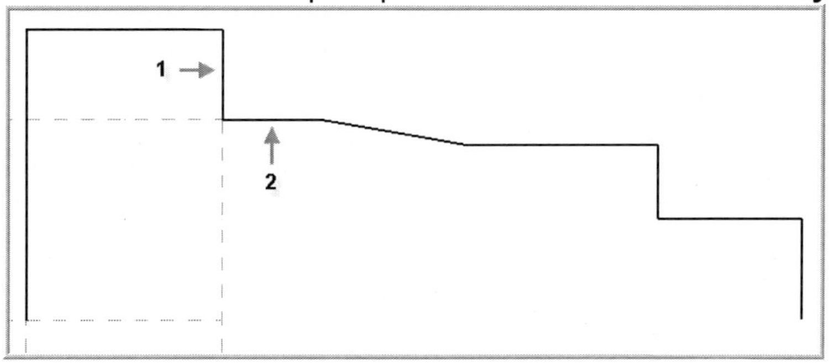

5. Click on the **OK** icon  to complete this feature.

➲ The completed fillet is shown below:

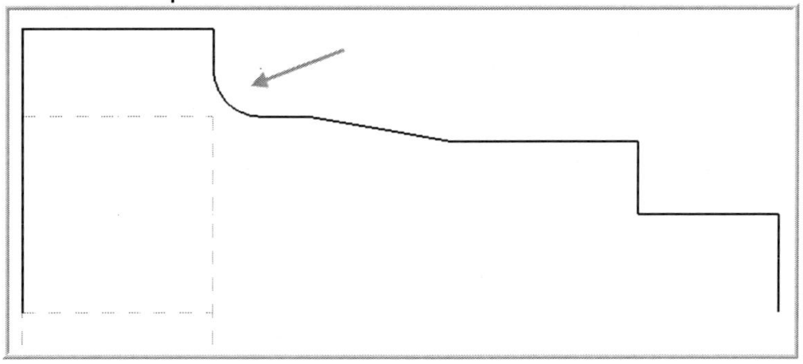

➲ **Create the 45° x 1/32" (.03125) Chamfer.**

6. Select the **WIREFRAME** tab at the top of the screen and in the **Modify** section click on **Chamfer Entities**.

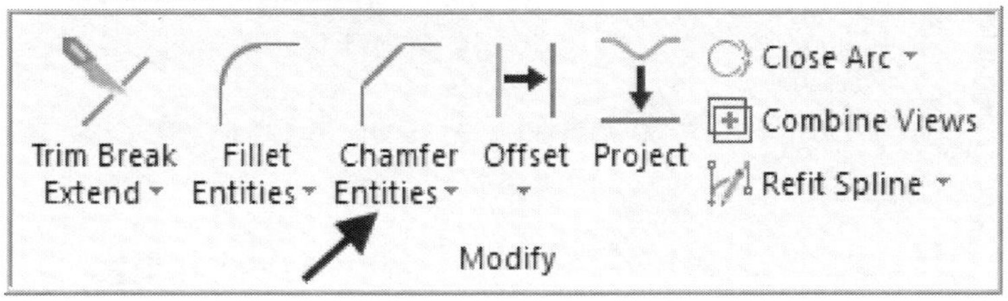

7. The **Chamfer Entities** panel appears. The chamfer you are creating is 1/32" x 45°, if required activate the **Style** to **1 distance.**
8. Click in the space for **distance 1** and input **1/32** and then hit the enter key.
9. Ensure the **Trim entities** box at the bottom of the panel is check marked to turn the trim on.

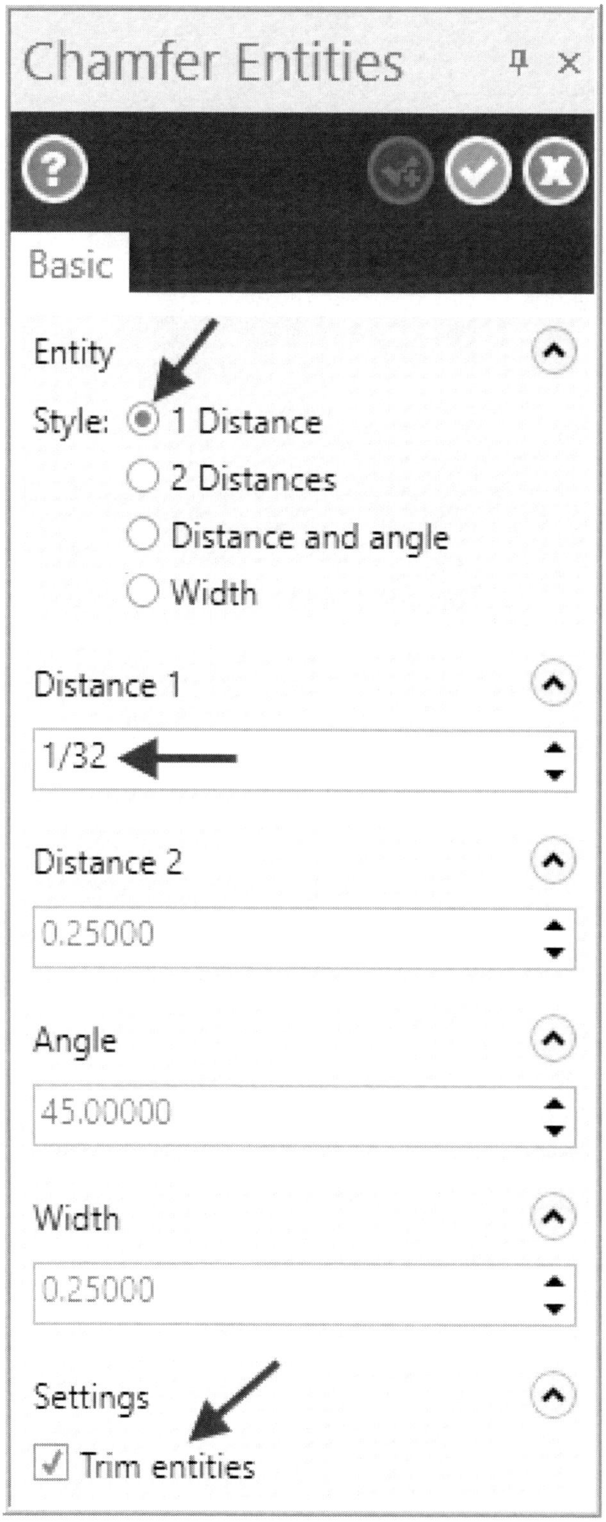

Style:
Defines chamfer style. Choose to create the chamfer style based on distance or width as defined below:

1 Distance - Sets the distance from the intersection of the two selected lines that each endpoint of the chamfer is positioned. Activates only the Distance 1 field for input. Both chamfer endpoints are positioned equal distances from the intersection.

2 Distances - Sets the distances from the intersection of the two selected lines that each endpoint of the chamfer is positioned. This allows you to set two separate distances. The value in the Distance 1 field sets the distance from the endpoint of the first line you select. The value in the Distance 2 field sets the distance from the endpoint of the second line you select.

Distance and Angle - Sets the distance from the intersection of the entity you select first, and an angle that determines the angle of the chamfer. When you are prompted to select the second entity, your cursor will snap to recognized chamfers that meet the conditions of both the Distance 1 and Angle fields. If those conditions cannot be met, you will not be able to create a chamfer.

Width - Sets the width of the chamfer and positions its endpoints along the two selected lines accordingly.

10. Click on **Line 1** and then click on **Line 2** as shown below:

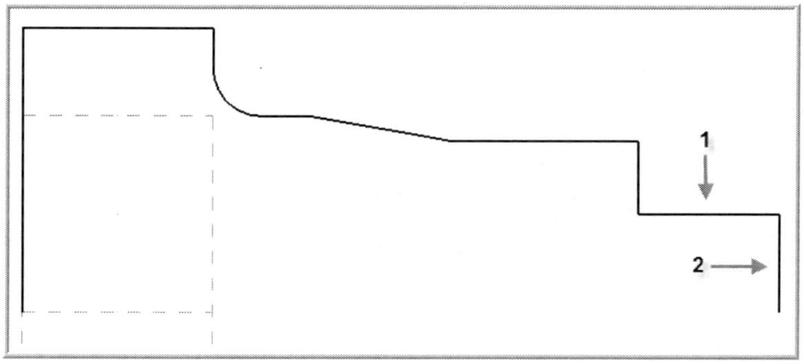

11. Click on the **OK** icon  to complete this feature.

➲ The Chamfer should look like the figure below:

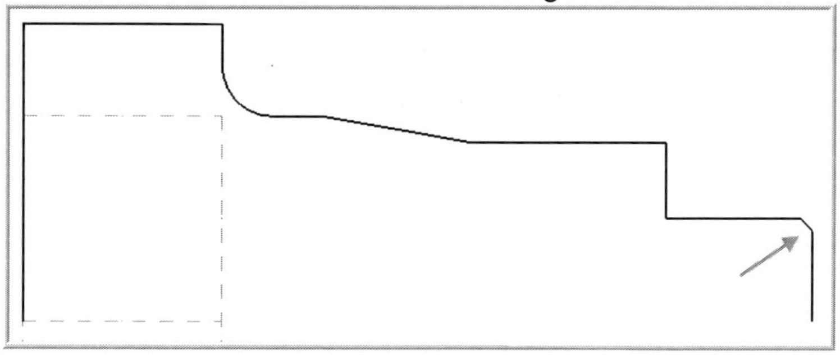

12. This completes the geometry for this part.

TASK 5:
SAVE THE DRAWING

1. Select **File.**
2. Select **Save As…**
3. Click on the **Browse** icon.
4. In the **"File name"** box, type **"LATHE-LESSON-2".**
5. Browse to an appropriate location.
6. Select **the Save** button **to save the file and complete this function**.

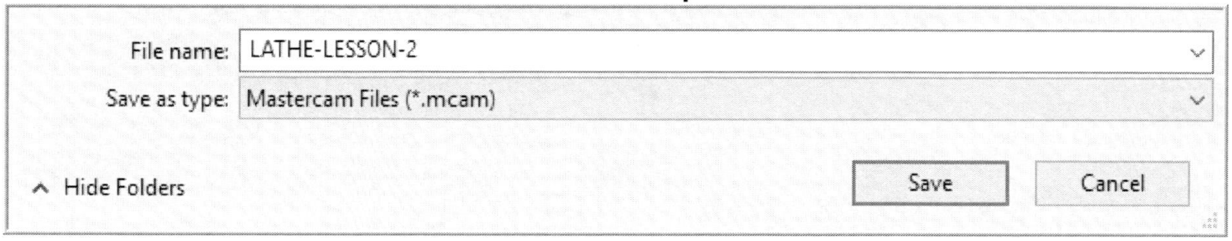

Toolpath Creation

TASK 6:
DEFINING THE STOCK AND CHUCK PARAMETERS

1. Select the **VIEW** tab at the top of the screen.
2. Select the **Fit** icon in the **Zoom** section. Next select **Unzoom 50%** to shrink the display.

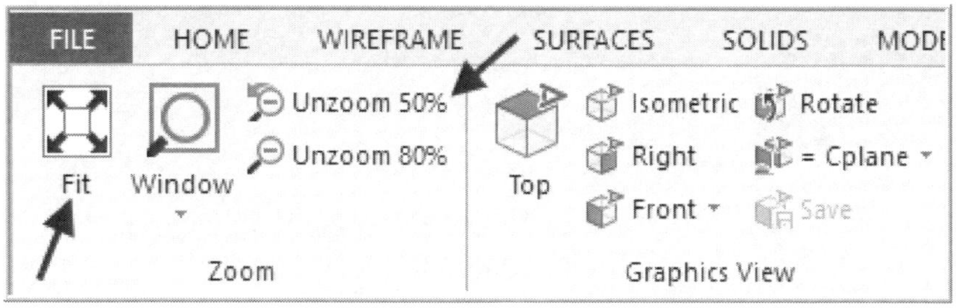

3. Still on the **View tab** and click on **Toolpaths** to display the Toolpaths Manager.

4. Ensure your screen looks like the image below:
   a. The Toolpaths Manager is open.
   b. The Properties icon displays **Lathe Default**. If it is not refer to **Setting the Environment** chapter at the beginning of the book.
   c. The **Lathe Lesson-2** Geometry is showing.

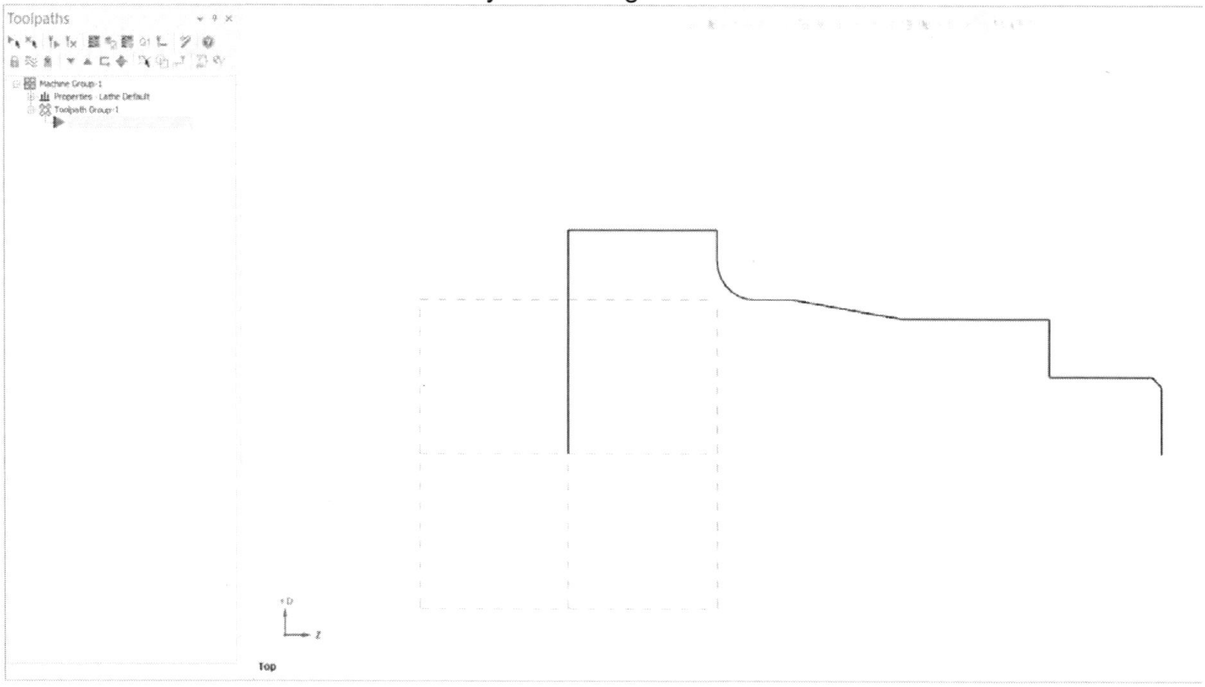

5. Click on the plus in front of **Properties** to expand the Machine Group Properties.

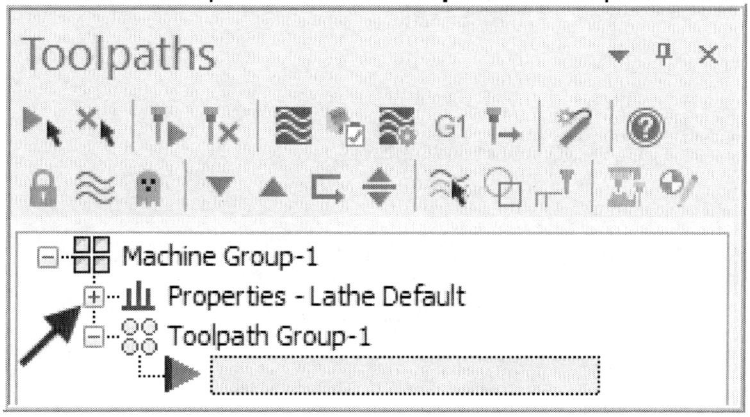

6. **This is Optional -** To expand the toolpaths manager window, click on the outside of the window with the left mouse button (hold the button down) and drag it to the right.

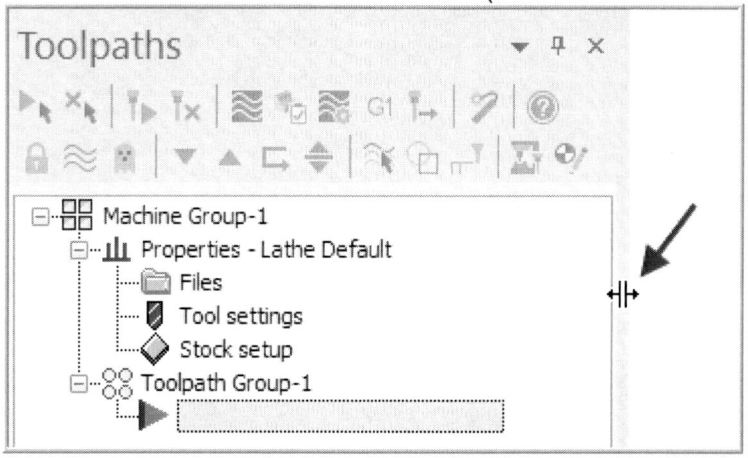

7. Click on **Stock setup** in the Toolpaths Manager window.

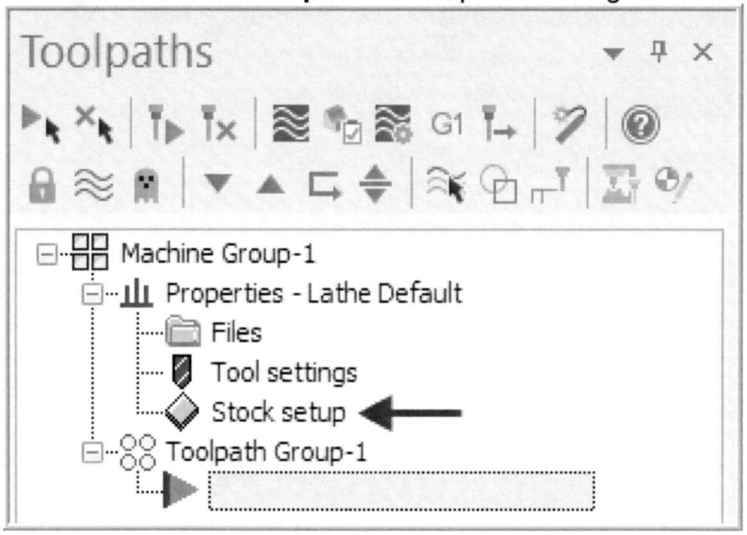

8. Select the **Stock Properties** button in the **Stock Setup** page as shown in the screenshot below:

Note: To learn more about Stock Setup refer to the Tips and Techniques content in the Online Course Instruction.

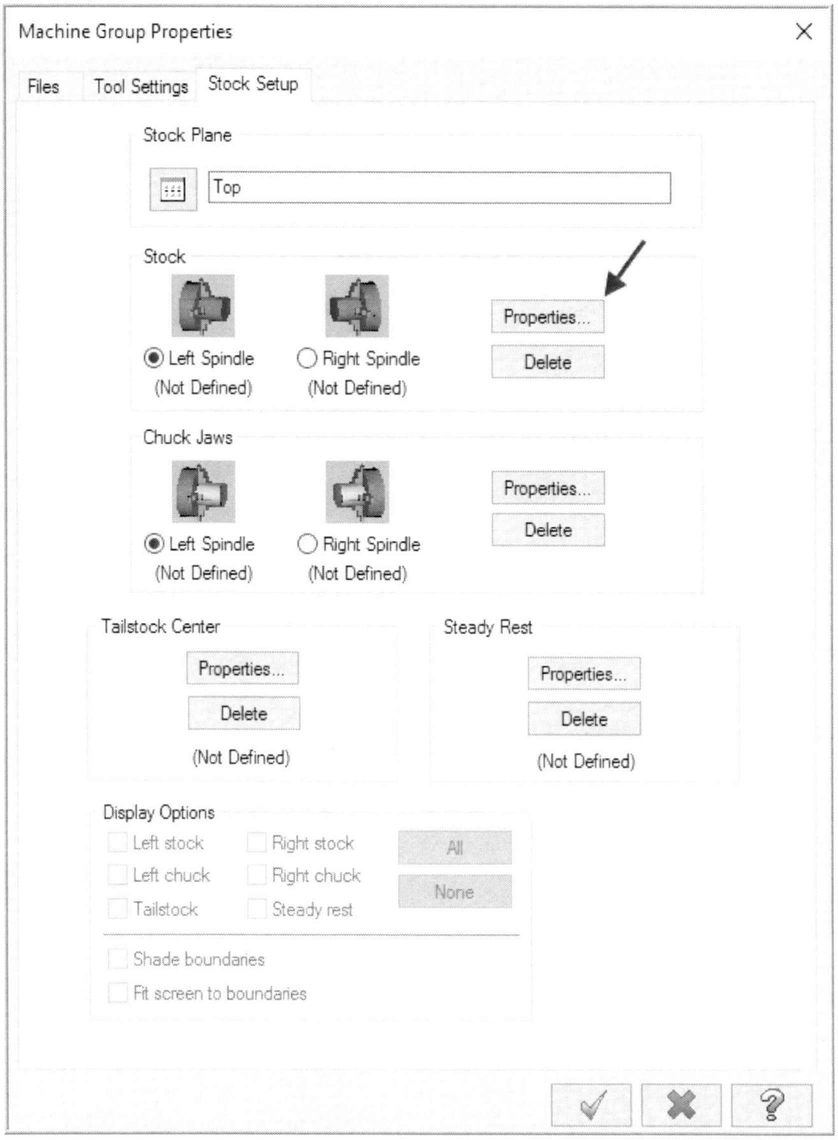

9. In the **Machine Component Manager-Stock** window click on the **Geometry** button and select **Cylinder** as shown below:

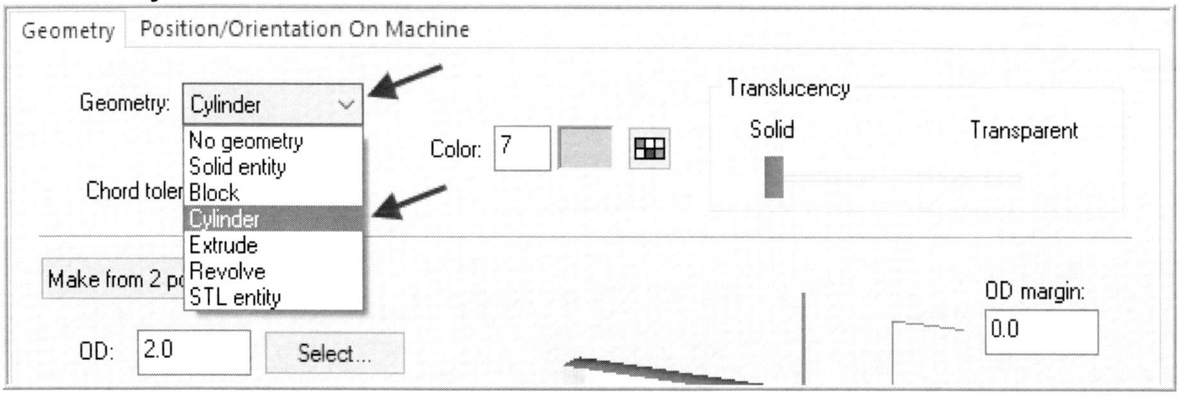

10. In the **Stock setup** set the values as shown below. **Axis is set to +Z**.

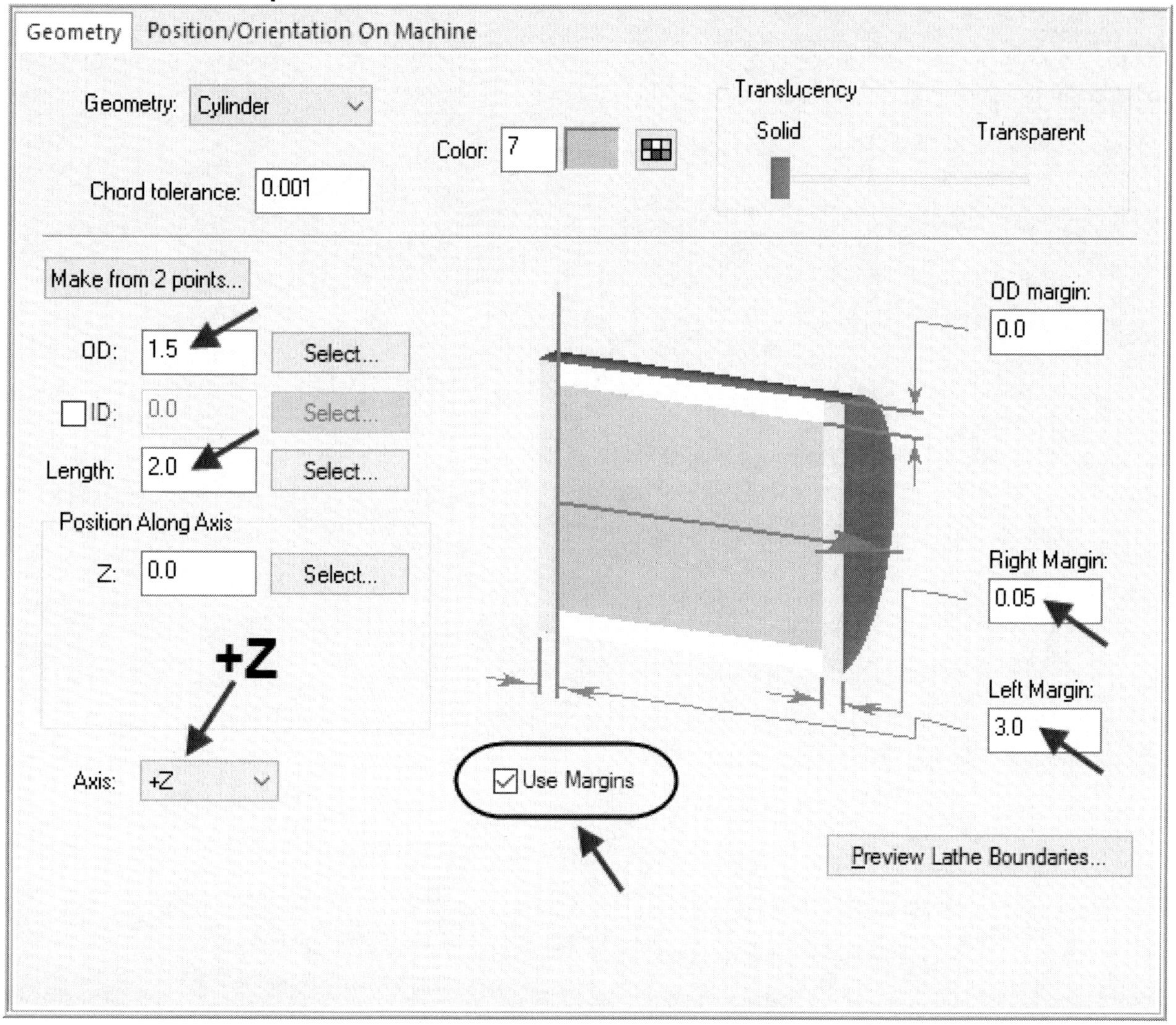

Use Margins Select this option to use stock margins. This is an extra safety feature; Mastercam will add the margin to the stock boundary when calculating the Tool Clearance warnings.

Axis Select the orientation and direction in which the cylinder will be generated relative to the Base Point.
Please note that these axis labels represent 3D world coordinates, not 2D lathe part coordinates. This means that to create stock aligned with a lathe Z axis for a typical turning application, you would choose either +X or -X.

OD Enter the value of the outer diameter, or click the Select button to choose a point from the graphic window.

Length Enter the length of the stock.

Position Along Axis Enter the location of the base point of the stock model or component or click the Select button to choose a point from the graphic window.
For a lathe stock model, this is typically a Z-axis position that represents either the left or right face of the stock.

11. Click on the OK icon  to complete this feature.

12. Still on the Stock Setup page activate **Fit screen to boundaries**.

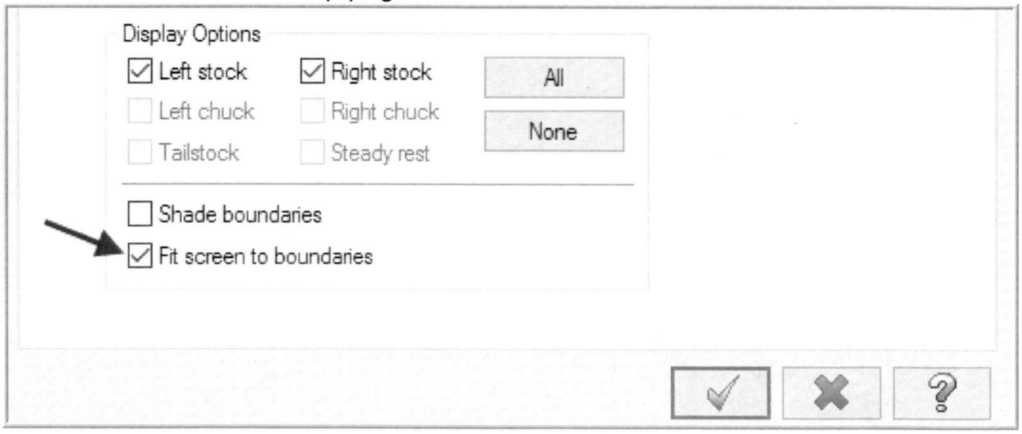

Fit screen to boundaries
Check to determine that the stock, chuck, and tailstock boundaries are included when fitting geometry to the graphics window

13. Select the **Chuck Properties** button in the **Stock Setup** page as shown in the screenshot below:

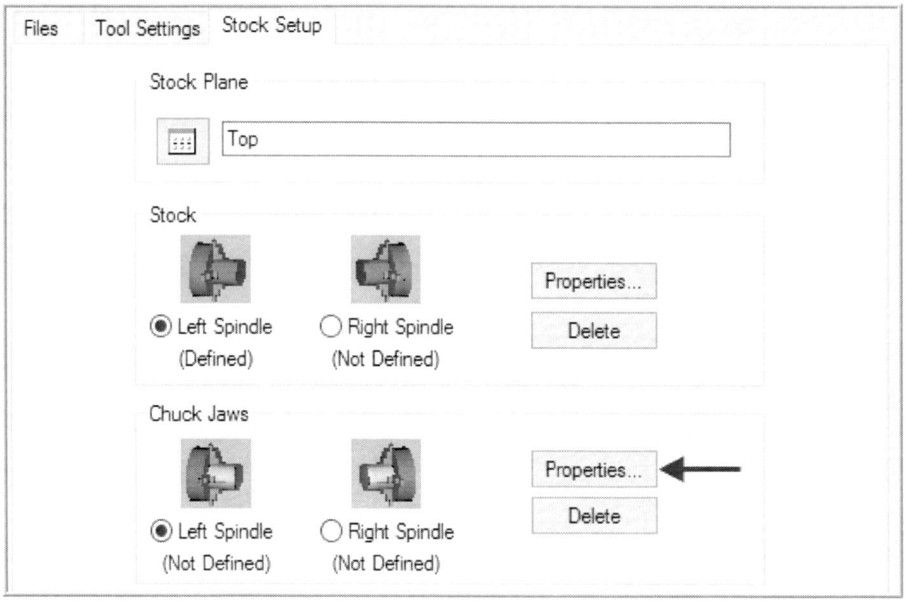

14. In the **Chuck Jaws** setup set the values as shown below:

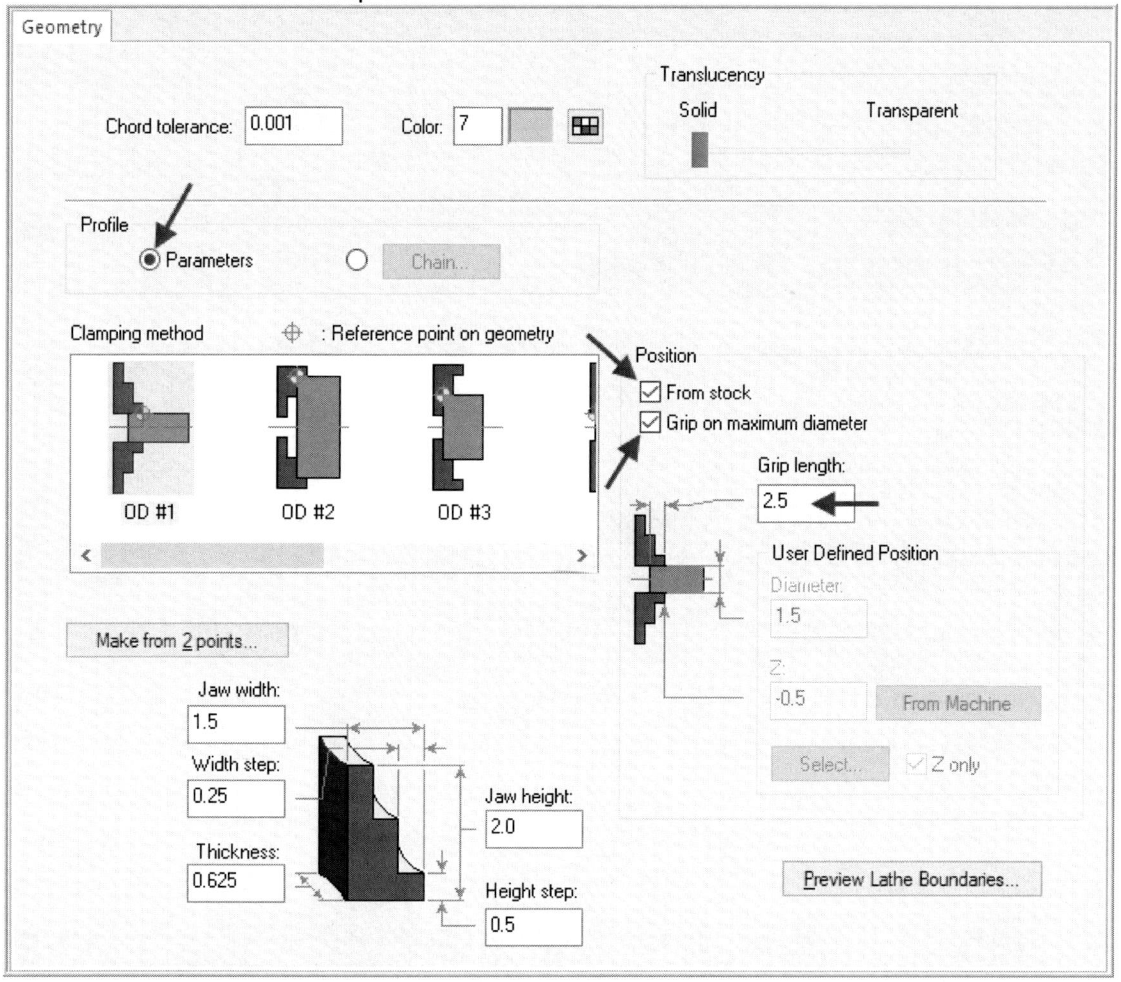

Chuck Jaws Geometry tab
Use this tab to define a set of chuck jaws for a machining operation. This locates the chuck in relation to the part and ensures that the tool will not make a move into the chuck.
To define the chuck jaw you need to:
- Define the chuck jaw's shape
- Select a clamping method
- Tell Mastercam where the chuck is located

Clamping method
Choose the picture which best represents how your chuck clamps the stock. The reference point is the point that represents the chuck position that is defined in the Position section of this dialog box and should be where the chuck clamps the stock.
Position - From stock
Check to have the system calculate the chuck jaw's position in space using the defined stock. You must have stock defined on the screen for this option to be enabled.
Grip on maximum diameter
Check to have the chuck jaw hold the stock at its maximum diameter. If cleared, the system calculates the chuck holding the stock at its minimum diameter. You must have stock defined on the screen for this option to be enabled.
Grip length
Enter a value to determine how much stock is being held by the chuck jaw.

15. Click on the **OK** icon  to complete this feature.

16. Click on the **Tool Settings** page and make changes as shown below:

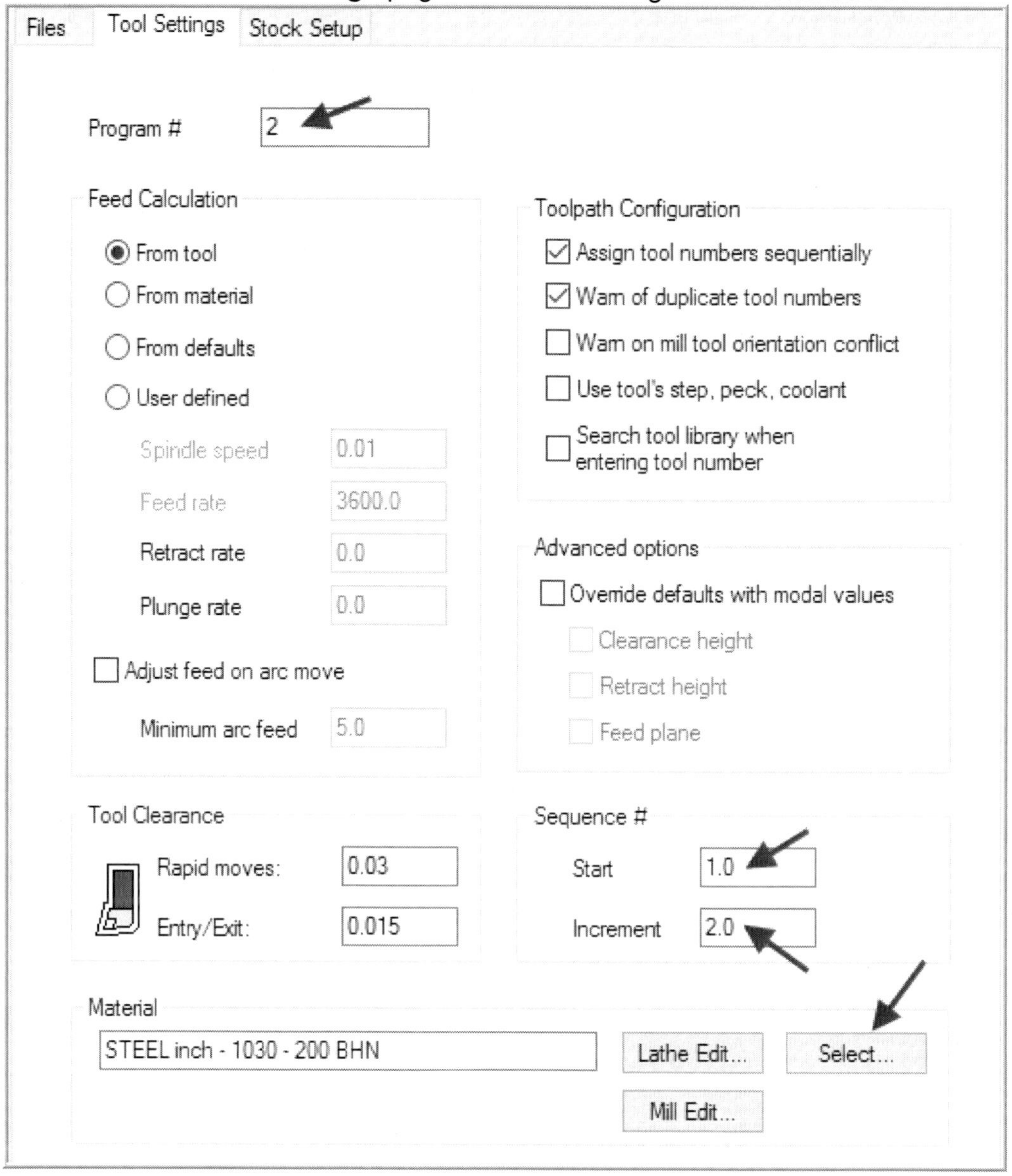

Tool Settings tab
Use this tab to control how Mastercam assigns tool numbers, tool offset numbers, and default values for feeds, speeds, coolant, and other toolpath parameters.

Program # The post processor will use this field if your machine tool requires a number for a program name.
From tool Uses the feed rate, plunge rate, retract rate, and spindle speed directly from the tool definition.
Assign tool numbers sequentially Assigns the next available tool number for new tools created or selected from the tool library. If you select this option, Mastercam overwrites the tool numbers stored in the tool definition with a sequential number.
Warn of duplicate tool numbers Informs you when duplicate tool numbers are entered and displays a description of the duplicate tool.
Sequence # (For the NC Code File) Enter the starting sequence number and the increment in the proper fields. The default values and specific format for these fields is determined by the **NC Output** section of the control definition.

17. To change the **Material** type to Aluminum 6061 now pick the **Select** button at the bottom of the Tool Settings page.
18. At the **Material List** dialog box open the Source drop down list and click on **Lathe–library.**

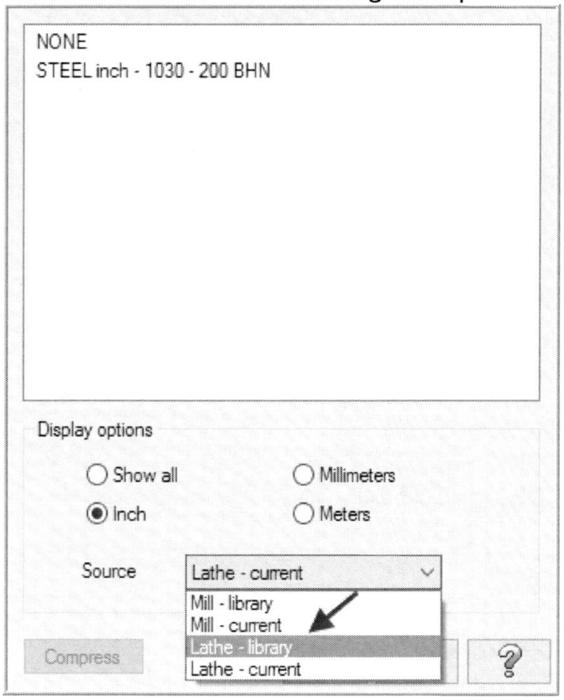

19. From the **Default Materials** list click on **ALUMINUM inch - 6061** and then click on [OK].

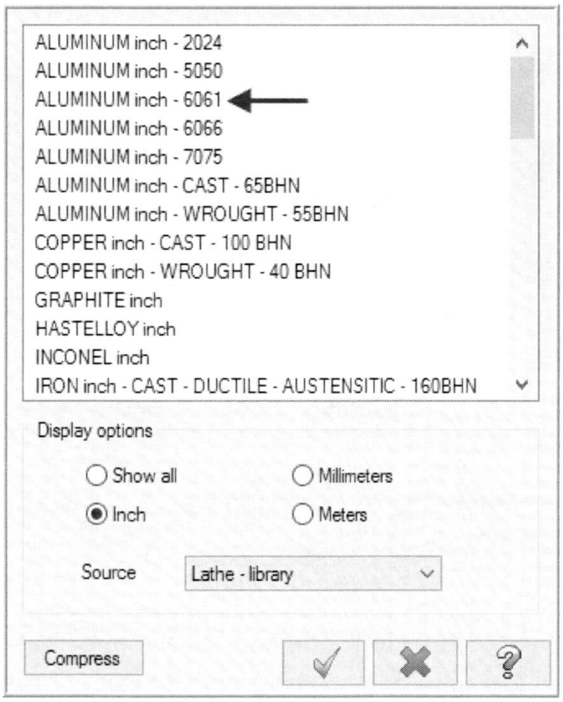

Material List dialog box
Use this dialog box to select materials and manage the materials list.

Right-click in the main window or on a material definition to see a menu of options.

These let you edit a material definition, create a new material, select different material libraries, and view the contents of a material library in different text formats.

Use the options in the **Source** list to display materials in the current part file or from a material library.

The **Compress** option reads a selected material library file and removes any deleted library entities. This decreases the size of the library file for more efficient storage.

20. Click on the OK button [OK] again to complete this Stock Setup function.

21. Right mouse click in the graphics area and click on the **Fit** icon .

➲ Notice the stock setup outline as indicated by broken lines as shown below:

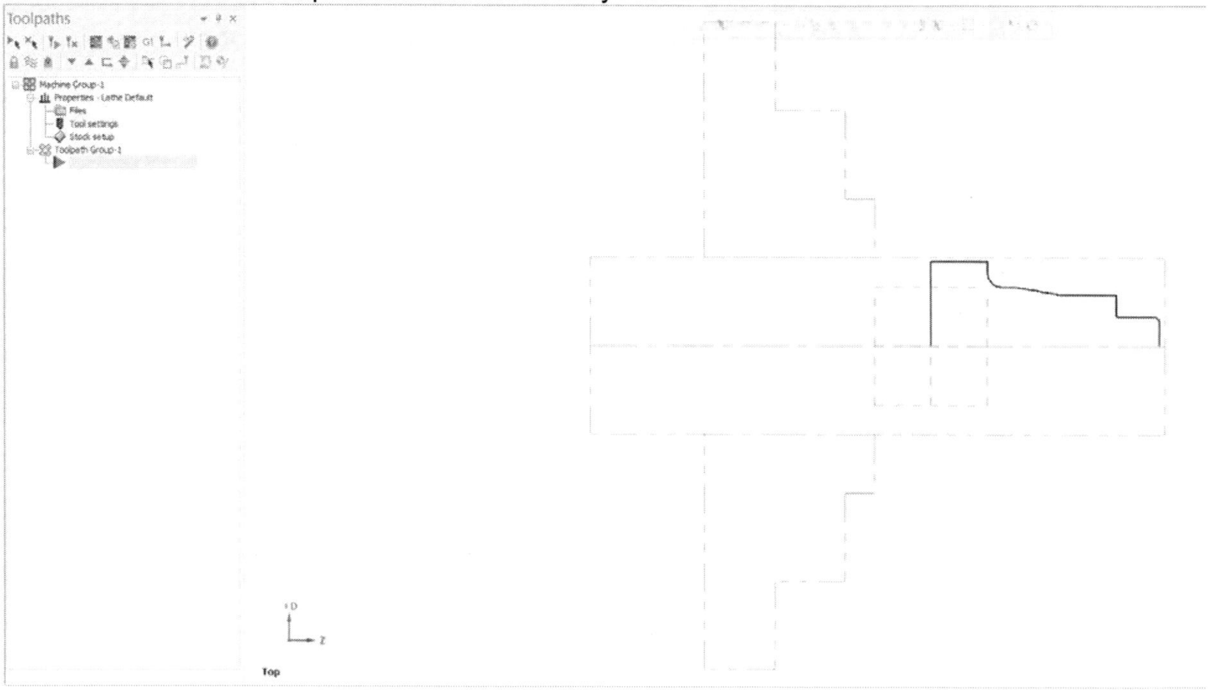

TASK 7:
FACE THE FRONT OF THE PART:

➲ In this task you will use a facing tool to face the front of the part in one cut.

1. If required right mouse click in the graphics area and click on the **Fit** icon.
2. Select the **TURNING** tab at the top right side of the screen.
3. Now select **Face** in the **General** section.

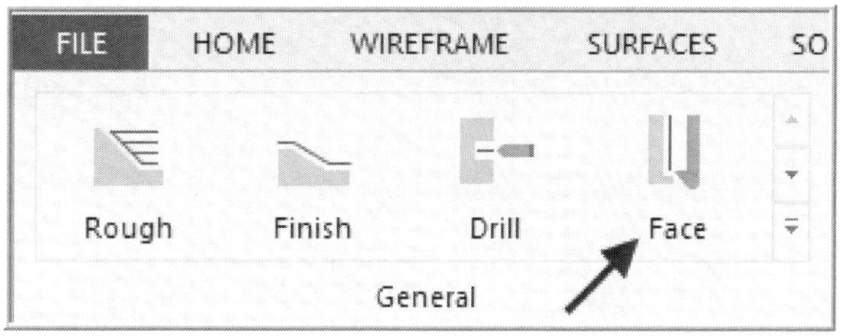

➲ After selecting the OK button you are confronted with **Toolpath parameters** page. The first task here will be to select **Tool #1 an OD Rough- Right – 80 deg.**

4. Click on **Tool #1** and make changes in the Toolpath parameters page as shown below.
5. Click on **Coolant,** open up the drop down menu for **Flood** and set it to **On.**

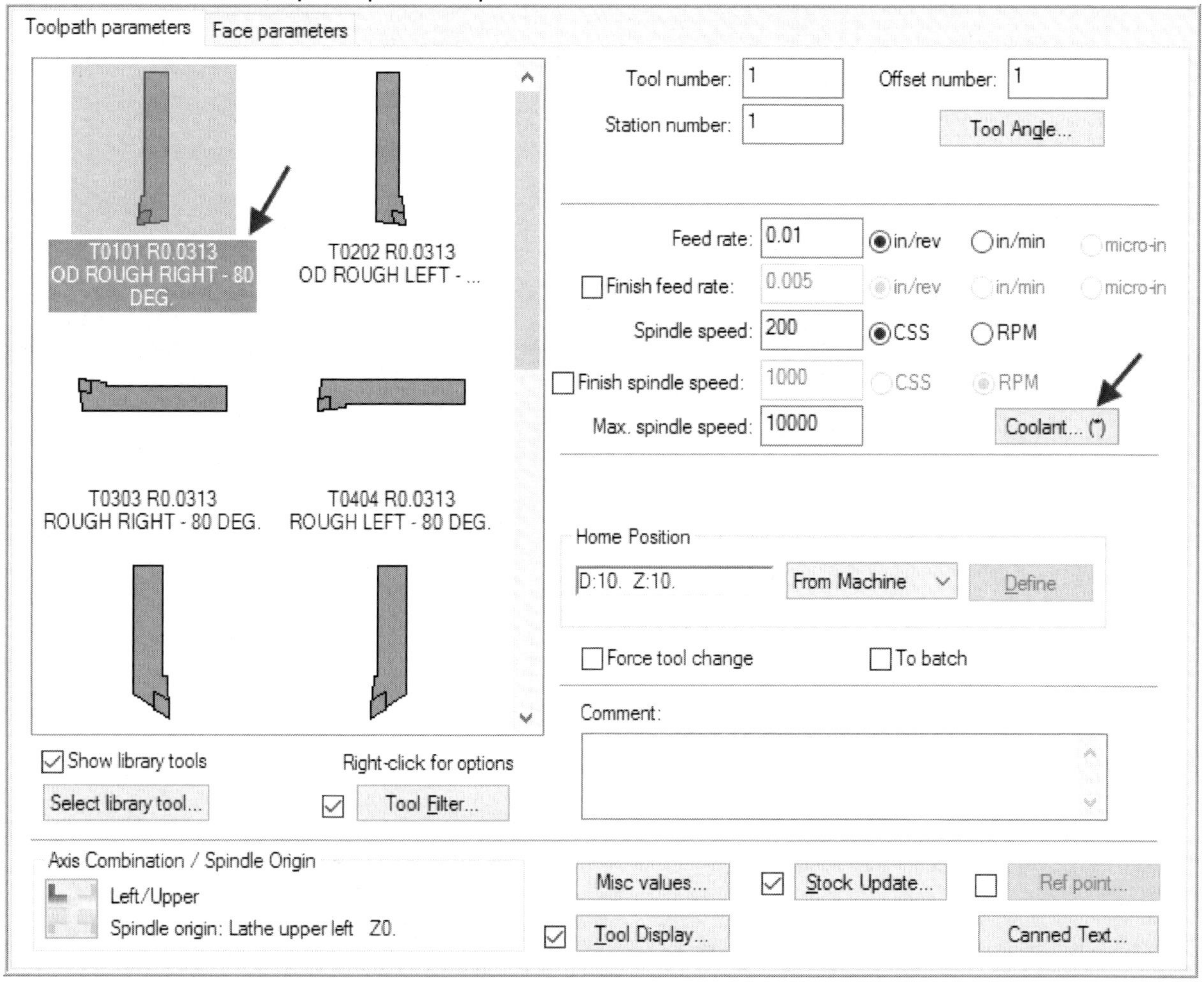

Use the Toolpath parameters tab to: Select a tool, set feeds and speeds, and set other general toolpath parameters. This tab is very similar for most Lathe toolpaths.

6. Select the **Face parameters** page and make changes as shown below.

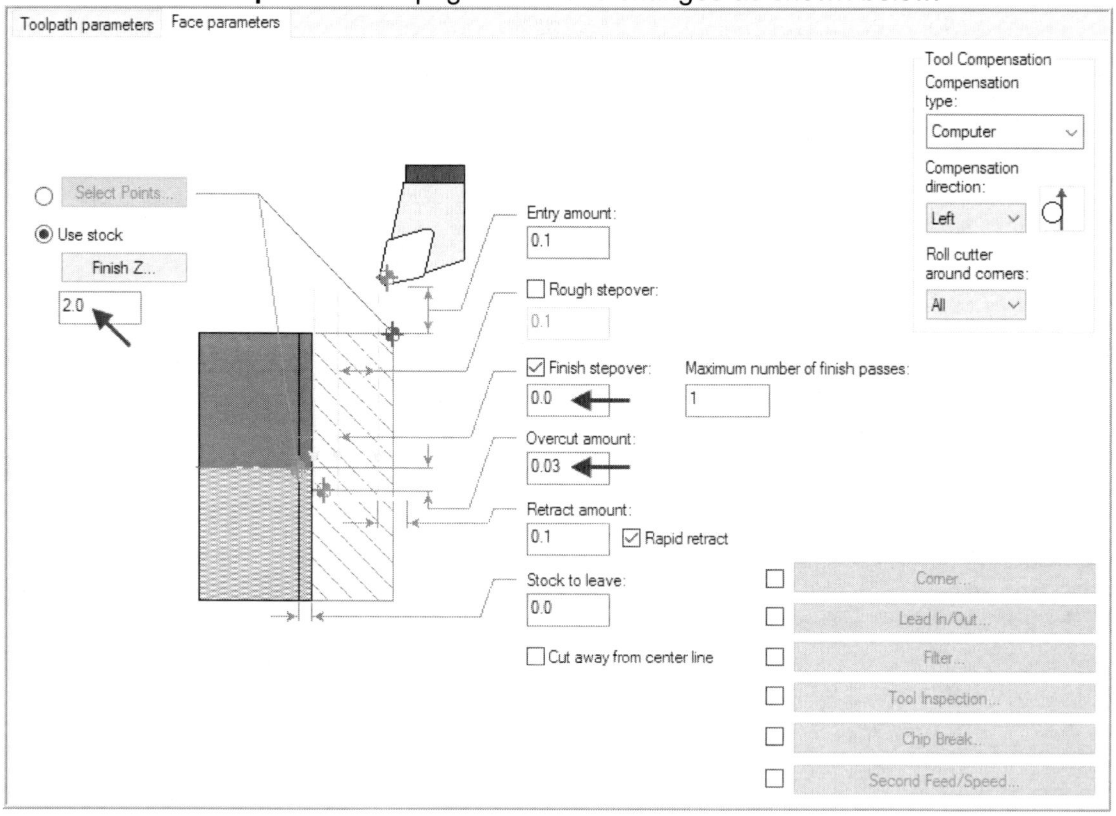

Finish stepover
Select this option to create one or more finish passes. Enter a stepover distance to define how much stock gets removed during each finish cut.
Overcut amount
A rectangle is used to define the material removed by the facing toolpath. The overcut amount determines how far past the rectangle the tool will cut. Typically this is a small distance that the **tool cuts past the part**

7. Select the OK button  to complete this **Lathe Face** operation.

➲ A new Toolpath called **1-Lathe Face** should be displayed as shown below:

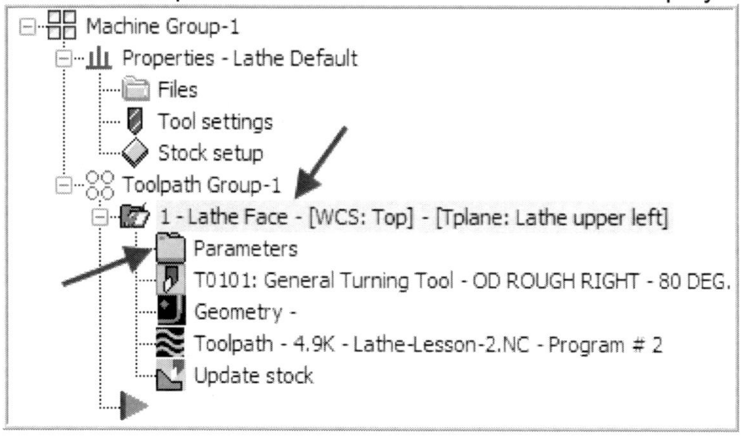

Note: The new Toolpath called **1-Lathe Face**. This is where all the toolpath information is kept. If changes are required to this toolpath just click on the parameter icon 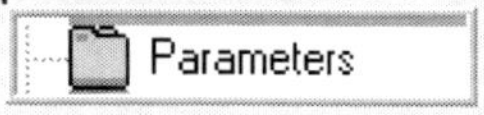

and the screens from steps 6 and 7 will be available. This is handy in case a mistake was made in setting the toolpath parameters or in case a modification needs to be made.

TASK 8:

ROUGH THE OUTSIDE DIAMETERS

➲ In this task you will use the same tool as used for the previous facing operation **Tool #1 an OD Rough- Right – 80 deg.**

1. On the **TURNING** tab select **Rough** in the **General** section.

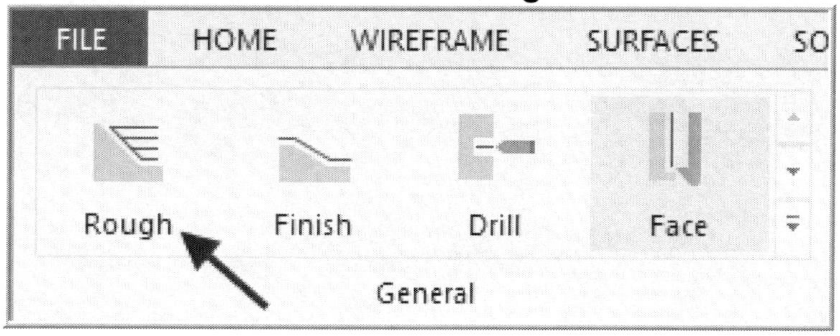

Rough toolpaths
Use rough toolpaths to quickly remove large amounts of stock in preparation for a finish pass. Roughing passes are typically straight cuts parallel to the Z-axis; however, you can set options for plunging into undercut areas. Standard rough toolpaths also include a semi-finish option, in which the roughing tool makes a final pass which follows the part contour, like a finish pass.
Mastercam includes several types of roughing toolpaths:
Standard rough toolpaths, which let you access all of Mastercam's roughing options.
Quick rough toolpaths, which let you quickly create simple rough toolpaths with fewer options.
Canned rough toolpaths, which use your machine tool's canned cycles to create the most efficient code (however, these do not offer as many options as the standard rough toolpaths).
Canned pattern repeat toolpaths, which create roughing passes in the shape of the part contour, rather than cutting parallel to the Z-axis.

2. In the **Chaining** window Chaining mode is set to **Partial** by default.

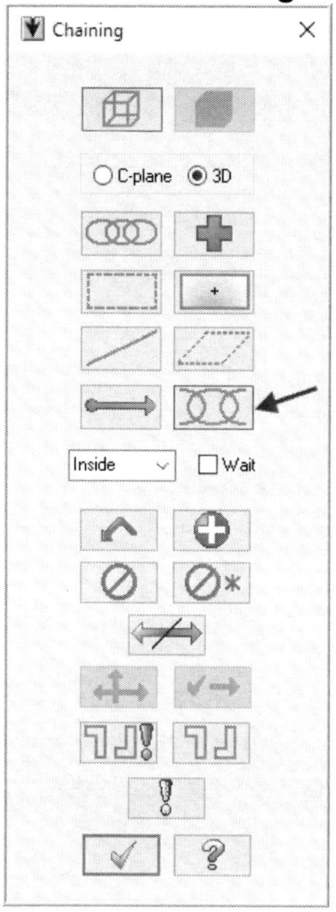

3. Click on the **chamfer** as shown below:

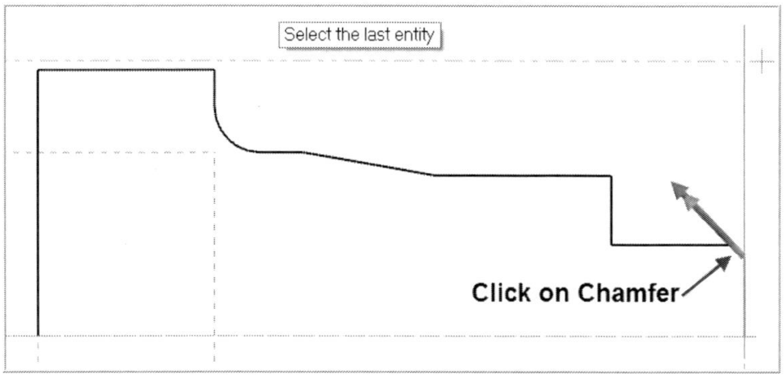

After you have selected the chamfer **ensure** that the arrows are pointing up and to the left of the part. If not select the reverse button in the Chaining dialog box.

4. Then select the Line shown below as the end entity in this chain.

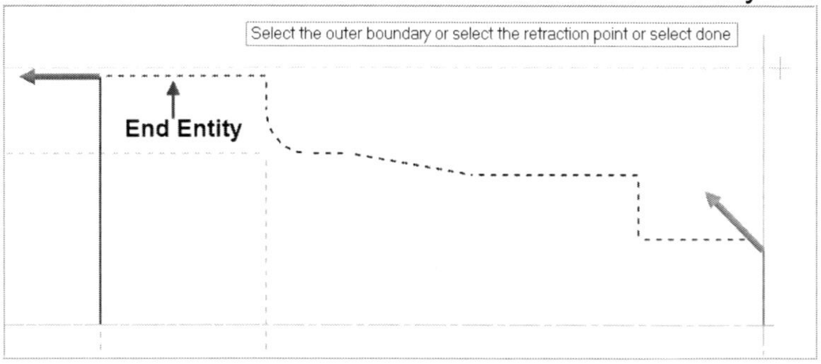

5. Select the OK button  to exit the Chaining dialog window.

6. In the **Toolpath parameters** page select the same tool used to face the part **Tool #1 an OD Rough- Right – 80 deg** and make changes as shown below.
7. Click on **Coolant,** open up the drop down menu for **Flood** and set it to **On.**

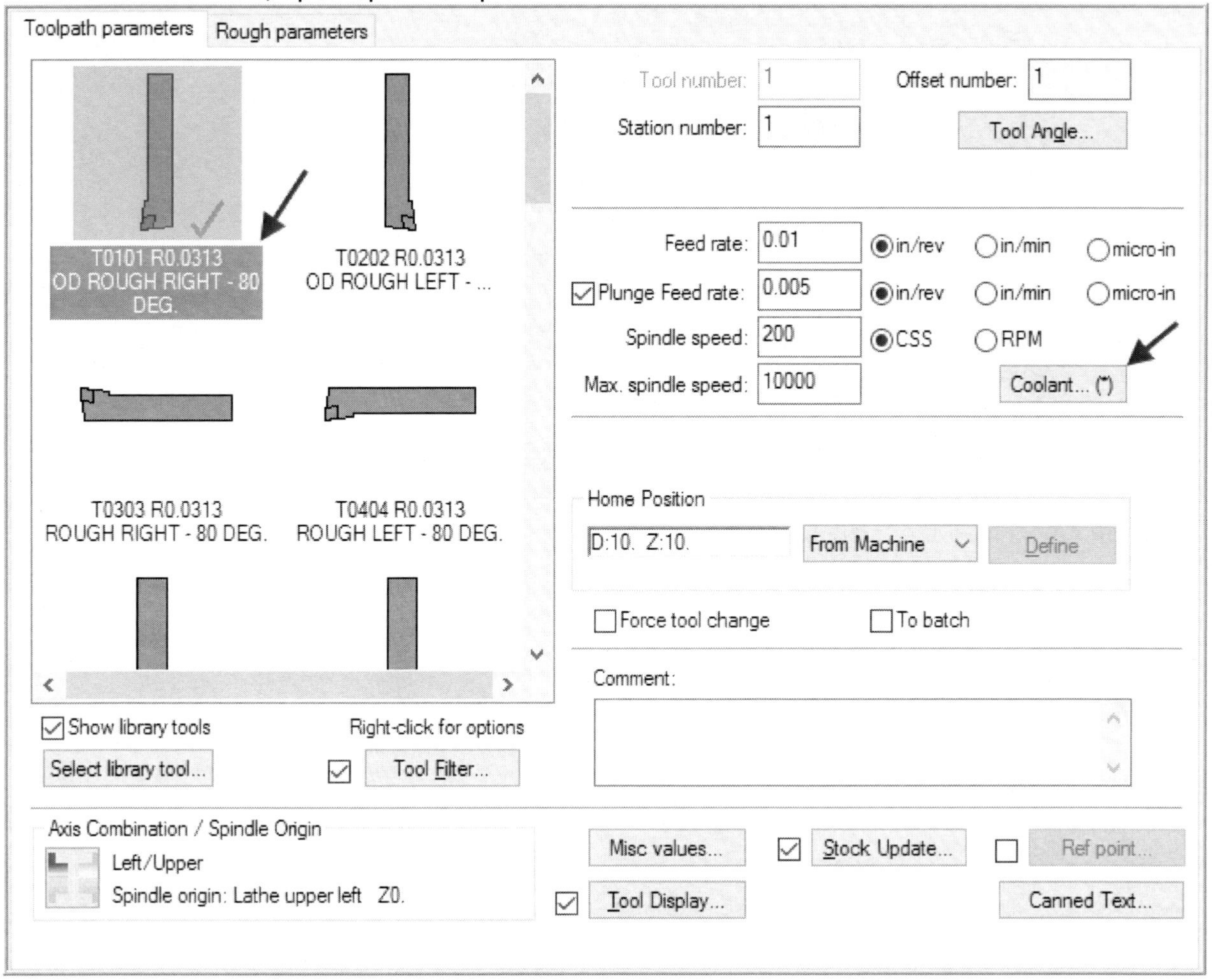

8. Select the **Rough parameters** page and make changes as shown below.

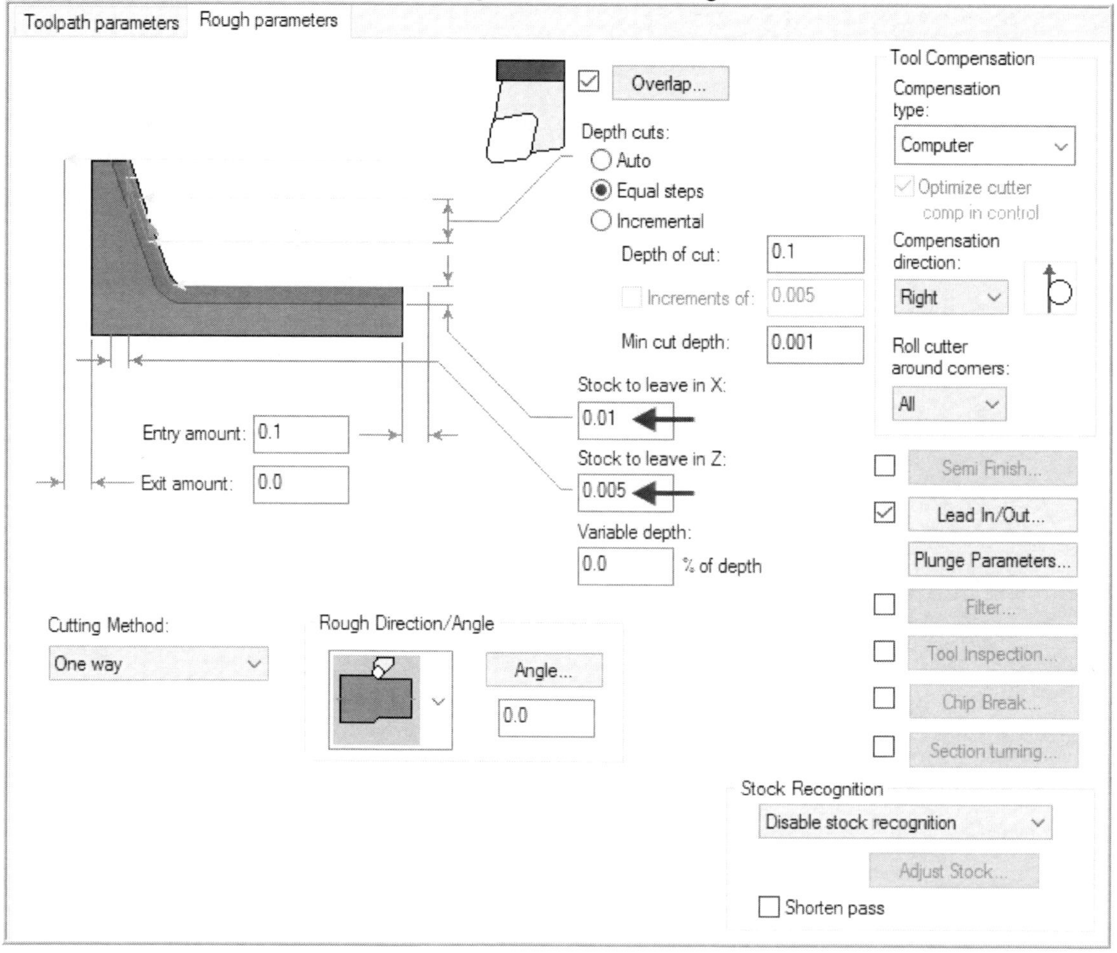

9. Select the **Lead In/Out** button, select the **Lead out** page and extend the contour by **0.2**.

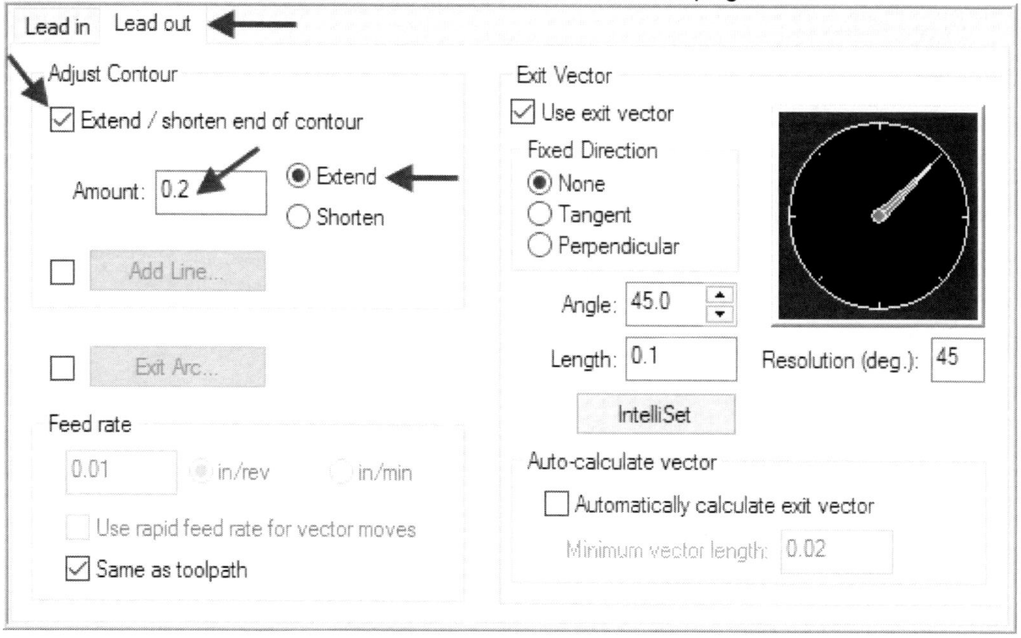

10. Select the OK button ✓ to exit this function.

11. Select the OK button ✓ to exit Rough Parameters.

TASK 9:
FINISH THE OUTSIDE DIAMETERS

➲ You will finish the outside diameters in one cut using **Tool #2 OD Finish Right – 35 DEG.**

1. On the **TURNING** tab select **Finish** in the **General** section.

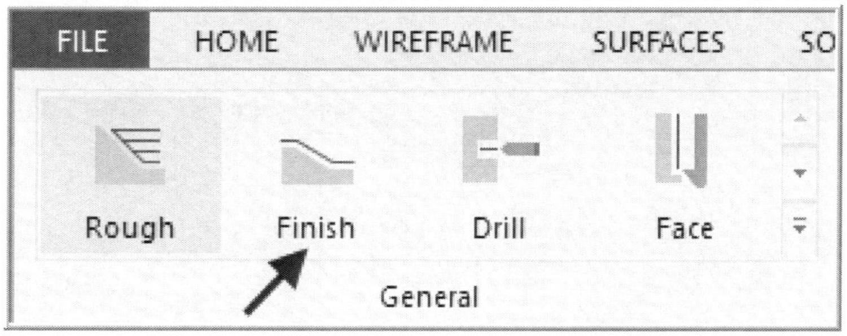

Finish toolpaths
Use finish toolpaths to have the tool follow the contour of chained geometry.

Typically, a finish toolpath follows a roughing toolpath, but this is not required.

You can create a finish toolpath even if no roughing operation has been created.

2. Select **Last** in the Chaining dialog box.

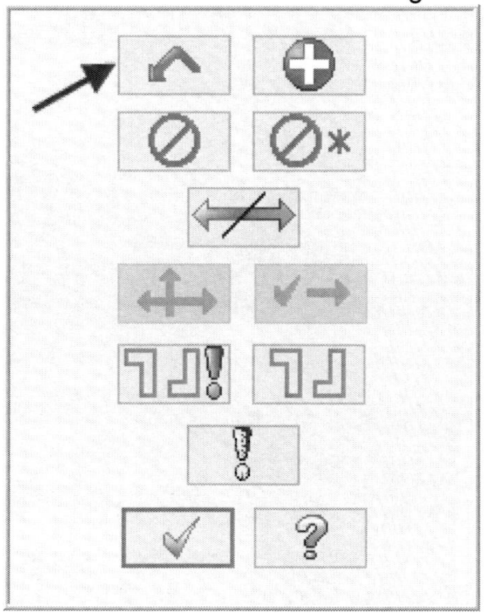

3. Select the **OK** button to complete the selection.

4. Select **Tool #2 OD Finish Right – 35 DEG** tool from the tool list and make changes as shown below. **Coolant Flood** is set to **On**.

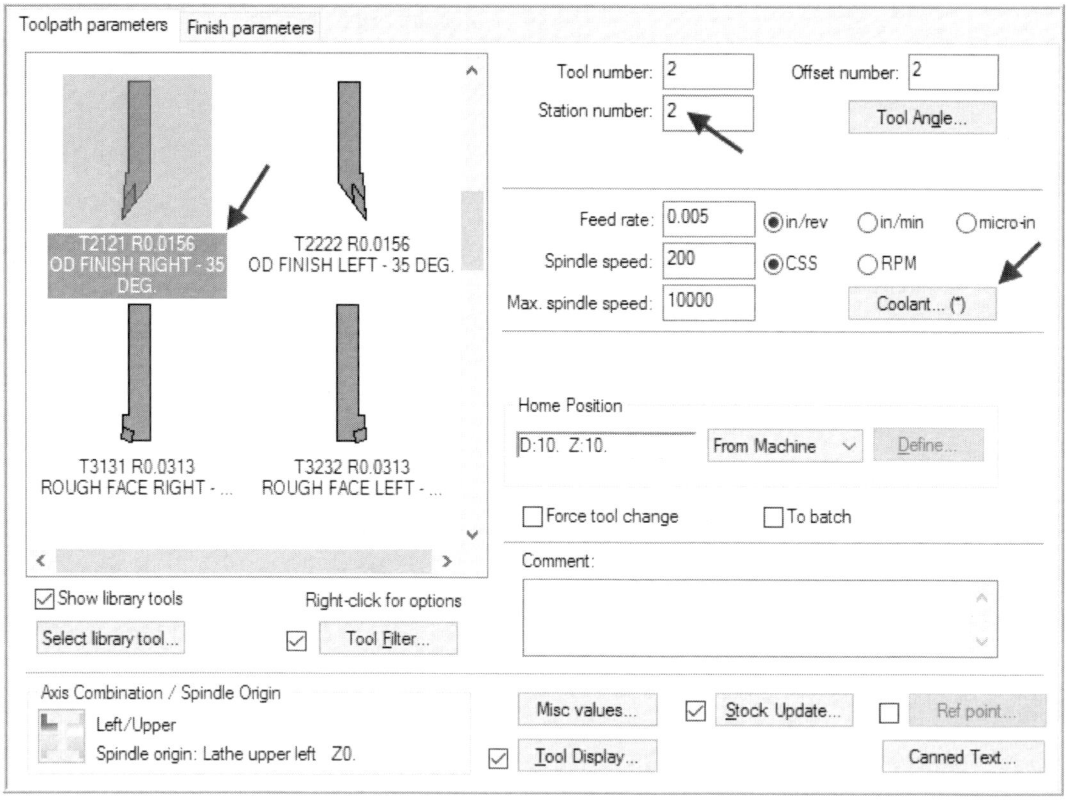

5. Select the **Finish parameters** page and make changes as shown below.

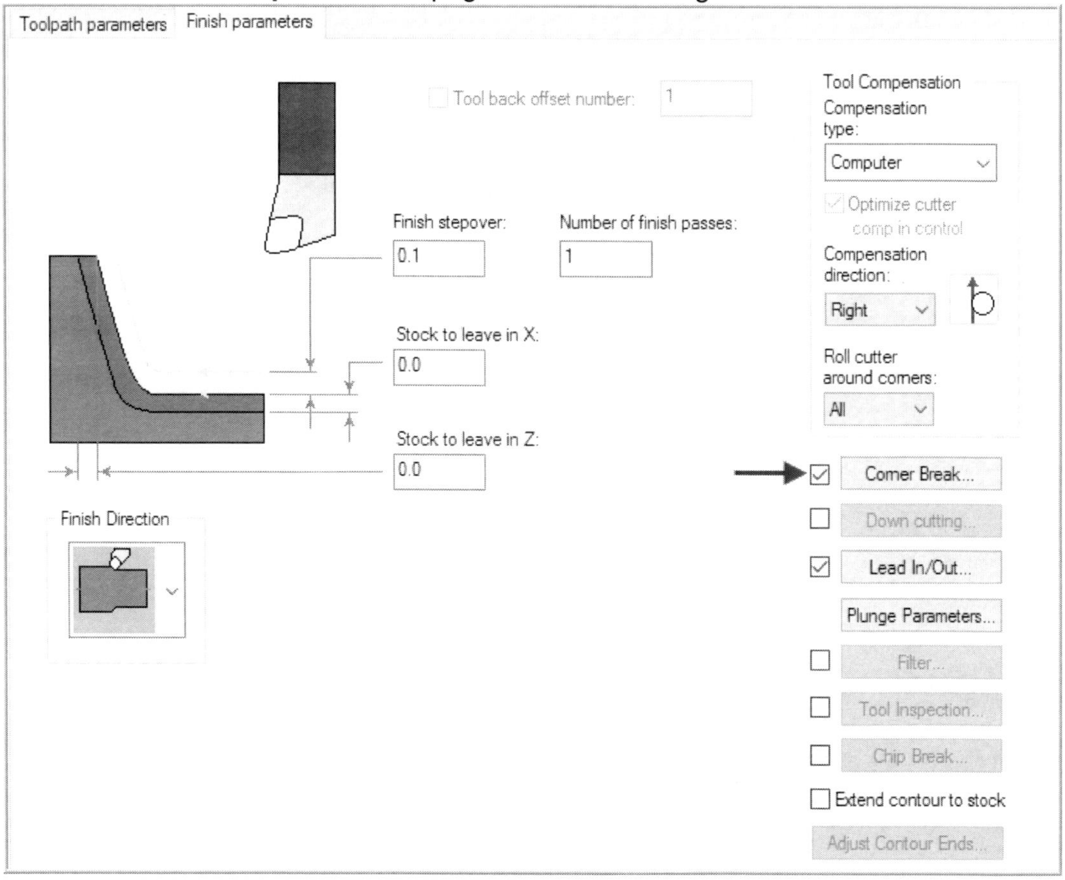

6. Select the **Corner Break** button and make changes as shown below if required:

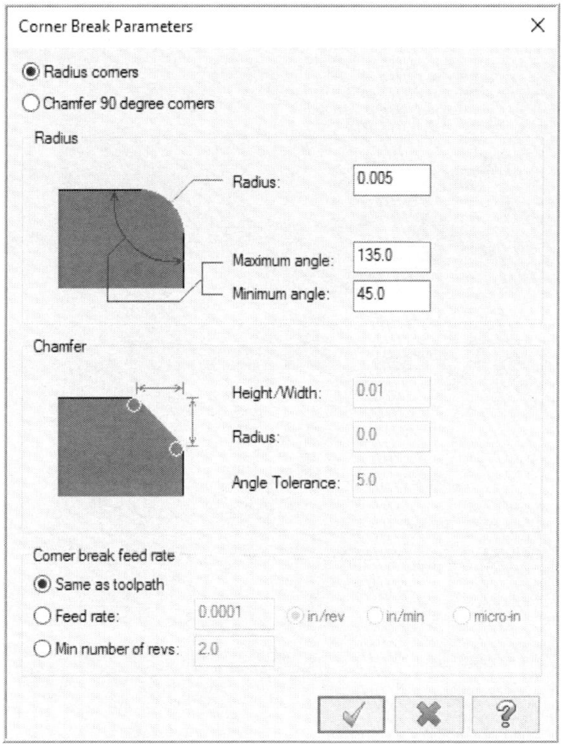

> **Corner Break**
> Use this dialog box to automatically create radii or chamfers on all outer corners of lathe finish toolpaths.
>
> You can also set the feed rate when the tool creates the radii or chamfers.

7. Select the OK button [✓] to complete this feature.
8. Select the **Lead In/Out** button select the **Lead in** page and change the **Fixed Direction** to **Tangent** as shown below:

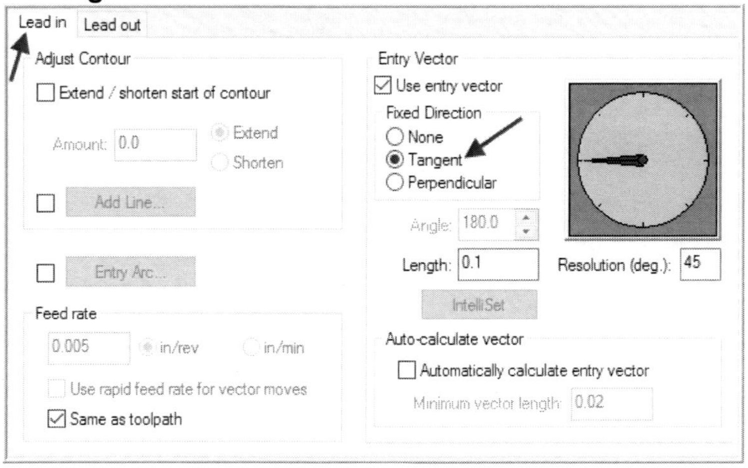

> **Lead In/Out dialog box**
> Use this dialog box to control how the tool approaches or retracts from the part for each pass in the toolpath. This eliminates the need to create extra geometry for this purpose
>
> **Fixed Direction Tangent**
> Force the vector to be tangent to either the first move in the toolpath, or the entry arc, if one is defined.

> **Lead In/Out dialog box**
> Use any of the following techniques:
> **Extend/Shorten** the geometry in the chained contour
> **Add Line** to the start of the chained contour
> **Create a tangent arc** move to the start of the toolpath
> **Manually define an Entry/Exit vector**, or let the system calculate a vector for you.
>
> The Lead In and Lead Out tabs have identical options for creating entry and exit moves, letting you set different values for each move.

9. **Select** the **Lead out** page and **extend** the contour by **0.2** as shown below:

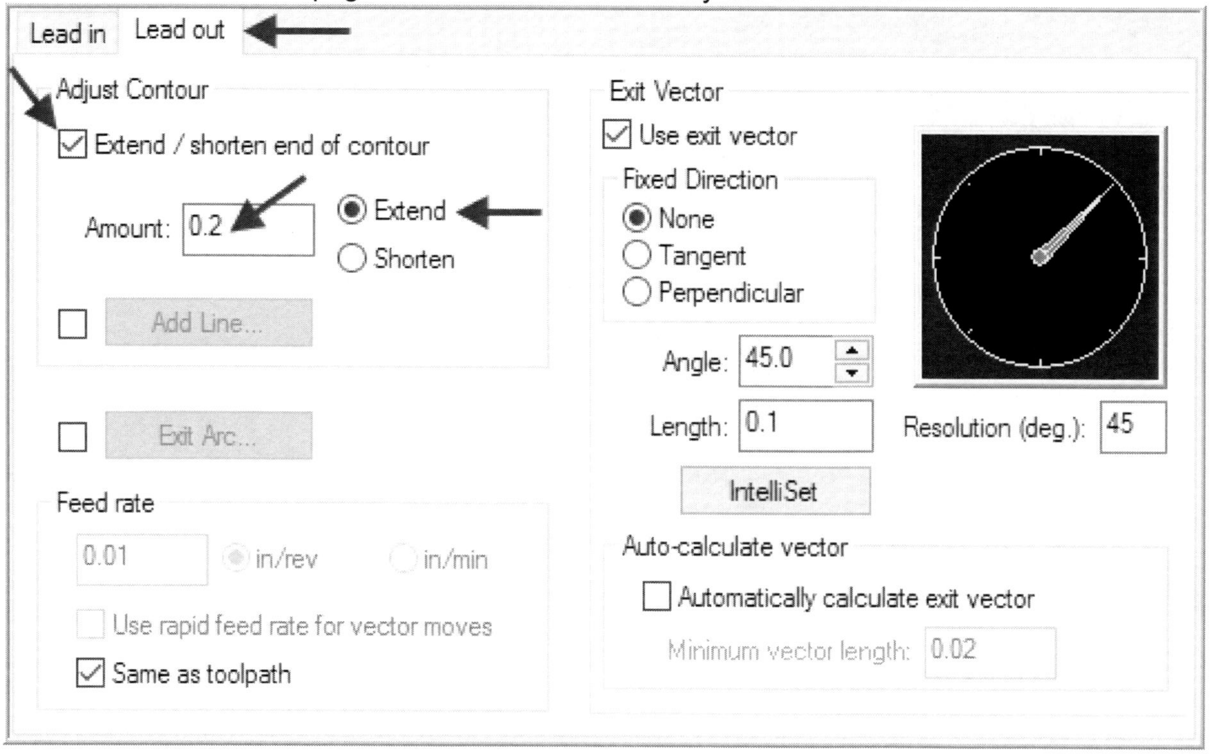

Lead In/Out dialog box
You can also combine different types of moves.

For example, you can extend a contour and lead in to it with a tangent arc.

10. Select the OK button  to exit **Lead In/Out.**
11. Select the OK button  to exit **Finish parameters.**

TASK 10:
CENTER DRILL THE .25" HOLE

➲ In this task you will center drill .2" depth using **Tool #3 Centre Drill - .25 diameter.**

1. Select **Drill** in the **General** section of the **Turning** tab.

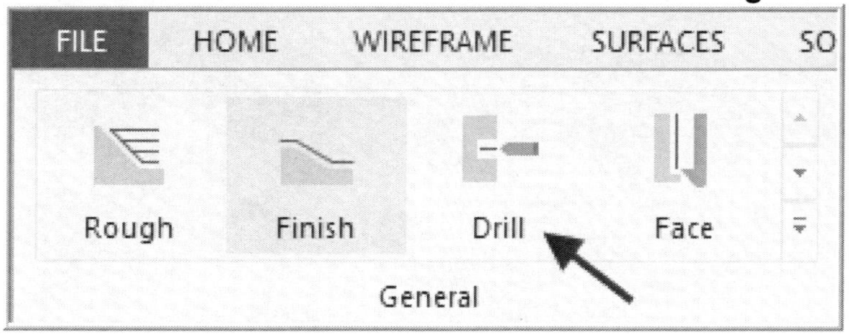

Lathe Drill Toolpaths
Mastercam Lathe offers several different types of drill cycles for drill toolpaths.

Lathe drill toolpaths typically drill into the face of the part along the centerline.

To drill off-center, in the side of the part, or in a different plane, use one of Mastercam's C-axis toolpaths.

You do not need to have any geometry or drill points in the graphics window to create a drill toolpath. Mastercam creates the toolpath entirely from parameters which you specify.

2. Scroll down and select the **Centre Drill .25 diameter** tool from the tool list and make changes as shown below. **Coolant Flood** is set to **On**.

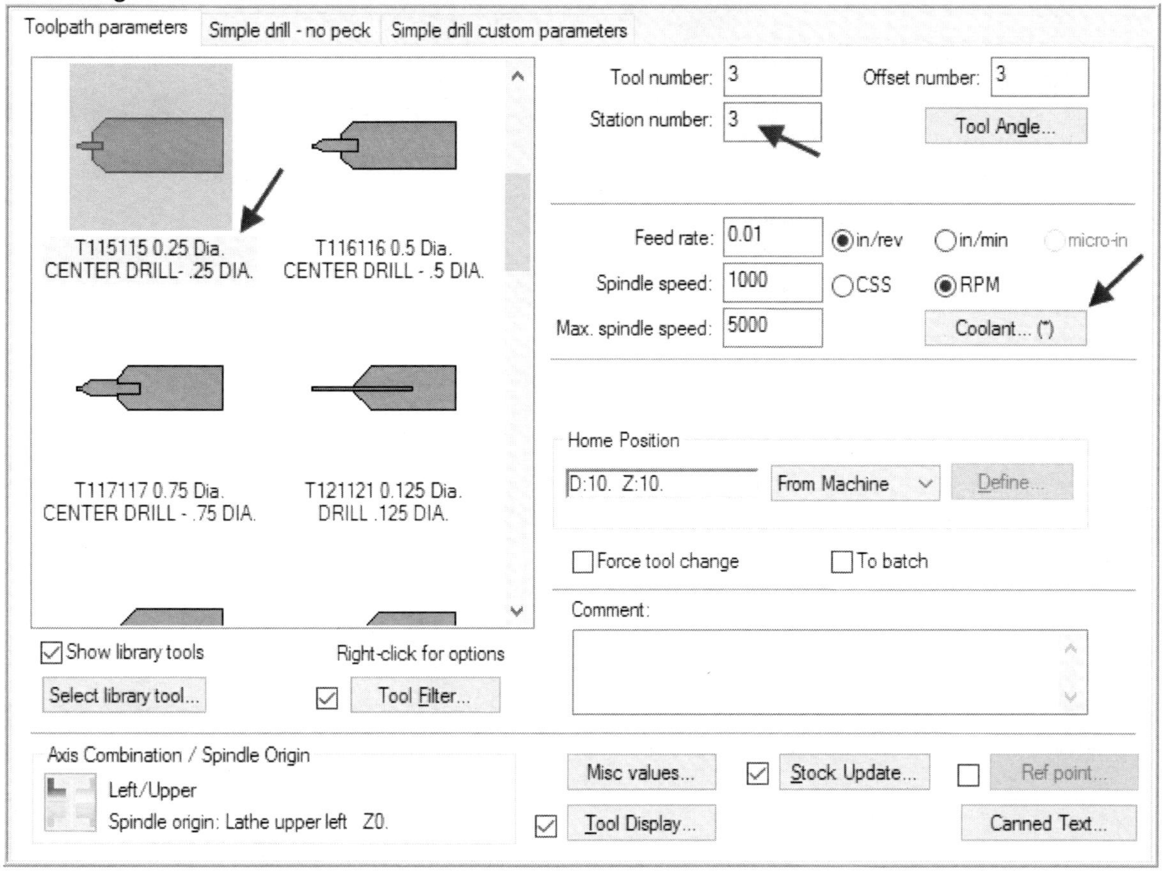

3. Select the **Simple drill – no peck** page and make changes as shown below:

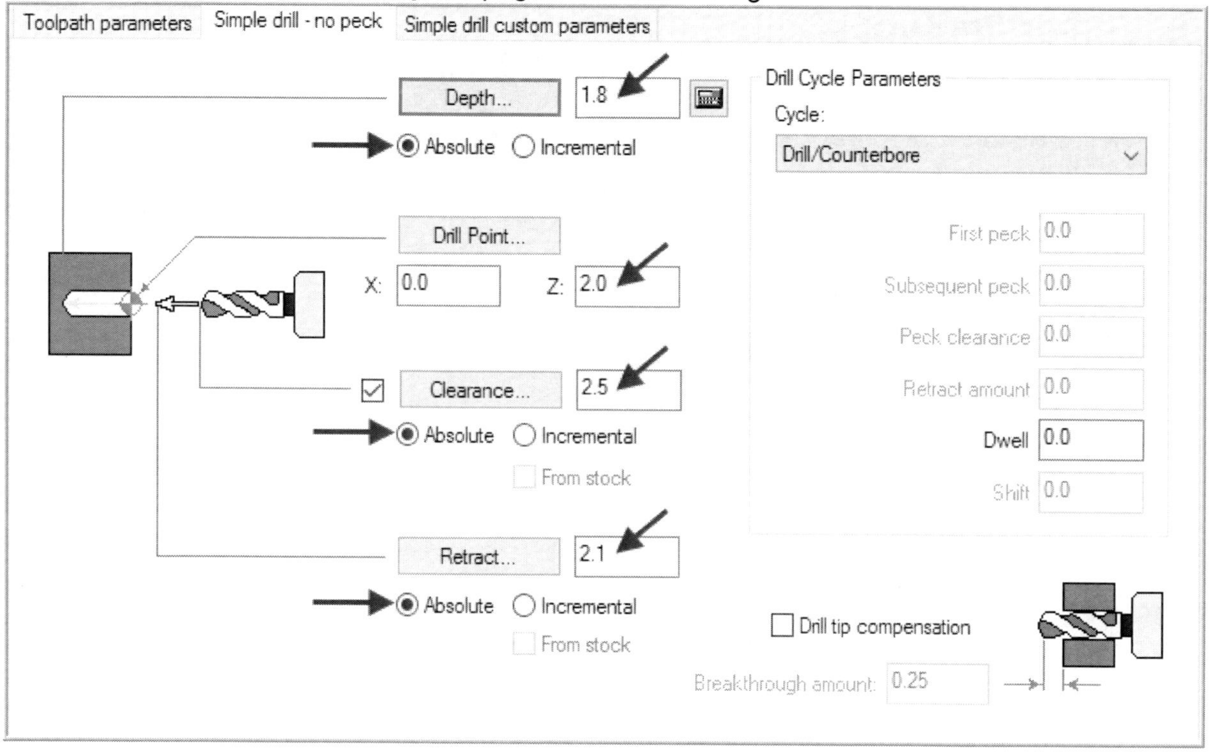

4. Select the OK button  to exit **Simple drill – no peck.**

TASK 11:
DRILL THE .25" HOLE

➲ In this task you will drill the .25" hole .75" depth using **Tool #4 Drill - .25 diameter.**

1. Select **Drill** in the **General** section of the **Turning** tab.

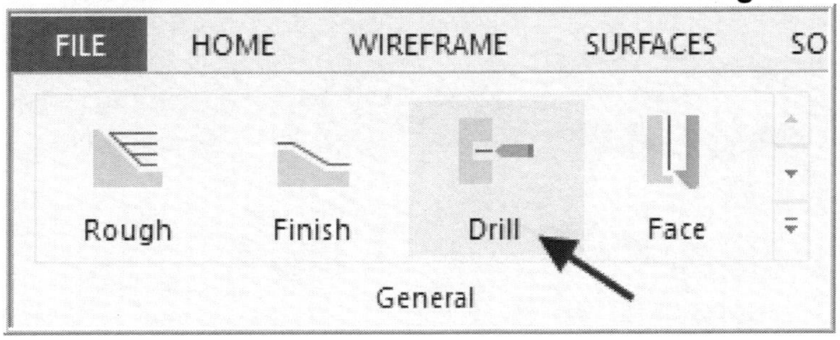

2. Scroll down and select the **Drill - .25 diameter** tool from the tool list and make changes as shown below. **Coolant Flood** is set to **On**.

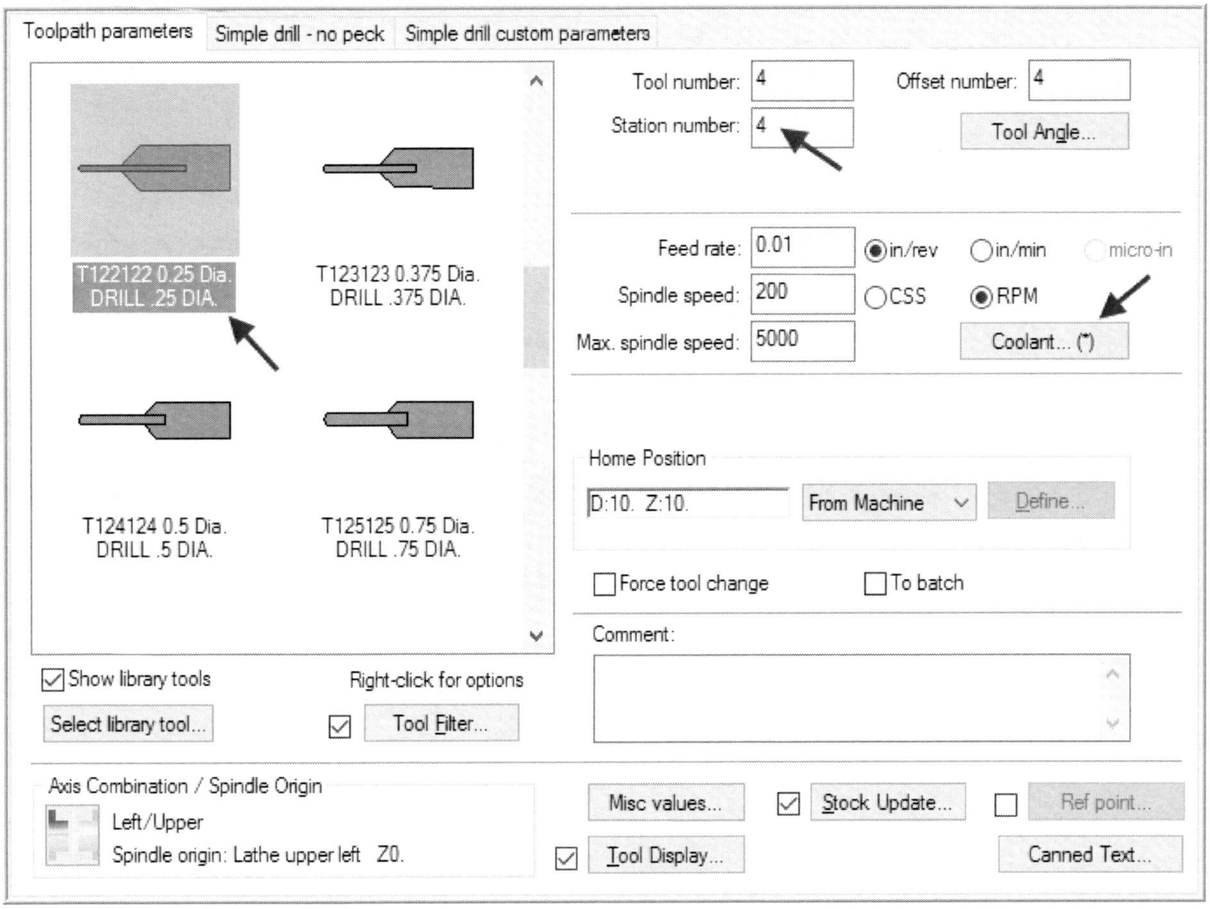

3. Select the **Single drill – no peck** page and make changes as shown below. This hole will be **peck drilled**. The **depth of the hole is .75 from the front face** so click in the space for depth and type in **1.25** and hit the enter key. Make changes as shown below:

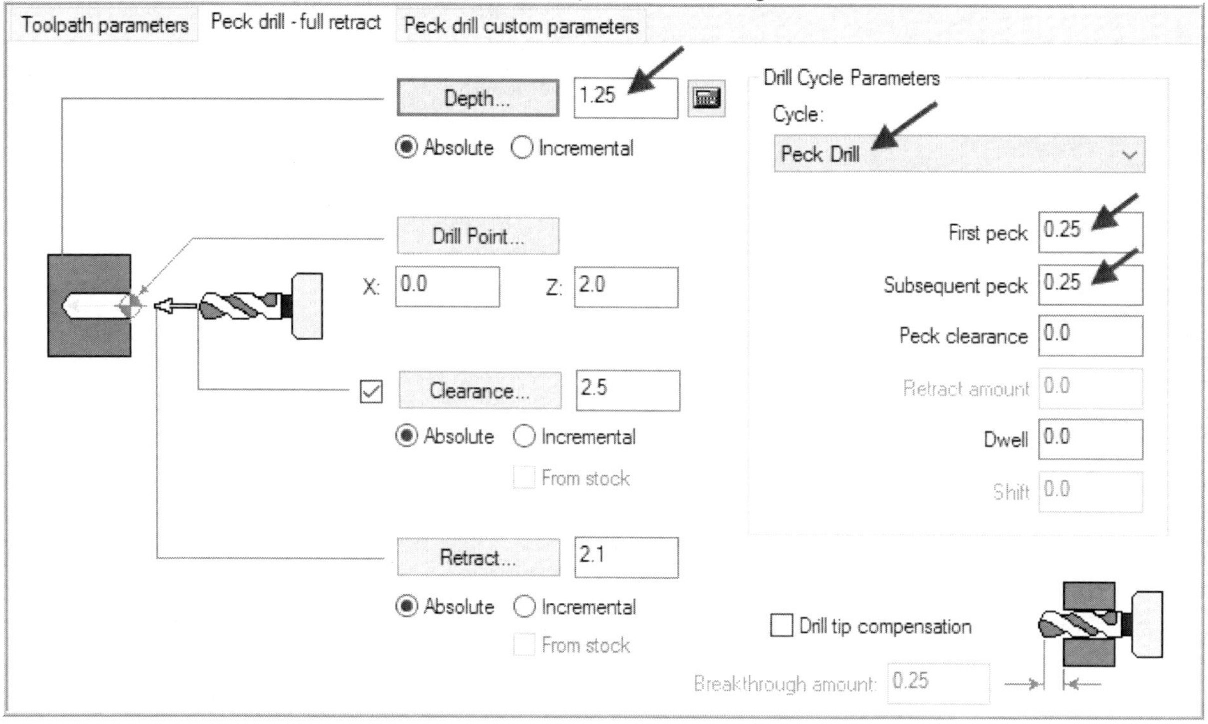

The hole depth on the drawing is dimensioned to .a depth of 0.75" at the full diameter of the hole. So the point of the drill will have to go deeper than 0.75"
You can use the depth calculator button to figure out the correct depth.

4. Select the **Depth Calculator** icon.

5. Make changes to the **Depth Calculator** as shown below, if required.

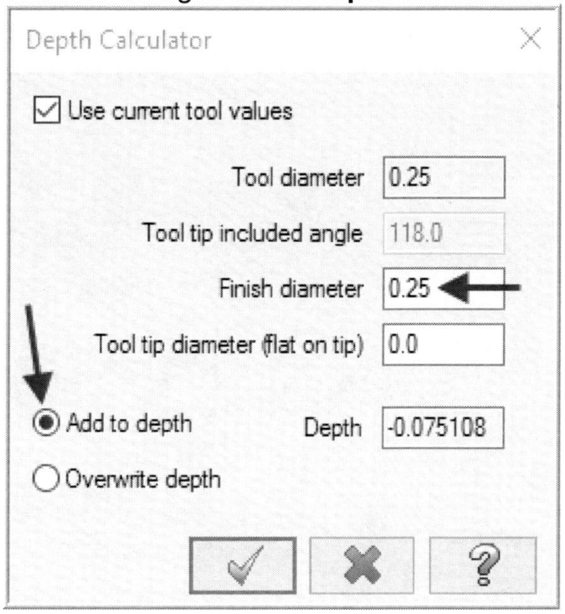

Use the **Depth Calculator** to calculate the proper drilling depth when the finish diameter of the hole is different from the drill diameter—for example, when countersinking a hole.

Mastercam automatically displays the Tool diameter, Tool tip included angle, and Tool tip diameter for the drill that has been selected for the operation.

Deselect Use current tool values to specify different values for these parameters.

6. Select the **OK** button  to exit **the Depth Calculator.**
7. The depth has now been updated.

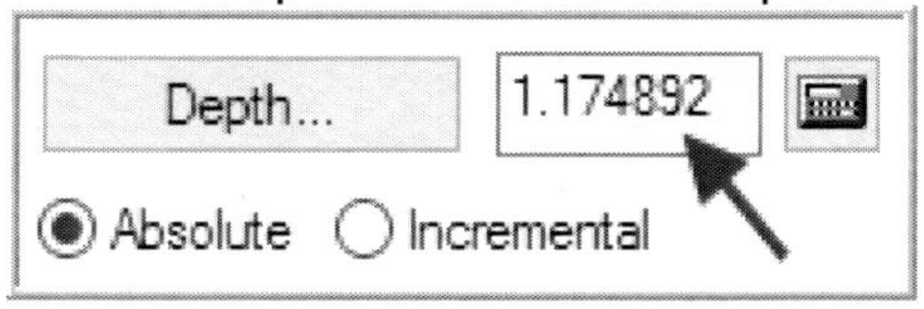

8. Select the **OK** button  to exit **Peck drill – full retract.**

TASK 12:
CUTOFF THE PART

➲ In this task you will cutoff the part using a .125 wide cutoff tool.

1. Click on the **Select all operations** icon .
2. Now click on the **Toggle display on selected operations**  button **or ALT and T** to show/hide the tool path.

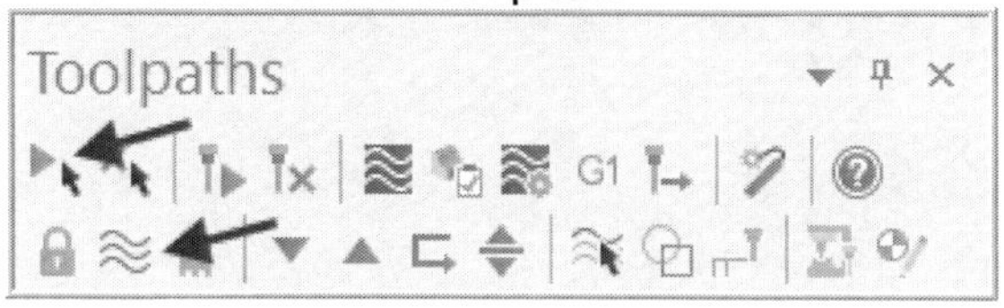

Toolpath Lines visible:

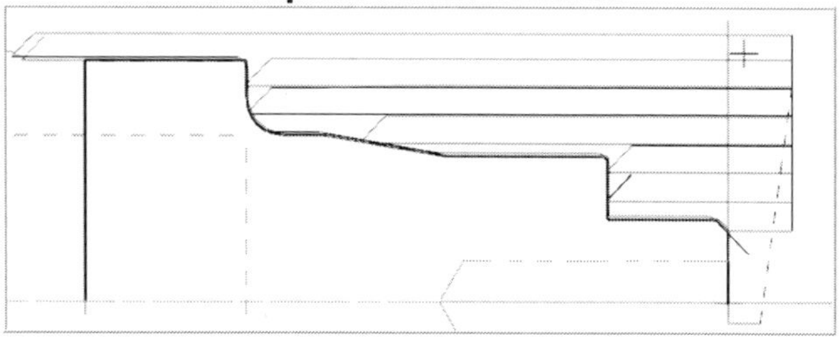

Press Alt T to hide toolpath Lines:

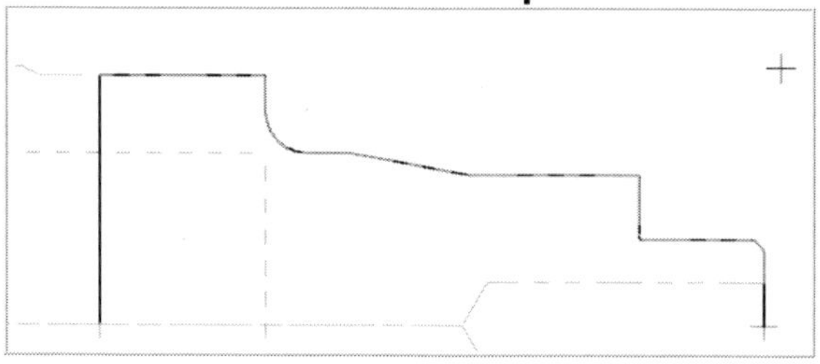

3. Click on the **Expand gallery** down arrow to view additional options in the **General** toolpath section.

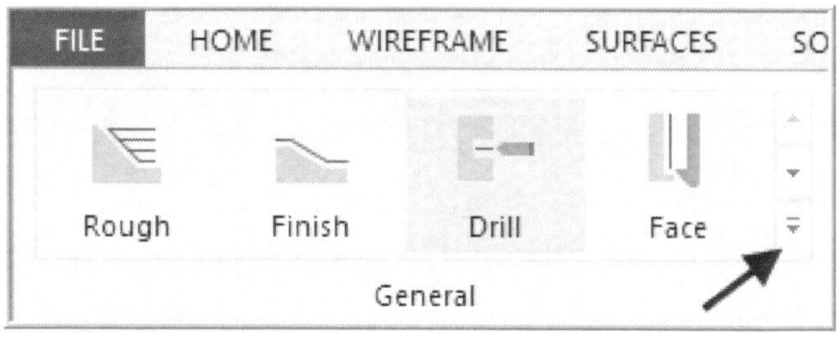

4. In the **General** section select **Cutoff.**

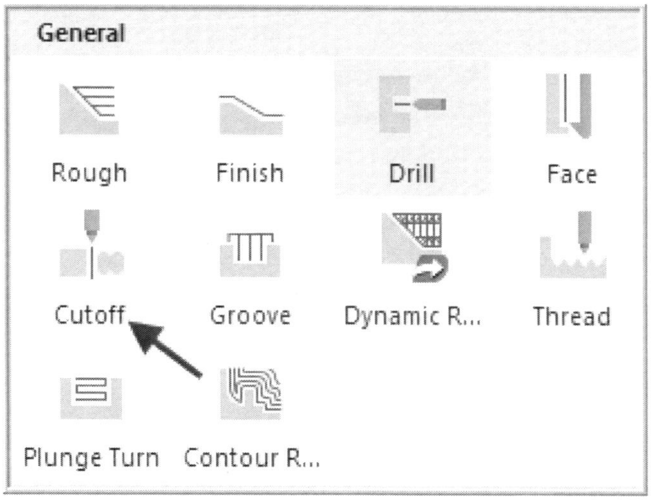

5. Pick where **Line 1 and Line 2** meet as shown below: (Move the cursor over the corner until the visual cue 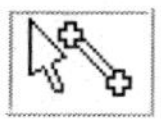 for End point displays and then click on this point.)

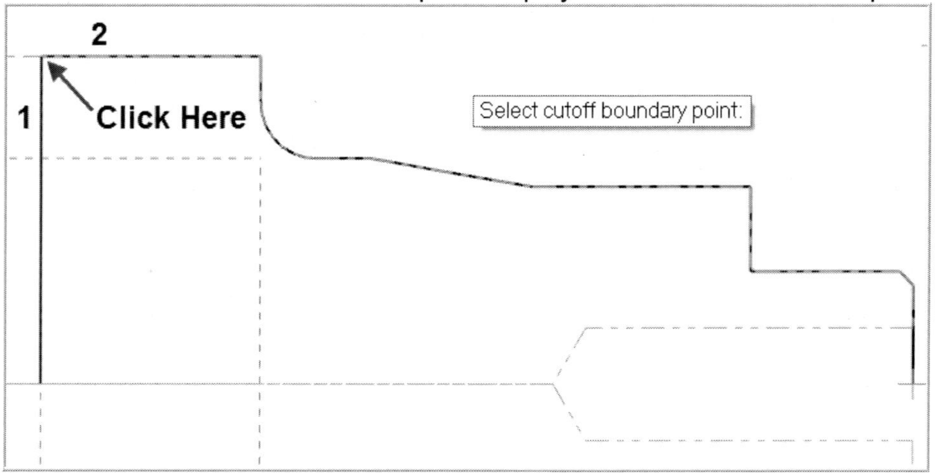

6. Scroll down the tool window and select the **OD Cutoff Right Width .125** tool and make changes as shown below in the **Toolpath parameters** page.

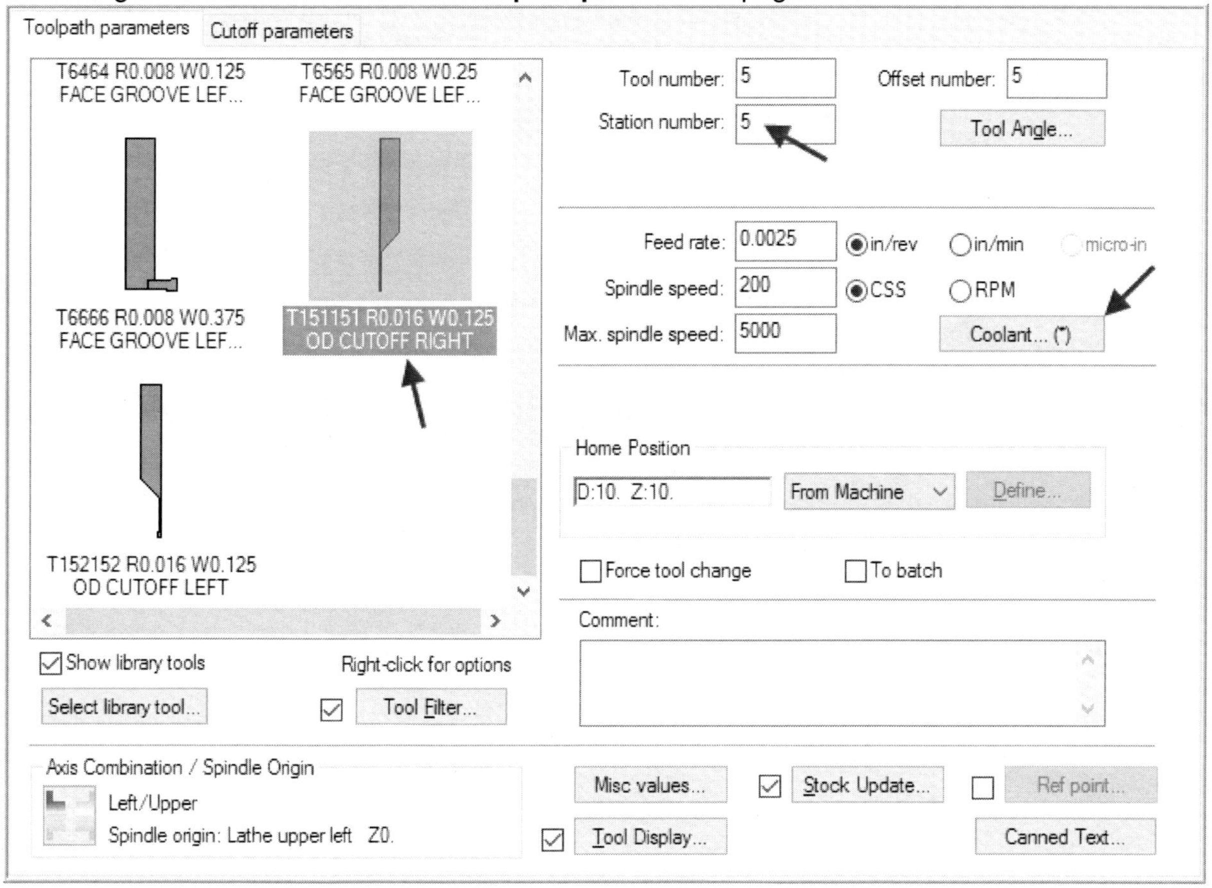

7. Click on the **Stock Update…** button.

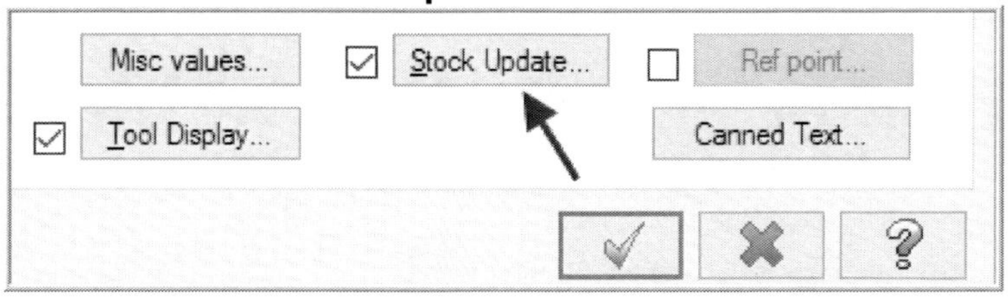

8. Activate **Keep both pieces**.

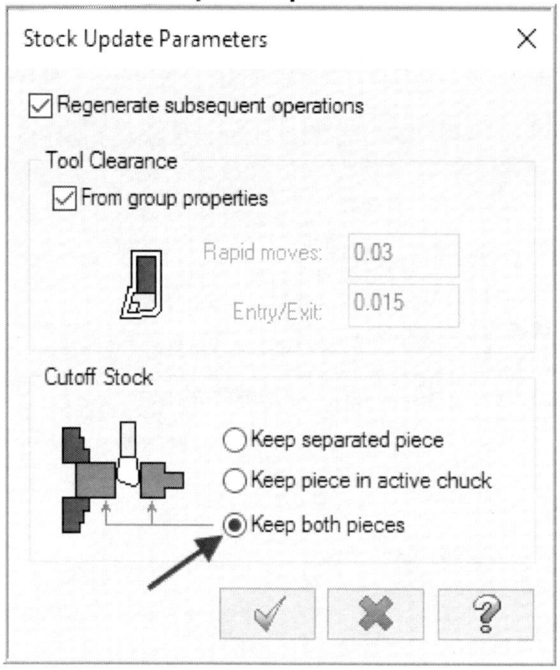

Keep separated piece
Select to display the part boundary after the part is cut off.

Keep piece in active chuck
Select to display the stock boundary after the part is cut off.

Keep both pieces
Select to display both the separated piece and the leftover piece. This is useful when the separated piece will be transferred to a sub spindle and you will be machining on both spindles at the same time.

These options are available only with cutoff operations.

9. Select the **OK** button to exit **Stock Update Parameters.**
10. Select the **Cutoff parameters** page and make sure the settings are as shown below:

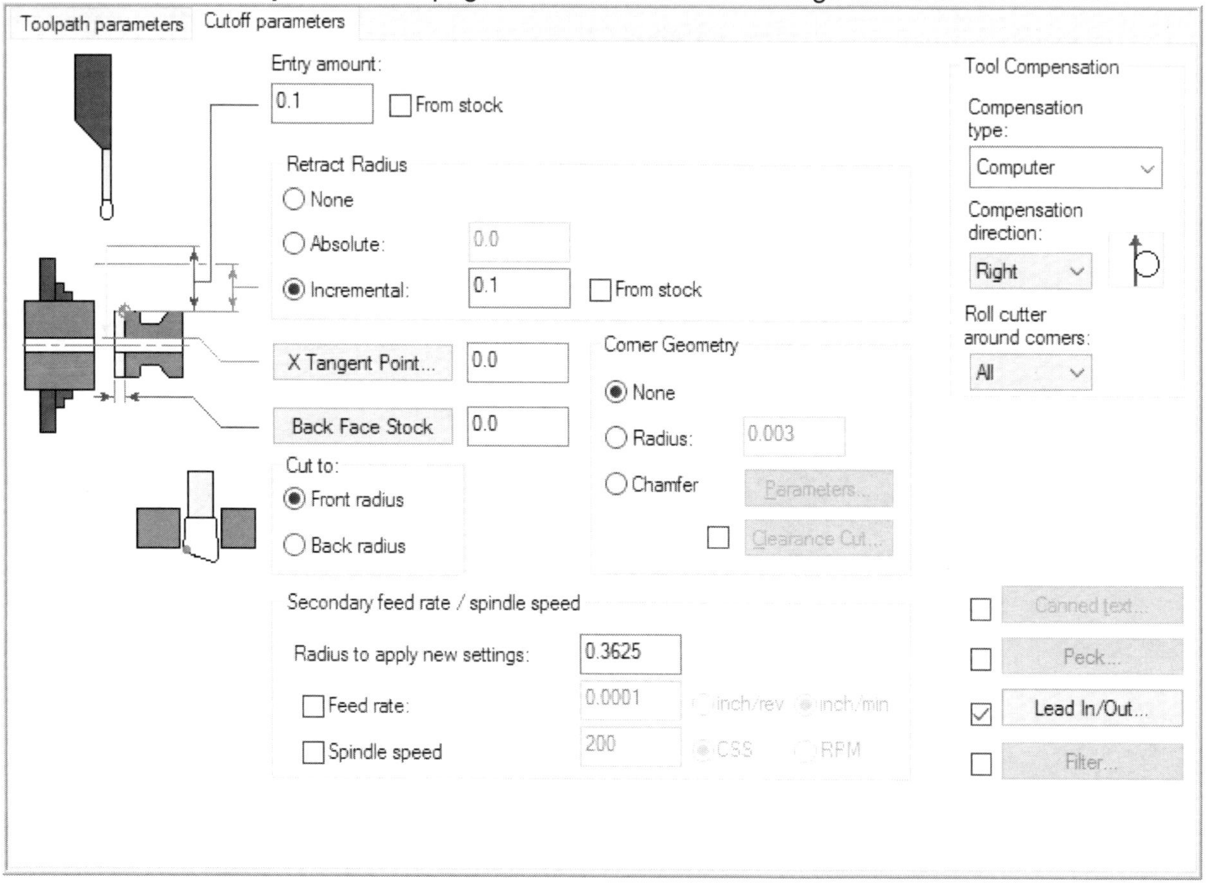

11. Select the OK button to exit **Cutoff parameters.**

TASK 13:
BACKPLOT THE TOOLPATH

- In this task you will use Mastercam's Backplot function to view the path the tools take to cut this part.
- Backplot will enable us to review the cutting motions and identify any problem areas when cutting the part.

1. Right mouse click in the graphics area and click on the **Fit** icon .

2. To pick all the operations to Backplot pick the **Select All** icon .

3. The next step is to select the **Backplot selected operations** icon shown below:

4. **Maximize** the Backplot/Verify window if required.
5. Select the **Home** Tab if required.

6. Activate the options shown below in the **Visibility** section of the Home tab.

Initial Stock
This displays the stock before machining.
Click to cycle through three states:
On
Translucent
Off

Tool
This displays the tool during Backplot or Verification. Click to cycle through three states as mentioned above

7. Activate the **Both** option in the **Toolpath section** of the **Home** tab.

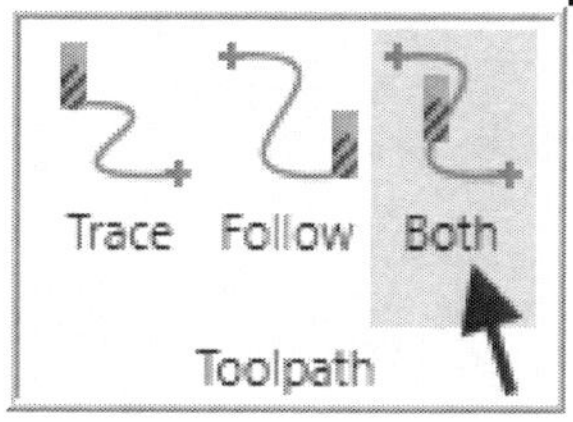

Both
This displays the entire toolpath and the tool as it travels over the displayed toolpath.

8. At the top of the screen select the **View** tab, the **Isometric** icon and then select **Fit**.

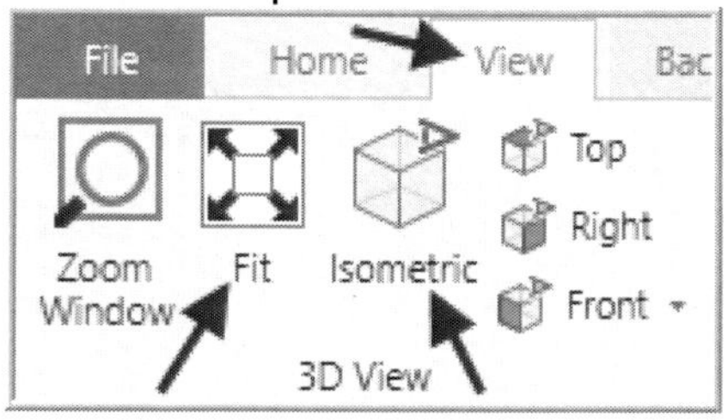

9. In the lower part of the screen now set the run **Speed** to slow by moving the slider bar pointer over to the left as shown below.

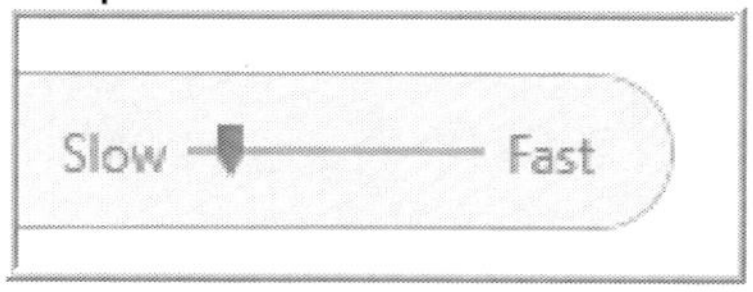

10. Now select the **Play Simulation** button to review the toolpaths.

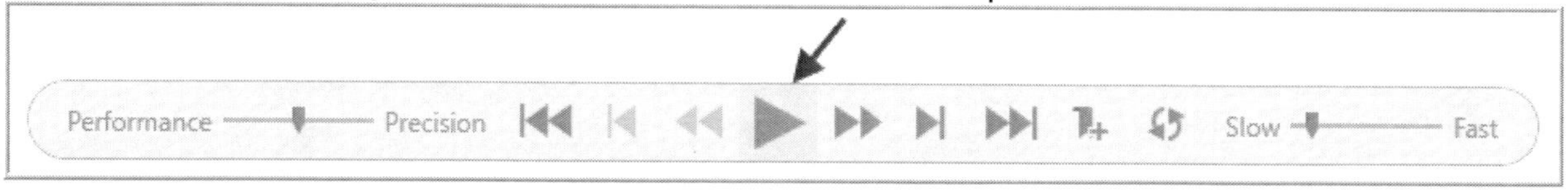

11. After reviewing the Backplot of the toolpaths select the Close button  to exit Backplot.

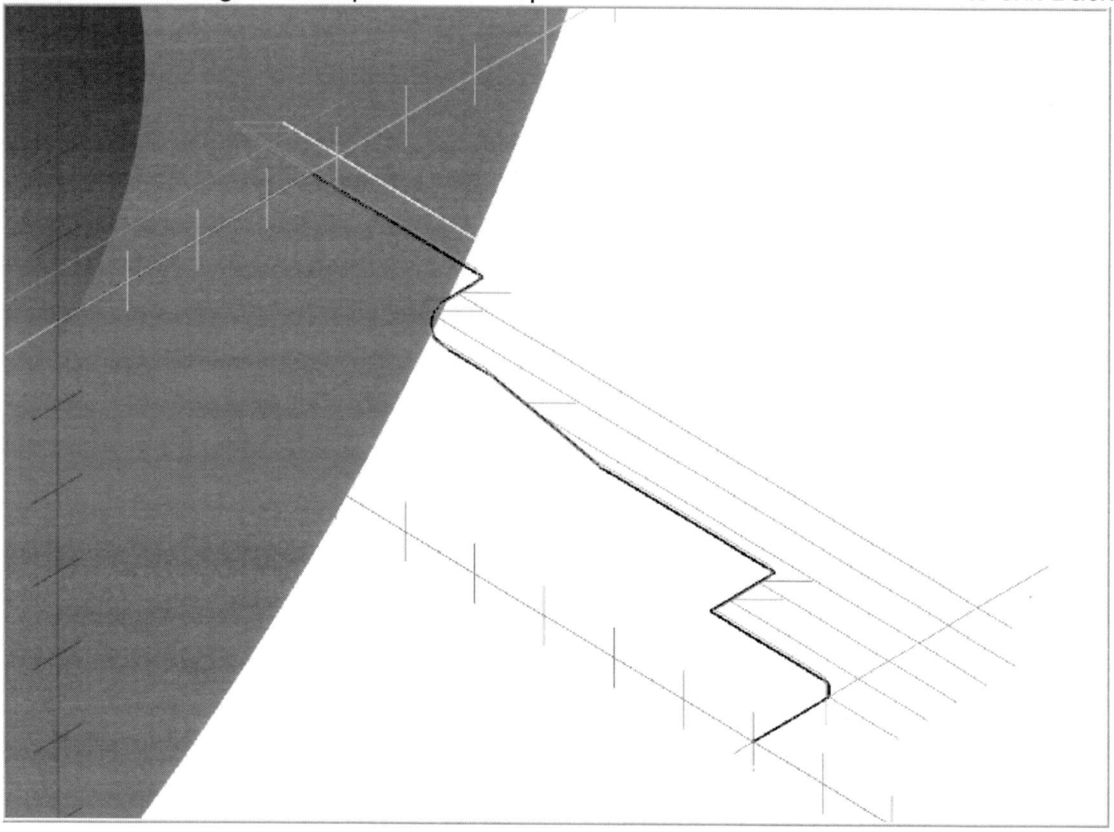

TASK 14:
VERIFY THE TOOLPATH

- Mastercam's Verify utility allows you to use solid models to simulate the machining of a part. The model created by the verification represents the surface finish, and shows collisions, if any exist.
- This allows you to identify and correct program errors before they reach the shop floor.
- Backplot and Verify are very similar. The differences between these two functions are that Backplot offers basic simulation options. Whereas Verify offers material removal, collision checking and precision control.
- **For more information on Verify refer to the Tips and Techniques content in the Online Course Instruction.**

1. In the Toolpaths Manager pick all the operations to Verify by clicking the **Select All** icon .
2. Select the **Verify selected operations** icon shown below:

3. **Maximize** the Backplot/Verify window if required.
4. Now select the **Home** Tab if required.

5. Activate the options shown below in the **Visibility** section of the Home tab. **Initial Stock not** activated.

6. At the top of the screen select the **View** tab, the **Isometric** icon and then select **Fit**.

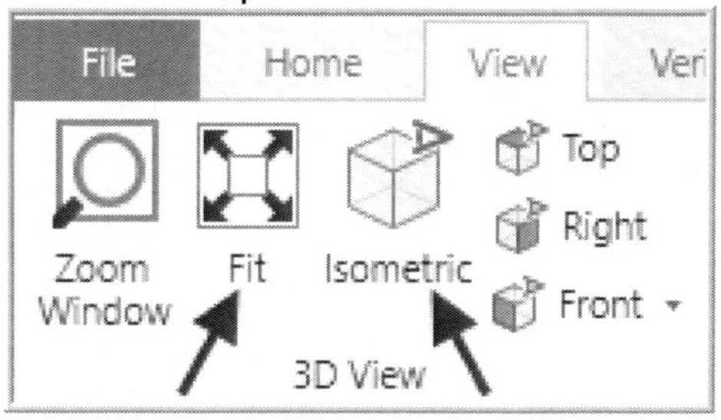

7. Select the **Verify** tab and activate the **Color Loop** to change the color of the tools for the verified part.

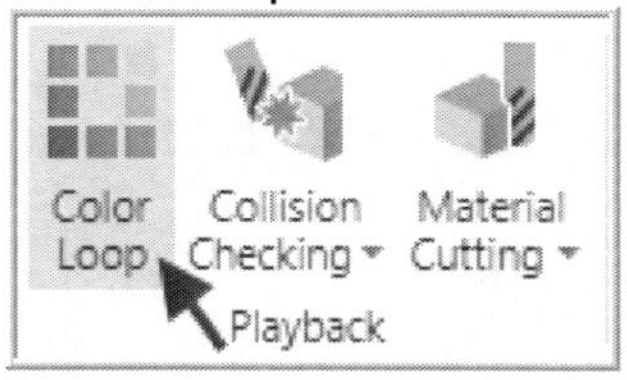

Color Loop
Changes the color of the toolpath or cut stock by operation or by tool change.

Choose **File Options** to set the colors.

8. In the lower part of the screen now set the run **Speed** to slow by moving the slider bar pointer over to the left as shown below.

9. Now select the **Play Simulation** button to review the toolpaths.

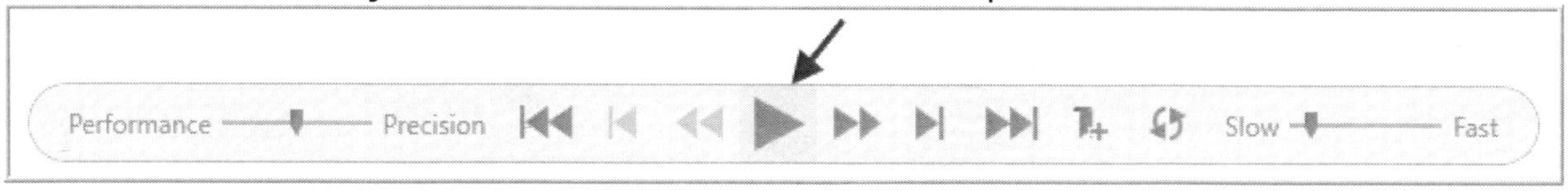

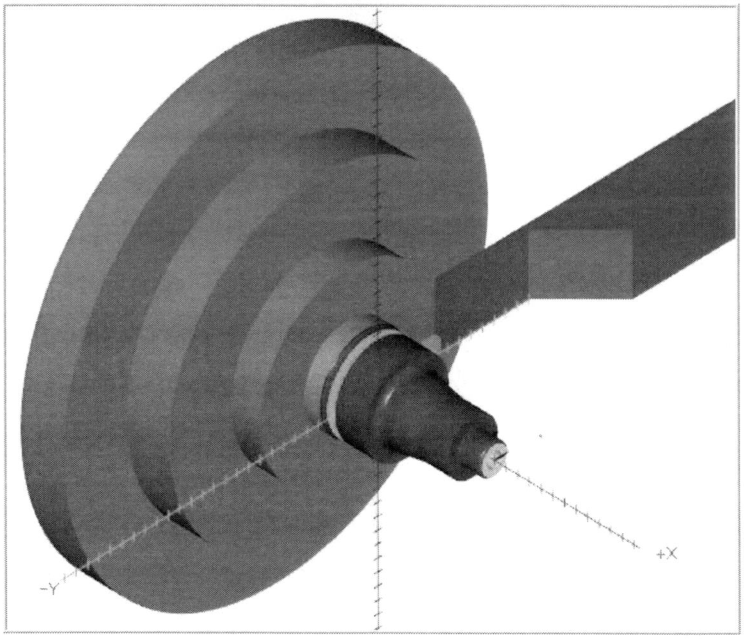

10. Select the **Close** button  in the top right hand corner to exit Verify.

TASK 15:
SAVE THE UPDATED MASTERCAM FILE

1. Select the **Save** icon from the **Quick Access** toolbar at the top left of the screen.

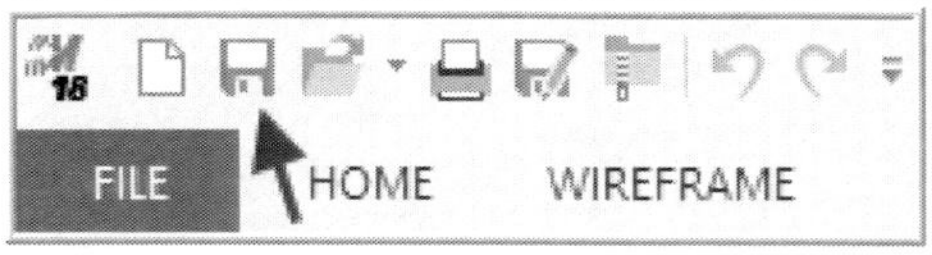

TASK 16:
POST AND CREATE THE CNC CODE FILE

1. Ensure all the operations are selected by picking the **Select All** icon from the Toolpaths manager.
2. Select the **Post selected operations** button from the Toolpaths manager.

➲ **Please Note:** If you cannot see **G1** click on the right pane of the Toolpaths manager window and expand the window to the right.

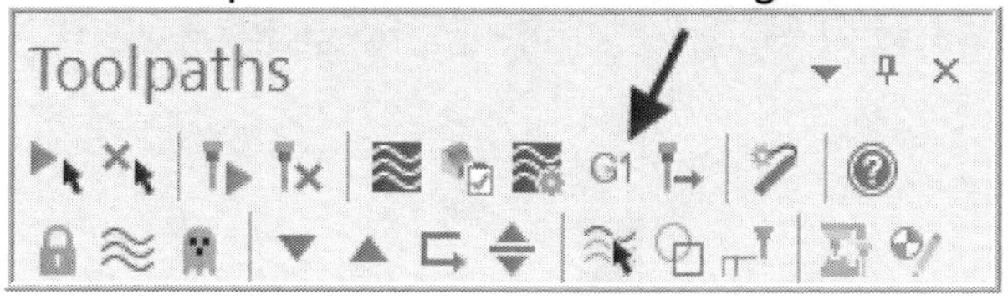

3. In the Post processing window, make the necessary changes as shown below:

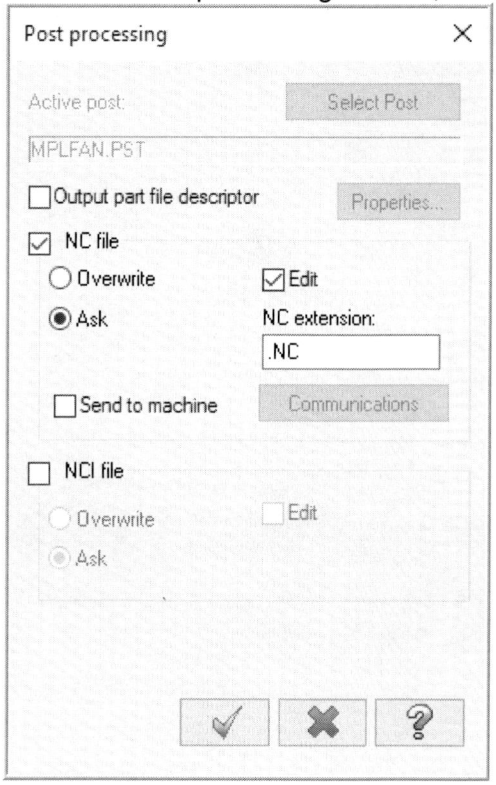

About Post Processing

NC file:
Select this option to save the NC file. The file name and extension are stored in the machine group properties for the selected operation. If you are posting operations from different machine groups or Mastercam files, or batch processing, Mastercam will create several files according to the settings for each machine group.

Edit:
When checked, automatically launches the default text editor with the file displayed so that you can review or modify it.

4. Select the OK button to continue.

5. Ensure the same name as your Mastercam part file name is displayed in the **NC File name** field as shown below:

6. Select the **Save** button.
7. The CNC code file opens up in the default editor.

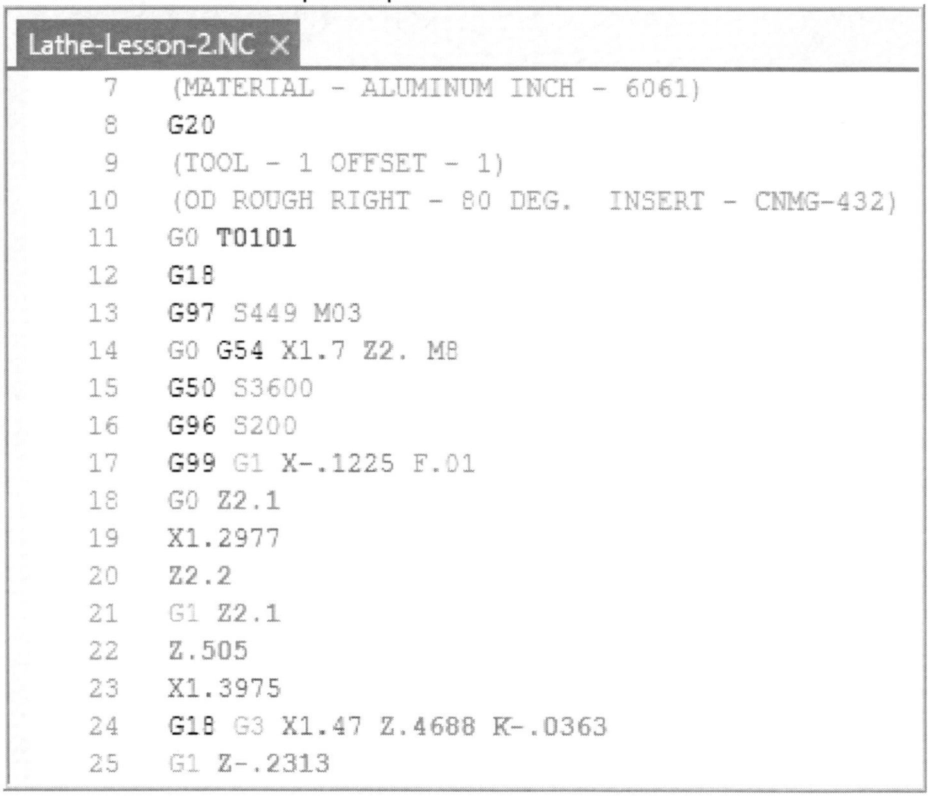

8. Select the  in the top right corner to exit the CNC editor.

➲ This completes Lathe-Lesson-2.

LATHE-LESSON-2 EXERCISE

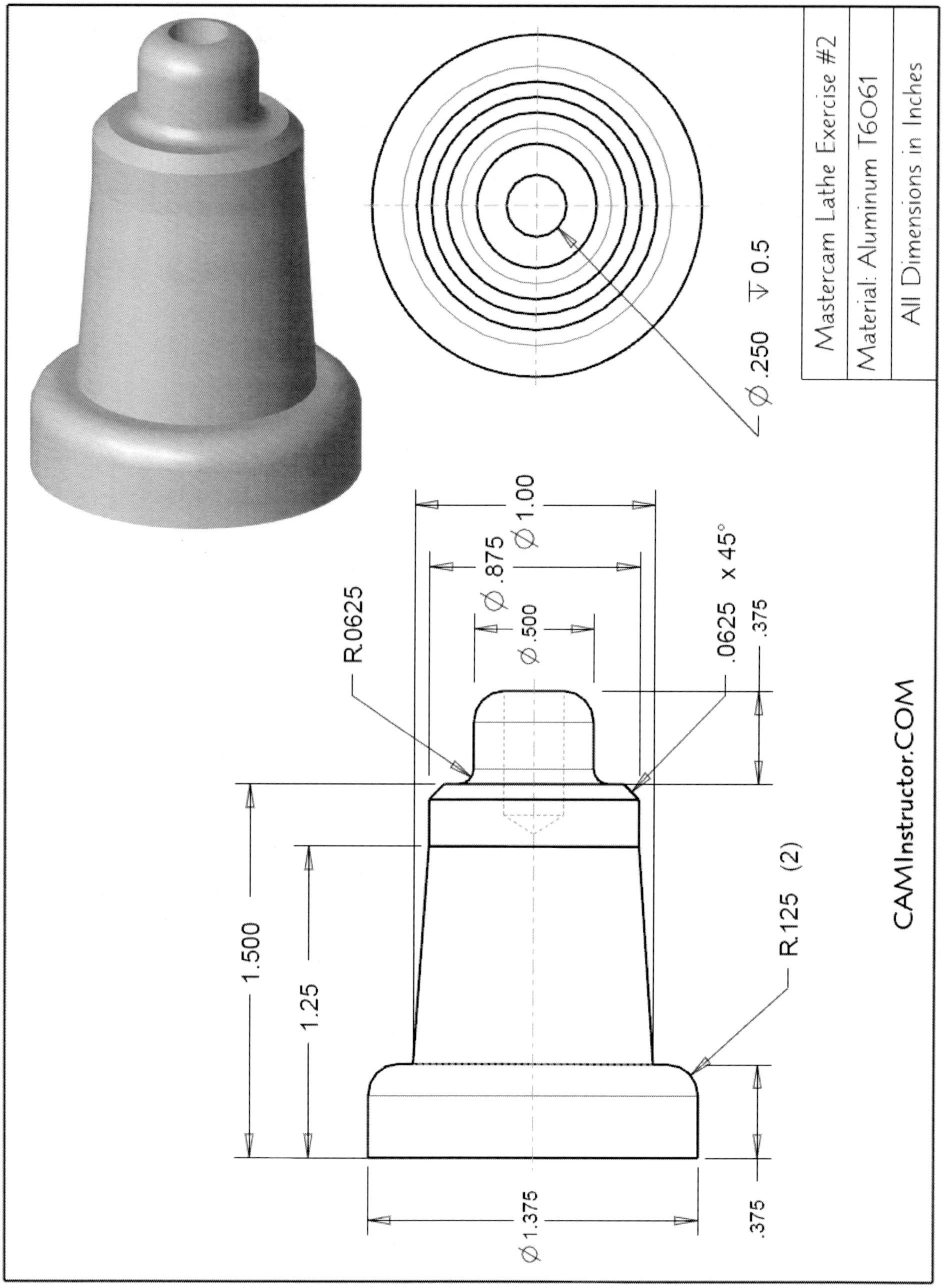

Mastercam® 2018

TRAINING GUIDE

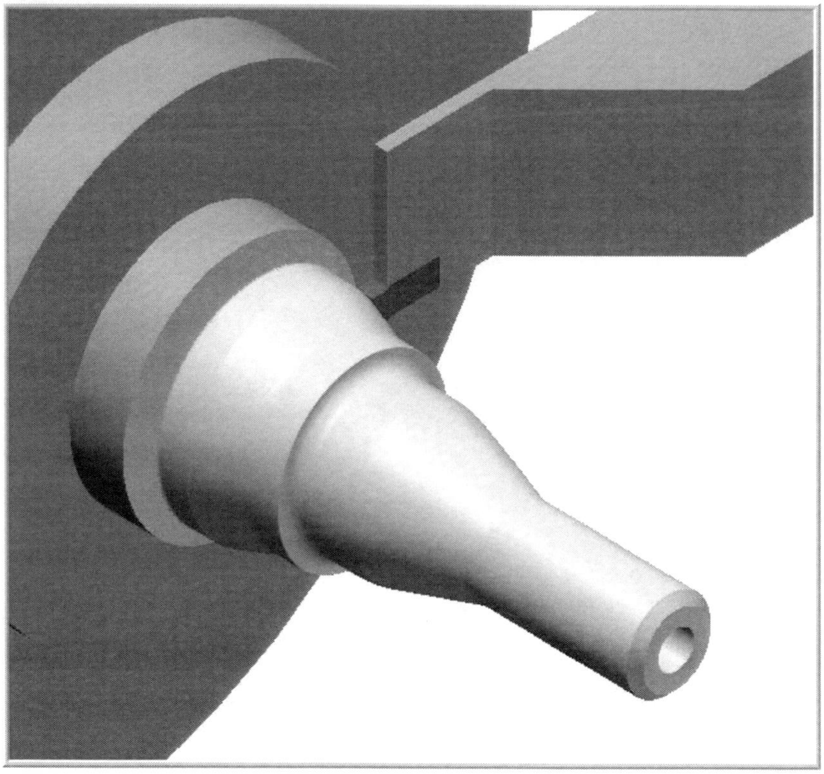

LATHE-LESSON-3

FACE, ROUGH, FINISH, DRILL, INTERNAL THREAD AND CUTOFF

camInstructor

Objectives

You will create the geometry for Lathe Lesson 3, and then generate a toolpath to machine the part on a CNC lathe. This lesson covers the following topics:

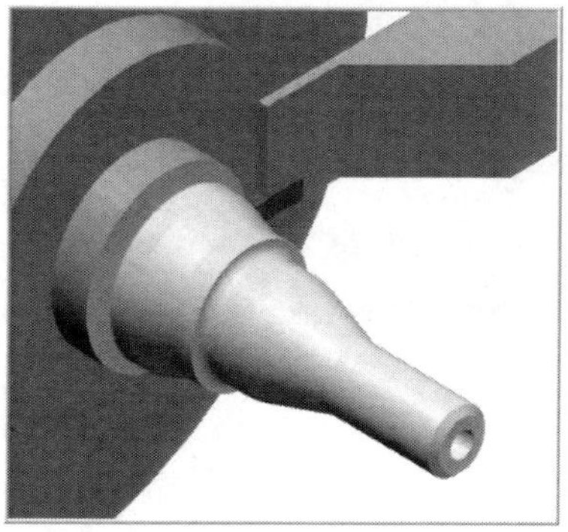

➲ **Create a 2-dimensional drawing by:**
Creating lines.
Creating fillets.
Creating chamfers.

➲ **Establish Stock and Chuck Setup settings:**
Stock size.
Chuck Configuration.
Material for the part.
Feed calculation.

➲ **Generate a 2-dimensional lathe toolpath consisting of:**
Lathe Face.
Lathe Quick Rough.
Lathe Quick Finish.
Lathe Drill and Thread.
Lathe Cutoff.

➲ **Inspect the toolpath using Mastercam's Verify and Backplot by:**
Launching the Verify function to machine the part on the screen.
Generating the NC- code.

LATHE - LESSON - 3 DRAWING

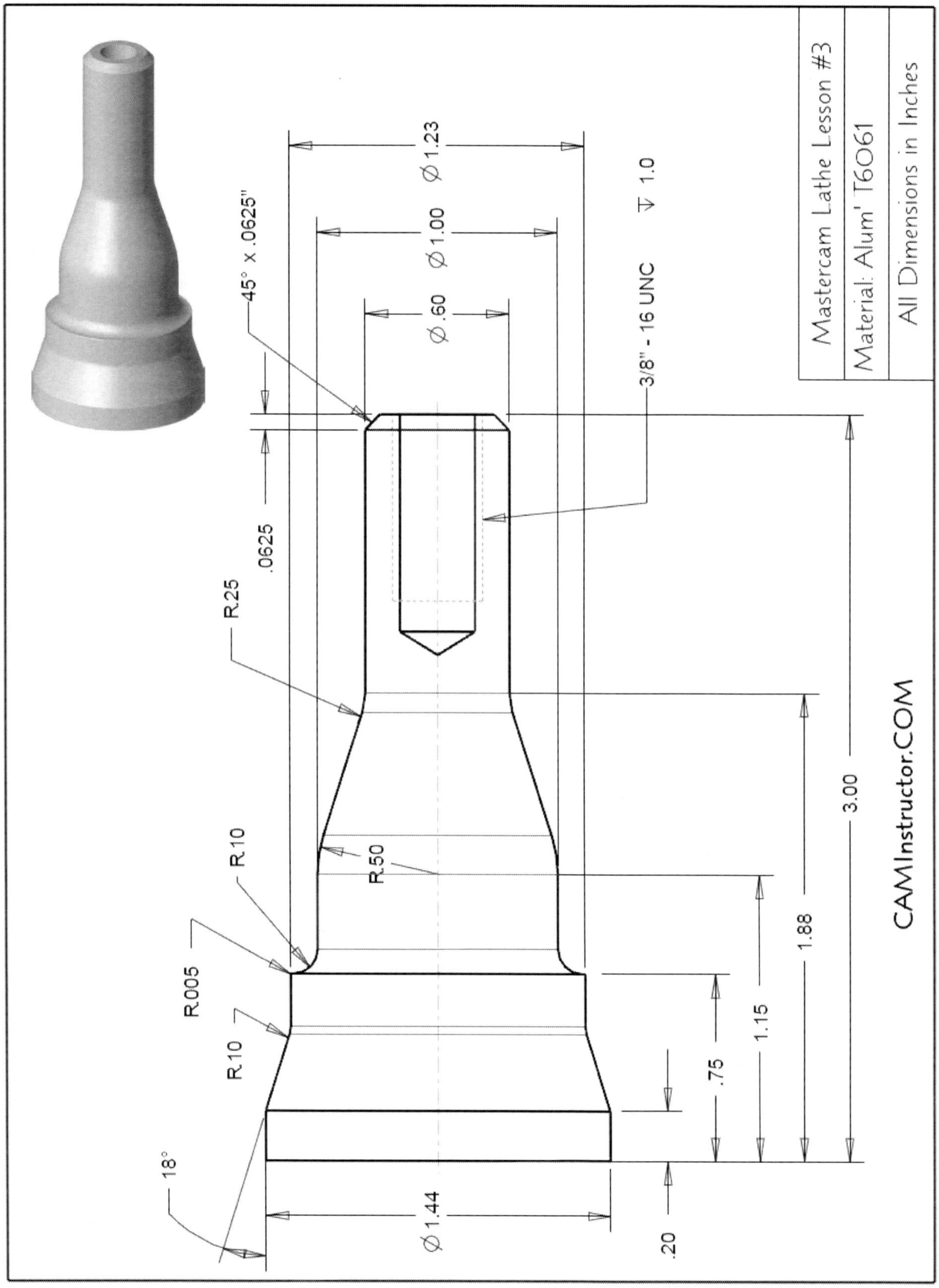

TOOL LIST

Six tools will be used to create this part.

- **Tool #1 Face and Rough the outside diameters**
  Holder: Outside Diameter Rough Right Hand - DCGNR-164D.
  Insert: 80 Degree Diamond Insert – CNMG-432

- **Tool #2 Finish the outside diameters**
  Holder: Outside Diameter Finish Right Hand - MVJNR-164D.
  Insert: 35 Degree Diamond Insert – VNMG-431.

- **Tool #3 Centre drill the hole**
  Centre Drill – body diameter 0.250”

- **Tool #4 Tap Drill the .3125 diameter hole**
  Drill 0.3125” diameter

- **Tool #5 Tap the .375-16 hole**
  Right Hand Tap 3/8”-16UNC

- **Tool #6 Cutoff the part**
  Holder: Outside Diameter Cut-off Right Hand.
  Insert: 0.125” Wide.

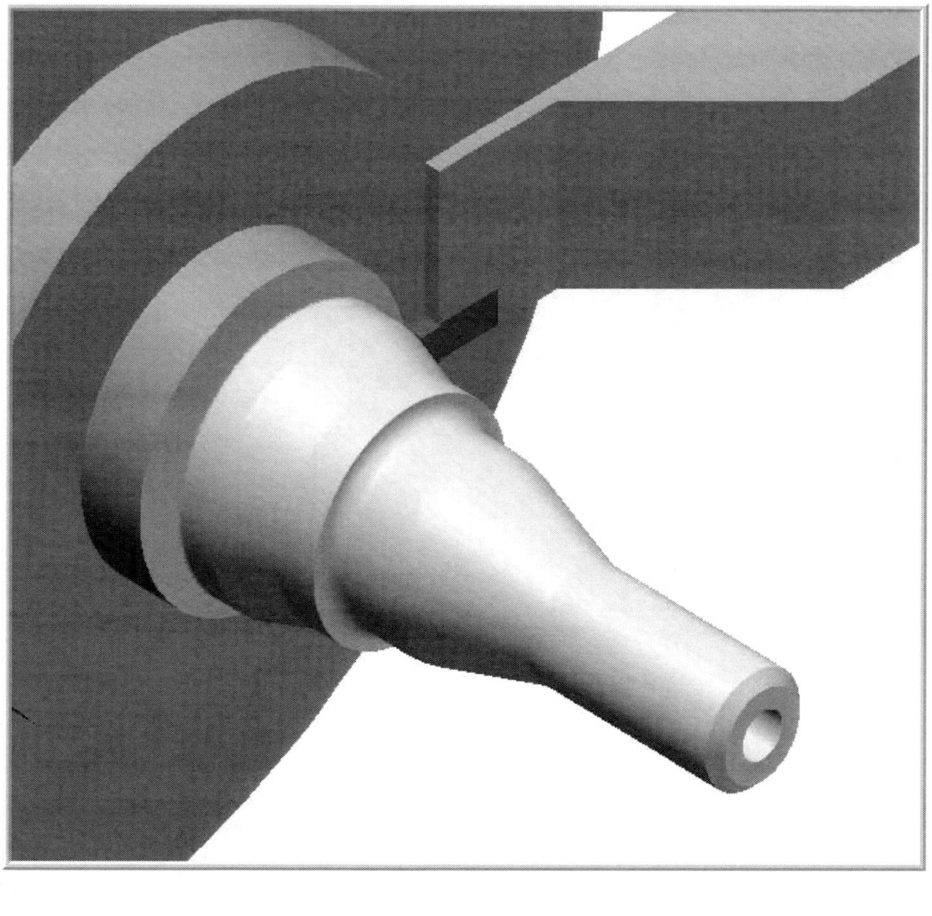

LESSON - 3 - THE PROCESS

Geometry Creation

TASK 1: Setting the Environment
TASK 2: Setting the Construction Planes
TASK 3: Create the Geometry
TASK 4: Create the 18 Degree Angle
TASK 5: Create the Fillets (Radius)
TASK 6: Create the Chamfer
TASK 7: Save the Drawing

Toolpath Creation

TASK 8: Define the Stock and Chuck Parameters
TASK 9: Face the Front of the Part
TASK 10: Rough the Outside Diameters
TASK 11: Finish the Outside Diameters
TASK 12: Center Drill the 5/16" Hole
TASK 13: Drill the 5/16" Hole
TASK 14: Tap the 3/8"-16 Hole
TASK 15: Cut off the Part
TASK 16: Verify the Toolpath
TASK 17: Save the Updated Mastercam File
TASK 18: Post and Create the CNC Code File

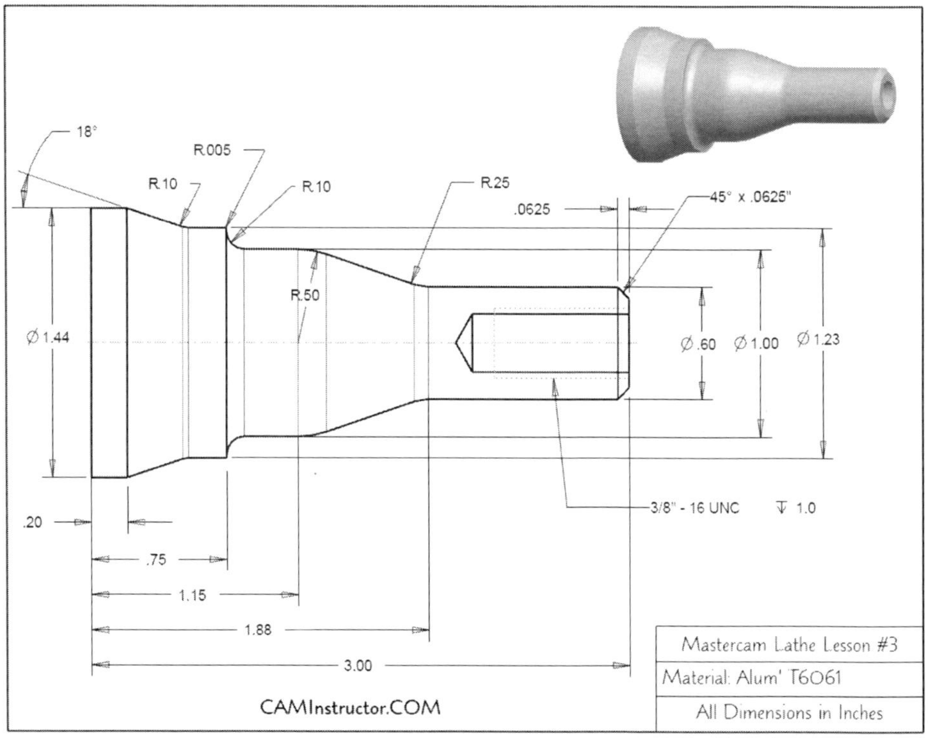

Geometry Creation

TASK 1:
SETTING THE ENVIRONMENT

Before starting the geometry creation you should set up the grid and machine type as outlined in the **Setting the Environment** section at the beginning of this text:

1. Set up the Grid. This will help identify the location of the origin.
2. Set the machine type to the default Lathe.

TASK 2:
SETTING THE CONSTRUCTION PLANES:

➲ **Set the Construction Plane to Lathe diameter +D +Z (WCS)**

1. Select the **View tab** and click on **Toolpaths** and **Solids** in the **Managers** section to **hide** them and toggle **only** the **Planes Manager to display**.

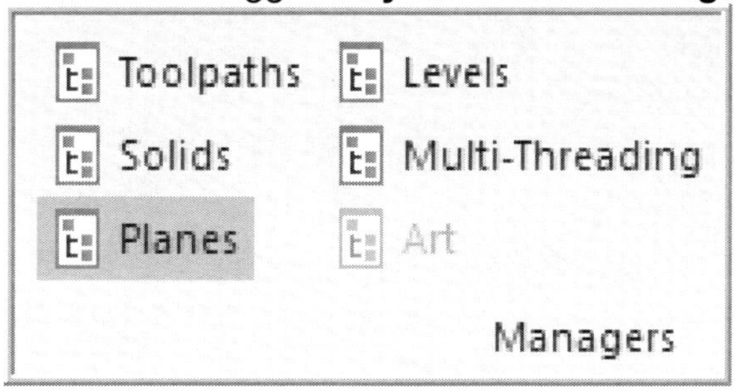

Once your machine is set up, Mastercam includes special lathe construction planes that let you work in **radius or diameter coordinates**.

For conventional 2D turning applications, use the Planes Manager to select the desired coordinate system, as shown below right. Choose to use either radius or diameter coordinates and then choose the desired X/D and Z directions.

2. Ensure the **C column** (Construction Plane) and **T column** (Tool Plane) are set to the **+D +Z Plane**. Just click in the C and T columns in the **+D +Z** row.

➲ Take note of the **Status bar** at the bottom of the screen **CPLANE: +D +Z TPLANE: +D +Z WCS:TOP** as shown below right.

3. To change the **Lathe Plane** open up the drop down menu for **Select lathe plane** and click on the required coordinate system as shown below right.
4. Select the **Close** button  in the top right hand corner to close the Planes Manager.

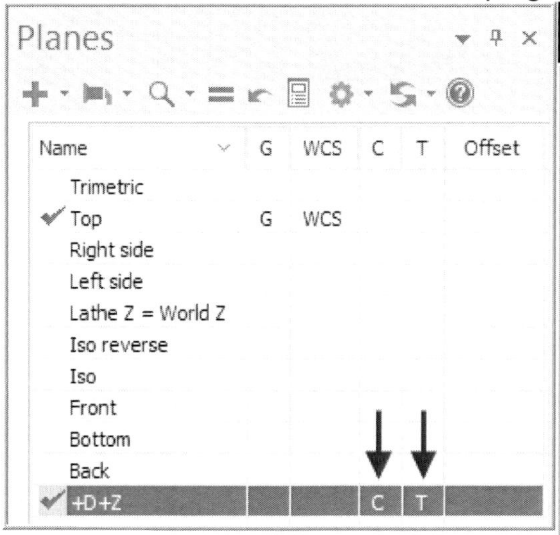

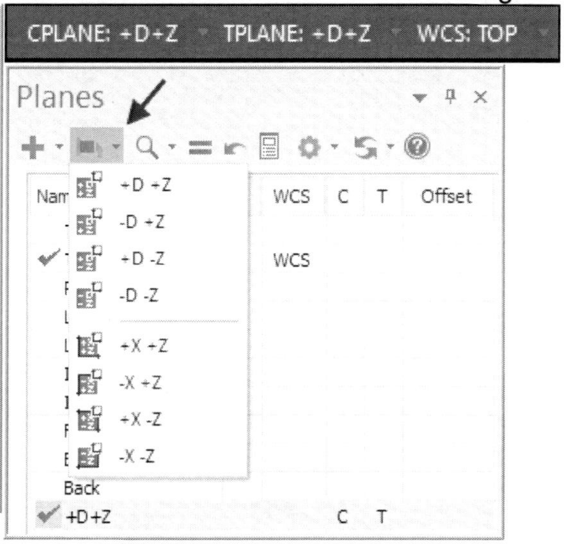

TASK 3:
CREATE THE GEOMETRY

- This task explains how to create the geometry of this part. In this lathe part you only need to create **half of the geometry**, the geometry above the center line.
- Lines 1 through 9 will be created first and then the fillet and chamfer will be created.

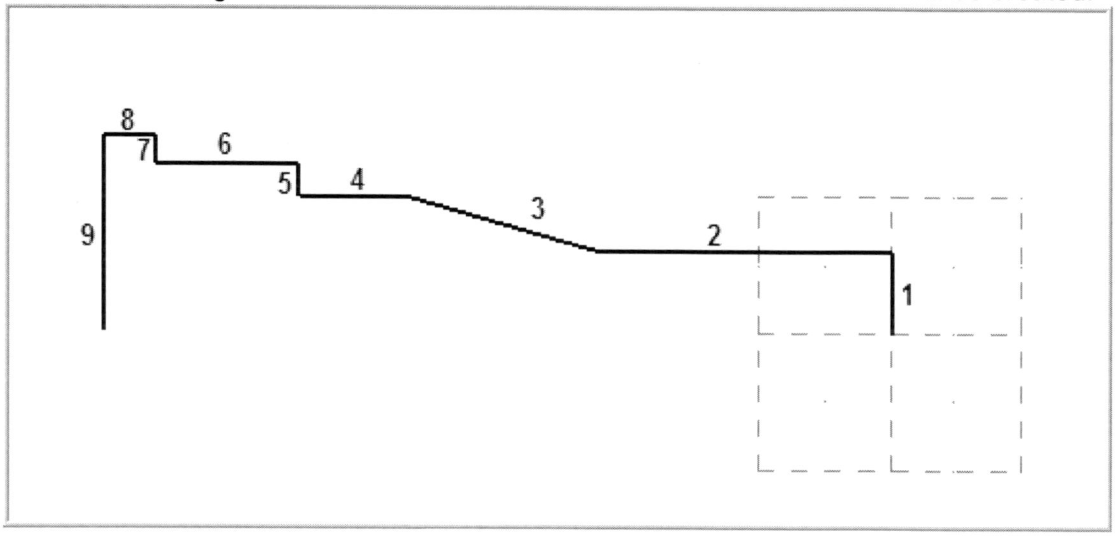

- **Create Line #1**

1. Select the **WIREFRAME** tab at the top of the screen and in the **Lines** section click on **Line Endpoints**.

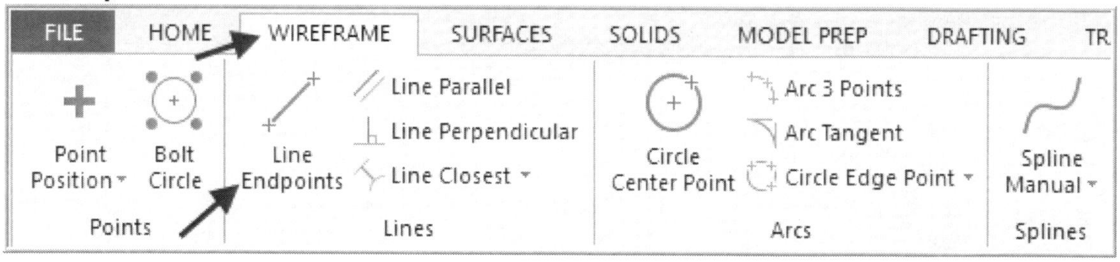

- On the graphics screen you are prompted: **Specify the first endpoint** and the Line Endpoints panel appears.

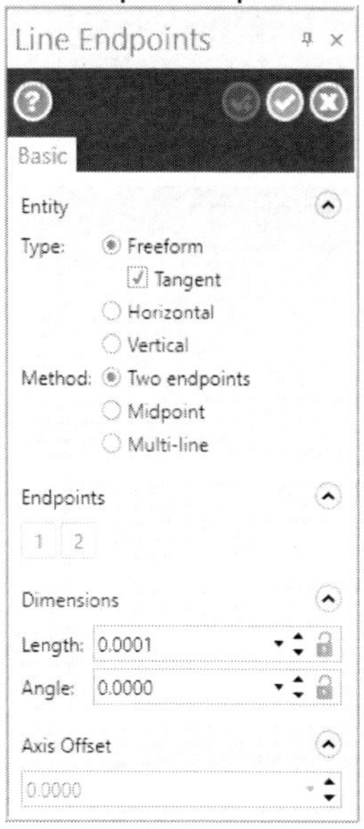

Line Endpoints
Use this function to create single lines with two endpoints, or multiple lines connected at their endpoints.

Simply click in the graphics window to set the two endpoints; or enter values in the Length and Angle fields, and then click in the graphics window to position the line.

2. Move the cursor over the **center of the grid** and as you get close to the origin a visual cue appears.  This is the cue that will allow you to snap to the **origin**. With this visual cue highlighted pick the **origin.**

> **AutoCursor:** Visual Cues detects and highlights endpoints and midpoints of curves, lines, arc center points, and point entities.
>
> In addition, AutoCursor can snap to angle, nearest, tangent, perpendicular, horizontal, and vertical conditions.

➲ The following are Mastercam Visual Cues:

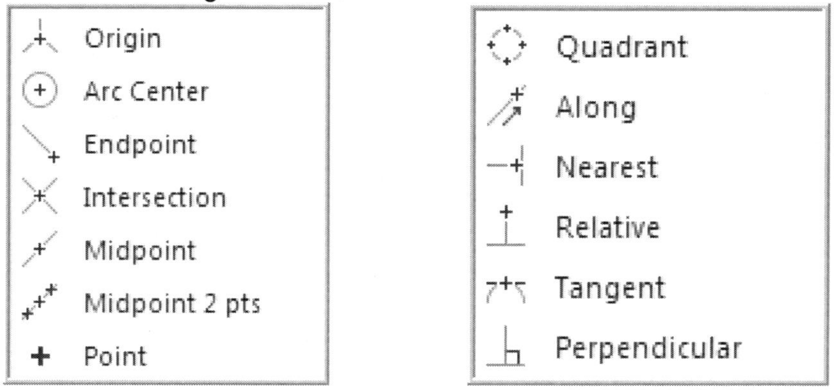

3. You are next prompted to **"Specify the second endpoint".** In the Line Endpoints panel activate **Multi-line and Freeform**.

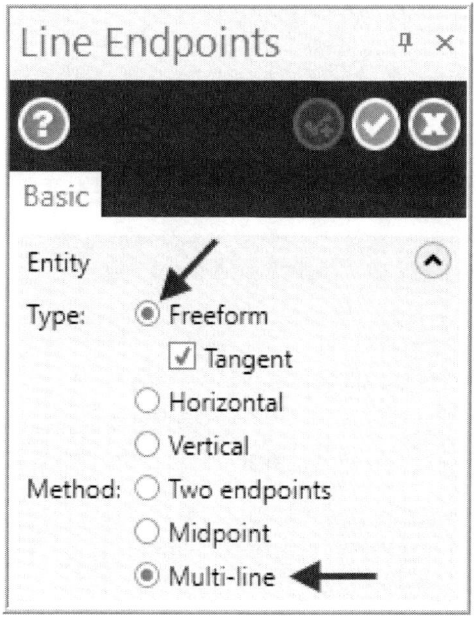

> **Multi-line**
> Let's you create multiple lines connected at their endpoints.
>
> Enter a point for the first endpoint of the first line and then a point for the second endpoint of the line. That second point becomes the first endpoint of the next line that you create.
>
> Double-click the last point or press Escape to end this function.
>
> **Freeform**
> Allows you to create the lien anywhere on the plane.

4. You are still prompted to **"Specify the second endpoint"**. **click the middle mouse button** and then **hit the spacebar** on your keyboard, the **Fastpoint** now opens. **Type 0.6,0**. This is **D0.6 Z0**. Hit the **Enter** key when done.

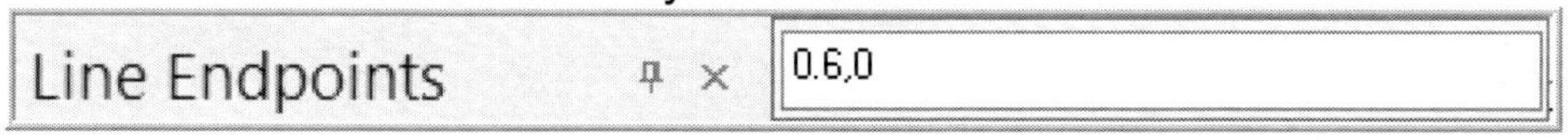

➲ A vertical line should be visible as shown below:

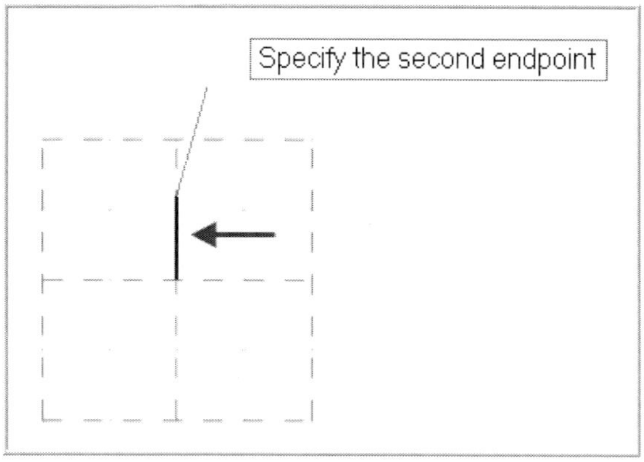

➲ **Create Line #2**

5. To satisfy the prompt **"Specify the second endpoint" just type** the coordinate, **type 0.6, -1.12** and hit the Enter key to complete this line.

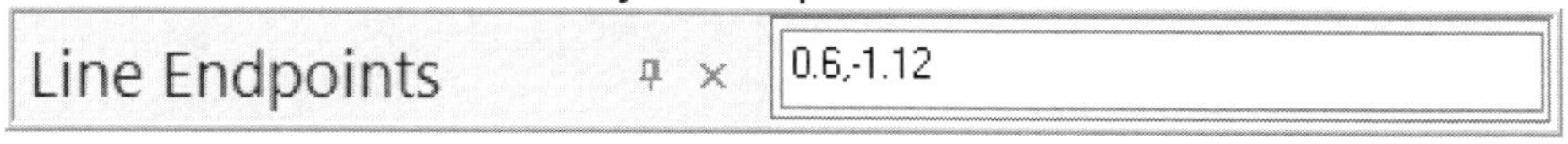

➲ **Create Line #3**

6. To satisfy the prompt **"Specify the second endpoint" just type** the coordinate, **type 1.0, -1.85** and hit the Enter key to complete this line.

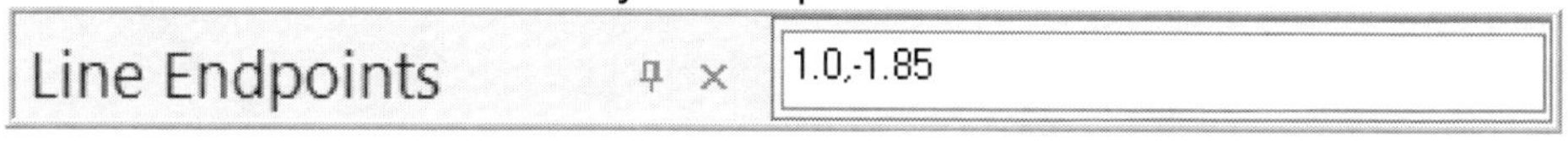

➲ **Create Line #4**

7. To satisfy the prompt **"Specify the second endpoint" just type** the coordinate, **type 1.0, -2.25** and hit the Enter key to complete this line.

➲ **Create Line #5**

8. To satisfy the prompt **"Specify the second endpoint" just type** the coordinate, **type 1.23, -2.25** and hit the Enter key to complete this line.

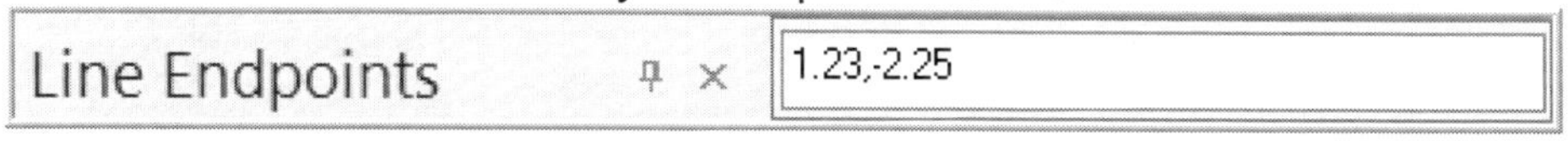

➲ **Create Line #6**

9. To satisfy the prompt **"Specify the second endpoint" just type** the coordinate, **type 1.23, -2.8** and hit the Enter key to complete this line.

10. Right mouse click in the graphics area and click on the **Fit** icon.
11. Right mouse click in the graphics area and click on **Unzoom 80%** to shrink the display.

➲ **Create Line #7**

12. To satisfy the prompt **"Specify the second endpoint" just type** the coordinate, **type 1.44, -2.8** and hit the Enter key to complete this line.

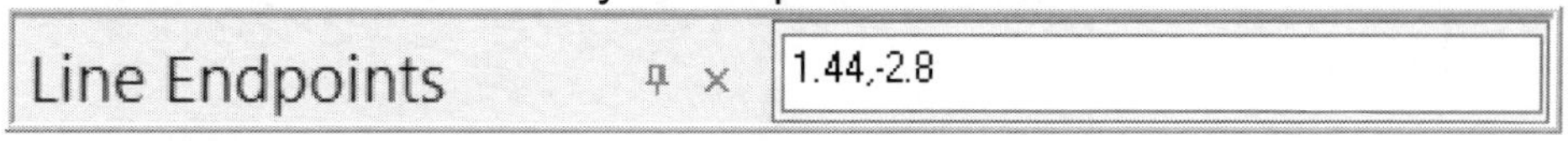

➲ **Create Line #8**

13. To satisfy the prompt **"Specify the second endpoint" just type** the coordinate, **type 1.44, -3.0** and hit the Enter key to complete this line.

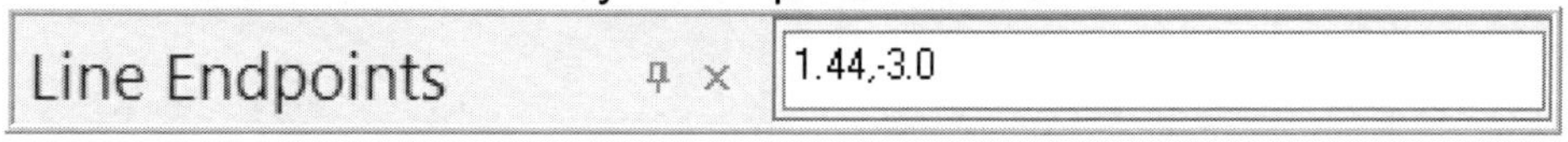

➲ **Create Line #9**

14. To satisfy the prompt **"Specify the second endpoint" just type** the coordinate, **type 0,-3.0** and hit the Enter key to complete this line.

15. Click on the **OK** icon to complete this feature.
16. Right mouse click in the graphics area and click on the **Fit** icon.

➲ Your geometry should look like the figure below.

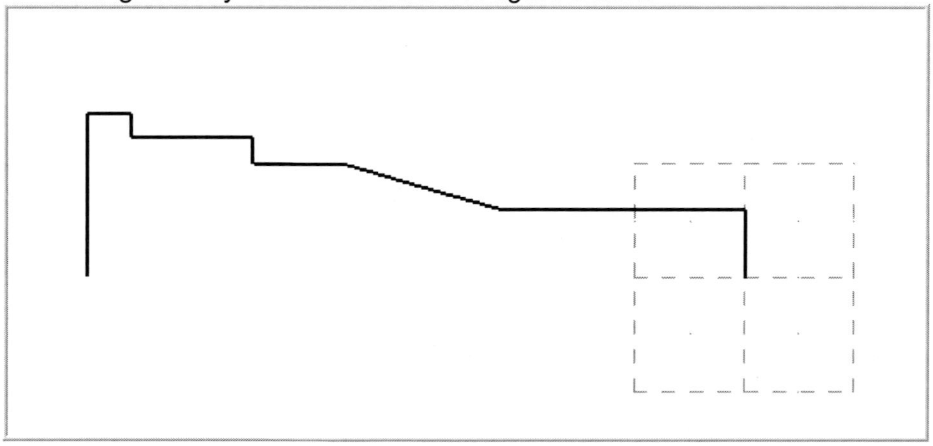

TASK 4:
CREATE THE 18 DEGREE ANGLE

➲ **Create the 18 Degree Angle.**

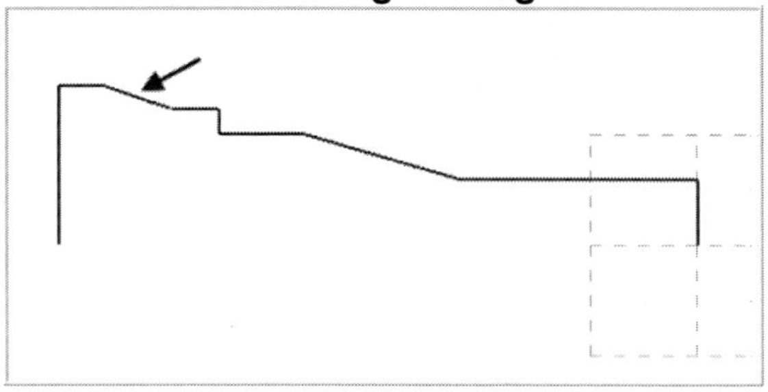

1. Click on **Line Endpoints** in the **Lines** section of the **WIREFRAME** tab.
2. In the Line Endpoints panel click in the space for **Length** and input **1.0. Hit the tab key** and for the **Angle** enter **-18.0** and hit **Enter**.

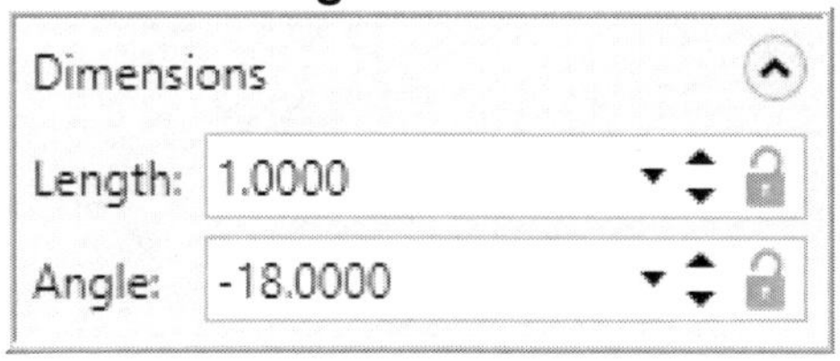

3. You are prompted to **"Specify the first endpoint".** Click on the endpoint of line 8 as shown below.

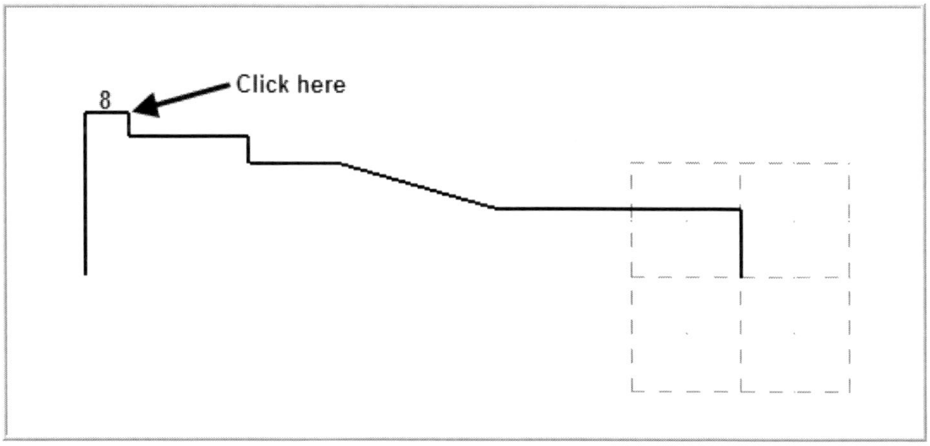

➲ A new line is drawn as shown below.

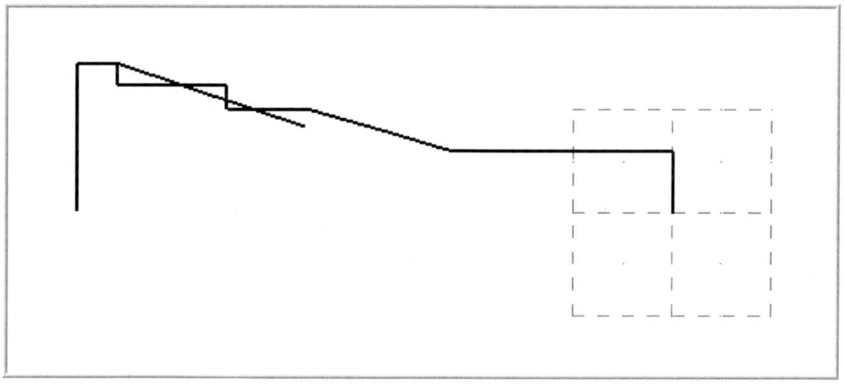

4. Click on the **OK** icon  to complete this feature.
5. In the **WIREFRAME** tab click on **Trim Break Extend** in the **Modify** section.

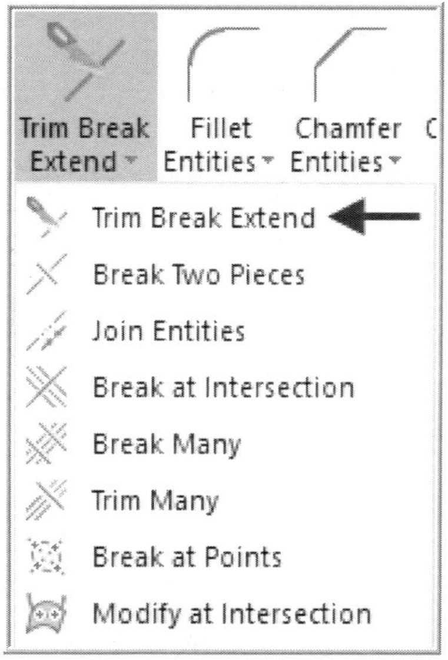

6. Activate **Trim 2 entities** as shown below.

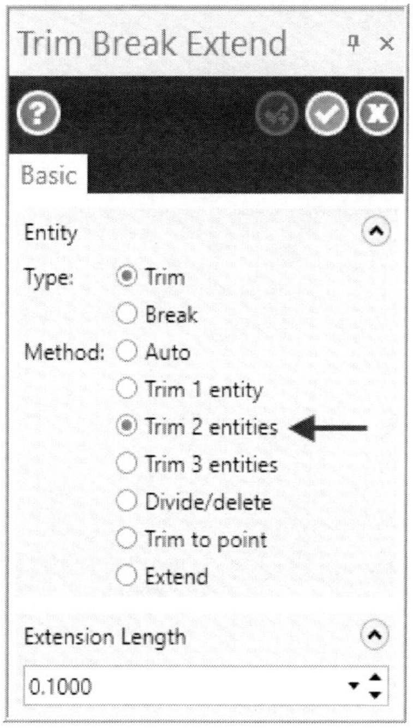

7. Click on **line 1** and then **line 2** as shown below.

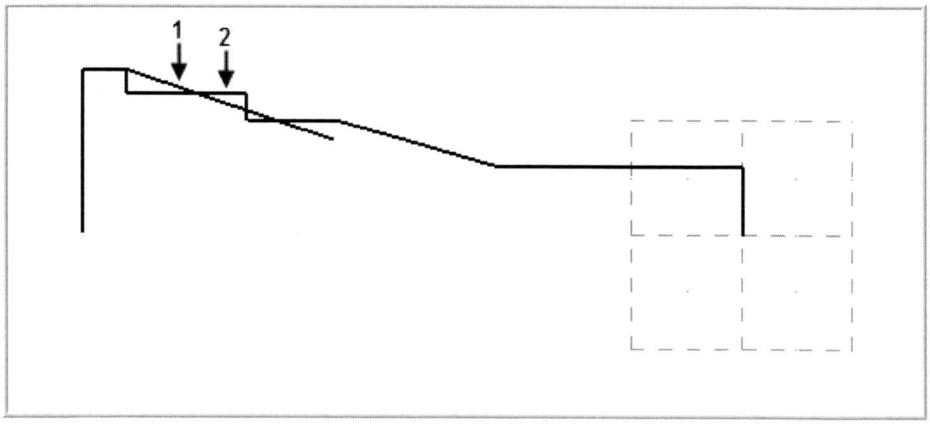

➲ The line is trimmed as shown below.

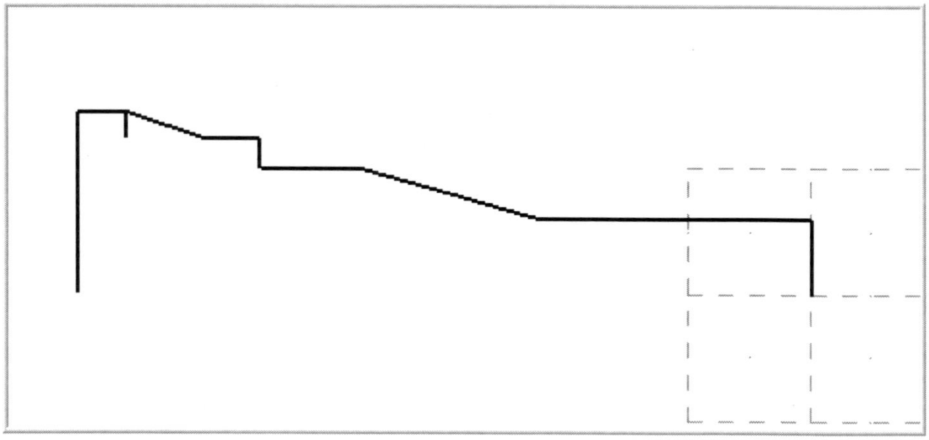

8. Click on the **OK** icon  to complete this feature.
9. Click on the line as shown below and hit the **Delete** key on your keyboard.

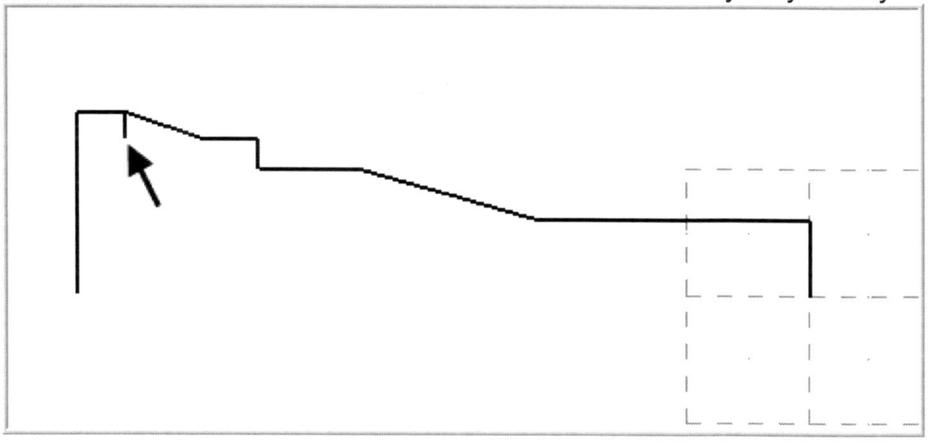

TASK 5:
CREATE THE FILLETS (RADIUS)

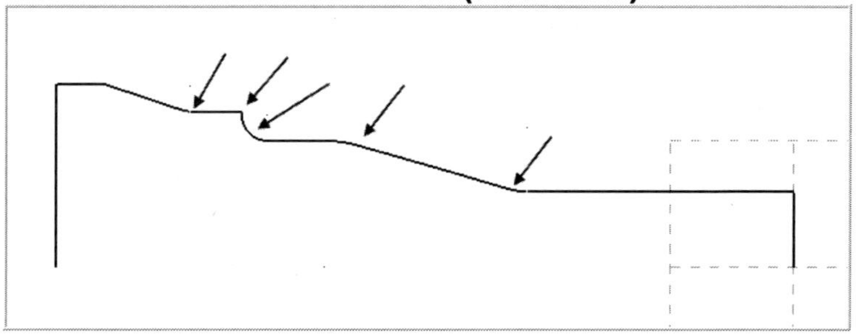

1. Select the **WIREFRAME** tab and in the **Modify** section click on **Fillet Entities**.

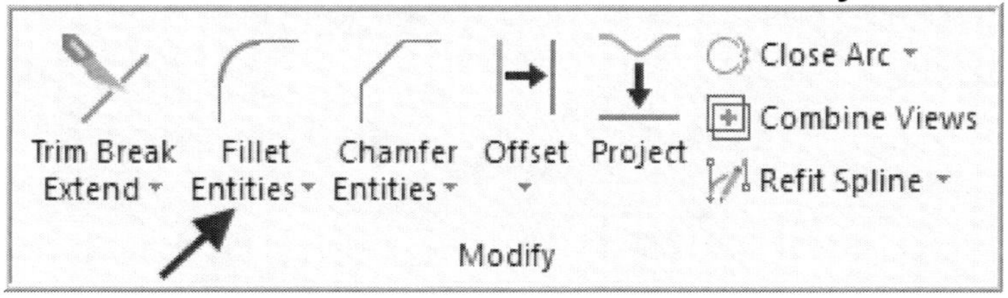

2. The **Fillet Entities** panel appears. If required activate the **Style** to **Normal** and enter a value of **0.1** for **Radius**.
3. Ensure the **Trim** entities box at the bottom of the panel is check marked to turn the trim on.

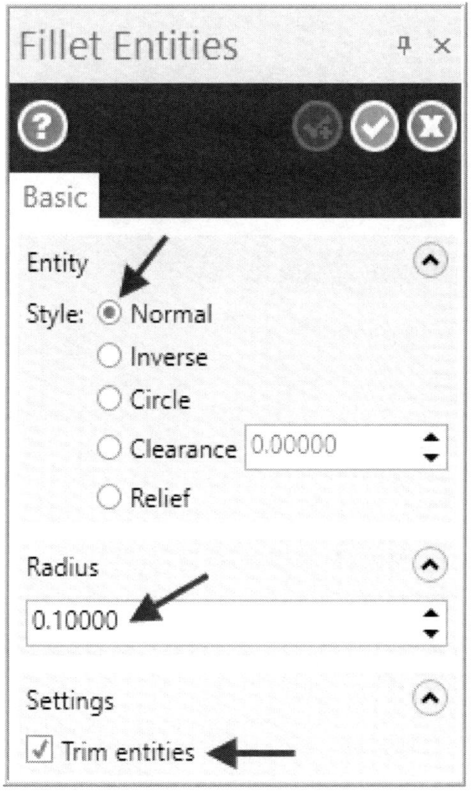

4. Move over to the graphic screen and for the prompt **"Fillet: Select an entity"** click on **Line 1** and then for the prompt **"Fillet: Select another entity"** click on **Line 2** as shown below.

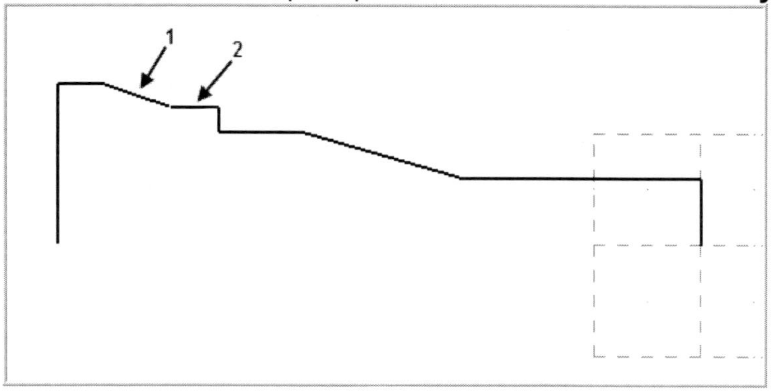

5. Click on the **OK and Create New Operation** icon.
6. Click in the space for **Radius**, input **0.005** and then hit the **Enter** key.

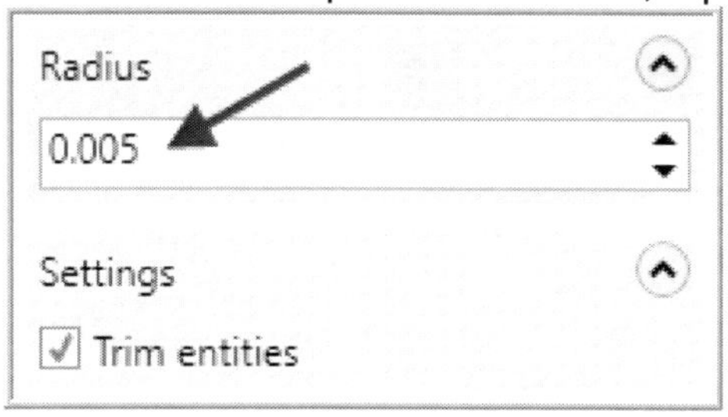

7. For the prompt **"Fillet: Select an entity"** click on **Line 1** and then for the prompt **"Fillet: Select another entity"** click on **Line 2** as shown below.

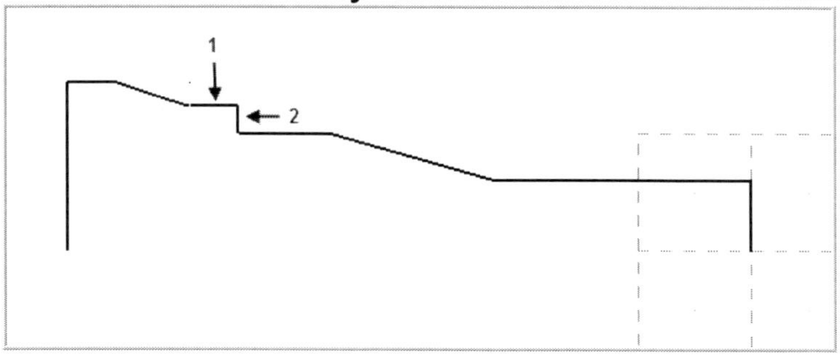

8. Click on the **OK and Create New Operation** icon.
9. Click in the space for **Radius**, input **0.1** and then hit the **Enter** key.

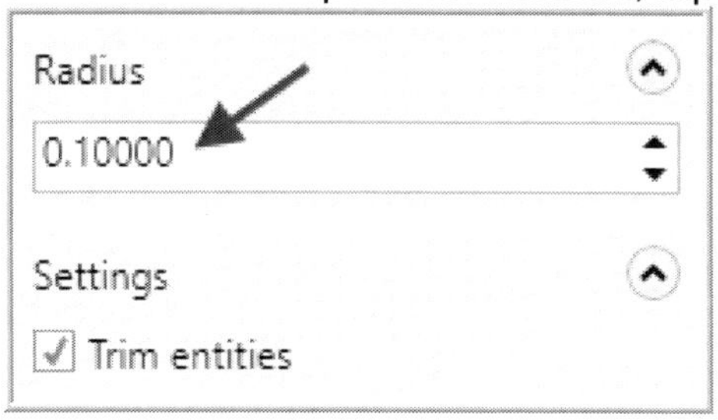

10. For the prompt **"Fillet: Select an entity"** click on **Line 1** and then for the prompt **"Fillet: Select another entity"** click on **Line 2** as shown below.

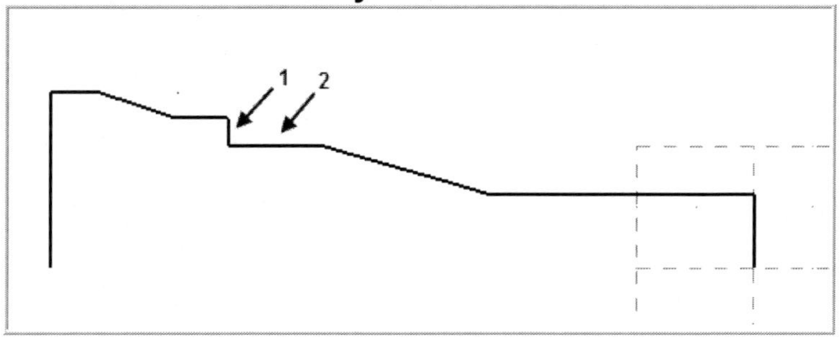

11. Click on the **OK and Create New Operation** icon .
12. Click in the space for **Radius,** input **0.5** and then hit the **Enter** key.

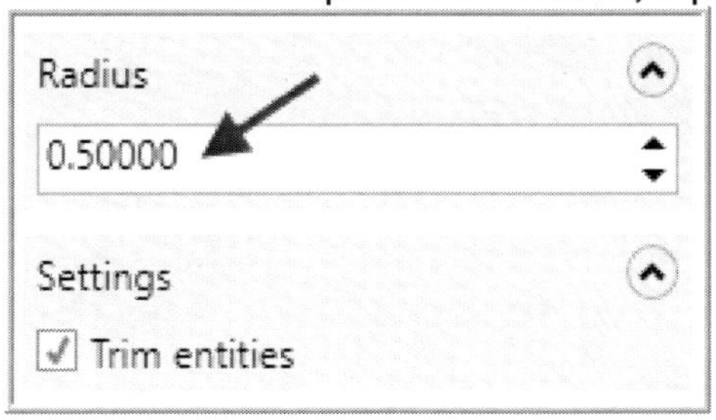

13. For the prompt **"Fillet: Select an entity"** click on **Line 1** and then for the prompt **"Fillet: Select another entity"** click on **Line 2** as shown below.

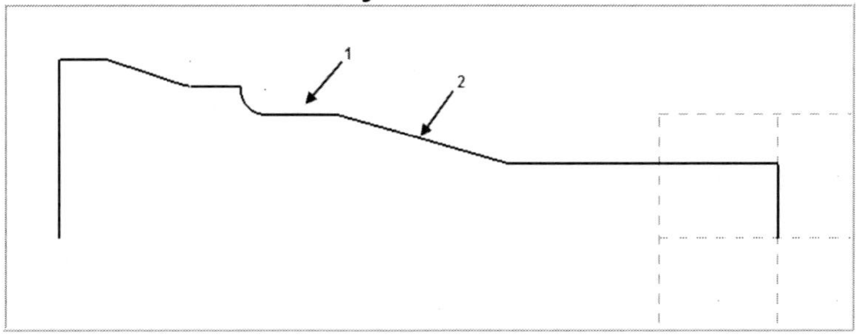

14. Click on the **OK and Create New Operation** icon .

15. Click in the space for **Radius**, input **0.2** and then hit the **Enter** key.

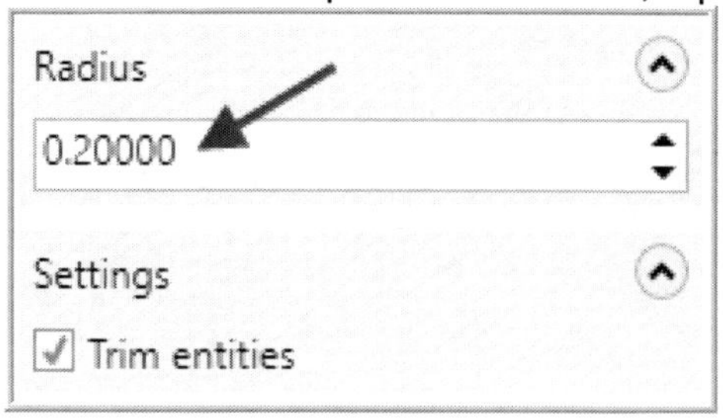

16. For the prompt **"Fillet: Select an entity"** click on **Line 1** and then for the prompt **"Fillet: Select another entity"** click on **Line 2** as shown below.

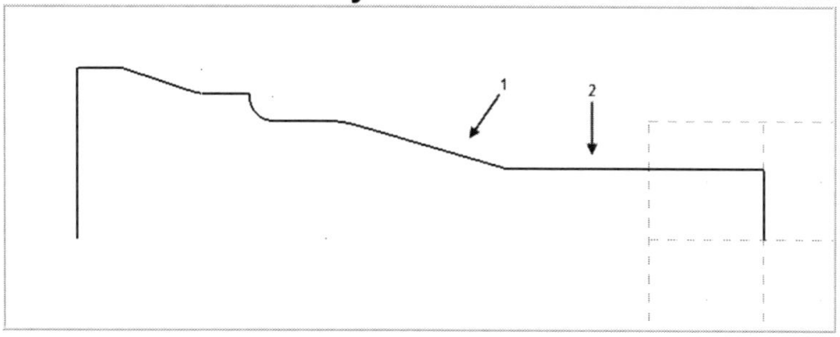

17. Click on the **OK** icon to complete this feature.

➲ The completed fillet is shown below.

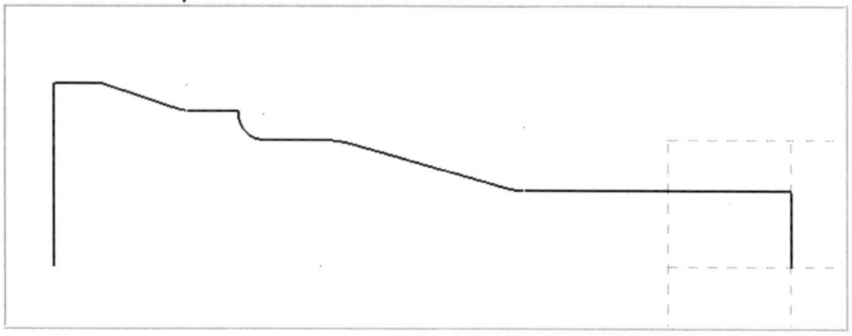

TASK 6:
CREATE THE CHAMFER

1. Select the **WIREFRAME** tab at the top of the screen and in the **Modify** section click on **Chamfer Entities**.

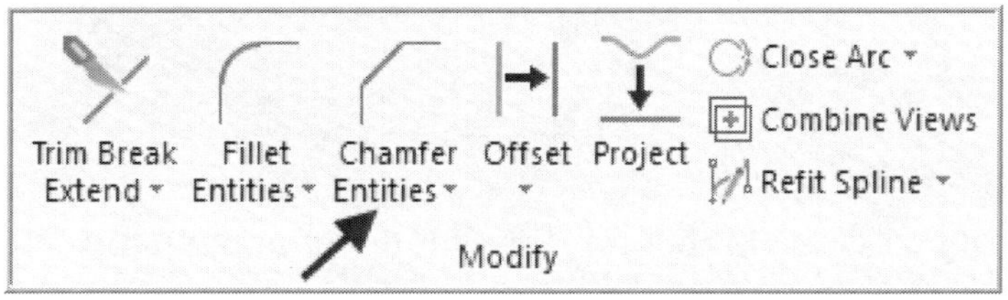

2. The **Chamfer Entities** panel appears. If required activate the **Style** to **1 Distance** and enter a value of **0.0625** for **Distance 1**.
3. Ensure the **Trim** entities box at the bottom of the panel is check marked to turn the trim on.

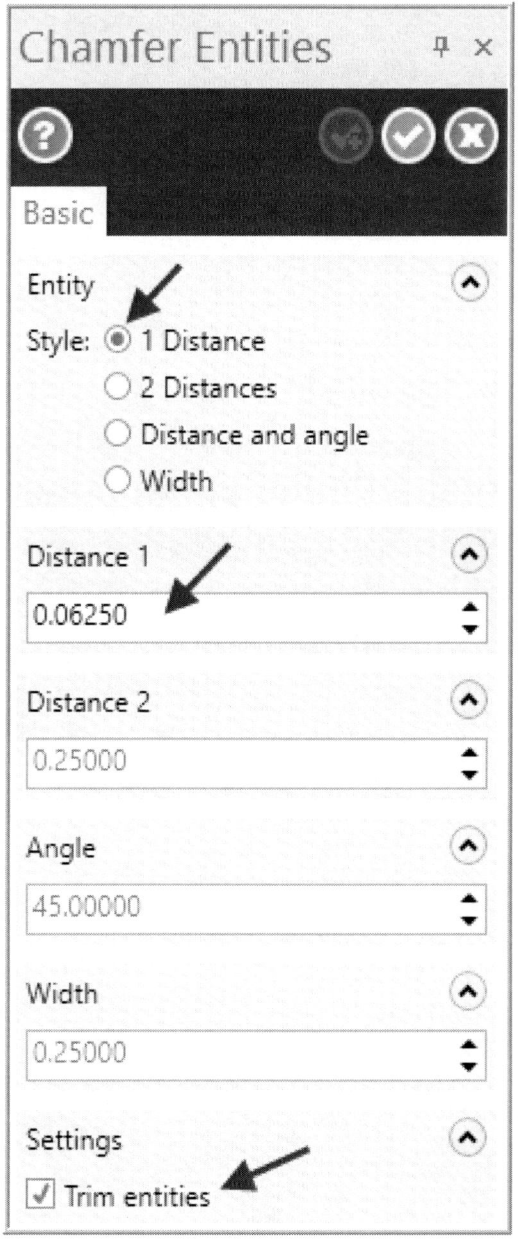

Style field
Defines chamfer style. Choose to create the chamfer style based on distance or width as defined below:

1 Distance - Sets the distance from the intersection of the two selected lines that each endpoint of the chamfer is positioned. Activates only the Distance 1 field for input. Both chamfer endpoints are positioned equal distances from the intersection.

2 Distances - Sets the distances from the intersection of the two selected lines that each endpoint of the chamfer is positioned. This allows you to set two separate distances. The value in the Distance 1 field sets the distance from the endpoint of the first line you select. The value in the Distance 2 field sets the distance from the endpoint of the second line you select.

Distance and Angle - Sets the distance from the intersection of the entity you select first, and an angle that determines the angle of the chamfer. When you are prompted to select the second entity, your cursor will snap to recognized chamfers that meet the conditions of both the Distance 1 and Angle fields. If those conditions cannot be met, you will not be able to create a chamfer.

Width - Sets the width of the chamfer and positions its endpoints along the two selected lines accordingly.

4. Move over to the graphic screen and for the prompt **"Select Line or arc"** click on **Line 1** and then for the prompt **"Select Line or arc"** click on **Line 2** as shown below.

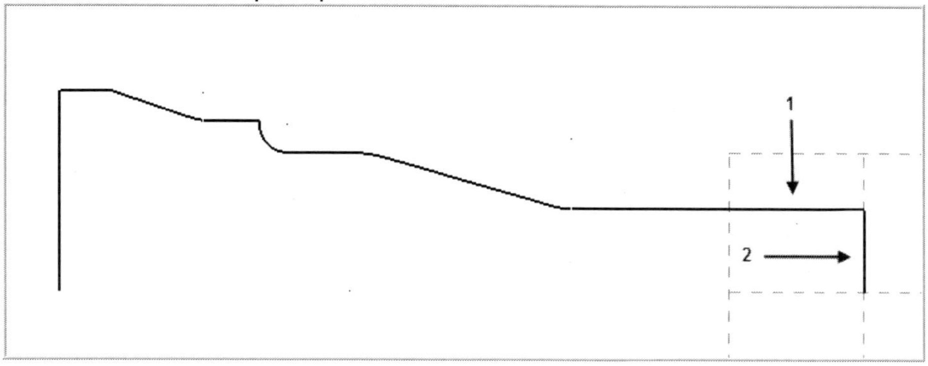

5. Click on the **OK** icon  to complete this feature.

➲ The Chamfer should look like the figure below.

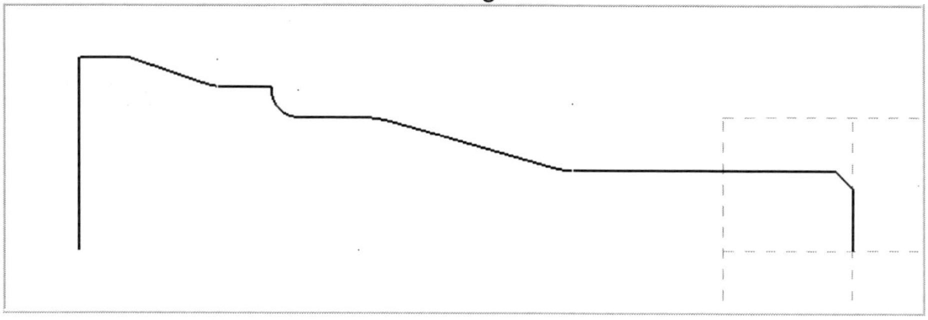

➲ This completes the geometry for this part.

TASK 7:
SAVE THE DRAWING

1. Select **File.**
2. Select **Save As…**
3. Click on the **Browse** icon.
4. In the **"File name"** box, type **"Lathe-Lesson-3".**
5. Browse to an appropriate location.
6. Select the **Save** button to save the file and complete this function.

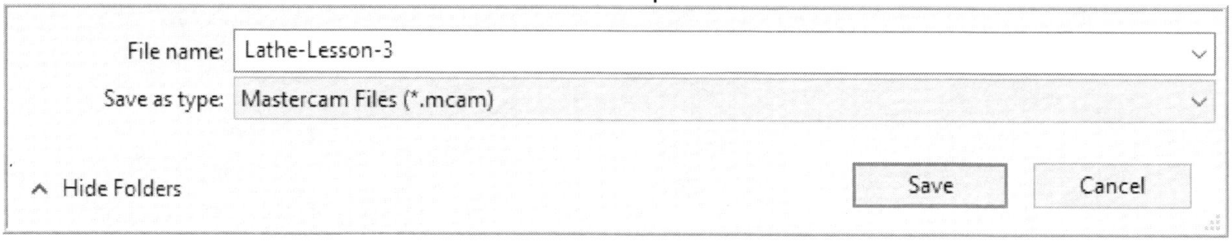

Toolpath Creation

TASK 8:
DEFINE THE STOCK AND CHUCK PARAMETERS

1. Select the **VIEW** tab at the top of the screen.
2. Select the **Fit** icon in the **Zoom** section. Next select **Unzoom 50%** to shrink the display.

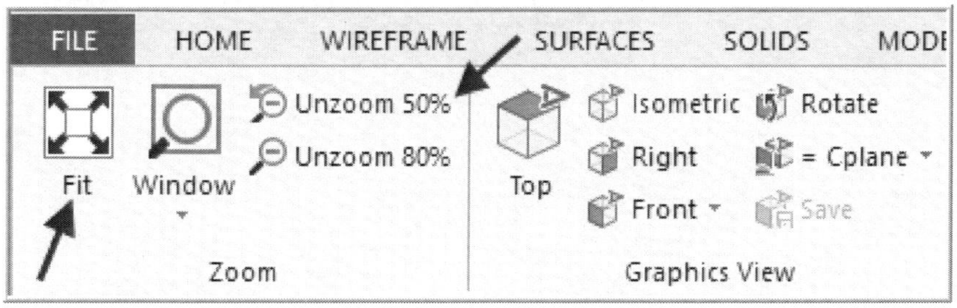

3. Still on the **View tab** and click on **Toolpaths** to display the Toolpaths Manager.

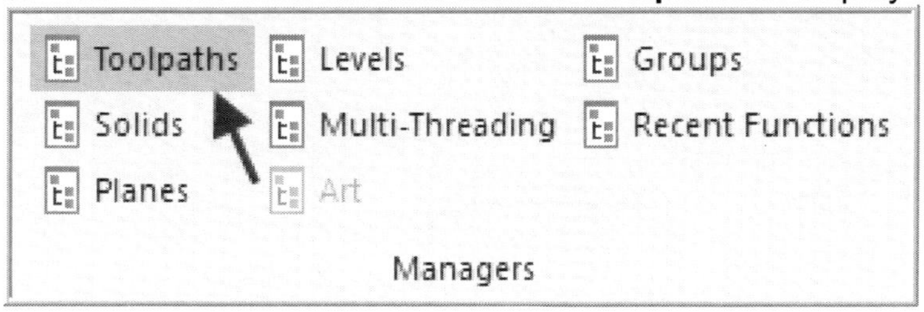

4. Ensure your screen looks like the image below:
   a. The Toolpath Manager is open.
   b. The properties icon displays Lathe Default. If it is not refer to **Setting the Environment** chapter at the beginning of the book.
   c. The Lathe Lesson-3 Geometry is showing.

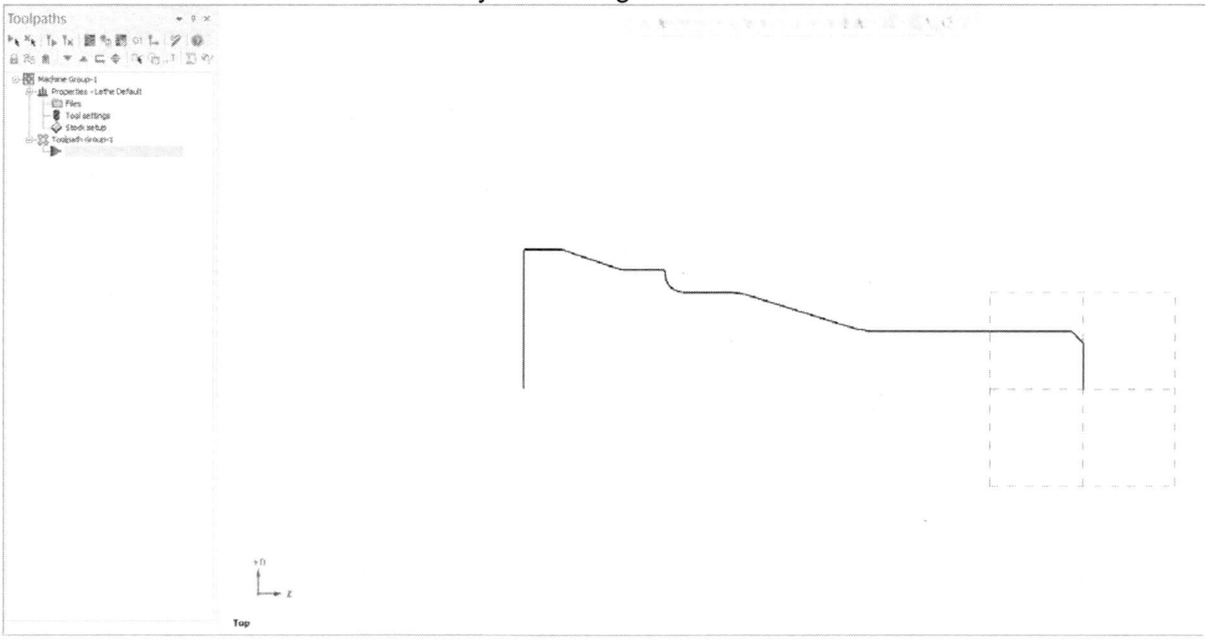

5. Select the plus in front of **Properties** to expand the Machine Group Properties, if required.

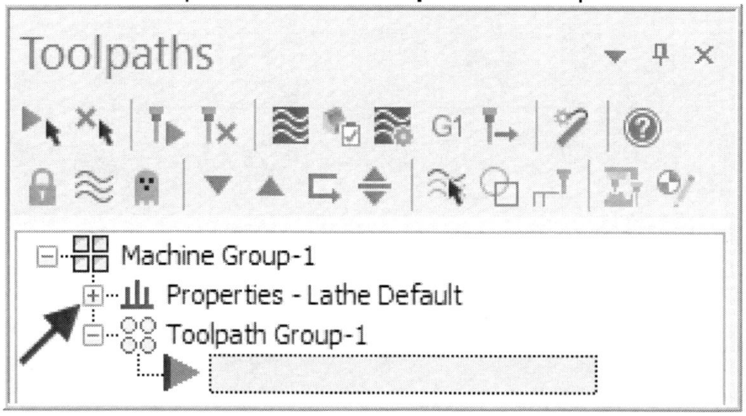

6. Select **Stock setup** in the toolpath manager window.

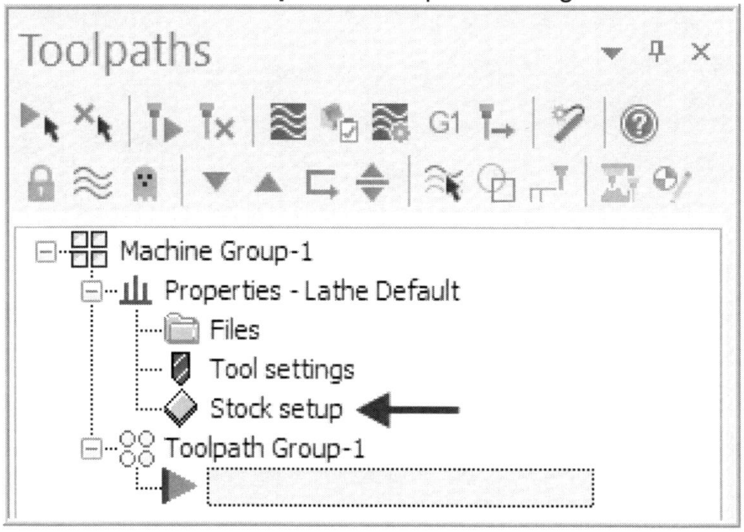

7. Select the **Stock Properties** button in the **Stock Setup** page as shown in the screenshot below:

Note: To learn more about Stock Setup refer to the Tips and Techniques content in the Online Course Instruction.

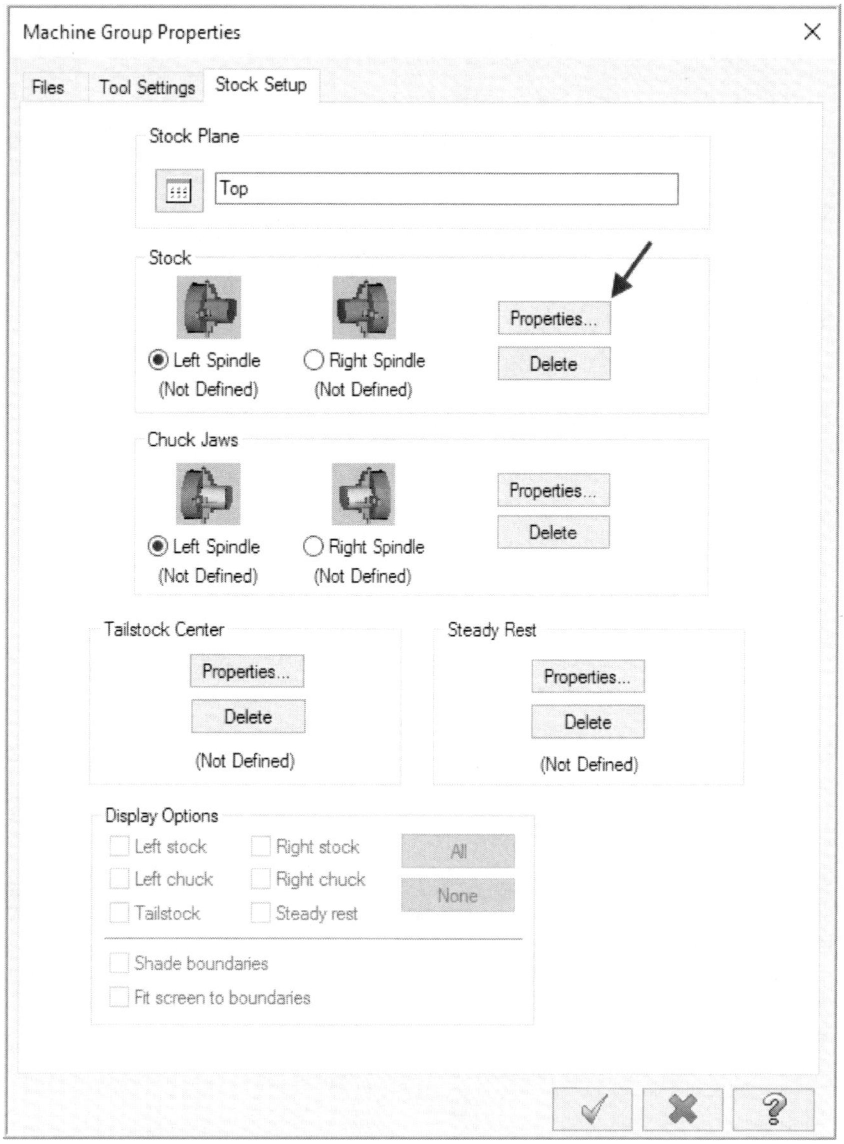

8. In the **Machine Component Manager-Stock** window click on the **Geometry** button and select **Cylinder** as shown below:

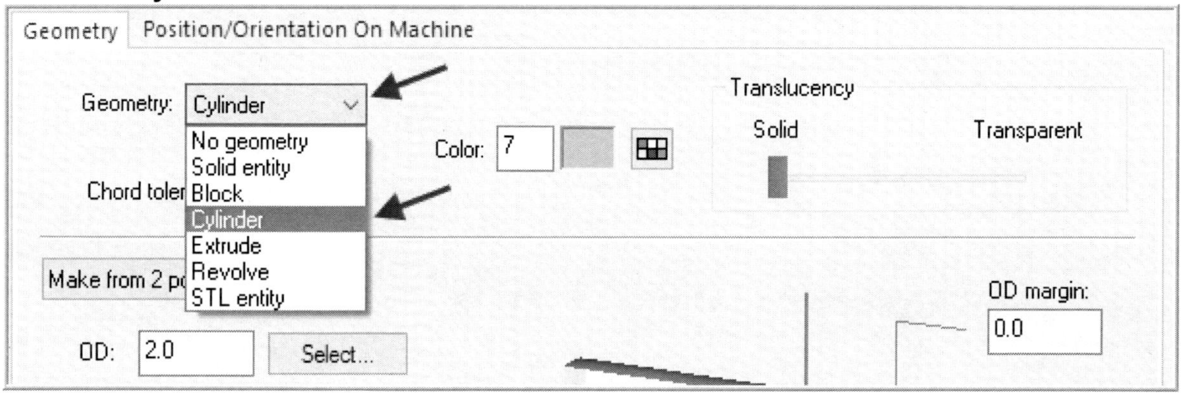

9. In the **Stock setup** set the values as shown below. **Axis is set to -Z**.

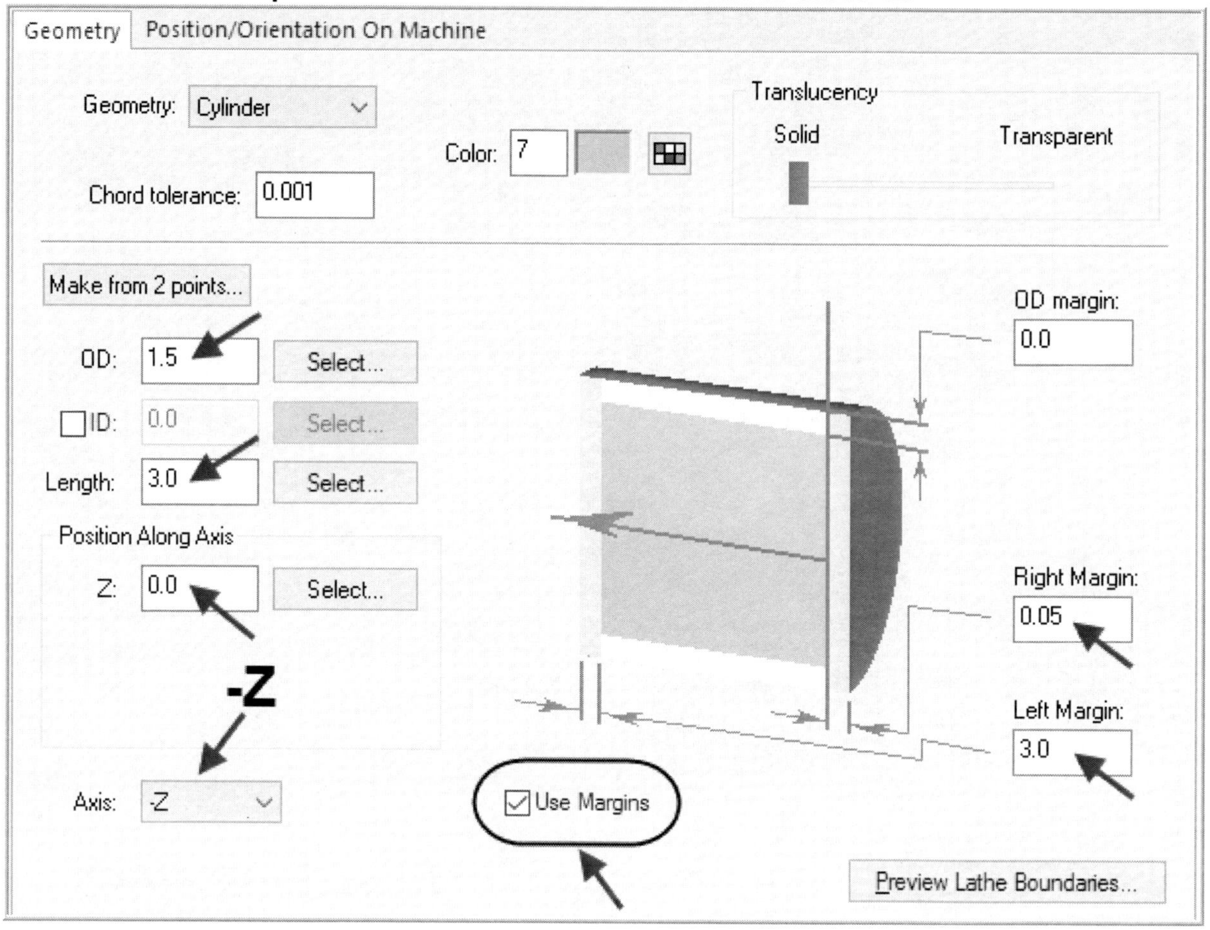

10. Click on the OK icon [OK icon] to complete this feature.
11. Still on the Stock Setup page activate **Fit screen to boundaries**.

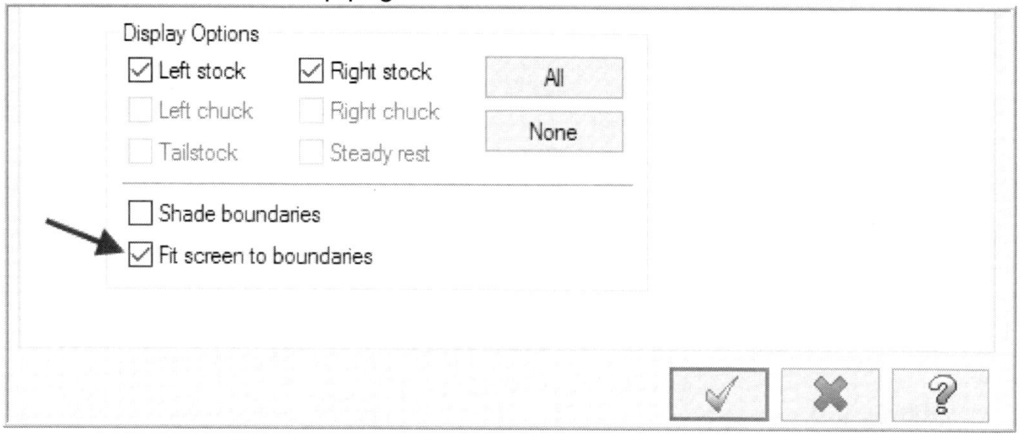

12. Select the **Chuck Properties** button in the **Stock Setup** page as shown in the screenshot below:

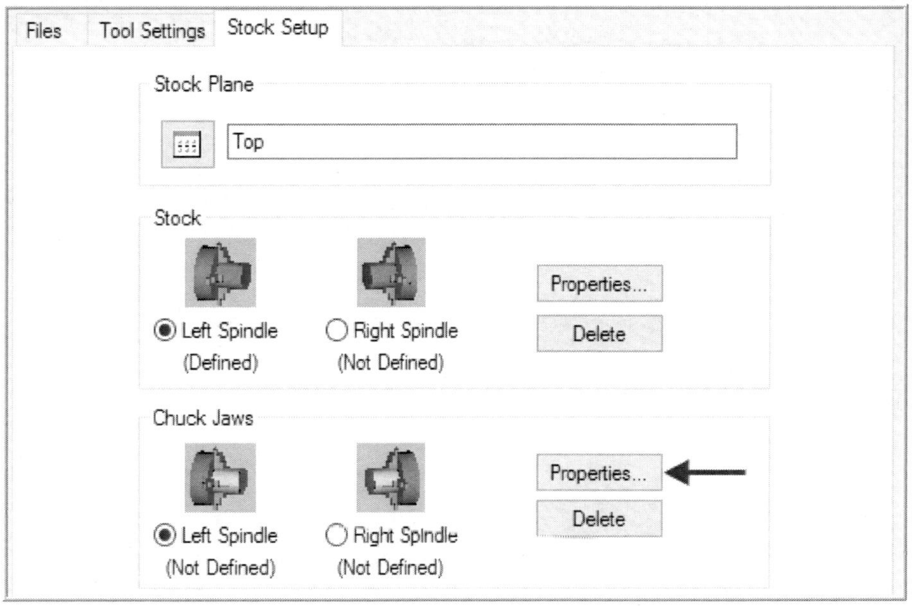

13. In the **Chuck Jaws** setup set the values as shown below.

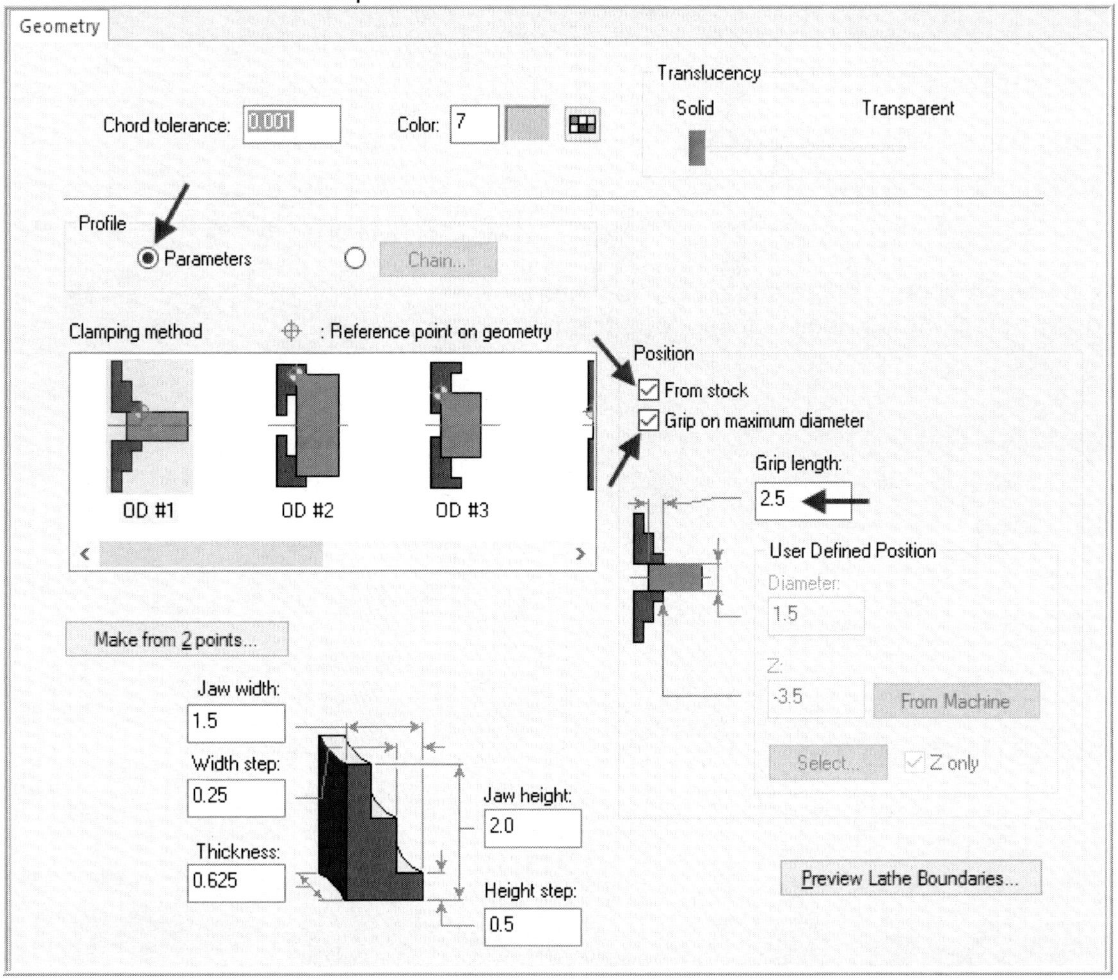

14. Click on the OK icon  to complete this feature.

15. Click on the **Tool Settings** page and make changes as shown below.

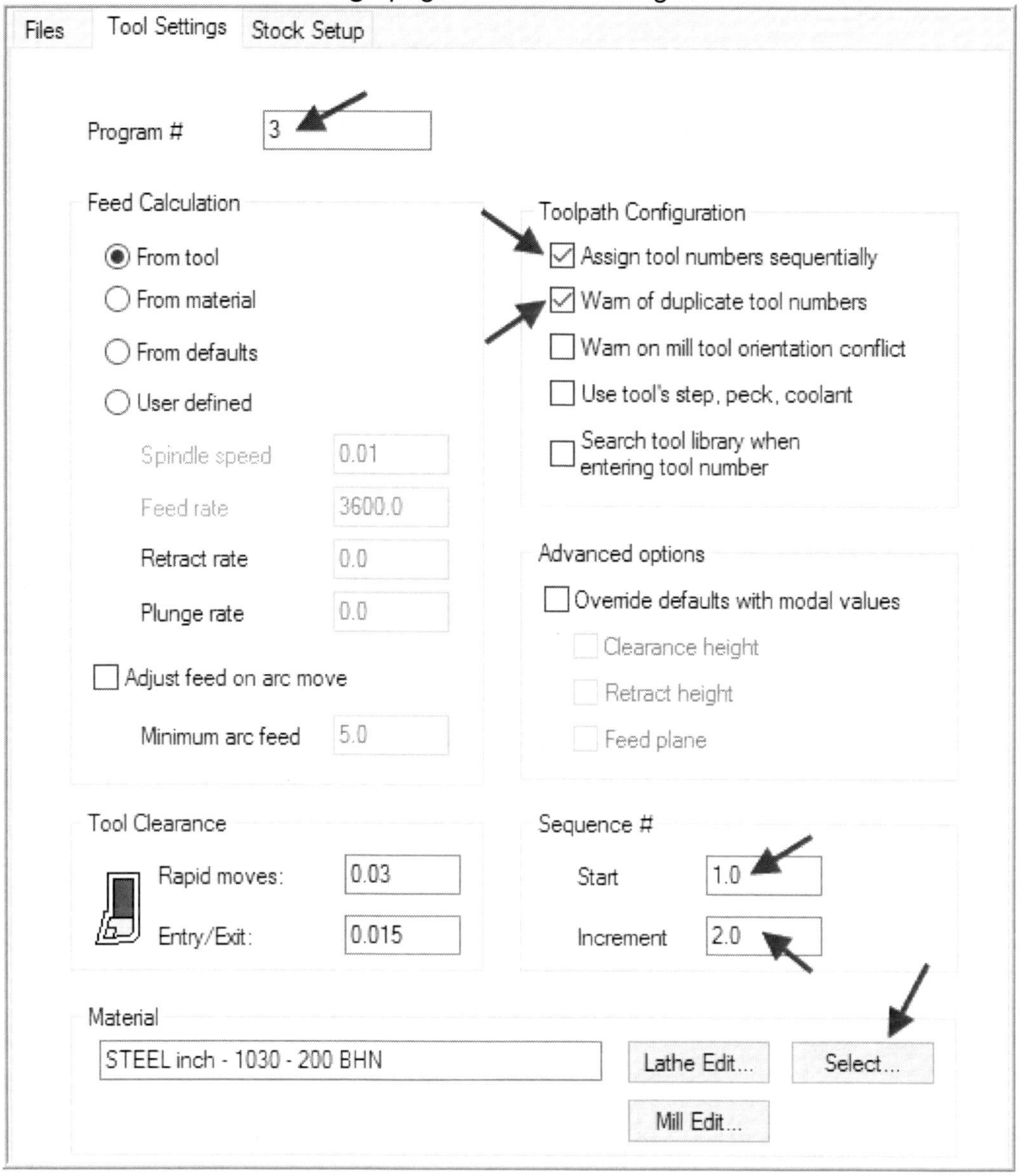

16. To change the **Material** type to Aluminum 6061 click on the **Select** button at the bottom of the Tool Settings page.

17. At the **Material List** dialog box open the Source drop down list and select **Lathe – library.**

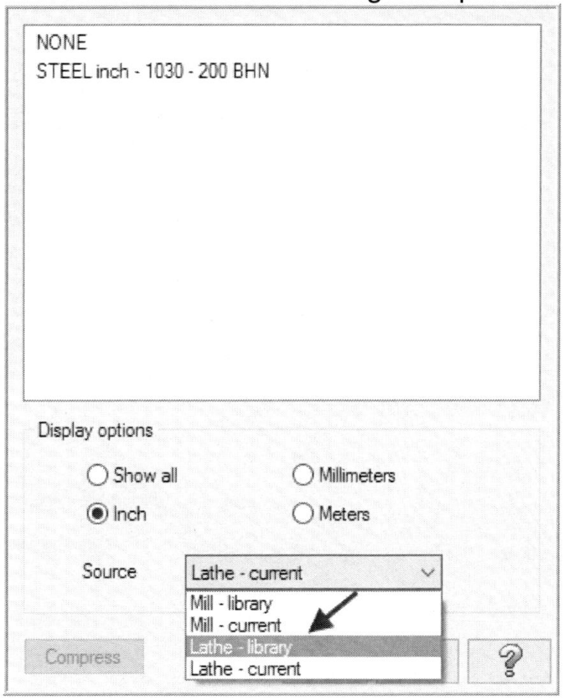

18. From the **Default Materials** list select **ALUMINUM inch - 6061** and then select .

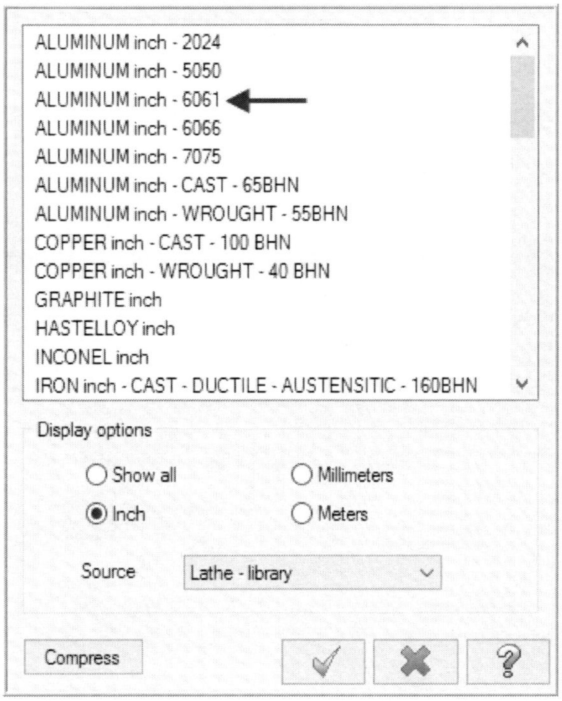

19. Select the OK button again to complete this Stock Setup function.

20. Right mouse click in the graphics area and click on the **Fit** icon .

➲ Note the stock setup outline as indicated by broken lines as shown below.

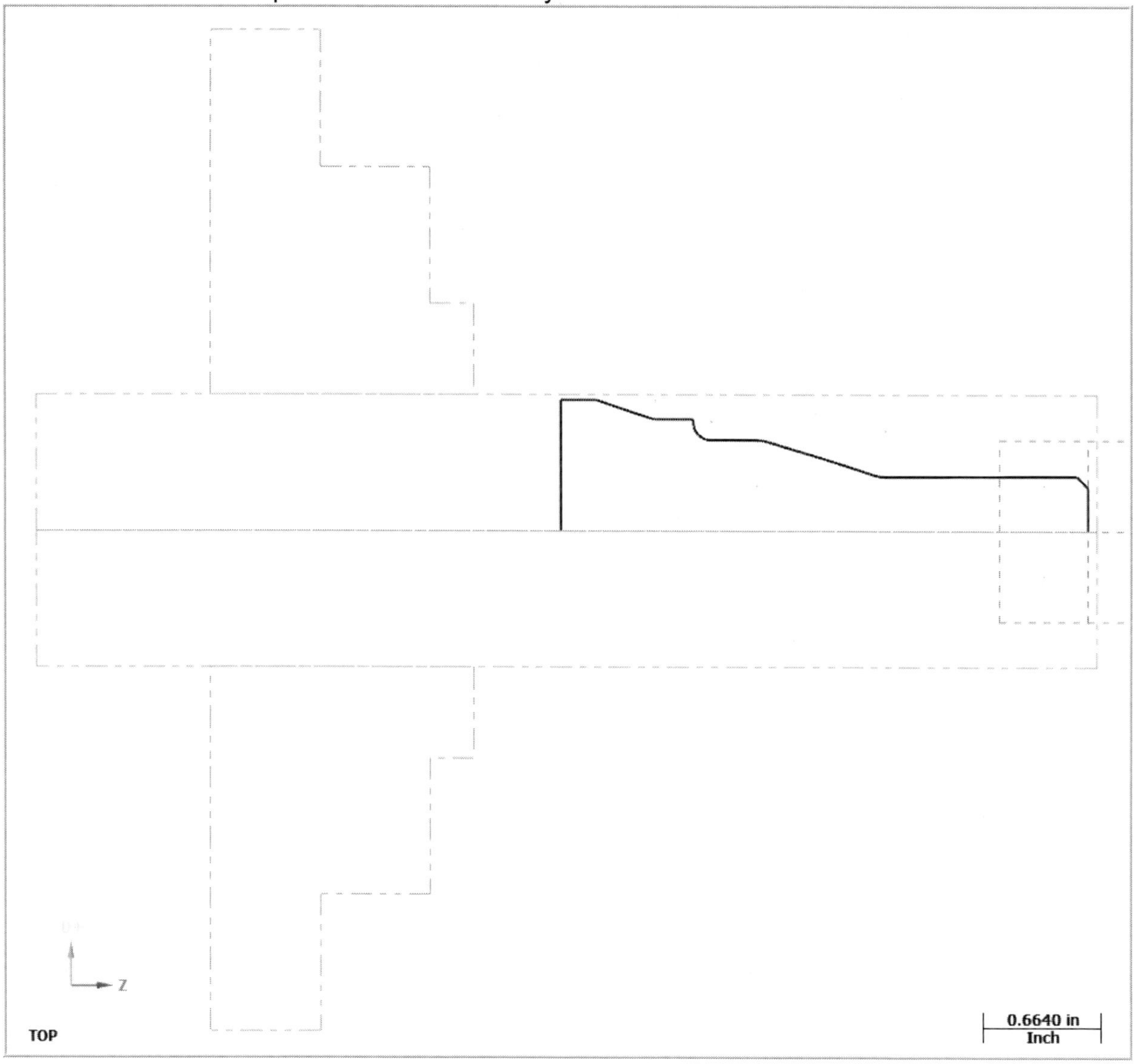

TASK 9:
FACE THE FRONT OF THE PART:

➲ In this task you will use a facing tool to face the front of the part in one cut.

1. If required right mouse click in the graphics area and click on the **Fit** icon.
2. Select the **TURNING** tab at the top right side of the screen.
3. Now select **Face** in the **General** section.

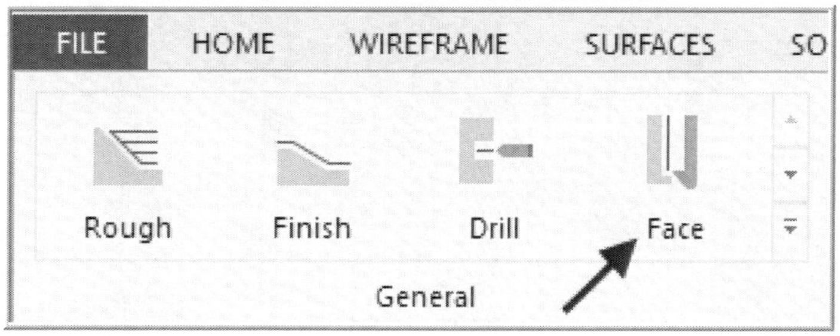

➲ After selecting the OK button you are confronted with **Toolpath parameters** page. The first task here will be to select **Tool #1 an OD Rough- Right – 80 deg.**

4. Click on **Tool #1** and make changes in the Toolpath parameters page as shown below.
5. Click on **Coolant,** open up the drop down menu for **Flood** and set it to **On.**

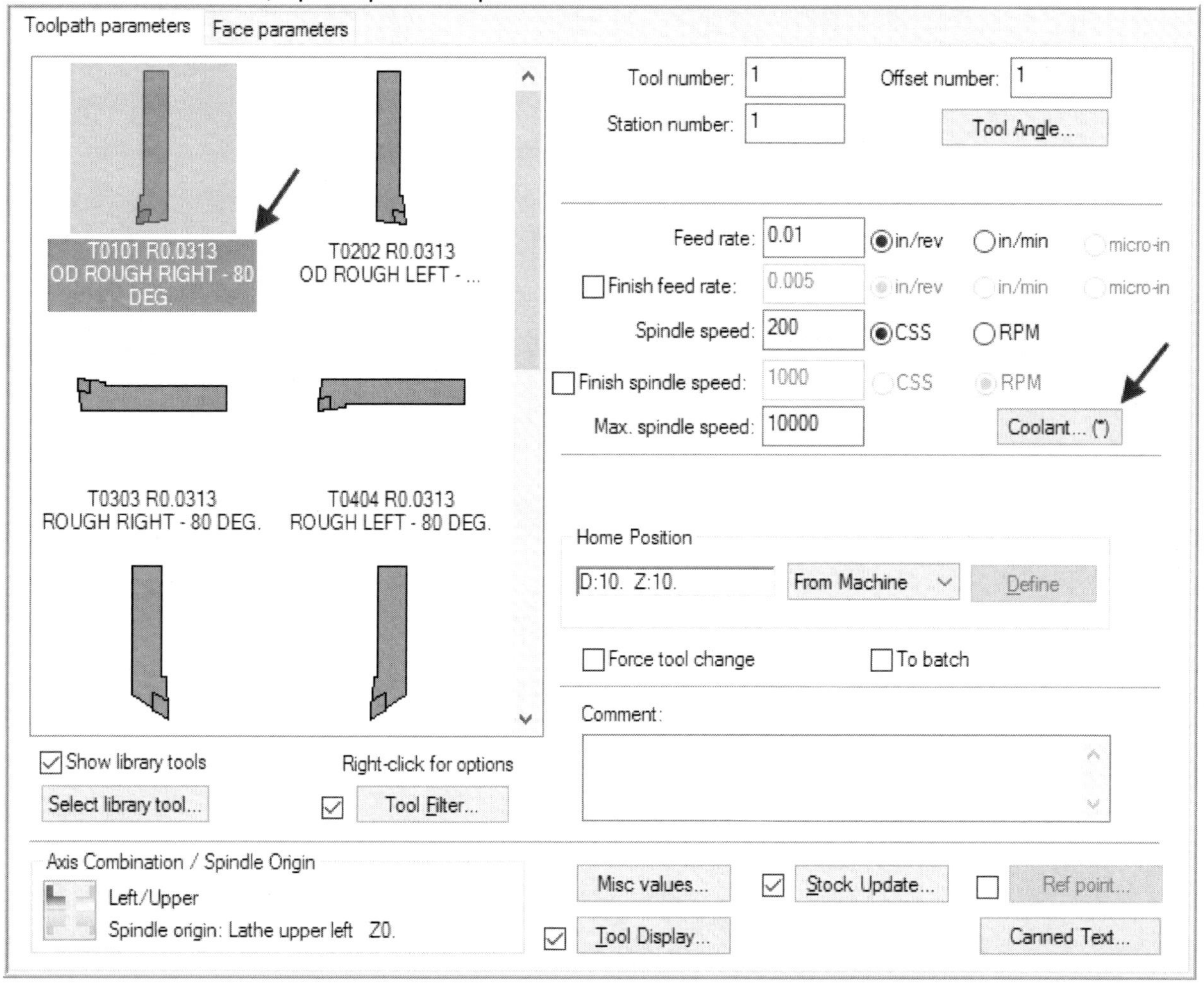

Use the Toolpath parameters tab to select a tool, set feeds and speeds, and set other general toolpath parameters. This tab is very similar for most Lathe toolpaths.

6. Select the **Face parameters** page and make changes as shown below.

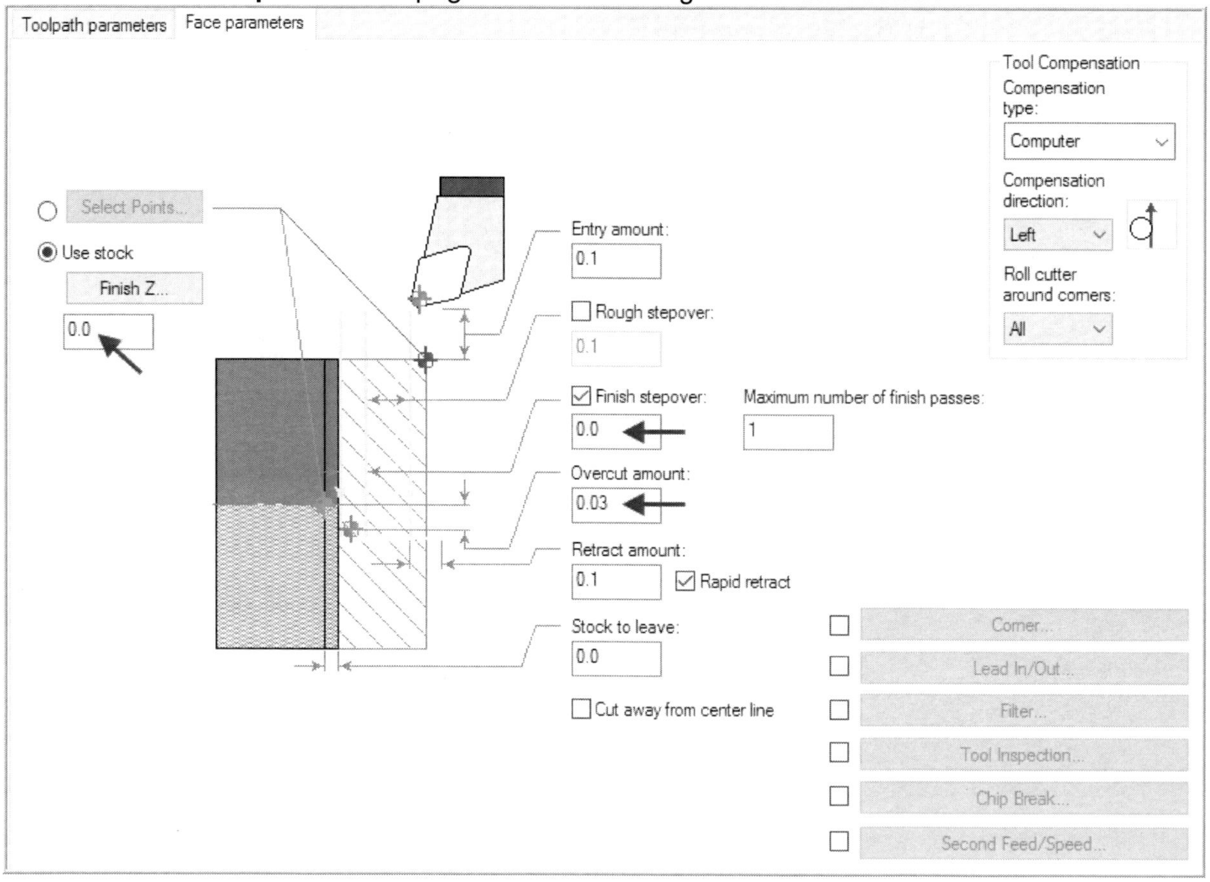

7. Select the OK button to complete this **Lathe Face** operation.

Finish stepover
Select this option to create one or more finish passes. Enter a stepover distance to define how much stock gets removed during each finish cut.

Overcut amount
A rectangle is used to define the material removed by the facing toolpath. The overcut amount determines how far past the rectangle the tool will cut.
Typically this is a small distance that the tool cuts past the part centerline.

TASK 10:
ROUGH THE OUTSIDE DIAMETERS

- ➲ In this task you will use a new Lathe toolpath called **Quick rough**.
- ➲ In this task you will use the same tool as used for the previous facing operation **Tool #1 an OD Rough- Right – 80 deg.**

1. Right mouse click in the white space of the **Toolpaths Manager** and select:
   Lathe toolpaths>Quick>Quick rough.

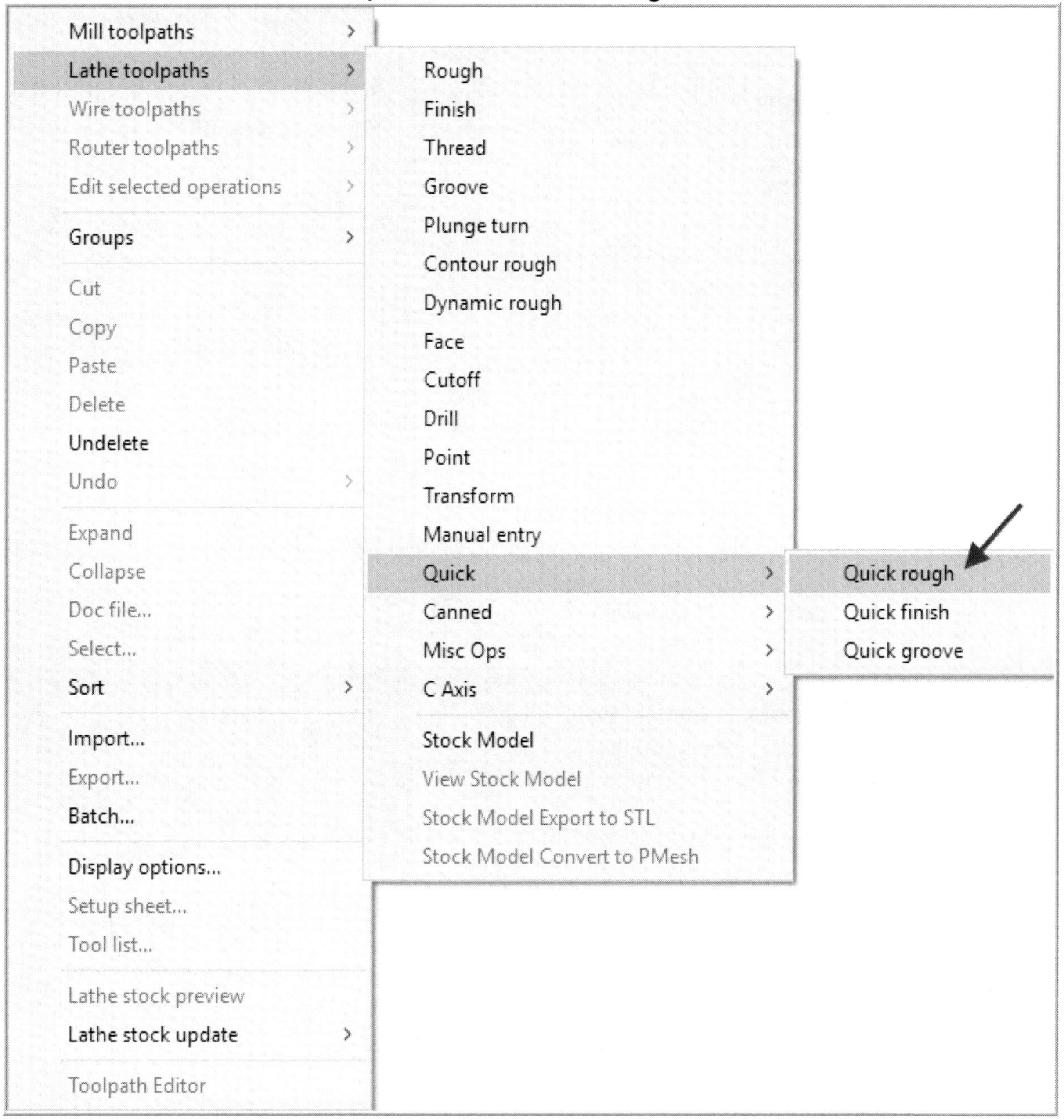

Quick rough toolpaths coarsely cut the part geometry in preparation for a finish toolpath.

Use this toolpath when you need to quickly create a simple roughing operation and don't need Mastercam's more advanced roughing features.

In addition, you have fewer options for creating entry and exit passes.

2. In the **Chaining** window chaining mode is set to **Partial** by default.

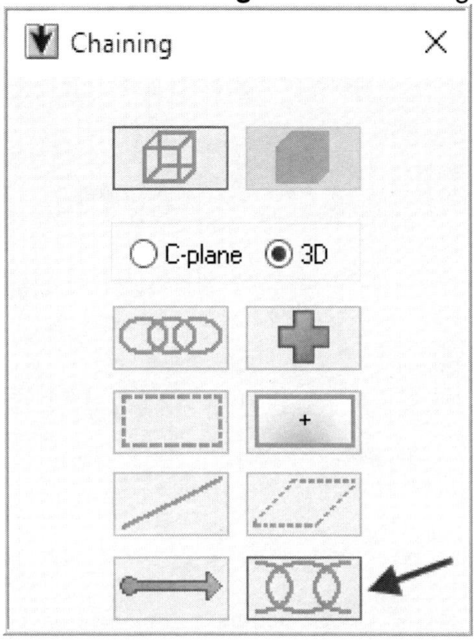

3. Select the chamfer, Line 1 as the start of the **Partial chain**.

After you have selected the chamfer **ensure** that the arrows are pointing up and to the left of the part. If it is not select the reverse button in the Chaining dialog box.

4. Then select Line 2 as the end entity in this chain.

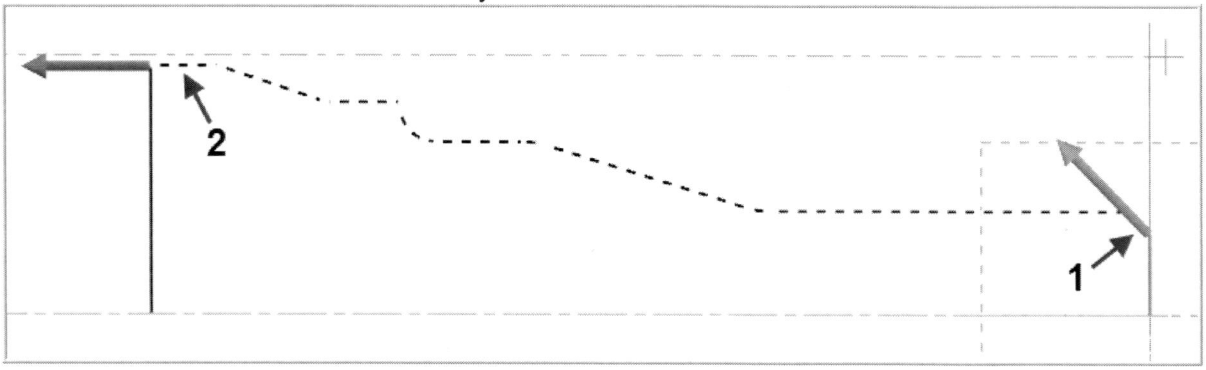

5. Select the OK button  to exit the Chaining dialog window.

6. In the **Toolpath parameters** page select the same tool used to face the part **Tool #1 an OD Rough- Right – 80 deg** and make any necessary changes as shown below.
7. Click on **Coolant,** open up the drop down menu for **Flood** and set it to **On.**

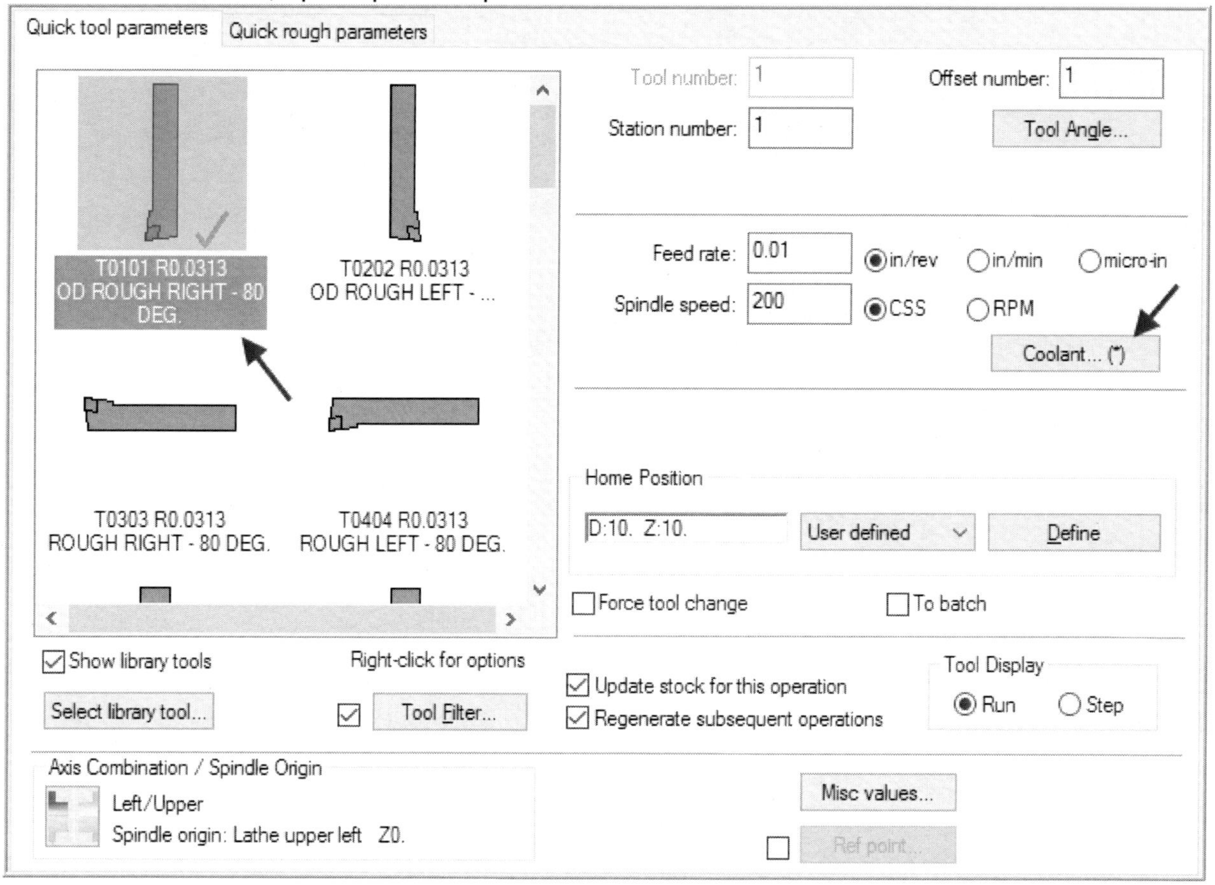

8. Select the **Quick rough parameters** page and make any necessary changes as shown below.

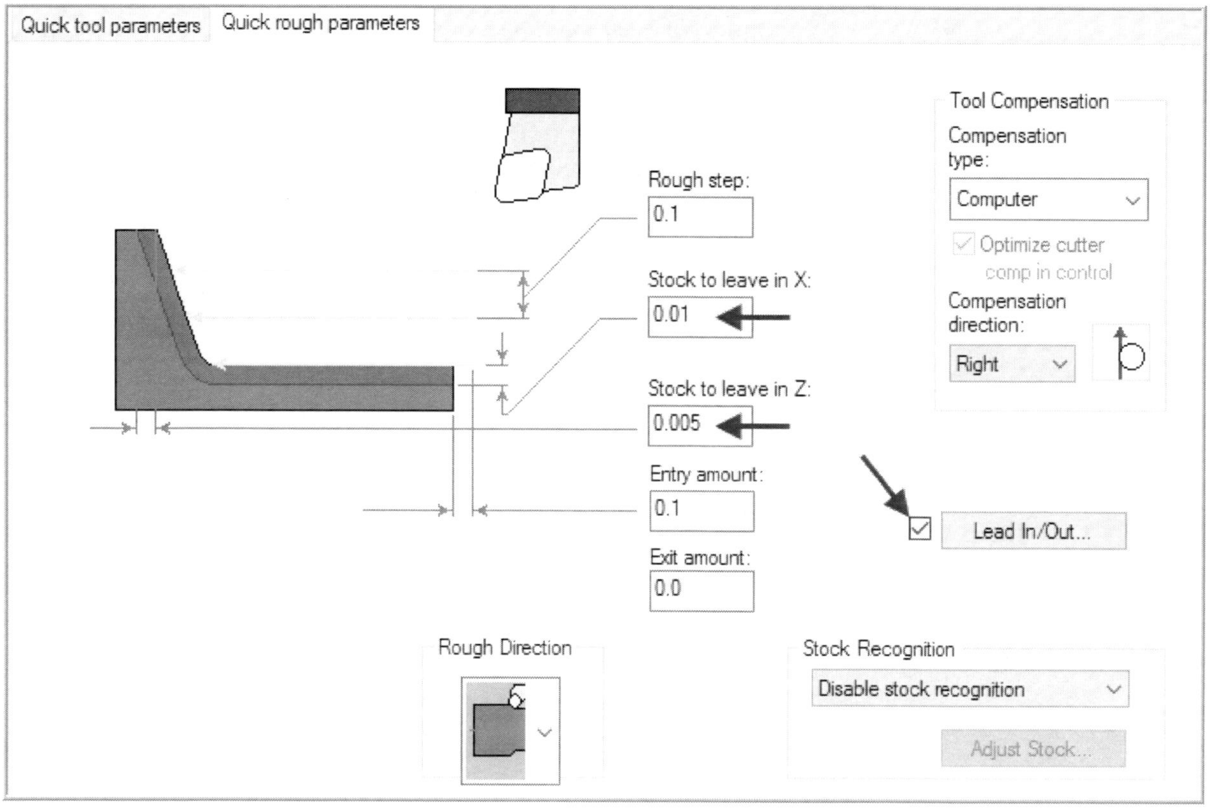

9. Select the **Lead In/Out** button select the **Lead out** page and **extend the contour by 0.2** as shown below.

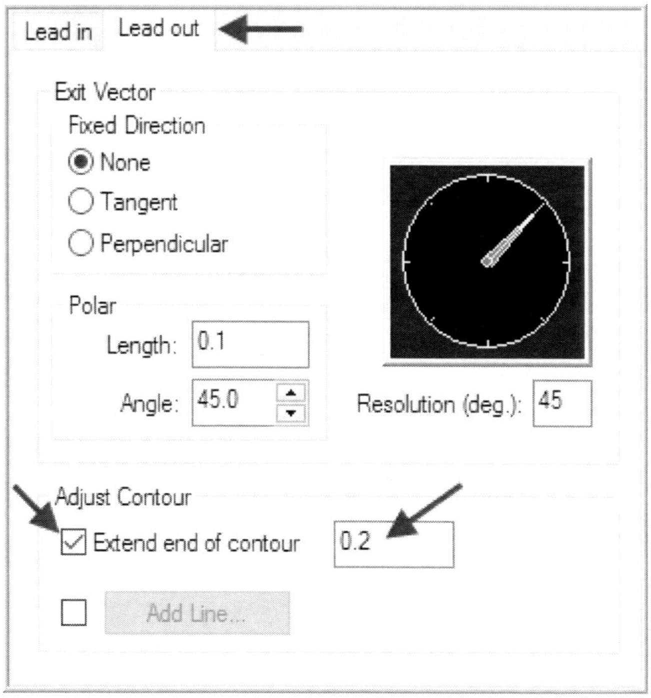

10. Select the OK button  to exit this function.

11. Select the **OK** button  to exit Quick rough Parameters.

TASK 11:
FINISH THE OUTSIDE DIAMETERS

➲ In this task you will finish the outside diameters in one cut using **Tool #2 OD Finish Right – 35 DEG.**

1. Right mouse click in the white space of the **Toolpaths Manager** and select:
   Lathe toolpaths>Quick>Quick finish.

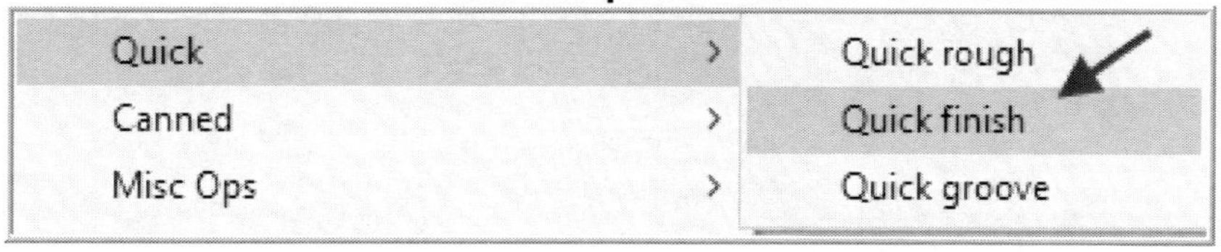

Quick finish toolpaths are useful for placing finish passes on an uncomplicated part where you don't need all of Mastercam's more advanced finishing options.

You can chain geometry for this toolpath or simply select an existing roughing operation

2. Select **Tool #2 OD Finish Right – 35 DEG** tool from the tool list and make any necessary changes as shown below. **Coolant Flood** is set to **On**.

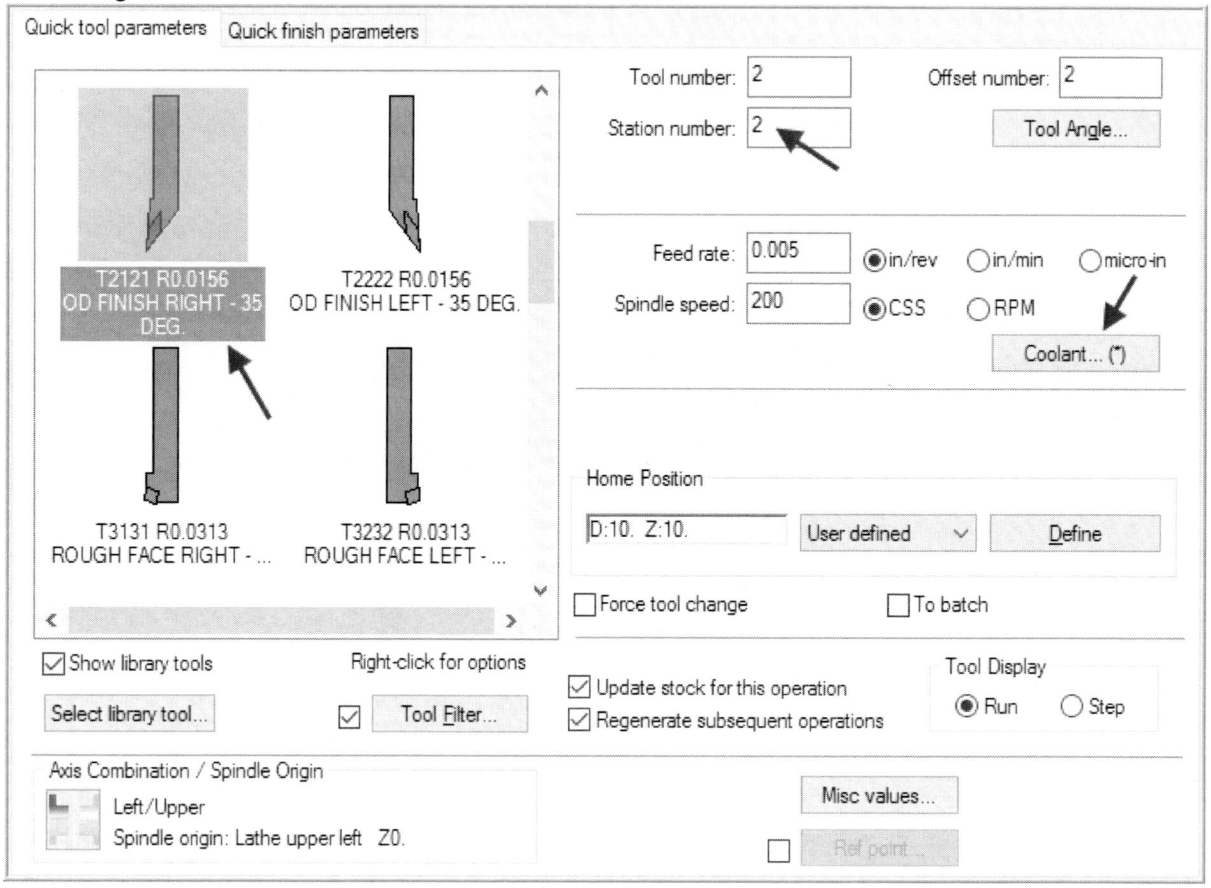

3. Select the **Quick finish parameters** page and make changes as shown below.

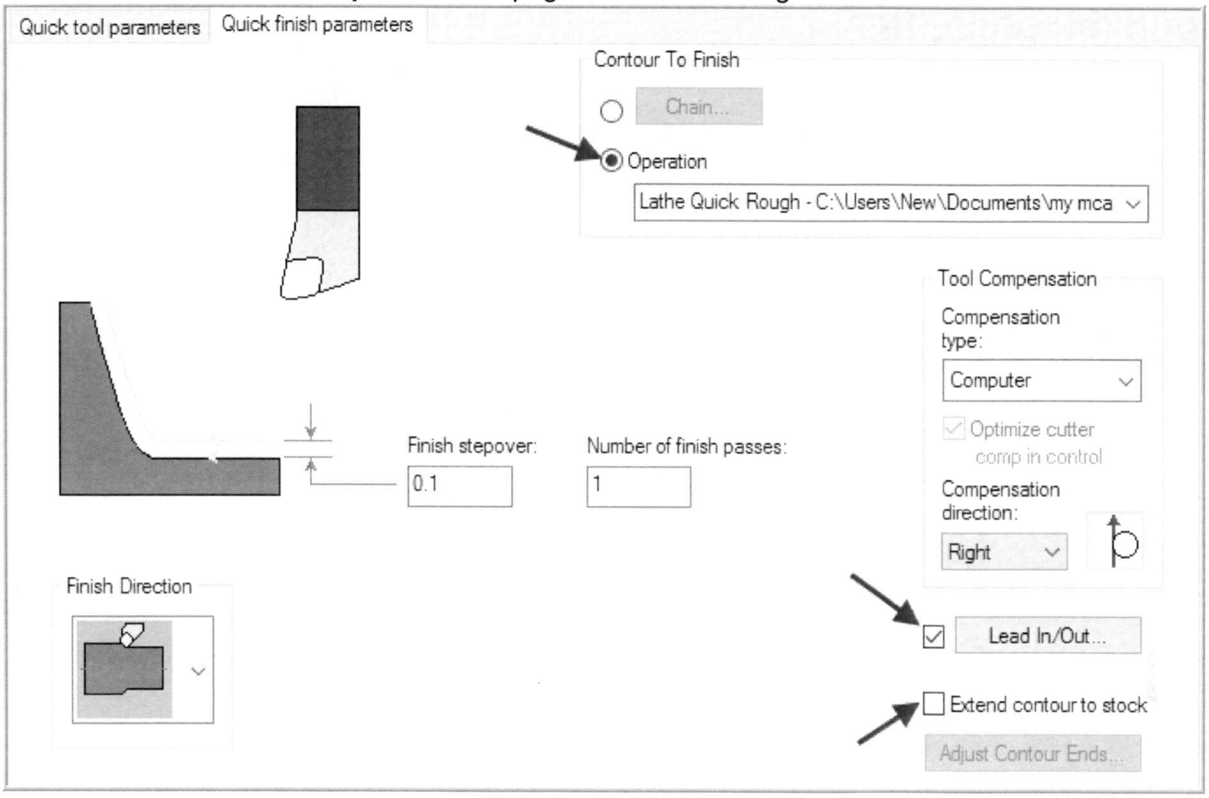

4. Select the **Lead In/Out** button select the **Lead out** page and extend the contour by .2 as shown below.

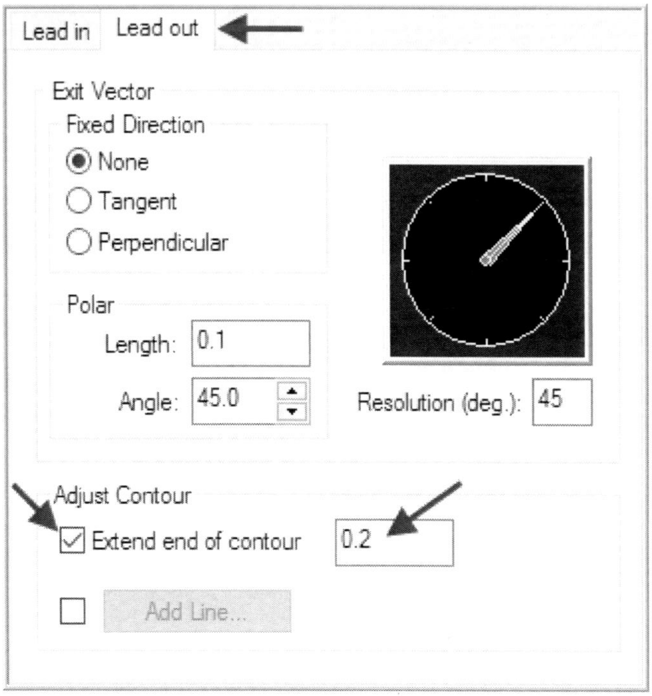

5. Select the OK button [✓] to exit this function.
6. Select the OK button [✓] to exit Quick finish parameters.

TASK 12:
CENTER DRILL THE HOLE

➲ In this task you will center drill .2" depth using **Tool #3 Centre Drill - .25 diameter.**

1. Select **Drill** in the **General** section of the **Turning** tab.

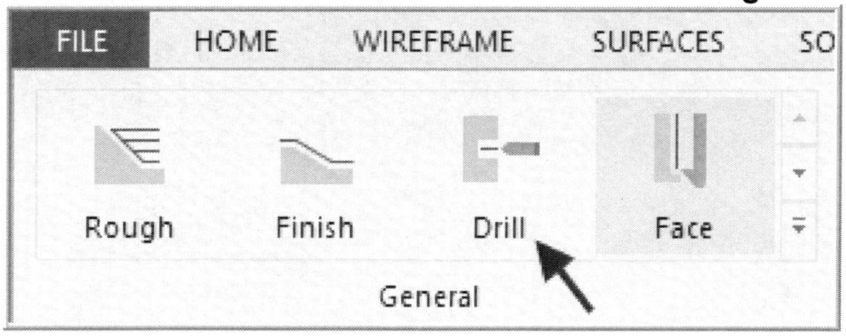

2. Select the **CENTER DRILL .25 DIAMETER** tool from the tool list and make changes as shown below. **Coolant Flood** is set to **On**.

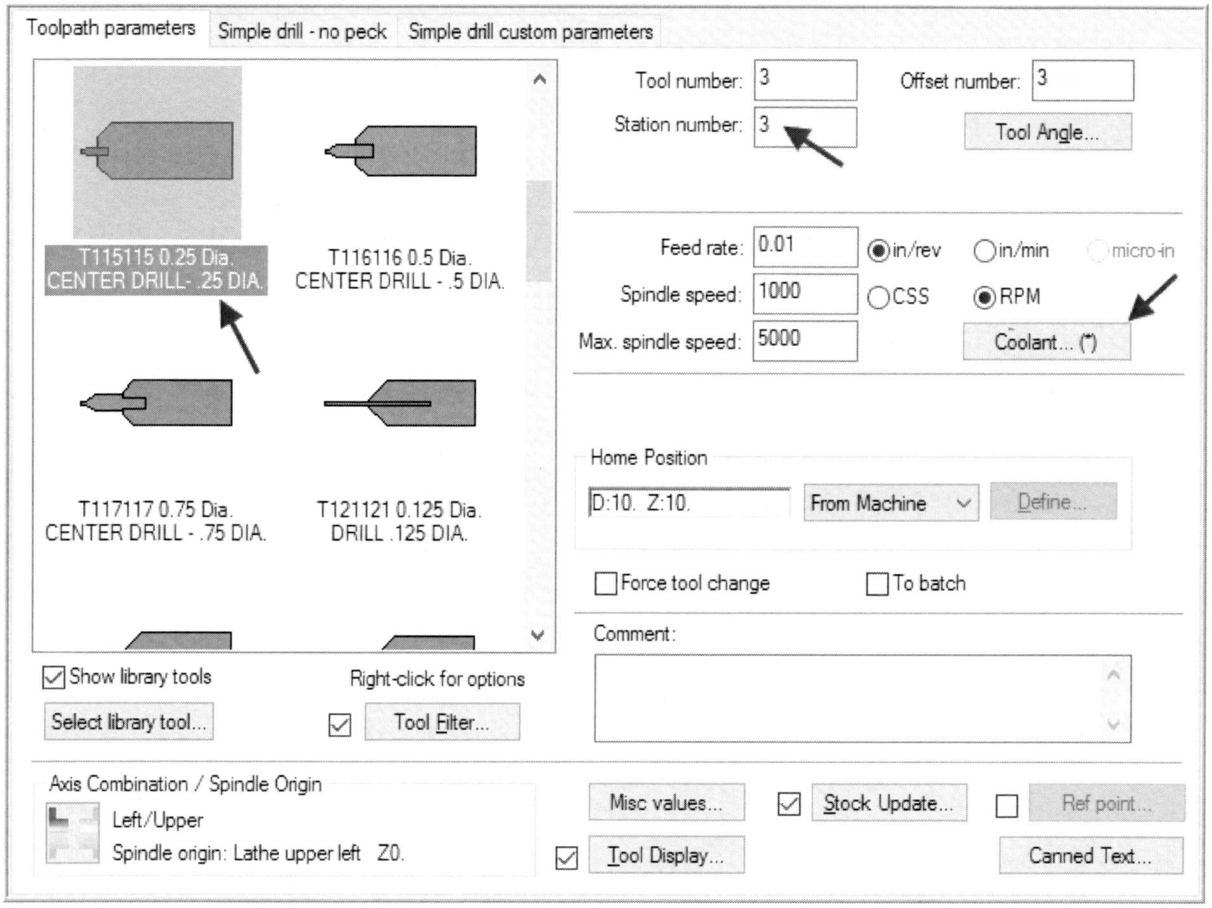

3. Select the **Simple drill – no peck** page and make changes as shown below.

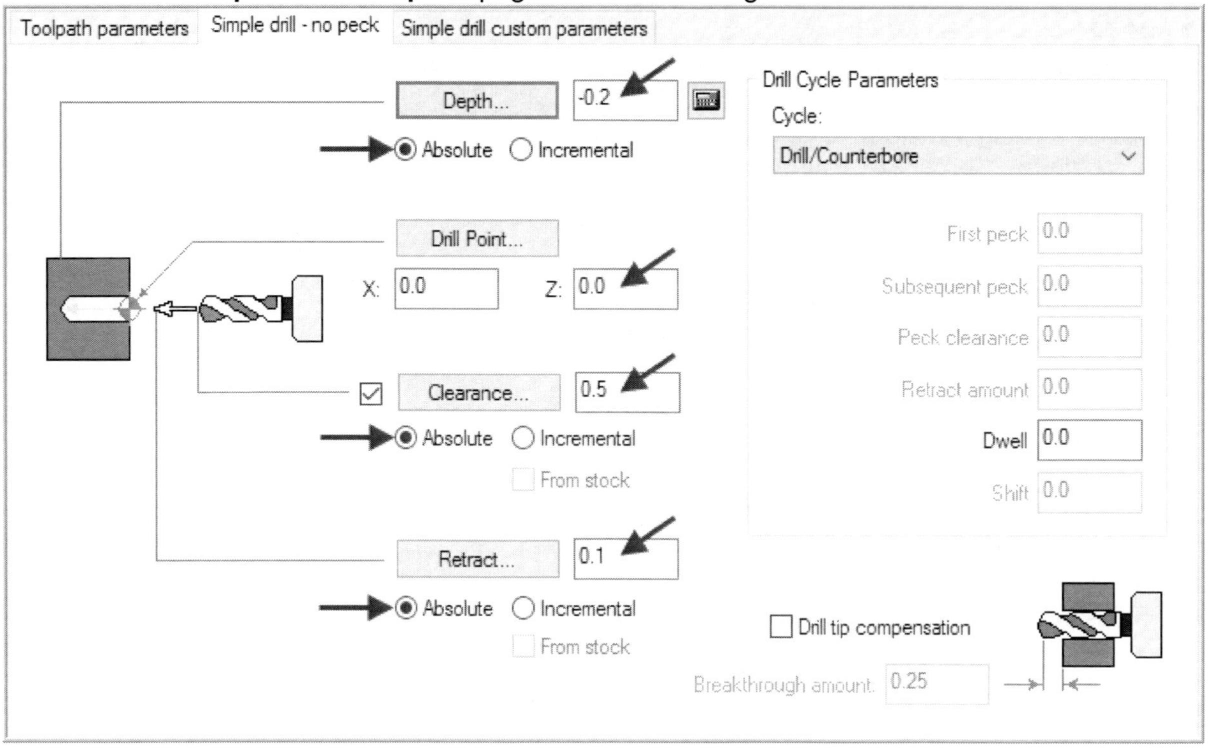

4. Select the OK button  to exit **Simple drill – no peck.**

TASK 13:
TAP DRILL THE 5/16" HOLE

➲ In this task you will drill the 5/16" hole .75" depth using a **0.3125 (5/16") Drill.**

1. Select **Drill** in the **General** section of the **Turning** tab.
2. Click on the **Select library tool…** button in the lower left corner of the Toolpath parameters page as shown below.

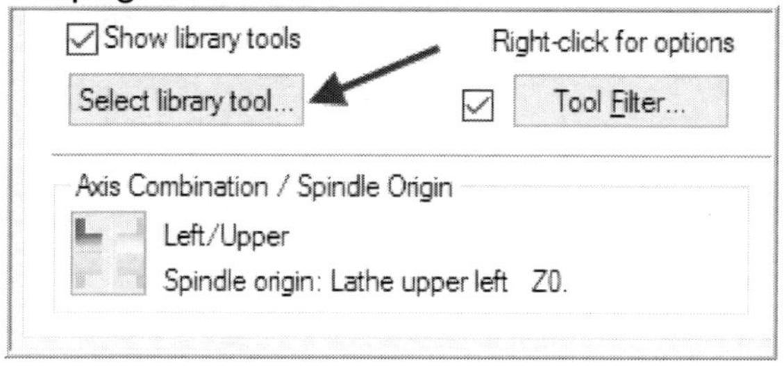

3. At the top left of this dialog box open up the Select new folder icon  to show the library tools list and select **LDRILLS.** Now click on the **Open button** to select **LDRILLS**.

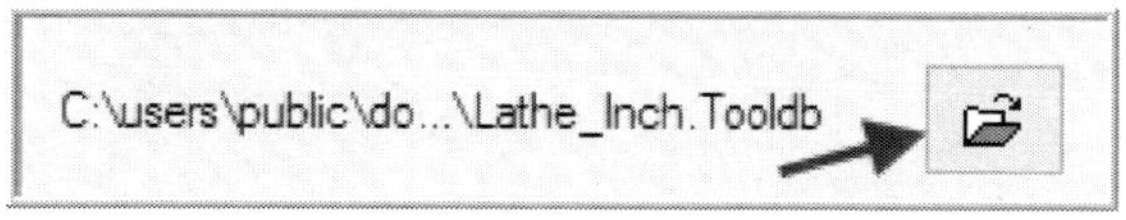

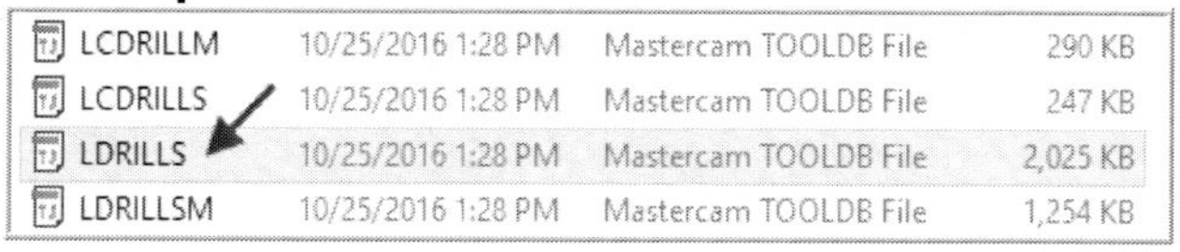

4. Scroll down and select the **0.3125 Dia. 5/16" DRILL** from the list.

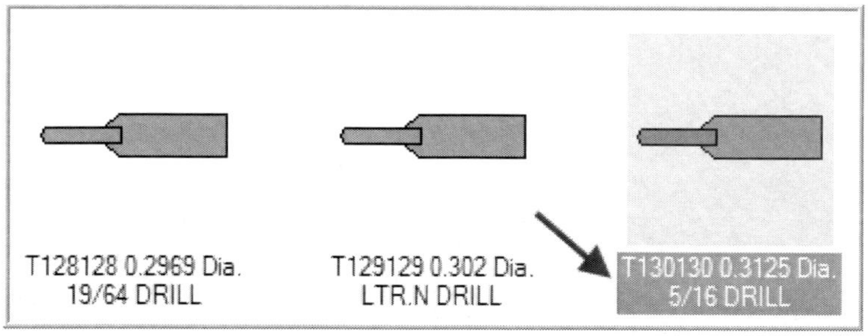

5. Select the OK button .

6. Ensure settings are as shown below. **Coolant Flood** is set to **On**.

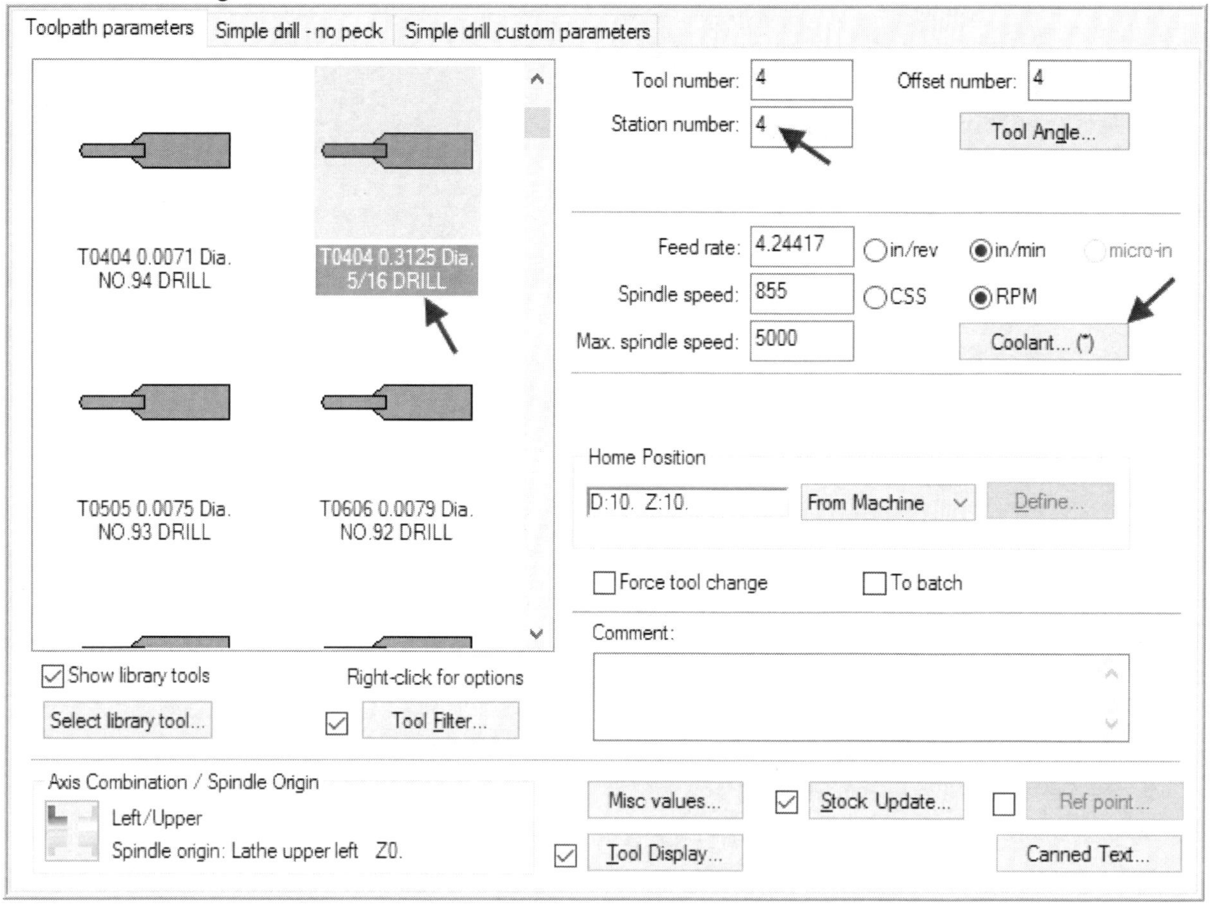

7. Select the **Simple drill – no peck** page and make changes as shown below. This hole will be **Peck Drilled**. The **depth of the hole is 1.00" from the front face** so click in the space for depth and type in **-1.0**.

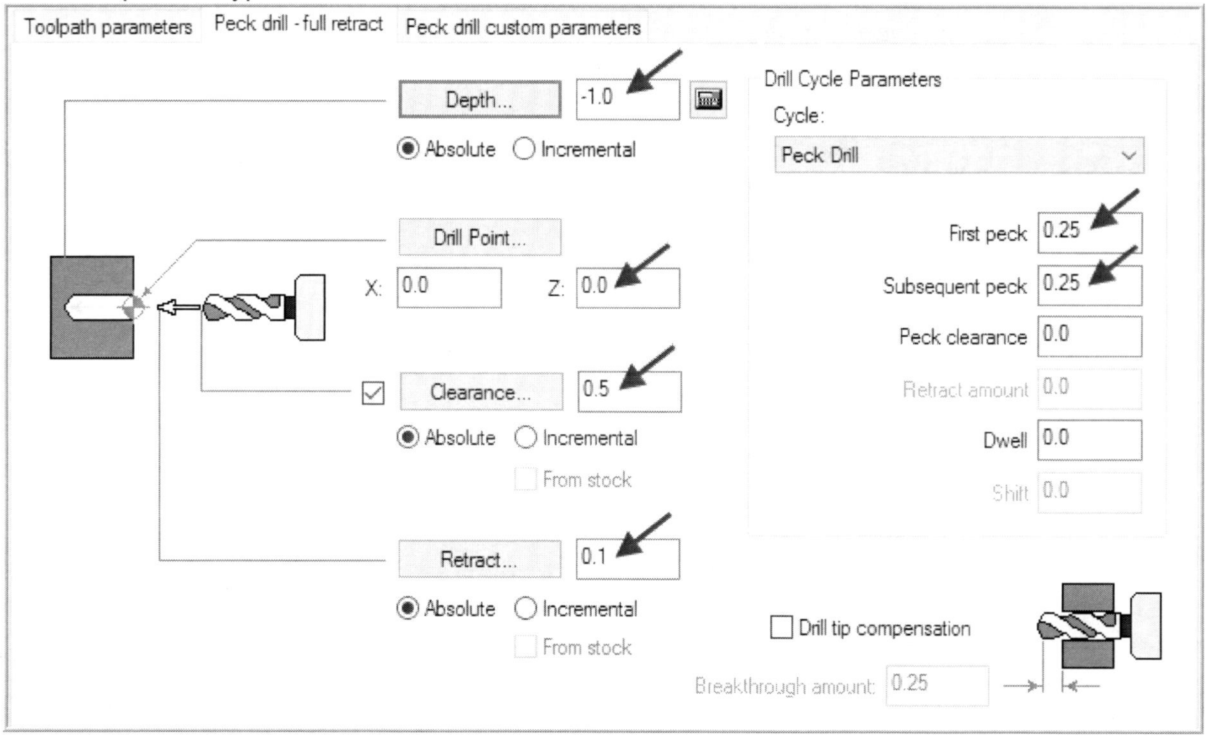

The hole depth on the drawing is dimensioned to .a depth of 1.0" at the full diameter of the hole. So the point of the drill will have to go deeper than 1.0"
You can use the depth calculator button to figure out the correct depth.

8. Select the **Depth Calculator** icon.

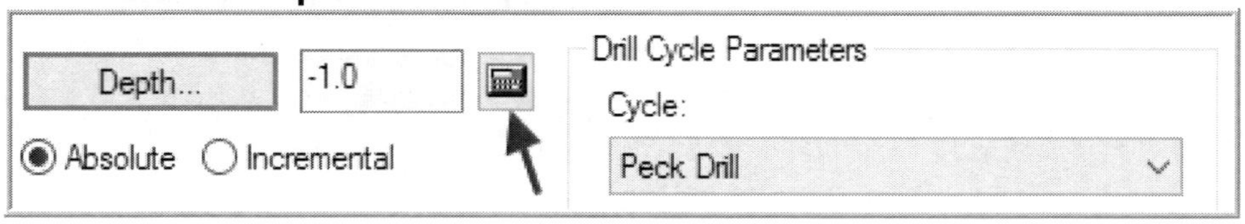

9. Make changes to the **Depth Calculator** as shown below.

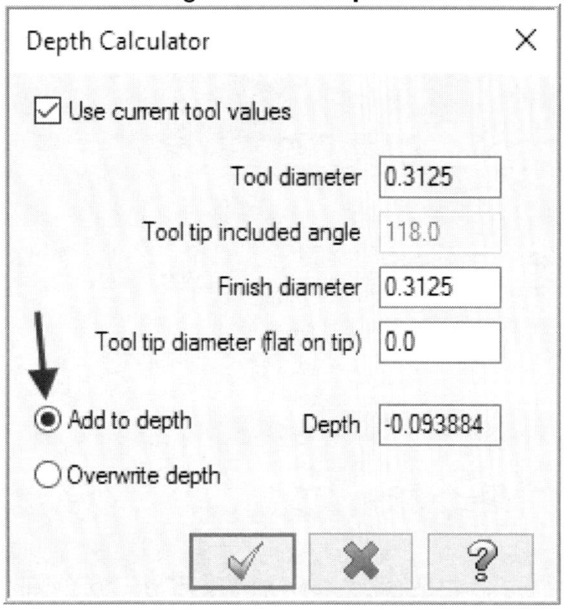

10. Select the OK button  to exit **the Depth Calculator.**
11. The depth has now been updated.

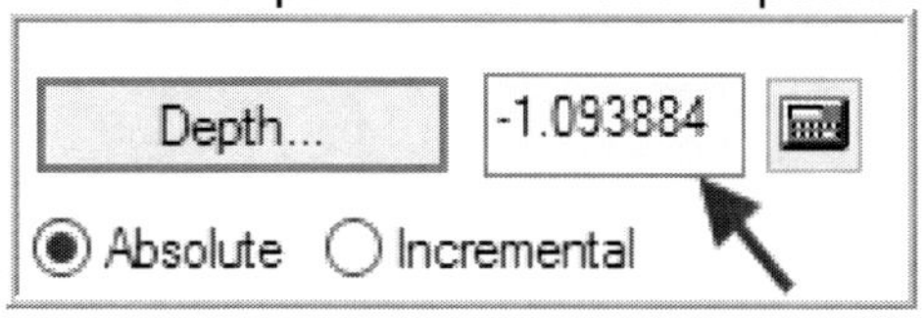

12. Select the OK button  to exit **Peck drill – full retract.**

TASK 14:
TAP 3/8" – 16 UNC

➲ In this task you will tap the 3/8"-16 hole 1" deep.

1. Select **Drill** in the **General** section of the **Turning** tab.
2. Click on the **Select library tool…** button in the lower left corner of the Toolpath parameters page as shown below.

3. Select the **select new folder** icon  at the top of the dialog box and then the **LTAPS** from the list as shown below. Now click on the **Open button** to select **LTAPS**.

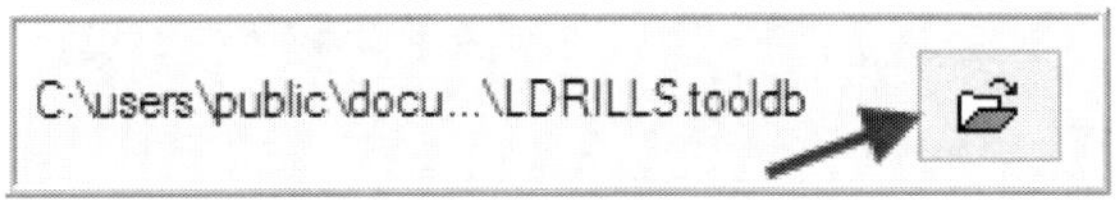

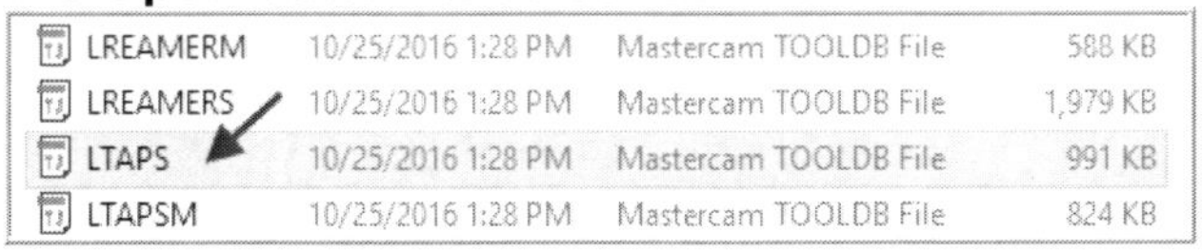

4. Scroll down and select **the 0.375 Dia. 3/8"-16 RH TAP** from the list.
5. Select the OK button .
6. Ensure necessary settings are as shown below. **Coolant Flood** is set to **On**.

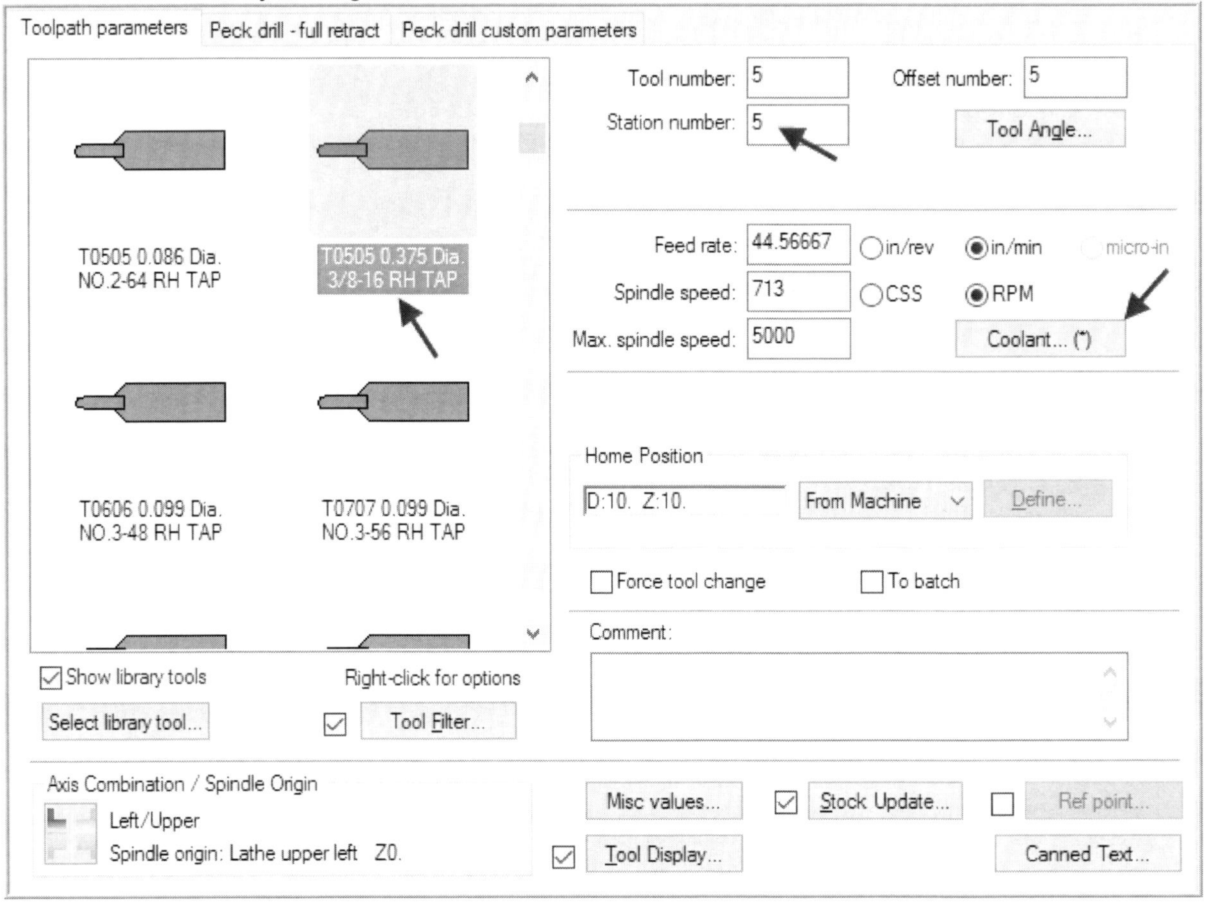

7. Select the **Peck drill – full retract** page and make changes to tap as shown below.

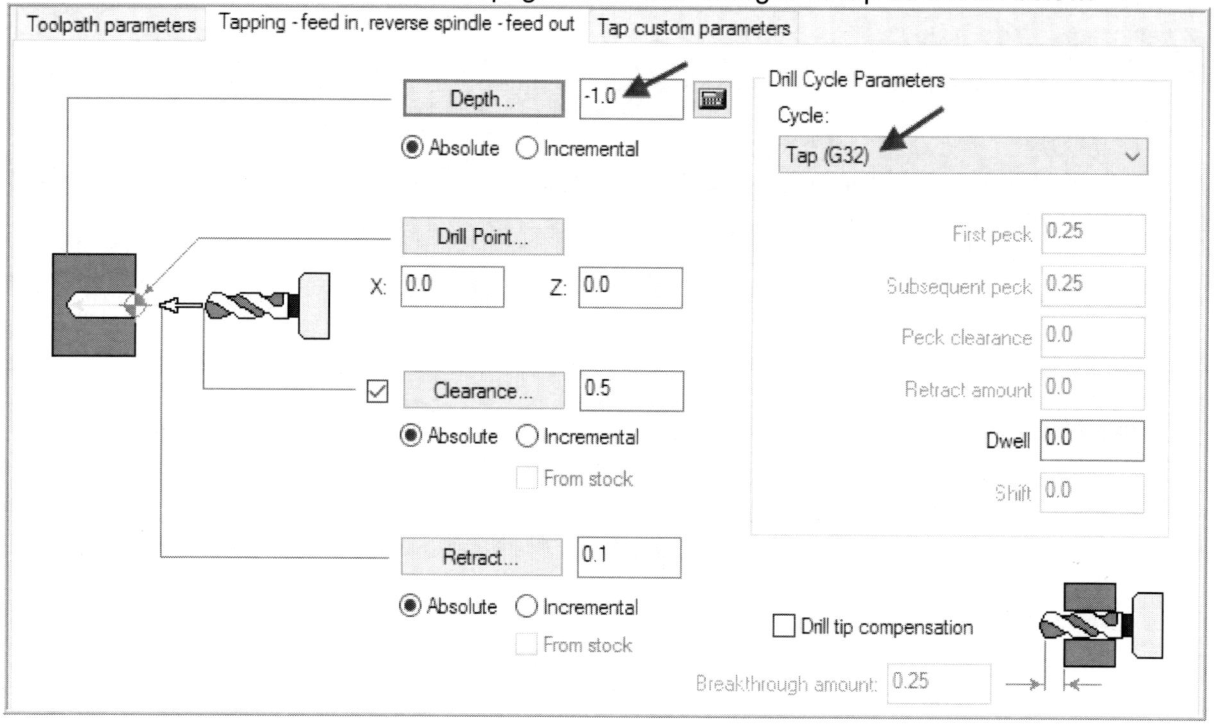

8. Select the OK button to exit **Tapping – feed in, reverse spindle – feed out.**

TASK 15:
CUT OFF THE PART

➲ In this task you will cut off the part using **Tool #6 - Cutoff Right - Width .125.**

1. Click on the **Select all operations** icon .
2. Now click on the **Toggle display on selected operations**  button **or ALT and T** to show/hide the tool path.

Toolpath Lines visible:

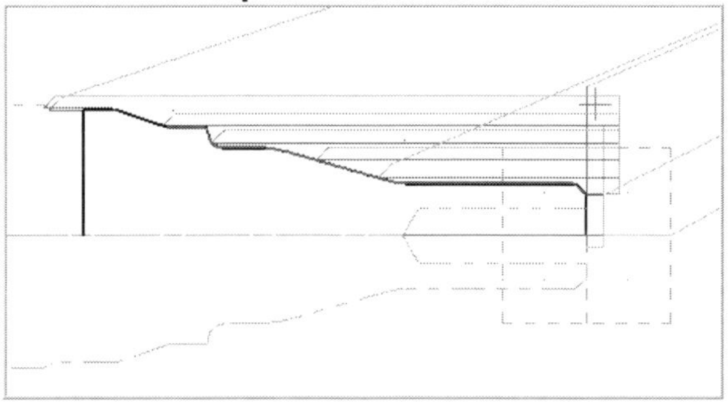

Press Alt T to hide toolpath Lines:

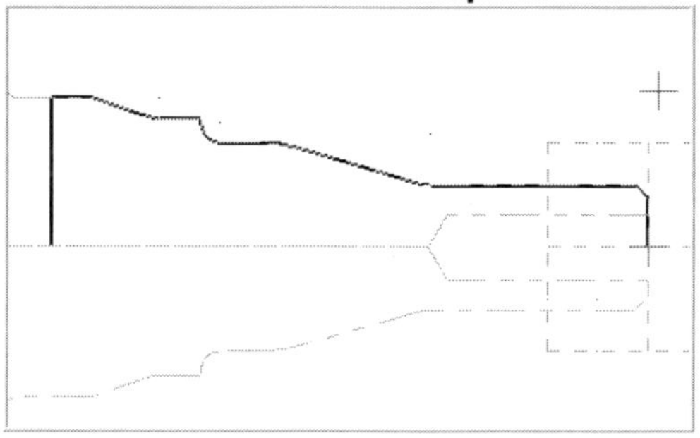

3. Click on the **Expand gallery** down arrow to view additional options in the **General** toolpath section.

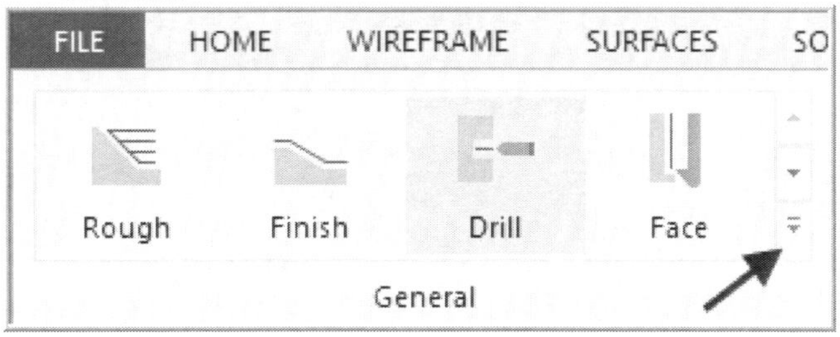

4. In the **General** section select **Cutoff.**

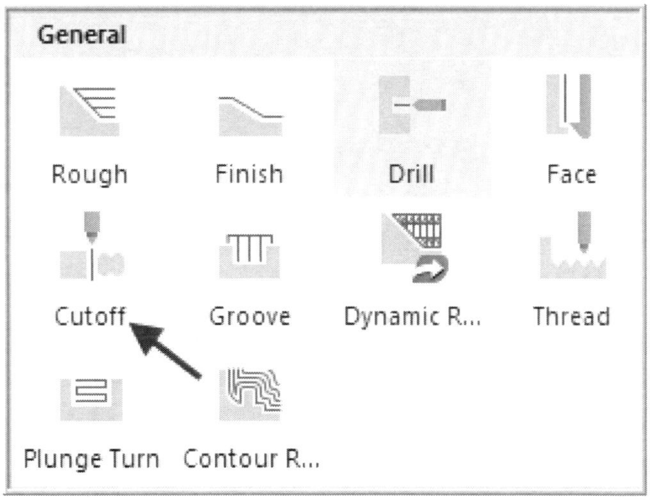

5. Pick where **Line 8 and Line 9** meet as shown below. (Move the cursor over the corner until the visual cue 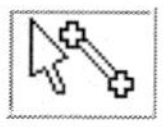 for End point displays and then click on this point.)

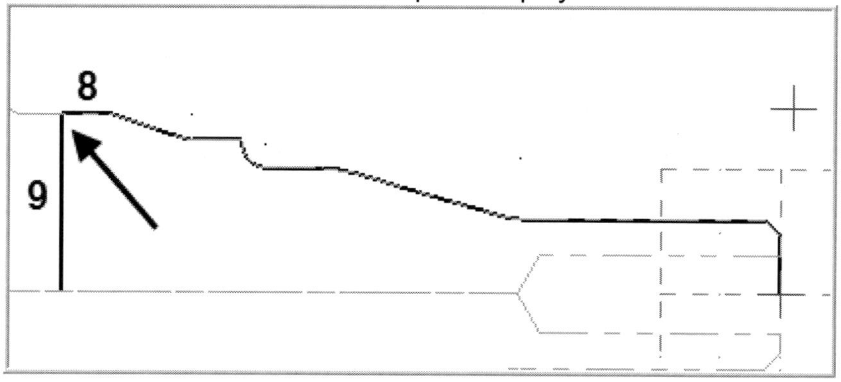

6. Click on the **Select library tool…** button.
7. Select the **select new folder** icon  at the top of the dialog box and then the **lathe_Inch** from the list as shown below. Now click on the **Open button** to select **lathe_Inch**.

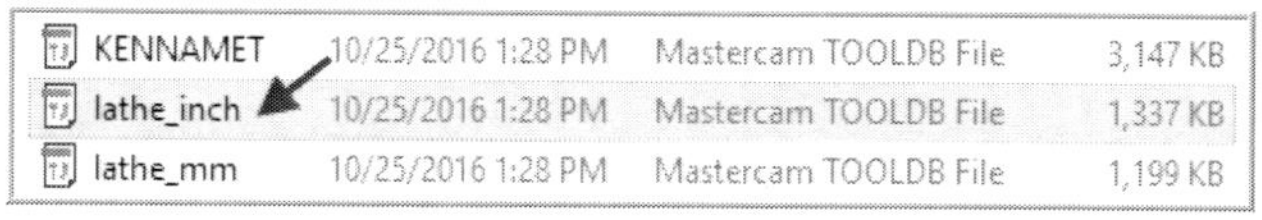

8. Scroll down and select **OD Cutoff Right Width .125** from the list.
9. Select the OK button .
10. Make changes as shown below in the **Toolpath parameters** page. **Coolant Flood** is **On**.

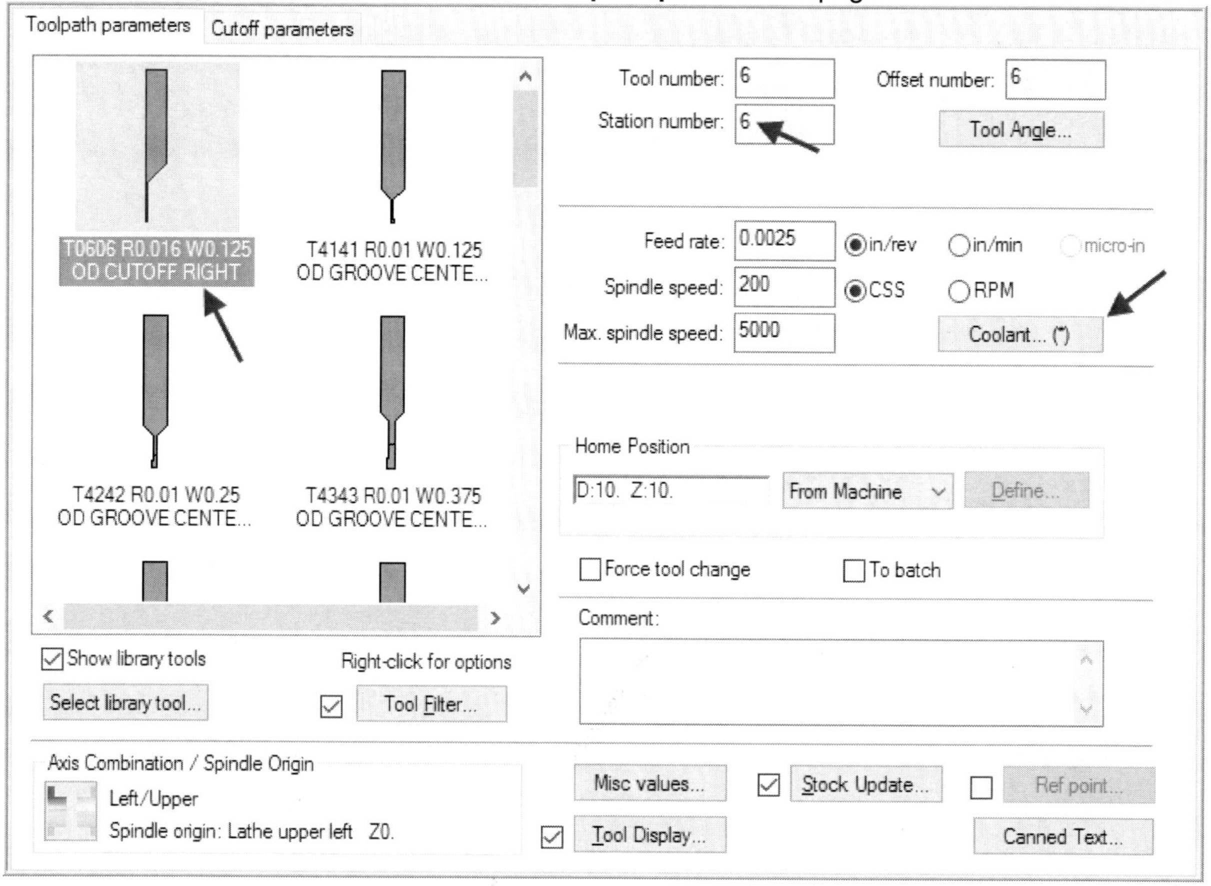

11. Click on the **Stock Update…** button.

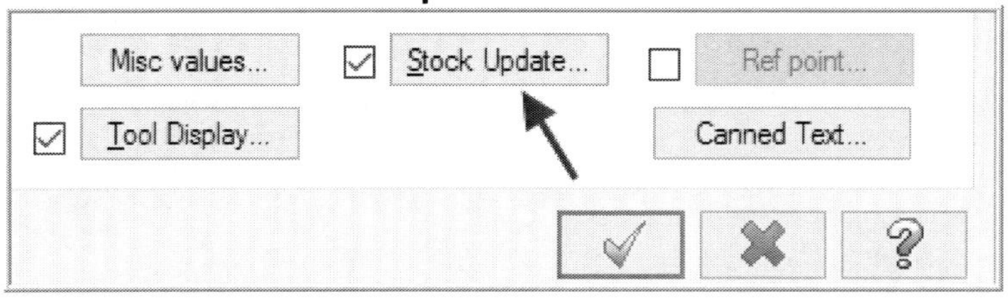

12. Activate **Keep both pieces**.

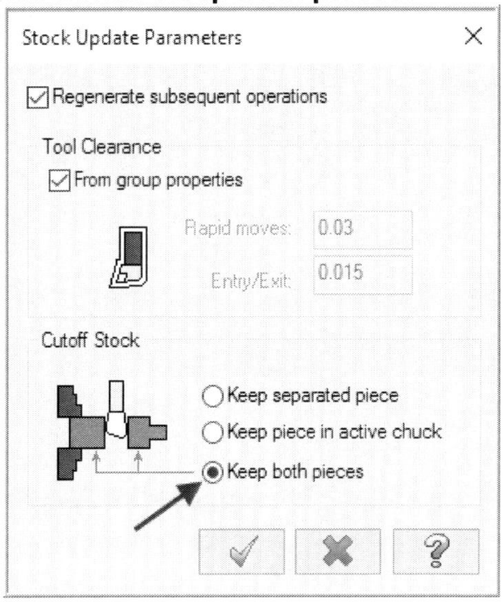

Keep separated piece
Select to display the part boundary after the part is cut off.
Keep piece in active chuck
Select to display the stock boundary after the part is cut off.

Keep both pieces
Select to display both the separated piece and the leftover piece. This is useful when the separated piece will be transferred to a sub spindle and you will be machining on both spindles at the same time.

These options are available only with cutoff operations.

13. Select the **Cutoff parameters** page and make sure the settings are as shown below.

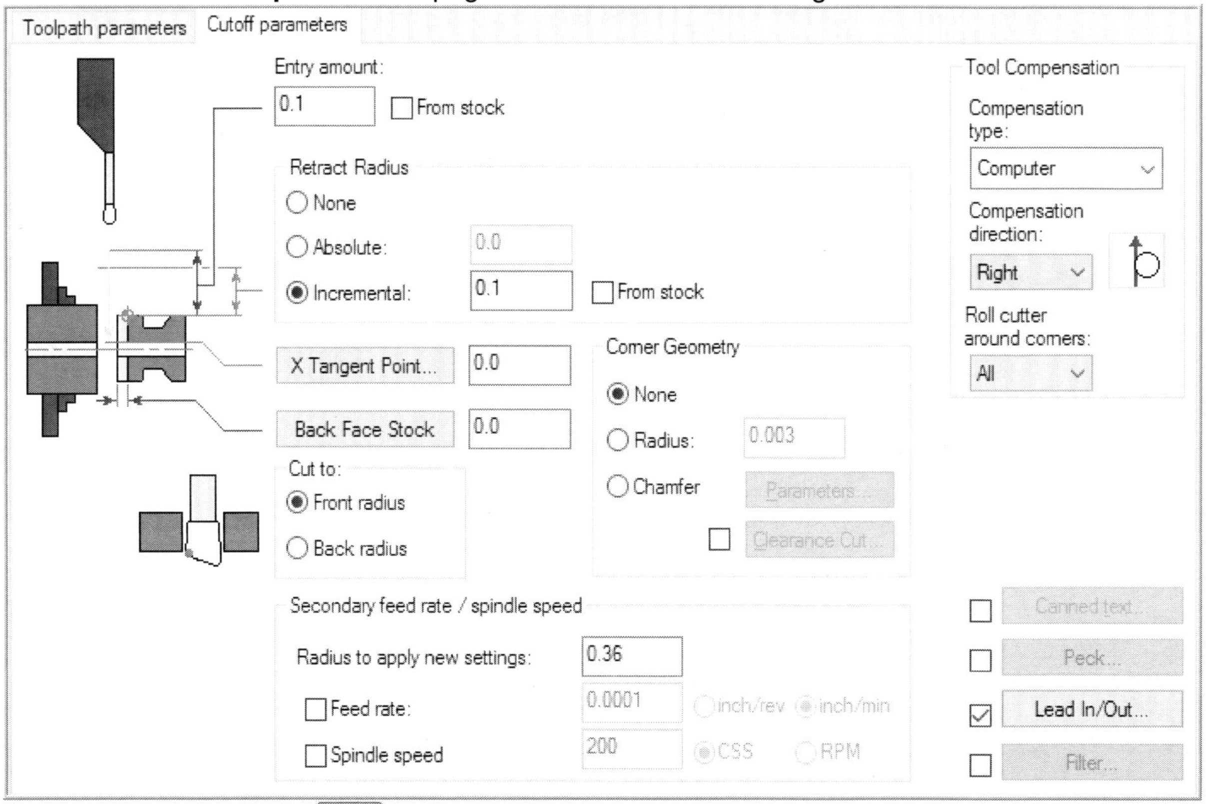

14. Select the OK button  to exit **Cutoff parameters.**

TASK 16:
VERIFY THE TOOLPATH

➲ Mastercam's Verify utility allows you to use solid models to simulate the machining of a part. The model created by the verification represents the surface finish, and shows collisions, if any exist.

1. Right mouse click in the graphics area and click on the **Fit** icon .
2. In the Toolpaths Manager pick all the operations to Verify by picking the **Select All** icon .
3. Select the **Verify selected operations** icon shown below.

4. **Maximize** the Backplot/Verify window if required.
5. Now select the **Home** Tab if required.

6. Activate the options shown below in the **Visibility** section of the **Home** tab. **Initial Stock not** activated.

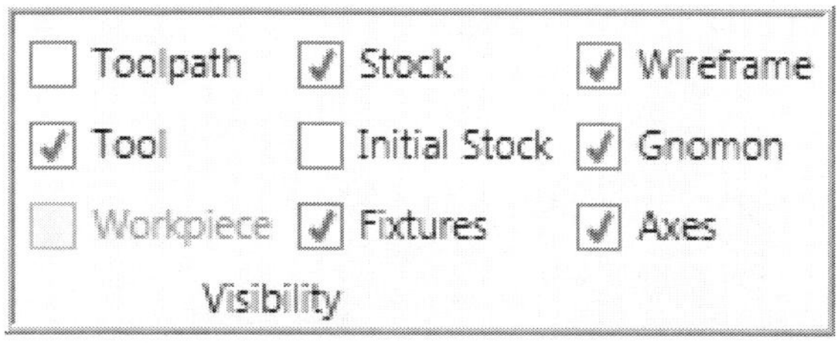

7. At the top of the screen select the **View** tab, the **Isometric** icon and then select **Fit**.

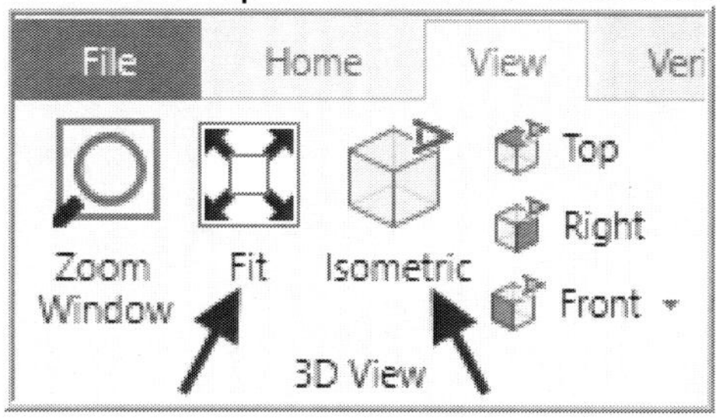

8. Select the **Verify** tab and activate the **Color Loop** to change the color of the tools for the verified part.

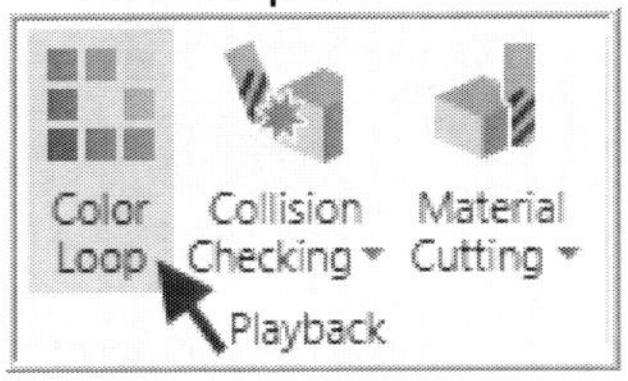

Color Loop
Changes the color of the toolpath or cut stock by operation or by tool change.

Choose **File Options** to set the colors.

9. In the lower part of the screen now set the run **Speed** to slow by moving the slider bar pointer over to the left as shown below.

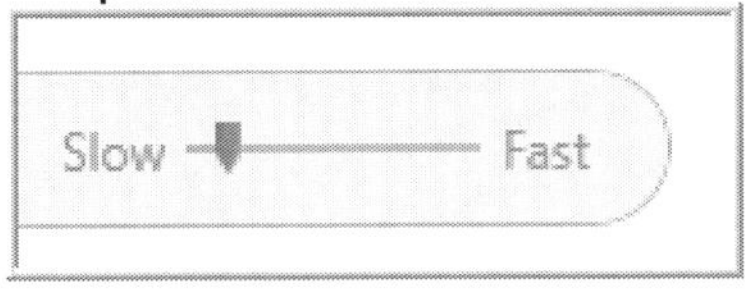

10. Now select the **Play Simulation** button to review the toolpaths.

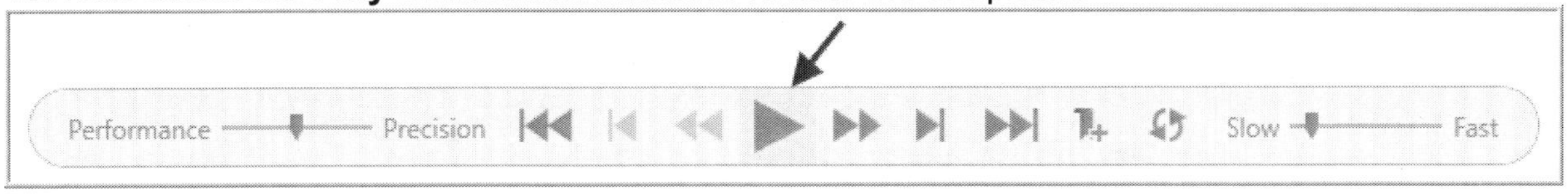

11. Select the **Close** button 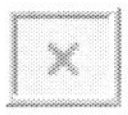 in the top right hand corner to exit Verify.

TASK 17:
SAVE THE UPDATED MASTERCAM FILE

1. Select the **Save** icon from the **Quick Access** toolbar at the top left of the screen.

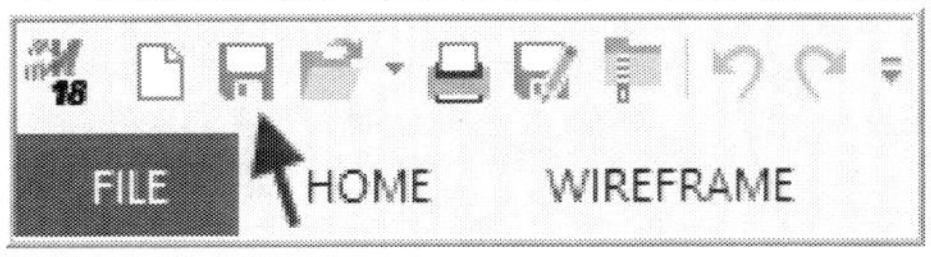

TASK 18:
POST AND CREATE THE CNC CODE FILE

1. Ensure all the operations are selected by picking the **Select All** icon from the Toolpaths manager.
2. Select the **Post selected operations** button from the Toolpaths manager.

➲ **Please Note:** If you cannot see **G1** click on the right pane of the Toolpaths manager window and expand the window to the right.

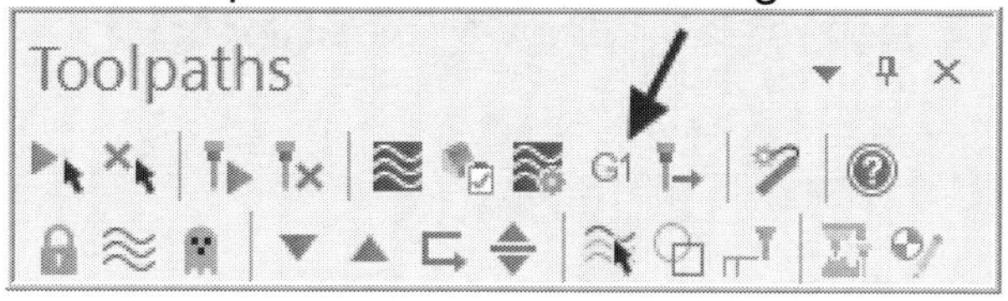

3. In the Post processing window, make the necessary changes as shown below.

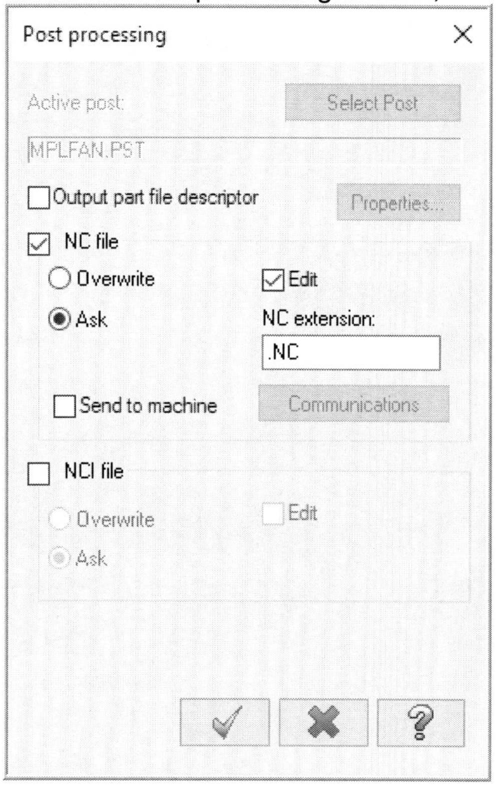

About Post Processing

NC file:
Select this option to save the NC file. The file name and extension are stored in the machine group properties for the selected operation. If you are posting operations from different machine groups or Mastercam files, or batch processing, Mastercam will create several files according to the settings for each machine group.

Edit:
When checked, automatically launches the default text editor with the file displayed so that you can review or modify it.

4. Select the OK button to continue.

5. Ensure the same name as your Mastercam part file name is displayed in the **NC File name** field as shown below.

6. Select the **Save** button.

➲ The CNC code file opens up in the default editor.

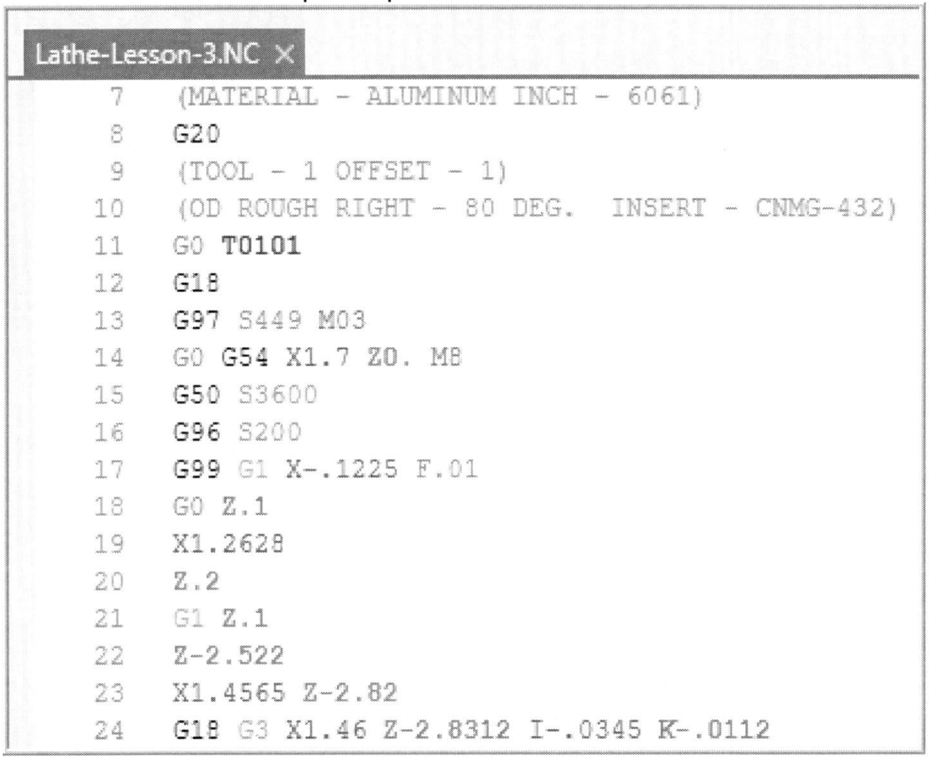

7. Select the [X] in the top right corner to exit the CNC editor.

➲ This completes Lathe-Lesson-3.

LATHE-LESSON-3 EXERCISE

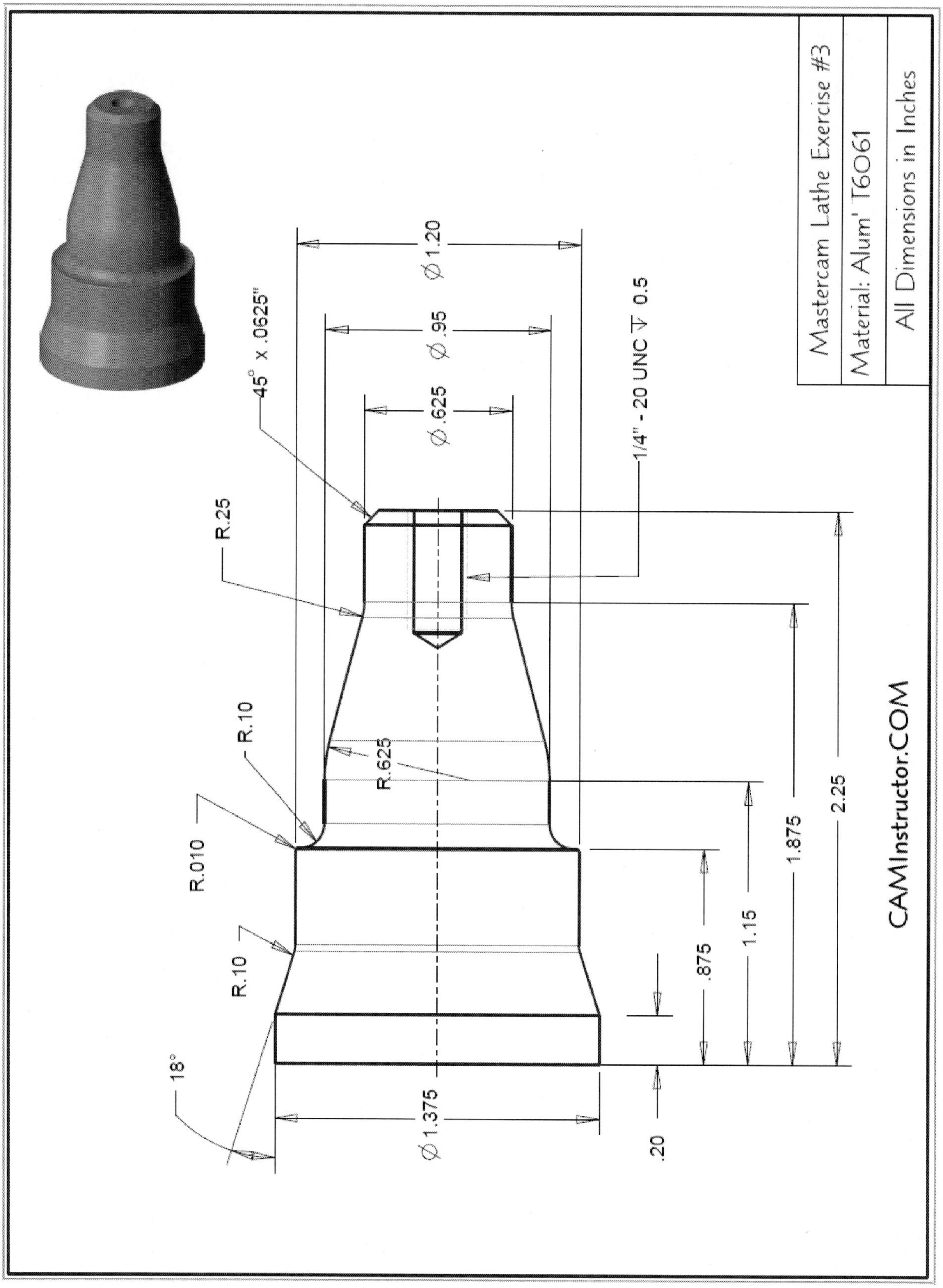

Mastercam® 2018
TRAINING
GUIDE

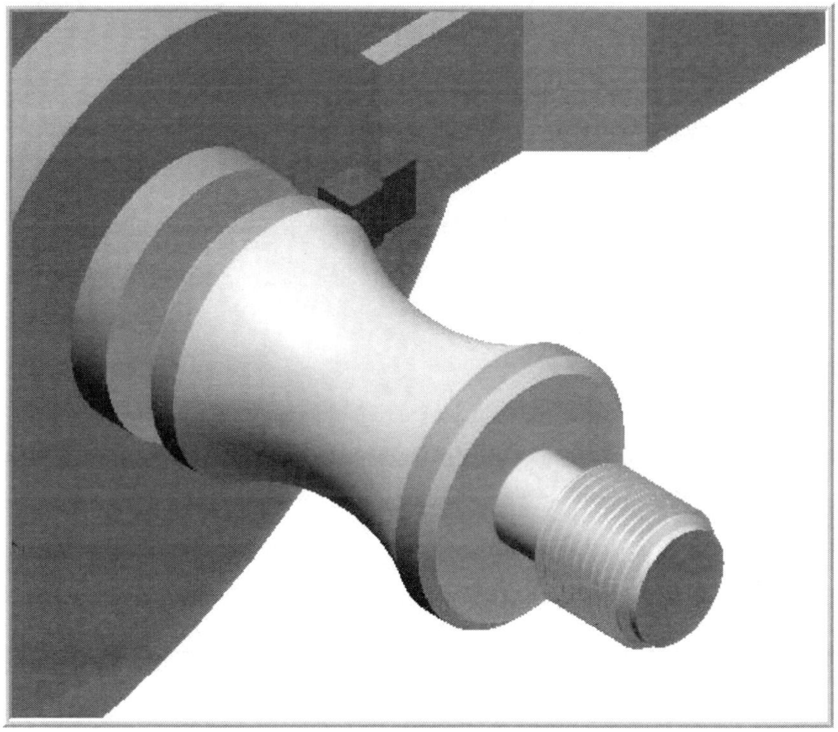

LATHE-LESSON-4
FACE, ROUGH, FINISH, GROOVE, THREAD AND CUTOFF

camInstructor

Objectives

You will create the geometry for Lathe Lesson 2, and then generate a toolpath to machine the part on a CNC lathe. This lesson covers the following topics:

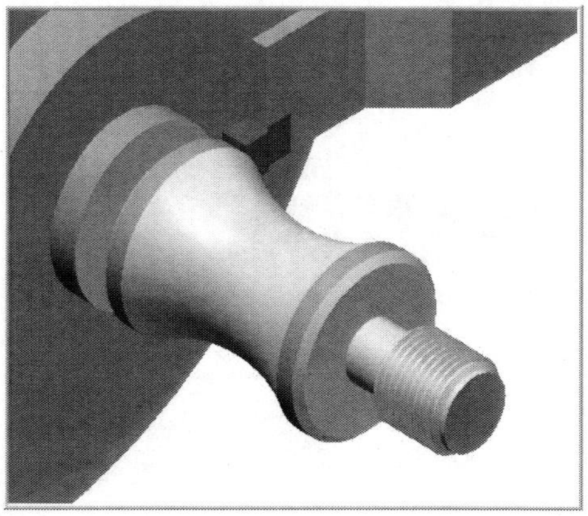

➲ **Create a 2-dimensional drawing by:**
Creating lines.
Creating chamfers.

➲ **Establish Stock and Chuck Setup settings:**
Stock size.
Chuck Configuration.
Material for the part.
Feed calculation.

➲ **Generate a 2-dimensional lathe toolpath consisting of:**
Lathe Face.
Lathe Quick Rough.
Lathe Quick Finish.
Lathe Groove.
Lathe Thread.
Lathe Finish.
Lathe Cutoff.

➲ **Inspect the toolpath using Mastercam's Verify and Backplot by:**
Launching the Verify function to machine the part on the screen.
Generating the NC- code.

LATHE - LESSON - 4 DRAWING

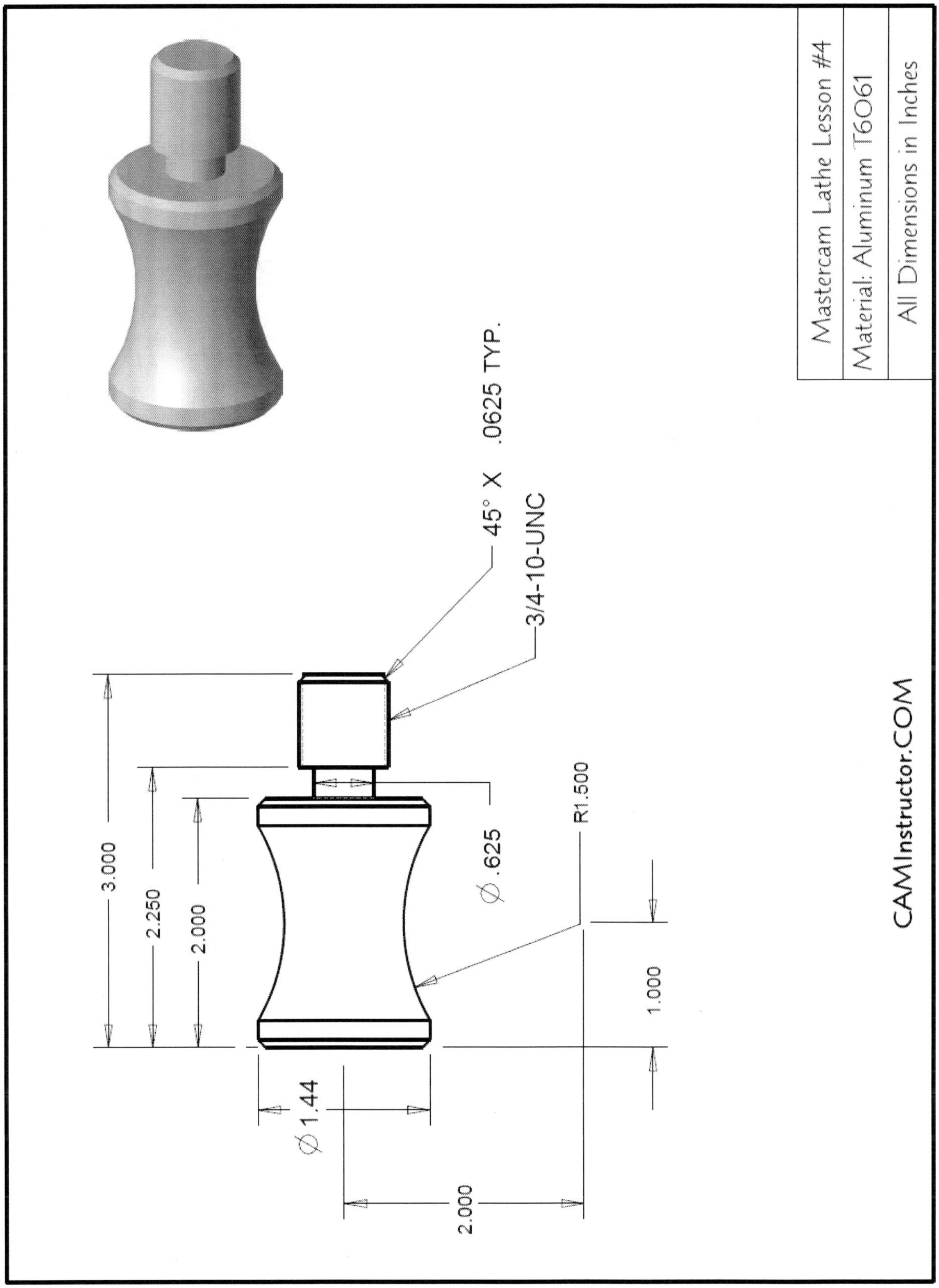

TOOL LIST

Five tools will be used to create this part.

➲ **Tool #1 Face and Rough the outside diameters**
Holder: Outside Diameter Rough Right Hand - DCGNR-164D.
Insert: 80 Degree Diamond Insert – CNMG-432

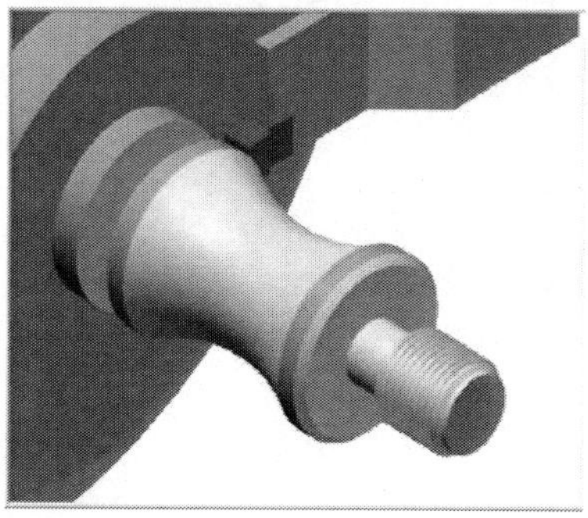

➲ **Tool #2 Finish the outside diameters**
Holder: Outside Diameter Finish Right Hand - MVJNR-164D.
Insert: 35 Degree Diamond Insert – VNMG-431.

➲ **Tool #3 Machine the Groove and Cut-Off the part**
Holder: Outside Diameter Groove Right Hand - Narrow.
Insert: 0.125" Wide - GC-4125

➲ **Tool #4 Machine the Thread**
Holder: Outside Diameter Thread Right Hand.
Insert: UN/NPT 60 Degree

➲ **Tool #5 Finish the 1.5" radius**
Holder: Outside Diameter - Cutting direction: Neutral
Insert: 35 Degree Diamond Insert – VNMG-431

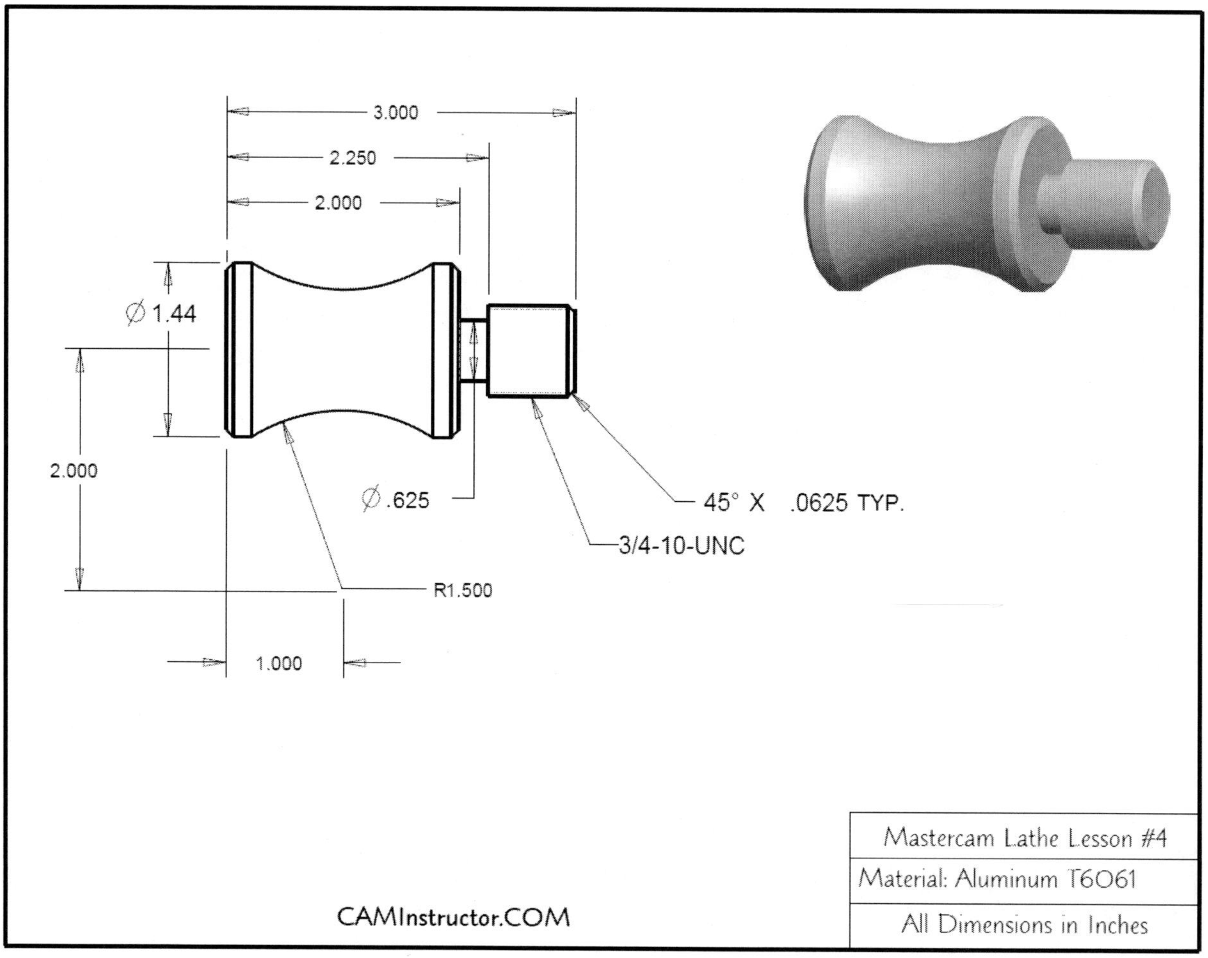

LESSON - 4 - THE PROCESS

Geometry Creation

TASK 1: Setting the Environment
TASK 2: Setting the Construction Planes
TASK 3: Create the Geometry
TASK 4: Create the 1.5" Radius
TASK 5: Create the Chamfers
TASK 6: Save the Drawing

Toolpath Creation

TASK 7: Define the Stock and Chuck Parameters
TASK 8: Face the Front of the Part
TASK 9: Rough the Outside Diameters
TASK 10: Finish the Outside Diameters
TASK 11: Cut the Groove
TASK 12: Cut the Thread
TASK 13: Finish the Radius
TASK 14: Cut off the Part
TASK 15: Verify the toolpath
TASK 16: Save the updated Mastercam file
TASK 17: Post and create the CNC code file

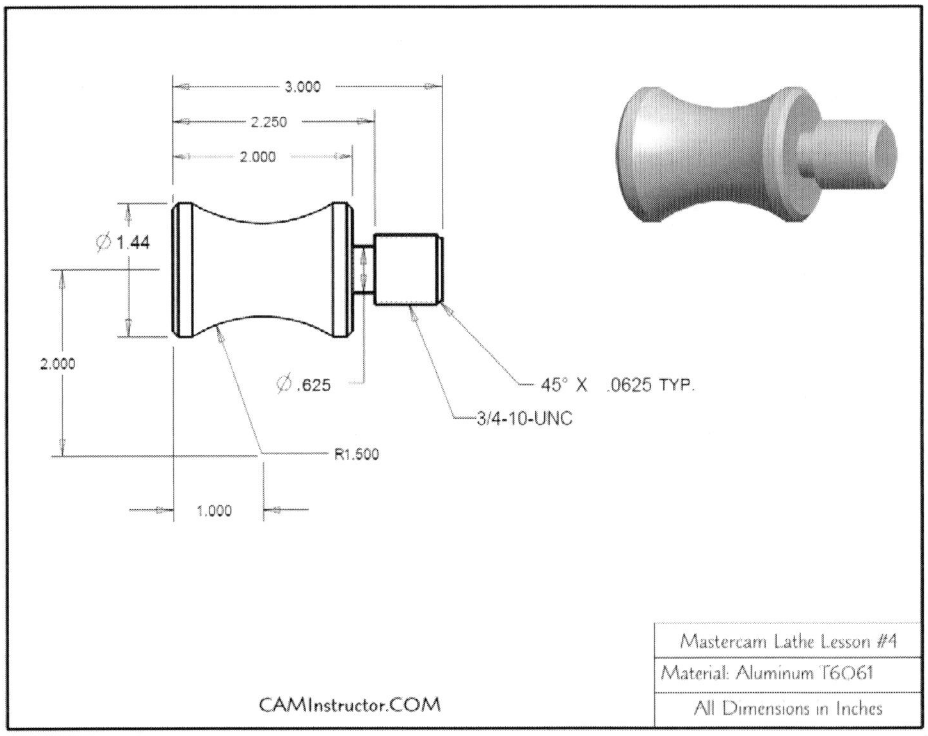

Geometry Creation

TASK 1:
SETTING THE ENVIRONMENT

Before starting the geometry creation you should set up the grid and machine type as outlined in the **Setting the Environment** section at the beginning of this text:

1. Set up the Grid. This will help identify the location of the origin.
2. Set the machine type to the default Lathe.

TASK 2:
SETTING THE CONSTRUCTION PLANES:

➲ **Set the Construction Plane to Lathe diameter +D +Z (WCS)**

1. Select the **View tab** and click on **Toolpaths** and **Solids** in the **Managers** section to **hide** them and toggle **only** the **Planes Manager to display**.

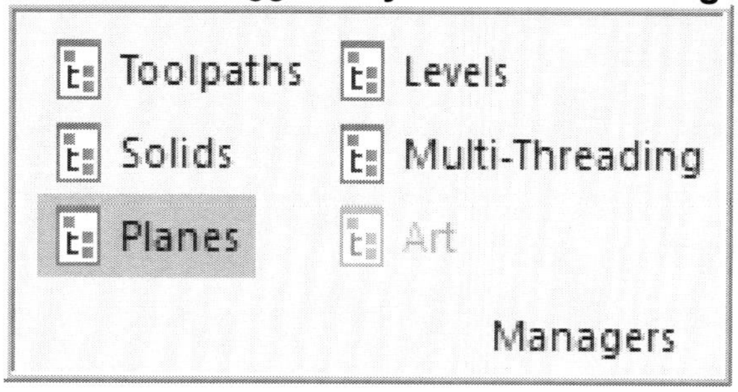

Once your machine is set up, Mastercam includes special lathe construction planes that let you work in **radius or diameter coordinates**.

For conventional 2D turning applications, use the Planes Manager to select the desired coordinate system, as shown below right. Choose to use either radius or diameter coordinates and then choose the desired X/D and Z directions.

2. Ensure the **C column** (Construction Plane) and **T column** (Tool Plane) are set to the **+D +Z Plane**. Just click in the C and T columns in the **+D +Z** row.

➲ Take note of the **Status bar** at the bottom of the screen **CPLANE: +D +Z TPLANE: +D +Z WCS:TOP** as shown below right.

3. To change the **Lathe Plane** open up the drop down menu for **Select lathe plane** and click on the required coordinate system as shown below right.
4. Select the **Close** button [X] in the top right hand corner to close the Planes Manager.

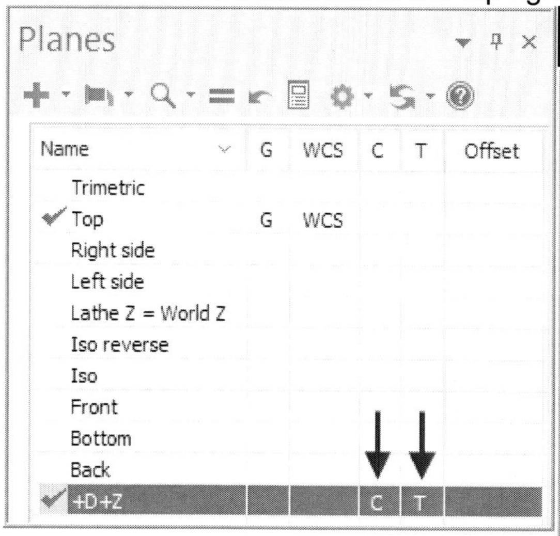

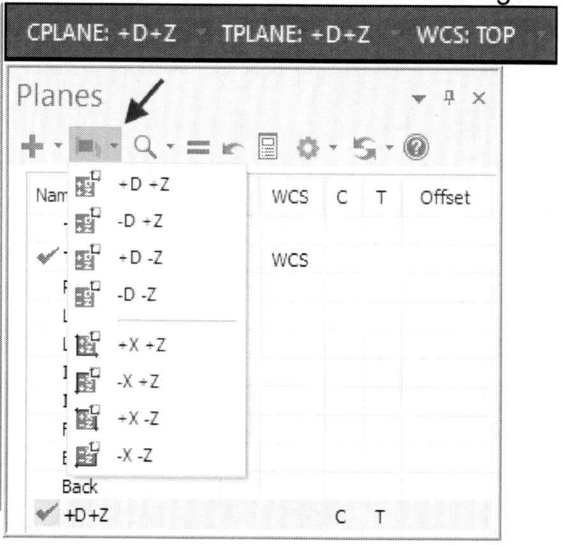

TASK 3:
CREATE THE GEOMETRY

- This task explains how to create the geometry of this part. In this lathe part you only need to create **half of the geometry**, the geometry above the center line.
- Lines 1 through 7 will be created first and then the radius and chamfer will be created.

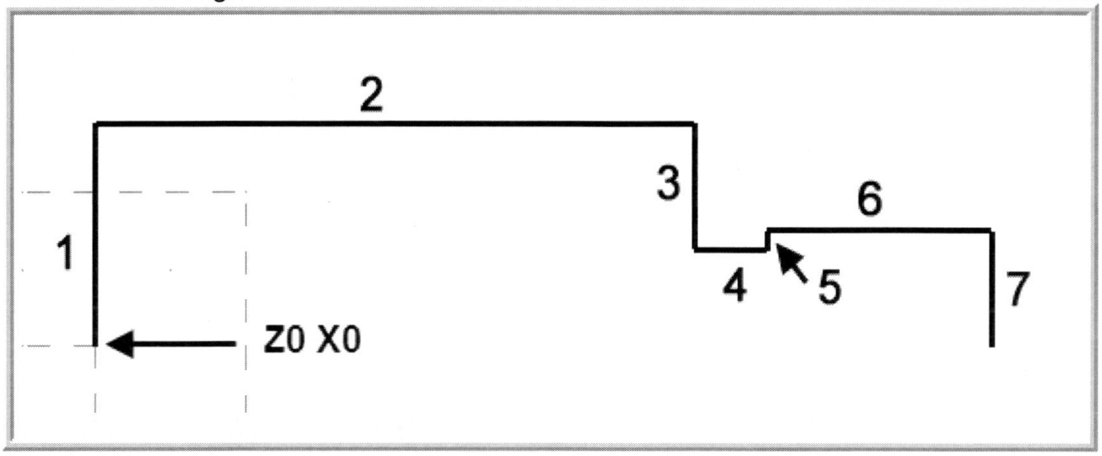

- **Create Line #1**

1. Select the **WIREFRAME** tab at the top of the screen and in the **Lines** section click on **Line Endpoints**.

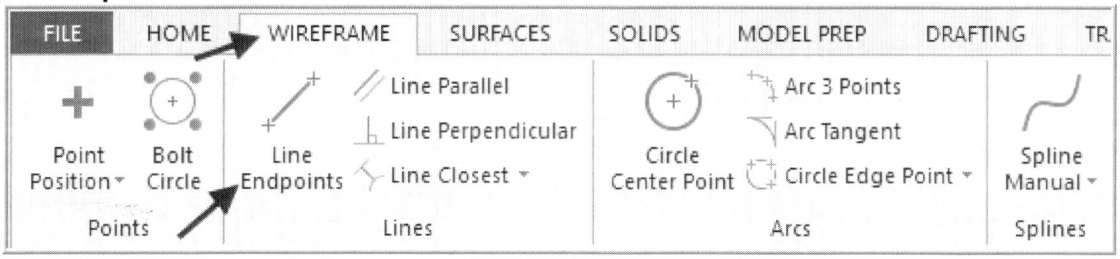

2. On the graphics screen you are prompted: **Specify the first endpoint** and the Line Endpoints panel appears. In the Line Endpoints panel activate **Multi-line and Freeform**.

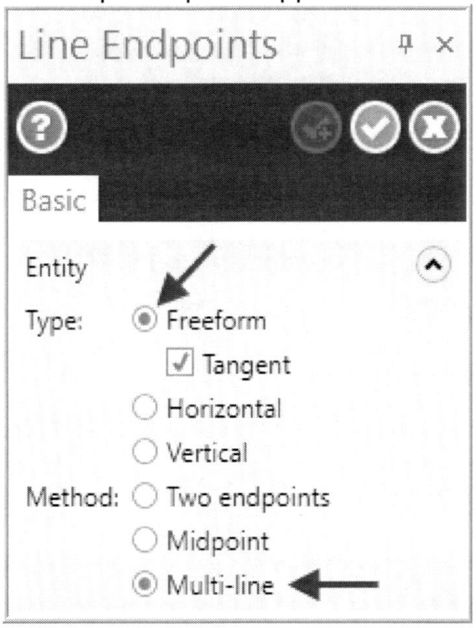

3. Move the cursor over the **center of the grid** and as you get close to the origin a visual cue appears.  This is the cue that will allow you to snap to the **origin**. With this visual cue highlighted pick the **origin.**
4. You are now prompted to **"Specify the second endpoint"**. To satisfy this prompt **just type** the coordinate, **type 1.44,0**. This is **D1.44 Z0**. As you begin to type the **Fastpoint** opens. Hit the **Enter** key when done.

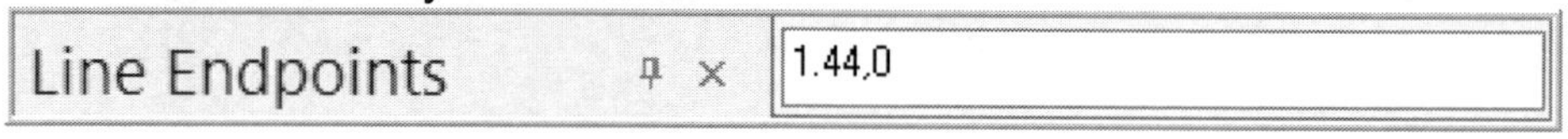

➲ A vertical line should be visible as shown below:

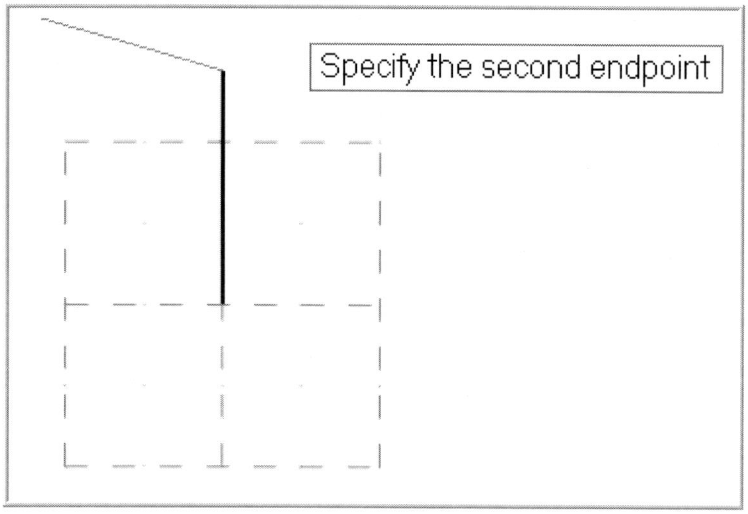

➲ **Create Line #2**

5. To satisfy the prompt **"Specify the second endpoint" type** the coordinate, **type 1.44,2.0** and hit the Enter key to complete this line.

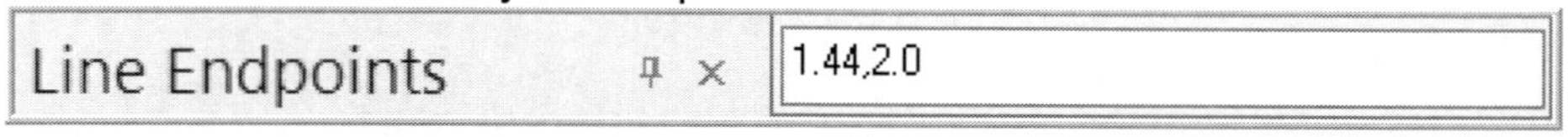

➲ **Create Line #3**

6. To satisfy the prompt **"Specify the second endpoint" type** the coordinate, **type 0.625,2.0** and hit the Enter key to complete this line.

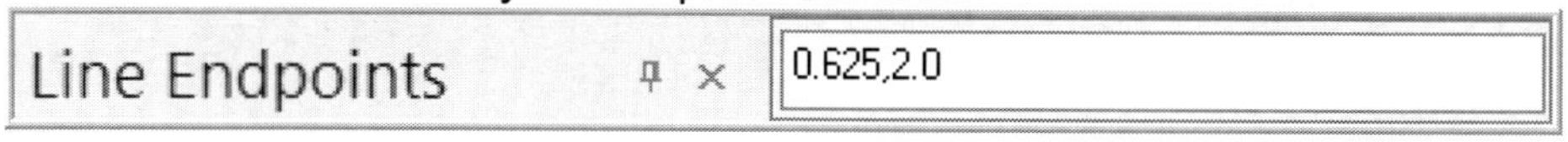

➲ **Create Line #4**

7. To satisfy the prompt **"Specify the second endpoint" type** the coordinate, **type 0.625,2.25** and hit the Enter key to complete this line.

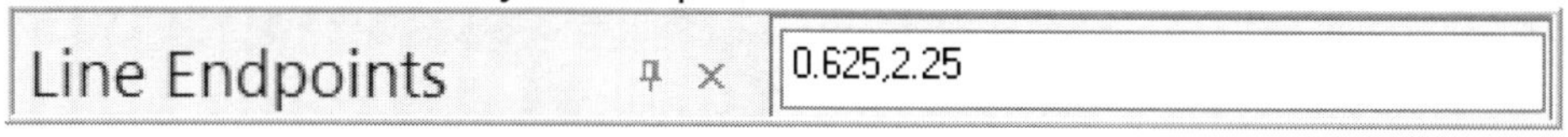

8. Right mouse click in the graphics area and click on the **Fit** icon .
9. Right mouse click in the graphics area and click on **Unzoom 80%** to shrink the display.

➲ **Create Line #5**

10. To satisfy the prompt **"Specify the second endpoint" type** the coordinate, **type 0.75,2.25** and hit the Enter key to complete this line.

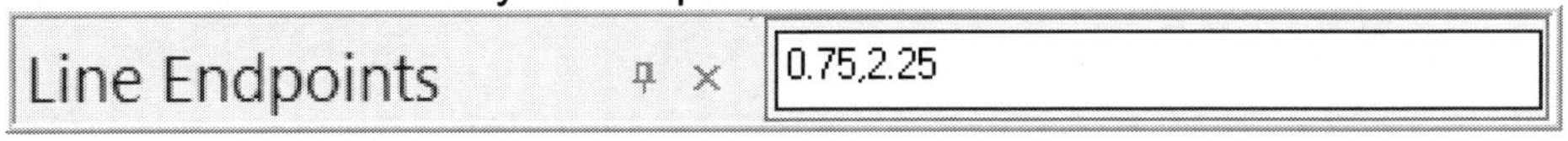

➲ **Create Line #6**

11. To satisfy the prompt **"Specify the second endpoint" type** the coordinate, **type 0.75,3.0** and hit the Enter key to complete this line.

➲ **Create Line #7**

12. To satisfy the prompt **"Specify the second endpoint" type** the coordinate, **type 0,3.0** and hit the Enter key to complete this line.

13. Click on the **OK** icon to complete this feature.

14. Right mouse click in the graphics area and click on the **Fit** icon.

➲ Your geometry should look like the figure below.

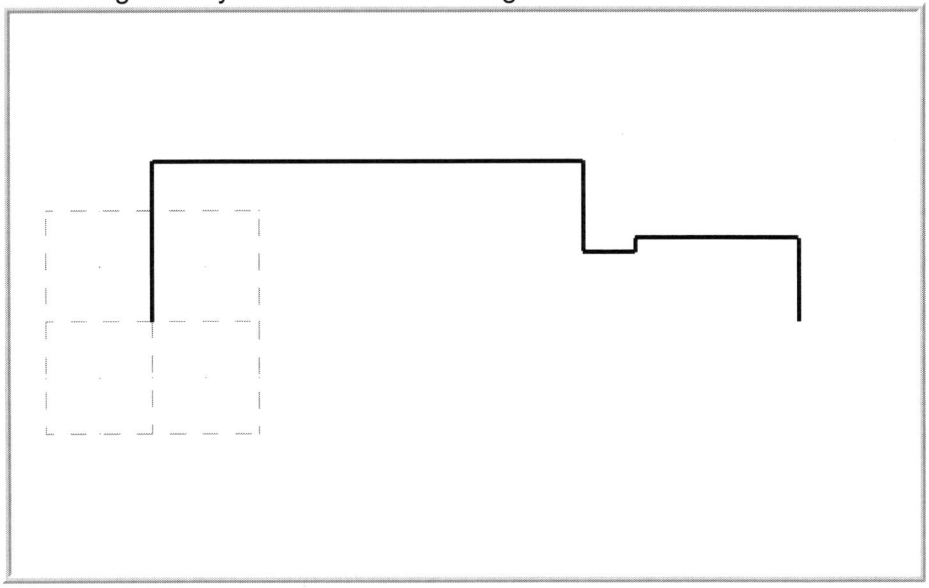

TASK 4:
CREATE THE 1.5" RADIUS

➲ **Create the Arc Center Point.**

1. On the **WIREFRAME** tab in the **Points** section click on **Point Position**.

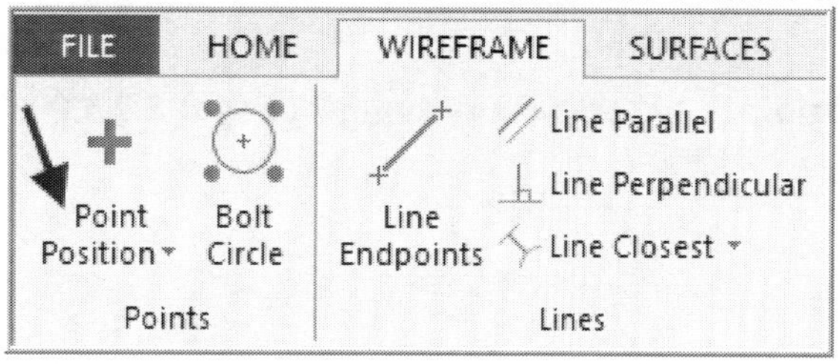

➲ On the graphics screen you are prompted: **Create point position** and the **Point Position** panel appears.

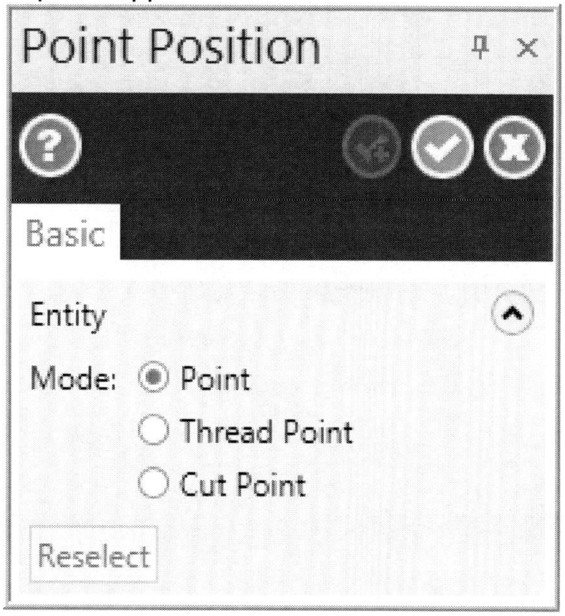

Point Position
Use this function to create a point, cut point, or thread point.

You can change the position of a point as long as it remains live.

Click the **Reselect** button, and click the new position in the graphics window.

2. To satisfy this first prompt **click the middle mouse button** and then **hit the spacebar** on your keyboard.
3. The **Fastpoint** box now opens. Input **4.0,1.0** and hit the Enter key.

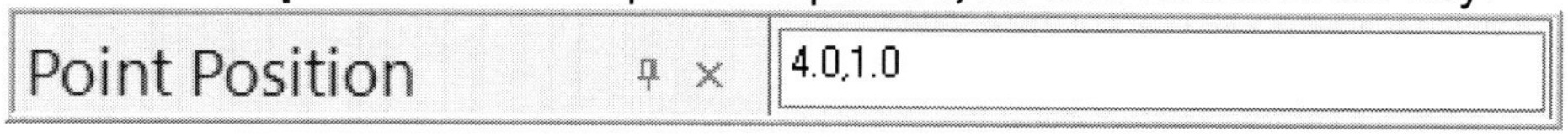

4. Click on the **OK** icon to complete this feature.

5. Right mouse click in the graphics area and click on the **Fit** icon .

➲ A point will be created as shown in the image below:

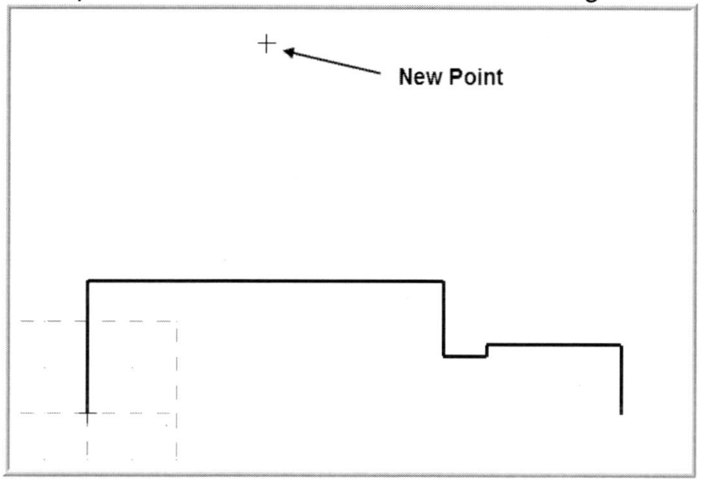

➲ **Create the 1.5" Arc**

6. On the **WIREFRAME** tab in the **Arcs** section select **Circle Center Point**.

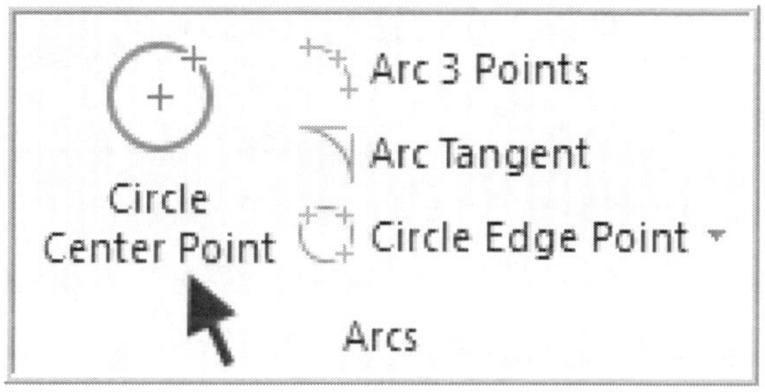

7. The **Circle Center Point** panel appears and you are prompted to **Enter the center point**. If required activate the **Mode** to **Manual.**
8. Enter a value of **1.5** for the **Radius** and hit the Enter key.

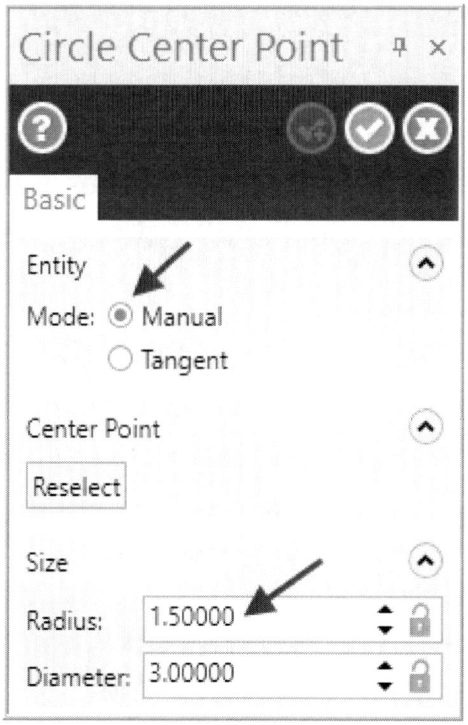

9. To satisfy the prompt **Enter the center point** move the cursor over the point you just created and as you get close to the point a **visual cue** appears. This is the cue that will allow you to snap to this point. With this visual cue highlighted pick the point.
10. Click on the **OK** icon to complete this feature.
11. Right mouse click in the graphics area and click on the **Fit** icon.

➲ A circle is created as shown below:

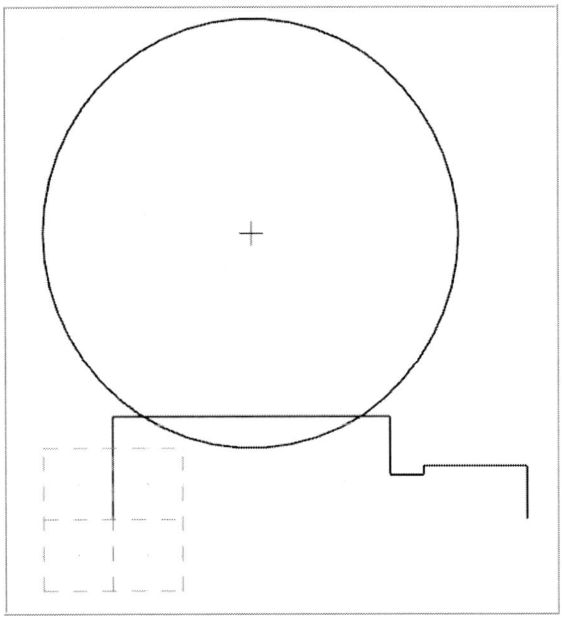

➲ **Trim the Circle**

12. In the **WIREFRAME** tab click on **Trim Break Extend** in the **Modify** section.

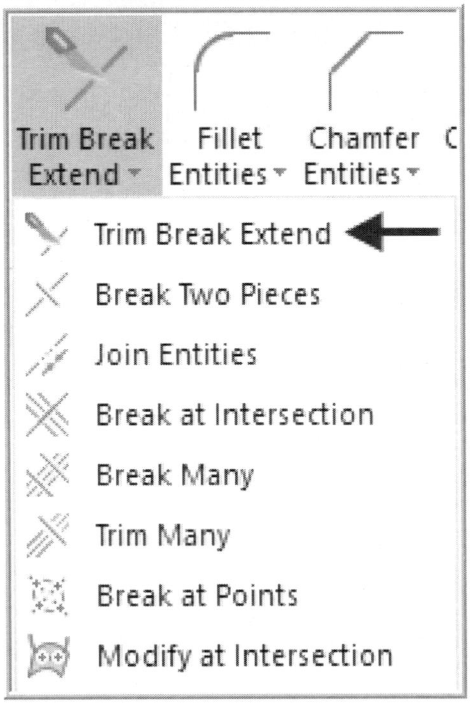

13. The **Trim Break Extend** panel appears. Activate **Divide/delete.**

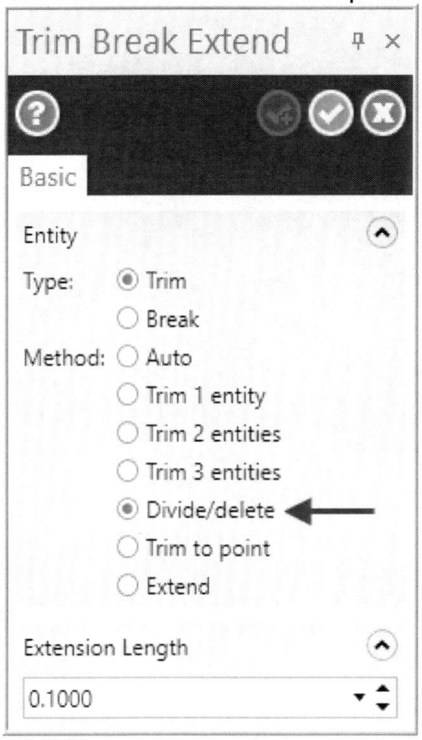

Divide/delete
This trims a line, arc, or spline into two disjointed segments by removing the segment that lies between two dividing intersections.

When you choose the Divide/delete and select an entity in the graphics window, Mastercam uses the nearest two intersections on each end to divide the entity.

14. You are prompted to **"Select the curve to divide / delete".** Click on the part of the entities you **DO NOT want to keep**; **Entity 1, Entity 2 and Entity 3** as shown below:

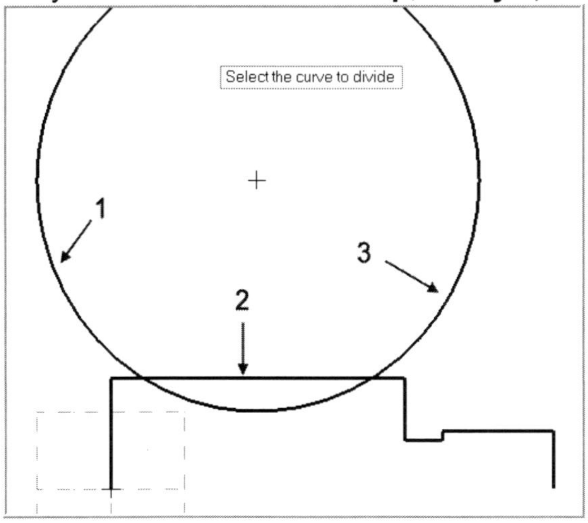

15. Click on the **OK** icon to complete this feature.

16. Right mouse click in the graphics area and click on the **Fit** icon.
17. Right mouse click in the graphics area and click on **Unzoom 80%** to shrink the display.

➲ The geometry should look like the image below:

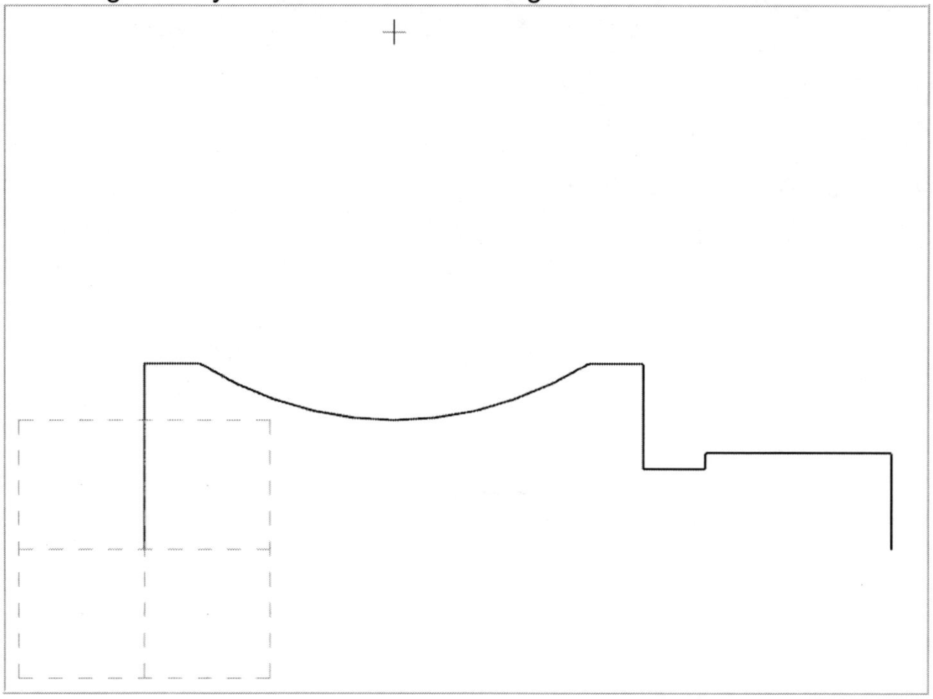

➲ **Delete the Point**

18. Select the point shown above. It should change color.
19. Hit the **Delete** key.
20. Right mouse click in the graphics area and click on the **Fit** icon .

TASK 5:
CREATE THE CHAMFERS

➲ **Create 3 Chamfers 45 degrees x .0625.**

1. Select the **WIREFRAME** tab at the top of the screen and in the **Modify** section click on **Chamfer Entities**.

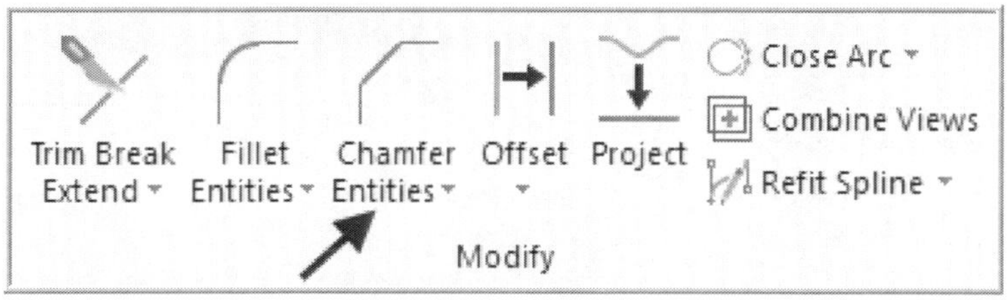

2. The **Chamfer Entities** panel appears. If required activate the **Style** to **1 Distance** and enter a value of **0.0625** for **Distance 1**.
3. Ensure the **Trim** entities box at the bottom of the panel is check marked to turn the trim on.

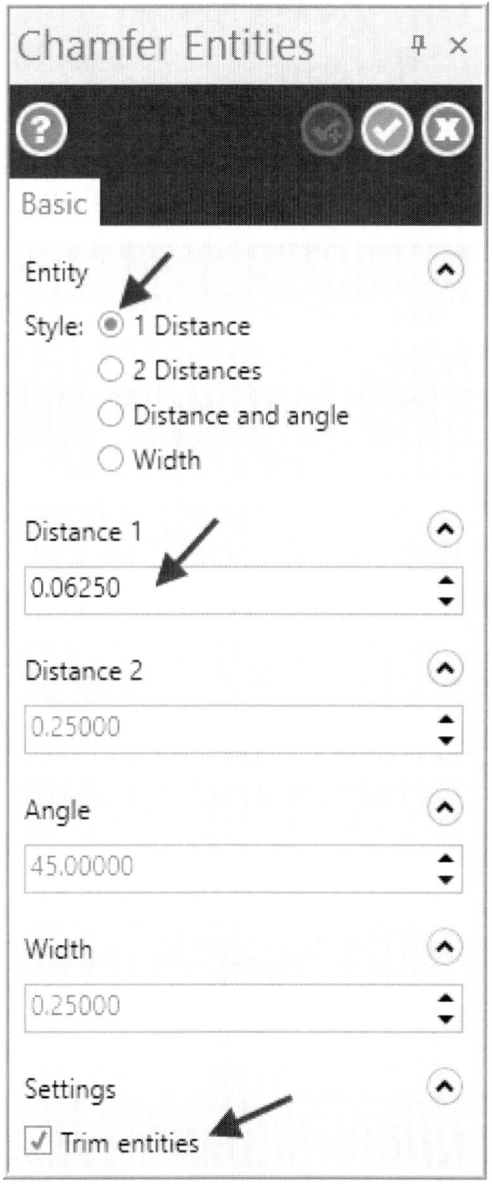

4. Click on **line 1** and then **line 2** as shown below:

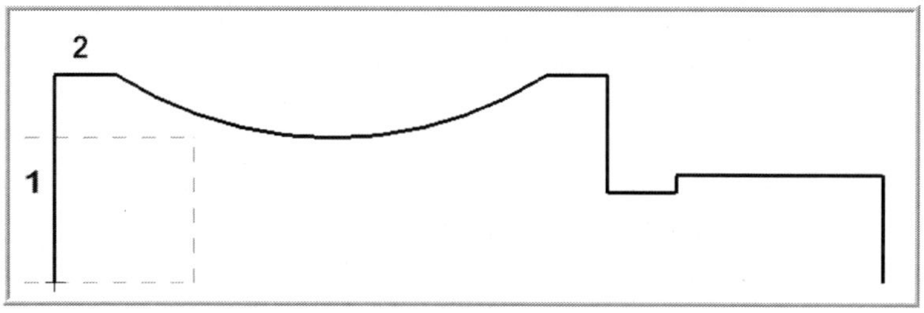

5. Click on **line 3** and then **line 4** as shown below:

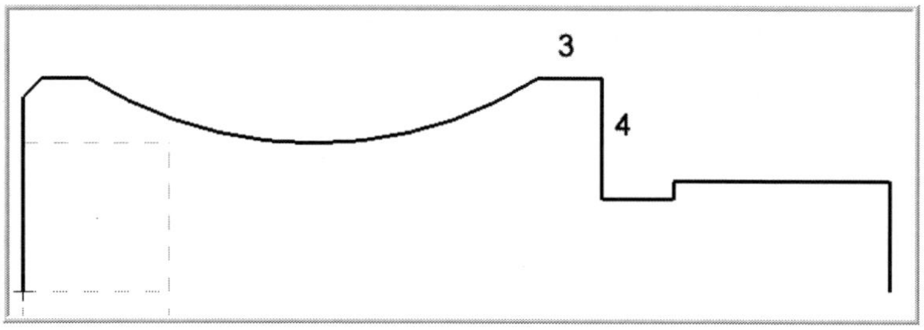

6. Click on **line 5** and then **line 6** as shown below:

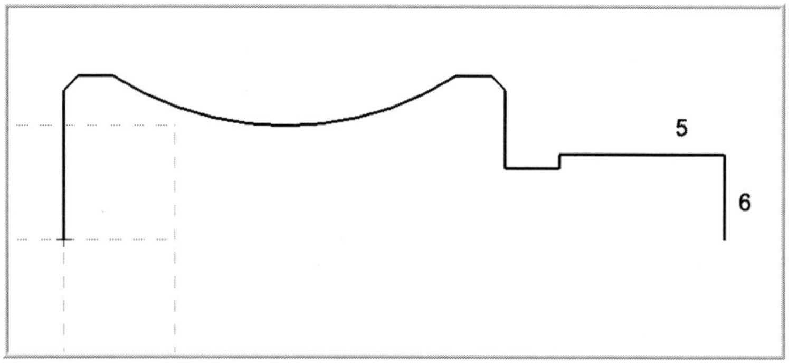

7. Click on the **OK** icon  to complete this feature.

➲ The completed geometry should look like the image below:

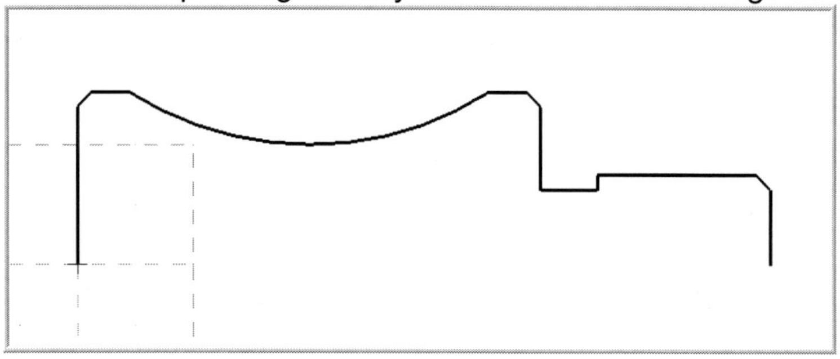

TASK 6:
SAVE THE DRAWING

1. Select **File.**
2. Select **Save As…**
3. Click on the **Browse** icon.
4. In the **"File name"** box, type **"Lathe-Lesson-4".**
5. Browse to an appropriate location.
6. Select **the Save** button to save the file and complete this function.

Toolpath Creation

TASK 7:
DEFINING THE STOCK AND CHUCK PARAMETERS

1. Select the **VIEW** tab at the top of the screen.
2. Select the **Fit** icon in the **Zoom** section. Next select **Unzoom 50%** to shrink the display.
3. Still on the **View tab** and click on **Toolpaths** to display the Toolpaths Manager.
4. Ensure your screen looks like the image below:
    a. The Toolpaths Manager is open.
    b. The properties icon displays **Lathe Default**. If it is not refer to **Setting the Environment** chapter at the beginning of the book.
    c. The **Lathe Lesson-4** Geometry is showing.

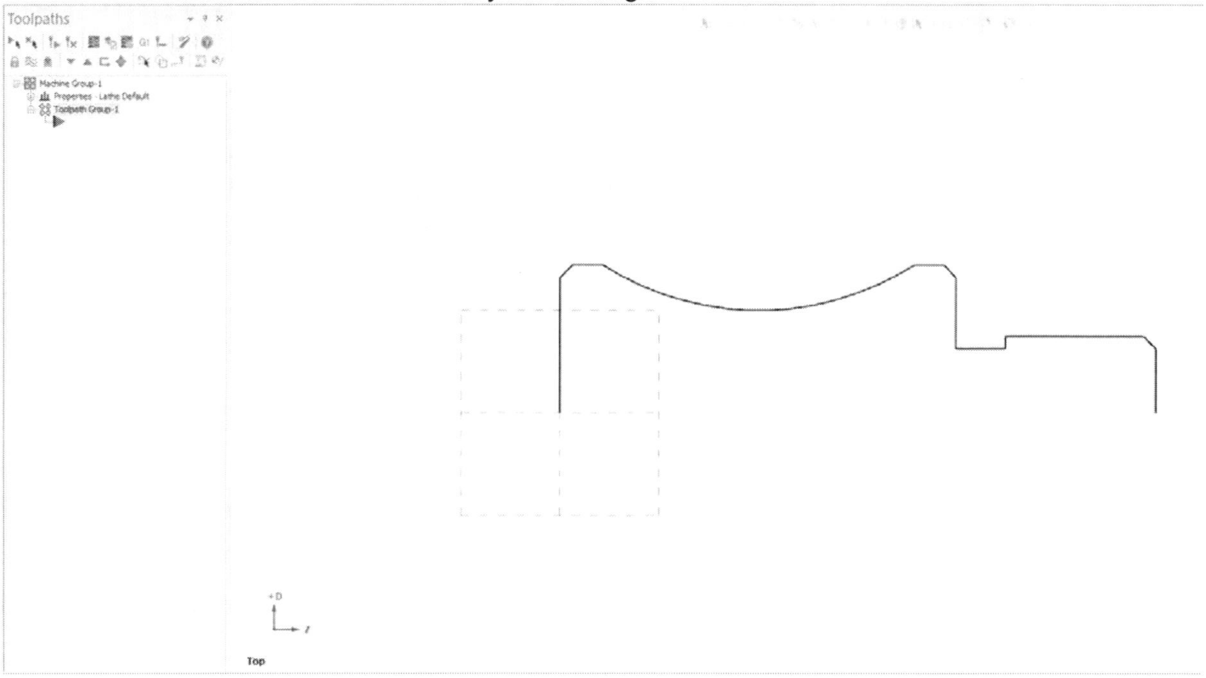

5. Select the plus in front of **Properties** to expand the Machine Group Properties, if required.

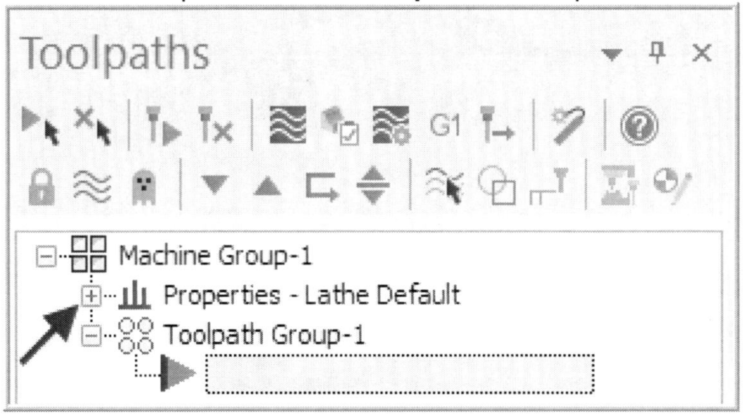

6. Select **Stock setup** in the Toolpaths Manager window.

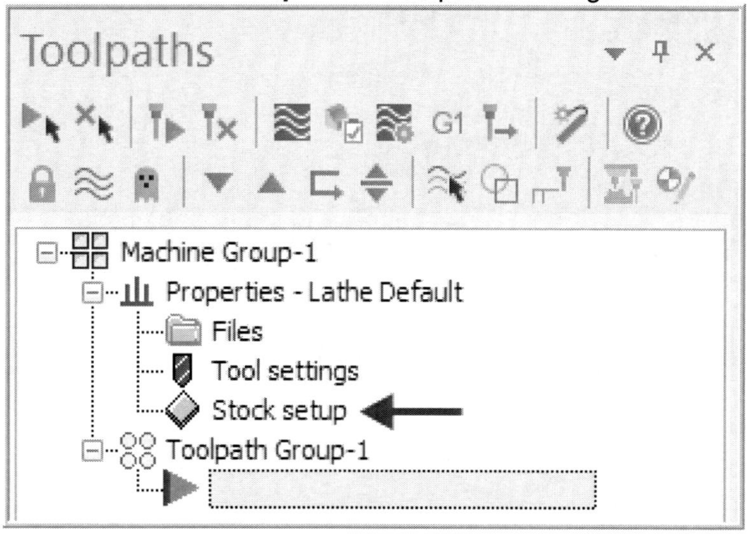

7. Select the **Stock Properties** button in the **Stock Setup** page as shown in the screenshot below.

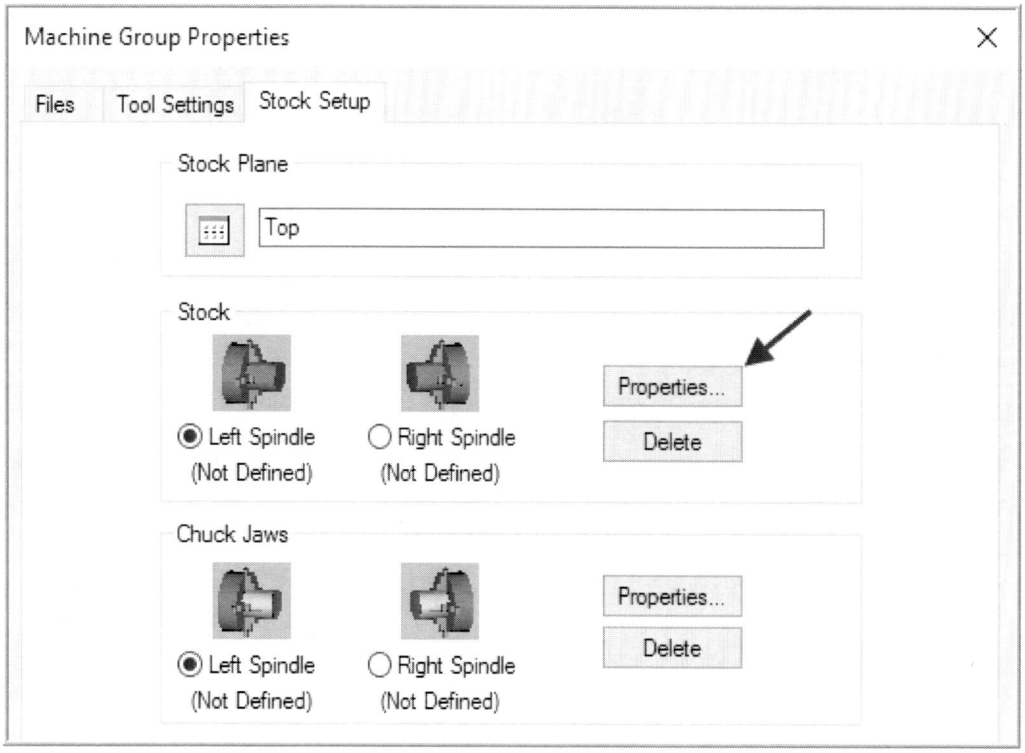

8. In the **Machine Component Manager**-**Stock** window click on the **Geometry** button and select **Cylinder** as shown below:

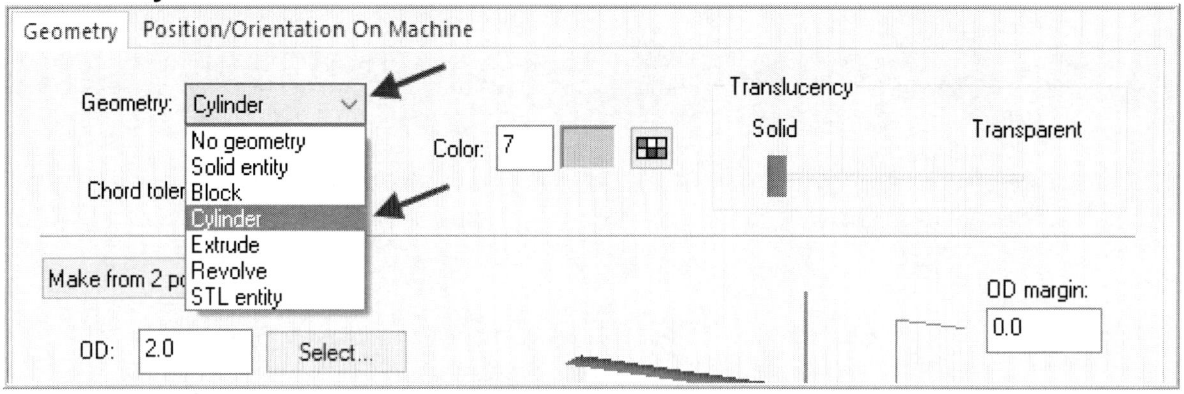

9. In the **Stock setup** set the values as shown below. **Axis is set to +Z**.

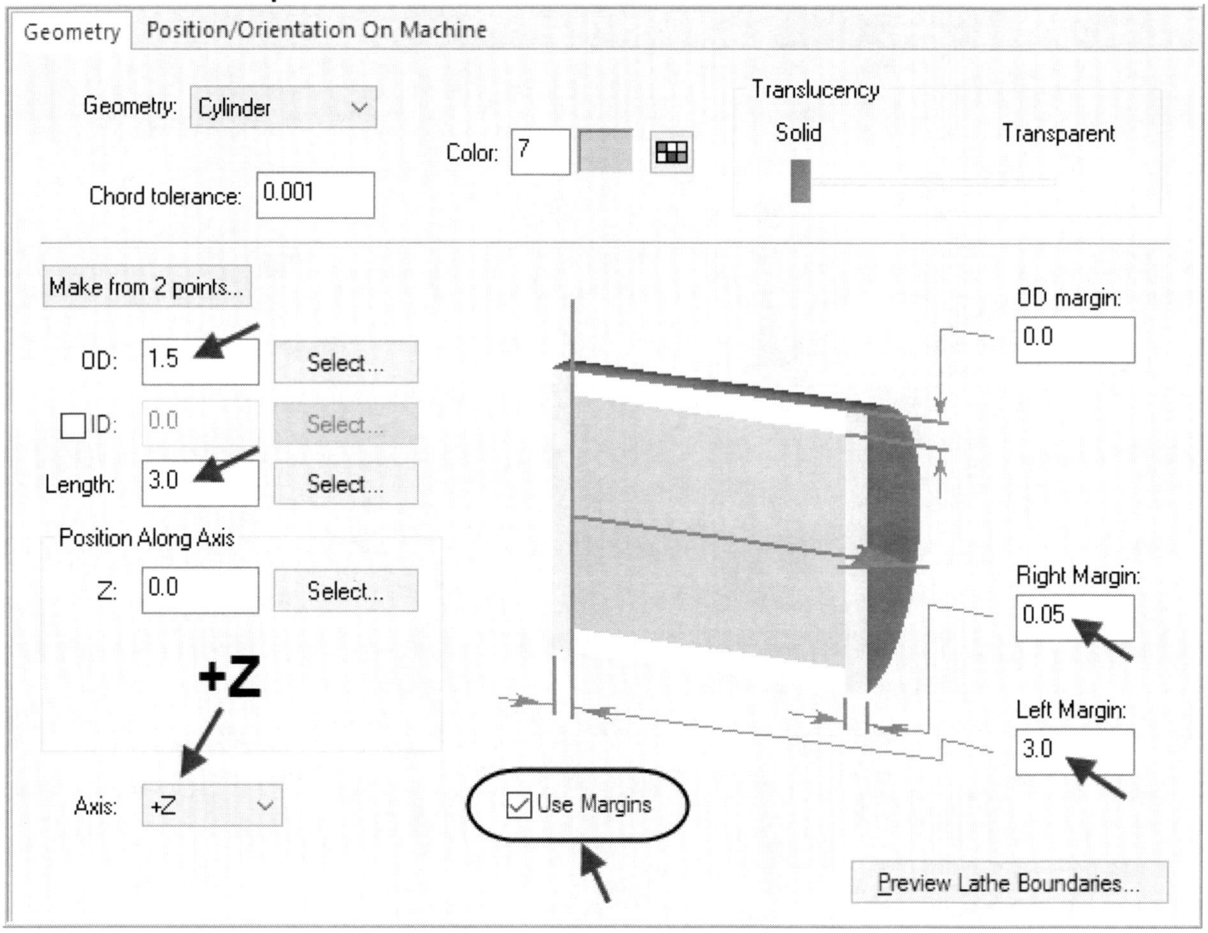

10. Click on the OK icon [OK icon] to complete this feature.

11. Still on the Stock Setup page activate **Fit screen to boundaries**.

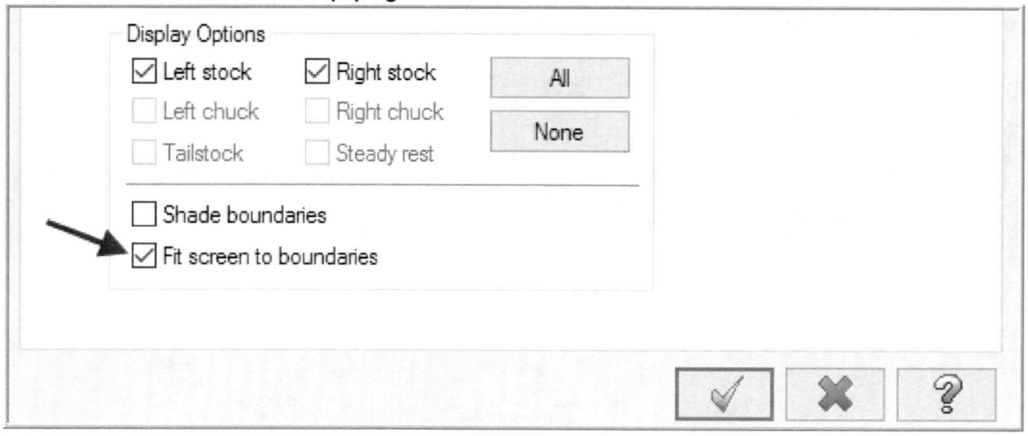

12. Select the **Chuck Properties** button in the **Stock Setup** page as shown in the screenshot below:

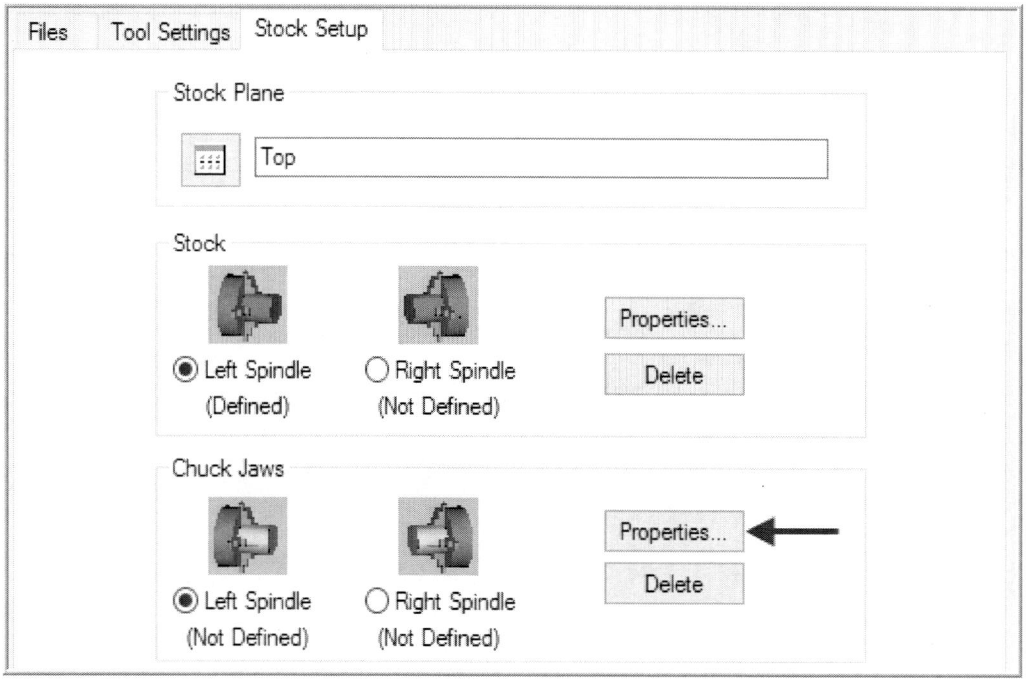

13. In the **Chuck Jaws** setup set the values as shown below:

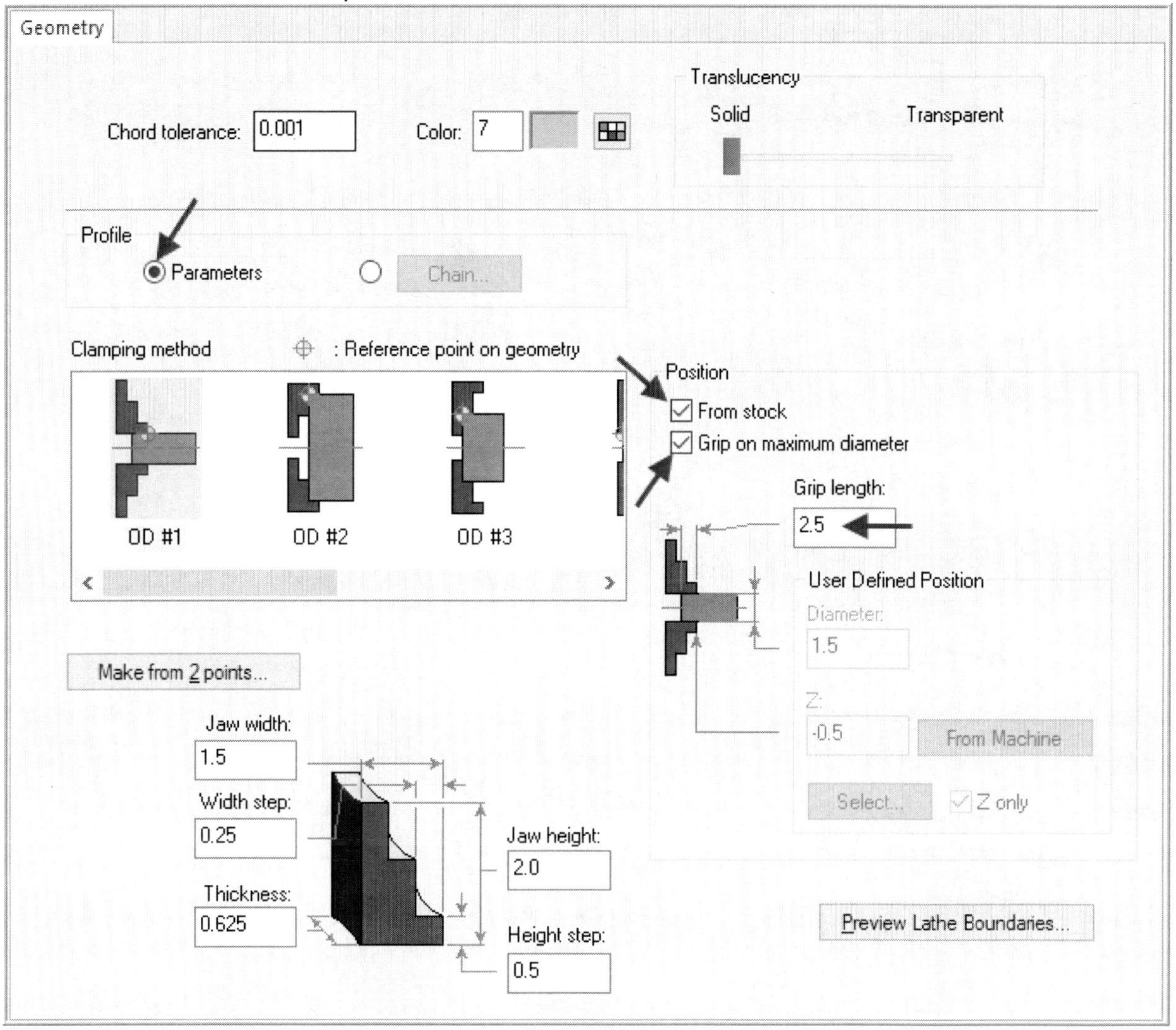

14. Click on the OK icon to complete this feature.

15. Click on the **Tool Settings** page and make changes as shown below:

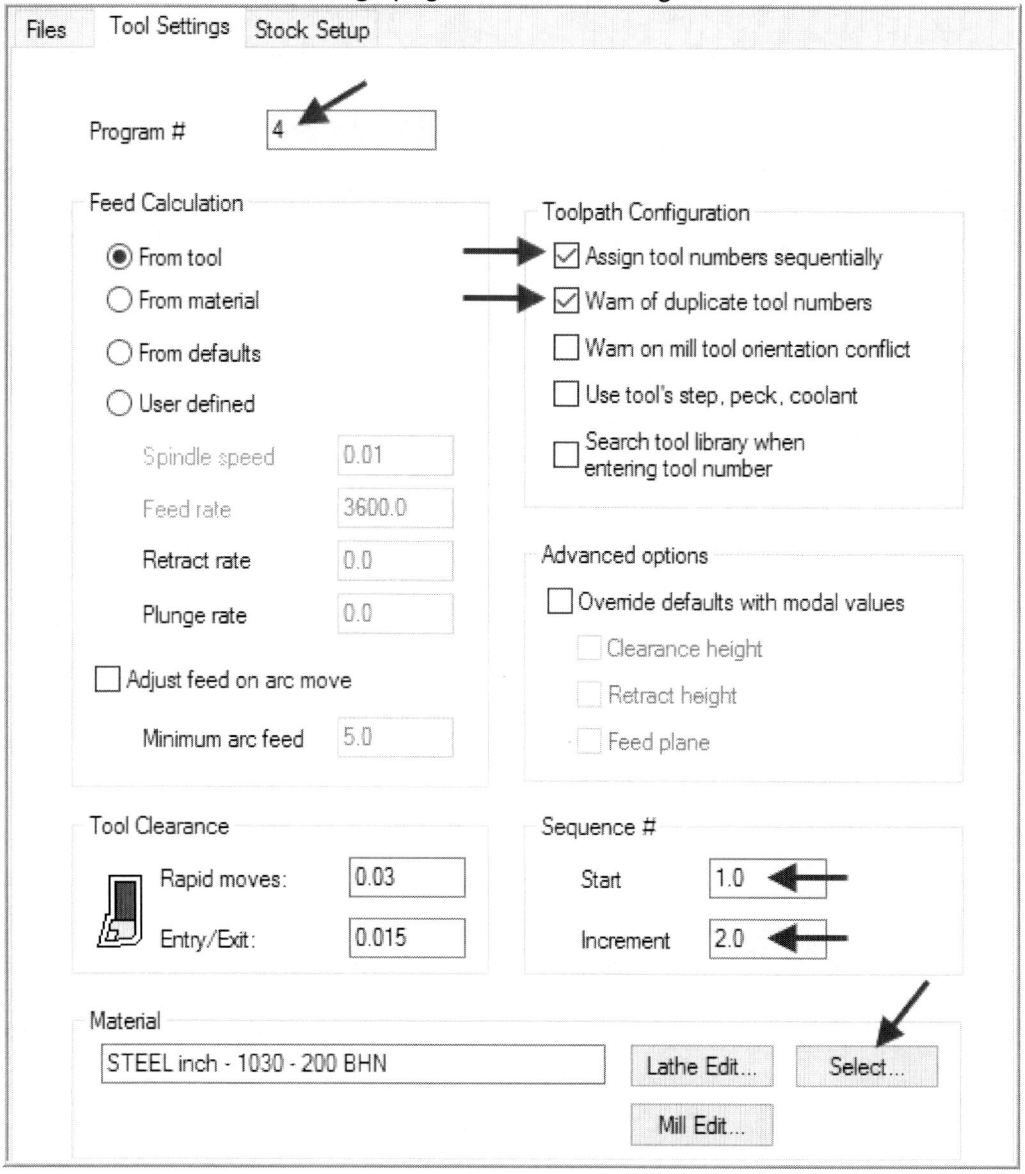

16. To change the **Material** type to Aluminum 6061 pick the **Select** button at the bottom of the Tool Settings page.

17. At the **Material List** dialog box open the Source drop down list and select **Lathe – library.**

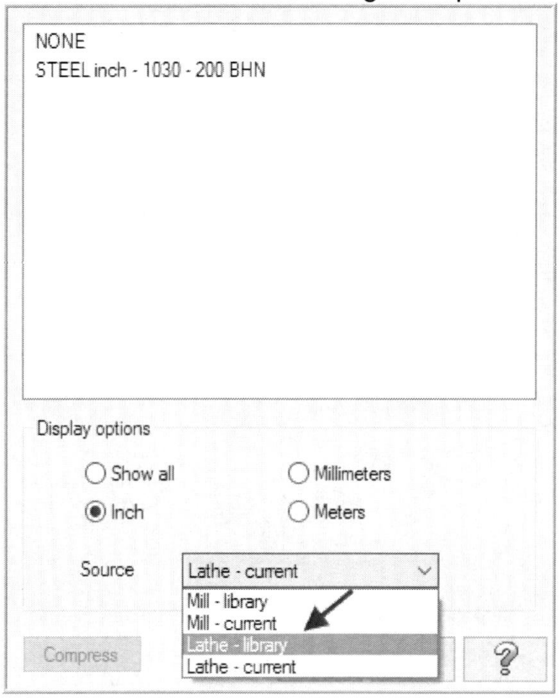

18. From the **Default Materials** list select **ALUMINUM inch - 6061** and then select .

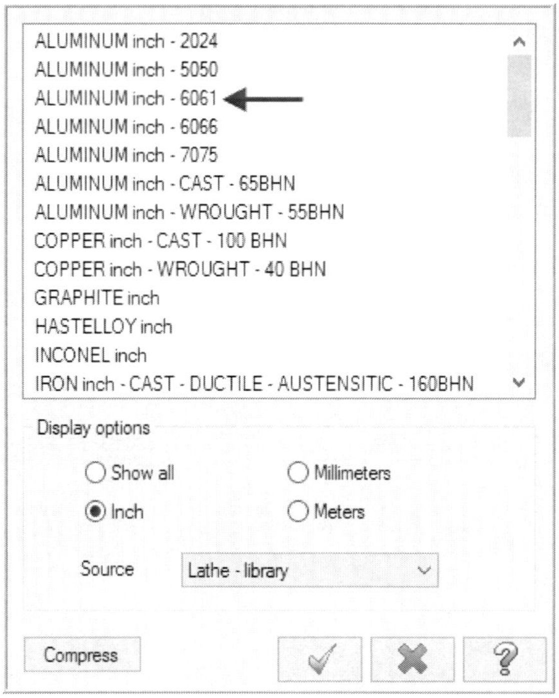

19. Select the OK button  again to complete this **Stock Setup** function.

20. Right mouse click in the graphics area and click on the **Fit** icon .

➲ Note the stock setup outline as indicated by broken lines as shown below:

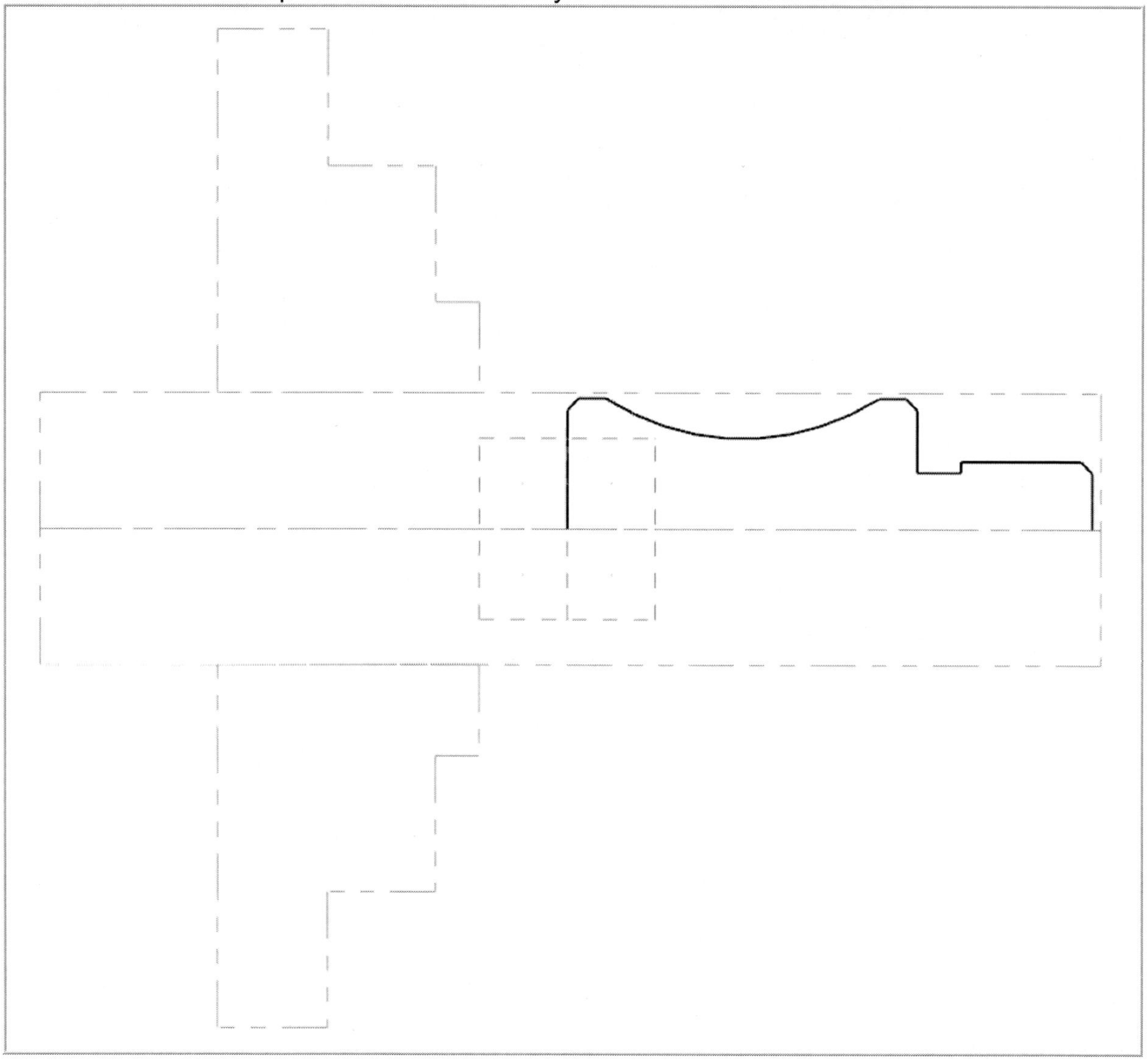

TASK 8:
FACE THE FRONT OF THE PART:

➲ In this task you will use a facing tool to face the front of the part in one cut.

1. If required right mouse click in the graphics area and click on the **Fit** icon.
2. Select the **TURNING** tab at the top right side of the screen.
3. Now select **Face** in the **General** section.

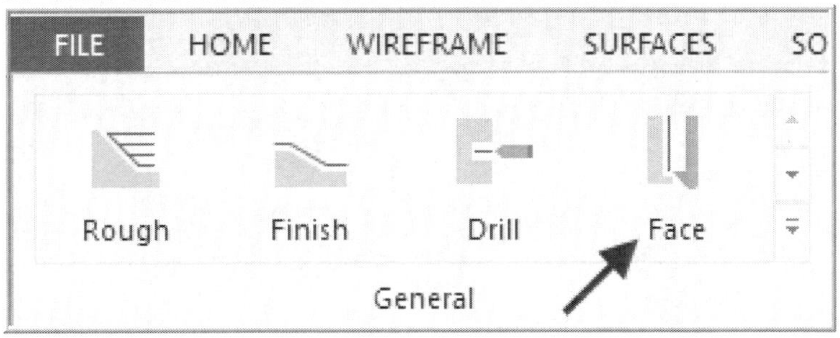

➲ After selecting the OK button you are confronted with **Toolpath parameters** page. The first task here will be to select **Tool #1 a Roughing – 80 deg.**

4. Click on **Tool 0101 Roughing – 80 degree** and ensure the settings are the same as in the Toolpath parameters page as shown below. **Coolant Flood** is set to **On**.

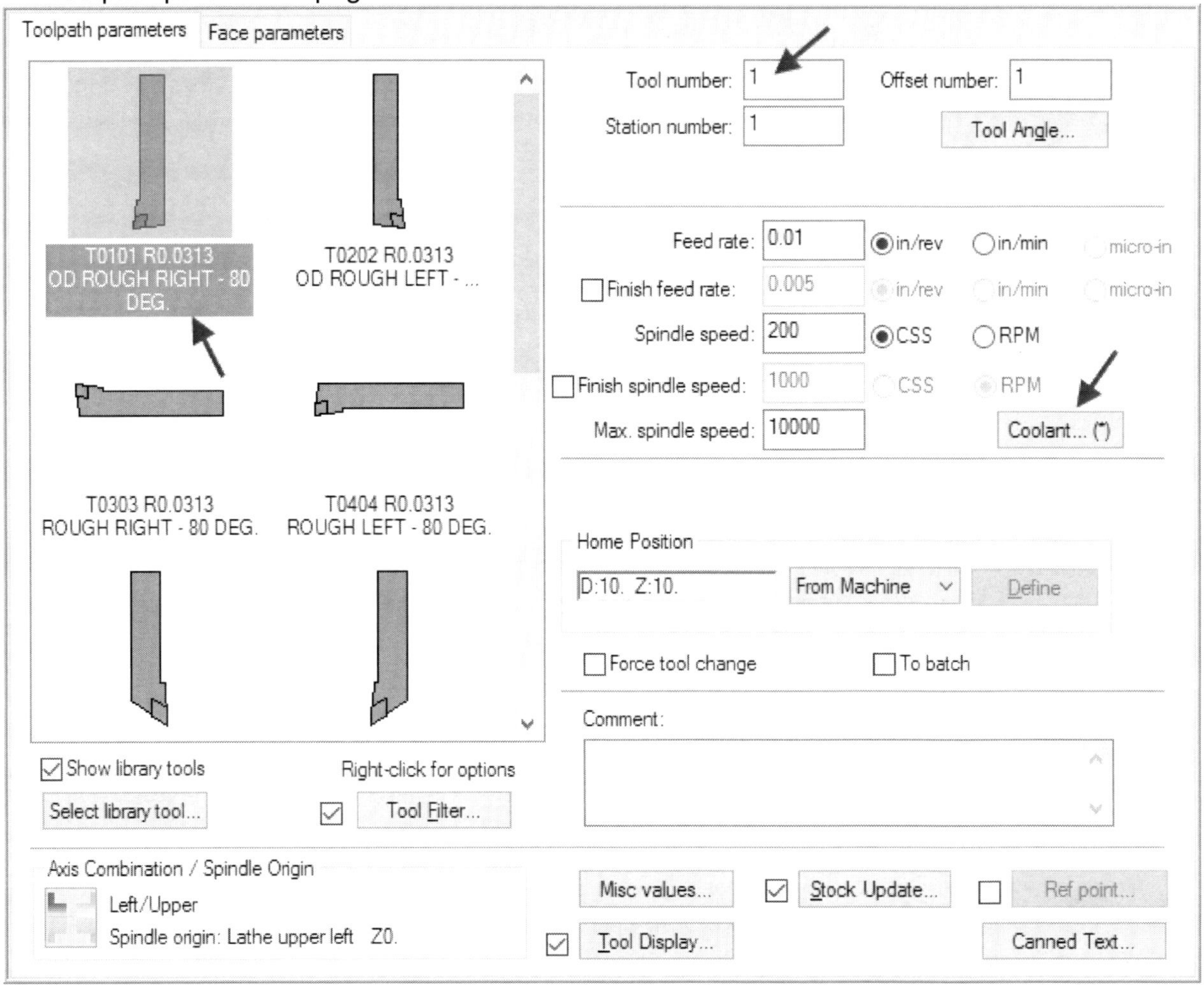

5. Select the **Face parameters** page and make changes as shown below:

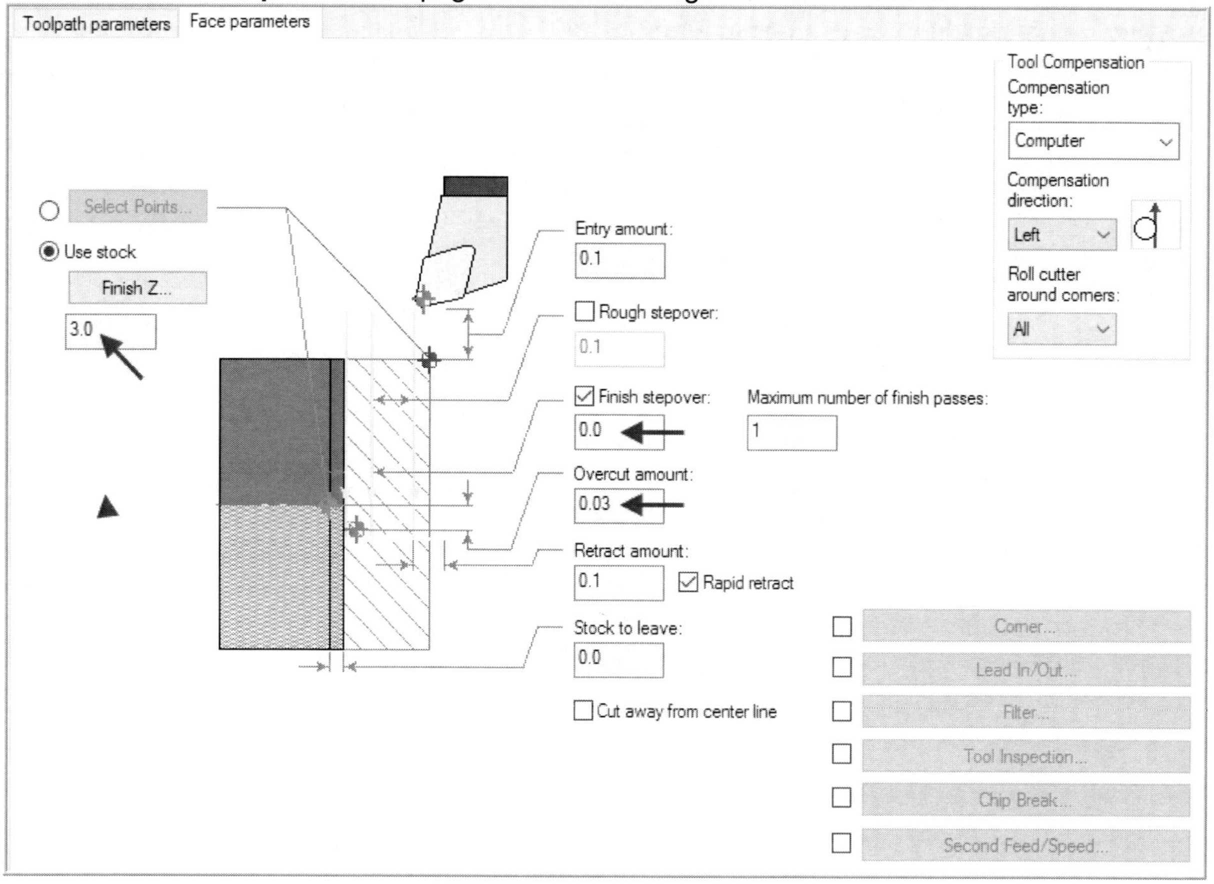

6. Select the OK button to complete this **Lathe Face** operation.

TASK 9:
ROUGH THE OUTSIDE DIAMETERS

➲ In this task you will use a Lathe toolpath called Lathe Quick rough.
➲ In this task you will use the same tool as used for the previous facing operation **Tool #1 an OD Rough- Right – 80 deg.**

1. Right mouse click in the white space of the **Toolpaths Manager** and select:
   Lathe toolpaths>Quick>Quick rough.

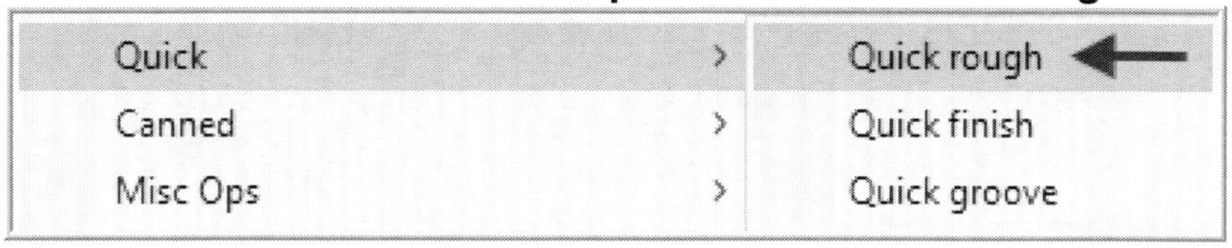

2. In the **Chaining** window Chaining mode is set to **Partial** by default.

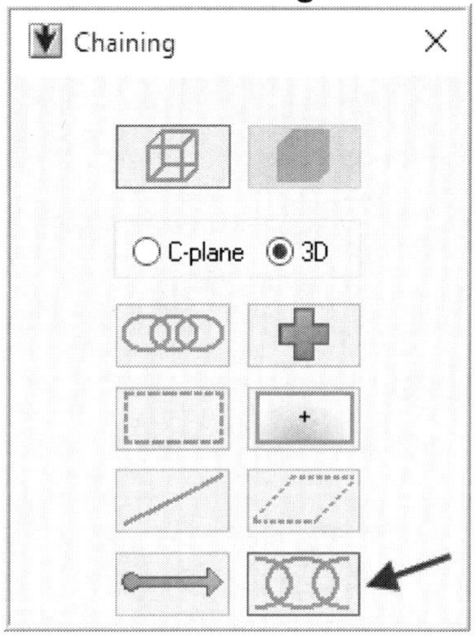

3. Select the chamfer, Line 1 as the start of the **Partial chain**.

After you have selected the chamfer **ensure** that the arrows are pointing up and to the left of the part. If it is not select the reverse button in the Chaining dialog box.

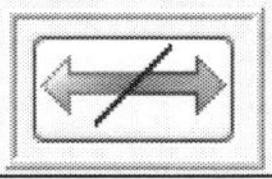

4. Then select the chamfer, Line 2 as the end entity in this chain.

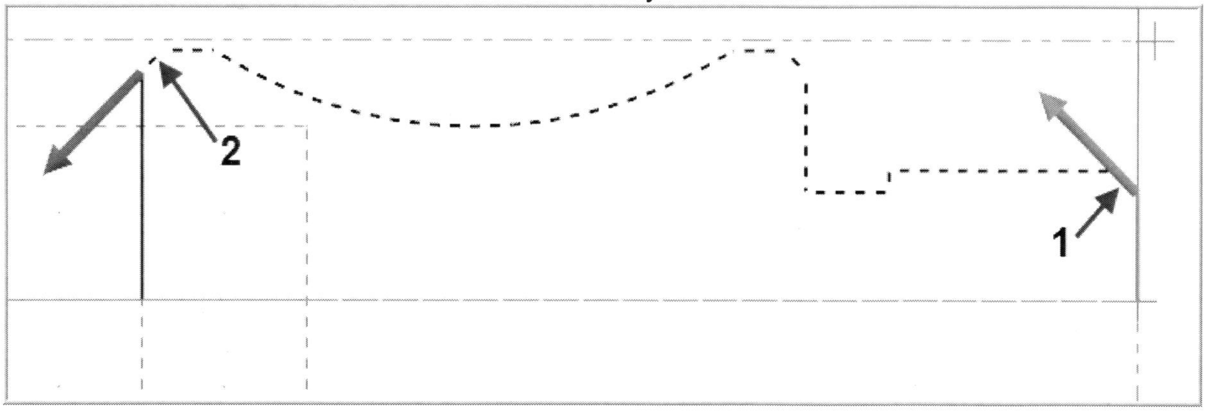

5. Select the OK button  to exit the Chaining dialog window.

6. In the **Quick tool parameters** page select the **Tool #1 an Roughing – 80 deg** and make any necessary changes as shown below. **Coolant Flood** is set to **On**.

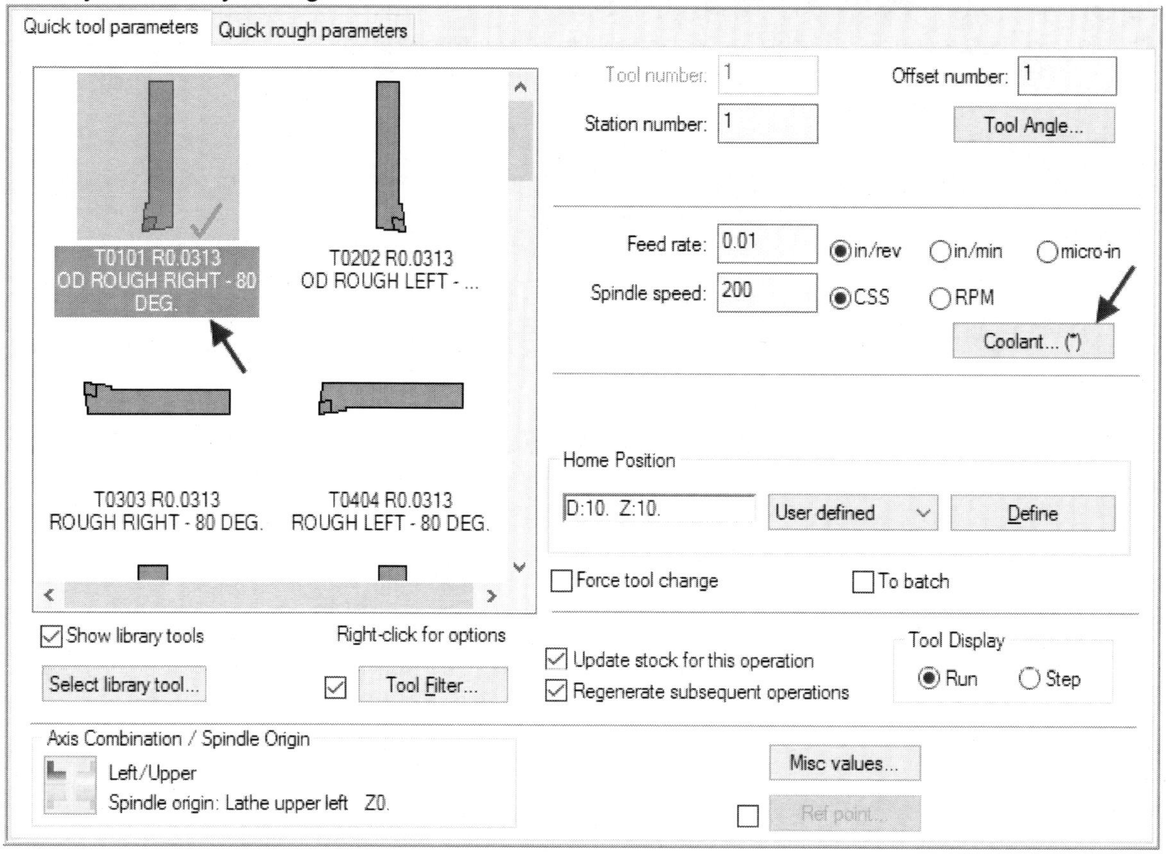

7. Select the **Quick Rough parameters** page and make changes as shown below:

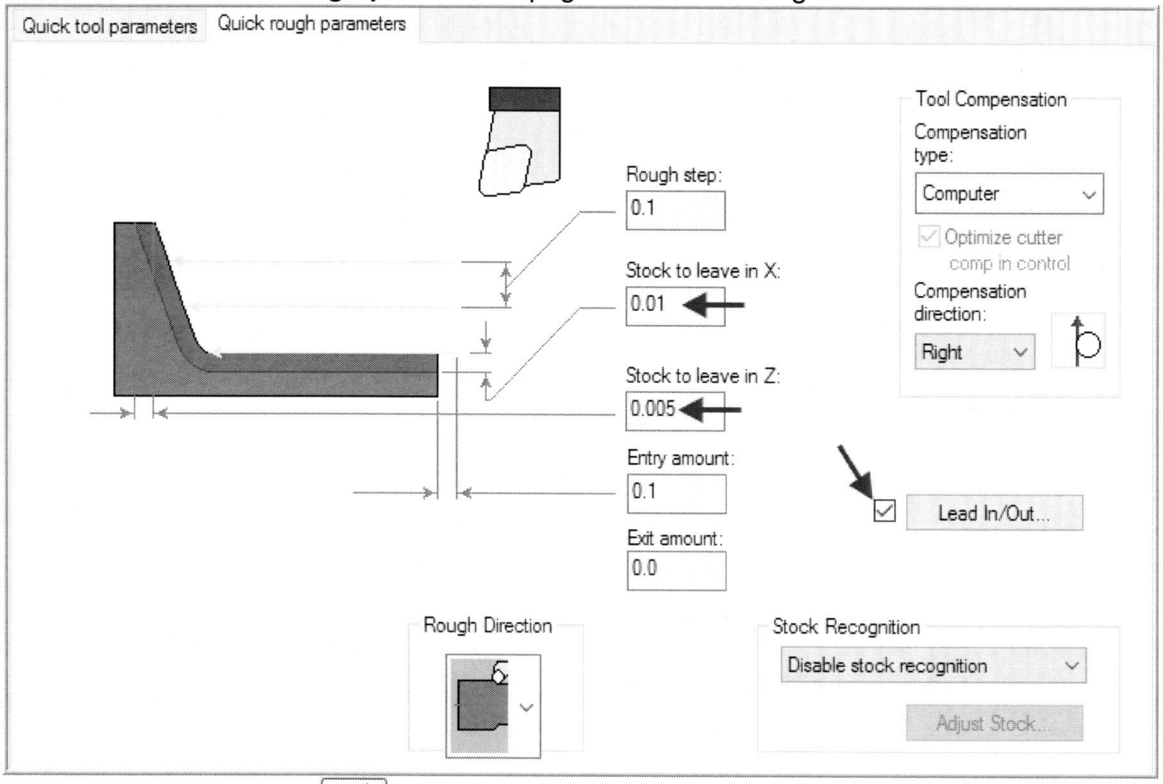

8. Select the OK button ✓ to exit Rough Parameters.

TASK 10:
FINISH THE DIAMETER

➲ In this task you will finish the diameter using **Tool #2 OD Finish Right – 35 DEG.**

1. Right mouse click in the white space of the **Toolpaths Manager** and select:
   Lathe toolpaths>Quick>Quick finish.

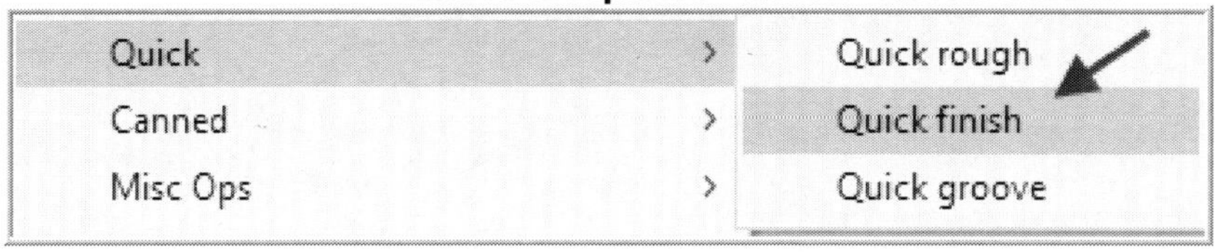

2. Select **Tool #2 OD Finish Right – 35 DEG** tool from the tool list and make any necessary changes as shown below. **Coolant Flood** is set to **On**.

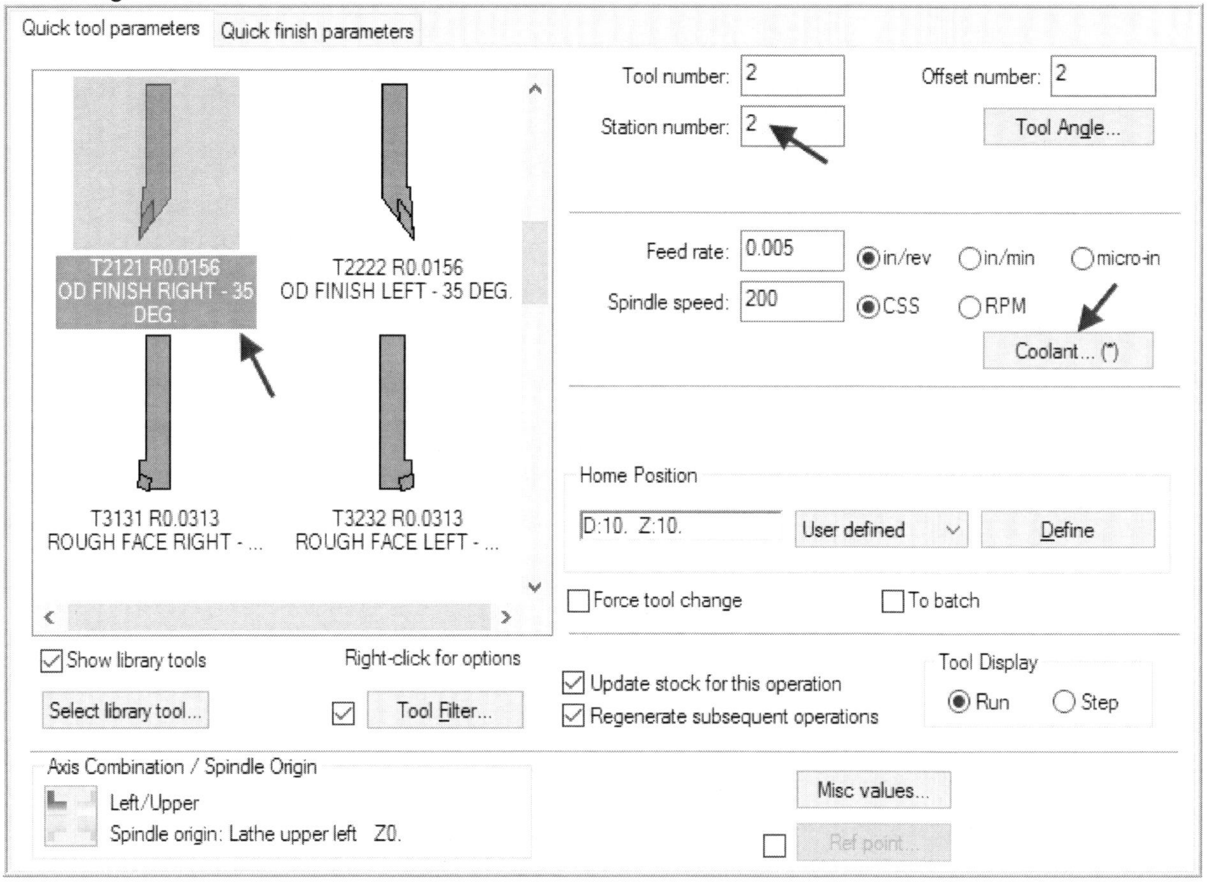

3. Click on the **Quick finish parameters** page and make changes as shown below:

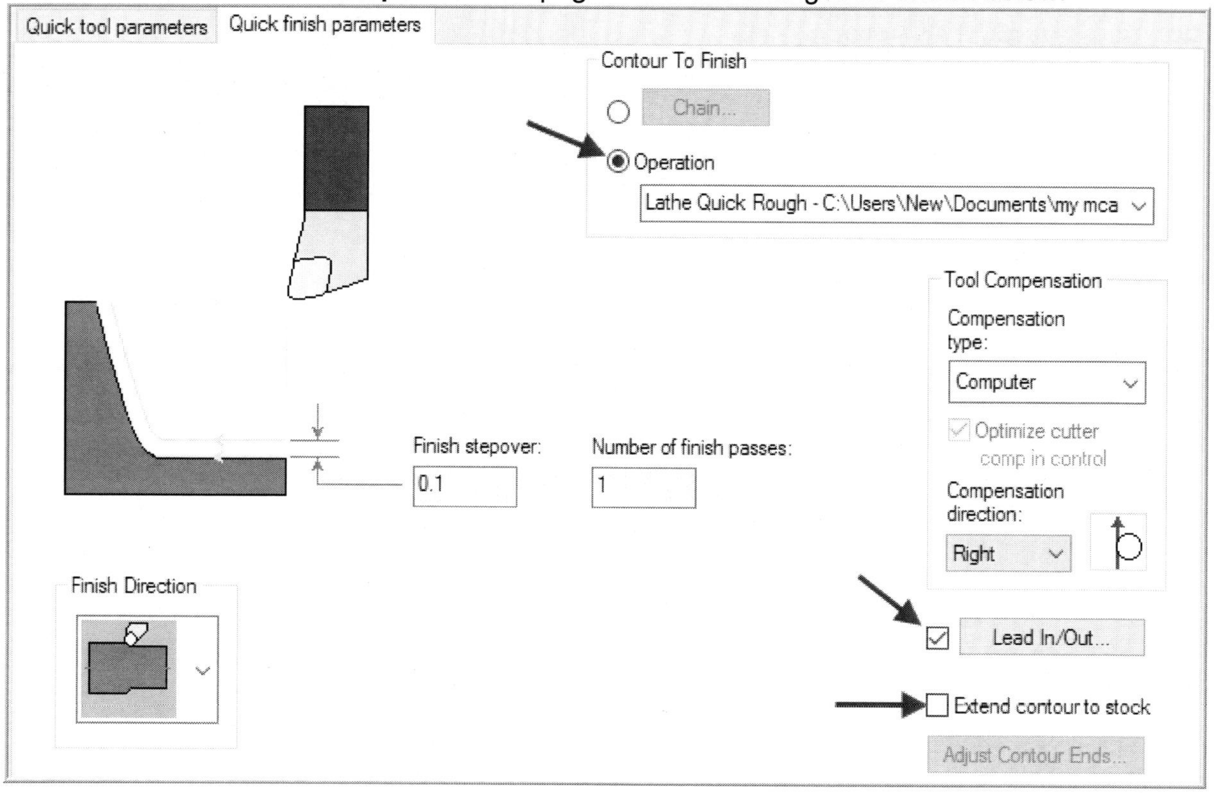

4. Click on the **Lead In/Out** button.
5. Make the necessary changes as shown below on the **Lead in** page. In order to adjust the **dial (#1),** click on the desired location of the arrow:

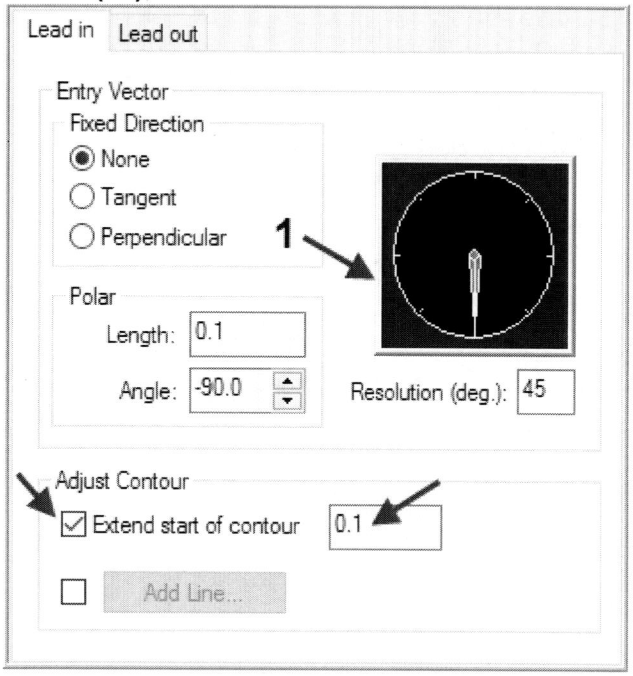

Extend start of contour
Select this option to create lead in/out moves by extending the beginning of the chained geometry.

After selecting the checkbox, you will be able to specify the amount of the adjustment.

Create the lead in and lead out moves separately on each tab.

Angle dial
Set the angle of the entry or exit vector by dragging the pointer to the desired orientation.

Mastercam will automatically enter the angle in the Angle field.

6. Select the OK button  to exit the **Lead In/Out** window.
7. Select the OK button  to exit the **Lathe Quick Finish** parameters.

TASK 11:
CUT THE GROOVE

➲ In this task you will use the Lathe Groove toolpath using **Tool #3 OD Groove Right Width .125.**

1. Click on the **Select all operations** icon .
2. Now **toggle the display of the toolpaths** by selecting **ALT and T** on your keyboard to hide the toolpaths display.
3. Click on the **Expand gallery** down arrow to view additional options in the **General** toolpath section. In the **General** section select **Groove.**

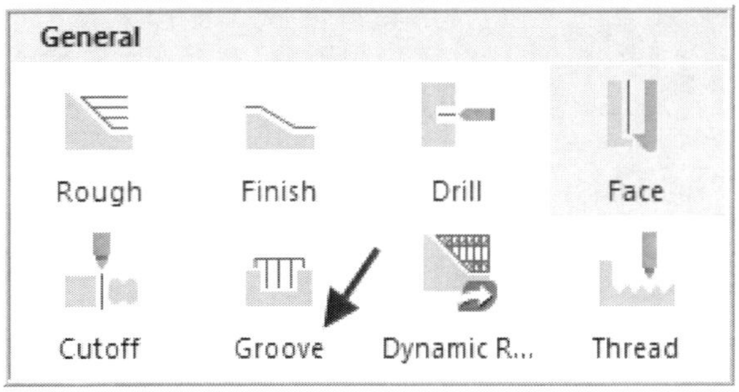

4. The **Grooving Options** window appears. Click on the **2 Points** option as shown below.

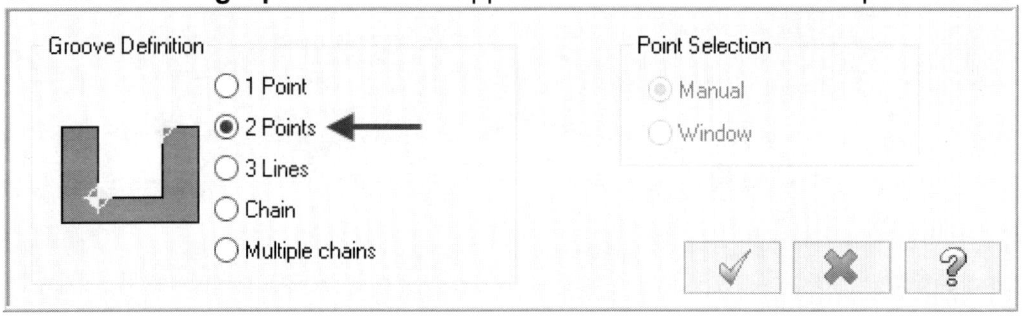

Grooving Options Use this dialog box to tell Mastercam how you will identify the grooves for a groove toolpath. You can identify grooves by one or both corner points, by three rectangular lines, or, for standard groove toolpaths, you can select a non-rectangular chain of curves. The **2 Points Groove Definition** will enable you to pick 2 points of the groove to define the groove.

5. Click on OK .

6. Click on the **2 points** as shown below.

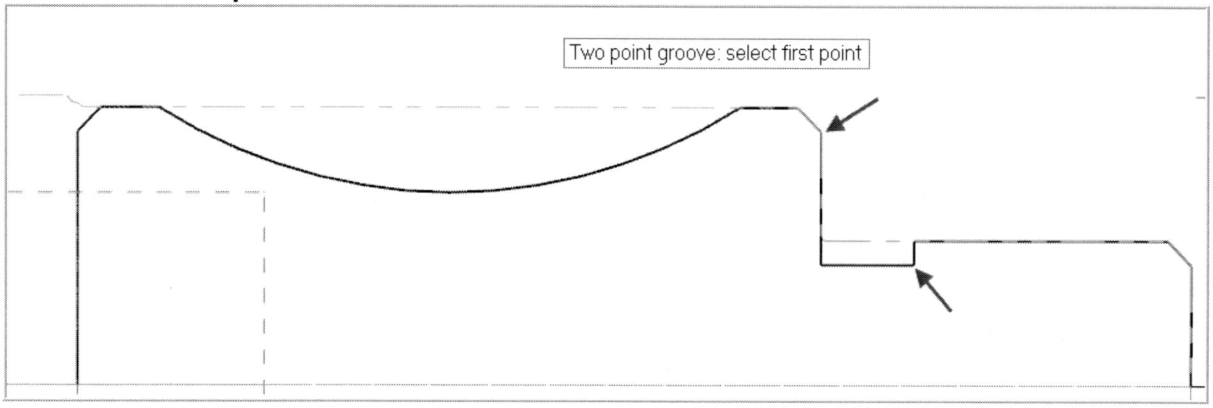

7. Hit **Enter** after selecting the two points.
8. Select **Tool #3 OD Groove Right Narrow - Width .125** tool from the tool list and make any necessary changes as shown below. **Coolant Flood** is set to **On**.

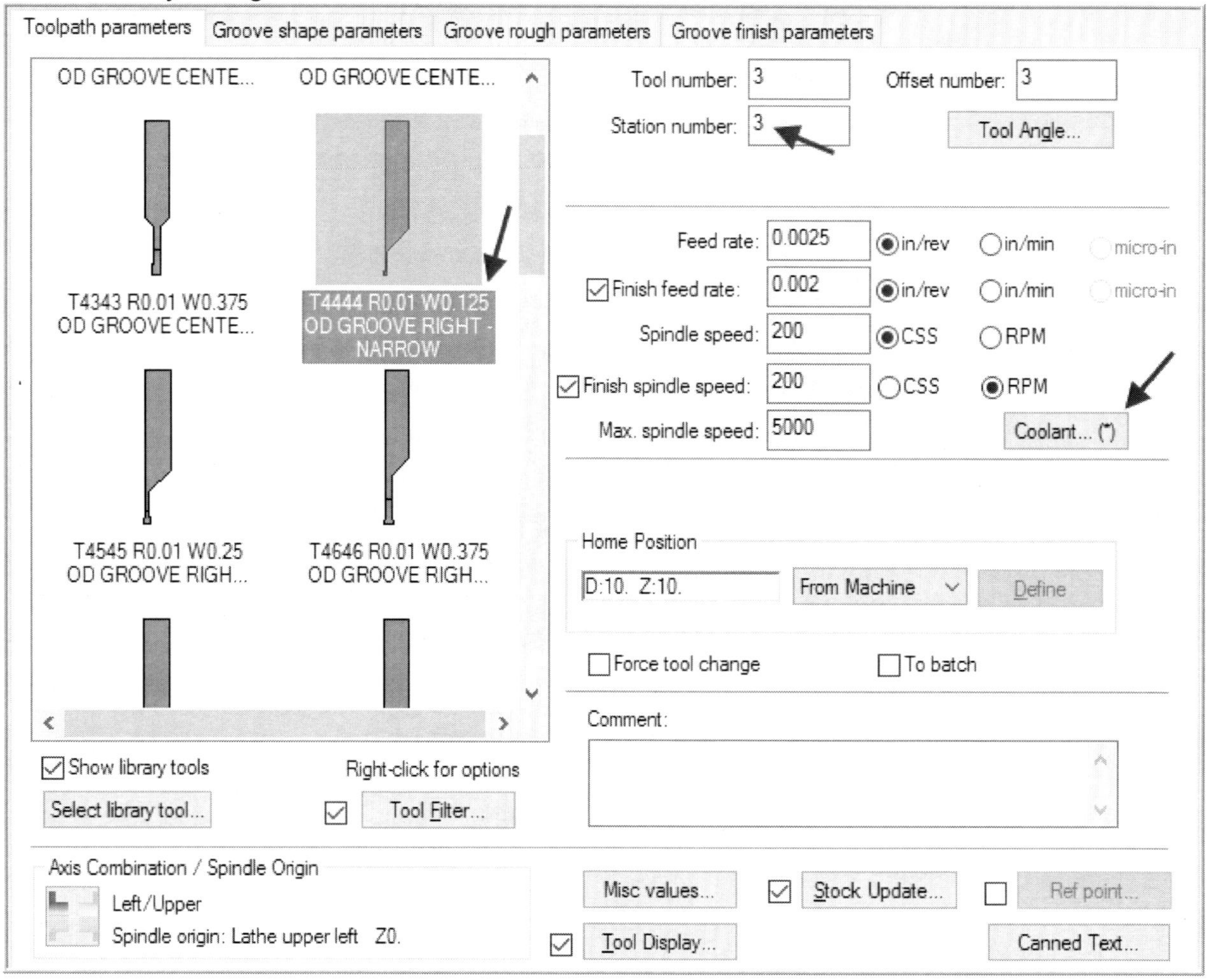

9. Click on the **Groove shape parameters** and take note of the settings. No changes will need to be made.

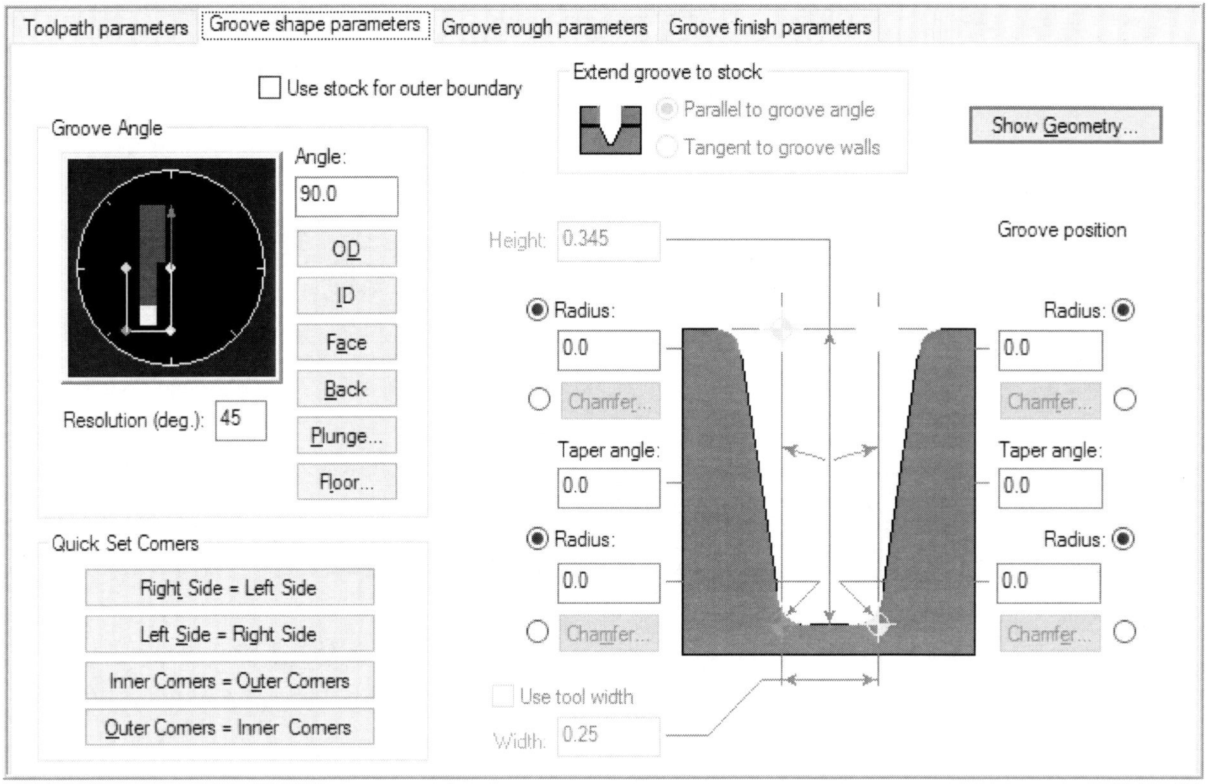

Groove shape parameters
Use this tab to tell Mastercam about the shape and orientation of the grooves in groove and plunge turn toolpaths. Because Mastercam does not need chained geometry to create these toolpaths, use the options on this tab to specify the groove boundaries. The settings you enter here will apply to all the grooves in the toolpath. There are several groups of settings.

Outer boundary
By default, the outer boundary of the groove will be a straight line between the outer corners. You can choose to use the stock boundary instead (if a stock model has been defined).

Groove angle
Use these settings to tell Mastercam how the groove is oriented on the part. Click a button to select a standard orientation or drag the dial to the desired angle.

Groove dimensions
Depending on how many points you selected to identify the groove locations, you might need to enter the height and width. You can also define radius and/or chamfer dimensions for each corner individually. The colored datum points represent the points you chose to identify the groove location.

10. Click on the **Groove rough parameters** and take note of the settings. No changes will need to be made.

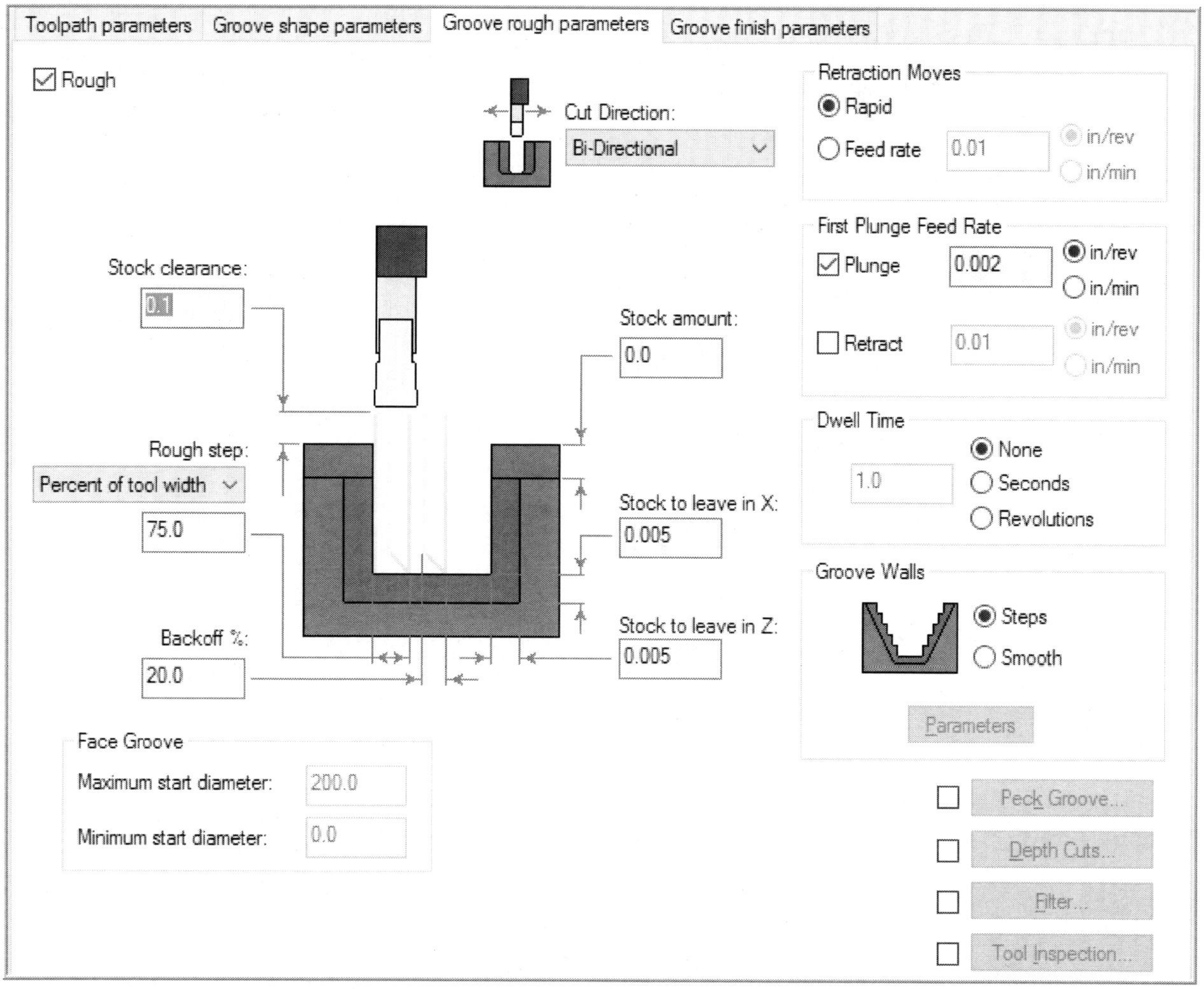

Groove rough parameters
Use this tab to create the roughing cuts for a groove toolpath. Select the Rough checkbox to activate the options on this tab and create a roughing pass. Leave this checkbox de-selected if you only want to create a finish operation.

Use the pictures on the tab as a guide to entering your roughing parameters. Select options on the right side of the tab to enable advanced grooving features, such as pecking, depth cuts, and toolpath filtering.

Note: There are no cutter comp options for groove roughing. Cutter comp in computer is always on and Mastercam determines the direction.

11. Click on the **Groove finish parameters** and take note of the settings. No changes will need to be made.

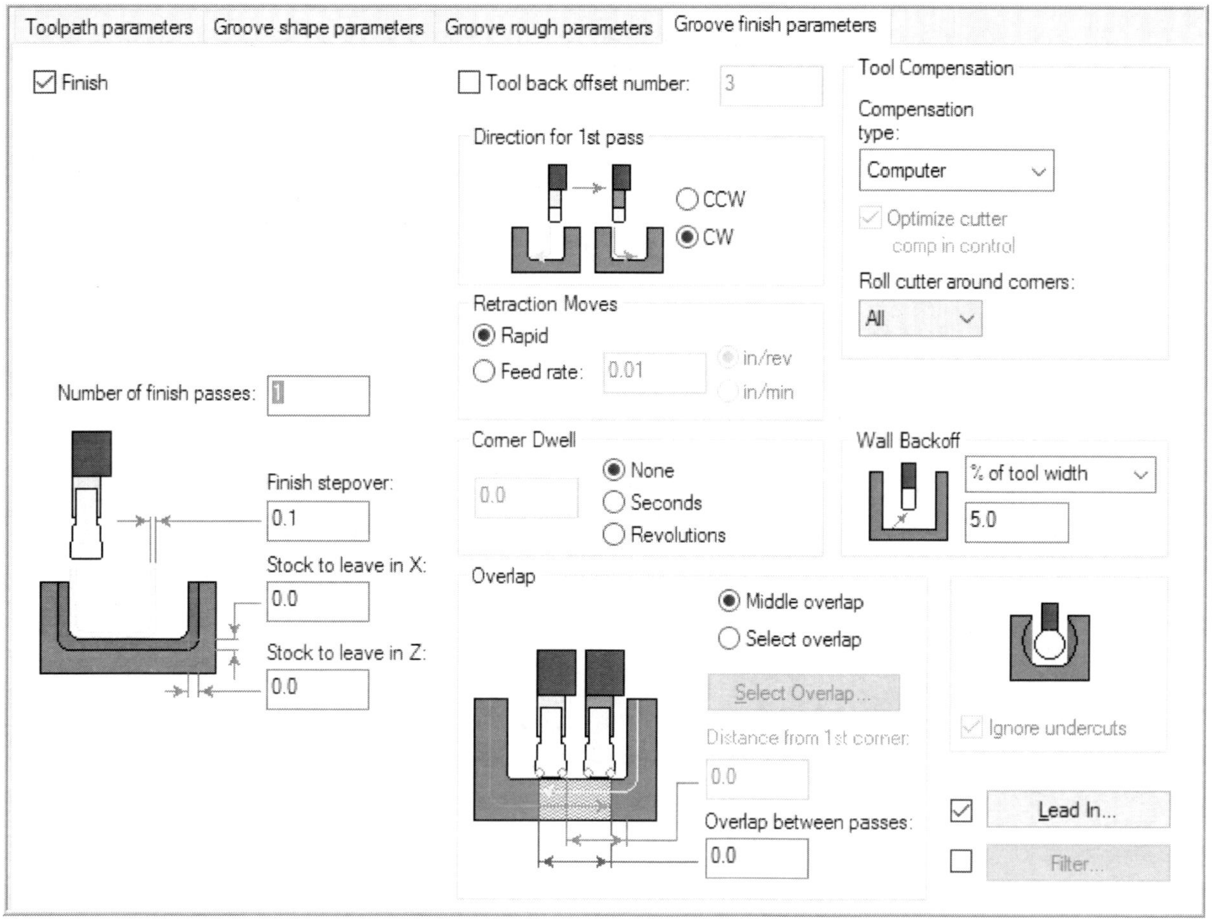

Groove finish parameters
Use this tab to create the finish passes for a groove toolpath. Select the Finish checkbox to activate the options on this tab and create finish passes. Leave this checkbox de-selected if you only want to create a roughing operation.

Use the pictures on the tab as a guide to entering your finishing parameters. Select options on the right side of the tab to enable advanced grooving features, such as lead in/out moves and toolpath filtering.

Note: With groove finish passes, if you set compensation in control to automatic. Mastercam changes the compensation in control direction for the clockwise and counter-clockwise cut directions.

12. Click on OK .

TASK 12:
THREAD THE PART

➲ In this task you will thread the outside diameter using **Tool #4 R0.0144 OD THREAD RIGHT.**

1. In the **General** toolpath section select **Thread**.

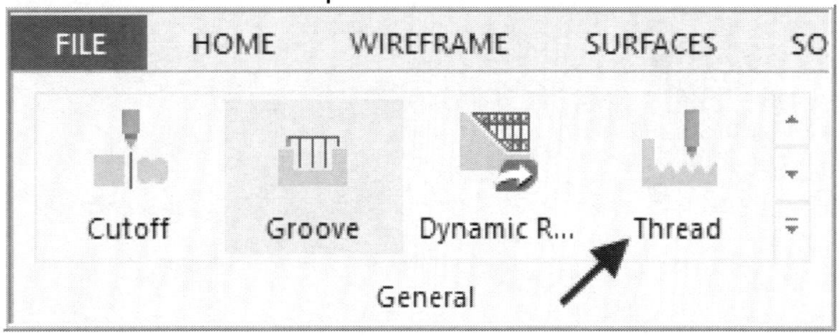

2. Scroll down the tool window if necessary and select the **Tool #4 R0.0144 OD THREAD RIGHT** tool and make changes as shown below in the **Toolpath parameters** page.
3. **Coolant Flood** is set to **On**.

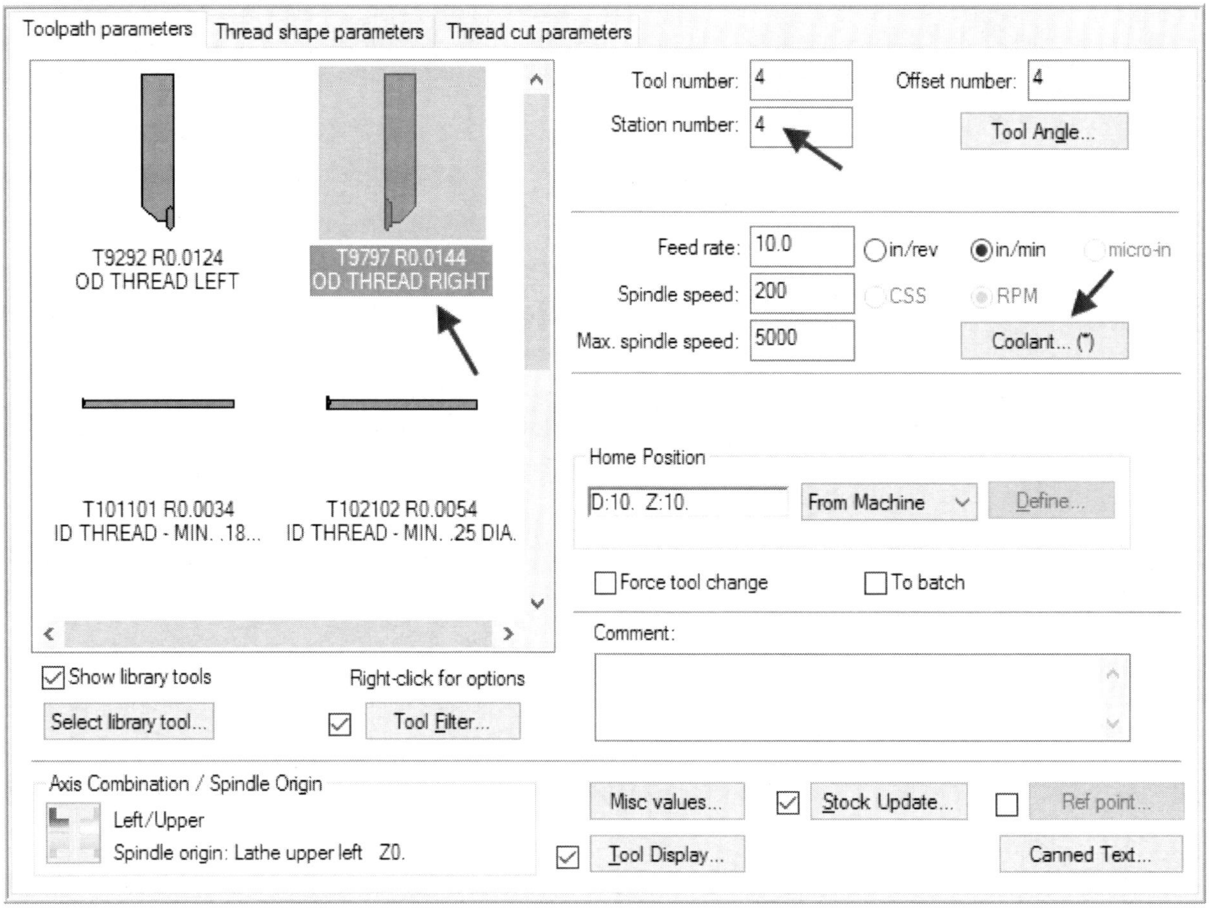

4. Click on the **Thread shape parameters** tab.
5. Click on **Select from table** as shown below.

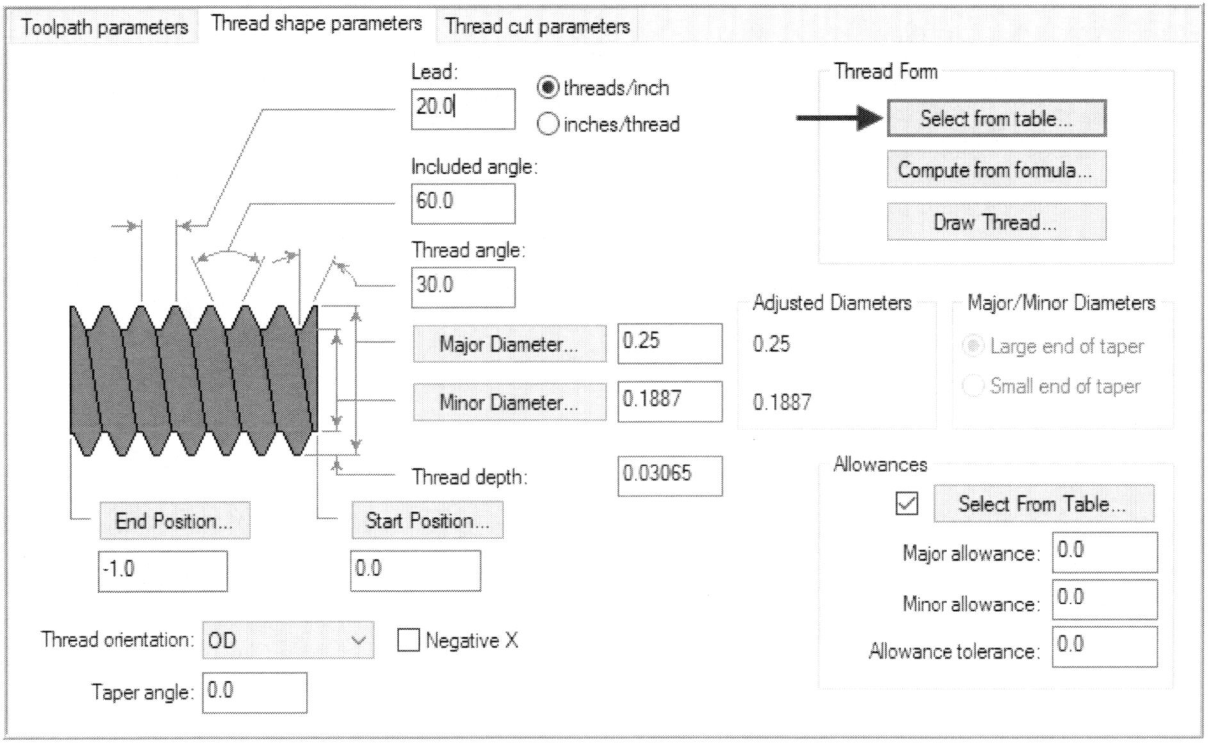

6. Click on the **Thread forms** drop down menu (1) and select **Unified – UNC, UNF** (2) as shown below.

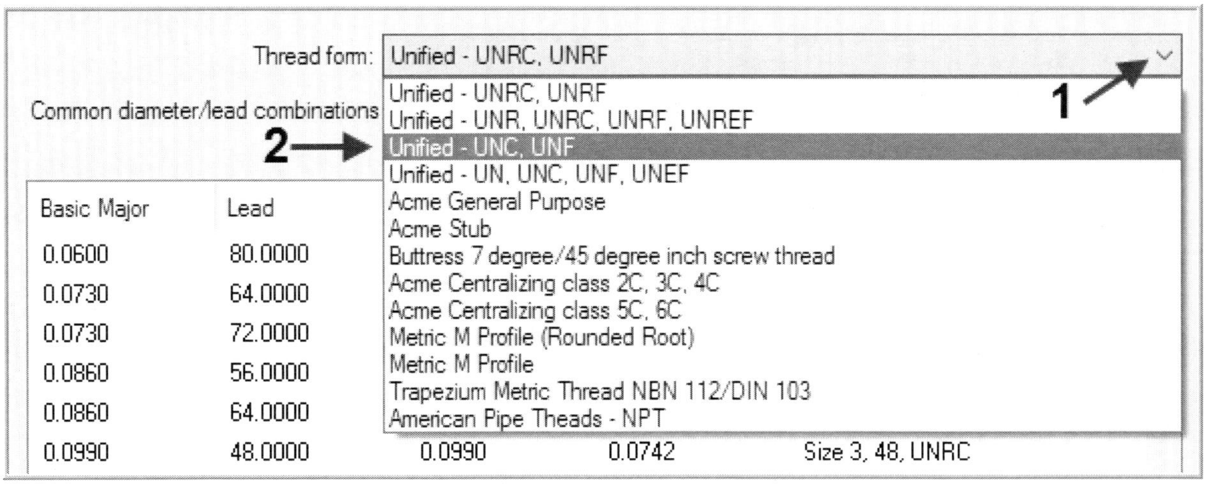

7. Scroll down and click on the **0.7500 10.000 (3/4, 10. UNC)** thread as shown below:

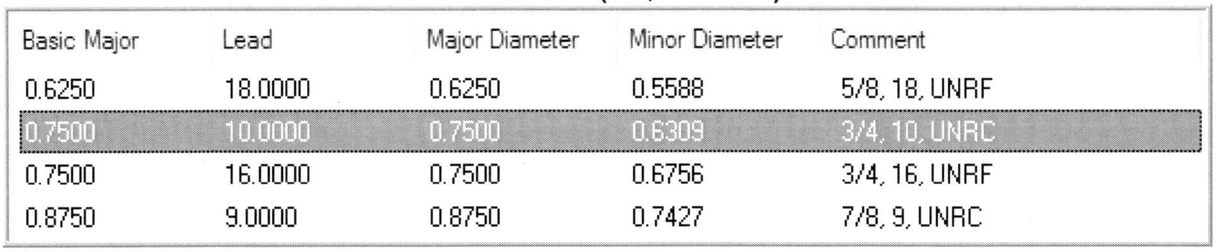

Basic Major	Lead	Major Diameter	Minor Diameter	Comment
0.6250	18.0000	0.6250	0.5588	5/8, 18, UNRF
0.7500	10.0000	0.7500	0.6309	3/4, 10, UNRC
0.7500	16.0000	0.7500	0.6756	3/4, 16, UNRF
0.8750	9.0000	0.8750	0.7427	7/8, 9, UNRC

8. Click on OK.

9. Click on the **Start Position** button (1) as shown below:

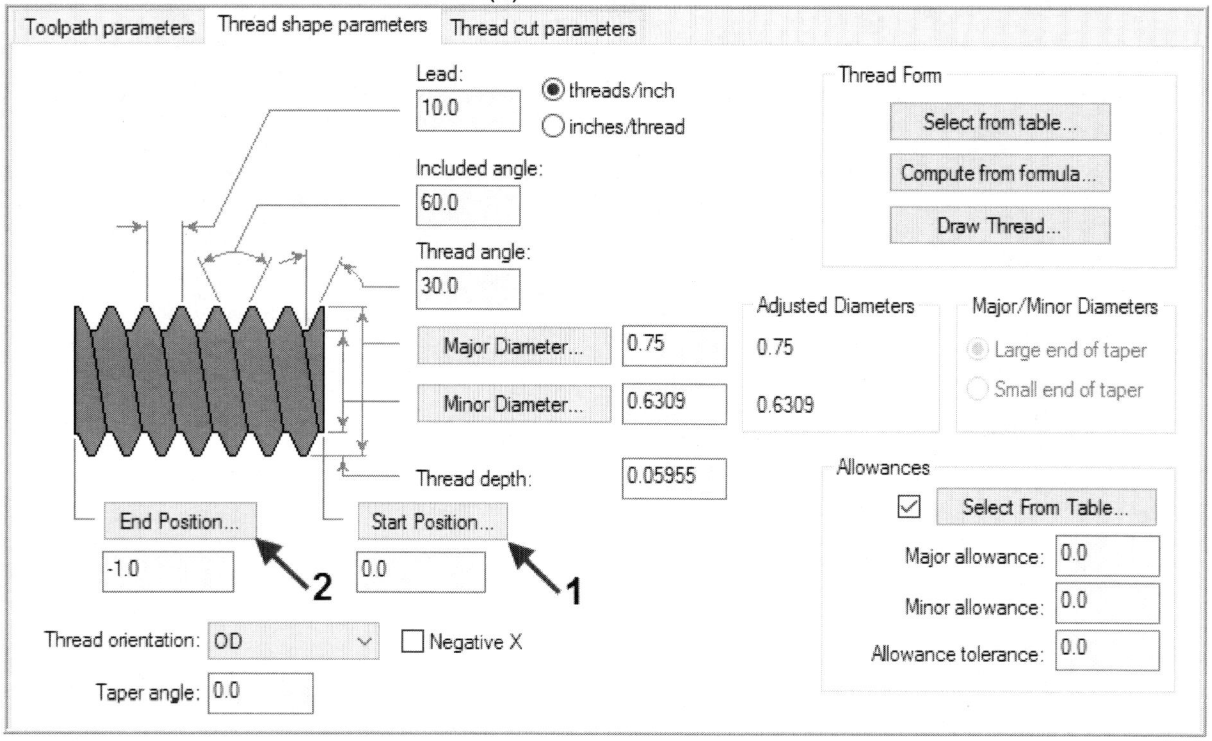

10. Click on the point as shown below:

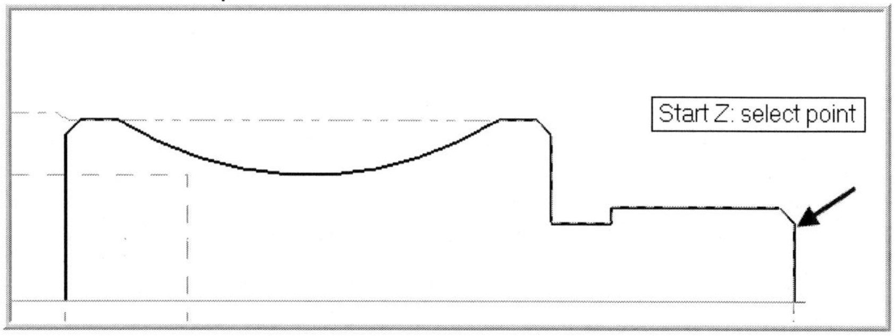

11. Click on the **End Position** button (2) as shown in step 9.
12. Click on the point as shown below:

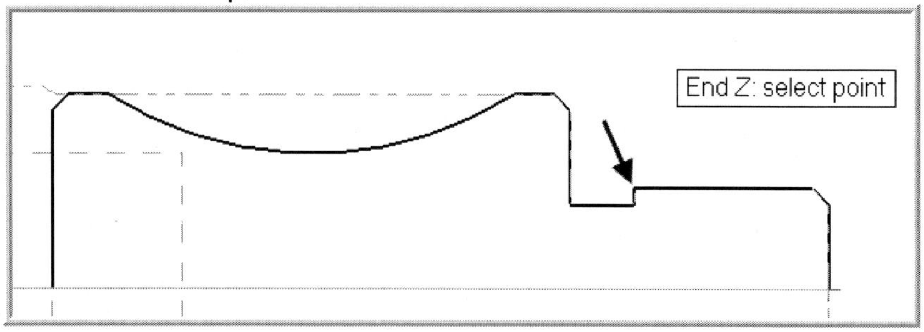

13. Your Start and End Positions should be as below:

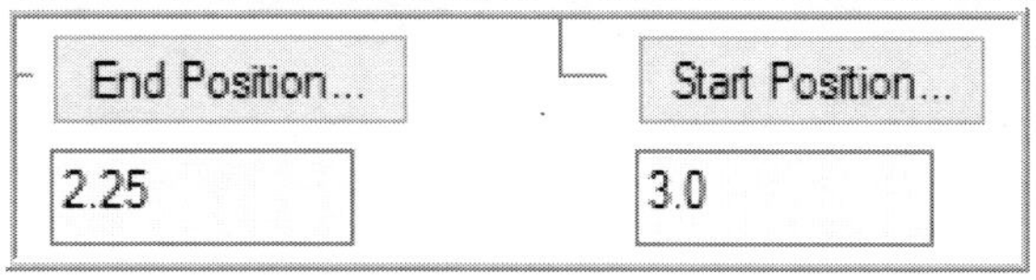

14. Click on the **Thread cut parameters** tab and makes changes as shown below:

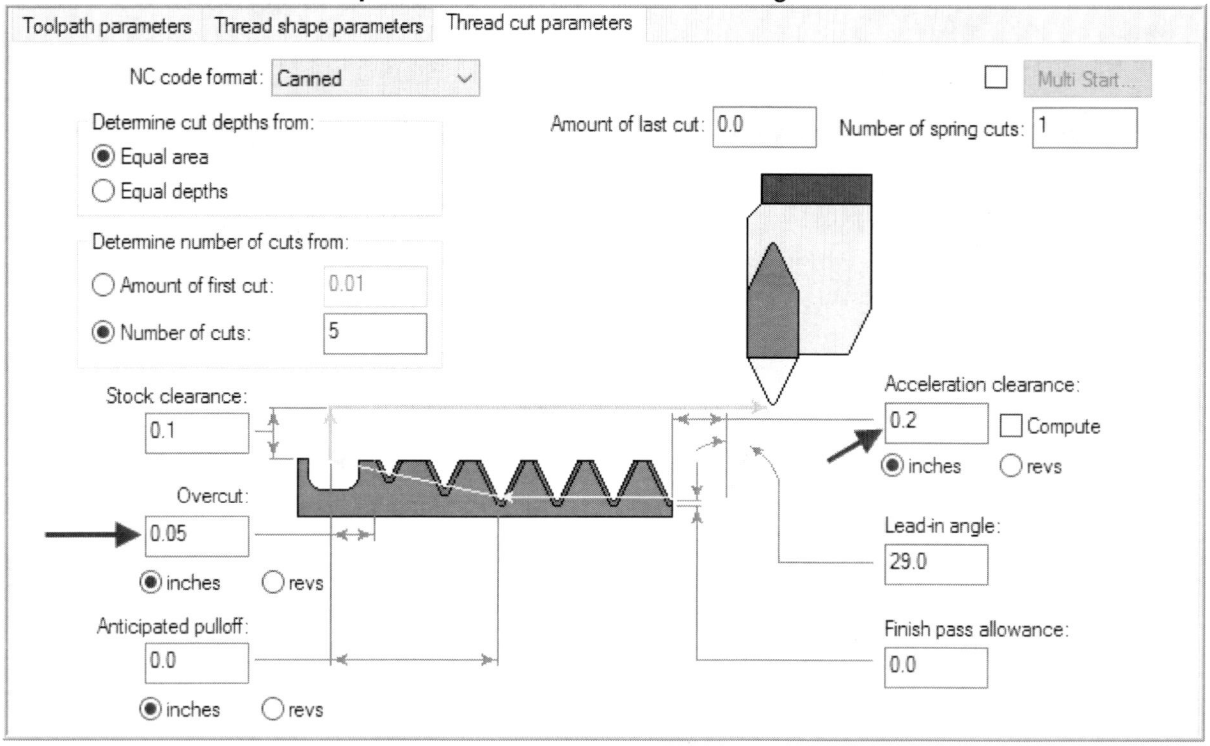

Overcut
Determines how far past the end of the thread the tool will go before retracting. Select units or revs to tell Mastercam which type of value you entered.

Acceleration clearance
Determines the distance necessary for the tool to accelerate to full speed in the Z direction before it starts cutting the thread. This is an incremental distance from the start of the thread along the Z axis.
The distance is set automatically if you check Compute.

15. Click on the OK icon .

TASK 13:
FINISH THE RADIUS

➲ In this task you will create a new Tool to machine and finish the 1.5" Radius.

1. Click on the **Expand gallery** down arrow to view additional options in the **General** toolpath section and in the **General** section select **Finish.**

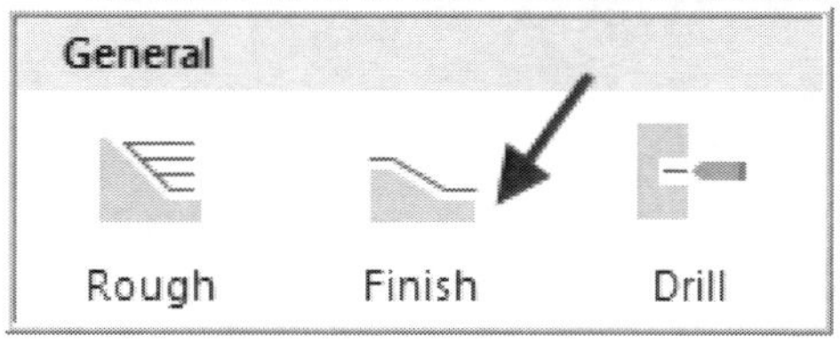

2. With the Chaining dialog box set to **Partial**, click on the radius as shown below:

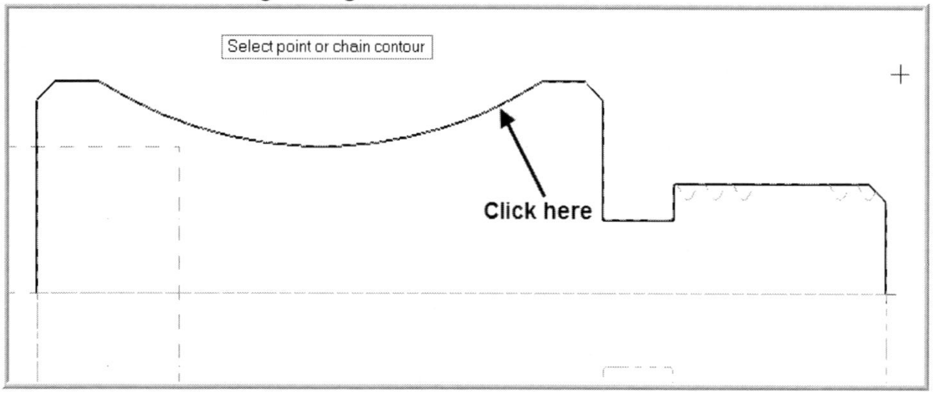

3. Click on the chamfer as shown below left: Arrows should be in the direction as shown below right after clicking on the chamfer.

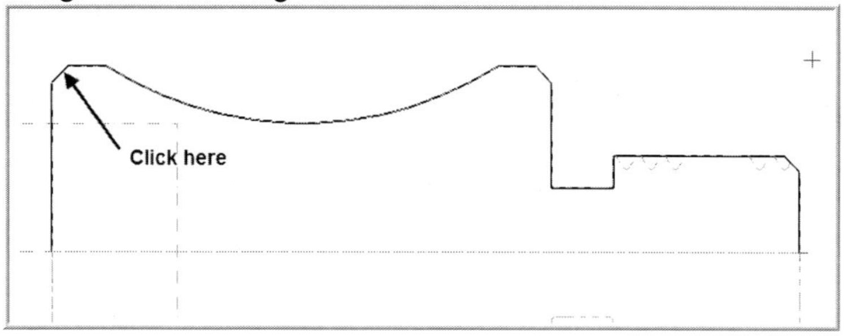

4. Click on OK  in the Chaining box.

5. Right Click the mouse in the white space as indicated by **arrow # 1** shown below.
6. Click on **Create new tool…** as indicated by **arrow # 2** as shown below.

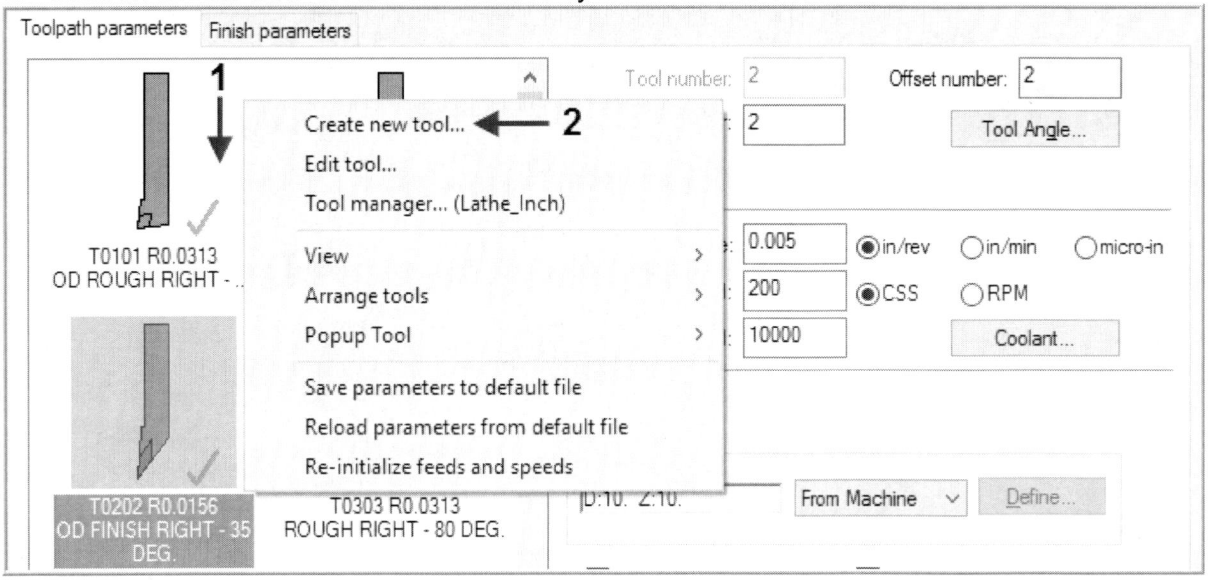

7. Click on the **General Turning** icon as shown below:

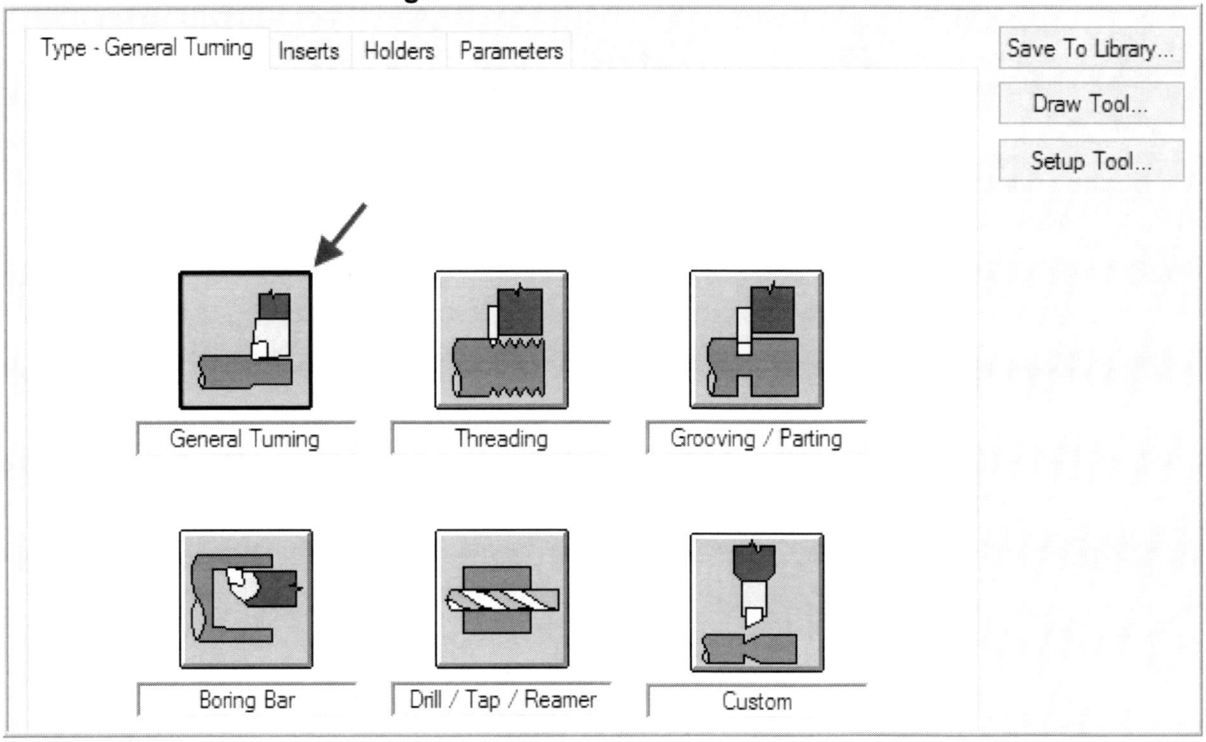

8. On the **Inserts** page click on the **V (35 deg. Diamond)** insert as shown below.

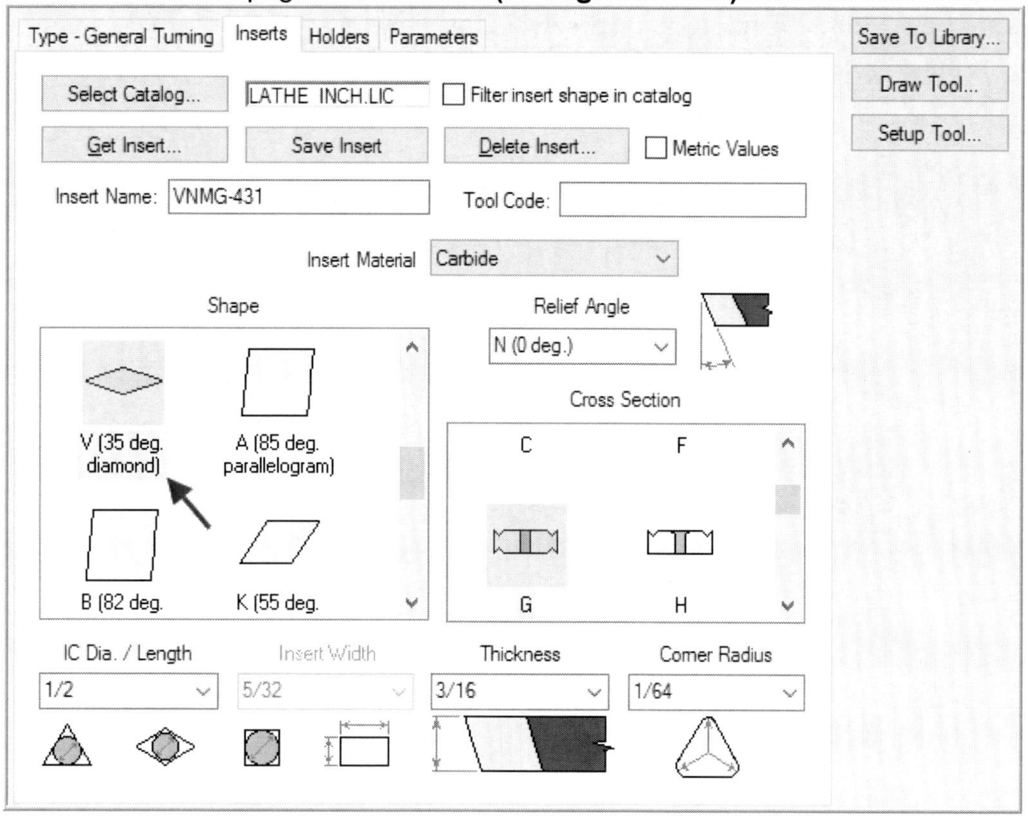

9. Click on the **Holders** Tab.
10. Scroll down and click on the **V (17.5 deg. Side clr.)** as shown below.

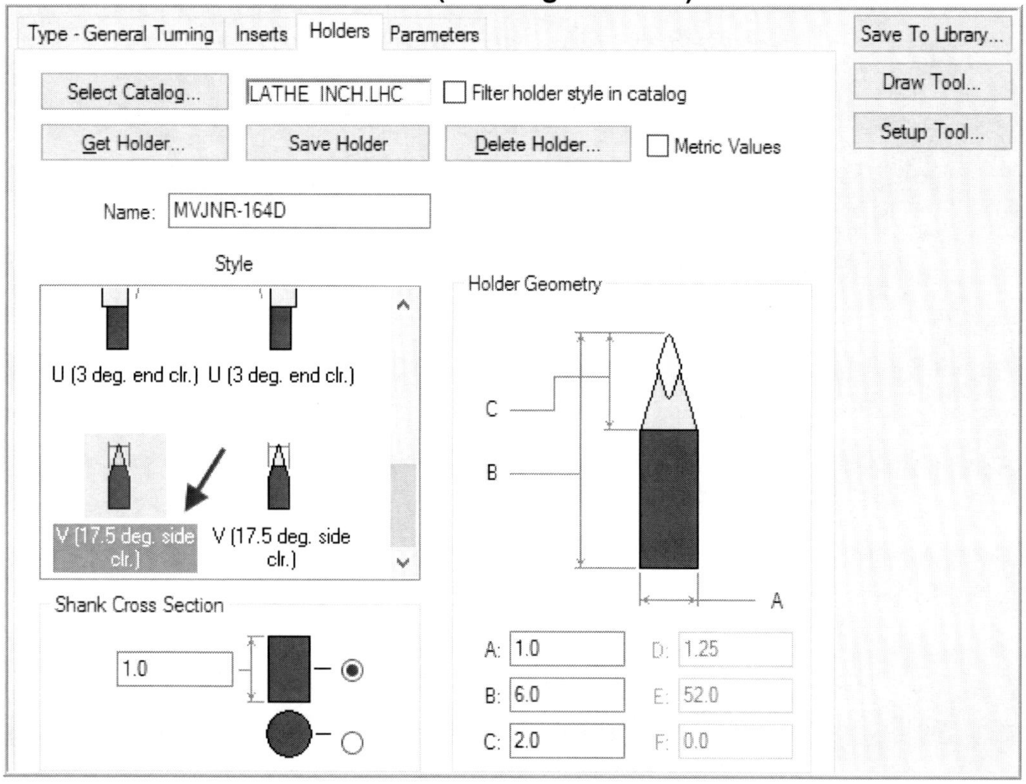

11. Click on the OK icon .

12. Make any necessary changes as shown below. **Coolant Flood** is set to **On**.

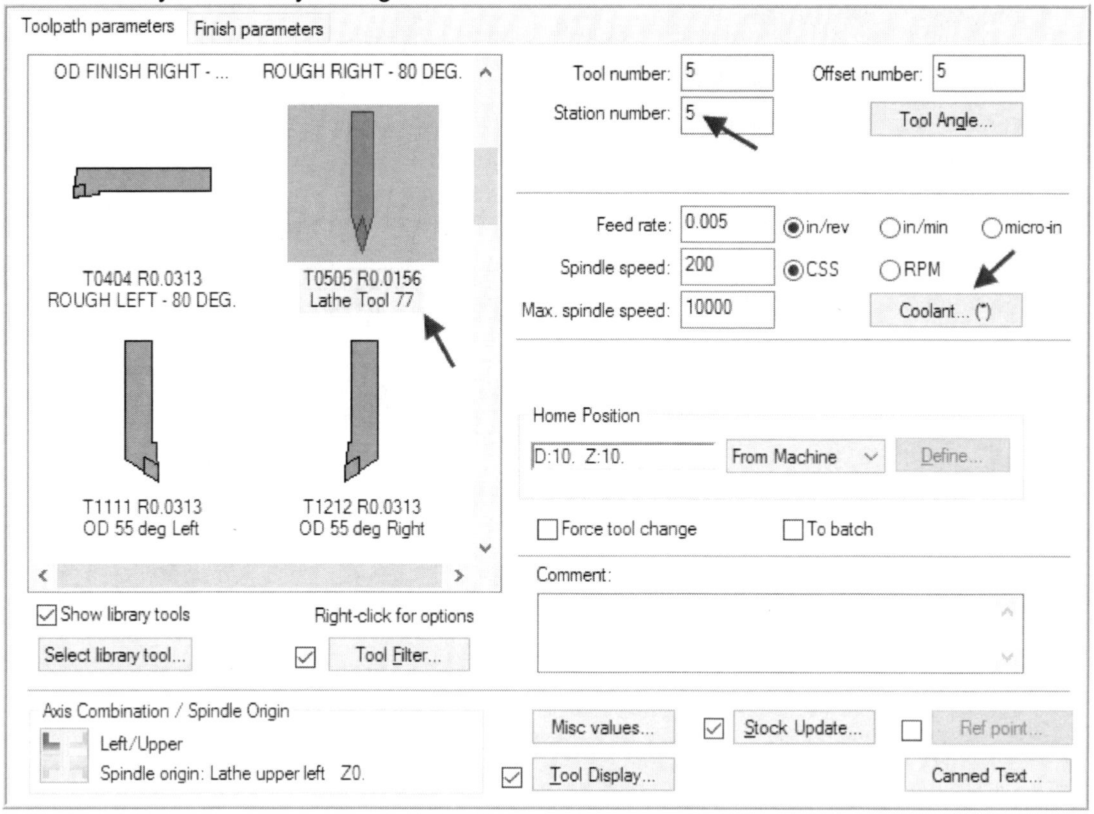

13. Click on the **Finish parameters** tab and make any necessary changes as shown below:

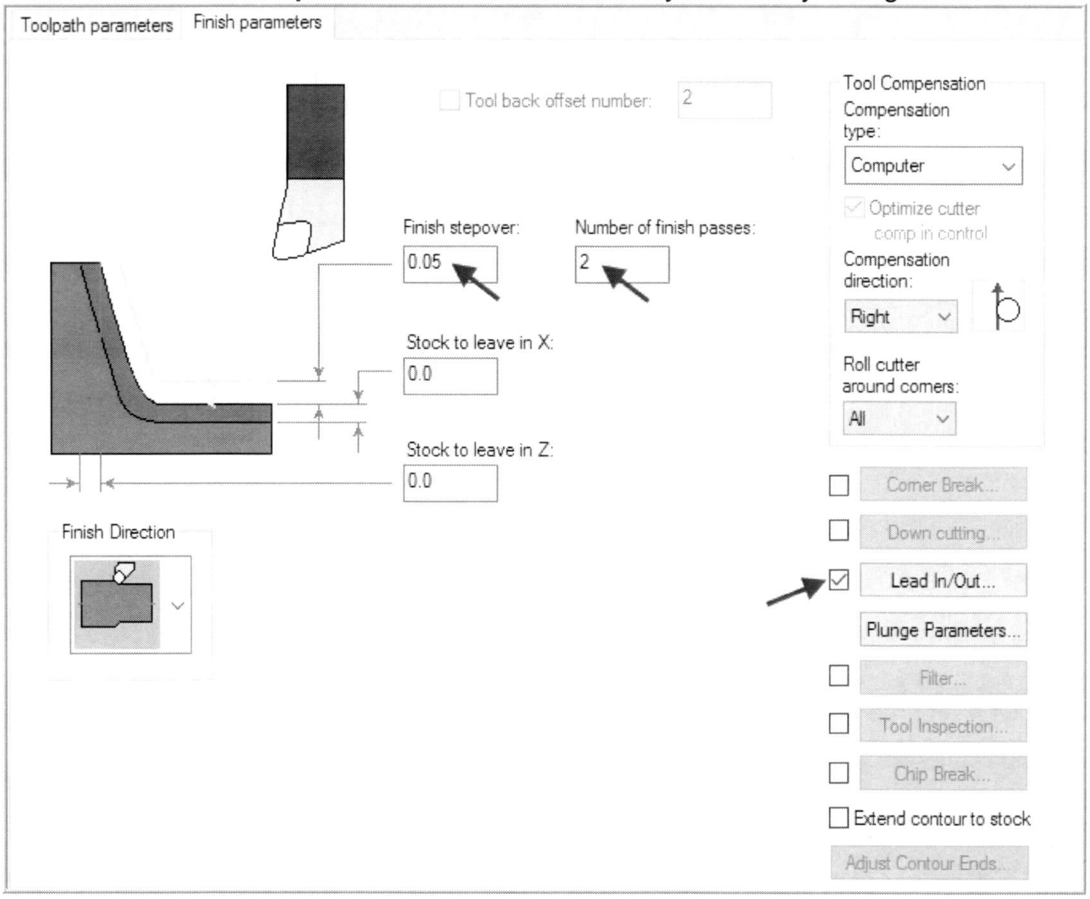

14. Click on the **Lead in/Out Button**.
15. On the **Lead in** page make the necessary changes as shown below. In order to adjust the dial (#1), click on the desired location of the arrow:

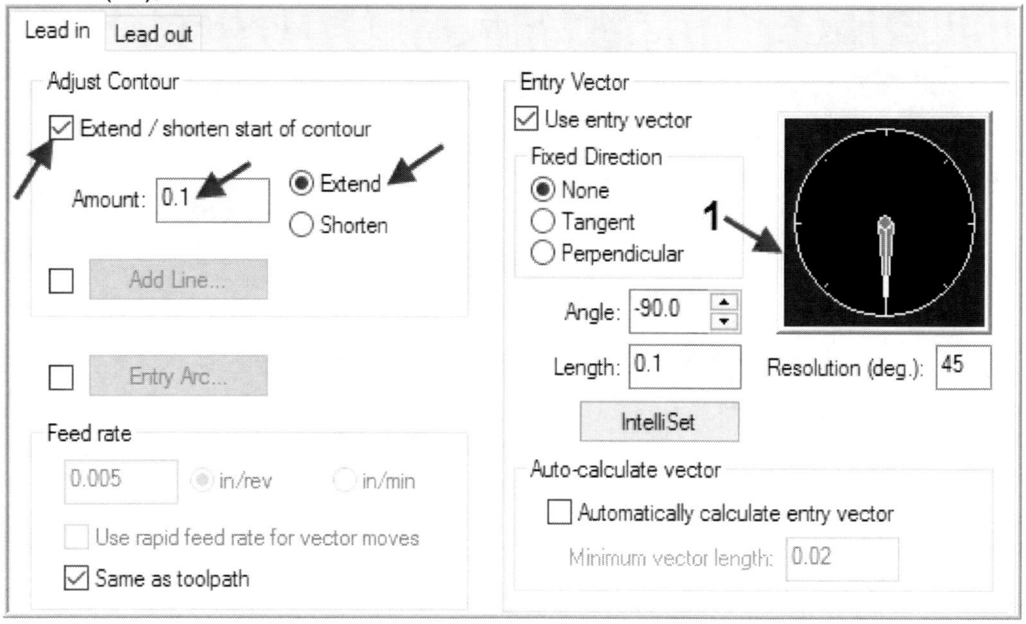

16. Click on the **Lead out Tab** and make the necessary changes as shown below:

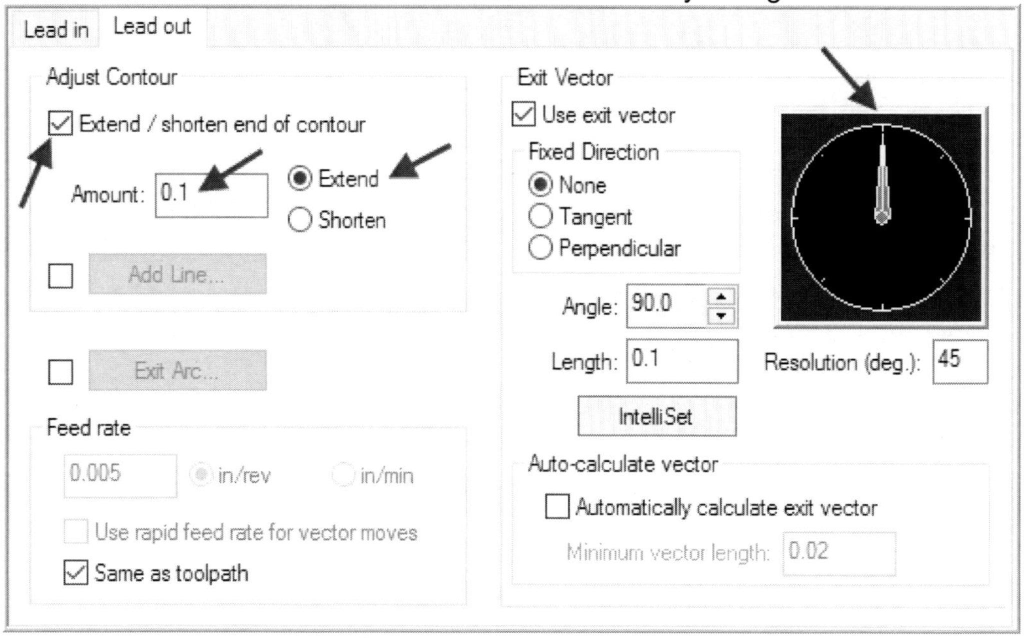

17. Click on OK  to exit the Lead In/out window.
18. Click on the **Plunge Parameters** button as shown below.

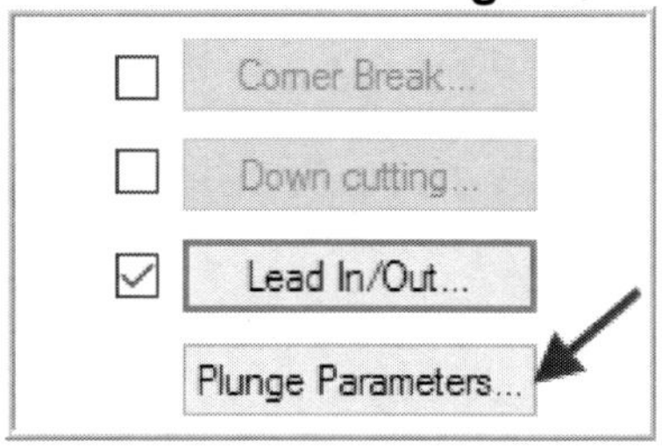

19. Make the necessary changes as shown below.

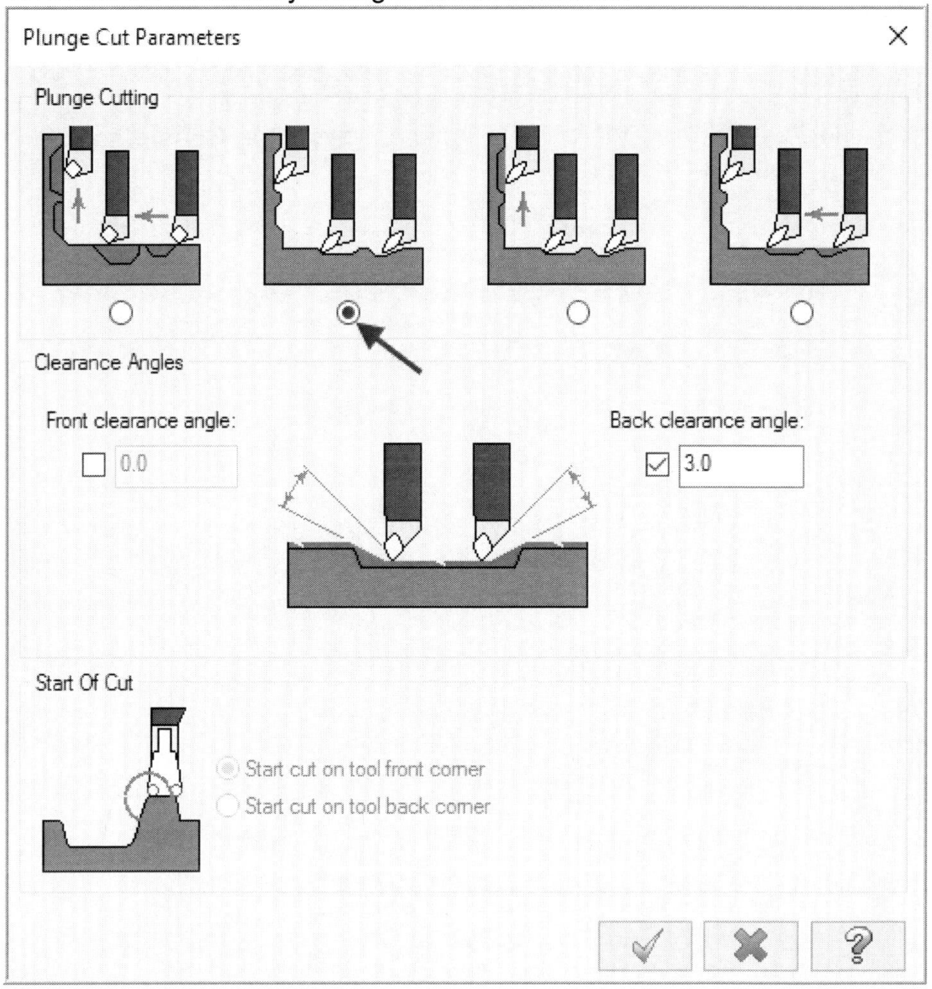

Plunge Cut Parameters dialog box
Use this dialog box to determine how you want the tool to handle undercuts along the toolpath. You can choose to plunge into undercuts in either X, Z, or both axes.

If you activate any of the plunge methods, use the other options to tell Mastercam how to begin the plunge move. Choose the options that fit best with your tool and part geometry.

You can choose whether or not to plunge at an angle for additional clearance at the undercut wall, and whether to start the plunge at the front or back of the tool.

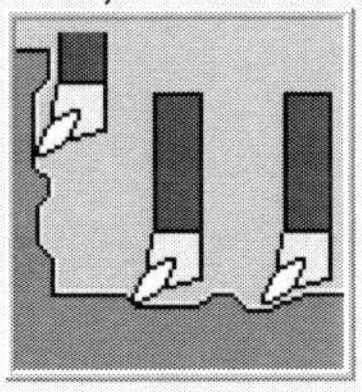
Allow plunging in both directions
The tool cuts into all undercuts on the chained path. Activates the Tool Width Compensation options. Not available for canned rough toolpaths.

20. Click on Ok 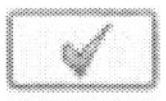 to exit the **Plunge Cut Parameters** window.
21. Click on Ok  to exit the **Lathe Finish parameters** window.

TASK 14:
CUT OFF THE PART

➲ In this task you will cut off the part using **Tool #3 0.125 OD GROOVE RIGHT HAND TOOL**

1. Click on the **Expand gallery** down arrow to view additional options in the **General** toolpath section. In the **General** section select **Cutoff.**

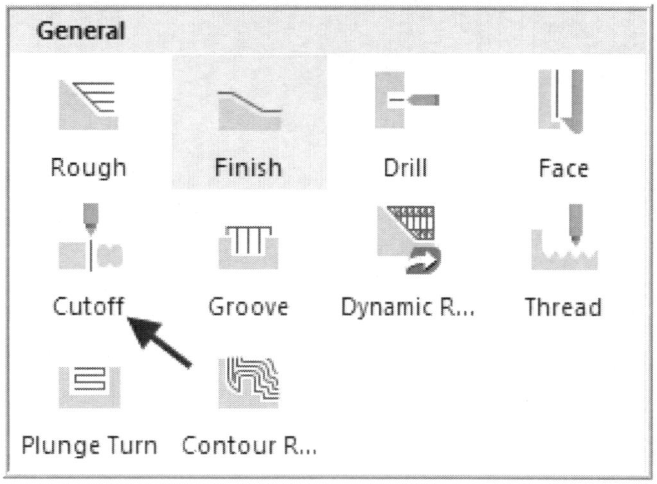

2. Pick the end point of the line shown below. Move the cursor over the corner until the visual cue for End point displays and then click on this point.

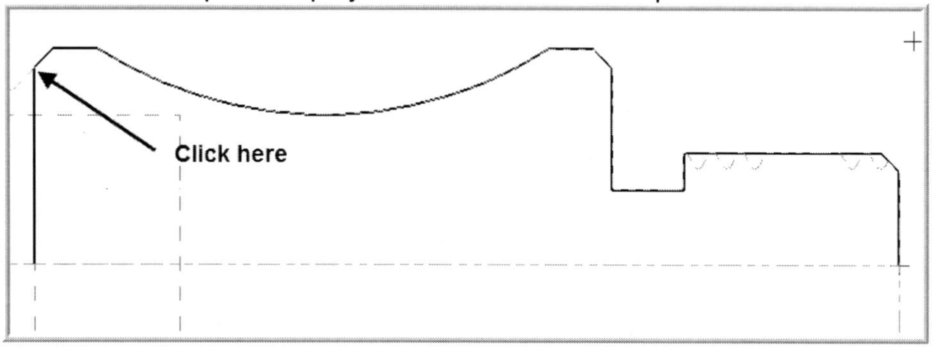

3. Select **Tool #3 OD GROOVE RIGHT WIDTH .125** tool from the tool list and make any necessary changes as shown below. **Coolant Flood** is set to **On**.

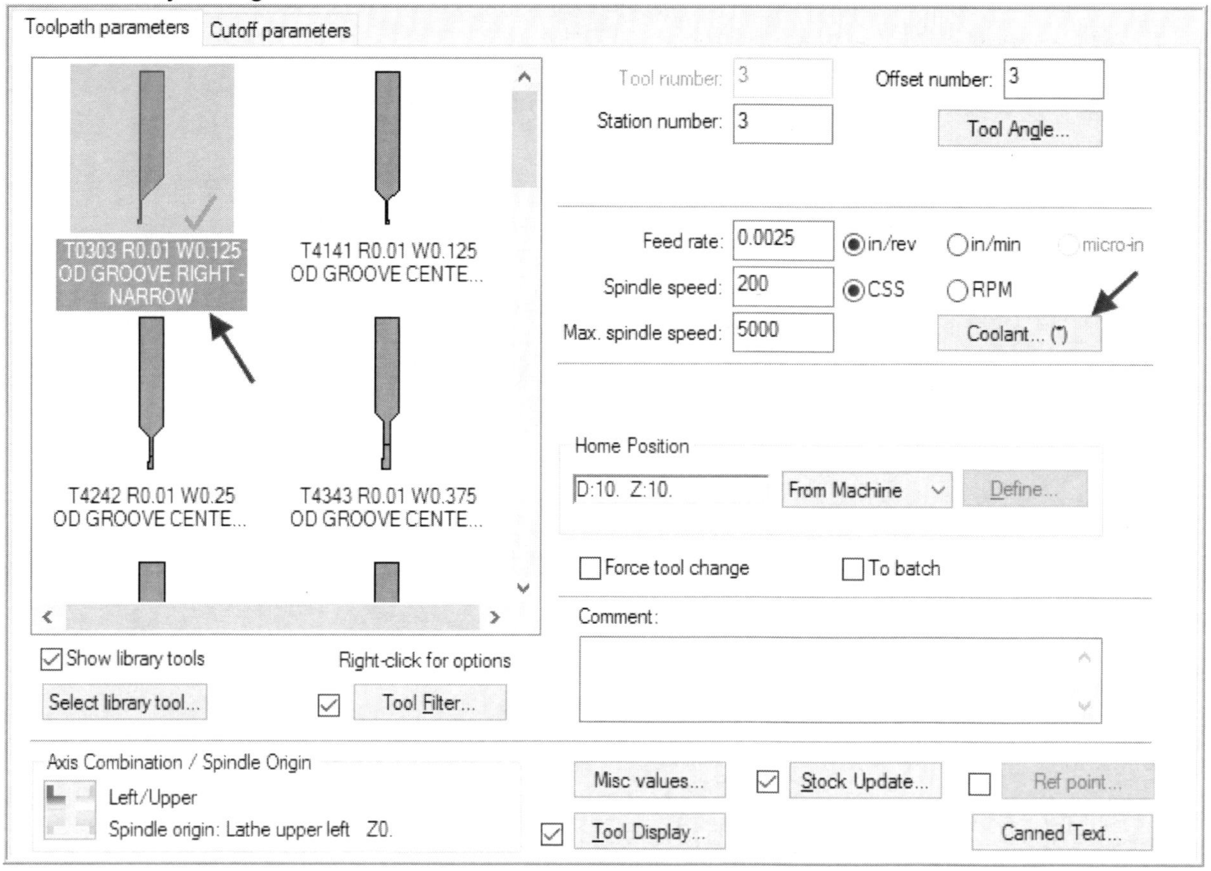

4. Still on the **Toolpath parameters** page click on the **Stock Update** button .

5. Ensure **Keep both pieces** is activated.

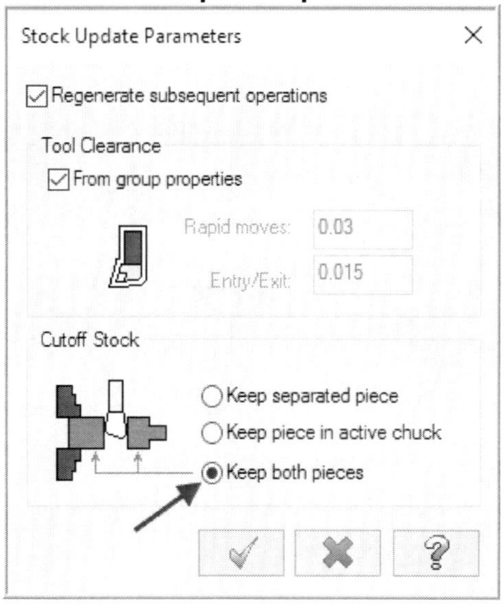

Keep separated piece
Select to display the part boundary after the part is cut off.
Keep piece in active chuck
Select to display the stock boundary after the part is cut off.

Keep both pieces
Select to display both the separated piece and the leftover piece. This is useful when the separated piece will be transferred to a sub spindle and you will be machining on both spindles at the same time.

These options are available only with cutoff operations.

6. Select the OK button  to exit **Stock Update Parameters**.

7. Select the **Cutoff parameters** page and make sure the settings are as shown below:

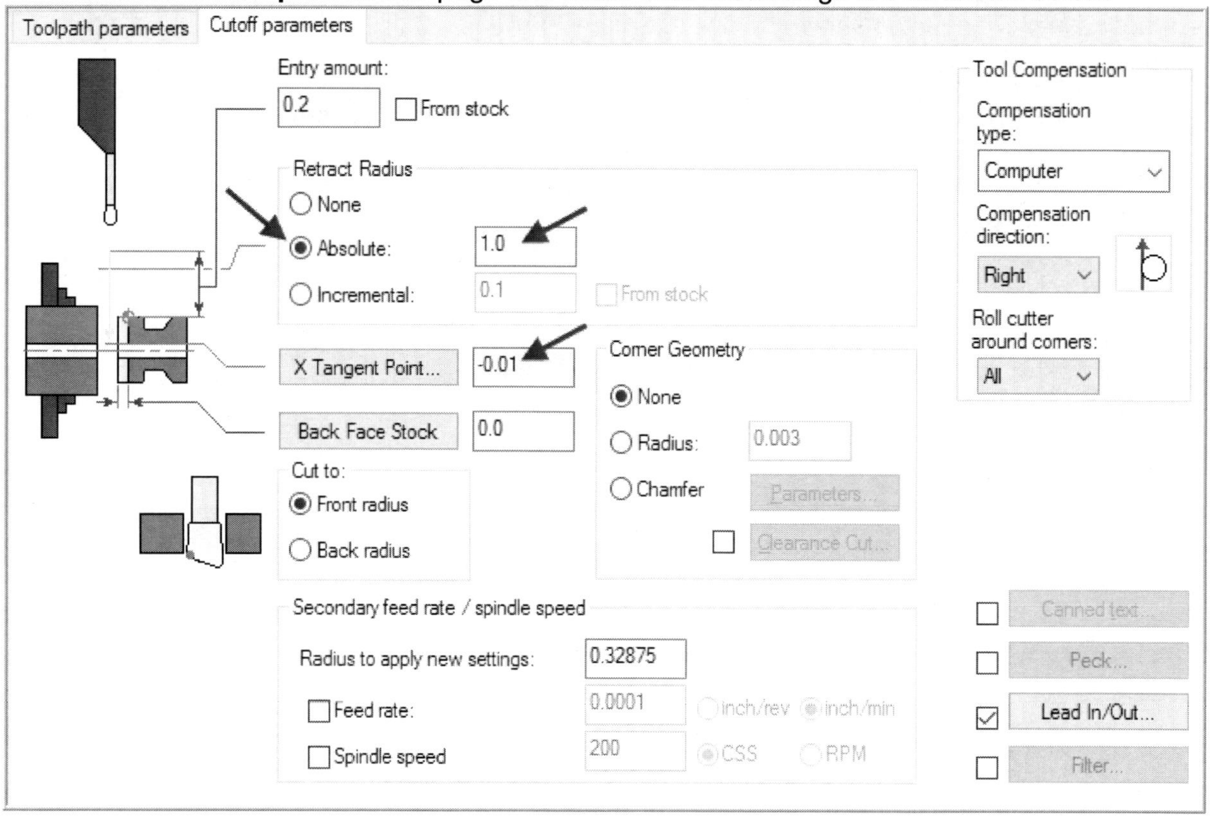

8. Select the OK button to exit **Lathe Cutoff parameters.**

Retract Radius
None - The tool will not retract before returning to the home position.

Absolute - Uses the exact value you enter to determine how far above the Z axis the tool will retract before moving to the home position..

Incremental - Determines how far above the Z axis the tool will retract before moving to the home position. Mastercam calculates this value relative to the current top of stock.

X Tangent Point
This determines the point on the part's radius to cut to. Choose the button and select a point on the geometry, or enter a value.
For example: when cutting a tube set this value to the ID radius of the tube.

TASK 15:
VERIFY THE TOOLPATH

➲ Mastercam's Verify utility allows you to use solid models to simulate the machining of a part. The model created by the verification represents the surface finish, and shows collisions, if any exist.

1. Right mouse click in the graphics area and click on the **Fit** icon .
2. In the Toolpaths Manager pick all the operations to Verify by picking the **Select All** icon .
3. Select the **Verify selected operations** icon shown below:

4. **Maximize** the Backplot/Verify window if required.
5. Now select the **Home** Tab if required.

6. Activate the options shown below in the **Visibility** section of the **Home** tab. **Initial Stock not** activated.

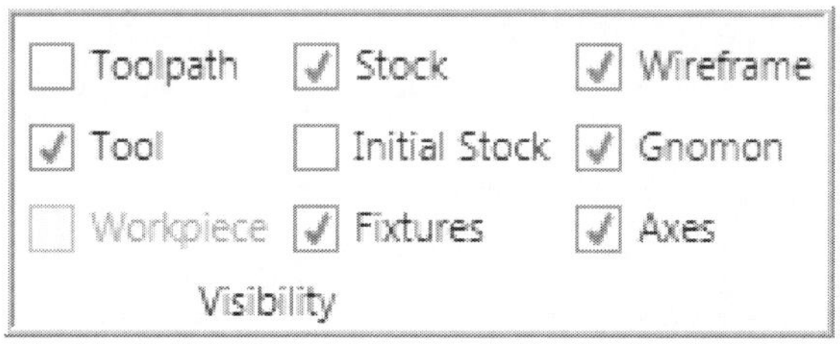

7. At the top of the screen select the **View** tab, the **Isometric** icon and then select **Fit**.

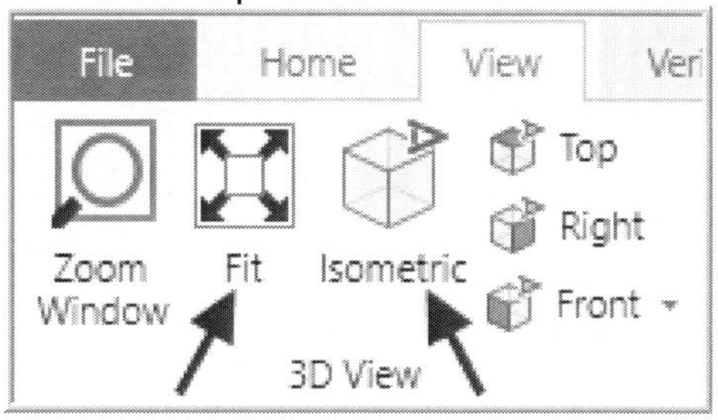

8. Select the **Verify** tab and activate the **Color Loop** to change the color of the tools for the verified part.

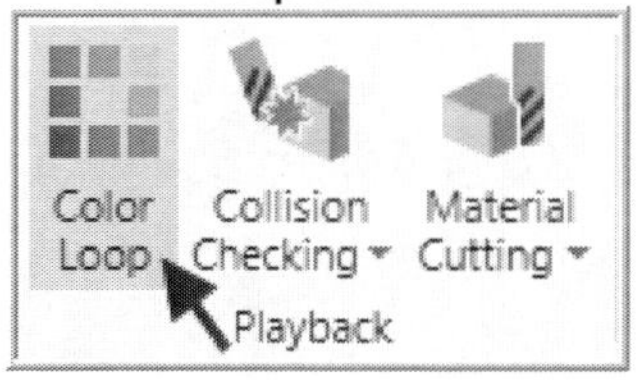

Color Loop
Changes the color of the toolpath or cut stock by operation or by tool change.

Choose **File Options** to set the colors.

9. In the lower part of the screen now set the run **Speed** to slow by moving the slider bar pointer over to the left as shown below.

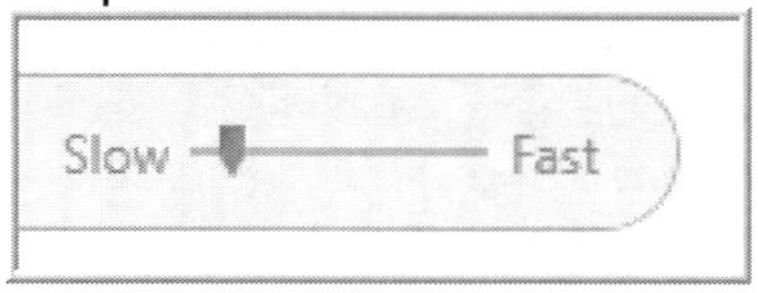

10. Now select the **Play Simulation** button to review the toolpaths.

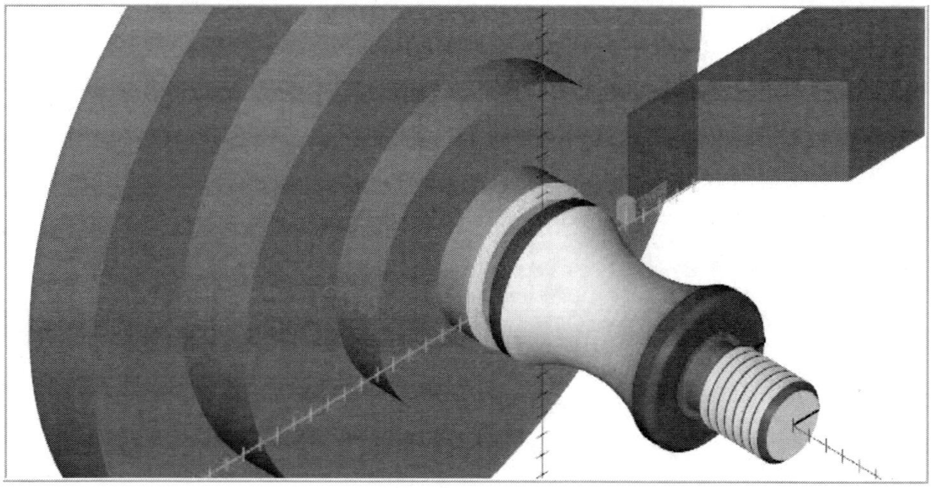

11. Select the Close button 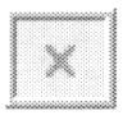 in the top right hand corner to exit Verify.

TASK 16:
SAVE THE UPDATED MASTERCAM FILE

1. Select the **Save** icon from the **Quick Access** toolbar at the top left of the screen.

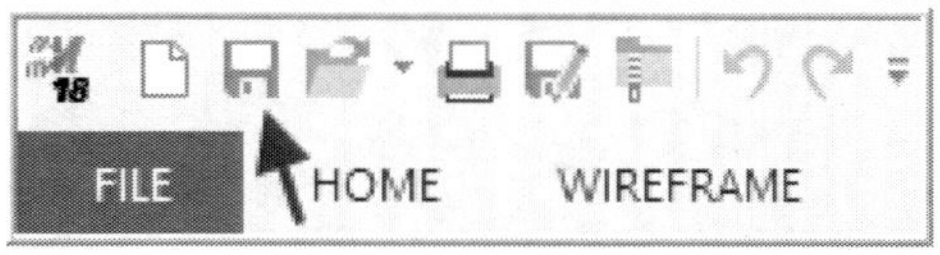

TASK 17:
POST AND CREATE THE CNC CODE FILE

1. Ensure all the operations are selected by picking the **Select All** icon  from the **Toolpaths manager.**
2. Select the **Post selected operations** button from the Toolpaths manager.

➲ **Please Note:** If you cannot see **G1** click on the right pane of the Toolpaths manager window and expand the window to the right.

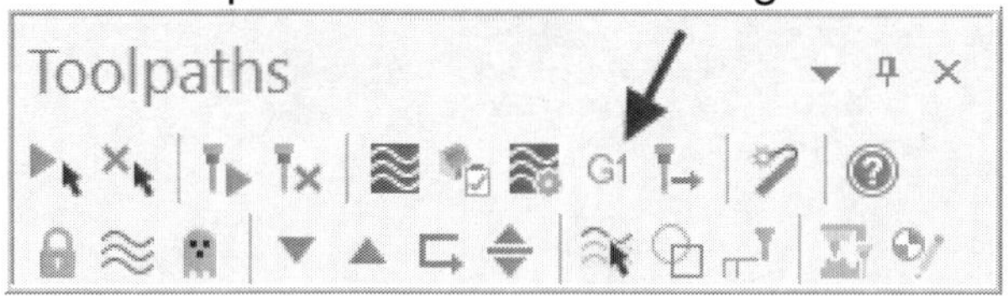

3. In the Post processing window, make the necessary changes as shown below:

About Post Processing

NC file:
Select this option to save the NC file. The file name and extension are stored in the machine group properties for the selected operation. If you are posting operations from different machine groups or Mastercam files, or batch processing, Mastercam will create several files according to the settings for each machine group.

Edit:
When checked, automatically launches the default text editor with the file displayed so that you can review or modify it.

4. Select the OK button  to continue.

5. Ensure the same name as your Mastercam part file name is displayed in the **NC File name** field.
6. Select the **Save** button.
7. The CNC code file opens up in the default editor.

Lathe-Lesson-4.NC ×

```
(MATERIAL - ALUMINUM INCH - 6061)
G20
(TOOL - 1 OFFSET - 1)
(OD ROUGH RIGHT - 80 DEG.  INSERT - CNMG-432)
G0 T0101
G18
G97 S449 M03
G0 G54 X1.7 Z3. M8
G50 S3600
G96 S200
G99 G1 X-.1225 F.01
G0 Z3.1
X1.2928
Z3.2
G1 Z3.1
Z2.0017
G18 G3 X1.3138 Z1.9944 I-.0151 K-.033
G1 X1.4388 Z1.9319
```

8. Select the  in the top right corner to exit the CNC editor.

➲ This completes Lathe-Lesson-4.

LATHE-LESSON-4 EXERCISE

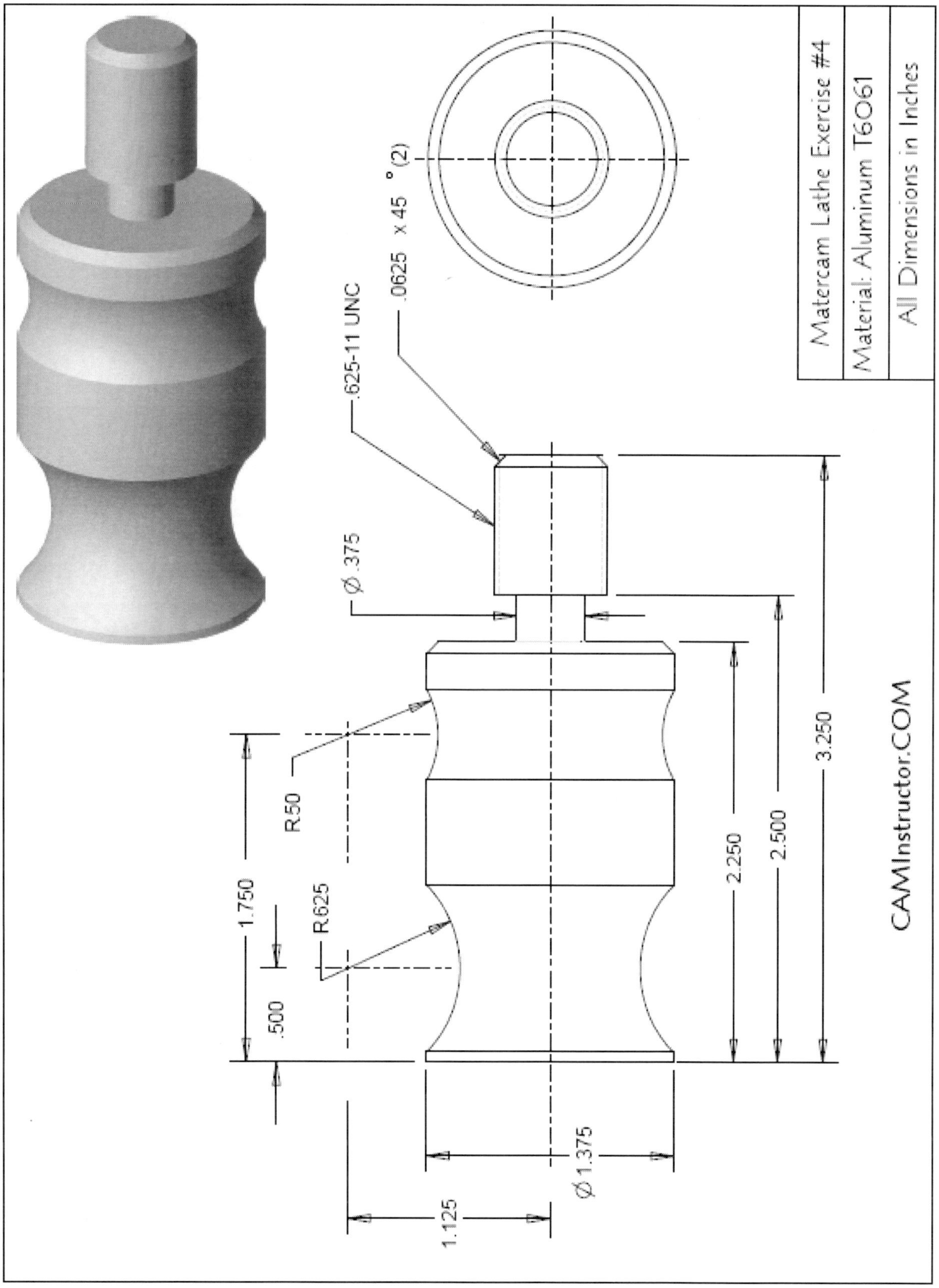

Mastercam® 2018

TRAINING GUIDE

LATHE-LESSON-5

FACE, ROUGH, FINISH, DRILL, BORE AND CUTOFF

camInstructor

Objectives

You will create the geometry for Lathe Lesson 5, and then generate a toolpath to machine the part on a CNC lathe. This lesson covers the following topics:

➲ **Create a 2-dimensional drawing by:**
Creating lines.
Creating fillets.
Creating chamfers.
Trimming geometry.

➲ **Establish Stock and Chuck Setup settings:**
Stock size.
Chuck Configuration.
Material for the part.
Feed calculation.

➲ **Generate a 2-dimensional lathe toolpath consisting of:**
Lathe Face.
Lathe Rough.
Lathe Finish.
Lathe Drill.
Lathe Cutoff.

➲ **Inspect the toolpath using Mastercam's Verify and Backplot by:**
Launching the Verify function to machine the part on the screen.
Generating the NC- code.

LATHE - LESSON - 5 DRAWING

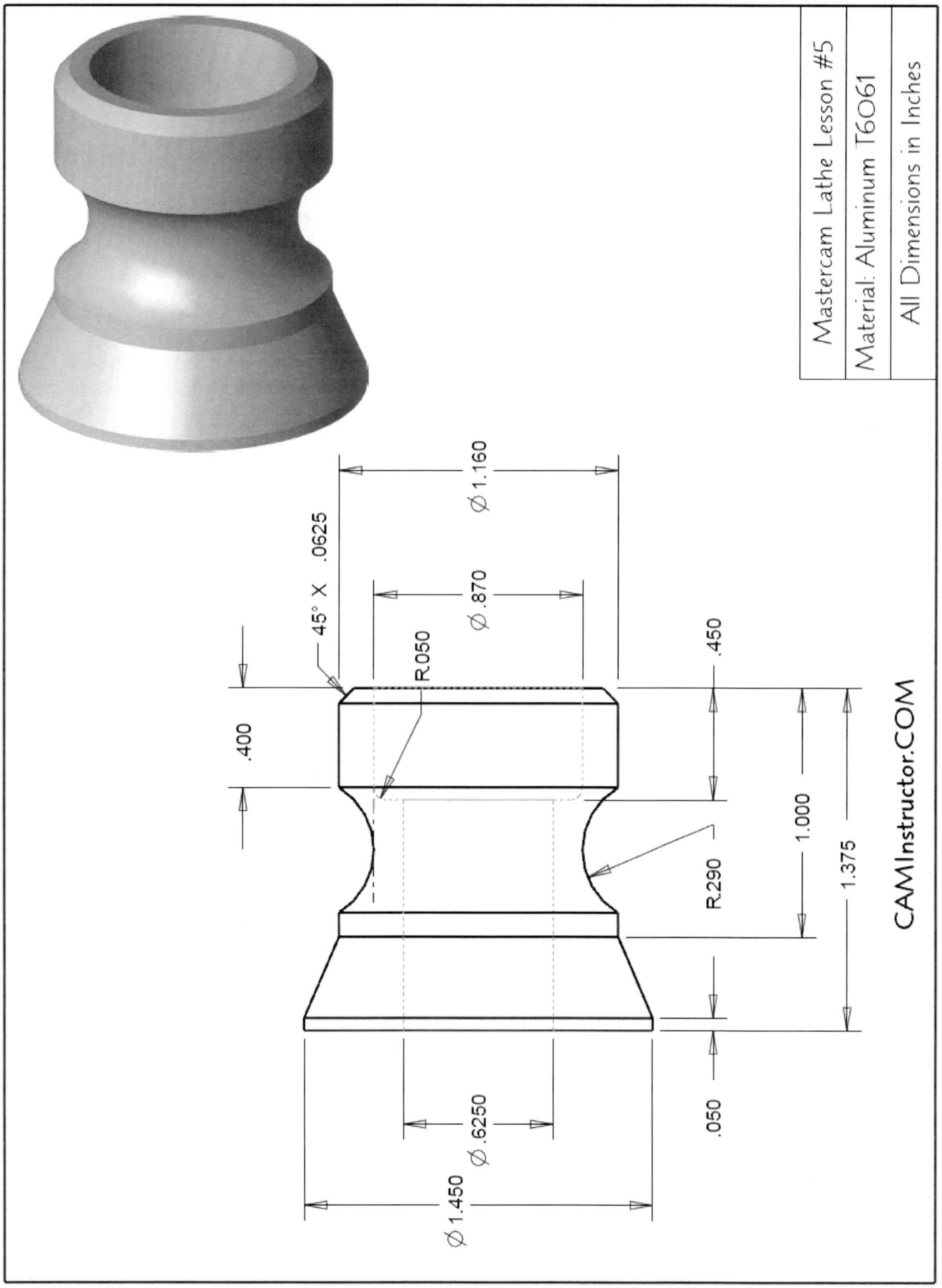

TOOL LIST

Seven tools will be used to create this part.

- **Tool #1 Face and Rough the outside diameters**
  Holder: Outside Diameter Rough Right Hand - DCGNR-164D.
  Insert: 80 Degree Diamond Insert – CNMG-432

- **Tool #2 Finish the outside diameters**
  Holder: Outside Diameter Finish Right Hand - MVJNR-164D.
  Insert: 35 Degree Diamond Insert – VNMG-431.

- **Tool #3 Center drill**
  Centre Drill – body diameter 0.250”

- **Tool #4 0.375 diameter drill**
  Drill 0.375” diameter

- **Tool #5 0.500 diameter drill**
  Drill 0.375” diameter

- **Tool #6 Boring tool**
  Holder: Boring Bar – minimum diameter 0.375”.
  Insert: 75 Degree Diamond Insert

- **Tool #7 Cutoff tool**
  Holder: Outside Diameter Groove Right Hand - Narrow.
  Insert: 0.125” Wide - GC-4125

LESSON - 5 - THE PROCESS

Geometry Creation

TASK 1: Setting the environment
TASK 2: Setting the construction planes
TASK 3: Create the geometry
TASK 4: Create the 0.290" radius
TASK 5: Create the geometry for the bore
TASK 6: Create the chamfers
TASK 7: Save the drawing

Toolpath Creation

TASK 8: Define the stock and chuck parameters
TASK 9: Face the front of the part
TASK 10: Rough the outside diameters
TASK 11: Finish the outside diameters
TASK 12: Center drill hole
TASK 13: Pre drill the 0.625" hole 0.375 diameter
TASK 14: Pre drill the 0.625" hole 0.5 diameter
TASK 15: Rough the bore
TASK 16: Finish the bore
TASK 17: Cut off the part
TASK 18: Verify the toolpath
TASK 19: Save the updated Mastercam file
TASK 20: Post and create the CNC code file

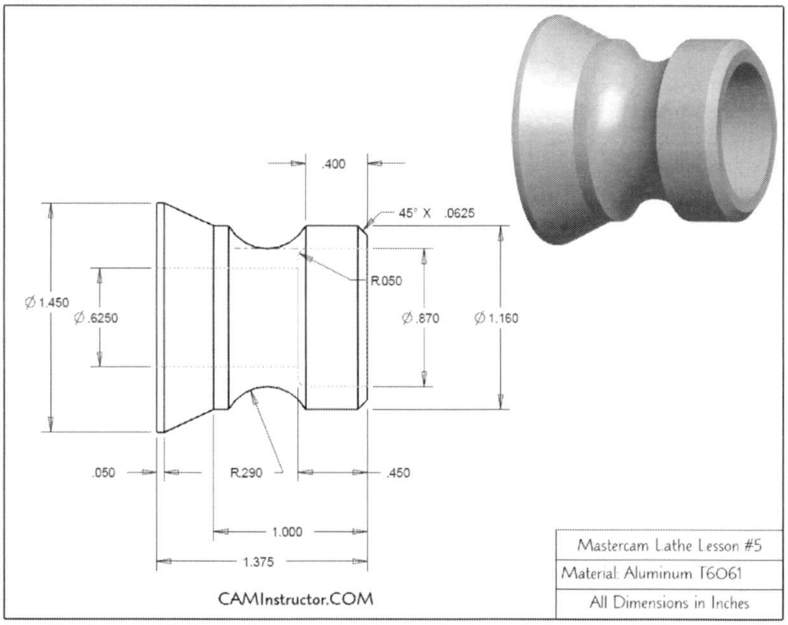

Geometry Creation

TASK 1:
SETTING THE ENVIRONMENT

Before starting the geometry creation you should set up the grid and machine type as outlined in the **Setting the Environment** section at the beginning of this text:

1. Set up the Grid. This will help identify the location of the origin.
2. Set the machine type to the default Lathe.

TASK 2:
SETTING THE CONSTRUCTION PLANES:

➲ **Set the Construction Plane to Lathe diameter +D +Z (WCS)**

1. Select the **View tab** and click on **Toolpaths** and **Solids** in the **Managers** section to **hide** them and toggle **only** the **Planes Manager to display**.

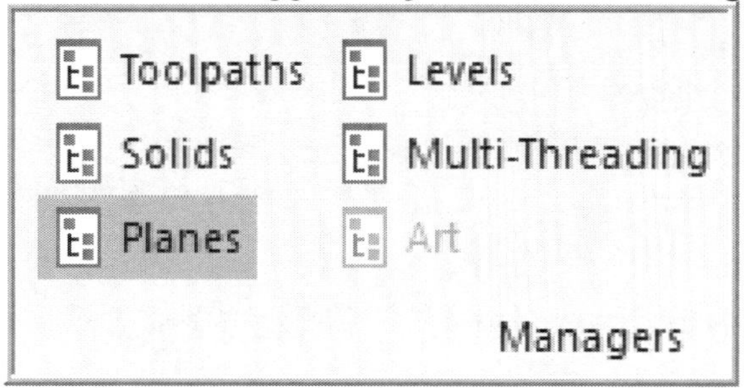

Once your machine is set up, Mastercam includes special lathe construction planes that let you work in **radius or diameter coordinates**.

For conventional 2D turning applications, use the Planes Manager to select the desired coordinate system, as shown below right.
Choose to use either radius or diameter coordinates and then choose the desired X/D and Z directions.

2. Ensure the **C column** (Construction Plane) and **T column** (Tool Plane) are set to the **+D +Z Plane**. Just click in the C and T columns in the **+D +Z** row.

➲ Take note of the **Status bar** at the bottom of the screen **CPLANE: +D +Z TPLANE: +D +Z WCS:TOP** as shown below right.

3. To change the **Lathe Plane** open up the drop down menu for **Select lathe plane** and click on the required coordinate system as shown below right.

4. Select the **Close** button ☒ in the top right hand corner to close the Planes Manager.

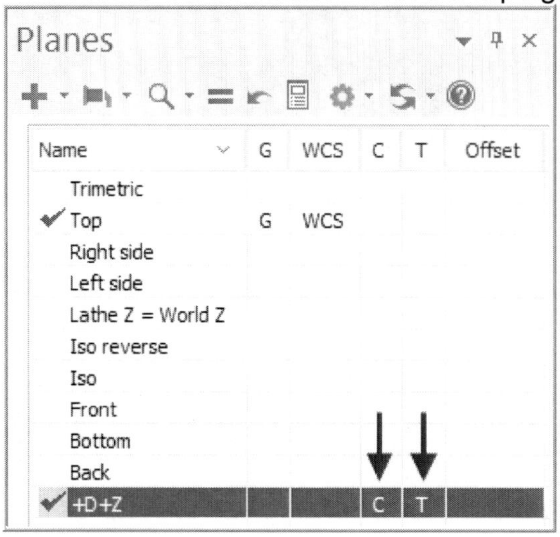

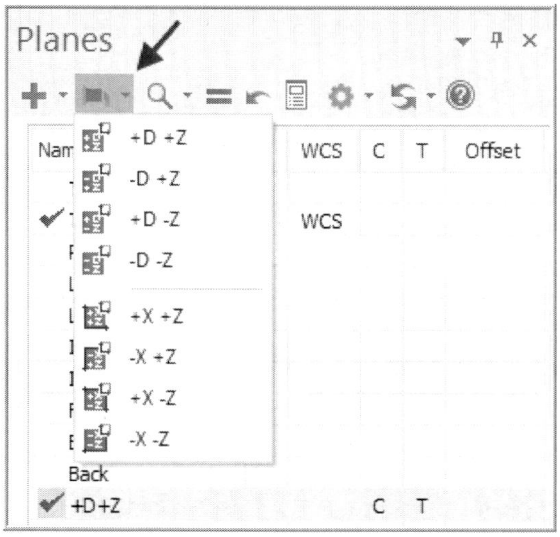

TASK 3:
CREATE THE GEOMETRY

➲ This task explains how to create the geometry of this part. In this lathe part you only need to create **half of the geometry**, the geometry above the center line.

➲ Lines 1 through 6 will be created first and then the radius and chamfer will be created.

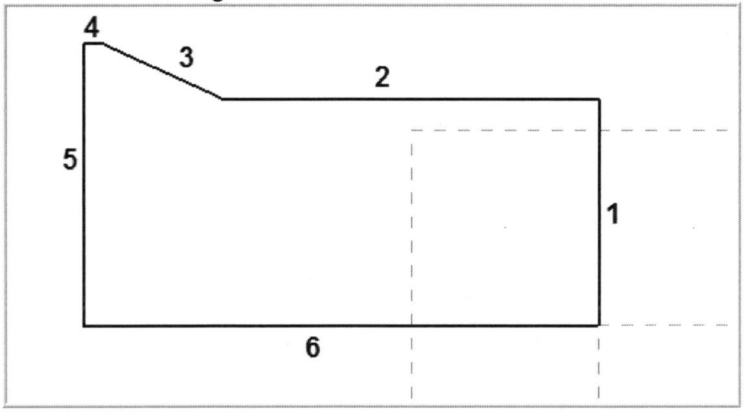

➲ **Create Line #1**

1. Select the **WIREFRAME** tab at the top of the screen and in the **Lines** section click on **Line Endpoints**.
2. On the graphics screen you are prompted: **Specify the first endpoint** and the Line Endpoints panel appears. In the Line Endpoints panel **activate Multi-line and Freeform**.

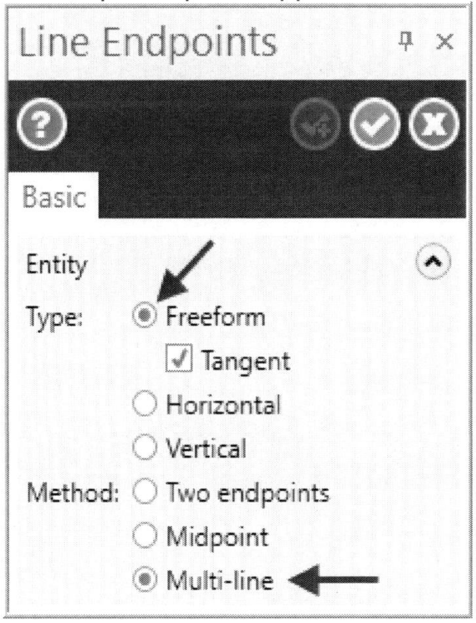

3. Move the cursor over the **center of the grid** and as you get close to the origin a visual cue appears. 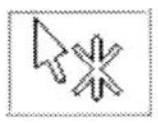 This is the cue that will allow you to snap to the **origin**. With this visual cue highlighted pick the **origin.**
4. You are now prompted to **"Specify the second endpoint"**. To satisfy this prompt **just type** the coordinate, **type 1.16,0**. This is **D1.16 Z0**. As you begin to type the **Fastpoint** opens. Hit the **Enter** key when done.

➲ A vertical line should be visible as shown below left.

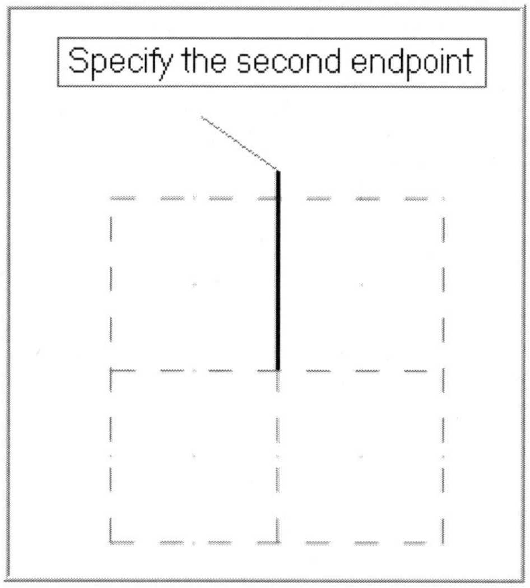

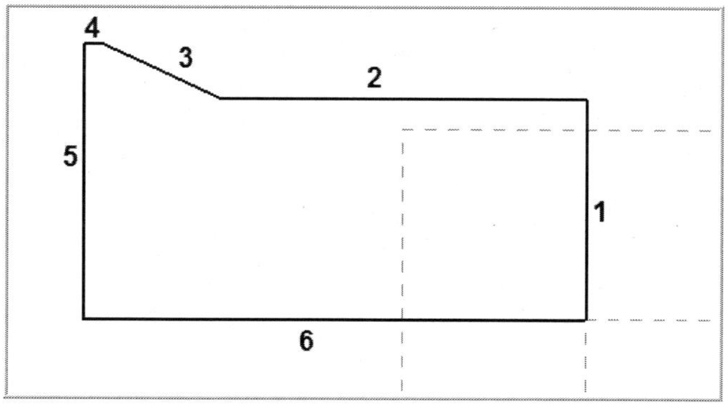

➲ **Create Line #2**

5. Type **1.16,-1.0** to satisfy the prompt **"Specify the second endpoint"** and hit the Enter key to complete this line.

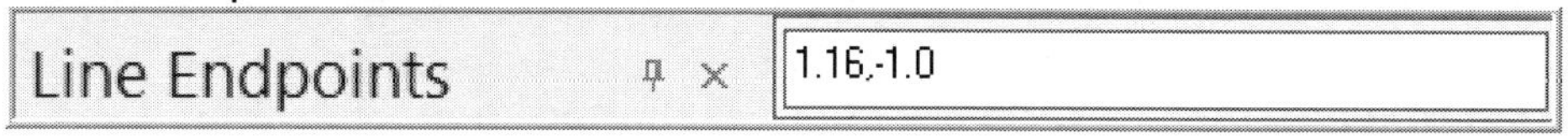

➲ **Create Line #3**

6. **Type 1.45,-1.325** to satisfy the prompt **"Specify the second endpoint"** and hit the Enter key to complete this line.

➲ **Create Line #4**

7. **Type 1.45,-1.375** to satisfy the prompt **"Specify the second endpoint"** and hit the Enter key to complete this line.

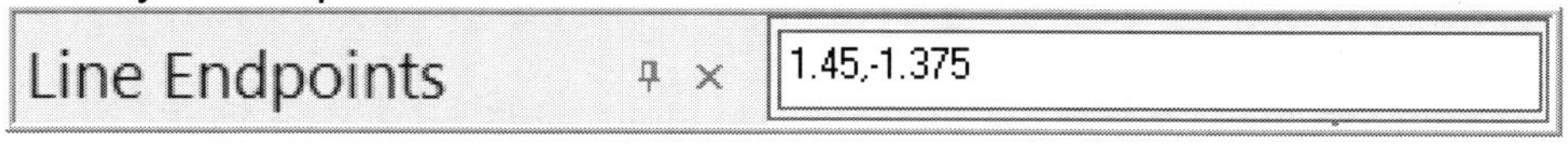

➲ **Create Line #5**

8. **Type 0,-1.375** to satisfy the prompt **"Specify the second endpoint"** and hit the Enter key to complete this line.

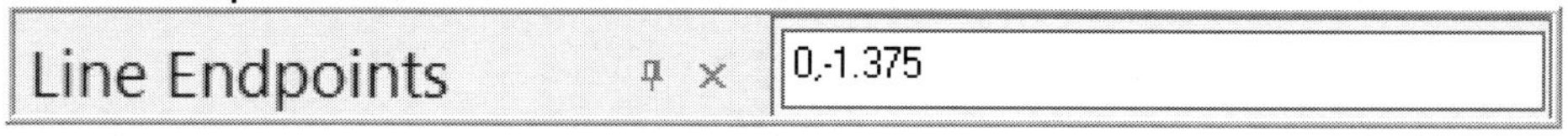

➲ **Create Line #6**

9. **"Specify the second endpoint";** Move the cursor over the **center of the grid** and as you get close to the origin a visual cue appears. 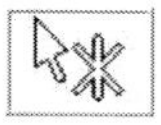 Click on this point.
10. Click on the **OK** icon  to complete this feature.
11. Right mouse click in the graphics area and click on the **Fit** icon .
12. Right mouse click in the graphics area and click on **Unzoom 80%** to shrink the display.

➲ Your geometry should now look like the figure above right at the top of the page.

TASK 4:
CREATE THE 0.290" RADIUS

➲ In this task you will create the 0.290 arc. It is an arc tangent to a line and passes through a point.

➲ **Create the line the arc is tangent to.**

1. Select the **WIREFRAME** tab if required and in the **Lines** section click on **Line Parallel**.

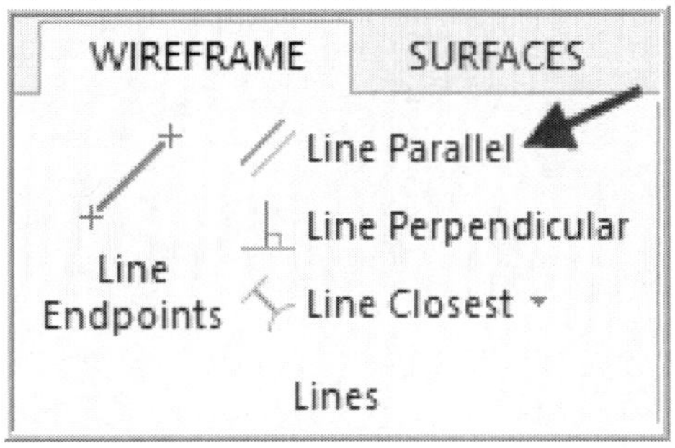

➲ On the graphics screen you are prompted: "**Select a line"** and the Line Parallel panel appears.

2. First click in the space for **Offset Distance** and input **0.4** then hit **Enter**.
3. To satisfy the prompt **Select a line**, select the line shown below.

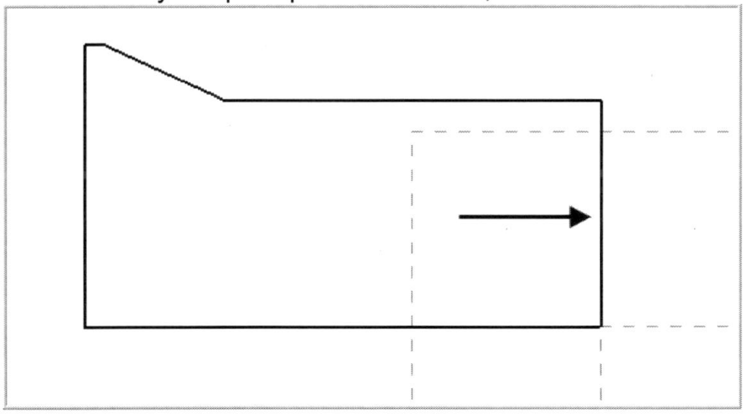

4. To satisfy the next prompt **Indicate the offset direction** move the cursor to the left of the line and pick a point.
5. Click on the **OK and Create New Operation** icon .

6. Click in the space for **Offset Distance** and input **0.870/2** then hit **Enter**.
7. To satisfy the prompt **Select a line**, select the line shown below.

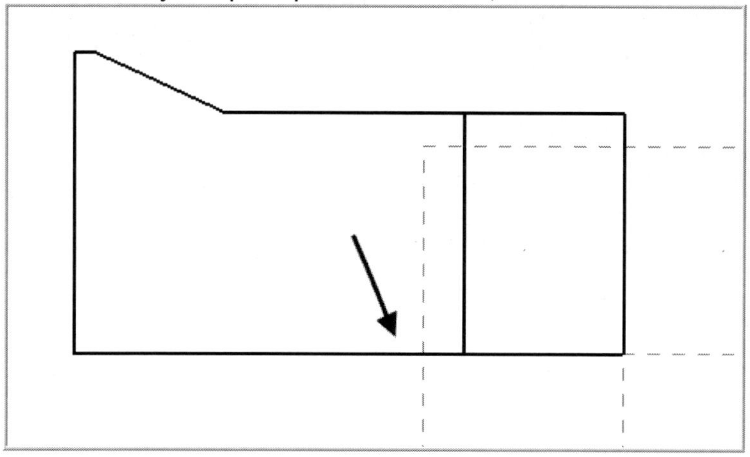

8. To satisfy the next prompt **Indicate the offset direction** move the cursor above the line and pick a point.
9. Click on the **OK** icon  to complete this feature.

➲ The completed geometry is shown below.

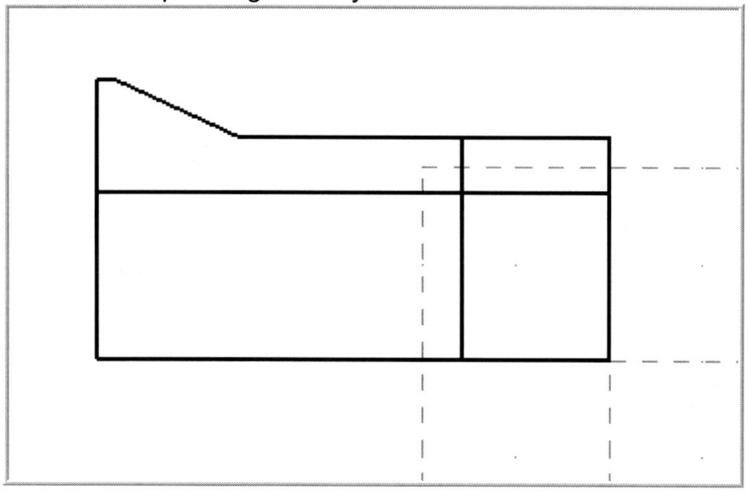

➲ **Create the 0.290" Arc**

10. In the **WIREFRAME** tab select **Arc Tangent** in the **Arcs** section.

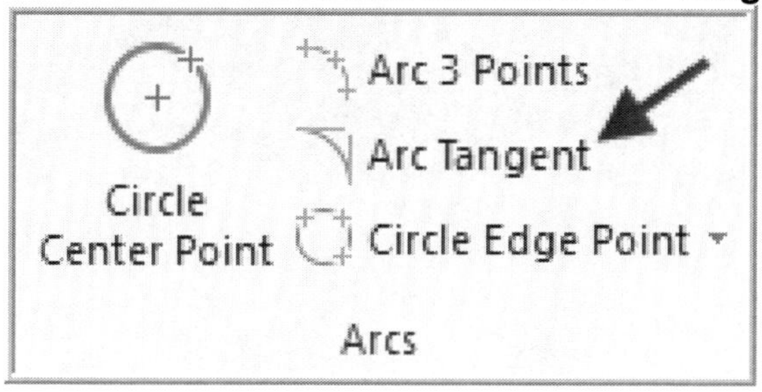

11. The **Arc Tangent** panel appears. Open up the drop down menu for **Mode** and select **Arc one point.** Click in the space for **Radius** and enter a value of **0.290** and then hit the **Enter** key.

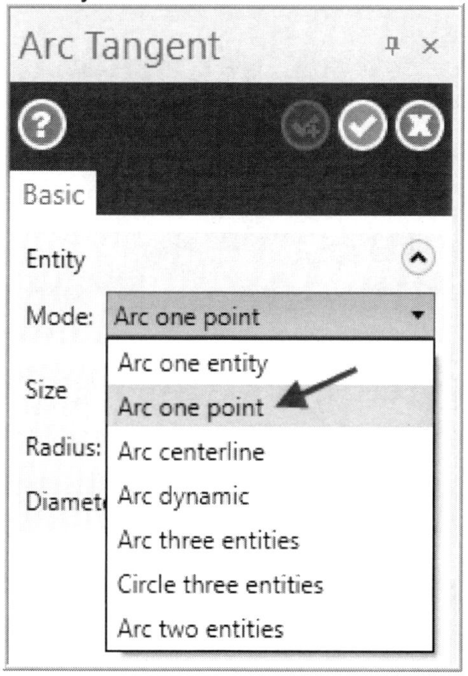

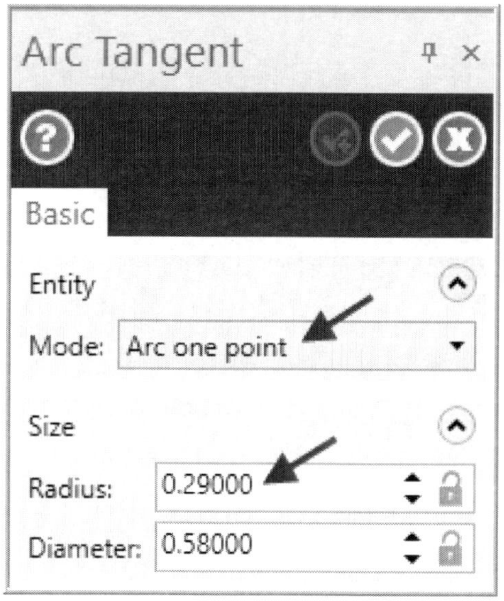

12. To satisfy the prompt **Select the entity that the arc is to be tangent to** move the cursor over the line shown below and select it:

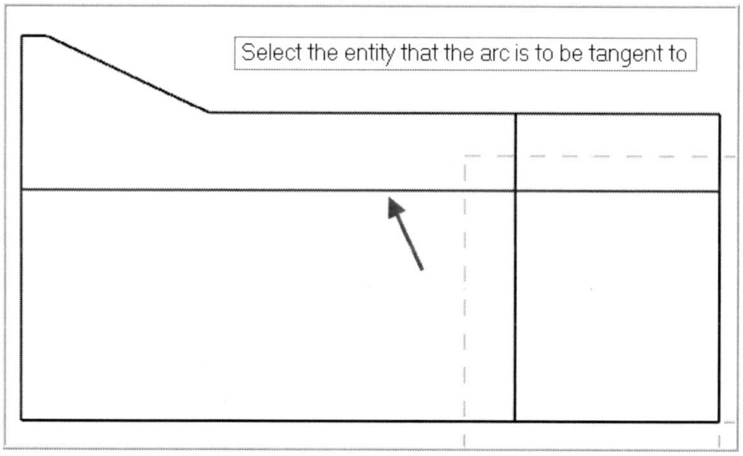

13. To satisfy the prompt **Specify the thru point** move the cursor over the endpoint of the line shown below. When the visual cue for endpoint appears click on this point.

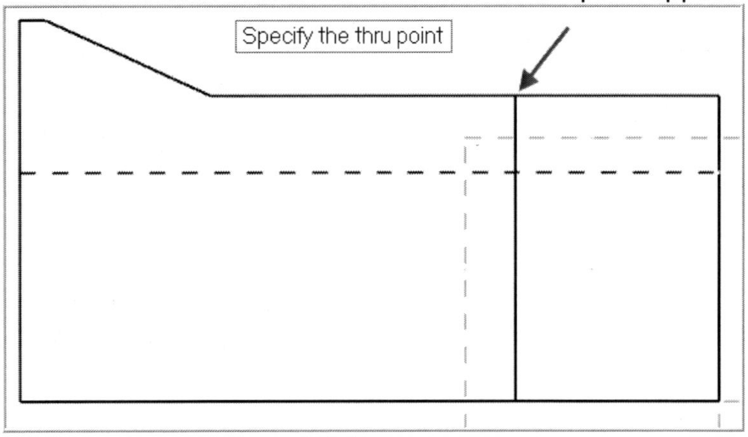

14. After selecting this endpoint you a confronted with a selection of arcs. The prompt changes to **Select an arc**. Select the arc in the position shown below:

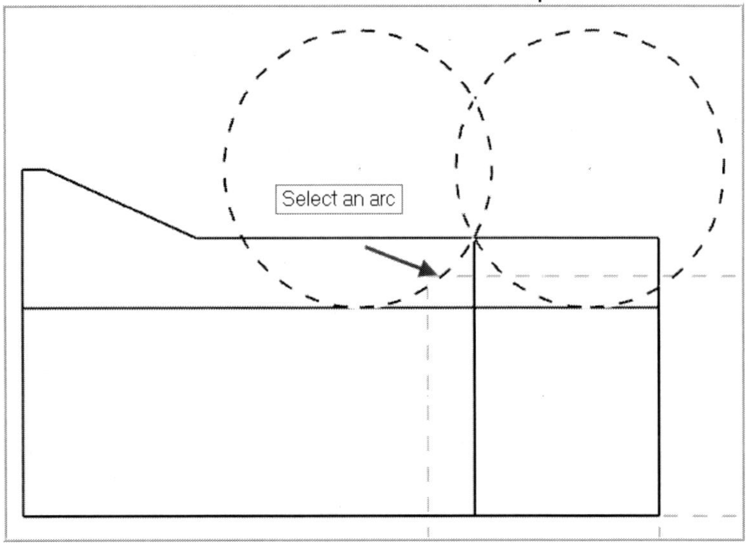

15. Click on the **OK** icon to complete this feature.

➲ The completed arc is shown below.

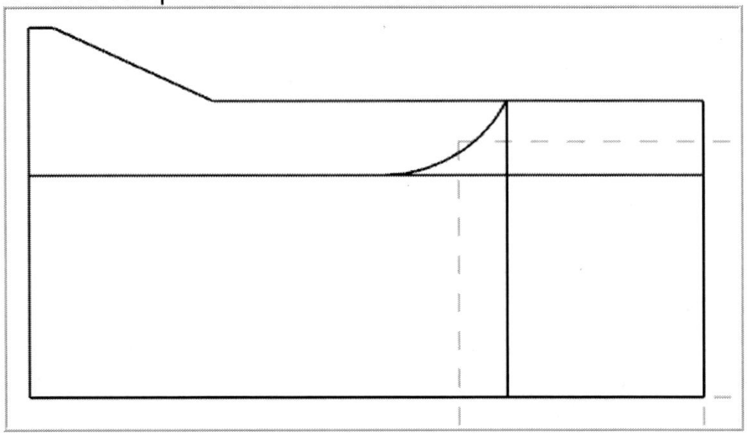

➲ **Trim the Arc**

16. In the **WIREFRAME** tab click on **Trim/Break/Extend** in the **Modify** section.

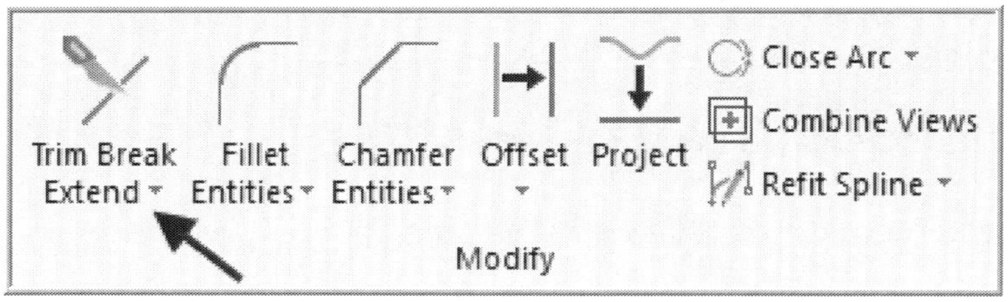

17. The Trim Break Extend panel appears. Activate **Trim 1 entity**.

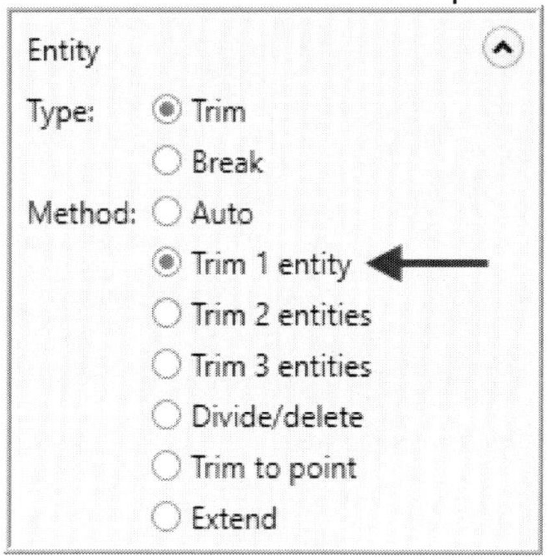

Trim Break Extend
Combines the most widely used wireframe editing tools into a single function with different modes.
For each mode, you have the option of trimming or extending entities, or breaking single entities into two pieces.

Auto-preview displays the results of the selected function as you move the mouse over the final entity selection.
A solid line represents what will be created. A dashed line represents what will be removed.

18. Now at the prompt **Select the entity to trim/extend** select the arc at **position 1**.
19. The prompt changes to **Select the entity to trim/extend to**, select the line at **position 2.**

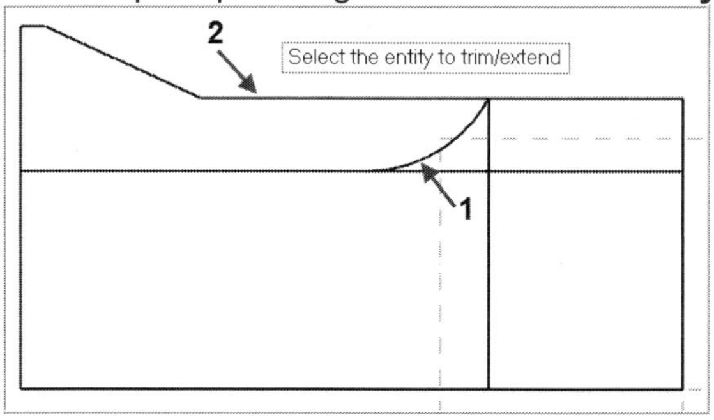

20. Click on the **OK** icon  to complete this feature.

➲ The geometry should look like the image below.

21. **Delete** the construction line shown below. Select the line and hit the **Delete key** on your keyboard.

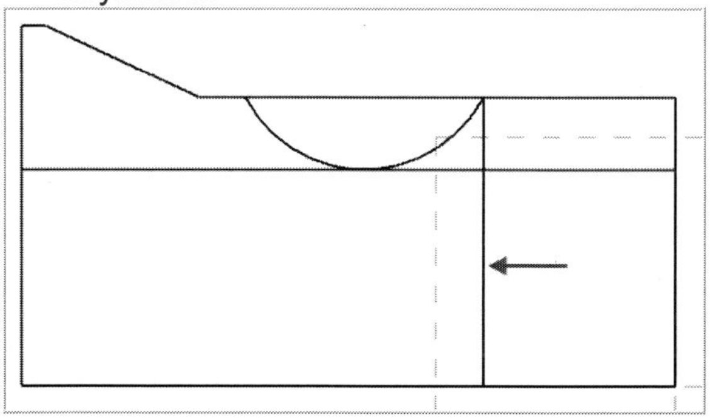

TASK 5:
CREATE THE GEOMETRY FOR THE BORE

➲ In this task you will create the geometry that make up the bore of this part

1. In the **WIREFRAME** tab click on **Line Parallel** in the **Lines** section.

➲ On the graphics screen you are prompted: Select a line and the Line Parallel panel appears.

2. First click in the space for **Offset Distance** and input **0.450** then hit **Enter**.
3. To satisfy the prompt **Select a line**, select the line shown below.

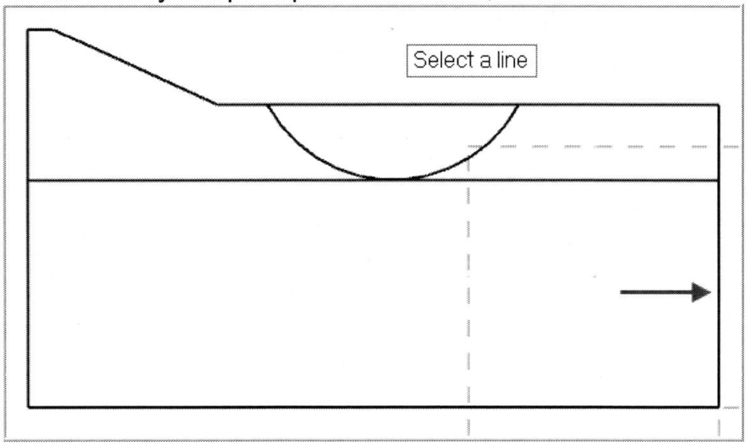

4. To satisfy the next prompt **Indicate the offset direction** move the cursor to the left of the line and pick a point.
5. Click on the **OK and Create New Operation** icon.
6. Click in the space for **Offset Distance** and input **0.625/2** then hit **Enter**.
7. To satisfy the prompt **Select a line**, select the line shown below.

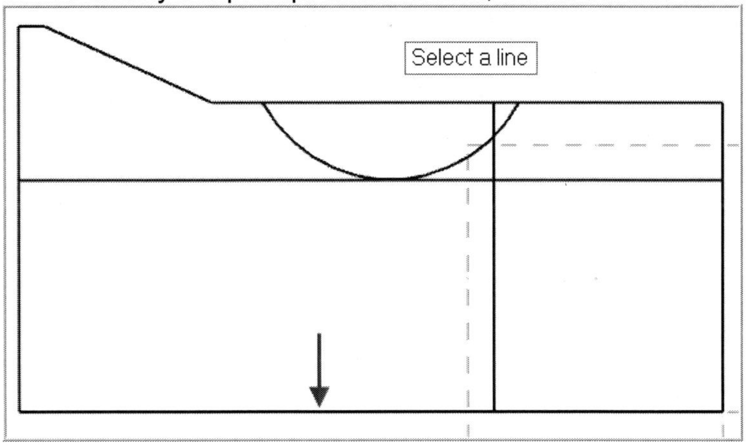

8. To satisfy the next prompt **Indicate the offset direction** move the cursor above the line and pick a point.
9. Click on the **OK** icon to complete this feature.

➲ **Create 0.050 fillet**

10. In the **WIREFRAME** tab click on **Fillet Entities** in the **Modify** section.

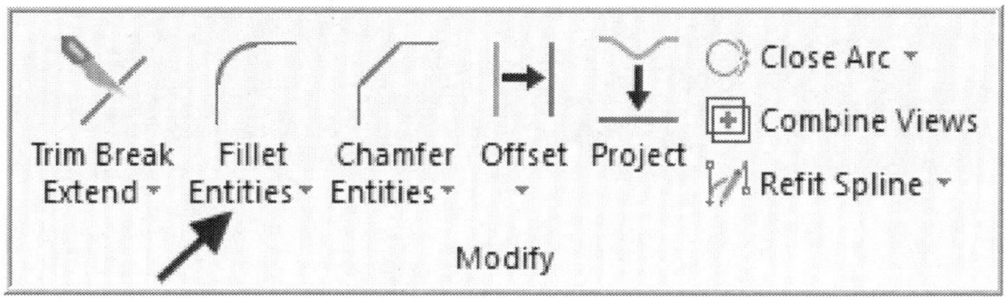

11. The **Fillet Entities** panel appears. If required activate the **Style** to **Normal** and enter a value of **0.05** for **Radius**.
12. Ensure the **Trim** entities box at the bottom of the panel is check marked to turn the trim on.

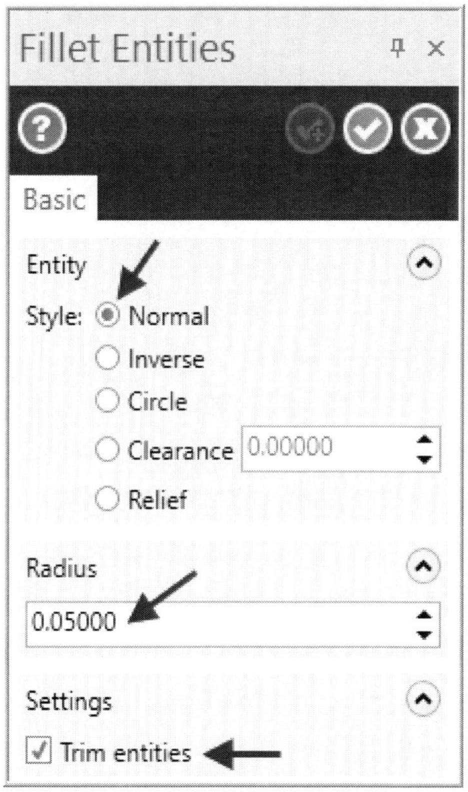

13. When prompted to **Fillet: Select an entity,** select Line 1 and 2 as shown below. The fillet radius appears at the corner of line 1 and 2.

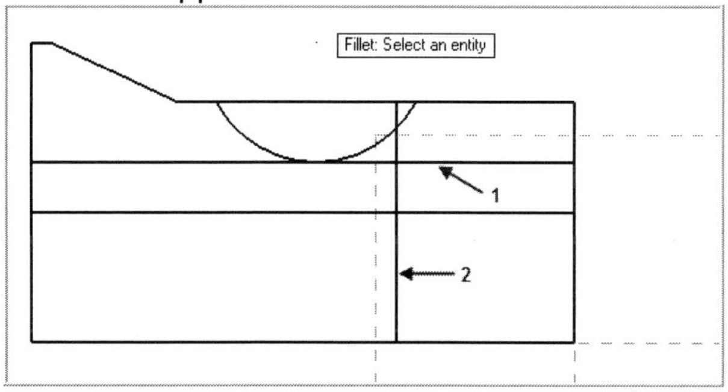

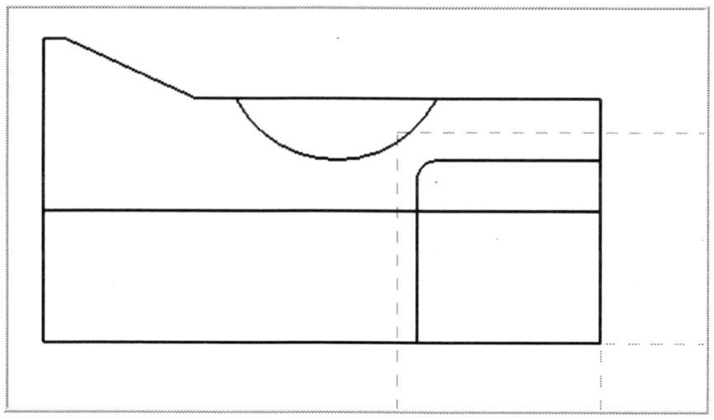

14. Click on the **OK** icon  to complete this feature.

➲ **Trim the bore**

15. In the **WIREFRAME** tab click on **Trim/Break/Extend** in the **Modify** section.

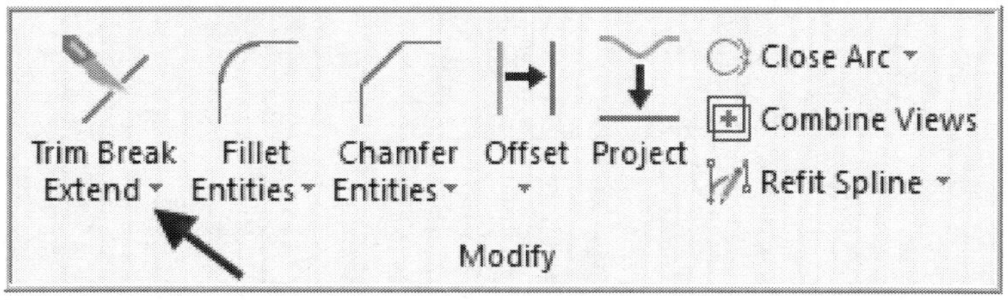

16. The Trim Break Extend panel appears. Activate **Trim 2 entities**.

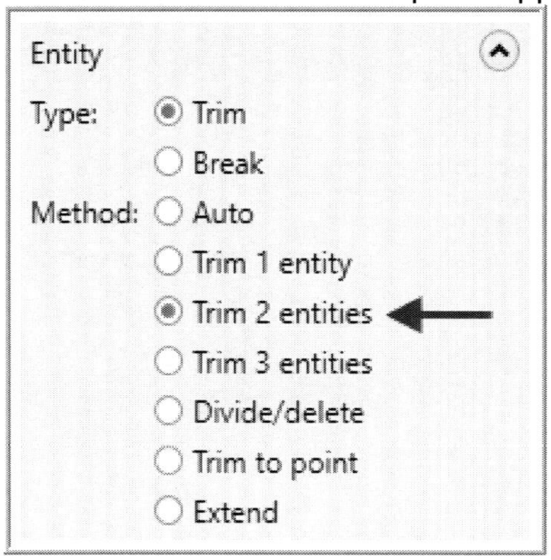

17. Now at the prompt **Select the entity to trim/extend** select the line at **position 1,**
18. The prompt changes to **Select the entity to trim/extend to**, select the line at **position 2.**

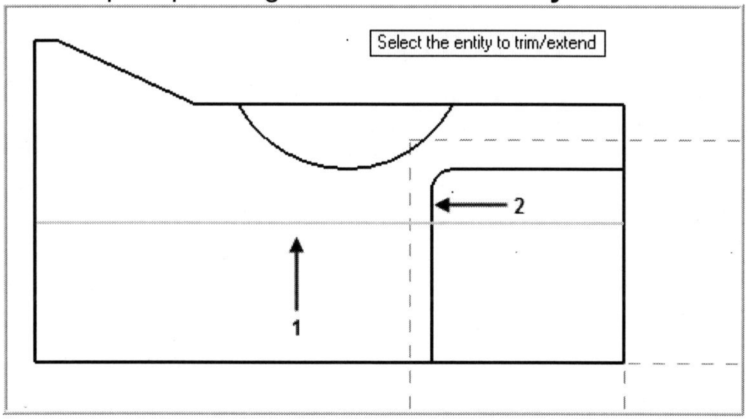

➲ The trimmed geometry should look like the image below.

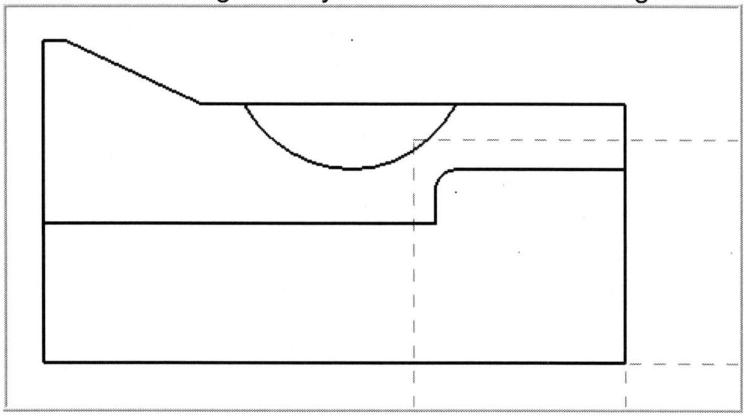

➲ **Trim the .290 arc**

19. Now activate **Divide/delete**.

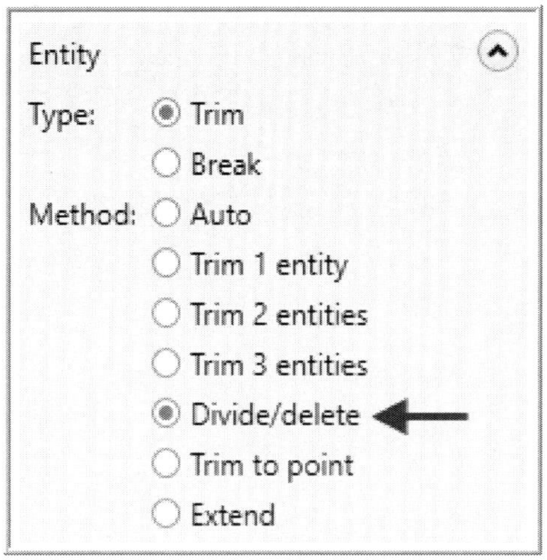

Divide/delete
Trims a line, arc, or spline into two disjointed segments by removing the segment that lies between two dividing intersections.

When you choose the Divide/delete function and select an entity in the graphics window, Mastercam uses the nearest two intersections on each end to divide the entity.

20. The prompt changes to **Select the curve to divide.** Move the cursor over the line and select it as shown below.

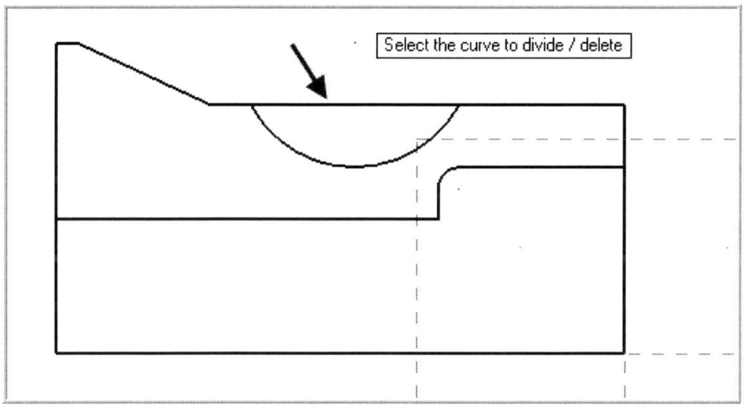

21. Click on the **OK** icon to complete this feature.

➲ The line is trimmed back to the two closest intersections as shown below.

22. **Delete** the construction line shown below. Select the line and hit the **delete key** on your keyboard.

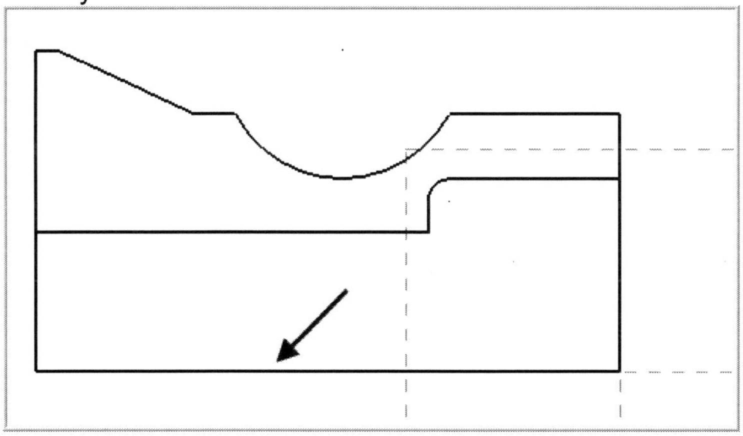

TASK 6:
CREATE THE CHAMFER

➲ **Create Chamfer 45 degrees x .0625.**

1. In the **WIREFRAME** tab click on **Chamfer Entities** in the **Modify** section.
2. The **Chamfer Entities** panel appears. If required activate the **Style** to **1 Distance** and enter a value of **0.0625** for **Distance 1**.
3. Click on line 1 and then line 2 as shown below:

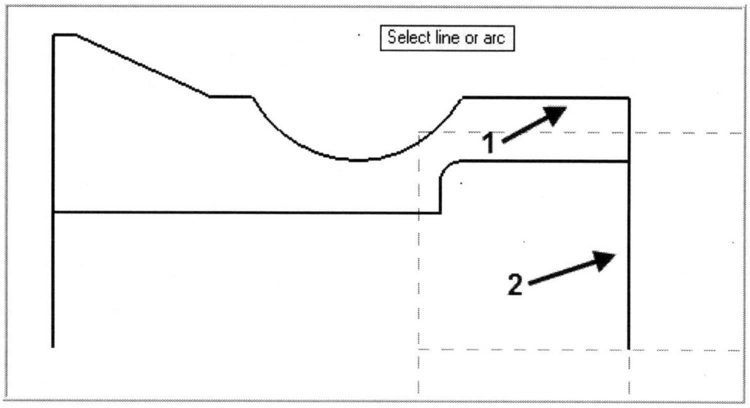

4. Click on the **OK** icon to complete this feature.

➲ The completed geometry should look like the image below:

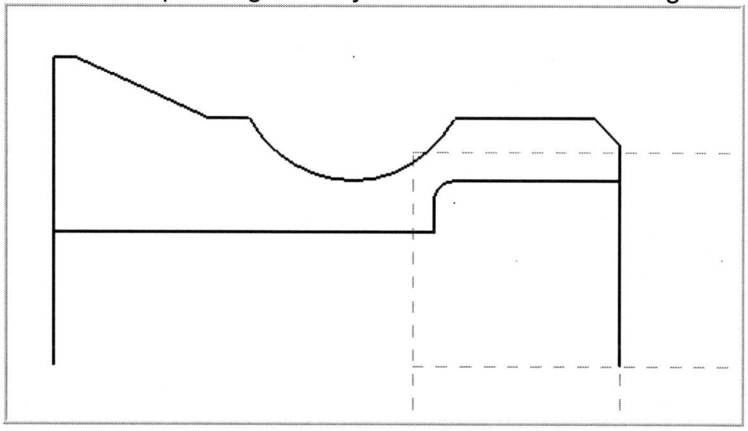

TASK 7:
SAVE THE DRAWING

1. Select **File.**
2. Select **Save As…**
3. Click on the **Browse** icon.
4. In the **"File name"** box, type **"Lathe-Lesson-5".**
5. Browse to an appropriate location.
6. Select the **Save** button to save the file and complete this function.

Toolpath Creation

TASK 8:
DEFINING THE STOCK AND CHUCK PARAMETERS

1. Select the **VIEW** tab at the top of the screen.
2. Select the **Fit** icon in the **Zoom** section. Next select **Unzoom 50%** to shrink the display.
3. Still on the **View tab** and click on **Toolpaths** to display the Toolpaths Manager.
4. Ensure your screen looks like the image below:
   a. The Toolpaths Manager is open.
   b. The properties icon displays Lathe Default. If it is not refer to **Setting the Environment** chapter at the beginning of the book.
   c. The Lathe Lesson-5 Geometry is displayed.

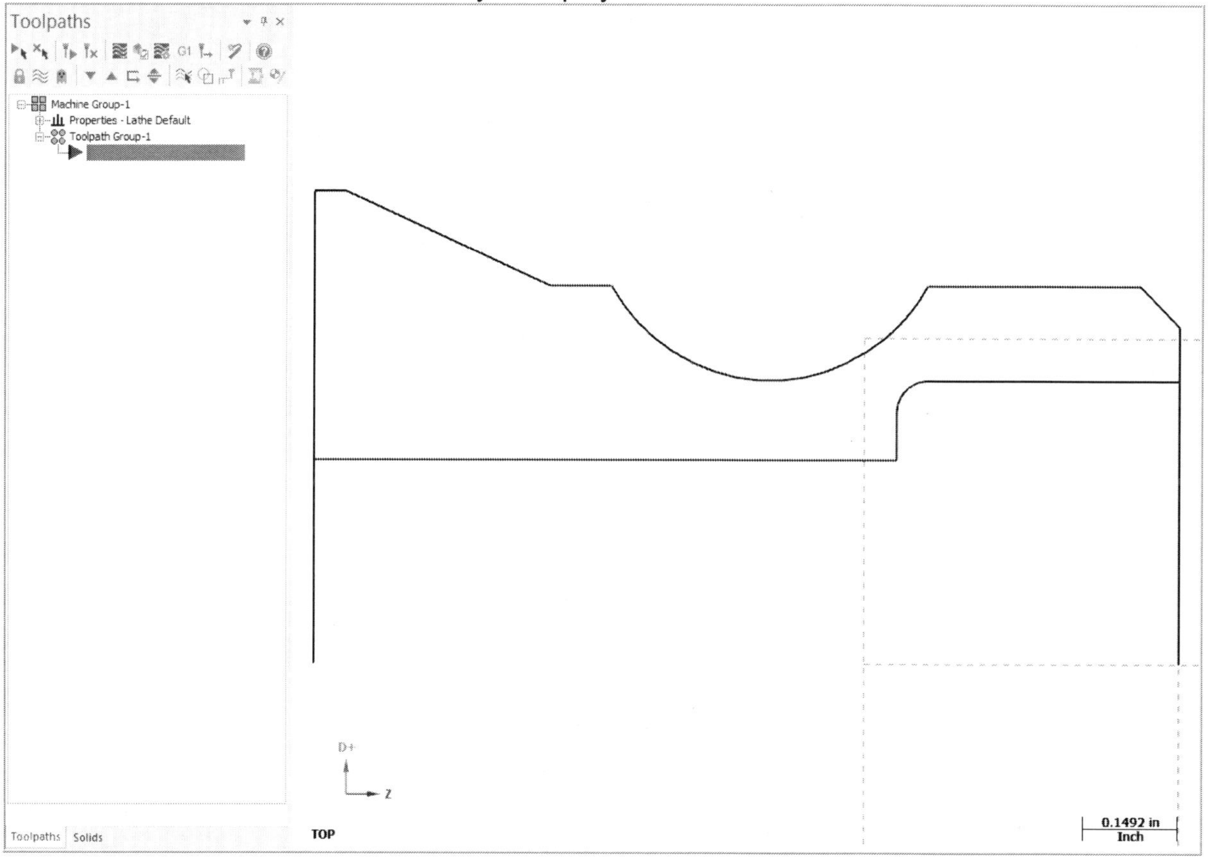

5. Select the plus in front of **Properties** to expand the Machine Group Properties.

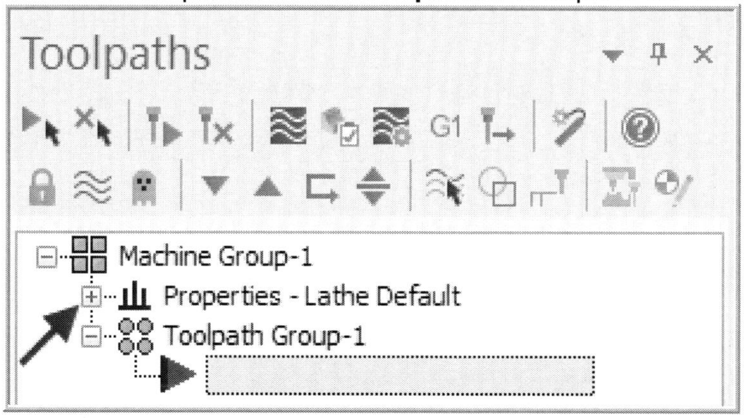

6. Select **Stock setup** in the Toolpaths Manager window.

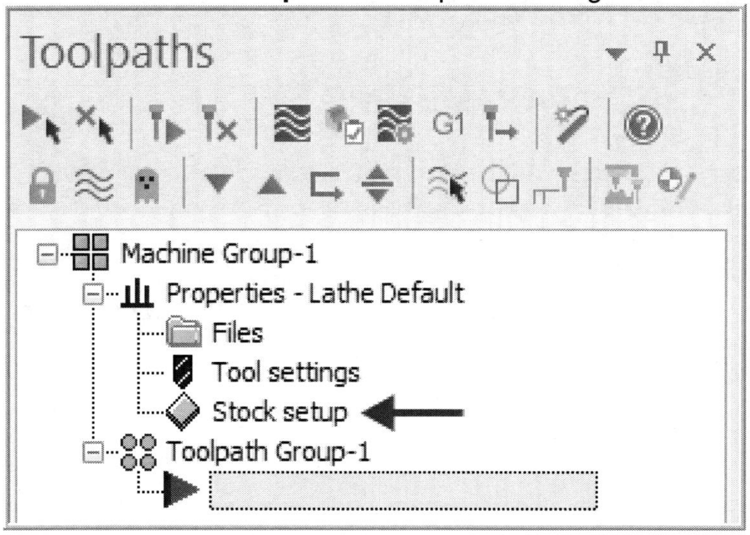

7. Select the **Stock Properties** button in the **Stock Setup** page as shown in the screenshot below.

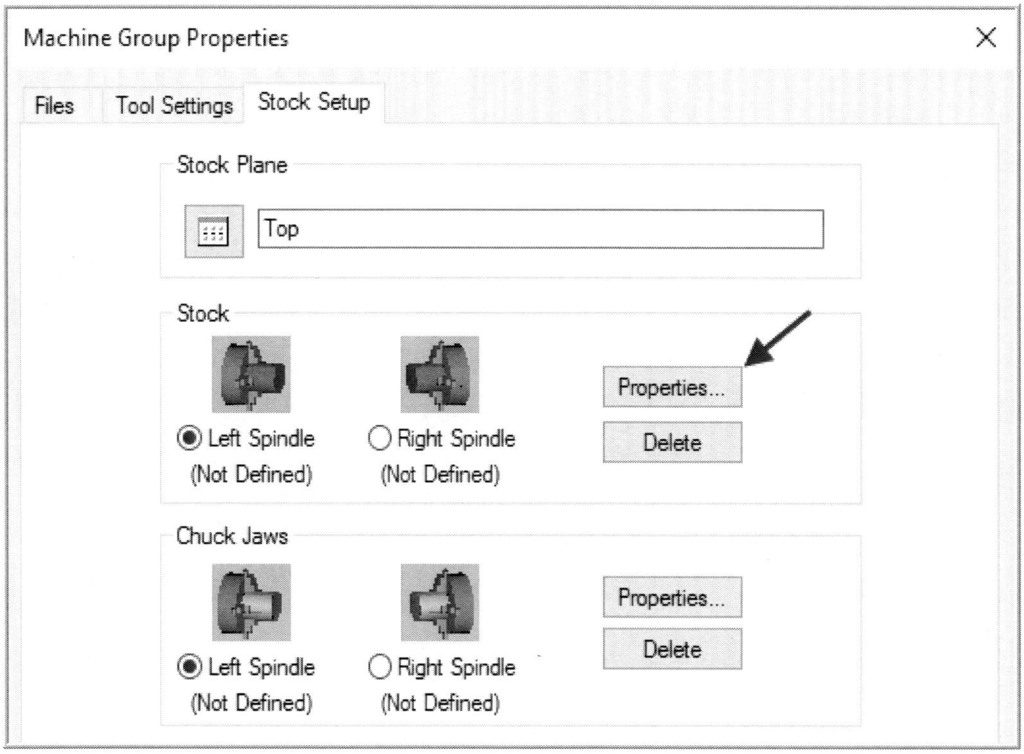

8. In the **Machine Component Manager-Stock** window click on the **Geometry** button and select **Cylinder** as shown below:

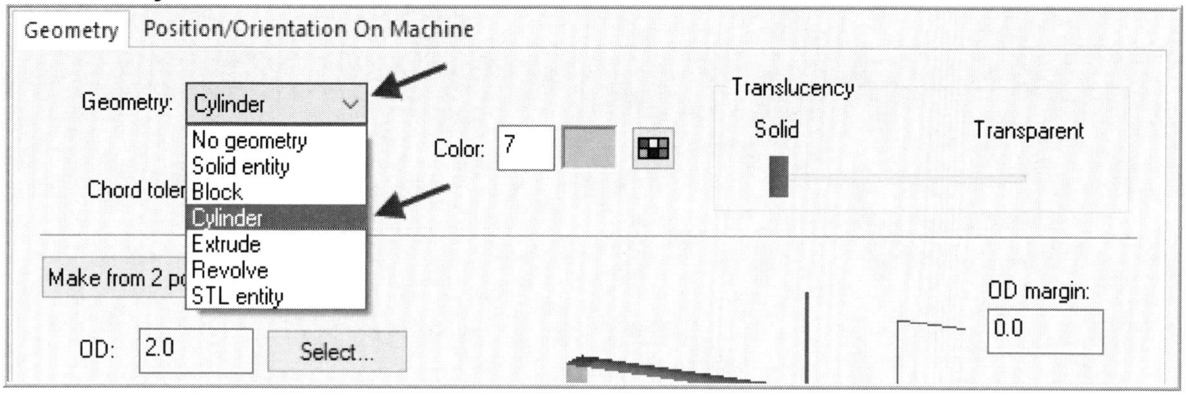

9. In the **Stock** setup set the values as shown below. **Axis is set to -Z**.

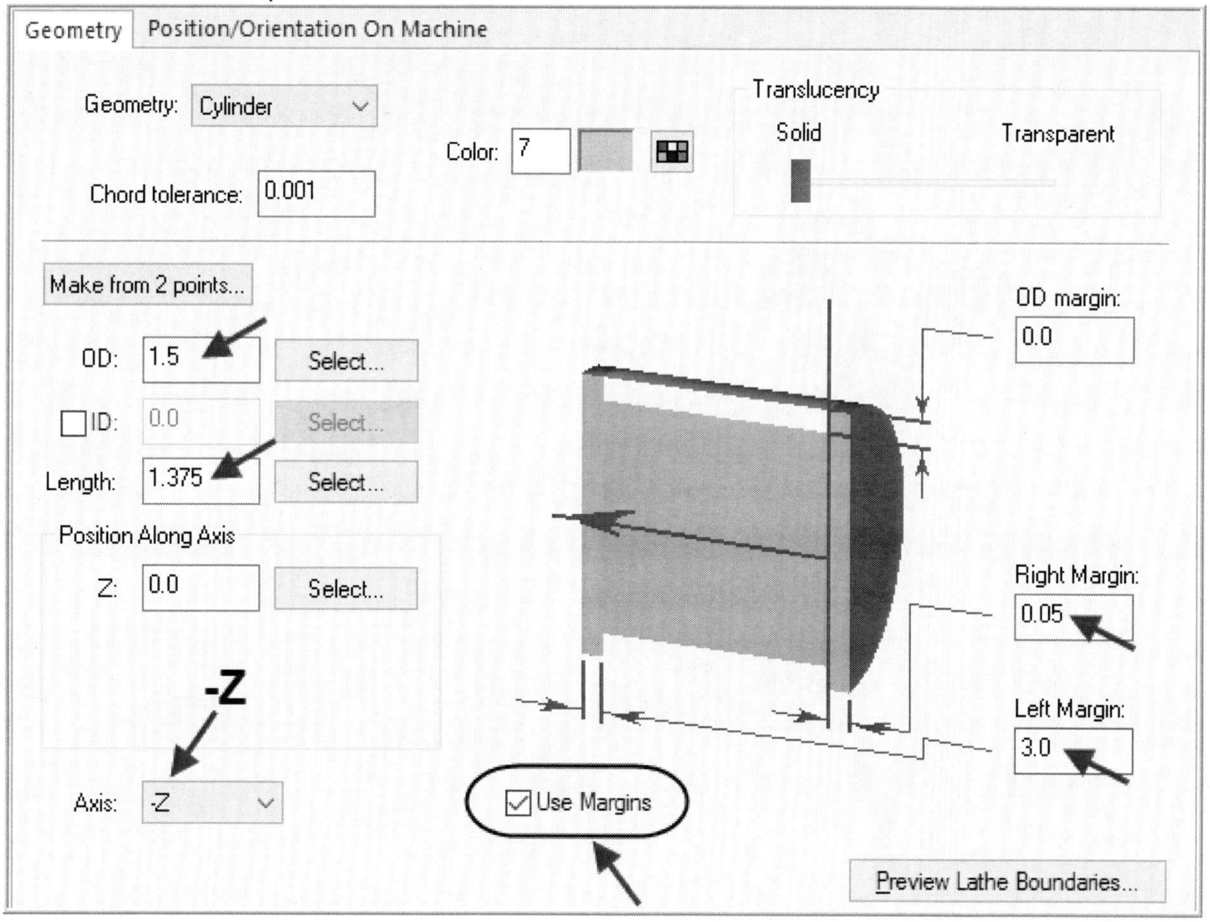

10. Click on the OK icon  to complete this feature.

11. Still on the Stock Setup page activate **Fit screen to boundaries**.

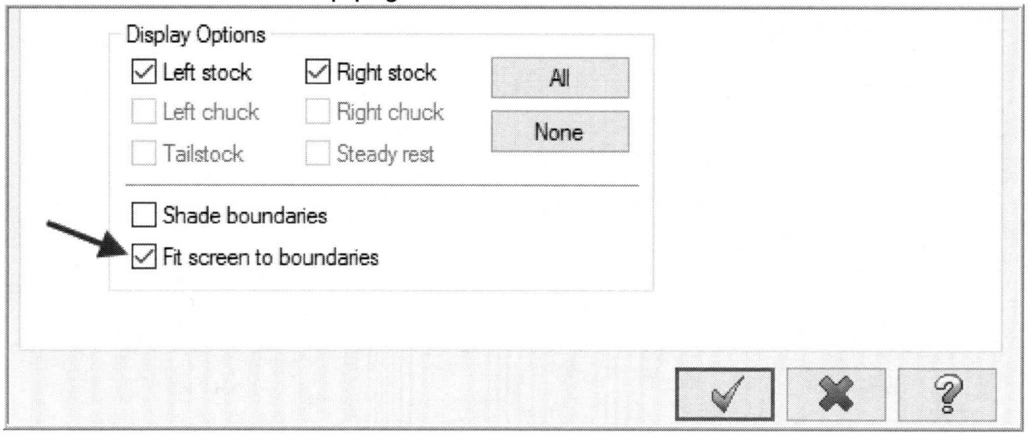

12. Select the **Chuck Properties** button in the **Stock Setup** page as shown below:

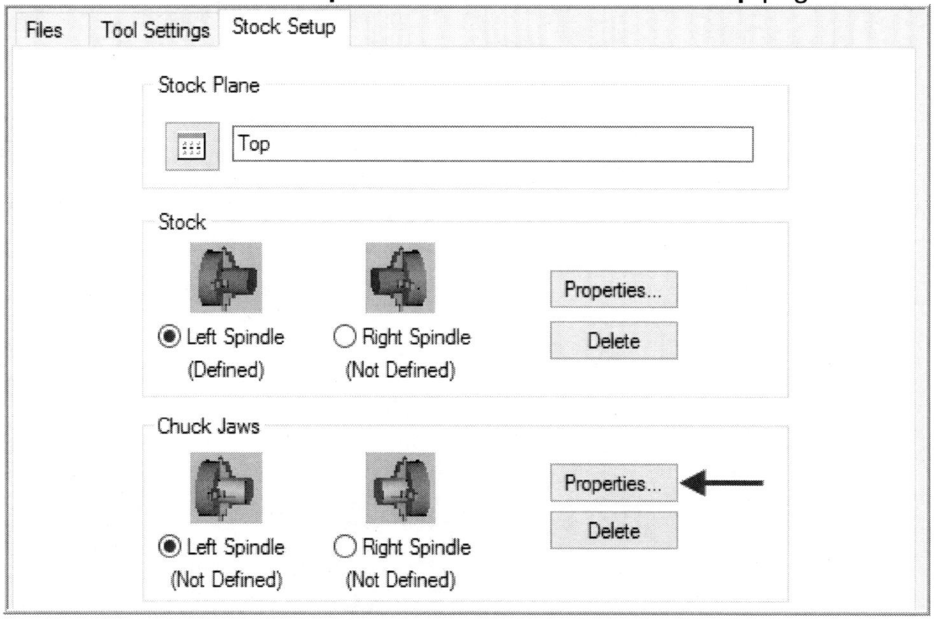

13. In the **Chuck Jaws** setup set the values as shown below:

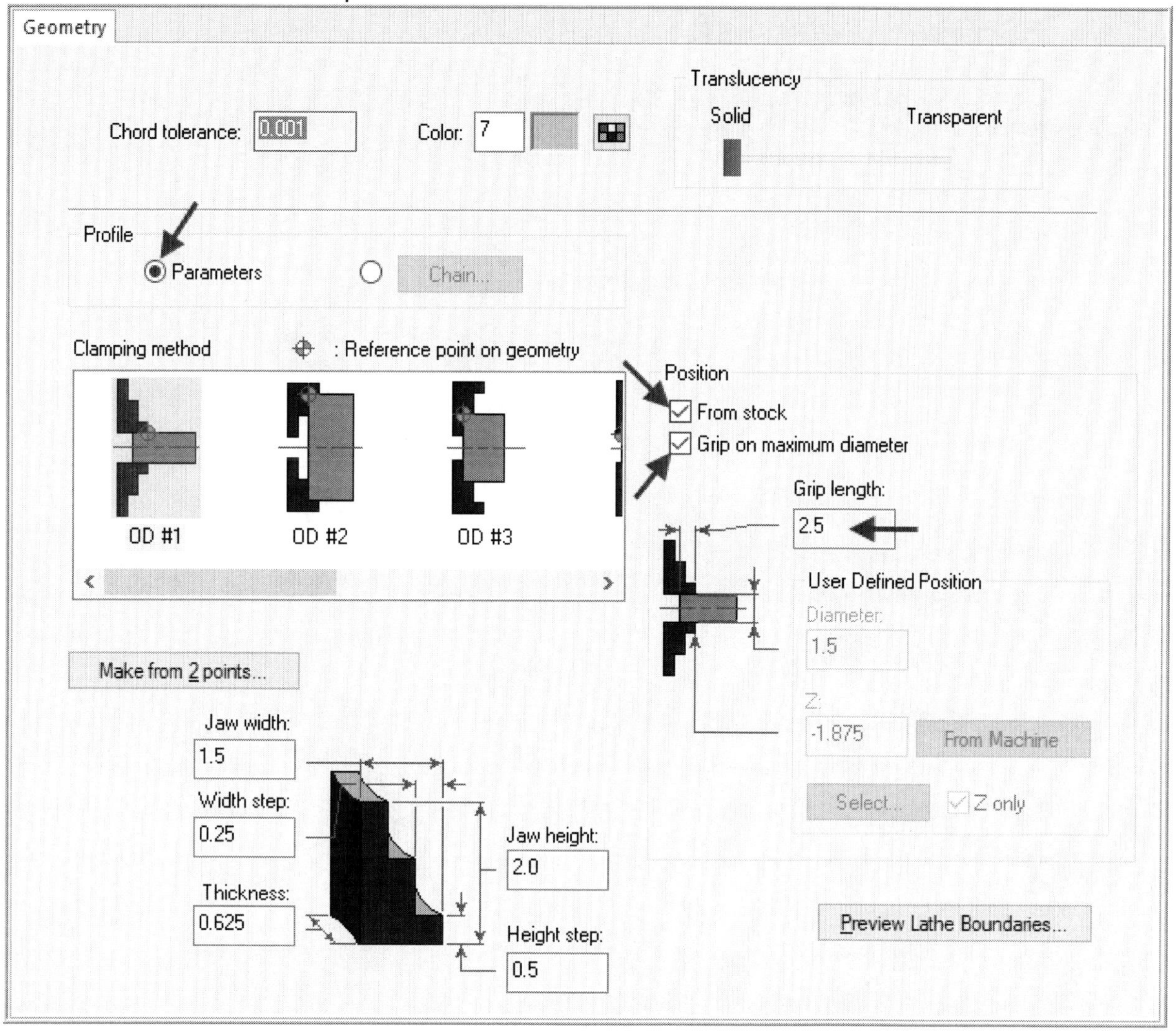

14. Click on the OK icon  to complete this feature.

15. Click on the **Tool Settings** page and make changes as shown below:

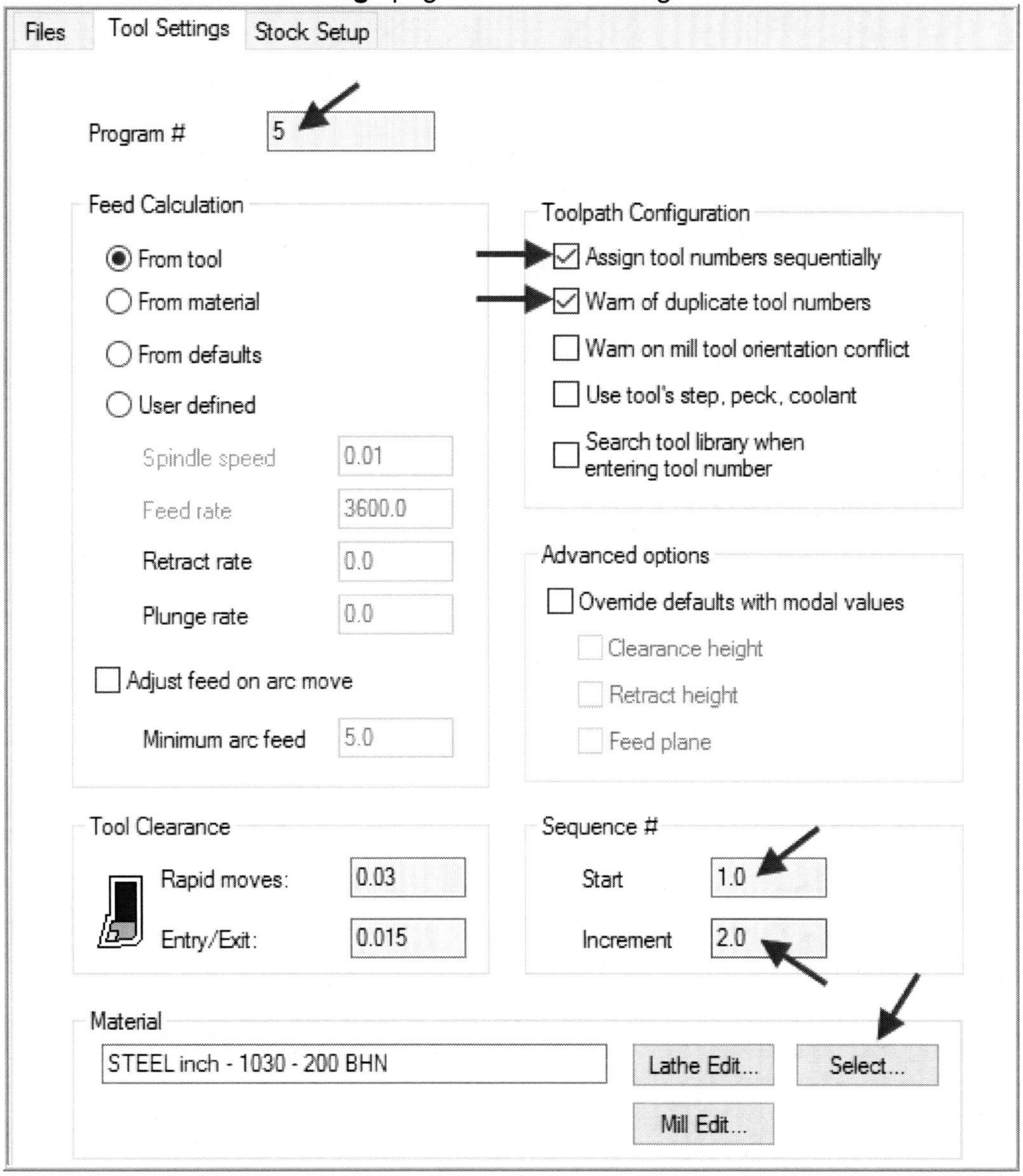

16. To change the **Material** type to Aluminum 6061 pick the **Select** button at the bottom of the Tool Settings page.

17. At the **Material List** dialog box open the Source drop down list and select **Lathe – library.**

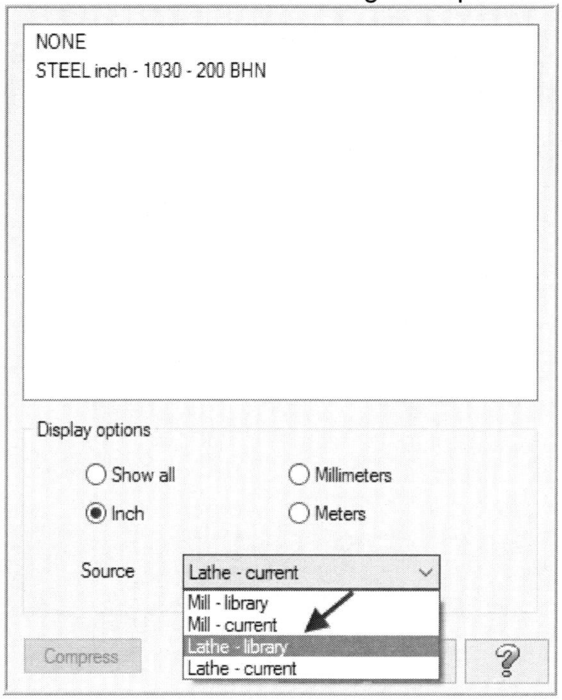

18. From the **Default Materials** list select **ALUMINUM inch - 6061** and then select.

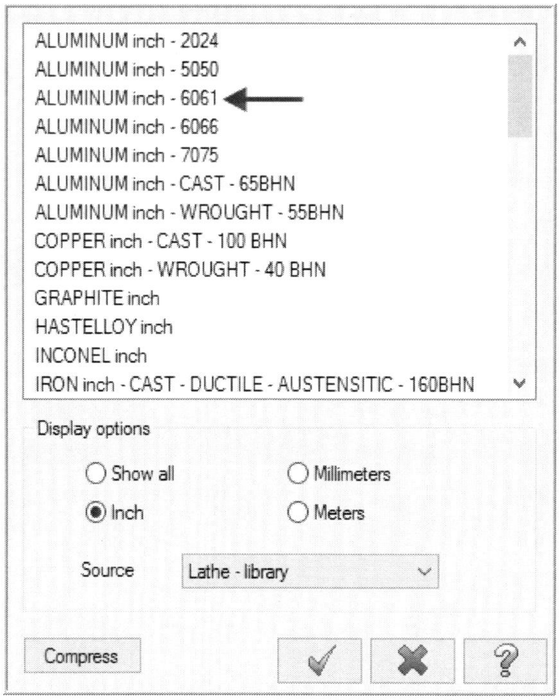

19. Select the OK button again to complete this Stock Setup function.

20. Right mouse click in the graphics area and click on the **Fit** icon.

➲ Note the stock setup outline as indicated by broken lines as shown below:

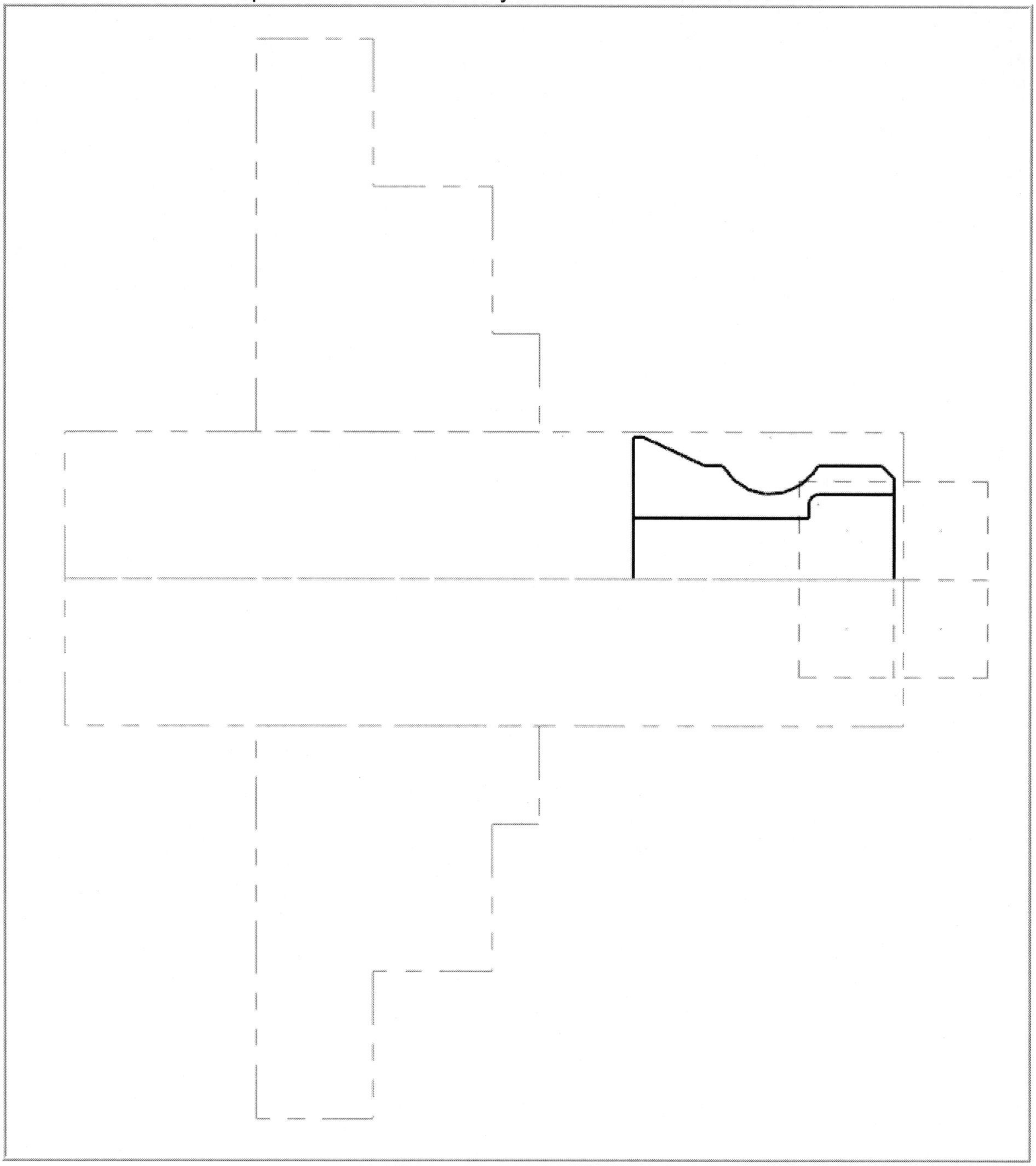

TASK 9:
FACE THE FRONT OF THE PART:

➲ In this task you will use a facing tool to face the front of the part in one cut.

1. Right mouse click in the graphics area and click on the **Fit** icon if required.
2. Select the **TURNING** tab at the top right side of the screen.
3. Now select **Face** in the **General** section.

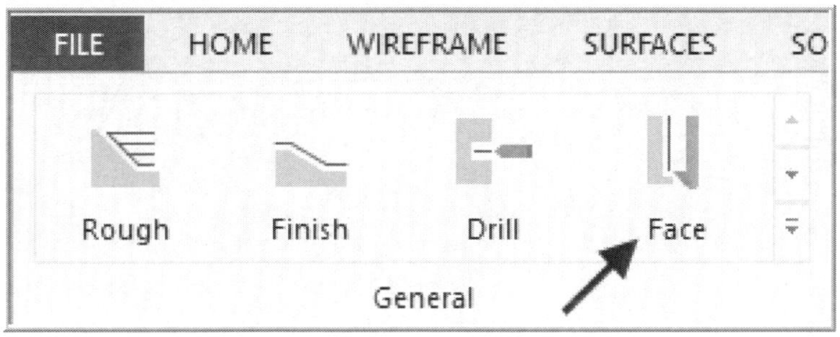

4. When prompted to **"Enter new NC name"** Ensure **Lathe-Lesson-5** is entered and then select the OK button.

➲ After selecting the OK button you are confronted with Toolpath parameters page. The first task here will be to select Tool #1 a Roughing – 80 deg.

5. Click on **Tool 0101 Roughing – 80 degree** and ensure the settings are the same as in the Toolpath parameters page as shown below. **Coolant Flood** is set to **On**.

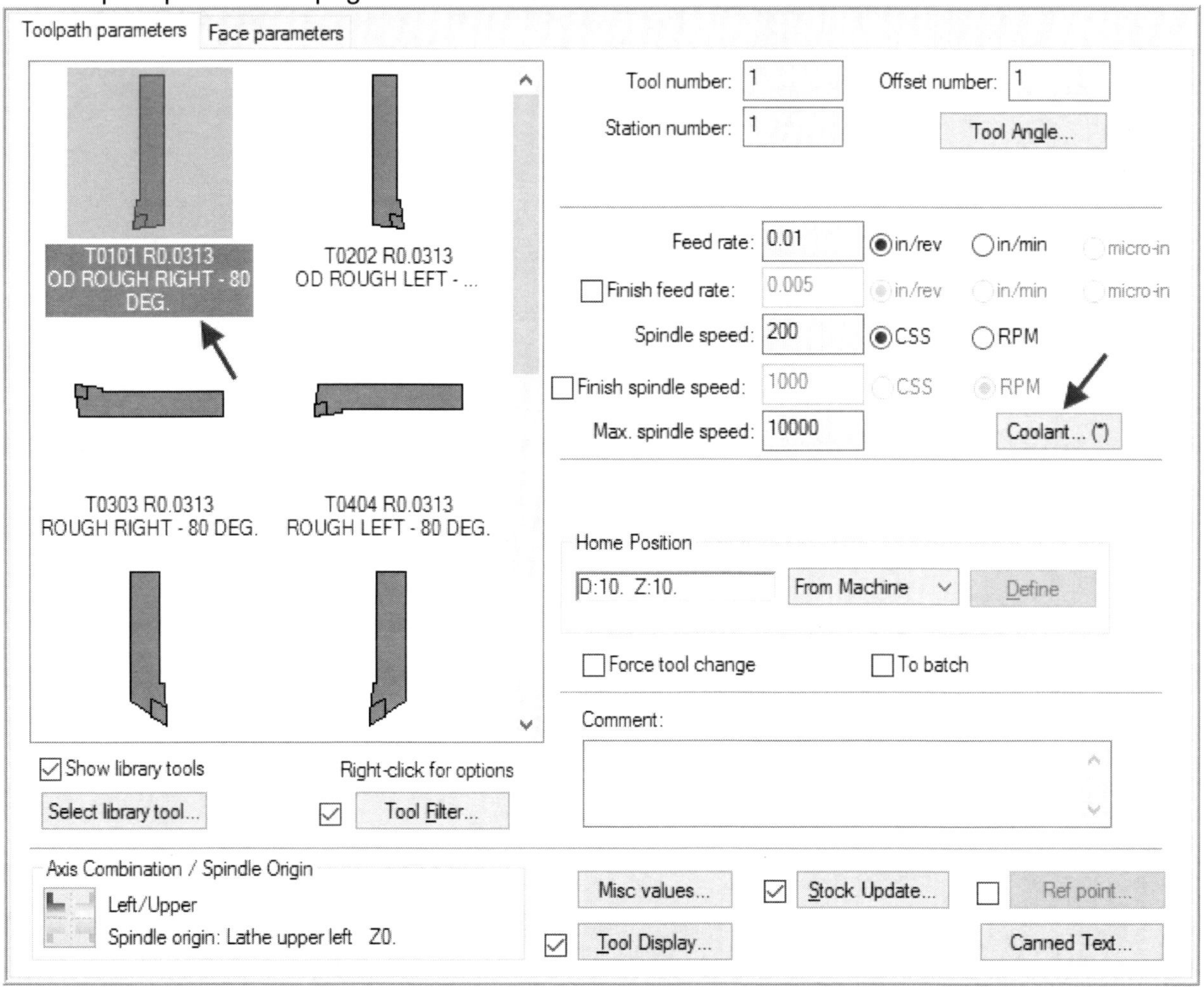

6. Select the **Face parameters** page and make changes as shown below.

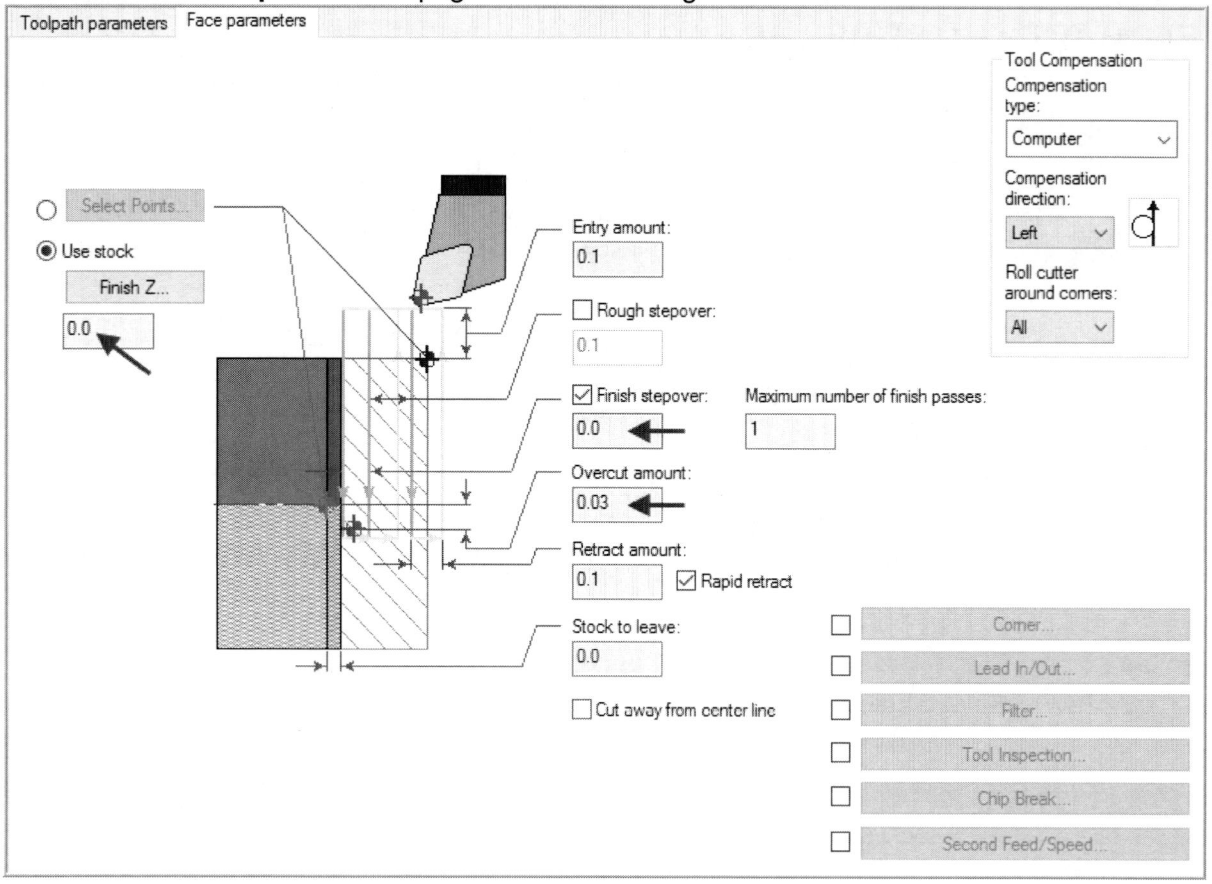

7. Select the OK button  to complete this **Lathe Face** operation.

TASK 10:
ROUGH THE OUTSIDE DIAMETERS

- In this task you will use a Lathe toolpath called Lathe Quick rough.
- You will use the same tool as used for the previous facing operation **Tool #1 an OD Rough-Right – 80 deg.**

1. Right mouse click in the white space of the **Toolpaths Manager** and select:
   Lathe toolpaths>Quick>Quick rough.

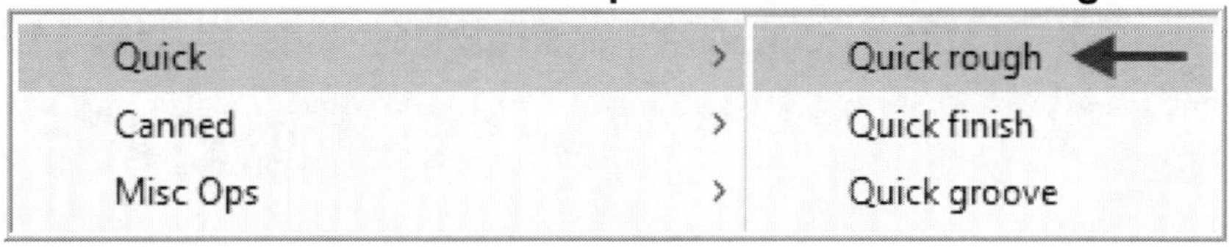

2. In the **Chaining** window Chaining mode is set to **Partial** by default.

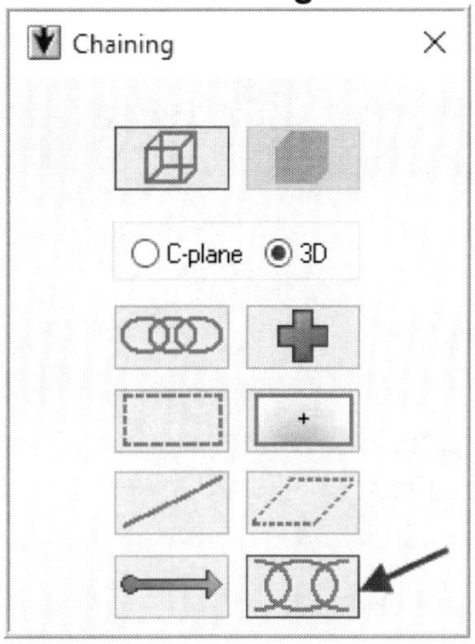

3. Select the chamfer, Line 1 as the start of the **Partial chain**.

After you have selected the chamfer **ensure** that the arrows are pointing up and to the left of the part. If it is not select the reverse button in the Chaining dialog box.

4. Then select Line 2 as the end entity in this chain.

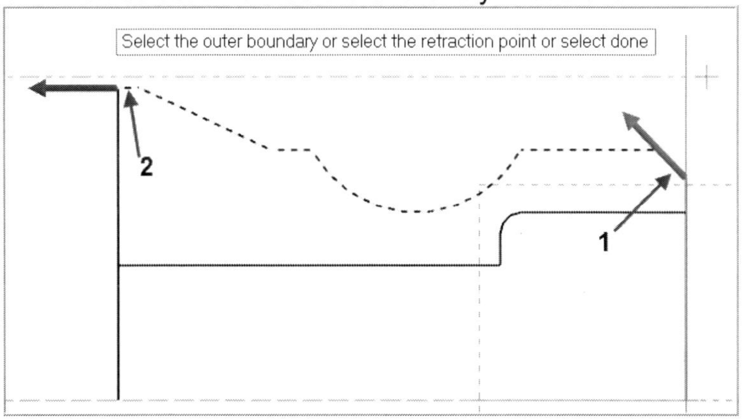

5. Select the OK button  to exit the Chaining dialog window.

6. In the **Quick tool parameters** page select the **Tool #1 an Roughing – 80 deg** and make any necessary changes as shown below. **Coolant Flood** is set to **On**.

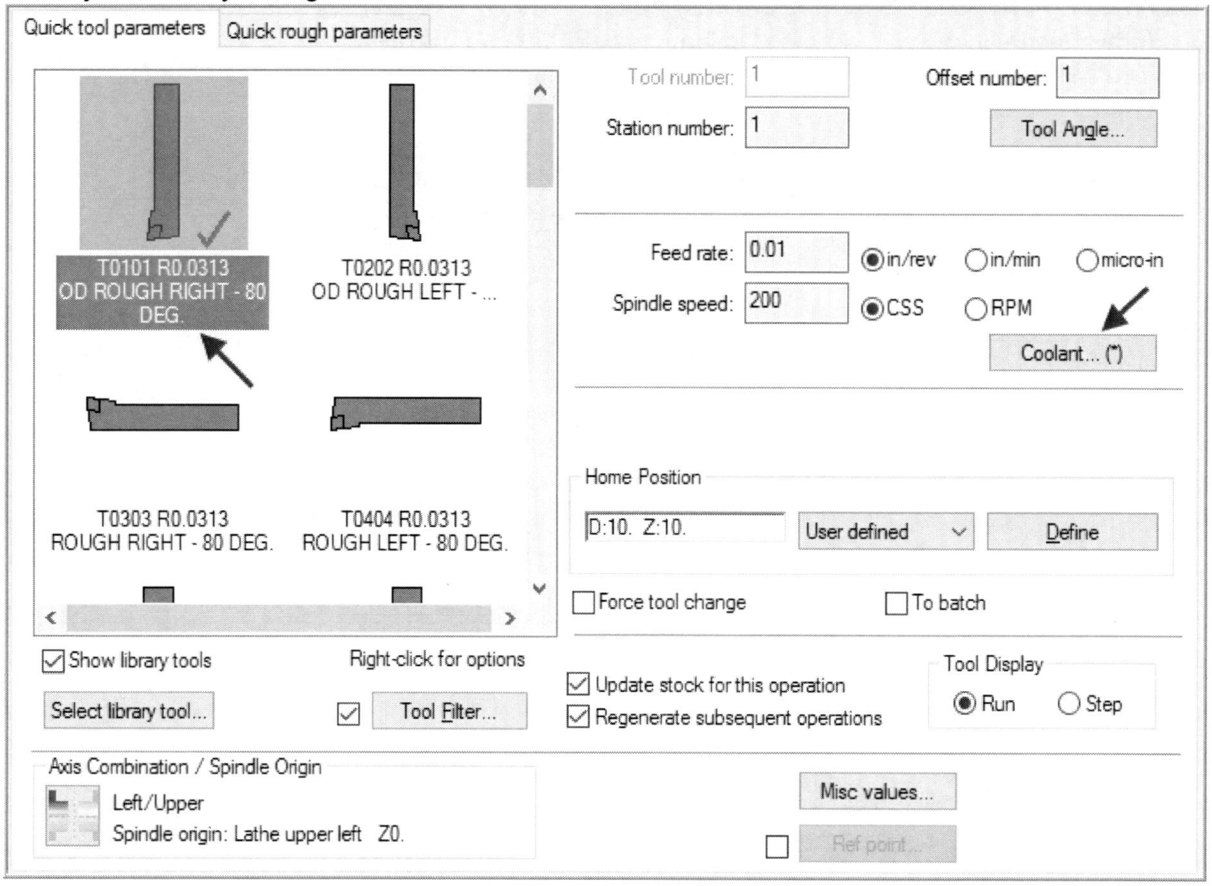

7. Select the **Quick Rough parameters** page and make changes as shown below.

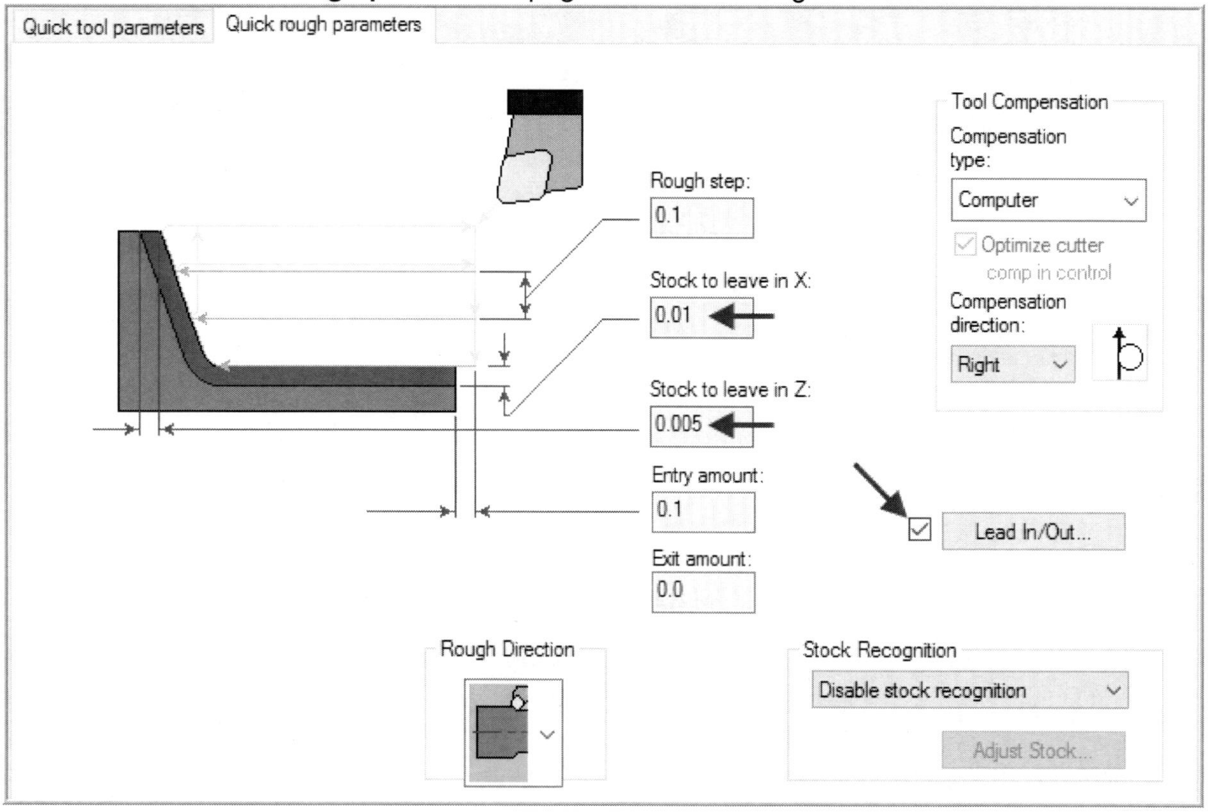

8. Select the **Lead In/Out** button, then select the **Lead out** page and extend the contour by **0.2** as shown below:

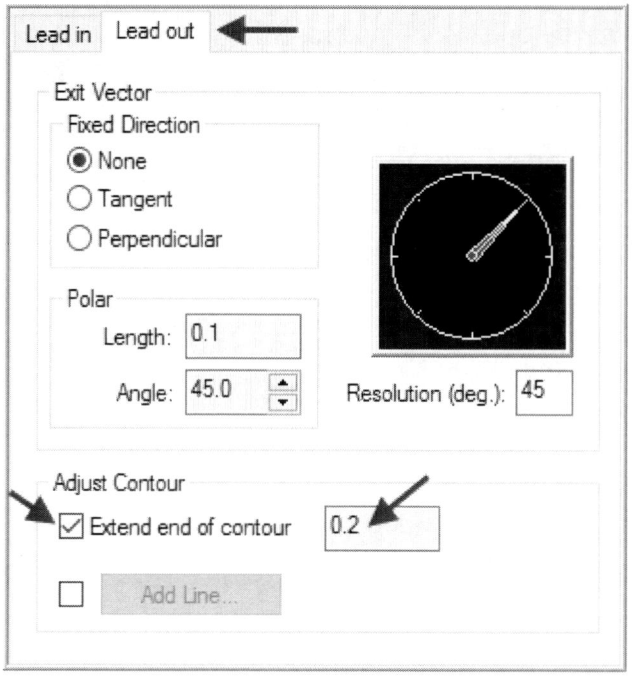

9. Select the OK button ✓ to exit this function.
10. Select the OK button ✓ to exit Rough Parameters.

TASK 11:
FINISH THE OUTSIDE DIAMETERS

➲ In this task you will create a new tool to finish the outside diameters.

1. On the **TURNING** tab select **Finish** in the **General** section.

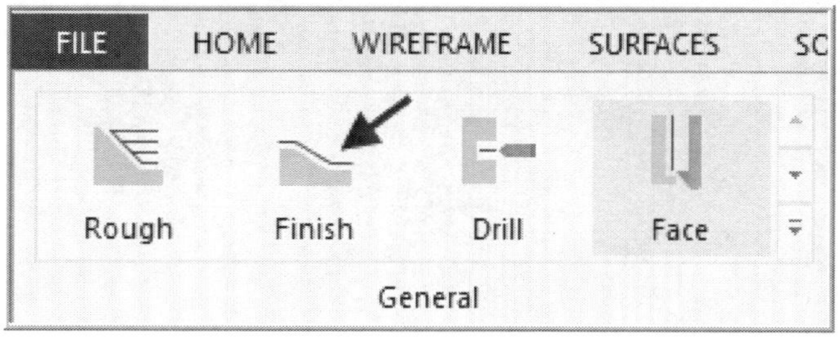

2. Click on the **Last** button  in the Chaining dialog box to select the previous chain.
3. Select the OK button  to exit the Chaining dialog window.
4. Right Click the mouse in the space as indicated by arrow **# 1** shown below:
5. Click on **Create new tool...** as indicated by arrow **# 2** as shown below.

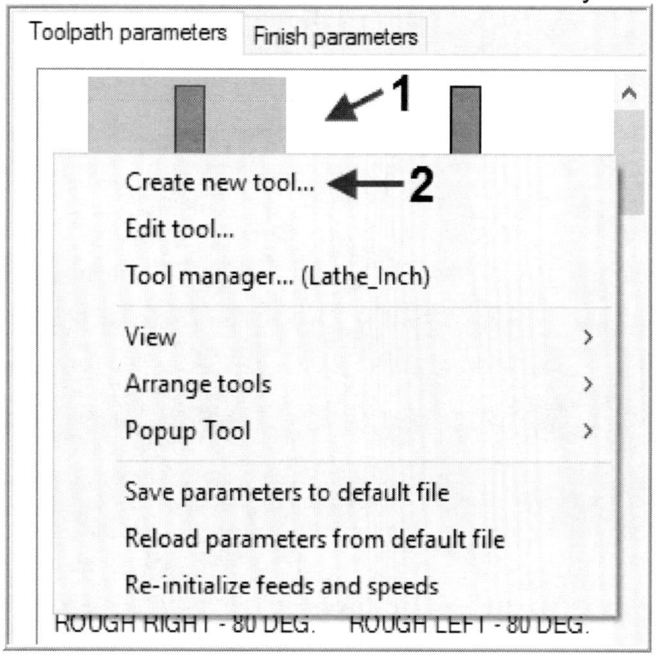

6. Click on the **General Turning** Button as shown below:

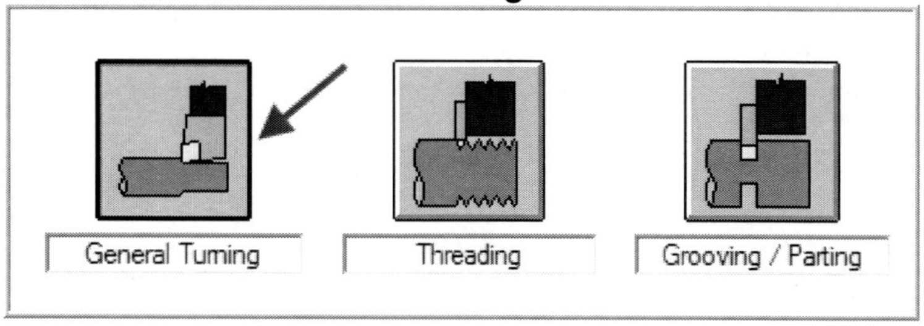

7. Scroll down and click on the **V (35 deg. Diamond)** insert as shown below:

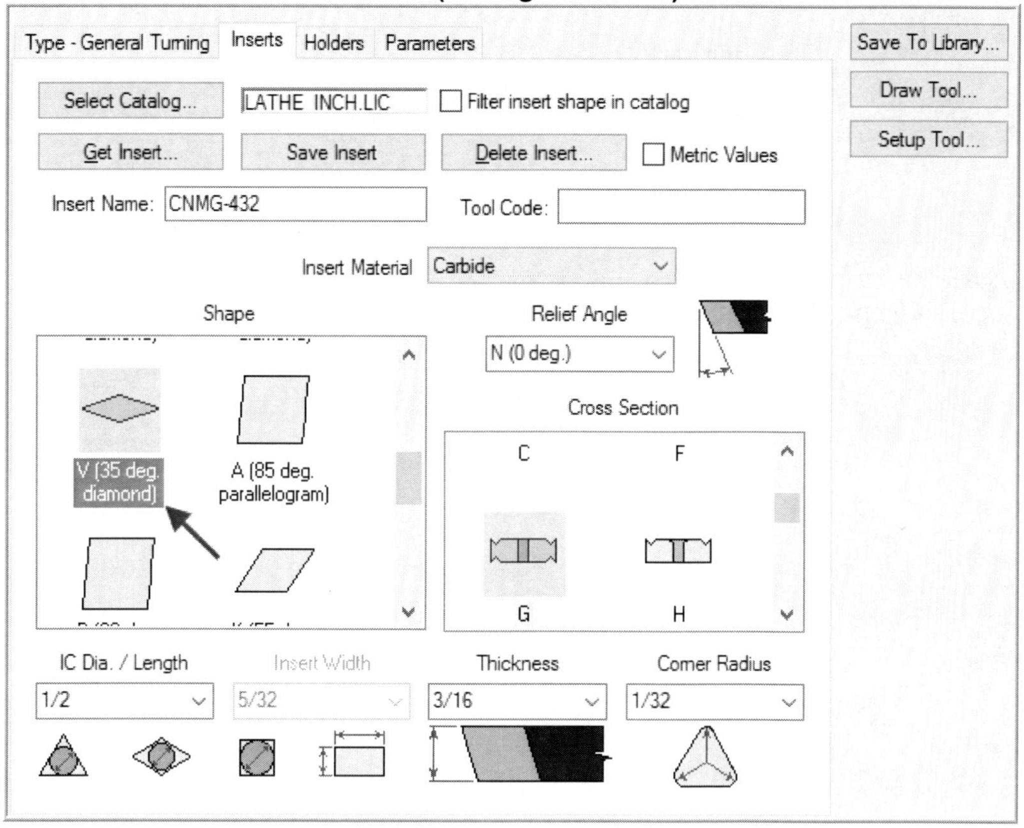

8. Click on the **Holders** Tab.
9. Scroll down and click on the **V (17.5 deg. Side clr.)** as shown below:

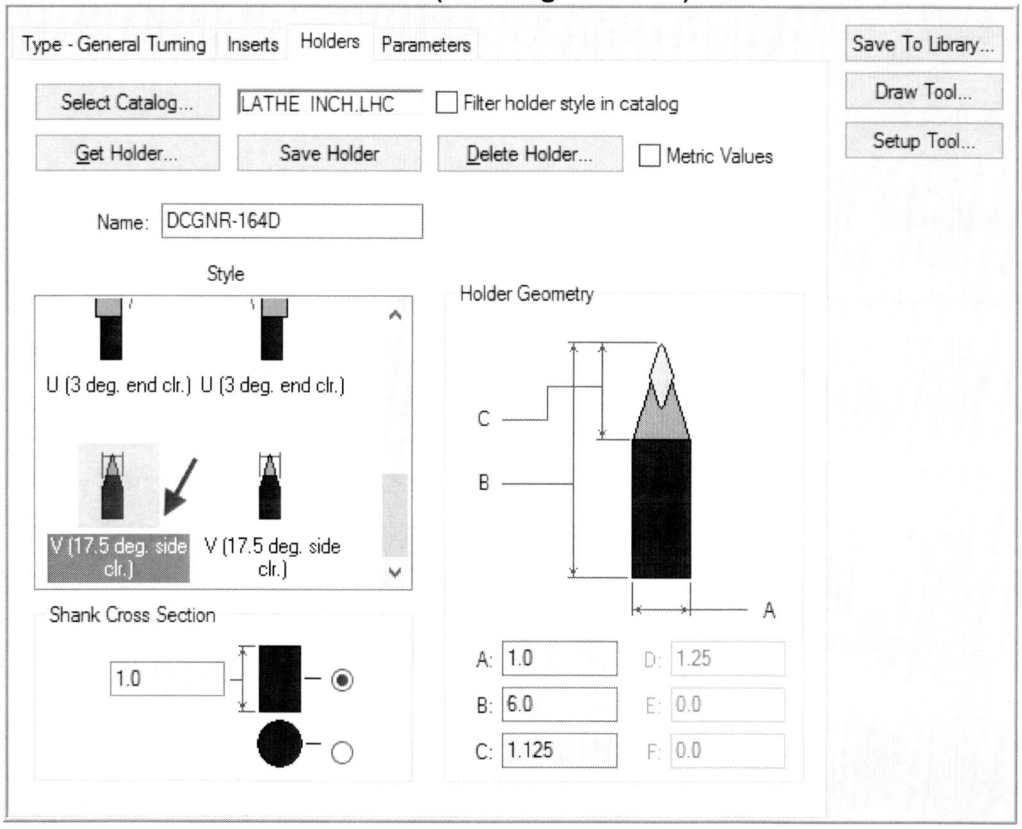

10. Click on the **Parameters** page and at the bottom of this page set the compensation for this tool as shown below:

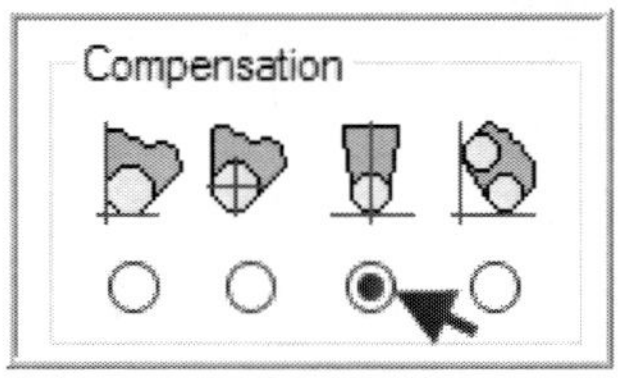

Compensation: Tip
The toolpath is programmed from the tip of the tool corner radius.

This is the only option available for threading tools, drills, taps, and reamers.

11. Click on the OK icon .
12. Make any necessary changes as shown below. **Coolant Flood** is set to **On**.

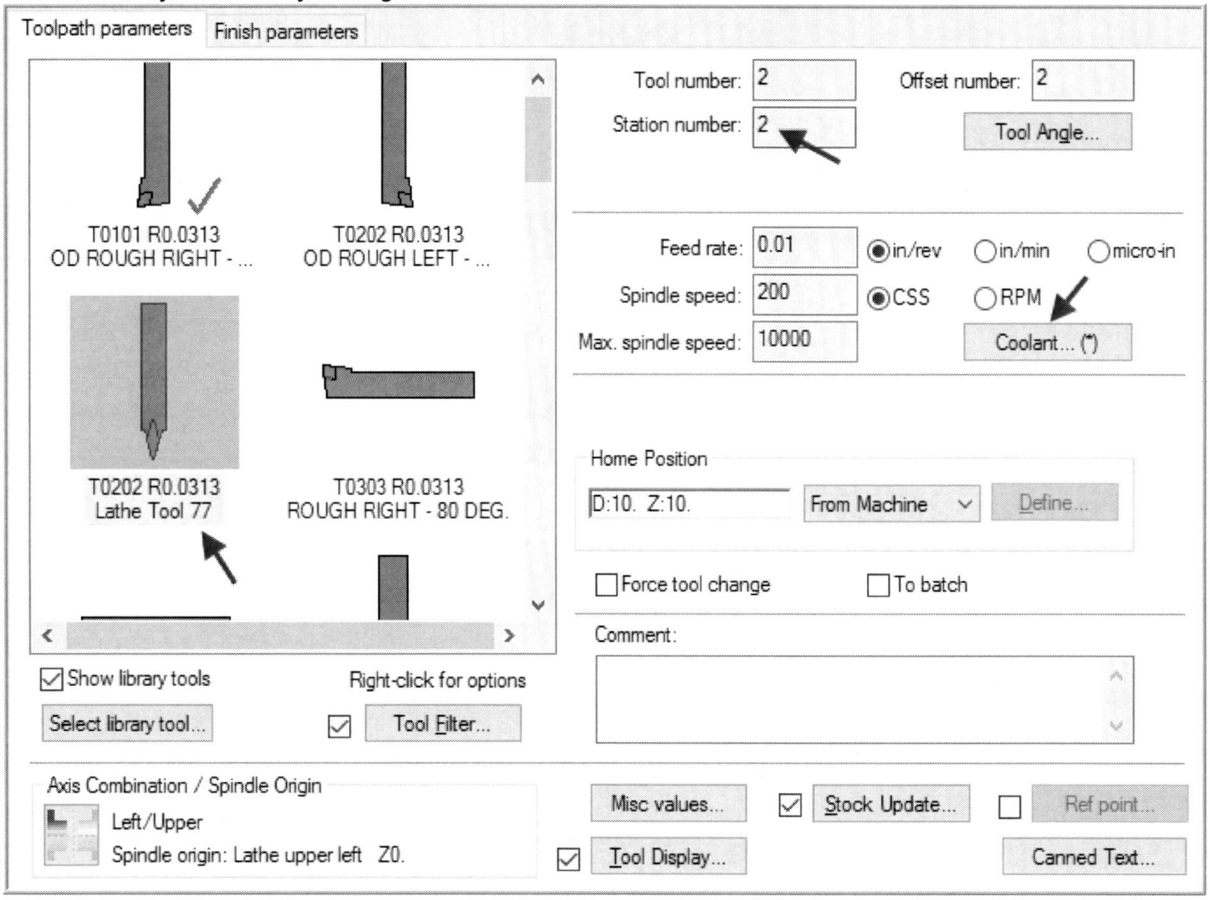

13. Click on the **Finish parameters** tab and make any necessary changes as shown below:

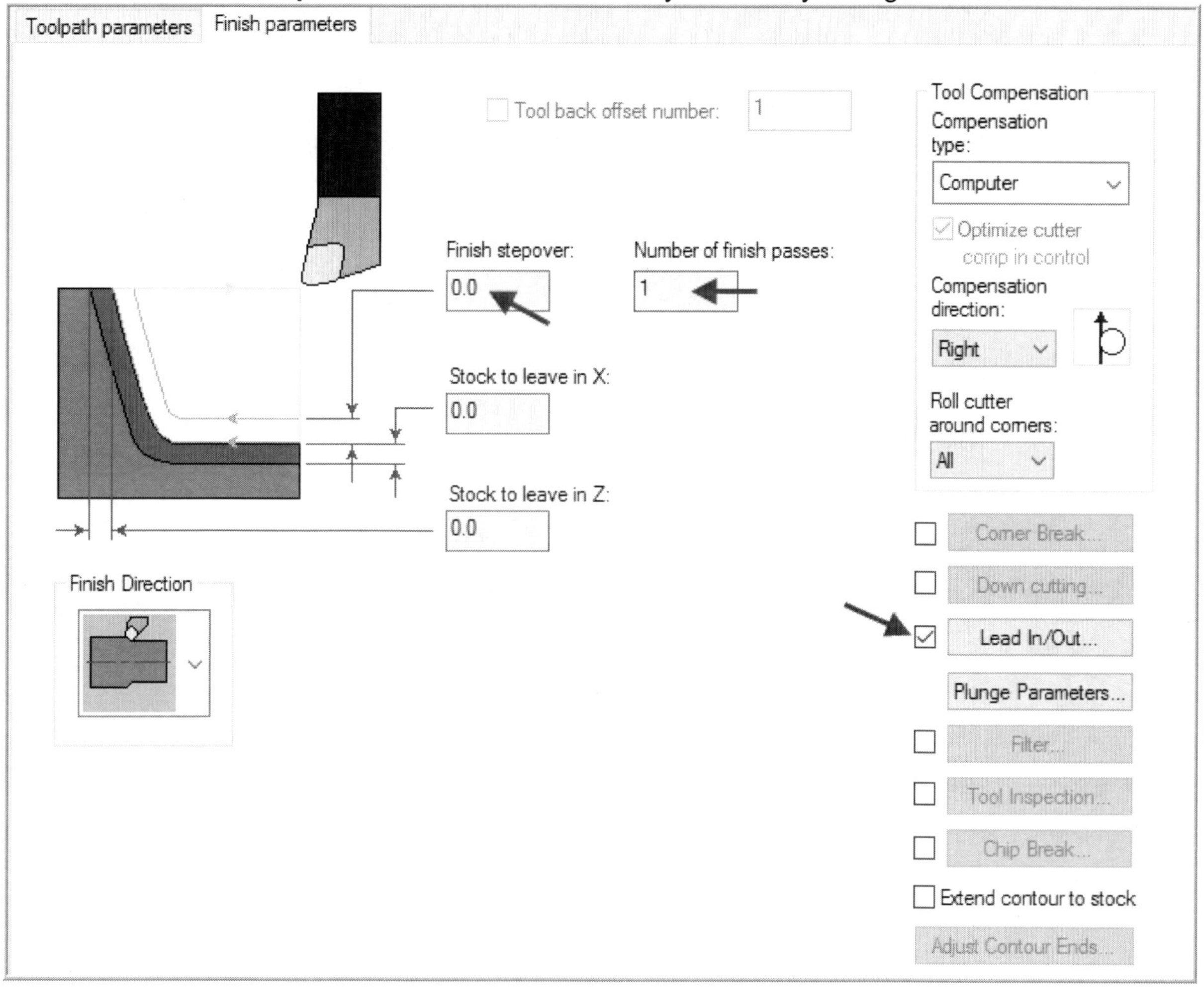

14. Click on the **Lead in/Out** button.
15. On the **Lead in** page make the necessary changes as shown below. In order to adjust the entry vector dial, click on the desired location of the arrow on the dial:

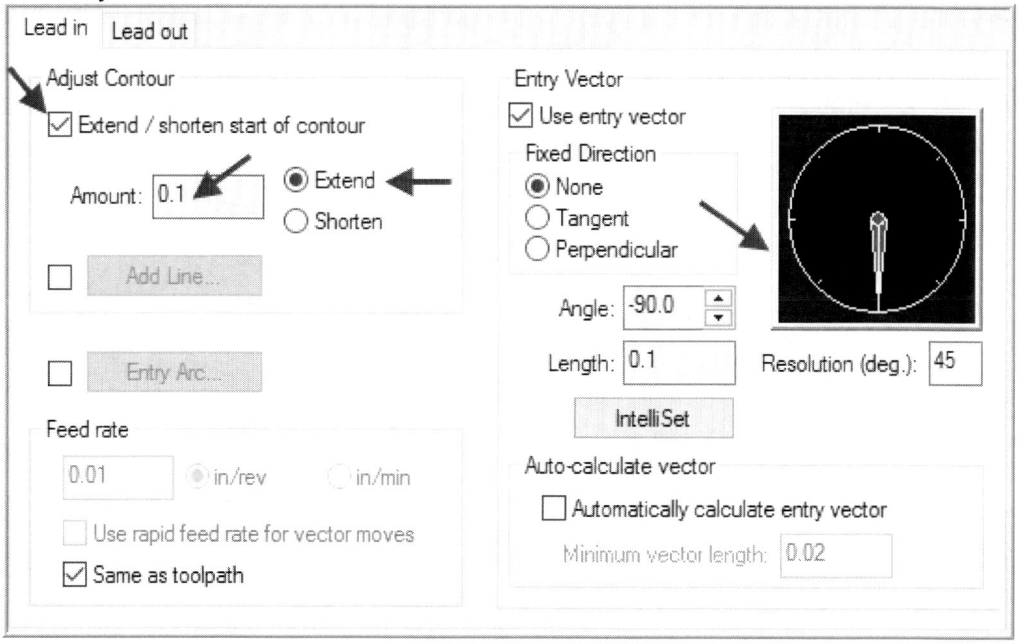

16. Click on the **Lead out** tab and make the necessary changes as shown below:

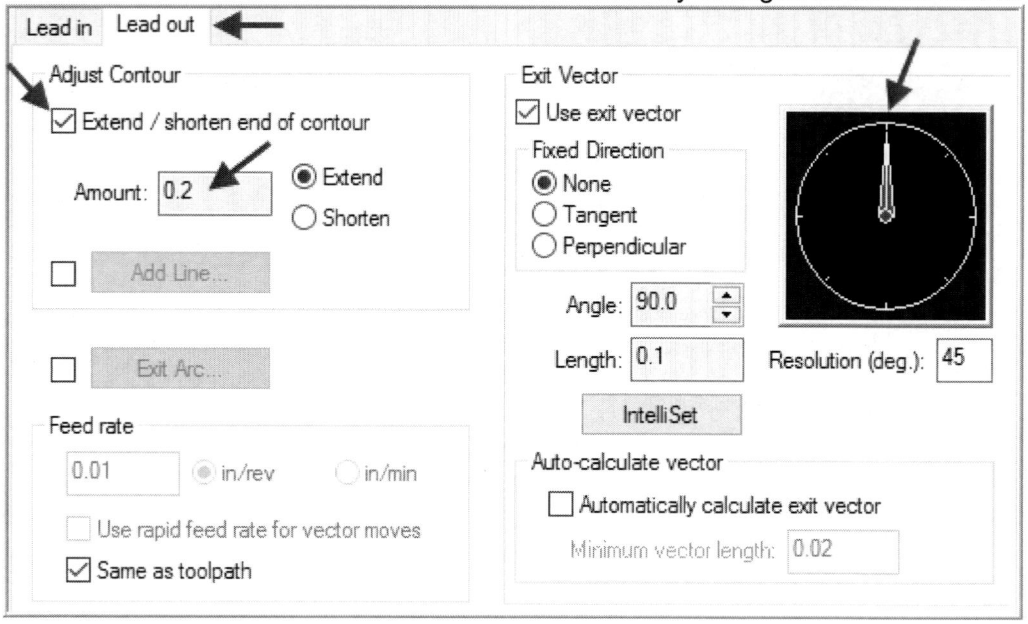

17. Click on OK to exit the Lead In/out window.

18. Click on the Plunge Parameters button Plunge Parameters... .

19. Make the necessary changes as shown below. **Activate** Allow Plunging In Both Directions.

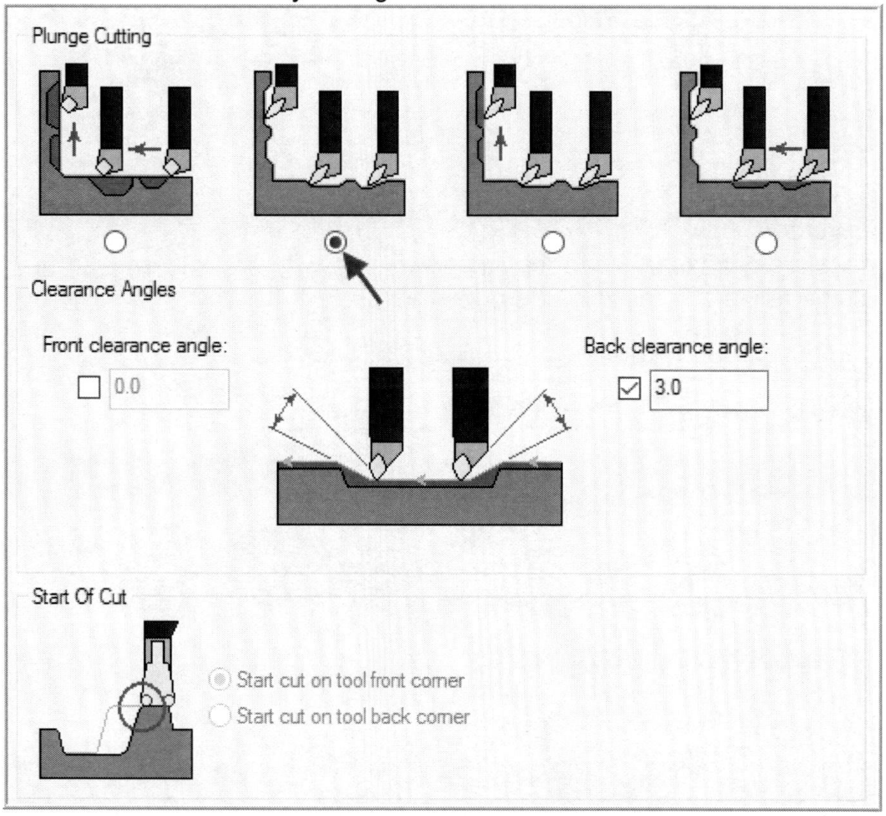

20. Click on **OK** to exit the **Plunge Cut parameters** window.

21. Click on OK to exit the Lathe Finish parameters window.

TASK 12:
CENTER DRILL HOLE

➲ In this task you will center drill .2" depth using **Tool #3 Centre Drill - .25 diameter.**

1. Select **Drill** in the **General** section of the **Turning** tab.

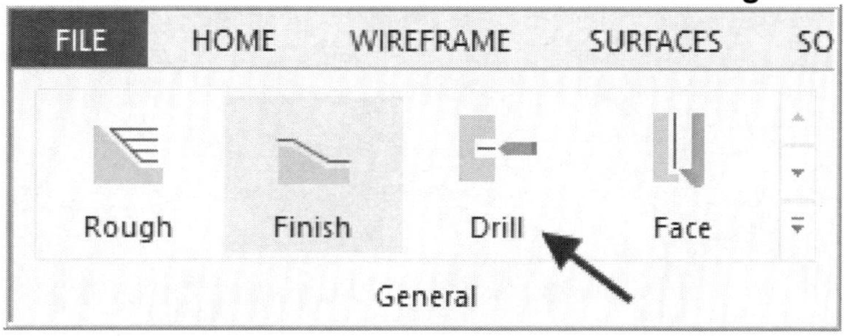

2. Select the **Centre Drill .25 diameter** tool from the tool list and make changes as shown below. **Coolant Flood** is set to **On**.

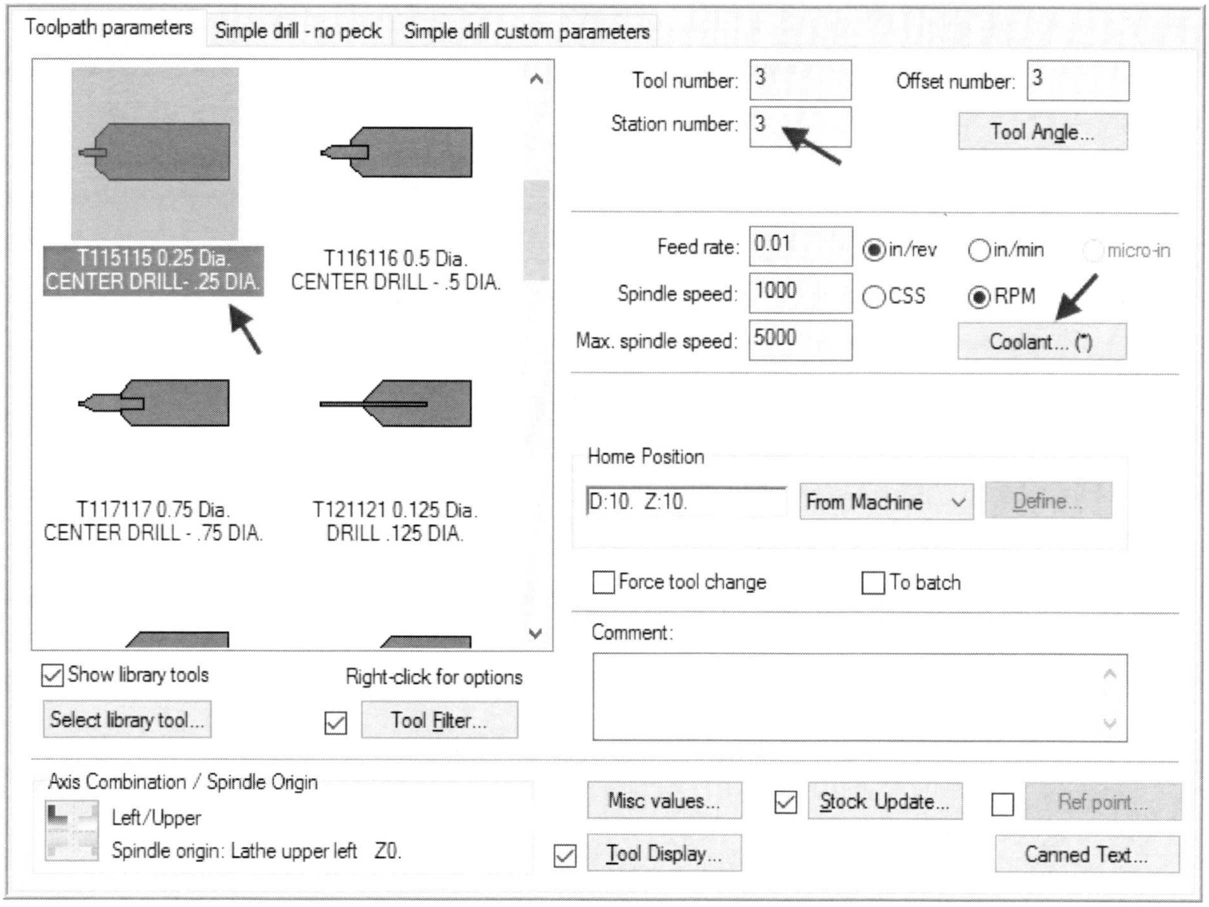

3. Select the Simple drill – no peck page and make changes as shown below:

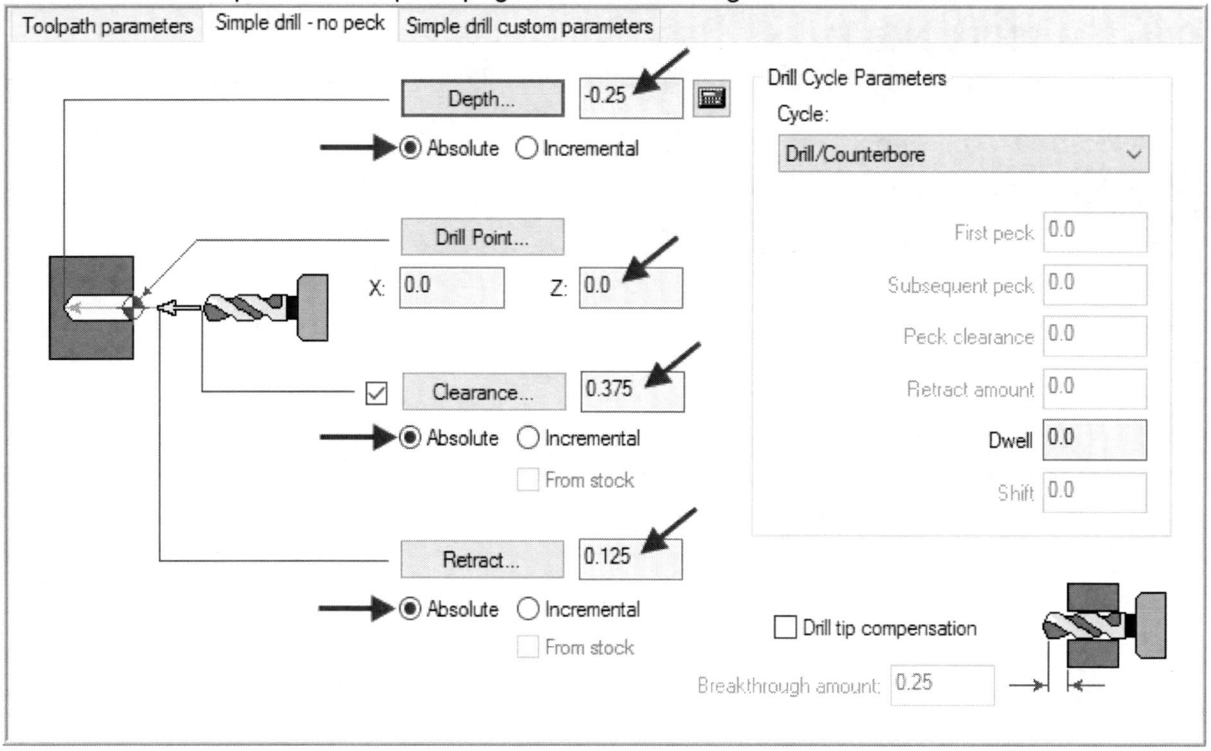

4. Select the OK button  to exit Simple drill – no peck.

TASK 13:
PRE DRILL THE 0.625" HOLE 0.375 DIAMETER

➲ In this task you will pre drill the .625" hole through the part using **Tool #4 Drill - .375 diameter.**

1. Select **Drill** in the **General** section of the **Turning** tab.
2. Scroll down and select the **Drill - .375 diameter** tool from the tool list and make changes as shown below. **Coolant Flood** is set to **On**.

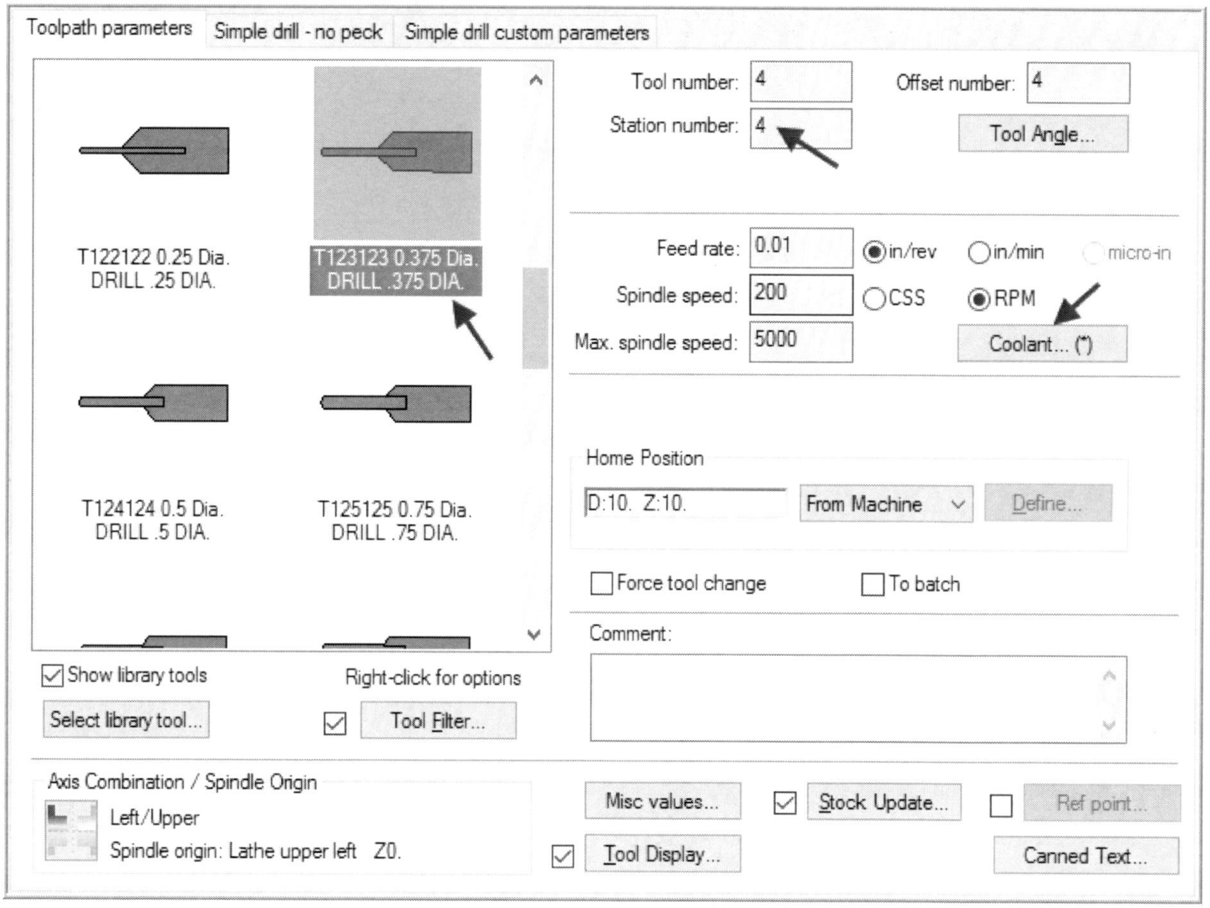

3. Select the **Simple drill – no peck** page and make changes as shown below. This hole will be **peck drilled through the part**. Make changes as shown below.

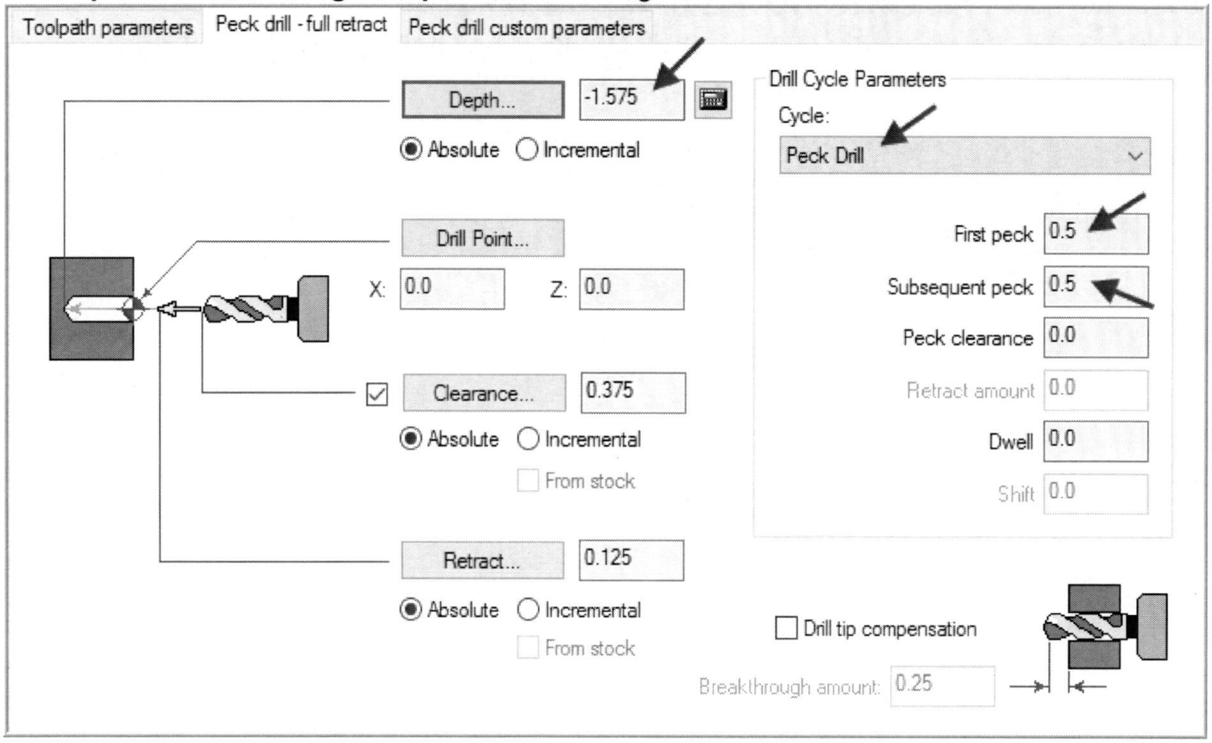

4. Select the OK button  to exit Peck drill – full retract.

TASK 14:
PRE DRILL THE 0.625" HOLE 0.5 DIAMETER

- ➲ In this task you will peck drill through the part with a 0.5 diameter drill prior to boring.
- ➲ You will copy the previous peck drill operation and then modify into this peck drilling operation.

1. On the left of the screen in the Toolpaths Manager the 0.375 drill peck drilling operation is the **fifth** operation. To copy this operation hold down the **Right mouse button** over the folder for this operation. Keep holding the right mouse button down and drag below the red arrow and release.
2. Select **Copy after** from this menu.

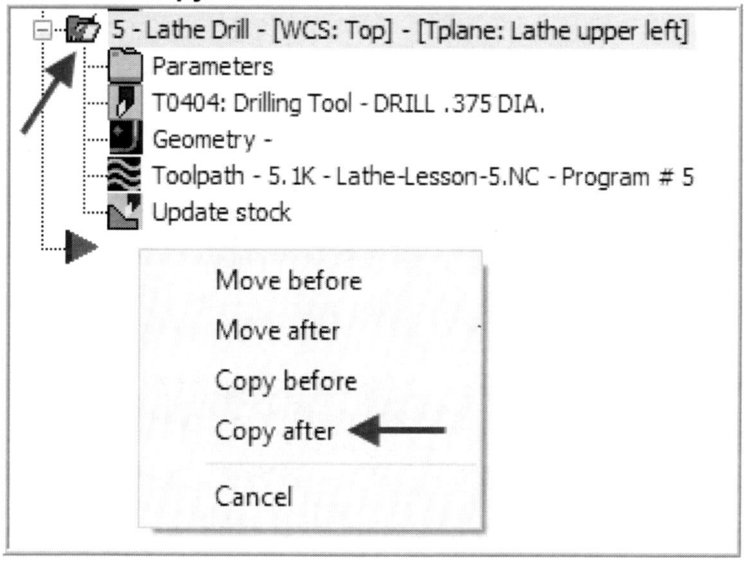

3. Move the Insert arrow 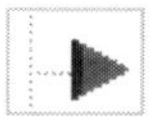 to the bottom of the list of operations by clicking the  icon on the Toolpaths Manager toolbar.
4. In the Toolpaths Manager click on the folder Parameters for the **sixth** operation as shown below:

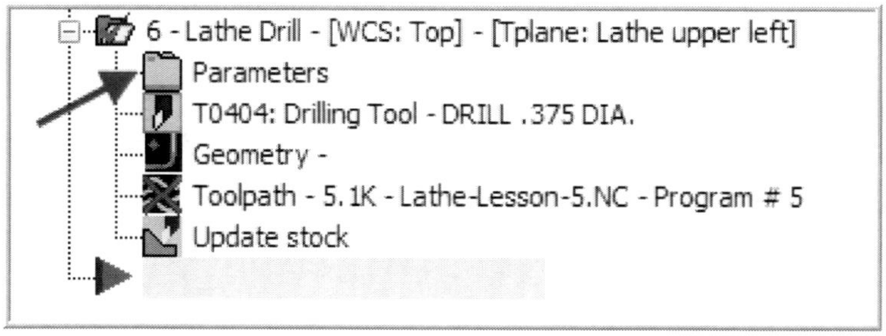

5. Select the **Toolpath parameters** page.
6. Scroll down and select the **.50 diameter drill**, as shown below.
7. Make changes to the Toolpath parameters page as shown below. **Coolant Flood** is already set to **On**.

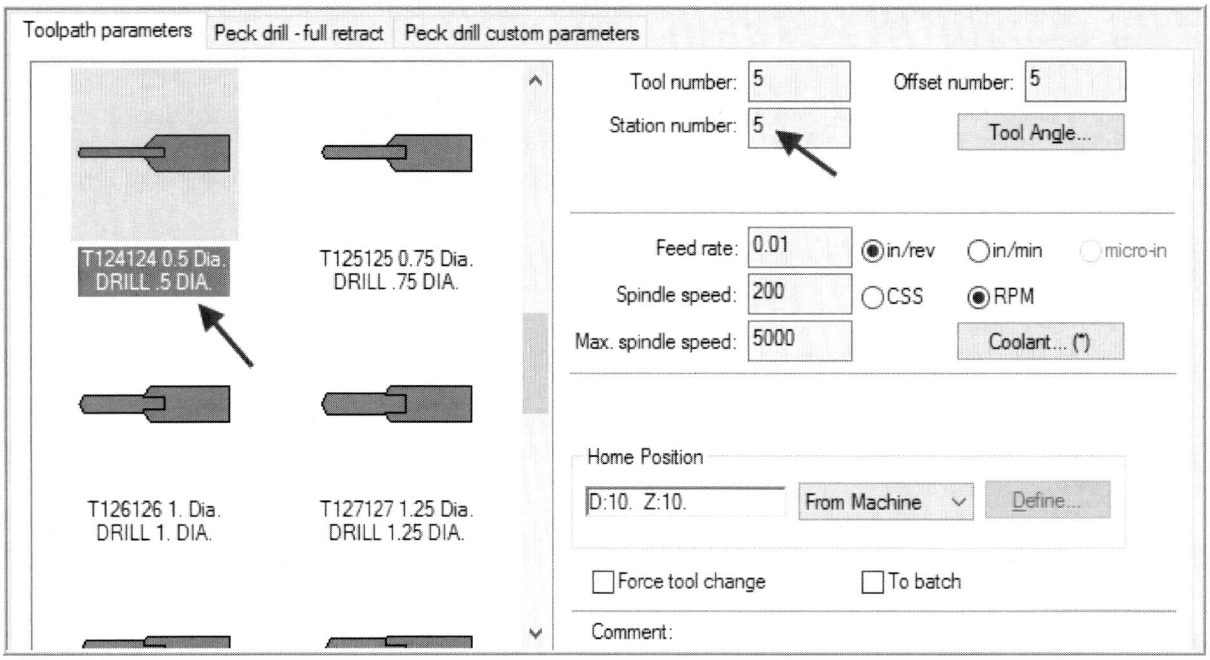

8. Select the **Peck drill – full retract** page and make changes as shown below.

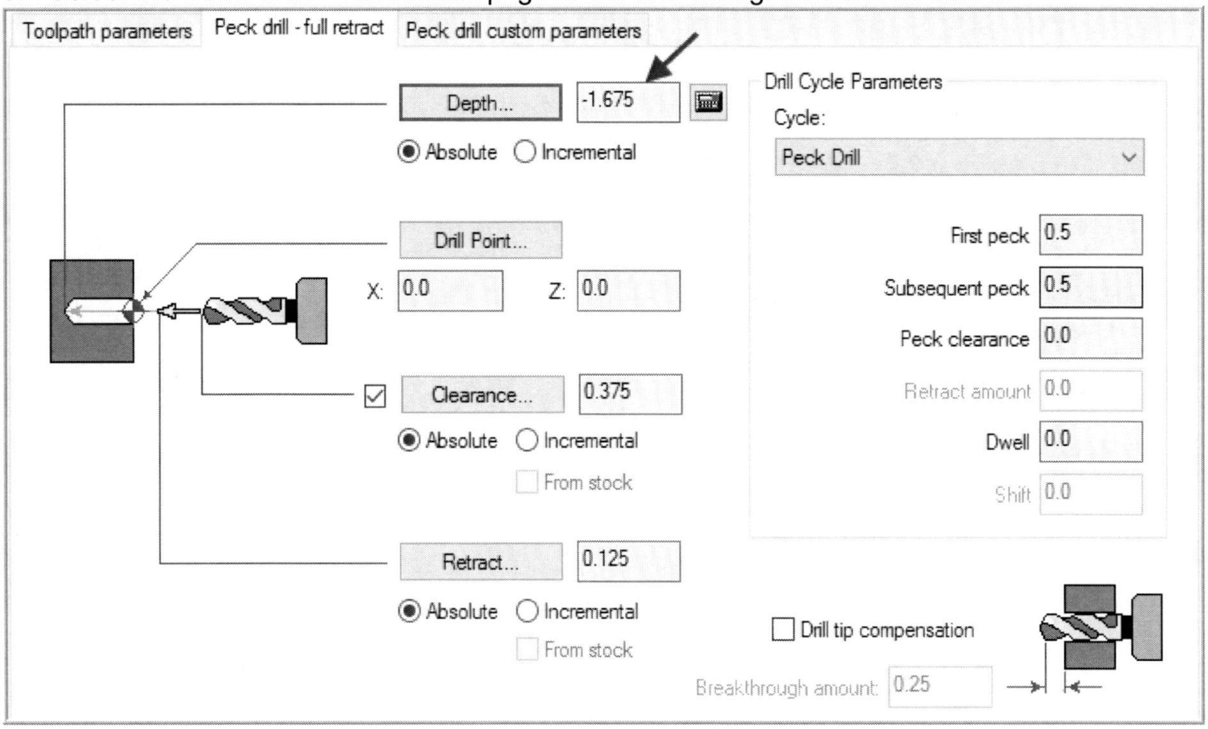

9. Select the OK button to exit Peck drill – full retract.

10. Select the **Regenerate all dirty operations** button to remove the red X from the drilling operation you have just edited. You need to update the toolpath with the new parameters you have just input.

TASK 15:
ROUGH THE BORE

➲ In this task you will use a boring tool to rough out the 0.870 and 0.625 diameter bores.

1. On the **TURNING** tab select **Rough** in the **General** section.
2. In the **Chaining** window Chaining mode is set to **Partial** by default.
3. Select **Line 1** as the start of the **Partial chain**.

> After you have selected the first line **ensure** that the arrow is pointing towards the part as shown below. If it is not select the reverse button in the Chaining dialog box
>
> 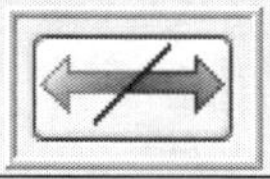

4. Then select Line 2 as the end entity in this chain.

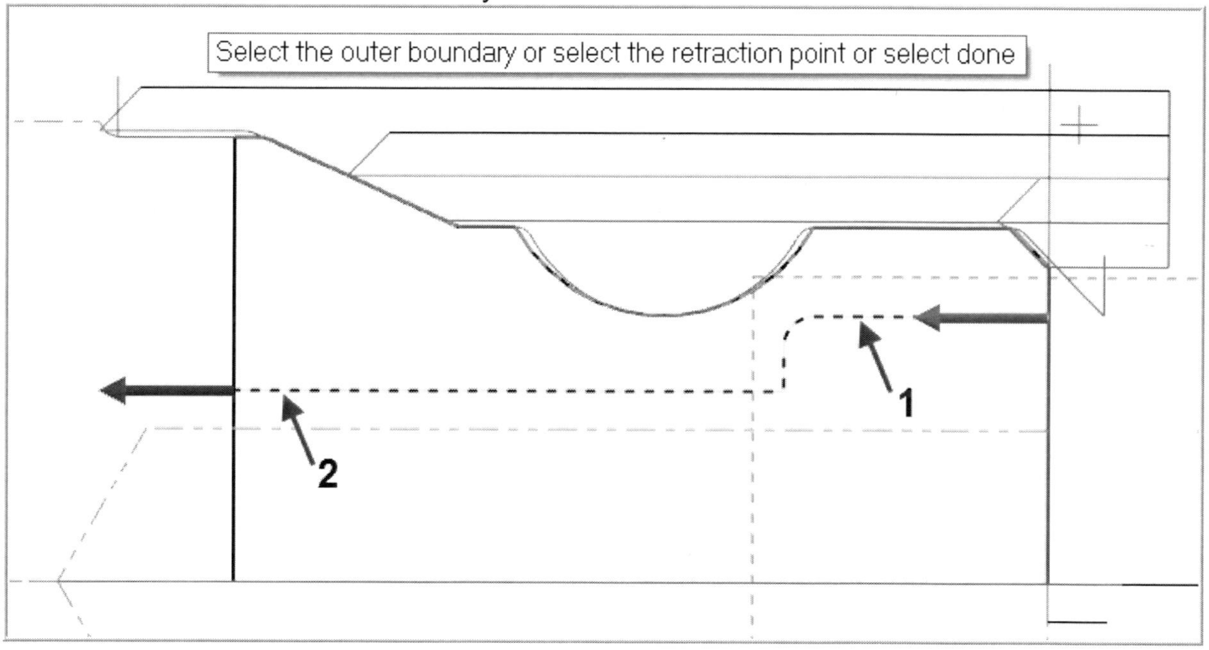

5. Select the OK button  to exit the Chaining dialog window.

6. In the **Toolpath parameters** page scroll down and select a boring tool **ID ROUGH MIN .375 DIA – 75 deg** and make any necessary changes as shown below. **Coolant Flood** is set to **On**.

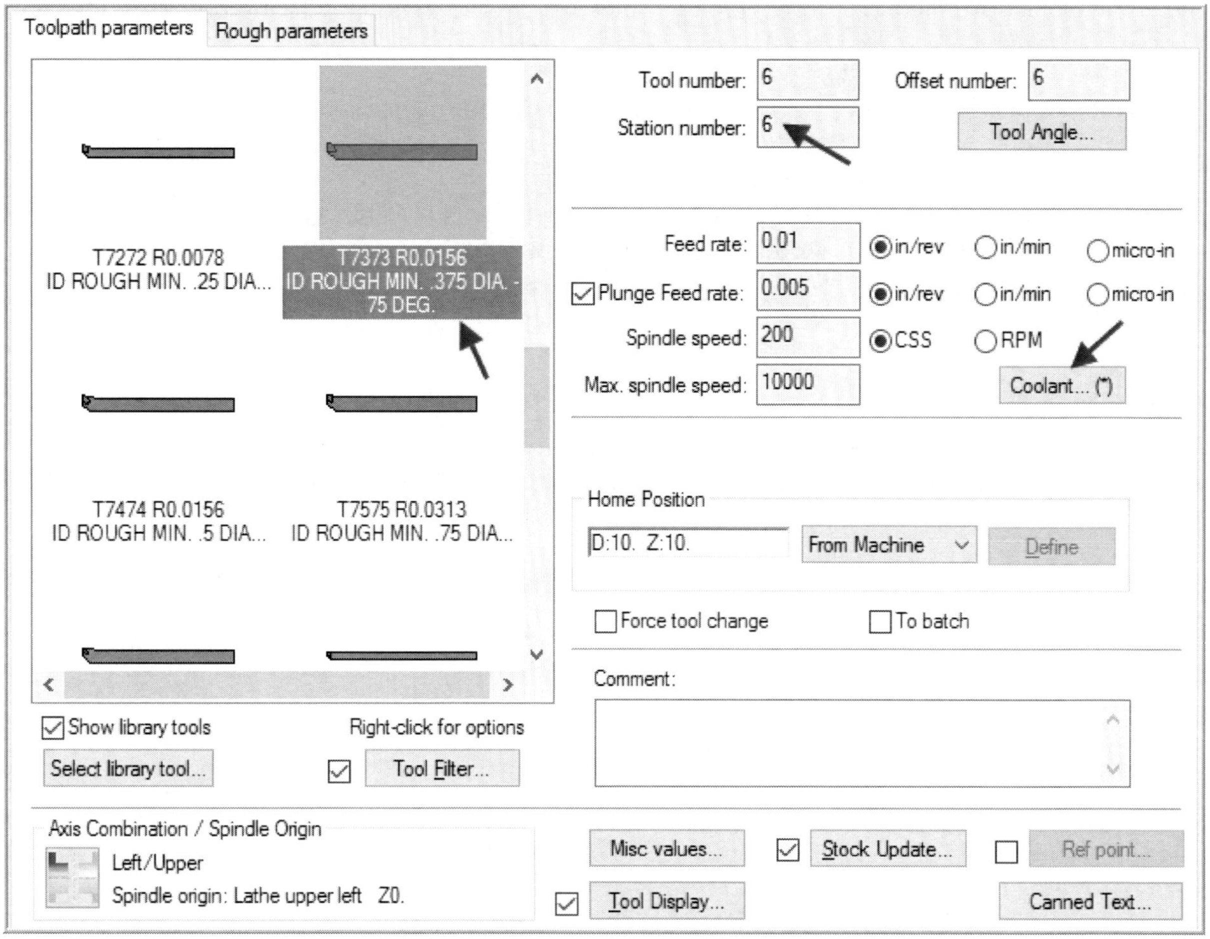

7. Double click on the picture 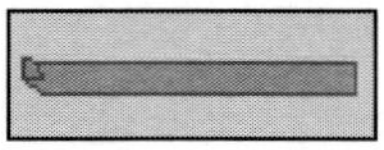 for this boring tool in the tool list window.

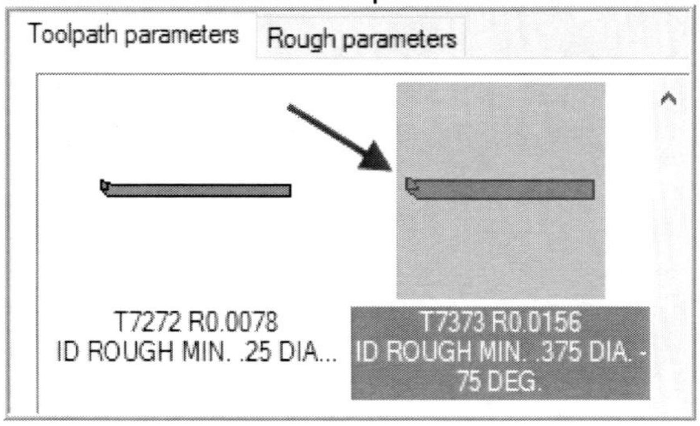

8. On the **Inserts** page change the **Thickness** of this insert to **1/32** as shown below.

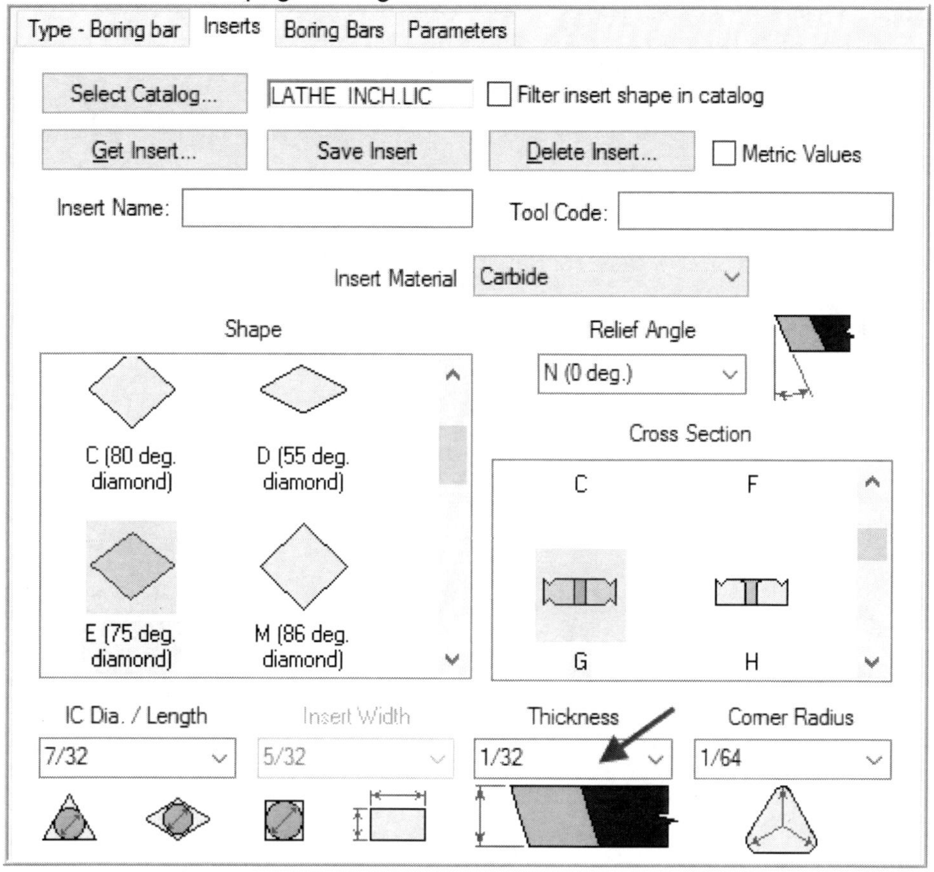

9. Select the OK button  to exit this function.

10. Select the Rough **parameters** page and make any necessary changes as shown below.

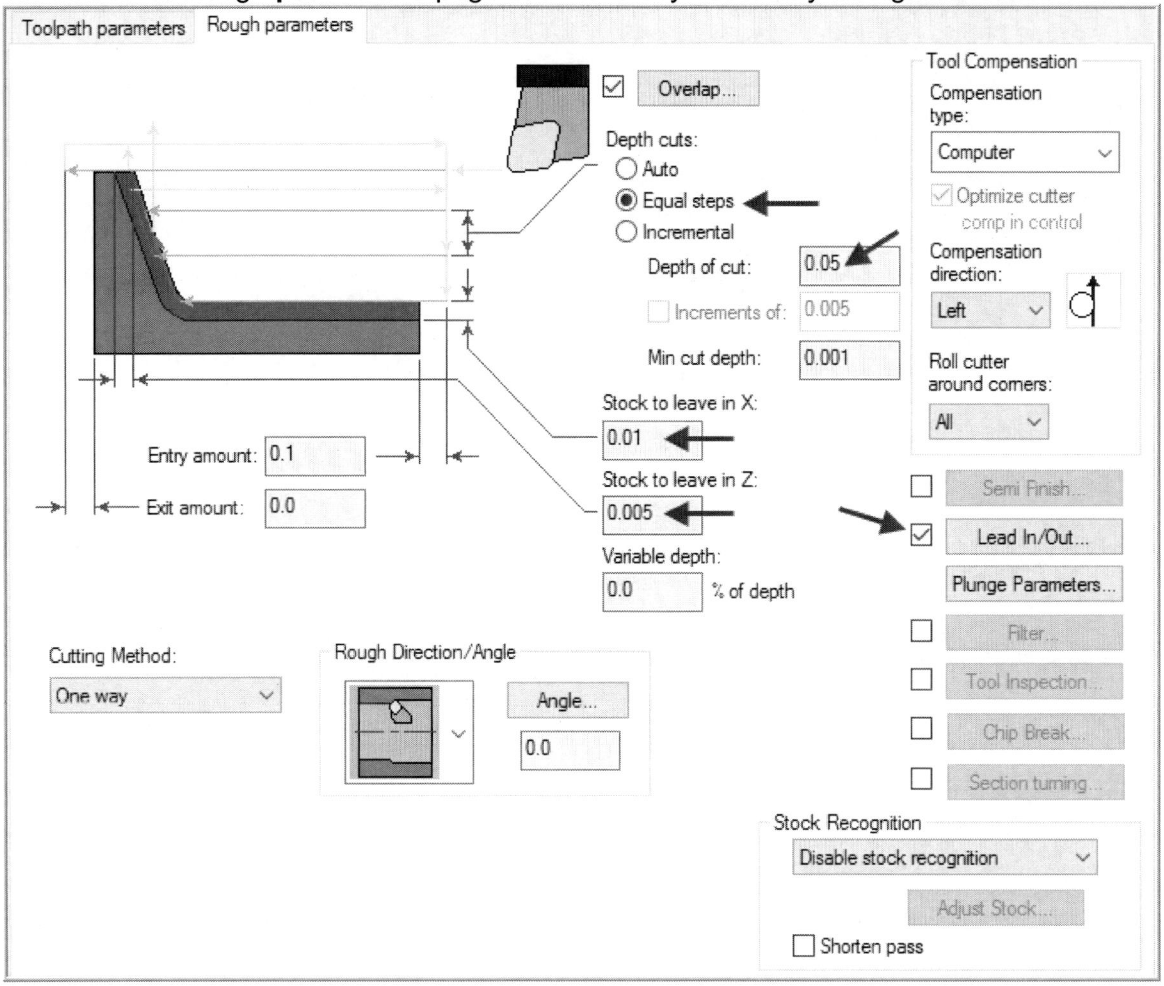

11. Select the **Lead In/Out** button select the **Lead out** page and extend the contour by **0.1** as shown below:

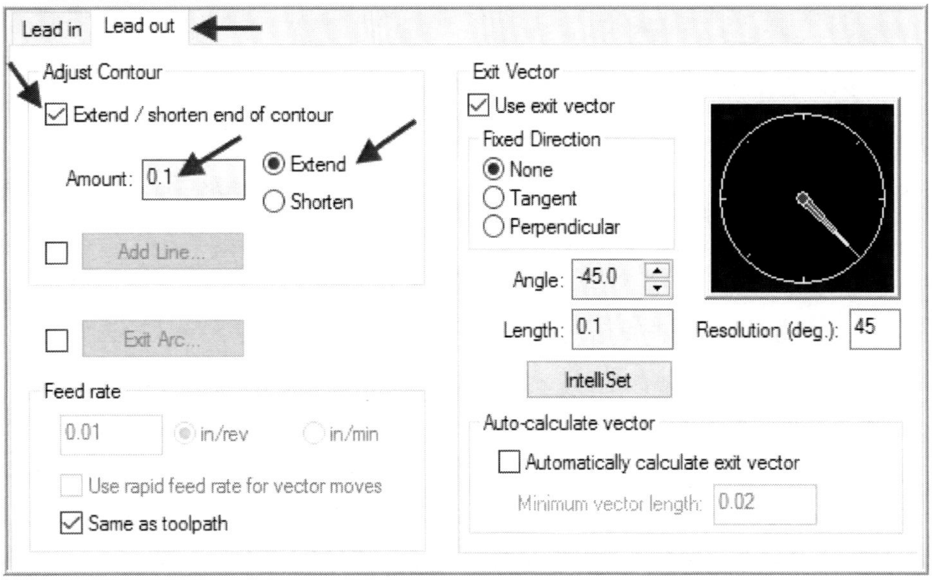

12. Select the OK button ✓ to exit this function.

13. Select the OK button ✓ to exit Rough Parameters.

TASK 16:
FINISH THE BORE

➲ In this task you will use the same boring tool as used for the previous rouging operation.

1. Right mouse click in the white space of the **Toolpaths Manager** and select:
Lathe toolpaths>Quick>Quick finish.

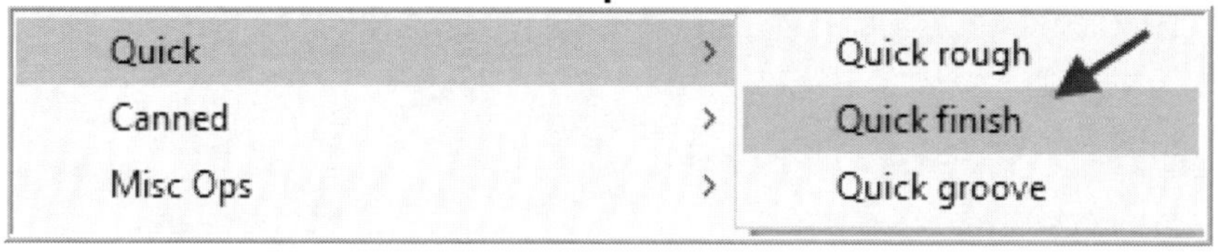

2. In the **Quick Toolpath parameters** page select **Tool #6 a boring tool ID ROUGH MIN .375 DIA – 75 deg** and make any necessary changes as shown below. **Coolant Flood** is set to **On**.

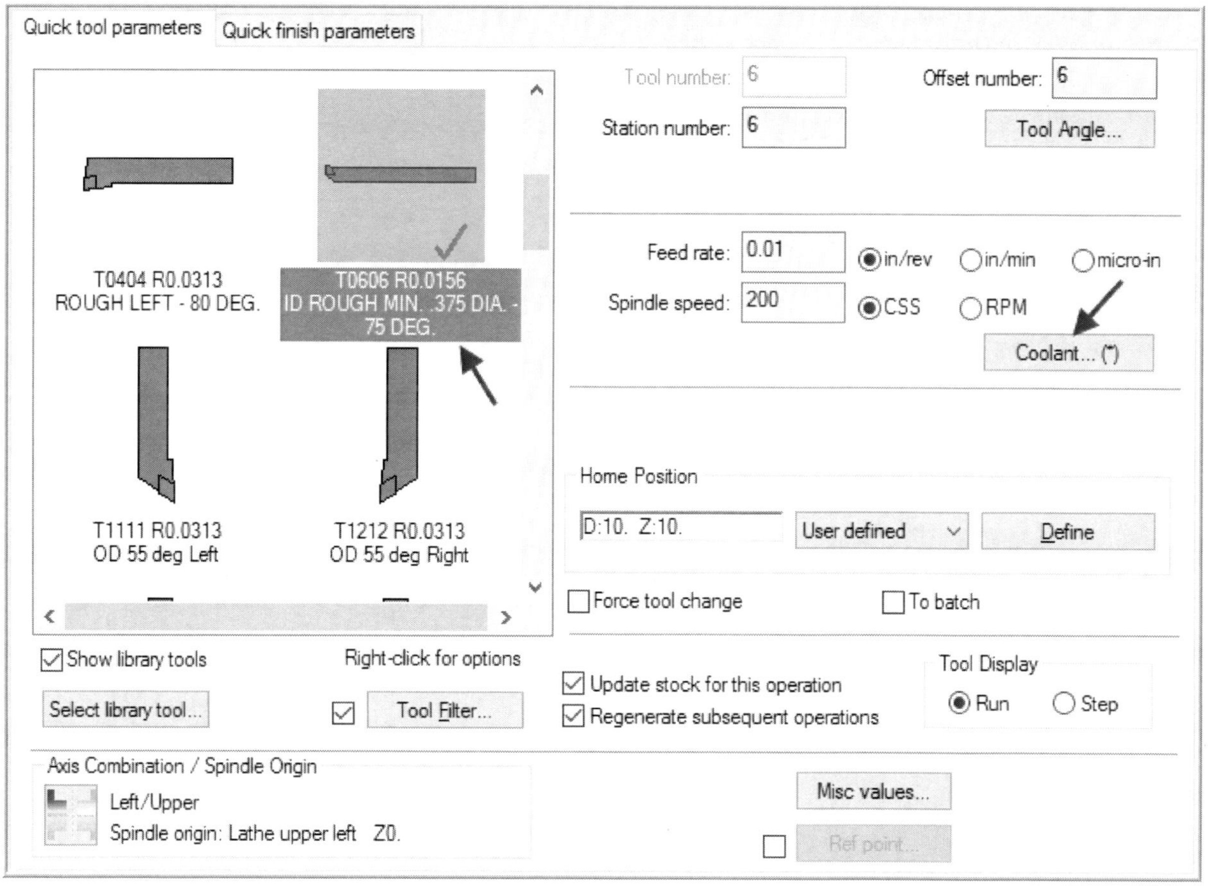

3. Select the **Quick finish parameters** page and in the lower left corner open up the drop down menu for **Finish Direction** and select **ID** from the four options listed here.

Finish Direction
Choose from which direction the tool will cut the toolpath: **ID** (inner diameter), **OD** (outer diameter), **Face** (front face), or **Back** (back face).

See the graphic representations for each below:

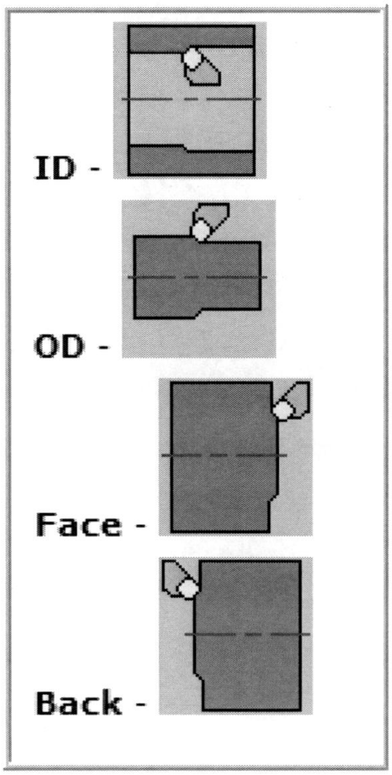

4. Select the **Quick finish parameters** page and make changes as shown below. Open up the drop down menu for operation and select the operation at the bottom of the list, this is the previous rough boring operation. **Compensation direction** is **Left**.

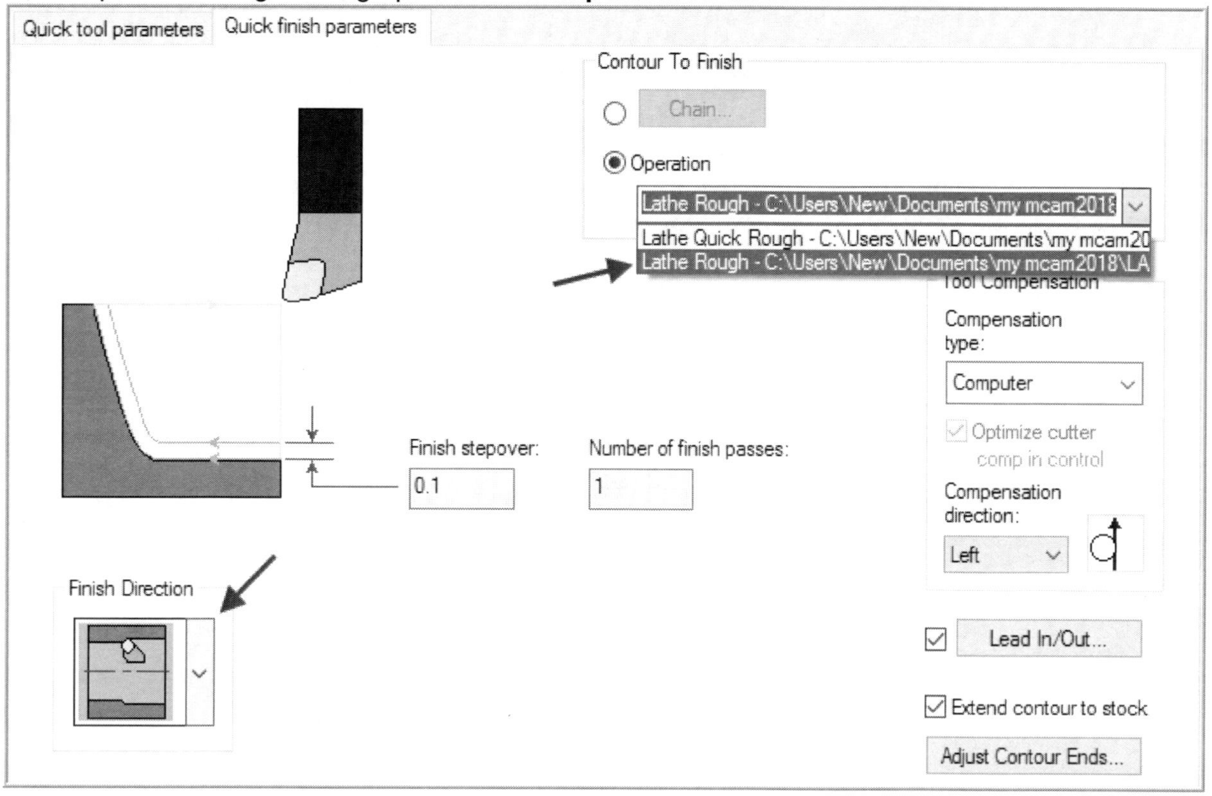

5. Select the **Lead In/Out button** select the **Lead out** page and extend the contour by .1 as shown below. **Exit Vector** is set at an angle of **-45**.

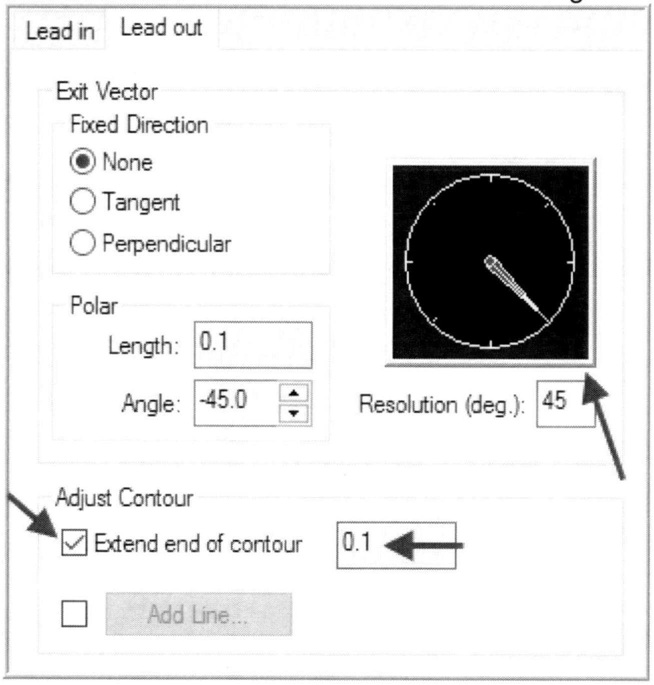

6. Select the OK button ✔ to exit this function.
7. Select the OK button ✔ to exit **Lathe Quick Finish** parameters.

TASK 17:
CUT OFF THE PART

➲ In this task you will cut off the part using **Tool #7 0.125 OD GROOVE RIGHT HAND TOOL**

1. Click on the **Select all operations** icon .
2. Now **toggle the display of the toolpaths** by selecting **ALT and T** on your keyboard to hide the toolpaths display.
3. Click on the **Expand gallery** down arrow to view additional options in the **General** toolpath section. In the **General** section select **Cutoff.**
4. When prompted to **Select cutoff boundary point** pick the end point of the line shown below. Move the cursor over the corner until the visual cue for End point displays and then click on this point.

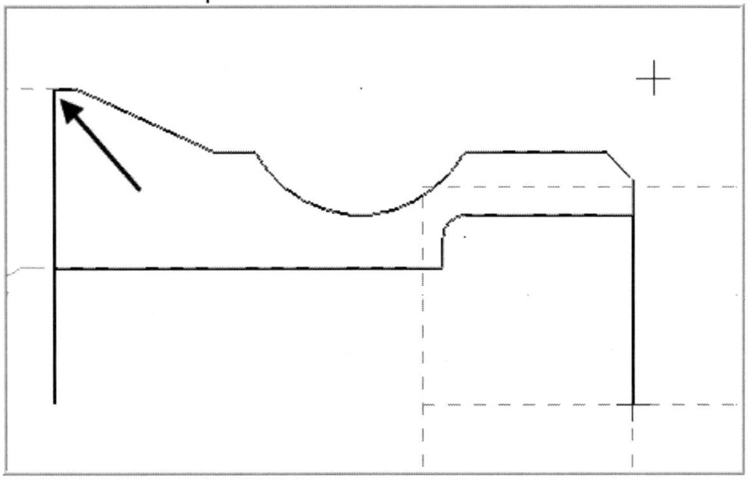

5. Select **OD GROOVE RIGHT WIDTH .125** tool from the tool list and make any necessary changes as shown below. **Coolant Flood** is set to **On**.

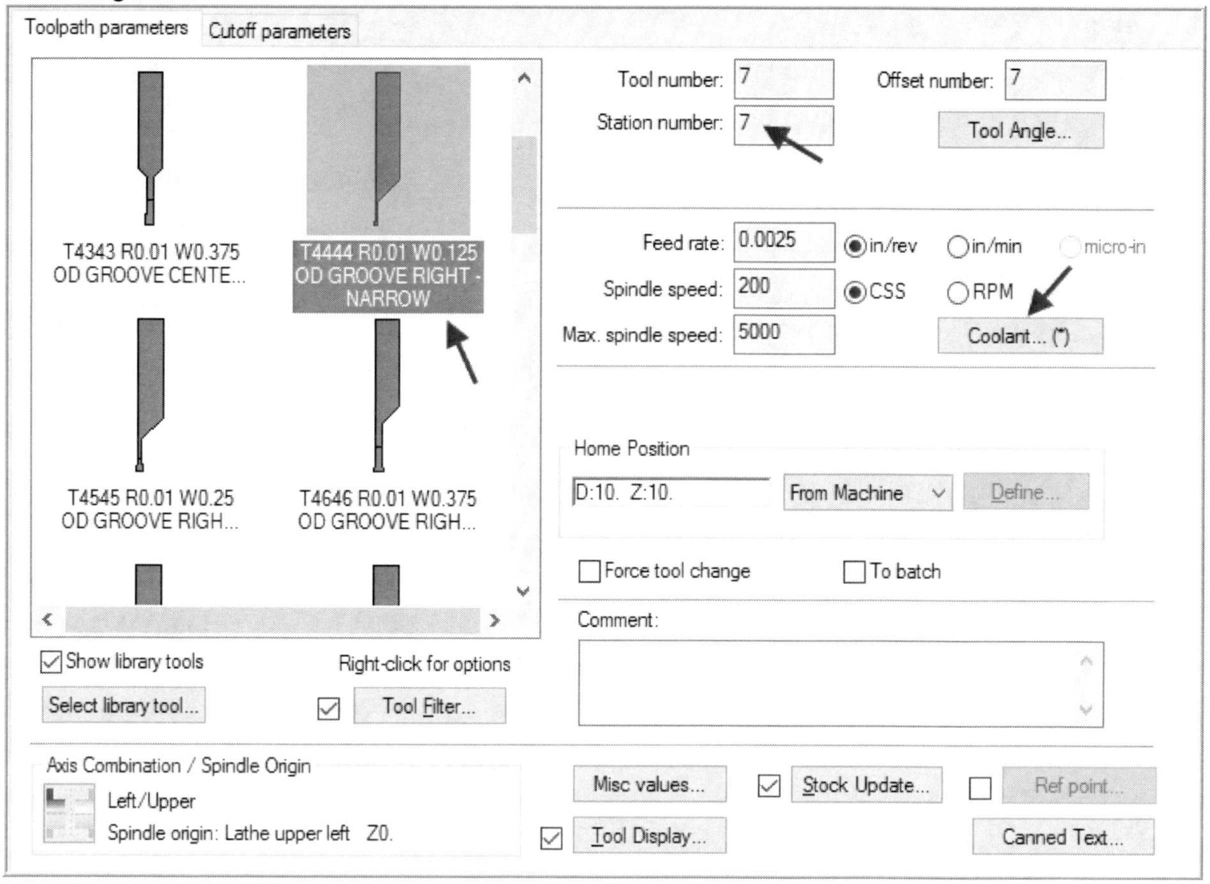

6. Still on the **Toolpath parameters** page click on the Stock Update button .

7. Ensure **Keep both pieces** is activated.

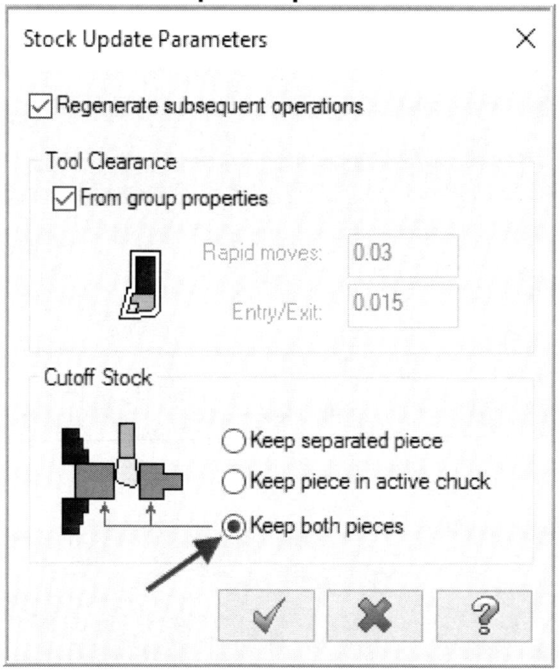

8. Select the **Cutoff parameters** page and make sure the settings are as shown below.

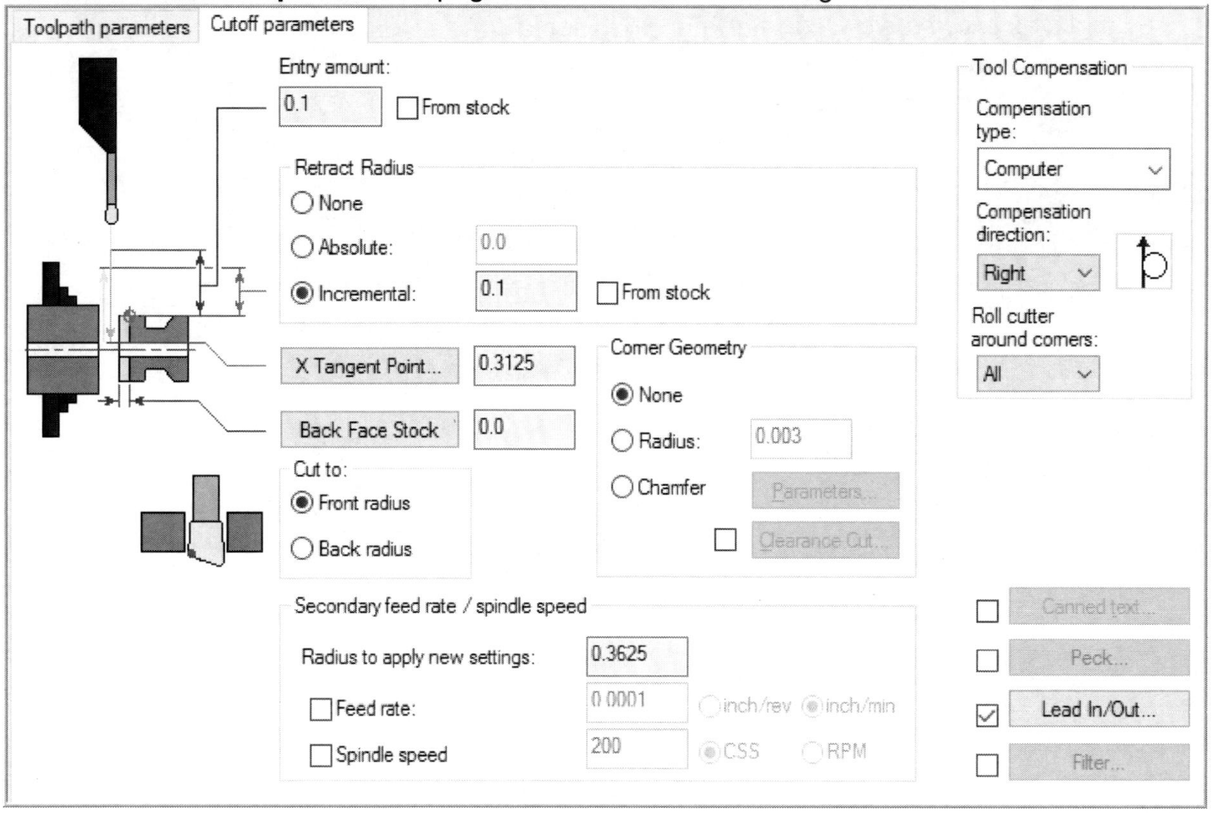

9. Select the OK button  to exit **Lathe Cutoff parameters.**

TASK 18:
VERIFY THE TOOLPATH

➲ Mastercam's Verify utility allows you to use solid models to simulate the machining of a part. The model created by the verification represents the surface finish, and shows collisions, if any exist.

1. Right mouse click in the graphics area and click on the **Fit** icon .
2. In the Toolpaths Manager pick all the operations to Verify by picking the **Select All** icon .
3. Select the **Verify selected operations** icon shown below:

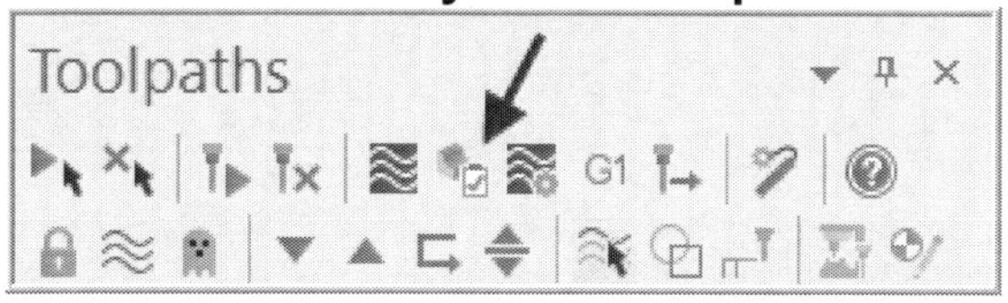

4. **Maximize** the Backplot/Verify window if required.
5. Now select the **Home** Tab if required.

6. Activate the options shown below in the **Visibility** section of the **Home** tab. **Initial Stock not** activated.

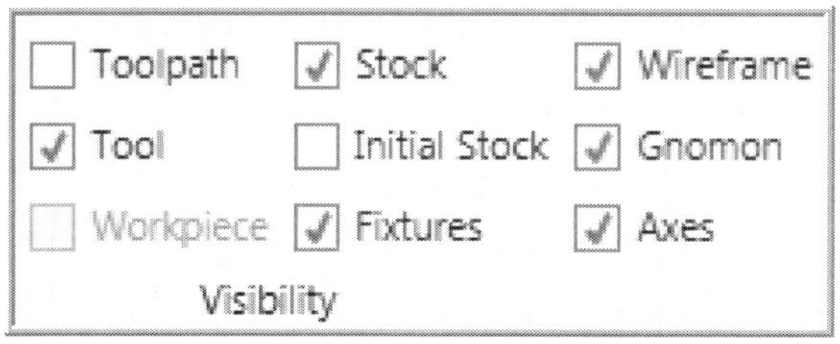

7. At the top of the screen select the **View** tab, the **Isometric** icon and then select **Fit**.

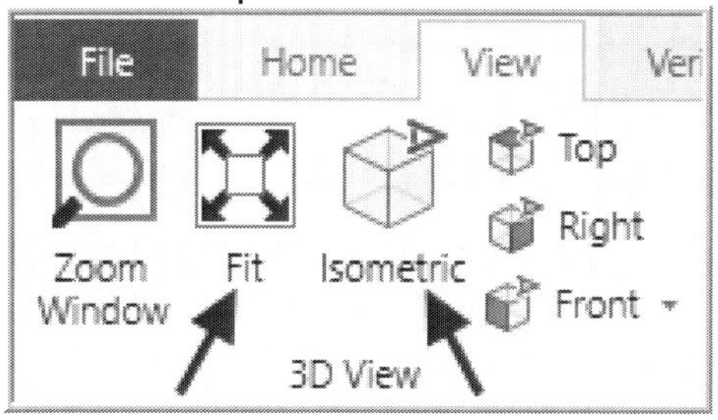

8. Select the **Verify** tab and activate the **Color Loop** to change the color of the tools for the verified part.

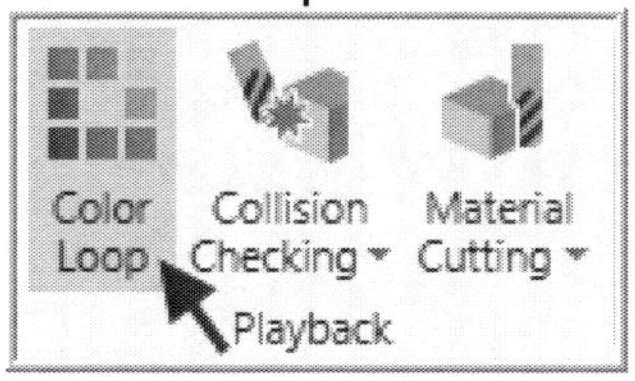

Color Loop
Changes the color of the toolpath or cut stock by operation or by tool change.

Choose **File Options** to set the colors.

9. In the lower part of the screen now set the run **Speed** to slow by moving the slider bar pointer over to the left as shown below.

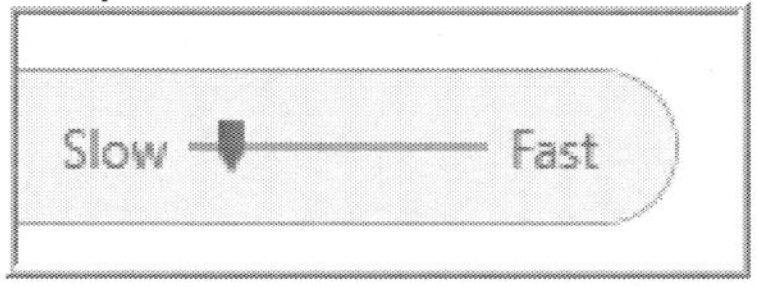

10. Now select the **Play Simulation** button to review the toolpaths.

11. **Select** the Close button 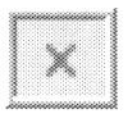 in the top right hand corner to exit Verify.

TASK 19:
SAVE THE UPDATED MASTERCAM FILE

1. Select the **Save** icon from the **Quick Access** toolbar at the top left of the screen.

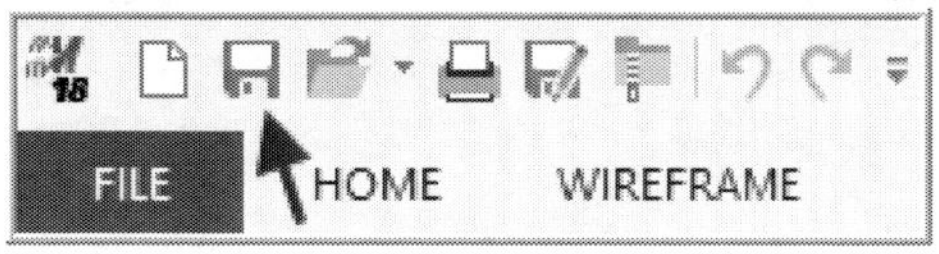

TASK 20:
POST AND CREATE THE CNC CODE FILE

1. Ensure all the operations are selected by picking the **Select All** icon from the Toolpaths manager.
2. Select the **Post selected operations** button from the Toolpaths manager.

➲ **Please Note:** If you cannot see **G1** click on the right pane of the Toolpaths manager window and expand the window to the right.

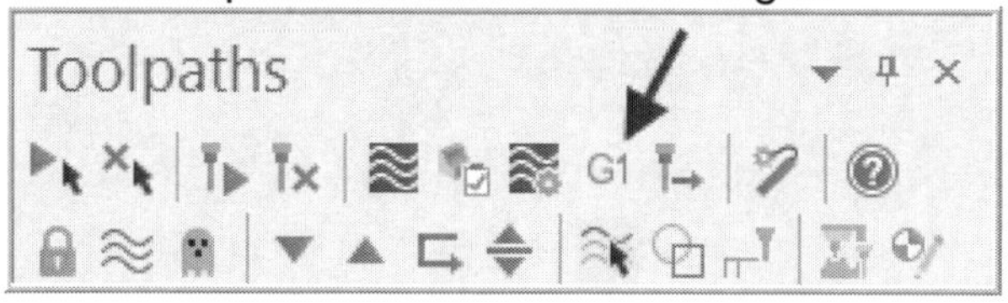

3. In the Post processing window, make the necessary changes as shown below:

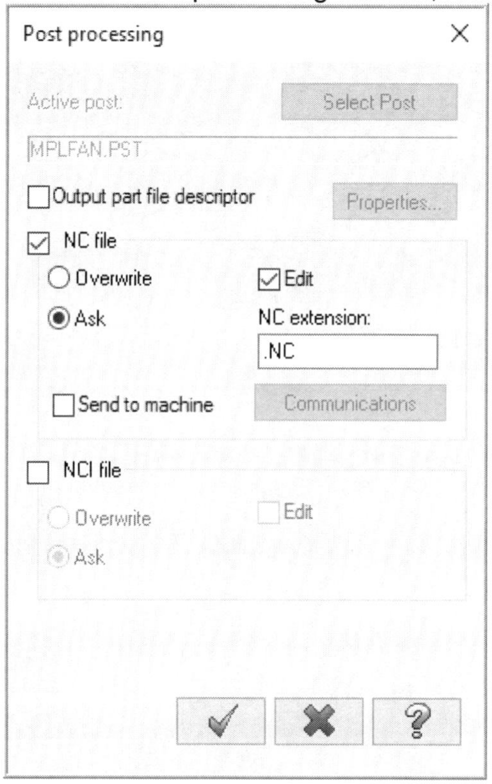

About Post Processing

NC file:
Select this option to save the NC file. The file name and extension are stored in the machine group properties for the selected operation. If you are posting operations from different machine groups or Mastercam files, or batch processing, Mastercam will create several files according to the settings for each machine group.

Edit:
When checked, automatically launches the default text editor with the file displayed so that you can review or modify it.

4. Select the OK button to continue.

5. Ensure the same name as your Mastercam part file name is displayed in the **NC File name** field.
6. Select the **Save** button.

➲ The CNC code file opens up in the default editor.

Lathe-Lesson-5.NC ×

```
(MATERIAL - STEEL INCH - 1030 - 200 BHN)
G20
(TOOL - 1 OFFSET - 1)
(OD ROUGH RIGHT - 80 DEG.  INSERT - CNMG-432)
G0 T0101
G18
G97 S449 M03
G0 G54 X1.7 Z0. M8
G50 S3600
G96 S200
G99 G1 X-.1225 F.01
G0 Z.1
X1.3246
Z.2
G1 Z.1
Z-1.1856
X1.4637 Z-1.3415
G18 G3 X1.47 Z-1.3563 I-.0331 K-.0148
G1 Z-1.6063
```

7. Select the  in the top right corner to exit the CNC editor.

➲ This completes Lathe-Lesson-5.

LATHE-LESSON-5 EXERCISE

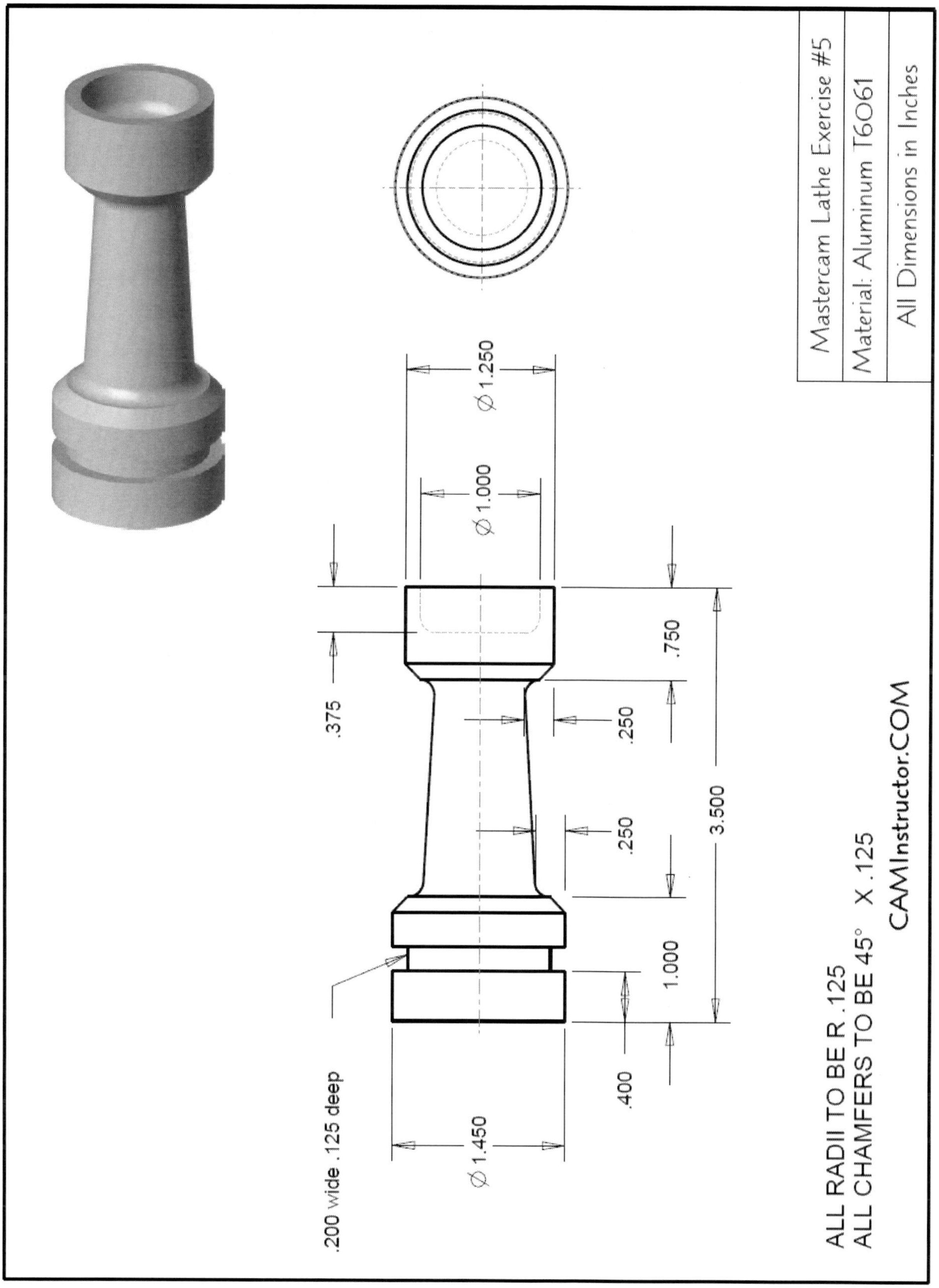

Mastercam® 2018

TRAINING

GUIDE

LESSON 5B

IMPORT A SOLID PART FILE

NOTE:
This Lesson is located on the **CamInstructor Course Site**.

1. Go to www.caminstructor.com and Log In.
2. Open the **Mastercam 2018 Lathe** course.
3. Click on **Lesson 5B Import & Toolpath a Solid.**

camInstructor

Mastercam® 2018

TRAINING

GUIDE

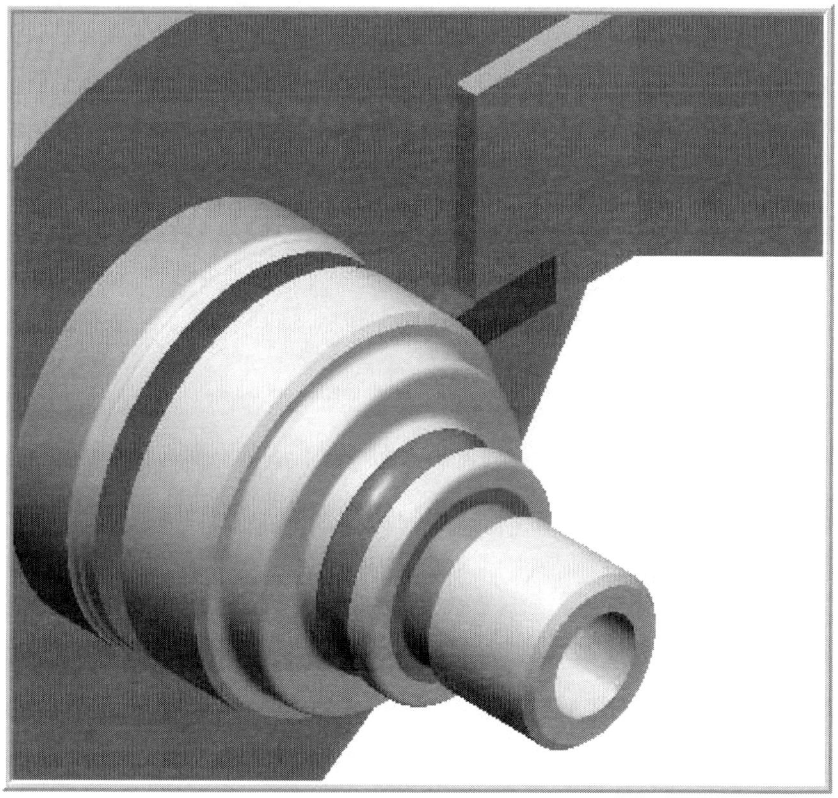

LATHE-LESSON-6

FACE, QUICK ROUGH AND FINISH, DRILL, GROOVE AND CUTOFF

camInstructor

Objectives

You will create the geometry for Lathe Lesson 6, and then generate a toolpath to machine the part on a CNC lathe. This lesson covers the following topics:

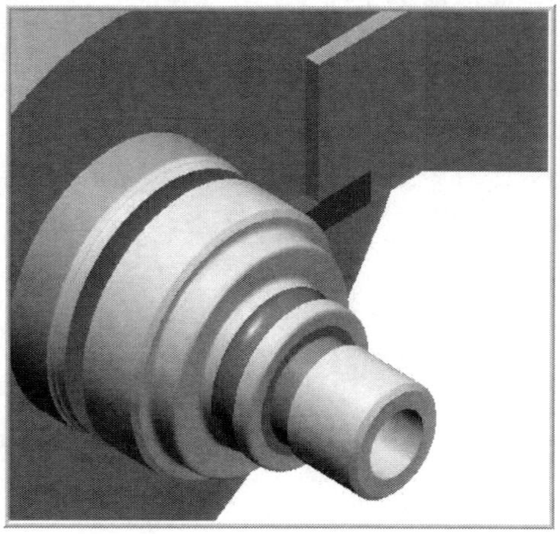

➲ **Create a 2-dimensional drawing by:**
Creating lines.
Creating fillets.
Creating chamfers.
Trimming geometry.

➲ **Establish Stock and Chuck Setup settings:**
Stock size.
Chuck Configuration.
Material for the part.
Feed calculation.

➲ **Generate a 2-dimensional lathe toolpath consisting of:**
Lathe Face.
Lathe Quick Rough.
Lathe Quick Finish.
Lathe Finish.
Lathe Drill.
Lathe Groove.
Lathe Cutoff.

➲ **Inspect the toolpath using Mastercam's Verify and Backplot by:**
Launching the Verify function to machine the part on the screen.
Generating the NC- code.

LATHE - LESSON-6 DRAWING

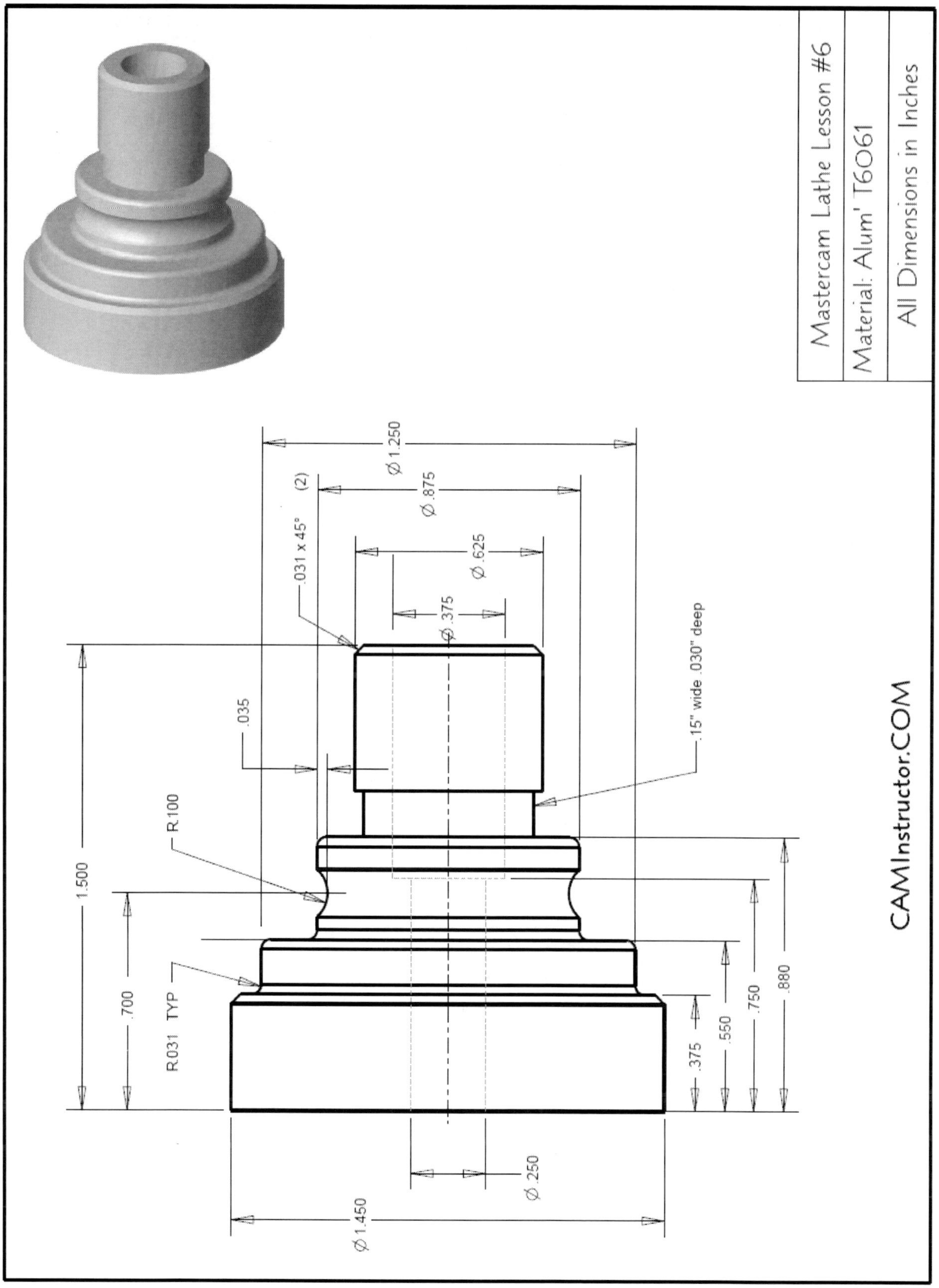

TOOL LIST

Six tools will be used to create this part.

- **Tool #1 Face, Rough and Finish the outside diameters**
  Holder: Outside Diameter Rough Right Hand - DCGNR-164D.
  Insert: 80 Degree Diamond Insert – CNMG-432

- Tool #2 Finish the 0.1 radius
  Holder: Offset Profiling.
  Insert: 0.1875 circular insert

- **Tool #3 Center drill**
  Centre Drill – body diameter 0.250"

- **Tool #4 0.250 diameter drill**
  Drill 0.25" diameter

- **Tool #5 0.375 End Mill**
  End Mill 0.375" diameter

- **Tool #6 Cutoff tool**
  Holder: Outside Diameter Groove Right Hand - Narrow.
  Insert: 0.125" Wide - GC-4125

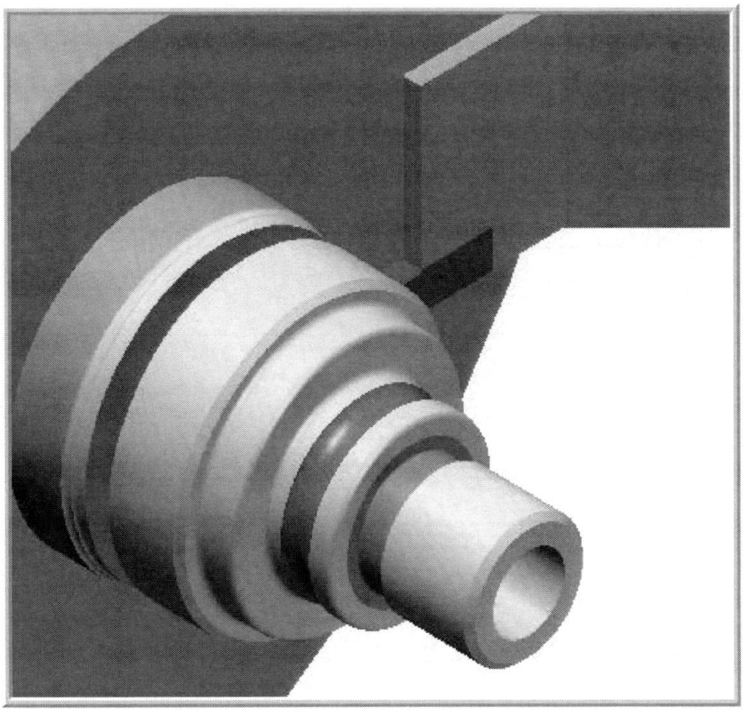

LESSON - 6 - THE PROCESS

Geometry Creation

TASK 1: Setting the environment
TASK 2: Setting the construction planes
TASK 3: Create the geometry
TASK 4: Create the 0.100" radius
TASK 5: Create the chamfers
TASK 6: Create the fillet radii
TASK 7: Create the geometry for the bore
TASK 8: Save the drawing

Toolpath Creation

TASK 9: Define the stock and chuck parameters
TASK 10: Face the front of the part
TASK 11: Rough the outside diameters
TASK 12: Finish the outside diameters
TASK 13: Finish the 0.1 radius
TASK 14: Center drill hole
TASK 15: Peck Drill the 0.250" Hole
TASK 16: Drill the 0.375" Hole
TASK 17: Cut the Groove
TASK 18: Cut off the part
TASK 19: Verify the toolpath
TASK 20: Save the updated Mastercam file
TASK 21: Post and create the CNC code file

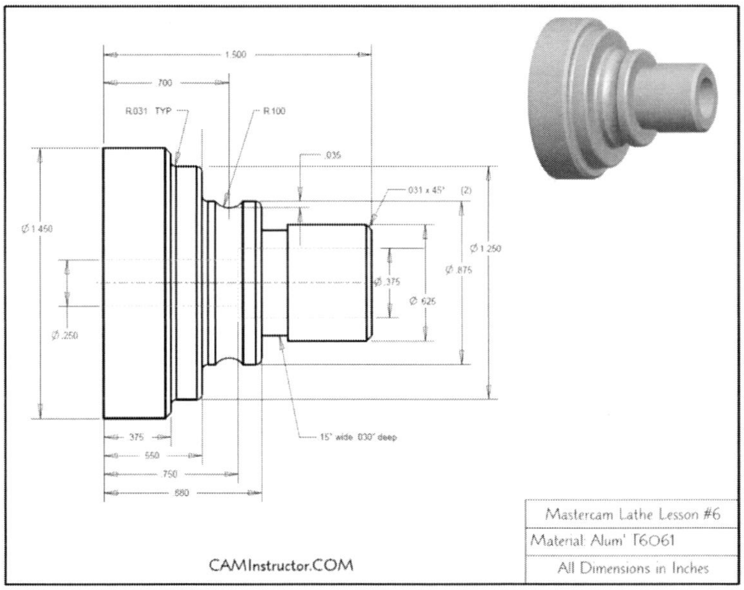

Geometry Creation

TASK 1:
SETTING THE ENVIRONMENT

Before starting the geometry creation you should set up the grid and machine type as outlined in the **Setting the Environment** section at the beginning of this text:

1. Set up the Grid. This will help identify the location of the origin.
2. Set the machine type to the default Lathe.

TASK 2:
SETTING THE CONSTRUCTION PLANES:

➲ **Set the Construction Plane to Lathe diameter +D +Z (WCS)**

1. Select the **View tab** and click on **Toolpaths** and **Solids** in the **Managers** section to **hide** them and toggle **only** the **Planes Manager to display**.

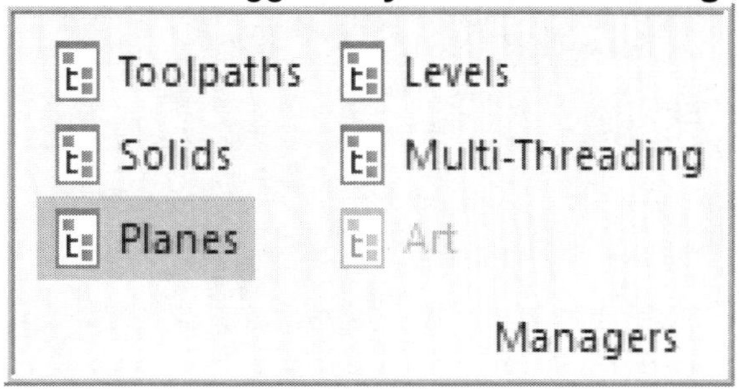

Once your machine is set up, Mastercam includes special lathe construction planes that let you work in **radius or diameter coordinates**.

For conventional 2D turning applications, use the Planes Manager to select the desired coordinate system, as shown below right. Choose to use either radius or diameter coordinates and then choose the desired X/D and Z directions.

2. Ensure the **C column** (Construction Plane) and **T column** (Tool Plane) are set to the **+D +Z Plane**. Just click in the C and T columns in the **+D +Z** row.

➲ Take note of the **Status bar** at the bottom of the screen **CPLANE: +D +Z TPLANE: +D +Z WCS:TOP** as shown below right.

3. To change the **Lathe Plane** open up the drop down menu for **Select lathe plane** and click on the required coordinate system as shown below right.

4. Select the **Close** button ☒ in the top right hand corner to close the Planes Manager.

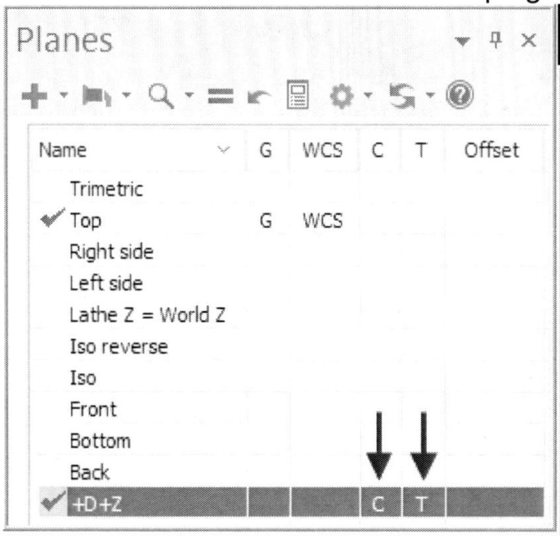

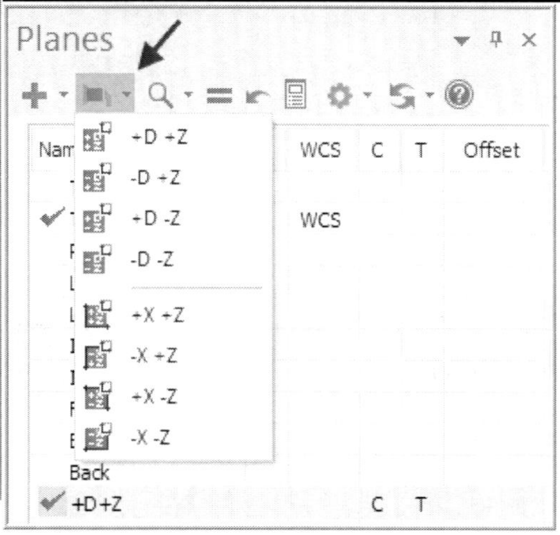

TASK 3:
CREATE THE GEOMETRY

- This task explains how to create the geometry of this part. In this lathe part you only need to create **half of the geometry**, the geometry above the center line.
- Lines 1 through 12 will be created first and then the radius and chamfer will be created.

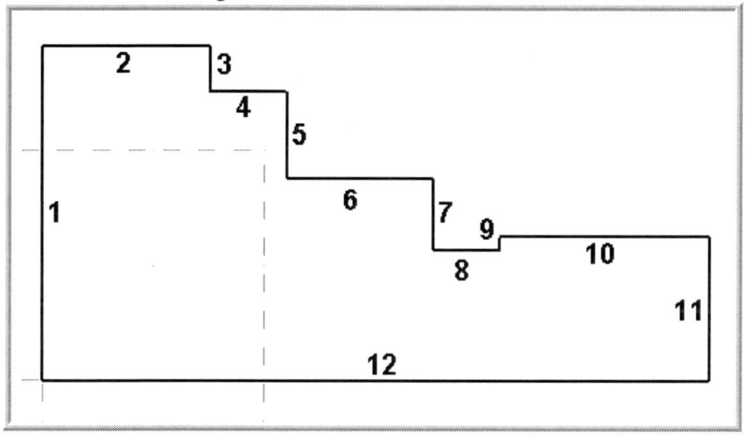

- **Create Line #1**

1. Select the **WIREFRAME** tab at the top of the screen and in the **Lines** section click on **Line Endpoints**.
2. On the graphics screen you are prompted: **Specify the first endpoint** and the Line Endpoints panel appears. In the Line Endpoints panel **activate Multi-line and Freeform**.

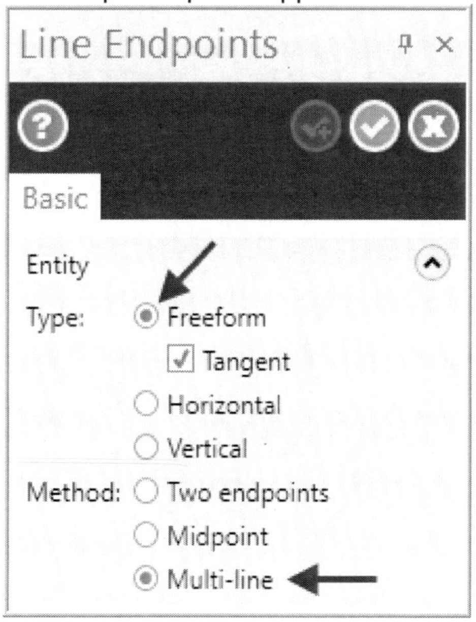

3. Move the cursor over the **center of the grid** and as you get close to the origin a visual cue appears.  This is the cue that will allow you to snap to the **origin**. With this visual cue highlighted pick the **origin.**
4. You are now prompted to **"Specify the second endpoint"**. To satisfy this prompt **just type** the coordinate, **type 1.45,0**. This is **D1.45 Z0**. As you begin to type the **Fastpoint** opens. Hit the **Enter** key when done.

➲ A vertical line should be visible as shown below:

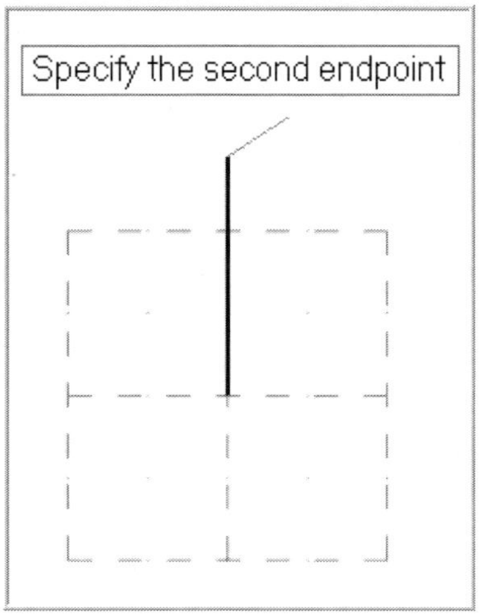

➲ **Create Line #2**

5. Type **1.45,0.375** to satisfy the prompt **"Specify the second endpoint"** and hit the Enter key to complete this line.

➲ **Create Line #3**

6. Type **1.25,0.375** to satisfy the prompt **"Specify the second endpoint"** and hit the Enter key to complete this line.

➲ **Create Line #4**

7. Type **1.25,0.55** to satisfy the prompt **"Specify the second endpoint"** and hit the Enter key to complete this line.

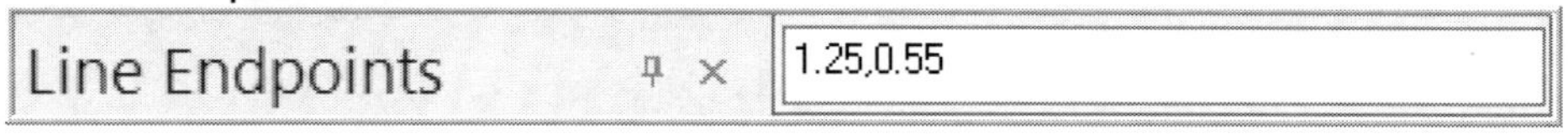

➲ **Create Line #5**

8. Type **0.875,0.55** to satisfy the prompt **"Specify the second endpoint"** and hit the Enter key to complete this line.

➲ **Create Line #6**

9. Type **0.875,0.88** to satisfy the prompt **"Specify the second endpoint"** and hit the Enter key to complete this line.

➲ **Create Line #7**

10. Type **0.565,0.88** to satisfy the prompt **"Specify the second endpoint"** and hit the Enter key to complete this line.

➲ **Create Line #8**

11. Type **0.625-0.06,0.880+0.15** to satisfy the prompt **"Specify the second endpoint"** and hit the Enter key to complete this line.

➲ **Create Line #9**

12. Type **0.625,0.880+0.15** to satisfy the prompt **"Specify the second endpoint"** and hit the Enter key to complete this line.

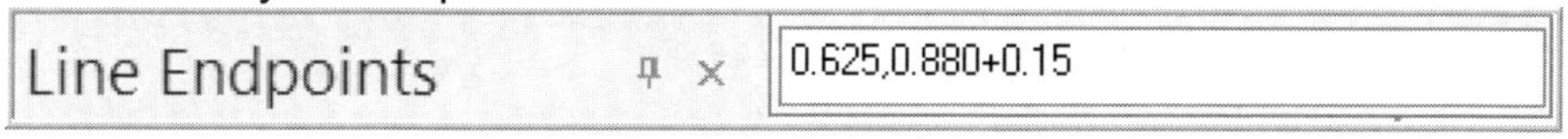

➲ **Create Line #10**

13. Type **0.625,1.5** to satisfy the prompt **"Specify the second endpoint"** and hit the Enter key to complete this line.

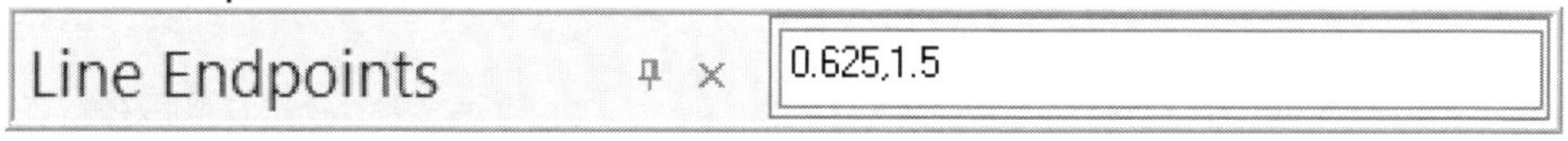

➲ **Create Line #11**

14. Type **0,1.5** to satisfy the prompt **"Specify the second endpoint"** and hit the Enter key to complete this line.

➲ **Create Line #12**

15. **"Specify the second endpoint";** Move the cursor over the **center of the grid** and as you get close to the origin a visual cue appears.  Click on this point.
16. Click on the **OK** icon  to complete this feature.
17. Right mouse click in the graphics area and click on the **Fit** icon .
18. Right mouse click in the graphics area and click on **Unzoom 80%** to shrink the display.

➲ Your geometry should look like the figure below:

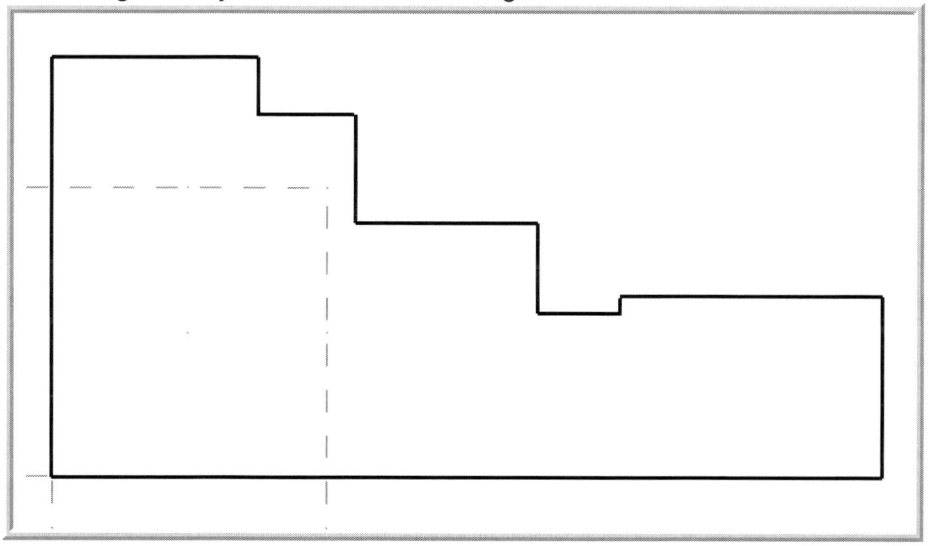

TASK 4:
CREATE THE 0.100" RADIUS

➲ In this task you will create the 0.100 arc. The center position and radius are known.

1. On the **WIREFRAME** tab and in the **Arcs** section open up the drop down menu and select **Arc Polar**.

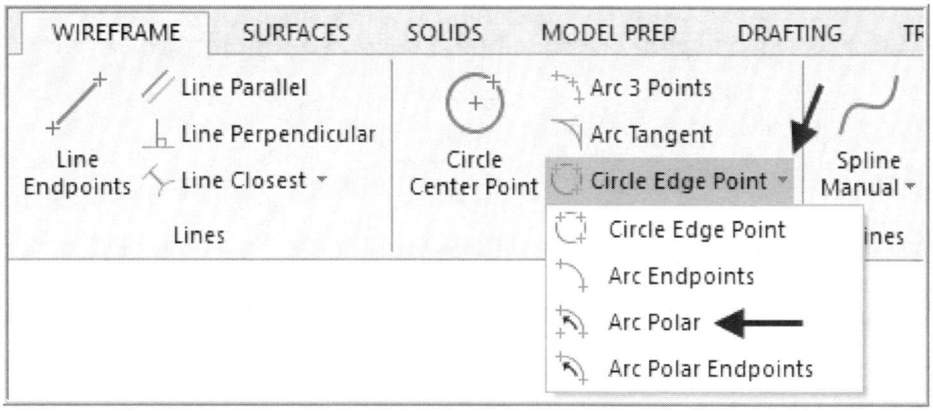

2. The **Arc Polar** panel appears and you are prompted to **Enter the center point**. If required activate the **Mode** to **Manual.**

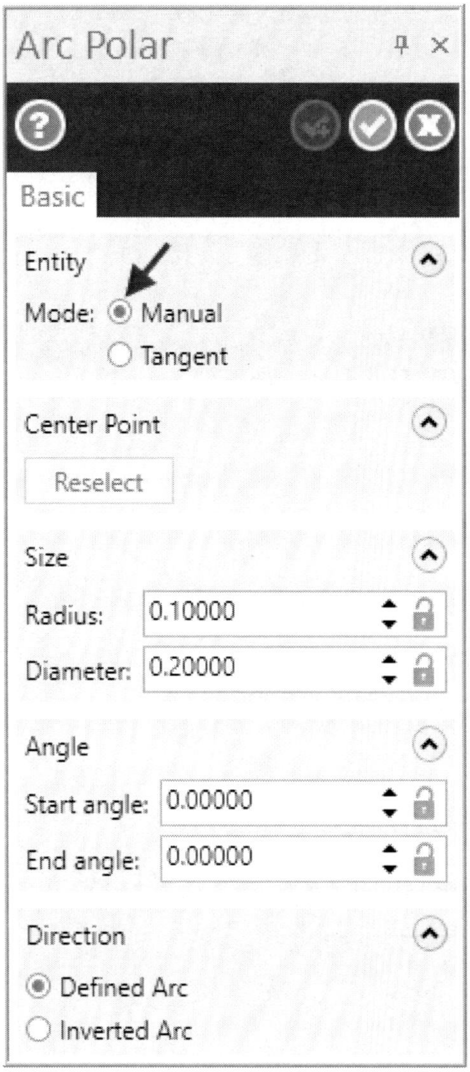

Arc Polar
Use this function to create polar arcs.

Click in the graphics window to set a center point and then click to set two edge points which define the radius, start point, and end angle.

No more than two of the points you select can be collinear.

Manual
Use this mode to select points in the graphics window.

Tangent
Use this mode to select existing entities to which you want your arc to be tangent to.

3. In the **Arc Polar** panel enter a value of **0.1** for **Radius**.
4. Set the **Start angle to 180** and the **End angle to 0** and hit the **Enter** key on your keyboard.
5. To satisfy this prompt "**Enter the center point" click the middle mouse button** and then **hit the spacebar** on your keyboard. Type **0.875-0.07+0.2,0.7** and hit the Enter key.

6. Activate **Inverted Arc** found at the bottom of the Arc Polar panel to position the arc in the correct position as shown below.

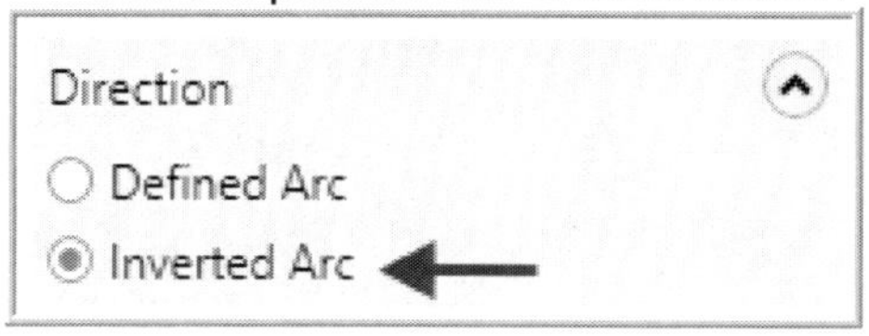

7. Click on the **OK** icon  to complete this feature.

➲ The completed arc is shown below:

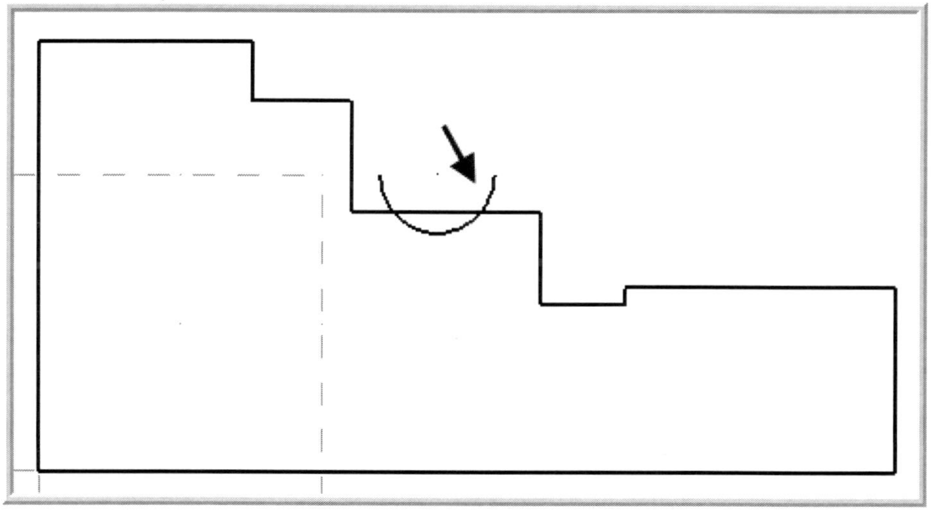

➲ **Trim the Arc**

8. In the **WIREFRAME** tab click on **Trim/Break/Extend** in the **Modify** section.

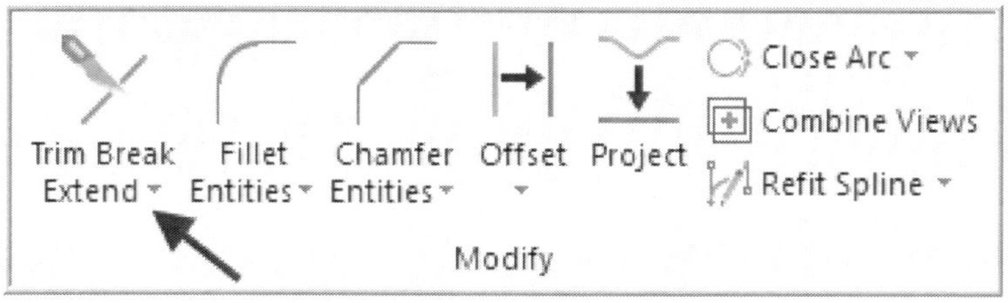

9. The Trim Break Extend panel appears. Activate **Trim 1 entity**.

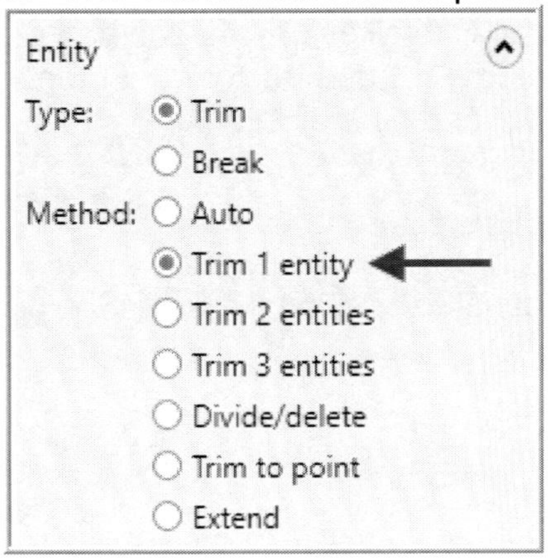

10. Now at the prompt **Select the entity to trim/extend** select the arc at position 1,
11. The prompt changes to **Select the entity to trim/extend** to, select the remaining entities in the order shown below.

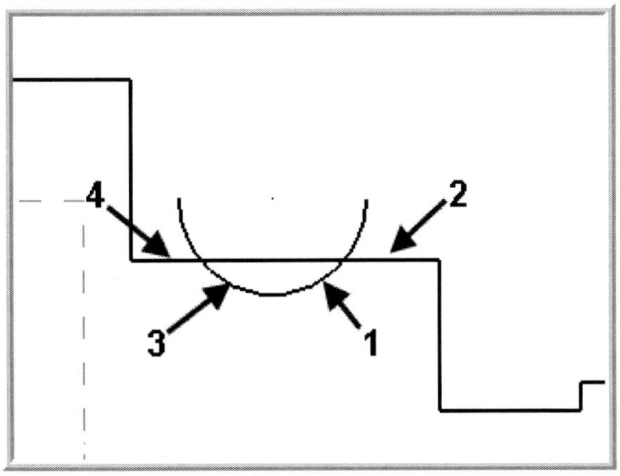

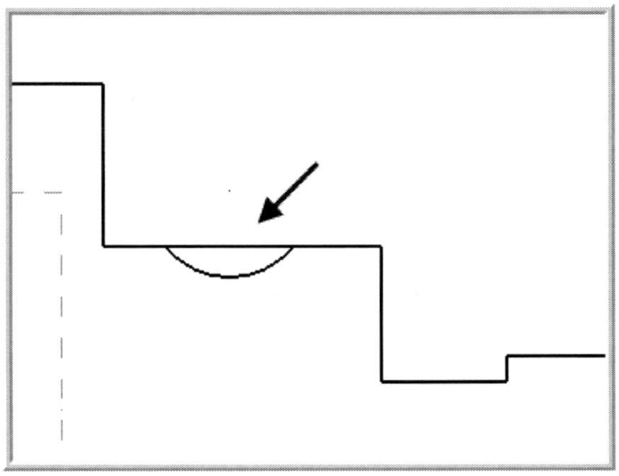

➲ The entities are trimmed as shown above right.

12. Now activate **Divide/delete**.
13. The prompt changes to **Select the curve to divide.** Move the cursor over the line and select it as shown below left.

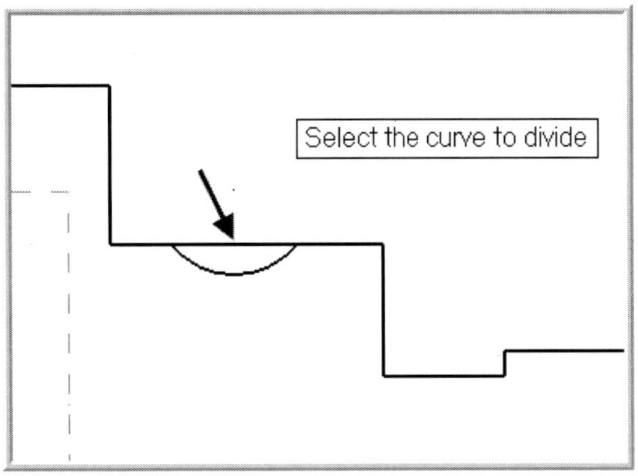

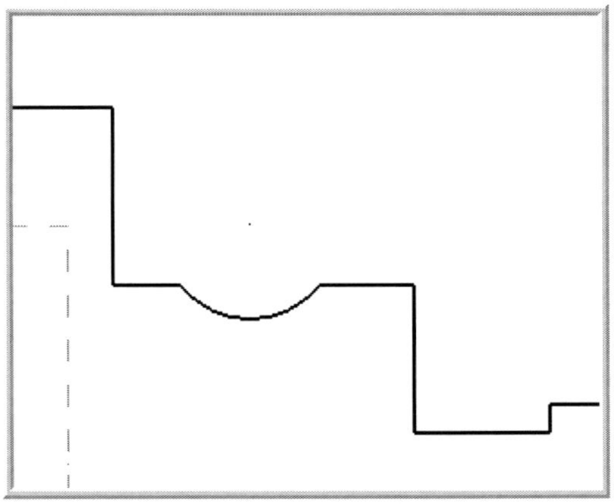

14. Click on the **OK** icon  to complete this feature.

➲ The line is trimmed back to the two closest intersections as shown above right:

TASK 5:
CREATE THE CHAMFERS

➲ **Create the two chamfers 45 degrees x .031.**

1. On the **WIREFRAME** tab and in the **Modify** section click on **Chamfer Entities**.

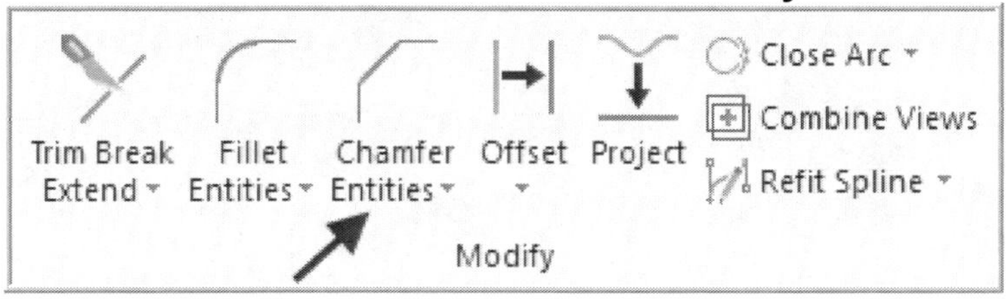

2. The **Chamfer Entities** panel appears. Activate the **Style** to **1 Distance** and enter a value of **0.031** for **Distance 1**.
3. Ensure the **Trim** entities box at the bottom of the panel is check marked to turn the trim on.

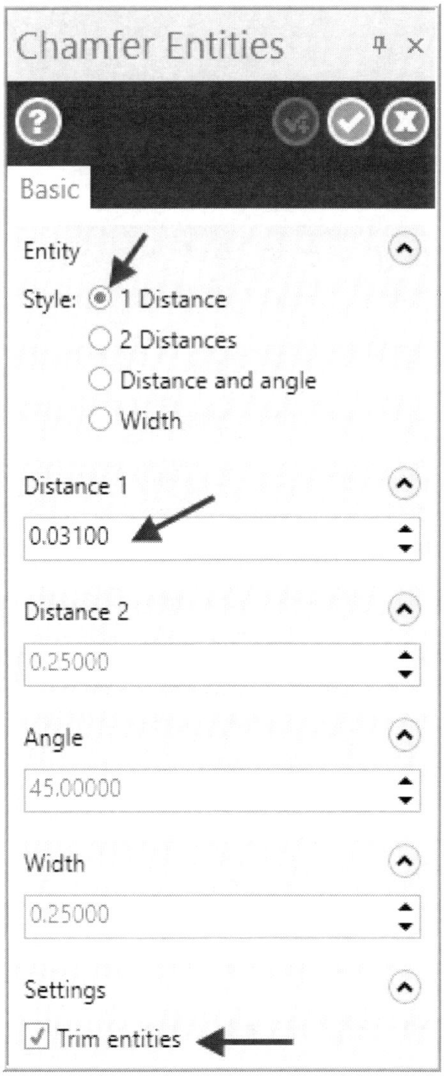

4. Now click on **line 1** and then **line 2** as shown below. Next on **line 3** and **line 4**.

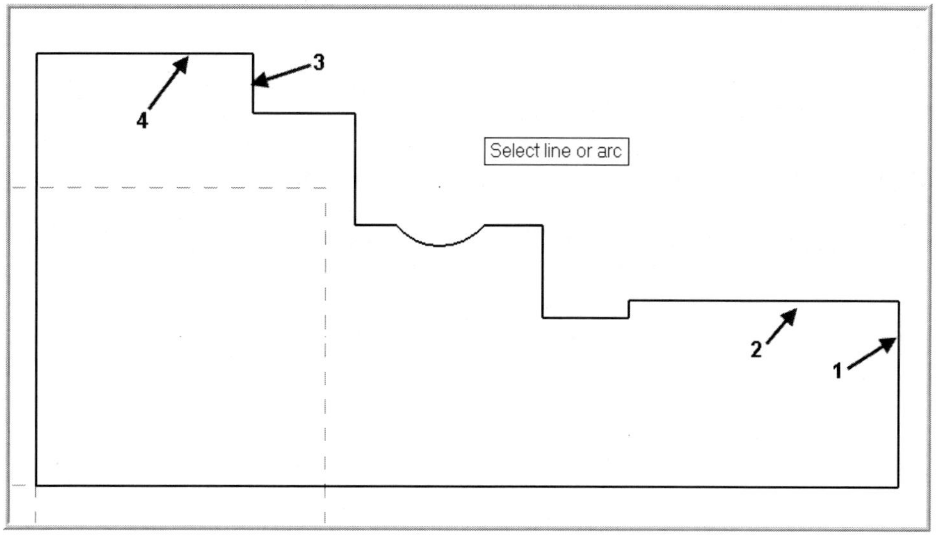

5. Click on the **OK** icon  to complete this feature.

➲ The completed geometry should look like the image below:

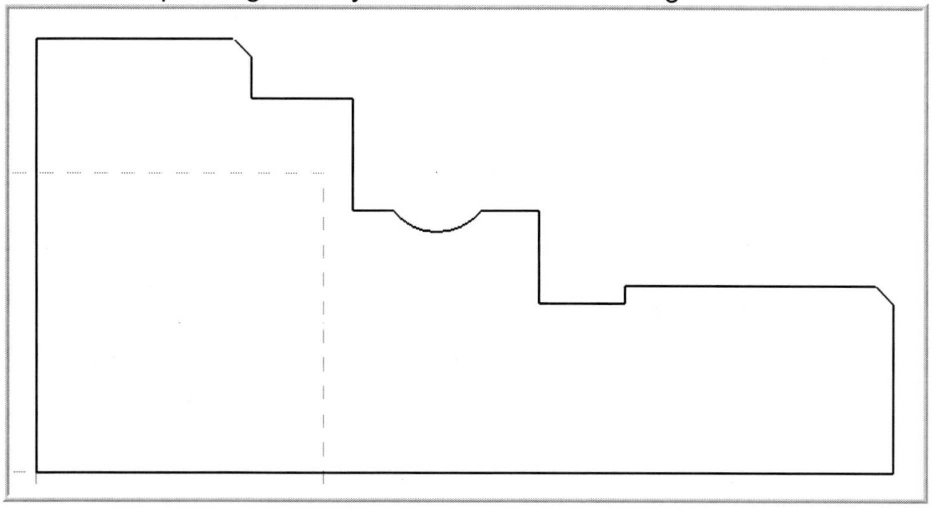

TASK 6:
CREATE THE FILLET RADII

➲ In this task you will create the 0.031 fillet radii in four places.

1. On the **WIREFRAME** tab and in the **Modify** section click on **Fillet Entities**.

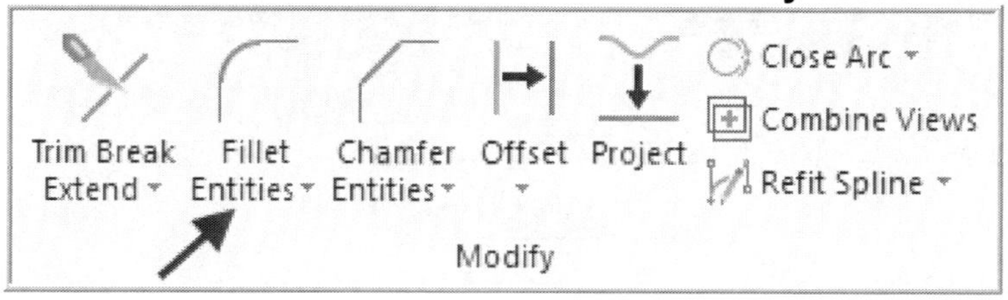

2. The **Fillet Entities** panel appears. Activate the **Style** to **Normal** and enter a value of **0.031** for **Radius**.
3. Ensure the **Trim** entities box at the bottom of the panel is check marked to turn the trim on.

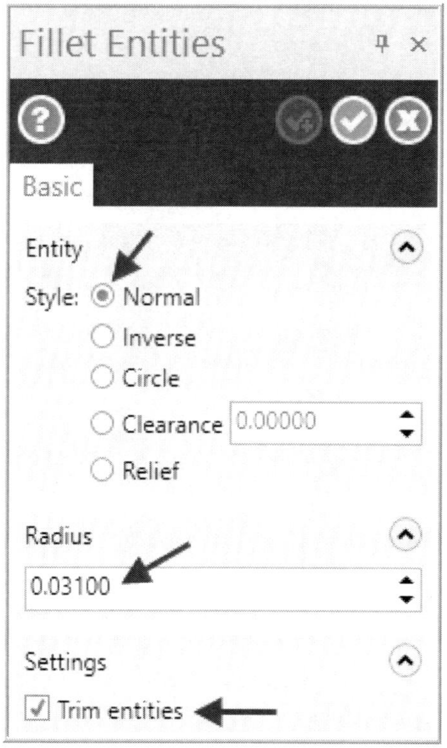

4. When prompted to **Fillet: Select an entity,** select **Line 1 and 2** and the select the remaining entities in the order shown below:

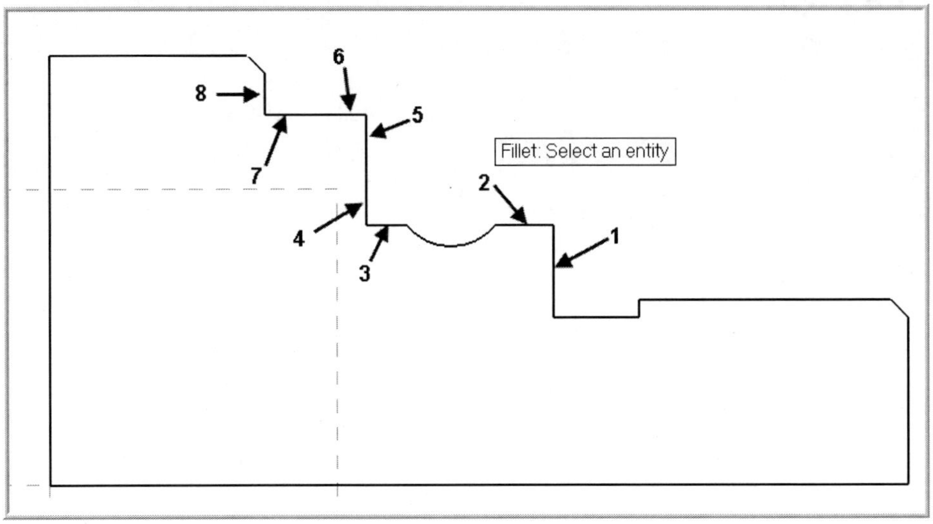

5. Click on the **OK** icon to complete this feature.

➲ The completed geometry is shown below:

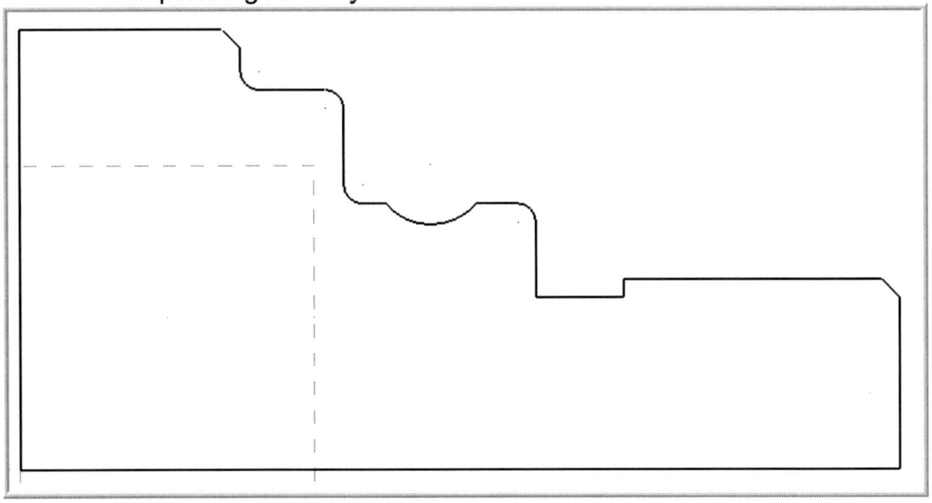

TASK 7:
CREATE THE GEOMETRY FOR THE BORE

➲ In this task you will create the geometry that make up the bore of this part

1. On the **WIREFRAME** tab and in the **Lines** section click on **Line Parallel**.

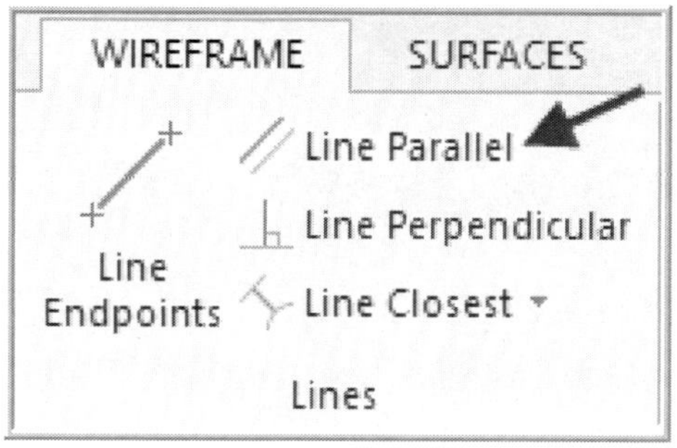

➲ On the graphics screen you are prompted: Select a line and the Line Parallel panel appears.
2. First click in the space for **Offset Distance** and input **0.75** then hit **Enter**.
3. To satisfy the prompt **Select a line**, select the line shown below.

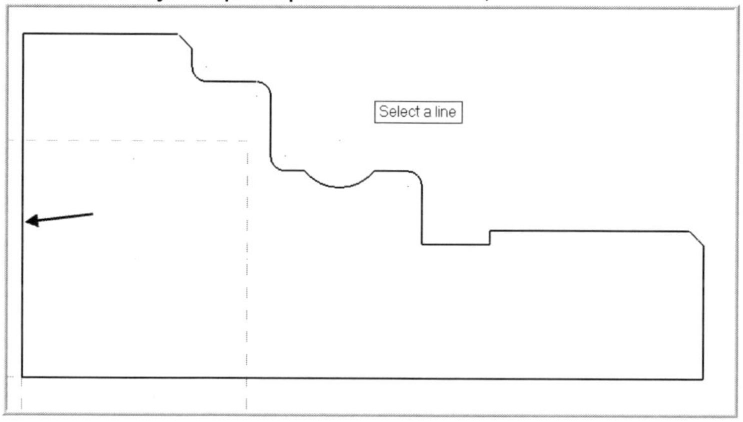

4. To satisfy the next prompt **Indicate the offset direction** move the cursor to the right of the line and pick a point.
5. Click on the **OK and Create New Operation** icon .
6. Click in the space for **Offset Distance** and input **0.250/2** then hit **Enter**.
7. To satisfy the prompt **Select a line**, select the line shown below.

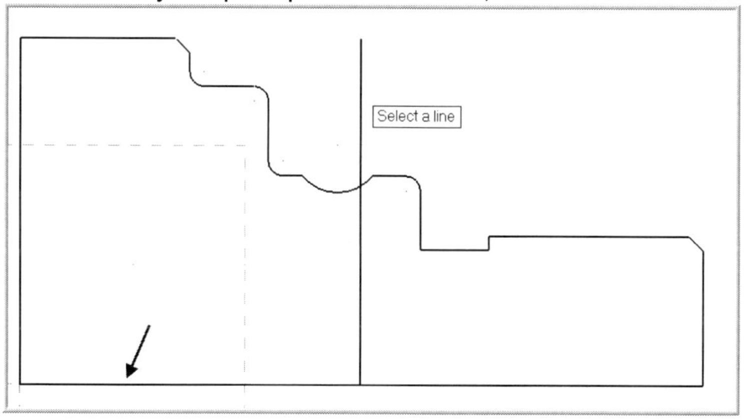

8. To satisfy the next prompt **Indicate the offset direction** move the cursor above the line and pick a point.

9. Click on the **OK and Create New Operation** icon .
10. Click in the space for **Offset Distance** and input **0.375/2** then hit **Enter**.
11. To satisfy the prompt **Select a line**, select the line shown below:

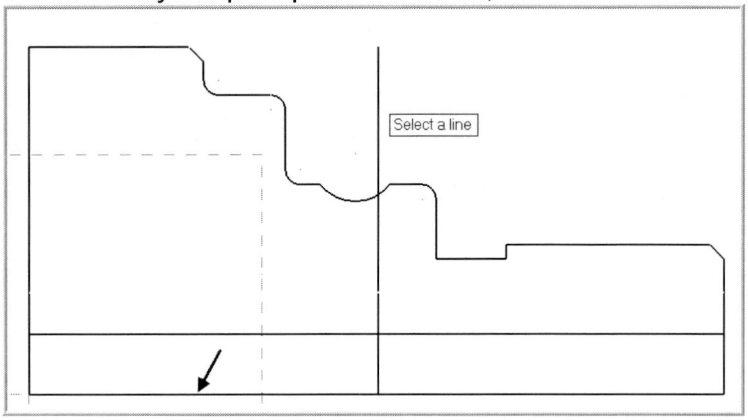

12. To satisfy the next prompt **Indicate the offset direction** move the cursor above the line and pick a point.
13. Click on the **OK** icon to complete this feature.

➲ The completed geometry is shown below:

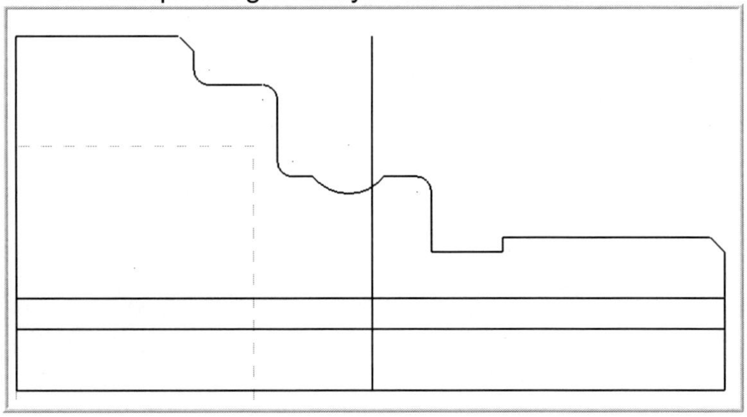

➲ Trim the bore

14. In the **WIREFRAME** tab click on **Trim/Break/Extend** in the **Modify** section.

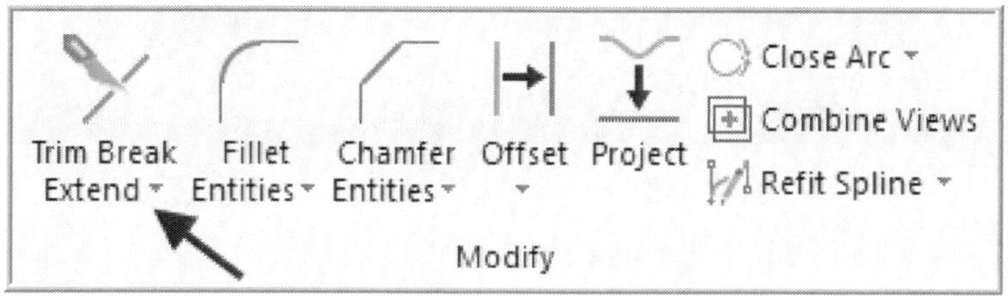

15. The Trim Break Extend panel appears. Activate **Trim 2 entities**.

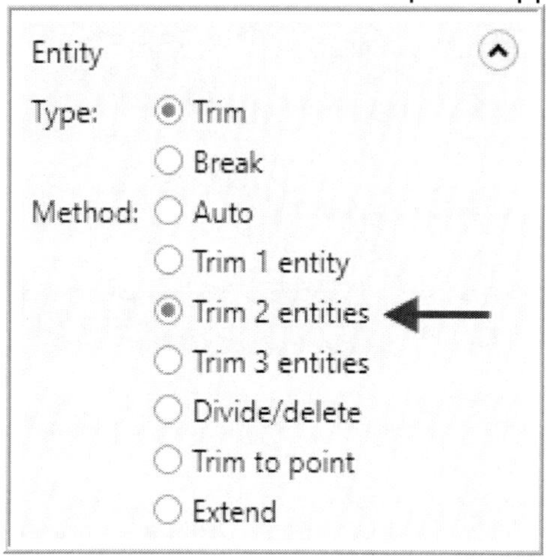

16. Now at the prompt **Select the entity to trim/extend** select the line at **position 1,**
17. The prompt changes to **Select the entity to trim/extend to**, select the line at **position 2**
18. Now at the prompt **Select the entity to trim/extend** select the line at **position 3,**
19. The prompt changes to **Select the entity to trim/extend to**, select the line at **position 4**

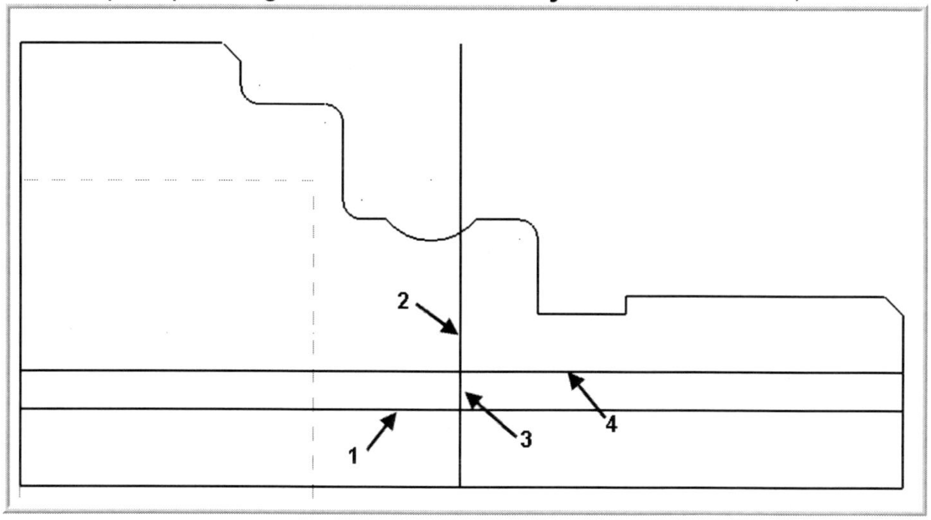

20. Click on the **OK** icon to complete this feature.

21. **Delete** the construction line shown below. Select the line and hit the **delete key** on your keyboard.

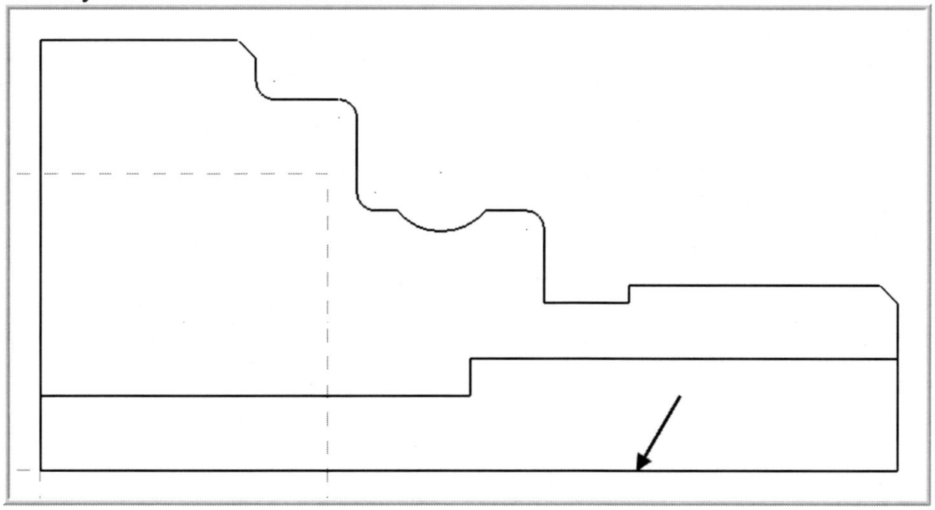

TASK 8:
SAVE THE DRAWING

1. Select **File.**
2. Select **Save As…**
3. Click on the **Browse** icon.
4. In the **"File name"** box, type **"Lathe-Lesson-6".**
5. Browse to an appropriate location.
6. Select the **Save** button to save the file and complete this function.

Toolpath Creation

TASK 9:
DEFINING THE STOCK AND CHUCK PARAMETERS

1. Right mouse click in the graphics area and click on the **Fit** icon .
2. Ensure your screen looks like the image below:
   a. The Toolpaths Manager is open.
   b. The properties icon displays Lathe Default. If it is not refer to **Setting the Environment** chapter at the beginning of the book.
   c. The Lathe Lesson-6 Geometry is displayed.

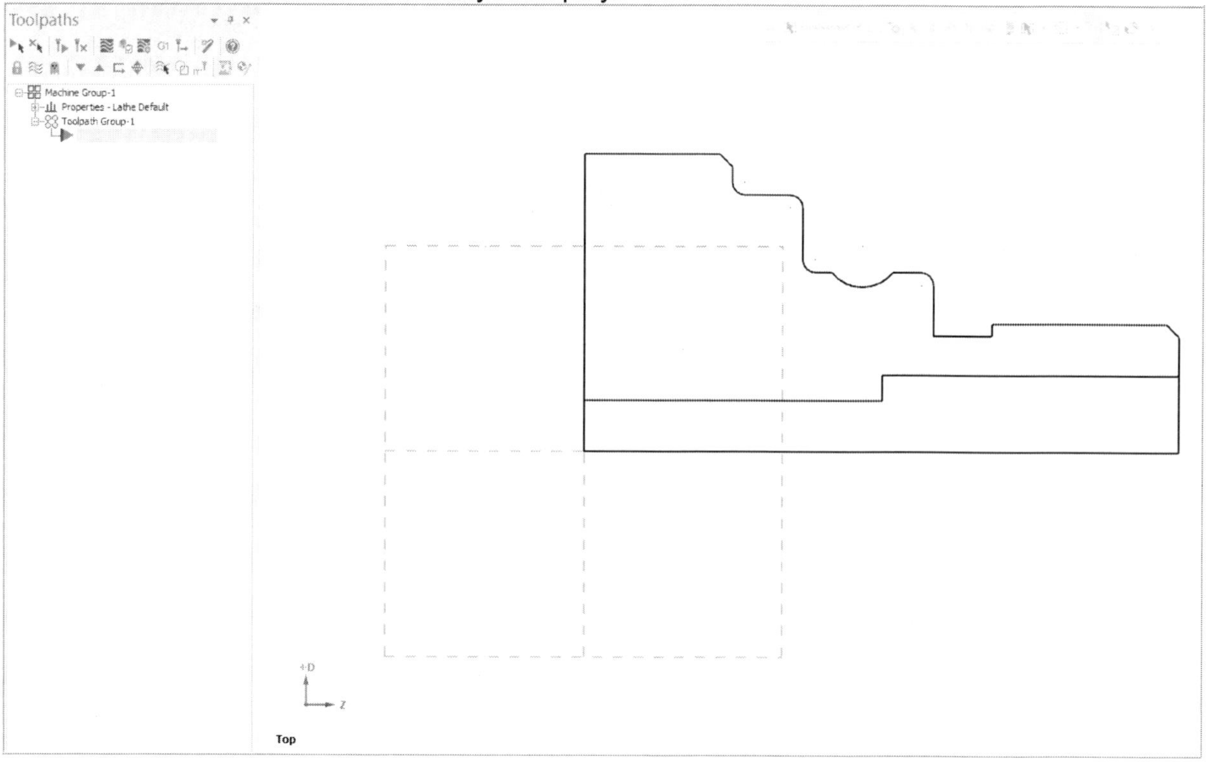

3. Select the plus in front of **Properties** to expand the Machine Group Properties.

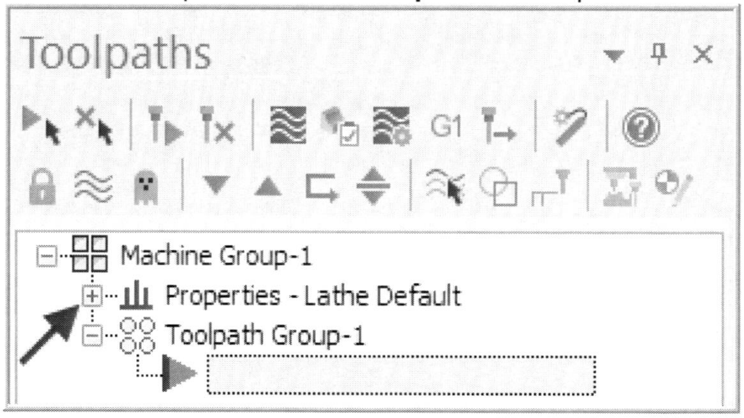

4. Select **Stock setup** in the Toolpaths Manager window.

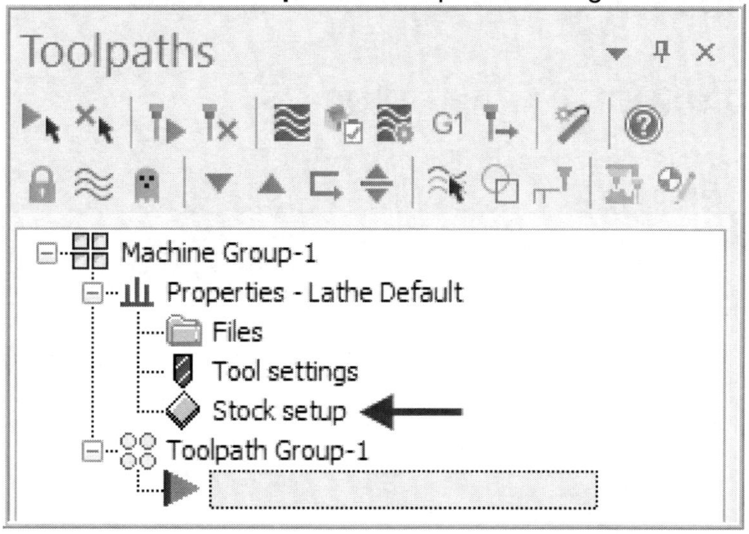

5. Select the **Stock Properties** button in the **Stock Setup** page as shown in the screenshot below.

Note: To learn more about Stock Setup refer to the Tips and Techniques content in the Online Course Instruction.

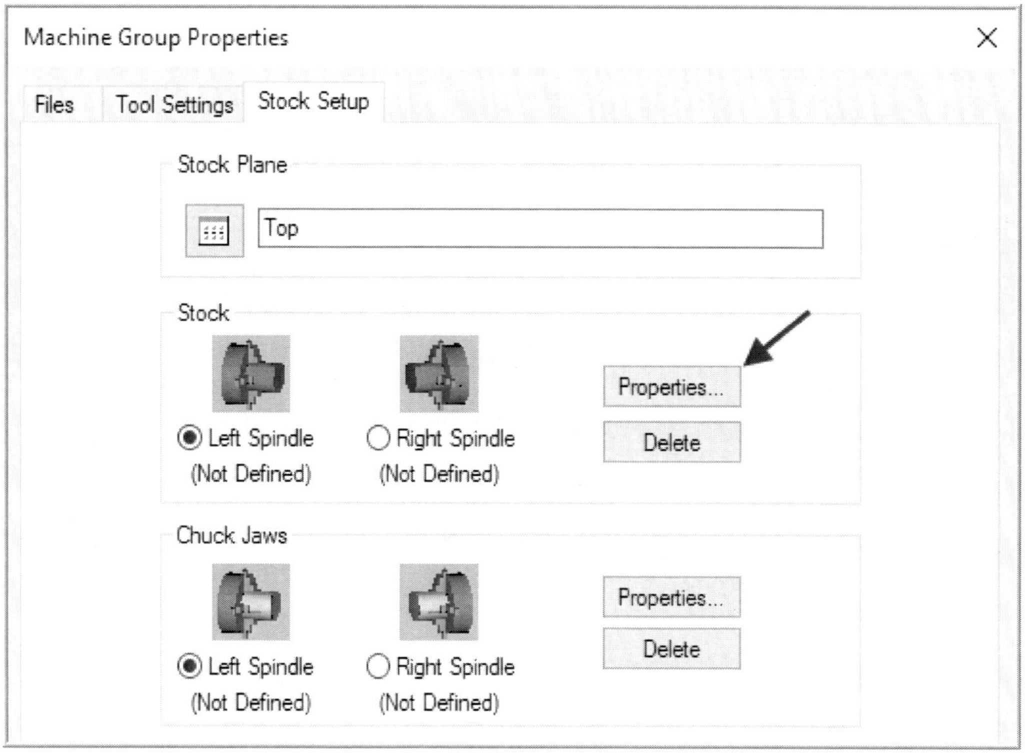

6. In the **Machine Component Manager-Stock** window click on the **Geometry** button and select **Cylinder** as shown below:

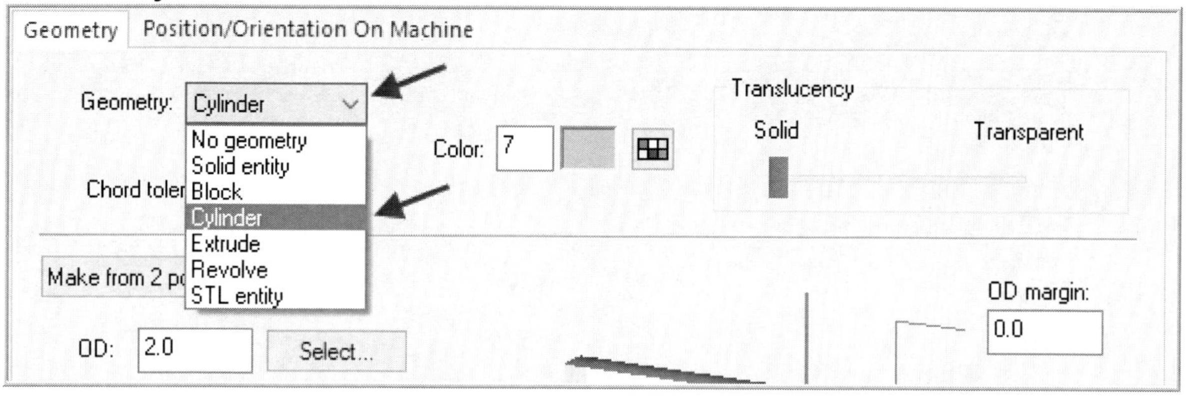

7. In the **Stock** setup set the values as shown below. **Axis is set to +Z**.

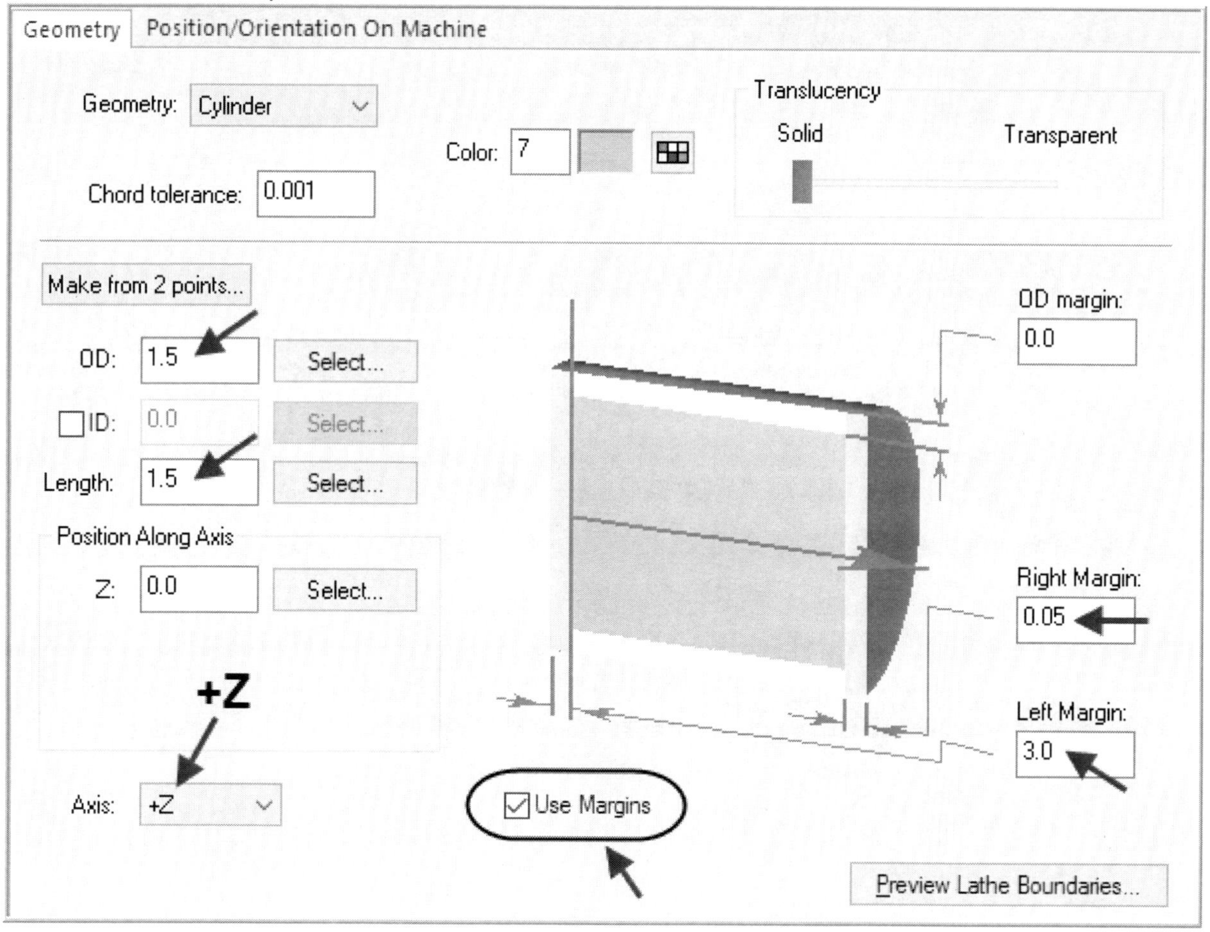

8. Click on the OK icon to complete this feature.

9. Still on the Stock Setup page activate **Fit screen to boundaries**.

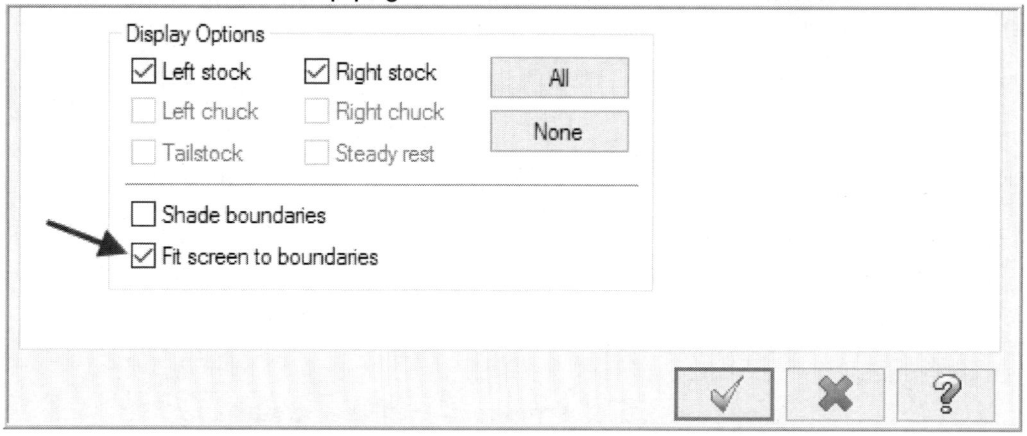

10. Select the **Chuck Properties** button in the **Stock Setup** page as shown below:

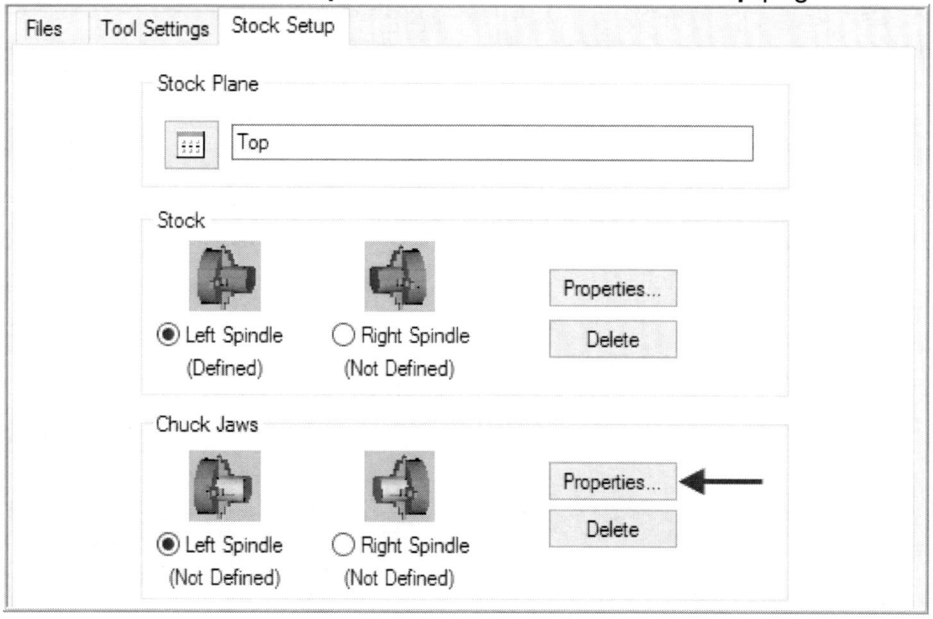

11. In the **Chuck Jaws** setup set the values as shown below:

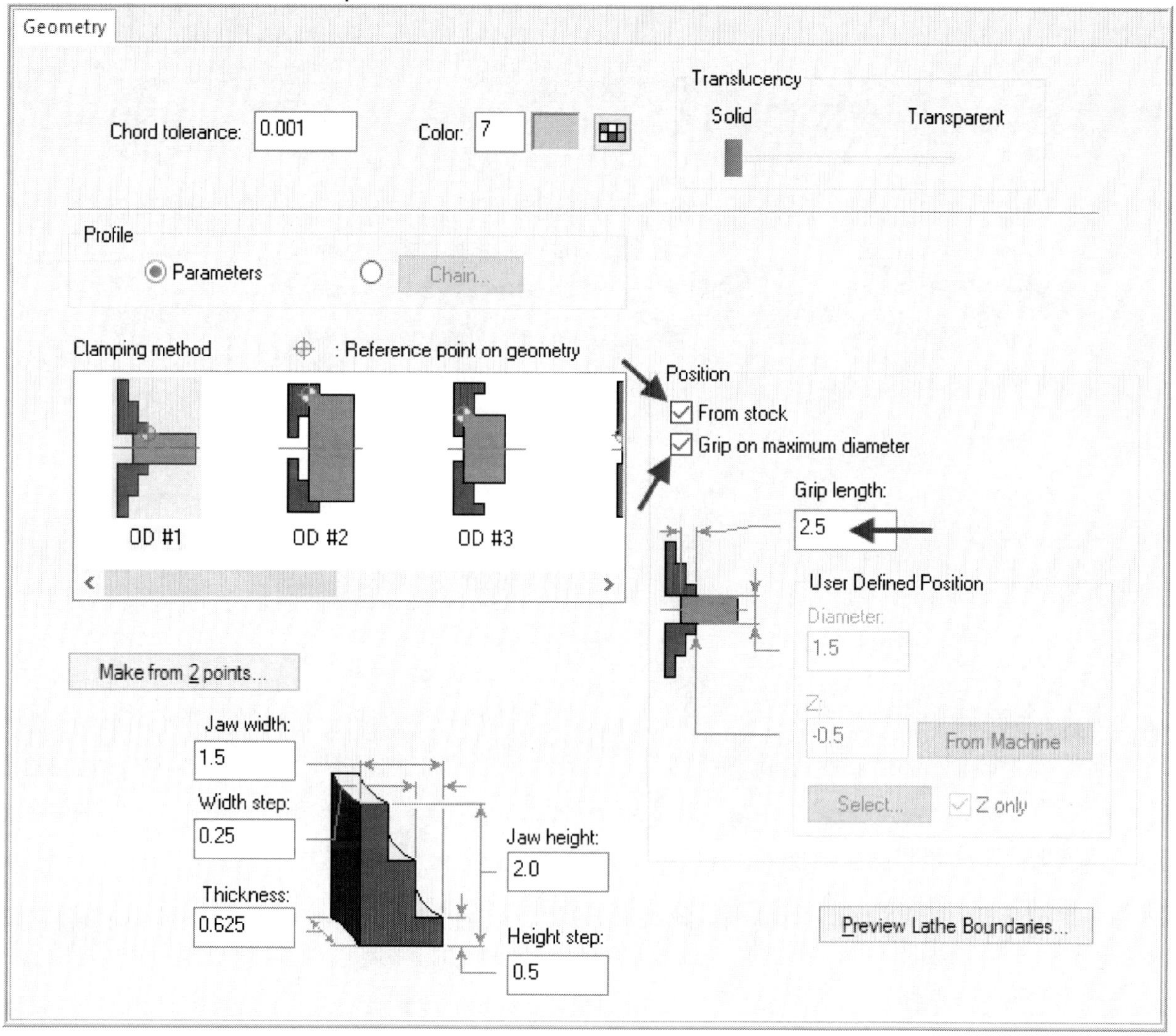

12. Click on the OK icon  to complete this feature.

13. Click on the **Tool Settings** page and make changes as shown below:

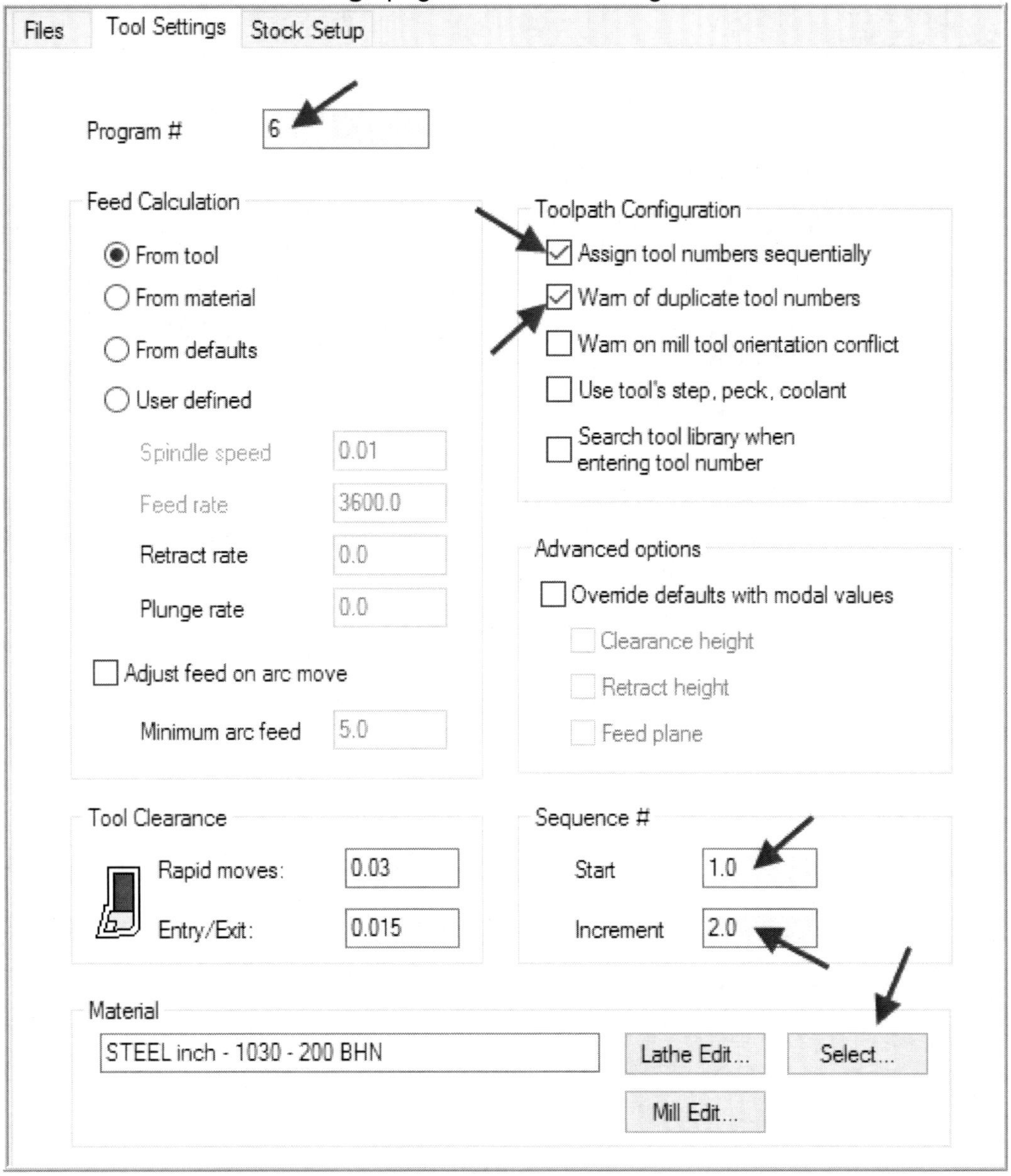

14. To change the **Material** type to Aluminum 6061 pick the **Select** button at the bottom of the Tool Settings page.

15. At the **Material List** dialog box open the Source drop down list and select **Lathe – library.**

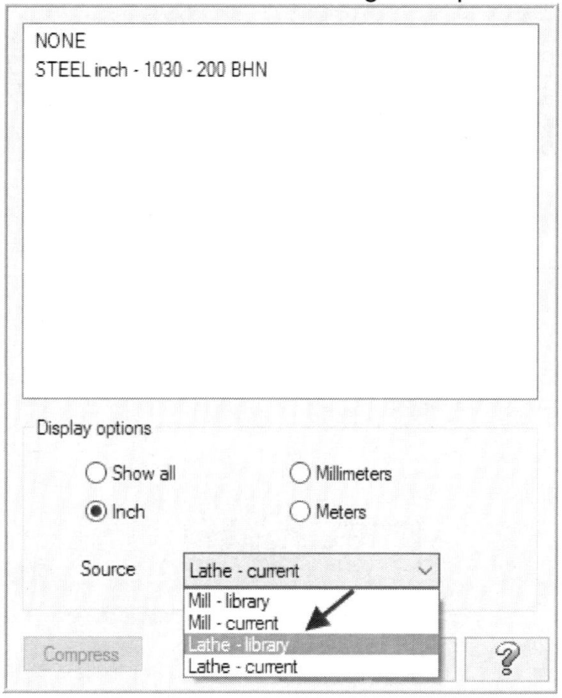

16. From the **Default Materials** list select **ALUMINUM inch - 6061** and then select .

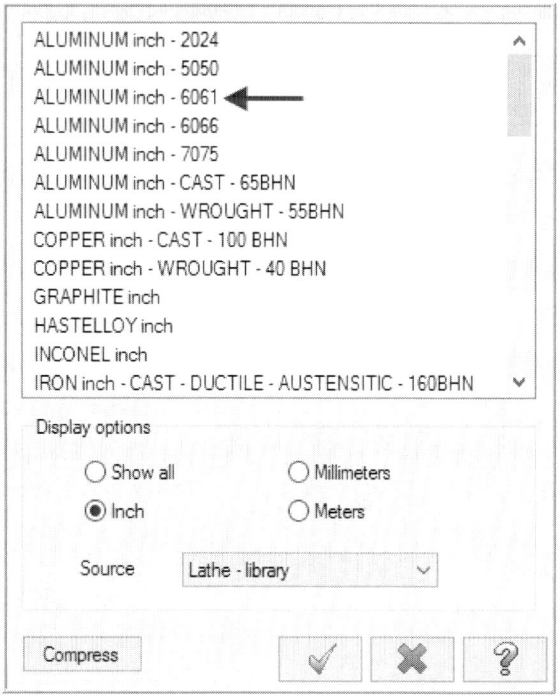

17. Select the OK button again to complete this Stock Setup function.

18. Right mouse click in the graphics area and click on the **Fit** icon .

➲ Note the stock setup outline as indicated by broken lines as shown below:

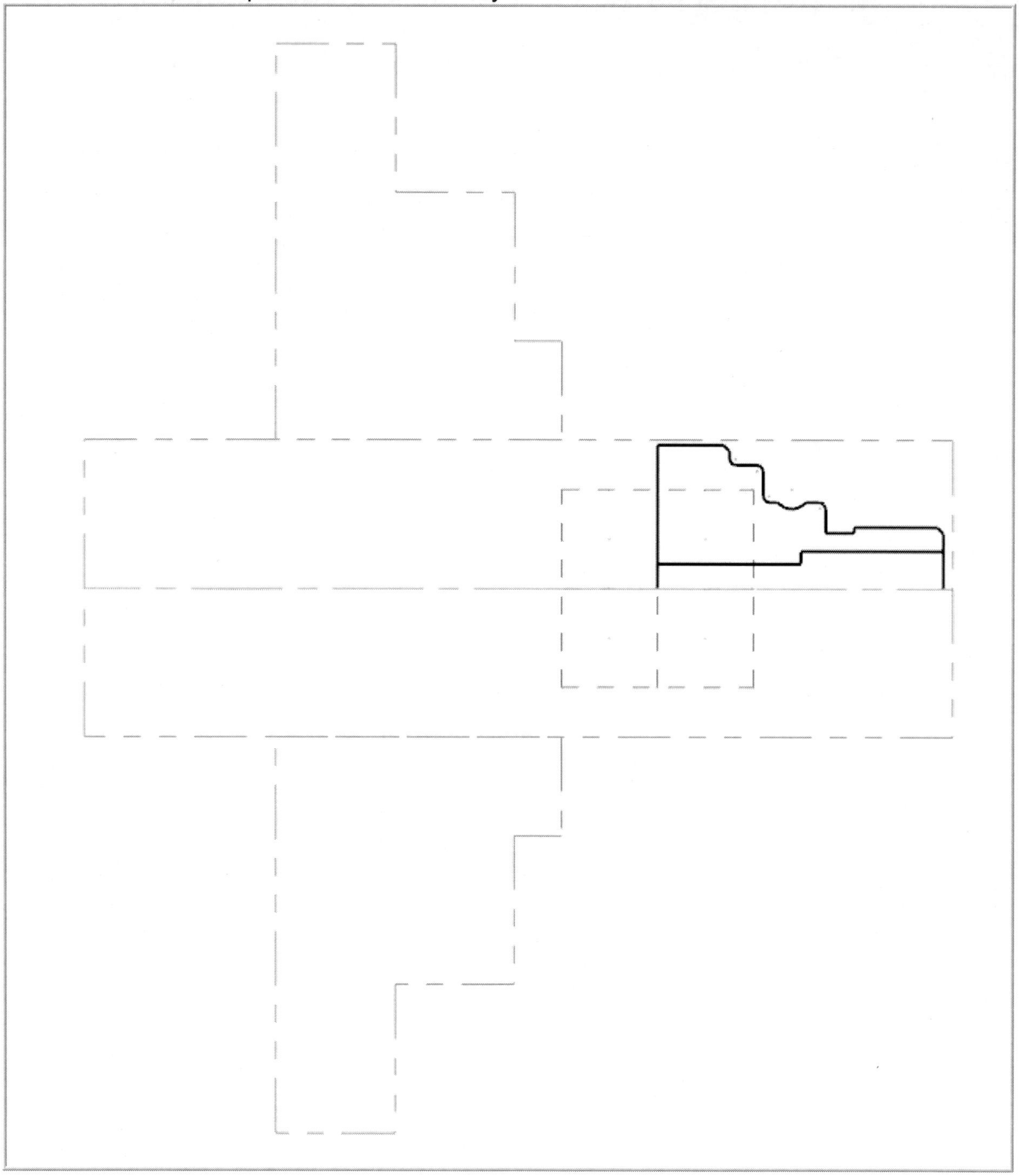

TASK 10:
FACE THE FRONT OF THE PART:

➲ In this task you will use a facing tool to face the front of the part in one cut.

1. Right mouse click in the graphics area and click on the **Fit** icon if required.
2. Select the **TURNING** tab at the top right side of the screen.
3. Now select **Face** in the **General** section.

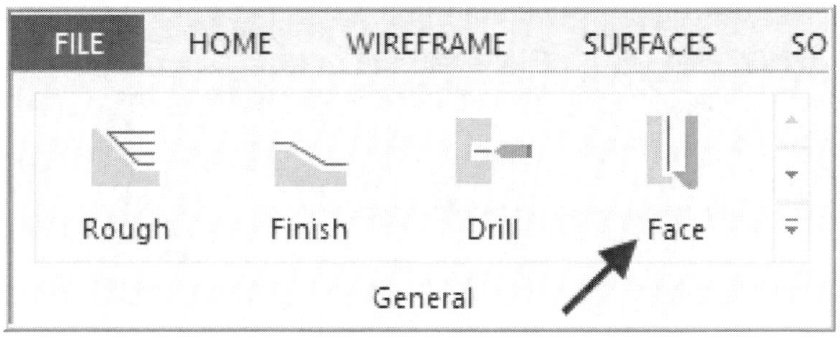

4. When prompted to **"Enter new NC name"** Ensure **LATHE-LESSON-6** is entered and then select the OK button.

➲ After selecting the OK button you are confronted with **Toolpath parameters** page. The first task here will be to select **Tool #1 a Roughing – 80 deg.**

5. Click on **Tool 0101 Roughing – 80 degree** and ensure the settings are the same as in the Toolpath parameters page as shown below. **Coolant Flood** is set to **On**.

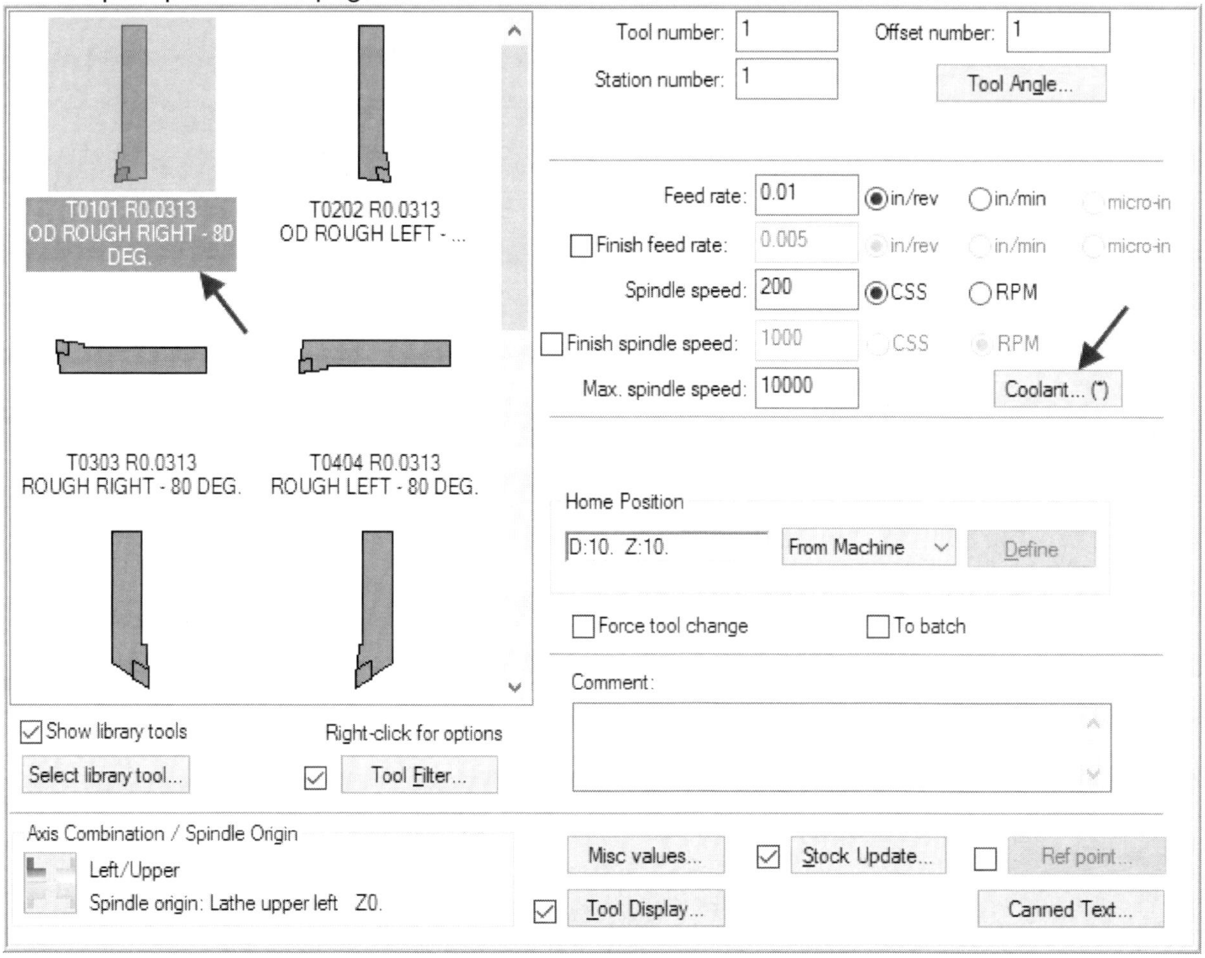

6. Select the **Face parameters** page and make changes as shown below.

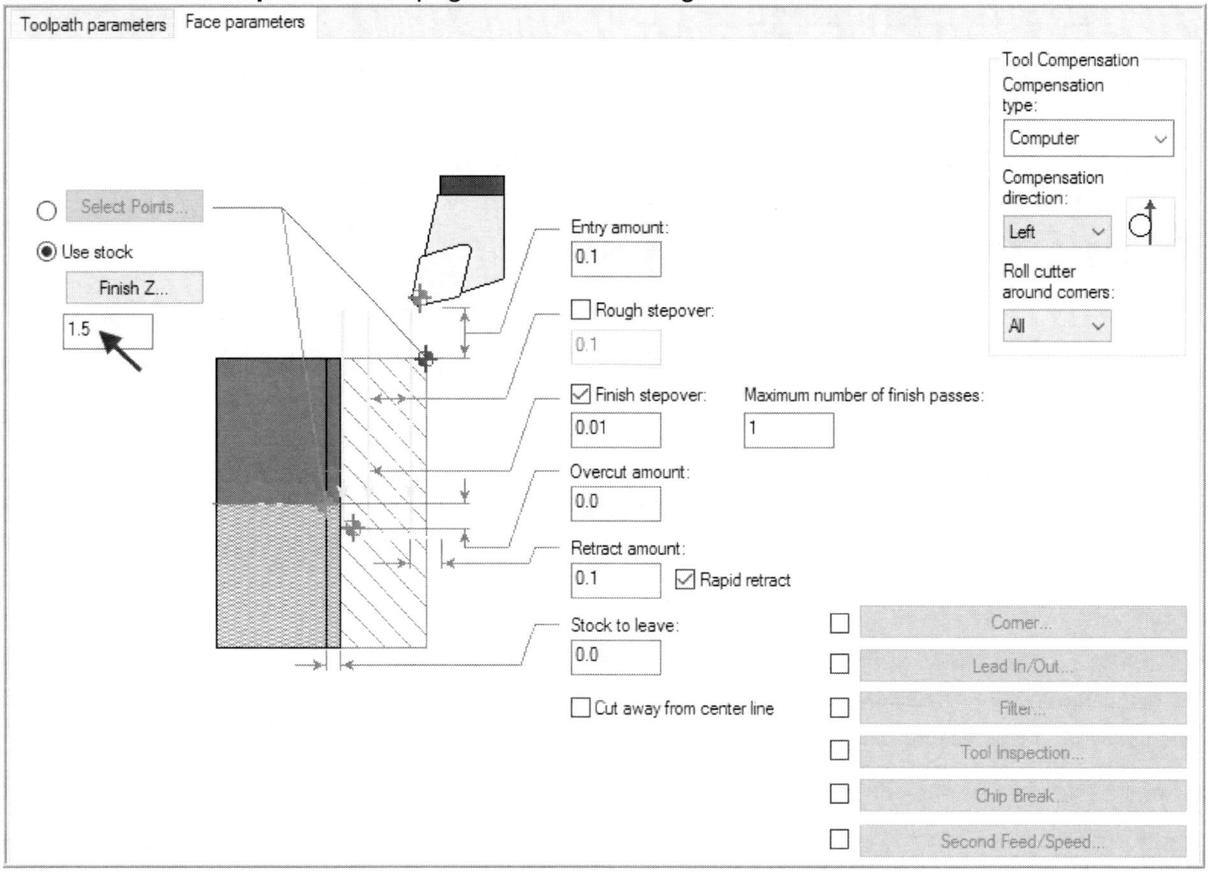

7. Select the OK button  to complete this **Lathe Face** operation.

TASK 11:
ROUGH THE OUTSIDE DIAMETERS

- In this task you will use a Lathe toolpath called Lathe Quick Rough Toolpath.
- You will use the same tool as used for the previous facing operation **Tool #1 an OD Rough-Right – 80 deg.**

1. Right mouse click in the white space of the **Toolpaths Manager** and select:
   Lathe toolpaths>Quick>Quick rough.

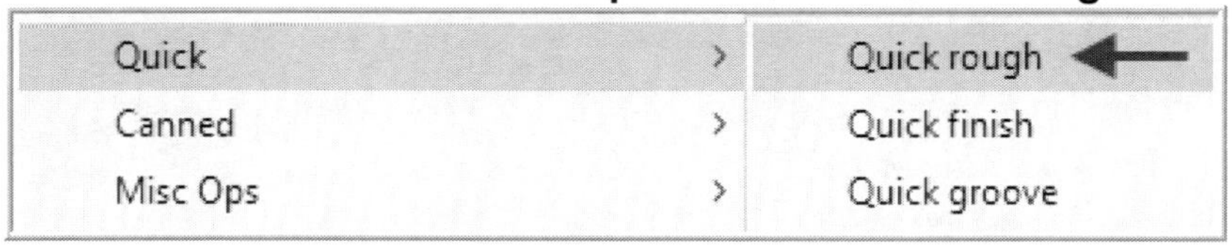

2. In the **Chaining** window Chaining mode is set to **Partial** by default.

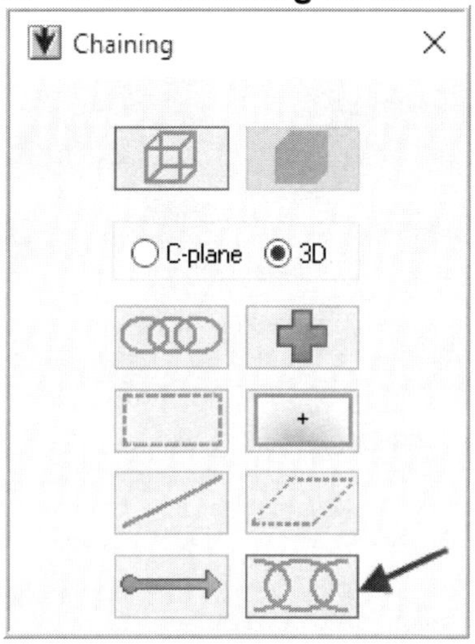

3. Select the chamfer, Line 1 as the start of the **Partial chain**.

After you have selected the chamfer **ensure** that the arrows are pointing up and to the left of the part. If it is not select the reverse arrow button in the Chaining dialog box.

4. Then select Line 2 as the end entity in this chain.

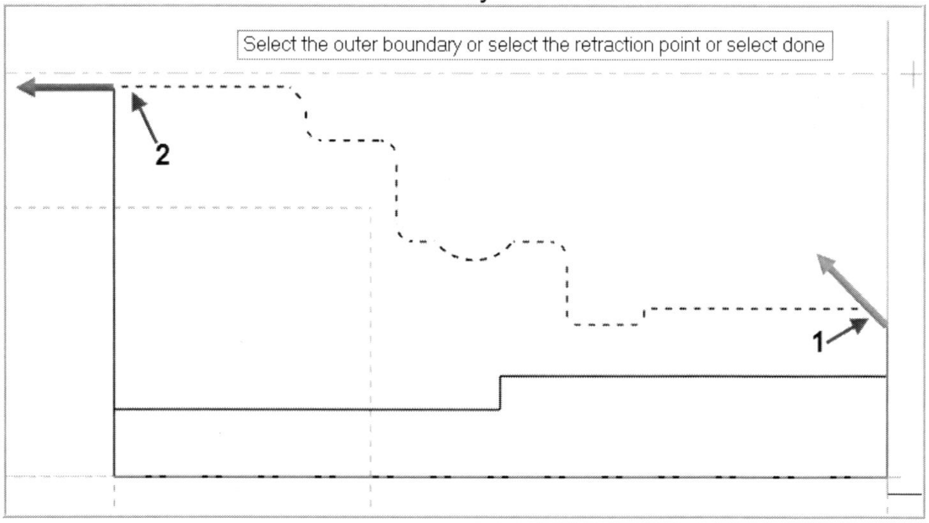

5. Select the OK button  to exit the Chaining dialog window.

6. In the **Quick Tool parameters** page select the **Tool #1 Roughing – 80 deg** and make any necessary changes as shown below. **Coolant Flood** is set to **On**

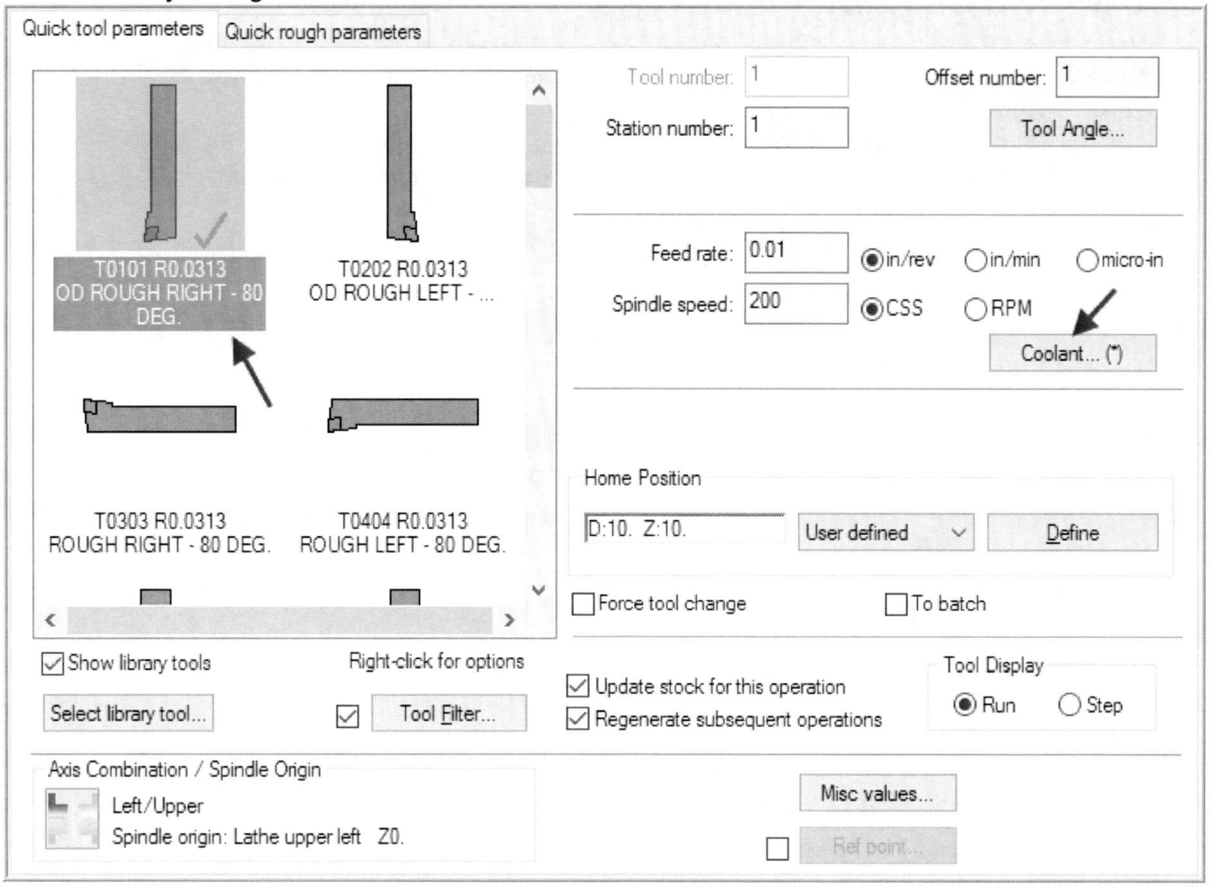

7. Select the **Quick Rough parameters** page and make changes as shown below.

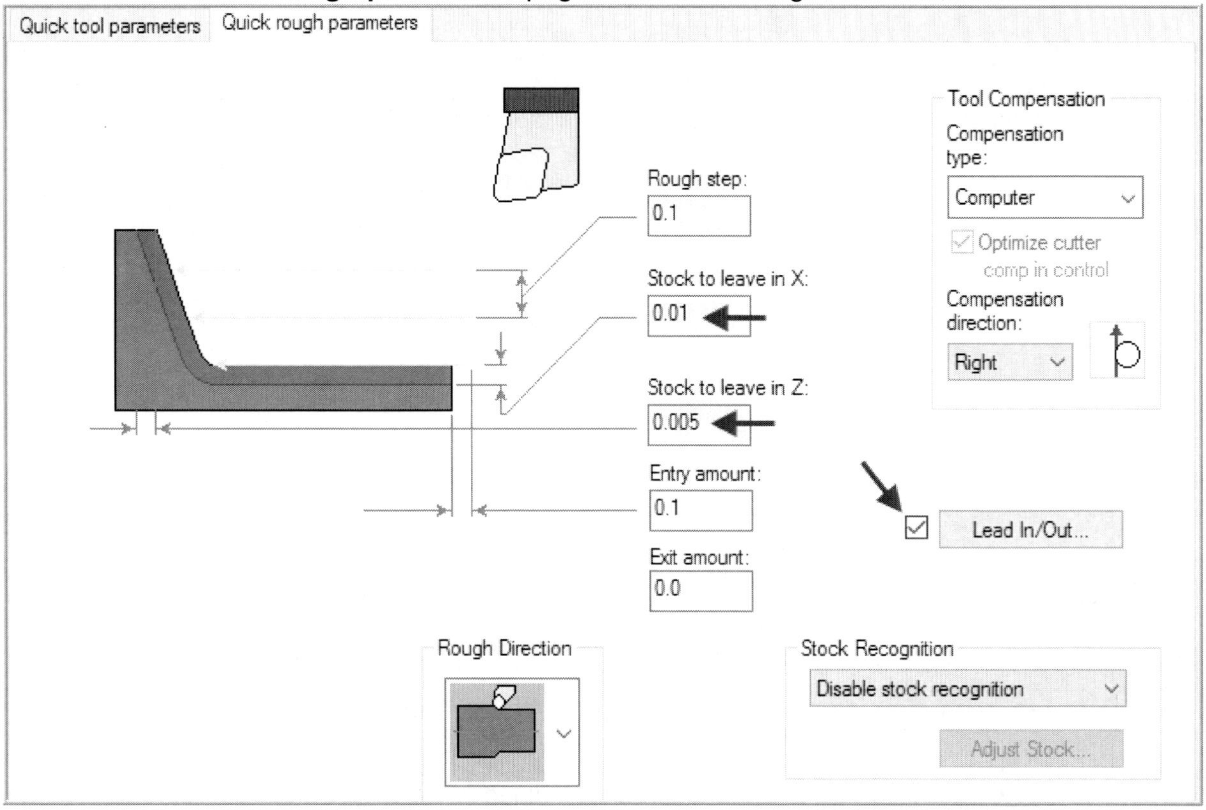

8. Select the **Lead In/Out** button, then select the **Lead out** page and extend the contour by **0.2** as shown below.

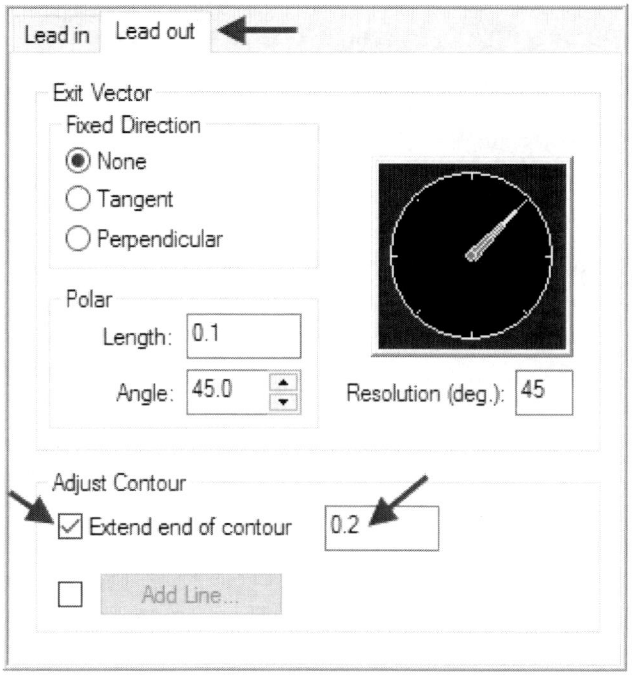

9. Select the OK button  to exit this function.
10. Select the OK button  to exit Quick Rough Parameters.

TASK 12:
FINISH THE OUTSIDE DIAMETERS

➲ In this task you will finish the outside diameters using Quick Finish. The tool you used for rouging will be used in this operation as well.

1. Right mouse click in the white space of the **Toolpaths Manager** and select:
Lathe toolpaths>Quick>Quick finish.

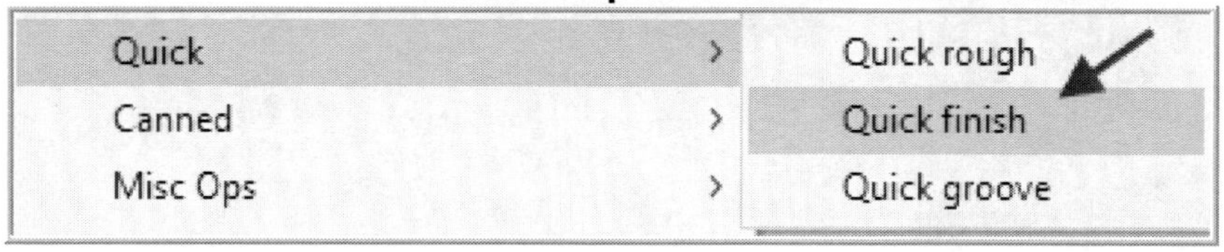

2. In the **Quick tool parameters** page select **Tool #1 Roughing – 80 deg** and make any necessary changes as shown below. **Coolant Flood** is set to **On**

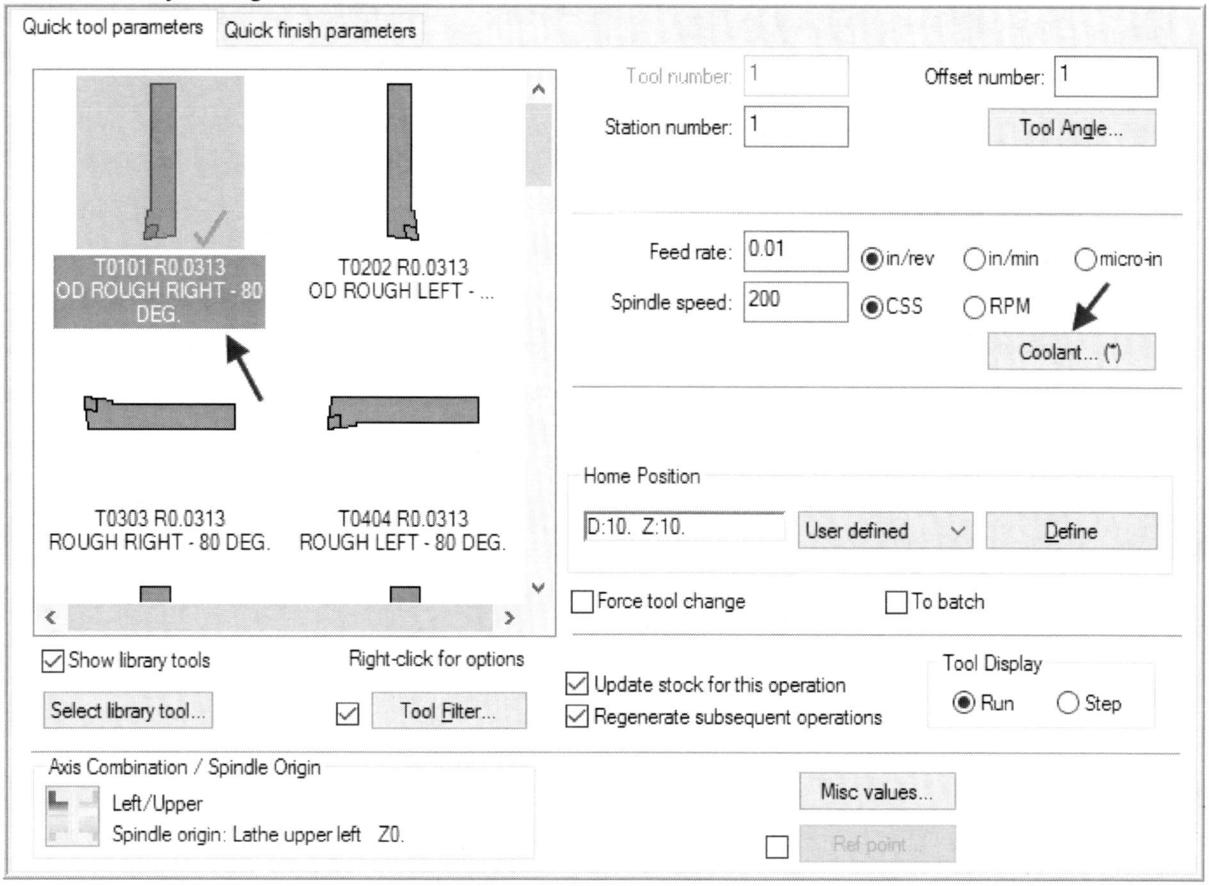

3. Select the **Quick finish parameters** page and make any changes as shown below:

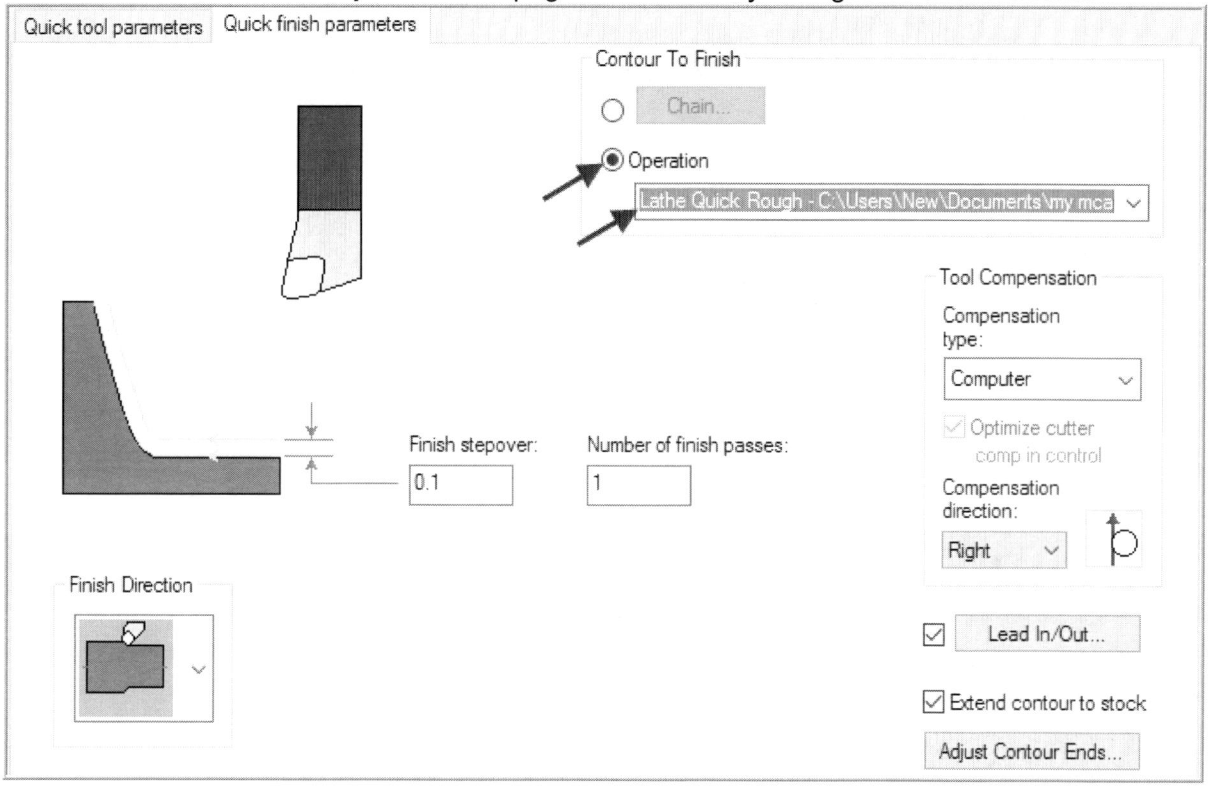

4. Select the **Lead In/Out** button select the Lead out page and extend the contour by **0.2** as shown below:

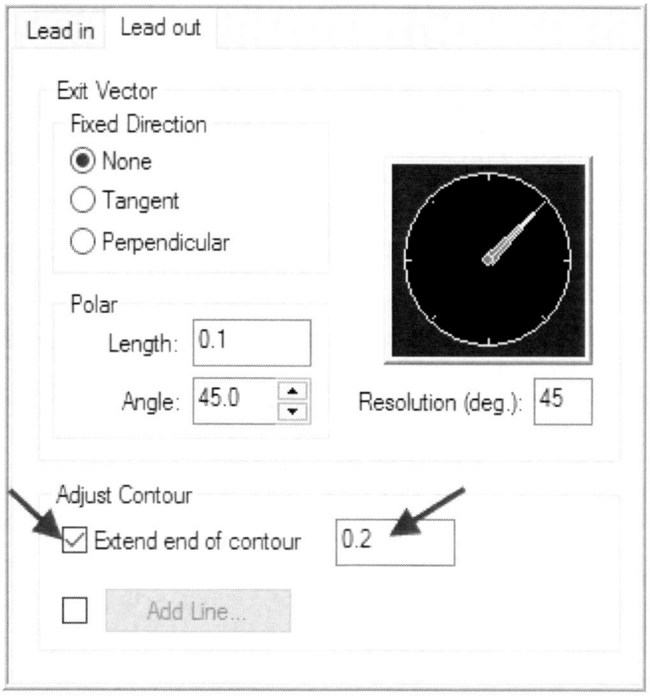

5. Select the OK button ✓ to exit this function.
6. Select the OK button ✓ to exit **Quick finish parameters**.

TASK 13:
FINISH THE 0.1 RADIUS

➲ In this task you will create a new Tool to machine the **0.1" Radius**.

1. On the **TURNING** tab select **Finish** in the **General** section.

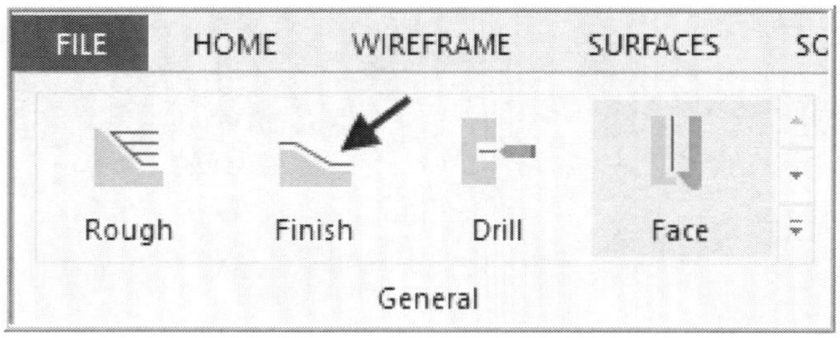

2. In the **Chaining** window click on the icon for **Single** 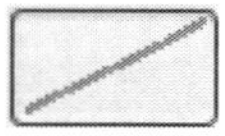
3. Select the **Arc** shown below. Pick the arc on the right hand side:

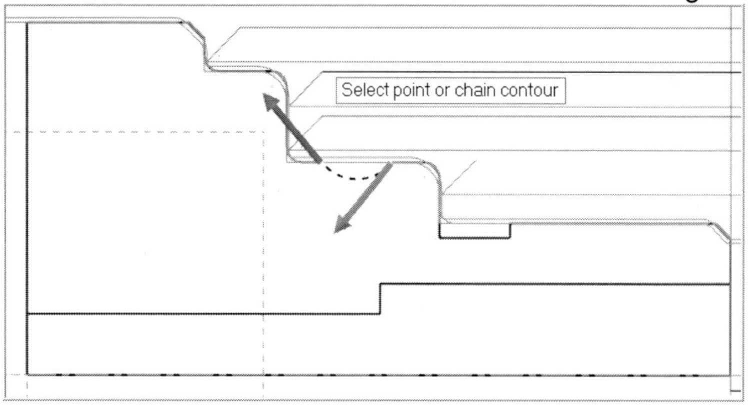

4. Select the OK button  to exit the **Chaining** dialog window.
5. Right Click the mouse in the space as indicated by **arrow # 1** shown below:
6. Click on **Create new tool...** as indicated by **arrow # 2** as shown below:

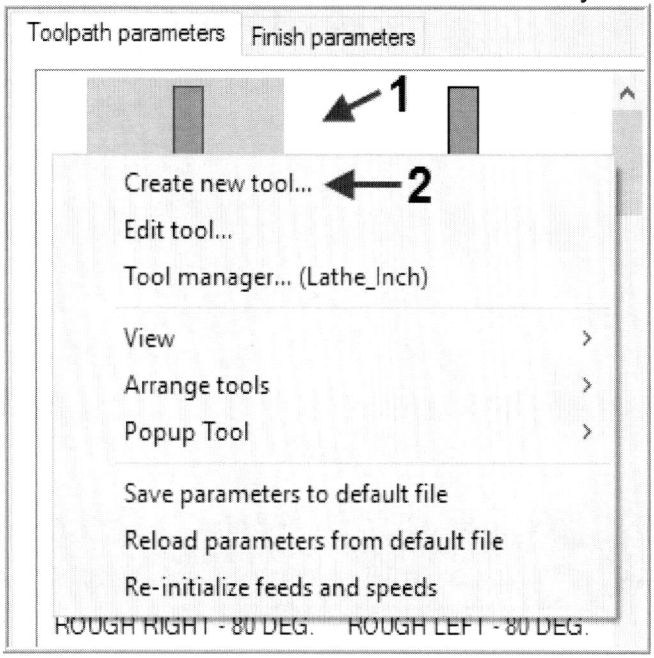

7. Click on the **General Turning** Button as shown below:

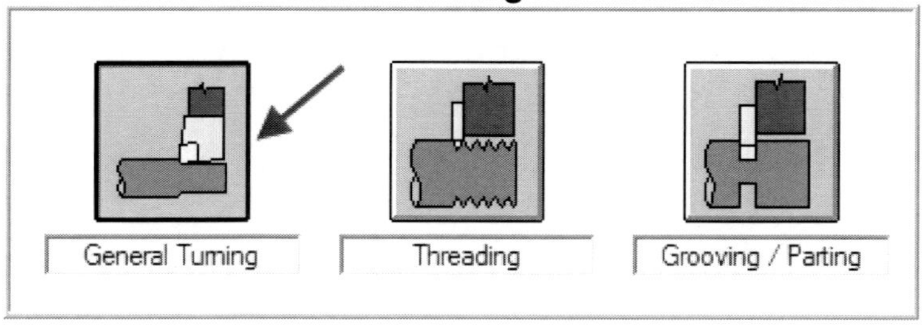

8. Click on the **Round** insert as shown below. Open up the drop down menu for **IC Dia / Length** and select **3/16**.

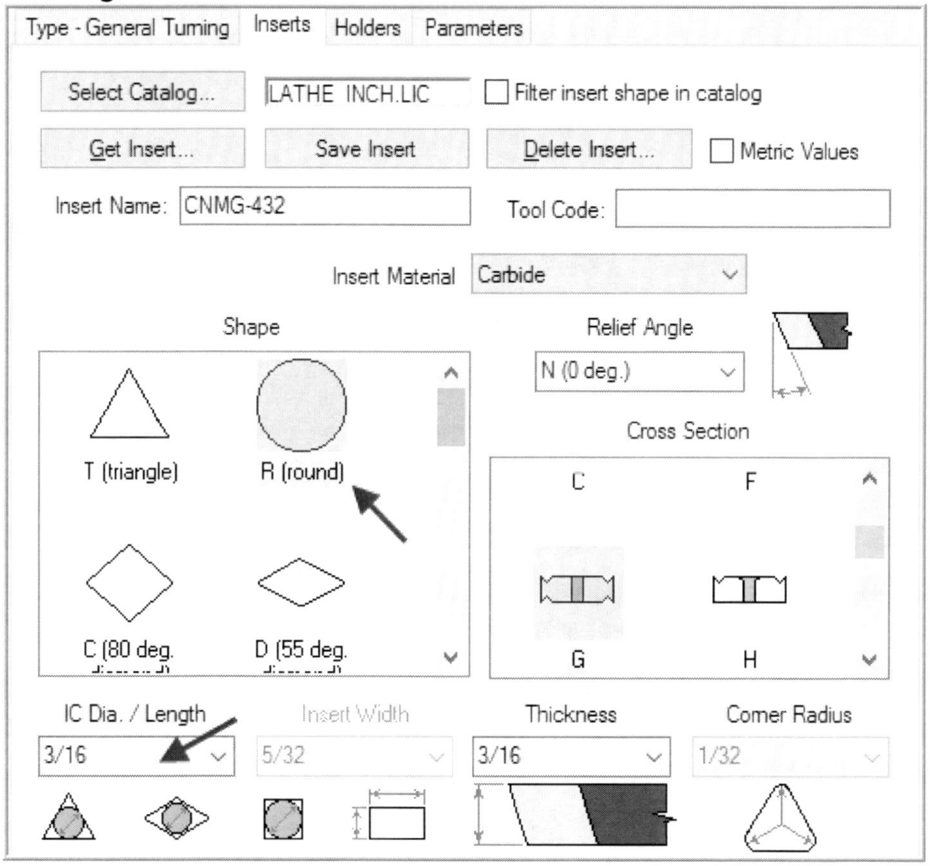

9. Click on the **Holders** Tab.
10. Scroll down and click on the **Offset Profiling** holder as shown below.

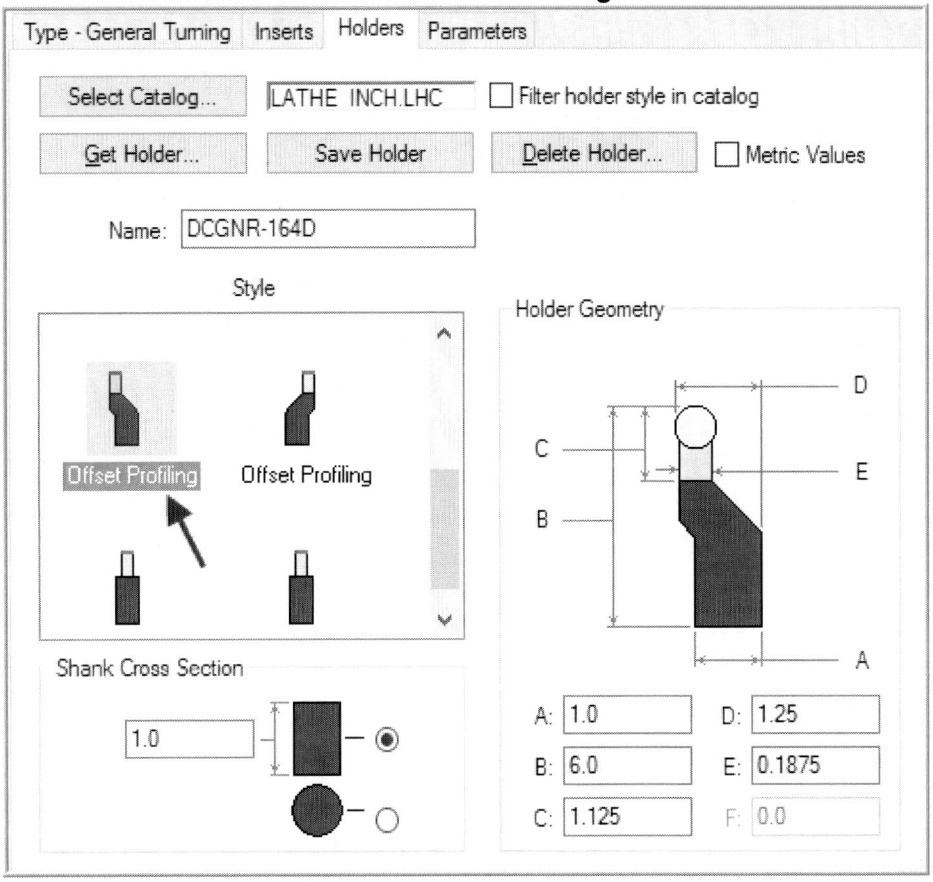

11. Click on the **Parameters** page and at the bottom of this page set the compensation for this tool as shown below:

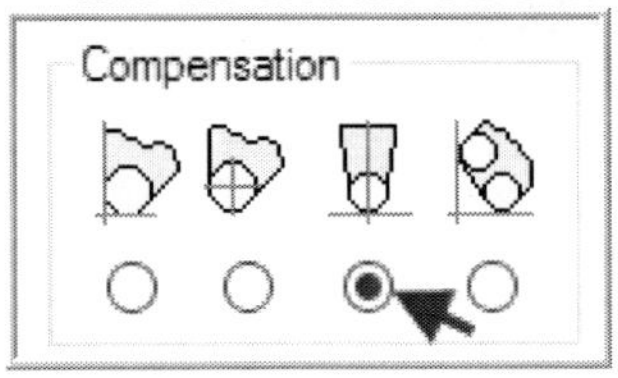

Compensation: Tip
The toolpath is programmed from the tip of the tool corner radius.

This is the only option available for threading tools, drills, taps, and reamers.

12. Click on the OK icon .

13. Make changes on the **Toolpath parameters** page. **Coolant Flood** is set to **On.**

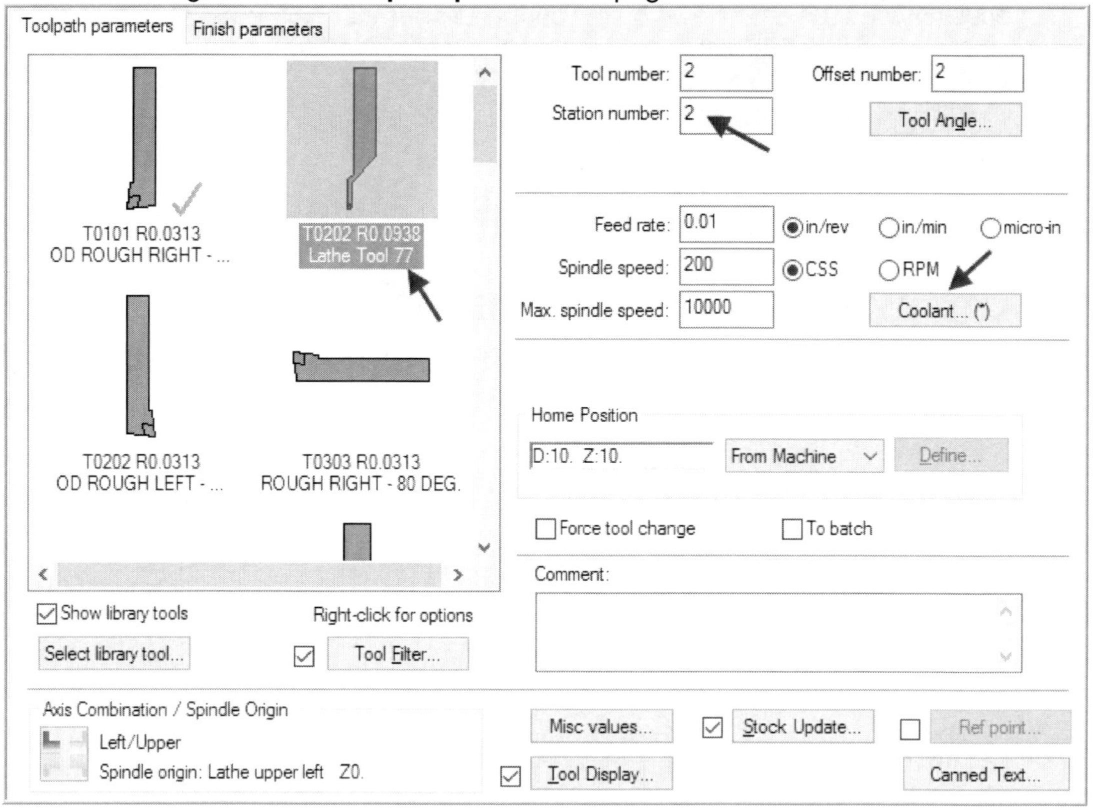

14. Click on the **Finish parameters** tab and make any necessary changes as shown below.

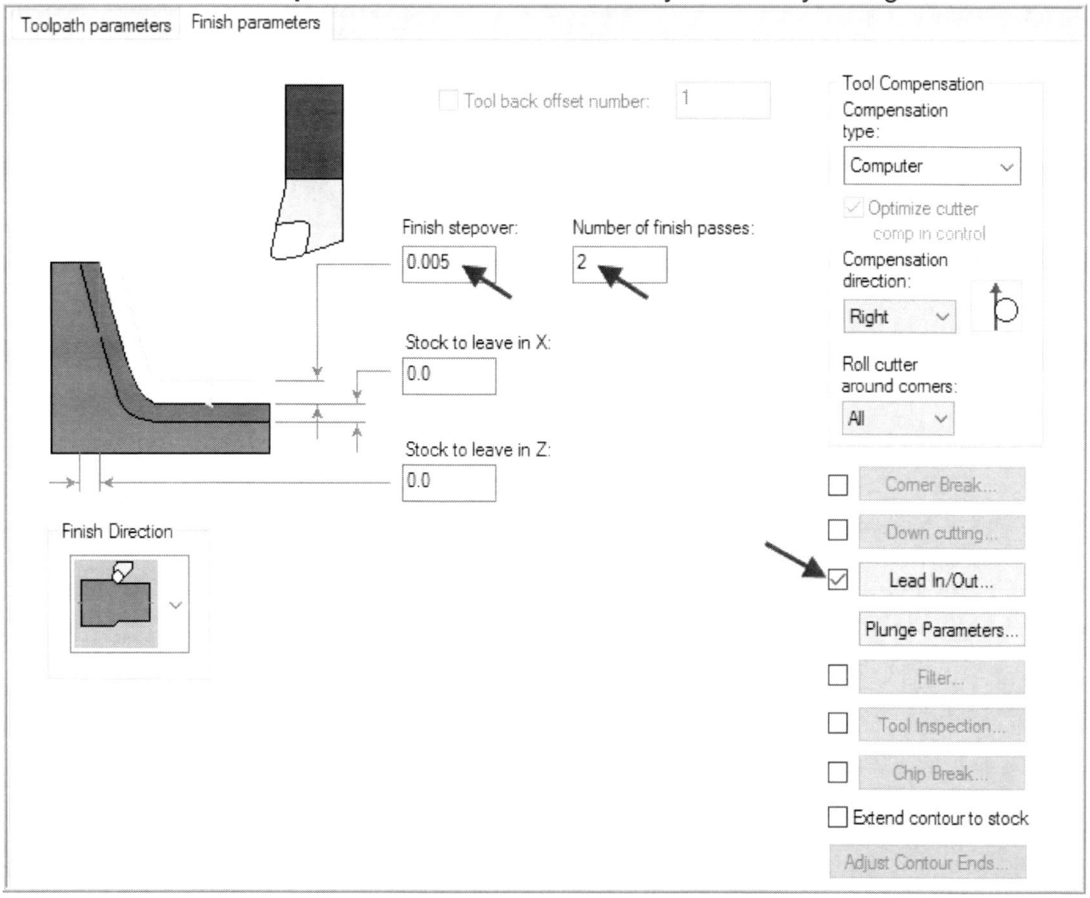

15. Click on the **Lead in/Out** button.
16. Make the necessary changes as shown below on the **Lead In** page. In order to adjust the dial click on the desired location of the arrow.

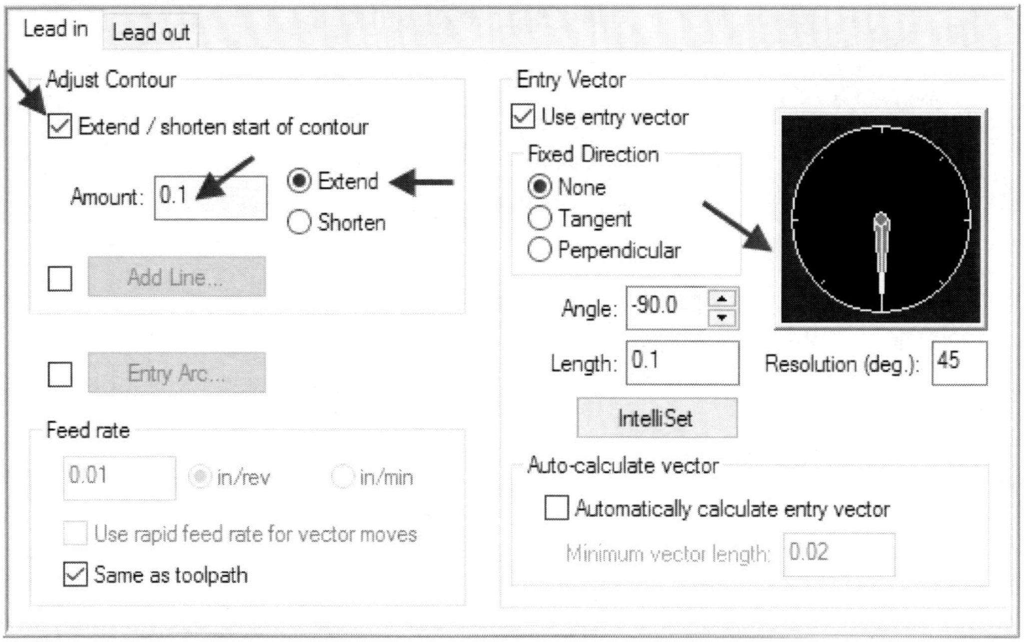

17. Click on the **Lead out** tab and make the necessary changes as shown below.

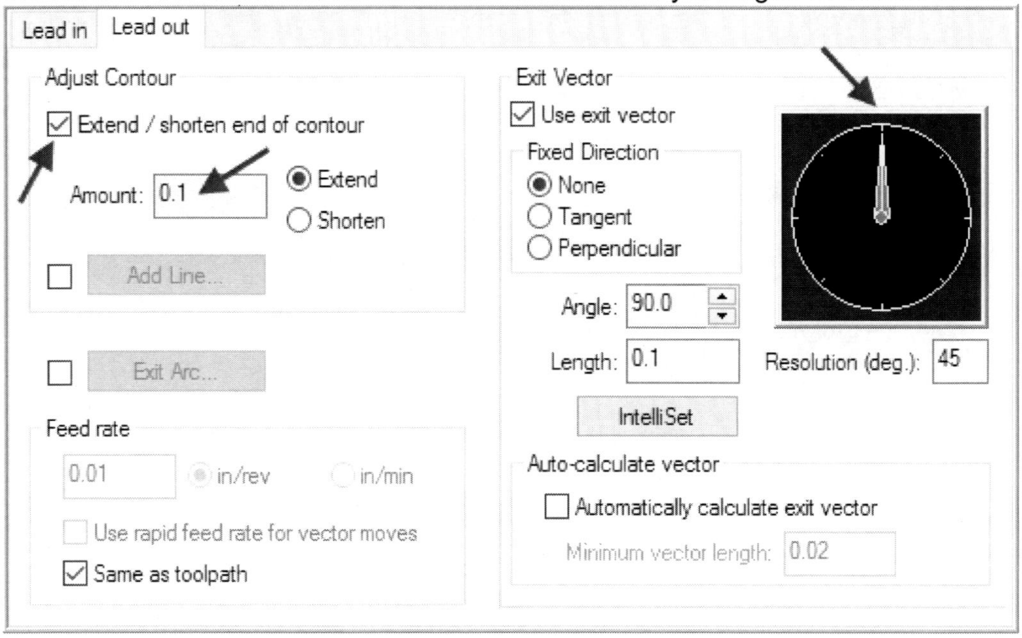

18. Click on OK  to exit the Lead In/out window.

19. Click on the **Plunge Parameters** button Plunge Parameters... .
20. Make the necessary changes as shown below.

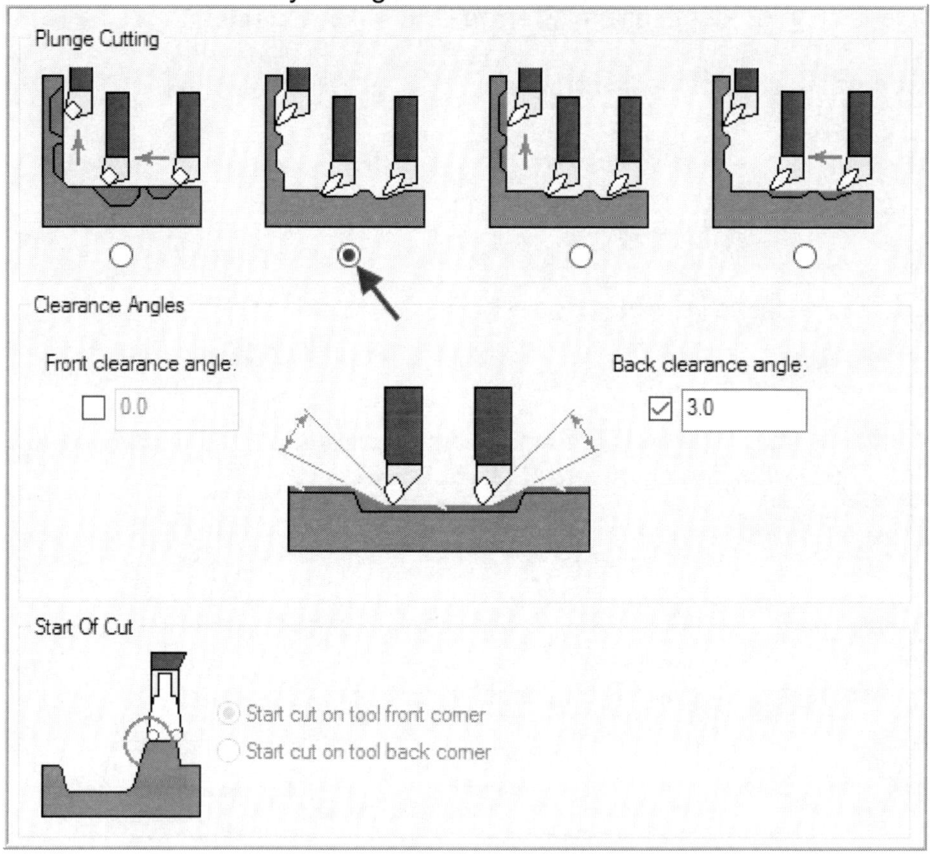

21. Click on Ok to exit the Plunge Cut Parameters window.
22. Click on Ok to exit the Lathe Finish parameters window.

TASK 14:
CENTER DRILL HOLE

➲ In this task you will center drill .2" depth using a **Centre Drill - .25 diameter.**

1. Select **Drill** in the **General** section of the **Turning** tab.

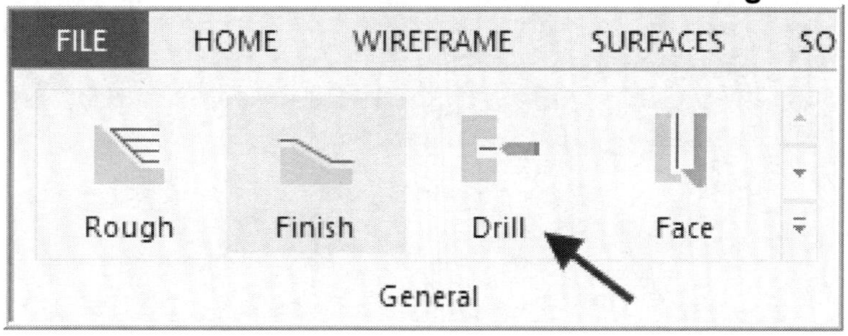

2. To achieve the tool list view shown below, right mouse button click in the white space and select **View>Details**. Then select the **Centre Drill .25 diameter.**

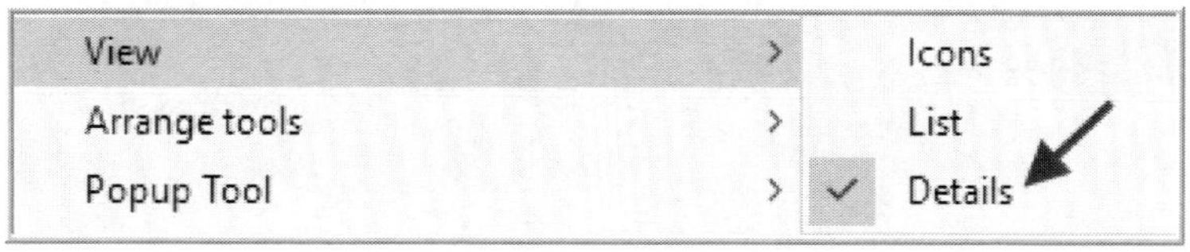

3. Make changes as shown below. **Coolant Flood** is set to **On**.

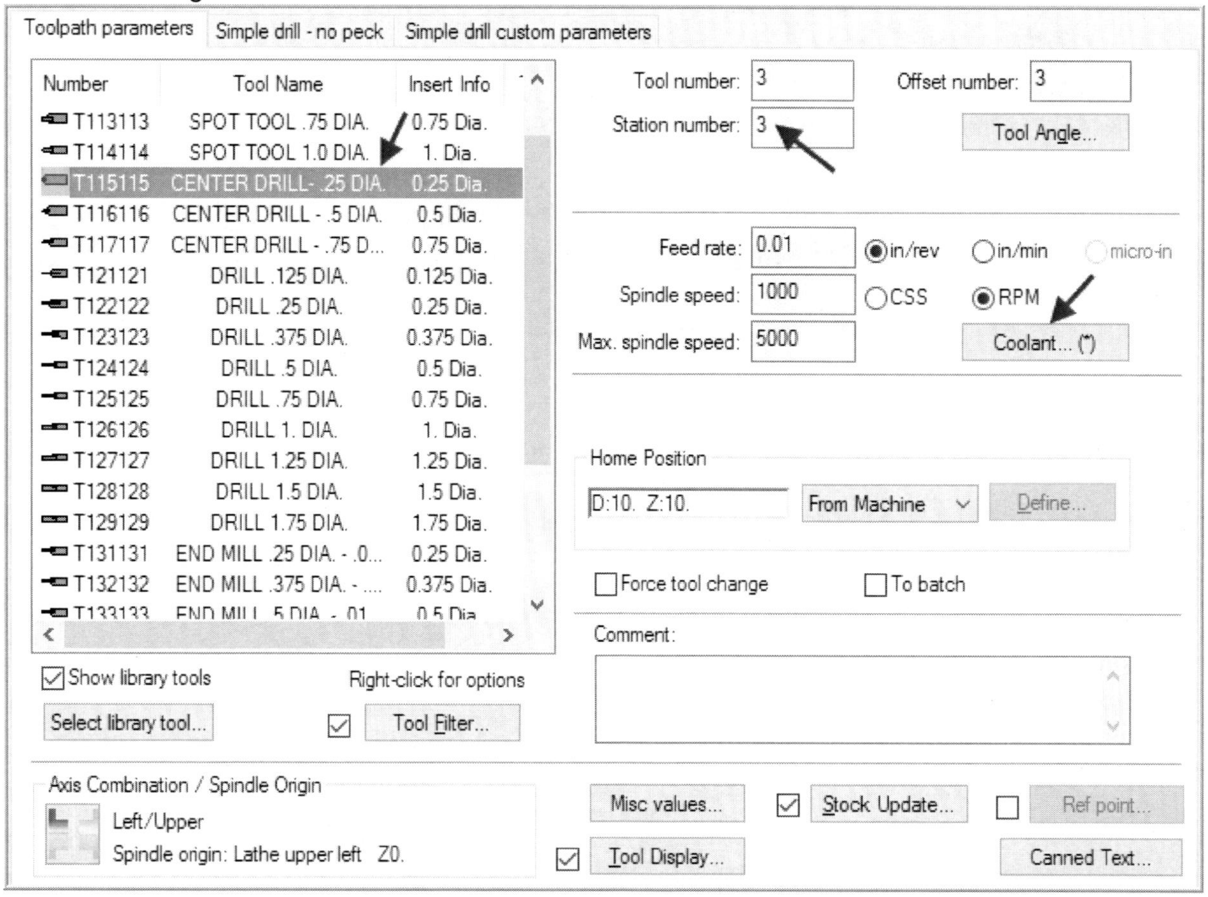

4. Select the **Simple drill** – no peck page and make changes as shown below:

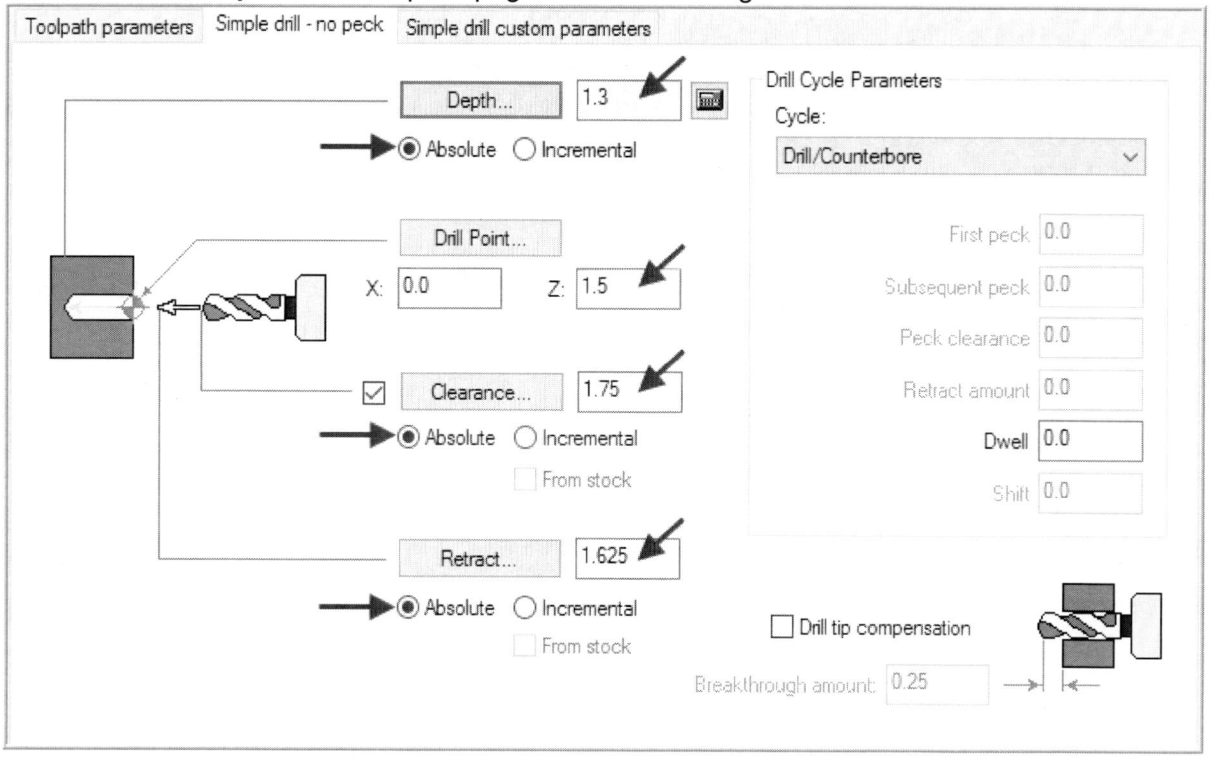

5. Select the OK button  to exit **Simple drill – no peck**.

TASK 15:
PECK DRILL THE 0.250" HOLE

➲ In this task you will peck drill the 0.25" hole through the part using **Drill - .250 diameter.**

1. Select **Drill** in the **General** section of the **Turning** tab.
2. Right mouse button click in the white space and select **View>Icons.**
3. Scroll down and select the **Drill .250 diameter** tool from the tool list and make changes as shown below. **Coolant Flood** is set to **On**.

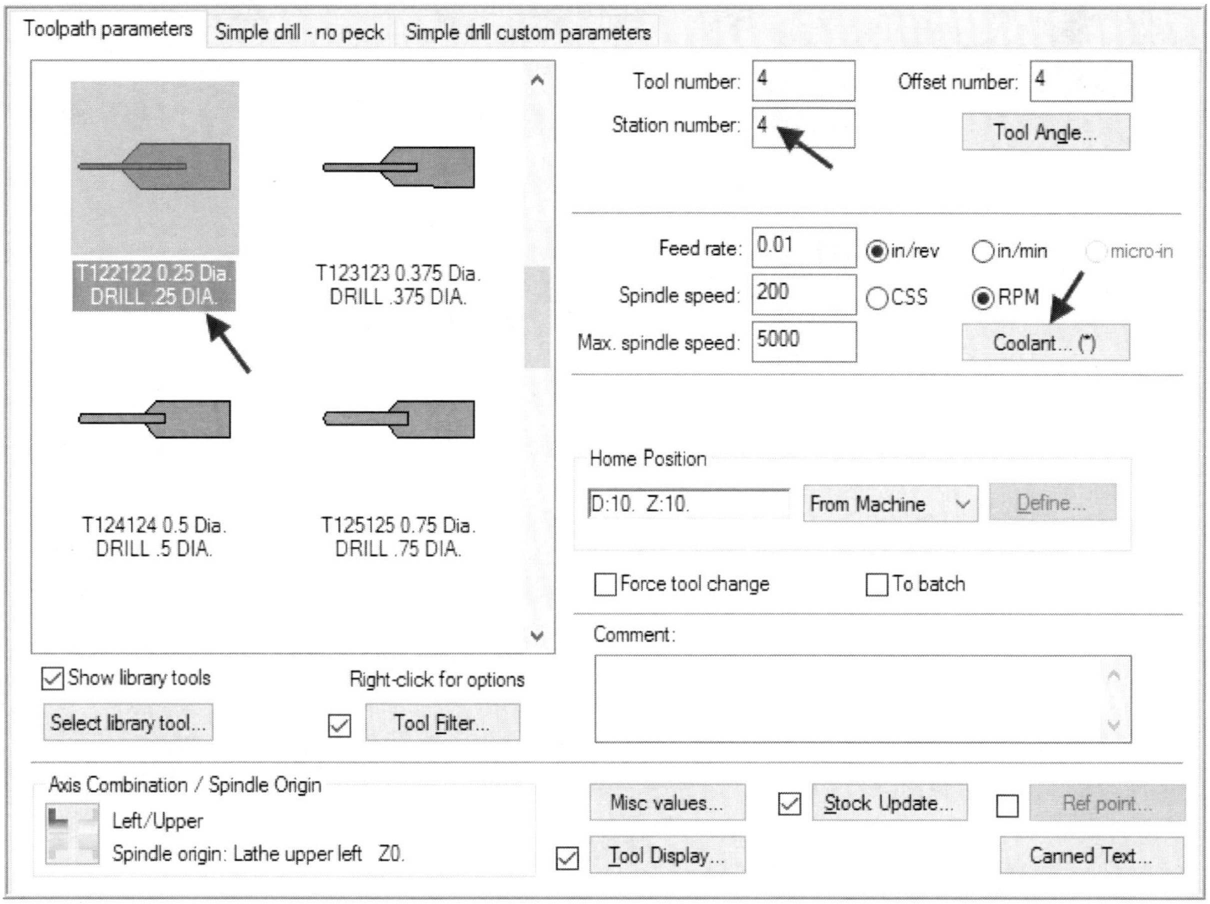

4. Select the **Simple drill – no peck** page and make changes as shown below. This hole will be **peck drilled through the part**. Make changes as shown below:

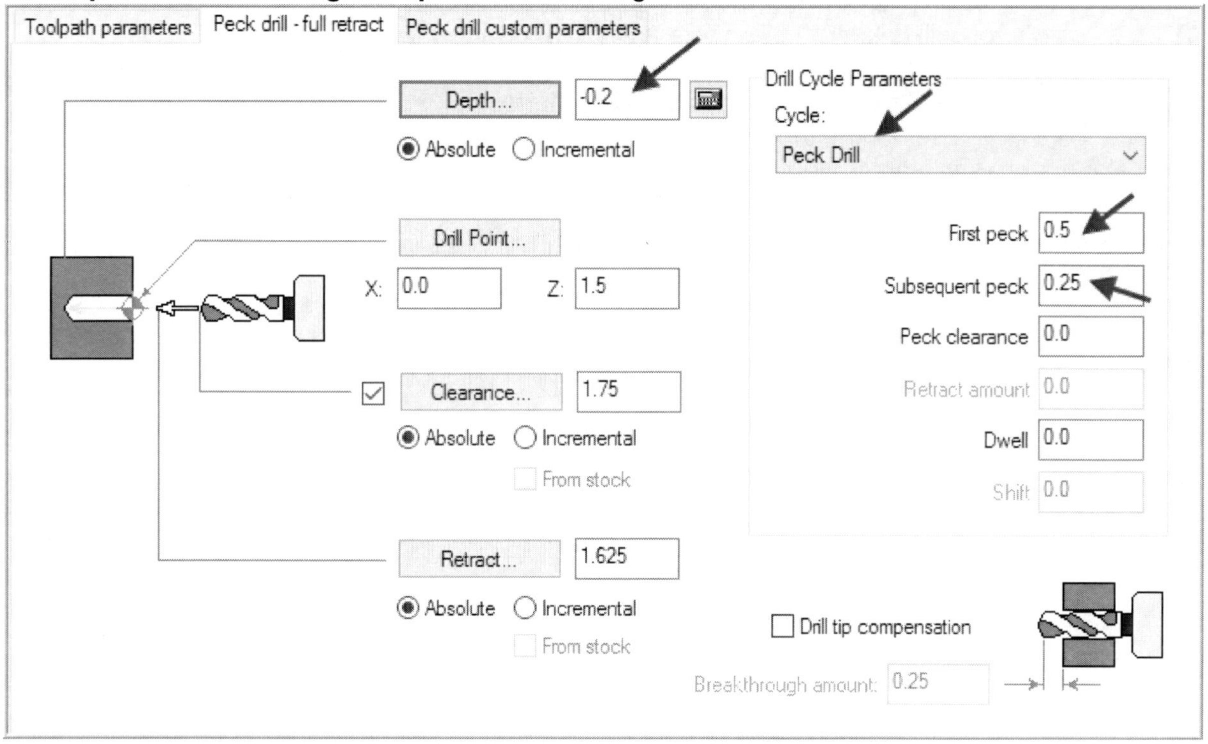

5. Select the OK button to exit Peck drill – full retract.

TASK 16:
DRILL THE 0.375" HOLE

➲ In this task you will drill the 0.375" hole using **0.375 diameter end mill.**

1. Select **Drill** in the **General** section of the **Turning** tab.
2. Scroll down and select the **0.375 DIA. - .007R diameter End Mill** tool from the tool list and make changes as shown below. **Coolant Flood** is set to **On**.

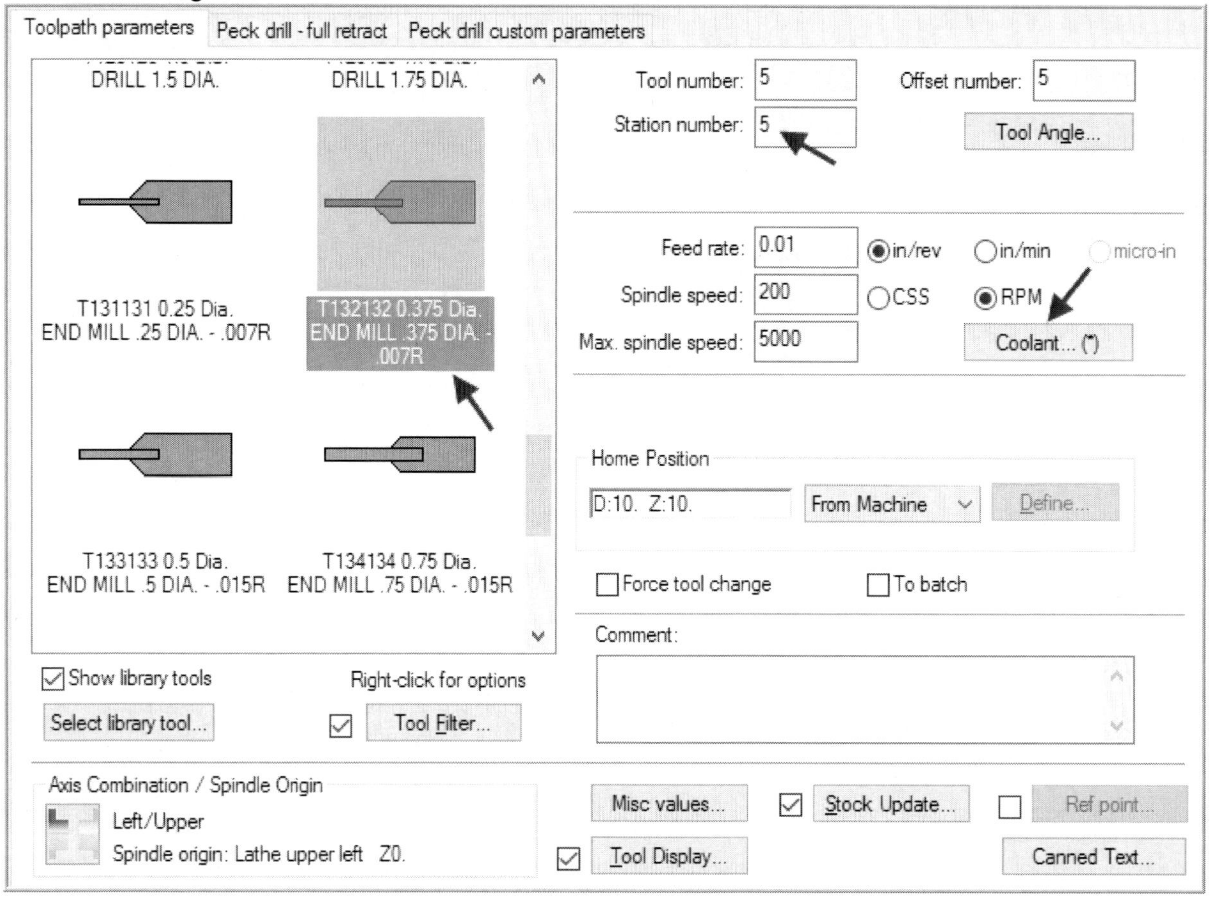

3. Select the second tab **Peck drill – full retract** and make changes as shown below**.** This is a **Simple drill – no peck** operation so change the **Cycle to Drill/Counterbore**.

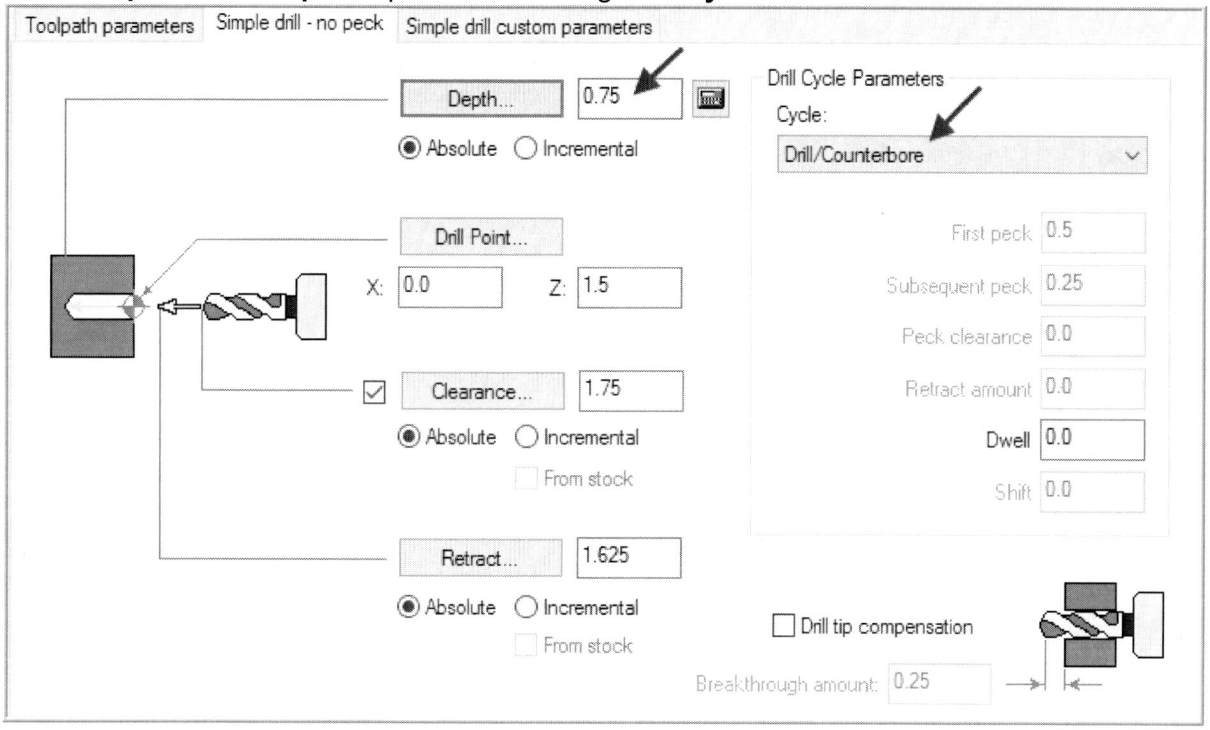

4. Select the OK button  to exit Simple drill – no peck.

TASK 17:
CUT THE GROOVE

➲ In this task you will use the Lathe Groove toolpath using an **OD Groove Right Width .125.**

1. Click on the **Select all operations** icon.
2. Now **toggle the display of the toolpaths** by selecting **ALT and T** on your keyboard to hide the toolpaths display.
3. Click on the **Expand gallery** down arrow to view additional options in the **General** toolpath section. In the **General** section select **Groove.**

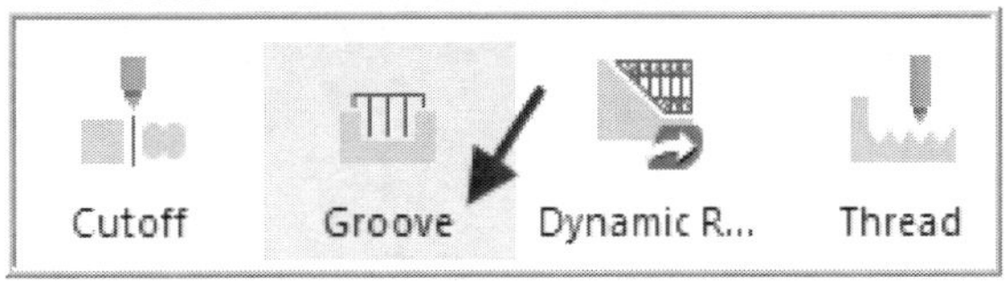

4. The Grooving Options window appears. Click on the **Chain** option as shown below:

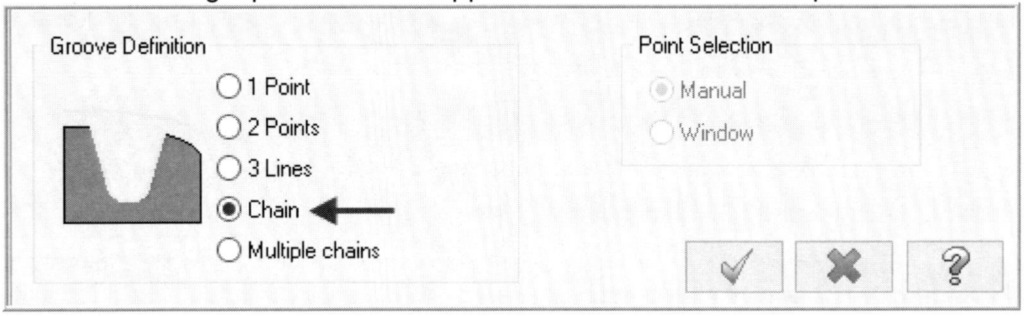

5. Click on OK.
6. Zoom in on the groove area as shown below:
7. In the **Chaining** window Chaining mode is set to **Partial** by default.
8. Select **Line 1** as the start of the **Partial chain**.

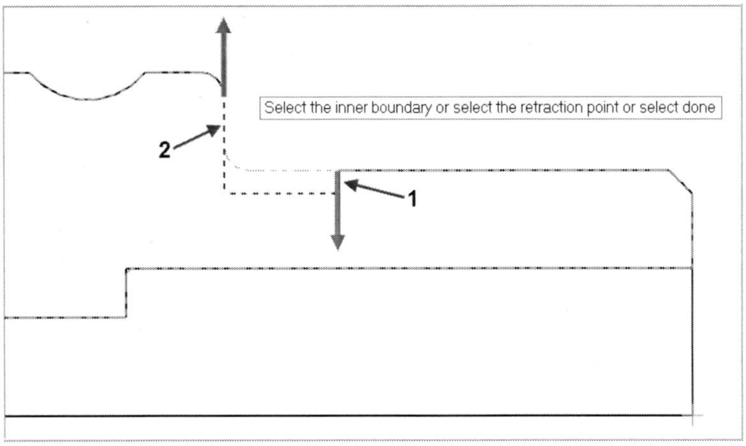

After you have selected line 1 **ensure** that the arrows are pointing downwards If it is not select the reverse button in the Chaining dialog box.

9. Then select **Line 2** as the end entity in this chain.
10. Select the OK button to exit the Chaining dialog window.

11. Select **OD Groove Right Width .125** tool from the tool list and make any necessary changes as shown below. **Coolant Flood** is set to **On**.

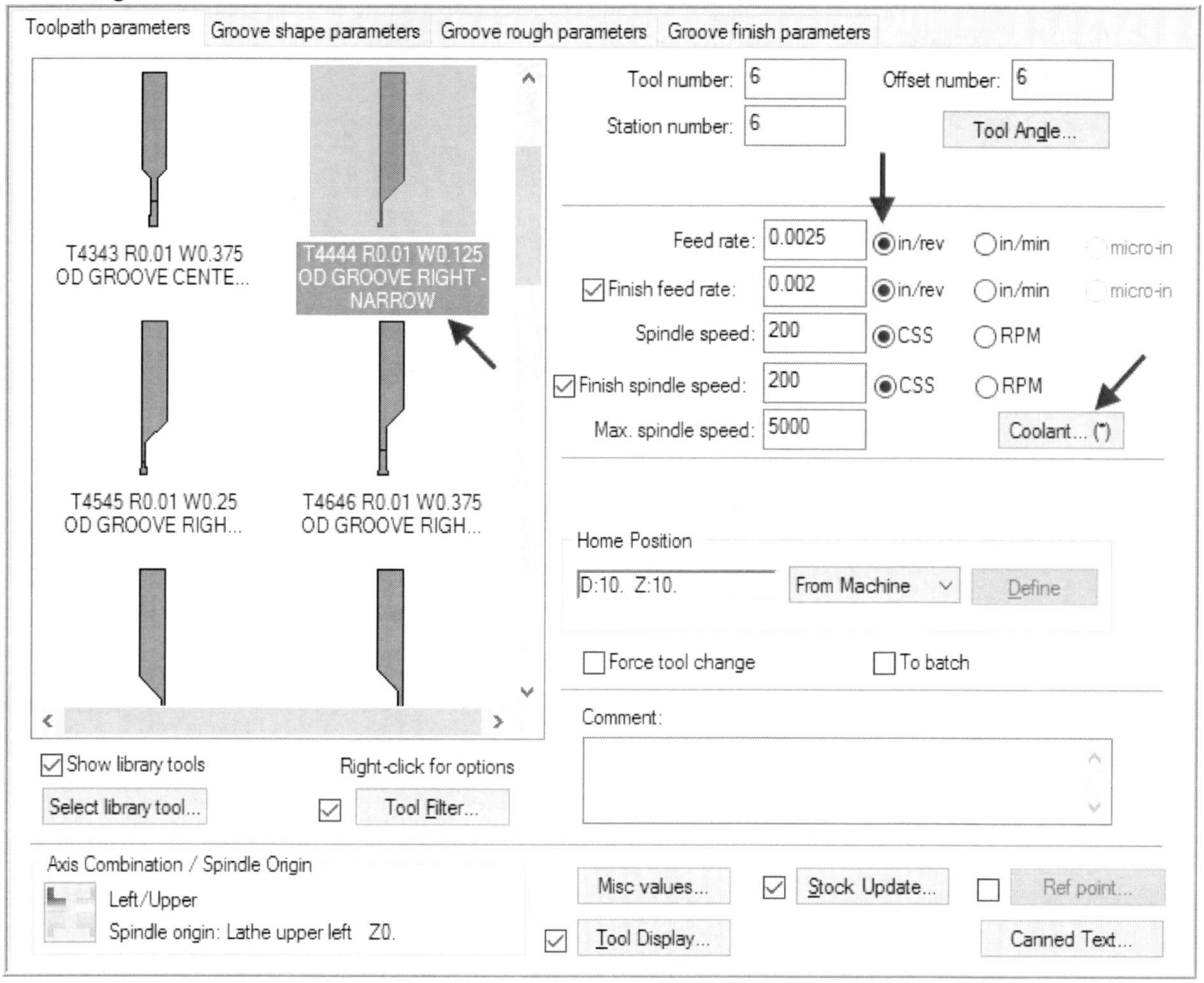

12. Select the **Groove finish parameters** page.

13. Click on the **Lead In** button Lead In... and make changes to the **Second pass Lead in** page as shown below.

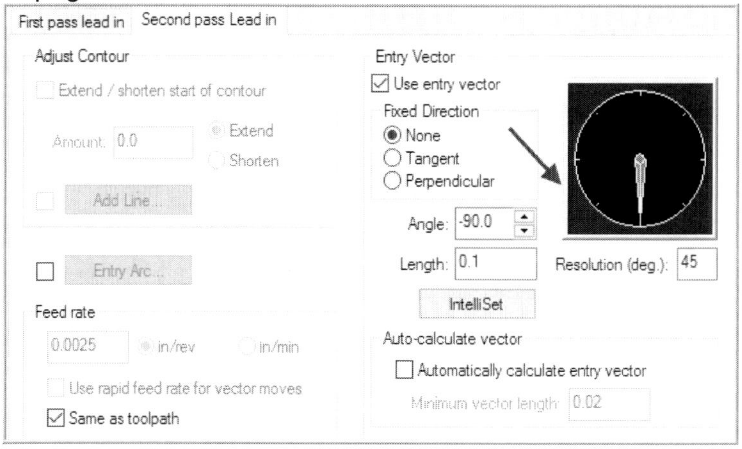

Note:
With grooving toolpaths, the tabs are called **1st Pass Lead In** or **2nd Pass Lead In**.

14. Select the OK button ✓ to exit Lead in.

15. Select the OK button ✓ to exit as no further changes are required.

TASK 18:
CUT OFF THE PART

➲ In this task you will cut off the part using **OD Groove Right Width .125** the same tool as the previous grooving operation.

1. Right mouse click in the graphics area and click on the **Fit** icon .
2. Click on the **Select all operations** icon .
3. Now **toggle the display of the toolpaths** by selecting **ALT and T** on your keyboard to hide the toolpaths display.
4. Click on the **Expand gallery** down arrow to view additional options in the **General** toolpath section. In the **General** section select **Cutoff.**
5. When prompted to **Select cutoff boundary point** pick the end point of the line shown below. Move the cursor over the corner until the visual cue for End point displays and then click on this point.

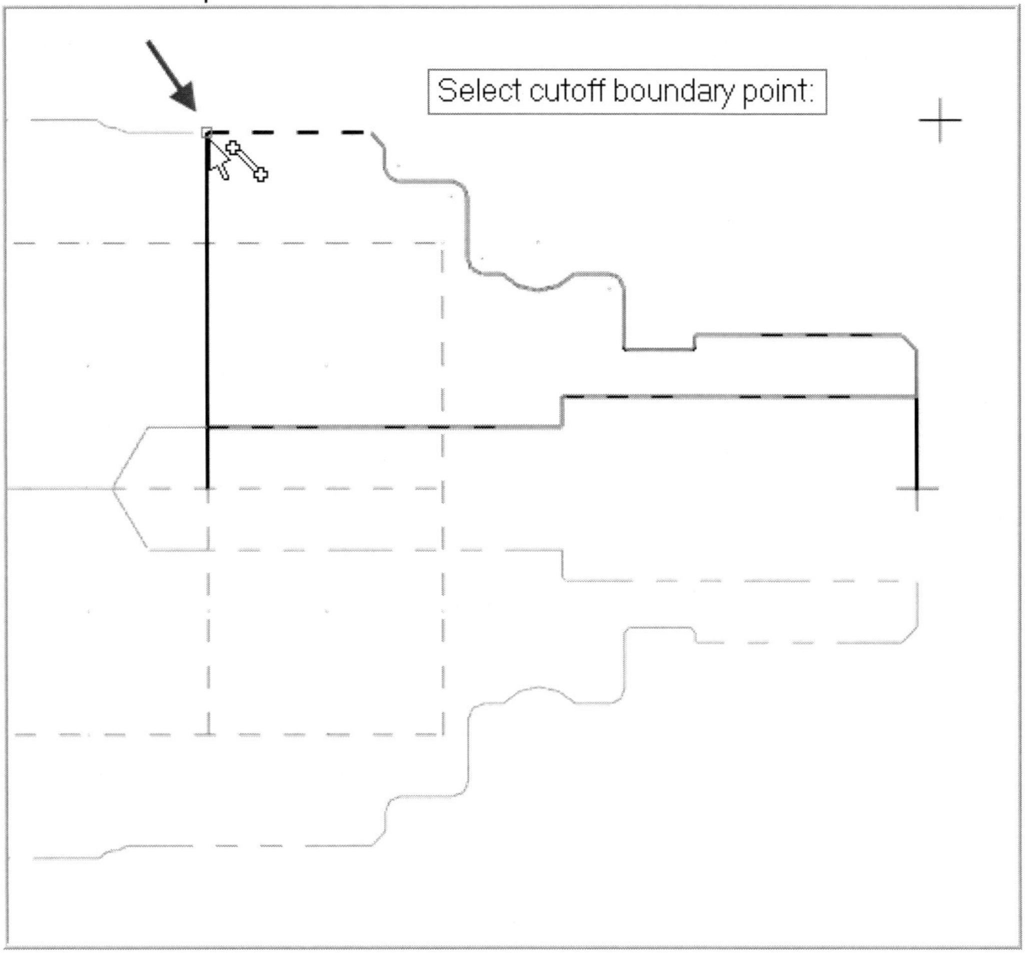

6. Select **OD GROOVE RIGHT WIDTH .125** tool from the tool list and make any necessary changes as shown below. **Coolant Flood** is set to **On**.

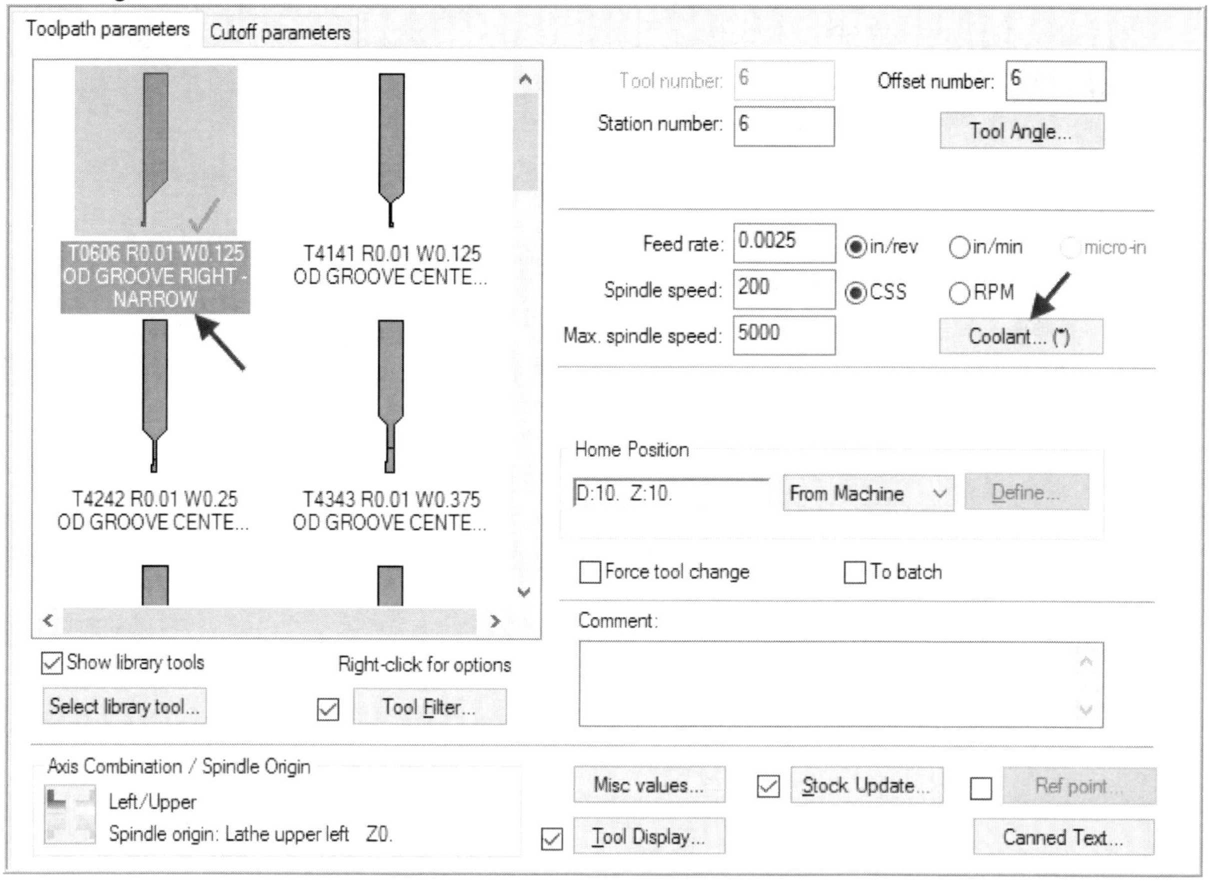

7. Still on the **Toolpath parameters** page click on the Stock Update button .
8. Ensure **Keep both pieces** is activated.

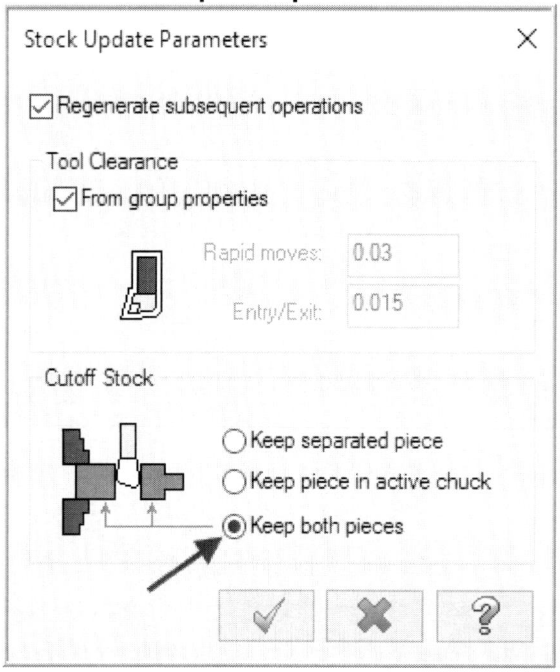

9. Select the **Cutoff parameters** page and make sure the settings are as shown below.

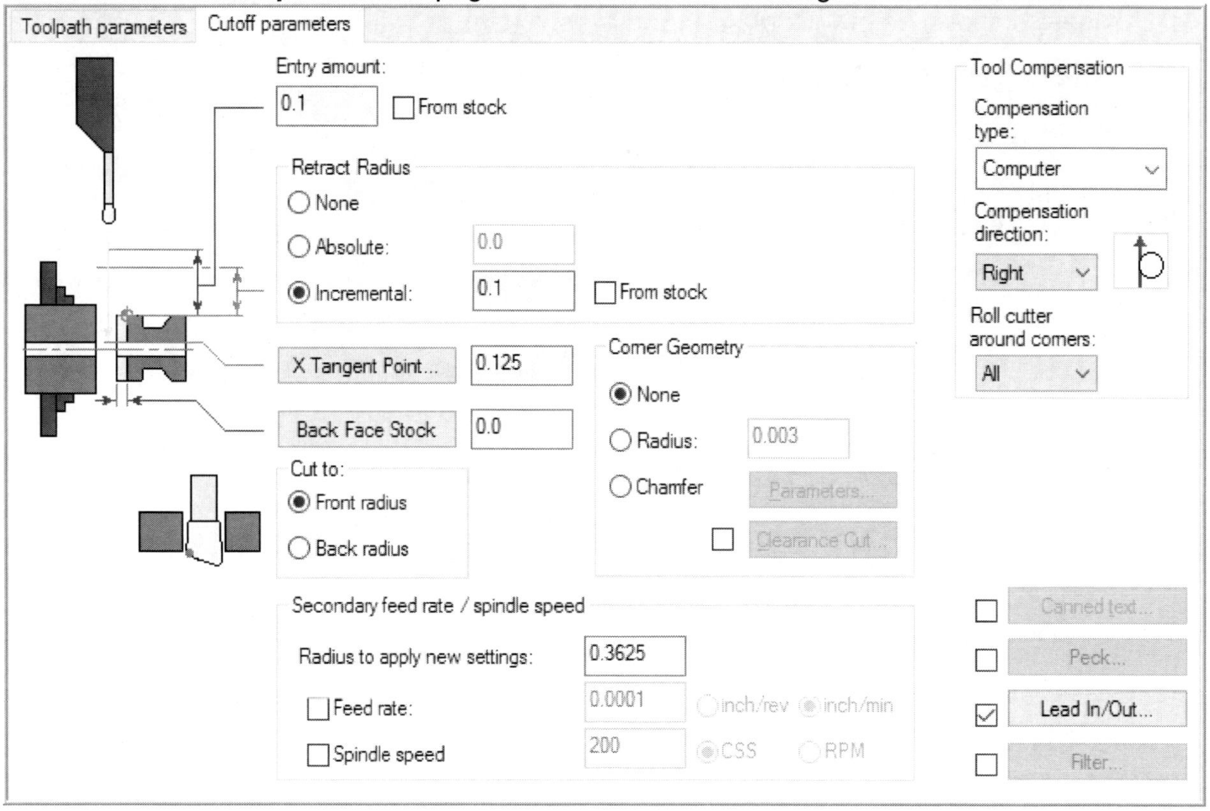

10. Select the OK button  to exit Lathe Cutoff parameters.

TASK 19:
VERIFY THE TOOLPATH

➲ Mastercam's Verify utility allows you to use solid models to simulate the machining of a part. The model created by the verification represents the surface finish, and shows collisions, if any exist.

1. Right mouse click in the graphics area and click on the **Fit** icon .
2. In the Toolpaths Manager pick all the operations to Verify by picking the **Select All** icon .
3. Select the **Verify selected operations** icon shown below:

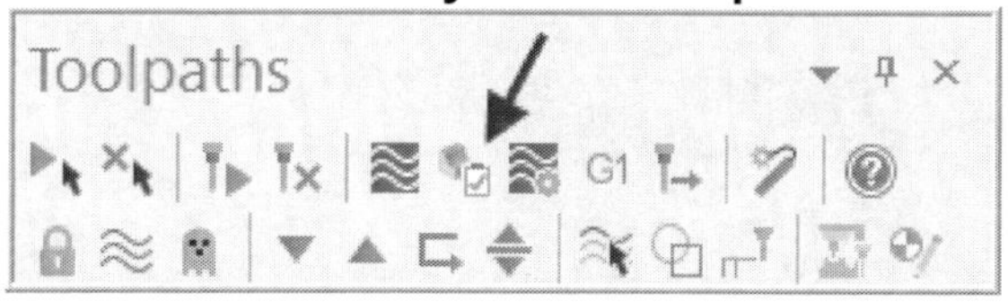

4. **Maximize** the Backplot/Verify window if required.
5. Now select the **Home** Tab if required.

6. Activate the options shown below in the **Visibility** section of the Home tab. **Initial Stock not** activated.

7. At the top of the screen select the **View** tab, the Isometric icon and then select **Fit**.

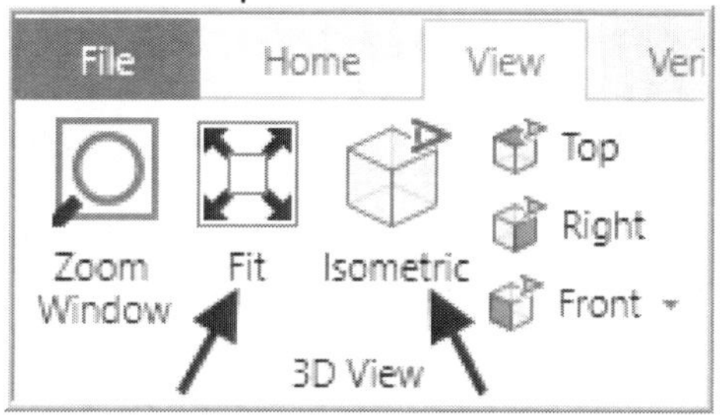

8. Select the **Verify** tab and activate the **Color Loop** to change the color of the tools for the verified part.

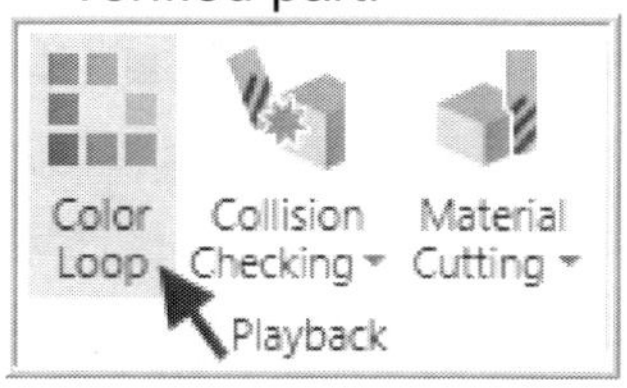

Color Loop
Changes the color of the toolpath or cut stock by operation or by tool change.

Choose File Options to set the colors.

9. In the lower part of the screen now set the run **Speed** to slow by moving the slider bar pointer over to the left as shown below.

10. Now select the **Play Simulation** button to review the toolpaths.

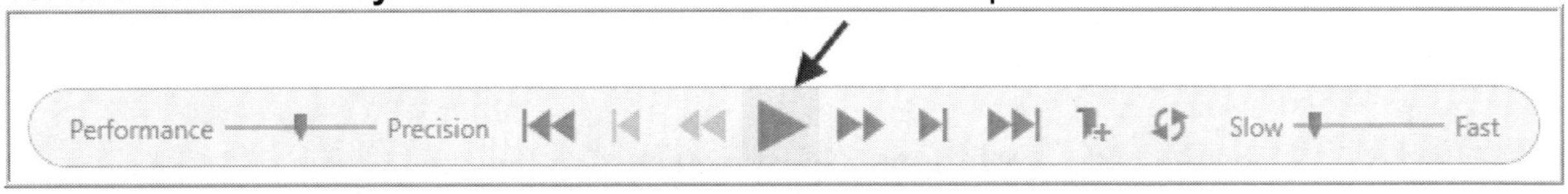

11. Select the Close button  in the top right hand corner to exit Verify.

TASK 20:
SAVE THE UPDATED MASTERCAM FILE

1. Select the **Save** icon from the **Quick Access** toolbar at the top left of the screen.

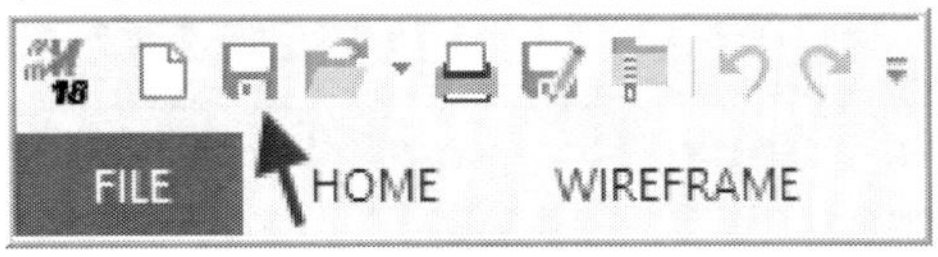

TASK 21:
POST AND CREATE THE CNC CODE FILE

1. Ensure all the operations are selected by picking the **Select All** icon  from the Toolpaths manager.
2. Select the **Post selected operations** button from the Toolpaths manager.

➲ **Please Note:** If you cannot see **G1** click on the right pane of the Toolpaths manager window and expand the window to the right.

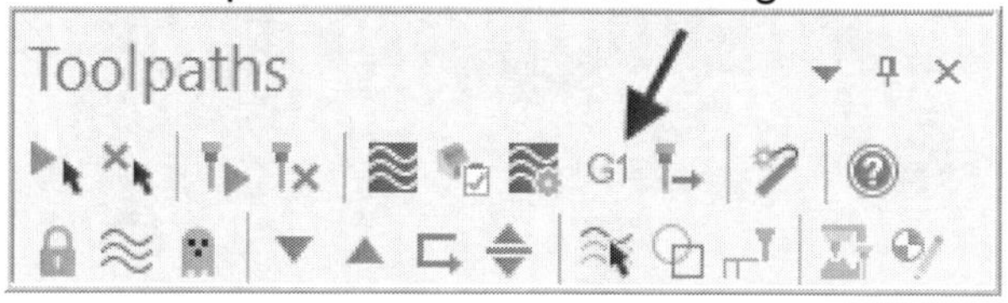

3. In the Post processing window, make the necessary changes as shown below:

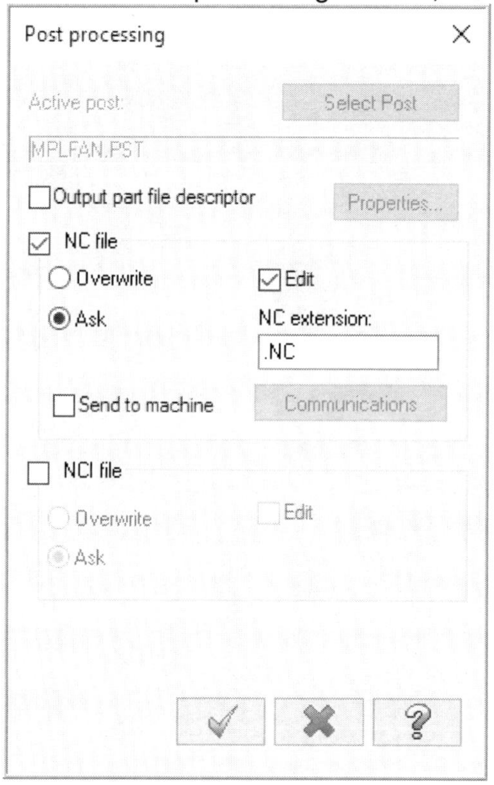

About Post Processing

NC file:
Select this option to save the NC file. The file name and extension are stored in the machine group properties for the selected operation. If you are posting operations from different machine groups or Mastercam files, or batch processing, Mastercam will create several files according to the settings for each machine group.

Edit:
When checked, automatically launches the default text editor with the file displayed so that you can review or modify it.

4. Select the OK button  to continue.

5. Ensure the same name as your Mastercam part file name is displayed in the **NC File name** field.
6. Select the **Save** button.

➲ The CNC code file opens up in the default editor.

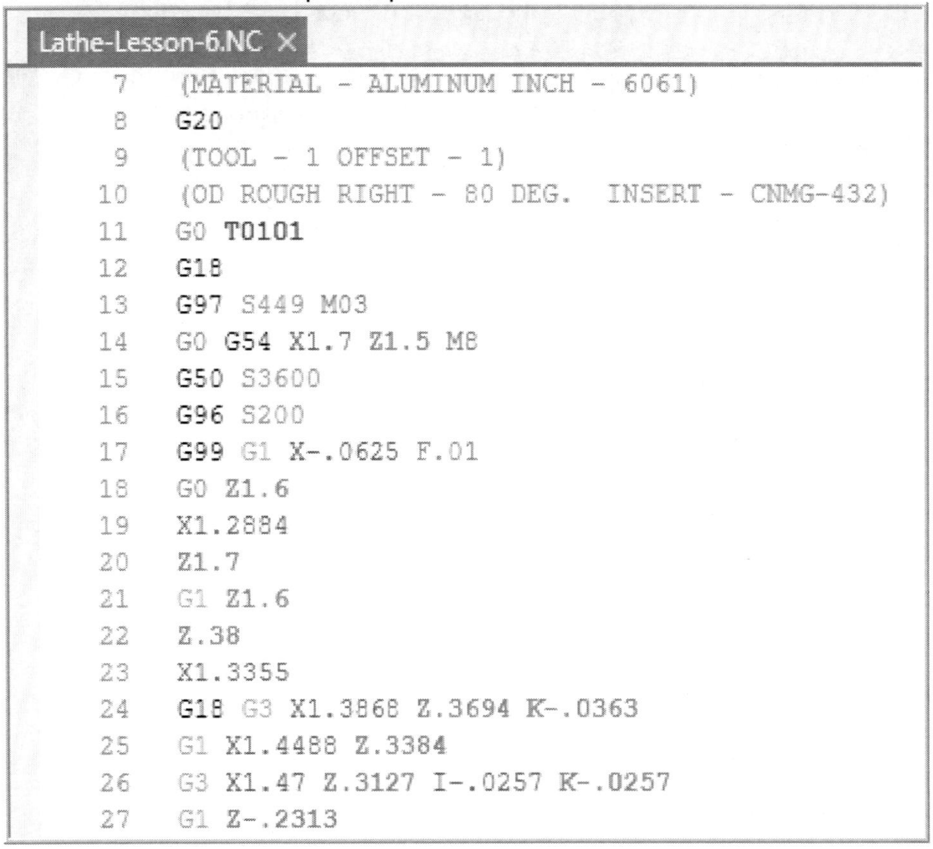

Lathe-Lesson-6.NC ×

```
(MATERIAL - ALUMINUM INCH - 6061)
G20
(TOOL - 1 OFFSET - 1)
(OD ROUGH RIGHT - 80 DEG.  INSERT - CNMG-432)
G0 T0101
G18
G97 S449 M03
G0 G54 X1.7 Z1.5 M8
G50 S3600
G96 S200
G99 G1 X-.0625 F.01
G0 Z1.6
X1.2884
Z1.7
G1 Z1.6
Z.38
X1.3355
G18 G3 X1.3868 Z.3694 K-.0363
G1 X1.4488 Z.3384
G3 X1.47 Z.3127 I-.0257 K-.0257
G1 Z-.2313
```

7. Select the × in the top right corner to exit the CNC editor.

➲ This completes Lathe-Lesson-6.

LATHE-LESSON-6 EXERCISE

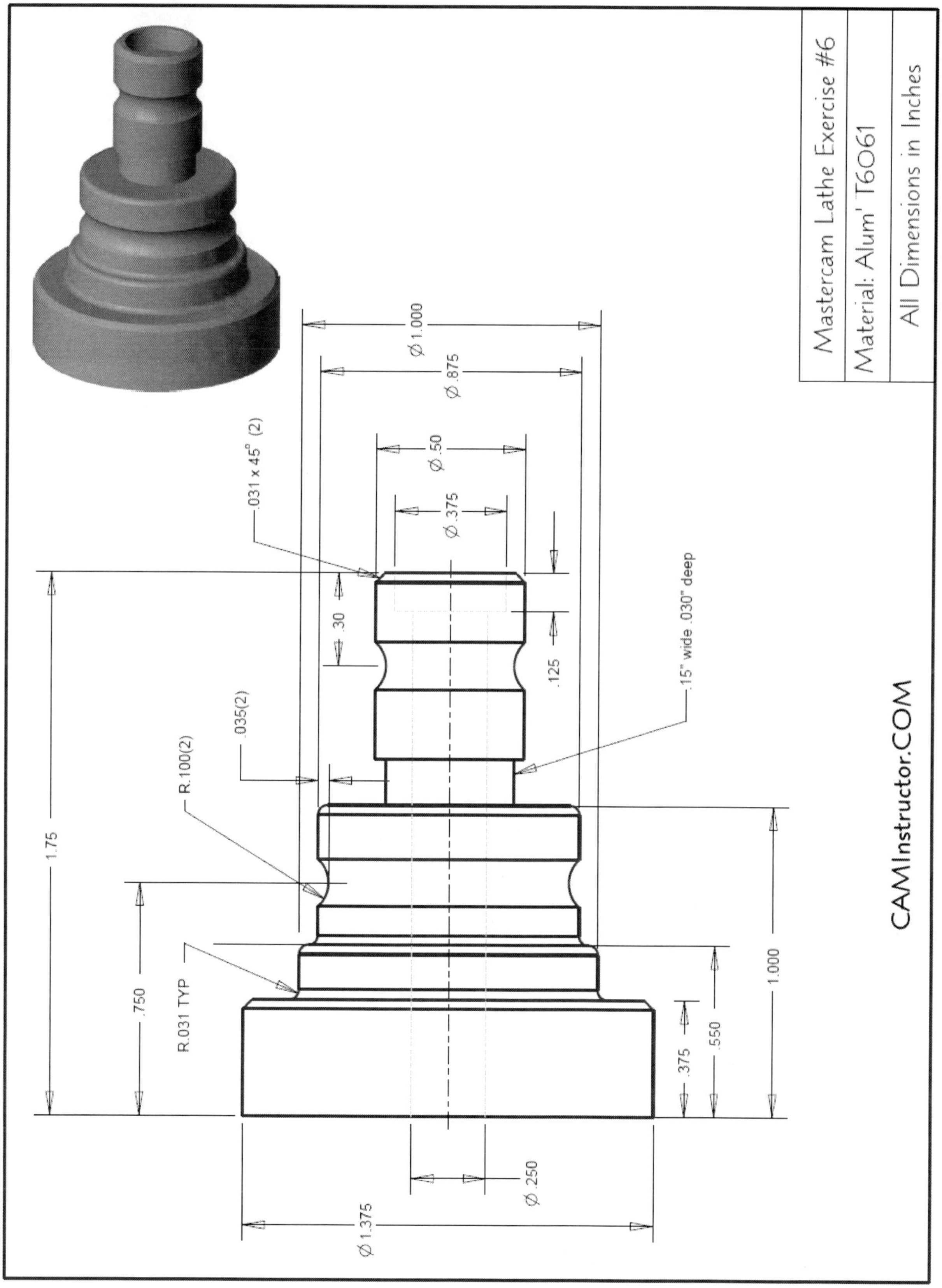

Mastercam® 2018

TRAINING GUIDE

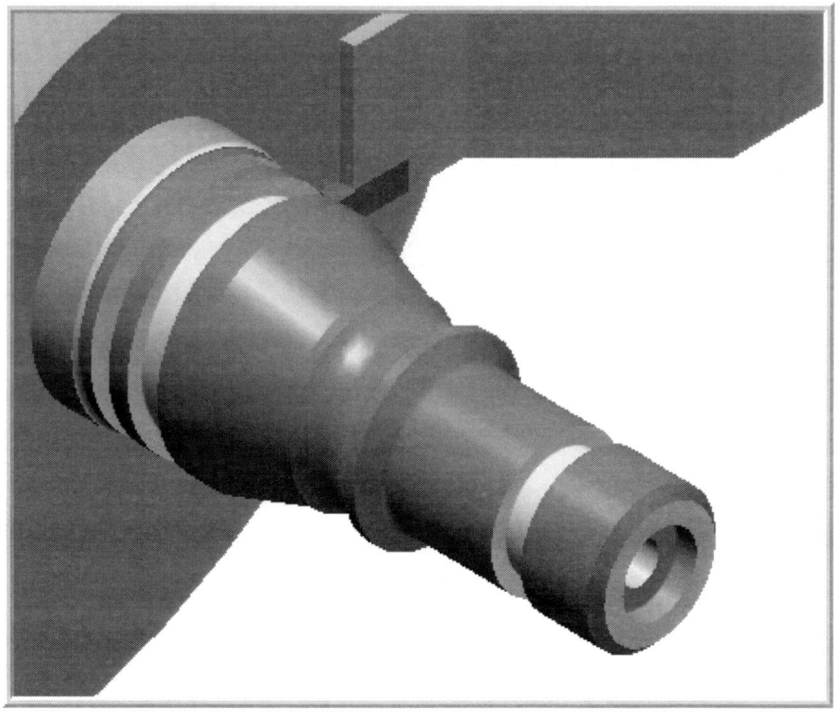

LATHE-LESSON-7

FACE, QUICK ROUGH AND FINISH, DRILL, TAP, GROOVE AND CUTOFF

camInstructor

Objectives

You will create the geometry for Lathe Lesson-7, and then generate a toolpath to machine the part on a CNC lathe. This lesson covers the following topics:

➲ **Create a 2-dimensional drawing by:**
Creating lines.
Creating fillets.
Creating chamfers.
Trimming geometry.

➲ **Establish Stock and Chuck Setup settings:**
Stock size.
Chuck Configuration.
Material for the part.
Feed calculation.

➲ **Generate a 2-dimensional lathe toolpath consisting of:**
Lathe Face.
Lathe Quick Rough.
Lathe Quick Finish.
Lathe Finish.
Lathe Drill.
Lathe Groove.
Lathe Cutoff.

➲ **Inspect the toolpath using Mastercam's Verify and Backplot by:**
Launching the Verify function to machine the part on the screen.
Generating the NC- code.

LATHE - LESSON-7 DRAWING

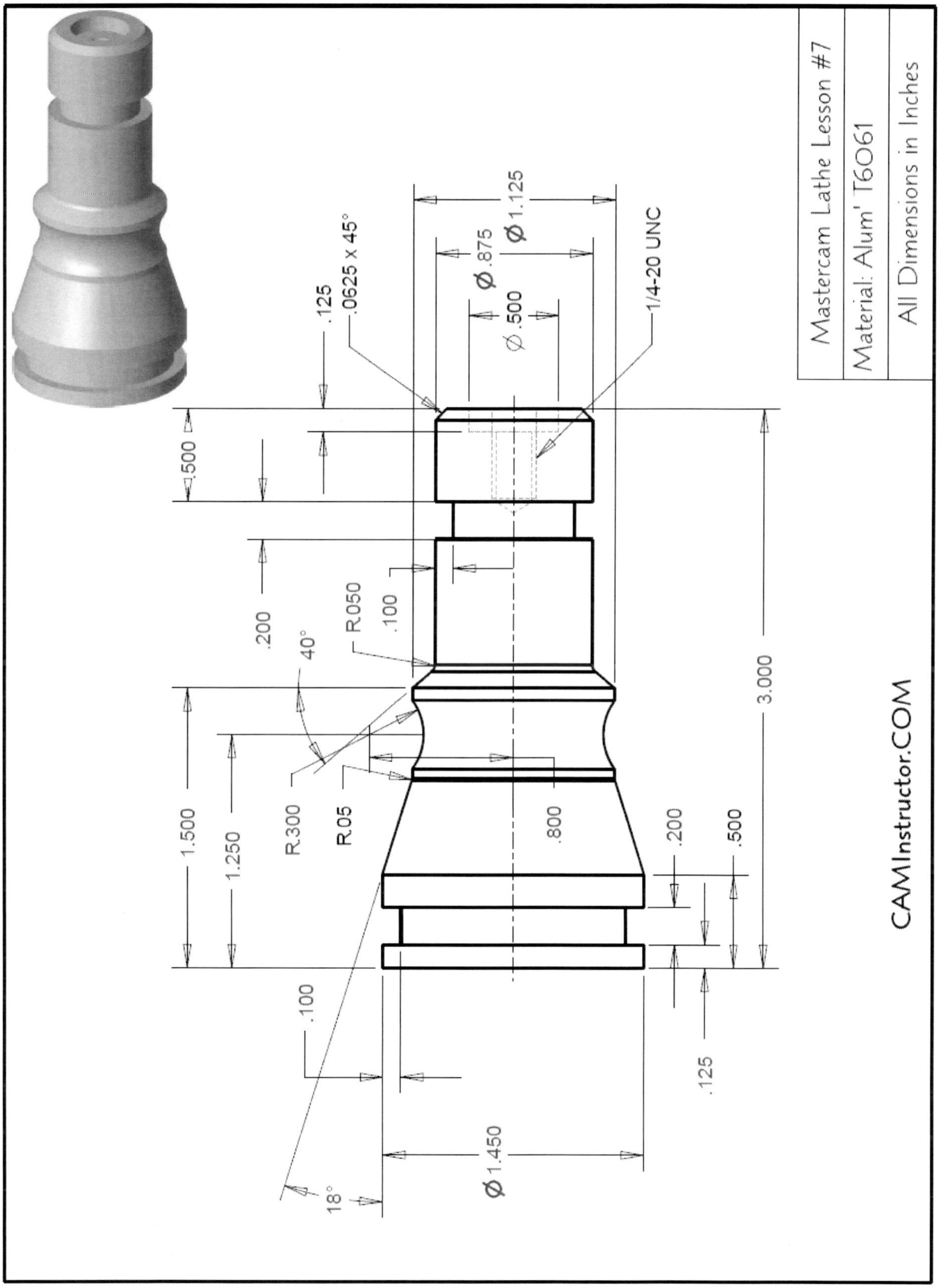

TOOL LIST

Seven tools will be used to create this part.

- **Tool #1 Face, Rough the outside diameters**
  Holder: Outside Diameter Rough Right Hand - DCGNR-164D.
  Insert: 80 Degree Diamond Insert – CNMG-432

- **Tool #2 Finish the outside diameters**
  Holder: Outside Diameter Finish Right Hand - MVJNR-164D.
  Insert: 35 Degree Diamond Insert – VNMG-431.

- **Tool #3 Center drill**
  Centre Drill – body diameter 0.250"

- **Tool #4 13/64 diameter drill**
  Drill 13/64" (0.2031)" diameter

- **Tool #5 ¼-20 UNC tap**
  Tap ¼"-20 UNC

- **Tool #6 Boring tool**
  Holder: Boring Bar – minimum diameter 0.1875".
  Insert: 75 Degree Diamond Insert

- **Tool #7 Cutoff tool**
  Holder: Outside Diameter Groove Right Hand - Narrow.
  Insert: 0.125" Wide - GC-4125

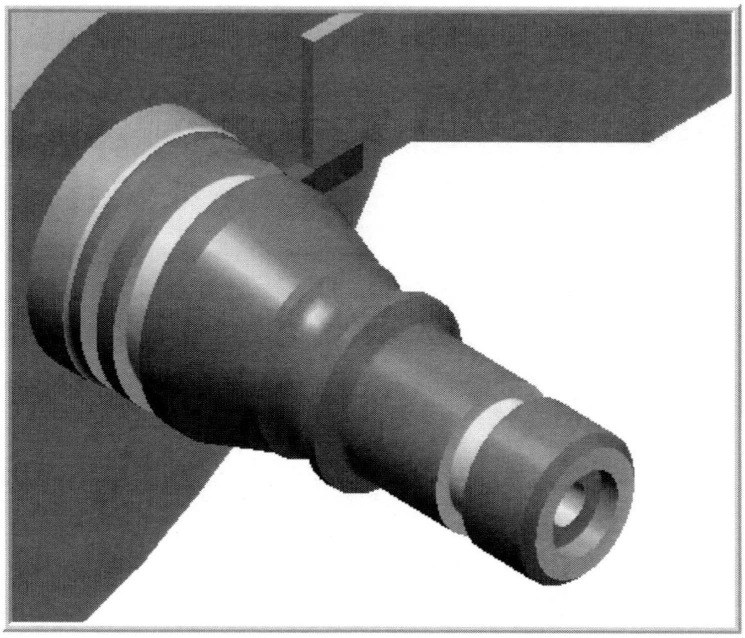

LESSON - 7 - THE PROCESS

Geometry Creation

TASK 1:	Setting the environment
TASK 2:	Setting the construction planes
TASK 3:	Create the geometry – Part 1
TASK 4:	Create the geometry – Part 2
TASK 5:	Create the 40 degree line and 0.050 fillets
TASK 6:	Create the chamfer on right side of part
TASK 7:	Create the 0.300" Radius
TASK 8:	Trim the Geometry
TASK 9:	Create the geometry for the bore
TASK 10:	Trim the geometry for the bore
TASK 11:	Save the drawing

Toolpath Creation

TASK 12:	Define the stock and chuck parameters
TASK 13:	Face the front of the part
TASK 14:	Rough the outside diameters
TASK 15:	Finish the outside diameters
TASK 16:	Finish the 0.3 radius
TASK 17:	Center drill hole
TASK 18:	Tap Drill 13/64" diameter
TASK 19:	Tap the ¼-20 UNC Hole
TASK 20:	Rough the bore
TASK 21:	Finish the bore
TASK 22:	Cut the Grooves
TASK 23:	Cut off the part
TASK 24:	Verify the toolpath
TASK 25:	Save the updated Mastercam file
TASK 26:	Post and create the CNC code file

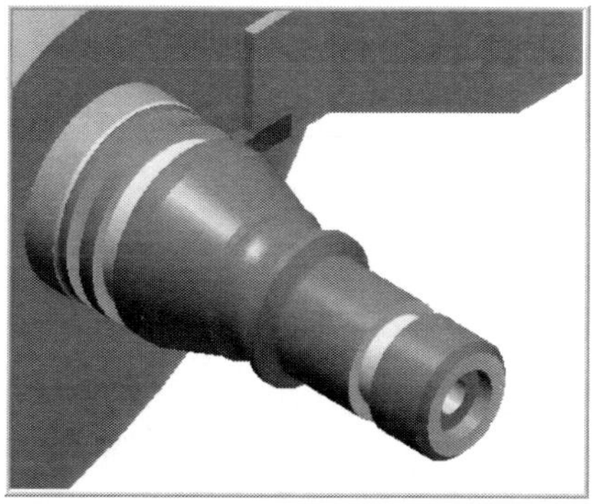

Geometry Creation

TASK 1:
SETTING THE ENVIRONMENT

Before starting the geometry creation you should set up the grid and machine type as outlined in the **Setting the Environment** section at the beginning of this text:

1. Set up the Grid. This will help identify the location of the origin.
2. Set the machine type to the default Lathe.

TASK 2:
SETTING THE CONSTRUCTION PLANES:

➲ **Set the Construction Plane to Lathe diameter +D +Z (WCS)**

1. Select the **View tab** and click on **Toolpaths** and **Solids** in the Managers section to hide them and toggle **only** the **Planes Manager** to display.

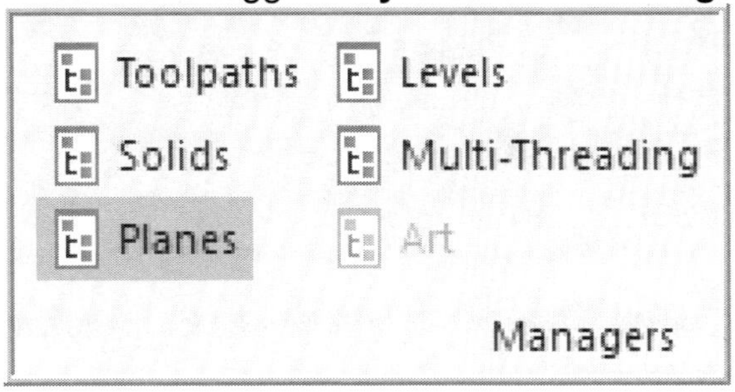

Once your machine is set up, Mastercam includes special lathe construction planes that let you work in **radius or diameter coordinates**.

For conventional 2D turning applications, use the Planes Manager to select the desired coordinate system, as shown below right. Choose to use either radius or diameter coordinates and then choose the desired X/D and Z directions.

2. Ensure the **C column** (Construction Plane) and **T column** (Tool Plane) are set to the **+D +Z Plane**. Just click in the C and T columns in the **+D +Z** row.

➲ Take note of the **Status bar** at the bottom of the screen **CPLANE: +D +Z TPLANE: +D +Z WCS:TOP** as shown below right.

3. To change the **Lathe Plane** open up the drop down menu for **Select lathe plane** and click on the required coordinate system as shown below right.
4. Select the **Close** button in the top right hand corner to close the Planes Manager.

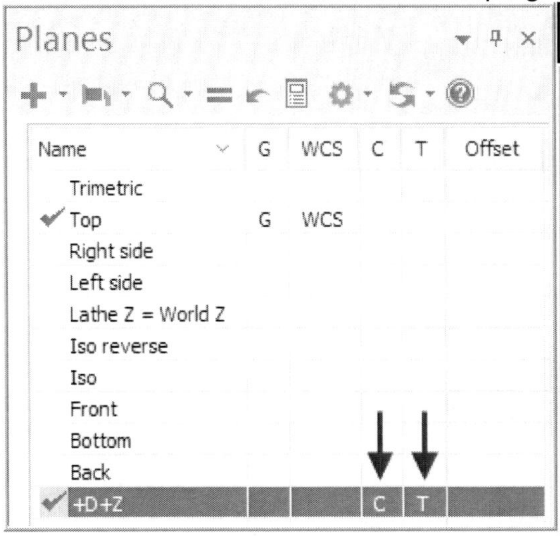

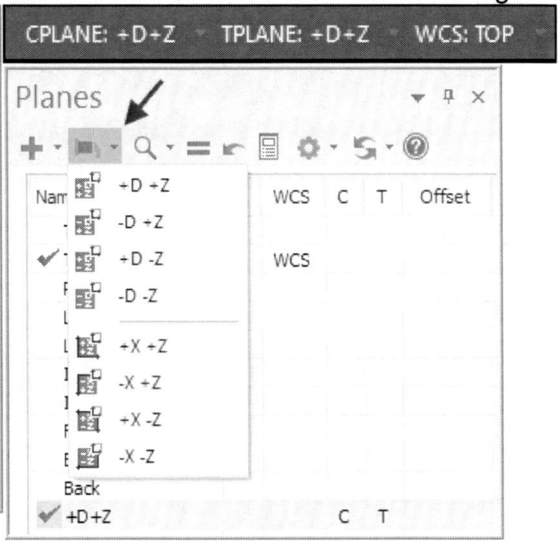

TASK 3:
CREATE THE GEOMETRY – PART 1

- This task explains how to create the geometry of this part. In this lathe part you only need to create half of the geometry, the geometry above the center line.
- Lines 1 through 8 will be created in this task.

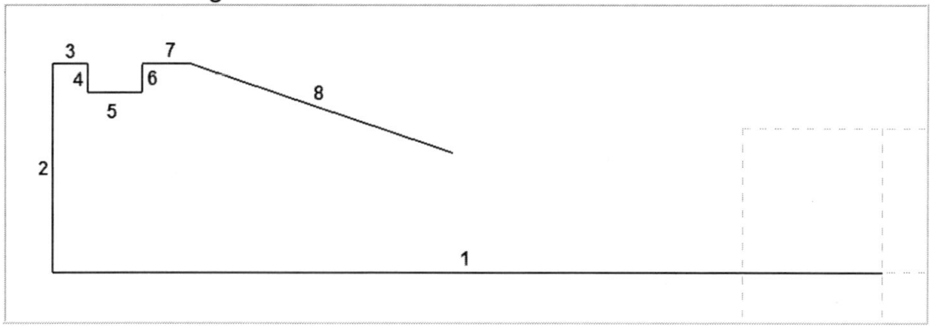

- **Create Line #1**

1. Select the **WIREFRAME** tab at the top of the screen and in the **Lines** section click on **Line Endpoints**.
2. On the graphics screen you are prompted: **Specify the first endpoint** and the Line Endpoints panel appears. In the Line Endpoints panel **activate Multi-line and Freeform**.

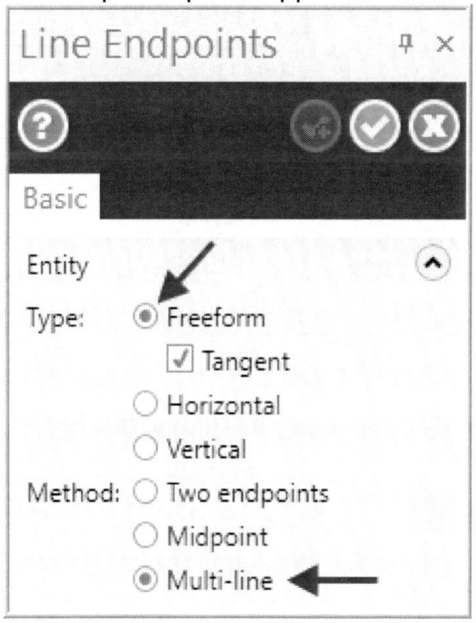

3. Move the cursor over the **center of the grid** and as you get close to the origin a visual cue appears. This is the cue that will allow you to snap to the **origin**. With this visual cue highlighted pick the **origin**.
4. You are now prompted to **"Specify the second endpoint"**. To satisfy this prompt **just type** the coordinate, **type 0,-3.0**. This is **D0 Z-3.0**. As you begin to type the **Fastpoint** opens. Hit the **Enter** key when done.

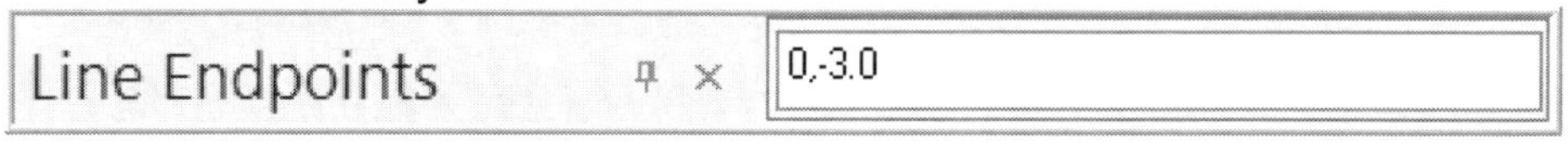

➲ **Create Line #2**

5. Type **1.45,-3.0** to satisfy the prompt **"Specify the second endpoint"** and hit the Enter key.

6. Right mouse click in the graphics area and click on the **Fit** icon .

➲ **Create Line #3**

7. Type **1.45,-3.0+0.125** to satisfy the prompt **"Specify the second endpoint"** and hit the Enter key.

➲ **Create Line #4**

8. Type **1.45-0.2,-3.0+0.125** to satisfy the prompt **"Specify the second endpoint"** and hit the Enter key.

➲ **Create Line #5**

9. Type **1.45-0.2,-3.0+0.125+0.2** to satisfy the prompt **"Specify the second endpoint"** and hit the Enter key.

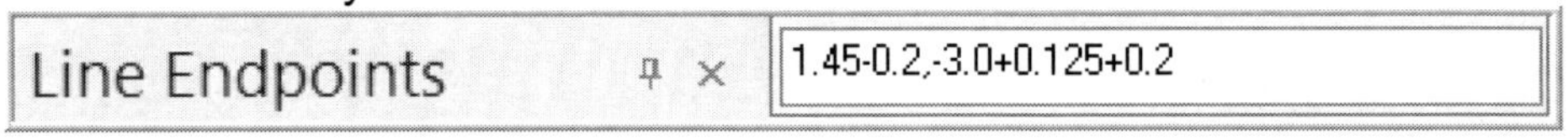

➲ **Create Line #6**

10. Type **1.45,-3.0+0.125+0.2** to satisfy the prompt **"Specify the second endpoint"** and hit the Enter key.

➲ **Create Line #7**

11. Type **1.45,-3.0+0.5** to satisfy the prompt **"Specify the second endpoint"** and hit the Enter key.

➲ **Create Line #8**

12. Now click in the space for **Length** and enter a value of **1.0** and hit the **Enter** key.
13. Now click in the space for **Angle** enter a value of **-18.0** and hit the **Enter** key.

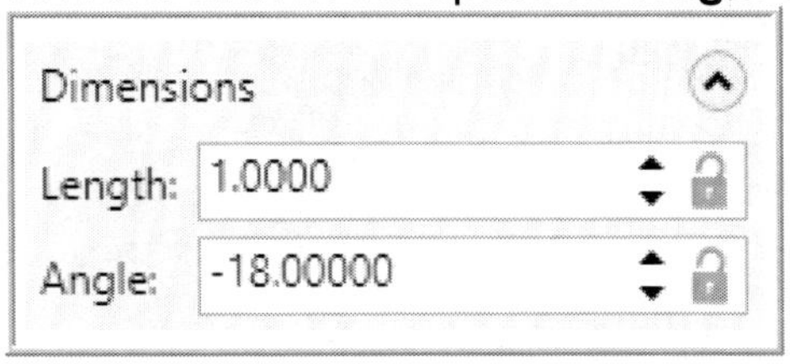

14. Click on the **OK** icon to complete this feature.

TASK 4:
CREATE THE GEOMETRY – PART 2

➲ This task explains how to create the geometry of this part.
➲ Lines 9 through 15 will be created using **Line Parallel**.

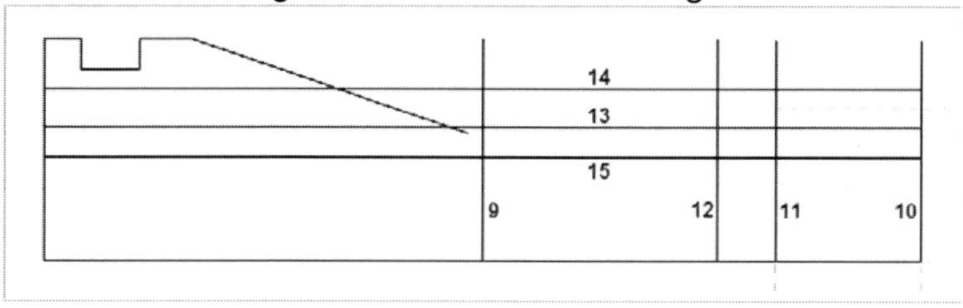

1. Right mouse click in the graphics area and click on the **Fit** icon .
2. Your geometry should look like the figure below:

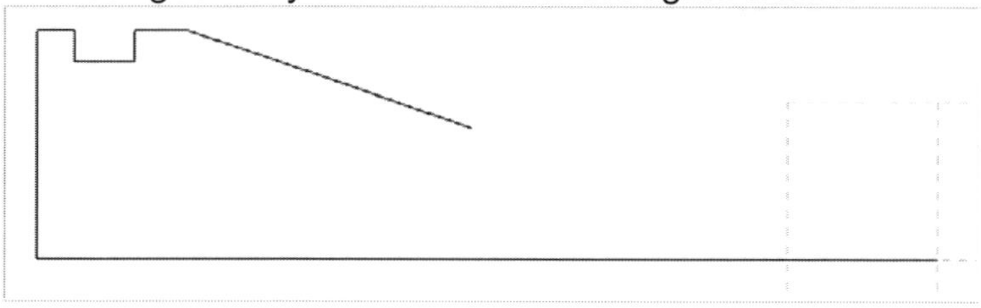

➲ **Create Line #9**

3. On the **WIREFRAME** tab and in the **Lines** section click on **Line Parallel**.

➲ You are prompted "Select a line" and the Line Parallel panel appears.

4. First click in the space for **Offset Distance** and input **1.5** then hit **Enter**.
5. To satisfy the prompt **Select a line**, select the line shown below:

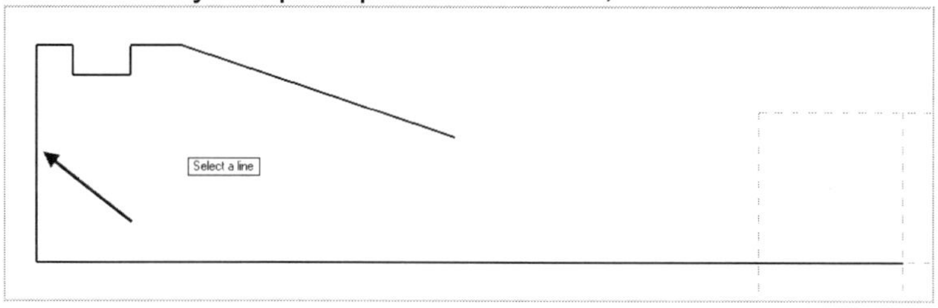

6. To satisfy the next prompt **Indicate the offset direction** move the cursor to the right of the line and pick a point.
7. Click on the **OK and Create New Operation** icon .

➲ **Create Line #10**

8. Click in the space for **Offset Distance** and input **3.0** then hit **Enter**.
9. To satisfy the prompt **Select a line**, select the line shown below:

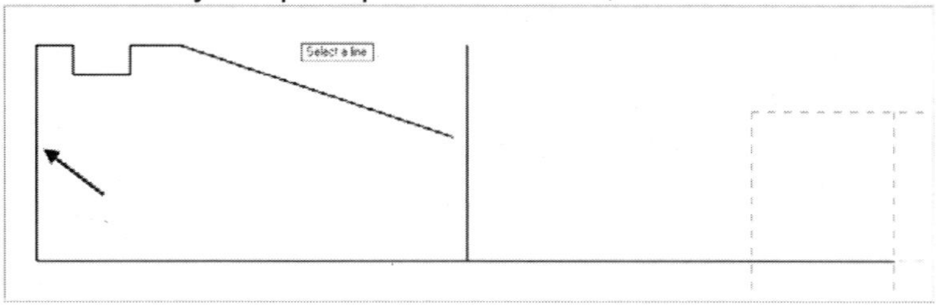

10. To satisfy the next prompt **Indicate the offset direction** move the cursor to the right of the line and pick a point.
11. Click on the **OK and Create New Operation** icon .

➲ **Create Line #11**

12. Click in the space for **Offset Distance** and input **0.500** then hit **Enter**.
13. To satisfy the prompt **Select a line**, select the line shown below:

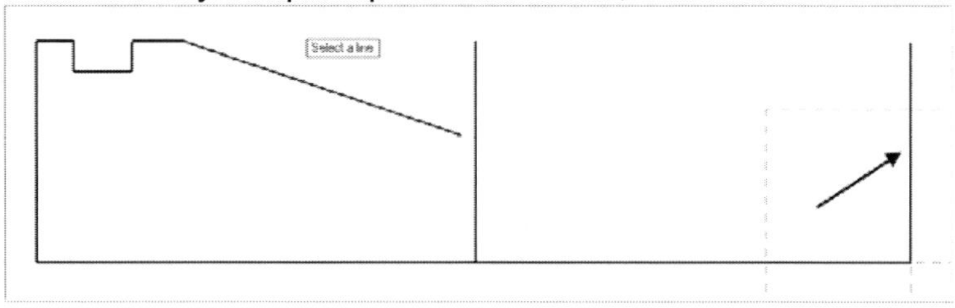

14. To satisfy the next prompt **Indicate the offset direction** move the cursor to the left of the line and pick a point.
15. Click on the **OK and Create New Operation** icon .

➲ **Create Line #12**

16. Click in the space for **Offset Distance** and input **0.200** then hit **Enter**.
17. To satisfy the prompt **Select a line**, select the line shown below:

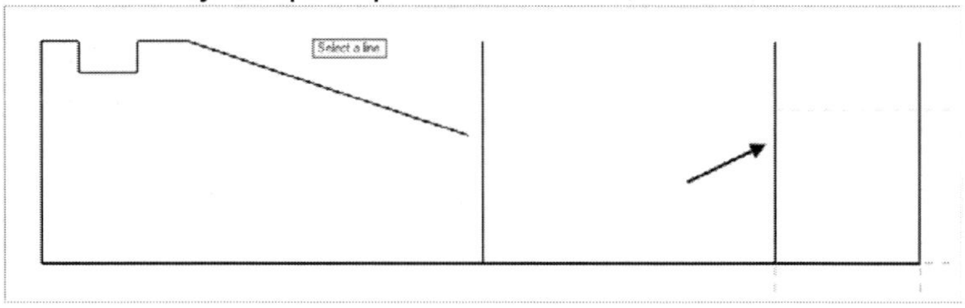

18. To satisfy the next prompt **Indicate the offset direction** move the cursor to the left of the line and pick a point.
19. Click on the **OK and Create New Operation** icon .

➲ **Create Line #13**

20. Click in the space for **Offset Distance** and input **0.875/2** then hit **Enter**.
21. To satisfy the prompt **Select a line**, select the line shown below:

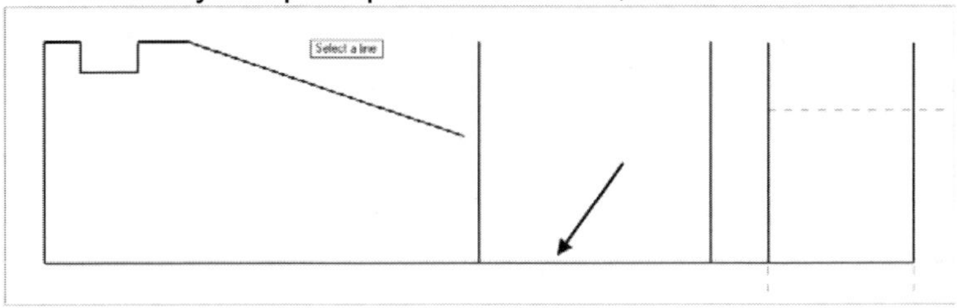

22. To satisfy the next prompt **Indicate the offset direction** move the cursor above the line and pick a point.
23. Click on the **OK and Create New Operation** icon .

➲ **Create Line #14**

24. Click in the space for **Offset Distance** and input **1.125/2** then hit **Enter**.
25. To satisfy the prompt **Select a line**, select the line shown below:

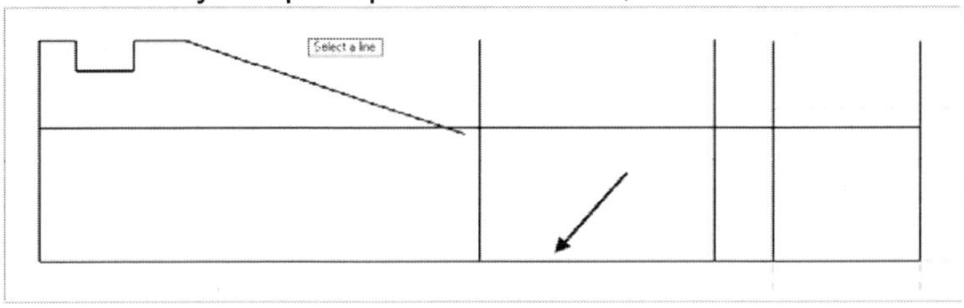

26. To satisfy the next prompt **Indicate the offset direction** move the cursor above the line and pick a point.
27. Click on the **OK and Create New Operation** icon .

➲ **Create Line #15**

28. Click in the space for **Offset Distance** and input **0.1** then hit **Enter**.
29. To satisfy the prompt **Select a line**, select the line shown below:

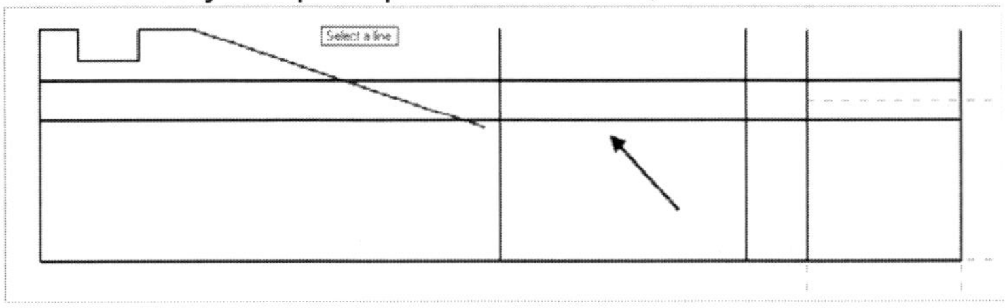

30. To satisfy the next prompt **Indicate the offset direction** move the cursor below the line and pick a point.
31. Click on the **OK** icon to complete this feature.

➲ The completed geometry is shown below:

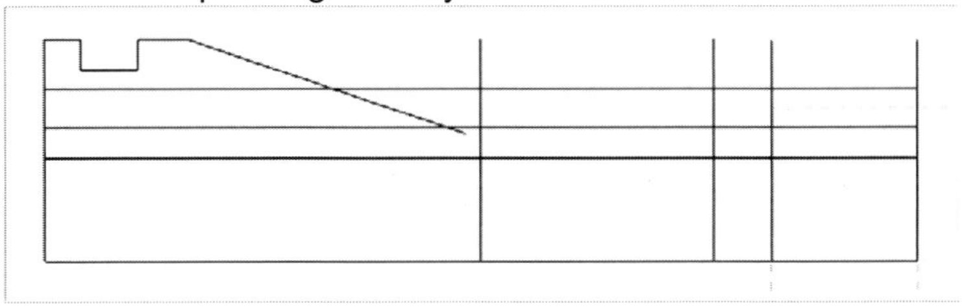

TASK 5:
CREATE THE 40 DEGREE LINE AND 0.050 FILLETS

1. On the **WIREFRAME** tab in the **Lines** section click on **Line Endpoints**.
2. You are prompted **Specify the first endpoint** and the Line Endpoints panel appears. Now click in the space for **Length** and enter a value of **0.25** and hit the tab key to move over to the Angle value.
3. For **Angle** enter a value of **-50.0 (90-40 degrees)** and hit the **Enter** key.

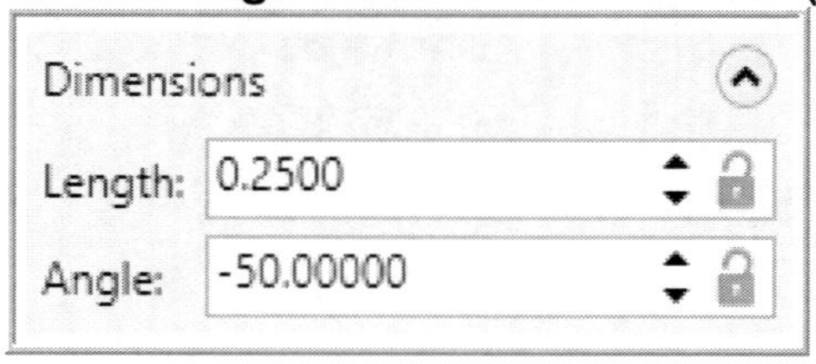

4. To satisfy the prompt to **Specify the first endpoint.** Move the cursor over the intersection of the two lines shown below and when the visual cue for intersection  appears pick this point.

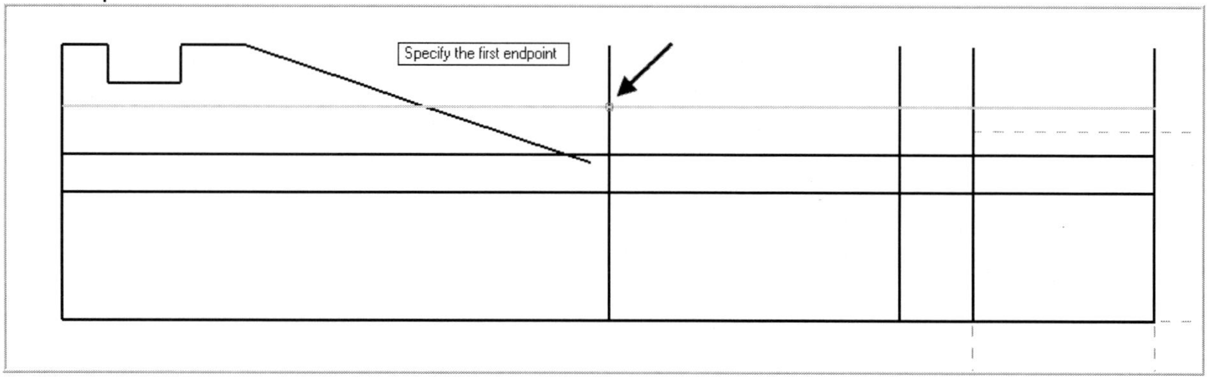

5. Click on the **OK** icon  to complete this feature.

➲ Your geometry should look like the figure below:

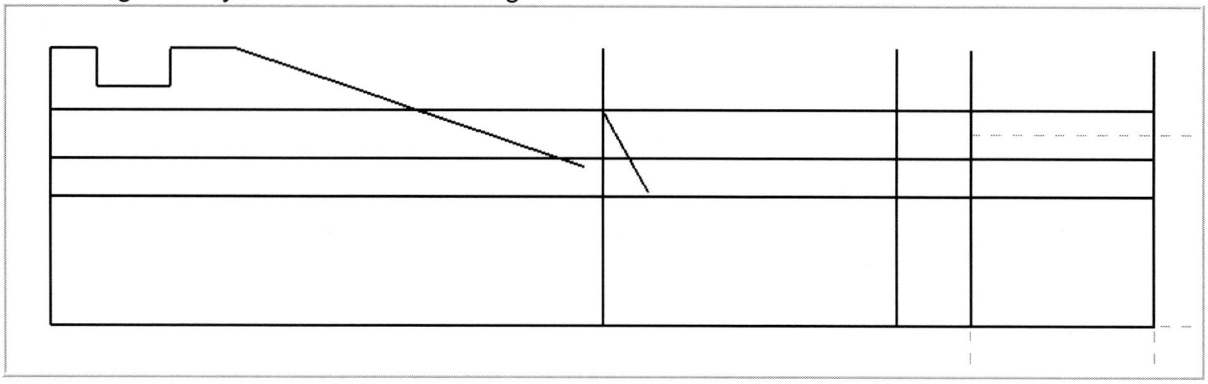

➲ **Create 0.050 fillet**

6. On the **WIREFRAME** tab and in the **Modify** section click on **Fillet Entities**.

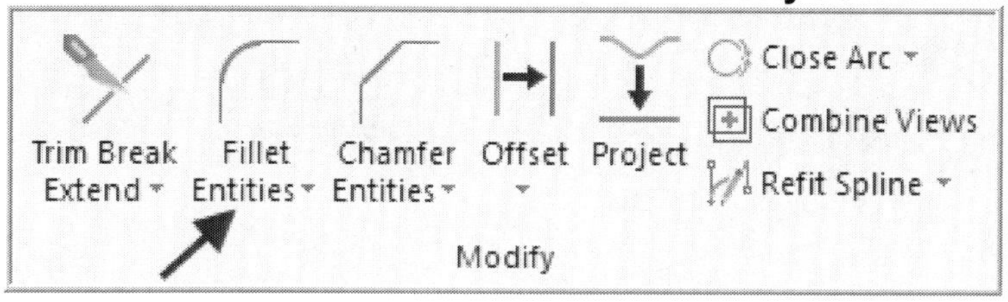

7. The **Fillet Entities** panel appears. Activate the **Style** to **Normal** and enter a value of **0.050** for for **Radius**.
8. Ensure the **Trim** entities box at the bottom of the panel is check marked to turn the trim on.
9. When prompted to **Fillet: Select an entity,** select Line 1 and 2 as shown below:
10. When prompted to **Fillet: Select an entity,** select Line 3 and 4 as shown below:

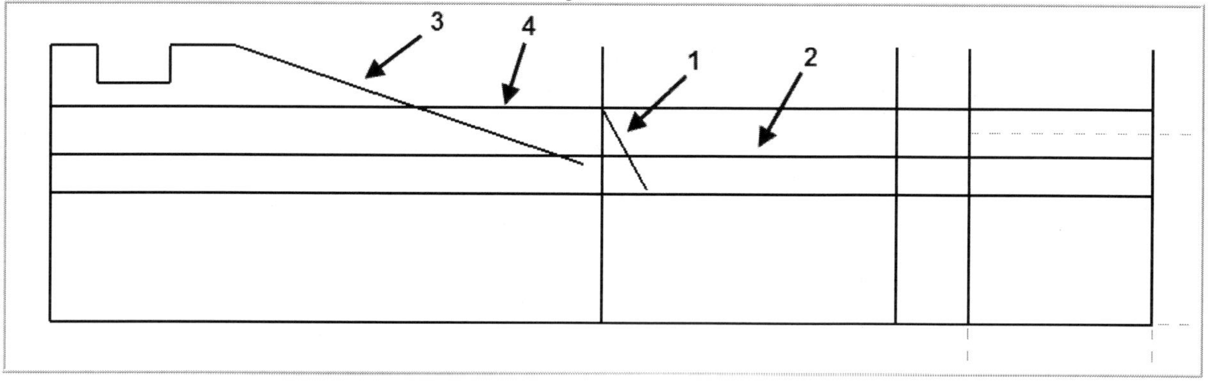

11. Click on the **OK** icon  to complete this feature.

➲ The completed geometry is shown below:

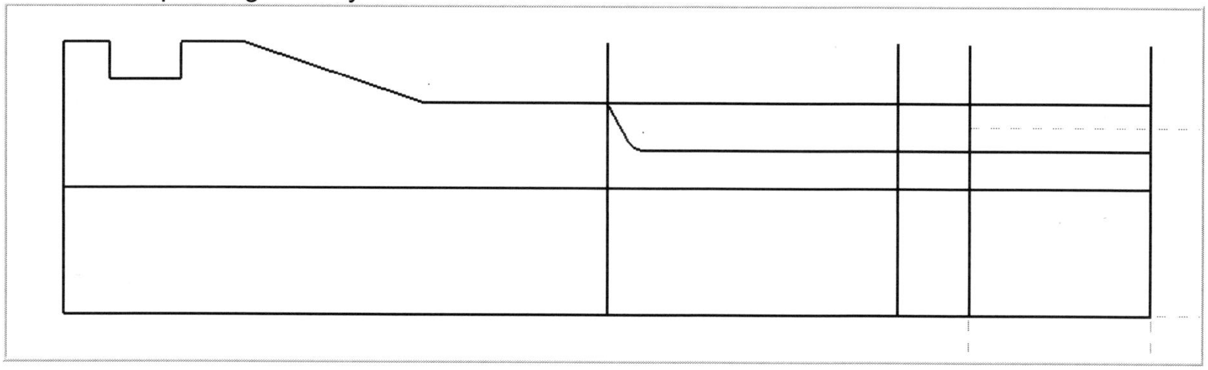

TASK 6:
CREATE THE CHAMFER ON RIGHT SIDE OF PART

➲ Create the chamfer 45 degrees x .0625.

1. On the **WIREFRAME** tab and in the **Modify** section click on **Chamfer Entities**.

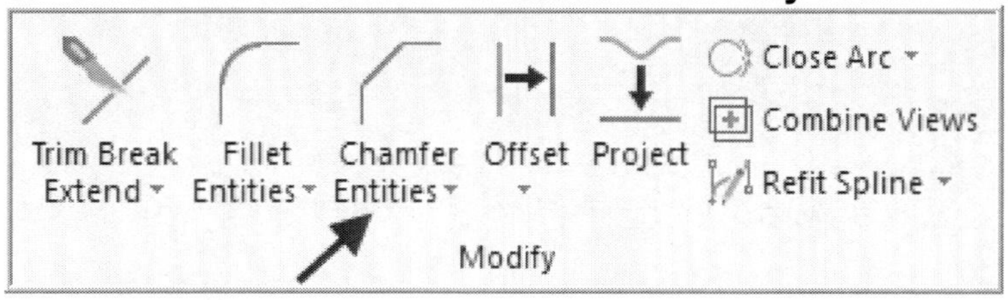

2. The **Chamfer Entities** panel appears. Activate the **Style** to **1 Distance** and enter a value of **0.0625** for **Distance 1**.
3. Ensure the **Trim** entities box at the bottom of the panel is check marked to turn the trim on.
4. Click on line 1 and then line 2 as shown below on the right side of the part.

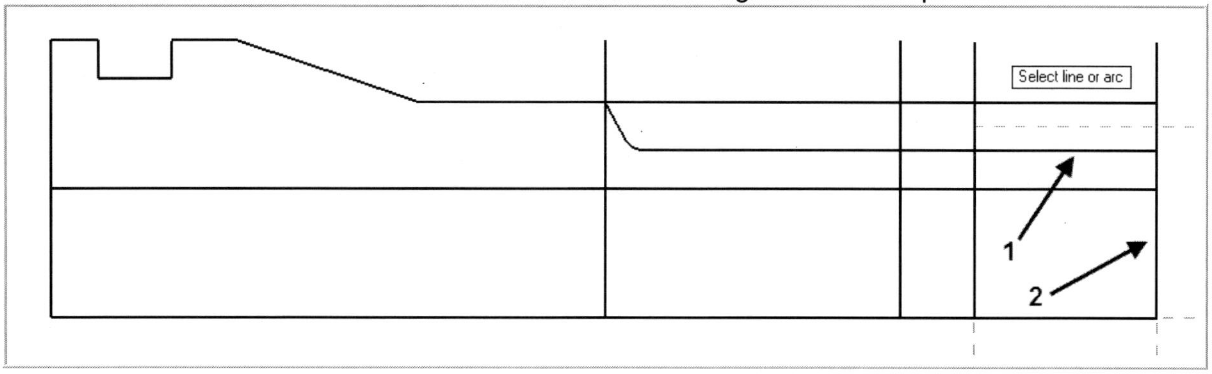

5. Click on the **OK** icon  to complete this feature.

➲ The completed geometry should look like the image below:

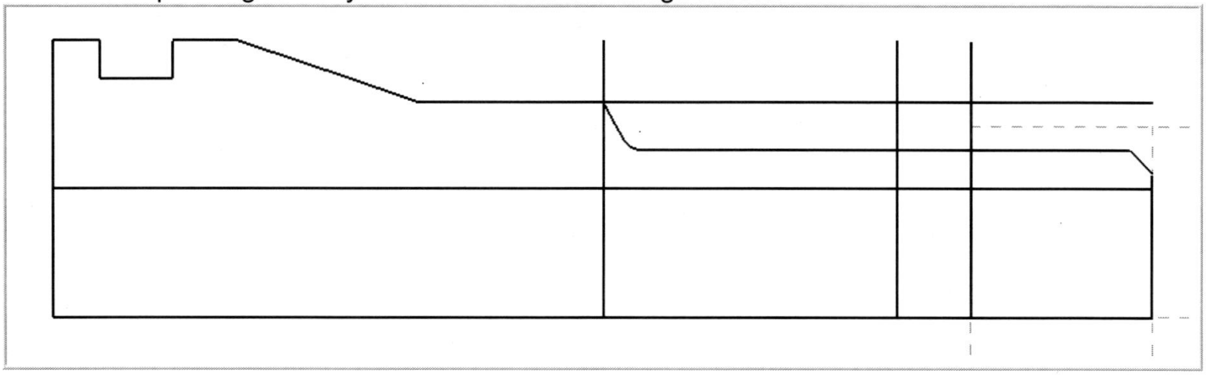

TASK 7:
CREATE THE 0.300" RADIUS

➲ In this task you will create the 0.300 arc. The center position and radius are known.

1. On the **WIREFRAME** tab and in the **Arcs** section open up the drop down menu and select **Arc Polar**.

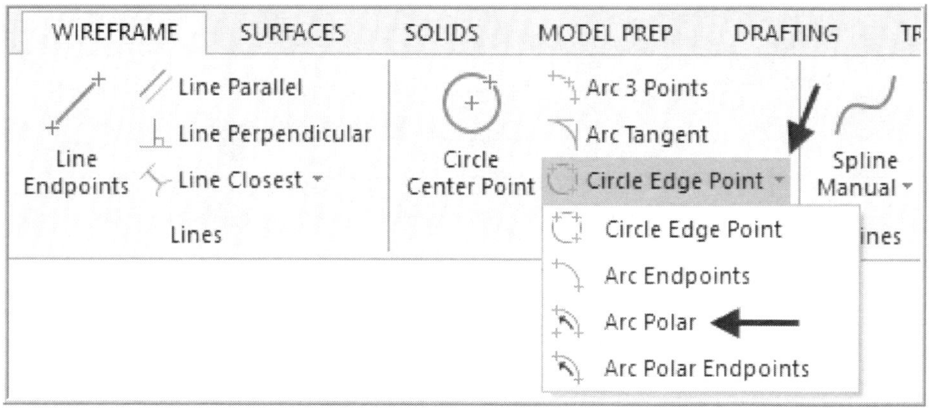

2. The **Arc Polar** panel appears and you are prompted to **Enter the center point**. If required activate the **Mode** to **Manual.**
3. In the **Arc Polar** panel enter a value of **0.3** for **Radius**.
4. Set the **Start angle to 180** and the **End angle to 0** and hit the **Enter** key on your keyboard.
5. Type **1.6,-1.75** to satisfy the prompt "**Enter the center point"** and hit the Enter key.

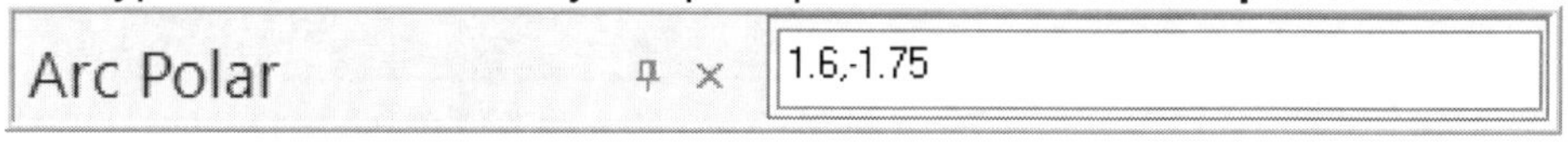

6. Activate **Inverted Arc** found at the bottom of the Arc Polar panel to position the arc in the correct position as shown below.

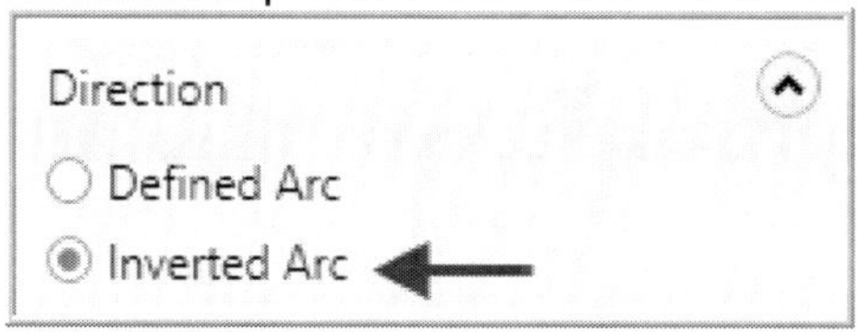

7. Click on the **OK** icon  to complete this feature.

➲ The completed arc is shown below:

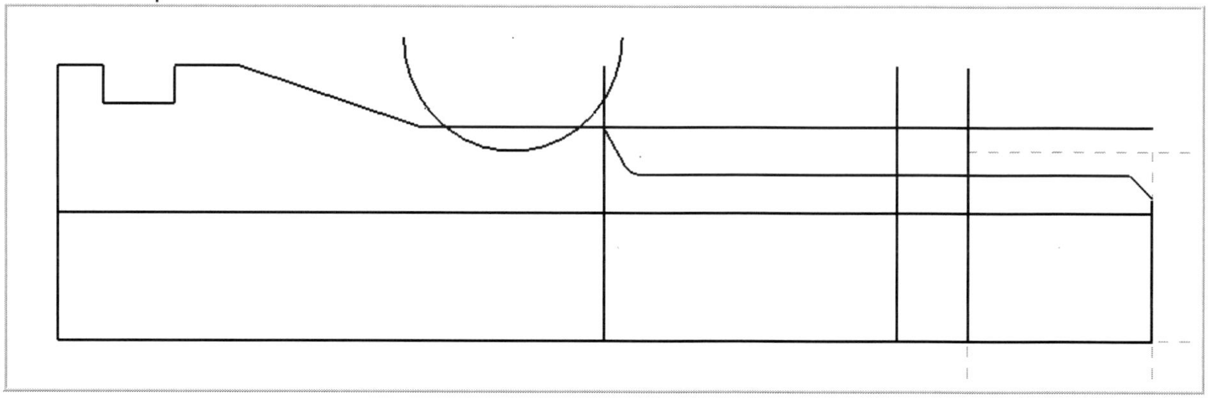

TASK 8:
TRIM THE GEOMETRY

➲ In this task you will use **Divide/delete** to trim the entities.

1. **Delete** the line shown below: Select the line and hit the **Delete** key on your keyboard.

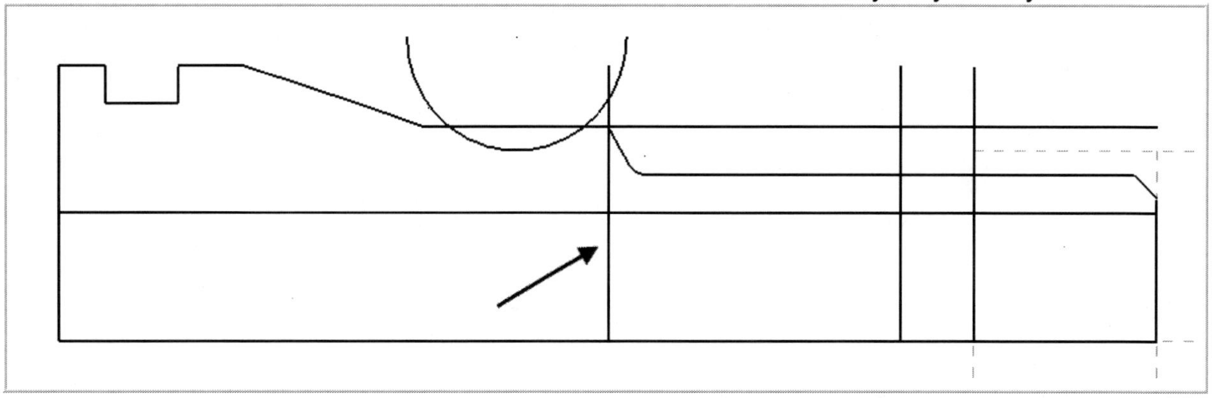

2. In the **WIREFRAME** tab click on **Trim/Break/Extend** in the **Modify** section.
3. The Trim Break Extend panel appears. Activate **Divide/delete**.
4. The prompt changes to **Select the curve to divide/delete.** Move the cursor over the various entities and select in the order and position shown below:

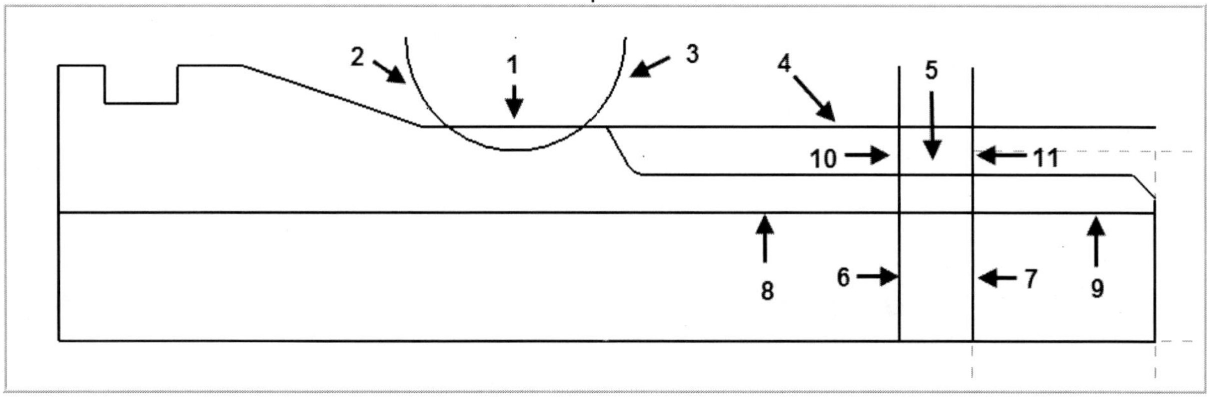

5. Click on the **OK** icon to complete this feature.
6. **Delete** the three lines shown below: Select the three lines and then hit the **Delete** key on your keyboard.

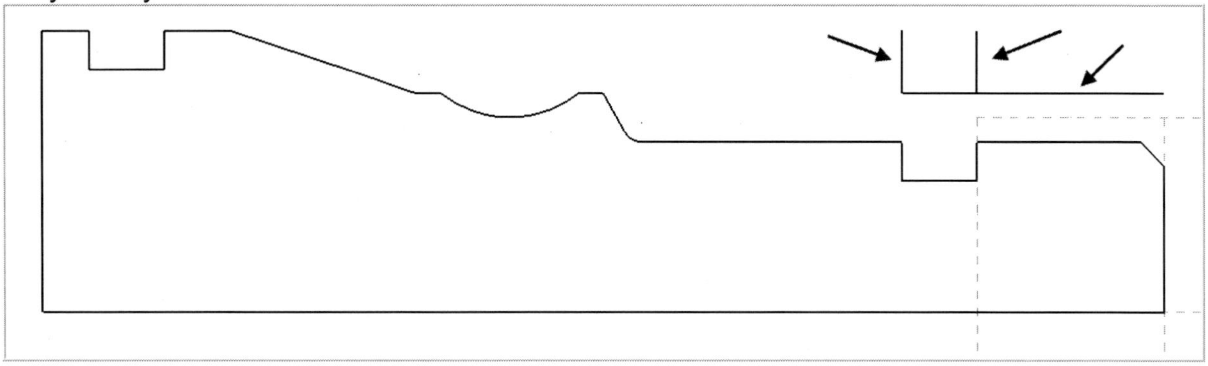

TASK 9:
CREATE THE GEOMETRY FOR THE BORE

➲ In this task you will create the geometry that make up the bore of this part

1. On the **WIREFRAME** tab and in the **Lines** section click on **Line Parallel**.

➲ You are prompted "Select a line" and the Line Parallel panel appears.

2. First click in the space for **Offset Distance** and input **0.125** then hit **Enter**.
3. To satisfy the prompt **Select a line**, select the line shown below:

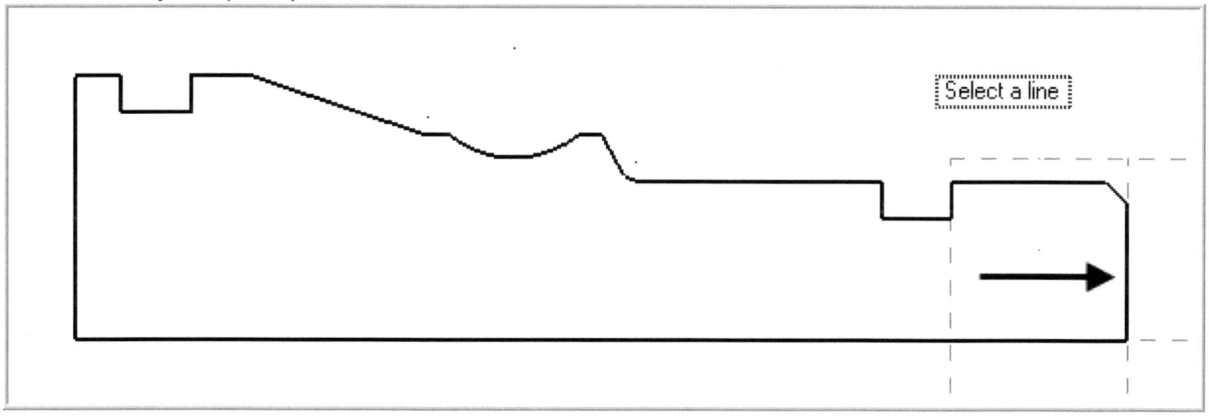

4. To satisfy the next prompt **Indicate the offset direction** move the cursor to the **left** of the line and pick a point.
5. Click on the **OK and Create New Operation** icon.
6. Click in the space for **Offset Distance** and input **0.5/2** then hit **Enter**.
7. To satisfy the prompt **Select a line**, select the line shown below:

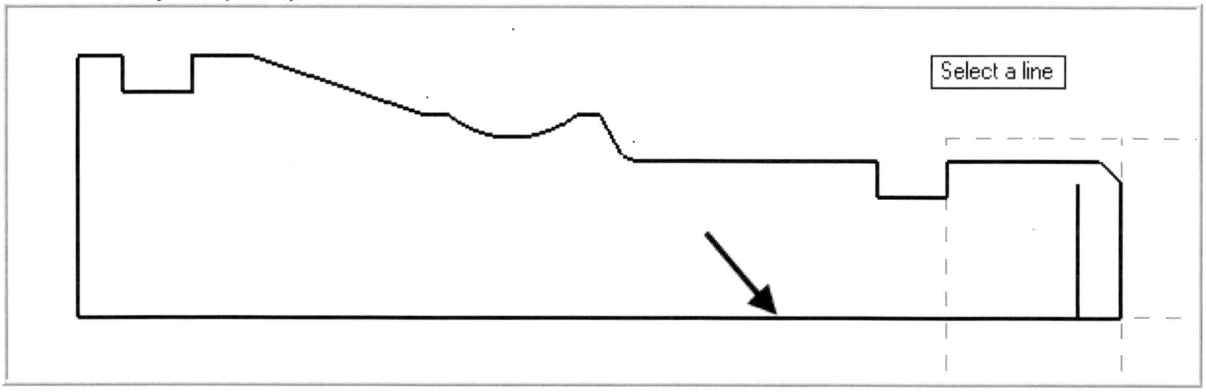

8. To satisfy the next prompt **Indicate the offset direction** move the cursor **above** the line and pick a point.
9. Click on the **OK and Create New Operation** icon.

10. Click in the space for **Offset Distance** and input **0.250/2** then hit **Enter**.
11. To satisfy the prompt **Select a line**, select the line shown below:

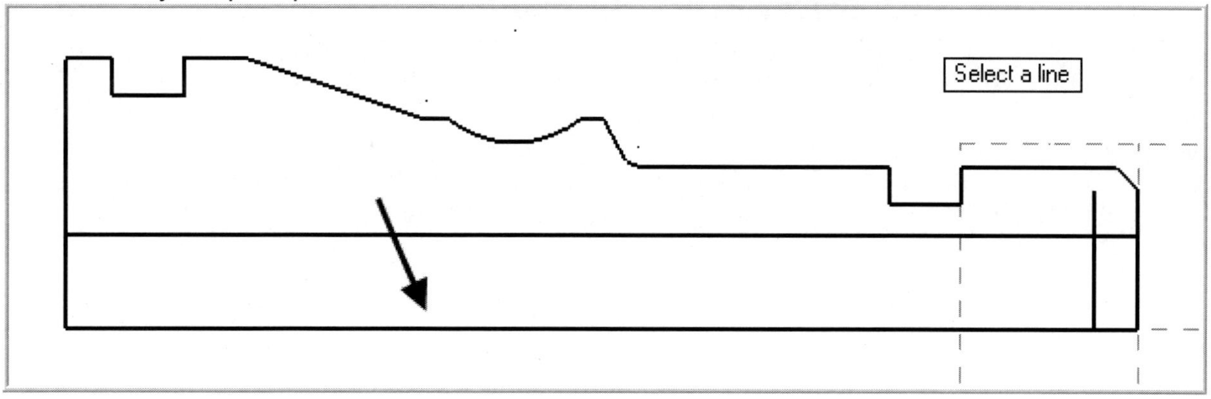

12. To satisfy the next prompt **Indicate the offset direction** move the cursor **above** the line and pick a point.
13. Click on the **OK** icon  to complete this feature.

➲ The completed geometry is shown below:

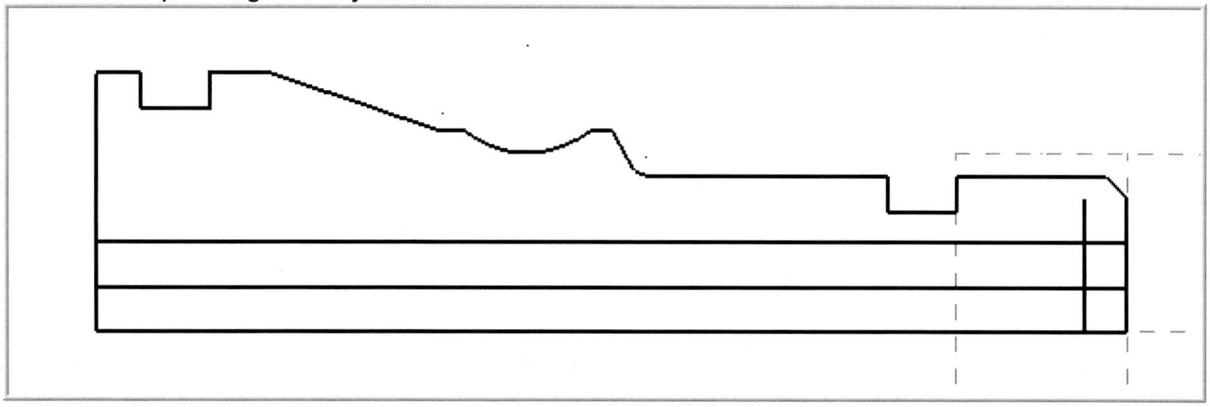

TASK 10:
TRIM THE GEOMETRY FOR THE BORE

1. In the **WIREFRAME** tab click on **Trim/Break/Extend** in the **Modify** section.
2. The Trim Break Extend panel appears. Activate **Divide**.
3. The prompt changes to **Select the curve to divide/delete.** Move the cursor over the various entities and select in the order and position shown below:

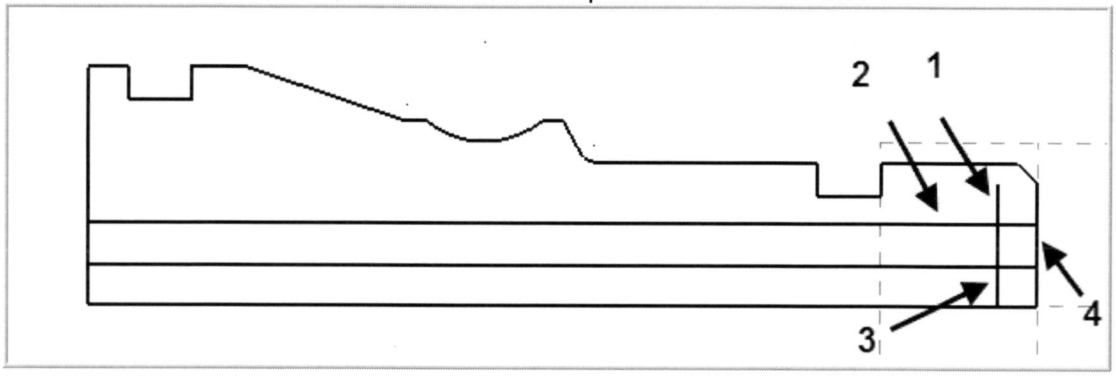

4. Click on the **OK** icon  to complete this feature.
5. **Delete** the three lines shown below: Select the three lines and then hit the **Delete** key.

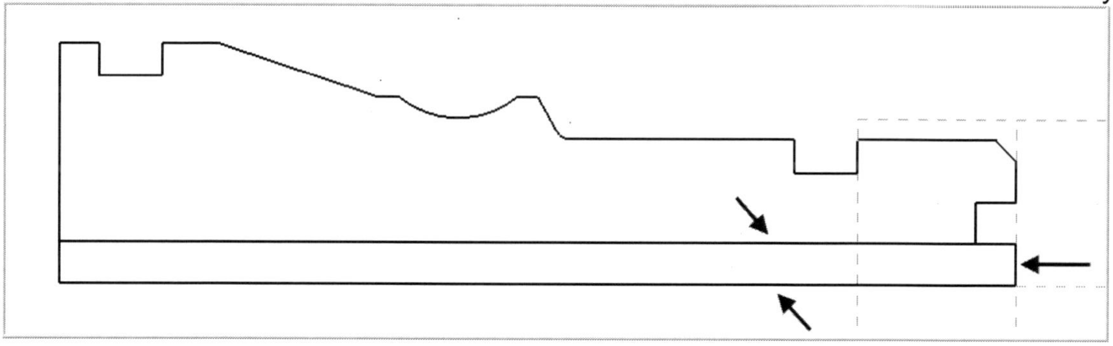

➲ The completed geometry is shown below:

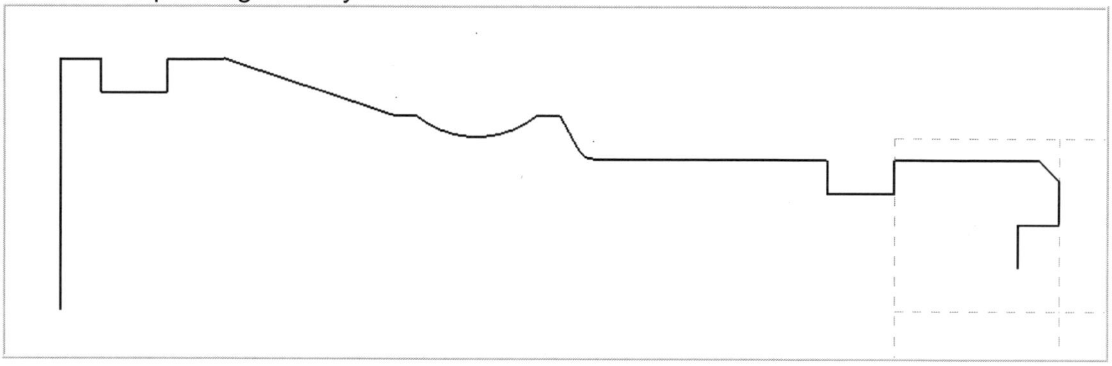

TASK 11:
SAVE THE DRAWING

1. Select **File.**
2. Select **Save As.**
3. Click on the **Browse** icon.
4. In the **"File name"** box, type **"Lathe-Lesson-7".**
5. Browse to an appropriate location.
6. Select the **Save** button to save the file and complete this function.

Toolpath Creation

TASK 12:
DEFINING THE STOCK AND CHUCK PARAMETERS

1. Right mouse click in the graphics area and click on the **Fit** icon .
2. Ensure your screen looks like the image below:
   a. The **Toolpaths Manager** is open.
   b. The properties icon displays Lathe Default. If it is not refer to **Setting the Environment** chapter at the beginning of the book.
   c. The **Lathe Lesson-7** Geometry is displayed.

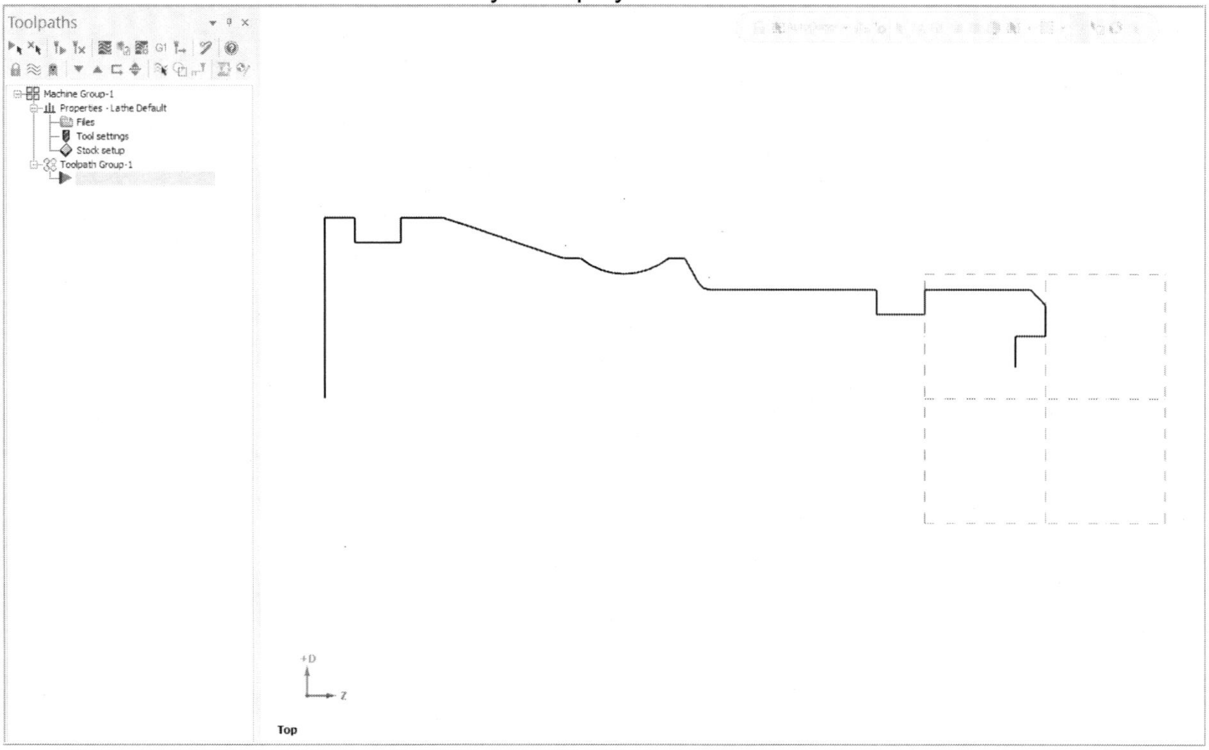

3. Select the plus in front of **Properties** to expand the Machine Group Properties.

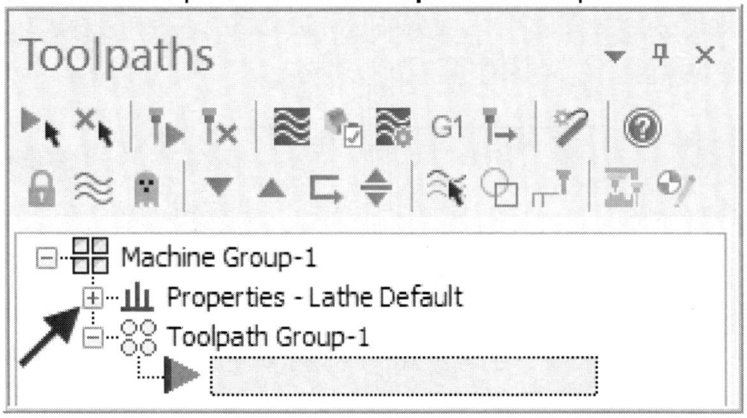

4. Select **Stock setup** in the Toolpaths Manager window.

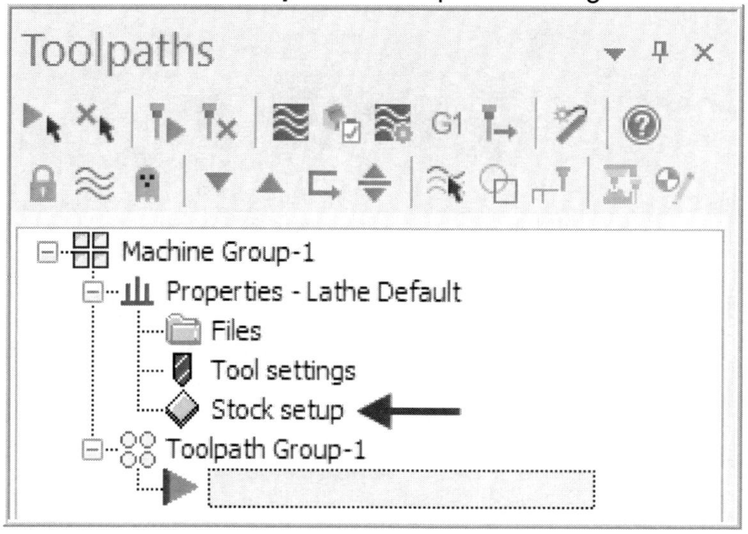

5. Select the **Stock Properties** button in the **Stock Setup** page as shown in the screenshot below:

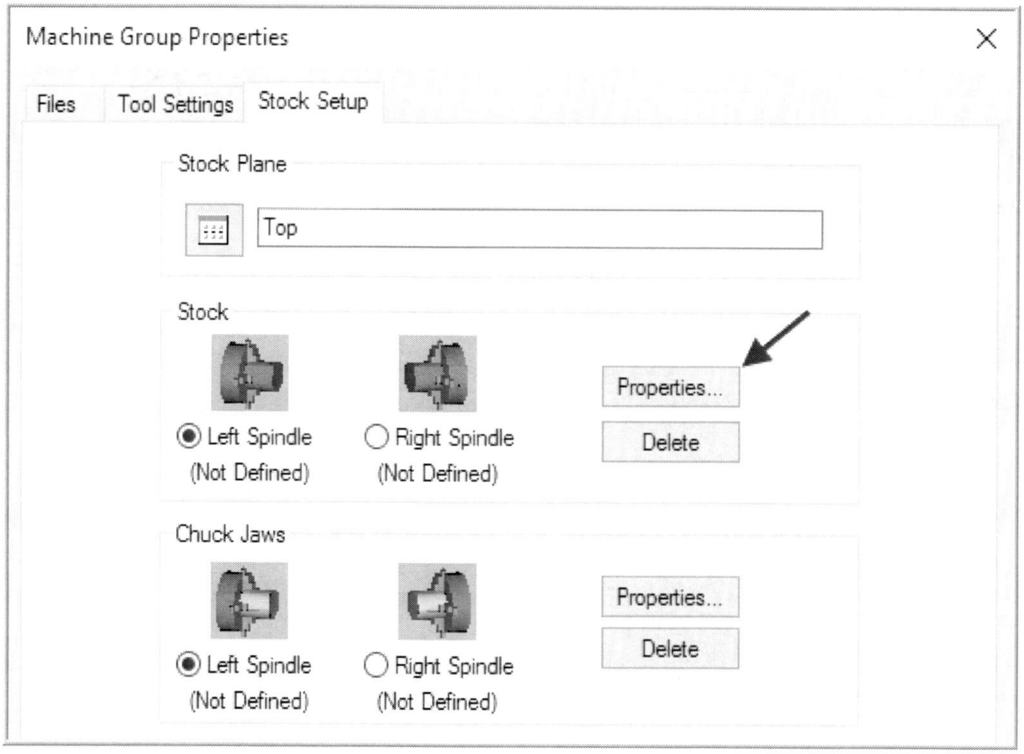

6. In the **Machine Component Manager-Stock** window click on the **Geometry** button and select **Cylinder** as shown below:

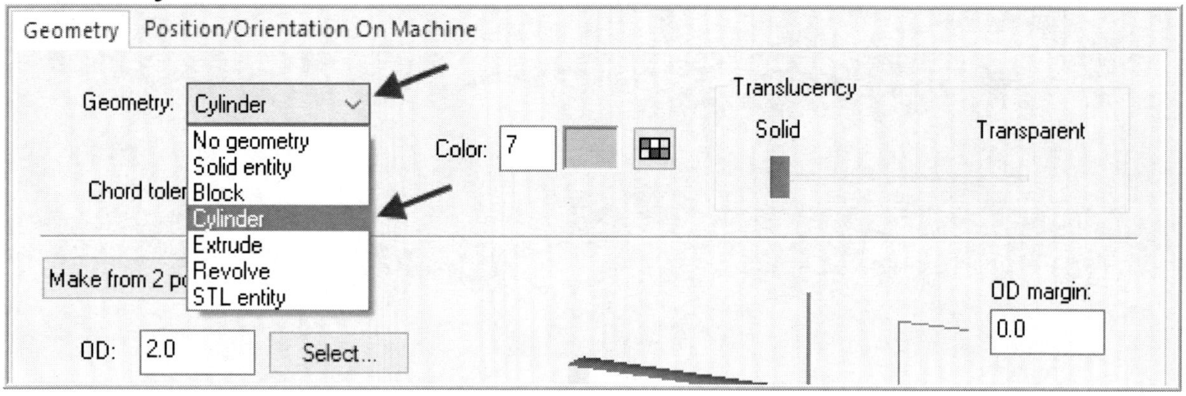

7. In the **Stock setup** set the values as shown below. **Axis is set to -Z**.

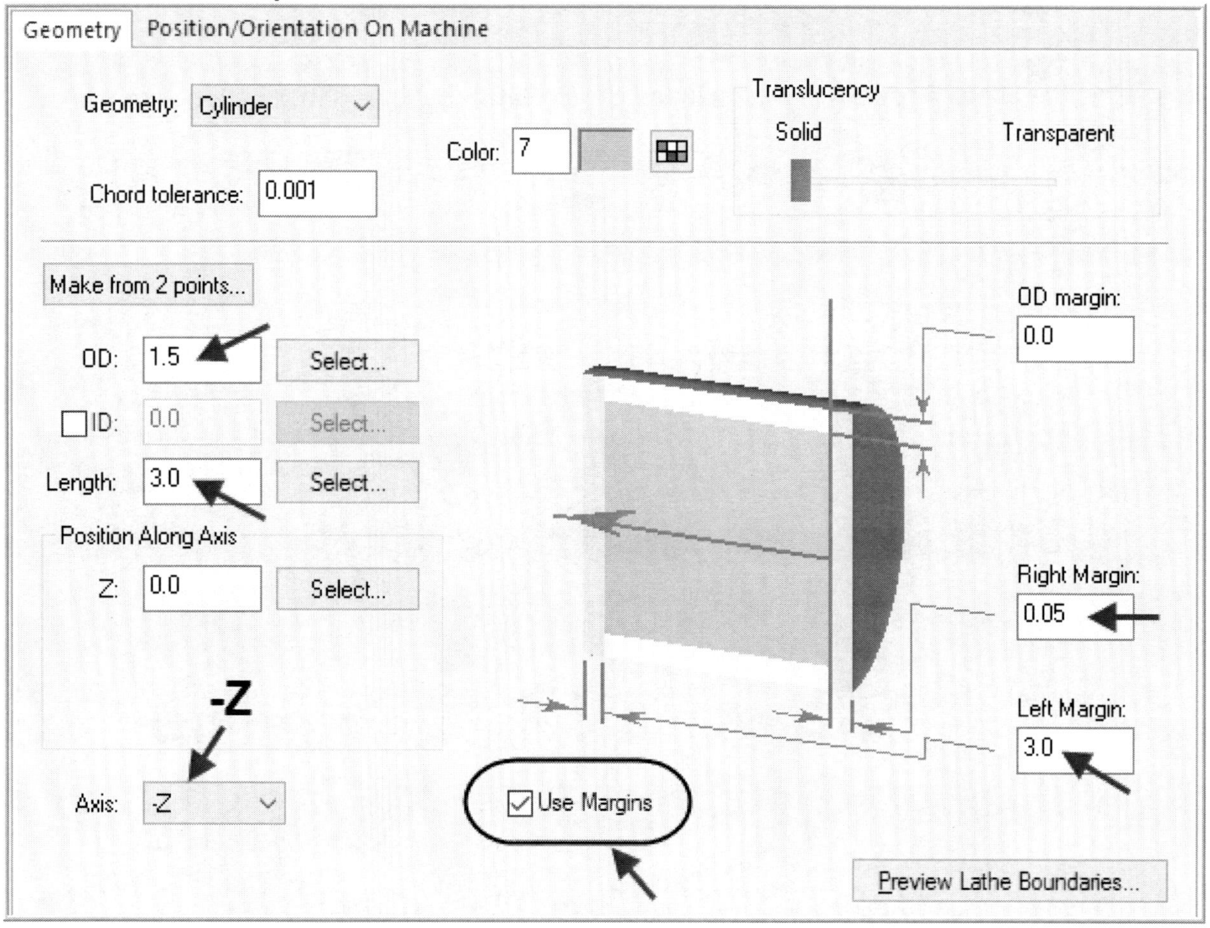

8. Click on the OK icon to complete this feature.

9. Still on the Stock Setup page activate **Fit screen to boundaries**.

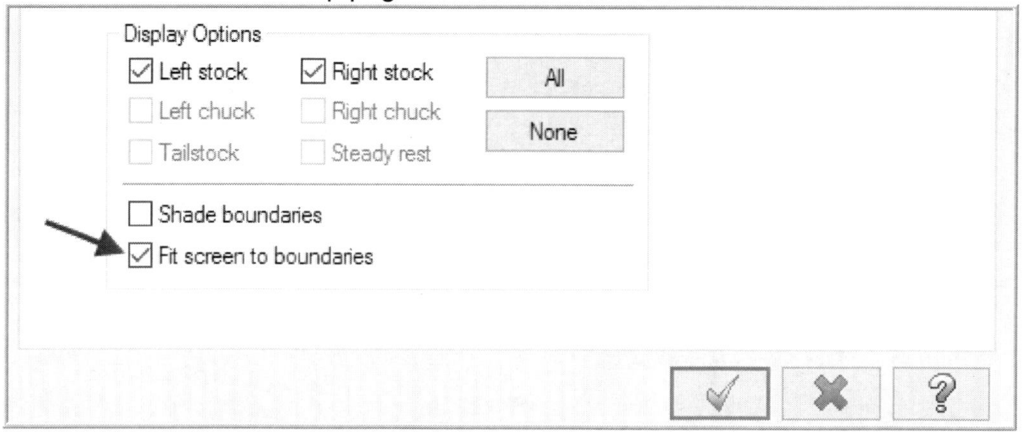

10. Select the **Chuck Properties** button in the **Stock Setup** page as shown in the screenshot below:

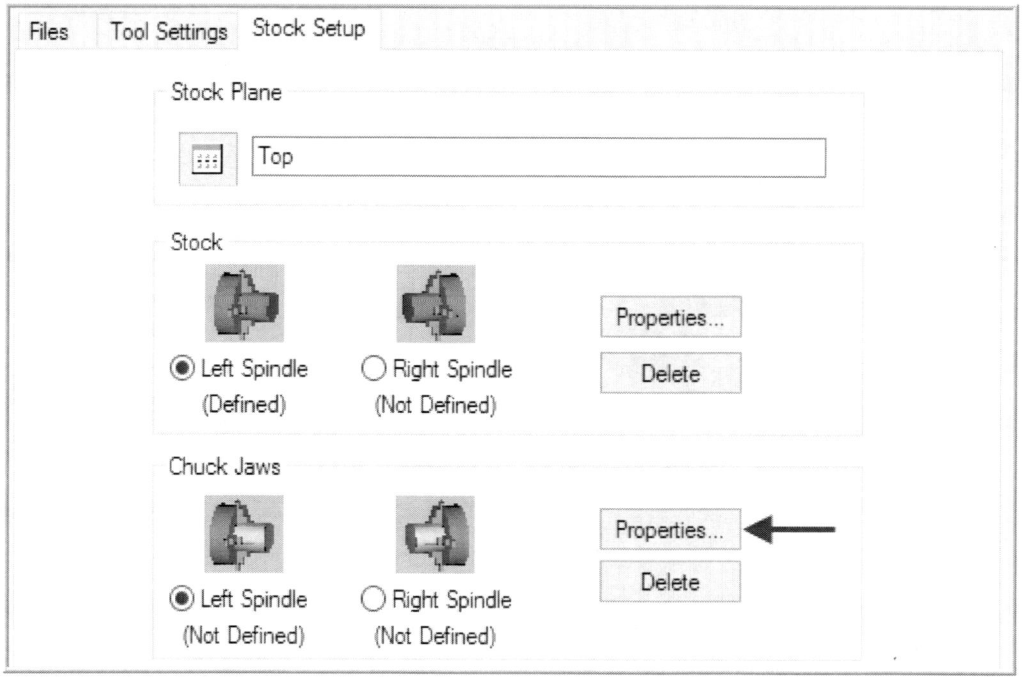

11. In the **Chuck Jaws** setup set the values as shown below:

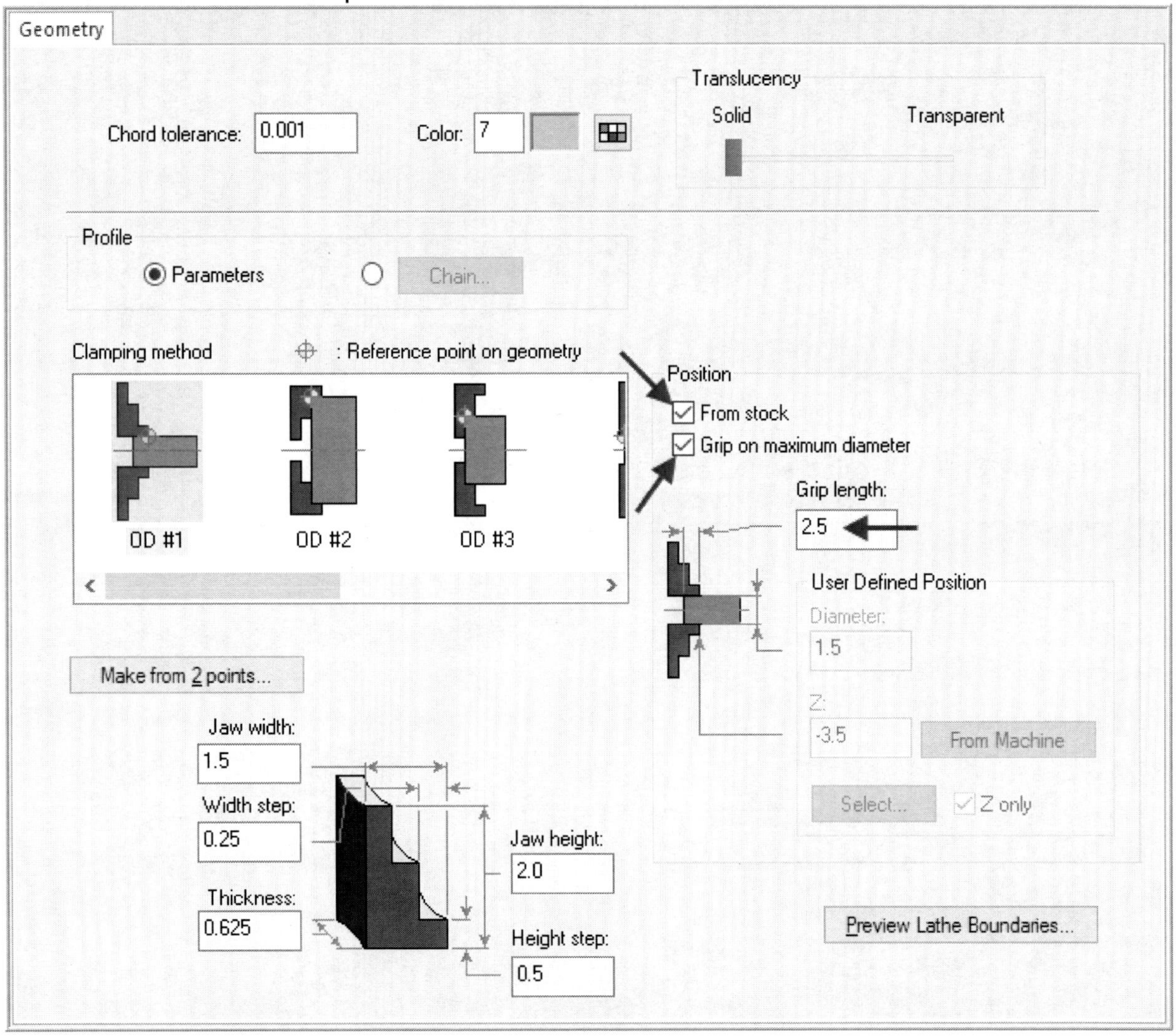

12. Click on the OK icon  to complete this feature.

13. Click on the **Tool Settings** page and make changes as shown below:

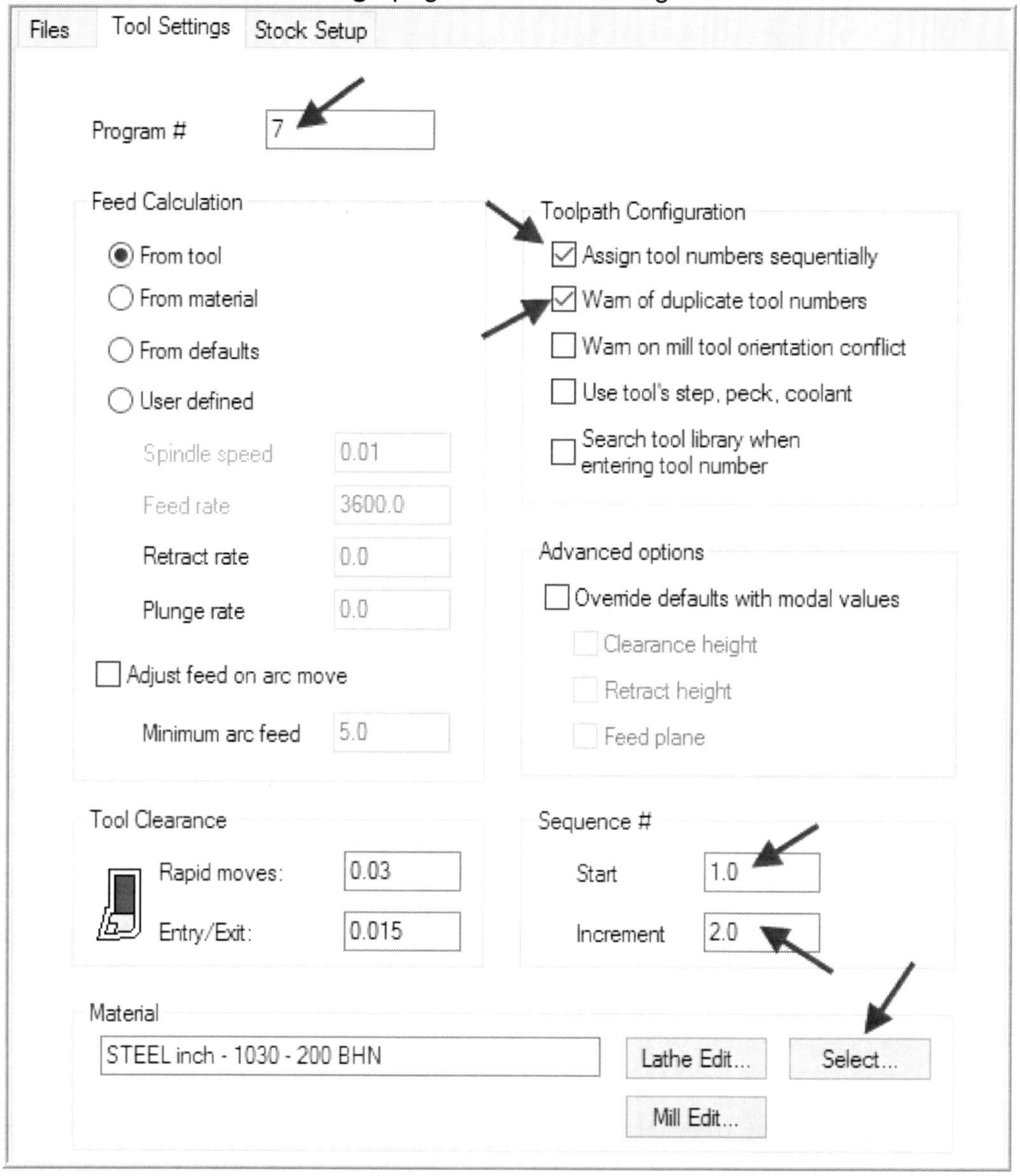

14. To change the **Material** type to Aluminum 6061 pick the **Select** button at the bottom of the Tool Settings page.

15. At the **Material List** dialog box open the Source drop down list and select **Lathe – library.**

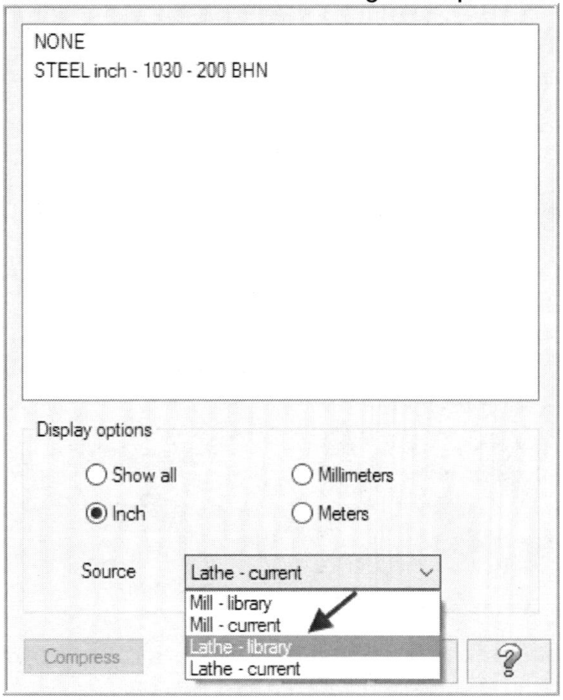

16. From the **Default Materials** list select **ALUMINUM inch - 6061** and then select .

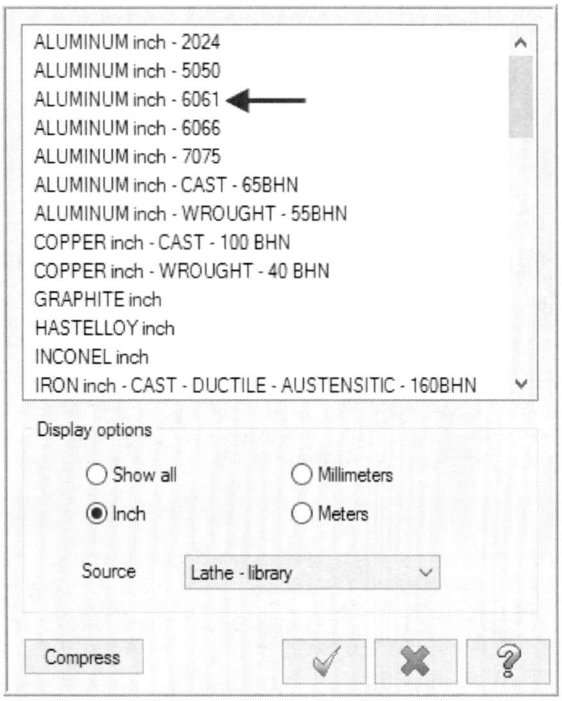

17. Select the **OK** button again to complete this Stock Setup function.

18. Right mouse click in the graphics area and click on the **Fit** icon .

➲ Note the stock setup outline as indicated by broken lines as shown below.

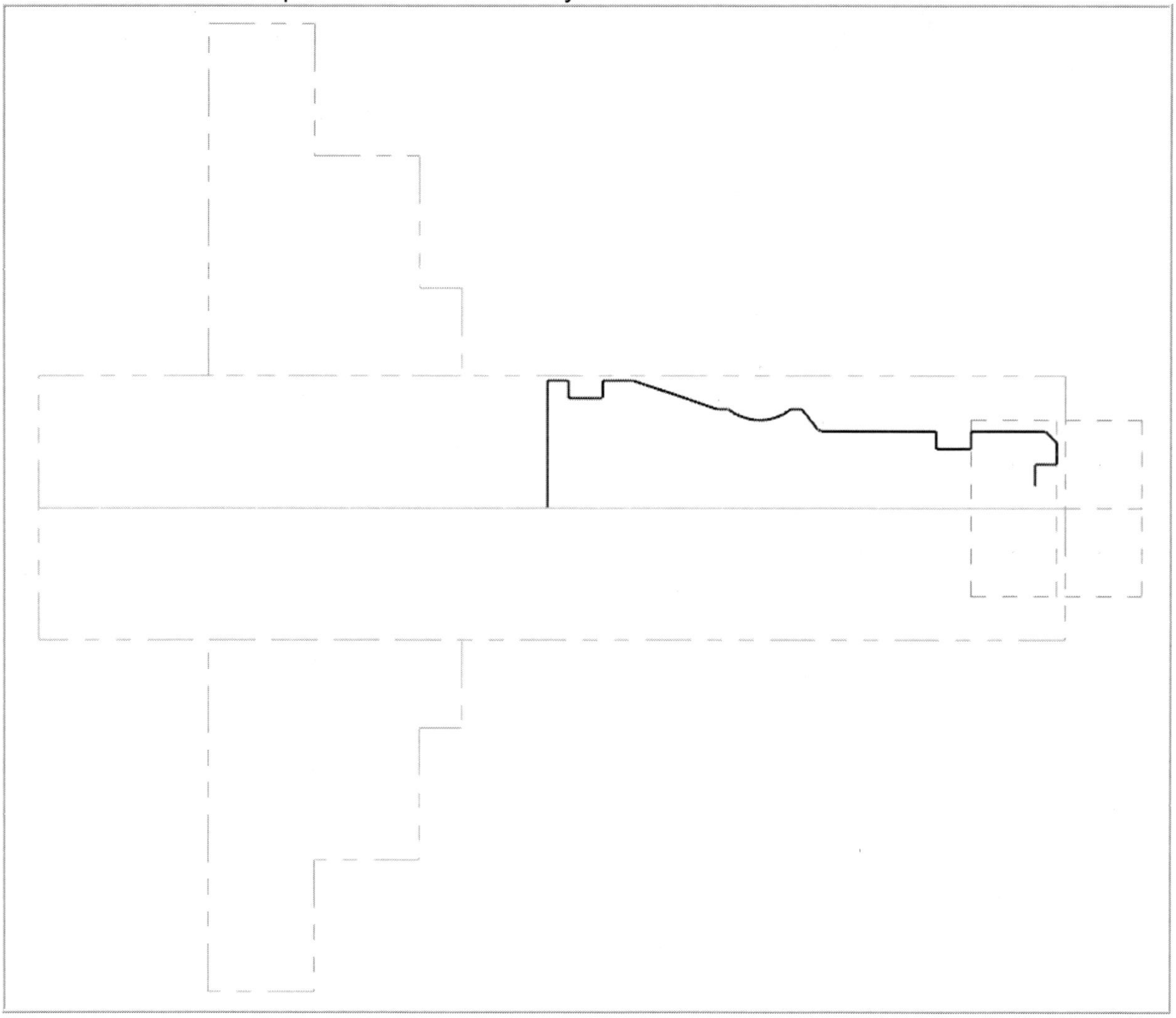

TASK 13:
FACE THE FRONT OF THE PART:

➲ In this task you will use a facing tool to face the front of the part in one cut.

1. Right mouse click in the graphics area and click on the **Fit** icon.
2. Select the **TURNING** tab at the top right side of the screen.
3. Now select **Face** in the **General** section.

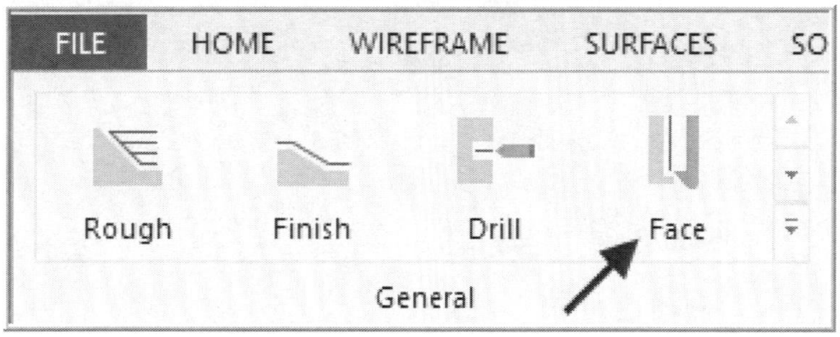

➲ After selecting the **OK** button you are confronted with **Toolpath parameters** page. The first task here will be to select **Tool #1 a Roughing – 80 deg.**

4. Click on **Tool 0101 Roughing – 80 degree** and ensure the settings are the same as in the Toolpath parameters page as shown below. **Coolant Flood** is set to **On**.

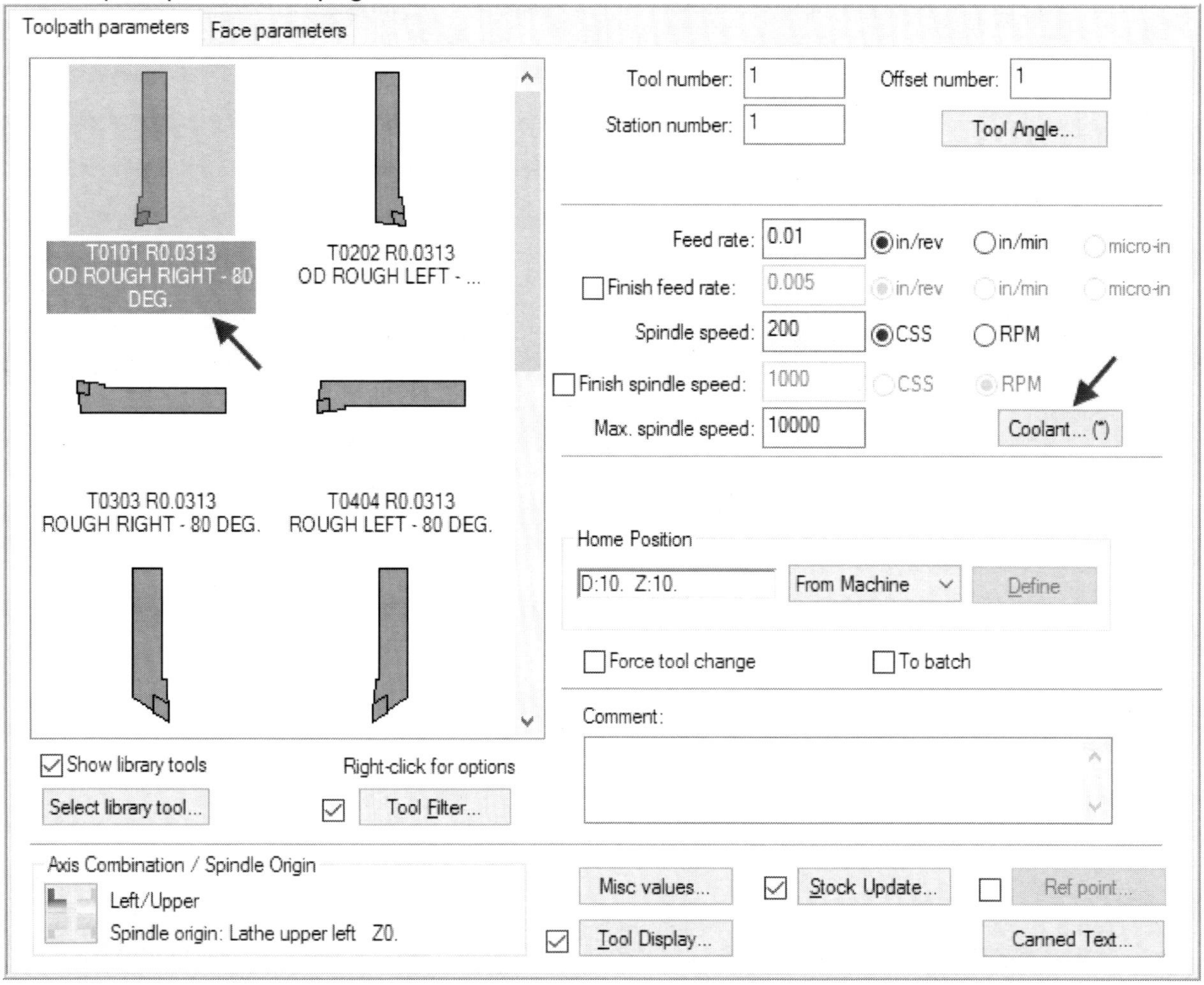

5. Select the **Face parameters** page and make changes as shown below.

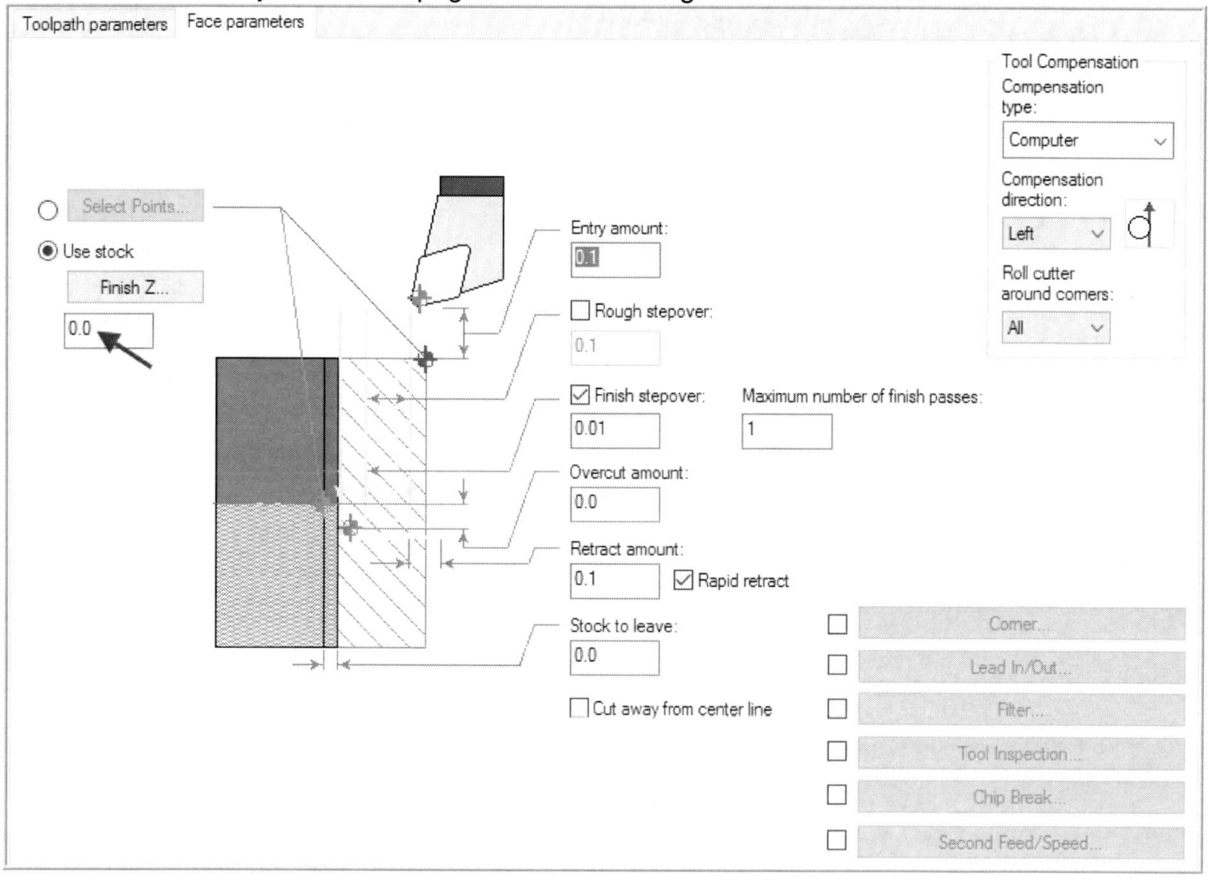

6. Select the **OK** button  to complete this **Lathe Face** operation.

TASK 14:
ROUGH THE OUTSIDE DIAMETERS

➲ In this task you will use Lathe Quick Rough Toolpath to rough the outside diameters.
➲ You will use the same tool as used for the previous facing operation Tool #1 an OD Rough-Right – 80 deg.

1. Right mouse click in the white space of the **Toolpaths Manager** and select:
   Lathe toolpaths**>Quick>Quick rough.**

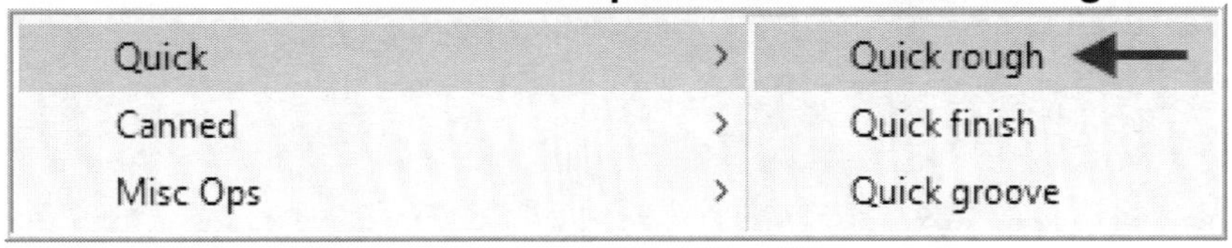

2. In the **Chaining** window Chaining mode is set to **Partial** by default.

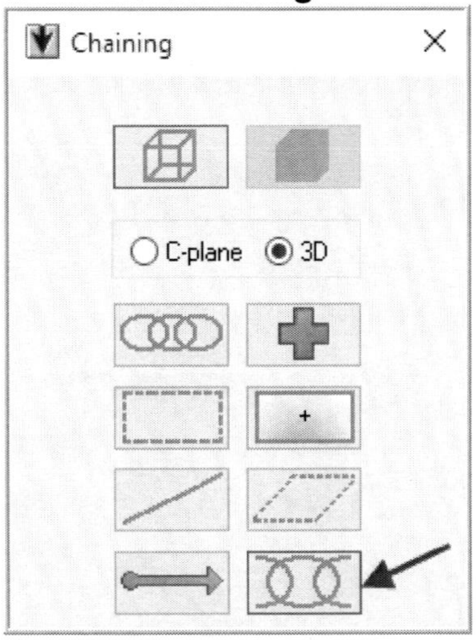

3. Select the chamfer, Line 1 as the start of the Partial chain.

After you have selected the chamfer **ensure** that the arrows are pointing up and to the left of the part. If it is not select the reverse button in the Chaining dialog box.

4. Then select Line 2 as the end entity in this chain.

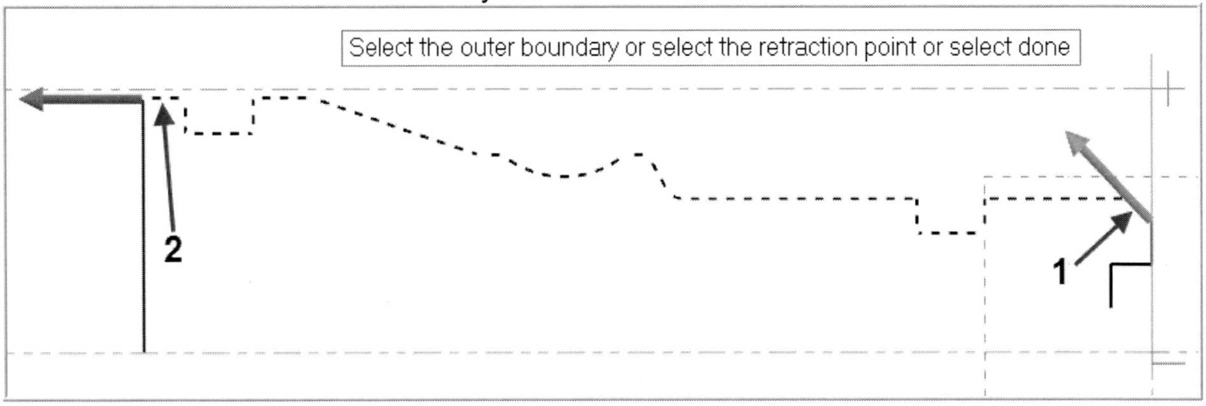

5. Select the OK button  to exit the Chaining dialog window.

6. In the Quick Toolpath parameters page select the Tool #1 Roughing – 80 deg and make any necessary changes as shown below. Coolant Flood **is set to** On.

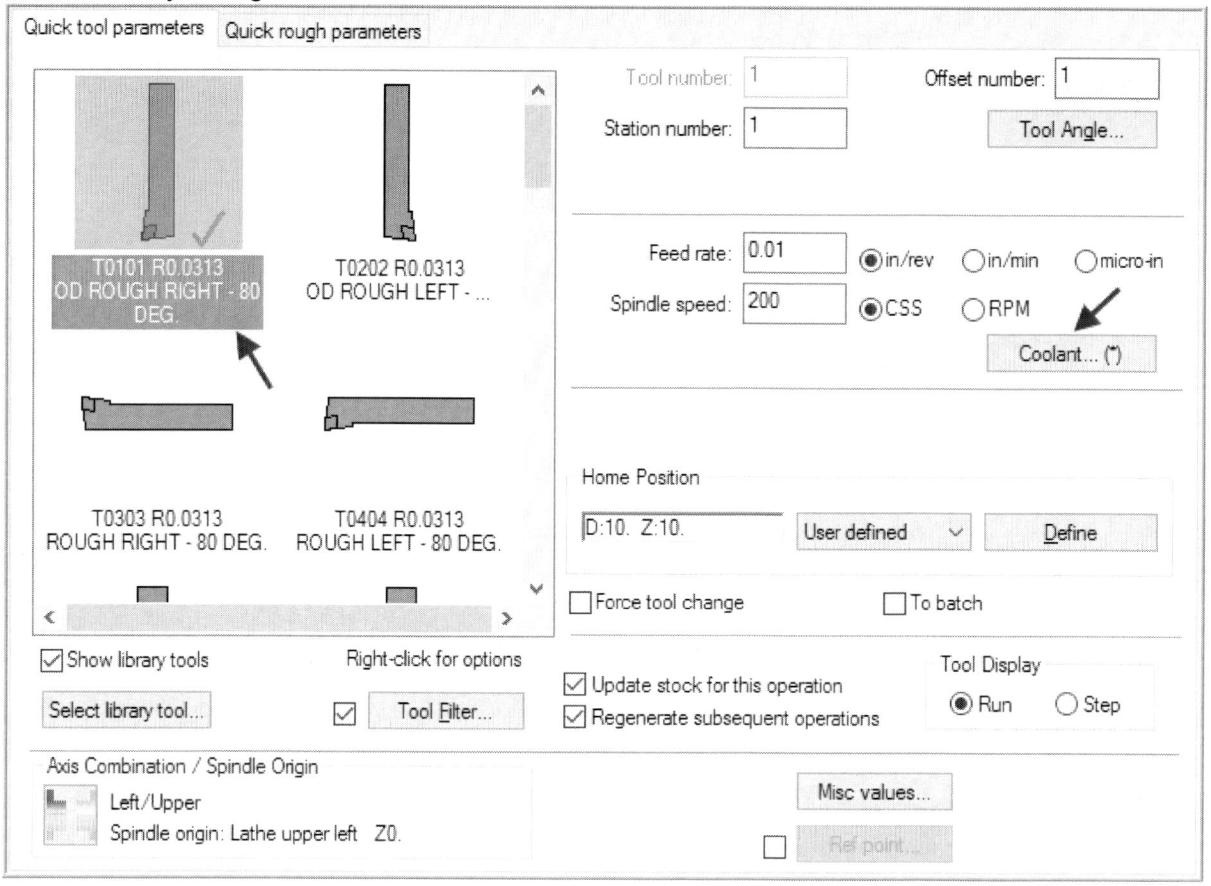

7. Select the **Quick Rough** parameters page and make any necessary changes.

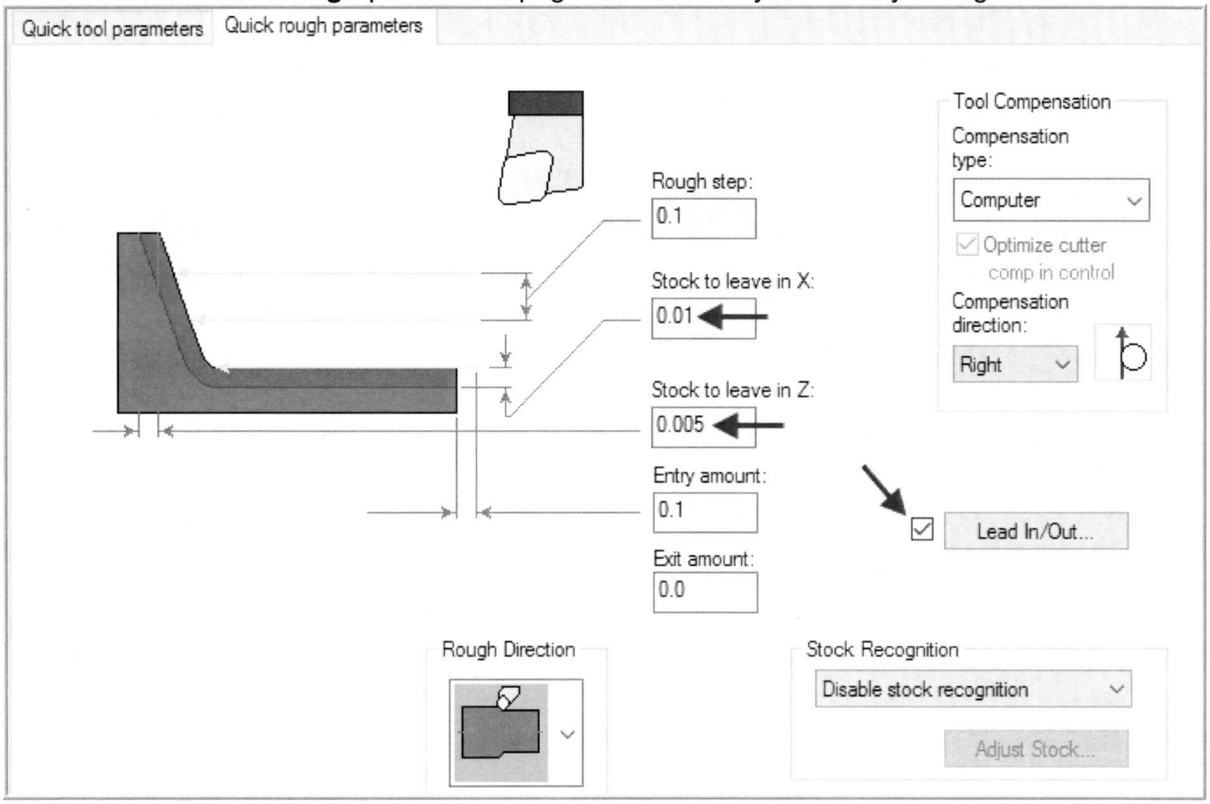

8. Select the **Lead In/Out** button, then select the **Lead out** page and extend the contour by **0.2** as shown below:

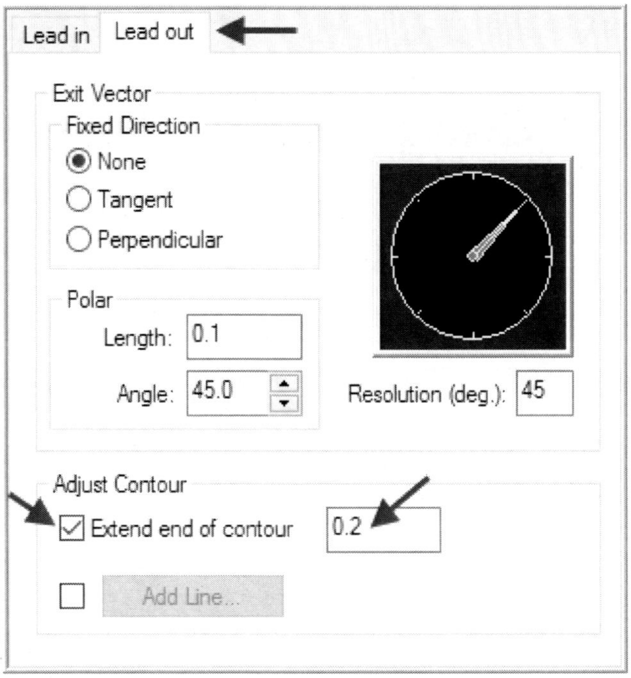

9. Select the **OK** button to exit this function.
10. Select the **OK** button to exit Quick Rough Parameters.

TASK 15:
FINISH THE OUTSIDE DIAMETERS

➲ In this task you will finish the outside diameters using Lathe Quick Finish Toolpath. The tool will be Tool #2 Finish – 35 deg.

1. Right mouse click in the white space of the **Toolpaths Manager** and select:
   Lathe toolpaths>Quick>Quick finish.

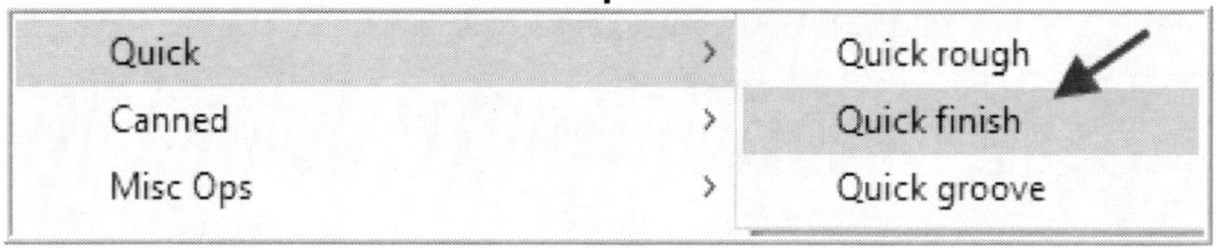

2. In the Quick tool parameters page **scroll down and locate the tool: OD Finish Right – 35 deg**. **<u>Then double click on this tool.</u>**

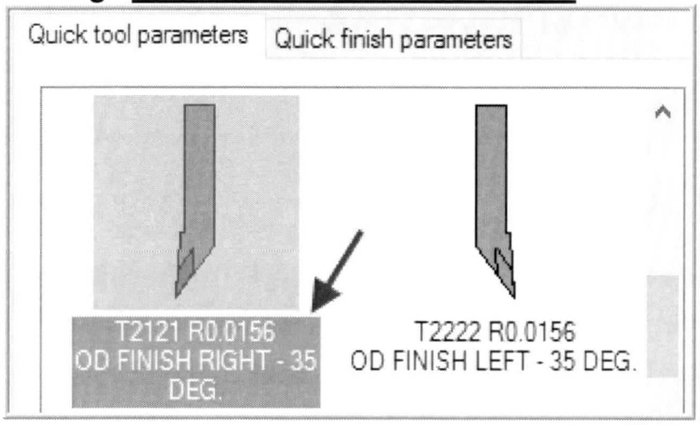

3. Click on the **Parameters** page and at the bottom of this page set the compensation for this tool as shown below:

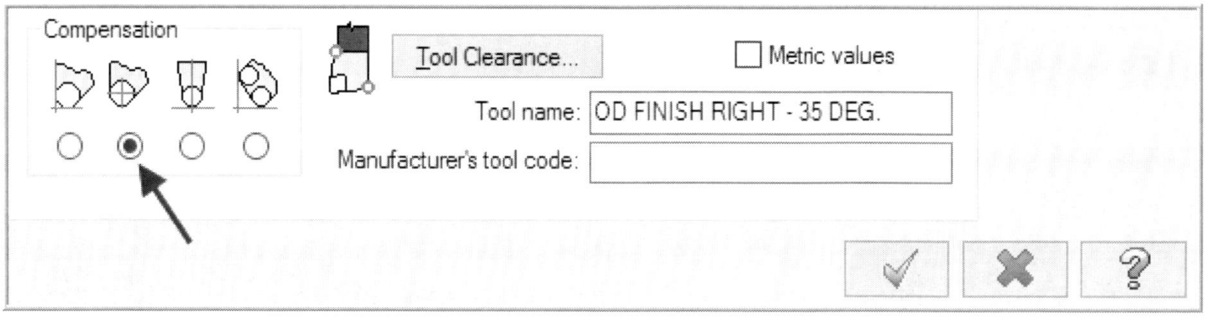

4. Click on the **OK** icon .

5. Back in the **Toolpath parameters** page make any necessary changes as shown below. **Coolant Flood** is set to **On**.

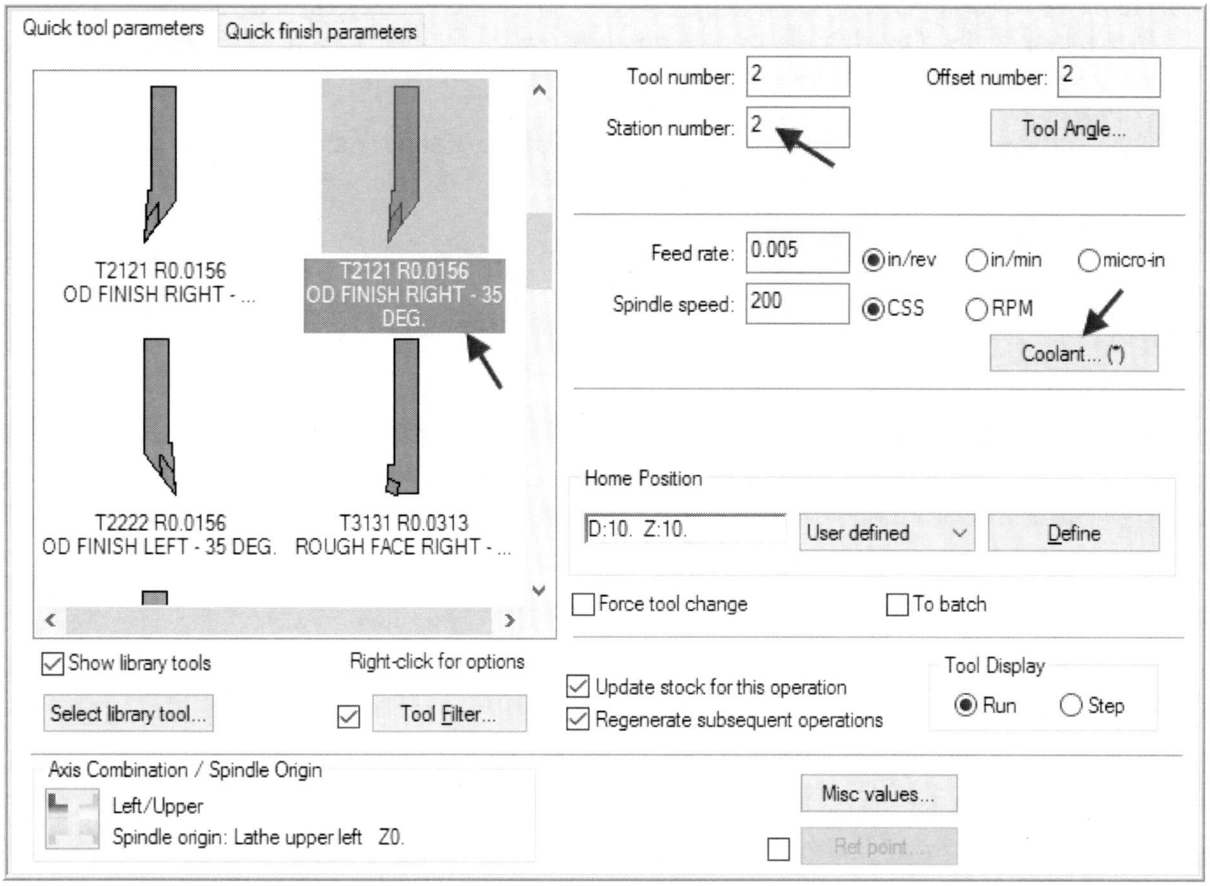

6. Select the **Quick Finish** parameters page and make changes as shown below:

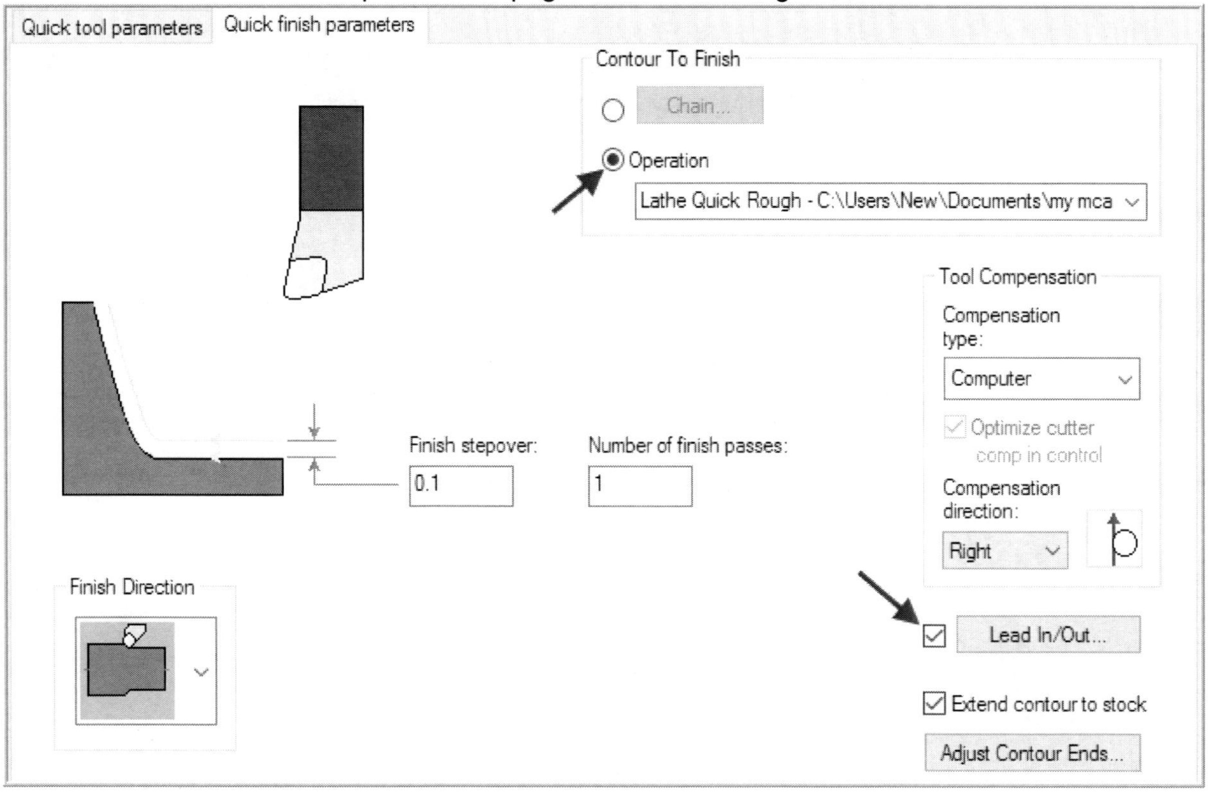

7. Select the **Lead In/Out** button select the **Lead out** page and extend the contour by **0.2** as shown below:

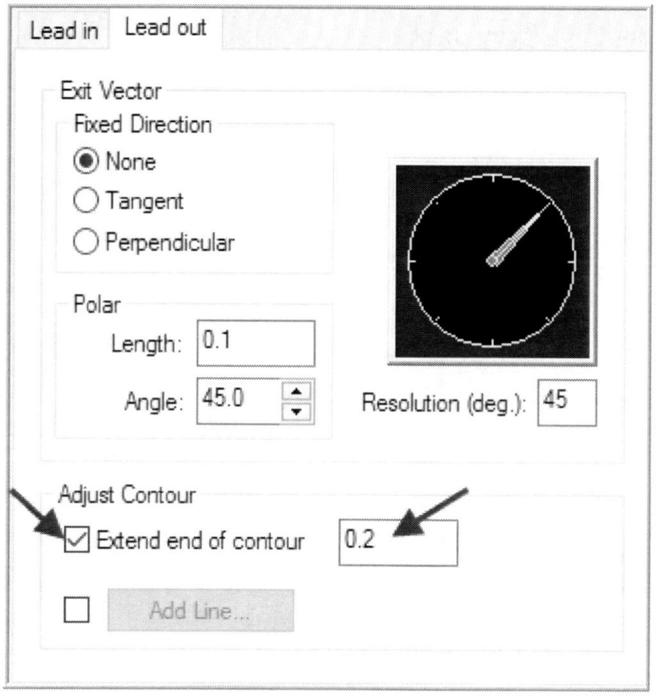

8. Select the **OK** button to exit this function.
9. Select the **OK** button to exit **Quick finish parameters**.

TASK 16:
FINISH THE 0.3 RADIUS

➲ In this task you will finish the 0.3 radius using the same tool you used for finishing a **Tool #2 Finish – 35 deg**.

1. On the **TURNING** tab select **Finish** in the **General** section.
2. In the **Chaining** window click on the icon for **Single** 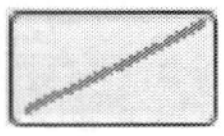
3. Select the Arc in the position shown below

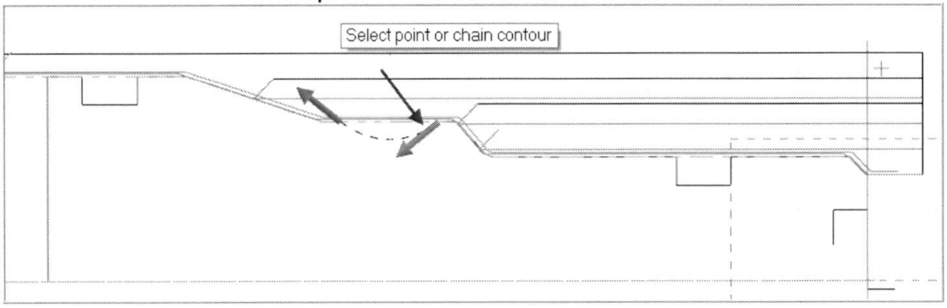

4. Select the **OK** button  to exit the Chaining dialog window.
5. In the **Toolpath parameters** page select **Tool #2 Finish – 35 deg** and make any necessary changes as shown below. **Coolant Flood** is set to **On**.

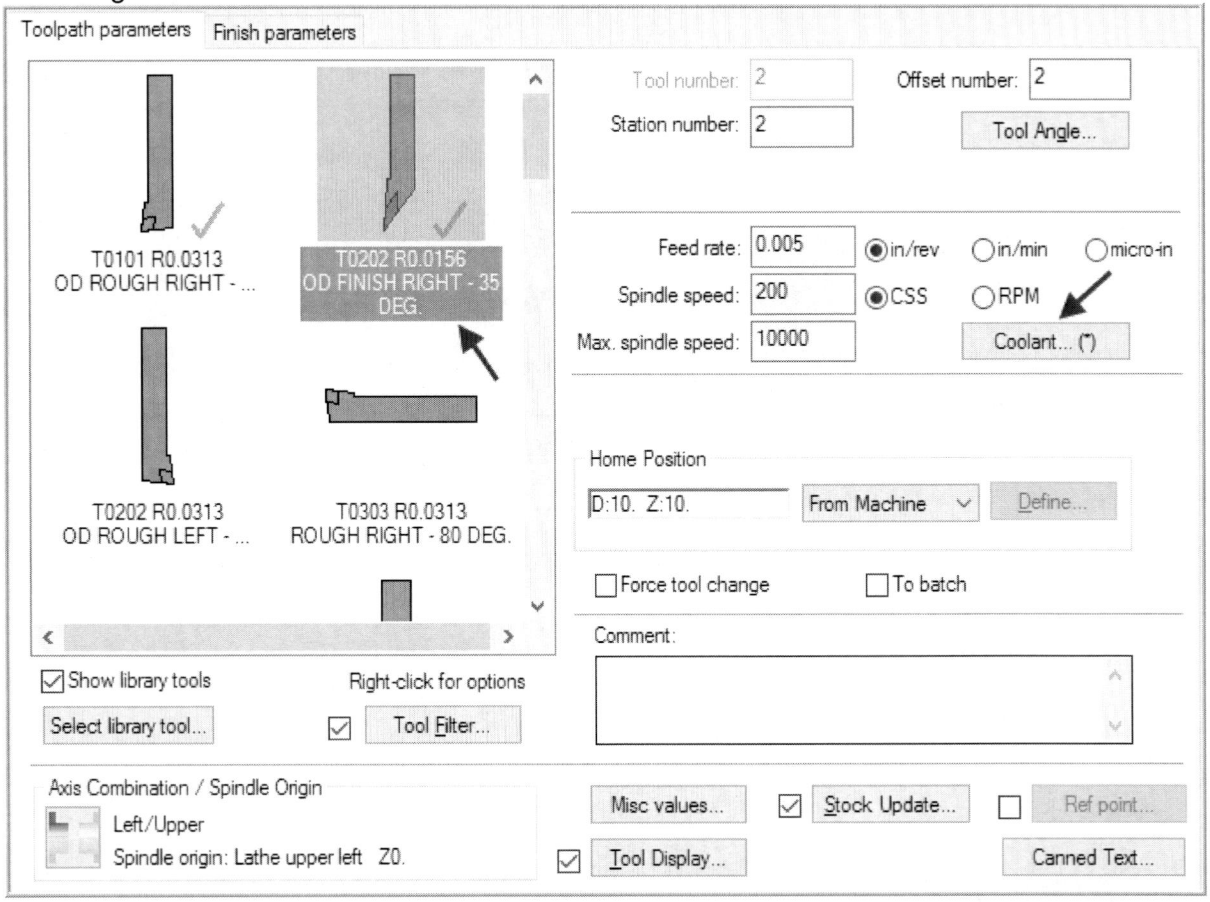

6. Click on the **Finish parameters** tab and make any necessary changes as shown below.

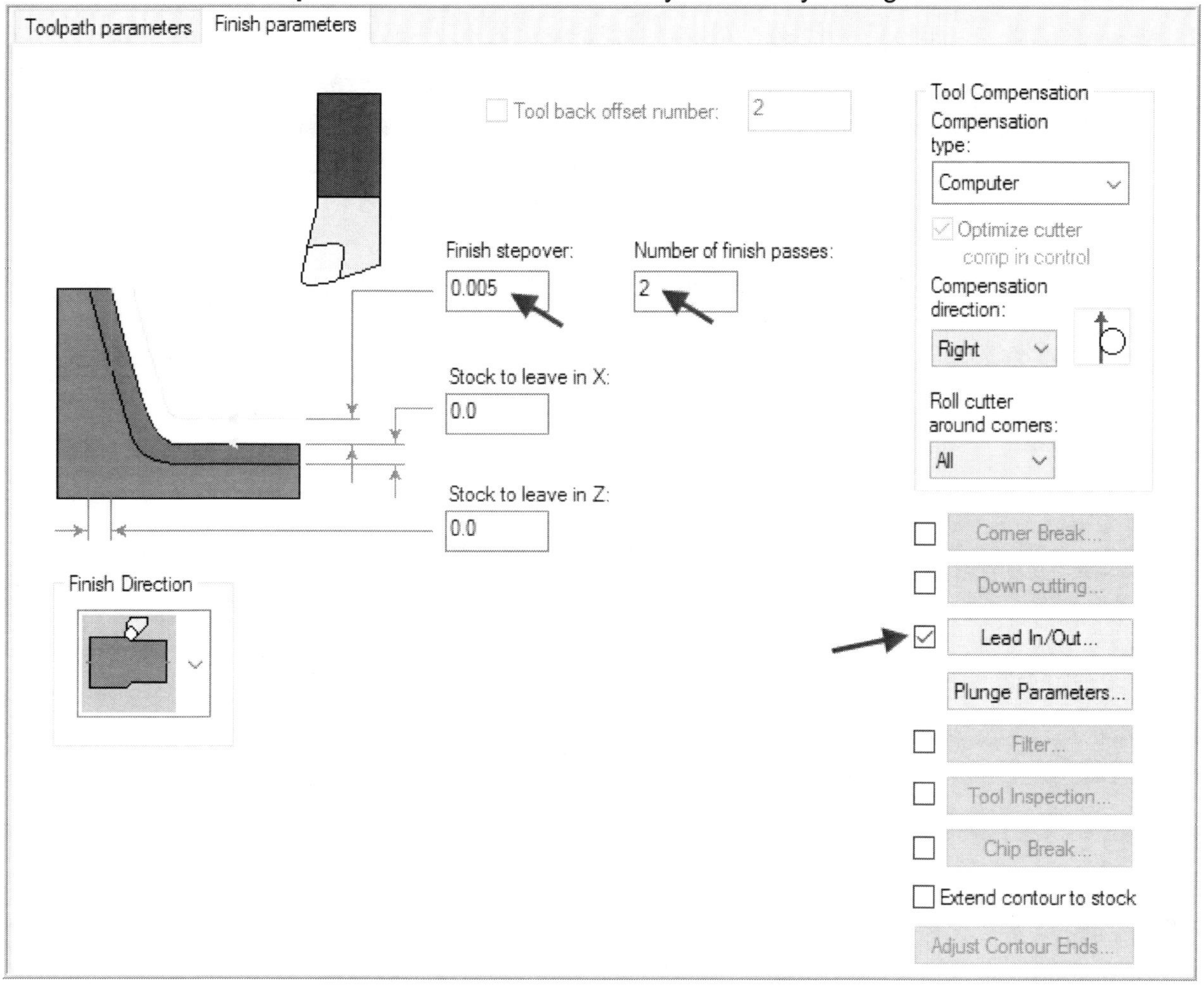

7. Click on the **Lead in/Out** button as shown above:
8. Make the necessary changes as shown below on the **Lead In** page. In order to adjust the dial click on the desired location of the arrow.

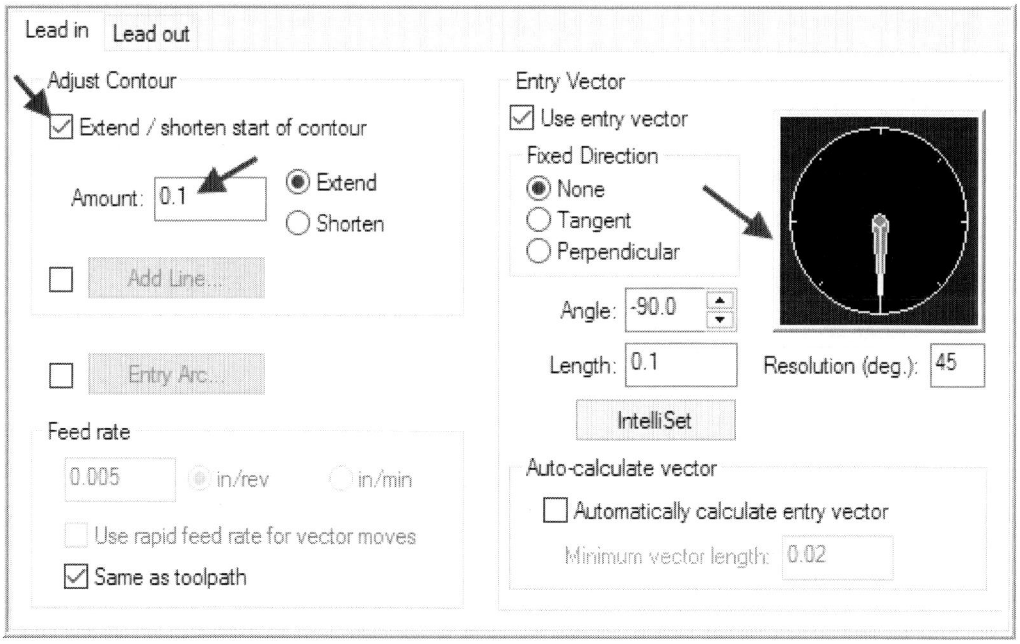

9. Click on the **Lead out** tab and make the necessary changes as shown below:

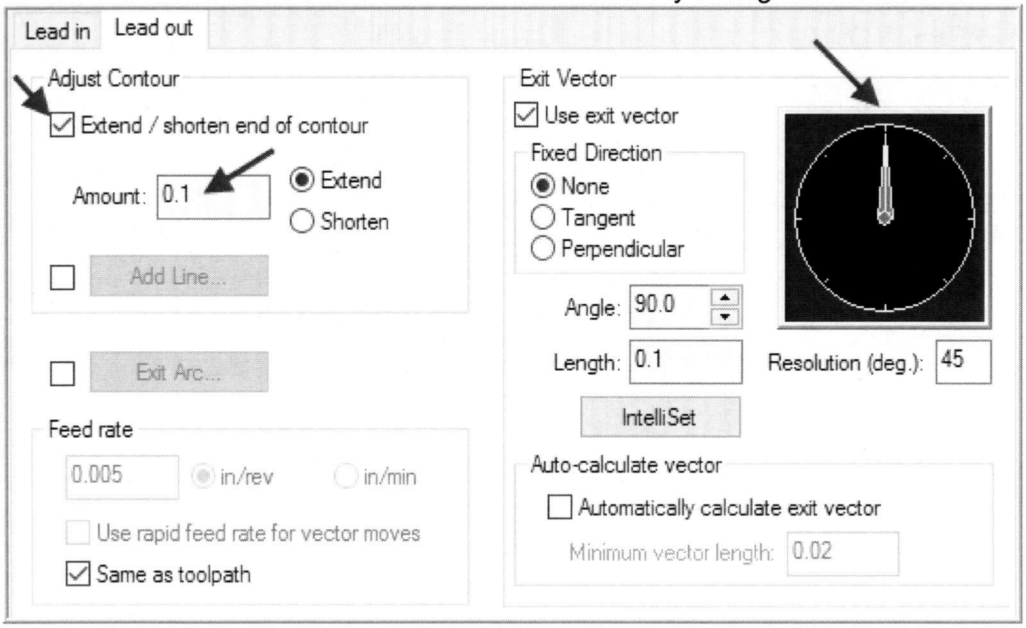

10. Click on **OK** to exit the Lead In/out window.

11. Click on the **Plunge Parameters** button Plunge Parameters... .

12. Make the necessary changes as shown below.

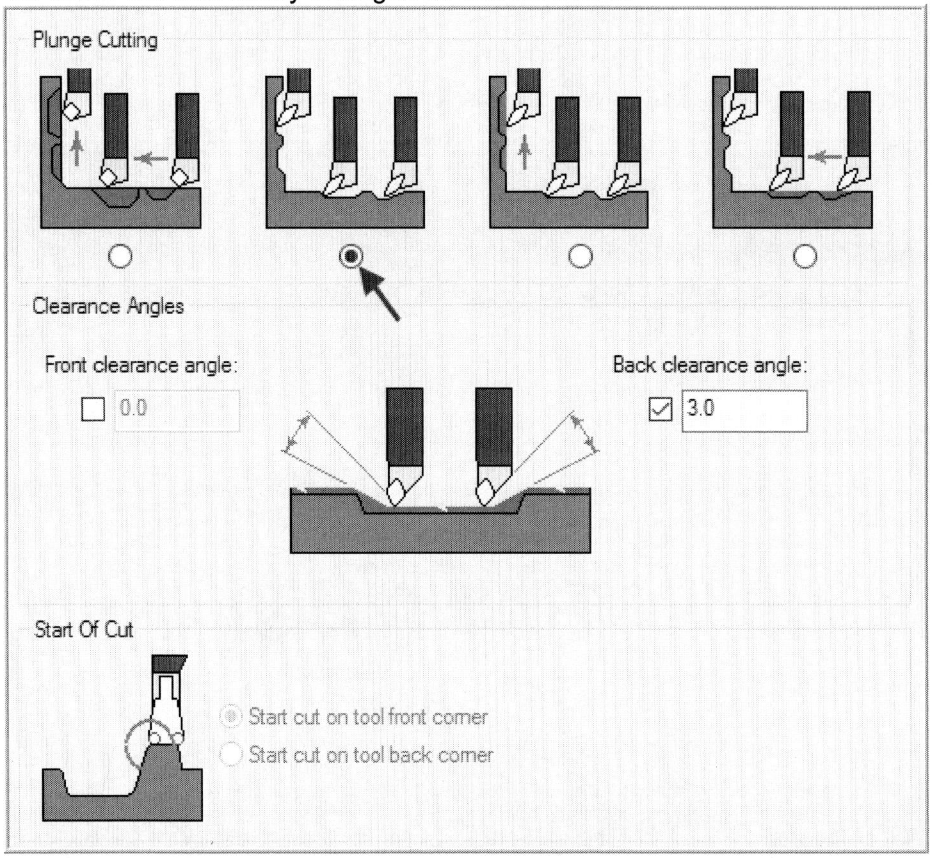

13. Click on Ok to exit the **Plunge Cut** Parameters window.

14. Click on Ok to exit the **Lathe Finish** parameters window.

TASK 17:
CENTER DRILL HOLE

➲ In this task you will center drill .2" depth using a **Centre Drill - .25 diameter.**

1. Select **Drill** in the **General** section of the **Turning** tab.

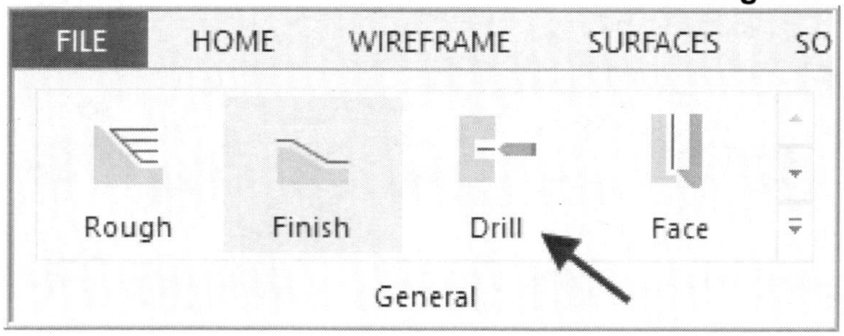

2. In the **Toolpath parameters** page select **Center Drill - .25 Dia.** and make any necessary changes as shown below. **Coolant Flood** is set to **On**.

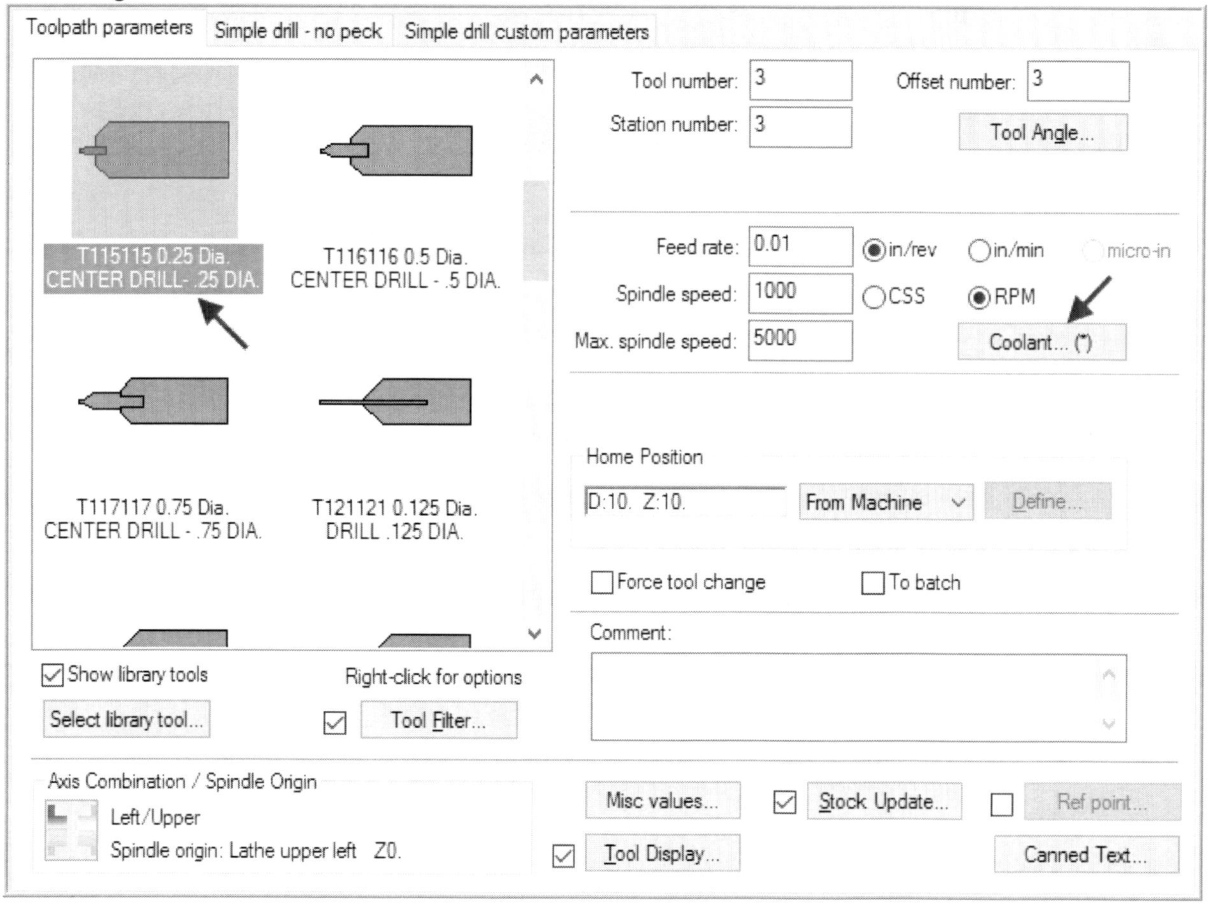

3. Select the **Simple drill – no peck** tab and make changes as shown below:

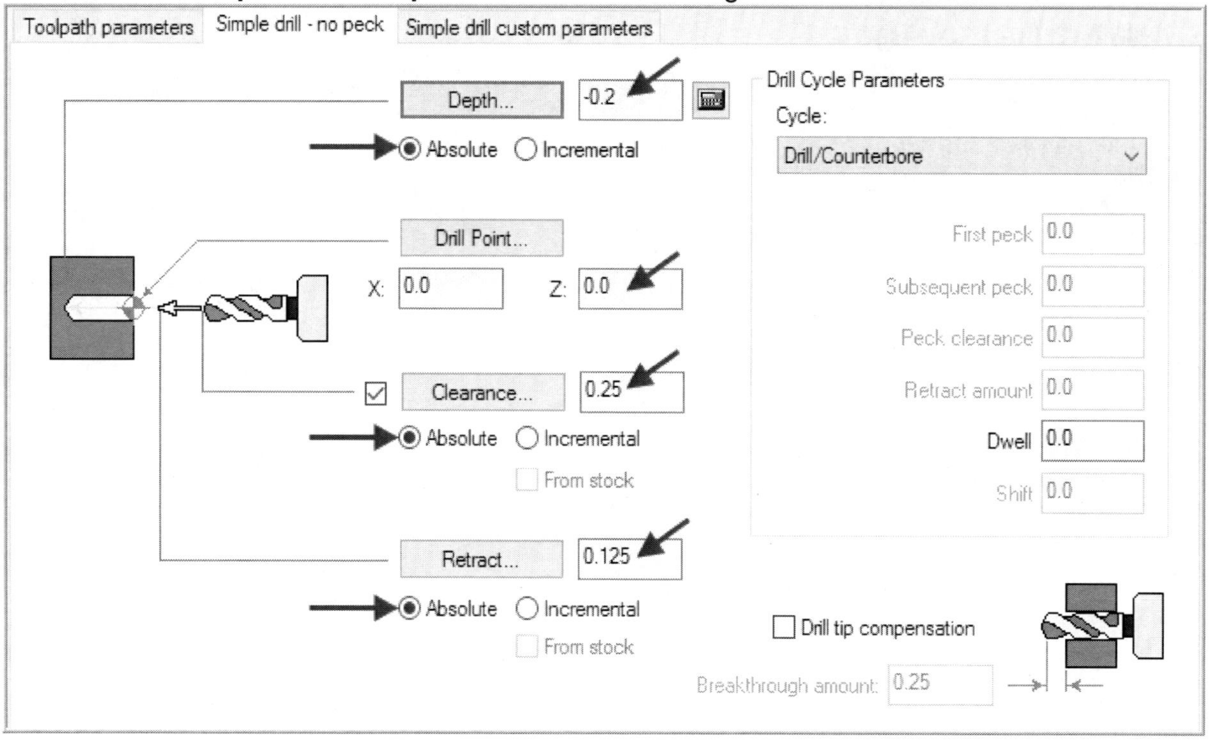

4. Select the **OK** button  to exit **Simple drill – no peck**.

TASK 18:
TAP DRILL THE 0.25-20 UNC TAPPED HOLE 13/64 DIAMETER

➲ In this task you will tap drill the 0.25-20 UNC hole using **13/64 diameter drill** this will be a peck drill operation.

1. Select **Drill** in the **General** section of the **Turning** tab.

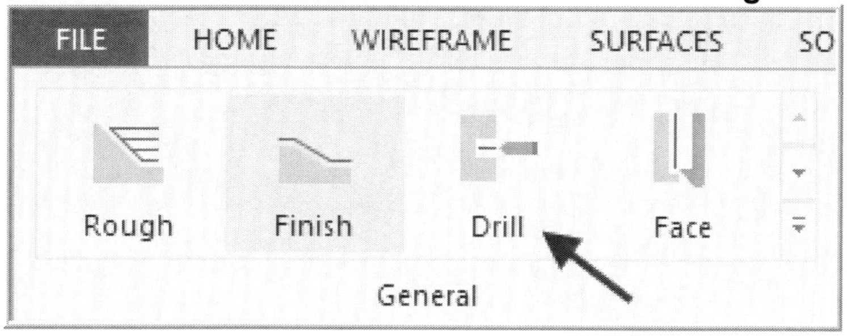

2. At the **Toolpath** parameters page click on the Select library tool button Select library tool... .
3. At the top left of this dialog box open up the **Select new folder** icon to show the library tools list and select **LDRILLS** and then click on **Open.**

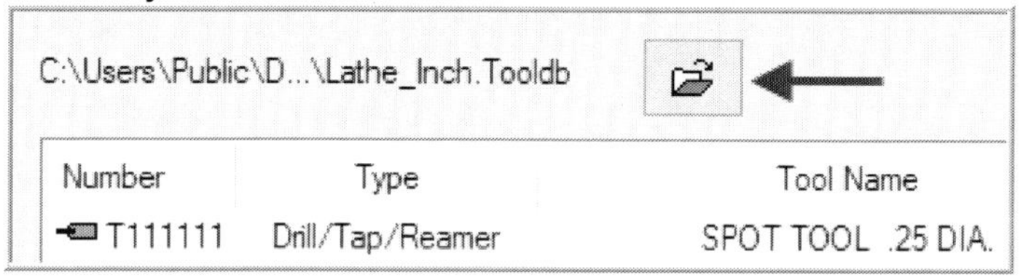

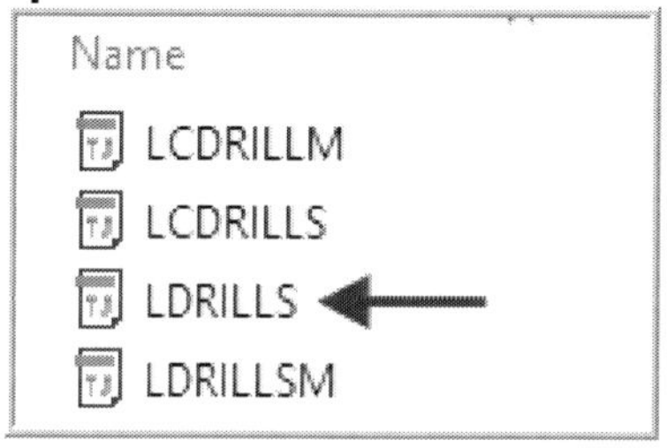

4. Scroll down and select the **13/64 drill** from the list. Right Mouse click and select **View>Details**.

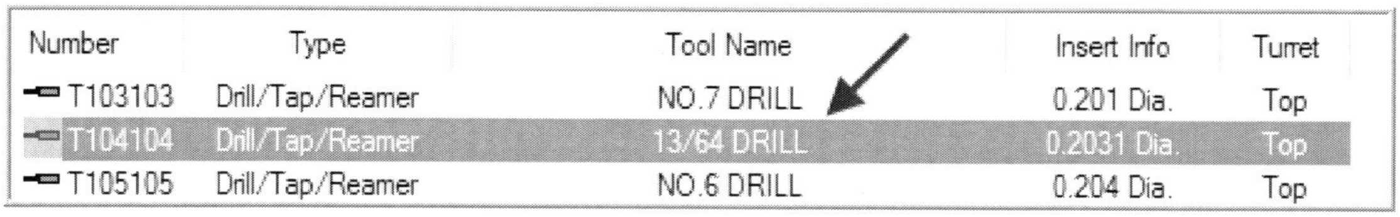

5. Select the **OK** button to exit the tool selection.

6. Make changes as shown below. **Coolant Flood** is set to **On**.

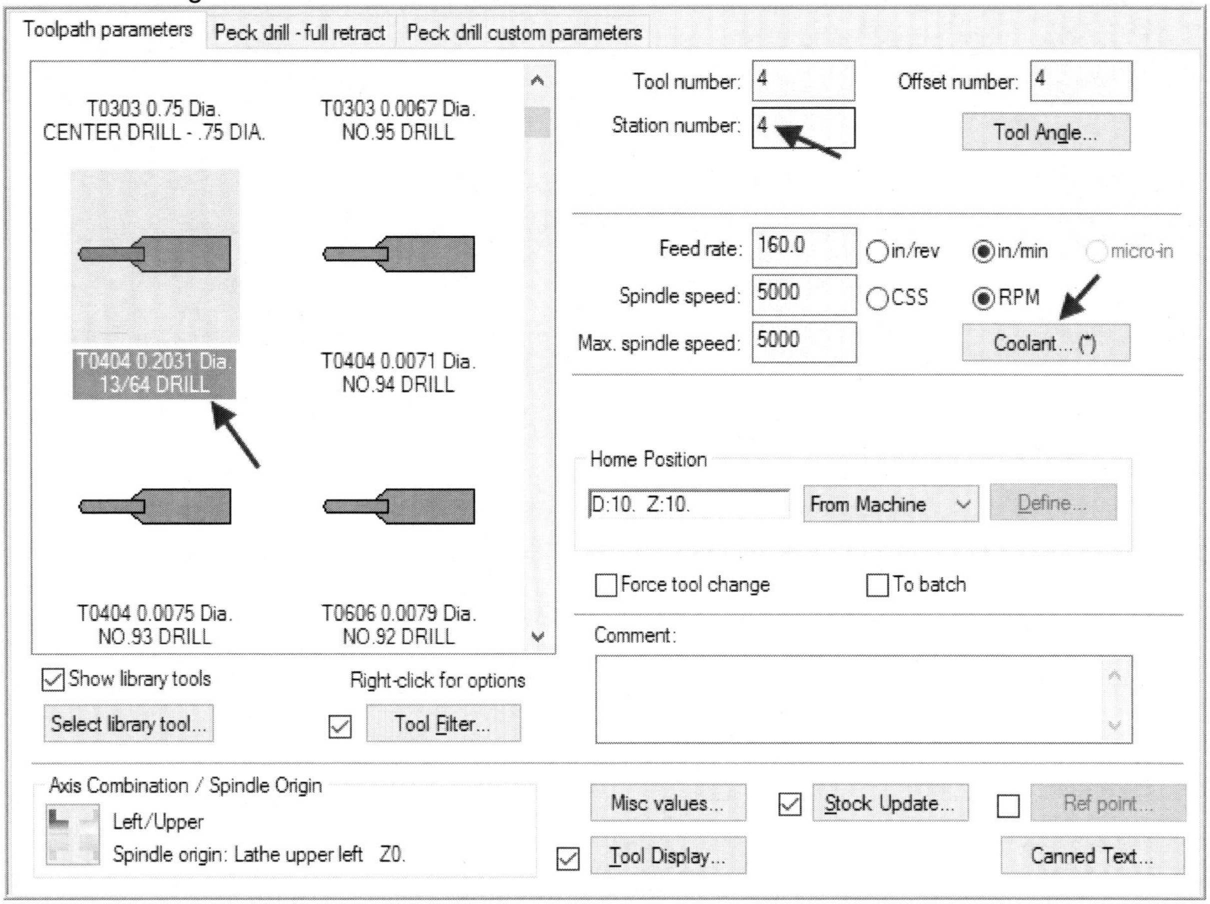

7. Select the **Simple drill – no peck** page and make changes as shown below: This hole will be peck drilled so **select the Cycle as Peck Drill** Make changes as shown below:

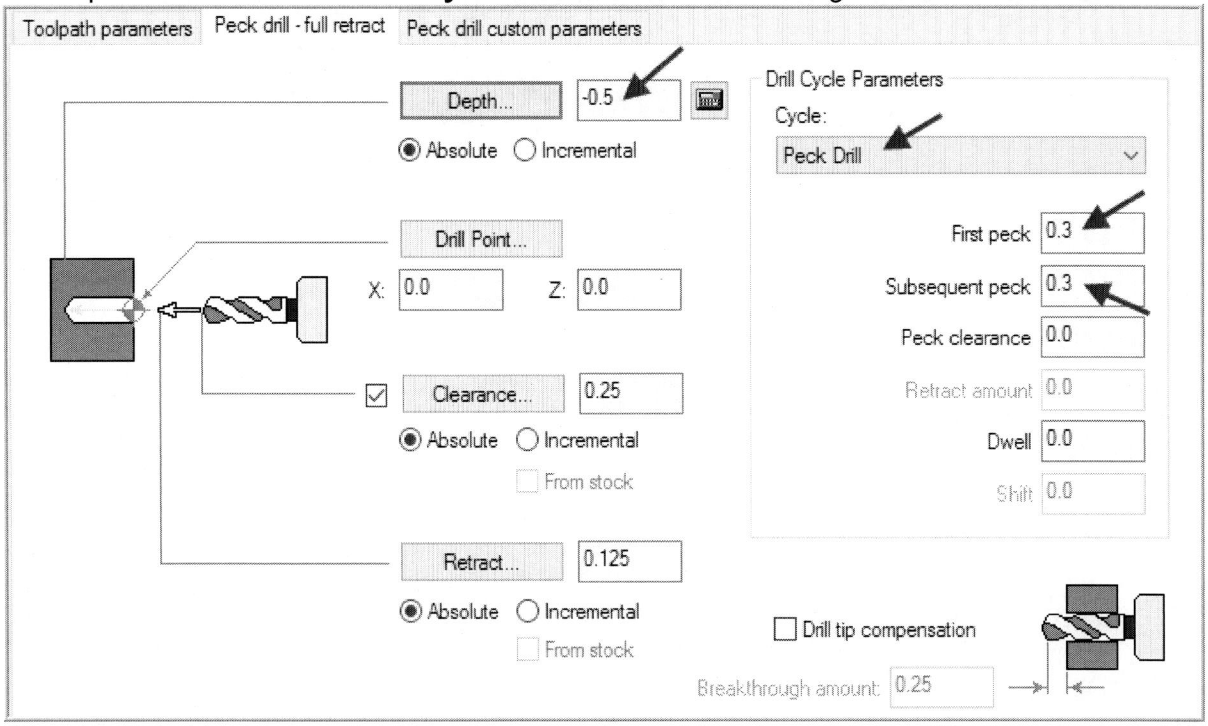

➲ As the drawing specifies the depth of 0.5 from the front face at full diameter you will now use the **Depth calculator** to calculate the true depth, taking into account the tip angle of this drill.

8. Click on the **Depth calculator** icon. 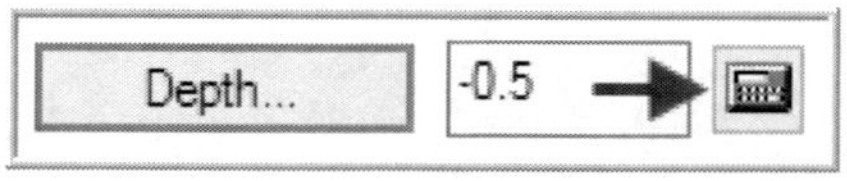

9. At the Depth Calculator dialog box activate the radio button for **Add to depth**.

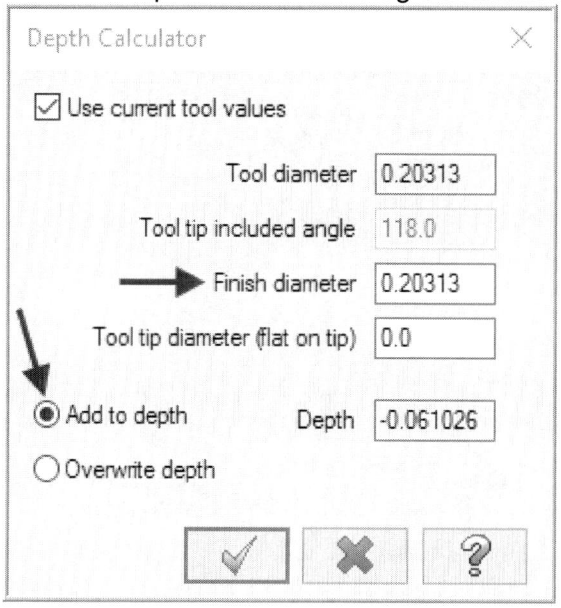

Use the **Depth Calculator** to calculate the proper drilling depth when the finish diameter of the hole is different from the drill diameter—for example, when countersinking a hole.
Mastercam automatically displays the **Tool diameter**, **Tool tip included angle**, and **Tool tip diameter** for the drill that has been selected for the operation. Deselect **Use current tool values** to specify different values for these parameters.
Once you calculate the depth, you have two options:
Choose **Overwrite depth** to replace the existing depth value on the parameter page.
Choose **Add to depth** to add the calculated depth to the existing depth value on the parameter page.

10. Select the **OK** button  to exit Depth Calculator.

➲ Notice how now the depth has been changed

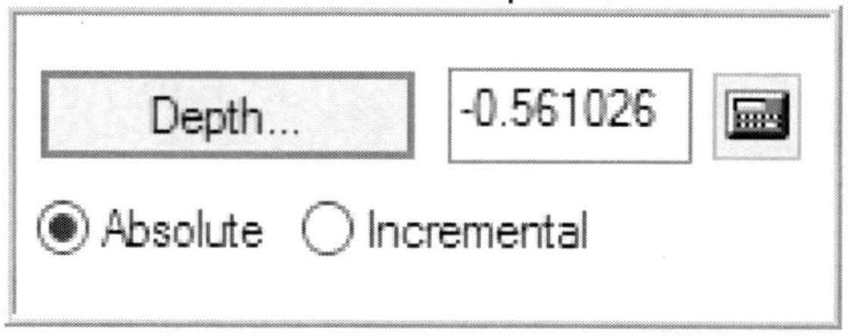

11. Select the **OK** button  to exit Peck drill – full retract.

TASK 19:
TAP THE 0.25-20 UNC TAPPED HOLE

➲ In this task you will tap the 0.25-20 hole.

1. Select **Drill** in the **General** section of the **Turning** tab.
2. At the Toolpath parameters page click on the **Select library** tool button .

3. Select the **select new folder** icon  at the top of the dialog box and then the **LTAPS** from the list as shown below and then click on **Open**.

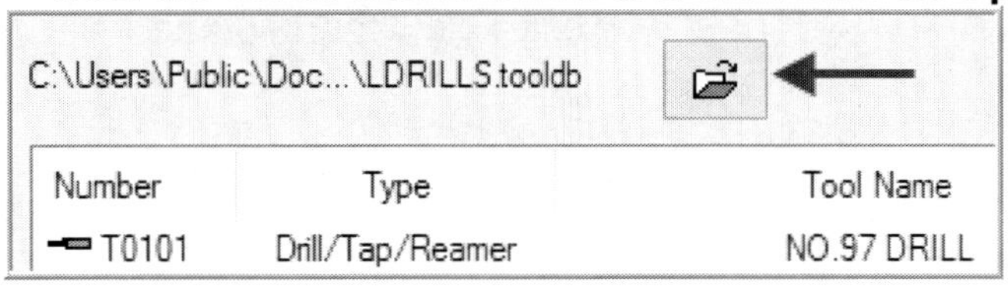

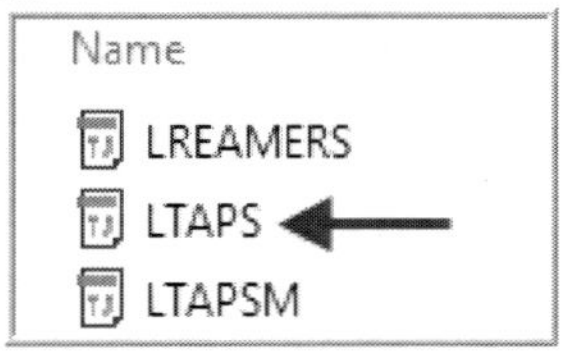

4. Select the **1/4-20 RH TAP** from the list:

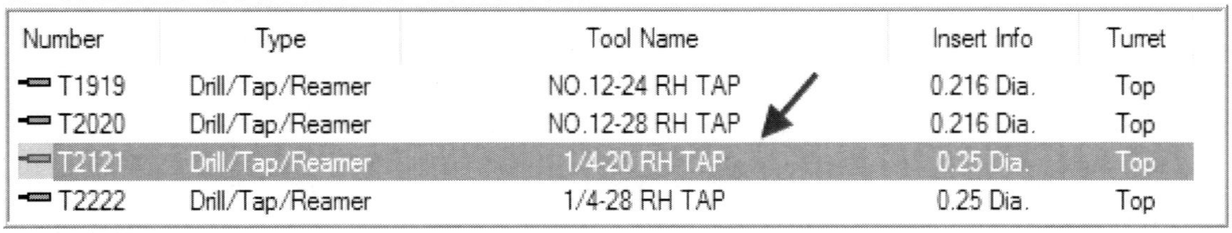

Number	Type	Tool Name	Insert Info	Turret
T1919	Drill/Tap/Reamer	NO.12-24 RH TAP	0.216 Dia.	Top
T2020	Drill/Tap/Reamer	NO.12-28 RH TAP	0.216 Dia.	Top
T2121	Drill/Tap/Reamer	1/4-20 RH TAP	0.25 Dia.	Top
T2222	Drill/Tap/Reamer	1/4-28 RH TAP	0.25 Dia.	Top

5. Select the **OK** button  to exit the tool selection.
6. <u>**Double**</u> **click** on the **1/4-20 tap** in the **Tool parameters** page.

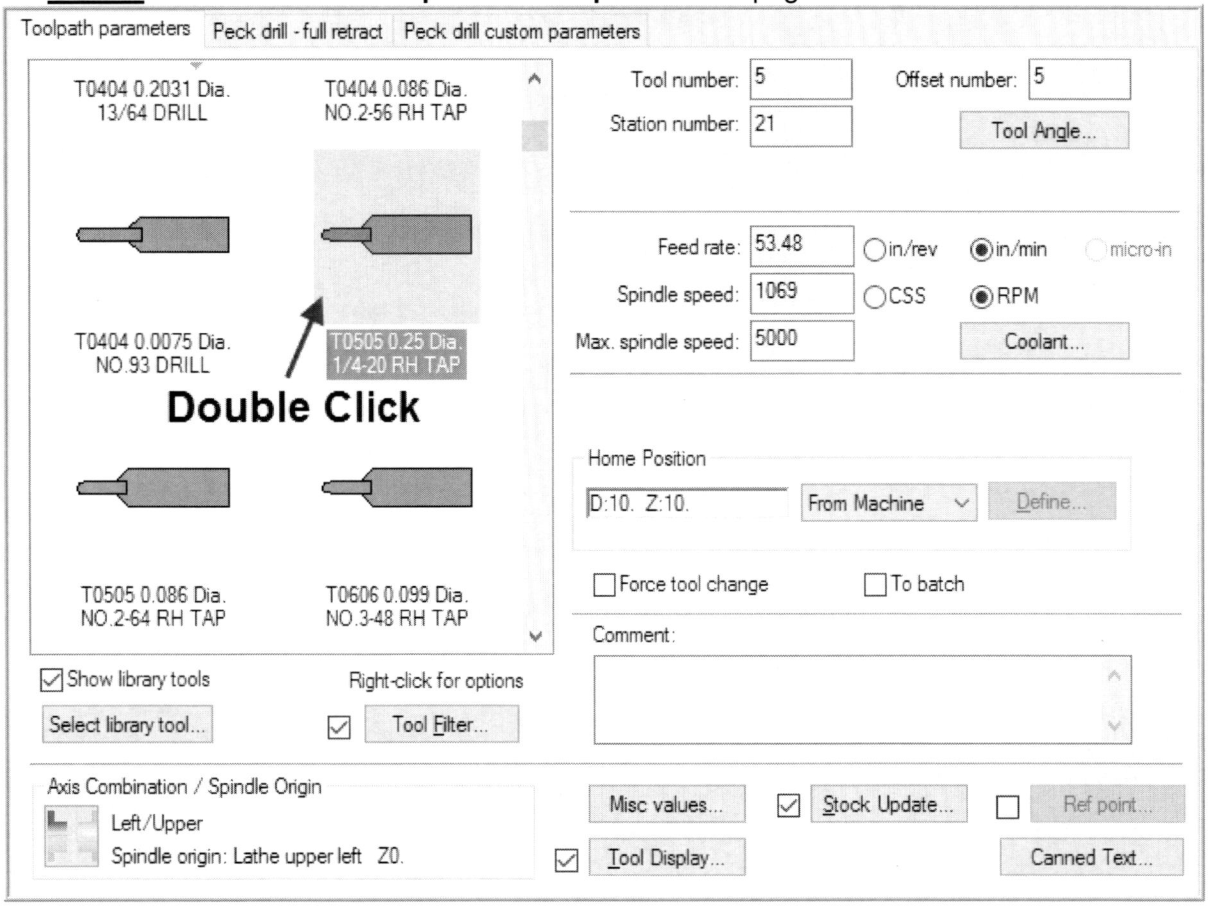

7. At the lower right corner of the screen activate the radio button for **Bottoming**.

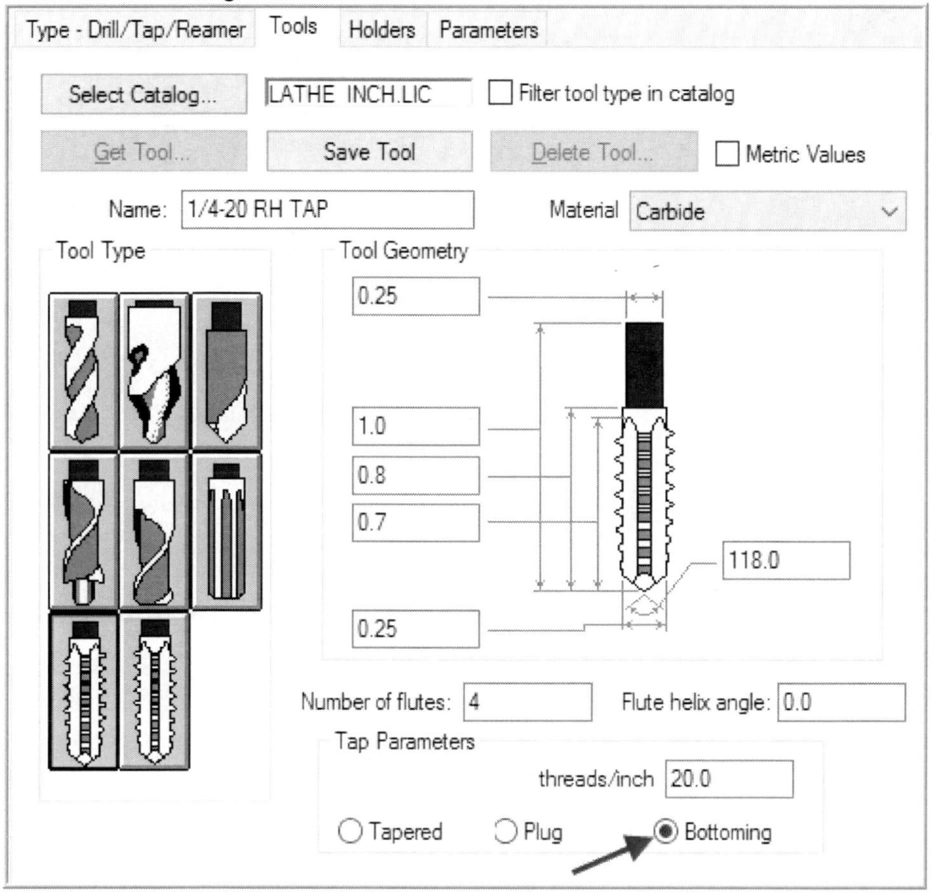

Bottoming
Select this option if you want the tap to have the same diameter all the way down.

This type of tap is used to cut threads through the bottom of the hole.

8. Select the **OK** button  to exit the Tools page.

9. Make changes as shown below: The **Spindle Speed** and **Feedrate** are synchronized for a **1/40-20 tap**. **Coolant Flood** is set to **On**.

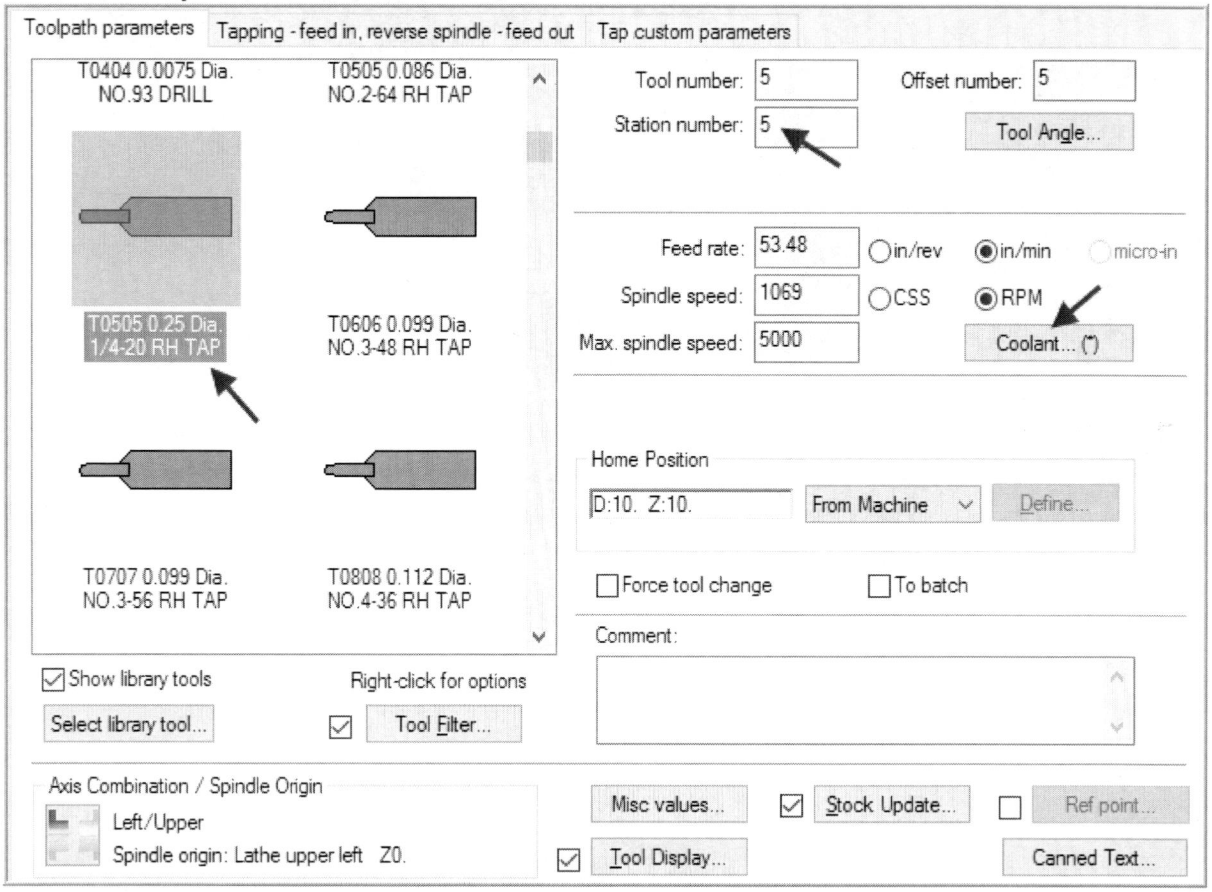

10. Select the **Peck drill – full retract** page and make changes as shown below: This hole will be tapped so **select the Cycle as Tap(G32)** Make changes as shown below:

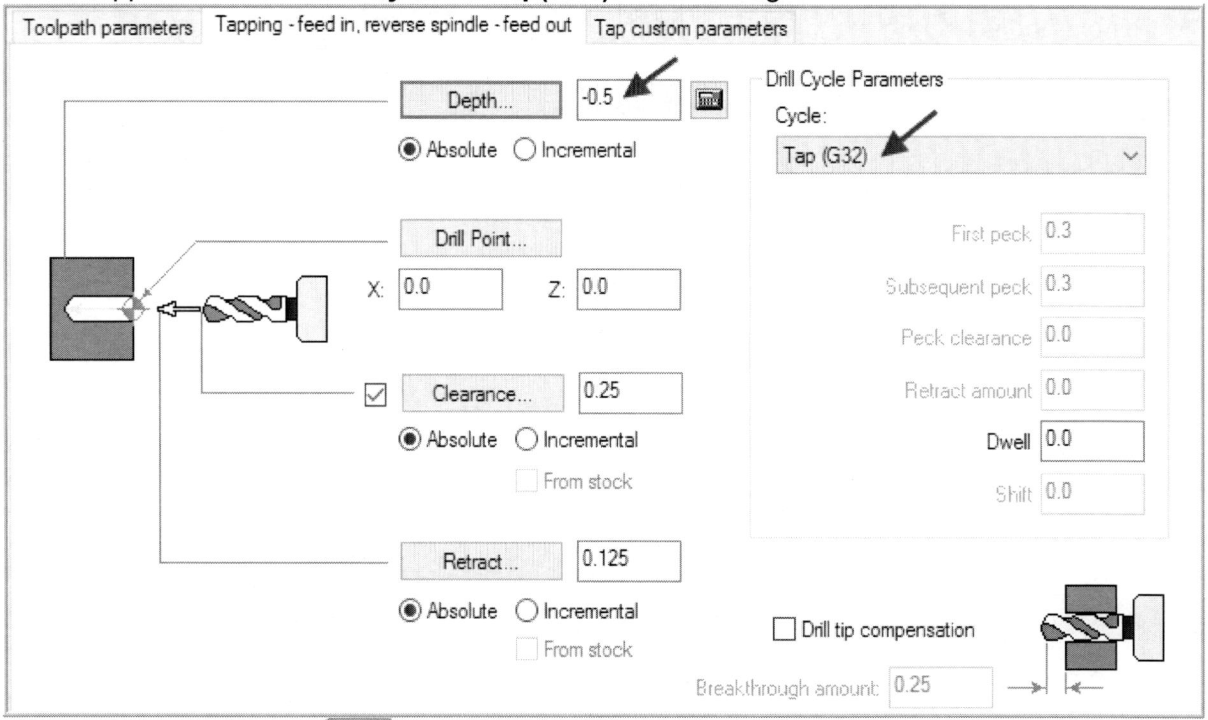

11. Select the **OK** button to exit Tapping – feed in, reverse spindle – feed out.

TASK 20:
ROUGH THE BORE

➲ In this task you will use a boring tool to rough out the 0.500 diameter bore.

1. Click on the **Select all operations** icon.
2. Now **toggle the display of the toolpaths** by selecting **ALT and T** on your keyboard to hide the toolpaths display.
3. Right mouse click in the white space of the **Toolpaths Manager** and select:
   Lathe toolpaths>Quick>Quick rough.

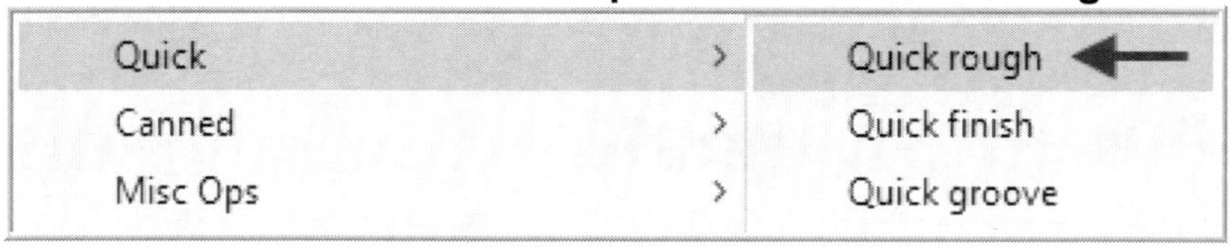

4. In the **Chaining window** Chaining mode is set to Partial by default.
5. Select **Line 1** as the **start** of the Partial chain.

After you have selected the first line **ensure** that the arrows are pointing towards the part as shown below: If it is not select the reverse button in the Chaining dialog box

6. Then select **Line 2** as the **end** entity in this chain.

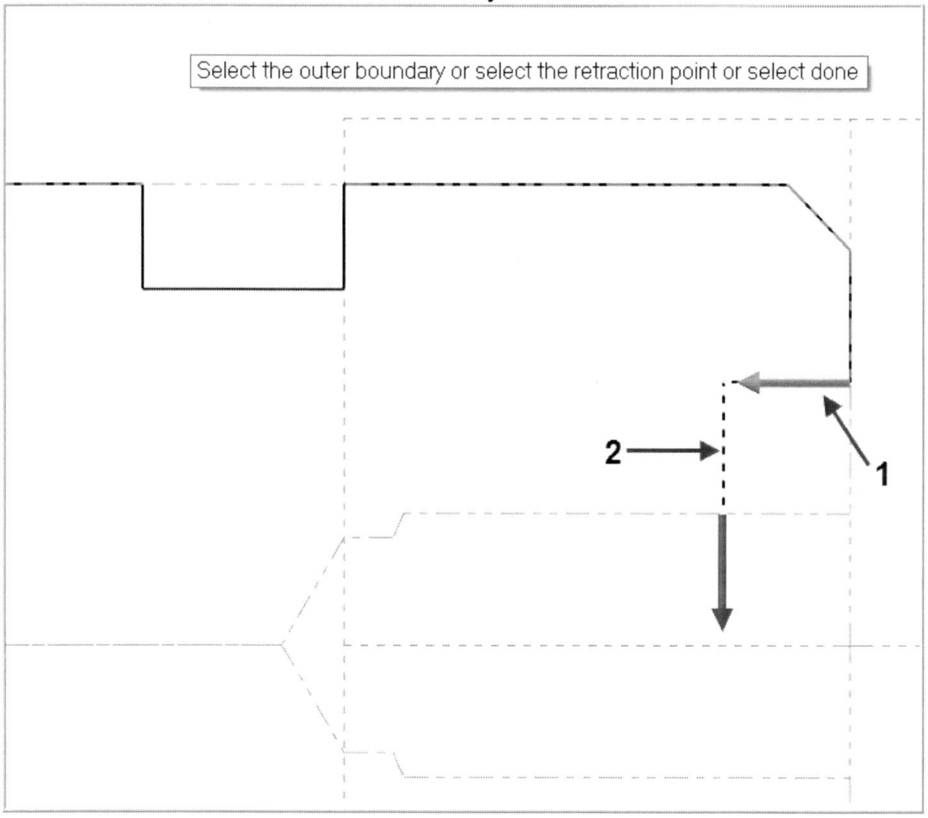

7. Select the **OK** button to exit the Chaining dialog window.

8. At the **Toolpath parameters** page click on the **Select library tool** button Select library tool... .

9. At the top left of this dialog box open up the Select new folder icon to show the library tools list and select **Lathe_Inch** and then click on **Open**.

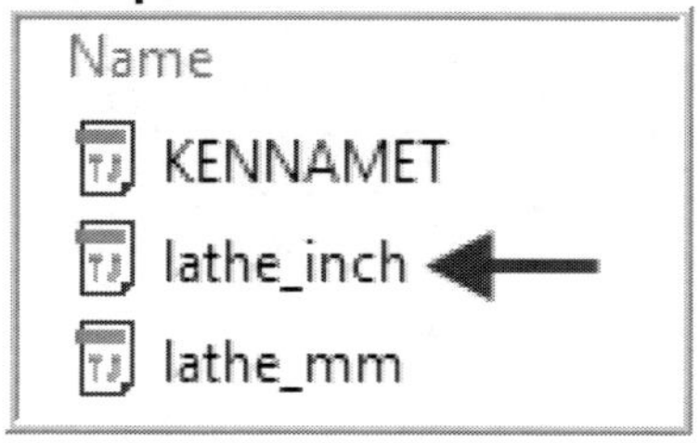

10. Select the boring bar **ID ROUGH MIN .1875 – 75 DEGREE**.

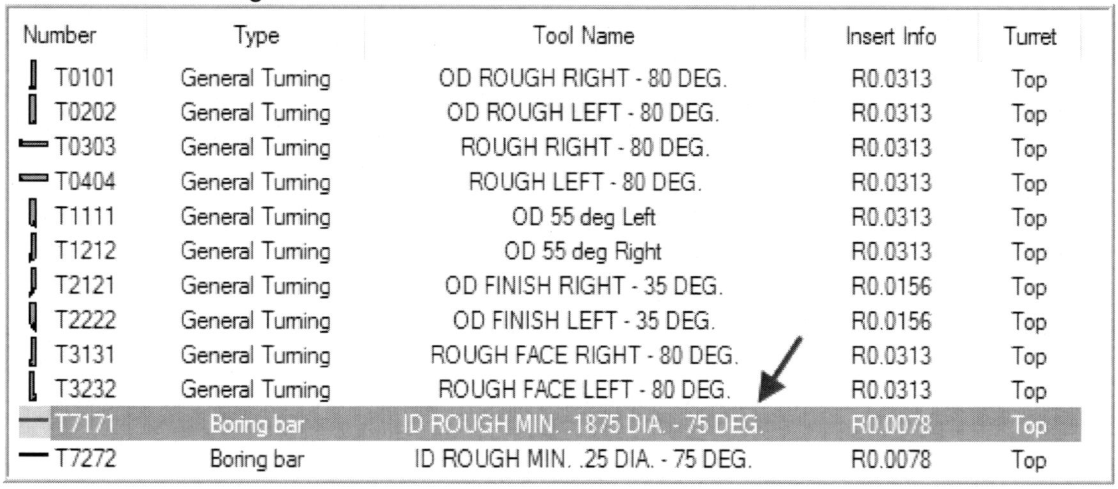

Number	Type	Tool Name	Insert Info	Turret
T0101	General Turning	OD ROUGH RIGHT - 80 DEG.	R0.0313	Top
T0202	General Turning	OD ROUGH LEFT - 80 DEG.	R0.0313	Top
T0303	General Turning	ROUGH RIGHT - 80 DEG.	R0.0313	Top
T0404	General Turning	ROUGH LEFT - 80 DEG.	R0.0313	Top
T1111	General Turning	OD 55 deg Left	R0.0313	Top
T1212	General Turning	OD 55 deg Right	R0.0313	Top
T2121	General Turning	OD FINISH RIGHT - 35 DEG.	R0.0156	Top
T2222	General Turning	OD FINISH LEFT - 35 DEG.	R0.0156	Top
T3131	General Turning	ROUGH FACE RIGHT - 80 DEG.	R0.0313	Top
T3232	General Turning	ROUGH FACE LEFT - 80 DEG.	R0.0313	Top
T7171	Boring bar	ID ROUGH MIN. .1875 DIA. - 75 DEG.	R0.0078	Top
T7272	Boring bar	ID ROUGH MIN. .25 DIA. - 75 DEG.	R0.0078	Top

11. Select the **OK** button to exit the selection of this tool.

12. Make any necessary changes as shown below. **Coolant Flood** is set to **On**.

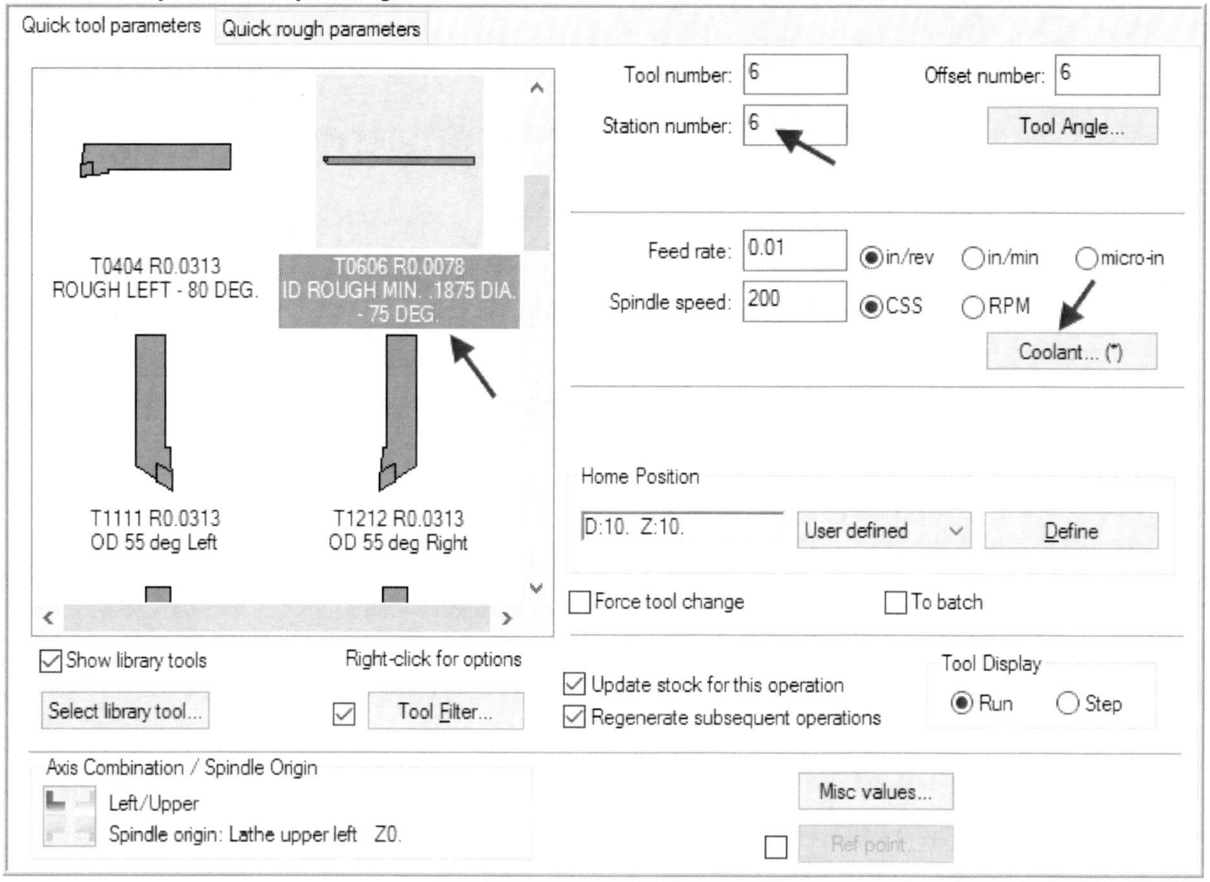

13. Select the **Quick rough parameters** page and make changes as shown below:

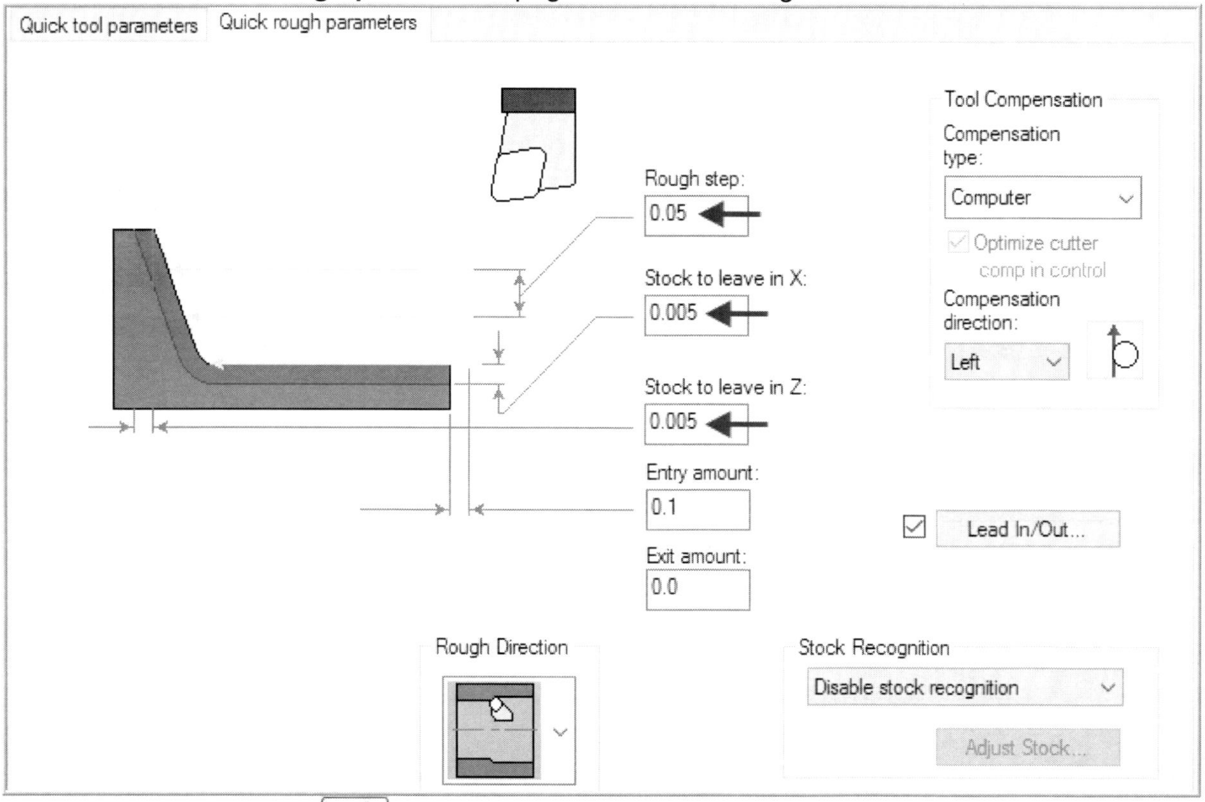

14. Select the **OK** button to exit Rough Parameters.

TASK 21:
FINISH THE BORE

➲ In this task you will use the same boring tool as used for the previous rouging operation.

1. Right mouse click in the white space of the **Toolpaths Manager** and select:
Lathe toolpaths**>Quick>Quick finish.**

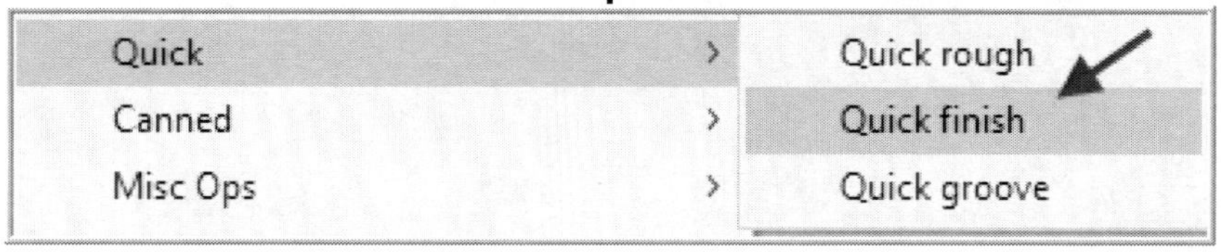

2. In the Quick Toolpath parameters page select **Tool #6 a boring tool ID ROUGH MIN .1875 DIA – 75 deg** and make any necessary changes as shown below. **Coolant Flood** is set to **On**.

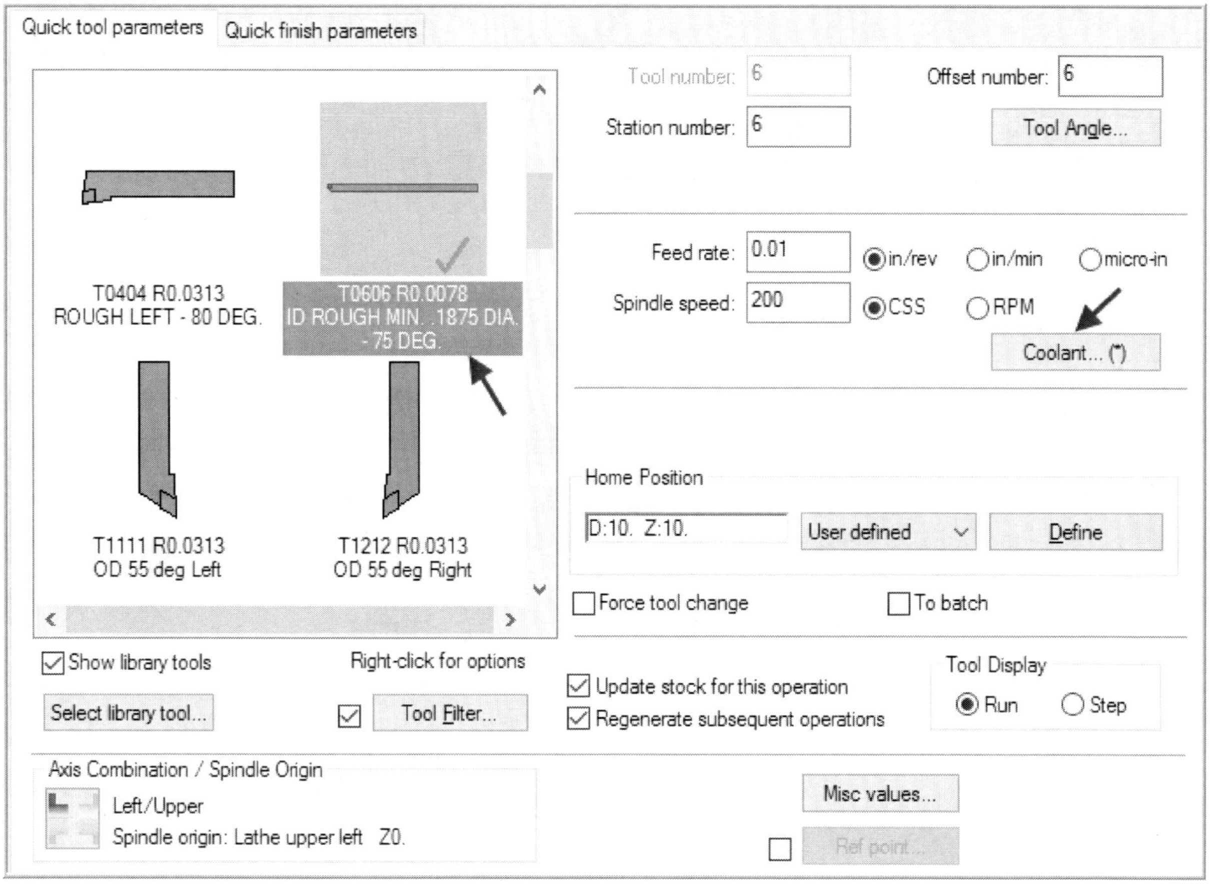

3. Select the **Quick finish parameters** page and make any necessary changes as shown below: Open up the drop down menu for operation and select the operation at the **bottom of the list**, this is the previous rough boring operation.
4. Open up the drop down menu for **Finish Direction** and set to **ID**.
5. **Compensation direction** is set to **Left**.

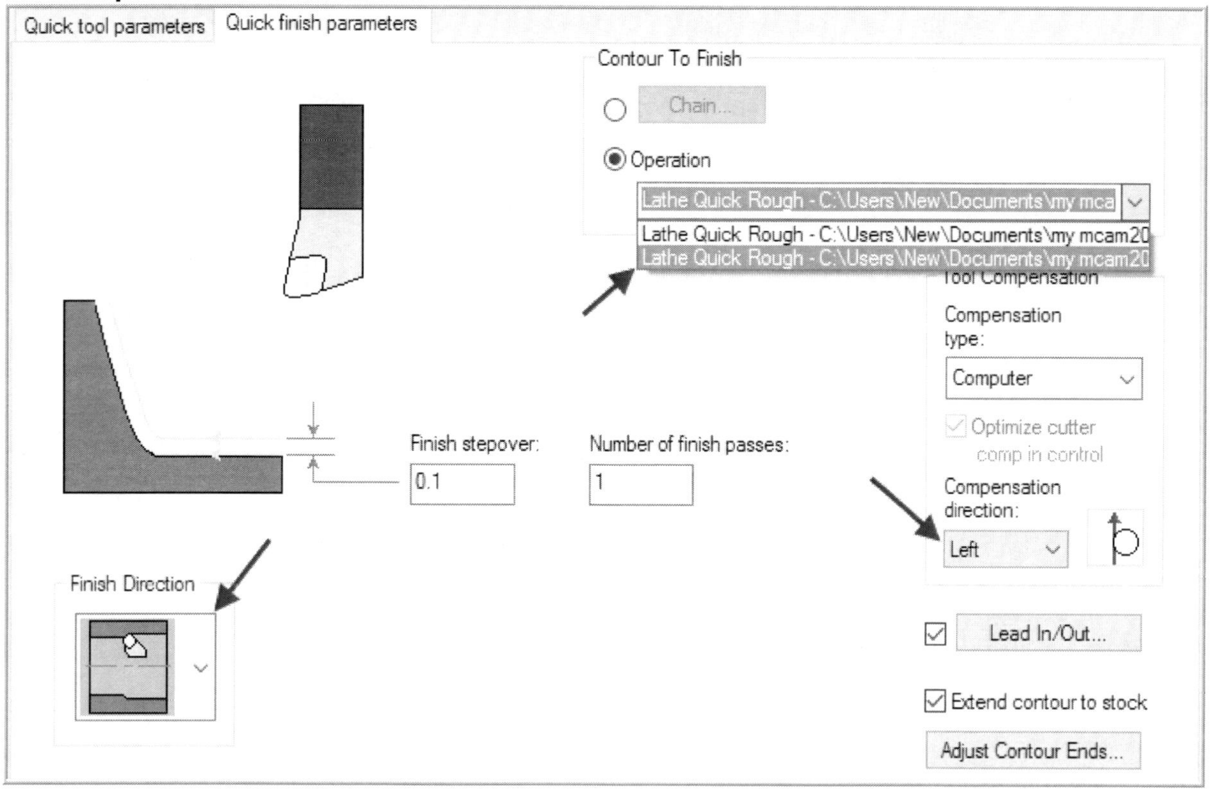

6. Select the **OK** button to exit Quick finish parameters.

TASK 22:
CUT THE GROOVES

➲ In this task you will use the Lathe Quick Groove toolpath using an **OD Groove Right Width .125 tool.**

Quick groove toolpaths
Lathe Quick groove toolpaths are useful when you need to create simple, symmetrical grooves. Quick groove toolpaths offer you a subset of Mastercam's grooving options.

Some of the differences between quick groove and regular groove toolpaths include:

- **No options** for chaining geometry or window chaining points. Your grooves must be defined by one, two, or three points.
- **Symmetrical grooves only**; no ability to individually set the chamfer or radius for each corner independently.
- **No tapered walls** or groove orientation options.
- **Fewer options** for roughing the groove walls, such as smoothing, separate stock to leave amounts for X and Z, and simpler pecking options.
- **Simpler lead in/out** and retract options.

If you need to use any of these features, consider creating a standard groove toolpath instead.

To create a quick groove toolpath, right mouse click in the Toolpaths Manager and select Quick, Groove from the menu. You will be prompted to select the corner points of the grooves (you can select multiple sets of points to define several grooves). Press Enter when you have identified all the grooves. Use the Lathe Quick groove dialog box to select a tool and enter the quick groove parameters.

1. Click on the **Select all operations** icon .
2. Now **toggle the display of the toolpaths** by selecting **ALT and T** on your keyboard to hide the toolpaths display.
3. Right mouse click in the white space of the **Toolpaths Manager** and select:
   Lathe toolpaths>Quick>Quick groove.

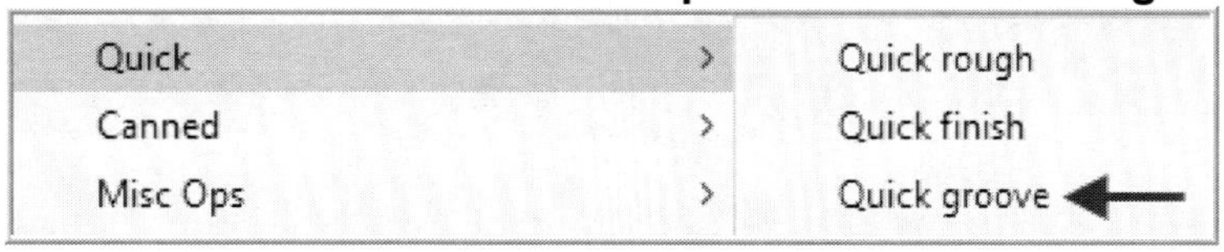

4. The **Groove Options** window appears. Click on the **2 Points** option as shown below.

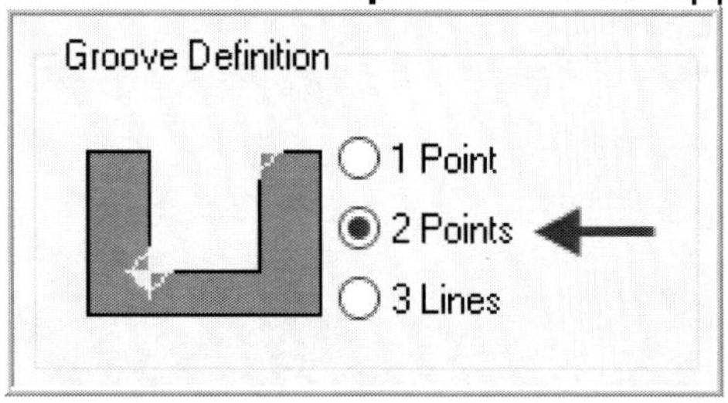

5. Click on **OK** .

6. Zoom in on the groove areas as shown below:
7. Select **Point 1 and Point 2** for the first groove. Move the cursor over the corner until the visual cue for End point displays and then click on the various points.
8. Then Select **Point 3 and Point 4** for the second groove.

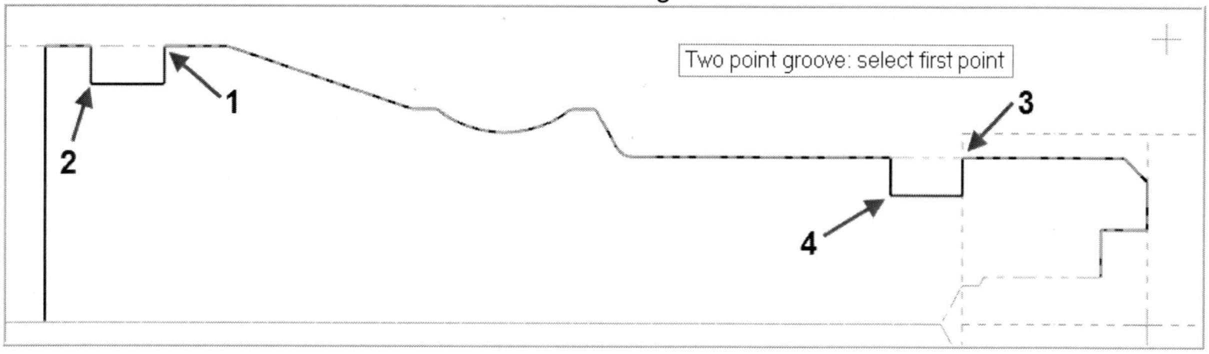

9. Press the **Enter** key when done.
10. Select **OD Groove Right Width .125** tool from the tool list and make any necessary changes as shown below. **Coolant Flood** is set to **On**.

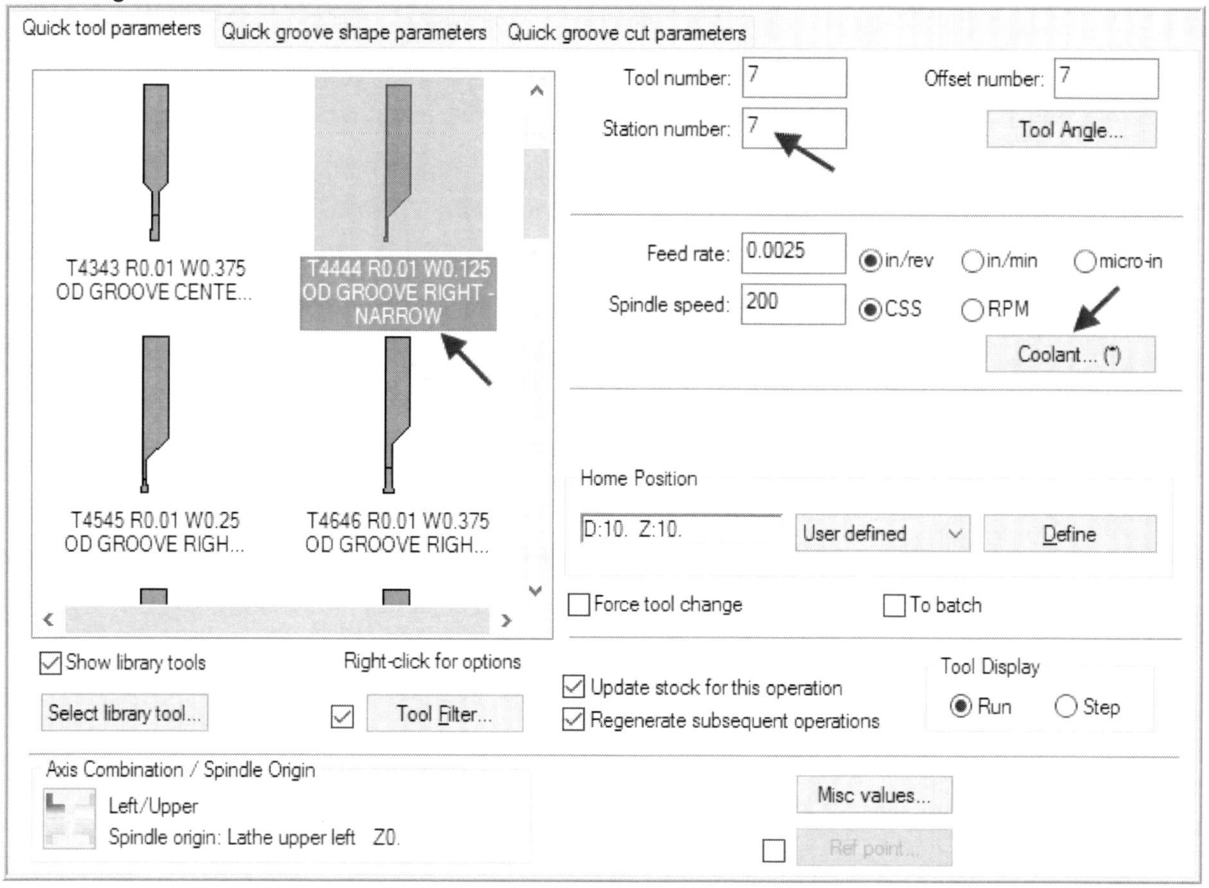

11. Select the **OK** button [OK] to exit as no further changes are required.

TASK 23:
CUT OFF THE PART

➲ In this task you will cut off the part using **OD Groove Right Width .125** the same tool as the previous grooving operation.

1. Right mouse click in the graphics area and click on the **Fit** icon .
2. Click on the **Expand gallery** down arrow to view additional options in the **General** toolpath section. In the **General** section select **Cutoff.**
3. When prompted to **Select cutoff boundary point** pick the end point of the line shown below: Move the cursor over the corner until the visual cue for End point displays and then click on this point.

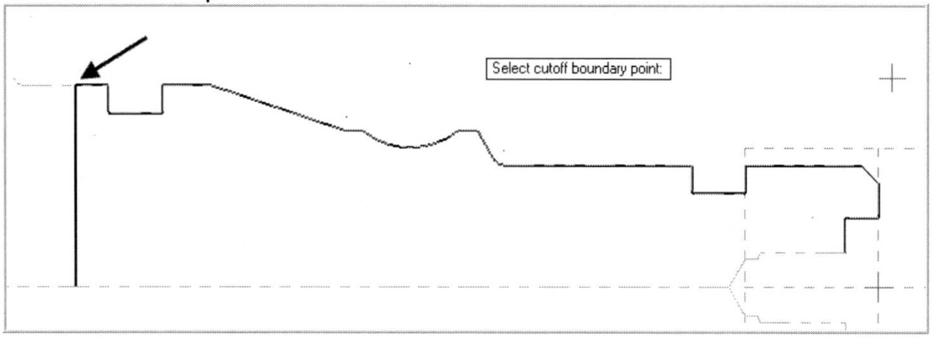

4. Select **OD GROOVE RIGHT WIDTH .125** tool from the tool list and make any necessary changes as shown below. **Coolant Flood** is set to **On**.

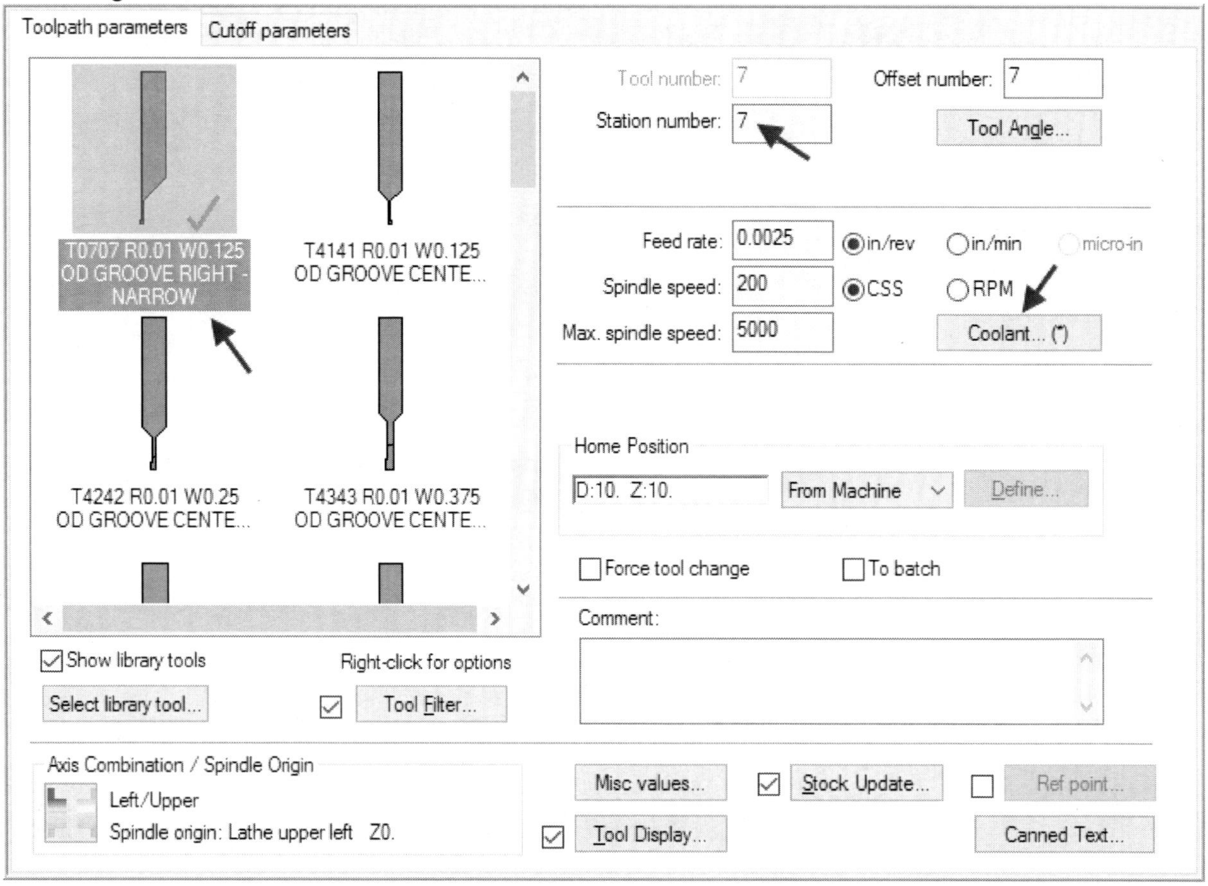

5. Still on the **Toolpath parameters** page click on the Stock Update button .

6. Ensure **Keep both pieces** is activated.

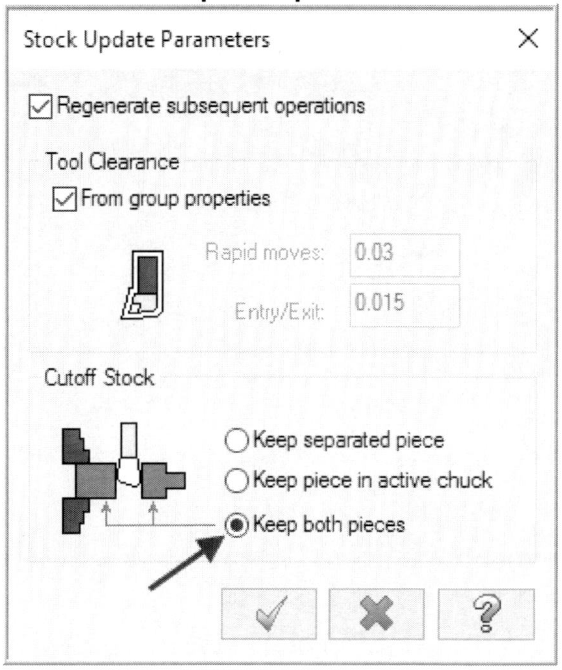

7. Select the **Cutoff parameters** page and make sure the settings are as shown below.

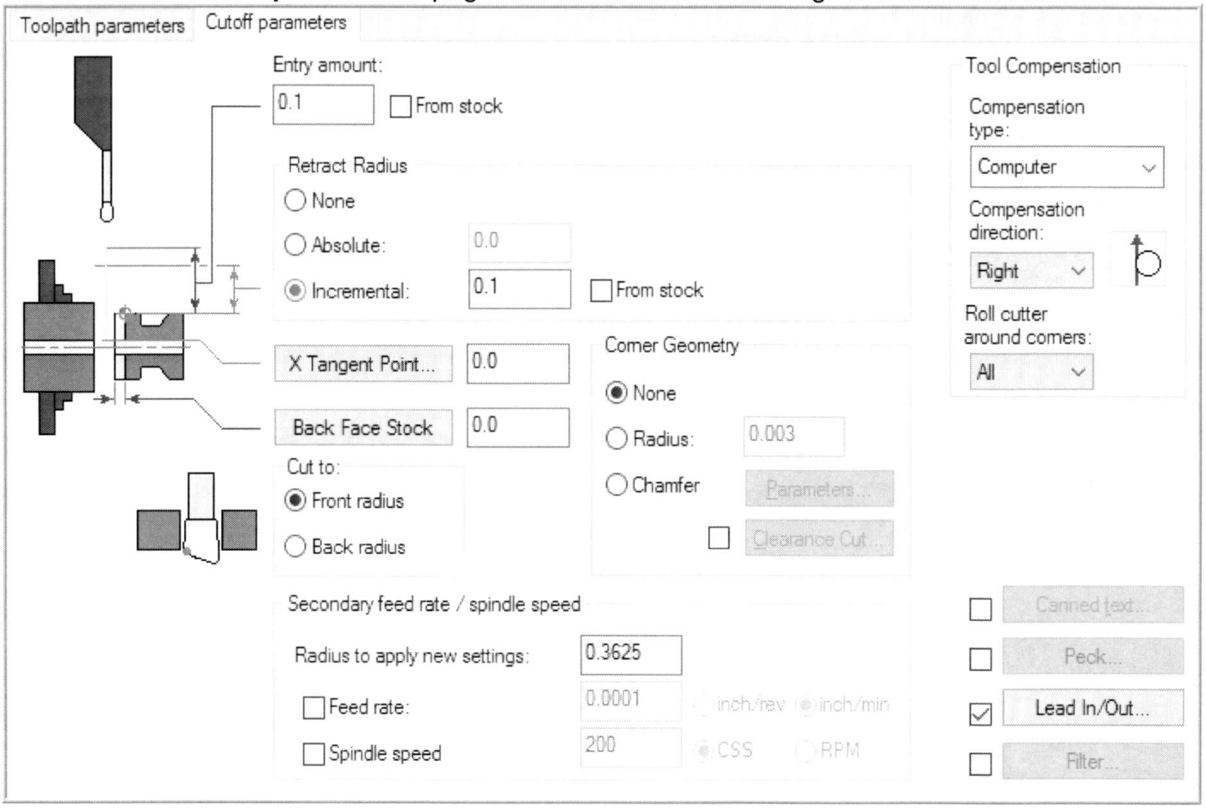

8. Select the **OK** button  to exit **Lathe Cutoff parameters.**

TASK 24:
VERIFY THE TOOLPATH

➲ Mastercam's Verify utility allows you to use solid models to simulate the machining of a part. The model created by the verification represents the surface finish, and shows collisions, if any exist.

1. Right mouse click in the graphics area and click on the **Fit** icon .
2. In the Toolpaths Manager pick all the operations to Verify by picking the Select All icon .
3. Select the **Verify selected operations** icon shown below:

4. **Maximize** the Backplot/Verify window if required.
5. Now select the **Home** Tab if required.

6. Activate the options shown below in the **Visibility** section of the Home tab. **Initial Stock not** activated.

7. At the top of the screen select the **View** tab, the Isometric icon and then select **Fit**.

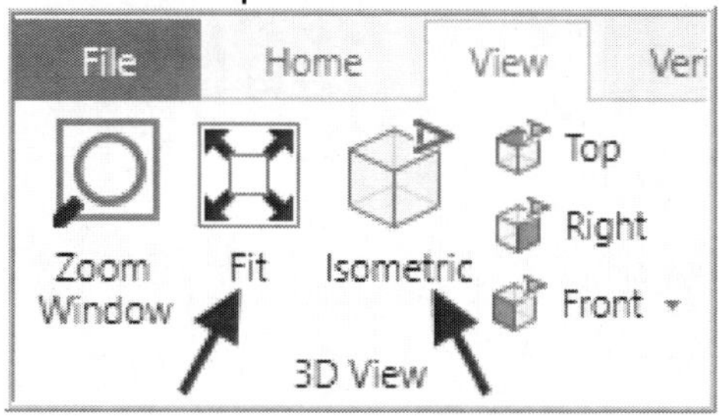

8. Select the **Verify** tab and activate the **Color Loop** to change the color of the tools for the verified part.

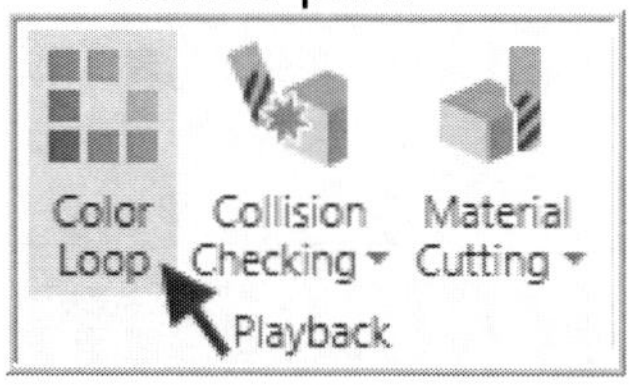

9. In the In the lower part of the screen now set the run **Speed** to slow by moving the slider bar pointer over to the left as shown below.

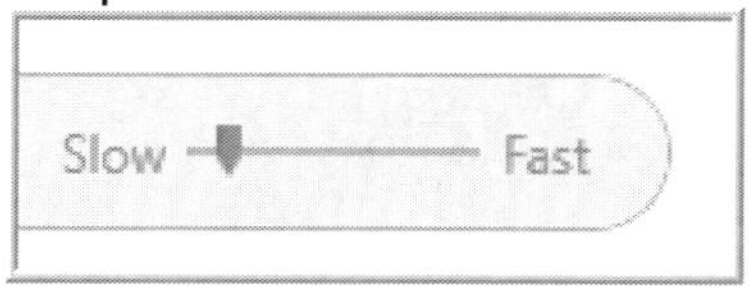

10. Now select the **Play Simulation** button to review the toolpaths.

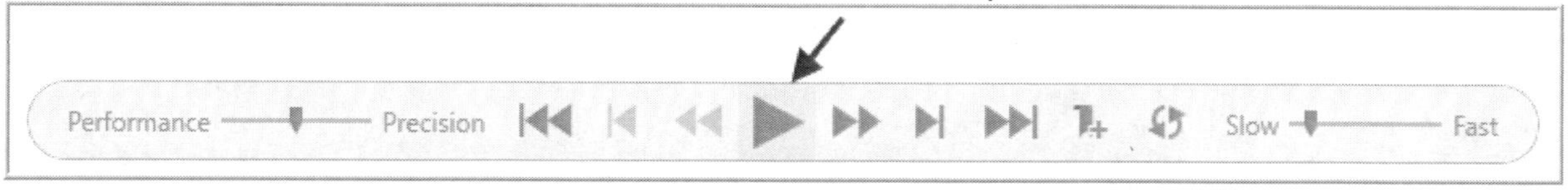

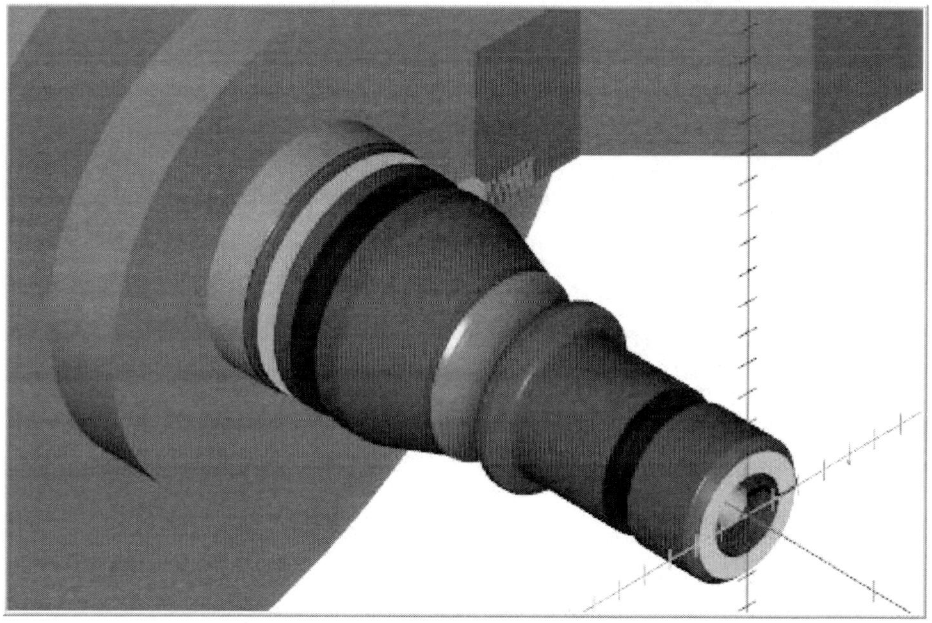

11. Select the **Close** button  in the top right hand corner to exit Verify.

TASK 25:
SAVE THE UPDATED MASTERCAM FILE

1. Select the **Save** icon from the **Quick Access** toolbar at the top left of the screen.

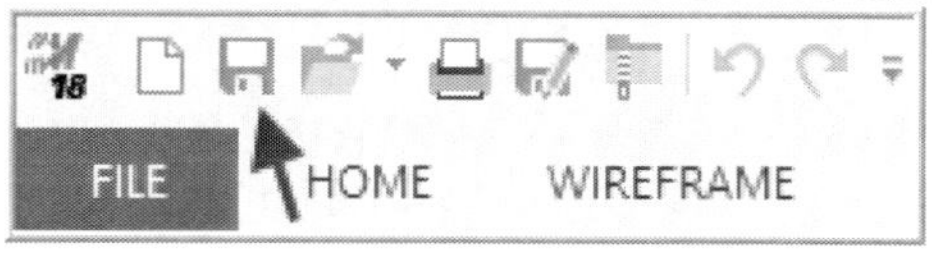

TASK 26:
POST AND CREATE THE CNC CODE FILE

1. Ensure all the operations are selected by picking the **Select All** icon  from the Toolpaths manager.
2. Select the **Post selected operations** button from the Toolpaths manager.

➲ **Please Note:** If you cannot see **G1** click on the right pane of the Toolpaths manager window and expand the window to the right.

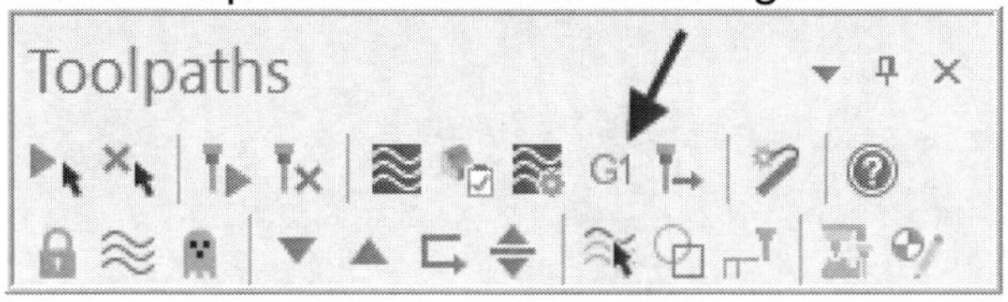

3. In the Post processing window, make the necessary changes as shown below:

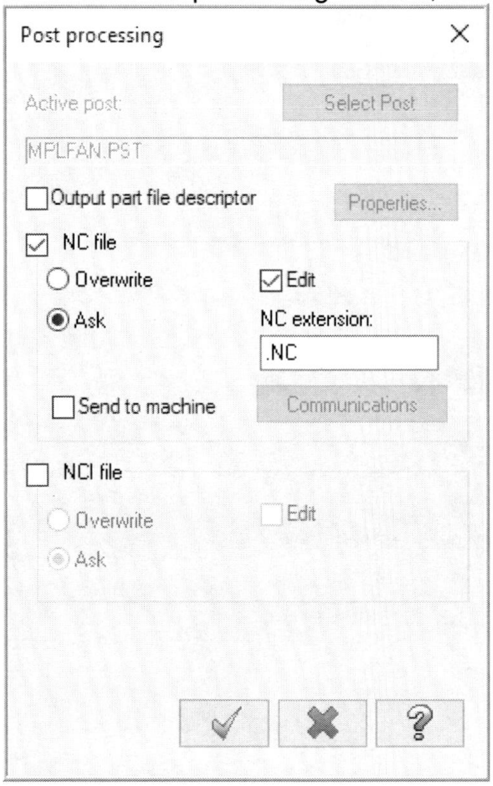

About Post Processing

NC file:
Select this option to save the NC file. The file name and extension are stored in the machine group properties for the selected operation. If you are posting operations from different machine groups or Mastercam files, or batch processing, Mastercam will create several files according to the settings for each machine group.

Edit:
When checked, automatically launches the default text editor with the file displayed so that you can review or modify it.

4. Select the OK button  to continue.

5. Ensure the same name as your Mastercam part file name is displayed in the **NC File name** field.
6. Select the **Save** button.
7. The CNC code file opens up in the default editor.

Lathe-Lesson-7.NC ×

```
(MATERIAL - ALUMINUM INCH - 6061)
G20
(TOOL - 1 OFFSET - 1)
(OD ROUGH RIGHT - 80 DEG.  INSERT - CNMG-432)
G0 T0101
G18
G97 S449 M03
G0 G54 X1.7 Z0. M8
G50 S3600
G96 S200
G99 G1 X-.0625 F.01
G0 Z.1
X1.2897
Z.2
G1 Z.1
Z-2.248
X1.4665 Z-2.52
G18 G3 X1.47 Z-2.5313 I-.0345 K-.0112
G1 Z-2.7062
```

8. Select the × in the top right corner to exit the CNC editor.

➲ This completes Lathe-Lesson-7.

LATHE-LESSON-7 EXERCISE

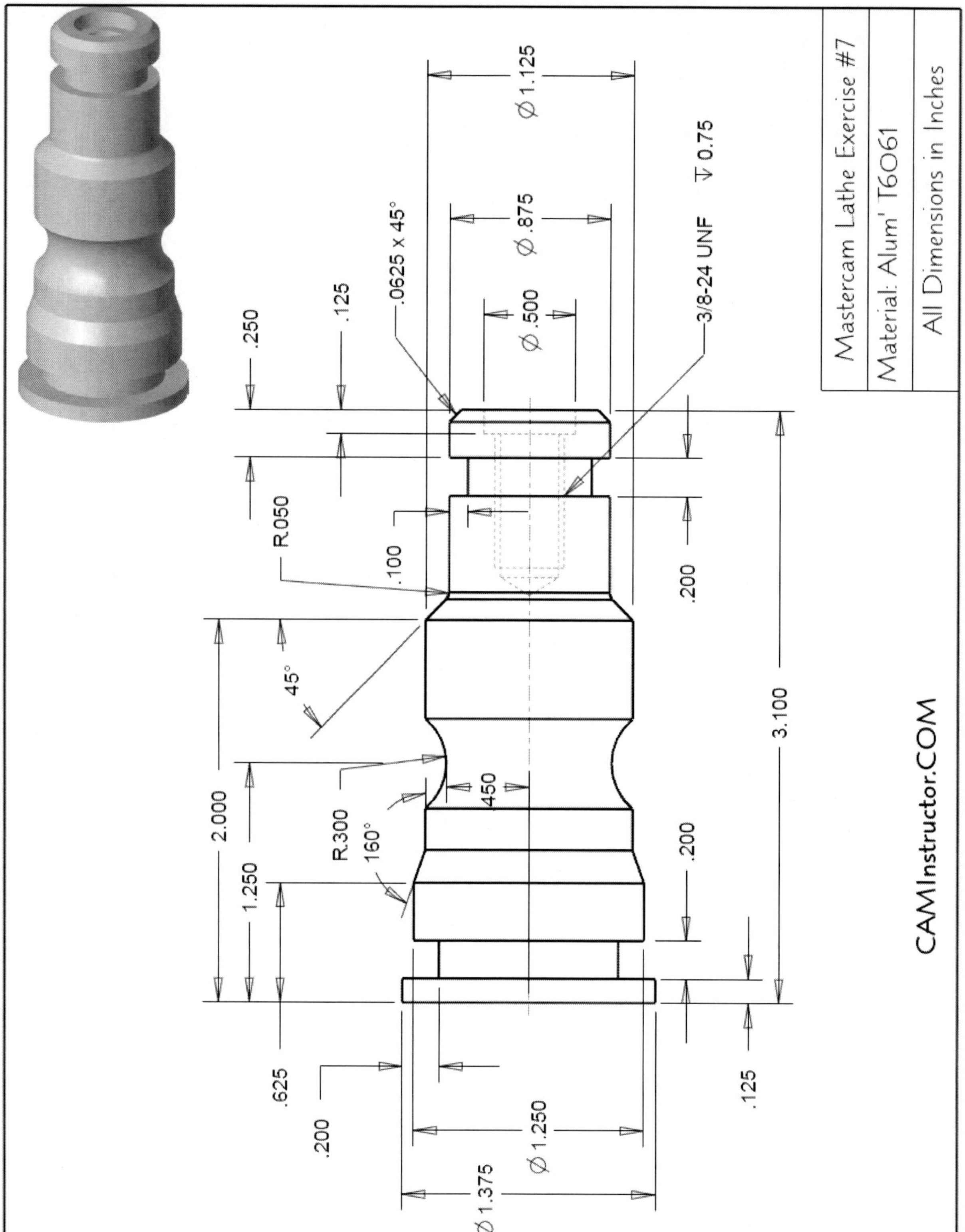

Mastercam® 2018

TRAINING

GUIDE

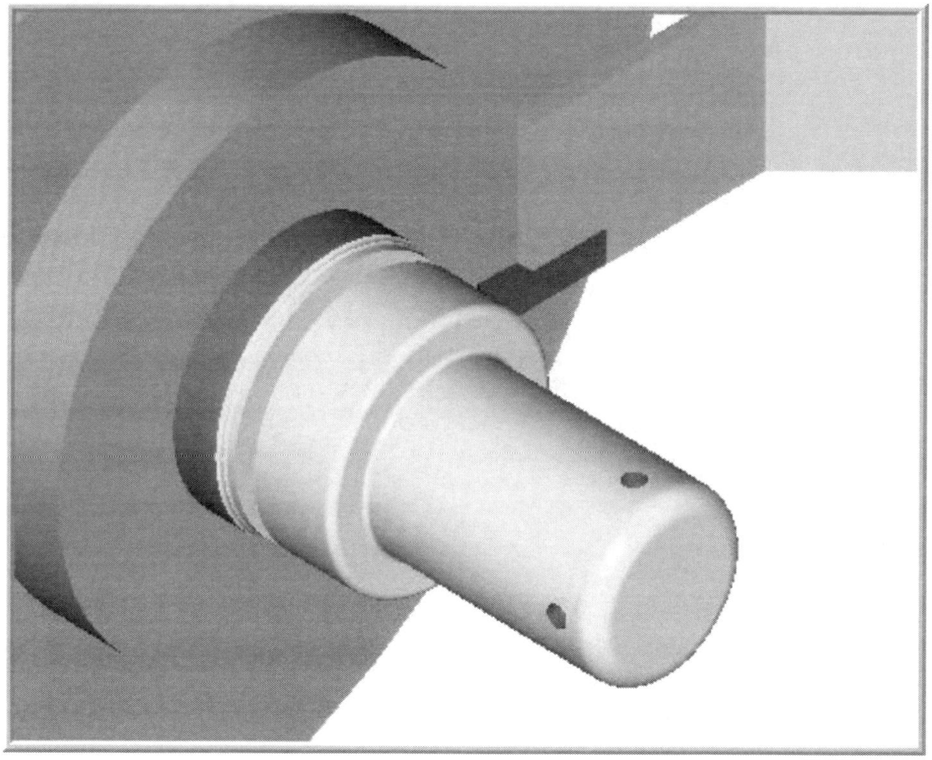

LATHE-LESSON-8

C-AXIS PART

camInstructor

Objectives

You will open an existing file: Lathe Lesson 1 and create the geometry for Lathe-Lesson-8. If you do not have the Mastercam file for Lathe Lesson 1 it is available Online. The file can be downloaded in one of the steps in the Lesson. The geometry creation for this part will involve the creation of a series of points that will be used to machine the four holes using the C-Axis.

You will then generate a toolpath to machine the part on a CNC lathe. This lesson covers the following topics:

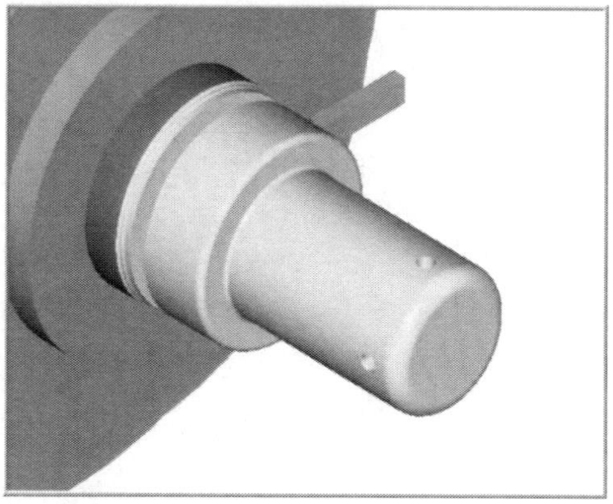

➲ **Create a 2-dimensional drawing by:**
Creating points.

➲ **Establish Stock and Chuck settings:**
Stock size.
Chuck Configuration.
Material for the part.
Feed calculation.

➲ **Generate a C-Axis lathe toolpath consisting of:**
C-Axis Drill.

➲ **Inspect the toolpath using Mastercam's Verify and Backplot by:**
Launching the Verify function to machine the part on the screen.
Using Backplot to identify the correctness of the toolpaths.
Generating the NC- code.

LATHE-LESSON-8 DRAWING

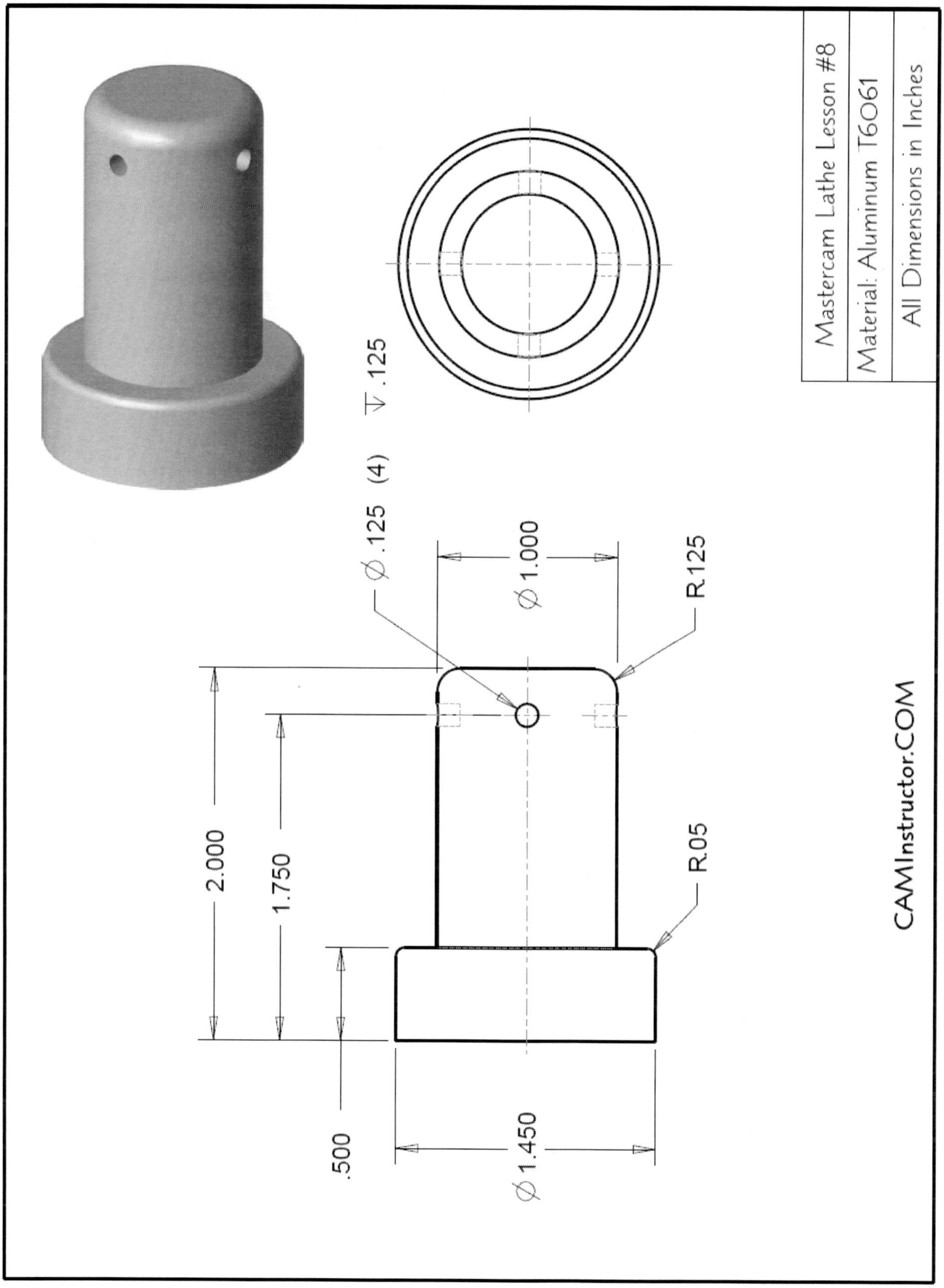

TOOL LIST

Three tools will be used to create this part.

➲ **Tool #1 Face, Rough and Finish the outside diameters**
Holder: Outside Diameter Rough Right Hand - DCGNR-164D.
Insert: 80 Degree Diamond Insert – CNMG-432.

➲ **Tool #2 Cutoff the part**
Holder: Outside Diameter Cut-off Right Hand.
Insert: 0.125" Wide.

➲ **Tool #3 Drill the part**
Center cutting End Mill 0.125" diameter

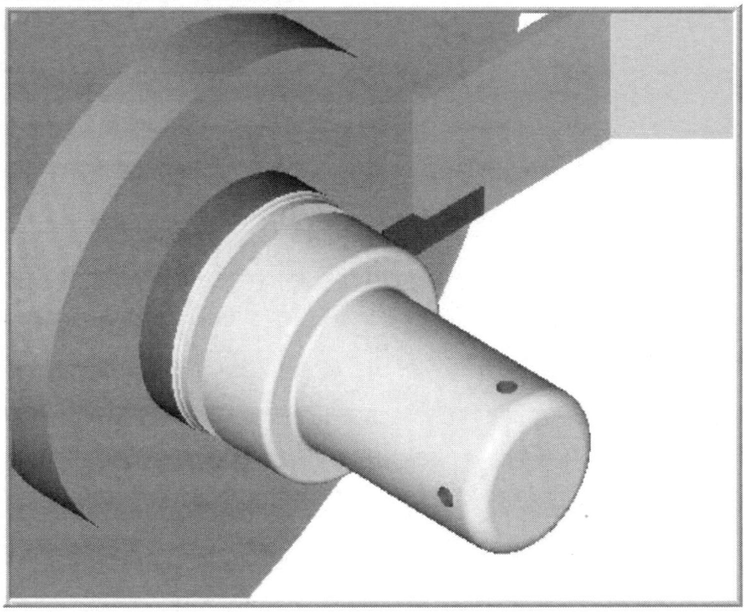

LATHE - LESSON - 8 - THE PROCESS

Geometry Creation

TASK 1: Duplicate Lathe-Lesson-1 for Lathe-Lesson-8
TASK 2: Setting the Environment
TASK 3: Create the Points
TASK 4: Save the Drawing

Toolpath Creation

TASK 5: Drill the Points using C-Axis toolpath
TASK 6: Backplot the Toolpath
TASK 7: Verify the Toolpath
TASK 8: Save the Updated Mastercam File
TASK 9: Post and Create the CNC Code File

Geometry Creation

TASK 1:
DUPLICATE LESSON-1 FOR LESSON-8

In this lesson you will use Lathe-Lesson-1 to complete Lathe-Lesson-8. If you do not have the Mastercam file for Lathe Lesson 1 it is available Online. The file can be downloaded in one of the steps in the Lesson.

1. Click on **File>Open>Lathe-Lesson-1.**
2. The screen should look like the one below:

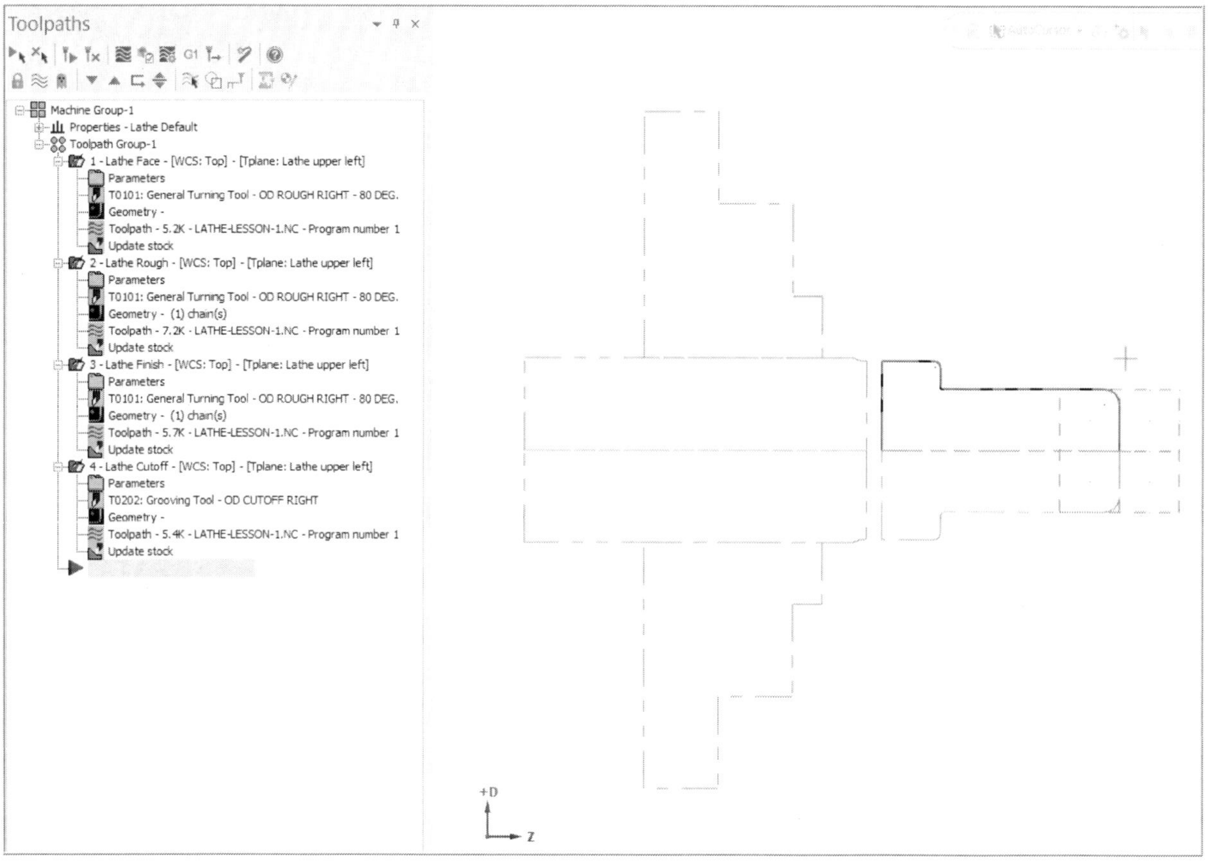

3. Select **File.**
4. Select **Save As**.
5. Click on the **Browse** icon.
6. In the **"File name"** box, type **"Lathe-Lesson-8".**
7. Browse to an appropriate location.
8. Select the **Save** button to save the file and complete this function**.**

TASK 2:
SETTING THE ENVIRONMENT

Before starting the geometry creation you should set up the grid and machine type as outlined in the **Setting the Environment** section at the beginning of this text:

1. Set up the Grid. This will help identify the location of the origin.
2. To set the machine type to **the C Axis Slant Bed Lathe** select the plus in front of **Properties** to expand the Machine Group Properties.

3. Click on **Files** as shown below:

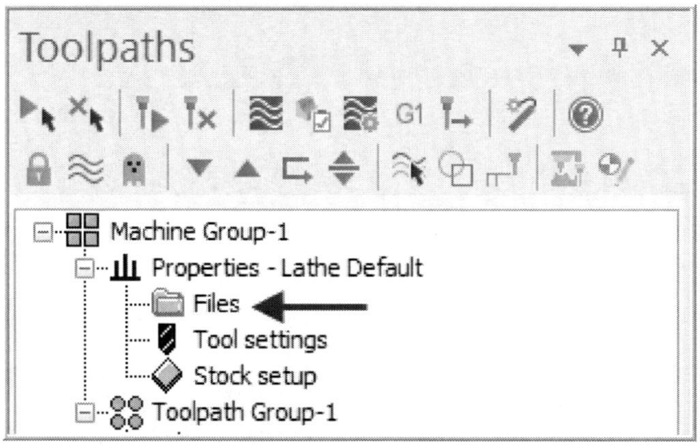

4. Click on the **Replace** icon as shown below:

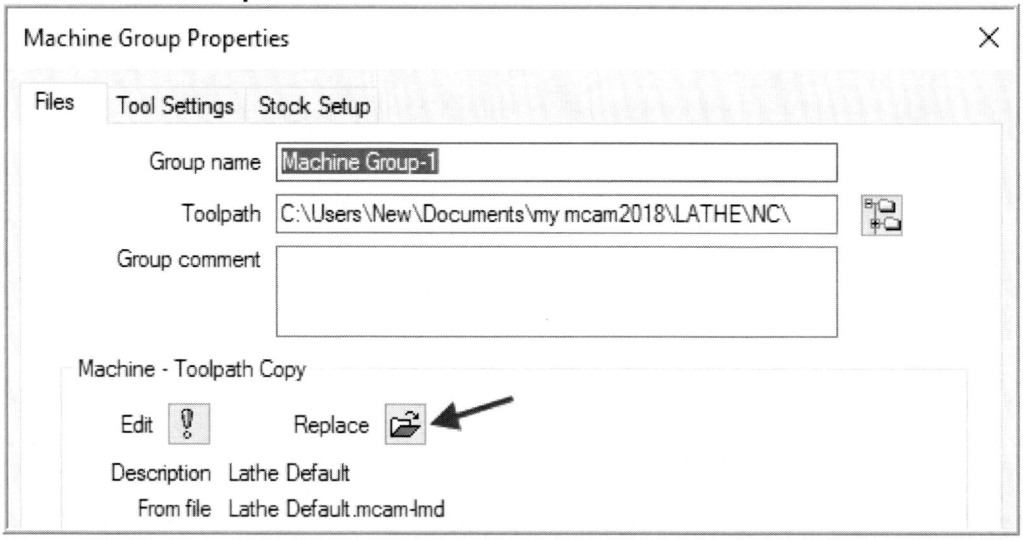

5. Select **Lathe C-AXIS SLANT BED** from the list of files and then click on **Open**.

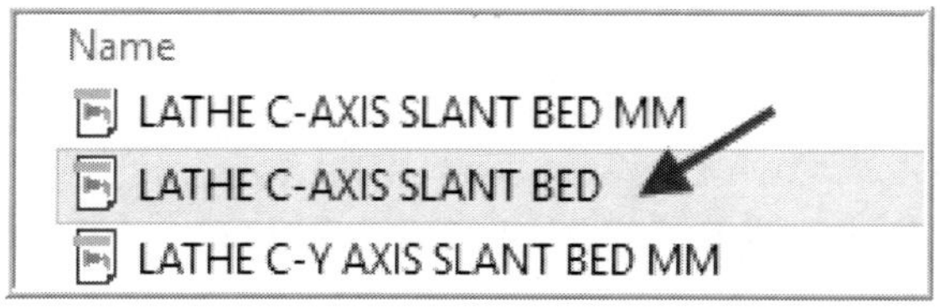

6. Click on the OK icon in the **Replace Group Machine** window.

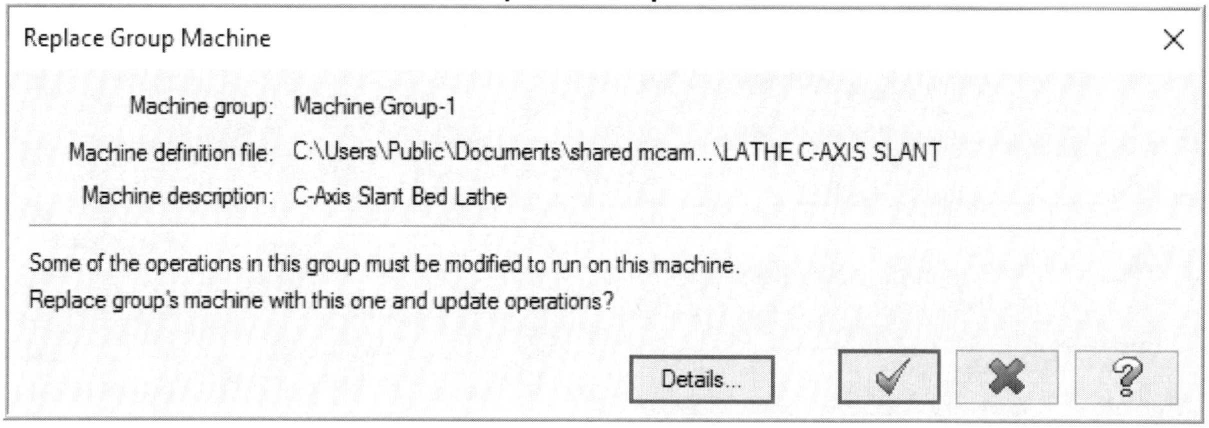

7. Click on the OK icon once again at the Machine group Properties page to exit.

8. Select the Regenerate all dirty operations button to remove the red X from the operations.

TASK 3:
CREATE THE POINTS

1. Select the **Home** tab and click on **Wireframe Color** down arrow in the **Attributes** section.
2. In the **Default Colors** section click on the **Cyan** color. **Note:** this will change the color of the points that you will be creating.

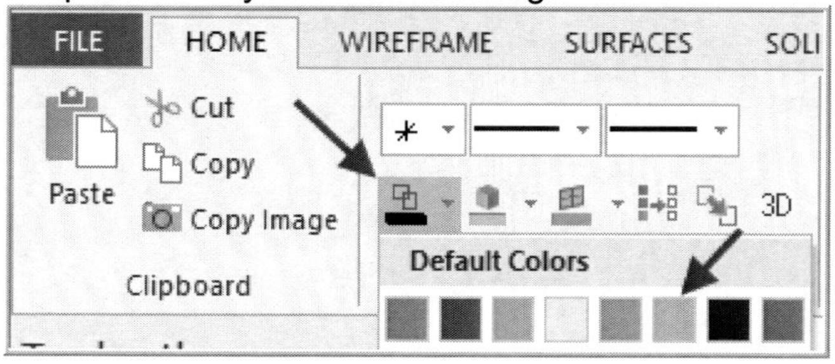

3. Click on the **Select all operations** icon .
4. Now **toggle the display of the toolpaths** by selecting **ALT and T** on your keyboard to hide the toolpaths display.
5. Select the **WIREFRAME** tab and in the **Points** section click on **Point Position**.

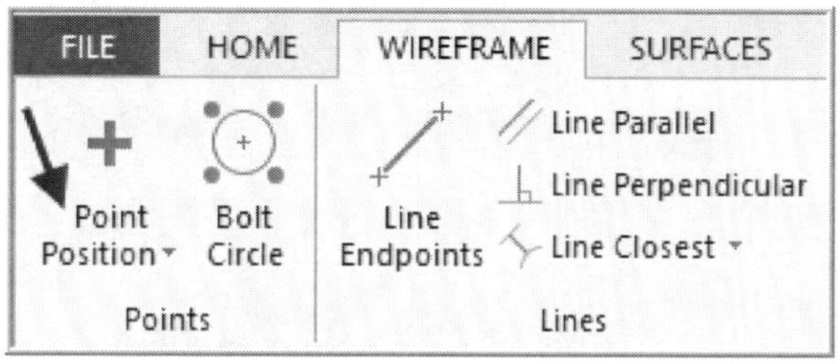

➲ On the graphics screen you are prompted: **Create point position** and the **Point Position** panel appears.

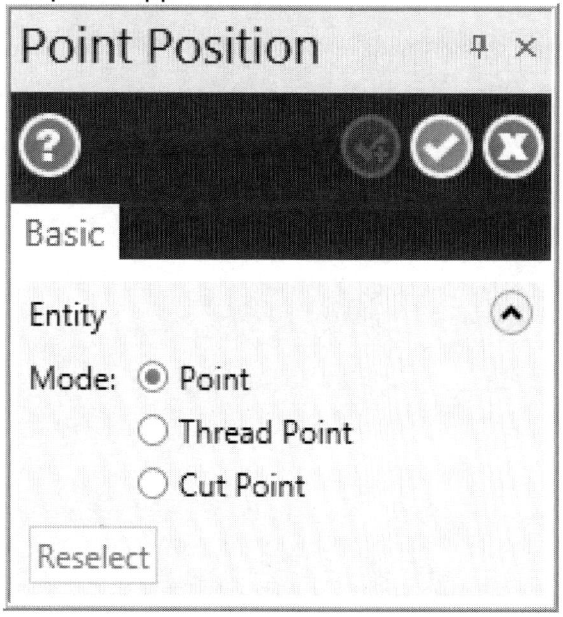

Point Position
Use this function to create a point, cut point, or thread point.

You can change the position of a point as long as it remains live.

Click the **Reselect** button, and click the new position in the graphics window.

6. You are now prompted to **"Create a point position"**. To satisfy this prompt **just type** the coordinate, **1.0,-0.25**. As you begin to type the **Fastpoint** opens. Hit the **Enter** key when done.

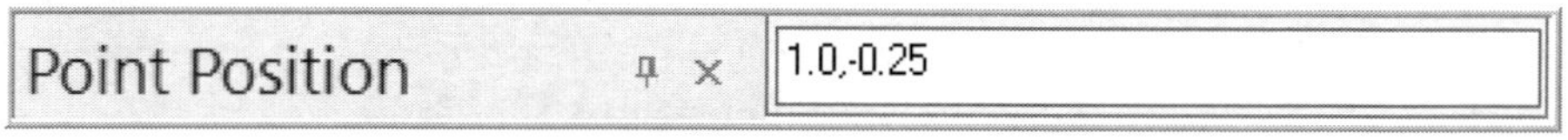

7. Click on the **OK** icon  to complete this feature.

➲ A point will be displayed on the geometry like the diagram shown below:

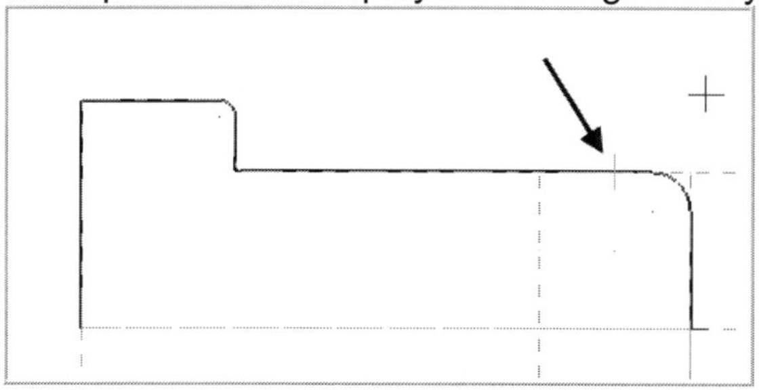

7. Right mouse click in the graphics area and click on **Isometric**.
8. Right mouse click in the graphics area and click on the **Fit** icon .
9. Selects the **TRANSFORM** tab and in the **Position** section select **Rotate**.

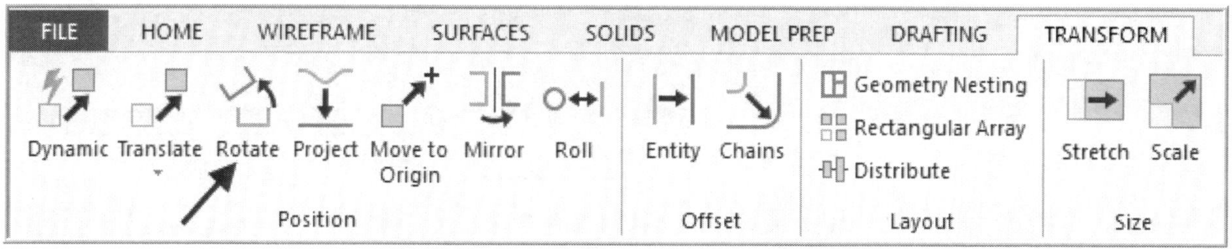

10. You are prompted to Select **entities**. First select the **Select only advanced** button on the right of your screen.

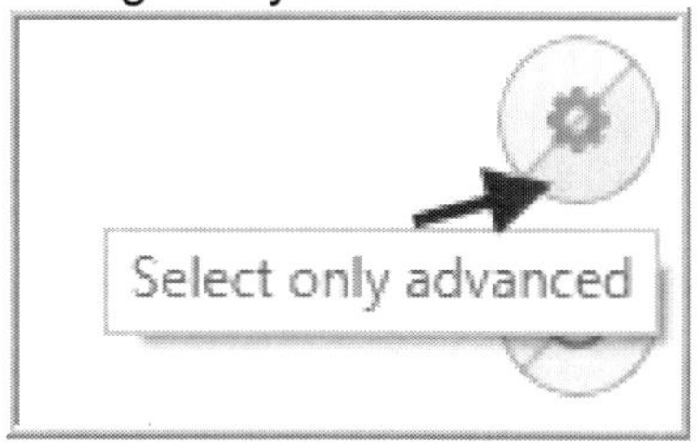

Select All and Select Only dialog boxes
Select the **left side** to open the **Select All** dialog box and select the **right side** to open the **Select Only** dialog box.
These two dialog boxes look very similar. The main difference is that the Select All dialog box has an extra section (Options buttons) at the top that does not appear in the Select Only dialog box.

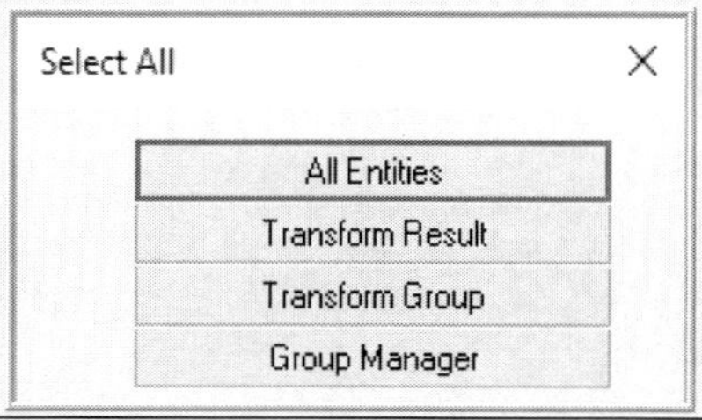

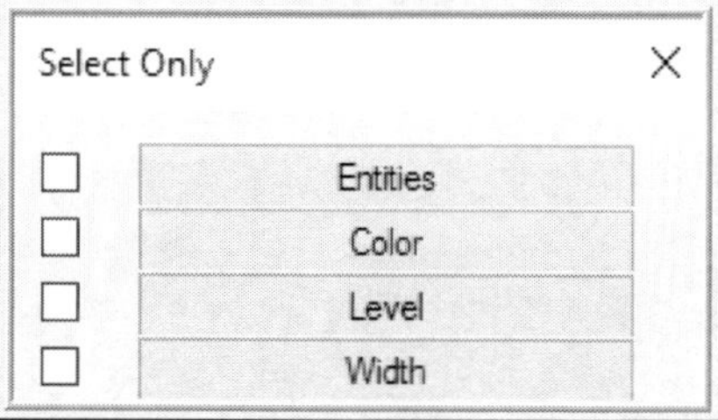

11. Activate checkmark for **Entities**. Click on **Points** and **OK** as shown below: **Note**: this will ensure only the point is selected and not the line attached to the point.

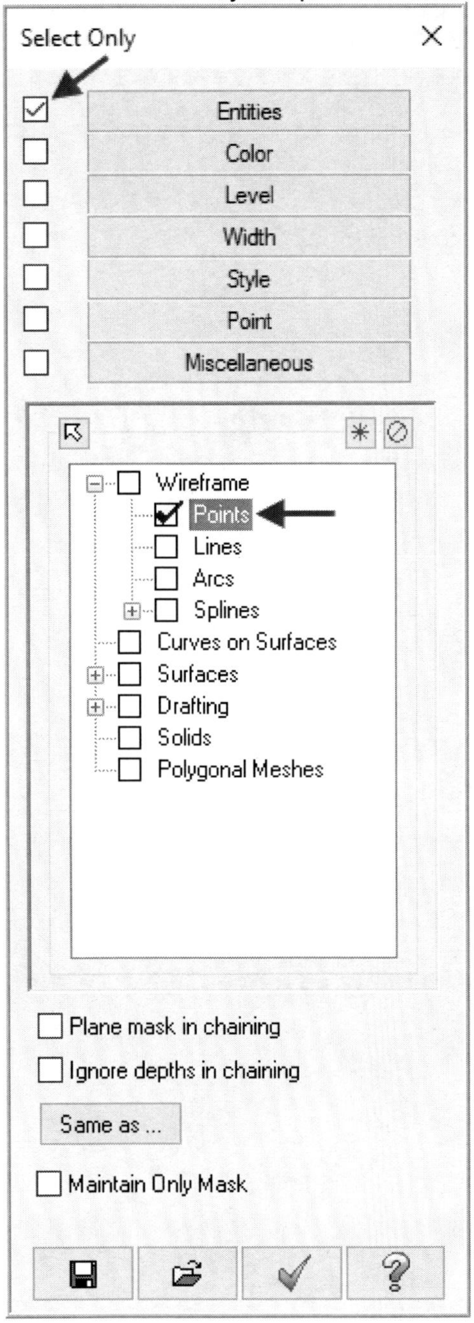

Select Only dialog box
Use this dialog box to set selection masks, which restrict entity selection to defined sets of criteria.

Set the criteria and choose the OK button. This closes the dialog box and lets you manually select any entities in the graphics window that meet the criteria.

This masking method prohibits you from selecting entities that do not match your criteria.

Entities button
Restricts the entities that you can select based on the type of entity.
When you click the Entities checkbox or button, the corresponding entity selections display in the Criteria List area.

Choosing an entity type in the Criteria List area will disable selection of any other type of entity.

For example, choosing Wireframe enables you to select points, lines, arcs, and splines but disables the selection of surfaces, solids, and other entity non-wireframe types.

12. Select the **Point** as shown below:

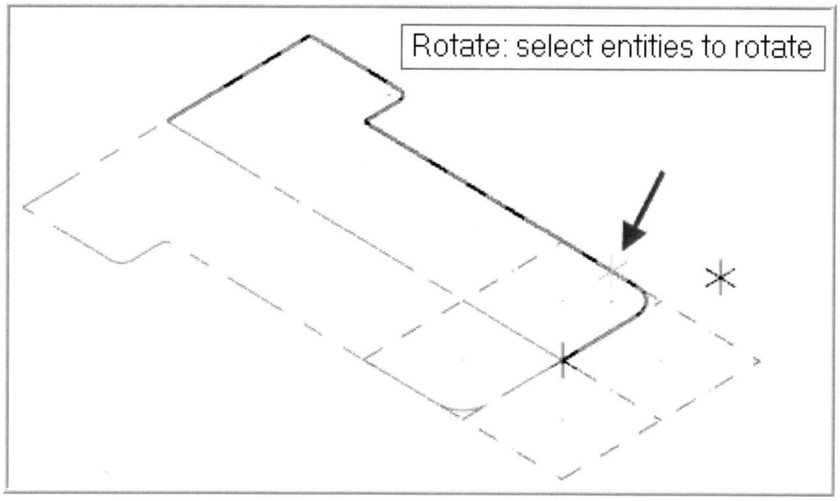

13. To move onto the next step you now need to pick the **End Selection** icon.

14. The **Rotate** panel appears. Make the changes as shown in the diagram below.

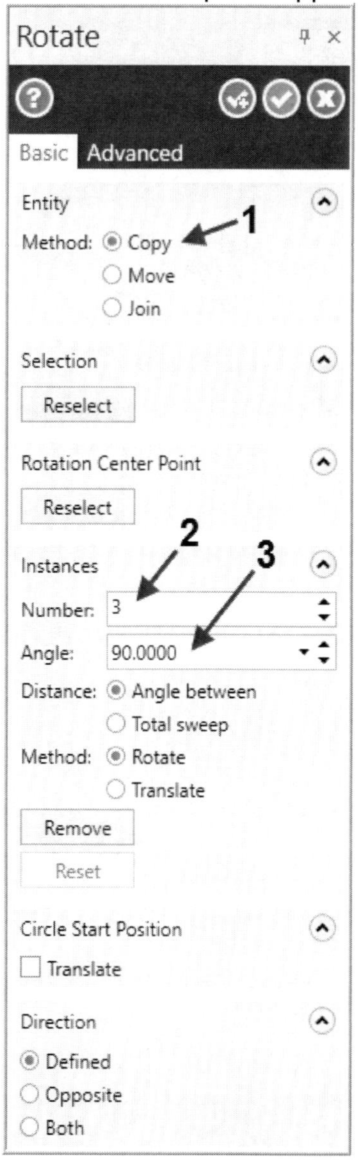

#1 Copy
Copies the points rather than moves them.

#2 Instances Number
The number of points to add, in this case we will be adding **3** more points.

#3 Angle
How many degrees each point is rotated from the other point.
Since a circle is 360 degrees and we are putting 4 points equally spaced around the diameter of the part, then each point will be **90 degrees**.
(360 / 4 = 90)

15. Right mouse click in the graphics area and click on the **Fit** icon.

➲ Notice the points are in the **wrong position** as shown in **Diagram 1** below. They should be in the position as shown in **Diagram 2** below.

Diagram 1 – Incorrect Point Position

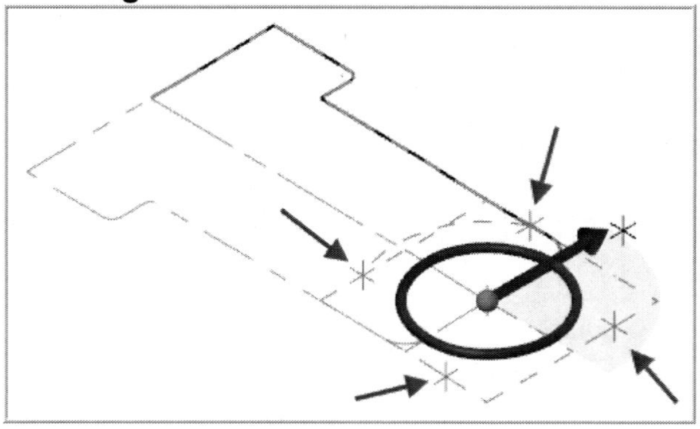

Diagram 2 – Correct Point Position

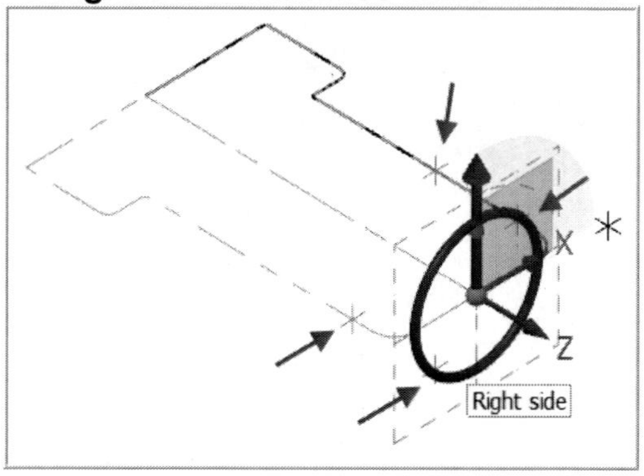

To put the points in the correct position you will now set the **Construction Plane** to **Right Side**. Changing the **Construction Plane** to **Right** will ensure the points are created around the diameter of the workpiece. Notice how the points change to the proper position.

16. Select the **View** tab and toggle the **Planes Manager** to display.

17. Now click in the **C column (Construction Plane)** for the **Right side** plane. The view is still set to Isometric but construction of the geometry will now take place on the Right side plane.

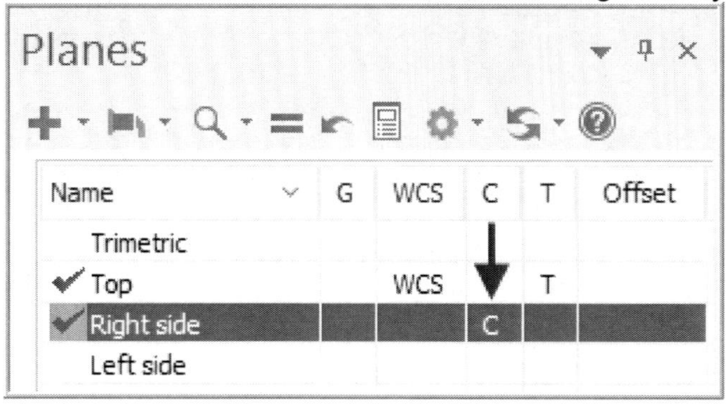

18. Click on **OK** in the **Rotate** panel.

19. Right mouse click in the graphics area and click on the **Clear Colors** icon.
20. Right mouse click in the graphics area and click on **Right (WCS)**. Notice the location of the points.
21. Right mouse click in the graphics area and click on **Isometric**.

22. Right mouse click in the graphics area and click on **Dynamic Rotation.**
23. When prompted to **Pick a point to begin dynamics** select the **origin** of the part.
24. After picking the origin move the mouse around to view the geometry at a different angle. Notice the location of the points now in the correct position. When finished with Dynamic Rotation **"Click a mouse button when done"**.
25. Right mouse click in the graphics area and click on **Top**.
26. Right mouse click in the graphics area and click on the **Fit** icon .
27. In the **Planes Manager** set the **C column** (Construction Plane) and **T column** (Tool Plane) to the **+D +Z Plane**. Just click in the C and T columns in the **+D +Z** row.

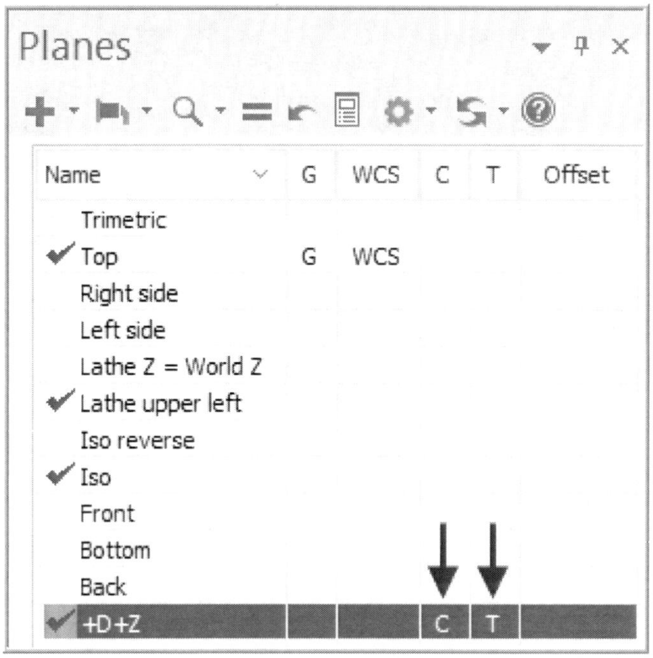

28. Select the **Close** button in the top right hand corner to close the Planes Manager.

TASK 4:
SAVE THE UPDATED MASTERCAM FILE

1. Select the **Save** icon from the **Quick Access** toolbar at the top left of the screen.

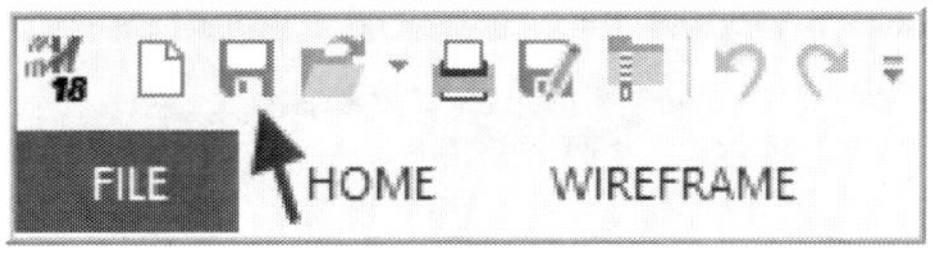

Toolpath Creation

TASK 5:
DRILL THE POINTS USING C-AXIS DRILL

1. Right mouse click in the graphics area and click on **Isometric**.
2. Right mouse click in the graphics area and click on the **Fit** icon.
3. In the Toolpaths Manager move the red **Insert arrow before the Cutoff operation** as shown below. Use the **Arrow icons** shown below right to position the Insert arrow up or down.

The insert arrow controls where new operations will be inserted.
Its default position is at the bottom of the list of operations

4. Select the **TURNING** tab at the top right side of the screen.
5. Click on the **Expand gallery** down arrow to view additional options in the **C-axis** toolpath section and select **C-axis Drill.**

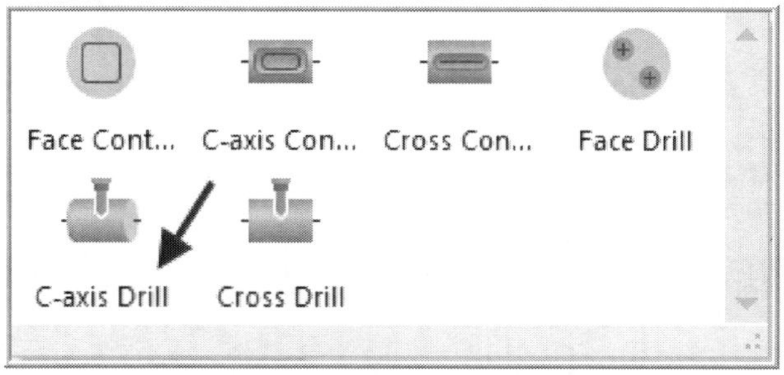

C-axis drill toolpaths
Use C-axis drill toolpaths in Mastercam Lathe to drill holes perpendicular to the part's spindle axis, as when drilling holes in a cylinder. You can choose points which are already in their correct 3D positions around the Z axis, or you can choose points which are in the top construction plane and let Mastercam roll them around the axis of rotation.

The toolpath is then created by converting the X coordinate of each point in the top Cplane to an angle about the Z axis. The position is determined by the rotary axis diameter entered in the in the Rotary Axis Control property page. The resulting toolpath is then displayed in its rolled state.

If the points are already in their correct 3D positions, you must check Unroll. Even if the points lie in different planes, you can select all the points that you want to drill at the same time without having to specify the tool plane for every hole.

C-axis drill toolpaths are similar to cross drill toolpaths. The difference is how they produce the rotary motion.

6. You are prompted to **Select Points, press Escape when finished**. Make sure the **Select Drill point position in graphics screen** button is selected as shown below:

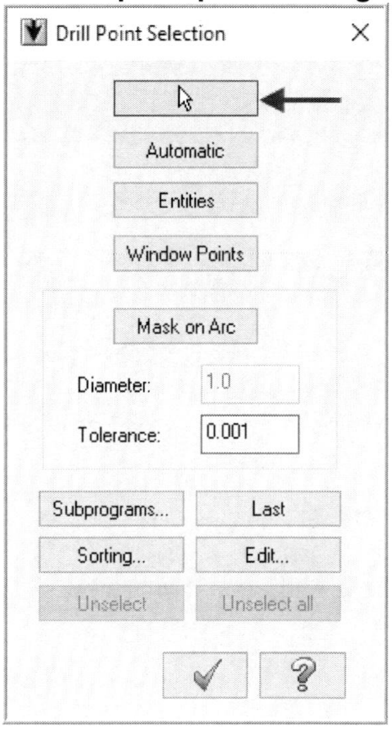

7. Click on the **4 points** in the order as shown below.

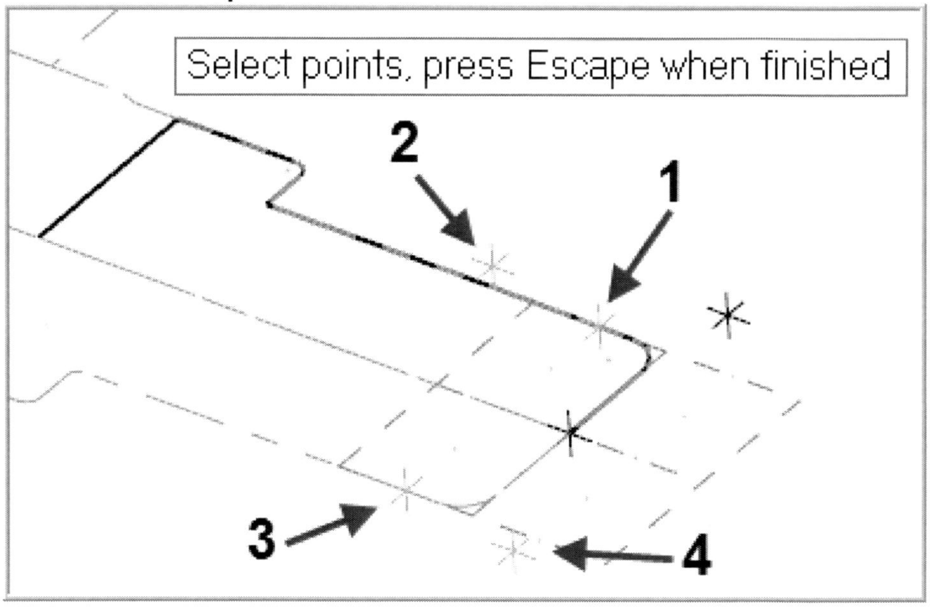

8. Click **OK** .

9. Select the **Tool** page and then click on **Select library tool…** as shown below.

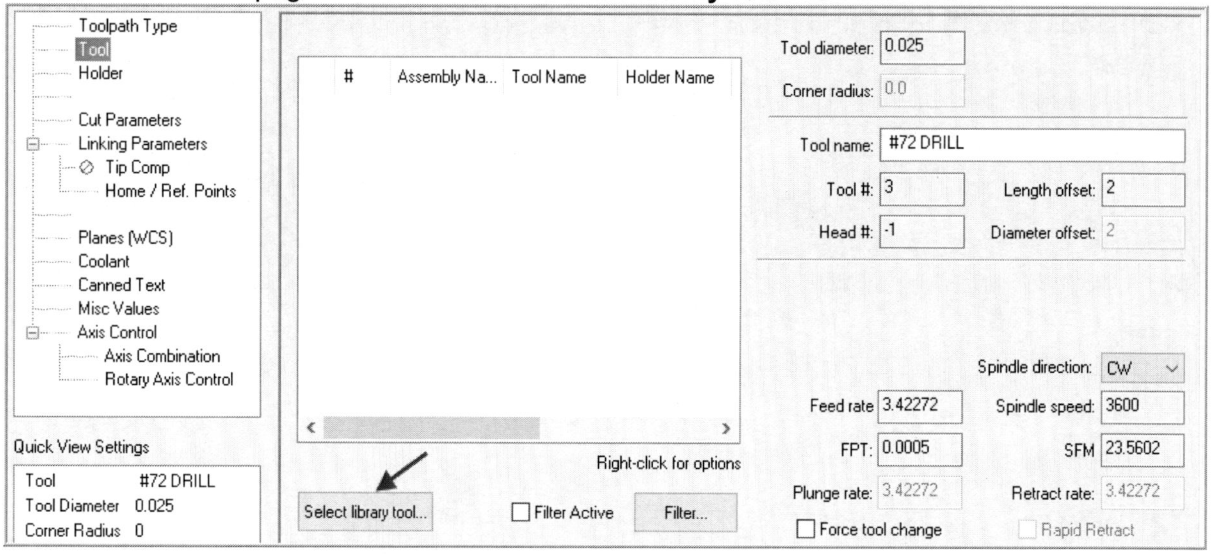

10. Scroll down the Tool Selection window and select the **1/8 Flat End Mill** as shown below:

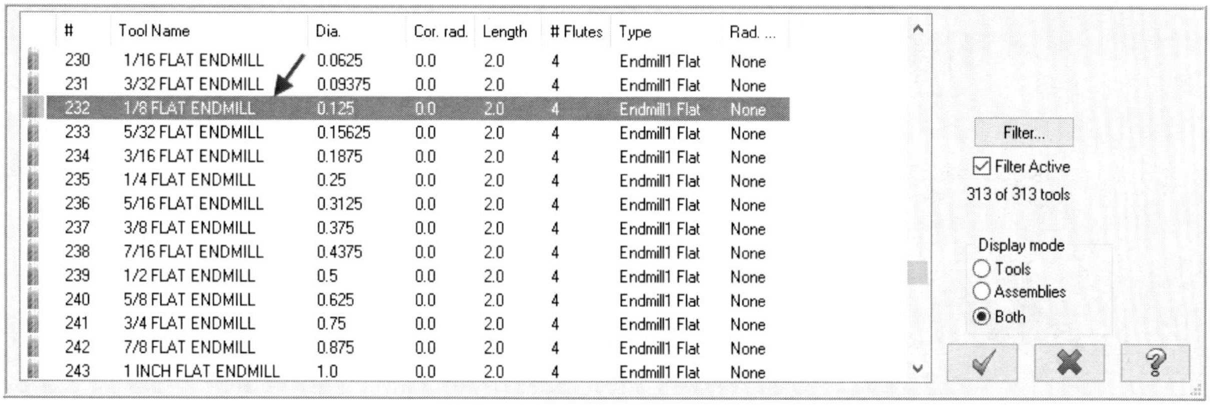

11. Click on **OK** .

12. Make the changes as shown below.

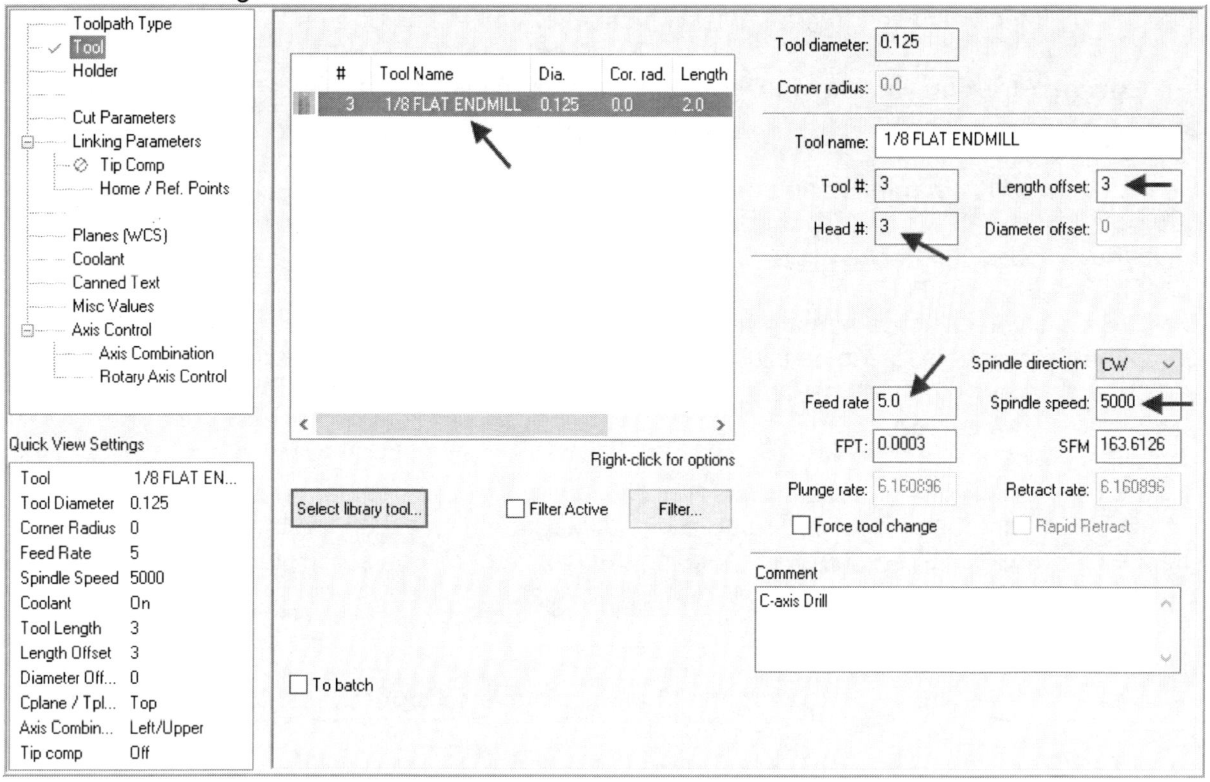

13. Expand the **Axis Control** menu and select **Rotary Axis Control.** Change the **Rotary Diameter** to **1.0** in the **Rotary Axis dialogue screen** as shown below: **Note:** this is the diameter of the part that the holes will be drilled into.

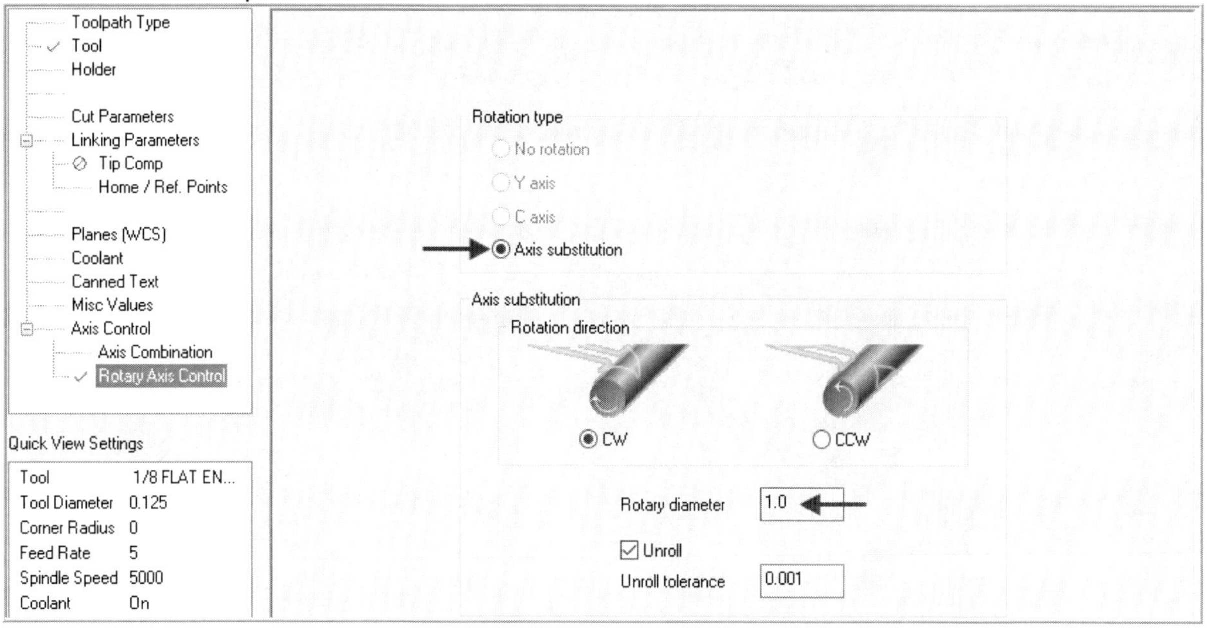

Rotary Axis Control (Lathe) page
Use this dialog box to configure rotary axis motion for Lathe applications.

For **axis substitution**, you need to tell Mastercam more information about how to wrap the geometry.

Select the direction of rotation and the diameter of the cylinder around which to wrap the geometry. Being able to specify these parameters in this dialog box means you do not have to have the cylinder created as geometry in your part file.

Note: Before you can create rotary axis motion, you need to configure the rotary axis components in your machine definition. You will only be able to select rotary axis options which are supported by your machine definition.

Unroll
Unrolls geometry wrapped on a cylinder so it lies flat on a plane. Cutter compensation and retract moves are then calculated relative to the flat geometry. When the toolpath posts, the geometry wraps back onto the cylinder using the Axis substitution and Rotary Diameter parameters. Only available for contour and drill toolpaths.

14. Click on the **Linking Parameters** menu and change the **Depth to -0.125** as shown below:

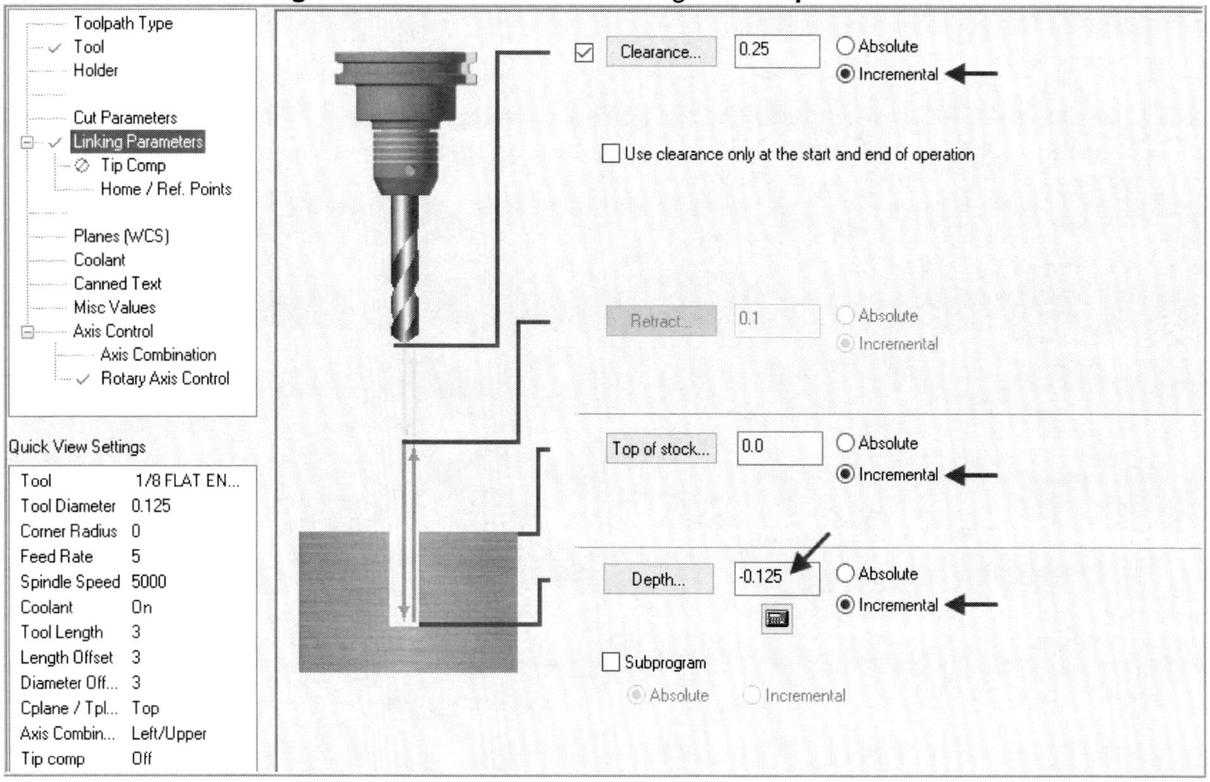

15. Set **Coolant Flood** to **On**.

16. Click **OK** .

17. In the Toolpaths Manager move the red **Insert arrow** after the Cutoff operation. Use the red Arrow icons to position the Insert arrow up or down
18. Right mouse click in the graphics area and click on the **Fit** icon .

➲ The C-axis Drill toolpath around the part should look like the diagram shown below.

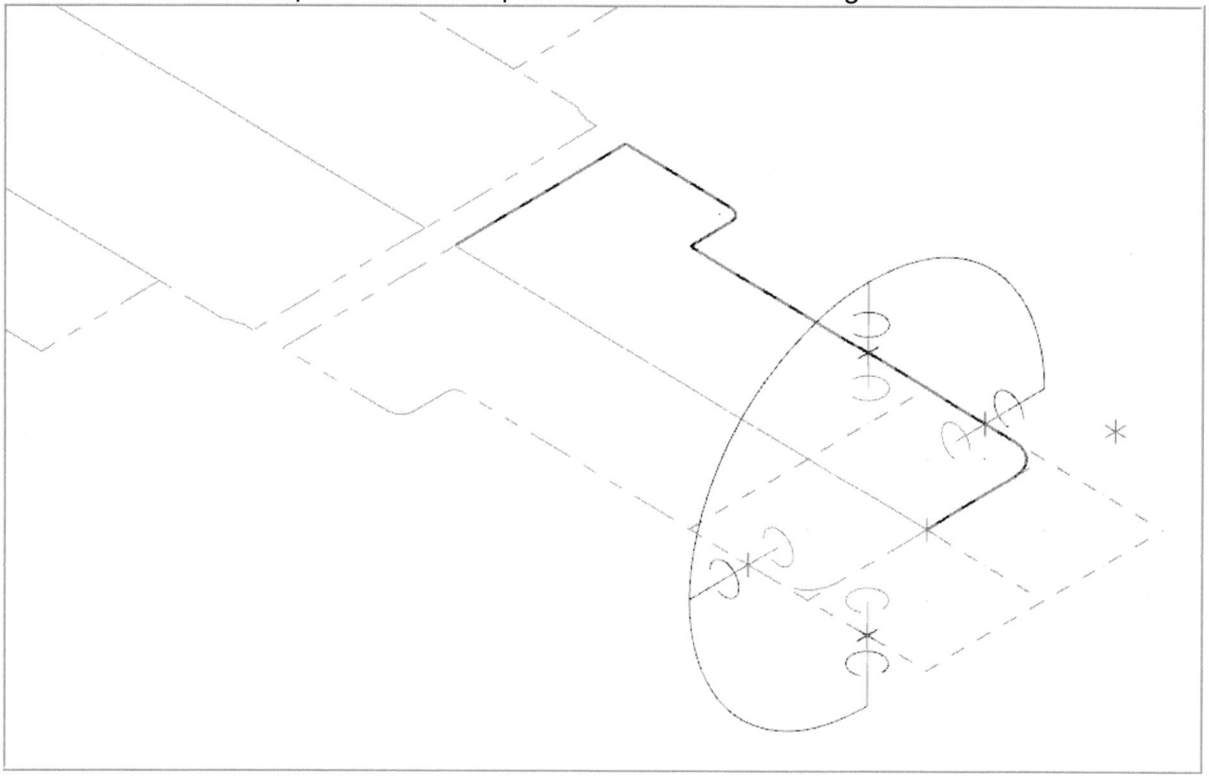

TASK 6:
BACKPLOT THE TOOLPATH

- In this task you will use Mastercam's Backplot function to view the path the tools take to cut this part.
- Backplot will enable us to review the cutting motions and identify any problem areas when cutting the part.

1. To pick all the operations to Backplot pick the **Select All** icon .
2. The next step is to select the **Backplot selected operations** icon shown below:

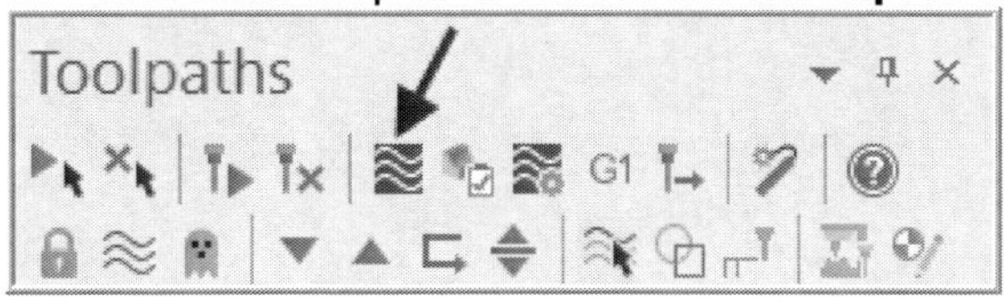

3. **Maximize** the Backplot/Verify window if required.
4. Select the **Home** Tab if required.
5. Activate the options shown below in the **Visibility** section of the Home tab.

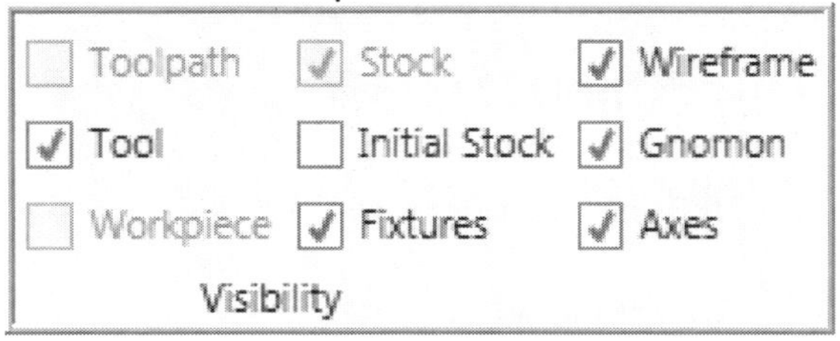

6. Activate the **Both** option in the **Toolpath section** of the **Home** tab.

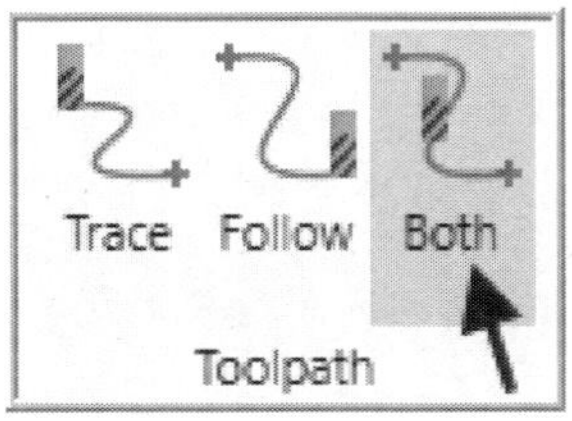

Both
This displays the entire toolpath and the tool as it travels over the displayed toolpath.

7. At the top of the screen select the **View** tab, the **Isometric** icon and then select **Fit**.

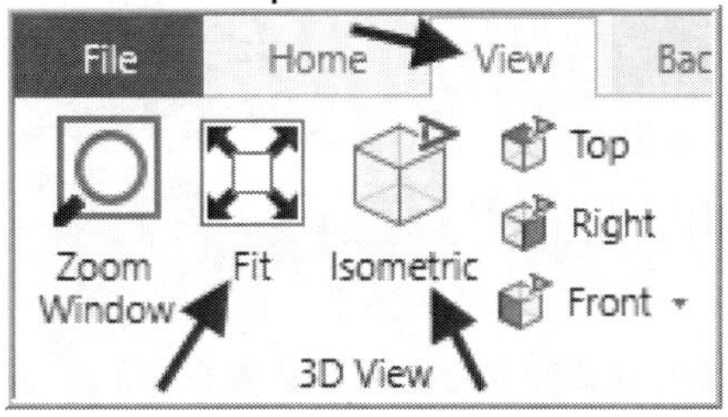

8. In the lower part of the screen now set the run Speed to slow by moving the slider bar pointer over to the left as shown below.

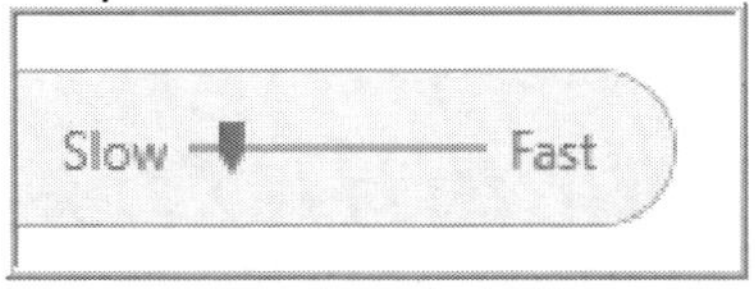

9. Now select the Play Simulation button to review the toolpaths.
10. After reviewing the Backplot of the toolpaths select the **Close** button to exit Backplot.

TASK 7:
VERIFY THE TOOLPATH

➲ Mastercam's Verify utility allows you to use solid models to simulate the machining of a part. The model created by the verification represents the surface finish, and shows collisions, if any exist.

1. In the **Toolpaths Manager** pick all the operations to verify by picking the **Select All** icon.
2. Select the **Verify selected operations** icon shown below:

3. **Maximize** the Backplot/Verify window if required.
4. Now select the Home Tab if required.
5. Activate the options shown below in the **Visibility** section of the Home tab. Initial Stock not activated.

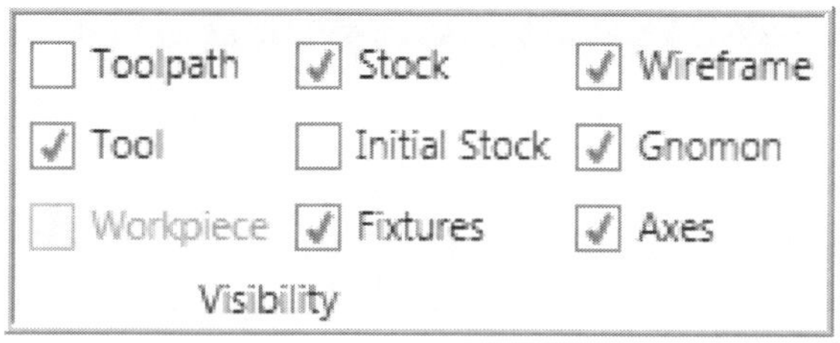

6. Select the **Verify** tab and activate the **Color Loop** to change the color of the cut stock.
7. In the lower right corner of the screen now set the run **Speed** to slow by moving the slider bar pointer over to the left.
8. Now select the **Play Simulation** button to review the toolpaths.

9. Select the **Close** button  in the top right hand corner to exit Verify.

TASK 8:
SAVE THE UPDATED MASTERCAM FILE

1. Select the **Save** icon from the **Quick Access** toolbar at the top left of the screen.

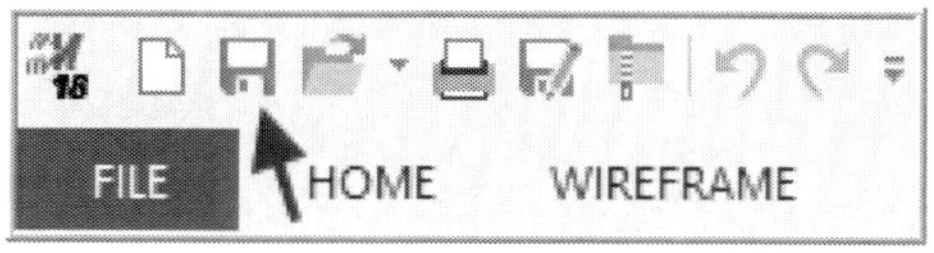

TASK 9:
POST AND CREATE THE CNC CODE FILE

1. Before you post the code enlarge the **Toolpaths Manager** window to the right as shown below. Click on the **right hand pane** and **slide to the right**.

➲ At present the **Program** number is set to 1 and the toolpath data file is set to **Lathe-Lesson-1.NC** because we initially made a duplicate of Lathe-lesson-1. You will now change the 1 to 8 for both of these as this is Lesson 8.

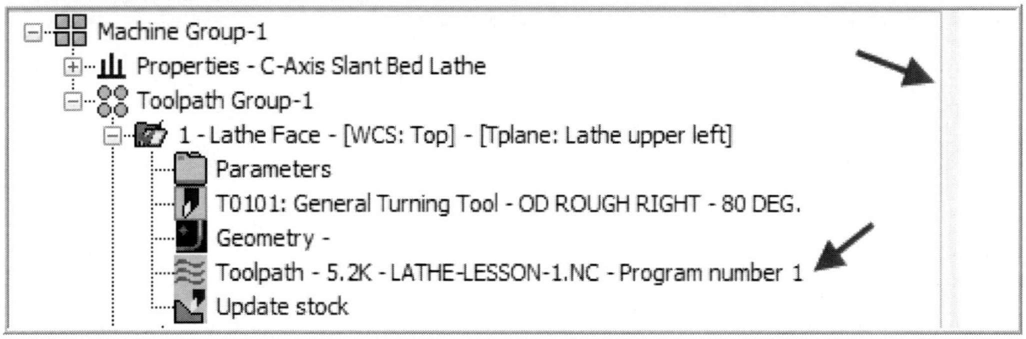

2. Right mouse click over the first operation folder. Select **Edit selected operations** and then pick **Change Program #.**

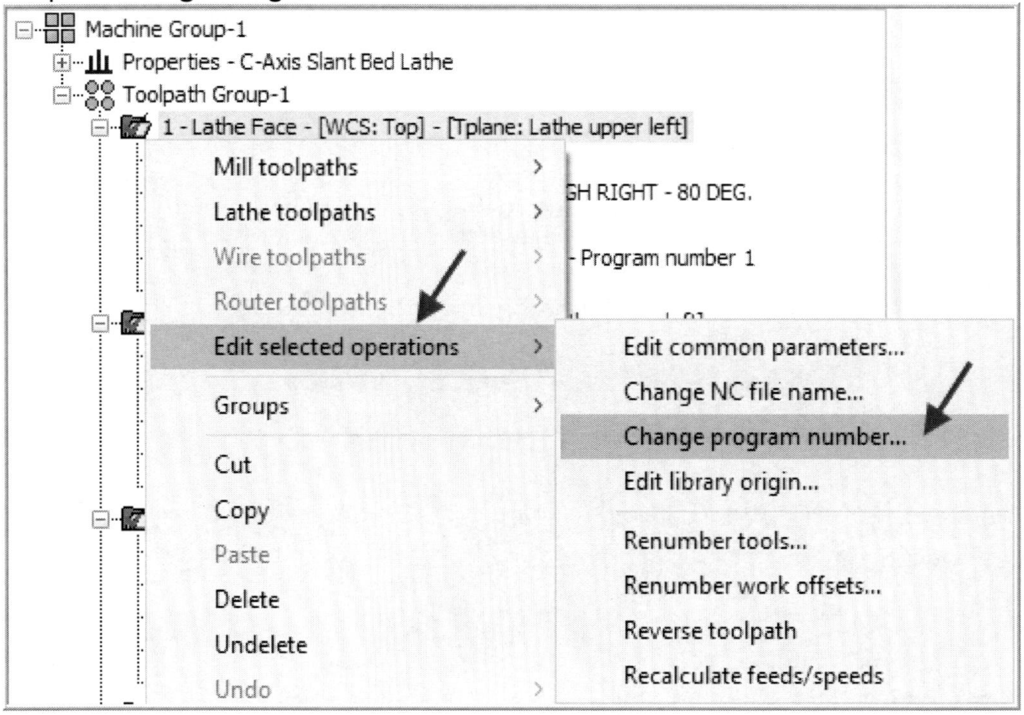

3. Enter **8** for the new Program number as shown below and clock **OK** .

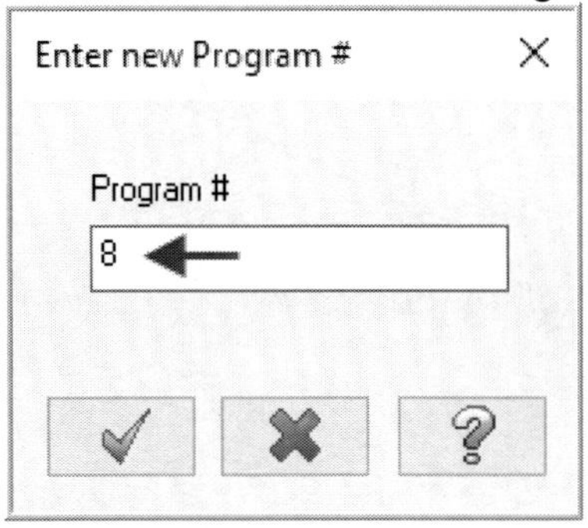

4. Right mouse click over the first operation folder. Select **Edit selected operations** and then pick **Change NC file name.**

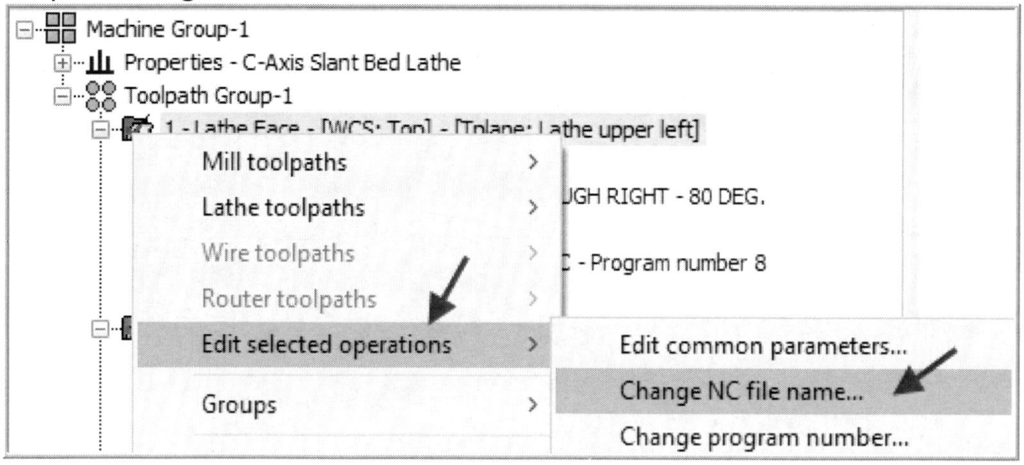

5. Enter **LATHE-LESSON-8** for the new NC name as shown below.

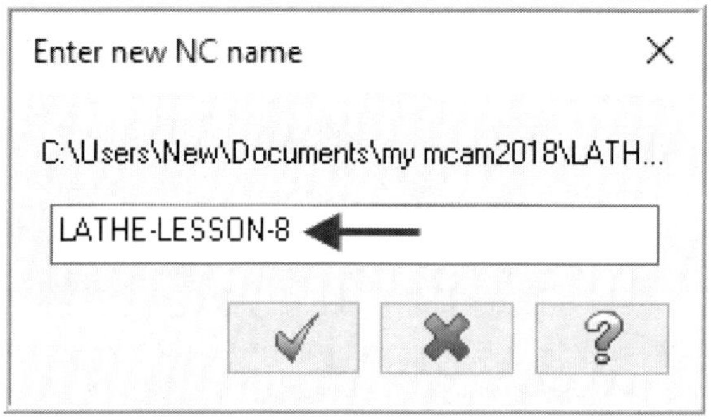

6. Ensure all the operations are selected by picking the **Select All** icon  from the **Toolpaths Manager.**
7. Select the **Post selected operations** button from the **Toolpaths Manager.**
8. In the Post processing window, make the necessary changes as shown below:

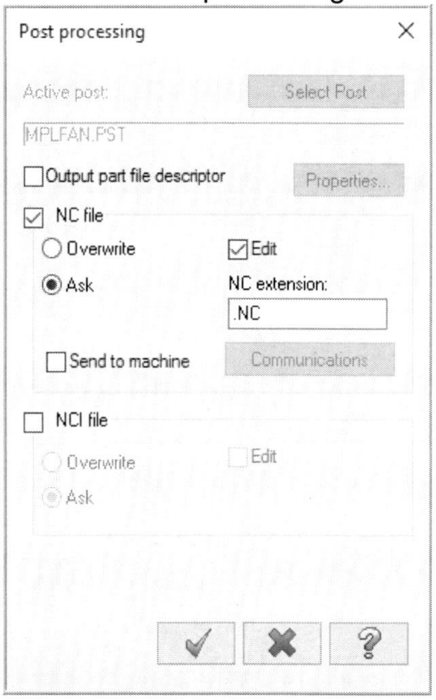

9. Select the **OK** button  to continue.

10. Enter the same name as your Mastercam part file name in the **NC File name** field **LATHE-LESSON-8.**
11. Select the **Save** button.
12. The CNC code file opens up in the default editor.

LATHE-LESSON-8.NC ×

```
(MATERIAL - ALUMINUM INCH - 6061)
G20
(TOOL - 1 OFFSET - 1)
(OD ROUGH RIGHT - 80 DEG.  INSERT - CNMG-432)
G0 T0101
M8
G97 S449 M03
G0 G54 X1.7 Z0.
G50 S3600
G96 S200
G99 G1 X-.0625 F.01
```

13. Scroll down the CNC code until you locate the commands to rotate the chuck (C-Axis) when drilling the four holes.

```
(TOOL - 3 OFFSET - 0)
( 1/8 FLAT ENDMILL)
(C-AXIS DRILL)
G0 T0300
M23
M8
G0 G55 X1.5 Z-.25
C0.
G97 S2500 M51
G81 X.75 R1.2 F5.
C90.
C180.
C270.
G80
M9
G28 U0. W0. H0. M55
T0300
M01
```

14. Select the 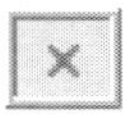 in the top right corner to exit the CNC editor.

➲ This completes LATHE-LESSON-8.

LATHE-LESSON-8 EXERCISE

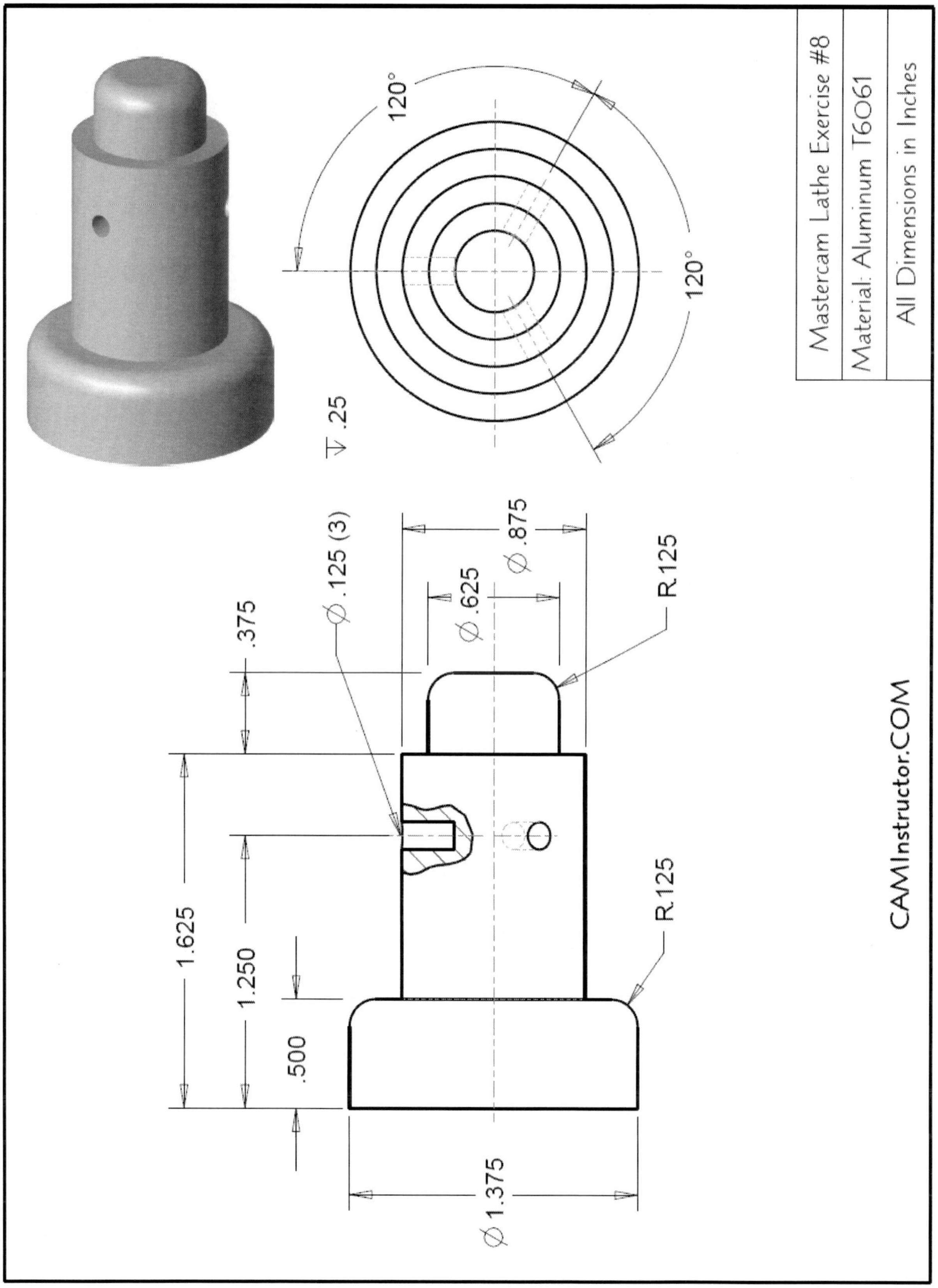

Mastercam® 2018

TRAINING GUIDE

LATHE-LESSON-9

C-AXIS CROSS CONTOUR

camInstructor

Objectives

You will create the geometry for Lathe-Lesson-9, and then generate a toolpath to machine the part on a CNC lathe. This lesson covers the following topics:

➲ **Create a 2-dimensional drawing by:**
Creating lines.
Creating fillets.
Creating lines rotated about the diameter.

➲ **Establish Stock and Chuck settings:**
Stock size.
Chuck Configuration.
Material for the part.
Feed calculation.

➲ **Generate a C-Axis lathe toolpath consisting of:**
Lathe Face.
Lathe Rough.
Lathe Finish.
Lathe Drill.
Lathe Bore.
C-Axis Cross Contour.
Lathe Cutoff.
Modify geometry and update toolpath operations

➲ **Inspect the toolpath using Mastercam's Verify and Backplot by:**
Launching the Verify function to machine the part on the screen.
Using Backplot to identify the correctness of the toolpaths.
Generating the NC- code.

LATHE-LESSON-9 DRAWING

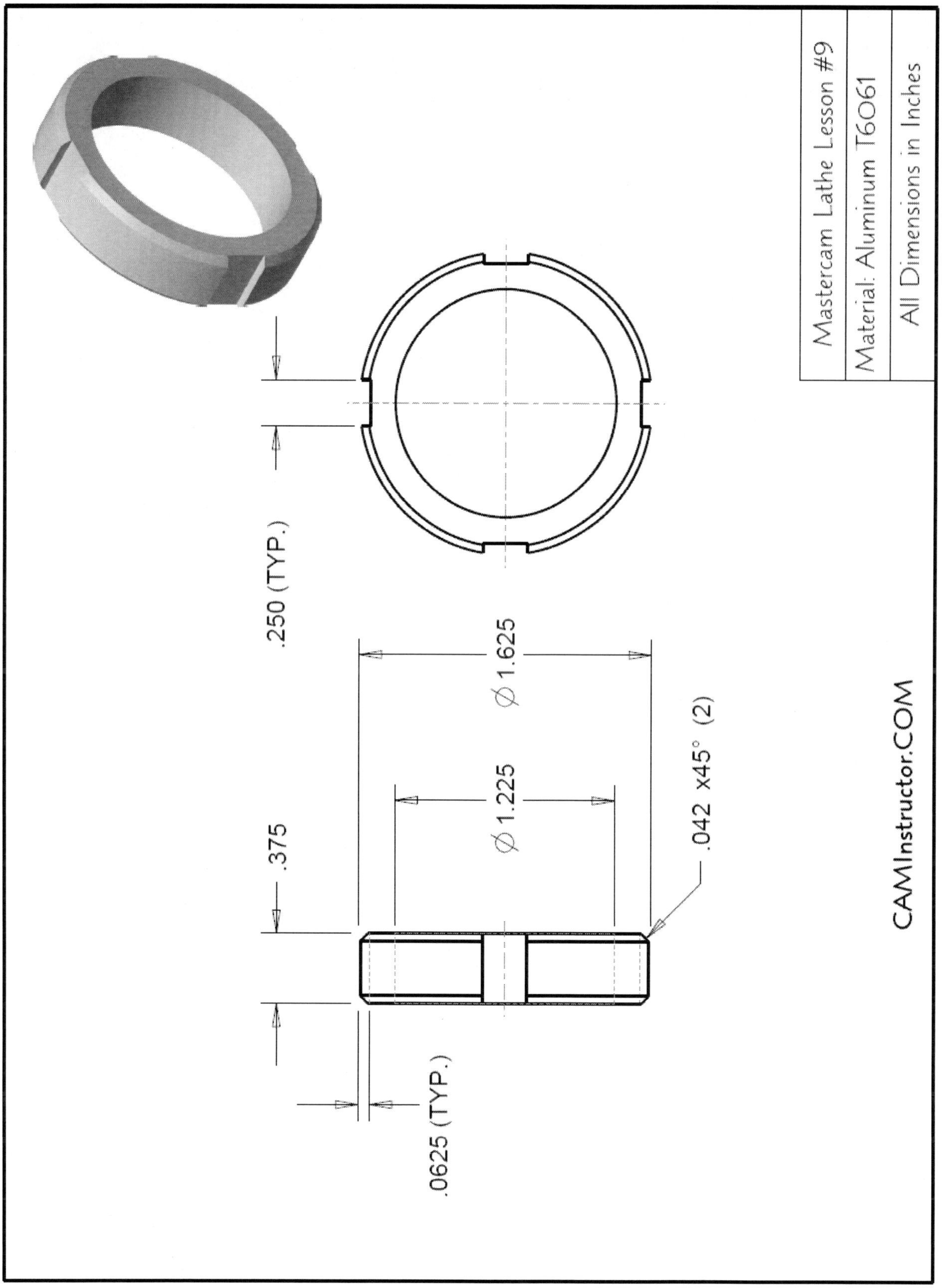

TOOL LIST

Eight tools will be used to create this part.

- **Tool #1 Face and Rough**
  Holder: Outside Diameter Rough Right Hand - DCGNR-164D.
  Insert: 80 Degree Diamond Insert – CNMG-432

- **Tool #2 Finish the outside diameter**
  Holder: Outside Diameter Finish Right Hand - MVJNR-164D.
  Insert: 35 Degree Diamond Insert – VNMG-431

- **Tool #3 Center drill**
  Centre Drill – body diameter 0.250"

- **Tool #4 0.375 diameter drill**
  Drill 0.375" diameter

- **Tool #5 0.500 diameter drill**
  Drill 0.5" diameter

- **Tool #6 Boring Tool**
  Holder: Boring Bar – minimum diameter 0.375".
  Insert: 75 Degree Diamond Insert

- **Tool #7 ¼" Flat End Mill**
  End Mill 0.25" diameter

- **Tool #8 Cutoff tool**
  Holder: Outside Diameter Groove Right Hand - Narrow.
  Insert: 0.125" Wide - GC-4125

LATHE - LESSON - 9 - THE PROCESS

Geometry Creation

TASK 1: Setting the Environment
TASK 2: Setting the Construction Planes
TASK 3: Create the Geometry
TASK 4 Create the Chamfers
TASK 5: Save the Drawing

Toolpath Creation

TASK 6: Define the Stock and Chuck Parameters
TASK 7: Face the Front of the Part
TASK 8: Rough the Outside Diameters
TASK 9: Finish the Outside Diameters
TASK 10: Center Drill the hole
TASK 11: Pre drill the 1.125" hole 0.375" diameter
TASK 12: Pre drill the 1.125" hole 0.500" diameter
TASK 13: Rough the bore
TASK 14: Finish the bore
TASK 15: Machine the first slot using C-axis Cross Contour
TASK 16: Machine the remaining three Slots using Transform Toolpath
TASK 17: Cut off the Part
TASK 18: Modify 1.625" diameter and regenerate operations
TASK 19: Backplot the Toolpath
TASK 20: Verify the Toolpath
TASK 21: Save the Updated Mastercam File
TASK 22: Post and Create the CNC Code File

Geometry Creation

TASK 1:
SETTING THE ENVIRONMENT

➲ Before starting the geometry creation you should set up the grid and machine type as outlined in the **Setting the Environment** section at the beginning of this text:

1. Set up the Grid. This will help identify the location of the origin.

➲ Set the Machine type to the **LATHE C-AXIS SLANT BED**.

2. Select the **Machine** tab, open up the **Lathe** drop down menu in the **Machine Type** section and click on **LATHE C-AXIS SLANT BED.MCAM-LMD**. If the machine type is not displayed, follow the step 3-6.

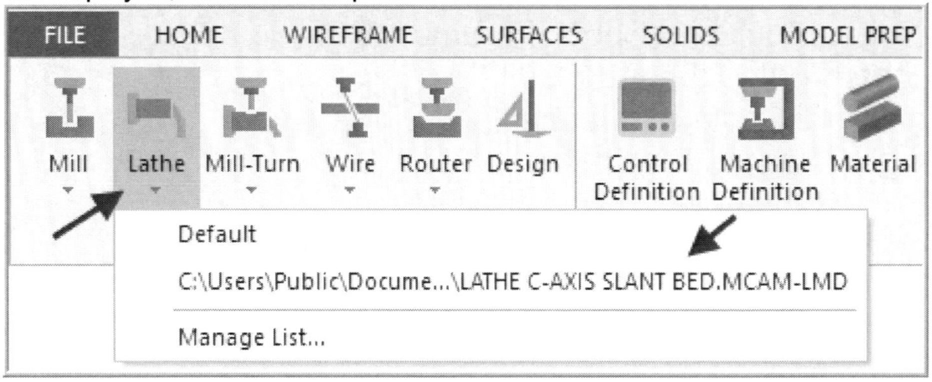

3. Select the **Machine** tab, open up the **Lathe** drop down menu in the **Machine Type** section and click on **Manage List** .

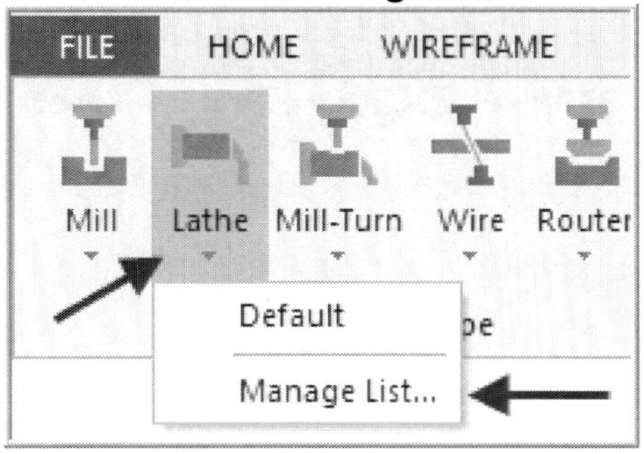

4. The **Machine Definition Menu Management** window appears. Select **LATHE C-AXIS SLANT BED.MCAM-LMD** from the list and click on **Add** button Add as shown below:

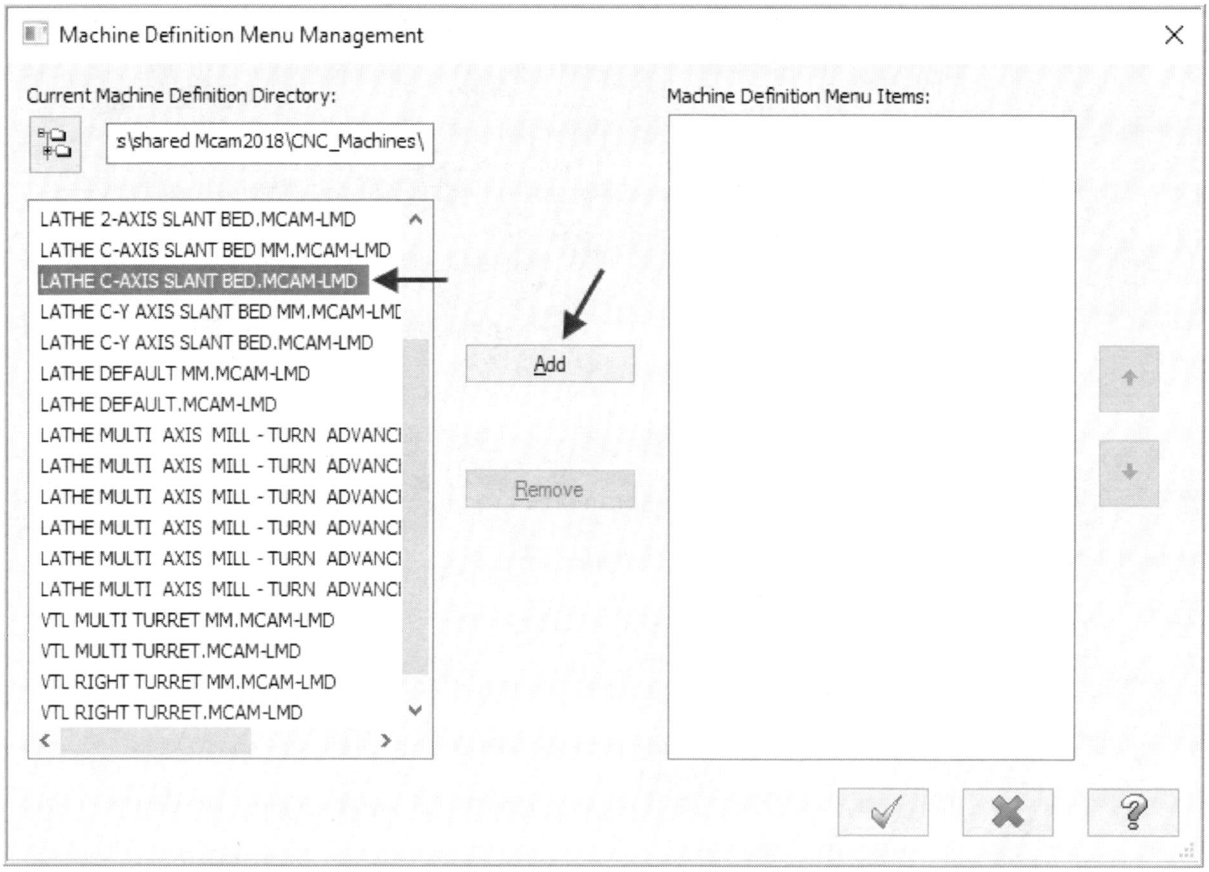

5. Click on the OK icon.
6. On the **Machine** tab, open up the **Lathe** drop down menu in the **Machine Type** section and click on **LATHE C-AXIS SLANT BED.MCAM-LMD**.

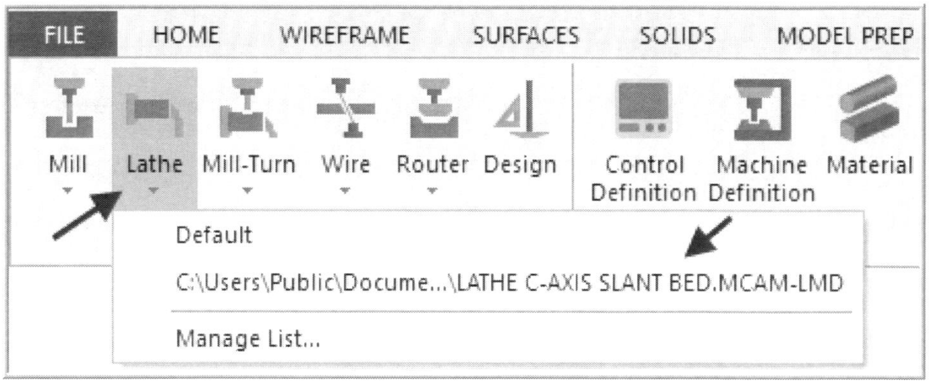

TASK 2:
SETTING THE CONSTRUCTION PLANES:

➲ **Set the Construction and Tool Plane to Lathe diameter +D +Z (WCS)**

1. Select the **View tab** and click on **Toolpaths** and **Planes** in the Managers section to display.

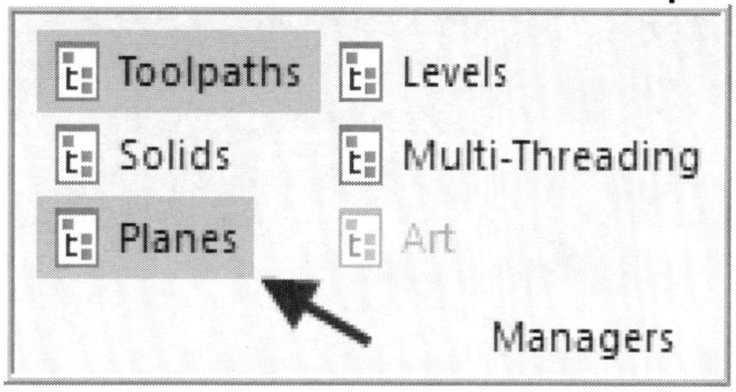

Once your machine is set up, Mastercam includes special lathe construction planes that let you work in **radius or diameter coordinates**.
For conventional 2D turning applications, use the Planes Manager to select the desired coordinate system, as shown below right. Choose to use either radius or diameter coordinates and then choose the desired X/D and Z directions.

2. To change the **Lathe Plane** open up the drop down menu for **Select lathe plane** and click on **+D +Z** as shown below, **if required**.

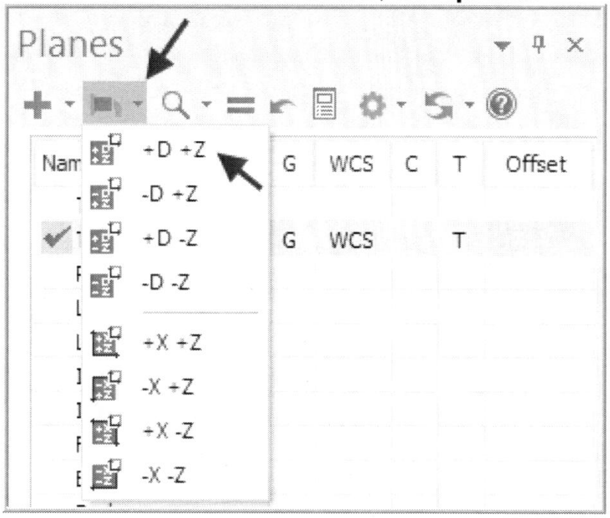

3. Ensure the **C column** (Construction Plane) and **T column** (Tool Plane) are set to the **+D +Z Plane**. Just click in the C and T columns in the **+D +Z** row.

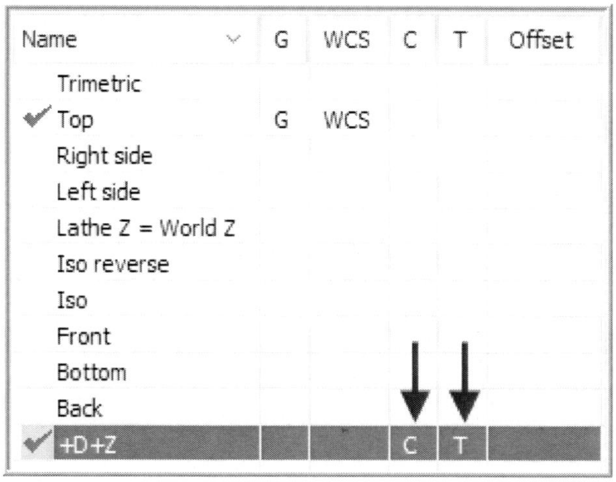

4. Select the **Close** button  in the top right hand corner to close the Planes Manager.

TASK 3:
CREATE THE GEOMETRY – THE RIGHT HAND FACE IS AT Z0

➲ This task explains how to create the geometry of this part. In this lathe part you only need to create **half of the geometry**, the geometry above the center line.
➲ Lines 1, 2 and 3 will be created using the **Rectangular Shapes** command.
➲ Lines 4 and 5 will be created using the **Offset** command.
➲ The Chamfers will be created last.

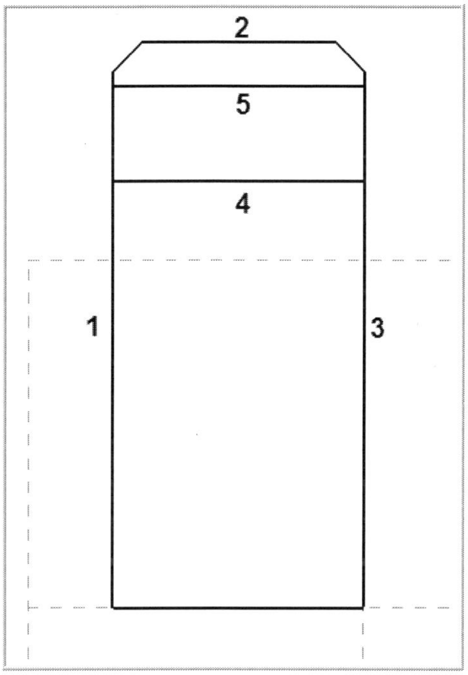

➲ **Create Lines 1, 2 and 3**

1. On the **WIREFRAME** tab in the **Shapes** section click on the drop down menu arrow under **Rectangle** and select **Rectangular Shapes**.

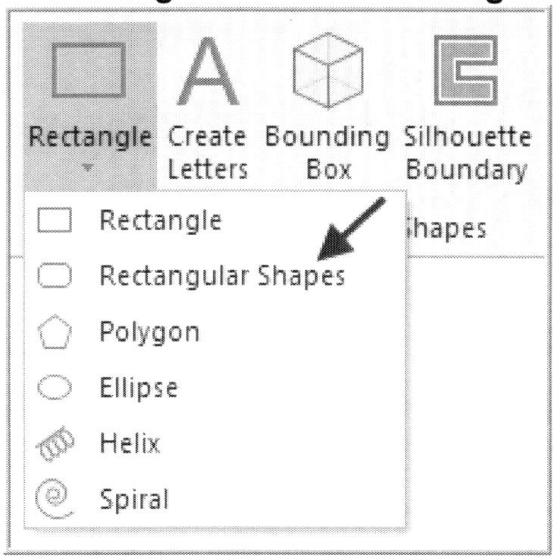

Use **Rectangular Shapes** to create rectangles using a base point or 2-point method.

Either method can create wireframe geometry only or wireframe geometry and a surface.

The options change depending on the method you select.

Both methods let you set a corner fillet radius, rotation angle, general shape, and surface creation.

2. The **Rectangular Shapes** panel appears and you are prompted to **Select position of base point**. Set the following values.

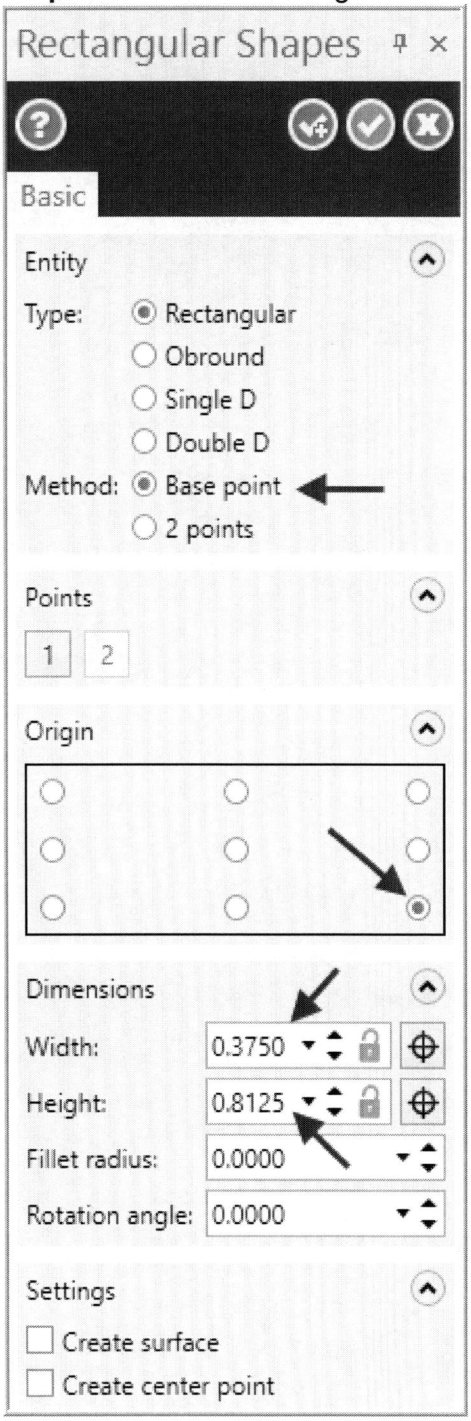

3. To satisfy the prompt **"Select position of base point".** Move the cursor over the **center of the grid** and as you get close to the origin a visual cue appears.  This is the cue that will allow you to snap to the **Origin**. With this visual cue highlighted pick the **Origin** as shown below:

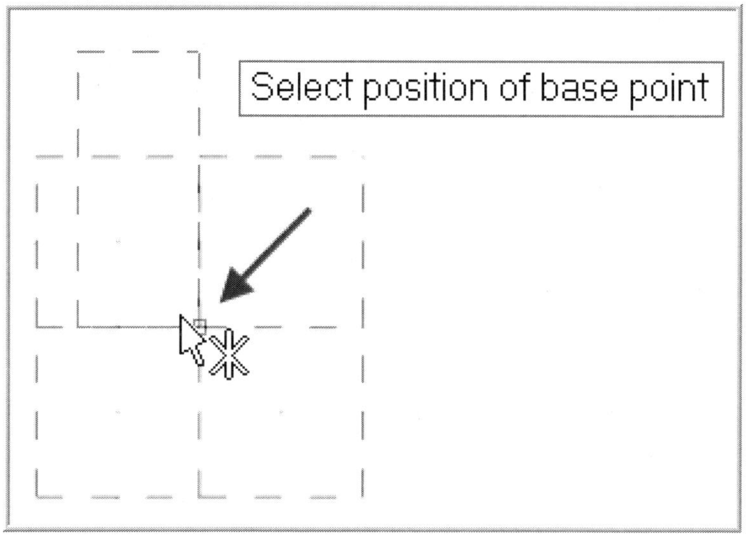

4. Click on **OK** .
5. Right mouse click in the graphics area and click on the **Fit** icon .
6. Right mouse click in the graphics area and click on **Unzoom 80%** to shrink the display.

➲ A rectangle should be visible as shown below:

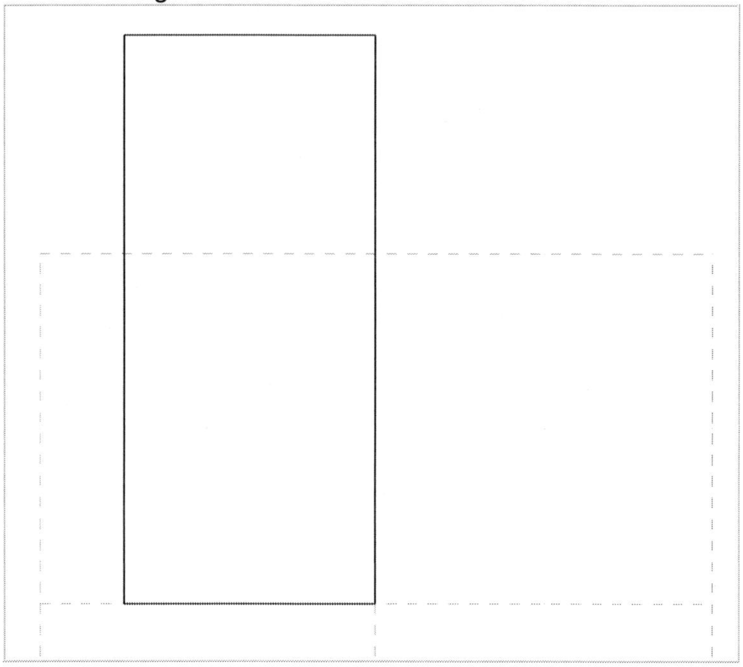

➲ **Create Lines 4 and 5 using the Offset command.**

7. In the **WIREFRAME** tab click on **Offset** in the **Modify** section.

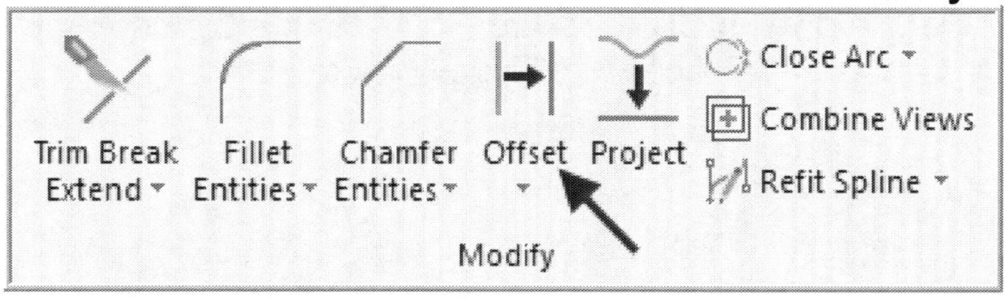

8. The **Offset Entity** panel appears and you are next prompted to **"Select the line, arc, spline or curve offset".** Make the necessary changes in the **Offset parameters** window as shown below:

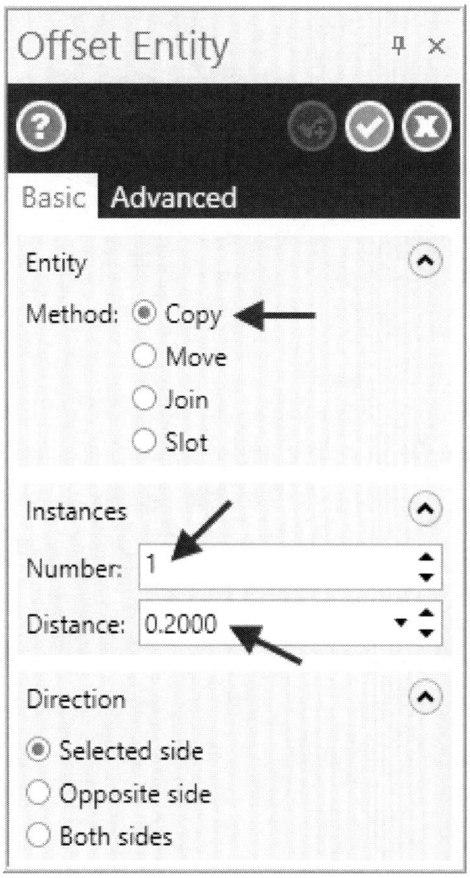

9. To satisfy the prompt **"Select the line, arc, spline or curve offset"** click on **line 2**
10. To satisfy the next prompt **"Indicate the offset direction"** move the cursor **below line 2** and click the **left mouse button** as shown below left:

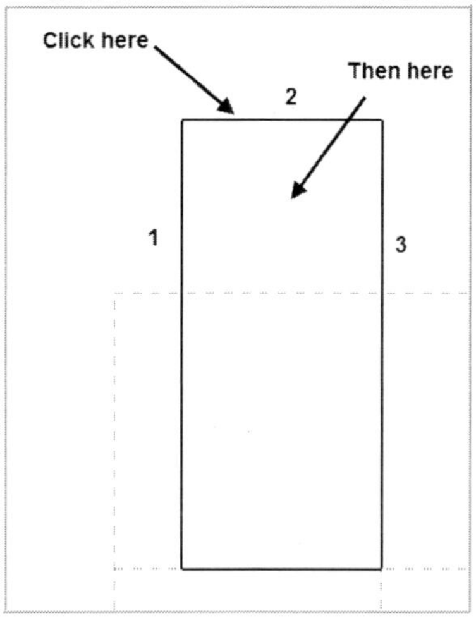

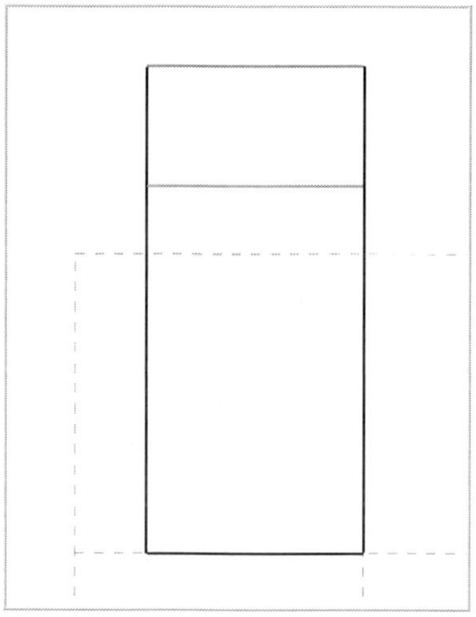

➲ A new line should be created just below line 2 as shown above right.

11. Click on the **OK and Create New Operation** icon .
12. Make the necessary changes in the **Offset Entity** panel as shown below. **Offset Distance is set to 0.0625**.

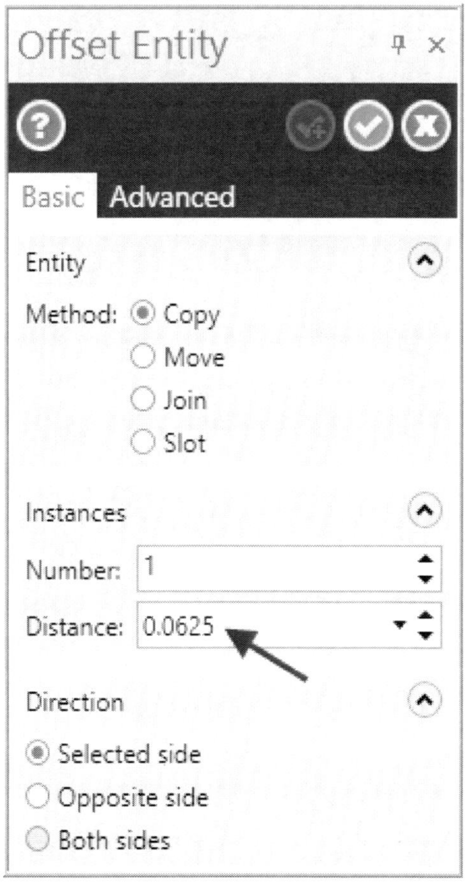

13. Click on **line 2** and move the cursor **below line 2** and click the **left mouse button** as shown below left:

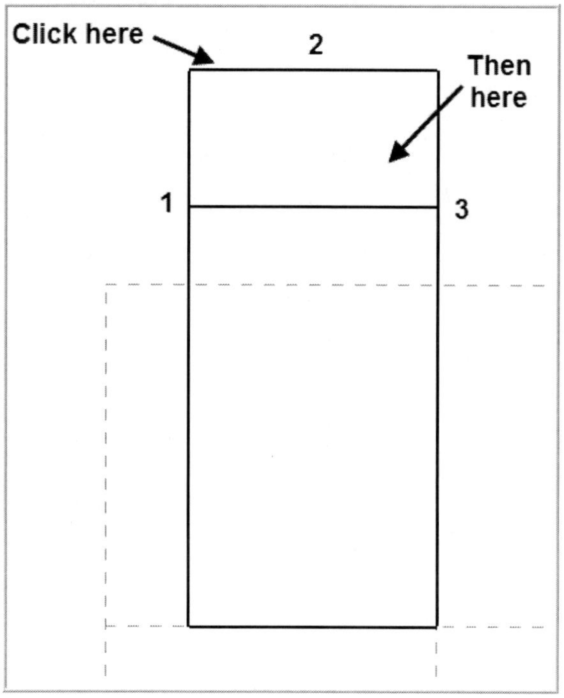

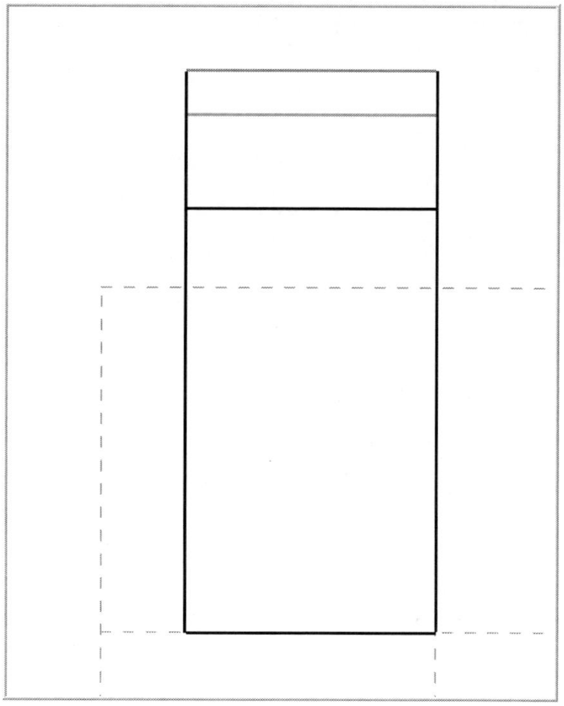

➲ A new line should be created just below line 2 as shown above right:

14. Click on the **OK** icon  to complete this feature.
15. Right mouse click in the graphics area and click on the **Clear Colors** icon .

TASK 4:
CREATE THE CHAMFERS

➲ **Create the .042 chamfer**

1. On the **WIREFRAME** tab and in the **Modify** section click on **Chamfer Entities**.

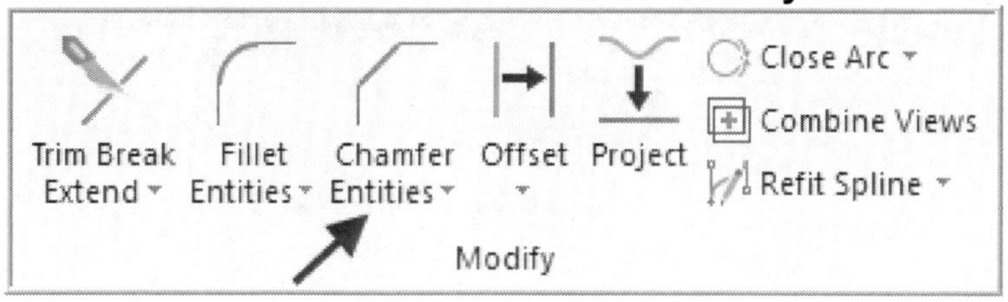

2. The **Chamfer Entities** panel appears. Activate the **Distance and angle** and enter a value of **0.042** for **Distance 1**. Ensure the **Trim** entities box at the bottom of the panel is check marked to turn the trim on.

3. Click on **line 1** and then click on **line 2** as shown below:

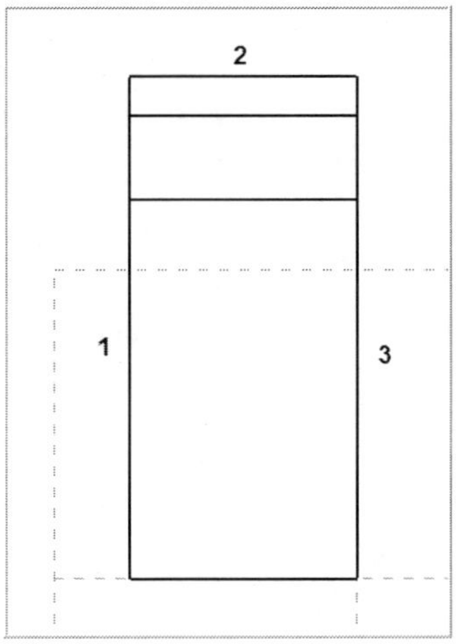

4. Click on **line 2** and then click on **line 3** as shown above.
5. Click on the **OK** icon to complete this feature.

➲ The completed chamfers are shown below.

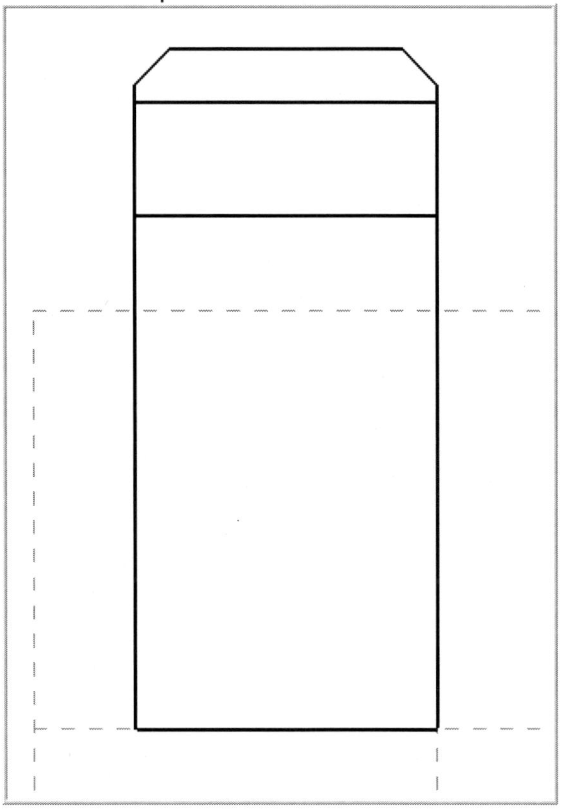

TASK 5:
SAVE THE DRAWING

1. Select **File.**
2. Select **File.**
3. Select **Save As.**
4. Click on the **Browse** icon.
5. In the **"File name"** box, type **"Lathe-Lesson-9".**
6. Browse to an appropriate location.
7. Select the **Save** button to save the file and complete this function.

Toolpath Creation

TASK 6:
DEFINING THE STOCK AND CHUCK PARAMETERS

1. Select the plus in front of **Properties** to expand the **Machine Group Properties**.

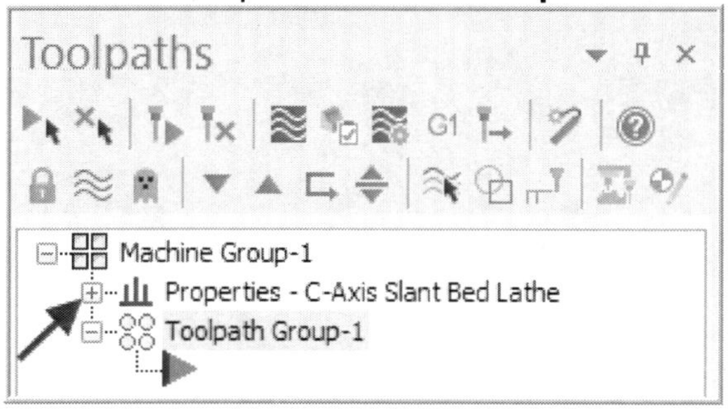

2. Select **Stock setup** in the Toolpaths Manager window.

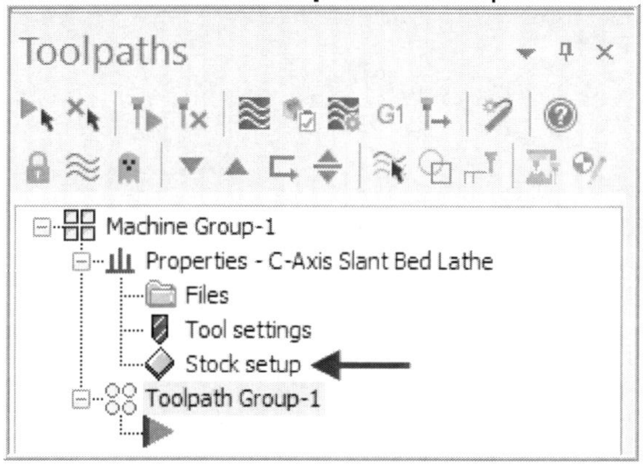

3. Select the **Stock Properties** button in the Stock Setup page as shown in the screenshot below:

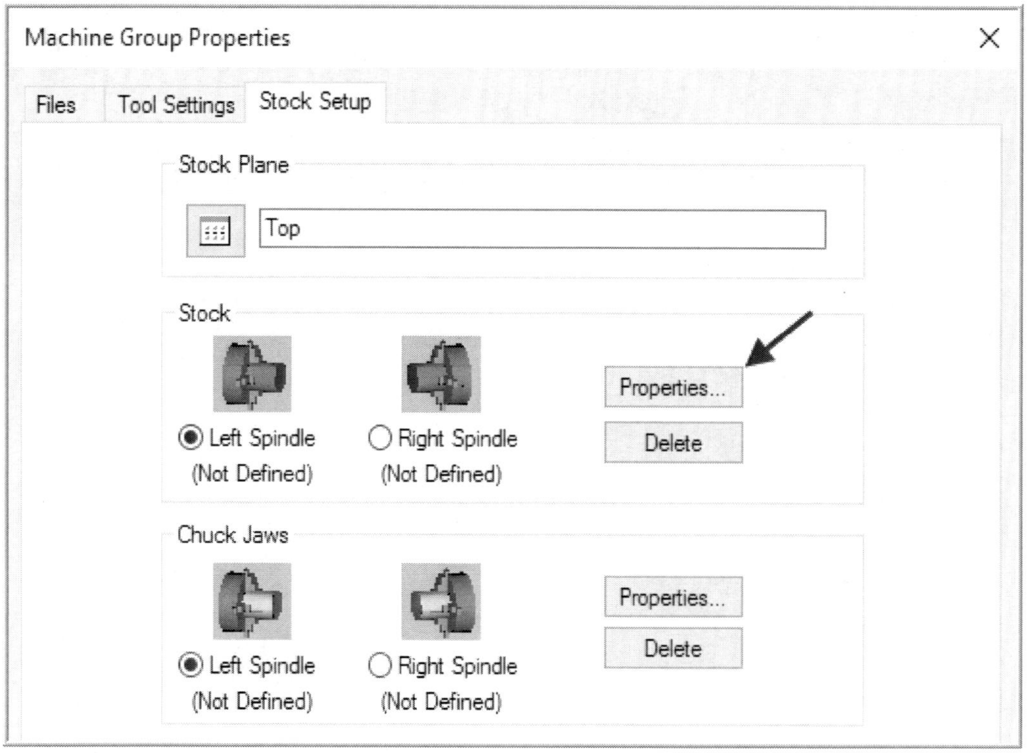

4. In the **Machine Component Manager-Stock** window click on the Geometry button and select Cylinder as shown below:

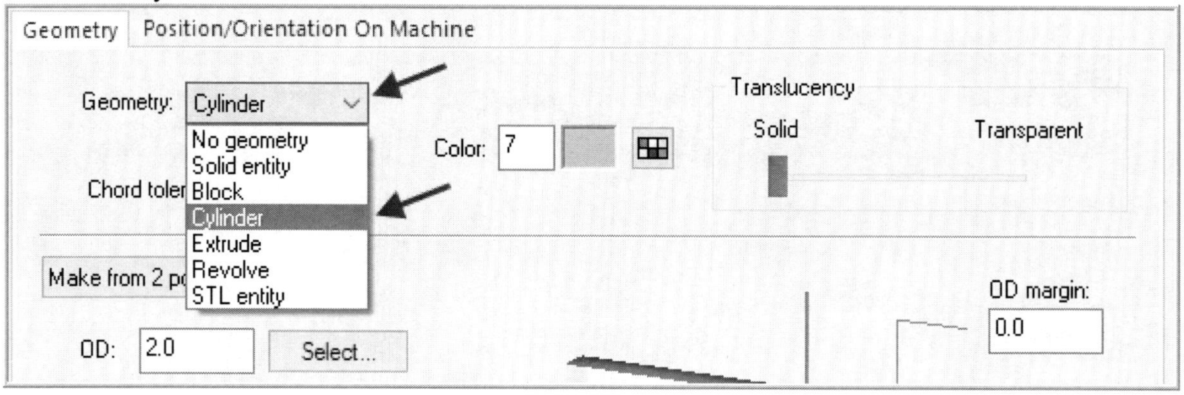

5. In the **Stock** setup set the values as shown below. **Axis is set to -Z**.

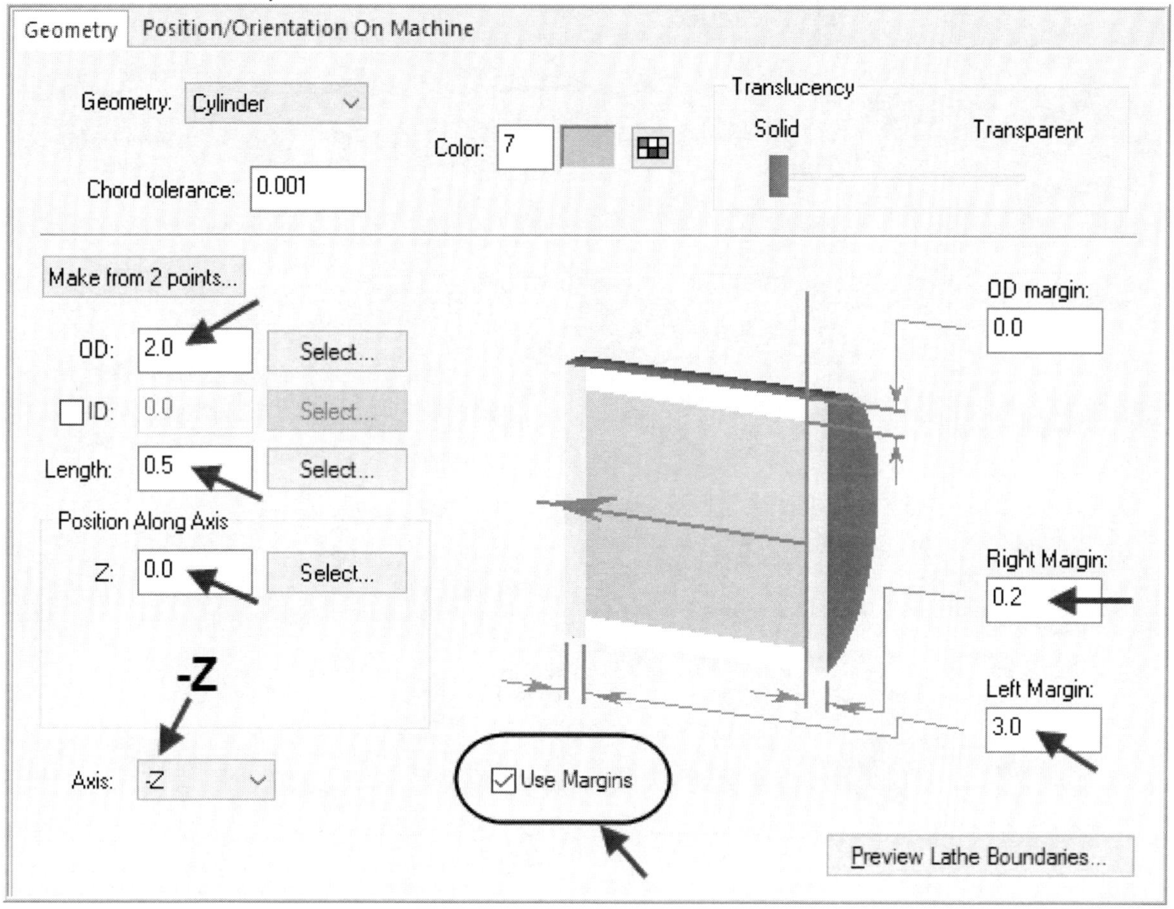

6. Click on the **OK** icon to complete this feature.
7. Still on the Stock Setup page activate **Fit screen to boundaries**.

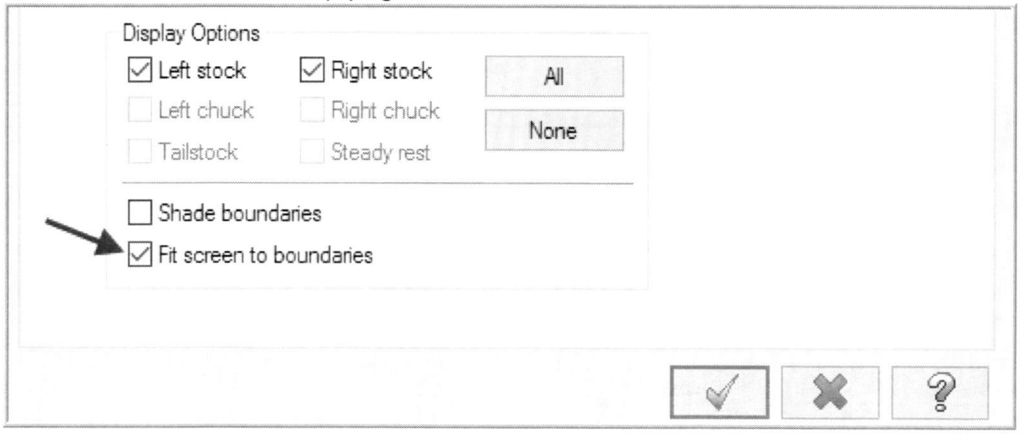

8. Select the **Chuck Properties** button in the Stock Setup page as shown below.

9. In the **Chuck Jaws** setup set the values as shown below:

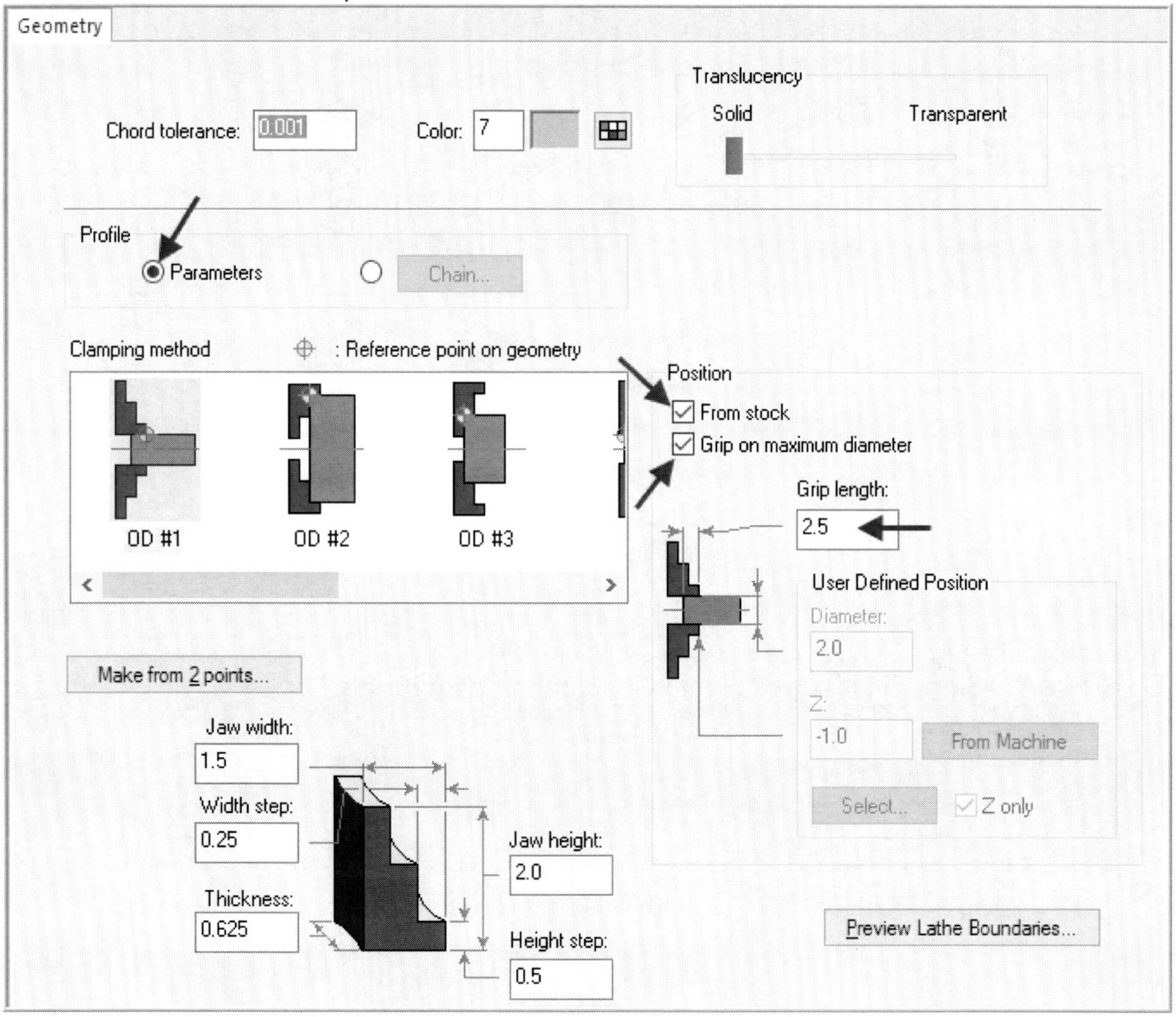

10. Click on the **OK** icon to complete this feature.

11. Click on the **Tool Settings** page and make changes as shown below.

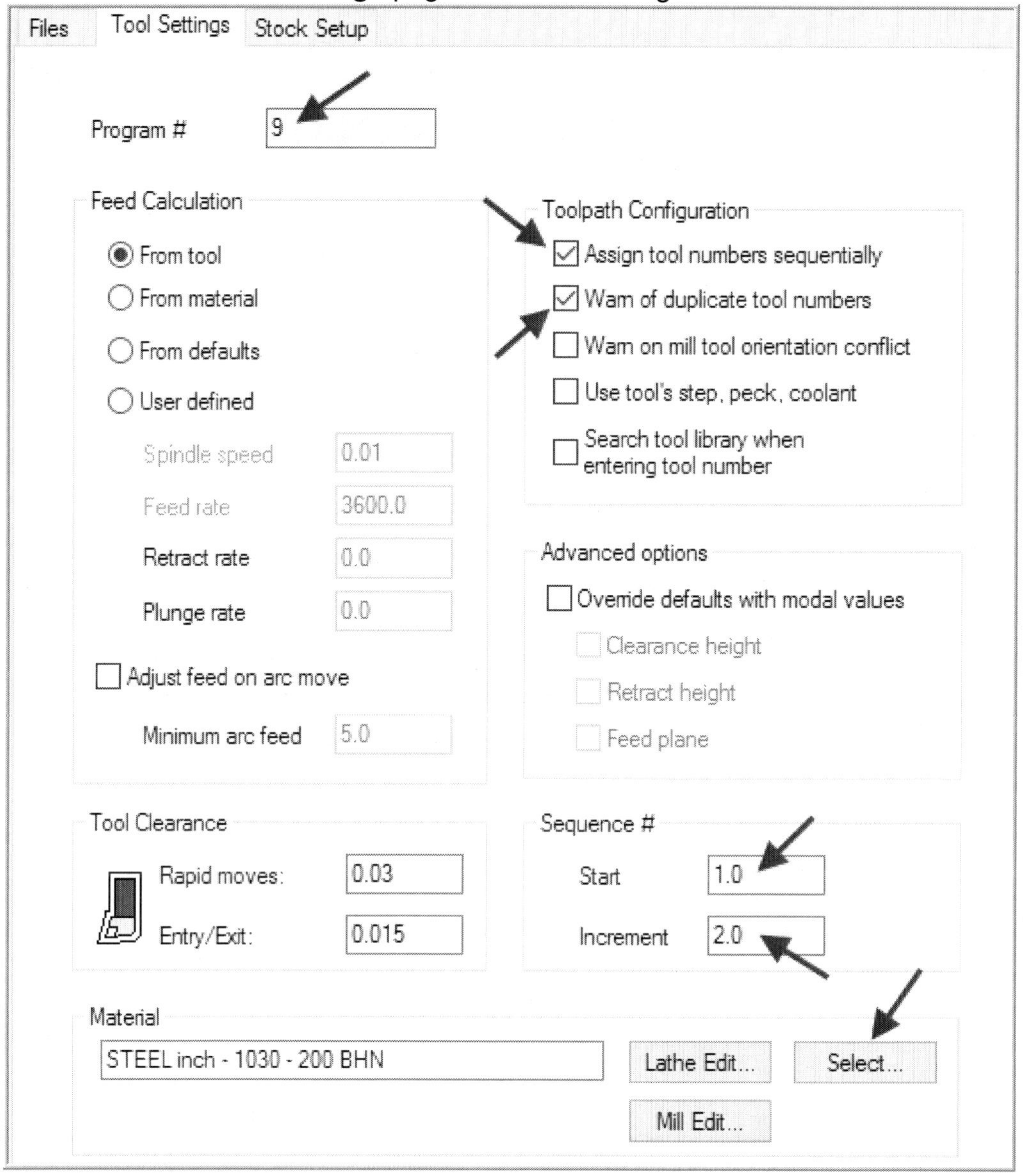

12. To change the **Material** type to Aluminum 6061 pick the **Select** button at the bottom of the Tool Settings page.

13. At the **Material List** dialog box open the Source drop down list and select **Lathe – library.**

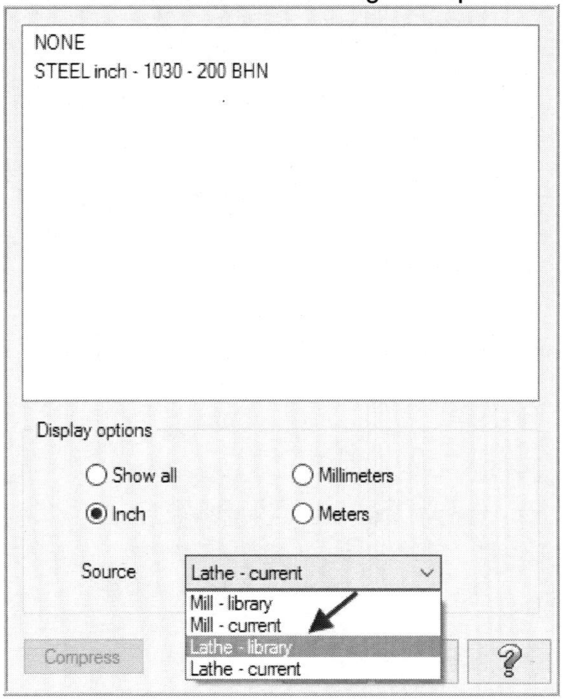

14. From the **Default Materials** list select **ALUMINUM inch - 6061** and then select .

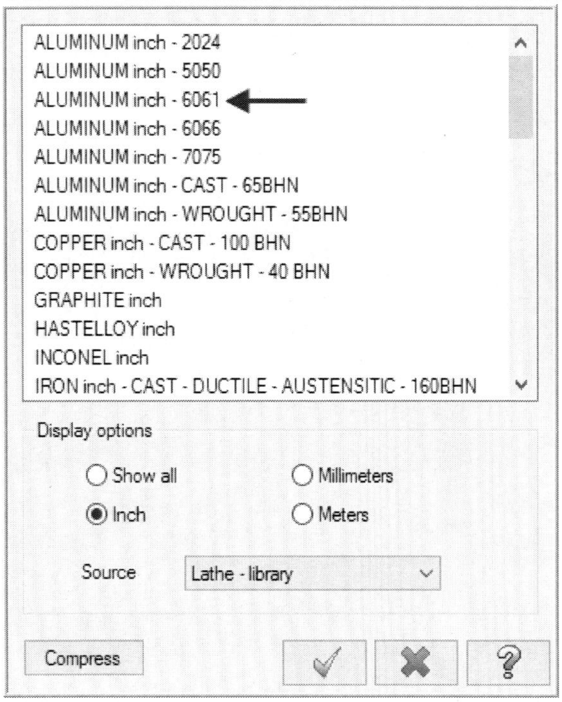

15. Select the **OK** button again to complete this Stock Setup function.

16. Right mouse click in the graphics area and click on the **Fit** icon .

➲ Note the stock setup outline as indicated by broken lines as shown below.

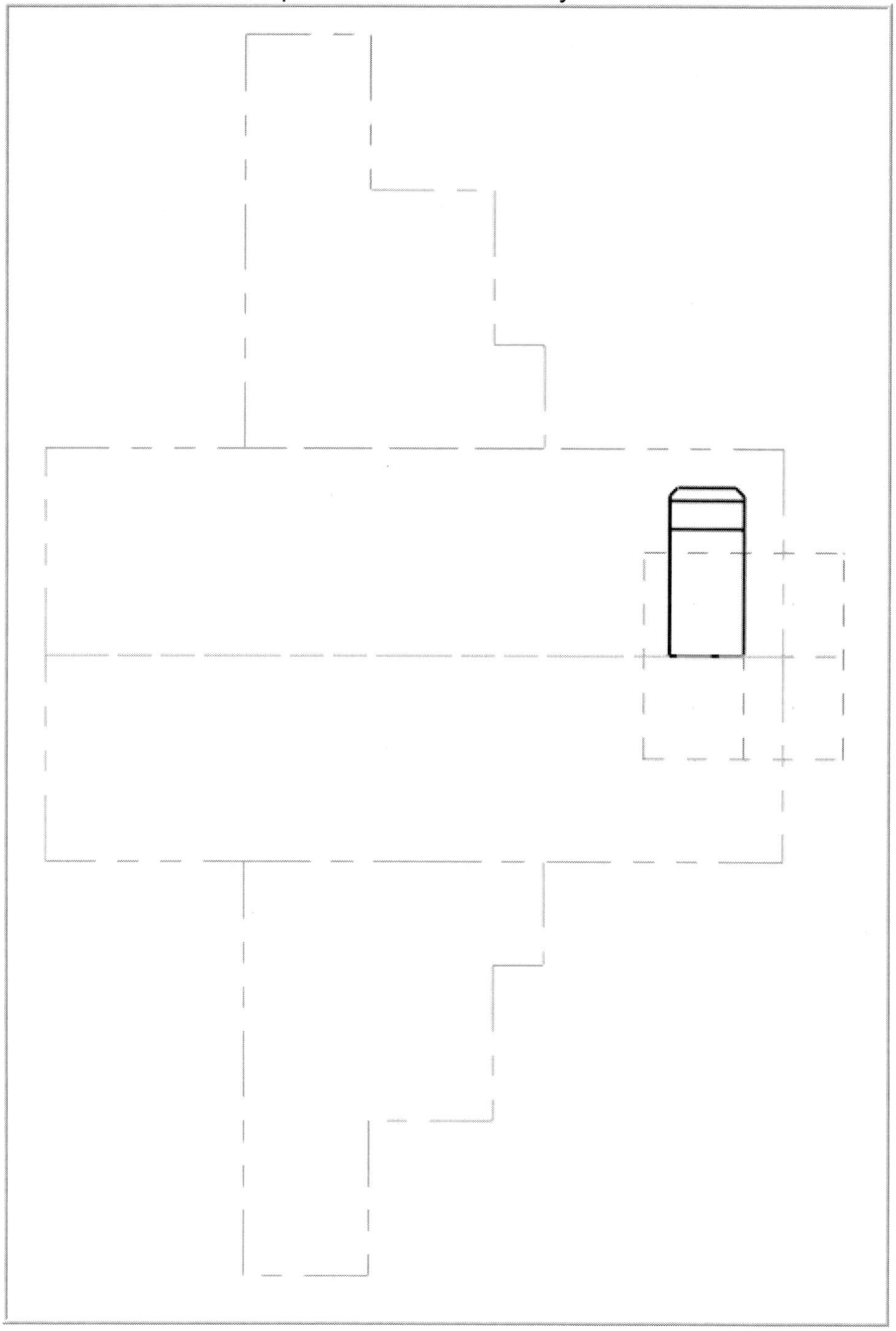

TASK 7:
FACE THE FRONT OF THE PART:

➲ In this task you will use a facing tool to face the front of the part in one cut.

1. Select the **TURNING** tab at the top right side of the screen.
2. Now select **Face** in the **General** section.

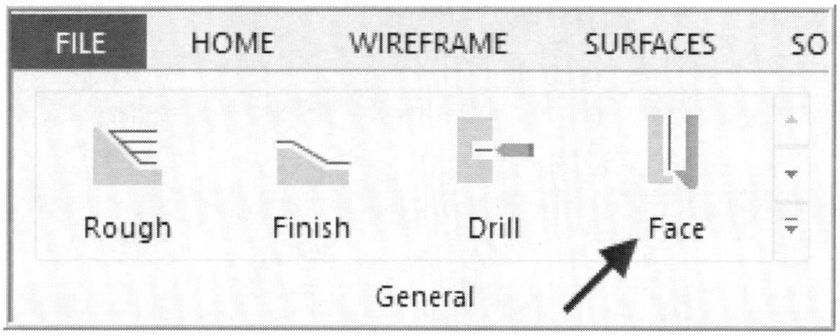

➲ After selecting the OK button you are confronted with **Toolpath parameters** page. The first task here will be to select **Tool #1 an OD Rough- Right – 80 deg.**

3. Click on **Tool #1 OD ROUGH RIGHT** and make changes in the **Toolpath parameters** page as shown below. **Coolant Flood** is set to **On**.

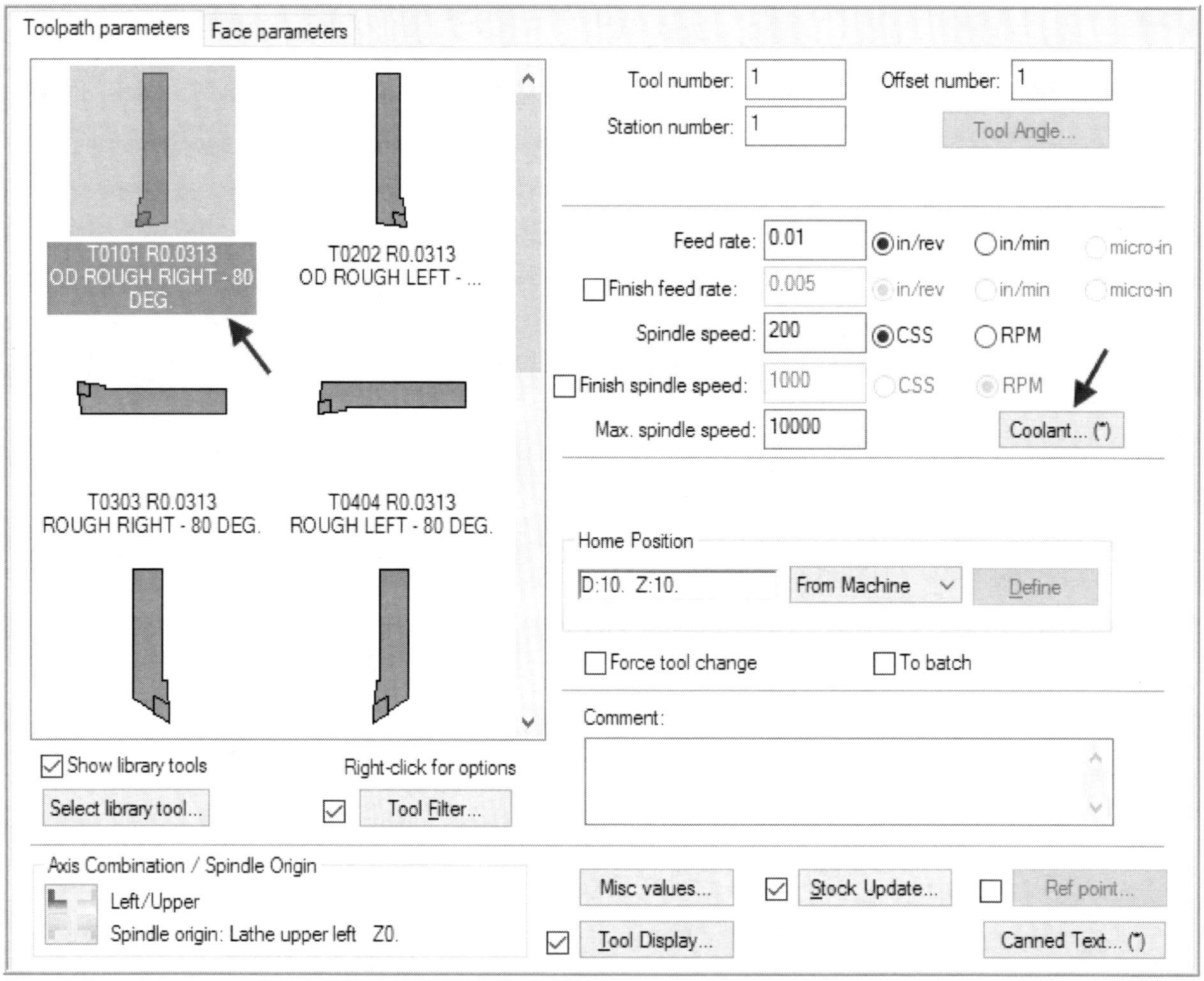

4. Select the **Face parameters** page and make changes as shown below, if required.

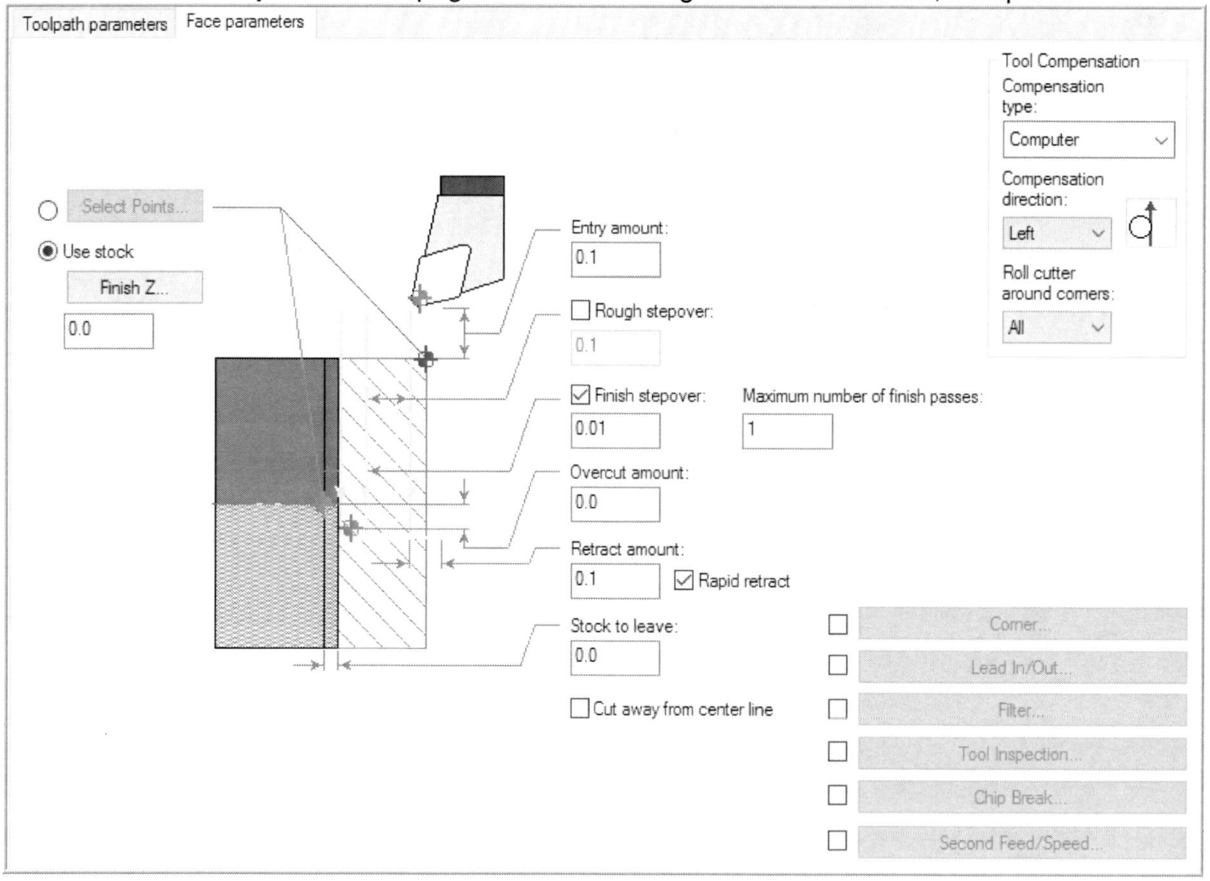

5. Select the OK button  to complete this **Lathe Face** operation.

TASK 8:
ROUGH THE OUTSIDE DIAMETERS

➲ In this task you will use the same tool as used for the previous facing operation **Tool #1 an OD Rough- Right – 80 deg.**

1. On the **TURNING** tab select **Rough** in the **General** section.

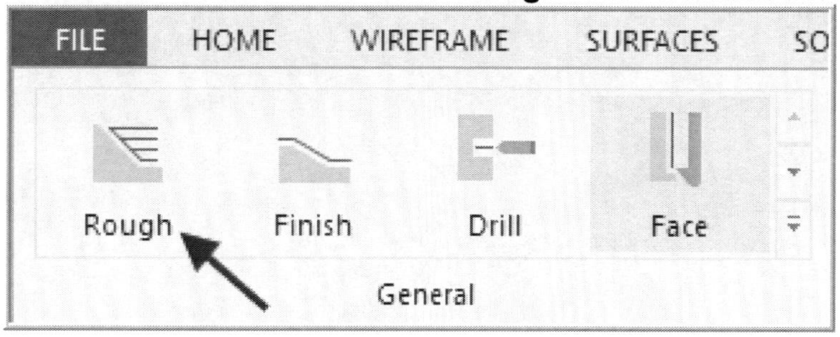

2. In the **Chaining** window Chaining mode is set to **Partial** by default.

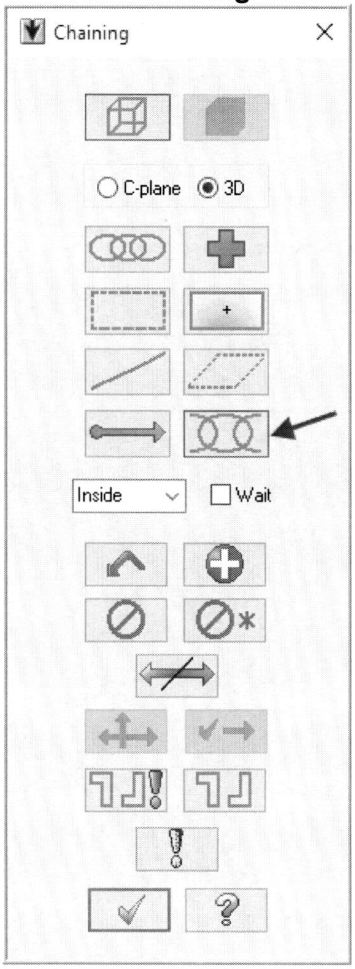

3. **Zoom** the part so it looks similar to the diagram below: **Note:** You can Zoom by using one of the following methods:
    a. By clicking on the **View Tab** and selecting the **Window** icon in the **Zoom** section.
    b. By **Scrolling the wheel** on your mouse (if your mouse has a wheel)
    c. Using the **Page Up** key on your keyboard. (The **Page Down** key un-zooms the part).

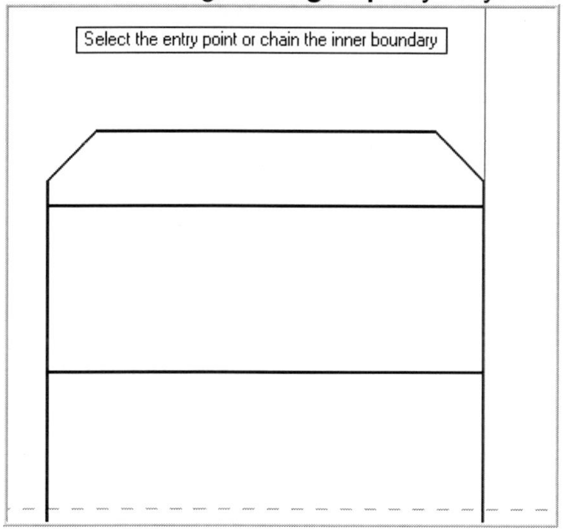

4. Select **Line 1** as the start of the **Partial chain**.

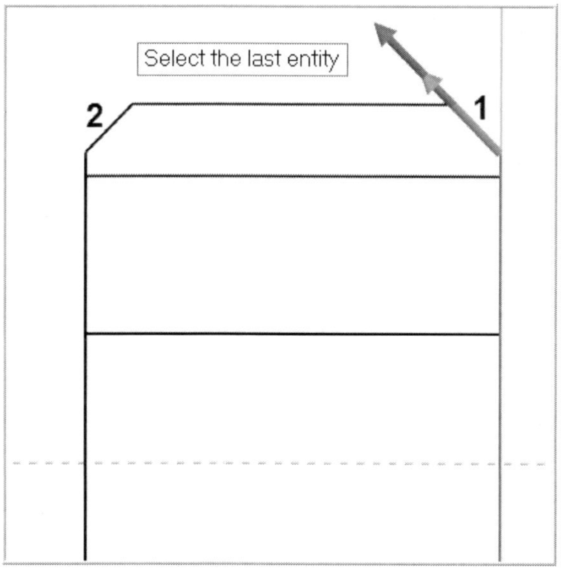

After you have selected the line **ensure** that the arrows are pointing up as shown above on **line 1**. If it is not, select the **reverse button** in the **Chaining dialog box**:

5. Then select **Line 2** as the end entity in this chain as shown above.

6. Select the **OK** button  to exit the Chaining dialog window.

7. In the **Toolpath parameters** page select the same tool used to face the part **Tool #1 OD ROUGH RIGHT** and make sure the settings are the same as shown below. **Coolant Flood** is set to **On**.

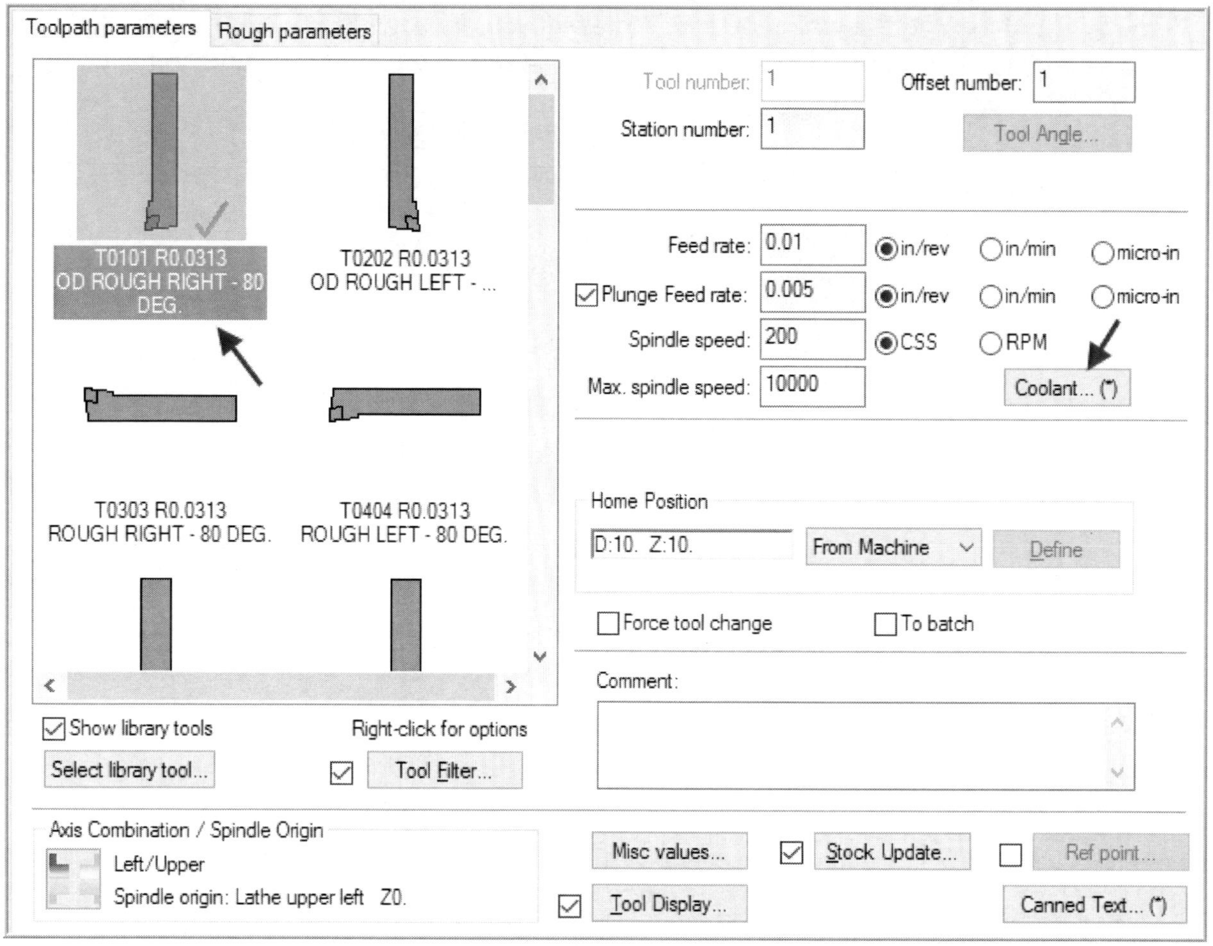

8. Select the **Rough parameters** page and make changes as shown below.

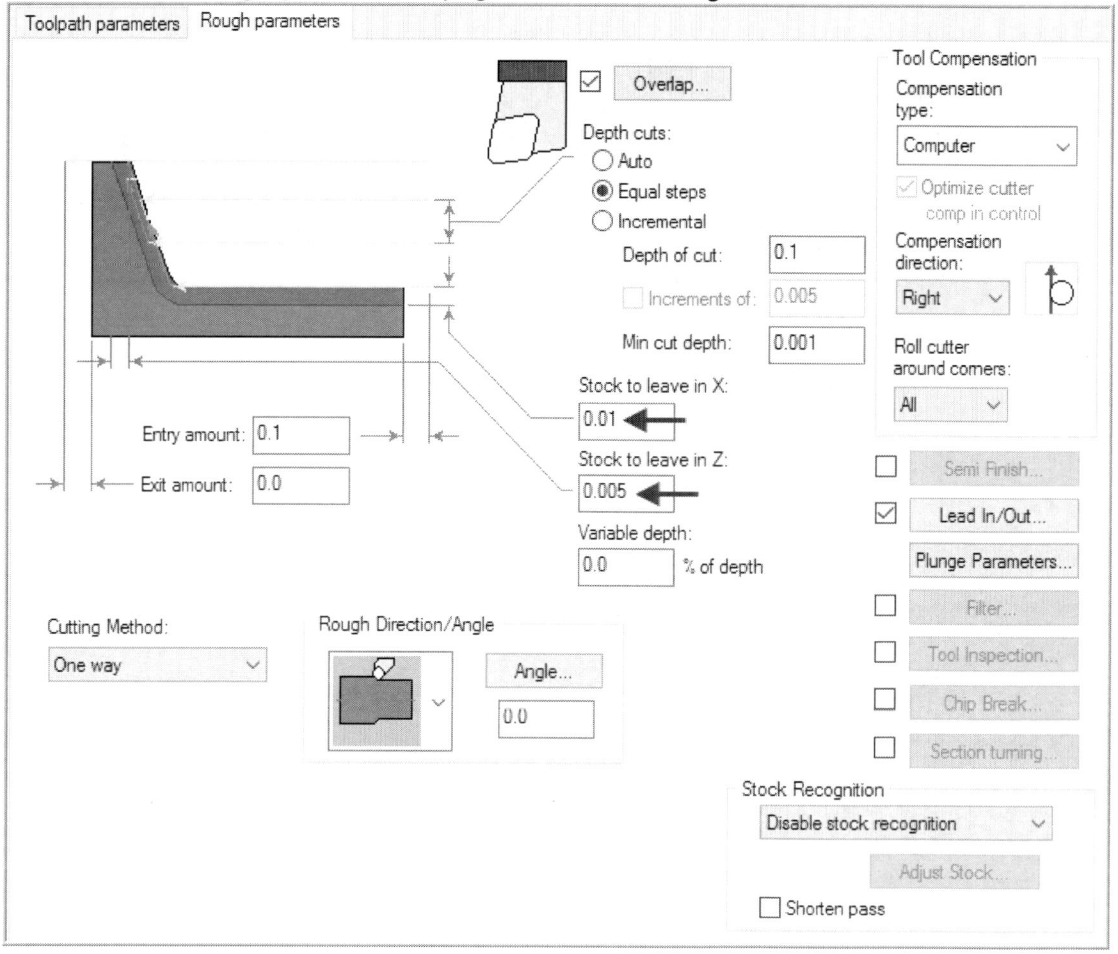

9. Select the **Lead In/Out** button, select the **Lead out** page and extend the contour by **0.2**.

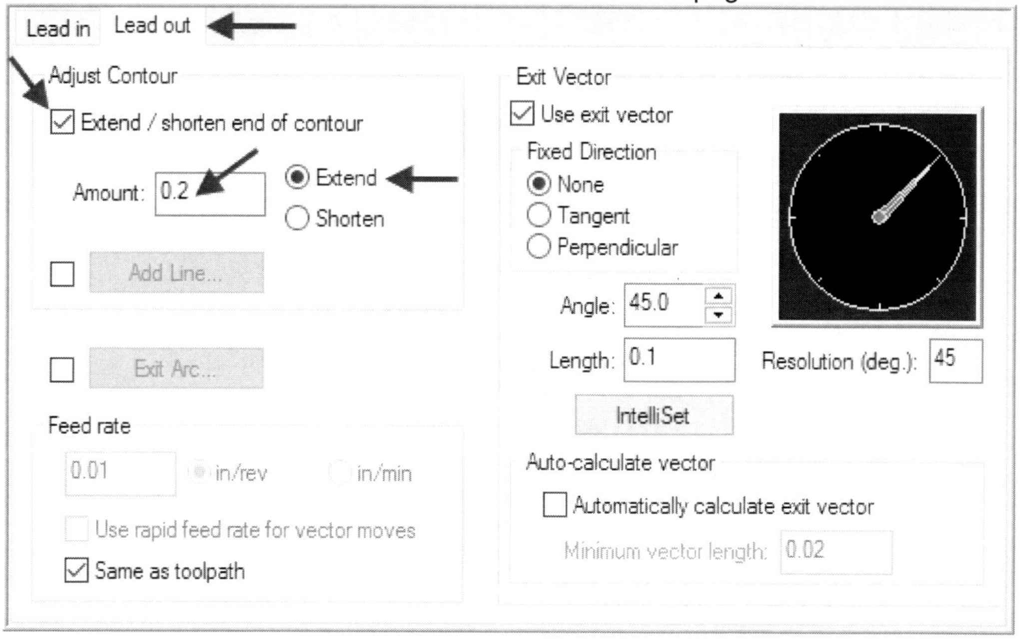

10. Select the **OK** button  to exit this function.

11. Select the **OK** button  to exit Rough parameters.

TASK 9:
FINISH THE OUTSIDE DIAMETER

➲ In this task you will finish the outside diameters in one cut using **Tool #2 an OD Finish-Right – 35 deg.**

1. On the **TURNING** tab select **Finish** in the **General** section.

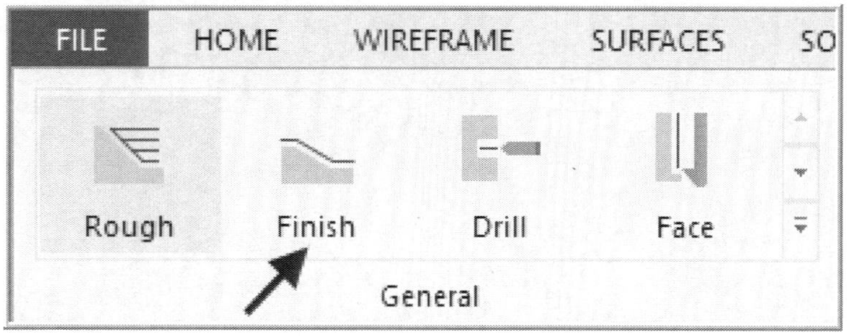

2. Select **Last** in the **Chaining dialog box**.

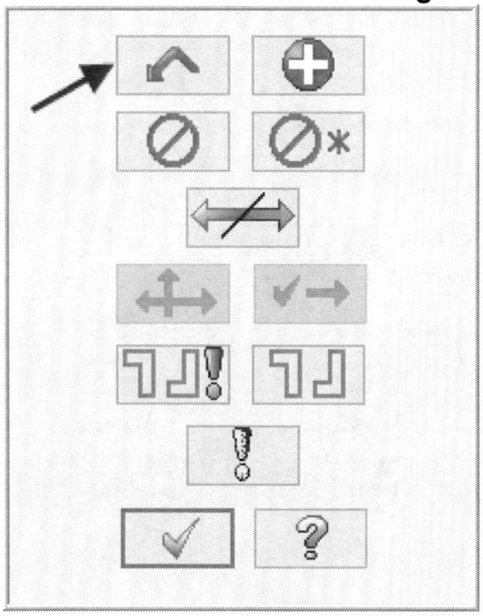

3. Select the **OK** button  to complete the selection.

4. Select **R0.0156 OD Finish Right 35 DEG** tool from the tool list and make changes as shown below. **Coolant Flood** is set to **On**.

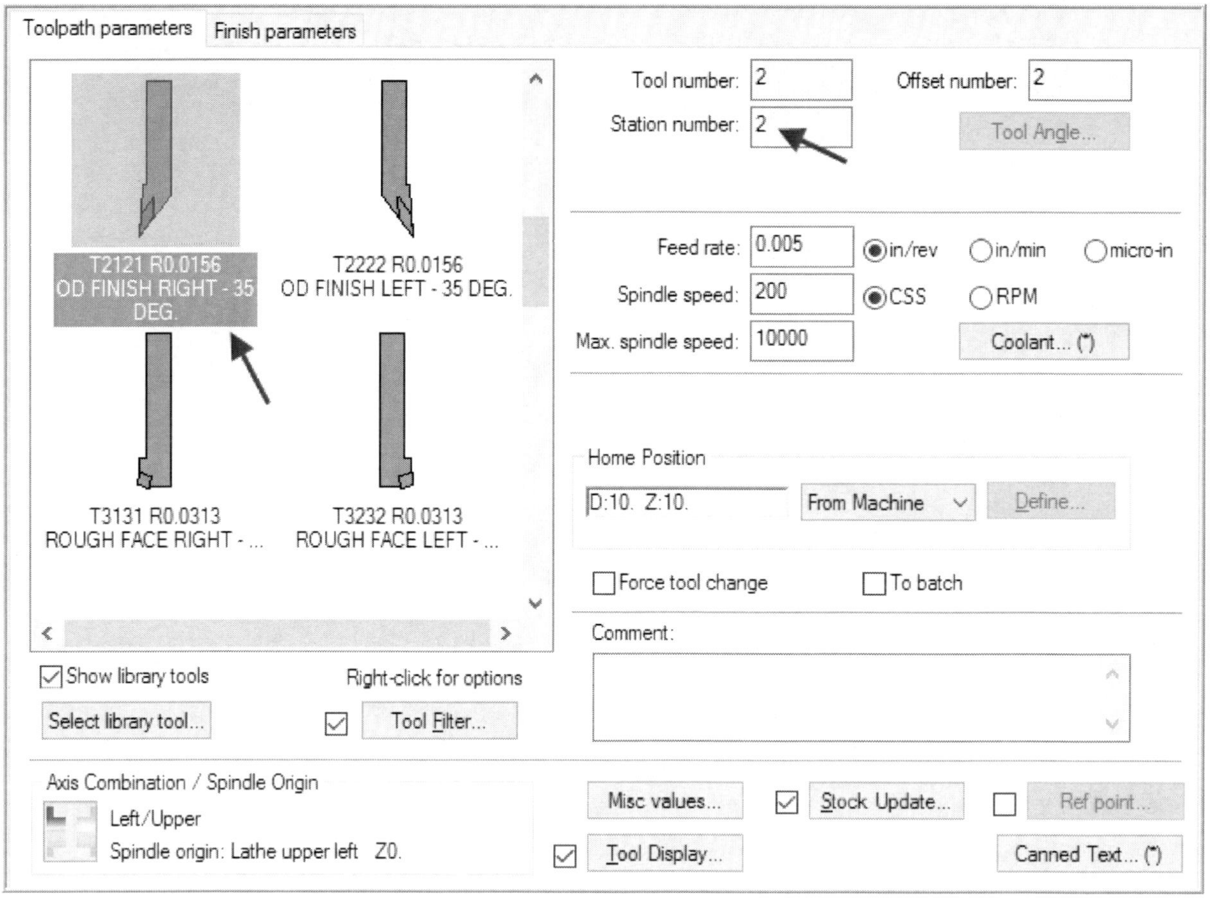

5. Select the **Finish parameters** page and make changes as shown below:

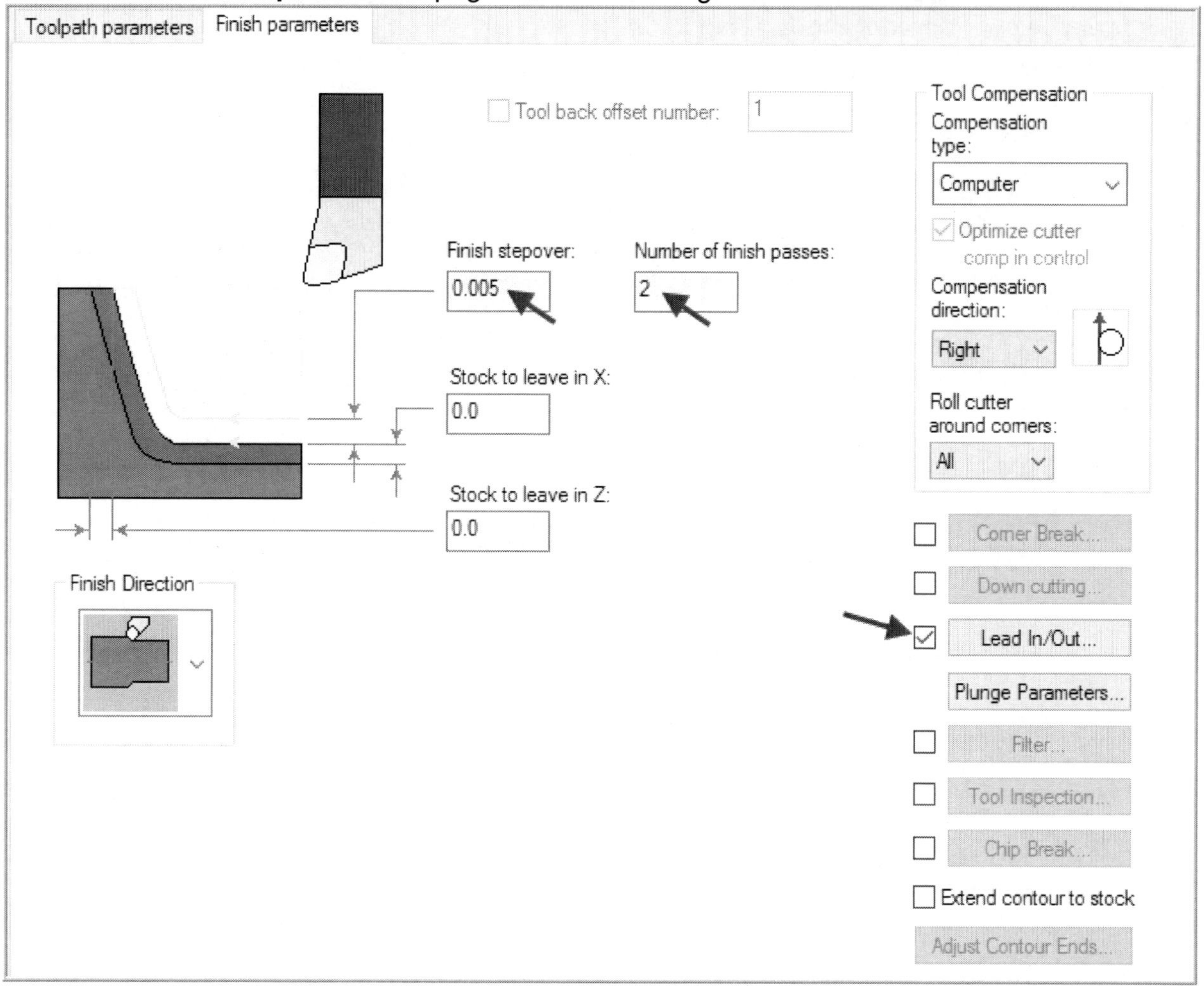

6. Select the **Lead In/Out** button select the **Lead out** page and **extend** the contour by **0.01** as shown below:

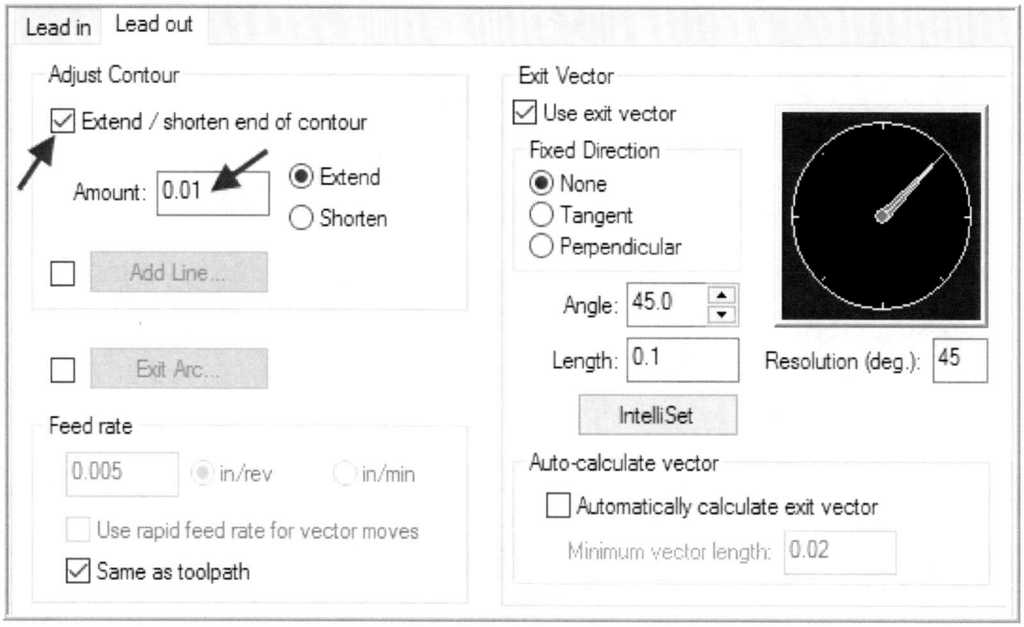

7. Select the **OK** button  to exit this function.

8. Select the **Plunge Parameters...** button Plunge Parameters... .
9. Make the necessary changes as shown below.

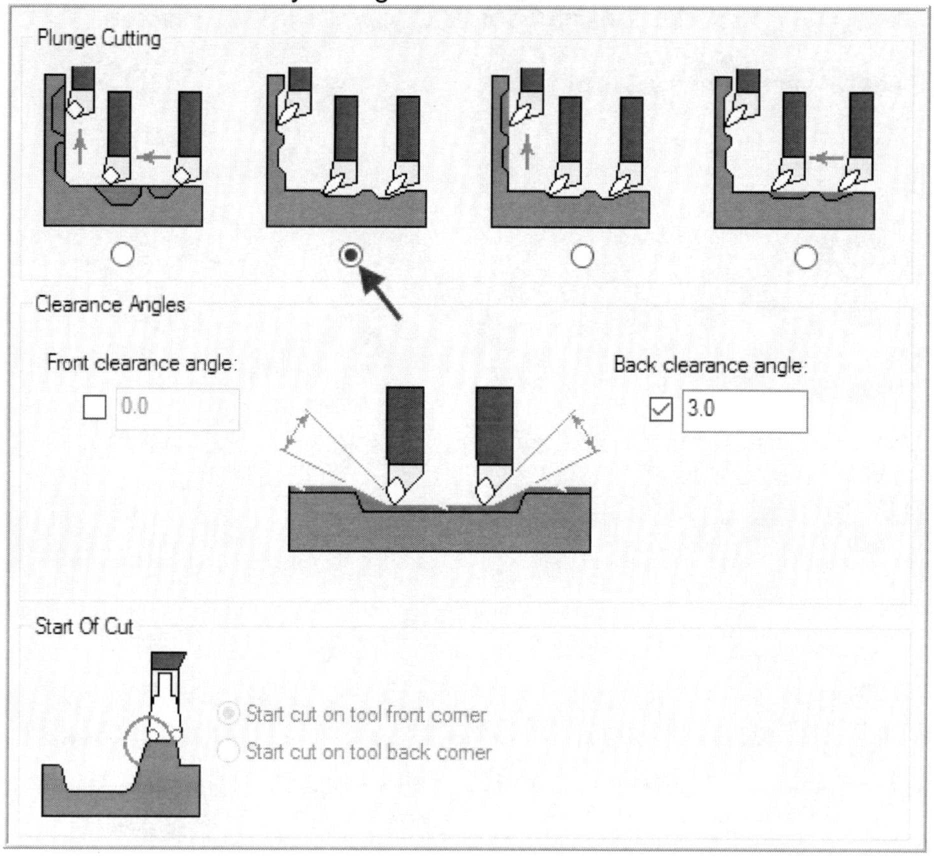

10. Select the **OK** button to exit this function.
11. Select the **OK** button to exit **Finish parameters**.

TASK 10:
CENTER DRILL HOLE

➲ In this task you will center drill **.125"** depth using **Tool #3 Centre Drill - .25 diameter.**

1. Select **Drill** in the **General** section of the **Turning** tab.

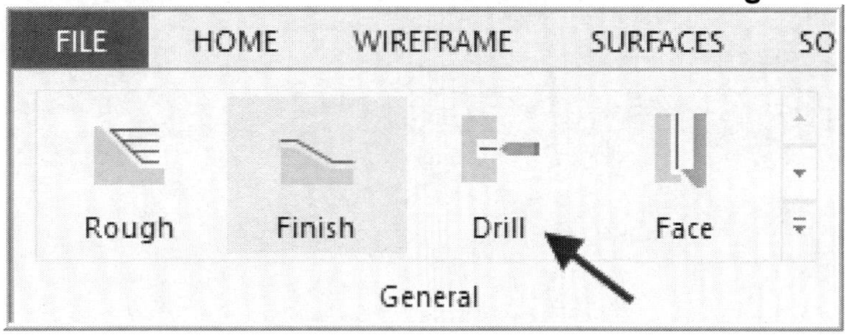

2. Select the **Centre Drill .25 diameter** tool from the tool list and make changes as shown below. **Coolant Flood** is set to **On**.

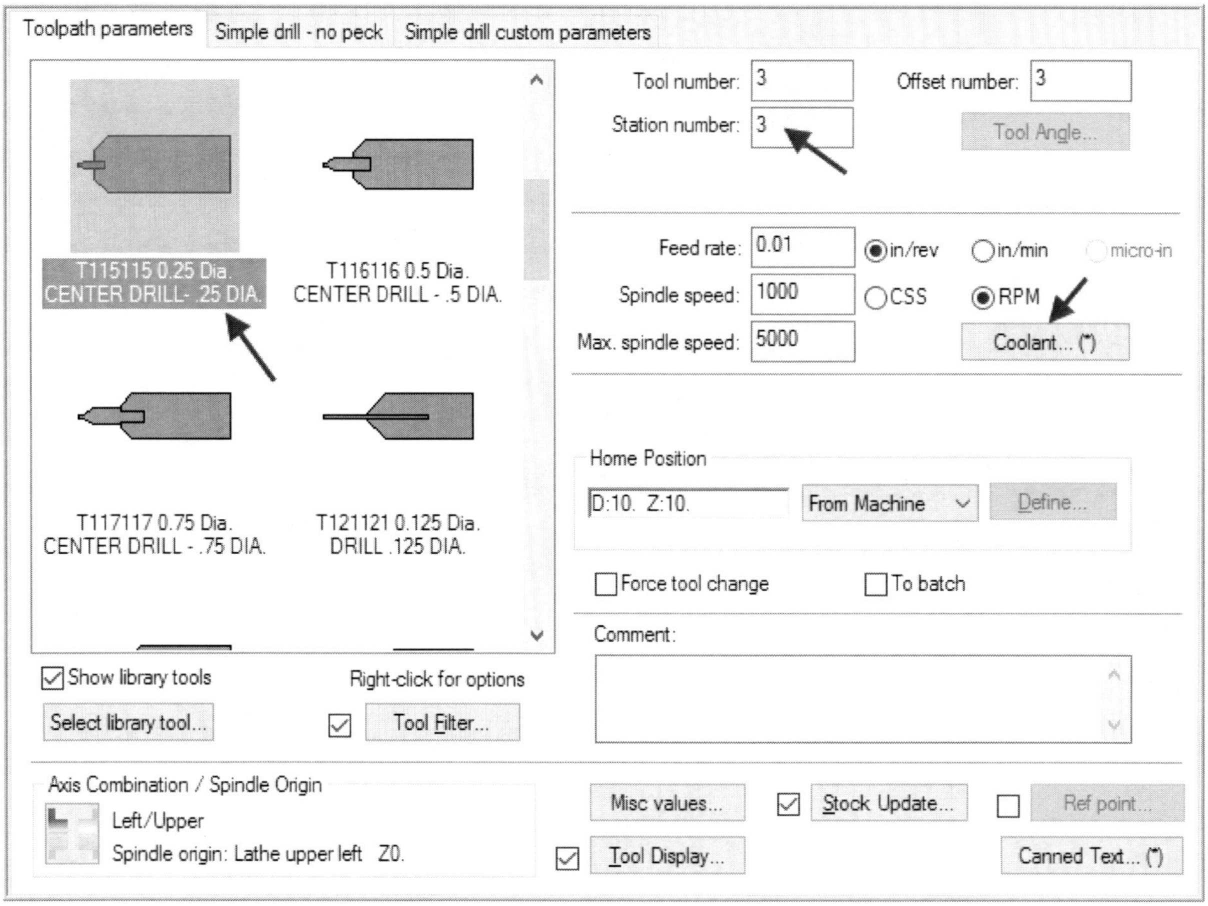

3. Select the **Simple drill – no peck** page and make changes as shown below:

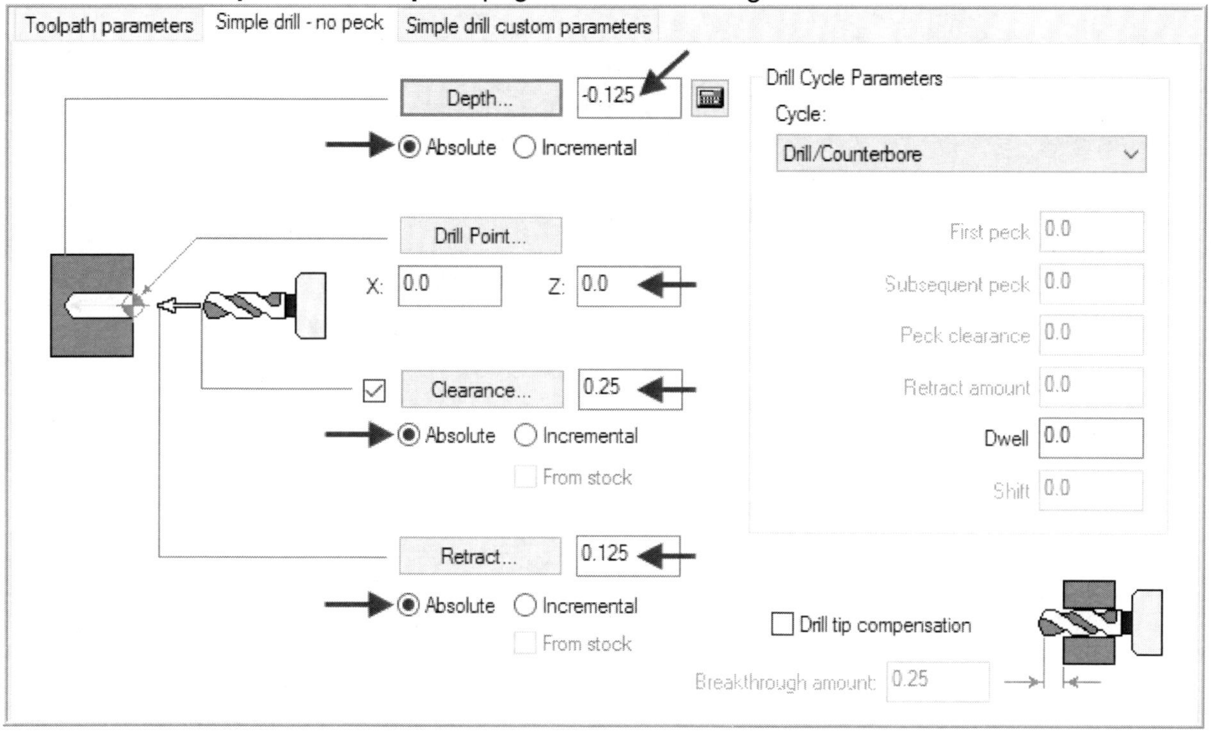

4. Select the **OK** button to exit **Simple drill – no peck**.

TASK 11:
PRE DRILL THE 1.125" HOLE 0.375 DIAMETER

➲ In this task you will pre drill the 1.125" hole through the part using **Tool #4 Drill - .375 diameter.**

1. Select **Drill** in the **General** section of the **Turning** tab.
2. Scroll down and select the **Drill - .375 diameter** tool from the tool list and make changes as shown below. **Coolant Flood** is set to **On**.

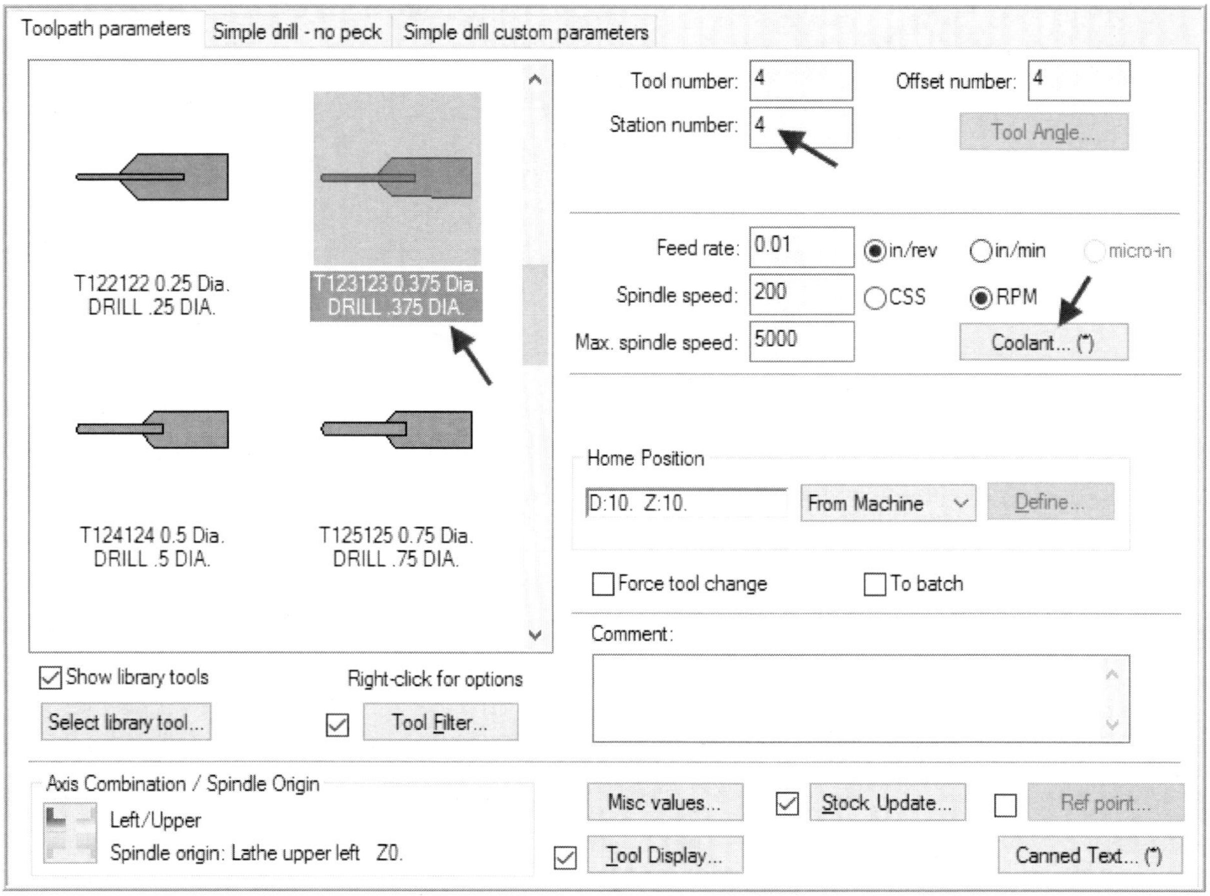

3. Select the **Simple drill – no peck** page and make changes as shown below. This hole will be **peck drilled through the part**. Make changes as shown below:

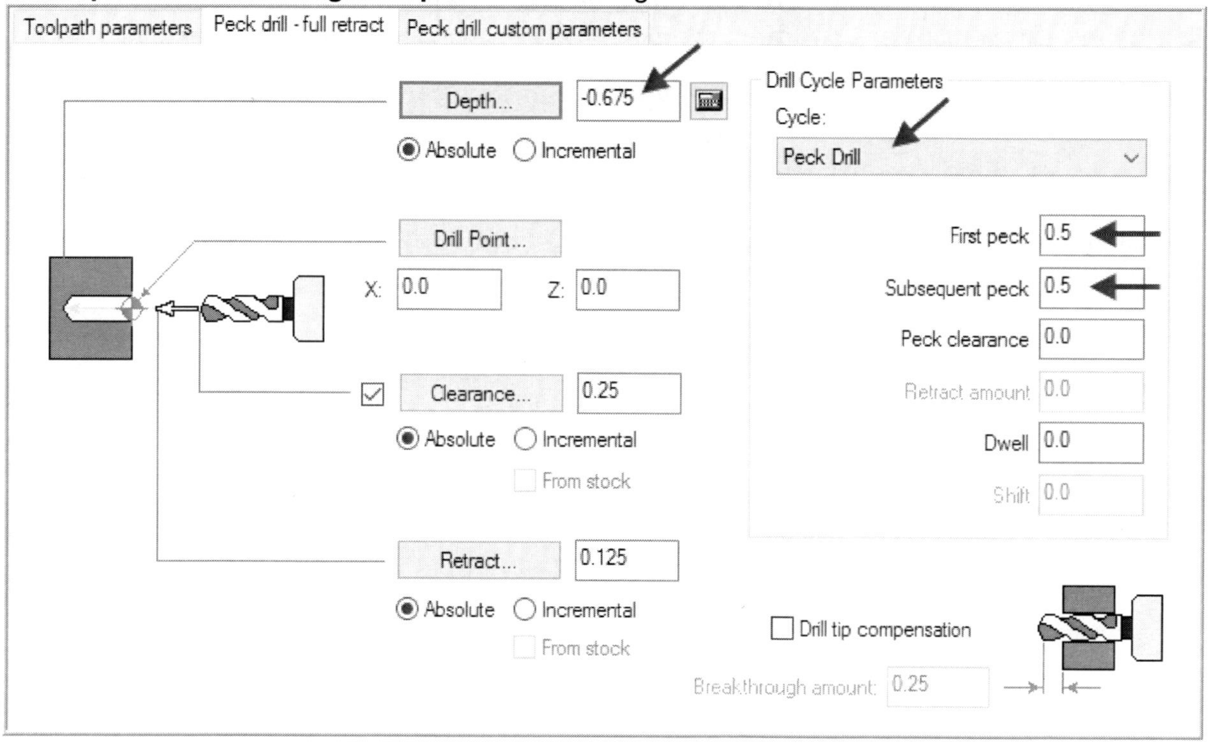

4. Select the **OK** button  to exit **Peck drill – full retract**.

TASK 12:
PRE DRILL THE 1.225" HOLE 0.5 DIAMETER

- In this task you will peck drill through the part with a 0.5 diameter drill prior to boring.
- You will copy the previous peck drill operation and then modify into this peck drilling operation.

1. On the left of the screen in the Toolpaths Manager the 0.375 drill peck drilling operation is the **fifth** operation. To copy this operation hold down the **Right mouse button** over the folder for this operation. Keep holding the right mouse button down and drag below the red arrow and release.
2. Select **Copy after** from this menu.

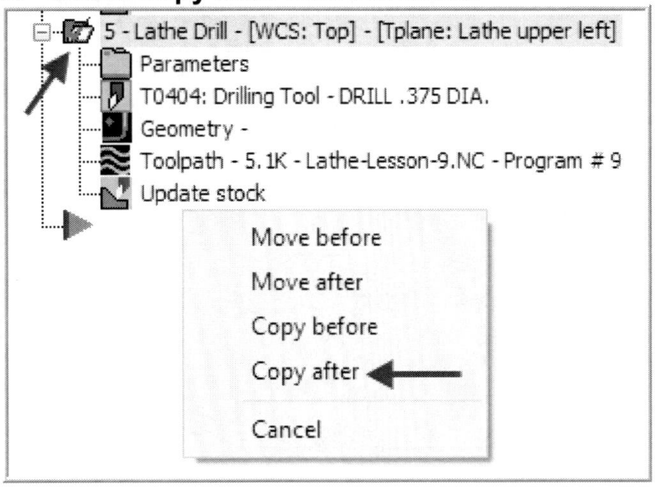

3. Move the Insert arrow 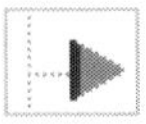 to the bottom of the list of operations by clicking the  icon on the Toolpaths Manager toolbar.
4. In the Toolpaths Manager click on the folder Parameters for the **sixth** operation as shown below:

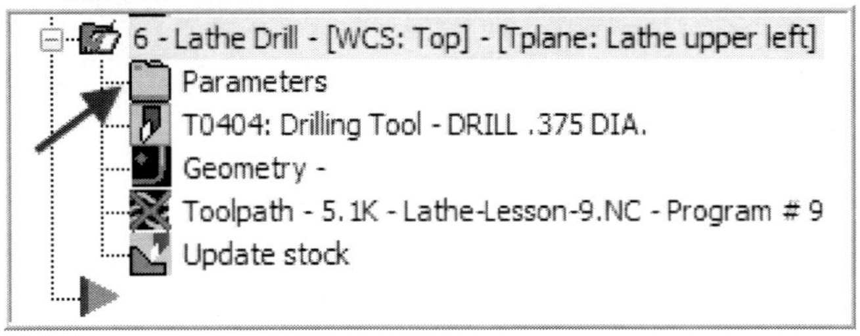

5. Select the **Toolpath parameters** page.

6. In the Toolpath parameters page select the **0.5 Dia Drill**, make changes as shown below.

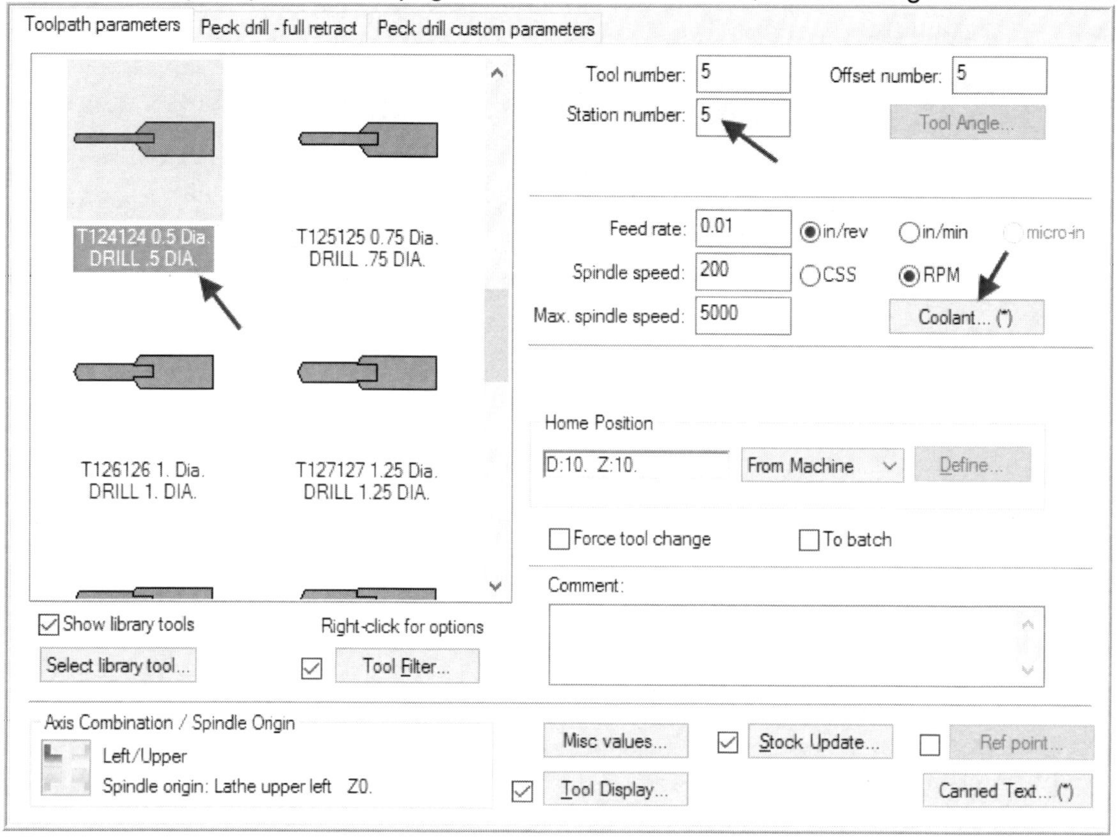

7. Select the **Peck drill – full retract** page and make changes as shown below.

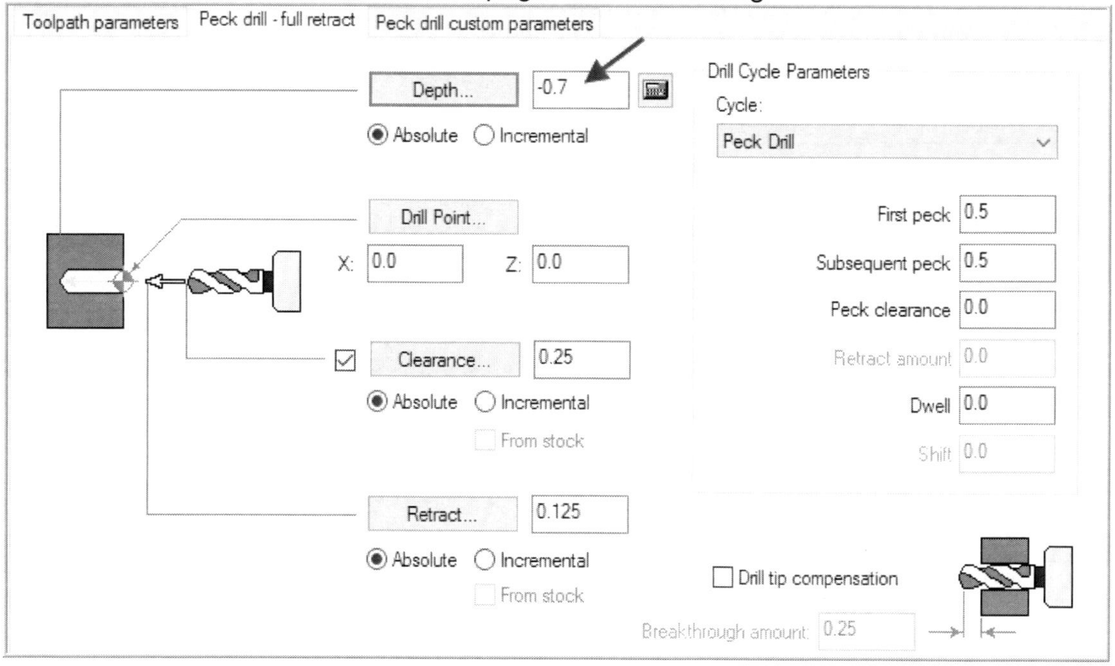

8. Select the **OK** button to exit **Peck drill – full retract**.

9. Select the **Regenerate all dirty operations button** to remove the red X from the drilling operation you have just edited. You need to update the toolpath with the new parameters you have just input.

TASK 13:
ROUGH THE BORE

➲ In this task you will use a boring tool to rough out the 1.225" diameter bore.

1. On the **TURNING** tab select **Rough** in the **General** section.
2. In the **Chaining** window Chaining mode is set to **Partial** by default.
3. Select **Line 1** as the start of the **Partial chain**.

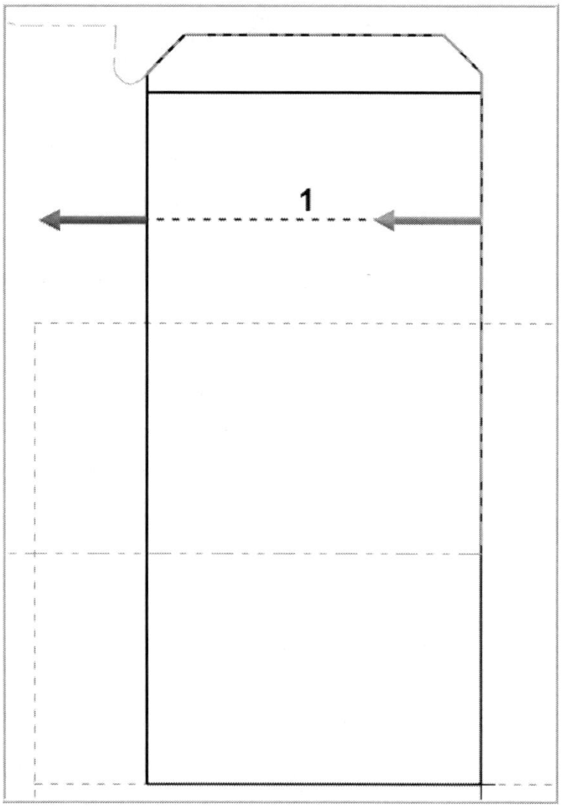

After you have selected the line ensure that the arrows are pointing towards the part as shown above. If it is not select the reverse button in the Chaining dialog box

4. Select the **OK** button  to exit the **Chaining dialog window**.
5. In the **Toolpath parameters** page scroll down and select a boring tool **ID ROUGH MIN .375 DIA – 75 deg**.

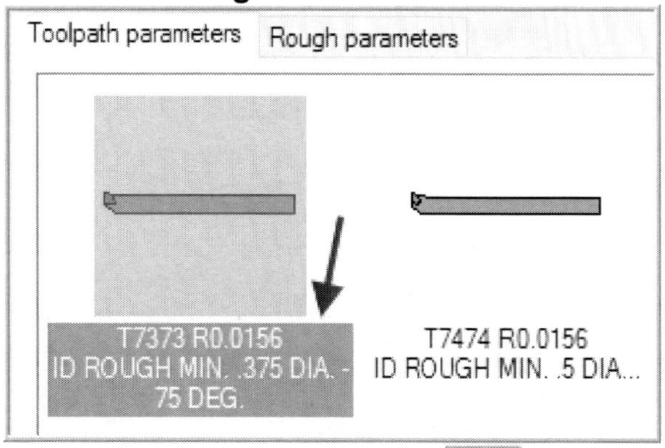

6. Double click on the picture  for this boring tool in the tool list window.

7. On the **Inserts** page change the thickness of this insert to 1/32 as shown below:

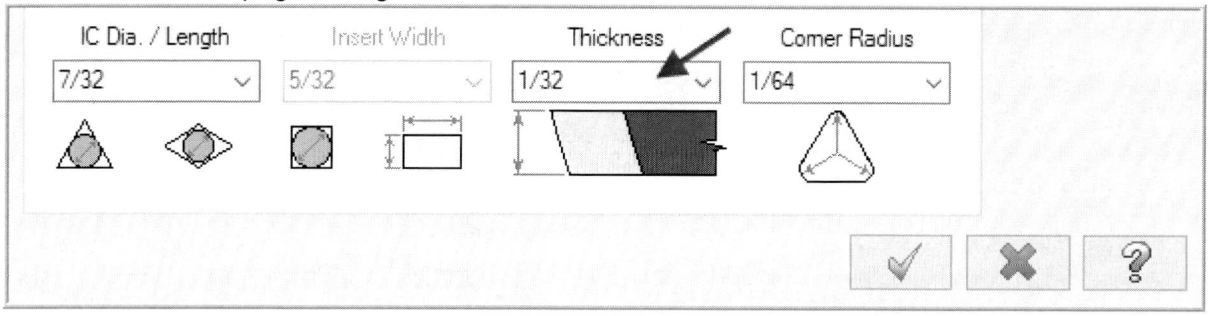

8. Select the **OK** button to exit the **Inserts** page.
9. In the **Toolpath parameters** page make any necessary changes as shown below. **Coolant Flood** is set to **On**.

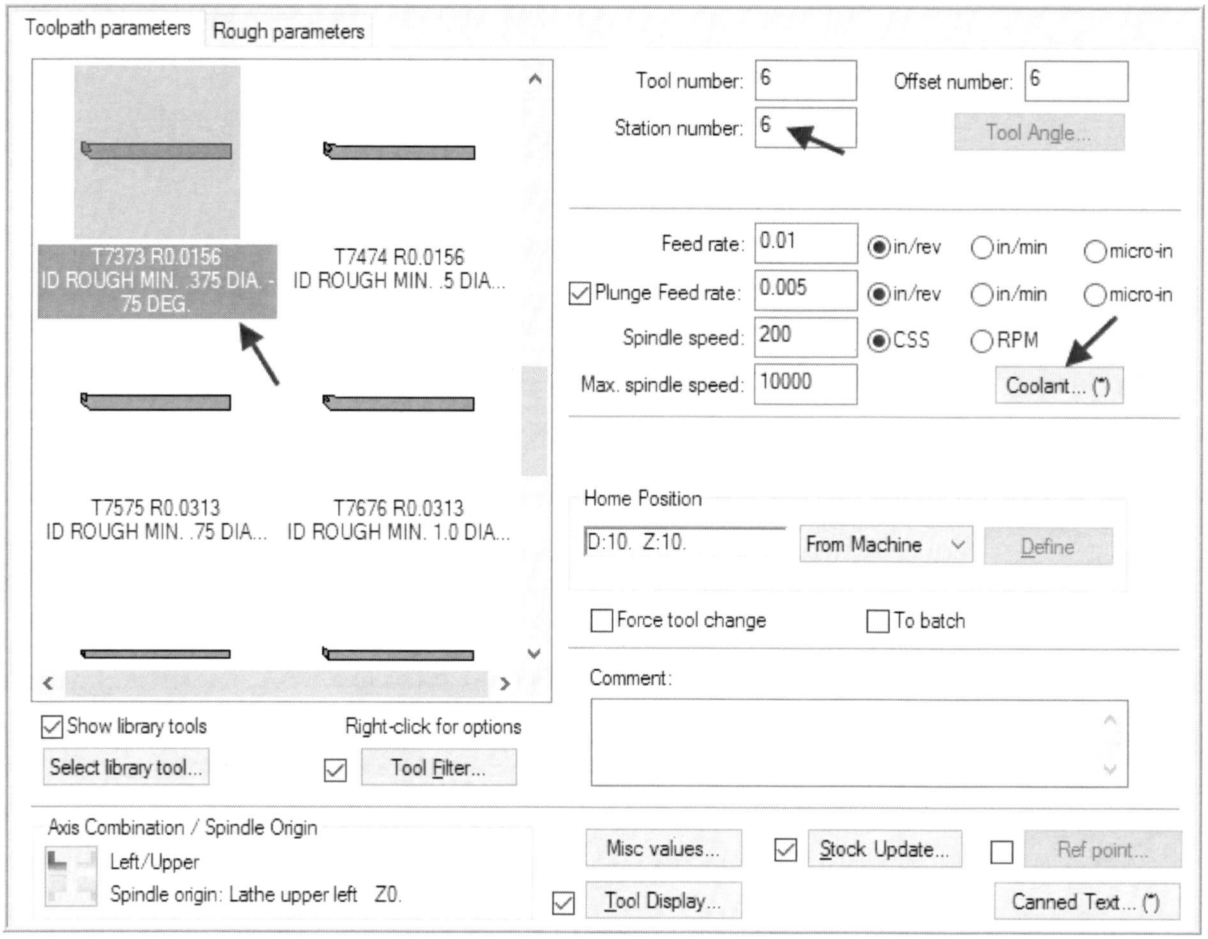

10. Select the **Rough parameters** page and make any necessary changes as shown below:

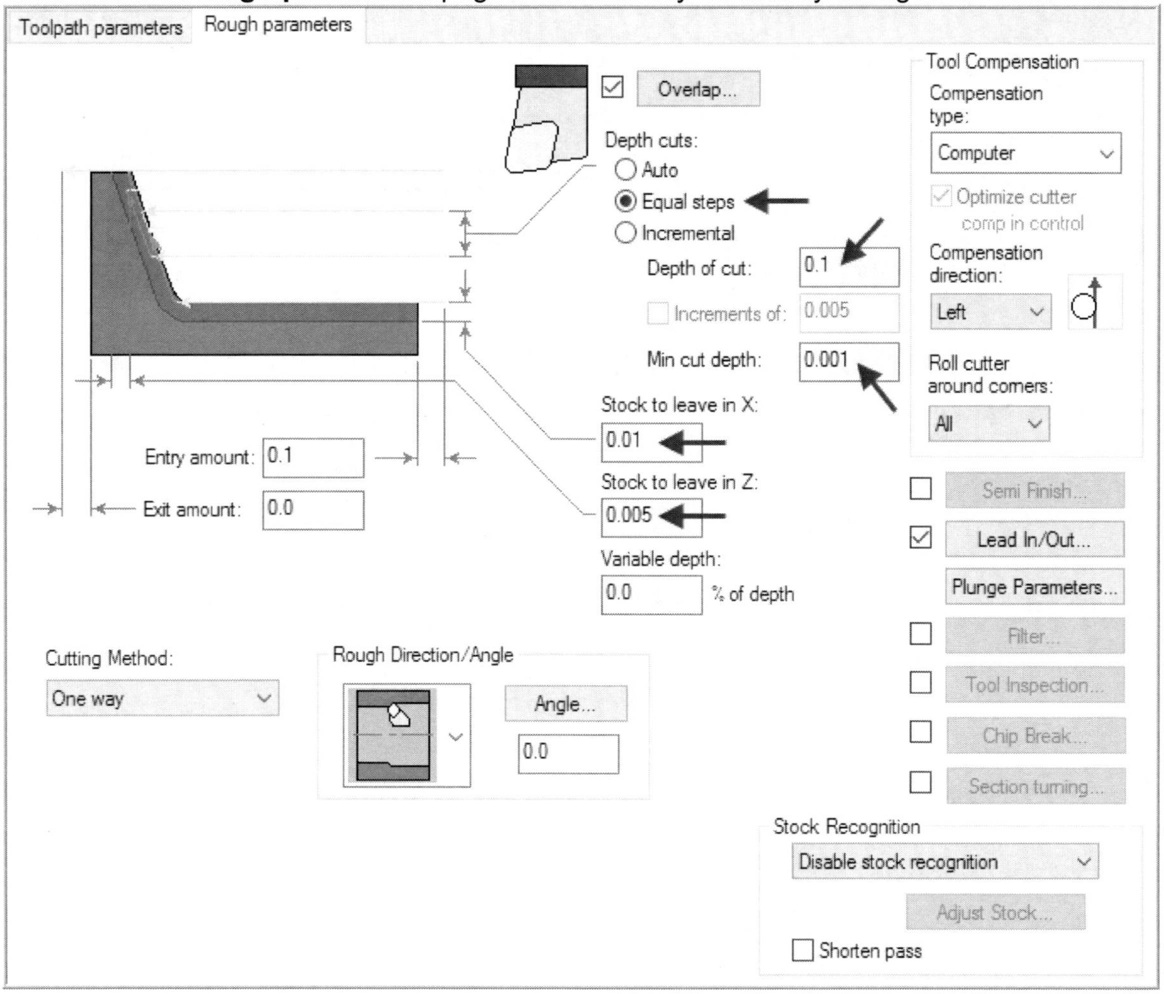

11. Select the **Lead In/Out** button select the **Lead out** page and extend the contour by **0.05** as shown below:

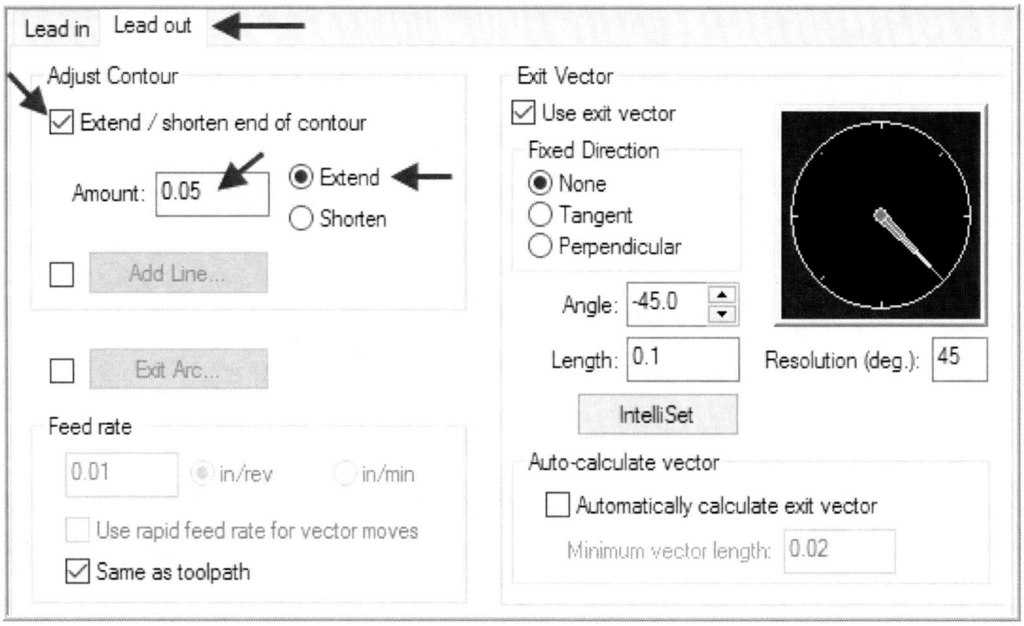

12. Select the **OK** button ✓ to exit this function.

13. Open up the **Stock Recognition** drop down menu and select **Use stock for outer boundary**.

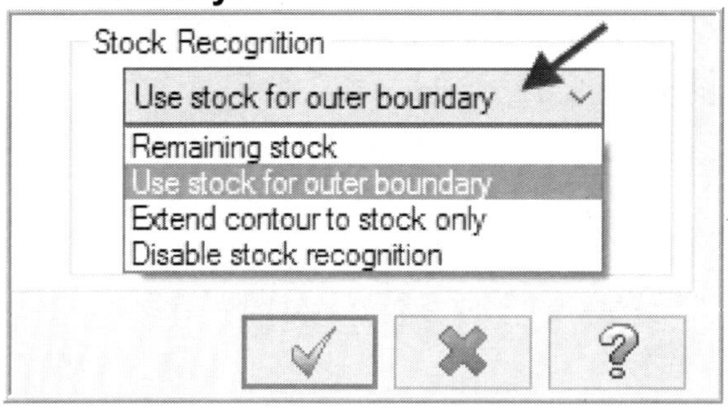

14. Now Click on the **Adjust Stock....** button.

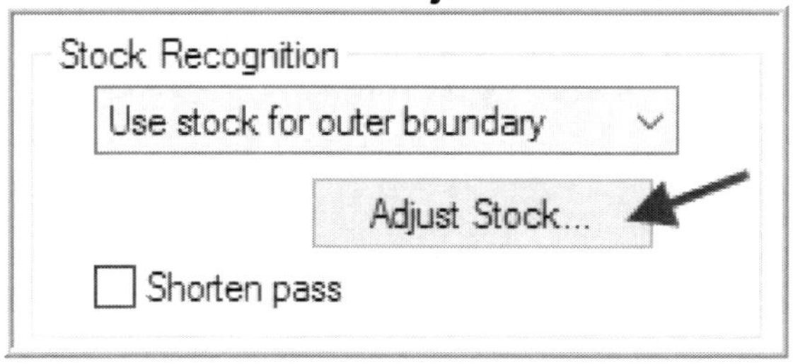

Adjust Stock dialog box
Use these options to tell Mastercam how to integrate the contour that you've chained for the toolpath with the stock boundary, so that the tool will approach and come off the part the way you intend to.
First, select an End to Adjust. The first radio button lets you adjust the start of the toolpath, the second lets you adjust the end. You can adjust the stock individually for each.
Then, for each end of the toolpath, select a stock adjustment method. Each option results in an imaginary line from the selected end of the toolpath to the stock boundary, in either of the following orientations:
- tangent to the toolpath
- perpendicular to the Z axis
- to the Z axis
The area of remaining stock between the stock boundary and chained contour is highlighted in orange. A yellow point indicates the start of the chained contour, while a red point indicates the end of the chained contour.
As you select different options, you will see them previewed on the screen. If the dialog box is in the way, choose Auto hide and it will hide when you move the cursor over the graphics window.

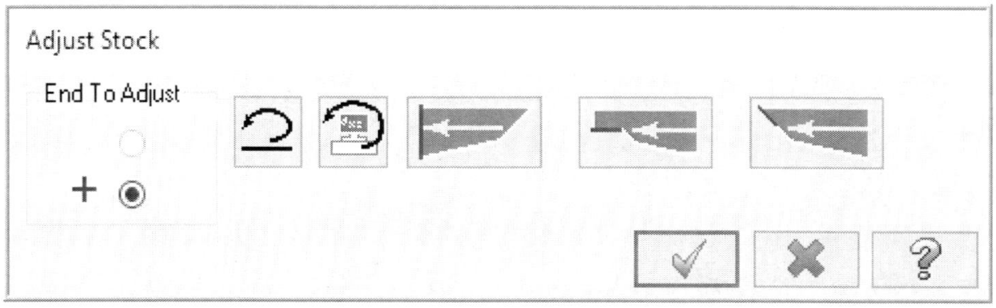

15. Select the **OK** button  to exit Adjust Stock.
16. Select the **OK** button  to exit Rough Parameters.

TASK 14:
FINISH THE BORE

➲ In this task you will use the same boring tool as used for the previous rouging operation.

1. Right mouse click in the white space of the **Toolpaths Manager** and select:
   Lathe toolpaths>Quick>Quick finish.

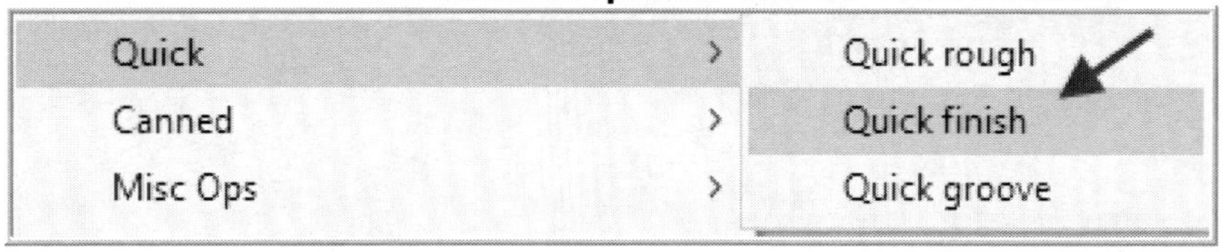

2. In the **Quick Toolpath parameters** page select **Tool #6 a boring tool ID ROUGH MIN .375 DIA – 75 deg** and make any necessary changes as shown below. **Coolant Flood** is set to **On**.

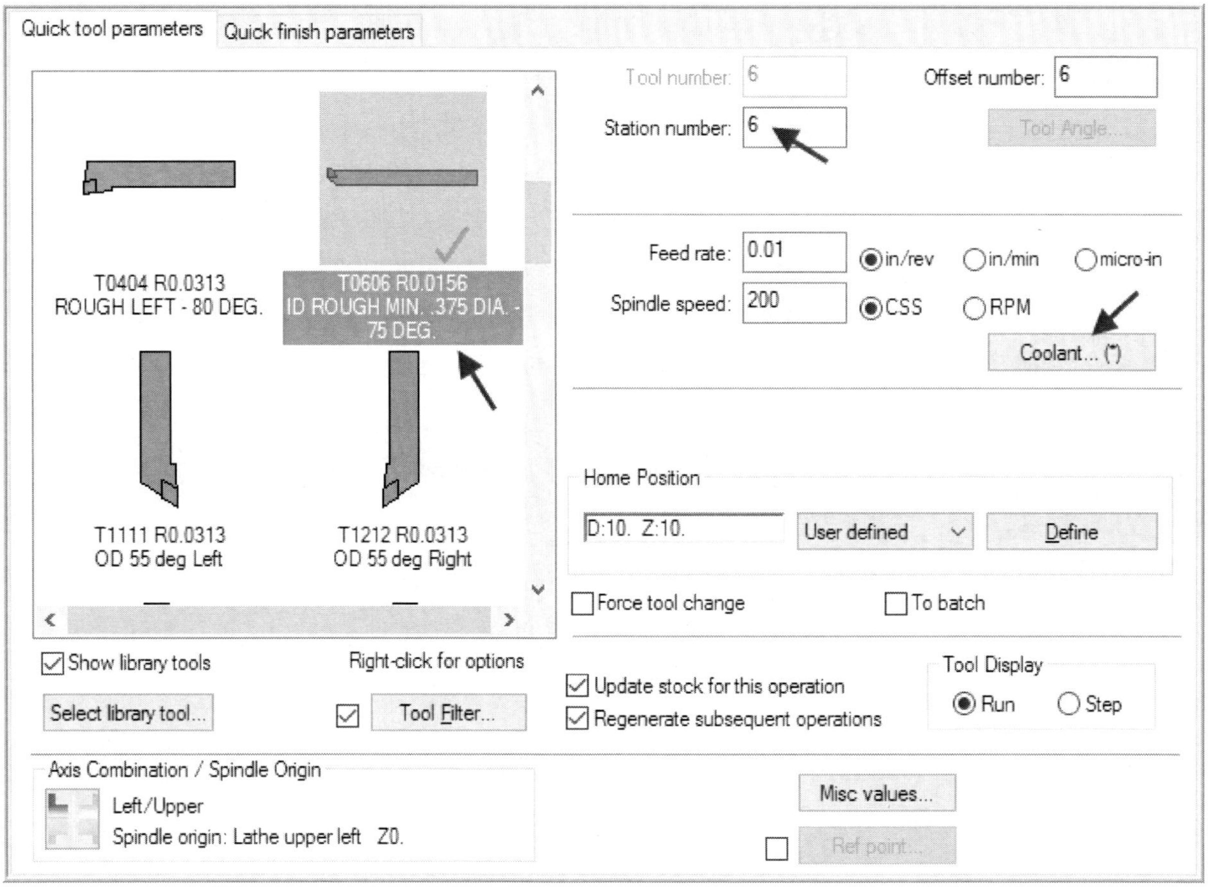

3. Select the **Quick finish parameters page** and in the lower left corner open up the drop down menu for **Finish Direction** and select **ID** from the four options listed here.

4. Still on the **Quick finish parameters** page and make any necessary changes as shown below. Open up the drop down menu for operation and select the operation at the **bottom of the list**, this is the previous rough boring operation.
5. Set the **Compensation direction** to **Left**.

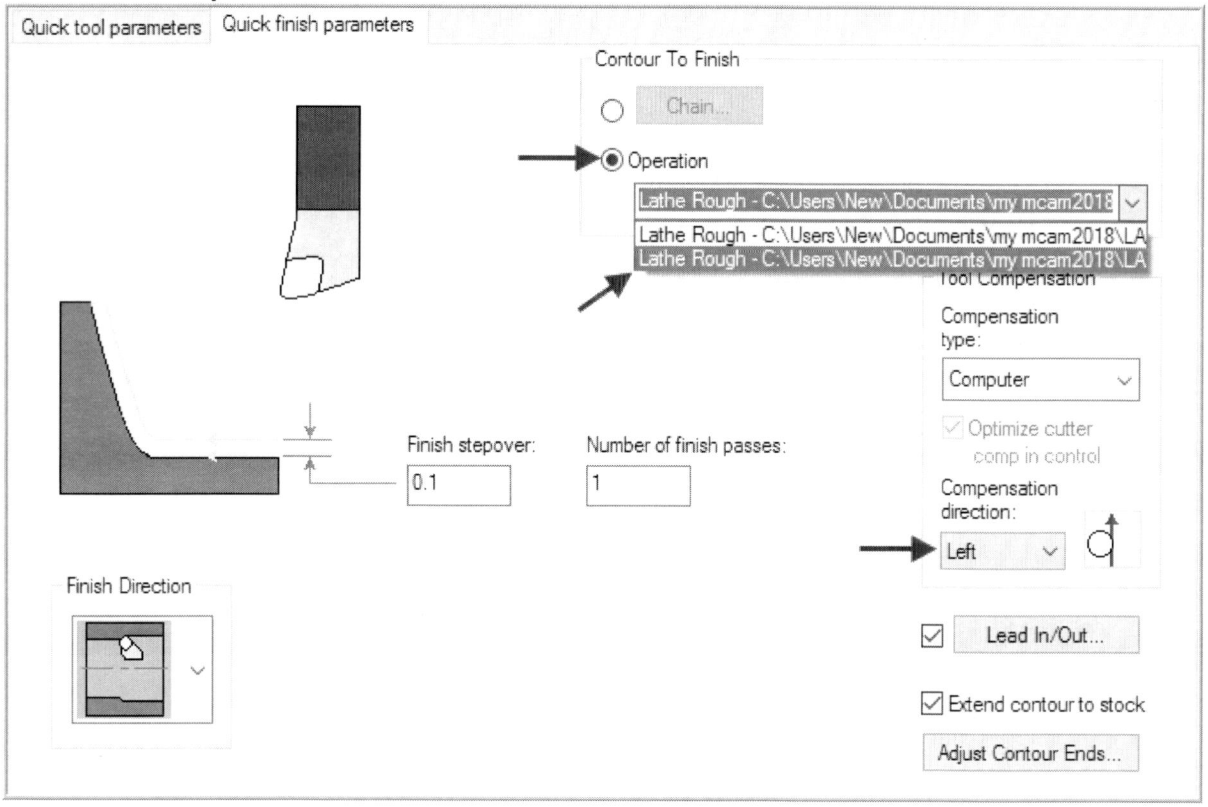

6. Select the **Lead In/Out button** select the **Lead out** page and extend the contour by **0.05** as shown below. Adjust **Exit Vector dial** to -45.

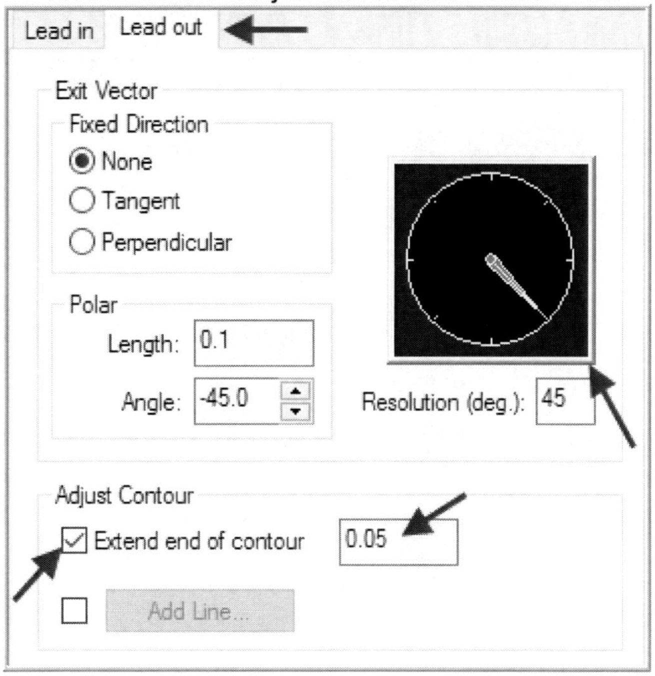

7. Select the **OK** button  to exit this function.
8. Select the **OK** button  to exit **Quick finish** parameters.

TASK 15:
MACHINE THE FIRST SLOT USING C-AXIS CROSS CONTOUR

1. Click on the **Select all operations** icon.
2. Now **toggle the display of the toolpaths** by selecting **ALT and T** on your keyboard to **hide** the toolpaths display.
3. Right mouse click in the graphics area and click on **Isometric**.
4. Right mouse click in the graphics area and click on the **Fit** icon.
5. Click on the **Expand gallery** down arrow to view additional options in the **C-axis** toolpath section and select **Cross Contour**.

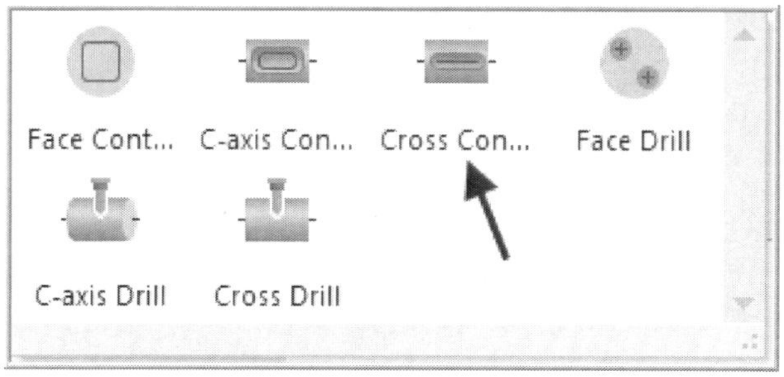

Cross contour toolpaths
Use Mastercam Lathe cross contour toolpaths to cut parallel to the axis of rotation.

These toolpaths are most often used to cut slots. Mastercam sets the tool plane (Tplane) and construction plane (Cplane) so that the tool is placed perpendicular to the axis of rotation (typically the part spindle).

Choosing this toolpath also sets the default cutter **compensation** to **Off** so that the center of the tool follows the chained geometry.

6. You are prompted to **Select Contour chain 1** and the Chaining parameter window appears. Select the **Single** button as shown below left:

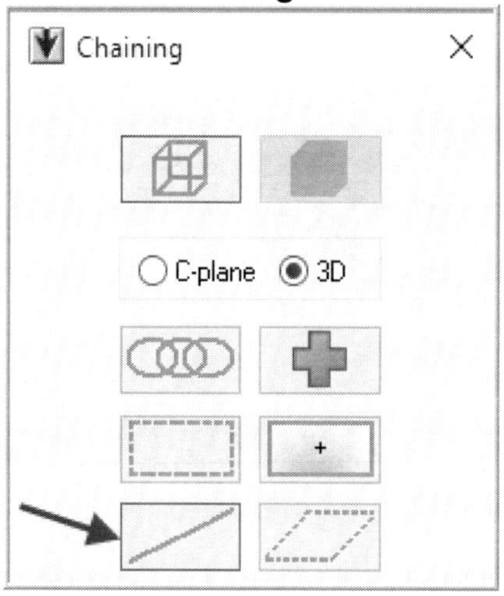

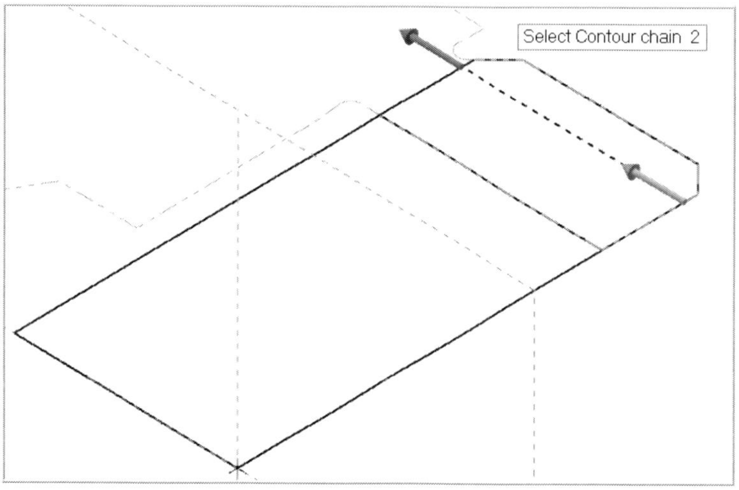

7. To satisfy the prompt click on the right end of the line as shown above right. Arrows are pointing towards the part.
8. Click **OK** in the Chaining dialog box.

9. Select the **Tool** page and then click on **Select library tool…** 

.

10. Select the **1/4 FLAT END MILL** as shown below:

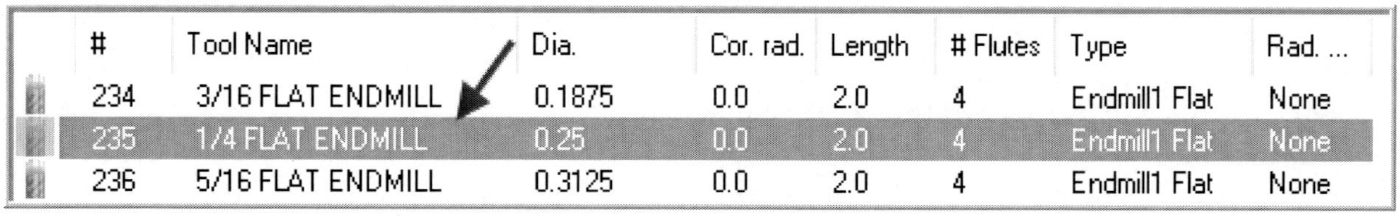

#	Tool Name	Dia.	Cor. rad.	Length	# Flutes	Type	Rad. ...
234	3/16 FLAT ENDMILL	0.1875	0.0	2.0	4	Endmill1 Flat	None
235	1/4 FLAT ENDMILL	0.25	0.0	2.0	4	Endmill1 Flat	None
236	5/16 FLAT ENDMILL	0.3125	0.0	2.0	4	Endmill1 Flat	None

11. Click on **OK**  for the selection of the 0.25" Flat End Mill.

12. Make the changes in the **Toolpath parameters** screen as shown below:

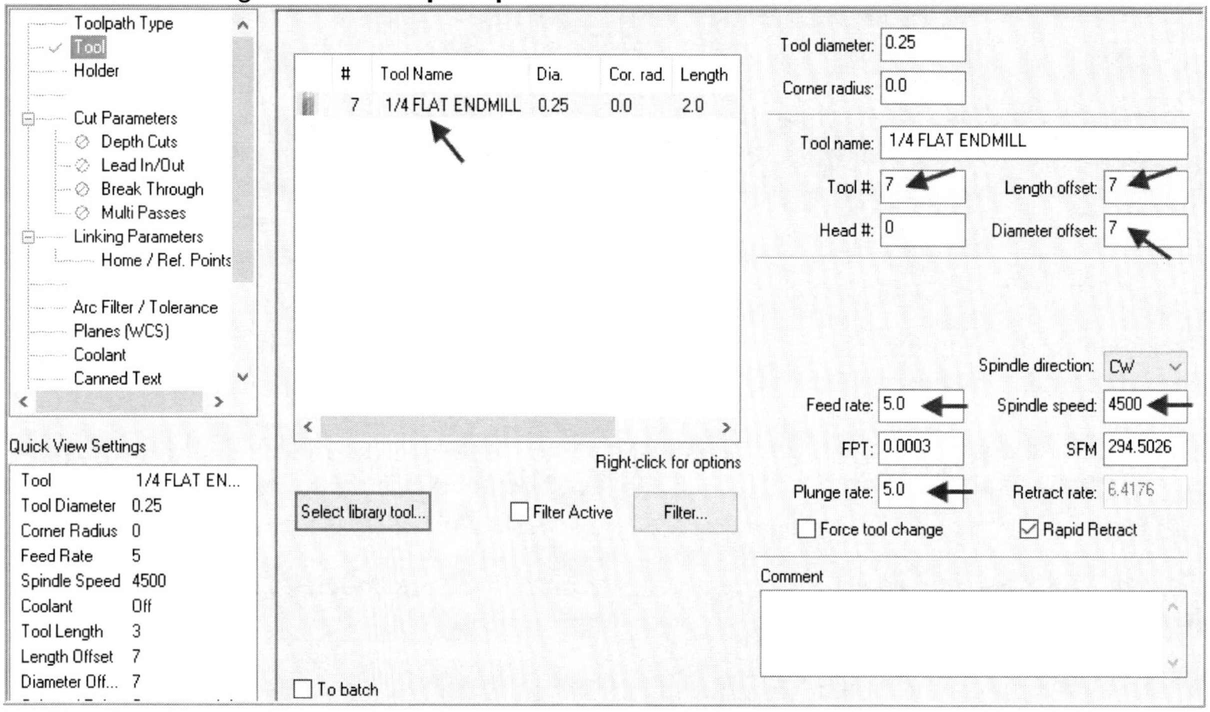

13. Select **Lead In/Out** and make changes as show below. **Tangent is activated**. **Exit is not activated**.

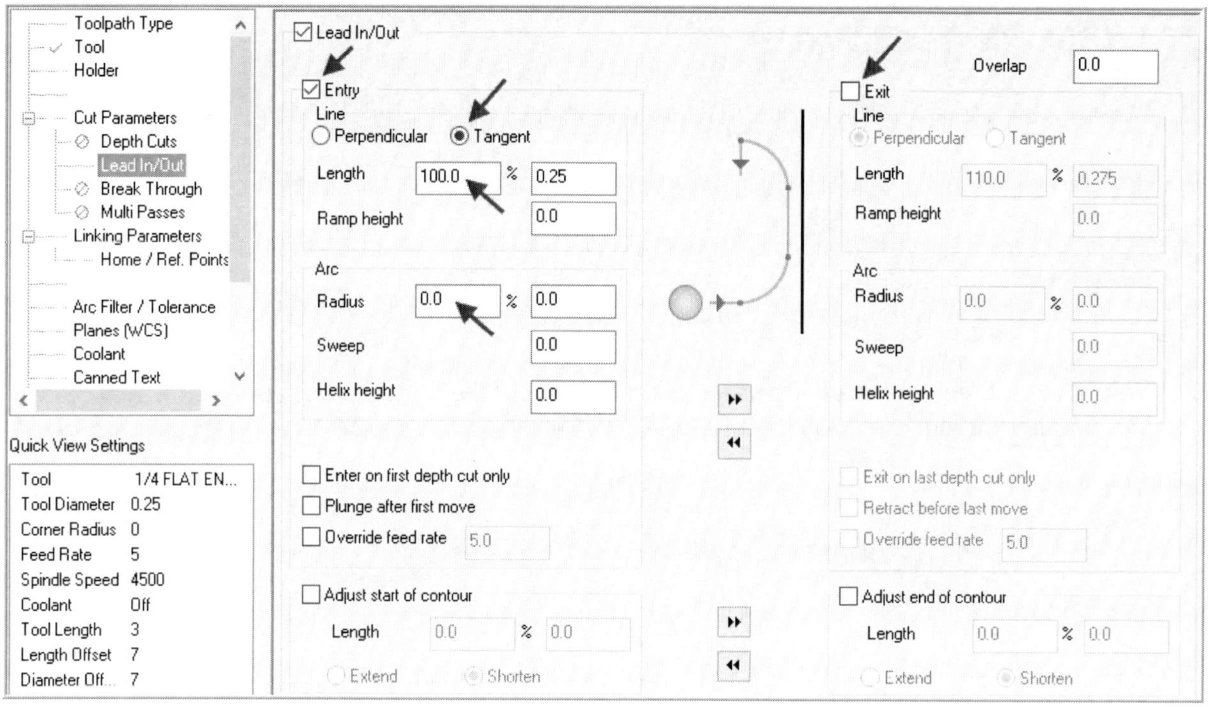

14. **Coolant Flood** is set to **On**.

15. Click **OK** .

➲ The screen should look like the image shown below.

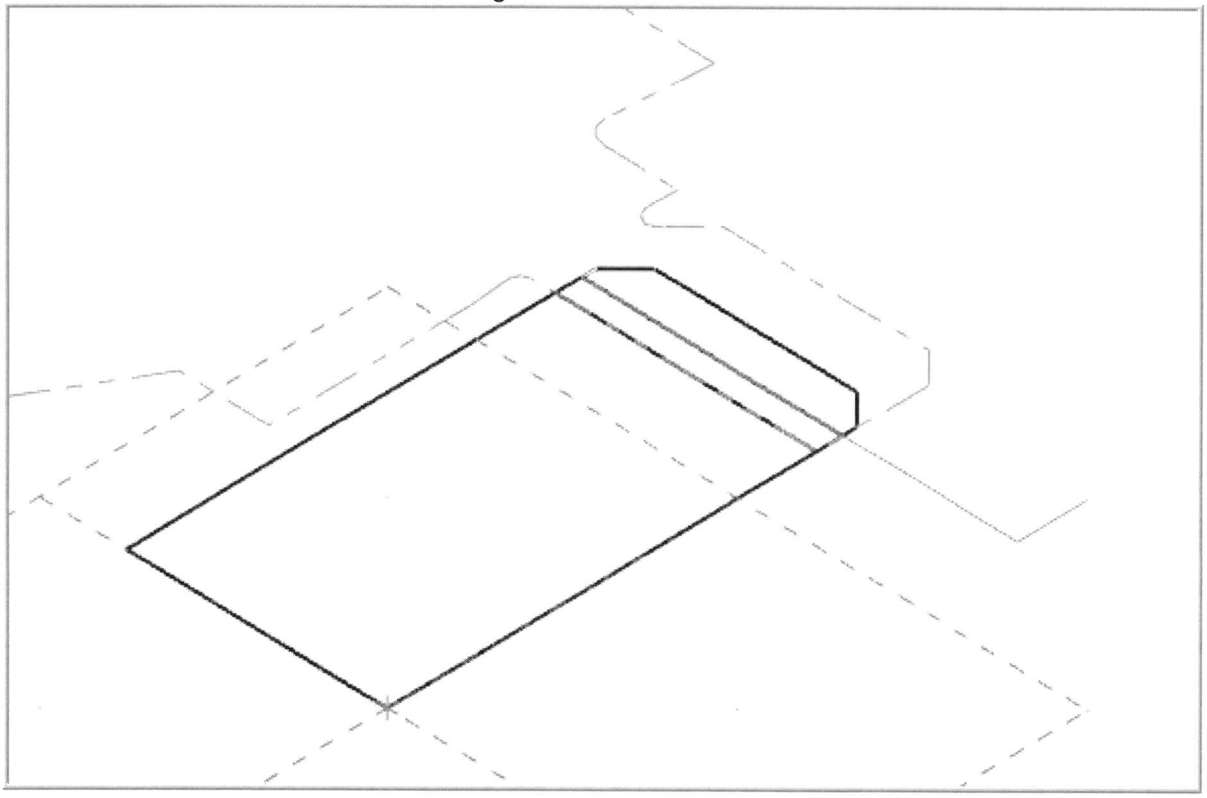

TASK 16:
MACHINE THE REMAINING THREE SLOTS USING TRANSFORM TOOLPATH

1. Select the **View** tab and toggle the **Planes Manager** to display.

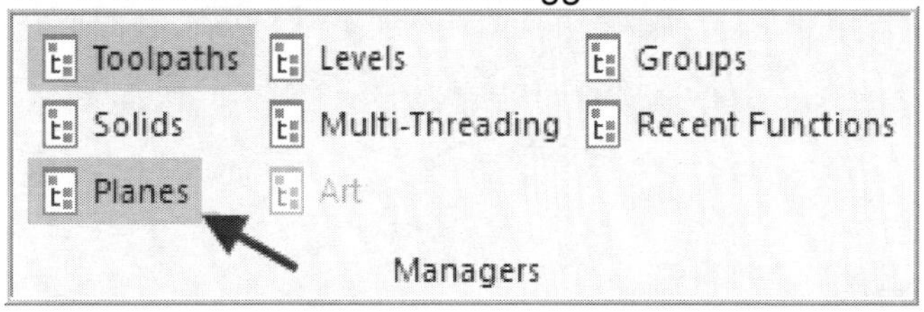

2. Now click in the **C column (Construction Plane)** for the **Right side** plane. The view is still set to Isometric but construction of the geometry will now take place on the Right side plane.

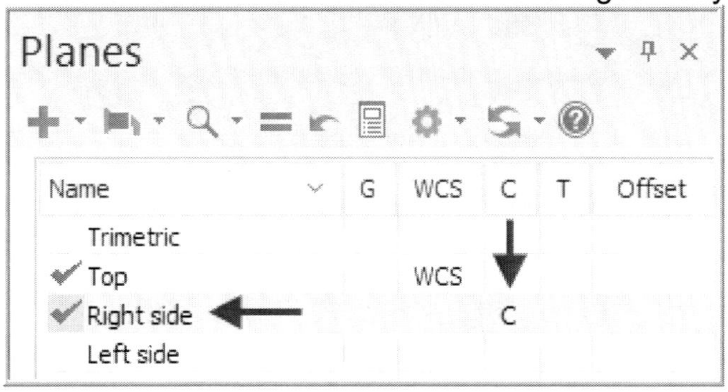

Changing the **Construction Plane** from **Top** to **Right** will allow the toolpath to be rotated correctly.

3. On the **TURNING** tab select **Toolpath Transform** in the **Utilities** section.

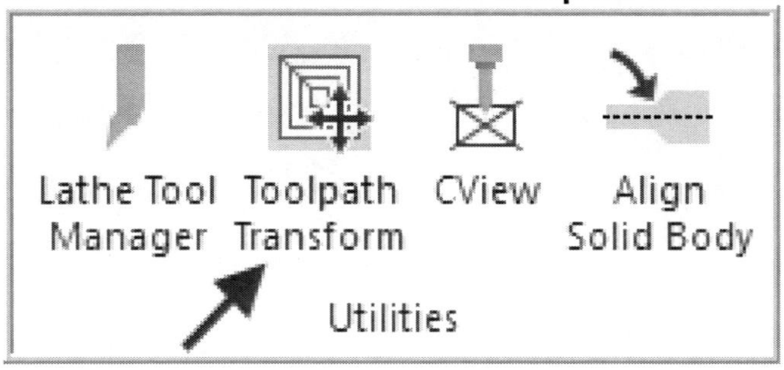

4. The **Transform Operation Parameters** dialog box appears. In the **Source operations** list ensure you have a check mark on only the **C-Axis** operation. Activate the radio button for **Method** to **Tool Plane**. Activate the radio button for **Type** to **Rotate**. Cancel any warning messages.

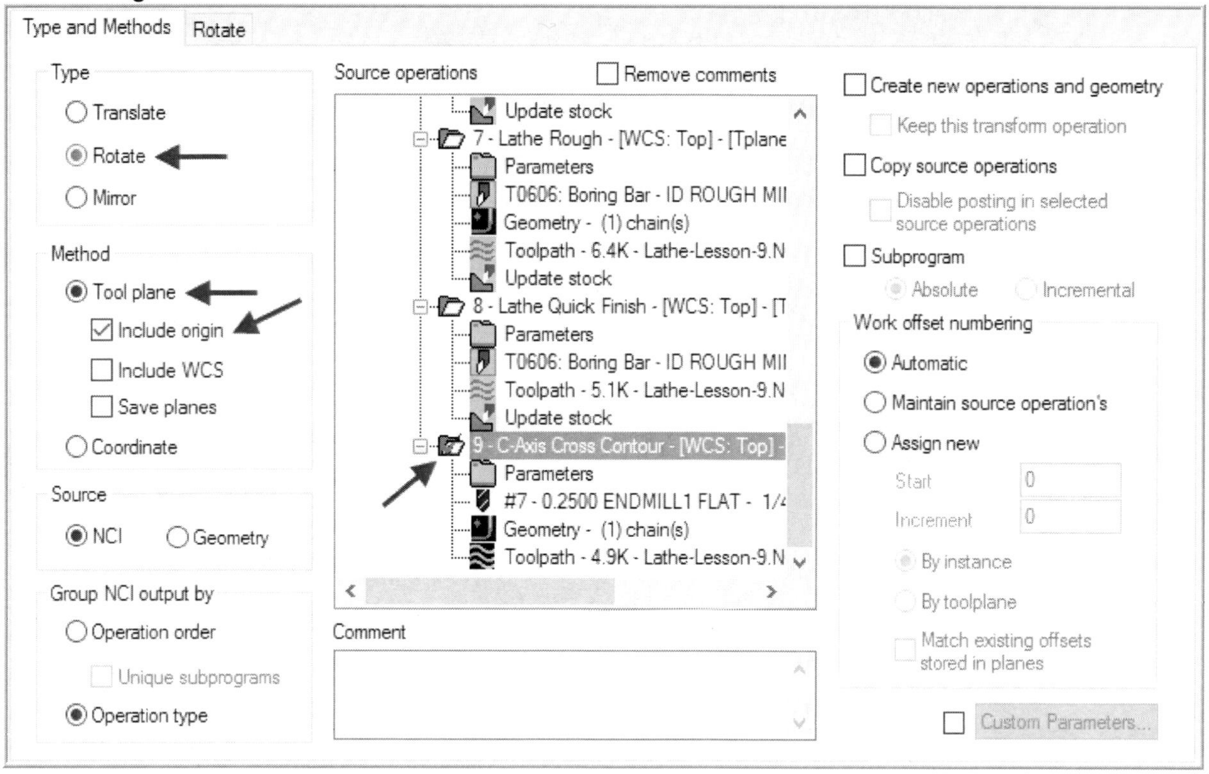

Transform Operation Parameters dialog box
Use this dialog box to begin creating a transform operation.

Here you can select the source operations, the type of transform, and how you want to organize the toolpaths which result.

After you select the type of transformation, choose only one of the remaining dialog box tabs to complete the operation. For example, if you choose a Rotate transformation, the Translate and Mirror tabs will be unavailable.

5. Click on the **Rotate** tab at the top of the dialog box and set the following as shown below:

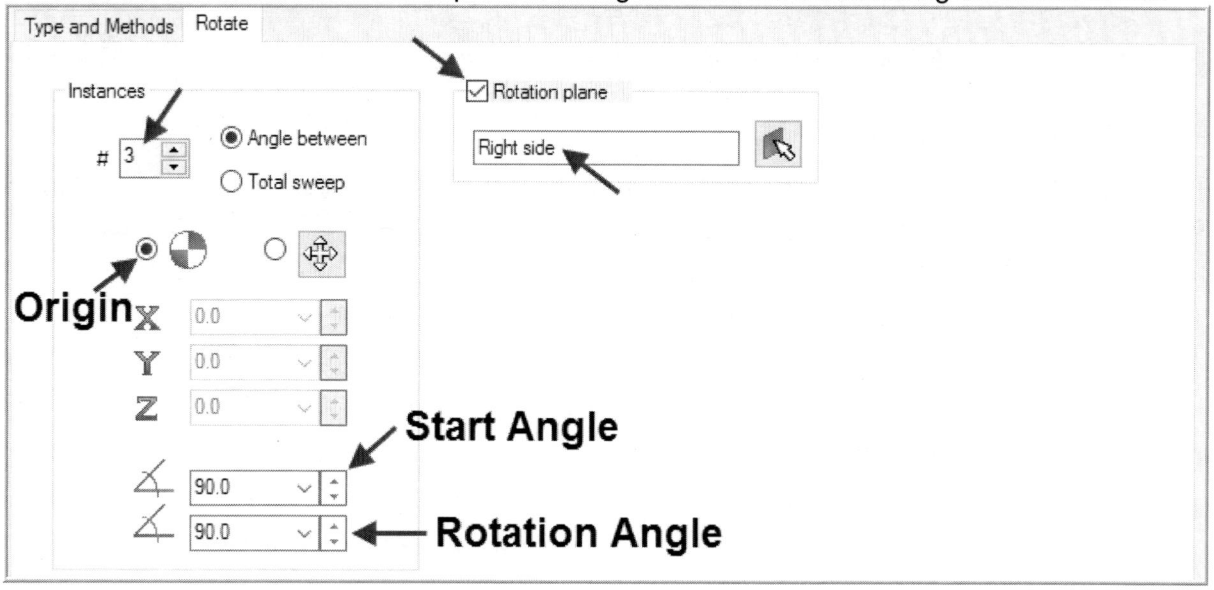

6. Select the OK button  to complete this function.

➲ The screen should look like the image shown below.

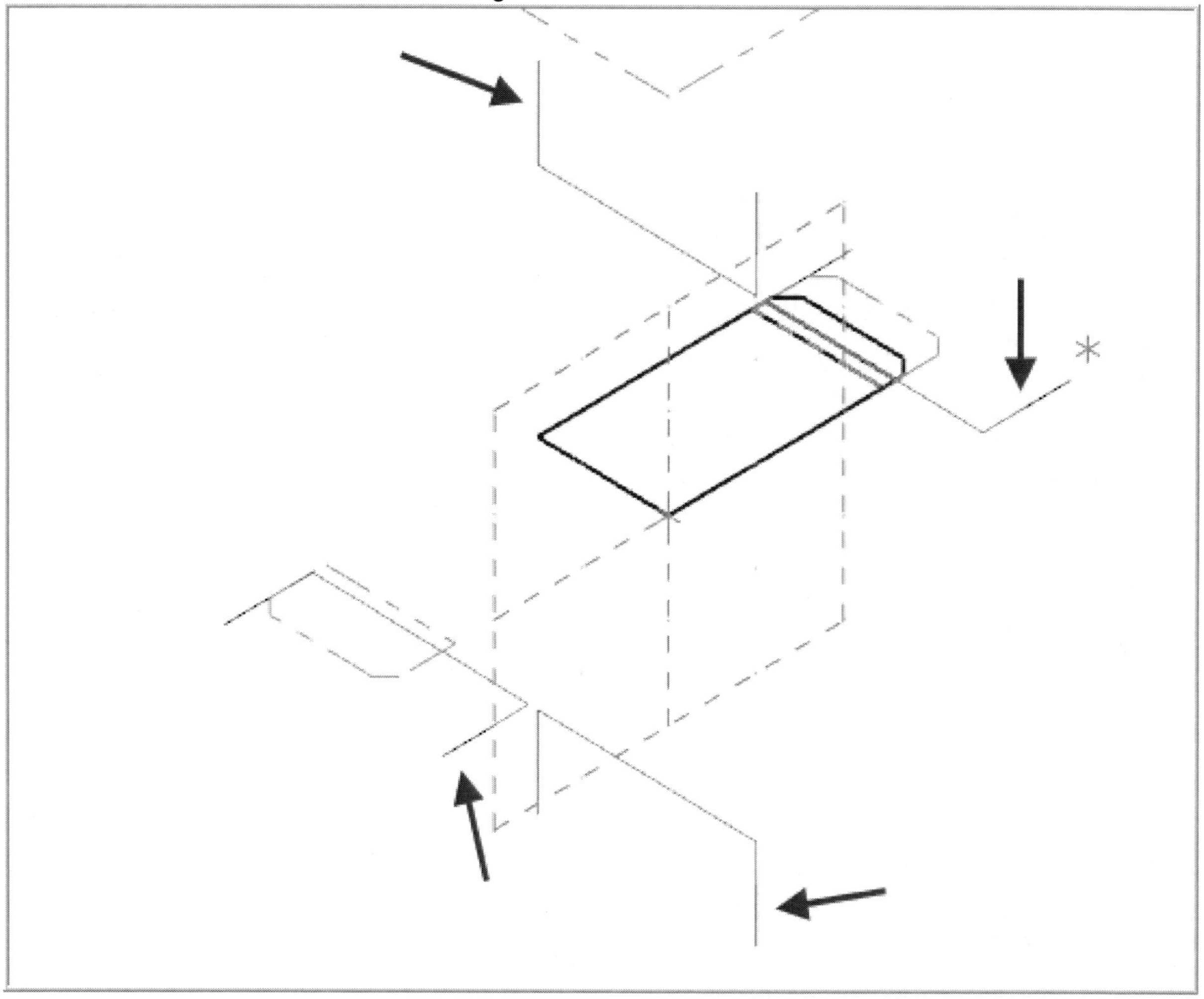

TASK 17:
CUTOFF THE PART

➲ In this task you will cutoff the part using a **0.125" wide cutoff tool**.

1. In the **Planes Manager** set the **C column** (Construction Plane) to the **+D +Z Plane**. Just click in the C column in the **+D +Z** row.

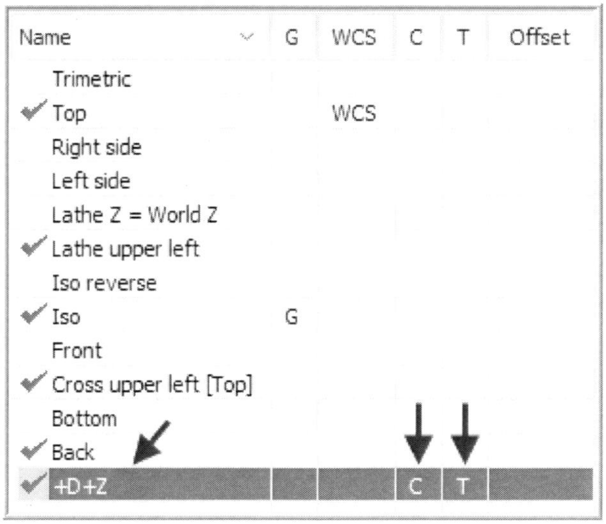

2. Select the **Close** button in the top right hand corner to close the Planes Manager.
3. Right mouse click in the graphics area and click on **Top**.
4. Click on the **Select all operations** icon.
5. Now click on the **Toggle the display of the toolpaths** button to **hide** the display of toolpaths.
6. Click on the **Expand gallery** down arrow to view additional options in the **General** toolpath section. In the **General** section select **Cutoff.**
7. Move the cursor over the corner until the visual cue for **End point** displays and then click on this point as shown below:

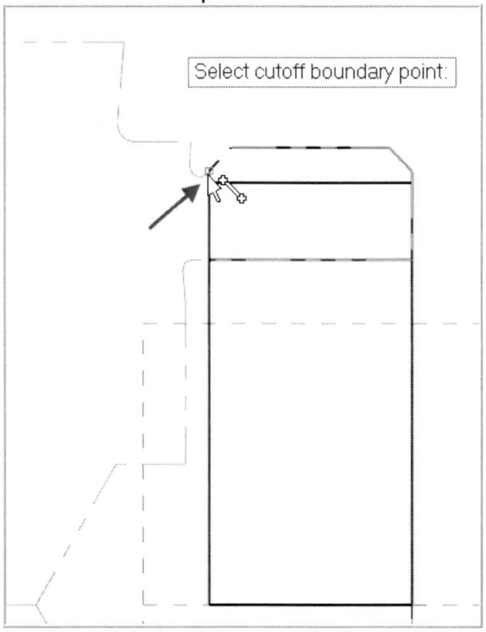

8. Scroll down the tool window and select the **OD Groove Right Width .125** tool and make changes as shown below in the **Toolpath parameters** page. **Coolant Flood** is set to **On**.

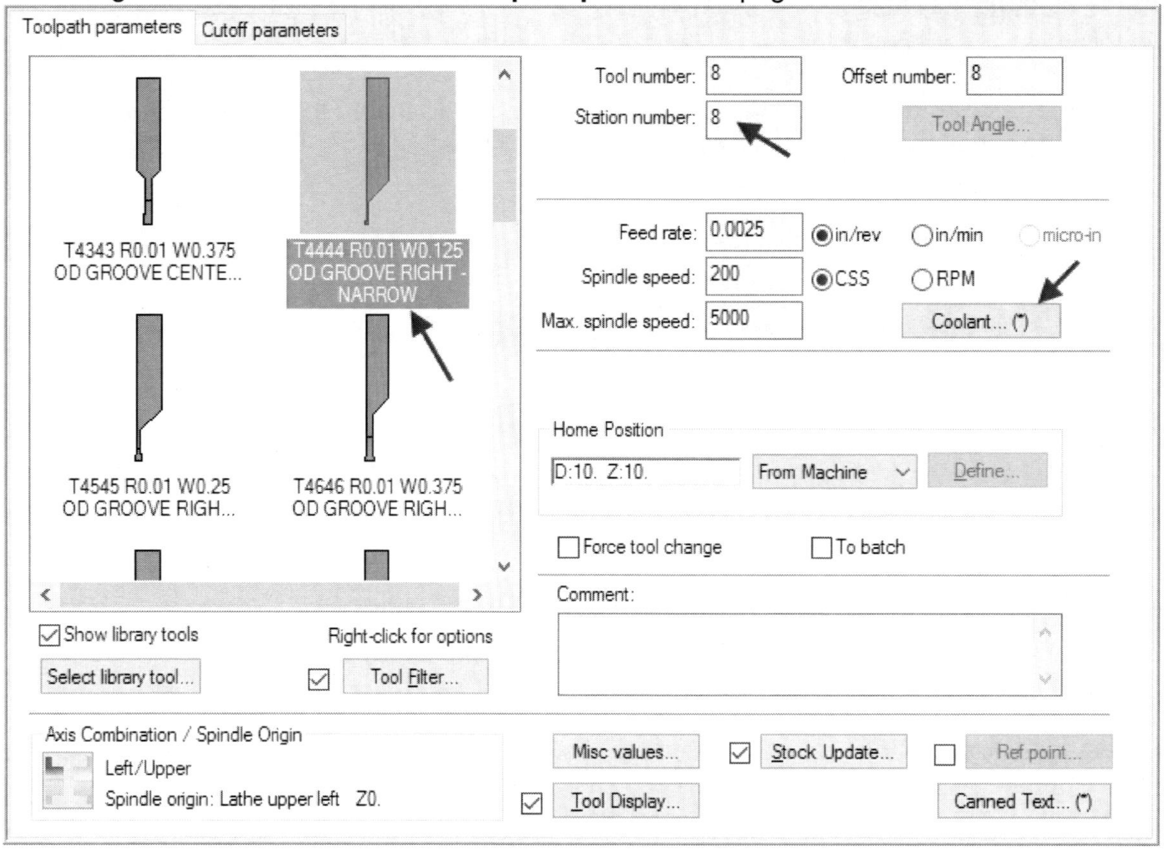

9. Still on the **Toolpath parameters** page click on the Stock Update button .

10. Activate **Keep both pieces**.

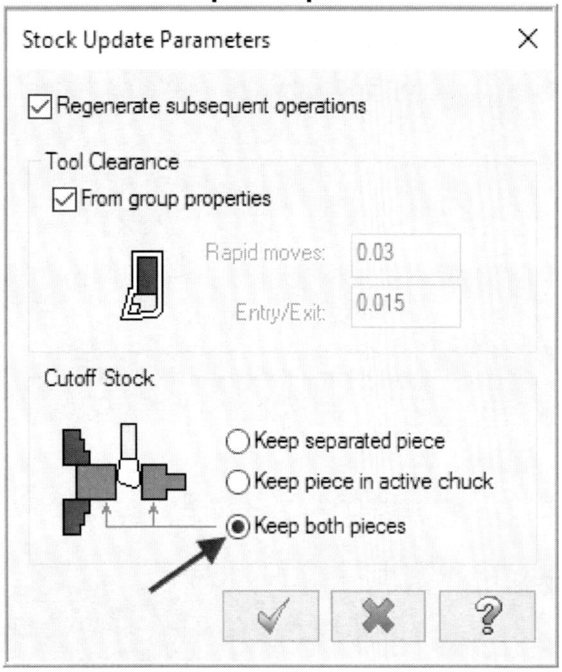

11. Select the **Cutoff parameters** page and make changes as shown below, if required.

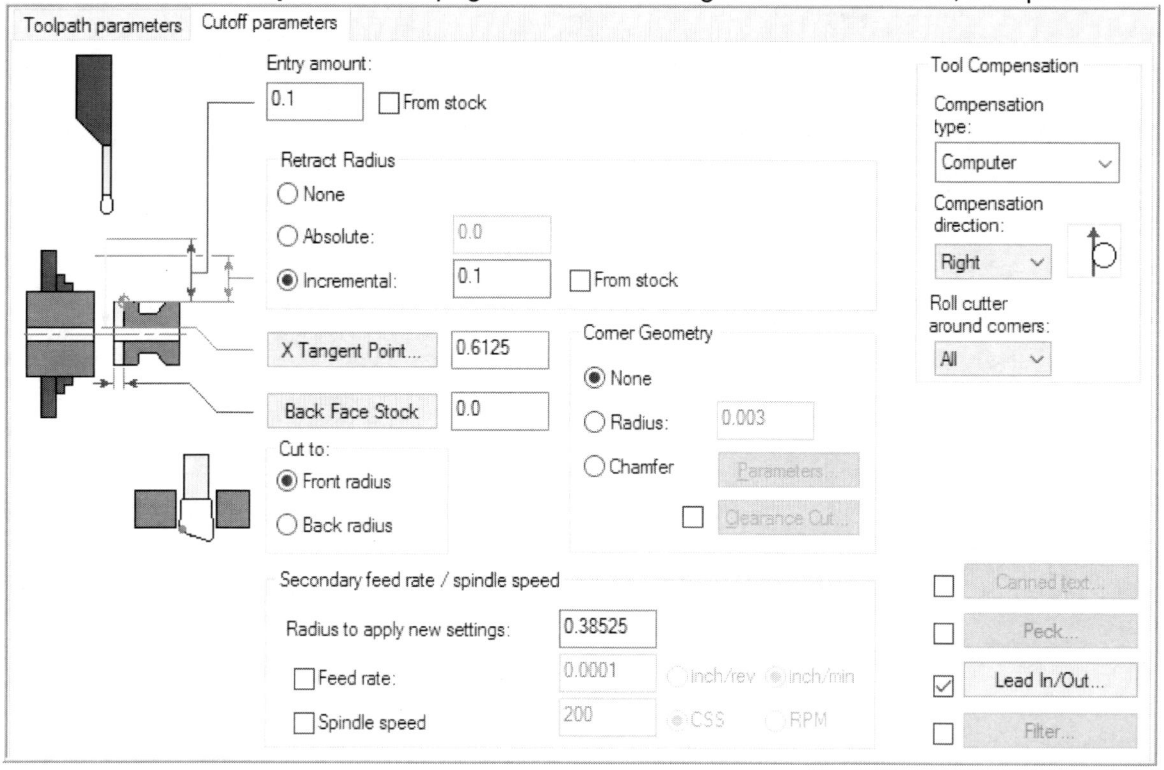

12. Select the **OK** button  to exit **Cutoff parameters.**

TASK 18:
MODIFY 1.625" DIAMETER AND REGENERATE OPERATIONS

- **Newsflash**: The engineering office has just contacted you with a change to this part.
- The 1.625" diameter has been changed from 1.625" to 1.425".
- In this task you will modify the geometry using **Transform Stretch** and then update the machining operations to reflect this change.
- Mastercam is fully associative, so after regenerating all the toolpaths the operations will now reflect this geometry modification.

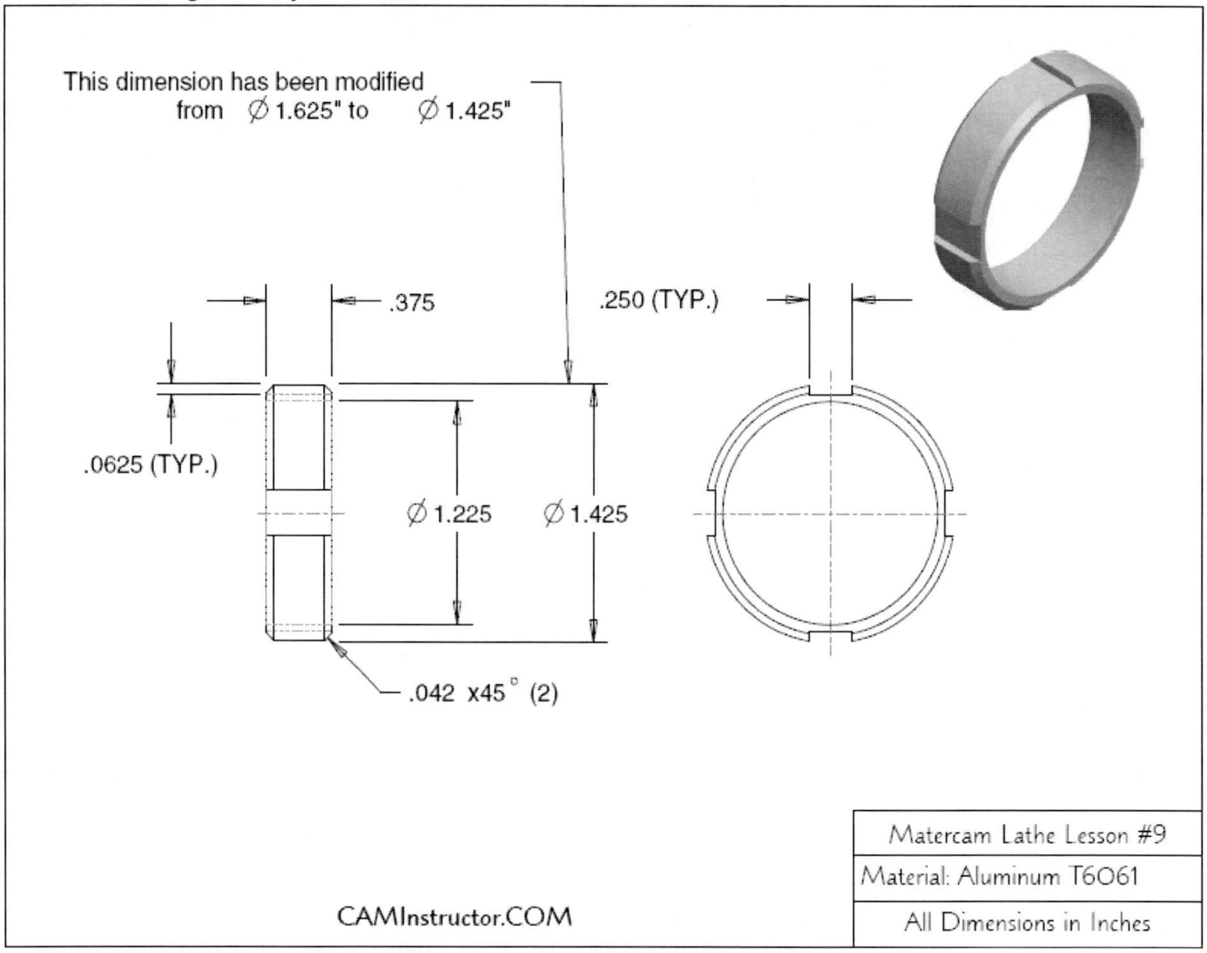

1. Select the **Transform** tab and in the **Size** section select **Stretch**.

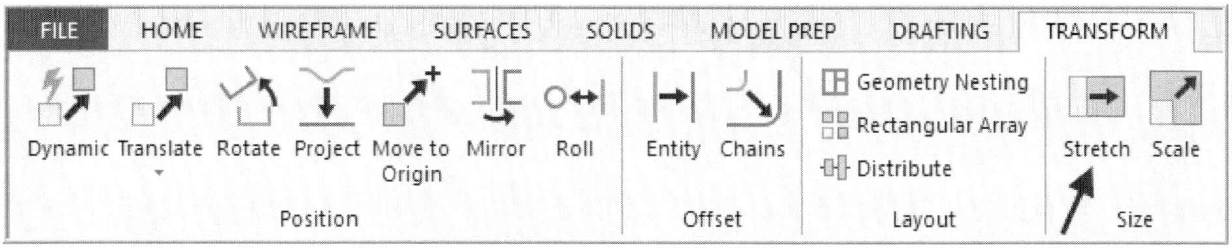

Use **Stretch** to move (translate) entities or one or more copies of the entities to new positions and optionally lengthen or shorten selected lines. Lines are stretched when they cross or intersect the window used to select the entities. The line endpoints that lie within the selection window are translated, while the endpoints that lie outside the selection window maintain their original positions. You can select all geometric and drafting entities within the Stretch function.

2. You are prompted to **Stretch: Window intersect entities to stretch.** Now draw a window around the entities by first picking a point at **position 1** and then dragging the window to **position 2** and then pick this point.

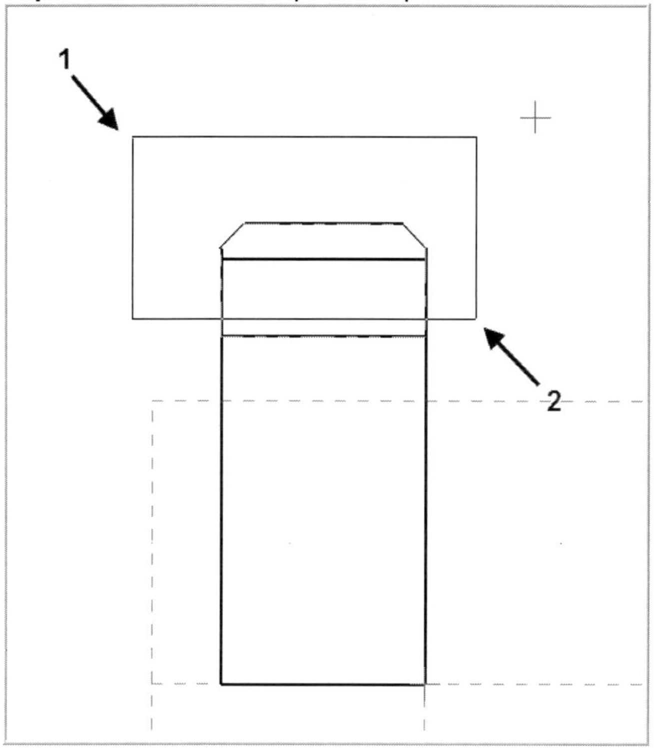

3. Click on **End Selection**  to move onto the next step**.**

4. The **Stretch** panel appears. Make the changes as shown in the diagram below:

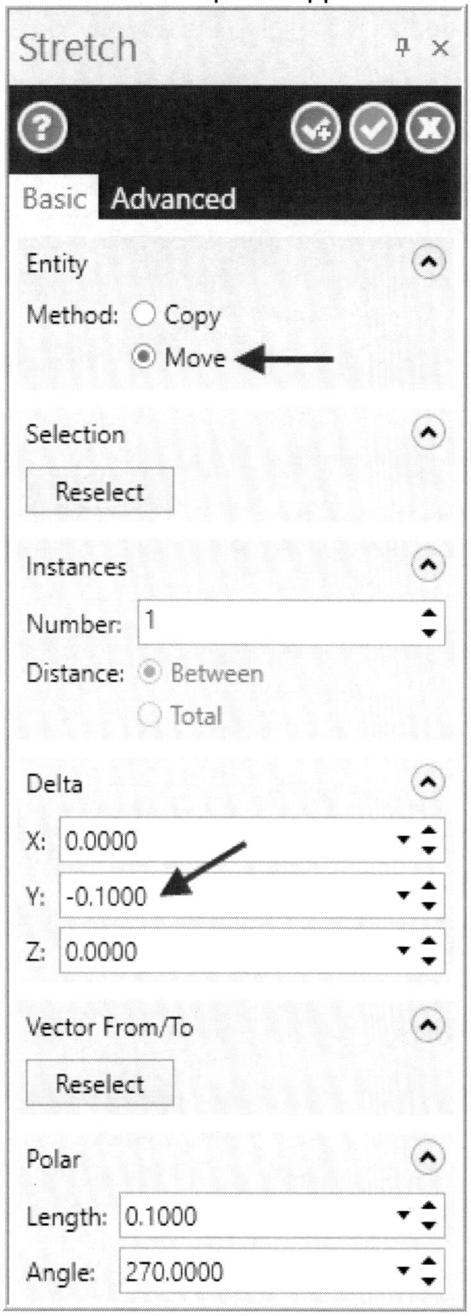

5. Click on **OK** in the **Stretch** panel.
6. Right mouse click in the graphics area and click on the **Clear Colors** icon.
7. Now pick all the operations by selecting the **Select All** icon as shown below:
8. Select the **Regenerate all dirty operations button** to remove the red X from the machining operations that have been modified by this geometry change.

TASK 19:
BACKPLOT THE TOOLPATH

➲ In this task you will use Mastercam's Backplot function to view the path the tools take to cut this part.

➲ Backplot will enable us to review the cutting motions and identify any problem areas when cutting the part.

1. Right mouse click in the graphics area and click on **Isometric**.
2. To pick all the operations to Backplot pick the **Select All** icon .
3. The next step is to select the **Backplot selected operations** icon shown below:

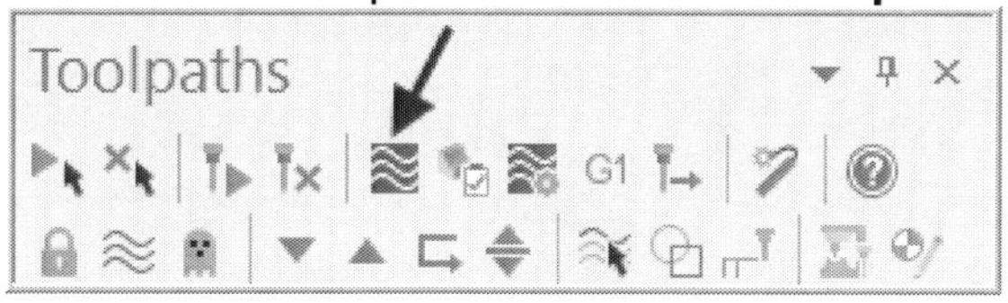

4. **Maximize** the Backplot/Verify window if required.
5. Select the **Home** Tab if required.
6. Activate the options shown below in the **Visibility** section of the **Home** tab.

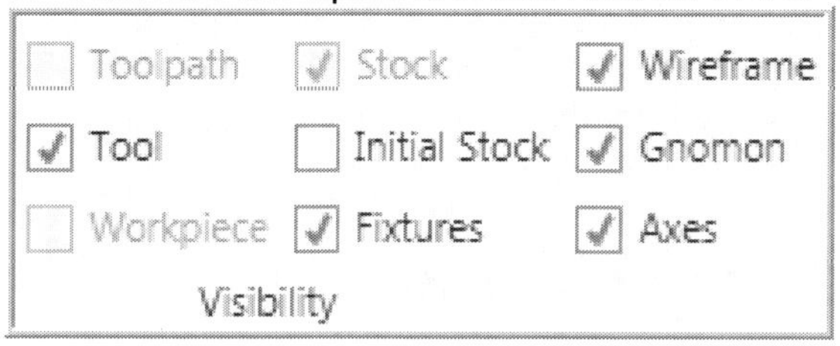

7. Activate the **Both** option in the **Toolpath** section of the **Home** tab.

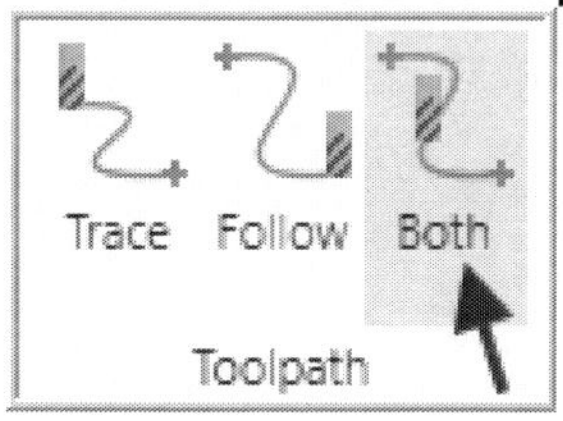

Both
This displays the entire toolpath and the tool as it travels over the displayed toolpath.

8. In the lower part of the screen now set the run Speed to slow by moving the slider bar pointer over to the left.
9. Now select the **Play Simulation** button to review the toolpaths.
10. After reviewing the Backplot of the toolpaths select the **Close** button 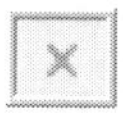 to exit Backplot.

TASK 20:
VERIFY THE TOOLPATH

➲ Mastercam's Verify utility allows you to use solid models to simulate the machining of a part. The model created by the verification represents the surface finish, and shows collisions, if any exist.

1. In the Toolpaths Manager pick all the operations to Verify by picking the **Select All** icon.
2. Select the **Verify selected operations** icon:
3. **Maximize** the Backplot/Verify window if required.
4. Activate the options shown below in the **Visibility** section of the **Home** tab. Initial Stock not activated.

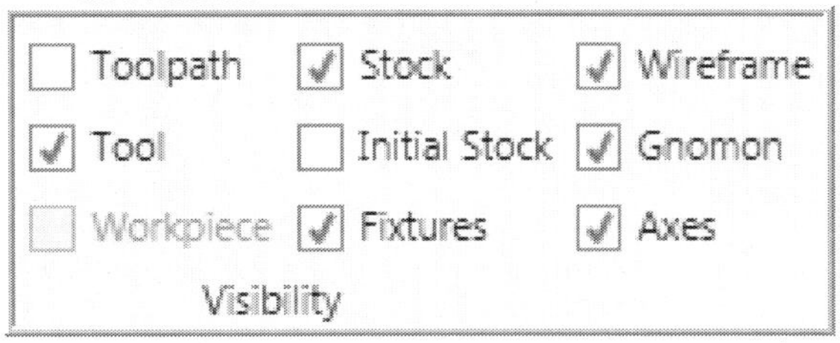

5. Select the Verify tab and activate the **Color Loop** to change the color of the cut stock for the verified part.
6. At the top of the screen select the **View** tab, the **Isometric** icon and then select **Fit**.
7. In the lower part of the screen now set the run **Speed** to slow by moving the slider bar pointer over to the left.
8. Now select the **Play Simulation** button to review the toolpaths.

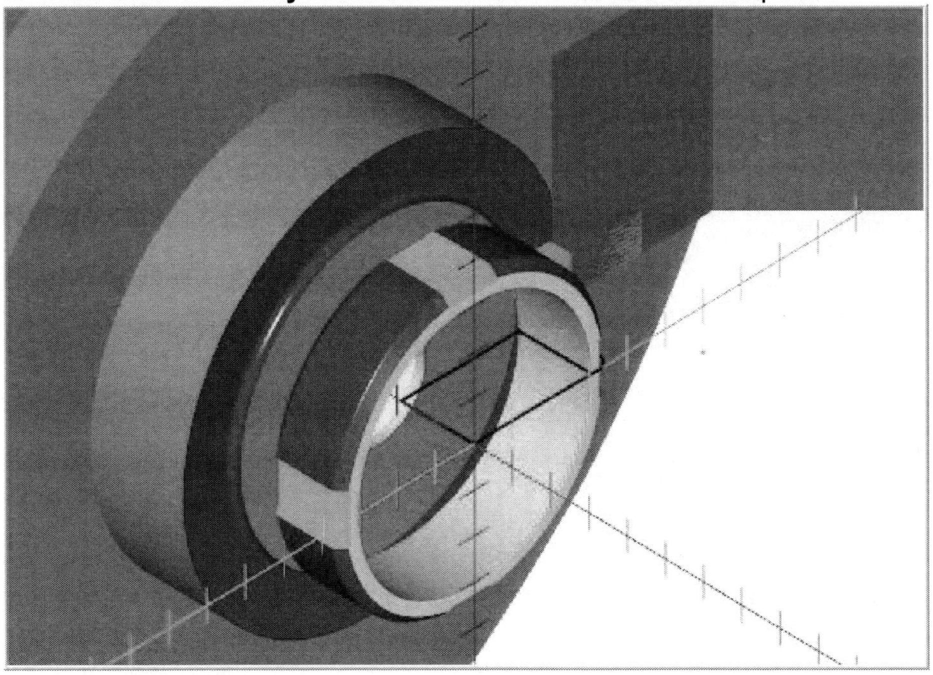

9. Select the **Close** button 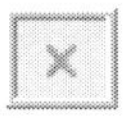 in the top right hand corner to exit Verify.

TASK 21:
SAVE THE UPDATED MASTERCAM FILE

1. Select the **Save** icon from the **Quick Access** toolbar at the top left of the screen.

TASK 22:
POST AND CREATE THE CNC CODE FILE

1. Ensure all the operations are selected by picking the **Select All** icon from the **Toolpaths Manager.**
2. Select the Post selected operations button from the **Toolpaths Manager.**
3. In the Post processing window, make the necessary changes as shown below:

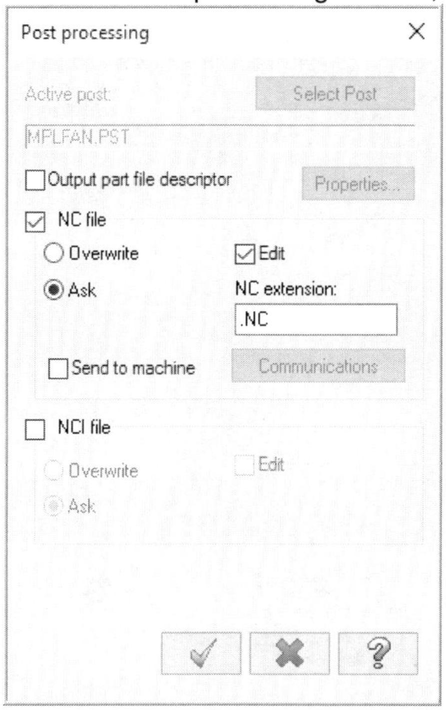

4. Select the **OK** button to continue.
5. Enter the same name as your Mastercam part file name in the **NC File name** field **LATHE-LESSON-9.**
6. Select the **Save** button.

➲ The CNC code file opens up in the default editor.

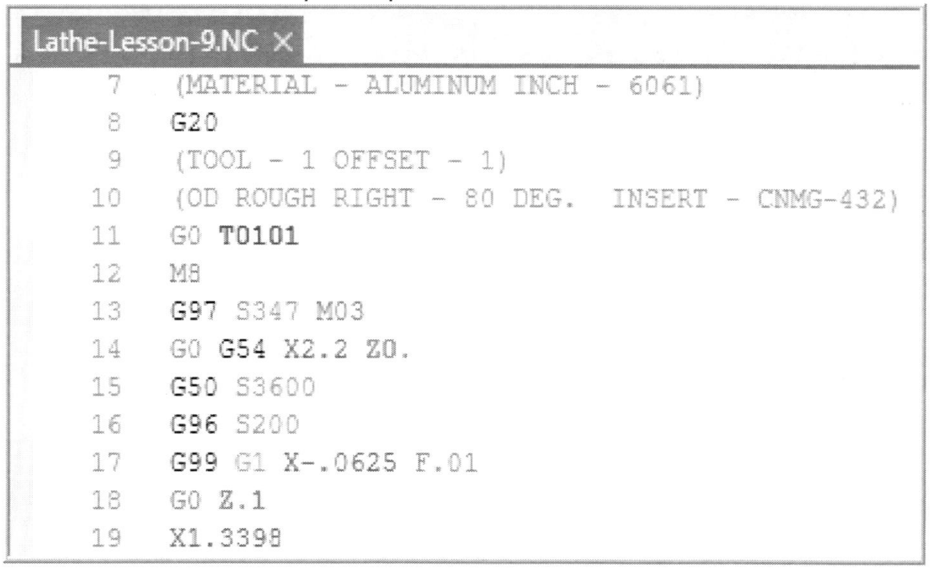

7. Scroll down the CNC code until you locate the commands to rotate the chuck (C-Axis) when machining the slots.

```
M01
(TOOL - 7 OFFSET - 0)
( 1/4 FLAT ENDMILL)
G0 T0700
M23
M8
G0 G55 X1.8 Z0.
C0.
G97 S2500 M51
X1.5
G98 G1 X1.3 F5.
Z-.375
G0 X1.8
G56 X1.8 Z0. C90.
X1.5
G1 X1.3
Z-.375
G0 X1.8
G57 X1.8 Z0. C180.
X1.5
G1 X1.3
Z-.375
G0 X1.8
G58 X1.8 Z0. C270.
```

8. Select the × in the top right corner to exit the CNC editor.

➲ This completes Lathe-Lesson-9.

LATHE-LESSON-9 EXERCISE

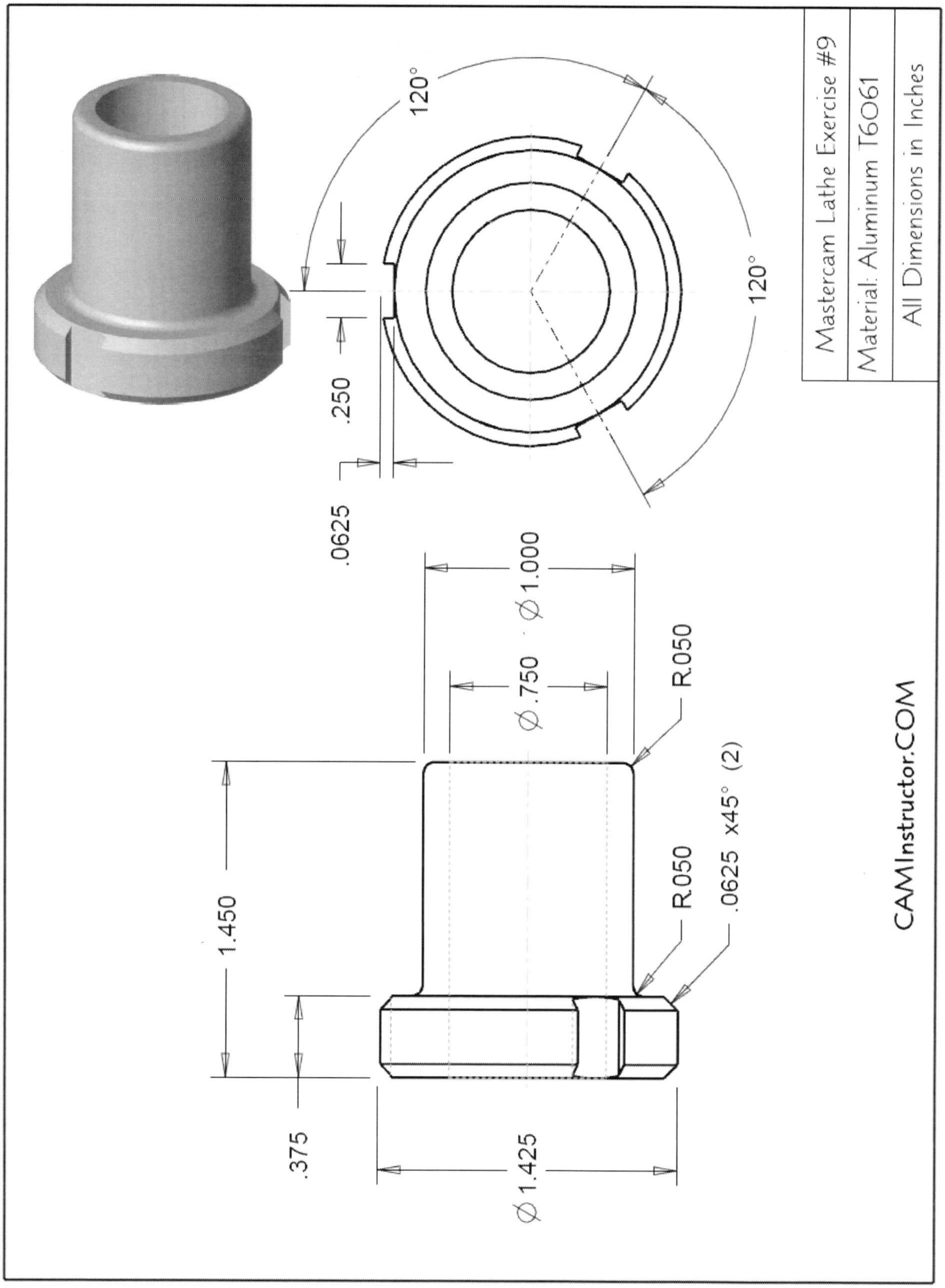

Mastercam® 2018
TRAINING
GUIDE

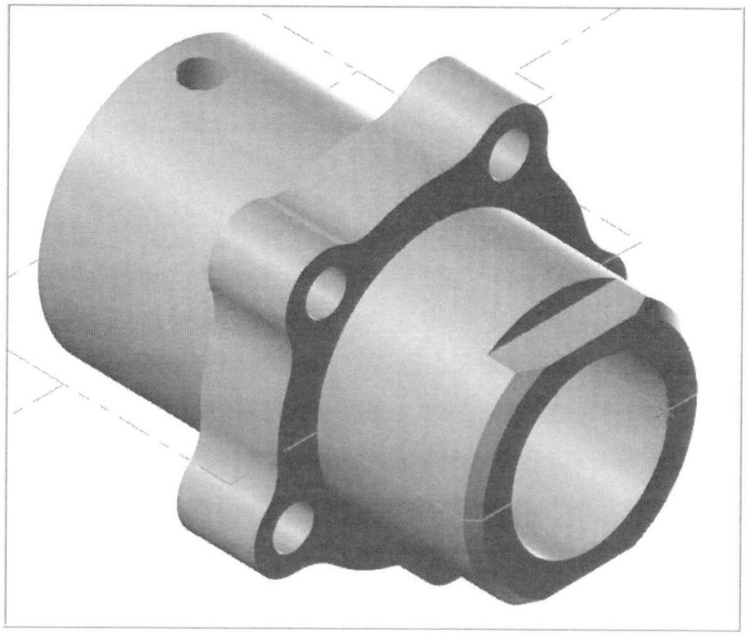

LATHE-LESSON-10

NOTE:
This Lesson is located on the **CamInstructor Course Site**.
1. Go to www.caminstructor.com and Log In.
2. Open the **Mastercam 2018 Lathe** course.
3. Click on **Lesson 10.**
4. Click on **Lesson 10 Instructions (PDF file)**.
5. The Lesson can be printed or you can follow the instructions on the computer screen.

camInstructor

camInstructor